Blackwell Handbook of Childhood Cognitive Development

Blackwell Handbooks of Developmental Psychology

This outstanding series of handbooks provides a cutting-edge overview of classic research, current research and future trends in developmental psychology.

- Each handbook draws together 25–30 newly commissioned chapters to provide a comprehensive overview of a sub-discipline of developmental psychology.
- The international team of contributors to each handbook have been specially chosen for their expertise and knowledge of each field.
- Each handbook is introduced and contextualized by leading figures in the field, lending coherence and authority to each volume.

The *Blackwell Handbooks of Developmental Psychology* will provide an invaluable overview for advanced students of developmental psychology and for researchers as an authoritative definition of their chosen field.

Blackwell Handbook of Infant Development
Edited by Gavin Bremner and Alan Fogel

Blackwell Handbook of Childhood Cognitive Development
Edited by Usha Goswami

Blackwell Handbook of Childhood Social Development
Edited by Peter K. Smith and Craig H. Hart

Blackwell Handbook of Adolescence
Edited by Gerald Adams and Michael D. Berzonsky

Blackwell Handbook of Childhood Cognitive Development

Edited by

Usha Goswami

BLACKWELL PUBLISHING
350 Main Street, Malden, MA 02148-5020, USA
9600 Garsington Road, Oxford OX4 2DQ, UK
550 Swanston Street, Carlton, Victoria 3053, Australia

The right of Usha Goswami to be identified as the Author of the Editorial Material in this
Work has been asserted in accordance with the UK Copyright, Designs, and Patents Act 1988.

First published 2002 by Blackwell Publishing Ltd
First published in paperback 2004

3   2006

Library of Congress Cataloging-in-Publication Data

Blackwell handbook of childhood cognitive development / edited by Usha Goswami.
        p. cm.—(Blackwell handbooks of developmental psychology)
    Includes bibliographical references and index.
    ISBN 0-631-21840-8 (hbk) — ISBN 0-631-21841-6 (pbk)
        1. Cognition in children. I. Goswami, Usha. II. Series.

    BF723.C5 B5 2002
    155.413—dc21

                                              20002023054

ISBN-13: 978-0-631-21840-1 (hbk) — ISBN-13: 978-0-631-21841-8 (pbk)

A catalogue record for this title is available from the British Library.

Set in 10.5 on 12.5 pt Adobe Garamond
by SNP Best-set Typesetter Ltd, Hong Kong
Printed and bound in Singapore
by C.O.S. Printers Pte Ltd

The publisher's policy is to use permanent paper from mills that operate a sustainable forestry
policy, and which has been manufactured from pulp processed using acid-free and elementary
chlorine-free practices. Furthermore, the publisher ensures that the text paper and cover board
used have met acceptable environmental accreditation standards.

For further information on
Blackwell Publishing, visit our website:
www.blackwellpublishing.com

To Ella Elisabeth Thomson
For making me interested in childhood cognitive
development all over again

Contents

Acknowledgments

I would like to thank my contributors for making my editorial duties in preparing this volume so enjoyable. The outstanding quality of their contributions and of their writing made the technical side of my job extremely easy, and their willingness to meet deadlines and to respond promptly to editorial requests was remarkable. I have also learned a tremendous amount from reading what they had to say! My thanks also to Jennifer Smith for her secretarial support.

List of Contributors

Renée Baillargeon, Department of Psychology, University of Illinois at Champaign-Urbana, 603 East Daniel, Champaign, IL 61820, USA. Email rbaillar@s.psych.uiuc.edu.

Simon Baron-Cohen, Departments of Experimental Psychology and Psychiatry, University of Cambridge, Downing Street, Cambridge CB2 3EB, UK.

Patricia J. Bauer, Institute of Child Development, 51 East River Road, University of Minnesota, Minneapolis, MN 55455-0345, USA. Email pbauer@tc.umn.edu.

Peter Bryant, Department of Experimental Psychology, University of Oxford, South Parks Road, Oxford OX1 3UD, UK.

Sharon Crosbie, Department of Speech, King George VIth Building, University of Newcastle, Newcastle upon Tyne NE1 7RU, UK.

Judy S. DeLoache, Psychology Department, PO Box 400400, University of Virginia, Charlottesville, VA 22904-4400, USA.

Barbara Dodd, Department of Speech, King George VIth Building, University of Newcastle, Newcastle upon Tyne NE1 7RU, UK.

Susan A. Gelman, Department of Psychology, University of Michigan, Ann Arbor, MI 48109, USA.

György Gergely, Institute for Psychology, Hungarian Academy of Psychology, H-1394 Budapest, PO Box 398, Hungary. Email 113524.2623@compuserve.com.

Usha Goswami, Faculty of Education, University of Cambridge, Shaftesbury Road, Cambridge CB2 2BX. Email ucg10@cam.ac.uk.

Rick Griffin, Departments of Experimental Psychology and Psychiatry, University of Cambridge, Downing Street, Cambridge CB2 3EB, UK.

Graeme S. Halford, School of Psychology, University of Queensland, 4072, Australia. Email gsh@psy.uq.edu.au.

Jacqueline Hill, Departments of Experimental Psychology and Psychiatry, University of Cambridge, Downing Street, Cambridge CB2 3EB, UK.

Susanne Huber, Friedrich Miescher Laboratory of the Max Planck Society, Spremannstrasse 34, 72076 Tübingen, Germany.

Annette Karmiloff-Smith, Neurocognitive Development Unit, Institute of Child Health, 30 Guildford Street, London WC1N 1EH, UK. Email A.Karmiloff-Smith@ich.ucl.ac.uk.

Barbara Koslowski, Human Development, Cornell University, Ithaca, NY 14853, USA.

Deanna Kuhn, Box 119, Teachers College Columbia University, New York, NY 10027, USA. Email dk100@columbia.edu.

John Lawson, Departments of Experimental Psychology and Psychiatry, University of Cambridge, Downing Street, Cambridge CB2 3EB, UK.

Lynn S. Liben, Department of Psychology, Pennsylvania State University, University Park, PA 16802, USA. Email liben@psu.edu.

Angeline Lillard, Psychology Department, PO Box 400400, University of Virginia, Charlottesville, VA 22904-4400, USA.

Amy Masnick, Department of Psychology, Carnegie Mellon University, 369 Baker Hall, Pittsburgh, PA 15213, USA.

Andrew N. Meltzoff, Center for Mind, Brain, and Learning, CHDD Rooms 357 and 373, University of Washington (Box 357920), Seattle, WA 98195, USA. Email Meltzoff@u.washington.edu.

Ulrich Müller, Department of Psychology, University of Toronto, 100 St. George Street, Toronto, Ontario, Canada M5S 3G3.

Larry P. Nucci, College of Education M/C 147, University of Illinois at Chicago, 1040 West Harrison Street, Chicago, IL 60607, USA.

Terezinha Nuñes, Psychology Department, Oxford Brookes University, Gipsy Lane Campus, Headington, Oxford OX3 0BP, UK.

John E. Opfer, Department of Psychology, Carnegie Mellon University, Baker Hall 331, Pittsburgh PA 15213-3890, USA.

Paul C. Quinn, Department of Psychology, Washington and Jefferson College, 60 South Lincoln Street, Washington, PA 15301, USA. Email pquinn@washjeff.edu.

Shawn M. Rowe, Department of Education, Washington University in St. Louis, USA.

Wolfgang Schneider, Institute of Psychology, University of Würzburg, Wittelsbacher-platz 1, Würzburg D-97074, Germany.

Leslie Smith, Department of Education, University of Lancaster, Bailrigg, Lancaster LA1 4YF, UK.

Margaret J. Snowling, Department of Psychology, University of York, Heslington, York YO10 5DD, UK. Email MJS19@york.ac.uk.

Robert J. Sternberg, Department of Psychology, Yale University, Box 208205, New Haven, CT 06520-8205, USA.

Michael S. C. Thomas, Neurocognitive Development Unit, Institute of Child Health, 30 Guildford Street, London WC1N 1EH, UK. Email M.Thomas@ich.ucl.ac.uk.

Sandra R. Waxman, Department of Psychology, Northwestern University, 2029 Sheridan Road, Evanston, IL 60208-2710, USA.

Henry M. Wellman, Centre for Human Growth and Development, University of Michigan, 300 North Ingalls Building, 10th floor, Ann Arbor, MI 48109-0406, USA.

James V. Wertsch, Department of Education, Washington University in St. Louis, USA.

Sally Wheelwright, Departments of Experimental Psychology and Psychiatry, University of Cambridge, Downing Street, Cambridge CB2 3EB, UK.

Friedrich Wilkening, Psychologisches Institut, University of Zurich, Attenhoferstrasse 9, CH-8032 Zurich, Switzerland.

Philip David Zelazo, Department of Psychology, University of Toronto, 100 St. George Street, Toronto, Ontario, Canada M5S 3G3. Email zelazo@psych.utoronto.ca.

PART I

Infancy: The Origins of Cognitive Development

The infant brain doubles in size during the first year of life. Although fetuses show both learning and memory (Hepper, 1992), most of the 1,000 trillion connections in the adult brain are formed during infancy and childhood (Gopnik, Meltzoff & Kuhl, 1999a). The number of actual brain cells (neurons) is virtually identical in infant and adult. What changes is the wiring. At birth, each neuron in the cerebral cortex has around 2,500 synapses. By the age of 2–3 years, each neuron has a staggering 15,000 synapses. By 2 years of age, the brain is already consuming glucose at adult levels. By 3, the little child's brain is actually twice as active as the adult's. It remains so until the child is 9 or 10. But pruning is as important as forming connections. Development consists of furious growth in connectivity and an associated pruning of old connections as the brain adapts itself to its surroundings and becomes more specialized.

This book is about how different aspects of cognitive development unfold during this period of peak sensitivity for learning. The plasticity of the child's brain is often remarked upon, but equally remarkable is the similarity in cognitive development across cultures and social contexts. In this first section on infancy, the authors focus on the basic kinds of knowledge that are central in human cognitive development. These are knowledge about social cognition, self and agency (Meltzoff, Gergely), knowledge about the physical world of objects and events (Baillargeon), and knowledge about the kinds of things in the world – conceptual knowledge (Quinn). These "foundational" domains (naïve psychology, physics, and biology) also depend on the development of memory (Bauer) and language (Waxman). Babies' experiences of the world continually lead them to enrich their possibly innate rudimentary understandings, to revise and modify them, and even to replace them with new understandings. Language and memory help them in this process.

The first chapter in this handbook considers the classical problem of how we come to know others as persons like ourselves. Based on his pioneering work in infant imitation, Meltzoff argues that the first common code between self and other is the ability to map the actions of other people onto the actions of our own bodies. He suggests that this imitative ability is innate, and argues that basic aspects of the representation of action must therefore also be innate. Furthermore, infants' ability to connect the seen acts of others with movements of their own (that they *feel* rather than see themselves make) is good evidence that certain cross-modal equivalences are present from birth. Meltzoff then summarizes the empirical evidence for early imitation. He shows that imitation is not simply an immediate mimicry of another's actions without any representation of those actions. It is not due to arousal, and it cannot be dismissed as a biologically based response that is released in the presence of certain signs. Rather, infant imitation is creative and open to modulation, and can occur hours or even days after the modeled event. Infants prefer to imitate people, not machines, and they can even associate certain people with certain imitative acts. Meltzoff argues that infants use information about whether a given person acts in a certain way to keep track of who that person is. Infants can also read the intention behind some adult acts by the age of around 18 months. At this point in development, they can watch unsuccessful actions and yet produce the intended target behavior. The idea that there is a language of human acts that is central to the development of human social cognition is an intuitively appealing one. Meltzoff's view is that seeing others as "like me" is central to the development of our ability to know other minds.

In his chapter on the development of understanding of the self as a causal agent, Gergely presents different evidence relevant to the same problem of knowing other minds. He addresses the traditional notion (stemming from Freud) that young infants are initially unable to distinguish themselves from their environments. He shows elegantly how unlikely this is, and argues that very simple cognitive skills such as the ability to detect contingency between events may underlie the development of an understanding of self and agency. Coupled with a probably innate propensity to attend to and interact with people, sensitivity to contingency may allow the infant to develop conscious awareness of their own emotional states and of how they are related to the actions of their caregivers. An important advance is thought to occur at around 9 months, when joint attention skills first start to appear, resulting in a new level of social-cognitive understanding of goal-directed rational action. This is at first focused only on the interpreter's own representations of reality, but eventually enables the development of an understanding of agency and of intentional mental states in others, which requires an understanding of the representations of other minds. Children become increasingly able to think in terms of mental causation during the second year onwards. Other people are represented in terms of generalized and enduring intentional properties, and this in turn brings about new levels of self-understanding. A cognitive representation of the self as an objective entity with enduring properties emerges at around the end of the second year. A full cognitive self-concept (possession of an abstract, temporally extended historical-causal concept of the autobiographical self) may not emerge until age 4 or 5, however.

Baillargeon summarizes current knowledge about infants' understanding of the physical world in eight "lessons" capturing the most recent findings from her laboratory. She discusses both the kinds of knowledge that infants possess, and the possible ways in which they might attain this knowledge. She suggests that infants first learn about physical events (such as occlusion, support, and collision) by forming rather specific primitive all-or-none rules consistent with innate core principles such as *solidity* and *continuity* and tied to their actual experience. With further concrete experience, they revise and elaborate these simple rules, taking account of different variables and reaching a more adult-like understanding of physical events. To demonstrate the critical role of experience, Baillargeon presents successful "teaching" experiments in which infants are given experiences that enable them to extract new variables at an earlier age than normally occurs. However, she also shows that they cannot extract arbitrarily manipulated variables that they cannot make sense of in terms of their prior physical knowledge. Baillargeon then considers whether the development of physical knowledge in infancy is best captured by a correlation-based model whereby infants absorb statistical regularities in the environment, or whether it is better described by a model of knowledge acquisition based on the detection of causal regularities. Given her teaching experiments, she argues that learning in infancy is "explanation-based," dependent on the ability of infants to construct causal explanations for new phenomena on the basis of their prior knowledge. As we will see in later chapters, older children appear to acquire knowledge of many kinds on much the same basis.

The absorption of statistical regularities in the environment can nevertheless be an important source of learning in infancy, as shown in the chapters by Quinn and Waxman. Quinn considers how infants go about the task of dividing the unlabeled world into like entities, which are then stored mentally as categorical representations. He begins from the premise that the perceptual world has structure in the form of bundles of statistically correlated attributes. Attention to these correlations may enable infants to carve up the world into entities such as dogs, people, cars, and trees. Quinn considers whether initial attention to correlation is at the "basic" categorical level of dogs and cars, or at the "super-ordinate" categorical level of animals and vehicles. Via a series of carefully controlled experiments, he demonstrates that very young infants proceed from more general ("animals") to more specific ("dogs," "cats") categorical representations. Quinn then develops a connectionist model of early categorization which suggests that this developmental sequence reflects the nature of perceptual learning. The learning process is very rapid, and basic-level categories dominate conceptual development by 3 to 4 months. These basic-level categories are very important for language acquisition, as of course the world is not really unlabeled for the infant. Caretakers are providing labels all the time, particularly for objects and actions, and such "open class" words are linguistically perceptually more salient too, receiving greater stress and having more interesting melodic contours.

Waxman, who makes this last point in her chapter, considers the close interaction between early conceptual development and early linguistic development in detail. She argues that a parsimonious explanation of the highly similar forms that conceptual and linguistic development take across very different cultures is that infants are born equipped with an innate expectation that words will refer to commonalities among objects. These commonalities can be of many kinds, for example taxonomic (dogs, cats), functional (pulls, cuts), thematic (bread goes with butter), or property-based (has wings, is red). As in Baillargeon's account, the initial core expectation is assumed to be fine-tuned via experience. As in Gergely's account, there is also a causal role for infants' innate propensity to attend to and interact with other people. Infants show a special interest in "people sounds" – the sounds of language. They rapidly become perceptually tuned to the phonologic, prosodic, and morphologic elements characterizing their native language, and very soon, novel words guide attention to objects and highlight commonalities and differences between them. Language itself plays a role in what is attended to: Waxman shows that infants learn that novel nouns signify categories of objects (balls), and that novel adjectives signify properties of objects (red). There is also a role for the understanding of agency: Waxman argues that infants can only map words to their referents if they can infer that the speaker *intended* to name the designated object. She then illustrates how naming promotes the formation of object categories, and demonstrates the importance of the "basic level" of object categorization in this process. Waxman ends by agreeing with Quinn that basic-level categories are probably *not* perceptually based.

The acquisition of all the different kinds of knowledge covered in these first chapters relies on infants having relatively well-functioning memories. Bauer's chapter discusses the relevant evidence. She demonstrates that the traditional view (stemming from Piaget) that infants were unable to represent information that was not currently available to their senses was misguided. This view stemmed partly from the lack of suitable paradigms within which to examine infant memory. Bauer shows that the development of new paradigms such as infant habituation and deferred imitation has enabled the documentation of really quite remarkable mnemonic capacities in infancy. Although very young infants appear to form very specific memories for events (as in Baillargeon's experiments), older infants of around 6 months form more general memories based on categorical information. Temporally ordered recall memory is present by at least 9 months, which is thought to be an important age for the development of long-term recall ability on the basis of electrical evoked potential evidence (note that this is the same age at which Gergely described a social-cognitive revolution in understanding goal-directed actions). Infants can benefit from cues designed to facilitate recall by at least 18 months, and with contextual support 2-year-olds can recall events that occurred around six months previously. By 3 years of age, children can provide verbal reports of events that occurred when they were 20 months old. Bauer demonstrates that some of these developments probably depend on the maturation of different brain structures. Memory functions subserved by the medial temporal lobes may develop relatively early, whereas those subserved by the association areas may develop more slowly. She concludes that there is great continuity in memory from infancy to early childhood and beyond.

Indeed, continuity seems to be the rule rather than the exception in all of the developmental domains discussed in this section. Each chapter illustrates ways in which the foundational domains of cognition are functioning from the earliest months. In contrast to traditional theories, current cognitive developmental psychology does not characterize the newborn as incapable of distinguishing self from other, incapable of forming representations and incapable of retaining memories. Rather, newborns are characterized as active learners, equipped with certain innate expectations which, although quite primitive, enable them to benefit hugely from experience. Experience of the physical and social worlds allows infants to enrich and revise these initial expectations, and even to replace them with new understandings. A number of potentially innate or very early-developing abilities are outlined in this section. These abilities include imitation, the perception of contingency, attending to people, assuming physical principles such as solidity and continuity, and expecting words to refer to commonalities among objects. Three learning mechanisms are also discussed: (1) the absorption of statistical regularities from the environment, as in conceptual learning and perceptual tuning to language; (2) making relational mappings, as in mapping the actions of other people onto the actions of one's own body, or mapping the responses of another person to one's own emotional states; and (3) "explanation-based" learning, comprising the detection of causal regularities in environmental information and the seeking of explanations for them. As we will see, these themes concerning innate or core principles of knowledge and likely mechanisms of learning (perceptual, motor/action-based, and cognitive/reflective) recur in many later chapters as well.

CHAPTER ONE

Imitation as a Mechanism of Social Cognition: Origins of Empathy, Theory of Mind, and the Representation of Action

Andrew N. Meltzoff

There is a kinship between the philosophical problem of "other minds" and the psychological problem of imitation. Philosophers are struck by the fact that people experience their own mental states differently than they register mental states in others. We experience our own internal thoughts, plans, and feelings but do not see ourselves from the outside. We perceive visual and auditory signals emanating from others, but do not directly experience their feelings. "Only connect!" (E. M. Forster), but how can we connect when we know each other in such incommensurate ways?

For developmental scientists and neuroscientists, imitation poses the other 'minds' problem in action. Infants can see an adult's face, but cannot see their own faces. They can feel their own face move, but have no access to the feeling of movement in others. How can infants connect the seen movements of others with acts of their own they only feel themselves make?

For the newborn, "only connect" is a matter of life and death. Which entities out there are conspecifics and what is the lingua franca of connectivity? What is the common code between self and other?

Classical theories of human development from Freud and Piaget to Skinner all agree on one axiom. Newborn infants have no inkling of the similarity between self and other.

I thank Keith Moore, Alison Gopnik, Patricia Kuhl, Jean Decety, and Rechele Brooks for insightful discussions on the topics raised here. I owe a special gratitude to Rechele for turning my attention to infant gaze-following. Preparation of this chapter was supported by a grant from NIH (HD-22514) and by funding from the Talaris Research Institute to the Center for Mind, Brain, and Learning.

Correspondence concerning this chapter should be addressed to Andrew N. Meltzoff, Center for Mind, Brain, and Learning, Box 357920, University of Washington, Seattle, WA 98195. Email: Meltzoff@u.washington.edu; Fax: 206-221-6475.

A primary task of cognitive development is to build a connection to others, causing the child to realize they are "one of us" and share desires, intentions, and emotions with other humans. The progression is from social isolate to social partner.

New empirical work has shaken this classic view to its foundations. It suggests that evolution provides the newborn with a grasp that others are "like me" and an innate propensity to imitate them. This innate foundation in turn provides an engine and mechanism for the growth of social cognition. It has bidirectional developmental effects. As infants' knowledge of themselves expands, they use this new psychological structure as a framework for interpreting others. Reciprocally, novel acts of others change the infant's mind and brain because the self is modeled on others right from birth. The result is a child who discovers facets of other minds through analogy with their own mind and who simultaneously discovers powers and possibilities of the self through observing others.

This chapter will link the imitative nature of the newborn and the developing theory of mind of the toddler. *The developmental hypothesis is that Nature's solution to the imitation problem gives babies the tools they need to crack the problem of other minds.* Imitative experience with other people serves as a "discovery mechanism" for social cognition, engendering interpersonal understanding that outstrips the innate givens and leads to empathy, perspective-taking, and theory of mind. Moreover, there are intriguing parallels between young children's growing cognition about people and their understanding about inanimate things. The focus of this chapter is social cognition, but as we shall see, the lessons apply much more broadly to general theories of developmental psychology (see also Gopnik, Meltzoff, & Kuhl, 1999b; Meltzoff & Moore, 1998b).

Classical Views of Newborns

On classical views of human development, the newborn is cut off from others. Freud and his followers proposed a distinction between a physical and psychological birth. When the baby is born there is a physical birth but not yet a birth of the mind (Freud, 1911; Mahler, Pine, & Bergman, 1975). The baby is like an unhatched chick within an eggshell, incapable of interacting as a social being because a "barrier" leaves the newborn cut off from external reality. Freud's powerful metaphor for the newborn – which influenced generations of psychoanalysts – is as follows:

> A neat example of a psychical system shut off from the stimuli of the external world. . . . is afforded by a bird's egg with its food supply enclosed in its shell; for it, the care provided by its mother is limited to the provision of warmth. (Freud, 1911, p. 220)

Piaget's newborn is similar, although Piaget reaches for a philosophical rather than ornithological metaphor. Piaget (1952c, 1954) claimed the baby is "solipsistic." The neonate has only a few reflexes to work with (e.g. sucking, grasping), and other people are registered only to the extent that they can be assimilated to these action schemes. The baby only knows his or her own actions. The child battles its way out of solipsism by 18 months. This is a very long road to understanding other people:

> During the earliest stages the child perceives things like a solipsist . . . This primitive rela-
> tion between subject and object is a relation of undifferentiation . . . when no distinction is
> made between the self and the non-self. (Piaget, 1954, p. 355)

Skinner (1953), an animal behaviorist, gave his blank-slate infant even less to work
with. One cannot really quote from Skinner about how children crack the puzzle of
social cognition, because, in a sense, he does not think they ever do. Even adults are
conceptualized as reacting to behaviors but not knowing the minds of their interactive
partners. Human beings have exquisite contingency detectors and that is all there is. To
use Skinner's phrase, social cognition is largely a "matter of consequences" (Skinner,
1983).

Two Types of Nativism

Empirical work over the past 25 years revealed a much richer innate state than
Freud, Piaget, and Skinner had posited. The nativists won the battle over the newborn's
mind and this applies both to infants' understanding of people (Gergely, ch. 2, and
Wellman, ch. 8, this volume) and things (Baillargeon, ch. 3 this volume). But two
distinct schools of nativism have emerged and the distinction is especially pronounced regarding social cognition. One view, "starting-state nativism," argues that
radical conceptual revision begins at birth (e.g., Gopnik & Meltzoff, 1997; Meltzoff &
Moore, 1998b). The other, "final-state nativism," argues that the initial state is equivalent to the final state. As a final-state nativist, Fodor believes that the adult theory of mind
is innate:

> Here is what I would have done if I had been faced with this problem in designing Homo
> sapiens. I would have made a knowledge of commonsense Homo sapiens psychology innate;
> that way nobody would have to spend time learning it . . . The empirical evidence that God
> did it the way I would have isn't, in fact, unimpressive . . . (Fodor, 1987, p. 132)

Fodor thinks the newborn innately posses the mature theory of mind. Why spend time
learning it? Spelke is also a final-state nativist, chiefly concerning infants' reasoning about
physical objects (e.g., Spelke, Breinlinger, Macomber, & Jacobson, 1992). She argues that
infants have the same core knowledge as adults and that age-related behavioral change is
due to biological maturation and the lifting of performance constraints which block
infants from expressing their true knowledge.

In the starting-state view, infants have innate knowledge and are endowed with
tools for constructing an adult-like theory – but the newborn does not innately
possess the adult theory. Evolution has provided the newborn with powerful discovery
procedures for developing adult cognition, but the final state is not specified at birth
or achieved through constraint removal. The view is not standard Piaget, because
the innate toolkit is wholly different, with far-reaching implications for the trajectory of
development.

Jump-Starting Theory of Mind

If the infant is not born with the adult model of mind, how do they come to it? Skinnerian blank slates, Freudian isolated eggs, and Piagetian solipsism won't get us from the newborn to the adult, because there is not enough innate structure to make good use of the experience received in social interaction.

Starting-state nativism proposes that three factors give human infants a jump-start on developing a theory of mind.

(a) *Innate equipment.* Newborns detect equivalences between observed and executed acts. When newborns see adult biological motion, including hand and face movements, these acts are mapped onto the infant's body movements. This mapping is manifest by newborn imitation. Newborn imitation suggests an innate common coding of human acts whether these body transformations are performed by self or observed in other (Meltzoff & Moore, 1997; Meltzoff & Prinz, 2002).

(b) *First-person experience.* Through everyday experience infants map the relation between their own bodily states and mental experiences. For example, there is an intimate relation between "striving to achieve a goal" and the concomitant facial expression of concentration and effortful bodily acts. Infants experience their own unfulfilled desires and their own matching facial/postural/vocal reactions. They experience their own inner feelings and outward facial expressions and construct a detailed bidirectional map linking mental experiences and behavior. In other words, they learn quite a bit about themselves in everyday life.

(c) *Inference to others.* When infants see others acting in a way that is similar to how they have acted in the past, acting "like me," infants project that others have the mental experience that is concomitant with those behavioral states themselves. This gives infants a window into understanding others before spoken language can be used.

Infants would not need the adult theory of mind preloaded. Infants could infer the internal states of others through an analogy to the self. This is not Fodorian nativism – newborns do not possess the adult theory. But they use special neural-cognitive machinery, coupled with experience with their own acts, to structure their interpretations of others. Infants' understanding of their own internal states and bodily acts, coupled with their innate grasp that others are "like me," kick starts their understanding of other minds. The remainder of this chapter grounds this general argument in new empirical work from infancy and cognitive neuroscience.

Facial Imitation: The Representation of Human Actions

Early imitation suggests that infants can detect the equivalences between self and other. Of course, the idea that infants have a rapport with other people is not a new one. It is expressed in Trevarthen's (1980) idea of "primary intersubjectivity" and extended by Stern (1985), Bruner (1983), Hobson (1989), and Jaffee, Beebe, Feldstein, Crown, & Jasnow (2001). However, these authors see the origins of intersubjectivity in the timing of infant-adult turn-taking and gestural "dances." Timing is important, but it is not everything: There seems no clear reason why temporal contingencies, by themselves, should lead infants to think of other people as like themselves in deep ways. Other entities can move as a consequence of my movements and still not be like me in any fundamental way. Similarly, some theorists believe that infants are innately endowed with a special visual attentiveness to the human face (Johnson & Morton, 1991). However, facial pattern detectors, in themselves, also do not provide a link between the self and the other. The adult face may be a particularly arresting visual entity, but why should infants think of this visual entity as someone connected to themselves?

Starting-state nativists seek the origins of social cognition in the representation of human acts. We propose that *infants' connection to others emerges from the fact that the bodily movement patterns they see others perform are coded as like the ones they themselves perform.* Twenty-five years of research on imitation has revealed quite a bit about the nature of this innate interpersonal mapping. The power of what has been discovered about the innate state cannot be grasped without a synopsis of the data, to which we now turn.

Nature and scope of early imitation

Meltzoff and Moore found that 12- to 21-day-old infants imitated tongue protrusion, mouth opening, lip protrusion, and hand movements. Infants responded differentially to two types of lip movements (mouth opening vs. lip protrusion) and two types of protrusion actions (lip protrusion vs. tongue protrusion). More recent research demonstrated that infants differentiated two different types of tongue protrusions from one another, straight tongue protrusion versus tongue out to the side of the mouth (Meltzoff & Moore, 1994, 1997). Thus the response was quite specific; it was not a global or a general arousal reaction.

There is also evidence that early matching is not simply restricted to immediate mimicry. In one study a pacifier was put in infants' mouths as they watched the display so that they could only observe the adult demonstration but not duplicate the gestures. After the infant observed the display, the adult assumed a passive face pose and only then removed the pacifier. After the pacifier was removed, the infants imitated the earlier displays (Meltzoff & Moore, 1977). Other research documents imitation after the memory delay is as long as one day. Six-week-old infants came in on one day, observed the gestures, and went home. They then returned the next day and were presented with the experimenter sitting motionless with a passive face. Infants successfully imitate based on their remembrance of things past (Meltzoff & Moore, 1994). If yesterday's adult had shown mouth opening, the infants initiated that gesture; if the adult had shown tongue protrusion, infants greeted him with that gesture.

Research also reveals that the response is not rigidly fixed or stereotypic. Infants correct their imitative attempts so that they more and more closely converge on the model demonstrated. For example, if the adult shows a novel gesture such as tongue-protrusion-to-the-side-of-the-mouth, infants will begin with ordinary tongue protrusions. They use the proprioceptive feedback from their own actions as the basis for guiding their response to the target (Meltzoff & Moore, 1994). Also, there was a revealing error that occurred significantly more often to the tongue-to-the-side display than any control gestures. Infants poked out their tongues and simultaneously turned their heads to the side (Meltzoff & Moore, 1997). Although the literal movements were very different, the goals are similar. Tongue protrusion + head turn was not the work of a mindless reflex. It was a creative error.

The subjects in the previous studies were 2 to 6 weeks old. At first glance this seems young enough to justify claims about an innate capacity. But perhaps neonates had been conditioned to imitate during the first weeks of life. Perhaps imitation was dependent upon earlier mother–infant interaction. To resolve the point, Meltzoff and Moore (1983) tested 40 newborns in a hospital setting. The average age of the sample was 32 hours old. The youngest infant was only 42 minutes old. The results showed that the newborns imitated both of the gestures shown to them, mouth opening and tongue protrusion. These findings were subsequently replicated using different gestures in newborns under 72 hours old (Meltzoff & Moore, 1989). Nativist claims are, of course, commonplace in the literature, but there are few cognitive capacities that have actually been demonstrated to be present at birth. You can't get much younger than 42 minutes old. These data demonstrate that a primitive capacity to imitate is part of the normal child's biological endowment.

Beyond arousal or an automatic sign-released response

Although early imitation was initially considered a surprise, the effect has now been replicated and extended in more than 25 different studies from 13 independent labs, including those from the US, England, Canada, France, Switzerland, Sweden, Israel, Greece, Japan, and even in rural Nepal (for literature reviews see Meltzoff & Moore, 1994, 1997). This research effort has uncovered several interesting characteristics of early imitation (table 1.1). Collectively, these characteristics contradict attempts to explain the imitative effects as (a) arousal or (b) a sign-released response. They show that – no matter how difficult for theory – we must abandon the classical theories of neonatal "solipsism."

Three well-replicated findings disprove the arousal interpretation.

(a) Proponents of arousal assume that a tongue protrusion display has a special arousal property. They predict it should be the only gesture imitated. The empirical findings worldwide demonstrate that a range of gestures can be imitated, including both facial and manual gestures, which directly counters the arousal interpretation (see table 1.1, point 1).
(b) Infants imitate static poses. This contradicts the notion that the visual movement alone is stirring up the response through arousal (table 1.1, point 2).
(c) Infants can imitate from memory in the absence of the (purportedly) arousing stimulus. No arousal is possible in this case because the infant is watching a passive face (table 1.1, point 3).[1]

Table 1.1   Characteristics of early imitation

Evidence that early imitation is not due to arousal

1. Infants imitate a range of acts, not just tongue protrusion
    Field, Goldstein, Vaga-Lahr, & Porter, 1986; Field et al., 1983; Field, Woodson, Greenberg, & Cohen, 1982; Fontaine, 1984; Heimann et al., 1989; Heimann & Schaller, 1985; Kugiumutzakis, 1985; Maratos, 1982; Meltzoff & Moore, 1977, 1989, 1994; Vinter, 1986
2. Nonmoving gestures can be imitated
    Field et al., 1986; Field et al., 1983; Field et al., 1982; Meltzoff & Moore, 1992
3. Perceptually absent stimuli are imitated
    Fontaine, 1984; Heimann et al., 1989; Heimann & Schaller, 1985; Legerstee, 1991; Meltzoff & Moore, 1989, 1992, 1994

Evidence that early imitation is not an automatically triggered, released response

4. Novel and unfamiliar acts can be imitated
    Fontaine, 1984; Meltzoff & Moore, 1994, 1997
5. Infants make errors on movements, but accurately recruit correct body part
    Kugiumutzakis, 1985; Meltzoff & Moore, 1983, 1994, 1997
6. Infants correct their imitative efforts
    Kugiumutzakis, 1985; Maratos, 1982; Meltzoff & Moore, 1994, 1997
7. Infants imitate from memory in the absence of the trigger stimulus
    Fontaine, 1984; Heimann et al., 1989; Heimann & Schaller, 1985; Legerstee, 1991; Meltzoff & Moore, 1989, 1992, 1994

Three replicated sets of findings are incompatible with the releaser interpretation:

(a) Infants imitate novel gestures and commit creative errors, demonstrating remarkable flexibility and lack of automaticity (table 1.1, points 4 and 5).
(b) Infants correct their responses to more faithfully match the model, thus showing feedback modulation, not the triggering of a fixed reaction (table 1.1, point 6).
(c) Infants can imitate from memory. The trigger for the (purported) reflex is nonexistent. It makes no sense to say that yesterday's stimulus triggered today's reflex after a 24-hour pause (table 1.1, point 7).

For most developmentalists interested in imitation, the key for the future lies in exploring the neural and psychological mechanisms underlying this early matching behavior and the role it serves in the infant's *Umwelt*. Excellent progress has been made.

Psychological mechanism

Meltzoff and Moore suggested that imitation is based on infants' capacity to register equivalences between the body transformations they see performed by other people and the body transformations they only feel themselves make. On this account, facial imitation involves crossmodal matching. Infants can, at some primitive level, recognize an equivalence between the acts they see others do and the acts they do themselves. There appears to be a very primitive and foundational "body scheme" that allows the infant to unify the seen acts of others and their own felt acts into one common framework. The infant's own facial gestures are invisible to them, but they are monitored by proprioception. Conversely, the adult's acts are not felt by proprioception but they can be seen. Infants can link observation and execution through a common "supramodal" coding of human acts. This is why they can correct their imitative movements. It is why they sometimes make interesting errors. And it is why they can imitate from memory: infants store a representation of the adult's act and it is the target against which they compare their own acts. Imitation is intentional, goal-directed activity. A detailed description of the metric infants use for establishing the crossmodal "common framework" between self and other is provided elsewhere (Meltzoff & Moore, 1997).

Brain bases

Recently, the work on neonatal imitation has been buttressed by neuroscience research, which has uncovered remarkably compatible findings. The new neuroscience research shows that a certain set of brain regions (in frontal and posterior parietal lobes) is activated both by observing and by performing motor movements, the so-called "mirror system" (Decety, 2002 ; Decety et al., 1997; Decety & Grèzes, 1999; Fadiga et al., 1995; Meltzoff & Decety, 2003; Rizzolatti et al., 1996). Thus, there are two lines of research documenting a close coupling between seeing and doing acts: (a) modern neuroscience showing that specific neural regions subserve both observation and execution of movements, and (b) developmental research showing that newborns execute certain motor acts based on observation. Taken together, these converging lines of research validate the idea that imitation is fundmental to humans' mental makeup (for neuroimaging studies on adult imitation making a similar point, see: Chaminade, Meltzoff, & Decety, 2002; Decety, Chaminade, Grèzes & Meltzoff, 2002; Iacoboni, Woods, Brass, Bekkering, Mazziotta, & Rizzolatti, 1999)

People as Individuals: Imitation and Numerical Identity

There are some basic aspects of social cognition that neonates don't grasp. One of their most surprising immaturities concerns the understanding of the *identity* of people. Keeping track of the identity of individuals is fundamental to adult social cognition. In *Star Trek*, the Borg are not individuals but a collective; but for human mortals, social relationships are not an oceanic feeling of connectedness to an undifferentiated universe of others. Adult social cognition arises from one's relation to specific others, each valued for their individuality. There is evidence showing that infants are very concerned about tracking the identity of individual people across changes in time and space.

Identity is most often discussed in relation to inanimate objects (e.g., Meltzoff & Moore, 1998b; Spelke, Kestenbaum, Simons, & Wein, 1995; Xu & Carey, 1996).

However, the same issue arises with regard to people. Here it is crucial to distinguish two meanings of "sameness" or "identity." One meaning of "the same" concerns an entity being the self-same individual over different encounters in space and time. This is often called "numerical identity," because there is one object that meets the definition of "this same object." A different meaning concerns an object's appearances or features. This is often referred to as "qualitative" or "featural identity." Identical twins differ in numerical identity but are featurally identical. My soft-drink can and yours can be featurally indistinguishable; yet they are different individuals. Investigations of object permanence are typically concerned with numerical identity – "Is this the self-same object again?" (Meltzoff & Moore, 1998b; Moore & Meltzoff, 1999); investigations of categorization are chiefly concerned with qualitative identity – "Is this exemplar the same kind as the other?" (Quinn, ch. 4 this volume).

Using imitation to keep track of people

Although the role of qualitative identity in social cognition has long been recognized (e.g., infants' ability to categorize happy vs. angry faces or male vs. female faces – and their social responses to those general categories), the importance of numerical identity to social cognition has been underappreciated. Attachment and romantic love (not to mention custodianship of bank accounts) depend on distinguishing numerical versus qualitative person identity. How does an infant individuate one person from another and re-identify a person as the "same one" again after a break in perceptual contact – as someone with whom I have this relationship? This can be posed as a baby-sized problem.

In one study, we presented 6-week-old infants with people who were coming and going in front of them, as would happen in real-world interaction. The mother appeared and showed one gesture (say, mouth opening). Then she exited and was replaced by a stranger who showed a different gesture (say, tongue protrusion). The experiment required that infants keep track of the two different people and their gestures (Meltzoff & Moore, 1992).

When infants visually tracked these exchanges they imitated each person without difficulty. But we also discovered an interesting error. If the mother and stranger surreptitiously changed places without the infant visually tracking the movements, infants did not differentially imitate the two actors. Instead, infants stared at the new person . . . paused (often with wrinkled brow) . . . and then intently produced the *previous* person's gesture. It appeared that in the absence of clear spatiotemporal evidence of twoness (visual tracking of the entrances and exits), infants were faced with an ambiguity: is it the same person with a different appearance, or a new person in the old place?

What can a young infant do to resolve this identity confusion? I believe that when infants are ambiguous about the identity of a person they see (e.g., because of a break in spatiotemporal contact), they are motivated to test whether this person *acts* in a certain way. For young infants, body-actions and expressive behavior of people are identifiers of who people are. Infants use these *functional* criteria in addition to spatiotemporal and featural criteria for determining numerical identity.

I think infants deployed imitative reactions to sort out their questions about the identity of the person they saw. That is why they stared at the new person and did the old person's signature gesture. It is their way of asking: "Are you the same person I saw before? Are you the one who does *x*?" Other studies on imitation and identity reinforce this point (Meltzoff & Moore, 1994, 1995, 1998b). Distinctive behavior and interactive games serve as markers of people's identity. Identity questions motivate the imitative re-enactment and imitation of people's acts.

People as Perceivers: Infant Gaze-following

We do not live in a world solely of people. We are surrounded by objects and many of our thoughts and wants are directed toward these objects. Neonates enjoy something like a conceptual Garden of Eden – populated by self and others paying attention to and imitating each other. But this Eden soon ends. The child becomes aware that their caretakers sometimes attend to third parties, including inanimate objects, despite the infant's own charming bids for attention.

In the adult psychological framework, head and eye movements have special significance. We realize that others direct their attention toward objects, picking up information about them from afar, despite the spatial gap between attender and target. We ascribe intentionality to the gazer who turns his head. Do infants understand this body movement in the same way? Or are head turns interpreted as nothing more than physical motions (even biological movements) with no notion that they are *directed toward* the external object – no referential value? If they start off meaningless, how do simple bodily movements come to gain such value?

Research has been aimed at understanding these issues. The data demonstrate that young infants follow another's gaze, but there is debate about the mechanism mediating this behavior (Baron-Cohen, 1995; Baldwin & Moses, 1994; Bruner, 1999; Butterworth, 1991; Moore, 1999; Moore & Dunham, 1995; Scaife & Bruner, 1975). Proponents of a conservative stance argue that infant gaze-following is based on their being attracted to the spatial hemi-field toward which the adult's head is moving. A young infant visually tracks the adult's head rotation and thereby swings its own head to the correct half of space without any notion of the adult's "attention to an object" (e.g., Butterworth & Cochran, 1980; Butterworth & Jarrett, 1991; Moore & Corkum, 1994). On this view, infants do not really process the adult as a perceiver/looker, but simply process the salient movement of the head regardless of what the genuine organs of attention – the eyes – are doing (Corkum & Moore, 1995; Farroni, Johnson, Brockbank, & Simion, 2000; Moore & Corkum, 1998).

Interpreting gaze-following

We recently focused on the question of whether infants understand the "object directedness" or referential value of adult attentive movements (Brooks & Meltzoff, 2002). In the study, two identical objects were used, and the adult turned in silence with no verbal or emotional cues. The infants were 12, 14, and 18 months of age. The interesting manipulation was that the adult turned to the target object with *eyes open* for one group and with *eyes closed* for the other group. In each case infants interacted contingently with the adult before the trial. If infants relied on gross head motions (Butterworth & Jarret, 1991), they should turn regardless of whether the adult's eyes were open or closed, because the head movement was identical. If they relied on an abstract rule to look in the same direction as a "contingent interactant" (Johnson, Slaughter, & Carey, 1998), they should also look whether the adult's eyes were open or closed, because the adult's interactive behavior was identical in both groups.

The findings showed that the infants turned selectively – they looked significantly more often toward the target object when the adult turned toward it with eyes open than eyes closed. The results were significant at each age group taken alone. One interpretation is that as early as 12 months infants begin to realize that the same person may either be looking/attending or not, depending on the status of his or her perceptual systems.

Closing one's eyes is a body movement performed by the adult. Infants have a good deal of experience with closing their own eyes and thereby cutting off their own visual perception. Perhaps this gives them leverage for understanding this act in others. Eye closure is only one way that a person's view can be blocked. Inanimate obstacles can also block one's view. Brooks and Meltzoff (2002) ran another experiment, duplicating all aspects of the first, but using a headband and a blindfold. When the adult turns to look at a target with the headband on, she is attending to it; when she turns with a blindfold on, she cannot be attending to it. The results showed that the 14- and 18-month-olds turned selectively to the appropriate target object only in the headband case. Interestingly, the 12-month-olds turned to look at the target even when the adult wore a blindfold that blocked her eyes. They did not seem to interpret the blindfold in the same way as eye closure. One interpretation is that infants may understand eye closure earlier (12 months) than blockage by an inanimate screen (14 months) in part because of experience with their own eyes.

In fact, Brooks and I noticed two responses that have not been systematically investigated in the joint visual attention literature. We think that these responses provide critical clues about the mechanism underlying gaze-following. First, we discovered that infants pointed to the target object significantly more often if the adult looked at it with open versus closed eyes. This supports the idea that it was not simply adult head movements dragging the child's head movements. The infant's response involved a different motor movement than the adults'. The goal was the same, making reference to an object, but the means was different.

Second, we selected those trials with accurate looking and measured the duration of infants' visual examination of the target object. Infants visually inspected the object longer when they were guided there by the adult with open eyes versus closed eyes. Of course the object, in itself, is the same toy in both cases. The physical object has not changed, but the infant's attention to it significantly changes. We propose that the object takes on special valence because it is the object-of-someone-else's-attention. Infants visually inspect the object longer when it is referenced by another attender.

Taken together, the pointing and visual examination data suggest that infants are not simply observing meaningless motions. Infants are not simply coding physical motions, but are making a psychological attribution to the gazer. The findings do not prove that infants ascribe to the adult an "internal experience of attending," but they certainly move beyond the most conservative stances about infant gaze-following. At minimum, they suggest that infants in the second year represent the "object-directedness" of adult gaze. They see the head movements as directed toward the external world and not as mere bodily movements without significance (see also Brooks, 1999; Brooks & Meltzoff, 2002; Butler, Caron, & Brooks, 2000; Johnson, 2000; Wellman & Phillips, 2001; Woodward, Sommerville, & Guajardo, 2001). In the conclusions of this chapter, we will propose a theory of how infants' own experience with cutting off and re-accessing the visual world through their own eye opening-closing could contribute to their understanding of the role of eyes in the visual perception of others.

People as Intenders: Understanding Goals of Acts

In the mature adult social cognition, other people not only act "like me," and have perceptual experiences "like me," they also enjoy a palette of other mental states, including beliefs, emotions, and intentions (Goldman, 1993, 2001; Searle, 1983; Stich, 1983). Intentions are particularly interesting for developmentalists. Indeed, a first question is whether infants have any inkling of the distinction between the actions someone performs and their intention in performing these actions. This is not an easy conceptual distinction. Wittgenstein (1953) makes it clear with a blunt question: "What is left over if I subtract the fact that my arm goes up from the fact that I raise my arm?" Answer: intention.

As Wittgenstein's example shows, intentions are not reducible to bodily movements. Intentions are mental states and bodily movements are physical events in the world. The two have an intimate relation because intentions underlie and cause bodily movements, and reciprocally, one can read intentions from body movements. But the intentions themselves are not directly seen, heard, tasted, or smelled. The developmental problem is clear and irresistible: Is there any evidence that infants read below the surface behavior and understand the intentions that lie behind them? How do they come to this interpretation of bodily acts?

To address these questions, it is not enough to explore whether young children act intentionally themselves; we need to investigate whether they understand the intentions of others. There is excellent research on this topic using verbal tests with 3- and 4-year-old children (Zelazo, Astington, & Olson, 1999; Flavell, 1999; Malle, Moses, & Baldwin, 2001; Moses, 1993; Taylor, 1996). Many investigators are now examining the origins of intention-reading using nonverbal techniques.

Reading people's goals

The "behavioral re-enactment procedure" was designed to provide a nonverbal technique for exploring intention-reading (Meltzoff, 1995a). The procedure capitalizes on children's natural tendency to re-enact or imitate, but uses it in a more abstract way to investigate whether infants can read below the literal surface behavior to something like the goal or intention of the actor.

The experimental procedure involves showing infants an unsuccessful act. For example, the adult accidentally under- or overshoots his target, or he tries to pull apart a dumb-bell-shaped toy but his hand slips off the ends and he is unsuccessful. Thus the goal-state is not achieved. To an adult, it is easy to read the actor's intentions although he never fulfills them. The experimental question is whether children read through the literal body movements to the underlying goal or intention of the act. The measure of how they interpreted the event is what they choose to re-enact, in particular whether they choose to produce the intended act despite the fact that it was never present to the senses. In a sense, the "correct answer" is to not copy the literal movement, but the intended act that remains unfulfilled and invisible.

Meltzoff (1995a) showed 18-month-old infants an unsuccessful act, a failed effort. The study compared infants' tendency to perform the full target act in several situations: (a) after they saw the full-target act demonstrated, (b) after they saw the unsuccessful attempt to perform the act, and (c) after it was neither shown nor attempted. The results showed that 18-month-olds can infer the unseen goals implied by unsuccessful attempts. Infants who saw the unsuccessful attempt and infants who saw the full-target act both produced target acts at a significantly higher rate than controls. Infants seemed to read through the surface behavior to the underlying goals or intentions of the actor. Evidently, toddlers can understand our goals even if we fail to fulfill them.

At what age does this understanding of others emerge? The results suggest that it develops between 9 and 15 months of age. I have found that 15-month-olds behaved much like the 18-month-olds in the original 1995 study, but 9-month-olds did not respond above baseline levels to the failed-attempt demonstrations (Meltzoff, 1999). Importantly, control conditions indicated that 9-month-olds succeeded if the adult demonstrated successful acts. Thus, the 9-month-olds imitated visible acts on objects, but gave no evidence of inferring intentions beyond the visible behavior itself. This finding of a developmental change in infants' understanding of others' goals and intentions has been documented in other studies as well (Bellagamba & Tomasello, 1999; Wellman & Phillips, 2001; Woodward et al., 2001). So there is converging evidence for an important developmental change between 9 and 15 months.

If infants can pick up the underlying goal or intention of the human act, they should be able to achieve the act using a variety of means. This was tested in a study of 18-month-olds using a dumb-bell-shaped object that was too big for the infants' hands. The adult grasped the ends of the dumb-bell and attempted to yank it apart, but his hands slid off so he was unsuccessful in carrying out his intentions. The dumb-bell was then presented to the child. Interestingly, the infants did not attempt to imitate the surface behavior of the adult. Instead they used novel ways to struggle to get the gigantic toy apart. They might put one end of the dumb-bell between their knees and use both hands to pull it upwards, or put their hands on inside faces of the cubes and push outwards, and so on. They used different means than the experimenter, but toward the same end. This fits with Meltzoff's (1995a) hypothesis that infants had inferred the goal of the act, clearly differentiating it from the literal surface behavior that was observed.

Other techniques assessing goal-reading in infants.   The foregoing analysis focuses on the behavioral re-enactment procedure, but for completeness, it is worth noting that this is not the only technique used in the preverbal period. Other researchers have used the visual habituation procedure to investigate infants' understanding of goal-directed actions (e.g., Gergely, ch. 2 this volume; Woodward et al., 2001; Wellman, ch. 8 this volume). The habituation procedure differs from the behavioral re-enactment procedure in a couple of interesting ways. First, it does not measure infant re-creations of events in *action*; it tests whether they choose to *look* longer at one display or another (the former is like an essay exam and the latter like a multiple choice). Second, the habituation procedure does not ask precisely the same questions as the behavioral re-enactment approach. For example, Woodward (1998, 1999) showed infants an adult grasping an object that appeared in either of two locations. The question was whether infants treated the object as the "goal of the reach." Note that the "goal" of the reach is the *seen* physical object (a toy ball or bear). This differs from the re-enactment procedure in which the goal is an *unseen* act the adult was "trying" to achieve but did not. In the behavioral re-enactment procedure the goal is not visible and has to be inferred; in Woodward's habituation technique, the goal object is visible to the infant.

Similarly, Tomasello investigated goal-reading, and also used an approach that is distinct from the behavioral re-enactment procedure (Tomasello & Barton, 1994; Tomasello, 1999). He showed infants well-formed successful acts versus ill-formed accidental-looking acts. The results showed that infants choose to imitate the former. Tomasello interpreted the data as showing that intentionality has a special valence for infants; they prefer to imitate intentional actions. A more conservative reading might be that infants preferentially imitate well-formed acts just because they are cleaner motor sequences – less messy and jerky than the "accidental" ones. If so, infants could preferentially imitate without understanding the intentionality behind these acts. Also note that in Tomasello's paradigm infants imitate what they see, and the question is which of two acts they see they prefer to copy. Again, the special characteristic of the re-enactment procedure is that the goal was never displayed; the intended goal of the actor had to be inferred by infants and recreated by them, although it was never presented to the senses.

These methodological and theoretical differences are actually productive for the field because they provide independent tests of infants' understanding using a variety of techniques. We can be more confident that infants are beginning to understand goals and intentions before language, inasmuch as the results from a variety of paradigms point in this direction. Moreover, the various procedures all point to an important developmental change in infants' reading of goals and intentions between about 9 and 15 months of age.

The goals of people: the motions of inanimate objects

Are there constraints on the types of entities that are interpreted to act in a goal-directed, intentional fashion? In the adult framework, only certain types of objects are ascribed intention. Chairs rock, and boulders roll, but their motions are not seen as intentional. Most prototypically, human acts are the types of movement patterns that are seen as caused by intentions. (Animals and computers present more borderline cases.) What do infants think?

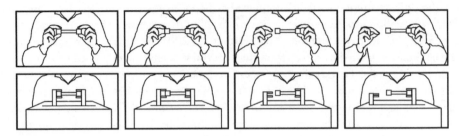

Figure 1.1   Human demonstrator (*top panel*) and inanimate device performing the movements (*bottom panel*) (from Meltzoff, 1995a)

To begin to examine this, Meltzoff (1995a) tested how 18-month-olds responded to a mechanical device that mimicked the same movements as the actor in the failed-attempt paradigm. An inanimate device was constructed that had poles for arms and mechanical pincers for hands. It did not look human but it could move very similarly to the human (figure 1.1, bottom panel). For the test, the pincers "grasped" the dumbbell at the two ends just as the human hands did. One mechanical arm was then moved outwards, just as in the human case, and its pincer slipped off the end of the dumbbell just as the human hand did. The movement patterns of machine and man were closely matched in terms of a purely spatiotemporal description of movements in space.

The results showed that infants did not attribute a goal or intention to the movements of the inanimate device. Although they were not frightened by the device and looked at it as long as at the human display, they simply did not see the sequence of actions as implying a goal. Infants were no more (or less) likely to pull apart the toy after seeing the failed attempt of the inanimate device than in baseline conditions when they saw nothing.

Another study pursued this point. In this study the inanimate device succeeded. The inanimate device held the dumb-bell from the two ends and successfully pulled it apart. When infants were given the dumb-bell, they too pulled it apart. It thus appears that infants can pick up certain information from the inanimate device (they pull it apart after seeing the device do so), but they cannot pick up other information (concerning failed attempts).

I think 18-month-olds interpret the person's actions within a psychological framework that differentiates between the surface behavior of people and a deeper level involving goals and intentions. When they see a person's hands slip off the ends of the dumb-bell they infer what the adult was "trying" to do (which is different from what he did do). When they see the inanimate device slip off the end of the dumb-bell, they see it as mechanical slippage and sliding with no implications for purposiveness.

It is possible that displays can be constructed that fool infants, as they do adults. Is a computer intentional? (*Mine* seems to know about grant deadlines and sabotage.) We do not know the necessary and sufficient conditions for ascribing intentions to entities. There is research, however, indicating that in certain circumstances infants see purposiveness in the actions of pretend humans (stuffed animals and puppets, Johnson, 2000) and dynamic displays that may be ambiguous as to animacy (e.g., some researchers have used 2-D spots that leap and move spontaneously on a TV screen: Gergely, ch. 2 this volume; Gergely, Nádasdy, Csibra, & Bíró, 1995).[2] This does not run against the thesis suggested here, but underscores the need for research on boundary conditions. The inanimate 3-D object used by Meltzoff (1995a) gives a lower boundary (infants fail) and real people give an upper boundary (infants succeed). There is a lot of room in between for more empirical research (and of course the conception of animate-inanimate changes with development, see Gelman & Opfer, ch. 7 this volume).

Human acts versus mechanical motions

On the basis of these findings it is useful to introduce a distinction that will be picked up later in the chapter. We wish to distinguish between construing the behaviors of others in purely physical versus psychological terms. To help keep this distinction clear we call the former *motions* and the latter *human acts*. The behavior of another person can be described using either physics or psychology. We can say, "Alison's hand contacted the cup, the cup fell over and the tea splattered" or "Alison was trying to pick up the cup (and disaster struck, as usual)." Strict behaviorists stick to the former description precisely because they eschew appealing to invisible psychological states. By 18 months old, infants are no longer behaviorists, if they ever were so. They do not construe the behavior of others simply as, "hold the dumb-bell and then remove one hand quickly" but rather construe it as an effort at pulling. Moreover, the work with the inanimate device shows that infants have a differentiation in the kinds of attributions they make to people versus things. By 18 months of age children have begun to adopt a fundamental aspect of a mature folk psychology – persons are understood within a framework involving goals and intentions.

Origins of Social Cognition: Toward Developing a New Theory

The problem

The puzzle of social cognition stems from the fact that persons are more than physical objects. Enumerating a person's height, weight, and eye color, does not exhaust our description of that person. We have skipped over their psychological makeup. If a self-mobile, human-looking body was devoid of psychological characteristics it would not be a person at all, but a robot or, to use the philosopher's favorite, a zombie. A fundamental issue is how we come to know others as persons like ourselves. Each of us has the phenomenological experience that we are not alone in the world, not the unique bearer of psychological properties. We know that we perceive, feel, and intend, and we believe others have psychological states just like ours.

Philosophers seek to justify the inference that the observed moving mounds of flesh are animated by psychological states. They contemplate whether this is a fiction and assemble criteria for knowing whether it is or is not (e.g., Russell, 1948; Ryle, 1949; Strawson, 1959). Developmental psychologists ask different questions. We inquire how such a view takes hold (regardless of whether it is logically justified). Is it innately specified? Does the child's understanding of mental states transform with age and social experience?

The starting-state: the primacy of human acts

The thesis of this chapter is that infant imitation provides an innate foundation for social cognition. Imitation indicates that newborns, at some level of processing no matter how primitive, can map actions of other people onto actions of their own body. When infants imitate they are linking the visual appearance of other people to their own internal kinesthetic feelings. They connect the visible bodily actions of others and their own internal states. Human acts are especially relevant to infants because they look like the infant feels himself to be and because they are events infants can intend. When a human act is shown to a newborn, it may provide the first recognition experience. "Lo! Something familiar! That seen event is like this felt event."

According to the thesis presented here, the starting-state parsing of the world by newborns is distinct from that proposed in other theories. The salient distinction for newborns is not the one between "animate versus inanimate" or "self-propelled versus moved-by-a-seen force." I would argue, instead, that the most salient distinction for newborns is the cut between "human acts versus other events" or possibly "acts that I can intend versus other events."

Privileged understanding of people

Infants' construing certain movements in the environment in terms of human acts that can be imitated has cascading developmental effects. First, the world of material objects is then divisible into those entities that perform these acts (people) and those that do not (things). Second, having made the division in the external world, new meanings are possible. Because human acts are seen in others and performed by the self, the infant can grasp that the other is at some level "like me." The other acts like me and I can act like the other. The crossmodal knowledge of what it feels like to do the act that was seen provides a privileged access to people not afforded by things. Newborns bring it to their first interactions with people, and it provides an interpretive framework for understanding the meaning that lies behind the perceived movements.

Using the "like me" analogy to attribute mental states to others

That young infants can interpret the acts of others in terms of their own acts and experiences provides them with enormous leverage and an engine for development. For example, the infant knows that when it wants something it reaches out and grasps it. The infant experiences her own internal desires and the concomitant bodily move-ments (hand extension, finger movements, etc.). The experience of grasping to satisfy desires gives infants leverage for making sense of the grasping behavior of others. When the child sees another person reaching for an object, she sees the person extending his hand in the same way, complete with finger curlings. *Object-directed, grasping move-ments can be imbued with goal-directedness, because of the child's own experience with these acts.*

One reason that such experienced-based "projection to others" has not been ascribed to the youngest infants is that classical theories thought them incapable of mapping their own manual movements to those they see others perform. After all, the child's hand is smaller than the adult's, seen from a different perspective, and so on. (Once again, the self and other seem to be known in such different ways.) But the research on imitation has established that young infants in the first half-year of life imitate manual gestures, including hand opening and closing (Meltzoff & Moore, 1997; Vinter, 1986). The data prove they can detect the similarity between their own manual movements and those they see adults perform. Self and other are known via a common code. A basic "like me" analogy may explain Woodward et al.'s (2001) fascinating findings that the amount of goal-directed reaching experience infants have predicts whether they succeed on tests evaluating their understanding of the reaches of others.

A similar argument applies to the goal-directed "striving" and "try and try again" behavior used in Meltzoff's (1995a) studies based on the behavioral re-enactment proce-dure. Infants have goals and act intentionally. They have experienced their own failed plans and unfulfilled intentions. Indeed in the second half-year of life they are obsessed with the success and failure of their plans: They mark such self-failures with special labels ("uh-oh," "no," or as once recorded in a British subject, "oh bugger" – see Gopnik & Meltzoff, 1986). More strikingly, they actually experiment with failed efforts by repeat-ing the solution (and the failure) numerous times until it comes under voluntary control (Gopnik & Meltzoff, 1997; Gopnik, Meltzoff, & Kuhl, 1999b). During such episodes of testing plans and why they failed, infants often vary the means and "try and try again." When an infant sees another act in this same way, the infant's self-experience could suggest that there is a goal, plan, or intention beyond the surface behavior. Thus infants would come to read the adult's unsuccessful attempts, and the behavioral envelope in which they occur, as a pattern of "strivings," rather than ends in themselves.

Even understanding another's looking behavior could benefit from self-generated expe-rience – in this case, experience of oneself as a looker/perceiver. Infants in the first year of life can imitate head movements and eye-blinking (Meltzoff, 1988a; Meltzoff & Moore, 1989; Piaget, 1962a). As unlikely as it seems at first, these data indicate that infants can map between the head movements they see others perform and their own head move-ments, and between adults' eyelid closures and their own eye closures. Infants' subjective experiences gained from "turning in order to see" could be used to make sense of the head movements of others who are orienting toward an object. Moreover, the infant's experi-ence is that eye closure cuts off the infant's own perceptual access. If an infant can map the eye closures of others onto his own eye closures (something infants manifest in imitating blinking), these mappings may provide data for developing inferences about perception in others.

This also makes sense of the fact that young infants have more advanced understanding of eye-closure than obstacle-blocking (Brooks & Meltzoff, 2002). Certainly, 1-year-olds have had months of practice with voluntary looking away and eye-closing to cut off unwanted stimuli. This bodily act is well understood. However, it is only around this age that infants begin to play peek-a-boo and develop a facile manual search for occluded objects. Manual search for hidden things indicates an understanding of the relation between self, object, and occluder. Moreover, at about 12 to 14 months old infants first begin actively experimenting with this relation, as when they find and then repeatedly rehide objects from themselves, seemingly to master the problem (Moore & Meltzoff, 1999; Gopnik & Meltzoff, 1997; Gopnik, Meltzoff, & Kuhl, 1999b). One prediction is that intervention experience with occluders and the self could accelerate infants' understanding of blindfolds on other people.

Summary

Piaget (1952c) argued that the infant is born a "solipsist"; Fodor (1987) supposed that an innate theory of mind was hardwired into the human brain. Starting-state nativism offers a third perspective. It grants far more to the newborn than the first view, while stopping short of the second. My thesis is that a starting point for social cognition is that human acts are represented within a common code that applies to self as well as others. Newborns bring this representation of human acts to their very first interactions with people, and it provides an interpretive framework for understanding the behavior they see. Put succinctly, seeing others as "like me" is our birthright.

It has long been appealing to think that "like me" and the perception of self–other equivalences are vitally involved in adult social understanding. Empathy, role-taking, and all manner of putting yourself in someone else's shoes emotionally and cognitively seem to rest on the connection between self and other. The stumbling-block for classical theories was that the self–other equivalence was postulated to be late developing and therefore could not play a formative role. Nearly a quarter century of research on infant imitation stands this proposition on its head. It indicates that young infants can represent the acts of others and their own acts in commensurate terms. They can recognize crossmodal equivalences between the acts they see others perform and their own tactile-kinesthetic sense of self. *The recognition of self–other equivalences is the starting point for social cognition, not its culmination.*

Given this facile self–other mapping, input from social encounters is more interpretable than supposed by Freud, Skinner, and even the ingenious Mr. Piaget. Infants have a storehouse of knowledge on which to draw: They can use the self as a framework for understanding the subjectivity of others. We begin to "only connect" via a common code, a lingua franca, that does not depend on words. It is more fundamental than spoken language. This common code is the language of human acts.[3] The neuro-cognitive machinery of imitation lies at the origins of empathy and developing a theory of mind. Through understanding the acts of others, we come to know their souls.

Notes

1. Proponents of the arousal interpretation also argue that certain visual displays aside from tongue protrusion can elicit a tonguing response, and therefore that all imitation is due to arousal. But this argument is logically flawed. Suppose we wanted to show that school-age children can imitate the act of hand raising. They do so after seeing us perform the gesture; this is imitation. But they also raise their hands in other circumstances and in response to other stimuli. For example, they raise their hands when they have a question to ask. They also do so when we give them a verbal command to "raise your hand." They may also do so when they want to change an overhead light bulb. As in many experiments in psychology, the claim that a stimulus (adult tongue protrusion) elicits a response (infant tongue protrusion) is not a statement that no other stimulus does so. A sufficient cause is not a necessary cause. The control conditions that Meltzoff and Moore used distinguish imitation versus arousal. Moreover, the factors in table 1.1 go far beyond the mere existence of infant tonguing; they strengthen the interpretation of imitation and have been left wholly unaddressed by proponents of arousal.

2. Gergely et al. (1995) can be interpreted as showing that 12-month-olds attribute primitive goal-directedness to inanimate objects. However, there are differences between this research and the Meltzoff studies, so there is no contradiction involved. The "goals" in the Gergely et al. work are spatial locations, physical endpoints (such as "next to the small object" or "in the left-hand corner of the screen"), see Gergely, ch. 2 this volume, for details. The re-enactment procedure measures the child's inferences about complex human actions on objects, such as striving to pull an object apart. It is possible that infants reason about spatial paths and *seen* goals (as in the Gergely experiments) before they can make inferences about endpoints that are never achieved, and therefore *un*seen, as in Meltzoff's behavioral re-enactment experiments (for a more extensive discussion about infants' reasoning about spatial trajectories and versus seen unseen events, see Meltzoff & Moore, 1998b).

3. If correct, species with more general imitative capacities (motor, face, hands, vocal) in infancy should develop more sophisticated forms of social cognition (Meltzoff, 1996). And conversely, a typical infants with profound deficits in imitative capacities and the sense that others are "like me," for example children with autism (e.g., Dawson, Meltzoff, Osterling, & Rinaldi, 1998; Dawson, Carver Meltzoff, Panagiotides, & McPartland, 2002; Meltzoff & Gopnik, 1993), will also have deficits in coming to understand the minds of others.

CHAPTER TWO

The Development of Understanding Self and Agency

György Gergely

The study of the development of understanding the self and others as causal agents has been revolutionized by recent advances in theory of mind research. It has been demonstrated that by 3–4 years of age children develop a sophisticated understanding of persons as "mental agents" whose actions are caused by intentional mind states such as desires, intentions, and beliefs. It has also been shown that this mentalistic understanding of self and agency has a complex developmental unfolding during the first years of life that is currently a much-researched field of study. Historically, however, this was not always so. For a long time, the study of the "self as a mental agent" received much less attention than the other major aspect of self-knowledge that James (1950) classically termed the "empirical self" or "Me." Today this is often called the "conceptual" or "categorical" self-concept or representation (Harter, 1999; Lewis & Brooks-Gunn, 1979; Neisser, 1988). These terms refer to the representation of the collection of those features and properties that the person believes to be true of him/herself (blue-eyed, handsome, good in math, poor goalkeeper, etc.) and that s/he has mostly inferred from the self-directed reactions of their social environment (for a recent review, see Harter, 1999).

The reason for the relative lack of interest in the development of the self as a mental agent has probably much to do with the strong conceptual influence of the Cartesian doctrine of "first-person authority," which claims that one has direct and infallible introspective access to one's own intentional mind states. Developmentally, this general view suggests that the conscious apprehension of our mind states through introspection is a basic, direct, and prewired ability of our mind. On this view, knowledge of the self as a mental agent is an innately given rather than a developing or constructed capacity. As we shall see, the Cartesian doctrine is still influential among many developmental researchers.

However, in current philosophy of mind, cognitive neuroscience, and developmental theory, the Cartesian view of the mind has been seriously challenged (Damasio, 1994; Dennett, 1991; Gopnik, 1993; Wegner & Wheatley, 1999). At the same time, recent philosophical (Davidson, 1980; Searle, 1983), cognitive and neuropsychological (Frith,

1992; Jeannerod, 1999; Pacherie, 1997; Prinz, 1997) models of the representation of intentional action indicate that the representation of intentional mind states has a complex internal structure whose conscious access may be absent or only partial, and may depend on a variety of factors (Dienes & Perner, 1999). This, together with evidence documenting a complex developmental unfolding of the understanding of different types of intentional mind states (such as desires, intentions, and beliefs) (Bartsch & Wellman, 1995; Perner, 1991), strongly indicates that the mature understanding of the self as a mental agent is also likely to be the product of complex developmental processes. This chapter will trace the different stages of the development of self-knowledge from early understanding of physical and social agency in infancy to the more mature understanding of the self as a mental agent in early childhood.

Early Development of the Self as a Physical Agent

Traditionally, it was believed (Freud, 1946; Piaget, 1952c) that infants at first are unable to differentiate between stimuli belonging to the self versus the environment. Such a differentiation, however, would seem to be a prerequisite for the development of a sense of physical agency which involves representing the causal relationships between the physical self and actions, on the one hand, and actions and the external world, on the other. More recently, researchers have uncovered a number of objective information sources and innate perceptual mechanisms that allow for the differentiation of the physical or "ecological self" (Butterworth, 1995; Neisser, 1988; Watson, 1995) from very early on. For example, infants as young as 2 months of age were shown to use visual proprioception to monitor their posture: when tested in a "moving room" (whose walls approach or recede) babies compensated for visually specified (but nonexistent) loss of balance by adjusting their body or head posture (Butterworth & Hicks, 1977; Lee & Aronson, 1974). Young infants also modify the position of their heads and/or blink when perceiving an object approaching on a collision course (Dunkeld & Bower, 1980; Pettersen, Yonas, & Fisch, 1980).

Numerous studies have also demonstrated that young infants are highly sensitive to the contingent relations between their motor responses and consequent stimulus events (Bahrick & Watson, 1985; Field, 1979a; Lewis, Alessandri, & Sullivan, 1990; Lewis & Brooks-Gunn, 1979; Papousek & Papousek, 1974; Rochat & Morgan, 1995; Watson, 1972, 1994). For example, Watson (1972) has shown that 2-month-olds increase their rate of leg-kicking when it results in a contingent stimulus event (the movement of a mobile), but not when they experience a similar, but noncontingent event. In fact, the detection of causal control proved positively arousing for these infants. After some experience with the contingency, the infants started to smile and coo at the contingent mobile (cf. Lewis et al., 1990).

Bahrick and Watson (1985) (see also Rochat & Morgan, 1995; Schmuckler, 1996) demonstrated that the perception of perfect contingency between the pattern of efferent motor activation and consequent proprioceptive and visual feedback can be used for self-detection and self-orientation as early as 3 months. Three- and 5-month-olds were seated in front of two monitors, so that they could freely move their legs. One monitor presented the video recorded live image of the subject's moving legs, providing a visual stimulus that was *perfectly contingent* with the infant's responses. The other monitor presented a previously recorded and, therefore, *noncontingent* image of the infant's moving legs. Five-month-olds and a subgroup of the 3-month-olds differentiated between the two displays, looking significantly more at the *noncontingent* image. This finding is in line with a number of other studies (Papousek & Papousek, 1974; Rochat & Morgan, 1995; Schmuckler, 1996) indicating that after 3 months infants differentiate self from other on the basis of response-stimulus contingencies and prefer to fixate *away* from the self. Interestingly, Bahrick and Watson found that while the other subgroup of 3-month-olds also differentiated between self and non-self, they showed the *opposite* preference for the perfectly contingent self image (cf. Field, 1979a).

Gergely and Watson (1999) proposed that this early sensitivity to contingency is mediated by an innate "*contingency detection module*" that analyzes the conditional probability structure of the contingent relations between responses and stimuli over time. Based on Watson's (1994) hypothesis they argue that during the first 2–3 months the initial target of the module is genetically set to seek out and explore perfectly response-contingent stimulation (hence the preference for the self image in one of the subgroups of Bahrick and Watson's 3-month-olds). The hypothesized evolutionary function of this initial attention bias is to develop *a primary representation of the bodily self* by identifying those stimuli that are the necessary sensory consequences of the body's motor actions and over which the infant exercises perfect control. Around 3 months the preferred target value of the contingency detection module is "shifted" towards high, but imperfect degrees of contingency typically provided by reactive social partners (hence the avoidance of the perfectly contingent self image by Bahrick and Watson's 5-month-olds and the other subgroup of their 3-month-olds).

Piaget (1952c) documented that from about 4 months, infants show a tendency to repeat motor actions that result in salient changes in the environment ("secondary circular reactions") in order to "make interesting things last." Habituation studies with 5–6-month-olds (Leslie, 1984; Woodward, 1998) suggest that by this age infants discriminate grasping hands from other (inanimate) physical objects, attributing to them special causal powers such as transporting objects through space.

In sum: there is converging evidence that infants during the first six months of life come to represent their bodily self as a differentiated object in space that can initiate action and can exert causal influence on the environment. However, while such a representation of the self as a physical agent certainly involves sensitivity to the causal relations that relate agents to actions on the one hand, and actions to outcomes on the other, this understanding is still restricted in important ways.

Early Understanding of the Self as a Social Agent

There is a large body of evidence indicating that infants from the beginning of life discriminate and actively orient towards people (Stern, 1985). They show a very early sensitivity to facial patterns (Fantz, 1963; Morton & Johnson, 1991), habituate to their mother's voice *in utero* and recognize it after birth (DeCasper & Fifer, 1980), prefer the exaggerated intonation pattern of infant-directed speech (Cooper & Aslin, 1990), and show neonatal imitation of facial gestures (Meltzoff and Moore, 1977, 1989). Young infants engage in bi-directional affective interactions with their caregivers that are characterized by a "protoconversational" turn-taking structure (Beebe, Jaffe, Feldstein, Mays, & Alson, 1985; Brazelton, Koslowski, & Main, 1974; Brazelton & Tronick, 1980; Stern, 1985; Trevarthen, 1979; Tronick, 1989). Many developmentalists hold that mother and infant form an affective communication system from the beginning of life (Bowlby, 1969; Brazelton et al., 1974; Hobson, 1993; Sander, 1970; Stern, 1977, 1985; Trevarthen, 1979; Tronick, 1989) in which the mother plays a vital interactive role in modulating the infant's affective states. During such interactions, caregivers often engage in facial and vocal mirroring of their baby's displays to regulate the infant's affects (Gergely & Watson, 1996, 1999; Malatesta & Izard, 1984; Papousek & Papousek, 1987; Stern, 1985).

Thus, infants exhibit a species-specific sensitivity to human facial/vocal displays and an innate propensity to engage in affective interactions. But how do young infants understand such early interactions and their own causal role in them as a social agent? There is a large spectrum of different theoretical views on this intriguing question.

First, there is the (Cartesian) view that I shall call the *"strong intersubjectivist" position.* This assumes (a) that infants are born with innate mechanisms to identify and attribute mental states such as intentions and feelings to the other's mind during early social interactions; (b) that from the beginning of life there is a relatively rich set of differentiated mental states of the self such as emotions, intentions, motives, and goals that are introspectively directly accessible to the infant; and (c) that such subjective mental self-states can be recognized as being similar to corresponding mental states of the other and, as such, are experienced as "being shared" with him/her (e.g., Braten, 1988, 1992; Stern, 1995; Trevarthen, 1979, 1993; for a recent collection of papers on intersubjectivity, see Braten, 1998).

For example, Trevarthen (1979) claims that the richly structured early affective exchanges between mothers and infants imply what he calls "primary intersubjectivity." A well-known study by Murray & Trevarthen (1985) with 6- to 12-week-olds is often cited as empirical support for this position. Infants were observed while interacting with their mother's live image through a TV monitor. After a certain period, the TV image was switched to a noncontingent image of the interacting mother recorded earlier. These very young infants were reported to have detected the change in the contingency structure of the interaction and reacted with dissatisfaction and negative affect to the loss of contingency. Based on such data, Trevarthen (1993) proposes that infants are born with a dialogic mind, with an innate sense of "the virtual other" (cf. Braten, 1988, 1992) and can interpret the other's affectively attuned interactions in terms of a rich set of underlying motives, feelings, intentions, and goals.

Meltzoff and his colleagues (Meltzoff & Gopnik, 1993; Meltzoff & Moore, 1997, 1998a) proposed a specific innate mechanism that underlies intersubjective attributions during early imitative interactions. The affective/intentional behavioral acts of the other are mapped onto the infant's "supramodal body scheme" that allows him/her to recognize the other person as "just-like-me." By imitating such acts infants generate the corresponding subjective intentional and/or feeling states in themselves. These are then introspectively accessed and attributed to the other by inference. In Meltzoff & Moore's (1998a) words: imitative interactions provide "grounds for an important realization by the infant: 'I intend to produce these acts, the adult performs these same acts, they are not chance events, therefore, the adult intends his acts'" (pp. 61–2).

In contrast to the "strong intersubjectivist" position, there are a number of researchers (e.g., Gergely & Watson, 1996, 1999; Thompson, 1998; Tomasello, 1999) who believe that the phenomena of early affective and imitative social interactions can be parsimoniously explained without assuming "primary intersubjectivity." In this view, innate attentiveness and reactivity to human facial/vocal displays together with an innate sensitivity to contingency are sufficient to explain the structured bi-directional nature of early affective interactions. These abilities can also account for young infants' reactions to experimentally induced perturbations of the flow of contingent exchanges such as the "still-face" procedure (Tronick, Als, Adamson, Wise, & Brazelton, 1978) or the delayed feedback procedure (Murray & Trevarthen, 1985).

First, as described above, while the detection of contingent control over a stimulus is positively arousing for young infants (Watson, 1972), loss of previously experienced contingency results in frustration and distress (even when the stimulus is not human) (Lewis et al., 1990). Thus, sensitivity to loss of contingent control would seem sufficient to explain the Murray and Trevarthen (1985) finding discussed above.

Second, though several studies have demonstrated this effect with 4- to 6-month-olds (Bigelow & DeCoste, 2000; Muir & Hains, 1999), it has proved difficult to replicate the original findings of Murray and Trevarthen (that was based on four 2-month-old infants only) with infants less than 3 months of age (Bigelow, 2000; Rochat, Neisser, & Marian, 1998). This pattern of findings is in line with Watson's (1994) "contingency switch" model discussed earlier, according to which the target value of the contingency analyzer is shifted around 3 months from an initial attention bias towards perfect contingencies to a preference for less-than-perfect social contingencies (cf. Watson, 1985). This maturational change functions to orient the infant after 3 months of age away from self-exploration (perfect contingencies) and towards *the exploration and representation of the social world* as presented by the (necessarily less than perfectly response-contingent) parental environment.[1] If this idea is correct, then infants before 3 months may yet be unable to detect the less-than-perfect contingencies of parental interactions. Therefore, in the delayed feedback procedure the degree of parental contingency may not be high enough for its disappearance to be detected by 2-month-olds during the noncontingent feedback phase. This in itself may explain the difficulty found in several studies to replicate the Murray and Trevarthen (1985) finding in less than 3-month-old infants (cf. Bigelow, 2000).

There are two alternative theoretical approaches to the "strong intersubjectivist" view: the first can be called the "weak intersubjectivist" position, while the second will be referred to as the "no starting-state intersubjectivism" position. The *"weak intersubjectivist" position* (e.g., Tomasello, 1999) accepts that the existence of early affective and imitative interactions reflects a specifically human biological adaptation to "identify" with other persons as "like me." In Tomasello's *simulation theory* this propensity for "identification" plays a crucial role in the developing understanding of other minds. However,

Tomasello (1999) emphasizes that "in attempting to understand other persons human infants apply what they already experience of themselves . . . [but] this experience of the self changes in early development, especially with regard to self-agency" (p. 70). Thus, Tomasello's (1999) views differ significantly from the "strong intersubjectivist" position in that he believes that before 9 months infants do not develop a differentiated understanding of their own subjective self-states such as intentions or goals, and so they cannot yet understand such mental states in others either by analogy to the self.

A further point of criticism concerns the type of *functional explanations* that proponents of initial state intersubjectivity attribute to early affective and imitative exchanges. It is often assumed that infants as well as caregivers engage in such interactions in order to "share or participate in" each other's subjective mental states or to "discover" the subjective world of intentions and feelings of the other (Meltzoff & Gopnik, 1993; Stern, 1985; Trevarthen, 1979). In contrast, the third alternative view, the *"no starting-state intersubjectivism" position* (Gergely & Watson, 1996, 1999; Gergely, Koós, & Watson, 2000) argues that there are plausible alternative evolutionary functions that early affective and imitative interactions may serve. First, the infant's innate preparedness to engage in affective interactions may function to establish and maintain proximity to the attachment figure (Bowlby, 1969) as such reactivity is highly reinforcing to the caregiver. Second, infants' innate propensity to engage parents in affective interchanges may contribute to affective self-regulation by maintaining positive arousal through the direct affect-regulative influence of parental interactions. To the degree that the level of contingent control over the parents' behaviors is detected (see above), this may also lead to feelings of causal efficacy. Finally, innate social reactivity may serve the evolutionary function of establishing and maintaining an "emotional-intentional scaffolding" environment (in the form of the infant-directed affect expressive mirroring displays of the parent). In this scaffolding environment learning about the dispositional displays of others, sensitization to intentional and affective self-states through processes of "social biofeedback," and the establishment of secondary representations for primary emotion states of the self are optimized.

Briefly, according to the "social biofeedback model" of affect mirroring (Gergely & Watson, 1996, 1999), during affect-regulative interactions caregivers repeatedly display attuned, exaggerated, and partially imitative "marked" reflections of their infant's affective/ intentional behaviors. The infant registers that such displays are markedly different from the caregiver's normative emotion expressions and so comes to represent them separately. S/he also comes to register through contingency detection that his/her own behavioral state-expressions exert high contingent control over the caregiver's mirroring displays. It is hypothesized that through contingency detection the infant becomes sensitive to the set of internal physiological and proprioceptive cues that are active while his/her affect-expressive behavior is controlling the adult's marked affect-mirroring expressions. This sensitizes the infant to the set of internal cues that covary with his/her – initially nonconscious – automatic and procedural emotional state expressions (sensitization function). Furthermore, it is assumed that the separate representations of the caregiver's affect-mirroring displays become associated as secondary representations with the infant's primary and procedural affective states (representation building function). Such secondary representations make the initially prewired and automatic primary emotion states more accessible to conscious introspection and form the basis of the development of emotional self-awareness and control (for details of the "social biofeedback model," see Gergely & Watson, 1996, 1999; Gergely, Koós, & Watson, 2000).

To conclude: it can be argued that there is no compelling evidence to support the intersubjectivist assumption that structured affective and imitative mother–infant interactions during the first months involve an ability on the part of young infants to introspectively access their own differentiated mental states. Similarly, there is no compelling evidence either for the view that young infants attribute corresponding subjective intentional and feeling states to the other's mind.[2]

When does "true" intersubjective understanding of other minds begin, then, in infancy? One clear sign of differentiated understanding of the other's subjective feeling states is the appearance of mature empathic reactions sometime during the second year (Hoffman, 2000; Thompson, 1998). Understanding intentional mental states of others, such as their attention, desire, or intention becomes also dominant during the second year of life (Bartsch & Wellman, 1995; Corkum & Moore, 1995; Wellman, ch. 8 this volume), though some of these abilities start to emerge already between 9 and 12 months when the set of so-called "joint attention" skills first start to appear (Carpenter, Nagell, & Tomasello, 1998).

An important theoretical question, then, concerns the way in which the innate human-specific propensity of infants to engage in affective and imitative interactions during the first six to nine months may be related to the later emergence of the intersubjective mentalistic stance starting around 1 year of age. We have reviewed three positions. First, the "strong intersubjectivist" view (Trevarthen, 1979) holds that such early affective communicative exchanges are examples of an already functioning mindreading capacity present from birth. Second, the "weak intersubjectivist" position considers these early affective interactions as evidence for the presence of a human-specific innate mechanism specialized to "identify" with the subjective perspective of other persons. This view, however, holds that the simulation of differentiated intentional mind states of others through this mechanism becomes possible only around 9 months. This is so because it is only by this age that some types of intentional self-states become differentiated and introspectively accessible (Tomasello, 1999). Third, the "no starting-state intersubjectivism" view holds that early affective and imitative interactions serve a number of important evolutionary functions (such as proximity maintenance or affect regulation), but do not involve an initial ability by the infant to read and attribute subjective mental states to others. One of the evolutionary functions of early affect regulative mirroring interactions, however, is hypothesized to be related to the later emerging intersubjective mentalistic stance. Attuned and contingent parental mirroring reactions to the infant's affective/intentional states provide an "emotional-intentional scaffolding" environment which, through the processes of contingency detection and social biofeedback, serve both a sensitization and a representation-building function (see Gergely & Watson, 1996, 1999 for details). This leads to the establishment of cognitively accessible representations of intentional and affective self-states that is a precondition for intersubjective understanding. However, the appearance of a truly mentalistic intersubjective stance during the second year emerges as a result of the maturation of representational abilities (theory of mind), which make the causal mentalistic interpretation of actions in terms of intentional mind states possible both for the other and for the self.

Understanding Self and Other as Teleological Agents: The 9-Month Social-Cognitive Revolution

There is a large body of evidence (e.g., Csibra, Gergely, Bíró, Koós, & Brockbank, 1999; Piaget, 1952c; Tomasello, 1999; Uzgiris and Hunt, 1975; Willatts, 1999) indicating that by 9 months of age a qualitatively new level of understanding of goal-directed action develops in infants. This involves the differentiation of goals from the means that bring them about, and an ability to choose among alternative means the one that brings about the goal in the most efficient manner. Recently, Csibra and Gergely (Csibra et al., 1999; Gergely & Csibra, 1998; Gergely, Nádasdy, Csibra, & Bíró, 1995; see also Woodward & Sommerville, 2000) have demonstrated that infants start to interpret other agents' intentional actions as goal-directed and rational at about the same time as they show means-end coordination in action production. For example, using visual habituation techniques, 9- and 12-month-olds (but not 6-month-olds) were shown to interpret the behavior of an abstract computer-animated figure as goal-directed and could infer its novel means action in a new situation.

As shown in figure 2.1, infants were habituated to an event in which a small circle repeatedly approached a large circle by "jumping over" a rectangle separating them. In the test phase, the "obstacle" was removed. The infants looked significantly longer if the small circle repeated its familiar jumping action (which, given the absence of the "obstacle," was not seen as a "sensible" goal approach any more) than if it took a novel (but more efficient) straight-line route (rational approach). No such looking-time differences were found in a control condition that differed only in that there was no "obstacle" in the habituation phase to start with. In this case, the small circle approached the large one in a nonrational manner as it was jumping over nothing. This comparison suggests that infants attributed the end state (contacting the large circle) as the goal of the action only if the action (the jumping approach) was evaluated as a rational or efficient means to bring about the outcome state given the constraints of the situation (presence or absence of the "obstacle").

Based on such results, Gergely and Csibra (1997; Csibra & Gergely, 1998a) proposed that by 9 months of age infants come to interpret goal-directed spatial behavior teleologically in terms of a *"teleological stance"* or a *"naïve theory of rational action."* Teleological explanations differ from causal ones in two respects. First, the explanatory element referred to is in a different *temporal* relation to the to-be-explained action. Teleological interpretations refer to the outcome that *follows* the action, while causal explanations point at some necessary condition that is *prior* to the event. Second, they use different *criteria* of acceptance. Causal explanations single out a prior condition that *necessitates* the action providing its generative source. In contrast, reference to the outcome state is accepted as a teleological explanation (reason) for a behavior in case it *justifies* it: i.e., when, given the constraints of reality, the behavior can be seen as a sensible way to bring about the goal state.

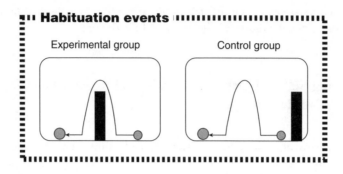

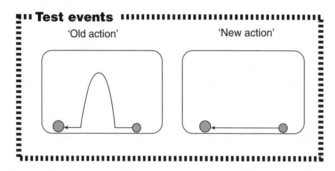

Figure 2.1   Schematic depiction of the habituation and test events used in Gergely, Nádasdy, Csibra, & Bíró. 1995

The infant's teleological stance (see figure 2.2) represents goal-directed action by establishing an explanatory relation among three representational elements: the action (A), the goal state (G), and the relevant constraints of physical reality (RC) (in the above case, the presence of an obstacle). Teleological representations are generated by the inferential *"principle of rational action"* that assumes that agents pursue their goals in the most rational or efficient manner available to them given the constraints of physical reality. In further studies, Csibra and Gergely have also demonstrated the inferential generativity and systematicity of the teleological stance by showing that, relying on the principle of rational action, 1-year-olds can infer any one of the three representational elements (A, G, or RC) given perceptual information about the other two (see Bíró, Gergely, Csibra, & Koós, 1996; Csibra, Gergely, Brockbank, Bíró, & Koós, 1998; Gergely & Csibra, 1998, 2000).

Adults tend to explain the goal-directed jumping action (figure 2.1) in *causal mentalistic* terms such as "it *wants* to get to the other circle and *thinks* that the obstacle is impenetrable, so it jumps over it" (cf. Heider & Simmel, 1944). Note, however, that such mentalistic attributions are not necessary for a viable teleological interpretation. The interpretation works even if it refers only to the relevant states of current reality (the presence of an obstacle) that constrain the goal approach, and to future reality (the goal state of

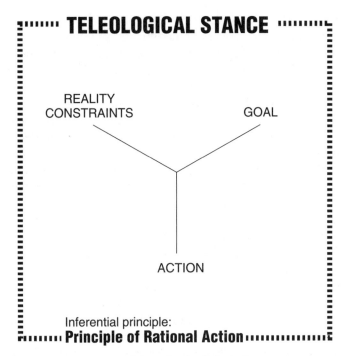

Figure 2.2   Schematic representation of the infants' teleological stance

contacting the large circle) as represented by the infant him/herself. Thus, even without attributing these representational elements to the actor's mind as causal intentional mental states (desires and beliefs) that are present prior to the action, infants could construct a viable teleological action interpretation or prediction. Gergely and Csibra (1997; Csibra & Gergely, 1998a) hypothesize, therefore, that the 1-year-old's teleological stance generates reality-based representations for goal-directed actions that are *neither mentalistic nor causal.*

The 9-month social-cognitive revolution also manifests itself in the emergence of goal-directed coordinated activities between infants and parents involving joint attention to objects or situations (Carpenter, Nagel, & Tomasello, 1998; Corkum & Moore, 1995; Tomasello, 1995, 1999; Trevarthen & Hubley, 1978). Infants start to reliably follow the adult's gaze (gaze-following), actively attend to the adult's attitude expressions in relation to objects or situations that are unfamiliar to them (social referencing), and imitate the actions on objects modeled by adults (imitative learning). They also begin to use communicative gestures themselves (such as pointing or object-showing) to direct adults' attention and behavior to objects. Carpenter, Nagel, and Tomasello (1998) demonstrated that this series of "joint attention skills" (including protoimperative and protodeclarative gestures, imitative learning, cooperative learning, and intentional teaching), emerge in a coordinated fashion between 9 and 15 months of age.

Tomasello (1995, 1999) proposes an alternative theory to capture the nature of infants' emerging capacity to interpret intentional goal-directed action. He suggests that at around

9 months, infants start using a qualitatively new mentalistic interpretational system that he calls the *"intentional stance."* Tomasello (1999) argues that the emerging joint attention skills (as well as infants' performance on the Csibra and Gergely type of habituation tasks) are different behavioral manifestations of the same underlying new level of understanding persons as mental agents with intentions.

According to Tomasello (1999), the emergence of the intentional stance is a function of two factors. First, it presupposes the ability to produce goal-directed actions in which goal states are differentiated from the means actions leading to them (Piaget, 1952c). It also presupposes the ability to choose the most rational or efficient action alternative available in a given situation to realize the goal (cf. Gergely et al., 1995). In Tomasello's view, as soon as infants start to show flexible means-end coordination in their own actions, they immediately become able to interpret other agents' goal-directed activities as well in terms of intentions and rational choice of means. This is made possible by the second, *simulationist* component of Tomasello's theory. He assumes that infants are born with a species-specific ability to "identify" with other humans who are perceived as "just like them." Starting from 9 months, this allows them to attribute subjective intentional states to others through analogy to their own self-experience.

When comparing Csibra and Gergely's "teleological stance" account with Tomasello's "intentional stance" account of the 9-month social-cognitive revolution, we can identify three (clearly related) theoretical issues that differentiate the two approaches. These concern (a) the role of simulation, (b) the mechanisms for understanding self versus other as goal-directed agents, and (c) the issue of mentalism.

The role of simulation in understanding others as goal-directed agents: full simulation versus default simulation

Simulationist theories tend to assume that attribution of intentional mind states to others takes place only in so far as the other's behavior is perceived as "just like me." An often cited example is Meltzoff's (1995a) demonstration that 18-month-olds infer and reenact an underlying intention when observing a human model's failed attempts at realizing it, but don't do so if the same acts are performed by a robot (that doesn't behave in a "just like me" manner). However, Gergely and Csibra (1998; Csibra et al., 1998) demonstrated that already at 12 months infants can infer the goal of an incomplete action even when the actor is not human but a computer-animated 2D disc with no facial features or biomechanical movement characteristics. In fact, Csibra et al. (1999) showed goal attribution as early as 9 months even when the actor's (again a 2D disc) behavior was lacking *all* animacy or agency cues such as self-propelled, irregular and biomechanical movement that could have triggered a "just like me" judgment. These findings suggest, therefore, that early goal attribution may *not* be restricted to humans or animate agents (see also Johnson, Slaughter, & Carey, 1998). This, in turn, suggests that simulation through analogy to the self may not be the only, or, for that matter, the most central mechanism through which the interpretation of goal-directed actions of others is mediated.

In contrast to Tomasello's theory, Csibra and Gergely's teleological stance is not based primarily on simulation. Rather, the infant's "naïve theory of rational action" is seen as equally applicable to goal-directed actions whether these are performed by the other or by the self. Through the principle of rational action the infant evaluates whether the observed action constitutes an efficient means to bring about the end state in the particular situation. This judgment is made in the light of the infant's available knowledge about the physical constraints of the situation and about perceived dispositional constraints that characterize the actor. To illustrate this latter point: while a straight-line approach to the goal may be judged as the most efficient means action in the case of a human actor, a hopping approach may be seen as more appropriate in the case of a kangaroo, assuming that knowledge about kangaroos' disposition to hop is available. Thus, relevant information about the dispositional properties of other agents can influence the evaluation of the rationality of action even if such properties do not correspond to those of the self.

At the same time, there is an important role for simulation to play in Csibra and Gergely's teleological model as well that can be called *"default simulation."* If no perceptual evidence is available about the dispositional constraints of the agent, the infant will simulate the other by default as being similar to the self. However, simulation is only a default option to fall back on when lacking relevant information about the other. In fact, Csibra and Gergely (1998b) have recently demonstrated that perceptual information about the agent's dispositions can, indeed, modify the infant's expectations about the type of goal approach the agent is expected to follow.

Understanding the self versus the other.   A corollary to Tomasello's simulationist account is his view that the self enjoys primacy over the other in the development of understanding goal-directed actions. It is proposed that means-end differentiation is first achieved in relation to the self's own actions primarily on the basis of introspective evidence (such as feelings of intentional effort) (Piaget, 1952c; Tomasello, 1999). For Tomasello, this is a representational precondition for simulating the other's behavior as goal-directed and intentional. Whether understanding intentional action is, indeed, achieved first in relation to the self rather than the other is difficult to ascertain, however. This is because the behavioral evidence suggesting such understanding emerges more or less simultaneously (somewhere between 7 and 9 months) both in producing and interpreting goal-directed intentional acts.

Tomasello's developmental account seems to imply that infants learn about intentional actions more readily through introspection of internal cues than by observation of exteroceptive cues. However, the literature on the ability of adults to rely on internal information (such as the activation of an efferent motor intention (Libet, 1985) or proprioceptive feedback from motor action) in making conscious agency judgments about perceived actions indicates a dominance of exteroceptive (e.g., visual) information over internal cues (Jeannerod, 1997, 1999; Pacherie, 1997). Similarly, there is evidence from 6- and 9-month-olds indicating the dominance of exteroceptive (visual) cues over proprioceptive (head orientation) cues in discriminative learning (Colombo, Mitchell, Coldren, & Atwater, 1990). Based on such evidence, Gergely and Watson (1996, 1999) argued that learning on the basis of exteroceptive stimuli may, in fact, have primacy in infancy. Introspective sensitivity to internal cues may be achieved more slowly as a function of the "emotional-intentional" scaffolding environment provided by parental mirroring of affective/intentional behavior and is mediated by the contingency detection mechanism and "social biofeedback" processes (see above).

Such data, together with the apparent simultaneity of the emergence of understanding intentional action in the self and in others are, therefore, compatible with the view that the development of self-knowledge does not enjoy primacy in the 9-month revolution. In this vein, Csibra and Gergely's teleological model holds that the emergence of the principle of rational action at this age brings about a new level of understanding goal-directed action simultaneously in the other and in the self (see also Dennett (1987, 1991) and Gopnik (1993) for arguments against the Cartesian notion of the primacy of "first-person authority" in understanding agency).

The origins of mentalism.   For Tomasello (1995, 1999) the 9-month-old's intentional stance marks the first appearance of understanding that the actions of agents are driven by causal *mental* states. Tomasello's evidence for this claim is twofold. First, he emphasizes that at least some of the joint attention skills emerging between 9 and 15 months (Carpenter, Nagel, & Tomasello, 1998), such as *protodeclarative gestures*, seem clearly to involve understanding (and influencing) another agent's intentional mind state (his/her attention) (cf. Leslie & Happé, 1989). Second, his simulationist view implies that 9-month-olds represent the other's intentional actions by reference to their own internally experienced subjective mental states (attention, intention) through which they simulate the mental causes of the other's behavior. For Tomasello this human-specific propensity for mental simulation is one of the preconditions (apart from means-end coordination) for the emergence of joint attention skills at the end of the first year.

In support of this view, Tomasello (1999) argues that the reason why primates do not acquire joint attention skills in their natural environment is not because they cannot achieve means-end coordination (they clearly do: see Tomasello & Call, 1997). Rather, what they are lacking is the human-specific biological adaptation to "identify" with the subjective perspective of other agents, i.e., they lack the ability for mental simulation.

In contrast, Gergely and Csibra (1997; Csibra & Gergely, 1998a) argue that the 9-month-old's understanding of goal-directed action can be parsimoniously modeled in terms of the teleological stance without attributing an ability to represent causal intentional *mental* states. In their view (Csibra & Gergely, 1998a; Gergely & Csibra, 2000) the representational requirements for a "purely" teleological interpretational system are less severe than the ones presupposed by later theory of mind. Teleological understanding does not require representing propositional attitude relations (Fodor, 1992; Leslie, 1987, 1994) or a comprehension of the representational nature of intentional mind states (Perner, 1991, 2000b). Thus, the teleological system is *ontologically more restricted* than theory of mind as its explanatory elements involve only the interpreter's *own* representations of (present and future) reality states. It is also *computationally simpler* as it does not involve the need to infer and attribute intentional mental states to the other. It can also work without understanding the causal conditions of belief fixation (Leslie, 1987, 1995) such as the fact that perception leads to knowledge. These differences may, in fact, help explain the remarkably early appearance of teleological interpretations by 9 months of age.

Of course, there is nothing in Csibra and Gergely's habituation results that would necessitate this "lean" nonmentalistic interpretation. Kelemen (1999a, 1999b) suggested that infants' early competence on such tasks may already reflect the attribution of mental states such as desires or intentions to the actors. How could one empirically differentiate between these views? Kelemen's mentalistic construal of teleological reasoning suggests that the infant's understanding of teleological relations and intentional mind states are not independent but are aspects of the same underlying innate ability to attribute causal mental states to agents. This view predicts that the two types of ability must be either present or absent concurrently in any organism or species. Therefore, a dissociation between the ability for teleological interpretation on the one hand, and understanding causal intentional mind states on the other, would represent potential counterevidence for this position.

In contrast, Csibra and Gergely's (1998a; Gergely & Csibra, 2000) "independent teleology" position holds that the teleological stance is a biological adaptation that may have evolved independently from theory of mind to interpret goal-directed action. The wide-ranging presence of goal-directed organization of behavior among numerous species (including rats, see Tolman, Ritchie, & Kalish, 1946) in the evolutionary environment may have exerted selective pressure for the evolution of a mechanism specialized for the discrimination and prediction of goal-directed action. In this view, the mentalistic "theory of mind" stance represents a further biological adaptation that leads to the ontological enrichment of the teleological stance to include, apart from representations of reality states, mental representations of *fictional* or *counterfactual* states as well in the form of mentally represented propositional attitude relations (Fodor, 1992; Leslie, 1987).

Therefore, the teleological stance may be a useful interpretational strategy only in the (restricted) domain of intentional actions that are driven by causal mental states that represent reality truthfully. This is so because in such cases teleological interpretation can be based directly on reality without considering the actor's mental representations of that reality. The teleological stance breaks down, however, in cases where the actor's causal mind states represent fictional or counterfactual realities such as in pretense- or false belief-based action. This predicts the possibility of dissociation within an organism or a species that could exhibit an intact (reality-based) teleological reasoning capacity, while lacking a mentalistic understanding of intentional action. There are, in fact, several types of dissociative evidence (Gergely & Csibra, 2000) that seem to favor the "independent teleology" position.

Dissociation 1: Intact teleological understanding, but impaired theory of mind in children with autism. Children with autism show a specific deficit in tests requiring the attribution of intentional mind states such as false beliefs (Baron-Cohen, Leslie, & Frith, 1985; Leslie & Thaiss, 1992). According to the "theory of mind deficit" account, childhood autism is caused by a genetic defect of the innate "theory of mind" module that is specialized for the representation of intentional mental states (Leslie, 1987). Therefore, if teleological interpretations always involved representing intentional mind states (cf. Kelemen, 1999a, 1999b), children with autism should be equally impaired in tests that require teleological reasoning, such as Csibra and Gergely's habituation studies. In contrast, the "independent teleology" position predicts that children with autism may have an intact reality-based "teleological stance" to interpret goal-directed actions, while due to their pervasive metarepresentational deficit (Leslie, 1994), they may be unable to onto-logically enrich their teleology to form a "proper" theory of mind.

A recent study by Abell, Happé, and Frith (in press) provides evidence for just this kind of dissociation. Briefly, these authors presented children with autism and matched controls with three types of computer-animated events involving abstract figures (such as triangles) to elicit verbal descriptions for these events. In their "Random" animations con-dition the triangles moved around purposelessly and independently of each other (float-ing in space; bouncing off the sides). Their "Goal-directed" sequences involved one of the triangles reacting to the other's behavior (e.g., following, chasing, or fighting). In their "Theory of Mind" sequences one character reacted to the other's mental state (e.g., seduc-ing, hiding and surprising, coaxing, or mocking). Normal adults predominantly used physicalist action descriptions for the "Random" sequences, teleological descriptions for the "Goal-directed" events, and mentalistic descriptions for the "Theory of Mind" sequences. High-functioning children with autism showed a deficit in providing accurate mentalistic descriptions for the "Theory of Mind" sequences when compared to matched controls. Interestingly, however, they showed no differential performance in physicalist or teleological descriptions. This indicates a dissociation between their intact capacity to interpret goal-directed interactions teleologically, and their impaired theory of mind.

Dissociation 2: Differential emergence of teleologically (but not mentalistically) based joint attention skills in enculturated apes.   As we have seen, Tomasello (1999) explains the lack of joint attention skills in nonhuman primates by their lack of the human-specific innate capacity to mentally simulate others through "identifying" with their subjective perspec-tive. Partly at odds with this theoretical view, Tomasello (1999; Call & Tomasello, 1996) documents that two "joint attention skills" ("protoimperative pointing" at objects in order to get them, and acquiring novel object-directed means actions through "imitative learn-ing") do emerge in chimpanzees raised by humans. In contrast, enculturation does not seem to result in the acquisition of the other joint attention behaviors (such as "pro-todeclarative gestures" or "intentional teaching").

By assuming that nonhuman primates do possess a nonmentalistic teleological stance one can provide a principled explanation for why exactly this subset (i.e., protoimpera-tives and imitative learning) of joint attention skills emerges in enculturated chimpanzees. Note that what differentiates these skills from, say, protodeclarative communication or intentional teaching is that they consist of goal-directed activities whose goals involve visible changes of external reality. In contrast, to interpret, say, a protodeclarative point correctly one needs to represent the goal-of-action as involving a *nonvisible intentional mind state* of the other. It is noteworthy that children with autism also show such a dis-sociation as they can produce and understand protoimperative pointing (which is a goal-directed act that can be teleologically interpreted), but fail to understand or produce protodeclarative pointing (that requires a mentalistic construal of goals) (Baron-Cohen, 1991b).

Their nonmentalistic teleological stance should allow apes to parse and represent pro-toimperative acts or new goal-directed actions modeled in imitative learning in terms of visible outcomes (as goals-of-action) differentiated from the means actions that bring them about. What enculturation training teaches them in addition (through modeling, shaping, selective reinforcement, etc.) is to specifically attend to and imitatively produce the means action modeled. This allows them to overcome their dominant natural tendency to attend to the salient outcome only (as evidenced in emulation). What enculturation *cannot* teach them, however, is to represent goals-of-action that are *nonvisible and mental* (such as inducing, sharing, or modifying an intentional mind state of the other): for that they would need to have the theory of mind capacity to represent intentional mental states.

To conclude: I have argued that the nonmentalistic "teleological stance" is an evolutionary adaptation for interpreting goal-directed action that is independent from the human-specific capacity to understand intentional mental states in others. This teleological interpretational system can parsimoniously account for 9-month-old infants' newly emerging abilities to produce goal-directed rational actions and to interpret such actions in others. We have reviewed evidence suggesting that the teleological stance is present not only in normal human infants, but also in nonhuman primates and children with autism. The latter two groups, however, seem to lack the mentalistic ability to represent causal intentional mind states that is likely to be an additional human-specific adaptation that has evolved to understand and communicate with other minds.

Understanding the Self and Other as Intentional Mental Agents

A clearly mentalistic understanding of intentional action is implied by the emerging ability during the second year to attribute *"prior intentions"* (Searle, 1983) to others. By this age infants show clear signs of understanding that the other can have a prior intention or desire before or without actually acting on it and can attribute such prior intentions to others from evidence other than observing the goal-directed action itself. The ability to predict goal-directed action from inferred prior intentions implies a capacity to think in terms of *mental causation.*

Evidence for such a *mentalistic* understanding of causal intentions by two years comes from a number of sources (Wellman & Phillips, 2001; Wellman, ch. 8 this volume). For example, Bartsch and Wellman (1995) demonstrated that 2-year-olds already speak about other persons' (or their own) specific desires (using mostly the word "want") even when the desire-based action has not yet been performed, or when the action executed did not fulfill the attributed desire. Such verbal references to desires or prior intentions also indicate that 2-year-olds can differentiate between their own versus other people's subjective desire states. Repacholi and Gopnik (1997) demonstrated that 18-month-olds when requested to give something to eat to the experimenter, provided her with the particular food item (broccoli vs. goldfish crackers) that she had previously expressed a liking for (by saying "yummy" or "yuk" when first seeing the food item). The infants generated their own goal-directed action (giving food to the experimenter) by considering the specific content of the desire they had attributed to the other previously (based on an earlier and different action) even when that desire was *different* from their own preference. In contrast, 14-month-olds gave the experimenter the item they themselves liked. In other words, these younger infants based their action on their *own* preference without being able to take into consideration the other's prior intention.

Mature empathic reactions of concern leading to prosocial acts also appear during the second year (Hoffman, 2000; Thompson, 1998; Zahn-Waxler & Radke-Yarrow, 1990). This indicates that infants of this age can attribute a subjective emotion state to the other and differentiate this state from their own felt emotion. This is shown by their capacity to devise a goal-directed prosocial act aimed at modifying the emotion state of the other.

Around the same time, young children also start to show some sensitivity to the systematic causal connections that exist between different types of intentional mental states. For example, they can infer that a desire that is unfulfilled by a given action triggers sadness or frustration rather than joy and is likely to lead to some alternative goal-directed action (Wellman & Phillips, 2000).

From two years on repeated experiences with similar types of goal-directed actions by significant others (such as caregivers or siblings) also lead to the attribution of *generalized intentions or attitudes* that become stable characteristics of agent representations. Such generalized and enduring intentional properties of particular persons will come to function as further constraining factors (in addition to situational and dispositional constraints) when the principle of rational action is applied to predict or interpret their behavior. At this point, a new principle of reasoning of naïve theory of mind, that can be called the "principle of mental coherence" (cf. Dennett, 1987), comes into play that assumes that a rational agent's causal intentions are not contradictory. In developmental psychopathology abusive and dissociating parental behavior, which provide inferential grounds to attribute contradictory generalized intentions to the caregiver, have been hypothesized to lead to a dysfunctional theory of mind leading to pathological patterns of self development involving disorganization and splitting (see Allen, 2001; Fonagy, Target, & Gergely, 2000; Gergely, 2000; Gergely et al., 2000).

Development of the self-concept during the second year.   This mentalistic "intentional stance" of the 2-year-old, which already involves representing agents in terms of generalized and enduring intentional properties, also brings about a new level of self-understanding. As Tomasello (1993, 1999) argues (in keeping with the long tradition of social constructivism in self development, see e.g., Allen, 2001; Baldwin, 1902; Cooley, 1912; Fonagy & Target, 1997; Mead, 1934) the intentional actions and attitudes repeatedly expressed towards the young child by caregivers and peers serve as the inferential basis for attributing generalized intentional properties to the self in an attempt to rationalize the social partners' self-directed behavior. This is how the establishment of a "categorical" self-concept or representation (the Jamesian "Me") originates (Harter, 1999; Lewis and Brooks-Gunn, 1979). For example, in developmental psychopathology unrealistically negative dysfunctional self-attributions are seen to arise from attempts to rationalize the abusive or seriously neglective child-directed behaviors of attachment figures (Allen, 2001; Cicchetti & Toth, 1994; Fonagy & Target, 1997; Fonagy et al., 2000).

The establishment of a cognitive representation of the self as an objective entity with enduring properties has also been linked to the end of the second year by the results of extended research on early *self-recognition in the mirror* (Amsterdam, 1972; Gallup, 1991; Gallup & Suarez, 1986; Lewis & Brooks-Gunn, 1979; Parker, Mitchell, & Boccia, 1994).

Between 18 and 24 months (but not before) infants recognize in the mirror an inadvertently placed rouge mark on their nose or forehead as belonging to themselves (as shown by their self-directed attempt to manually remove it). This indicates that, based on previous experience with their mirror image, infants have inferred and attributed to their self a representation of the (not directly perceivable) enduring visual features of their faces. The correct interpretation of this finding, however, has been subject to controversy (see Parker et al., 1994). For some (e.g., Bertenthal & Fisher, 1978; Menzel, Savage-Rumbaugh, & Lawson, 1985) mirror self-recognition can be accounted for in terms of increased perceptuomotor skills. At the other extreme Gallup (1991; Gallup & Suarez, 1986) argues that this capacity implies self-awareness and the achievement of a representational self-concept that is inherently linked to understanding intentional mind states of others. This strong mentalistic interpretation of mirror self-recognition has, however, been challenged on a number of grounds (e.g., Gergely, 1994; Mitchell, 1993; Povinelli, 1995; Povinelli & Simon, 1998). For example, mirror self-recognition is present in chimpanzees (Gallup, 1970) as well as in children with autism (Dawson and McKissick, 1984), both of whom seem to lack a theory of mind (Baron-Cohen et al., 1985; Call & Tomasello, 1999).

Recently, Howe and Courage (1993, 1997) argued that the cognitive self-concept as evidenced by mirror self-recognition is a precondition for the establishment of autobiographic memory for personally experienced events. They attribute the phenomenon of infantile amnesia to the lack of a cognitive self-concept before 2 years of age. They propose that the construction of the cognitive self-concept with enduring properties provides a common conceptual schema in terms of which the particular memory traces of personal experiences can become organized into an integrated and coherent memory structure that allows for later autobiographical recall. Below, however, we shall review some intriguing new findings that suggest that mirror self-recognition may indicate only a limited understanding of the self that is tied to the present (the "present self," see Povinelli, 1995). These findings suggest that the construction of a temporally "extended self" underlying autobiographical memory in which past events experienced by the self are causally integrated with the present self into a unified self concept (the "proper self," see James, 1950) seems to require some further developments in representational capacities and appears only around 4–5 years of age.

Understanding Self and Other as Representational Agents and the Development of the Autobiographical Self

A mature understanding of mental agency (i.e., naïve theory of mind) involves a number of further factors (see Fodor, 1992; Leslie, 1987; Wellman, ch. 8 this volume). Central among these is the child's understanding of the *representational* nature of beliefs that is evidenced by comprehending that actions can be caused by *false beliefs*. This ability arises around 4 years of age (Perner, 1991; Wimmer & Perner, 1983). Here I will focus on another aspect of the developing understanding of intentional mind states as "representational" that has been recently revealed by some intriguing correlations discovered between understanding false belief-based action (theory of mind) on the one hand, and showing mature self-control abilities in executive function tasks (Zelazo & Müller, ch. 20 this volume) and mastery of counterfactual reasoning tasks (Goswami, ch. 13 this volume) on the other.

To explain the correlated dramatic improvement in these rather different task domains around four years, Perner (2000a) argues that they all require an understanding that the intentional mental states they involve have the property of "*causal self-referentiality,*" a concept taken over from philosophy of mind (see Campbell, 1997; Searle, 1983). Briefly, this notion suggests that a proper representational understanding of a mental intentional state, say, an intention to act, involves not only that the intention represents some state of affairs, but also that it specifies (represents in its content) that the action be caused by the intention itself (Perner, 2000a, p. 300). (This forms the representational basis for our awareness or sense of agency and ownership of action.) Similarly, to be recalled as an item in autobiographical memory, the memory representation of a specific event that a person has experienced must not only specify the event itself but must also represent the fact that the memory has been caused by that event (memory for causal source of knowledge).

Perner (2000a) reviews evidence indicating that children before 4–5 years of age are notoriously bad at identifying the causal sources of their beliefs (for example, whether they have seen, were told about, or inferred what's in a box, see Wimmer, Hogrefe, & Perner, 1988; Gopnik & Graf, 1988; Wimmer, Hogrefe & Sodian, 1988). Executive function tasks (such as the Wisconsin Card-Sorting Task), in which failure by 3-year-olds (and by children with autism, see Hughes & Russell, 1993; Russell, 1997a) correlates with failure on theory of mind tasks, involve the need to inhibit a natural response tendency in favor of an adaptive response. It has been suggested (Pacherie, 1997; Perner, 2000a, 2000b; Russell, 1996, 1997a) that self-awareness of the causal power of the mental disposition that results in the prepotent response is a necessary prerequisite for the executive inhibition of such a response. Difficulties in self-monitoring of intentions have also been hypothesized to underlie the co-occurrence of self-control difficulties (and mistaken attributions of the contents of one's own intentions to external sources) and theory of mind problems in schizophrenia (Frith, 1992) as well as the co-occurrence of executive function problems and theory of mind difficulties in children with autism (Carruthers, 1996; Pacherie, 1997; Russell, 1996, 1997a; see also Zelazo & Müller, ch. 20, and Baron-Cohen et al., ch. 22, this volume).

The emergence of the autobiographical self.   Perner (2000a) also argues that the cause of infantile amnesia (the lack of genuine memories of personally experienced events that occurred prior to about 3–4 years of age, see Bauer, ch. 6 this volume) has to do with young children's inability to "encode personally experienced events *as personally experienced*" (p. 306), i. e., in terms of their causal informational source "as having been seen." Around 4–5 years of age, as the ability to represent the informational source as well as the content of knowledge emerges in theory of mind tasks, the autobiographic organization of memories as personally experienced events is also established.

Povinelli and his colleagues have demonstrated that young children have serious difficulties before 4–5 years of age in integrating self-related experiences into a coherent causal-temporal organization around a self-concept extended in time (Povinelli, 1995; Povinelli,

Landau, & Perilloux, 1996; Povinelli & Simon, 1998; Povinelli, Landry, Theall, Clark, & Castille, 1999). They have shown that recognition of the self on a briefly delayed video feedback is absent before 4–5 years of age. In one study (Povinelli & Simon, 1998), children were videotaped while playing a game with an experimenter who covertly placed a large sticker on the back of the child's head during the game. Three minutes later when the videotape was played back to the children, 3-year-olds failed to reach up to remove the sticker from their head, even though they generally managed to verbally "recognize" themselves by saying "it's me" or their proper name when asked who the child was on the video. (However, when asked where the sticker was, they tended to reply that "it's on *his* or *her* head" instead of their own!) They nevertheless did reach up to remove the sticker when presented with a mirror. In contrast, 4–5-year-olds could relate the delayed video feedback to their current self as shown by the fact that they removed the sticker when presented with the videotape.

Perner (2000a) explains this finding by arguing that "3-year-olds seem to lack an understanding of the causal link between recorded events and what they see on the video record" (p. 302). However, Povinelli et al. (1999) demonstrated that 3-year-olds do understand the equivalence between delayed video images and the real world, as they are able to witness an object being hidden on video and then successfully locate it (see also DeLoache, ch. 10 this volume). In Povinelli's theory (1995; Povinelli & Simon, 1998; Povinelli et al., 1999) the concept of an *"autobiographical self"* emerges around 4 years as a function of domain-general changes in the child's representational capacities. First, at the end of the second year infants develop the ability to hold a single representation or model of the world in mind (cf. Olson & Campbell, 1993; Perner, 1991) that they can compare to presently perceived aspects of reality. This underlies the ability to recognize the self in the mirror between 18–24 months: the single mental representation of the self's actions and physical features (the "present self") is compared to the mirror image with which an equivalence relation is assumed. At around 4 years, however, "children become able to hold in mind multiple representations or models of the world simultaneously" (Povinelli & Simon, 1998, p. 189). This makes it possible for the child to establish temporal and causal relations among memories of previously encoded experiences of the self: in particular, to causally "evaluate the relevance of previous states of the self to the present self" (p. 189). (Thus, 4–5-year olds can draw a causal inference that if a few minutes ago a sticker was placed on their head (as revealed by the videotape), their present state is likely to be affected by this past event so that the sticker is probably still on their head.) The ability to relate multiple representations, therefore, underlies the establishment of an abstract historical-causal self-concept (the "autobiographical stance") which integrates memories of previously unrelated states of the self into an organized, coherent, and unified autobiographical self representation.

Conclusions

In this chapter I have traced the complex and intricate development of the young child's emerging understanding of the self and others as agents in the environment starting from birth to about 5 years of age. I have focused on the ways in which the young child develops a representational understanding of the causal relations (both physical and mental) between persons and their actions, and between actions and consequent changes in the environment. Five different levels of the development of understanding agency and selfhood were distinguished: The first was *the self as a "physical agent,"* which involves the differentiated representation of the body as a separate, integrated, and dynamic entity that can cause physical changes in the environment. The second was *the self as a "social agent,"* which represents the species-specific affective interactions that infants and caregivers engage in already during the first months of life. The third was *the self as a "teleological agent,"* which refers to the qualitatively new, but still nonmentalistic understanding of goal-directed rational action emerging around 9 months of age. The fourth was *the self as an "intentional mental agent,"* which emerges during the second year and involves an already mentalistic understanding of some causal intentional mind states such as desires and intentions that are represented as existing prior to and separately from the actions they generate. Finally, I distinguished *the self as a "representational agent"* and *the emergence of the "autobiographical self"* between 4 and 5 years of age, which involves the ability to comprehend the "representational" and "causally self-referential" properties of intentional mind states leading, among other things, to the establishment of an abstract, temporally extended, historical-causal concept of the "autobiographical self."

Notes

1. Recently, Watson hypothesized (Gergely, Koós, & Watson, 2000; Gergely & Watson, 1999; Watson 1994) that the etiology of *childhood autism* may be related to a genetically based malfunctioning of the "switching mechanism" of the contingency detection module. In autistic individuals the contingency analyzer gets "stuck" for ever in its original (or close to original) setting of preferentially seeking out and processing perfectly self-contingent stimuli. As a result, children with autism continue to invest in perfect contingencies (generated by stereotypic self-stimulation or repetitive object-manipulation) throughout their lives, while showing a lack of interest in the less-than-perfect contingencies provided by their social environment (for some preliminary supporting evidence, see Gergely, Magyar, & Balázs, 1999; Gergely & Watson, 1999, pp. 125–30).

2. Of course, it is not denied that during early interactions mother and infant may experience similar subjective states. However, such "affect sharing" during empathic parental mirroring or infantile imitation of parental expressions can, at best, be called "objective intersubjectivity" in so far that the two subjective states thus generated become aligned. This, however, does not imply that the young infant is aware of sharing the subjective state with the other, or, for that matter, that the other experiences a subjective state at all.

CHAPTER THREE

The Acquisition of Physical Knowledge in Infancy: A Summary in Eight Lessons

Renée Baillargeon

As adults we possess a great deal of knowledge about the physical world. For example, we realize that an object continues to exist when placed behind a nearer object, that a wide object can be lowered inside a wide but not a narrow container, and that an object typically falls when released in midair. Piaget (1954) was the first researcher to examine whether infants, like adults, hold expectations about physical events. Analyses of infants' responses in various object-manipulation tasks led him to conclude that, during the first year of life, infants possess very little physical knowledge. For the next several decades, this conclusion was generally accepted (for reviews of this early research, see Bremner, 1985; Gratch, 1976; Harris, 1987; and Schubert, 1983). This state of affairs began to change in the 1980s, however, when evidence obtained with novel, more sensitive tasks revealed that even young infants hold at least limited expectations about physical events (e.g., Baillargeon, 1986; Baillargeon, Spelke, & Wasserman, 1985; Baillargeon & Graber, 1987; Diamond, 1985; Hood & Willatts, 1986; Leslie, 1982, 1984; Pieraut-Le Bonniec, 1985; Spelke & Kestenbaum, 1986).

In subsequent years, researchers began to explore many new facets of infants' physical knowledge, bringing to light new competences and developments (e.g., Arterberry, 1993; Clifton, Rochat, Litovsky, & Perris, 1991; Diamond, 1991; Goubet & Clifton, 1998; Kotovsky & Baillargeon, 1994; Lécuyer, 1993; Needham & Baillargeon, 1993; Oakes & Cohen, 1990; Spelke, Breinlinger, Macomber, & Jacobson, 1992). Today, investigators generally agree (with a few notable exceptions: e.g., Bogartz, Shinskey, & Speaker, 1997;

The preparation of this chapter was supported by a grant from the National Institute of Child Health and Human Development (HD-21104). I would like to thank Jerry DeJong, Cindy Fisher, Yuyan Luo, Kris Onishi, and Su-Hua Wang for many helpful discussions, comments, and suggestions. Correspondence concerning this chapter should be sent to: Renée Baillargeon, Department of Psychology, University of Illinois, 603 East Daniel, Champaign, IL 61820, USA (email: <rbaillar@s.psych.uiuc.edu>).

Haith & Benson, 1998; Rivera, Wakeley, & Langer, 1999) that young infants' physical world is far more sophisticated than Piaget (1954) – with the limited methodological tools at his disposal – would ever have thought possible.

In keeping with these advances, for the past 10 years my collaborators and I have been investigating the development of infants' physical knowledge. Our research has focused on two main questions: first, what knowledge do infants possess, at each age, about different physical events (e.g., occlusion, support, collision, and containment events);[1] and second, how do infants attain this knowledge? In this chapter, I summarize some of the main findings we have obtained to date. For ease of communication, I have organized this summary in eight "lessons." These lessons are of course still preliminary. Nevertheless, they are useful in providing a framework for what has been learned so far, and in making clear what needs to be studied next.

To give a brief overview, the first three lessons are concerned with the nature of the expectations infants acquire about physical events. The next three lessons deal with some of the factors and processes involved in the acquisition of these physical expectations. Finally, the last two lessons address the possible contributions of innate concepts to infants' physical reasoning.

Lesson 1: Infants Acquire Rules about Physical Events

The first lesson suggested by our research and that of other investigators is that infants acquire expectations or rules about physical events; these rules specify for them what are the likely outcomes of events (e.g., Aguiar & Baillargeon, 1999; Baillargeon, Graber, DeVos, & Black, 1990; Hespos & Baillargeon, 2001b; Kotovsky & Baillargeon, 2000; Lécuyer & Durand, 1996; Needham, 1998; Newcombe, Huttenlocher, & Learmonth, 1999; Wilcox, Nadel, & Rosser, 1996). When faced with events inconsistent with their rules, as in violation-of-expectation experiments (e.g., Baillargeon, 1995, 1998, 2000b), infants typically are surprised or puzzled, as evidenced by increased attention: under most circumstances, infants look reliably longer at events that violate, as opposed to confirm, their physical expectations.

Not surprisingly, in the initial stages of learning, infants' rules about physical events tend to be rather primitive or incomplete, so that they often err in determining what are the likely outcomes of events. Two types of errors have been documented to date. First, infants sometimes fail to view as unexpected events that adults perceive to be physically impossible (I will refer to such events as violation events). Second, infants sometimes view as unexpected events that adults perceive to be physically possible and indeed commonplace (non-violation events). Their lack of physical knowledge thus leads infants both (1) to respond to violation events as though they were expected and (2) to respond to non-violation events as though they were unexpected. To illustrate these two types of errors, I briefly describe new findings on 2.5-month-old infants' knowledge of occlusion events.

Occlusion events

Recent evidence suggests that, although 2.5-month-old infants recognize that an object continues to exist *after* it becomes occluded, they are rather poor at predicting *when* it should be occluded (e.g., Aguiar & Baillargeon, 1999; Hespos & Baillargeon, 2001b; Luo, 2000; Luo & Baillargeon, 2001a; Spelke et al., 1992; Wilcox et al., 1996). At 2.5 months of age, infants appear to follow a simple "behind/not-behind" rule when predicting the outcomes of occlusion events: they expect an object to be hidden when behind an occluder, and to be visible otherwise. At this stage, infants do not take into account information about the relative sizes of the object and occluder, or about the presence of openings in the occluder; *any* object is expected to be hidden when behind *any* occluder.

Because their knowledge of the conditions under which objects should and should not be occluded is very limited, 2.5-month-old infants often err in distinguishing between violation and non-violation occlusion events. A recent experiment by Yuyan Luo and myself clearly illustrates this point (Luo & Baillargeon, 2001a). This experiment built on prior findings by Aguiar and Baillargeon (1999) and examined infants' ability to determine whether an object should remain continuously hidden or become temporarily visible when passing behind a screen with a large opening in its midsection.

The infants were assigned to a cylinder-appears or a cylinder-does-not-appear condition (see figure 3.1). In both conditions, the infants first saw a familiarization event in which an upright cylinder moved back and forth along a track whose center was hidden by a screen; the cylinder disappeared at one end of the screen and reappeared, after an appropriate interval, at the other end. Next, the infants saw two test events. In one (separate-screens event), the entire midsection of the screen was removed to create two separate screens. In the other event (connected-screens event), the two screens remained connected at the top by a short strip. In both events, the cylinder moved back and forth along the track, as in the familiarization event. For the infants in the cylinder-appears condition, the cylinder appeared in the gap between the screens in each test event. For the infants in the cylinder-does-not-appear condition, the cylinder disappeared behind one screen and reappeared from behind the other screen *without* appearing in the gap between them.

As adults, we would expect the cylinder to appear both between the separate and the connected screens. What of the 2.5-month-old infants in the experiment, with their simple behind/not-behind rule? We predicted that, like adults, the infants should expect the cylinder to appear between the separate screens, because at that point the cylinder did not lie behind any occluder. Unlike adults, however, the infants should expect the cylinder *not* to appear between the connected screens: the infants should view these as a single occluder, and they should expect the cylinder to remain hidden when passing behind it.

The results supported our predictions: the infants in the cylinder-appears condition looked reliably longer at the connected- than at the separate-screens test event, whereas those in the cylinder-does-not-appear condition showed the reverse looking pattern. Together, these results suggested that the infants expected the cylinder to appear between the separate but not the connected screens, and were surprised when each of these expectations was violated.

To return to our first lesson: the infants' limited knowledge about occlusion events led them to err, in both conditions, in their response to the connected-screens event. The infants were not surprised when the cylinder failed to appear between the screens (a violation event), and they were surprised when it did appear (a non-violation event).

Cylinder-appears condition

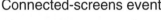

Connected-screens event

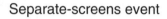

Separate-screens event

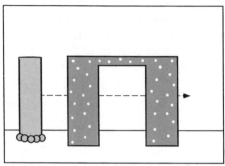

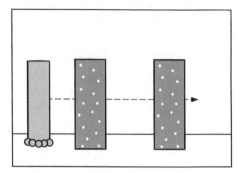

Cylinder-does-not-appear condition

Connected-screens event

Separate-screens event

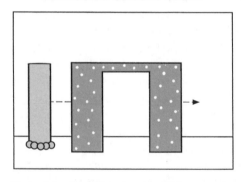

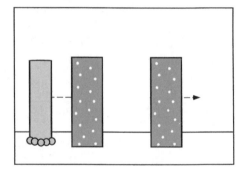

Figure 3.1   Schematic drawing of the test events in Luo and Baillargeon (2001a)

Additional remarks

It is not very surprising that infants detect far fewer physical violations than do adults. One would expect that, as infants' physical knowledge grows, the set of violation events they recognize gradually approximates that of adults. What is more intriguing is the fact that infants sometimes perceive physically possible, non-violation events as violation events (e.g., Baillargeon, DeJong, & Sheehan, 2001; Luo & Baillargeon, 2001a; Wang & Baillargeon, 2001a). Such findings provide strong evidence that infants are acquiring rules about physical events, rules that are initially limited and incomplete and as such can lead to false predictions. One is reminded here of the young child who produces such words as "goed" and "eated" in the course of acquiring the past-tense rule of English (e.g., Marcus, Pinker, Ullman, Hollander, Rosen, & Xu, 1992).

Some investigators have recently questioned the notion that infants acquire rules about physical events (e.g., Bogartz et al., 1997; Haith & Benson, 1998; Rivera et al., 1999; Thelen & Smith, 1994). For example, Bogartz et al. (1997) argued that the process of knowledge acquisition is essentially one of data collection. Infants collect and store "video-tapes" of physical events. When faced with an event, infants search through their "library" of videotapes, retrieve the most relevant, and compare the current and stored events; mismatches engage infants' attention and cause them to update the existing videotape or create a new one.

This approach can address why infants respond to violation events with increased attention – no videotape in their library would be likely to match these physically impossible events. However, what of the findings that infants also respond to physically possible, non-violation events with increased attention? Why would infants detect mismatches where there are none?

A more parsimonious explanation for the evidence currently available is that, in their attempts to make sense of physical events, infants formulate rules about how the events might operate. Initially, these rules tend to be rather primitive, with the result that infants often err in determining what are violation and non-violation events. Of course, these errors themselves may play a powerful motivating role in the development of infants' physical knowledge. The 2.5-month-old infant who notices that, contrary to his expectations, objects do become temporarily visible when passing behind occluders with central openings, is taking the first step toward improving his knowledge of the conditions under which objects should and should not be occluded. We return to this issue in Lesson 4.

Lesson 2: Infants' Rules Become More Sophisticated Over Time

The second lesson suggested by the research from our and other laboratories is that infants' rules become more sophisticated over time (e.g., Aguiar & Baillargeon, in press; Baillargeon, 1991; Dan, Omori, & Tomiyasu, 2000; Hespos & Baillargeon, 2001a; Kotovsky & Baillargeon, 1998; Needham, 1999; Sitskoorn & Smitsman, 1995; Wilcox, 1999). In fact, infants' rules about different physical events all seem to develop according to the same general pattern. Specifically, when learning about events such as occlusion, support, collision, and other events, infants typically first form an initial concept centered on a primitive, all-or-none distinction. With further experience, infants identify a sequence of variables – some discrete and others continuous – that revise and elaborate this initial concept, resulting in increasingly accurate predictions and interpretations over time. To illustrate this developmental pattern, I summarize the results of experiments from our laboratory on the development of infants' knowledge about occlusion and support events.

Occlusion events

In our experiments on the development of infants' expectations about occlusion events (e.g., Aguiar & Baillargeon, 1999, in press; Baillargeon & DeVos, 1991; Luo, 2000; Luo

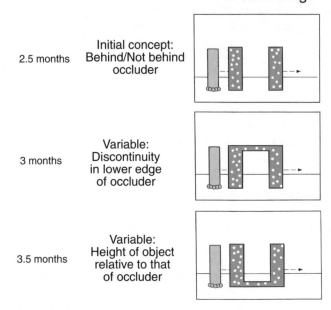

Figure 3.2   Schematic description of the development of infants' knowledge about occlusion events between 2.5 and 3.5 months of age

& Baillargeon, 2001a; for reviews, see Baillargeon, 1998, 1999), infants aged 2.5 to 3.5 months watched an object (e.g., a cylinder, a toy mouse, or a toy carrot) move back and forth behind a screen; next, a portion of the screen was removed, and the infants judged whether the object should remain hidden or become (at least partly) visible when passing behind the screen. The results of these experiments are illustrated in figure 3.2. By 2.5 months of age, as was discussed earlier, infants have formed an initial concept of occlusion centered on a simple *behind/not-behind* distinction. When the entire mid-section of the screen is removed to form two separate screens, infants expect the object to become visible in the gap between them. However, if the screens remain connected either at the top or at the bottom by a short strip, infants no longer expect the object to become visible: they view the connected screens as a single screen and expect the object to be hidden when behind it. Over the course of the next month, infants rapidly progress beyond their initial concept. At about 3 months of age, infants begin to consider the presence of a *discontinuity in the lower edge* of the screen. Although infants still expect the object to remain hidden when passing behind two screens that are connected at the bottom by a short strip, they now expect the object to become visible when passing behind two screens that are connected at the top by a short strip. Finally, at about 3.5 months of age, infants begin to consider the relative *heights* of the object and screen. When the object passes behind two screens that are connected at the bottom by a strip, infants expect the object to become partly visible if it is taller but not shorter than the strip.

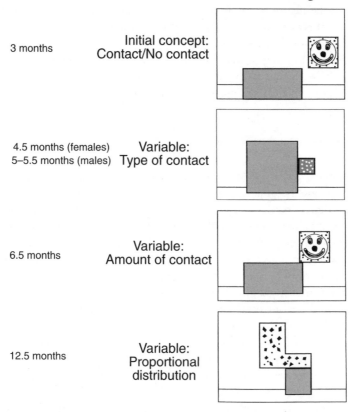

Figure 3.3   Schematic description of the development of infants' knowledge about support events between 3 and 12.5 months of age

Support events

In our experiments on the development of infants' knowledge about support events (e.g., Baillargeon, Needham, & DeVos, 1992; Needham & Baillargeon, 1993; for reviews, see Baillargeon, 1995, 1998, and Baillargeon, Kotovsky, & Needham, 1995), infants aged 3 to 12.5 months were presented with support problems involving a box and a platform; the box was held in one of several positions relative to the platform, and the infants judged whether the box should remain stable when released. The results of these experiments are summarized in figure 3.3. By 3 months of age, infants have formed an initial concept of support centered on a simple *contact/no-contact* distinction: they expect the box to remain stable if released in contact with the platform, and to fall otherwise. At this stage, any contact with the platform is deemed sufficient to ensure the box's stability. In the months that follow, infants identify a sequence of variables that progressively revise and elaborate their initial concept. At about 4.5 to 5.5 months of age (females precede males by a few weeks in this acquisition), infants begin to take into account the *type of contact* between the box and the platform. Infants now expect the box to remain stable when released on but not against the platform. At about 6.5 months of age, infants begin to consider the *amount of contact* between the box and the platform. Infants now expect the box to remain stable if a large but not a small portion of its bottom surface rests on the platform. Finally, at about 12.5 months of age, infants begin to attend to the *proportional distribution* of the box; they realize that an asymmetrical box can be stable only if the proportion of the box that rests on the platform is greater than that off the platform.

Additional remarks

The results summarized above all focus on infants' responses to *violation* events – what new violation infants become able to detect at each age, and how the total set of violations they can detect increases steadily with age. However, based on these same results, one can also predict how infants should respond to the converse *non-violation* events. In the case of occlusion events, it should be the case that 2.5-month-old infants, for example, are surprised when an object appears between two screens that are connected either at the top or at the bottom by a short strip. Similarly, in the case of support events, it should be the case that 3-month-old infants, for example, are surprised to see an object fall when deposited against a wall or on the edge of a table. Until now, most of the research on infants' physical reasoning has tended to focus on infants' responses to violation as opposed to non-violation events. However, as we saw in Lesson 1, evidence that infants perceive non-violation events as surprising is extremely useful in that it helps make clear the nature of the rules that underlie their interpretations of events.

The focus on violation as opposed to non-violation events has also tended to obscure certain developments in infants' physical knowledge: those in which the addition of a new variable does not lead to the detection of a new violation (as in figures 3.2 and 3.3). Recent research by Dan et al. (2000), Huettel and Needham (2000), and Wang and Baillargeon (2001a) suggests that, at about 8.5 months of age, infants add a new variable to their understanding of support events. Specifically, infants begin to distinguish between situations in which the *side or middle portion* of a box's bottom surface rests on a platform; they recognize that, in the latter case, when the box is balanced on a narrower platform, stability is possible even if less than half of the box's bottom surface is in contact with the platform. This development is interesting in that it does not allow infants to detect a novel violation (and hence does not easily fit into figure 3.3). Rather, it leads infants to regard events previously viewed as violation events (e.g., a box that remains stable when balanced on a narrow platform, with, say, only the middle 33 percent of its bottom surface supported) as non-violation events.

The findings summarized to this point do not, of course, represent all that infants learn about occlusion and support events. First, many more variables must be identified. For example, in the case of occlusion events, infants must also learn that wide objects can be fully hidden behind wide but not narrow occluders (e.g., Baillargeon & Brueckner,

2000; Wilcox, 1999; Wilcox & Baillargeon, 1998a, 1998b), that faster objects reappear sooner than slower objects from behind occluders (e.g., Spelke, Kestenbaum, Simons, & Wein, 1995; Wilcox & Schweinlee, 2001), and that opaque occluders function differently than do transparent occluders (e.g., Luo, 2001; Luo & Baillargeon, 2001b, 2001d).

Second, infants' reasoning about several of the variables they identify must undergo considerable refinement. For example, in the case of support events, preliminary data collected by Su-Hua Wang and myself suggest that when 6.5-month-old infants first identify amount of contact as a variable, they assume that an object will be stable if 66 percent but not 50 percent of its bottom surface is supported; over time, infants come to realize that 50 percent is typically sufficient to ensure stability. In the same vein, Dan et al. (2000) reported that after infants come to realize that an object can be stable when balanced on a narrower platform, they must still learn how wide the platform needs to be for the object to be stable.

Finally, other developments involve the transition from qualitative to quantitative reasoning. The distinction between quantitative and qualitative reasoning strategies is derived from computational models of everyday physical reasoning (e.g., Forbus, 1984). A strategy is said to be quantitative if it requires one to encode and use information about absolute quantities (e.g., object A is "this" tall, where "this" stands for some absolute measure of A's height). In contrast, a strategy is said to be qualitative if it requires one to encode and use information about only relative quantities (e.g., object A is taller than object B). There is now considerable evidence (for reviews, see Baillargeon, 1994, 1995) that, when infants first identify a continuous variable, they can reason about the variable qualitatively but not quantitatively: they are not able at first to encode and remember absolute information about the variable.

A recent experiment by Yuyan Luo and myself clearly illustrates this point (Luo & Baillargeon, 2001c). This experiment examined whether 5-month-old infants realize that the height of an object relative to that of an occluder determines not only (1) *whether* the object should appear above the occluder, but also (2) *how much* of the object should appear above the occluder. The infants were assigned to a qualitative or a quantitative condition (see figure 3.4). The infants in the qualitative condition first saw familiarization events in which a tall or a short cylinder moved back and forth along a track whose center was hidden by a screen; the tall cylinder was the same height as the screen (30 cm), and the short cylinder was 8 cm shorter (22 cm). The tall and short cylinders were shown on alternate trials. Next, a window was cut into the top midsection of the screen; the bottom of the window was located 14 cm above the screen's lower edge. The infants saw two test events in which the tall and short cylinders again moved back and forth along the track. In both events, the cylinder appeared in the window when passing behind the screen; and in both events, the cylinder extended to the top of the window. This last outcome was expected for the tall cylinder, which was as tall as the screen, but not for the short cylinder, which was 8 cm shorter and should have reached only the midpoint of the window. The infants in the quantitative condition saw similar familiarization and test events except that the screen was 8 cm taller. In this condition, both the tall and the short cylinders were shorter than the screen, and both reached a point 8 cm below the top of the window when passing behind the screen (this outcome was expected for

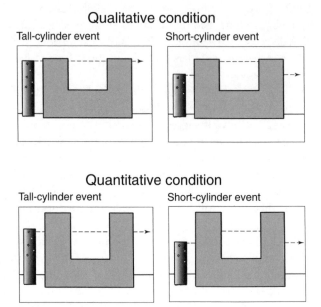

Figure 3.4   Schematic drawing of the test events in Luo and Baillargeon (2001c)

the tall cylinder, which was 8 cm shorter than the screen, but not for the short cylinder, which was 16 cm shorter).

The infants in the qualitative condition could succeed at detecting the violation in the short-cylinder test event by reasoning qualitatively about the event. As the short cylinder approached the screen, the infants could visually compare its height to that of the bottom and top of the window. Based on these comparisons, they could conclude that (1) since the short cylinder was taller than the bottom of the window, it would appear in the window; and (2) since the short cylinder was shorter than the top of the window, it would not reach the top of the window. This last expectation was violated when the short cylinder extended all the way to the top of the window.

In contrast, the infants in the quantitative condition could detect the violation in the short-cylinder test event only by engaging in quantitative reasoning. A qualitative comparison of the heights of the short cylinder and window could establish only that (1) the cylinder would appear in the window and (2) the cylinder would not reach the top of the window. To detect the violation in the short-cylinder event – that is, to detect that the short cylinder extended higher than it should have in the window – the infants had to engage in quantitative reasoning: they needed to encode the absolute height of the short cylinder as it approached the screen, and to compare this (represented) height to that of the cylinder in the window.

The infants in the qualitative condition looked reliably longer at the short- than at the tall-cylinder test event, whereas those in the quantitative condition tended to look equally at the two events. Together, these results suggested that 5-month-old infants can reason qualitatively but not quantitatively about height information in occlusion events. Further research is needed to determine at what age infants become able to engage in quantitative reasoning about this variable.

Lesson 3: Infants' Rules are Narrow in Scope

So far we have learned that infants form rules about physical events, and that these rules become richer and more complex with the identification of additional variables. In Lesson 3, we consider the following question: How general or specific are infants' rules about physical events? Do infants acquire *general* rules that are applied broadly to all relevant physical events, or more *specific* rules that remain tied to the events where they are first acquired?

Recent research suggests that the second possibility is more likely (e.g., Hespos, 1998, 2000; Hespos & Baillargeon, 2001a; Luo, 2001; Luo & Baillargeon, 2001b; Wang, Baillargeon, & Paterson, 2001; Wang & Paterson, 2000; Wilcox & Baillargeon, 1998a). Specifically, it appears that infants "sort" physical events into event categories, and learn separately how each category operates. A variable acquired in the context of one event category is not generalized to other relevant categories; it is kept tied to the specific category where it is first identified. As a result, infants must sometimes "relearn" in one event category a variable they have already acquired in another category. When weeks or months separate these two acquisitions, striking lags (or, to borrow a Piagetian term, décalages; e.g., Flavell, 1963) can be observed in infants' responses to events from the two categories. To illustrate such lags, I briefly describe the results of recent experiments on infants' reasoning about height and transparency information in occlusion, containment, and other events.

Height information

In a recent experiment, Sue Hespos and I compared 4.5-month-old infants' ability to reason about height information in containment and in occlusion events (Hespos, 1998; Hespos & Baillargeon, 2001a). Specifically, we asked whether infants this age realize that a tall object cannot be fully hidden when placed inside a short container or behind a short occluder.

The infants were assigned to a container or an occluder condition and saw two test events (see figure 3.5). At the start of each event shown in the container condition, an experimenter's gloved hand grasped a knob at the top of a tall cylindrical object; next to the object was a cylindrical container. The hand lifted the object and lowered it inside the container until only the knob protruded above the rim. The container used in the tall-container event was as tall as the cylindrical portion of the object; the container used in the short-container event was only half as tall, so that it should have been impossible for the cylindrical portion of the object to become fully hidden inside the container. Prior to the test trials, the infants received familiarization trials in which the containers were rotated forward so that the infants could inspect them. The infants in the occluder

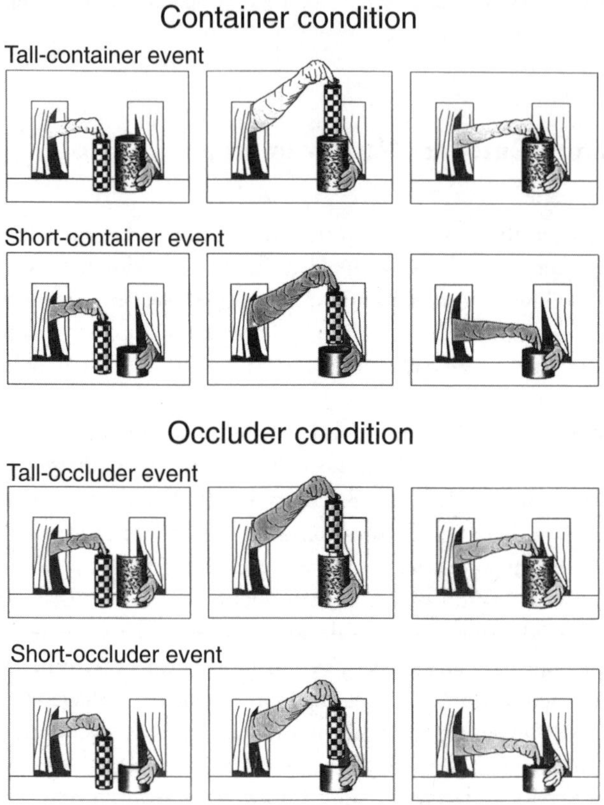

Container condition

Tall-container event

Short-container event

Occluder condition

Tall-occluder event

Short-occluder event

Figure 3.5   Schematic drawing of the test events in Hespos and Baillargeon (2001a)

condition saw similar familiarization and test events with one exception: the bottom and back half of each container were removed to create a rounded occluder.

The infants in the occluder condition looked reliably longer at the short- than at the tall-occluder test event, whereas those in the container condition looked about equally at the two events. Our interpretation of these results was that 4.5-month-old infants view occlusion and containment as two distinct event categories and do not generalize rules or variables acquired about occlusion to containment. Infants realize that the height of an object relative to that of an occluder determines whether the object can be fully or only partly hidden when behind the occluder, but they do *not* yet appreciate that the height of an object relative to that of a container determines whether the object can be fully or only partly hidden when inside the container.

This interpretation led to a striking prediction: infants shown the same test events as in the container condition but with the object lowered *behind* rather than *inside* each container should be able to detect the violation in the short-container test event. With the containers serving as mere occluders, infants' performance should mirror that of the infants in the occluder condition. This prediction was confirmed: when the object was lowered behind rather than inside each container, infants looked reliably longer at the short- than at the tall-container event. These and additional control results (Hespos & Baillargeon, 2001a) provided converging evidence that 4.5-month-old infants view occlusion and containment as distinct event categories and learn separately about each category. Infants consider the height of an object relative to that of a container when the object is lowered *behind* but not *inside* the container.

At what age do infants become able to reason about height in containment events? In an additional experiment, 5.5-, 6.5-, and 7.5-month-old infants were shown the container condition test events (Hespos & Baillargeon, 2001a). Only the 7.5-month-old infants looked reliably longer at the short- than at the tall-container event, suggesting that it is not until this age that infants begin to consider height information when reasoning about containment events.

It might be suggested that the 7.5-month-old infants were perhaps successful, not because they had – at long last – identified height as a containment variable, but because they had achieved a general ability to reason about height in different physical events. However, results obtained with other events cast doubts on such a possibility (e.g., Baillargeon, 1993; Wang & Paterson, 2000; Wang et al., 2001). For example, Wang and Paterson (2000), building upon the present results, compared 9-month-old infants' ability to reason about height information in containment and in covering events (in these events, the containers were turned upside down and lowered over the object). The infants succeeded in the container but not the cover condition: they were surprised when a tall object was fully lowered inside a short container, but not when a short cover was fully lowered over the same tall object. Recent results (Wang & Baillargeon, 2001b) indicate that it is not until infants are about 12 months of age that they begin to reason about height information in covering events. These findings make clear that infants do not acquire at 7.5 months of age a generalized ability to reason about height in physical events.

The results reported in this section (and converging results obtained with object-retrieval paradigms: Hespos, 1998; McCall, 2001) suggest that infants view events involving occluders, containers, and covers as belonging to separate categories, and do not generalize information acquired about one category to the others. Infants begin to consider height information in occlusion events at about 3.5 months of age (e.g., Baillargeon & DeVos, 1991), in containment events at about 7.5 months of age (e.g., Hespos, 1998; Hespos & Baillargeon, 2001a), and in events involving covers at about 12 months of age (e.g., McCall, 2001; Wang & Baillargeon, 2001b; Wang & Paterson, 2000; Wang et al., 2001).

Transparency information

In a recent experiment, Yuyan Luo and I compared 8.5-month-old infants' ability to reason about transparency information in containment and in occlusion events (Luo, 2001; Luo & Baillargeon, 2001b). More specifically, the experiment asked whether infants expect an object to be visible when lowered inside a transparent container or behind a transparent occluder.

The infants were assigned to a container or an occluder condition and saw two test events (see figure 3.6). At the start of each event shown in the container condition, a

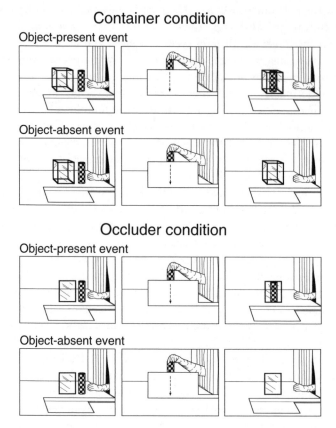

Figure 3.6   Schematic drawing of the test events in Luo and Baillargeon (2001b)

cylindrical object stood next to a rectangular container of the same height; the container was made of transparent Plexiglass and its edges were outlined with red tape (prior to the test session, an experimenter showed the container to the infants for a few seconds, so that they had the opportunity to inspect its surfaces). To start, a screen was raised to hide the container, and an experimenter's gloved hand grasped the object and lowered it inside the hidden container. Next, the screen was lowered to reveal the container with either the object standing inside it (object-present event), or no object inside it (object-absent event). The infants in the occluder condition saw similar test events except that the transparent container was replaced with a transparent occluder. This occluder was identical to the front of the container; a small Plexiglass base behind the occluder allowed it to stand upright.

The infants in the occluder condition looked reliably longer at the object-absent than at the object-present test event, whereas those in the container condition tended to look equally at the two events. These results suggested that 8.5-month-old infants expect an object to be visible when lowered behind a transparent occluder, but not when lowered inside a transparent container. In subsequent experiments (Luo & Baillargeon, 2001b), we found that it is not until infants are about 10 months of age that they begin to attend to transparency information in containment events.

These results (and additional results, some of which are discussed later; Luo & Baillargeon, 2001d) provide converging evidence that infants view occlusion and containment as distinct event categories, and learn separately how each category operates. As was the case with height (e.g., Hespos & Baillargeon, 2001a), infants identify transparency as a variable first in occlusion events, and only after some time in containment events.

Additional remarks

The findings reviewed in this section suggest that infants sort physical events into distinct categories, and learn separately about each category. Such a learning strategy must, overall, greatly facilitate infants' acquisition of physical knowledge; after all, breaking down the task of learning into smaller, more manageable components is a time-honored solution to the difficulties of knowledge acquisition.

The notion that infants acquire event-specific rather than event-general rules or expectations is consistent with an emerging theme in the developmental literature that infants' knowledge tends to be highly context-specific. For example, Adolph (1997) reported that infants learn to navigate steep slopes with caution in the first weeks of crawling – and again in the first weeks of walking; the knowledge that steep slopes can lead to falling is not generalized from crawling to walking but must be learned all over again. Similarly, Needham (in press) found that infants use featural information to segregate objects placed side by side several months before they succeed in doing the same with objects (even the same objects) placed one on top of the other. Finally, Onishi (2000) reported that 13-month-old infants correctly judge whether a stack of boxes should be stable when they are led to believe that the stack is composed of two but not three boxes; apparently, infants do not generalize the support rules they use when reasoning about stacks of two boxes to stacks of three boxes.

The evidence that infants form event categories raises many questions for future research. In particular, on what basis are categories generated? Why are occlusion and containment, for example, viewed as distinct categories? In many cases (and contrary to those studied here), occlusion and containment outcomes are different: for example, a wide object can be lowered behind a narrow occluder, but not inside a narrow container; and an object that has been lowered inside a container typically moves with it when displaced, but an object that has been lowered behind an occluder does not. It seems plausible that these clusters of interrelated causal relationships underlie infants' distinct event categories (e.g., Keil, 1991, 1995; Leslie, 1994, 1995; Pauen, 1999). We return to this issue in Lesson 6.

Lesson 4: The Acquisition of Rules is Triggered by Exposure to Unpredicted Outcomes

The evidence reviewed in the previous lessons suggests that infants sort physical events into distinct categories and, for each category, identify a sequence of variables that specify (rightly or wrongly) expected outcomes. One important issue that has not been discussed so far is infants' identification of variables in each event category. How does this process occur?

Before addressing this question, we need to consider more closely what variables are. My collaborators and I (e.g., Aguiar & Baillargeon, 1999; Baillargeon, in press; Hespos & Baillargeon, 2001b) have suggested that variables are akin to condition–outcome rules. A variable specifies, for a set of contrastive outcomes, what condition produces each outcome. For example, the containment variable width specifies that an object *can* be inserted into a container if it is *narrower* than the opening of the container, but *cannot* be inserted if it is *wider* than the opening. For each of the two contrastive outcomes (can or cannot be inserted into the container), the variable identifies the condition responsible for the outcome (narrower or wider than the opening of the container).[2]

How, then, do infants go about identifying variables? We have proposed that what typically triggers the identification of a variable in an event category is exposure to contrastive outcomes that are not predicted by infants' current knowledge of the category (e.g., Aguiar & Baillargeon, 1999; Baillargeon, in press; Hespos & Baillargeon, 2001b). When infants register these contrastive outcomes, they begin to seek out the conditions that are responsible for them. The identification of these condition–outcome relations signals the identification of a new variable.

To illustrate, consider once again the containment variable width. When reasoning about containment events, infants initially assume that any object can be inserted into any container with an open – as opposed to a closed – top (e.g., Hespos & Baillargeon, 2001b). After some time, however, infants begin to notice that objects sometimes can and sometimes cannot be inserted into containers with open tops. At that point, infants begin to search for the conditions that map onto these contrastive outcomes. Eventually, infants come to realize that objects can be inserted into containers whose openings are wider but not narrower than the objects (e.g., Aguiar & Baillargeon, 1998, 2000b, 2001; Baillargeon & Brueckner, 2000; Sitskoorn & Smitsman, 1995).

In many instances, as in the preceding example, contrastive outcomes will involve contradictions of infants' current knowledge. Infants will realize that, contrary to their expectations, objects do not always remain hidden when passing behind occluders, do not always move when hit, do not always remain stable when placed on supports, and so on. In each case, noticing these contradictions will lead to a revision of infants' rules – until the noticing of further contradictions brings forth further revisions. In other instances, however, contrastive outcomes may simply involve facets of events that had hitherto gone unnoticed. For example, infants seem to realize at some point in their development that objects not only move when hit, but move different distances depending on the sizes (or masses) of the objects hitting them (e.g., Kotovsky & Baillargeon, 1994, 1998). Such a realization does not contradict infants' prior knowledge about collision events, but still adds a new variable to this knowledge.

From the present perspective, what triggers the identification of new rules is thus exposure to some unpredicted variation in outcome, whether or not this variation conflicts with pre-existing rules. Is there any evidence for such a notion? Recent findings by Yuyan Luo and myself could be taken to support it (Luo & Baillargeon, 2001d). This experiment built on the results of the transparency experiment reported in Lesson 3 (Luo, 2001;

Luo & Baillargeon, 2001b), and asked at what age infants identify transparency as an occlusion variable. As we saw earlier, 8.5-month-old infants expect an object that is placed behind a transparent occluder to be visible through the occluder. We next tested 7.5-, 7-, and 6.5-month-old infants, using the same object-present and object-absent test events as before (see figure 3.6).

The results were unexpected. Like the 8.5-month-old infants in our previous experiment (Luo, 2001; Luo & Baillargeon, 2001b), both the 7.5- and the 6.5-month-old infants looked reliably longer at the object-absent than at the object-present test event. In contrast, the 7-month-old infants showed the *reverse* pattern: they looked reliably longer at the object-present than at the object-absent event.

Our interpretation for these results (and control results; Luo, 2001; Luo & Baillargeon, 2001b) is as follows. Prior to about 7 months of age, infants do not perceive the clear surface of the occluder: they see only an empty frame (remember that the edges of the occluder are outlined with red tape). Based on their knowledge of occlusion events, infants expect the object to be visible in this frame, and they are surprised in the object-absent test event when it is not. At about 7 months of age, infants' vision is sufficiently improved that they can now perceive the clear surface of the occluder. At this stage, infants are puzzled by the object-present event. Their knowledge of occlusion specifies that an object should be hidden, not visible, when placed behind a larger occluder (e.g., as when a small cup is placed behind a large cereal box); and yet infants can clearly see the object behind the occluder. How is this possible? In their daily lives, 7-month-old infants no doubt experience a range of similar experiences (e.g., when they notice people and objects through car or house windows). Infants then begin to search for the conditions that explain why objects behind larger occluders are sometimes visible and sometimes hidden. In essence, infants realize that an additional variable must be taken into account to explain these observations, and they set about discovering what it is. By 7.5 months of age (and thus in a very short time), infants have formed a new condition–outcome rule: they now expect objects to be hidden when behind larger occluders that are opaque but not transparent. Armed with this new knowledge, infants can now detect violations such as that in the object-absent event.

Support for the notion that infants' perception of transparent surfaces improves at about 7 months of age comes from an experiment by Johnson and Aslin (2000). They reported improvements at this age in infants' responses to a computer-animated display consisting of a transparent box suspended in front of an opaque rod. Johnson and Aslin suggested that this change might reflect gains in contrast sensitivity, which might in turn be tied to the maturation of the magnocellular system.

Additional remarks

The main claim made in Lesson 4 is that the identification of new variables or rules is typically triggered by exposure to unpredicted outcome variation. This claim makes strong predictions about the conditions under which learning about event categories should and should not occur. In particular, it predicts that where no variation is experienced, no learning should occur.

To illustrate, consider once again the variable width in containment events. What is being proposed is that in order to identify this variable, infants must see *both* objects being inserted into wider containers, and objects failing to be inserted into narrower containers. On the present view, seeing only objects being inserted into wider containers would not be sufficient for infants to abstract the variable width. Infants would not be able to reflect on these observations and detect the underlying regularity that the object inserted into the container is always narrower than its opening. For width to be identified as a variable, infants must experience variation in outcome – they must notice that objects sometimes can and sometimes cannot be inserted into containers – and thus be induced to search for the conditions responsible for these different outcomes.

One important caveat needs to be introduced here. The claim being made is *not* that infants can never learn facts about objects in the absence of outcome variation. Such a claim is blatantly false. As an illustration, consider the results of an experiment conducted by Laura Kotovsky and myself on 5.5-month-old infants' responses to collision events (Kotovsky & Baillargeon, 1998). The infants were first habituated to the following event: a cylinder rolled down a ramp and hit a wheeled toy bug, causing it to roll to the middle of a track. Following habituation, the infants saw two test events in which the same cylinder hit the bug, causing it to roll to either the middle (same event) or the end (different event) of the track. The infants looked reliably longer at the different than at the same event, suggesting that they had learned how far the bug rolled when hit by the cylinder and noticed when a change was introduced. Because the bug always traveled the same distance during the habituation trials, learning obviously occurred in the absence of any outcome variation, through some associative process.

What is being suggested, then, is that infants acquire their knowledge about objects through several learning mechanisms, each with its own requirements for learning. Facts about individual objects and events can be learned through repetition; but general and abstract facts that apply to entire event categories cannot. To return to our collision example above (Kotovsky & Baillargeon, 1998), infants can readily learn, through simple repetition of the cylinder-bug event, that the bug rolls to the middle of the track when hit by the cylinder. But infants could not learn, even with a million repetitions of the cylinder-bug event, the general rule that objects move farther when hit by larger (or heavier) than by smaller (or lighter) objects. Indeed, infants could not learn this rule even if they saw different objects hit different wheeled toys, all of which then rolled to the middle of the track. In order to learn such a rule, we believe, infants would need to see objects roll *different distances* when hit by different objects. Exposure to these contrastive outcomes would induce infants to search for the conditions responsible for them, resulting in the acquisition of a new condition–outcome rule.

To put the preceding arguments another way: infants are not designed to reflect on a collection of similar observations (e.g., a spoon being lowered into a cup, an apple being placed into a bowl, a toy car being dropped into a bucket), and abstract from them a general rule (e.g., "in every case, the object being lowered into the container is smaller than its opening"). Infants do not gratuitously compare events, in search of abstract truths. Rather, infants are designed to solve concrete problems: they look for abstract truths when challenged to do so through exposure to unpredicted contrastive outcomes: why sometimes this outcome, and sometimes not?

Lesson 5: The Ages at which Rules are Identified Depend in Part on Exposure to Appropriate Outcome and Condition Data

It was suggested in Lesson 4 that the acquisition of a variable typically begins with infants noticing contrastive outcomes they cannot predict based on their current knowledge, and then searching for the conditions that map onto these outcomes. This description leaves many questions unanswered about the processes involved in the identification of variables. Despite its limitations, however, this description does make clear some of the factors likely to affect the *ages* at which variables are identified in different event categories. Two such factors are discussed below.

Exposure to relevant outcomes

If it is true that infants begin the process of identifying a variable when they become aware of contrastive outcomes for the variable, then it follows that the age at which a variable is identified will depend in part on the age at which infants are exposed to and register contrastive outcomes for the variable.

We saw an example of this in Lesson 4 when discussing young infants' responses to transparent occluders (e.g., Johnson & Aslin, 2000; Luo & Baillargeon, 2001d). Infants younger than 7 months of age cannot register the contrastive outcomes for the variable transparency in occlusion events because they cannot *see* clear or transparent occluders. Only when the infants' visual system has matured sufficiently to enable them to detect such surfaces, at about 7 months of age, do they realize that objects can be visible *through* the surfaces.

In the preceding case, infants are exposed to the contrastive outcomes for a variable in their everyday life, but cannot register these outcomes because of visual limitations. In many other cases, however, infants possess sufficient visual ability to detect the contrastive outcomes for the variables – but it just so happens that they are rarely exposed to these outcomes in their daily lives.

To illustrate, consider the finding, discussed in Lesson 2, that infants do not identify the support variable amount of contact until about 6.5 months of age (e.g., Baillargeon et al., 1992). We have suggested that infants do not acquire this variable sooner because they are not exposed sooner to appropriate contrastive outcomes. In everyday life, infants often see their caretakers place objects on supports (e.g., plates on tables, pots on burners, or bottles on counters). However, in most instances, the objects remain stable when released; only in rare accidental cases do they fall. Hence, it is typically not until infants themselves begin to deposit objects on supports (after about 6 months of age, when they learn to sit independently; e.g., Rochat, 1992) that they have the opportunity to notice that objects placed on supports sometimes remain stable and sometimes do not. At that point, infants begin to seek out the conditions that are responsible for these different outcomes, and eventually come to the realization that an object on a support can be stable when a large but not a small portion of its bottom surface rests on the support.

Availability of data on relevant conditions

Another factor likely to affect the age at which infants identify a variable is how easy it is for them, after they are exposed to the relevant contrastive outcomes, to uncover the conditions that map onto these outcomes.

To illustrate, consider the finding, discussed in Lesson 3, that infants do not identify height as a containment variable until about 7.5 months of age (e.g., Hespos, 1998; Hespos & Baillargeon, 2001a). In order to identify this variable, infants must be able to encode information about the heights of objects and containers. As we saw in Lesson 2, prior research (e.g., Baillargeon, 1994, 1995) suggests that, when infants begin to reason about a continuous variable in an event category, they can do so qualitatively, but not quantitatively: they cannot encode and remember information about absolute amounts. To encode information about the heights of objects and containers qualitatively, infants must compare them as they stand side by side. Unfortunately, infants may witness relatively few instances in which objects are placed first next to and then inside containers; caretakers will more often insert objects directly into containers, allowing infants no opportunity to compare their heights.

In the scenario outlined here, infants would thus notice that objects placed inside containers sometimes do and sometimes do not protrude above the containers. However, infants would have few opportunities to gather data about the relative heights of the objects and containers, because they would rarely see (perhaps until they themselves begin placing objects inside containers) the objects standing next to the containers.

The preceding speculations suggest possible explanations for the décalages described in Lesson 3 in infants' identification of similar variables across event categories. Consider, for example, the findings that infants identify height as an occlusion variable at about 3.5 months of age (e.g., Aguiar & Baillargeon, in press; Baillargeon & DeVos, 1991), and as a containment variable at about 7.5 months of age (e.g., Hespos, 1998; Hespos & Baillargeon, 2001a). One possibility is, of course, that infants observe many more occlusion than containment events in their daily lives, and hence learn about occlusion events earlier. However, another possibility is that infants can more easily collect qualitative data about the relative heights of objects and occluders than of objects and containers. In the case of occlusion, infants will not only see objects being lowered from above behind occluders – they will also see objects being pushed from the side behind occluders (e.g., as when a parent slides a cup behind a teapot, or a sibling pushes a toy car behind a box). In these side occlusions, it will typically be possible for infants to qualitatively compare the heights of the objects and their occluders; infants will then be in a position to begin mapping conditions onto outcomes.

The importance placed here on the availability of qualitative observations for the identification of continuous variables makes a number of interesting predictions. For example, this approach suggests that, in containment events, infants should learn the variable *width* before height, because each time an object is lowered inside a container infants can compare their relative widths. And indeed, recent findings (e.g., Aguiar & Baillargeon, 2000, 2001; Baillargeon & Brueckner, 2000; Sitskoorn & Smitsman, 1995) indicate that infants do identify width before height as a containment variable, at about 4 months of age.

Additional remarks

The general approach adopted here makes a strong experimental prediction: in cases where infants cannot acquire a variable because they are rarely exposed in their daily lives to appropriate outcome or condition data for the variable, then deliberate exposure to such data in the laboratory should result in infants' acquisition of the variable. In other words, it should be possible to "teach" infants variables they have not yet had the opportunity to identify by showing them observations from which to abstract the variables.

To test this approach, my colleagues and I have undertaken a number of "teaching" experiments. In some of these experiments (Baillargeon et al., 2001; Baillargeon, Fisher, & DeJong, 2000; for reviews, see Baillargeon, 1998, 1999), we attempted to teach 11.5- and 11-month-old infants the variable proportional distribution in support events; as was discussed in Lesson 2, this variable is typically not identified until about 12.5 months of age (e.g., Baillargeon, 1995). In other, more recent experiments (Wang & Baillargeon, 2001e), we attempted to teach 9-month-old infants the variable height in covering events; as was mentioned in Lesson 3, this variable is usually not identified until about 12 months of age (McCall, 2001; Wang & Baillargeon, 2001b; Wang & Paterson, 2000; Wang et al., 2001). All of these experiments have yielded positive results; due to space constraints, however, only one of the support teaching experiments is described here.

In this experiment (Baillargeon et al., 2001), 11-month-old infants received three pairs of teaching trials; each pair of trials involved a box-stays and a box-falls event (see figure 3.7). In both events, an experimenter's gloved hand deposited an asymmetrical box on a platform in such a way that half of the box's bottom surface rested on the platform. In the box-stays event, the larger end of the box was placed on the platform, and the box remained stable when released. In the box-falls event, the smaller end of the box was placed on the platform, and the box fell when released. Three different asymmetrical boxes were used in the three pairs of teaching trials. Following these trials, the infants saw two static test displays involving a novel, L-shaped box on a platform. In each display, half of the box's bottom surface rested on the platform; either the larger end (adequate-support display) or the smaller end (inadequate-support display) of the box was supported. The experiment thus examined whether the infants could form a new condition–outcome rule during the teaching trials that would enable them to detect the violation in the inadequate-support test display.

After observing the six teaching trials, the infants looked reliably longer at the inadequate- than at the adequate-support test display. These results suggested that the teaching trials presented the infants with appropriate outcome and condition data from which to abstract the new variable proportional distribution. In each pair of trials, the infants saw contrastive outcomes they could not explain based on their current knowledge. They expected the box to remain stable in both the box-stays and box-falls events, because in each case half of the box's bottom surface was supported; and yet the box fell

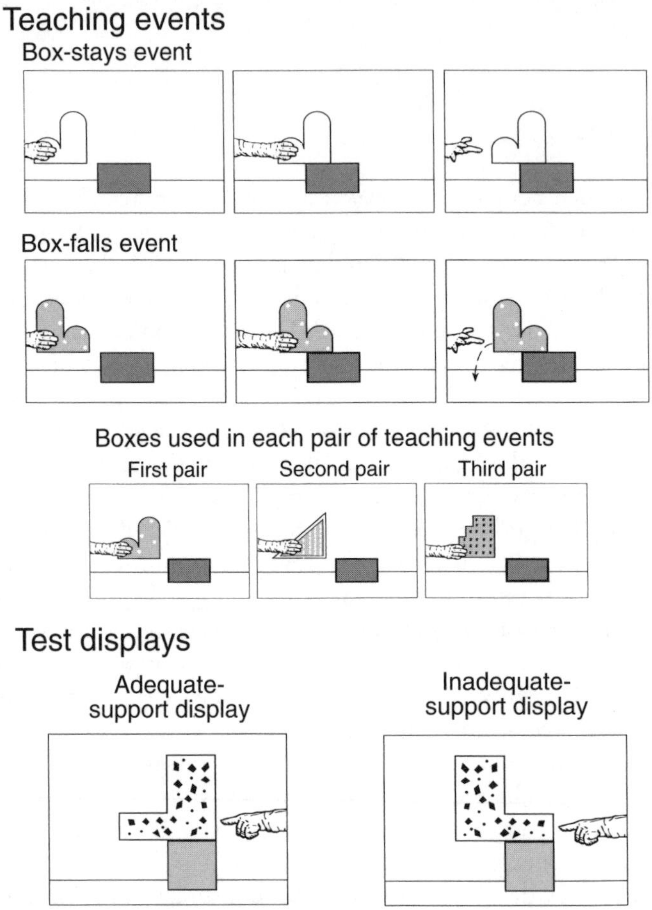

Teaching events
Box-stays event

Box-falls event

Boxes used in each pair of teaching events

| First pair | Second pair | Third pair |

Test displays

| Adequate-support display | Inadequate-support display |

Figure 3.7   Schematic drawing of the teaching events and test displays in Baillargeon et al. (2001)

in the box-falls event. How could this be? By comparing the box-stays and box-falls events, the infants could come to the realization that the box remained stable when the proportion of the entire box (not just of the box's bottom surface) resting on the platform was greater than that off the platform.

Much additional research is needed to flesh out these initial findings (for additional findings, see Baillargeon, 1998, 1999; and Baillargeon et al., 2000, 2001). For example, we need to find out whether the rules infants form in the laboratory are permanent or transitory. Would the same infants tested a week later still show an understanding of proportional distribution in support events? Furthermore, under what teaching conditions do infants show evidence of learning, and under what conditions do they not? Are we correct in saying that infants must be exposed to appropriate outcome and condition data in order to learn? Would infants fail in our support teaching experiment if shown, for example, only the box-stays or the box-falls events during the teaching trials? The answers to these and related questions should shed light on the conditions under which infants can and cannot add to their physical knowledge.

Lesson 6: New Rules are Integrated with Infants' Prior Knowledge

Up to this point, we have suggested that infants form narrow event categories and, for each category, identify a sequence of condition–outcome rules that enable them to predict and interpret outcomes more and more accurately over time. We have also proposed that the identification of rules depends in part on exposure to appropriate outcome data (learning is typically triggered by the detection of outcome variation not predicted by infants' current knowledge) and appropriate condition data (in order to identify the conditions that map onto the contrastive outcomes they have observed, infants must have access to qualitative condition data, for both discrete and continuous variables).

But is this all there is to infants' learning? Are there no limits or constraints on the condition–outcome rules they are capable of forming? Could infants acquire *any* new rule, as long as they were exposed to appropriate condition and outcome data? Could one successfully teach infants, for example, that tall objects can be hidden behind short but not tall occluders, that wide objects can be lowered inside narrow but not wide containers, or that asymmetrical objects can be stable when their smaller but not their larger ends are supported?

A recent experiment addressed this last question. In this experiment, we attempted to teach 11-month-old infants the *reverse* of the proportional distribution rule (Baillargeon et al., 2001). As before, the infants received three pairs of teaching trials; however, the box now fell when its larger end rested on the platform, and remained stable when its smaller end rested on the platform. Had the infants abstracted the reverse rule "an object on a support is stable when the proportion of the object off the support is greater than that on the support," they should have looked reliably longer at the adequate- than at the inadequate-support test display. However, the infants tended to look equally at the two displays, suggesting that they had *not* learned this reverse rule. Negative results were also obtained in a similar experiment with older, 11.5-month-old infants (Baillargeon et al., 2001).

What should one make of these results? It seems likely that the infants could not learn the reverse proportional distribution rule because they could not integrate it with the knowledge they brought to the laboratory. But how should this prior knowledge be characterized? Two very different interpretations are possible, depending on one's model of infants' knowledge acquisition process and the constraints that limit it.

A *first* model is that infants' knowledge acquisition process consists primarily in the detection of *statistical regularities* in the environment. On this view, there would be few constraints on the condition–outcome rules infants can learn, and these would involve mainly basic limitations in infants' perception, memory, and information-processing abilities (e.g., infants cannot learn regularities they cannot see, or see too infrequently to remember). According to this first, *correlation-based* model, it should in principle be possible for infants to learn that an asymmetrical object typically falls when its larger end is supported, or any such reverse rule, as long as they were exposed to the necessary condition and outcome data to learn it. The fact that the infants in our experiment failed to learn the reverse proportional distribution rule (Baillargeon et al., 2001) could be attributed to their having already begun accumulating observations about asymmetrical objects prior to coming to the laboratory. When shown novel observations *consistent* with their own (in our initial, successful teaching experiment), infants were able to abstract a new rule, presumably because they now possessed sufficient data to do so. However, when shown novel observations *inconsistent* with their own (in our reverse teaching experiment), infants could learn nothing – they could only note the inconsistency between their past and present observations.

A *second*, radically different model of infants' knowledge acquisition process is that it consists mainly in the detection of *causal regularities* (e.g., Keil, 1991, 1995; Leslie, 1994, 1995; Pauen, 1999; Wilson & Keil, 2000). On this view, only regularities for which infants could construct explanations based on their prior knowledge would be accepted as condition–outcome rules. These explanations would obviously tend to be shallow and incomplete; nevertheless, they would require some degree of causal analysis, which would place severe limits on the condition–outcome rules infants could learn. According to this second, *explanation-based* model, infants would be able to learn the proportional distribution rule because they could construct an explanation for it; and they would *not* be able to learn the reverse rule because they could not make sense of it in terms of their prior knowledge (for a discussion of explanation-based machine learning, see DeJong, 1988, 1993, 1997).

What causal analysis might have enabled the infants in our initial teaching experiment to identify proportional distribution as an acceptable rule? One possibility is that the infants brought to bear their knowledge of *weight*. Upon seeing the teaching trials, the infants might have reasoned along the following lines: (1) the larger end of each asymmetrical box very likely weighed more than the smaller end; (2) when off the platform, the heavier end of the box pulled downward, and pulled the lighter end downward as well, causing the box to fall; and (3) when off the platform, the lighter end of the box pulled downward, but could not pull the heavier end downward as well, so that the box remained stable. For the infants in the reverse teaching experiment, the fact that each asymmetrical box fell when its heavier end was supported and remained stable when not, would have been impossible to reconcile with their knowledge of weight and of the forces exerted by heavier and lighter objects, so that no learning could occur.

How could one decide between the correlation- and explanation-based interpretations of the results of our teaching experiments? As a first step, Su-Hua Wang, Cindy Fisher, Jerry DeJong, and I are planning to test the hypothesis, derived from the explanation-based interpretation, that the infants in our initial teaching experiment used their knowledge of weight to construct an explanation for the teaching trials. This new experiment will be identical to our initial experiment with one exception: prior to the test session, the infants will hold, one at a time, the three asymmetrical boxes used in the three pairs of teaching trials. For half of the infants (consistent condition), the larger end of each box will be heavier than the smaller end; for the other infants (inconsistent condition), the reverse will be true. Next, all of the infants will receive exactly the same teaching and test trials as in our initial teaching experiment.

Evidence that the infants in the consistent but not the inconsistent condition learn the proportional distribution rule (i.e., look reliably longer at the inadequate- than at the adequate-support test display) would be important for two reasons. First, it would suggest that infants do bring to bear weight information when attempting to make sense of the teaching trials. Second, and more generally, it would suggest that the acquisition of physical knowledge in infancy involves the detection of causal, rather than merely statistical, regularities. Such evidence would thus support an explanation-based, rather than a correlation-based, model of learning.

Additional remarks

What evidence is there that infants attend to the weights of objects, and hold different expectations for events involving objects of different weights? In a recent series of experiments, Su-Hua Wang and I examined 10-month-old infants' ability to reason about collision events involving heavier and lighter objects (Wang, 2001; Wang & Baillargeon, 2001d). The infants in one experiment were first given two cylinders to hold, one at a time. The cylinders were identical in size but differed in color: one was blue and one was yellow (see figure 3.8). For half of the infants (same-weight condition), the two cylinders were equally light; for the other infants (different-weight condition), the blue cylinder was again light but the yellow cylinder was much heavier (it was simply laid on the infants' lap, as they typically could not hold it up). All of the infants first saw a familiarization event in which the yellow cylinder rolled down a ramp and hit a box, causing it to move a short distance. Next, the infants saw a test event in which the blue cylinder rolled down the ramp and hit the same box, which now remained stationary.

The infants in the same-weight condition looked reliably longer during the test event than did those in the different-weight condition. This result suggested two conclusions. First, the infants in the same-weight condition (1) remembered that the yellow cylinder weighed about the same as the blue one and (2) reasoned that, if the yellow cylinder could displace the box, then the blue cylinder should also be able to do so. Second, the infants in the different-weight condition (1) remembered that the yellow cylinder was heavier than the blue one and (2) appreciated that the heavier yellow cylinder might be able to displace the box, and the lighter blue cylinder fail to do so.

Parallel results were obtained in a second experiment that was similar to our initial experiment with two exceptions: first, the infants no longer felt the cylinders, they could only inspect them visually; and second, the yellow cylinder was now either the same size as (same-size condition) or much larger than (different-size condition) the blue cylinder. In this experiment, the knowledge that the yellow cylinder was as light as (same-size condition) or heavier than (different-size condition) the blue cylinder thus had to be *inferred* – it was no longer available through direct proprioceptive feedback. Nevertheless, the results were analogous to those of the first experiment: the infants in the same-size condition looked reliably longer than did those in the different-size condition. This result

Familiarization event

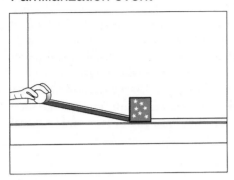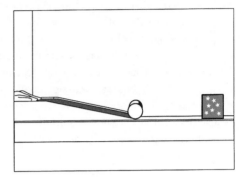

Test event

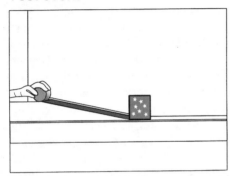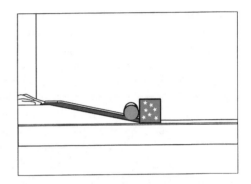

Figure 3.8   Schematic drawing of the test events shown in the same- and different-weight conditions in Wang and Baillargeon (2001d)

suggested that the infants in the same-size condition (1) inferred that the two cylinders were about the same weight and (2) reasoned that, if the yellow cylinder could displace the box, then the blue cylinder should be able to do so as well. For their part, the infants in the different-size condition (1) inferred that the large yellow cylinder was heavier than the smaller blue one and (2) recognized that the heavier yellow cylinder might be able to displace the box, and the lighter blue cylinder might not.

Consistent results were obtained in further experiments in which the weight of the box, rather than that of the cylinder, was manipulated (Wang, 2001; Wang & Baillargeon, 2001d). Together, the results of these experiments suggest that 10-month-old infants attend to and remember the weights of objects, and recognize that events may have different outcomes depending on the weights of the objects involved. In particular, infants appear to possess an expectation that heavier objects can both exert and resist greater forces than can lighter objects. In light of these findings, it does not seem implausible that older, 11-month-old infants should extend this expectation to make sense of support events involving asymmetrical objects, such as those in the teaching trials of our initial teaching experiment (Baillargeon et al., 2001).

Lesson 7: Innate Concepts Guide Infants' Interpretation of their Physical Representations

In our previous lessons, it was suggested that infants sort events into distinct categories and, for each category, identify a sequence of variables (or condition–outcome rules) that result in more and more accurate predictions and interpretations over time. Furthermore, the identification of a new variable may depend on (1) infants' exposure to appropriate outcome and condition data and (2) infants' ability to use their prior knowledge to construct a causal explanation for the variable. In Lesson 7, we begin to consider the possible contributions of *innate physical knowledge* to this acquisition process.

Several researchers (e.g., Carey & Spelke, 1994, 1996; Gelman, 1990; Gopnik & Wellman, 1994; Keil, 1991, 1995; Leslie, 1994, 1995; Spelke, 1994; Spelke et al., 1992; Wellman & Gelman, 1992, 1998) have proposed that infants' naïve physics is a foundational or core domain, and that as in other such domains (e.g., language, number, and naïve psychology), reasoning is facilitated by innate concepts. For example, Spelke (1994; Spelke et al., 1992; Spelke, Phillips, & Woodward, 1995) has proposed that core principles of *continuity* (objects exist and move continuously in time and space) and *solidity* (two objects cannot exist in the same space at the same time) constrain from birth infants' interpretations of physical events.

It might be argued that much of the evidence discussed in our previous lessons calls into question Spelke's (1994; Spelke et al., 1992; Spelke, Phillips, & Woodward, 1995) proposal. For if infants possessed core principles of continuity and solidity, shouldn't they detect all salient violations of these principles? And yet that is clearly not the case: as we have seen, infants often fail to detect what appear to adults to be marked continuity and solidity violations. To give a few examples, recall that 3-month-old infants are not surprised when a tall object becomes fully hidden behind a short occluder (Aguiar & Baillargeon, in press; Baillargeon & DeVos, 1991); that 6.5-month-old infants are not surprised when a tall object is fully lowered inside a short container (Hespos & Baillargeon, 2001a); that 8.5-month-old infants are not surprised when an object lowered inside a transparent container is not visible through the front of the container (Luo, 2001; Luo & Baillargeon, 2001b); and that 9-month-old infants are not surprised when a tall object becomes fully hidden under a short cover (Wang & Paterson, 2000; Wang et al., 2001). How could these negative findings be reconciled with the claim that core principles of continuity and solidity constrain infants' interpretations of events from birth?

My colleagues and I have suggested that such a reconciliation is in fact possible, and depends on a number of assumptions about the nature and development of infants' representations of physical events (e.g., Aguiar & Baillargeon, in press; Baillargeon, in press; Hespos & Baillargeon, 2001b). Below, I describe these assumptions, and then return to the issue of how core principles might contribute to infants' interpretations of events.

Three Assumptions about Infants' Physical Representations

My collaborators and I have arrived at three main assumptions about infants' representations of events (e.g., Aguiar & Baillargeon, in press; Baillargeon, in press; Hespos & Baillargeon, 2001b). First, we assume that, when observing physical events, infants build representations – which we call *physical representations* – that focus on the physical properties, displacements, and interactions of the objects and surfaces within the events.[3] Second, we assume that infants' physical representations of events are by no means faithful copies of the events: they are abstract descriptions that include some but not all of the physical information in the events. Third, we assume that how much information infants include in their physical representation of an event depends in large part on their knowledge of the variables likely to affect the event.

To put these assumptions more concretely, we suppose that, when watching an event, infants first categorize it, and then access their knowledge of the event category selected. This knowledge specifies what variables should be attended to, and thus what information should be included in the physical representation of the event. To illustrate, this means that 3.5-month-old infants who see an object being lowered behind a container (occlusion event) will include information about the relative heights of the object and container in their physical representation of the event, because they have already identified height as an occlusion variable (Aguiar & Baillargeon, in press; Baillargeon & DeVos, 1991). In contrast, 3.5-month-old infants who see an object being lowered inside a container (containment event) will not encode the relative heights of the object and container, because they have not yet identified height as a containment variable (Hespos & Baillargeon, 2001a).

According to the preceding assumptions, infants' physical representations would thus be initially very sparse. As infants discover the importance of different variables in predicting outcomes, they would begin to include this variable information, thus achieving richer and more detailed physical representations over time.

A Case of Impoverished Physical Representations

If one accepts the assumptions described in the previous section, then it becomes clear how infants might possess core continuity and solidity principles and still fail to detect salient violations of these principles. Infants' core principles, like all of their physical knowledge, can operate only at the level of their representations (infants, like adults, do not apply their knowledge directly to events, only to their representations of the events). It follows that infants can succeed in detecting violations of their continuity and solidity principles *only* when the key information necessary to detect these violations is included in their physical representations. Infants' principles can only guide the interpretation of information that has been included in their representations; information that has not been represented cannot be interpreted.

To illustrate how incomplete physical representations could lead infants to ignore violations of their continuity and solidity principles, consider one of the findings discussed in Lesson 2, that 3-month-old infants are not surprised when a tall object fails to appear between two screens connected at the bottom by a short strip (Aguiar & Baillargeon, in press; Baillargeon & DeVos, 1991). What is being suggested is that, when observing such an event, 3-month-old infants typically do not include information about the relative heights of the object and occluder in their physical representation of the event. Thus, when infants apply their continuity principle to their incomplete physical representation of the event, they have no basis for predicting that a portion of the object should be visible above the short strip between the screens.

Additional remarks

It was suggested above that young infants might possess core continuity and solidity principles and still fail to detect violations of these principles, because of sparse or incomplete physical representations. This approach makes a number of intriguing predictions. In particular, it suggests that if infants could be temporarily induced or "primed" to include key variable information in their representations of physical events, they should then be in a position to detect continuity or solidity violations they would otherwise have been unable to detect. On the present view, it should not matter whether infants include variable information in their physical representation of an event because (1) they have been primed to do so by some contextual manipulation or (2) they have already identified the variable as relevant to the event category. In either case, the information, once represented, should be subject to infants' continuity and solidity principles.

To test these ideas, Su-Hua Wang and I recently conducted a "priming" experiment with 8-month-old infants, focusing on the variable height in covering events (Wang & Baillargeon, 2001c). As we saw in Lesson 3, this variable is typically not identified until about 12 months of age (McCall, 2001; Wang & Baillargeon, 2001b; Wang & Paterson, 2000; Wang et al., 2001). In the experiment of Wang et al. (2001), for example, 9-month-old infants saw a tall- and short-cover test event. At the start of the tall-cover event, a tall cylindrical cover stood next to a tall cylindrical object. An experimenter's gloved hand grasped the cover, lifted it over the object, and lowered it to the apparatus floor, thereby fully hiding the object. The short-cover event was identical except that the cover was only half as tall, so that it should have been impossible for the cover to fully hide the object. The infants tended to look equally at the events, suggesting that they had not yet identified height as a covering variable.

The 8-month-old infants in our priming experiment (Wang & Baillargeon, 2001c) saw the same test events as in Wang et al. (2001) with one exception: each test event was preceded by a brief pretrial designed to prime the infants to include information about the relative heights of the cover and object in their physical representation of the covering event (see figure 3.9). Because infants aged 3.5 months and older attend to height information in occlusion events (Baillargeon & DeVos, 1991; Hespos & Baillargeon, 2001a), the pretrial presented the infants with an *occlusion* event involving the cover and object. At the start of each pretrial, the cover rested next to the object; after a pause, the

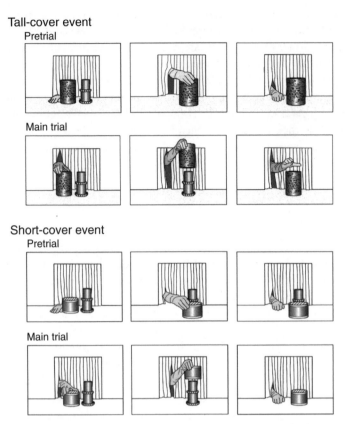

Figure 3.9   Schematic drawing of the test events shown in the experimental condition in Wang and Baillargeon (2001c)

hand grasped the cover, slid it in front of the object, and then returned to the apparatus floor. The tall cover occluded all of the object, the short cover only its bottom portion. The cover remained in its new position until the computer signaled that the infant had looked at the display for five cumulative seconds. The hand then returned the cover to its original position next to the object, and the test trial proceeded exactly as in Wang et al. (2001). Infants in a control condition received a similar pretrial at the start of each test event, except that the cover was simply slid forward and thus never occluded the object.

Our reasoning in designing the pretrials was as follows: after the infants in the experimental condition included the relative heights of the cover and object in their physical representation of the occlusion event, they might be inclined to do the same – or they might have this information still available – when forming their physical representation of the covering event. This information would then be subject to the infants' core principles of continuity and solidity, making it possible for them to detect – at a much younger age than they would otherwise – the violation in the short-cover test event.

As expected, the infants in the experimental condition looked reliably longer at the short- than at the tall-cover test event, whereas those in the control condition looked about equally at the events, like the 9-month-old infants in our original experiment (Wang & Paterson, 2000; Wang et al., 2001). These results are important for three reasons. First, they provide strong support for the notion that infants' failures to detect continuity and solidity violations reflect impoverished physical representations: what is not represented cannot be interpreted. Second, the results give weight to our analysis of infants' physical representations, and more specifically to our proposal that infants do not routinely include information about a variable in a physical representation of an event until they have identified the variable as pertinent to the event category. Finally, our results (see also Chapa & Wilcox, 1999, for a different type of priming experiment) raise many new questions about priming issues: for example, what manipulations are helpful for priming variables and what manipulations are not; what are the long-term effects of successful priming experiences; and finally, what are the similarities and differences between priming and teaching experiences (as in Baillargeon et al., 2001, which was discussed in Lesson 5).

Lesson 8: Innate Concepts Guide Even Very Young Infants' Interpretations of their Physical Representations

It was suggested in Lesson 7 that (1) principles of continuity and solidity constrain from birth infants' interpretations of physical events (e.g., Spelke, 1994; Spelke et al., 1992; Spelke, Phillips, & Woodward, 1995); (2) these principles operate at the level of infants' physical representations; and (3) because these representations are at first very limited – variables not yet identified as relevant to an event category are typically ignored – infants cannot detect continuity and solidity violations involving these variables. This approach makes one strong prediction: even very young infants should be able to detect continuity and solidity violations, as long as these do not involve variable information.

In the first months of life, infants' physical representations most likely include only basic spatial, temporal, and possibly mechanical (Leslie, 1994, 1995) information. As they grow older, infants certainly become better at representing this information (e.g., Arterberry, 1997; Yonas & Granrud, 1984). But the key point here is this: even very young infants should detect continuity and solidity violations that involve only the basic information they can represent.

Over the past ten years, evidence has been slowly but steadily accumulating that 2.5-month-old infants (the youngest that have been successfully tested to date with violation-of-expectation tasks) interpret a wide range of physical events in accord with continuity and solidity principles (e.g., Aguiar & Baillargeon, 1999, in press; Hespos & Baillargeon, 2001b; Spelke et al., 1992; Wilcox et al., 1996). Due to space constraints, only one experiment, on containment events, is described here.

Containment events

Sue Hespos and I recently asked whether 2.5-month-old infants realize that an object that has been lowered inside a container should move with the container when the latter is slid to a new location (Hespos & Baillargeon, 2001b).

Behind-container condition

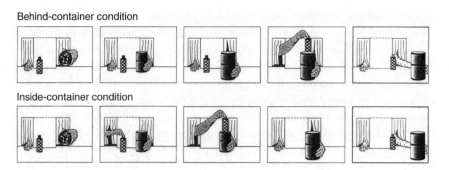

Inside-container condition

Figure 3.10   Schematic drawing of the test events in Hespos and Baillargeon (2001b)

The infants were assigned to a behind- or an inside-container condition and saw a single test event (see figure 3.10). At the start of the event shown in the *behind-container* condition, an experimenter's gloved right hand rested on an apparatus floor next to a cylindrical object; the same experimenter's gloved left hand grasped the midsection of a tall cylindrical container standing to the right of the object. To start, the left hand rotated the container forward so that the infants could see its open top and hollow interior. After a few seconds, the container was placed upright next to the object and then slid forward. Next, the right hand grasped the object, moved it above and behind the container, and lowered it until it disappeared behind the container. The left hand then moved the container to the right, revealing the object standing behind it. The infants in the *inside-container* condition saw the same test event except that the object was lowered inside the container before the latter was moved forward; hence, it should have been impossible for the object to be revealed when the container was moved to the right.

Prior to the test trials, the infants in the behind- and inside-container conditions received baseline trials identical to the test trials with one exception: the container was never moved to the right to reveal the object behind it. The baseline trials provided an assessment of whether the infants had an intrinsic preference for seeing the object being lowered behind or inside the container. The test events shown in the two conditions were perceptually identical except for the fact that in one condition the container was moved forward and the object was then lowered behind it, whereas in the other condition the object was lowered inside the container which was then moved forward. Because the baseline events also were perceptually identical except for this difference, the data from the baseline trials could be used to assess whether seeing the object lowered behind or inside the container was intrinsically more attractive to the infants.

During the baseline trials, the infants in the inside- and behind-container conditions tended to look equally; during the test trials, however, the infants in the inside-container condition looked reliably longer than did those in the behind-container condition. Together, these results suggested that the infants (1) believed that the object continued to exist after it disappeared from sight; (2) remembered whether it had been lowered inside or behind the container; (3) realized that the object, when lowered inside the container, could not pass through its closed sides and thus had to move with it when displaced; and therefore (4) expected the object to be revealed when the container was moved to the right in the behind- but not the inside-container condition.

It is certainly remarkable that infants as young as 2.5 months of age can detect the violation in the inside-container test event. However, to return to our earlier discussion, such a success is precisely what should be possible to young infants whose physical representations include only basic, pre-variable information, but whose interpretations of this information are guided by continuity and solidity principles. Detecting the violation in the inside-container test event required only keeping track of the locations of the object and container over time, and realizing that the object continued to exist when inside the container (an assumption that would be suggested by the infants' continuity principle), and moved with it when displaced (an assumption that would be suggested by the infants' solidity principle).

Additional remarks

In Lessons 7 and 8, we saw that whether infants succeed in detecting continuity and solidity violations depends on two main factors: first, what information infants include in their physical representations of events; and second, what information must be attended to for the violations to be detected. Thus, even very young infants may detect violations if these involve only the basic, pre-variable information they encode about events; and much older infants may fail to detect violations if these involve variables they have not yet identified and thus tend to ignore when forming their physical representations.[4]

In the preceding discussion, we have focused primarily on how infants' core principles of continuity and solidity might guide their interpretations of events. Here, I would like to consider another role for these and other innate concepts, one which is related to our discussion in Lesson 6 of the explanation-based approach to learning. According to this approach, infants only learn rules they can make sense of or explain in terms of their prior physical knowledge. To the extent that this prior knowledge includes innate concepts, then these concepts could also contribute to infants' acquisition of rules, by helping them build acceptable explanations for novel variables.

It is easy to see how infants' principles of continuity and solidity might contribute to their causal analyses of variables in occlusion, containment, covering, and other physical events. For example, it might be suggested that infants readily accept height as an occlusion variable (e.g., Aguiar & Baillargeon, in press; Baillargeon & DeVos, 1991), because it is highly consistent with their notion of continuity: if an object continues to exist when behind an occluder, and is taller than the occluder, then it should indeed extend above the occluder. Similarly, consider the variable width in containment events (e.g., Aguiar & Baillargeon, 1998, 2000b, 2001; Baillargeon & Brueckner, 2000; Sitskoorn & Smitsman, 1995): infants' notion of solidity would suggest that if an object is wider than the opening of a container, then it should not be possible for the object to be lowered through this opening, for to do so would mean passing through the solid body of the container.

Although we have focused here on Spelke's (1994; Spelke et al., 1992; Spelke, Phillips, & Woodward, 1995) core principles of continuity and solidity, other innate notions might also contribute to infants' explanations for novel variables. Consider, for example, Leslie's (1994, 1995) proposal that infants are born with a primitive notion of *force*. At about 5.5 to 6.5 months of age (e.g., Kotovsky & Baillargeon, 1994, 1998), infants come to realize that, in collision events, larger (heavier) objects displace stationary objects farther than do smaller (lighter) objects. One can see that such a rule (but not its reverse) would appear consistent with a simple notion of force as a unidirectional and incremental application of energy: all other things being equal, greater forces should yield greater effects. Infants' notion of force might also be implicated in their learning about support events. Recall our discussion, in Lesson 6, of how infants might have interpreted the teaching trials in our initial teaching experiment (Baillargeon et al., 2001). Implicit in this causal analysis is the notion that a heavier object (or portion of an object) can exert and resist a greater force than can a lighter object (or portion of an object). Other support variables might be interpreted by infants in similar terms. For example, consider the variable "middle or side contact," which is identified at about 8.5 months of age (Dan et al., 2000; Huettel & Needham, 2000; Wang & Baillargeon, 2001a), and was discussed in Lesson 2. Upon seeing that an object does not fall despite the fact that only its middle portion (e.g., the middle 30 percent of its bottom surface) is supported, a 6.5-month-old infant might assume that (1) the weight of the object is evenly distributed along its bottom surface and (2) when the middle portion of the object is supported, leaving two identical portions unsupported on either side, then each of these unsupported portions exerts an equal, and opposite, pull downward, thereby keeping the object balanced over the supported portion.

Pondering what causal analyses might underlie infants' acquisition of different variables, and what role innate notions of continuity, solidity, force, and so on, might play in these causal analyses, is a fascinating research exercise. But how can we determine whether our intuitions about infants' causal analyses are correct? As was discussed in Lesson 6, our current approach is to conduct teaching experiments in which infants (1) are exposed to appropriate outcome and condition data to learn a new variable, but (2) are given additional information that is either consistent or inconsistent with infants' hypothesized causal analysis of these outcome and condition data. We have already seen an example of such a teaching experiment, in Lesson 6: recall the experiment in which infants receive teaching trials on the support variable proportional distribution after holding asymmetrical boxes whose larger end is either heavier (consistent condition) or lighter (inconsistent condition) than their smaller end.

Parallel experiments can be designed for other variables. For example, consider once again the support variable middle or side contact discussed above. If our description of infants' causal analysis of this variable is correct, then it should be possible to teach infants that an object can remain stable (or balanced) with two *identical* unsupported portions extending on either side of a small supported portion; however, it should be very difficult to teach infants that an object can be stable with two *non-identical* unsupported portions extending on either side of a small supported portion. In the latter case, the object could in fact still be physically stable, but infants would no longer be able to produce a causal analysis in terms of two identical portions exerting equal and opposite downward pulls. A notion of center of mass is necessary to explain such cases of support, and children do not achieve such a notion until much later in development.

Conclusions

How do infants acquire their physical knowledge? The eight lessons discussed in this chapter point to the following picture. From birth, infants build specialized representations of physical events, which we termed physical representations. These physical representations initially include only limited spatial, temporal, and mechanical information. The interpretation of this information is guided by a few core principles, including continuity and solidity.

Over time, infants begin to form distinct event categories, such as occlusion, containment, and support events. For each category, infants identify a sequence of variables (condition–outcome rules) that enable them to predict outcomes more and more accurately over time. The identification of each variable depends on two main factors: (1) infants' exposure to appropriate outcome and condition data (exposure to contrastive outcomes not predicted by infants' current physical knowledge is thought to trigger the identification process; infants then seek out the conditions that map onto these outcomes); and (2) infants' ability to build a causal explanation for these condition–outcome data, based on their prior knowledge. This prior knowledge is presumed to include both the knowledge infants have already accumulated about the category, and the innate principles and concepts mentioned earlier.

The model just outlined shares many features in common with descriptions offered by other researchers. First, the notion that infants' naïve physics is a foundational or core domain, with its own innate concepts and specialized learning mechanism, is one with a long history in the field of conceptual development (e.g., Carey, 1985; Gelman, 1990; Keil, 1989; Spelke et al., 1992; Wellman & Gelman, 1992). Second, the idea that infants seek out causal rather than mere statistical regularities, and use their prior knowledge to build shallow explanations for these regularities, is highly consistent with the work of Keil, Leslie, Pauen, and their colleagues (e.g., Keil, 1991, 1995; Leslie, 1994, 1995; Pauen, 1999; Wilson & Keil, 2000). Finally, the notion that infants analyze the outcome and condition data to which they are exposed to abstract new rules about event categories is reminiscent of Mandler's proposal that infants analyze various data to form object categories (e.g., Mandler, 1992, 1998, 2000a; see also Quinn, ch. 4 this volume).

The model outlined here also differs from current models and descriptions in a number of important respects. First, it is not entirely consistent with the recent "theory theory" approach to knowledge acquisition (e.g., Gopnik & Wellman, 1994; Gopnik & Meltzoff, 1997). According to Gopnik and Wellman, for example, an important characteristic of scientists' as well as children's theories "is their coherence . . . changes in one part of the theory have consequences for other parts of the theory" (1994, pp. 260–261). As we saw in Lesson 3, however, the knowledge infants acquire about physical events during the first year of life is very piecemeal: infants' learning about height in occlusion events does not seem to have any consequence for their knowledge of containment or covering events (e.g., Hespos & Baillargeon, 2001a; McCall, 2001; Wang & Baillargeon, 2001b; Wang & Paterson, 2000; Wang et al., 2001); and infants' learning about transparency in occlusion events does not seem to have any distant effect on their knowledge of containment events (e.g., Luo, 2001; Luo & Baillargeon, 2001b, 2001d). In what sense can an infant who must learn the same variables separately in different event categories be said to possess a theory-like understanding of these categories? To attribute to infants a theory – even an incorrect theory – of the physical world, one would want to see many more generalizations, and many fewer décalages, than our research has actually revealed. Infants are in the business of acquiring physical rules – they are not (or not yet) in the business of building a coherent physical theory (see also Wilson & Keil, 2000).

Another feature of the present model that differs from other descriptions concerns the way in which innate concepts are thought to contribute to infants' interpretations of physical events. In our model, innate concepts play an important but still limited role. Infants must discover for themselves, event category by event category and variable by variable, much that is relevant to continuity, solidity, and so on. True, to the extent that several of these variables – say, transparency in occlusion events, width in containment events, and height in covering events – are implied in the principles of continuity and solidity, one can say that infants are doing no more than discovering what they already know. But this process of discovery is an important and a protracted one, and to dismiss it is to ignore much of what happens in the first year of life. Infants are not philosophers who reflect at leisure upon abstract principles and infer from them new truths. Infants are concrete thinkers who draw novel inferences – who discover what they already know – only when challenged to do so by reality, in the form of unexplained variation in outcome.

Notes

1. Occlusion events are events in which an object becomes at least partly hidden behind a nearer object or occluder (e.g., as when a cup is lowered behind a teapot). Support events are events in which an object becomes supported by another object (e.g., as when a plate is placed on a table). Collision events are events in which an object hits another object (e.g., as when a toy car hits a shoe). Finally, containment events are events in which an object is placed inside a container (e.g., as when a ball is lowered inside a box). From an adult perspective, containment of course often involves occlusion. However, this occlusion is of a different form than that defined above: the contained object is hidden because it is lowered inside, not behind, the container. As we will see in Lesson 3, this distinction appears to be crucially important to infants.
2. From the present perspective, a variable is thus tantamount to a dimension; conditions correspond to values on the dimension, with each value (or discernable range of values) being associated with a distinct outcome.
3. Infants no doubt build several representations simultaneously, for different purposes. For example, another representation might focus on the features of the objects in the events, and be used for object recognition and categorization purposes – to ascertain whether these particular objects, or similar objects, have been encountered in the past (e.g., Needham & Modi, 2000; Quinn & Eimas, 1996).
4. It might be suggested that principles of continuity and solidity could be learned in the first few weeks or months of life, as infants observe the world around them. For example, when fixating stationary objects such as a chair, a cup on a table, or a phone on a wall, infants could notice that these objects do not disappear and reappear capriciously, but persist through time, in their same locations. Similarly, when watching moving objects such as a ball rolling across a floor, a parent walking across a room, or even their own hand fluttering back and forth,

infants could notice that these objects follow smooth, continuous paths – they do not abruptly disappear at one point in space and reappear at a different one. On the basis of such, very common, observations, infants could conclude that objects exist and move continuously in time and space.

One difficulty with this alternative account is that it is not consistent with the learning mechanism described in Lessons 4 to 6. We have seen that the acquisition of rules seems to be triggered by exposure to unpredicted variation in outcome – contrastive outcomes not predicted or explained by infants' current knowledge. But in the case of continuity, for example, what contrastive outcomes could be involved? Stationary objects persisting through time, in their same locations, moving objects following continuous paths: such events involve no contrastive outcomes. A learning mechanism that must be triggered by variation in outcome would be incapable of detecting the abstract regularities in these events. Hence, one is left with the following two possibilities: either these general principles, which are present in very young infants and affect their physical reasoning very broadly, are innate, as Spelke (1994; Spelke et al., 1992; Spelke, Phillips, & Woodward, 1995) has suggested; or else they are acquired by a learning mechanism very different from that responsible for the bulk of infants' acquisitions about occlusion, containment, support, and other physical events. At the present time, the first possibility seems to us more compelling.

CHAPTER FOUR

Early Categorization: A New Synthesis

Paul C. Quinn

This chapter will begin with an introduction to the concept of *categorization*, a mental ability that Thelen and Smith (1994) have described as "the primitive in all behavior and mental functioning" (p. 143). The discussion will focus on how categories get started, so the chapter will proceed to a description of some historical and more contemporary perspectives on how categories are initially formed. Two contemporary approaches will be highlighted, that of Rosch on the one hand (e.g. Rosch, Mervis, Gray, Johnson, & Boyes-Braem, 1976), and Mandler on the other (e.g., Mandler & McDonough, 1998a). In addition, the data that have been used to support these positions will be reviewed. These data center on whether there is an order to category emergence and whether early categories are perceptually or conceptually based. The chapter will then turn to an account of more recent efforts to build a computational model that yields output that is consistent with the data, and to develop a computational approach to understanding infant categorization performance more generally (Mareschal, French, & Quinn, 2000; Quinn & Johnson, 1997, 2000). In accord with differentiation theory (Gibson & Gibson, 1955; Werner, 1957) and the theme of developmental continuity (Eimas, 1994), it will be suggested that infant category learning in the domain of objects may proceed from broad to narrow (or global to basic) as surface feature differences between categories are progressively extracted from visual input during the course of early experience. It will also be argued that each of the contemporary perspectives has at least one major advantage and disadvantage. The new synthesis attempts to retain the advantages and discard the disadvantages.

Preparation of this chapter was supported by National Science Foundation Research Grant BCS-0096300. The author thanks Peter Eimas for his comments on an earlier draft.

Correspondence concerning this chapter should be addressed to Paul C. Quinn, Department of Psychology, Washington & Jefferson College, 60 South Lincoln Street, Washington, PA, 15301. Electronic mail may be sent via the Internet to <pquinn@washjeff.edu>.

Categorization: A Foundation for Cognition

Gerald Edelman (1987), a Nobel prizewinner in molecular biology and immunology, has in recent years turned his attention to neuroscience and argued that "One of the fundamental tasks of the nervous system is to carry out perceptual categorization in an unlabeled world" (p. 7). This observation certainly speaks to the task facing young infants who must at some point during development come to organize objects encountered in the environment into groupings or categories such as dog, animal, chair, and furniture. The term categorization as used in the modern cognitive sciences literature refers to the recognition of discriminably different entities as members of the same category based on some internalized representation of the category that has been called a schema (Anderson, 1995; Mandler, 1997), concept (Smith & Medin, 1981), or categorical representation (Quinn & Eimas, 1997). In this chapter, the term categorical (or category) representation will be used to describe the mental structure under consideration. Perceptual schema seems not powerful enough a label given that it can be used to describe a representation for an individual object rather than a category of multiple objects (Quinn, Slater, Brown, & Hayes, 2001), whereas concept may be too strong a label given its connection with philosophical constructs such as essences (e.g., Medin & Ortony, 1989) and sortals (Xu & Carey, 1996). One can think of a categorical representation as a stored mental representation for like entities. A concrete way to think about categorical representations is to think about file folders. File folders are used to organize information, and many in the cognitive sciences believe that adult humans possess mental files or categorical representations to hold information about various object classes.

What are the advantages of having a mind-brain system that categorizes experience? First, categorization is important for reducing the diversity of the physical world. Color is a good example. It is estimated that there are 7,000,000 discriminable colors in our experience. Yet most languages collapse the wavelength continuum into a dozen or fewer basic categories (Bruner, Goodnow, & Austin, 1956). Think about how much more complex cognition and language would become if child language acquisition included the mapping of 7,000,000 color terms onto 7,000,000 color experiences.

A second advantage of categorization is that it provides for organized storage and efficient retrieval of information from memory (Quinn & Bomba, 1986). If all human observers did was to throw individual items encountered in the natural environment into their memories in no particular arrangement in a kind of "garbage truck" or "laundry basket" model of storage, then recognition would be slow and error-prone because it would require comparing each new stimulus to a huge number of stored items on a trial-and-error basis. It would be a bit like searching for a needle in a haystack. That recognition is often fast and accurate is consistent with the idea that memory is organized and most likely in terms of categories (Bauer, ch. 6 this volume).

A third advantage of categorization is our ability to respond equivalently to an indefinitely large number of examples from multiple categories including many instances never before experienced (Smith & Medin, 1981). Our days can include encounters with novel stimuli, for example, new furry, four-legged creatures that bark, and new moving, elongated, metallic objects on rubber discs. Yet, human perceivers generally do not walk around the world saying "What is this?" or "How should I respond to that?". Rather, observers say "This is a dog and that is a car." In other words, categories allow individuals to respond to the novel as if it is familiar, thereby preserving a presumed finite amount of cognitive resources for day-to-day mental activities including creative problem-solving, thinking, and reasoning.

Historical Perspective: Two Traditional Views and an Alternative

Because of the perceived importance of categories to mental life and the recognition that they have to start somewhere, there has been interest in *how categories develop* and there have been different historical perspectives on this issue. First, it needs to be acknowledged that Edelman (1987) may not have framed the problem correctly; maybe the world is labeled for the child. This in fact was the view taken by the famous American behaviorist Clark Hull. According to Hull (1920), "A young child finds himself in a certain situation . . . and hears it called 'dog'. After an indeterminate intervening period he finds himself in a somewhat different situation and hears that called 'dog' also . . . The 'dog' experiences appear at irregular intervals . . . At length the time arrives when the child has a meaning for the word 'dog'" (pp. 5–6). Hull's view implies that a young child may not recognize a previously unseen dog as a member of the category dogs until hearing the label "dog" associated with different dogs over an extended period of time. So, for example, a young child might go for a walk with her parents, see a dog, and hear the parents label it as a dog. The repetition of this experience over time, Hull believed, prompted the child to seek out characteristics common to dogs.

A second view about how categories emerge comes from the symbolic anthropology literature. Edmund Leach (1964) proposed that "The physical and social environment of a young child is perceived as a continuum . . . The child, in due course, is taught to impose upon this environment a kind of discriminating grid which serves to distinguish the world as being composed of a large number of separate things, each labeled with a name" (p. 34). According to Leach, the world has little or no natural order. To categorize, the child must learn through instruction to impose order on natural disorder.

These views are plausible, and there is certainly ample evidence that some of our skill at dividing our experiences into meaningful categories is derived from language and formal tuition (Anderson, 1991; Callanan, 1985; Gopnik & Meltzoff, 1987; Loose & Mareschal, 1997; Markman, 1989; Millikan, 1998; Waxman & Markow, 1995; Xu & Carey, 1996). The question is whether something even more fundamental might underlie the initial beginnings of categorization in young infants. A possible answer to this question emerges from an examination of the framework put forth by Eleanor Rosch and her colleagues. Rosch et al. (1976) advanced a position in between that of Edelman on the one hand, and Hull and Leach on the other. The major argument is that the world is not necessarily labeled for the child, but it does have structure, and that structure comes in the form of bundles of correlated attributes (Mervis & Rosch, 1981). In the Rosch view, categorization is highly determined because the world breaks down along lines of natural discontinuity. For example, objects like birds have feathers, beaks, two legs, and make chirping sounds, whereas objects like dogs have fur, snouts, four legs, and make barking sounds. Importantly, if the Rosch framework is correct, then an organism that can detect such regularities and correlations, and compile them into separate representations, is capable of categorization (e.g., Mareschal & French, 2000; Younger, 1990). And if that is true, then some of the abilities involved in recognizing that dogs are alike in ways that cats are not may be present before the emergence of language and formal instruction. Thus, by the Rosch account, it becomes important to understand the abilities prelinguistic infants might have to categorize their environment, as it may be from these abilities that the complex categories of the adult will develop.

At the time of Rosch's writings, the mid- to late 1970s, the procedures available to study infant perception and cognition had not yet been adapted to study categorization. But Rosch (1978) did have a view of natural category development, and that was another major part of her overall theory. Rosch et al. (1976) had argued that category knowledge is organized hierarchically into various levels, and the three that are most often discussed are the superordinate, basic, and subordinate levels. For example, subordinate categories like beagle and boxer are nested under the basic-level category of dog, which in turn lies below the superordinate categories of mammal and animal. Rosch et al. also claimed that the basic level in the hierarchy is the most functional: the level at which we do most of our thinking. Basic-level superiority occurs because members of basic-level categories tend to possess significant numbers of attributes in common, have similar shapes, and invoke similar motor movements.

Rosch et al. (1976) also suggested that basic-level categories might be the first to be acquired during development. To provide support for this suggestion, 3-year-olds participated in a task in which they were asked to identify which two of three objects were alike. The key finding was that the children succeeded in a basic-level task involving, for example, two airplanes and a dog, but performed poorly in a superordinate-level task involving, for example, an airplane, a car, and a dog. On this basis, Rosch et al. argued that object categories were initially represented at the basic level. Development thus consisted of (1) grouping together basic-level representations to form the superordinate level and (2) differentiation of basic-level representations to form the subordinate level.

Evidence of Categorization with Young Infants

At the time that I started to work on the problem of category development (Quinn & Eimas, 1986), the Rosch view of basic-to-superordinate category emergence was widely accepted, and there was also a methodology available to study infant perceptual discrimination and memory abilities that could be adapted to study categorization. This methodology is called the familiarization/novelty-preference procedure and is based on the established preference that infants have for novel stimulation. It was originally developed by Robert Fantz in the early 1960s (e.g., Fantz, 1964). As can be seen in the top half of figure 4.1, to determine if two stimuli are discriminable, infants are repeatedly presented with two copies of one stimulus and subsequently presented with the familiar stimulus paired with the other (novel) stimulus. A preference for the novel stimulus (that can be measured in looking time) implies both memory for the familiar stimulus and the ability to discriminate between it and the novel stimulus. As is shown in the bottom half of figure 4.1,

Discrimination using the familiarization/novelty-
preference procedure

	Familiarization		Novelty preference test	
	F	F	F	N

Categorization using the familiarization/novelty-
preference procedure

	Familiarization		Novelty preference test	
	F_1	F_2		
	F_3	F_4	F_{n+2}	N
	F_n	F_{n+1}		

Figure 4.1   Schematic depiction of familiarization/novelty-preference procedure used to test for discrimination (*top panel*) and categorization (*bottom panel*)

to study categorization in the infant, two modifications are necessary. First, a number of stimuli, all of which belong to the same category, are presented during familiarization. Second, two new stimuli are presented during what we call a novel category preference test – one is from the familiar category, and the other is from a novel category. If infants generalize their familiarization to a novel discriminably different exemplar from the familiar category, and display a preference for an equally discriminable exemplar from a novel category, then this pattern of responding is taken as evidence to infer that the familiar exemplars have in some manner been grouped together or categorized and that the representation of this category excludes the novel category exemplar. One view of the "kind" of representation that infants form in this type of procedure is that it is implicit, perceptually based (i.e., based on surface attributes of the stimuli), and formed on-line during the course of the experiment (Mandler, 1998; but see Quinn & Eimas, 1998).

Early studies of infant categorization utilizing one or another variant of the familiarization/novelty-preference procedure showed that 3- and 4-month-old infants could categorize local attributes of stimuli such as orientation (Bomba, 1984) and hue (Bornstein, 1981). Infants under 1 year of age were also shown to form category representations for more global visual patterns including angles (Slater, Mattock, Brown, & Bremner, 1991), forms (Bomba & Siqueland, 1983; Colombo, McCollam, Coldren, Mitchell, & Rash,

1990; Quinn, 1987; Younger & Gottlieb, 1988), and black-and-white schematic faces and animals (Roberts, 1988; Sherman, 1985; Strauss, 1979; Younger, 1990). This body of work has been reviewed in Bornstein (1984), Cohen and Younger (1983), Eimas and Miller (1990), Reznick (1989), and Reznick and Kagan (1983).

An issue that was not clear from the initial round of infant categorization studies was whether infants could form category representations for realistically appearing natural and artifactual objects that later come to be conceptually significant for children and adults (e.g., cat, table). Therefore, armed with the familiarization/novelty-preference procedure and with the Rosch view of basic-to-superordinate category development in mind, an initial investigation was undertaken to determine whether young infants, 3 to 4 months of age, could form separate category representations for cats, dogs, and birds chosen from the superordinate category animal (Quinn, Eimas, & Rosenkrantz, 1993). These categories seemed liked good candidates to begin the study of natural category formation by infants because some of the earliest words in the child's vocabulary refer to animals and include "dog," "kittie," and "bird" (Roberts & Cuff, 1989). The stimuli were 54 photographic exemplars from the categories (18 exemplars/category), and the exemplars were chosen to represent a variety of shapes, colors, and poses so as to approximate their variability in the environment. However, across the categories, stimuli were selected to be nearly the same size as possible. If size was not removed as a cue, and babies formed category representations of the animals, then the result would have been subject to the criticism that only simple size discrimination (rather than complex categorization) was demonstrated.

The first question asked was whether infants could form separate category representations for dogs and cats which were sufficiently differentiated to exclude instances of birds. As can be seen in the top half of figure 4.2, half of the infants were exposed to a dozen cats, and the other half were shown a dozen dogs. Infants in each group then entered into a novel category preference test. Those infants that saw cats were presented with a novel cat paired with a bird, and those infants that began with dogs were presented with a novel dog paired with a bird. Looking time to the stimuli was measured by trained observers who were naive to the hypotheses under investigation. The results were that those infants that saw dogs looked predominantly to the novel birds, and those that saw cats also looked mostly to the birds. A control experiment indicated that the preference for the bird stimuli was not due to an a priori preference for the birds, that is, infants did not simply like to look at birds more than dogs or cats. It was also determined that the bird preference could not be attributed to a failure to discriminate among the exemplars within the dog and cat categories. In other words, the infants could differentiate one dog from another and one cat from another. Within-category discrimination is important to show if one wants to claim that the infants have formed a representation for a category of discriminably different entities.

The next question asked was whether the infants could make the presumably more difficult categorical distinction between cats and dogs. Infants were familiarized as before with either cats or dogs, and then as shown in the bottom of figure 4.2, tested with a novel cat versus a novel dog. The findings were that infants familiarized with cats preferred dogs over novel cats, and infants familiarized with dogs preferred cats over novel dogs. It should be noted that the latter result occurs with certain limitations related to the variability of the dog exemplars and their overlap (i.e., inclusion relation) with the

Can young infants form categorical representations for
cats and dogs each of which excludes instances of
birds?

Familiarization	<u>Cats</u>		<u>Dogs</u>	
	C_1	C_2	D_1	D_2
	C_3	C_4	D_3	D_4
	•		•	
	•		•	
	•		•	
	C_{11}	C_{12}	D_{11}	D_{12}
Novel category preference test	C_{13-18}	B_{1-18}	D_{13-18}	B_{1-18}

Can young infants form categorical representations for
dogs and cats each of which excludes instances of the
other?

Novel category preference test	C_{13-18}	D_{1-18}	D_{13-18}	C_{1-18}

Figure 4.2   Schematic depiction of the experimental designs used by Quinn, Eimas, & Rosenkrantz (1993) to investigate whether 3- to 4-month-old infants could form individuated categorical representations for cats and dogs

cat exemplars (for further comment, see Mareschal, French, & Quinn, 2000; Oakes, Coppage, & Dingel, 1997). Nevertheless, the overall pattern of results indicated that young infants, 3 to 4 months of age, could form separate categorical representations for cats and dogs, each of which was structured to exclude instances of the other as well as birds (see also Eimas & Quinn, 1994, for further results of categorization of other animal species by young infants).

Global-to-Basic Category Development: Two Systems of Category Representation?

Although the work described thus far is consistent with the Rosch et al. (1976) idea that basic-level category representations can be evidenced readily and early in development, there is another line of evidence questioning the developmental superiority of the basic level. Mandler and Bauer (1988) published a paper entitled "The cradle of categorization: Is the basic-level basic?". In this paper, and a number of subsequent others, Mandler and colleagues have challenged the traditional view of category development by arguing that the critical sorting experiment of Rosch et al. (1976) was confounded in that the basic-level task could be solved on the basis of either basic-level knowledge (e.g., how much two airplanes are alike), superordinate-level knowledge (e.g., how much two airplanes are different from the dog), or both. The more appropriate test of the basic-to-superordinate hypothesis is to determine if children (or infants) can differentiate basic-level categories chosen from the same superordinate before they can differentiate two superordinates. Mandler's group have now reported a number of studies adopting this experimental design, and infants and toddlers between 7 and 24 months participating in both object-examining and sequential touching procedures (Oakes, Madole, & Cohen, 1991; Riccuiti, 1965) more readily formed global representations differentiating between animals and vehicles than basic-level representations distinguishing horses from dogs or cars from trucks (Mandler, Bauer, & McDonough, 1991; Mandler & McDonough, 1993; Mandler & McDonough, 1998a). One view of the "kind" of representation infants form in object-exploration procedures is that it is explicit and conceptually based (Mandler, 1998). That is, infant performance in such procedures may be guided by representations formed prior to participation in the experiment (but see Rakison & Butterworth, 1998).

At this point in the discussion, the reader might note that Mandler and Bauer's (1988) argument concerning the experimental design of Rosch et al. (1976) cannot be used to explain the findings of Quinn et al. (1993) because the young infants in the Quinn et al. study were presented with basic-level categories chosen from the same superordinate structure (i.e., cats and dogs). The fact that older infants performing in the object-exploration procedures do not make use of the information that younger infants apparently use to form basic-level categories is puzzling. Mandler and McDonough (1993) have suggested that the two outcomes can be explained if one assumes that the familiarization/novelty-preference procedure taps primarily a perceptual level of processing, whereas the object-exploration procedures tap a more conceptual level of processing. The suggestion is that cats and dogs can be categorically distinguished by young infants on a perceptual basis in the visual recognition procedure (via attributes found on the surfaces of the stimuli), whereas animals and vehicles can be differentiated by older infants on a conceptual basis in the object exploration procedures (via conceptual primitives – such as the recognition that animals are self-starters and vehicles are nonself-starters, Mandler, 1992). This suggestion makes the assumption that global or superordinate categories are too perceptually variable to be anchored by perceptual cues. On the basis of this reasoning, Mandler and McDonough (1993) have speculated, "Global categories such as animals and vehicles are highly perceptually variable, and it may not be possible to differentiate them by perceptual categorization . . . it should be difficult to show global categorization of animals and vehicles using the traditional looking time tests" (p. 315).

The major thrust of this "double dissociation" argument is that one possesses separate perceptual versus conceptual representations for each category of experience. That is, one has a perceptual category representation that gets deployed when engaged in lower-level tasks like identification and recognition, and a conceptual category representation that gets used in higher-level tasks involving inference and problem-solving. One concern with this view is whether the proposed system of dual representations for each category would be efficient and cognitively economical (Quinn & Eimas, 1997, 2000; see also Waxman, ch. 5 this volume). It is worth asking whether humans would have evolved a cognitive architecture in which one representation is used for perceiving an entity and a different representation is used for thinking about that same entity. The question is whether it would be adaptive to have two different representations for each object category, one based on perceptual inputs, the other based on more conceptual inputs, when it may be possible to have just a single representation that incorporates both perceptual and conceptual information. The perceptual/conceptual dissociation view would also seem to require a third system of representation to coordinate between the perceptual and conceptual systems (Schyns, 1991).

An additional issue for the perceptual/conceptual dissociation view of early category development has to do with the reliability of some of the proposed conceptual cues for category formation. Consider the idea that animals and vehicles are differentiated by the recognition that animals are self-starters and vehicles are not (Mandler, 1992; Gelman & Opfer, ch. 7 this volume). Also imagine a 7-month-old infant positioned to observe a street scene. A taxi comes into view, stops, the passenger door opens, and an individual exits the vehicle. The taxi then starts up again. Unless the infant has a complex theory of human–machine interaction, the departure of the taxi may appear as self-starting motion. Would the taxi thus be conceptualized by the infant as an animal?

Yet another concern for the perceptual/conceptual dissociation idea is that there is no formal or in-principle difference between the object-examining procedure that is hypothesized to tap conceptual processing, and the familiarization/novelty-preference procedure that is believed to tap perceptual processing (Quinn, in press-a). In both cases, infants are familiarized with exemplars and one determines whether familiarization is generalized to a novel exemplar from the familiar category and whether there is an increase in attention to the novel category exemplar. It is not clear why the two procedures would tap qualitatively different kinds of representations. However, there is one parametric difference between the way the two procedures have been used and it centers on the number of exemplars presented to support category formation, four in the case of the object-examining procedure (e.g, Mandler & McDonough, 1993) and 12 in the case of the familiarization/novelty-preference procedure (e.g., Quinn et al., 1993). This seemingly small quantitative difference could lead to an account of the findings that is rather different from the double dissociation model (see also Oakes, Plumert, Lansink, & Merryman, 1996), a point that will become clearer as the chapter proceeds.

Arguments aside, what creates the most difficulty for the perceptual/conceptual dissociation view of early category formation are the findings indicating that young infants participating in a familiarization/novelty-preference task *can* form global category representations (Behl-Chadha, 1996). In Behl-Chadha's study, 3- and 4-month-olds were familiarized with instances from a number of mammal categories and preference tested with instances of novel mammal categories not experienced during familiarization, non-mammalian animals (i.e., birds or fish), and furniture. A schematic depiction of the experimental design is presented in figure 4.3. The infants responded by generalizing their familiarization to the novel mammal category instances, and by displaying novel category preferences for the birds, fish, and furniture. The findings cast doubt on the idea that global representations are *necessarily* conceptually based and on the perceptual/conceptual dissociation view more generally. The age of the infants and the nature of the stimuli (i.e., static pictorial instances of the categories) make it improbable that the participants relied on conceptual knowledge about mammals and furniture to perform successfully in the

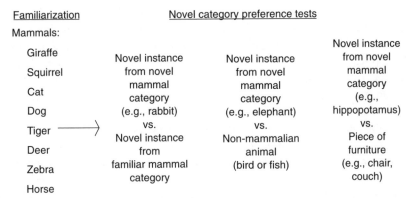

Familiarization	Novel category preference tests		

Mammals:

Giraffe

Squirrel

Cat

Dog

Tiger $\longrightarrow$

Deer

Zebra

Horse

Novel instance
from novel
mammal
category
(e.g., rabbit)
vs.
Novel instance
from
familiar mammal
category

Novel instance
from novel
mammal
category
(e.g., elephant)
vs.
Non-mammalian
animal
(bird or fish)

Novel instance
from novel
mammal
category
(e.g.,
hippopotamus)
vs.
Piece of
furniture
(e.g., chair,
couch)

Figure 4.3   Schematic depiction of the experimental design used by Behl-Chadha (1996) to investigate whether 3- to 4-month-old infants could form a categorical representation of mammals

task. Behl-Chadha's study therefore supports the position that both basic and global levels of representation can have a perceptual basis.

A Continuity-Based Approach to Understanding Early Categorization

If a double dissociation model does not provide a proper account of the infant categorization data, then might an alternative model based on developmental continuity accommodate the evidence (e.g., Eimas, 1994)? An important question for such a model is to explain why young infants form global and basic-level category representations in looking procedures (Behl-Chadha, 1996; Quinn et al., 1993), whereas older infants form predominantly global category representations in object-exploration procedures (Mandler & McDonough, 1993, 1998a). Also at issue is the course of category development in infants younger than 3 months of age. Are the earliest representations formed by infants more nearly global or basic in their exclusiveness? Does development consist of derivation of the specifics from the global level or grouping together of the specifics to form the global level?

In the tradition of differentiation theory (Gibson & Gibson, 1955; Werner, 1957), and in contrast to Rosch et al. (1976), it has recently been suggested that the early development of categorization may proceed from more general to more specific representations (Quinn, 1998, 1999; Quinn & Eimas, 1996, 1997). Although this view is similar to the one advanced by Mandler (1998) in emphasizing differentiation of broad category representations (i.e., global) to form narrower ones (i.e., basic-level), it attempts to account for this development with a single system of representation that becomes progressively differentiated during the course of experience (Quinn & Eimas, 2000; Quinn, Johnson, Mareschal, Rakison, & Younger, 2000; but see Mandler, 2000b). The proposal is that the information that differentiates many global categories such as mammals and vehicles from each other may be the presence versus absence of *perceptible surface features* such as faces, fur, and tails possessed by the mammals and not by the vehicles, and wheels, windshields, and shiny exteriors possessed by the vehicles and not by the mammals (for related proposals and supportive evidence, see Haith & Benson, 1998; Rakison & Butterworth, 1998; Smith & Heise, 1992; Van de Walle, Spelke, & Carey, 1997). This information may turn out to be more discriminable than the information that may be used to separate mammals from one another (or vehicles from one another) which may be the specific values of these same features. Such a suggestion is consistent with Murphy's (1982) argument that "superordinates . . . have more reliable cues than do the basic categories they include" (p. 176). Accordingly, global category distinctions may be more readily evidenced, whereas distinctions within a global category may be less likely. Although differentiation-based theories have sometimes been used to account for the development of conceptually based concepts (e.g., Keil, 1979; Mandler, 1998), the idea that global categories emerge before those at the basic (and presumably subordinate) levels through *perceptual learning* processes represents a new position in the literature (see also Schyns, Goldstone, & Thibaut, 1998, for a recent view of object concept representation with a similar developmental theme).

Connectionist Modeling of the Emergence of Category Representations

One way to attempt to better understand the formation of category representations by infants in a more formal way than in the past is to explore the emergence of global and basic-level category representations in computational learning systems. The value of computational modeling in developmental psychology is that it provides a means of testing hypotheses over and above empirical work with infants. It also makes theorizing more rigorous in that to implement a developmental theory as a computer program forces one to make explicit decisions about what environmental features infants may be sensitive to and also what internal constraints be built into the model (Mareschal & Shultz, 1996). As a class of computational models, connectionist models seem particularly well suited to simulating early category development because they are composed of interconnected processing units that form representations as connection strengths between units change with experience according to one or another learning mechanism (Thomas & Karmiloff-Smith, ch. 26 this volume; Elman, Bates, Johnson, Karmiloff-Smith, Parisi, & Plunkett, 1996). Moreover, as is hypothesized to be the case with infants, the models learn by progressive extraction of statistical regularities in the input. That is, the models pull apart categories more easily when quantitative inputs that separate those categories are characterized by large and clear value differences. Although connectionist networks have been used to model categorization (e.g., Feldman & Ballard, 1982; Knapp & Anderson, 1984), little work has focused on development of categorization from the period of early infancy.

Quinn and Johnson (1997, 2000) described a series of three-layered connectionist networks (i.e., input→hidden units→output) that were given the task of categorizing mammal and furniture stimuli at basic and global levels. Input included a number of dimensions measured from the surfaces of the mammal and furniture stimuli used in the familiarization/novelty-preference experiments cited earlier (e.g., leg length, horizontal extent). In terms of internal architecture, the number of hidden nodes was kept smaller than the number of inputs. The information compression created by this architectural feature is consistent with the idea that categorization exists in part to reduce physical diversity and serve cognitive economy. Although the original networks contained a back-propagation-based category-teaching signal and were subject to the criticism that this manner of simulation is an unrealistic way to model the presumed unsupervised category formation achieved by young infants, follow-up simulations were conducted with an autoassociative network architecture that did not contain a category-teaching signal. In the autoassociative network, inputs are simply mapped to outputs (which are copies of the inputs) through a layer of hidden (representational) units. The job of the network at the level of the hidden units is to extract enough of the statistical regularities in the input to reproduce the input as the output. This architecture stands in contrast to the backpropagation network in which inputs are mapped through a layer of hidden units to categories at the output.

A majority of the backpropagation- and autoassociative-based simulations produced a common result, namely, that global categories preceded basic-level categories in order of appearance. Other connectionist models of category formation have extended the general to specific learning sequence from global to basic to subordinate levels (McClelland, McNaughton, & O'Reilly, 1995; Rumelhart & Todd, 1993; Schyns, 1991). The strength of the modeling is that it provides an in-principle demonstration of the category representations that can be formed, their level of exclusiveness, and their relative time course of emergence, in a learning device with no category-teaching signal (in the case of the autoassociative network architecture) that receives inputs measured directly from the surfaces of the stimuli – inputs that young infants might conceivably be sensitive to. The modeling also provides a quantitative formalization of descriptive ideas contained in a differentiation theory of perceptual category learning. It should be noted that the global-to-basic-to-subordinate proposal is not at all obvious or trivial given the more traditional basic-to-superordinate view of category development (Rosch et al., 1976).

Implications of the Modeling

Another value of the modeling is that it sometimes yields novel perspectives that might have been difficult to achieve through purely descriptive theorizing. For example, through connectionist modeling of categorization processes, it is possible to examine how the internal (representational) resources of the network (i.e., the hidden nodes) interact with inputs to produce category representations at different levels of exclusiveness over different time courses. One problem for any descriptive theory or computational model of categorization in general is to reconcile why global category superiority is achieved under some circumstances (Mandler & McDonough, 1993), and why basic-level superiority is manifest in others (Rosch et al., 1976). Although some basic-level superiority might be attributable to experimental design flaws (Mandler & Bauer, 1988), it is not clear that the great variety of basic-level superiority effects observed in both children and adults can be explained in this way (Murphy & Lassaline, 1997).

The networks developed by Quinn and Johnson (1997) behaved in a way which may reconcile the differences in findings. Specifically, they displayed a tendency during initial learning to allocate a number of hidden nodes to coding the global level. Anywhere from 35 to 80 percent of the hidden nodes coded the global level, with the remaining nodes not yet committed. The early global-coding nodes quickly learned to represent large differences in a small number of attributes that distinguished the global level (i.e., the presence of face and tail attributes in the case of mammals, and the absence of them in the case of furniture). However, as learning proceeded, more and more of the network's hidden nodes became committed to encoding more subtle basic-level distinctions that were characterized quantitatively by smaller value differences along a variety of attributes (e.g., head width in the case of dogs vs. cats, leg length in the case of dressers vs. tables). Thus, what happened during the course of learning was a gradual decrease in the percentage of hidden nodes coding the global level (to 10 to 20 percent), and a gradual increase in the percentage of hidden nodes coding the basic level (to 80 to 90 percent).

This network behavior suggests that one might think of global representations as precursor representations from which basic-level (and eventually subordinate-level) representations evolve. Once basic-level structures emerge, however, they may display a variety of superiority effects, because more internal resources are committed to representing them. That generally younger participants (< 2.5 years) tend to show global or at least child-basic superiority (e.g., Mandler & McDonough, 1993; Mervis, 1987; but see Waxman & Markow, 1995), whereas older participants (> 2.5 years) tend to show basic-level superiority (e.g., Horton & Markman, 1980; Mervis & Crisafi, 1982; Murphy & Smith, 1982) is consistent with this idea. Furthermore, adults who become experts within a domain may come to represent subordinate-level categories as robustly as basic-level categories for that domain (Tanaka & Taylor, 1991). Finally, just as global-to-basic-to-subordinate may be the order in which category information is learned during development, subordinate-to-basic-to-global may be the order in which category information is lost in older adults with Alzheimer's disease (AD). According to a kind of "first in, last out" principle, patients with AD are often able to provide the global label for visually presented objects, but not the basic- or subordinate-level label (e.g., "animal" instead of "cow"; Bayles, Tomoeda, & Trosset, 1990; Tippet, McAuliffe, & Farah, 1995).

A global-to-basic sequence of category learning suggests that as infants are presented with increasing numbers of exemplars from a *single basic-level category*, the representation of these exemplars will initially be at the global level (for small numbers of exemplars), and only subsequently at the basic level (for larger numbers of exemplars). This time course of emergence could help reconcile why infants participating in object exploration procedures have been less likely to form basic-level categories when presented with a small number (n = 4) of exemplars (e.g., Mandler & McDonough, 1993), whereas infants participating in looking procedures have been more likely to form basic-level categories with a larger number (n = 12) of exemplars (e.g., Quinn et al., 1993). Note that this explanatory framework is very different from the perceptual/conceptual dissociation view discussed earlier. The overall pattern of findings might more parsimoniously be accommodated by a single representation that becomes progressively differentiated during the course of early experience.

It is important to recognize that changes in a single, quantitative variable like exemplar number can produce changes in the level of inclusiveness of the category representations formed (i.e., global vs. basic) – changes that lead to behavior that may appear to be qualitatively different (Mandler, 1998, 2000a). However, the argument presented here is that the development of these representations need not be driven by dissociations or discontinuities in underlying mental processes or knowledge structures. Sophisticated category representations may grow from a gradual accrual of information by means of many input systems. Perhaps an analogy can be made between this process and the kinds of self-organizing types of processes described by Thelen and Smith (1994). For example, with respect to the gait of a horse, if one changes speed slightly, the nature of the gait appears to undergo a very considerable change. Although this example comes from the domain of locomotion, the principle remains the same – quantitative changes in input can lead to apparently qualitative changes in behavior, but without discontinuity of underlying process.

Empirical Results Consistent with the Modeling

As has been described, 3- to 4-month-old infants will form perceptually based category representations for mammals and furniture at either a basic or global level (Quinn & Eimas, 1996). The question arises as to the levels of category representation available to younger infants. If what occurs in the connectionist simulations is analogous to what happens to infants during the developmental course of experience (i.e., both the network and the infant have more and more experiences with category instances over time), then the global-to-basic order of development observed in the simulations predicts that formation of global representations will precede formation of basic-level representations sometime during the first 3 months.

Because of this latter suggestion from the modeling, Quinn and Johnson (2000) recently reported a set of experiments designed to test the global-before-basic prediction in 2-month-olds. Specifically, the investigators examined whether 2-month-olds could form: (1) a global representation for mammals that excluded furniture, and (2) a basic-level representation for cats that excluded dogs, rabbits, and elephants. In the basic-level test, infants were familiarized with cats and then given two preference tests, one pairing a novel cat with either a rabbit or an elephant, the other pairing a novel cat with a dog. In the global test, a different group of infants was familiarized with mammals and then given two preference tests, one of which paired a novel member of a familiar mammal category with a novel member from a novel mammal category, whereas the other paired a novel member from a novel mammal category with a furniture exemplar. The expectation was that these younger infants might form a global representation for mammals, but not a basic-level representation for cats. This pattern of outcomes would be evidenced by (1) infants in the global test preferring furniture over novel mammal category exemplars, but not novel over familiar mammal category exemplars, *and* (2) infants in the basic-level test not responding preferentially to novel elephants, rabbits, or dogs over novel cats. The results were in accord with the predictions. For infants familiarized with cats, the preference scores for rabbits and elephants (combined) and for dogs were not reliably different from the chance preference of 50 percent. For infants familiarized with mammals, novel mammal category exemplars were not reliably preferred over familiar mammal category exemplars, but furniture exemplars were preferred to novel mammal category exemplars. Control experiments indicated that the preference for furniture was not attributable to a failure to discriminate within the mammal category or to an a priori preference for furniture.

The data indicated that the 2-month-olds formed a global representation of mammals that included instances of novel mammal categories, but excluded furniture; 2-month-olds did not, however, form a basic-level representation for cats that excluded instances of novel mammal categories. Given that 3- and 4-month-olds have been shown to form both global and child-basic category representations, the finding that 2-month-olds form only global category representations is consistent with the global-to-basic learning sequence observed in the connectionist simulations. The data also correspond with evidence of global category superiority obtained with older infants performing in object-exploration procedures (Mandler & McDonough, 1993, 1998a). As has been discussed, the studies with older infants have been interpreted as providing evidence that infants use "conceptual primitives" as a basis for global categories (Mandler, 1992), on the assumption that perceptual similarity is not sufficient to ground such categories. However, this interpretation may require a major revision because the simulation and experimental results obtained with young infants suggest that global category representations can also emerge on the basis of *perceptual* information. Younger and Fearing (1999, 2000) have recently reported further data supporting this conclusion: global-to-basic category development was observed in 4- to 10-month-old infants presented with the animal versus vehicle contrast in the context of the familiarization/novelty-preference procedure.

It has been suggested that infants' representation of the mammal versus furniture distinction reported by Quinn and Johnson (2000) and the animal versus vehicle distinction reported by Younger and Fearing (1999, 2000) might be isolated cases of perceptually based global-to-basic category learning (Mandler, 2000a, 2000b). For example, infants might just be representing entities with faces separately from entities without faces. Although the presence versus absence of face information would appear to be an ecologically valid cue for the category contrasts at issue, there is also evidence to indicate that global-to-basic category learning by young infants is a phenomenon of a more general nature. For example, Quinn et al. (2001) have examined the formation of geometric form categories (i.e., circles, crosses, squares, and triangles) by newborn versus 4-month-old infants. The categories and their exemplars are shown in figure 4.4. Infants were presented with exemplars from one form category and then preference tested with a novel exemplar from the familiar category paired with a novel exemplar from the novel category. The findings were that 4-month-old infants formed exclusive basic-like category representations (i.e., circles vs. crosses vs. squares vs. triangles), whereas newborns appeared to form category representations of open versus closed classes of forms (i.e., crosses vs. circles, squares, and triangles). These findings indicate that the trend from more global to more

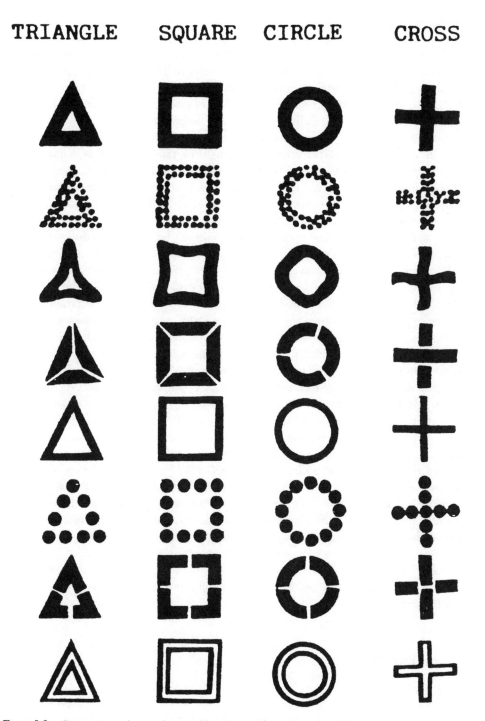

TRIANGLE   SQUARE   CIRCLE   CROSS

Figure 4.4   Categories and exemplars used by Quinn, Slater, Brown, & Hayes (in press) to examine form categorization by newborn and 4-month-old infants

specific category representations formed by young infants participating in looking-time tasks is not limited to category contrasts marked by the face versus no face distinction. It should also be noted that the limiting factor in these experiments is not immature sensory acuity, given that the infants in all of these studies were shown capable of discriminating individual instances within the categories (see also Mash, Quinn, Dobson, & Narter, 1998, for further comment on the lack of relation between sensory acuity and novel category preference of individual infants in the age range at issue).

Another concern that has been registered about reports of global category representations in young infants participating in looking-time tasks (e.g., Behl-Chadha, 1996; Quinn & Johnson, 2000) is their level of inclusiveness. For example, Behl-Chadha's (1996) stimuli were all typical-looking, four-legged mammals, and the representation excluded birds and fish. In contrast, the representations formed by older infants participating in object-exploration tasks have included such diverse exemplars as birds, fish, and turtles and are clearly closer to something like "animal." Because of this difference in the breadth of the representations, it has been suggested that young infants participating in looking-time tasks may show no categorization when presented with the varied exemplars that have been used with older infants in object-exploration tasks (Mandler, 2000a, 2000b). However, 3- and 4-month-old infants participating in the familiarization/novelty-preference procedure have been shown to form a global category representation inclusive of humans, mammals (i.e., cats and horses), and nonmammalian animals (i.e., fish), but exclusive of cars (Quinn & Eimas, 1998). This broad representation may have been based on the detection of a set of facial attributes (Johnson & Morton, 1991), adjoined to an elongated body axis with skeletal appendages (Zhu & Yuille, 1996). Moreover, the inclusion of humans as familiarization exemplars may have served as a magnet or attractor for nonhuman animals (cf. Kuhl, 1991; Miller & Eimas, 1996; Thelen & Smith, 1994).

Further results obtained on how infants represent humans permit consideration of the nature of the representation for categories and the possible role that experience might have on this representation. Quinn and Eimas (1998) found that under certain experimental conditions, 3- to 4-month-old infants represented individual humans as subordinate-level prototypes belonging to the same category (i.e., the infants have in effect become "human experts"), whereas nonhuman animal species (e.g., cats, horses) were represented by summary structures (e.g., basic-level prototypes). Given the greater experience that even 3- to 4-month-olds most likely have with humans relative to nonhuman animals, the experimental results are consistent with a basic-to-subordinate component in early category emergence, and imply that the full course of early category development may proceed in general from global to basic to subordinate representations.

Concluding Remarks

Although one view of category development suggested that basic-level representations emerge before those at the superordinate level (Rosch et al., 1976), there is evidence accumulating to indicate that global category representations actually emerge before those at the basic level (Mandler & McDonough, 1998a). The latest work suggests that this global-before-basic developmental sequence may come about at least initially through the operation of perceptual learning processes (Quinn & Johnson, 2000; Quinn et al., 2001; Younger & Fearing, 1999, 2000). The formation of perceptually based category representations by young infants has taken on increased significance in recent discussions of mechanisms of conceptual representation more generally. While it seems clear that perceptual categorization by infants may not easily be related to formation of certain goal-directed categories formed by adults, i.e., things to take from the house in case of fire (Barsalou, 1983), it is also the case that infant performance is consistent with Malt's (1995) suggestion that many object categories "seem to be strongly influenced by regularities in the input that are recognized by the categorizer" (p. 130). In addition, Millikan (1998) has argued that many object concepts of adults begin with a process of perceptual tracking of object categories by infants. Furthermore, even Xu, Tenenbaum, and Sorrentino (1998), writing from a quite different perspective, have agreed that "infants have a perceptual system that is similar to that of adults, so that infants carve up the world in more or less the same way adults do" (p. 89).

While the role that early perceptually based categorical representations play in support of inferences, beliefs, and theories remains controversial (Karmiloff-Smith, 1992; Mandler & McDonough, 1996, 1998b; Quinn et al., 2000; Xu & Carey, 1996), it is possible that some of the conceptual representations found later in life are informational enrichments of the original perceptually based categorical representations of young infants (Quinn & Eimas, 1996, 1997, 2000; Jones & Smith, 1993; Madole & Oakes, 1999). That is, the early parsing of the world, given its validity to reality, would permit the infant to begin to associate new knowledge with perceptually based categorical representations. For example, the information that dogs eat bones, give birth to puppies, and have dog DNA – information that is presumably acquired after the first few months of life by means of the input system of language and through formal and informal tuition – can be incorporated into the perceptually based representation of young infants and used to know dogs as a particular "kind of thing." Overall then, the significance of the work reviewed in this chapter is that the infant has the correct parse of the world to begin the process of further knowledge acquisition.

CHAPTER FIVE

Early Word-Learning and Conceptual Development: Everything had a Name, and Each Name Gave Birth to a New Thought

Sandra R. Waxman

How do infants begin to map words to their meaning? How do they discover that different types of words (e.g., noun, adjective) refer to different aspects of the same objects (e.g., object category, object property)? I have proposed that (1) infants begin the task of word-learning with a broad, universal expectation linking novel words to commonalities among objects, and that (2) this initial expectation is subsequently fine-tuned on the basis of infants' experience with the native language under acquisition. In this chapter, we examine this proposal, in light of recent evidence with infants and young children.

Introduction

Infants across the world's communities are exposed to vastly different experiences. Consider, for example, one infant being raised in a remote region of the Guatemalan rainforest, another growing up in the mountains of rural Switzerland, and a third being raised in Brooklyn, NY. Each infant will live in a world that is unimaginable to the others, surrounded by objects and events that are foreign to the others, and immersed in a language that the others cannot begin to understand. Yet in spite of such vast differences, infants across the world display striking similarities in the most fundamental aspects of their conceptual and language development.

Within the first year of life, each of these infants will form categories that capture both the similarities and differences among the objects they encounter. Most of these early object categories will be at the basic level (i.e., *dog*) and the more inclusive global level (i.e., *animal*) (see Quinn, ch. 4 this volume). Infants will begin to use these early object categories as an inductive base to support inferences about new objects that they encounter. They will also begin to relate categories to one another, implicitly, on the basis of taxonomic (e.g., dogs are a kind of animal), thematic (e.g., dogs chase tennis balls), functional (e.g., dogs can pull children on sleds), and other relations among them. Infants' early categories will provide a core of conceptual continuity from infancy through adulthood.

Concurrent with these conceptual advances, infants in each community will make remarkably rapid strides in language acquisition. Even before they begin to understand the words of their native language, infants show a special interest in the sounds of language. Newborns respond to the emotional tone carried by the melody of human speech (Fernald, 1992b), and prefer speech sounds to other forms of auditory input. Within the first six months, infants become perceptually attuned to the distinct prosodic, morphologic, and phonologic elements that characterize their native language (Jusczyk & Kemler Nelson, 1996; Kemler Nelson, Hirsh-Pasek, Jusczyk, & Cassidy, 1989; Morgan & Demuth, 1996; Shi, Werker, & Morgan, 1999; Werker, Lloyd, Pegg, & Polka, 1996). By their first birthdays, infants begin to produce their first words. These early words tend to refer to salient individual objects (e.g., "Mama"), categories of objects (e.g., "cup," "doggie"), social routines (e.g., "bye-bye"), and actions (e.g., "up"). Across languages, infants' earliest lexicons tend to show a "noun advantage," with nouns referring to basic-level object categories (e.g., cup, dog) being the predominant form. By their second birthdays, most infants have mastered hundreds of words of various grammatical forms (e.g., nouns, verbs, adjectives) and have begun to combine these into short, well-formed phrases that conform broadly to the syntactic properties of their native language.

This brief sketch illustrates several early milestones along the road of language and conceptual development. Infants naturally form *categories* to capture commonalities among objects and learn *words* to express them. Together with my colleagues, I have argued that these two advances do not proceed independently. Instead, there are powerful implicit links between them.

Links between early language and conceptual development: a view through the lens of word-learning

These links between early language and conceptual development are most clearly viewed through the lens of early word-learning. Perhaps more than any other developmental achievement, word-learning stands at the very intersection of language and cognition, and serves as the gateway to subsequent development in both domains. Early word-learning represents infants' entrance into a truly symbolic system and brings with it a means to establish reference. It supports infants' subsequent discovery of the fundamental syntactic properties of the native language (see Gillette, Gleitman, Gleitman, & Lederer, 1999; Snedeker & Gleitman, 1999; Waxman, 1999a, 1999b) as well as the evolution of increasingly abstract conceptual representations. Moreover, from the onset of acquisition the process of word-learning involves powerful, implicit links between the linguistic and conceptual systems. Even before infants begin to speak, novel words guide their attention to objects, and highlight commonalities and differences among them (Balaban & Waxman, 1997; Waxman & Markow, 1995; Xu, 1999).

My colleagues and I have made a developmental proposal regarding these links. We have proposed (1) that infants across the world's language communities begin the task of word learning equipped with an initially general and universal expectation, and (2) that this early expectation is then shaped by the structure of the particular language under acquisition. In our most recent work, which will be reviewed here, we have sought to uncover the origin and unfolding of these links (Klibanoff & Waxman, 2000; Waxman, 1998; Waxman & Booth, 2000a; Waxman & Booth, in press; Waxman & Markow, 1995). To amplify this topic, I will discuss what it takes to learn a word, to establish a mapping between the linguistic entities that we call *words* and the corresponding entities in the *world*. This exploration will underscore infants' implicit expectations, as well as their ability to recruit fundamental perceptual and conceptual capacities in the service of word-learning. The second section will be devoted to illustrating some of these links between word-learning and conceptual development in preschool-aged children. In the third section, the goal is to trace the origin and emergence of these links in infants.

What Does it Take to Learn a Word?

Perhaps the most celebrated example of word-learning comes from Helen Keller's autobiography. As Keller recounts,

> my teacher placed my hand under the spout. As the cool stream gushed over one hand she spelled into the other the word *water*, first slowly, then rapidly. I stood still, my whole attention fixed upon the motions of her fingers. Suddenly I felt a misty consciousness as of something forgotten – a thrill of returning thought; and somehow the mystery of language was revealed to me. I knew then that 'w-a-t-e-r' meant the wonderful cool something that was flowing over my hand. That living word awakened my soul, gave it light, hope, joy, and set it free! . . . I left the well-house eager to learn. Everything had a name, and each name gave birth to a new thought. (Keller, 1904, pp. 22–3)

This memorable passage poignantly conveys the obstacles in first establishing a correspondence between the abstract entities that we call *words* and their referents in the *world*. It also conveys the power of such *word-to-world* mappings, once they are attained. But the scenario in this passage differs in important ways from the more typical circumstances in which infants' first words are acquired. One important difference is the age of acquisition. Infants tend to produce their first words at approximately 1 year of age. Keller, in contrast, learned *water* at approximately 7 years of age.[1] A second difference is the extent to which names are deliberately "taught." Psycholinguists and anthropologists have conducted detailed observations of naming practices across cultures. In some cultures (e.g. Western, college-educated communities), caretakers do name objects deliberately for their infants, even before the infants themselves can speak. Yet in many other communities (e.g. Kahluli, see Ochs & Schieffelin, 1984), caretakers refrain from speaking directly to infants until the infants themselves have begun to speak. Clearly, then, infants can discover the meaning of novel words even in the absence of direct tutoring.

A third relevant difference is in the presentation of the new word. In the typical course of events, words are seldom, if ever, presented in isolation, as Keller's tutor presented the word *w-a-t-e-r*. Instead, words tend to be embedded in a fluent stream of continuous speech (e.g., "Look at the water! Oooh . . . it's so cold. Isn't that cold water?"), leaving it to the infant to parse the novel word. How do they succeed in these cases? At a most general level, it helps that infants devote special attention to human speech, for this puts them in a good position to begin to single out the novel words. Infants' preference for human speech over other sources of auditory input has been documented in studies using a variety of techniques, including the head-turn procedure (Jusczyk & Kemler Nelson, 1996). Another advantage is that in many cultures, caretakers use a special speech register (sometimes known as infant-directed speech or "motherese") when addressing infants and young children. Two characteristic features of this speech register – exaggerated pitch contours and phrase boundaries – help infants to identify words and phrases in the continuous speech stream (Gleitman & Wanner, 1988). In addition, whether or not words are presented in "motherese", infants as young as 8 months of age are especially attentive to words that come at the end of a sentence or phrase boundary (e.g., "See the *water*?") (Fernald, 1992b; Jusczyk & Aslin, 1995; Newsome & Jusczyk, 1994). In many languages (e.g., English, Spanish, French), nouns tend to occupy this privileged phrase-final position. However, in other languages (e.g., Mandarin Chinese (Tardif, 1996), Korean (Au, Dapretto, & Song, 1994; Choi & Gopnik, 1995), and apparently Tzeltal and Itzaj) this is less often the case. Yet, despite these variations, infants across the world's language communities begin to produce their first words at roughly the same age, and the composition of their early lexicons is roughly comparable, with nouns (that is, words that are classified as nouns in the adult language) being the predominant early form (Au et al., 1994; for a different interpretation see Bloom, 1993; Choi & Gopnik, 1995; Gentner, 1982; Gentner & Boroditsky, in press; Gleitman, 1990; Goldin-Meadow, Seligman, & Gelman, 1976; Huttenlocher & Smiley, 1987; Nelson, Hampson, & Shaw, 1993; Saah, Waxman, & Johnson, 1996; Tardif, 1996). Information regarding the composition of the early lexicon has been gleaned primarily from two types of survey-based research. In the first, researchers present a list of words and caretakers indicate which of these the infant comprehends and/or produces. The most commonly used list (the MacArthur Communicative Developmental Inventory) has been translated into several languages (Fenson, Dale, Reznick, Bates, et al., 1994). The second method involves direct observations of conversations between infants and their caretakers (Bloom, 1993; Braun, Balaban, Booth, & Waxman, 2001; Gelman, Coley, Rosengren, Hartman, & Pappas, 1998).

A fourth difference concerns the identification of the referent of the novel word. The referent is seldom available for inspection throughout the duration of the naming episode. Therefore, unlike Keller, infants must identify the referent of a novel word amidst an ever-changing current of events. In many cases, the referent may be absent entirely (e.g., "Let's call Daddy," uttered as the caretaker picks up a cordless telephone). In other cases, the referent may make only a fleeting appearance (e.g., "Look at the monkey," uttered as a monkey makes a fleeting appearance in its habitat at the zoo). And even if the referent is present throughout the naming episode, there is no guarantee that the infant will be attending to it at the time that the novel word is introduced (e.g., "Go find your teddy-bear," uttered as a caretaker tries (in vain) to pull the infants' attention away from the sleeping family cat).

The puzzle of word-learning

Thus, in the natural course of word-learning, an infant is faced with a difficult three-part puzzle. Typically, one individual (say, an adult) points to an object (say, a tapir) and provides its name ("Ila' a' tzimin~che' je'lo'" (in Itzaj Maya) or "Look, a tapir" (in English)). To succeed, the infant must (1) parse the relevant word (*tzimin~che* or *tapir*) from the ongoing stream of speech, (2) identify the relevant entity (the tapir) in the ongoing stream of activity in the world, and (3) establish a word-to-world correspondence. To put matters more formally, successful word-learning rests on the infant's ability to discover the relevant linguistic units, the relevant conceptual units, and the mappings between them.

Notice also that each piece in the word-learning puzzle is itself dependent on infants' ability to recruit other perceptual and psychological capacities. Consider, for example, the ability to parse words. We know that even newborns prefer to listen to human speech – and particularly infant-directed speech – as compared to other sources of auditory stimulation. However, the function of infant-directed speech appears to change during the first year of life (Fernald, 1992b). Initially, infant-directed speech serves primarily to engage and modulate the infant's attention. Toward the end of the first year, "words begin to emerge from the melody" (Fernald, 1992a, p. 403). By approximately 9 to 10 months, infants become increasingly sensitive to the cues (morphologic, phonetic, and prosodic cues) that mark word and phrase boundaries (Jusczyk & Aslin, 1995; Kemler Nelson et al., 1989).

Infants' growing sensitivity to these perceptual cues, which are available in the speech stream, permit them to distinguish two very broad classes of words: *open class* words (or, *content* words, including nouns, adjectives, verbs) and *closed class* words (or, *function* words, including determiners and prepositions) (Shi et al., 1999). Research using a preferential listening task reveals that 9- to 10-month old infants prefer to listen to open class words. This preference is likely related to the fact that these are perceptually more salient: they receive greater stress and more interesting melodic contours than closed class words. Since this preference exists well before infants begin to map words systematically to meaning, it is reasonable to assume that it is perceptually based and independent of meaning. Yet this perceptually based preference represents an important step on the way to word-learning, for it insures that infants attend to just those words (the open class, content words) that are required if they are to anchor their first word-to-world mappings (Jusczyk & Kemler Nelson, 1996; Morgan & Demuth, 1996; Werker et al., 1996).

Early word-learning also is dependent upon the infants' perceptual and conceptual ability to identify objects in their environment, and to notice commonalities among them.

During the first year, infants demonstrate a great deal of core knowledge about objects (Baillargeon, 2000a, and ch. 3 this volume; Spelke, 2000). They also form a repertoire of pre-linguistic concepts, including category-based (e.g., dog, bottle) and property-based (e.g., red, soft) commonalities (see Quinn, ch. 4 this volume). Since many of these concepts are formed before the advent of word-learning, it is reasonable to assume that they are independent of language and are universally available. Each object and concept is, in essence, a candidate for a word's meaning. The infants' task is to discover which candidate meaning maps to the word that they have parsed.

The third piece of the word-learning puzzle – grasping the symbolic and referential power of words – further requires infants to draw upon fundamental notions related to human behavior: inferring the goals and intentions of others (see Gergely, ch. 2 this volume). For example, the ability to establish a mapping between a word and its referent is predicated upon infants' capacity to infer that the speaker *intended to name* the designated object. Recent research reveals that by 10 months, infants have begun to make such connections (Baldwin & Baird, 1999; Guajardo & Woodward, 2000); they spontaneously follow a speaker's line of regard to identify the object to which an adult speaker is attending.

In addition to these three central elements, successful word-learning requires infants to go beyond a word-to-object mapping. For to use a word consistently over time, infants must be able to store in memory the correspondence between a word and its intended referent. They must also be able to generalize a newly learned word appropriately beyond the individual on which it was taught. Infants are exceptional word-learners (see Carey, 1978; Goldfield & Reznick, 1990; Heibeck & Markman, 1987; Waxman & Booth, 2000b; Waxman & Booth, 2001; Waxman & Hall, 1993; Woodward, Markman, & Fitzsimmons, 1994). For example, when a child applies the word *tapir* to a new, and (as yet) unlabeled object, that child has made an inference regarding its extension. Infants' spontaneous extensions indicate that they do not merely map words to the objects on which they were introduced. Infants go beyond *word-to-object* mappings to establish *word-to-category* mappings (Waxman & Booth, 2000b).

Different kinds of words highlight different aspects of a scene

To complicate matters further, even if an infant happens to be attending to the same scene as a speaker, and even if the infant takes notice of the novel word introduced in this context, there is no guarantee that the infant will successfully map the word correctly. In large part, this is because many different words – indeed many different *types* of words – may be offered in a naming episode. Importantly, each type of word highlights a different aspect of the same observed scene and supports a unique pattern of extension. For example, in English, count nouns ("Look, it's a *tapir*") typically refer to the named object itself and are extended spontaneously to other members of the same object kind (other tapirs); proper nouns ("Look, it's *Zeus*") also refer to the named individual, but these are not extended further; although adjectives can also be applied correctly to that individual ("Look, it's *furry*"), they do not refer to the individual itself, but to a property of the named individual, and are extended to other objects sharing that property.

An important feature of human language is that different kinds of words bring to the foreground different aspects of the very same observed scene. Considerable research has documented that by 2.5 to 3 years of age, children are sensitive to many of these links between kinds of words and kinds of relations among objects, and recruit these links in the process of word-learning (For a review, see Waxman, 1998). This establishes that preschool-aged children have the *linguistic* capacity to distinguish among the relevant syntactic forms (count noun vs. adjective) and the *conceptual* or *perceptual* ability to appreciate many different kinds of relations among objects (see Goswami, ch. 13 this volume), and a tacit expectation that these linguistic and conceptual abilities are interwoven.

Acquisition of word-to-world links: three theoretical possibilities

But how do infants acquire these specific word-to-world links? Which, if any, are available at the very onset of lexical acquisition, and how are these shaped over the course of development? There are three logically possible classes of answer.

Possibility 1.   One possibility is that early acquisition is guided by an a priori set of expectations, linking each type of word (e.g., noun, adjective, verb) to a particular type of meaning (e.g., object categories, object properties, actions). A review of the cross-linguistic literature casts serious doubt on this possibility, because the links between particular types of words (or grammatical forms) and meaning are not universal. Across languages, the grammatical form *noun* tends to refer to individual objects (Zeus) and to categories of objects (e.g., tapir). In contrast, there is considerable cross-linguistic variability in the mappings for most other grammatical forms, including adjectives, verbs, prepositions, and spatial terms (Bowerman, 1996b; Haryu & Imai, 1999; Imai & Gentner, 1993; Regier & Carlson, in press; Waxman, Senghas, & Benveniste, 1997). This cross-linguistic variability is directly related to the question at hand, for it reveals that infants' expectations linking particular grammatical forms to their meaning cannot be fixed from the outset. Instead, infants must discover how the various grammatical forms are mapped to meaning in the language under acquisition.

Possibility 2.   Perhaps, then, infants begin the task of word-learning as something of a *tabula rasa* (blank slate), equipped with no expectations to guide the acquisition of their first word-to-world mappings. On this view, any expectation regarding a word and its meaning must be acquired inductively, as infants notice the precise correlations between particular grammatical forms and particular types of meaning. Implicit in this account is the assumption that at the onset of lexical acquisition, word-learning is qualitatively different in nature than word-learning in older children, for only older children could have induced the appropriate correlations between types of words and types of meaning. Although this position has been argued forcefully (Smith, 1999), a review of the developmental literature casts serious doubt on its plausibility. There is now ample evidence that infants begin the task of word-learning with certain powerful, albeit general, expectations linking words with concepts (Balaban & Waxman, 1997; Waxman & Markow, 1995; Xu, 1999). The fact that these nascent expectations are in place in advance of word-learning makes it unlikely that they could have been induced from infants' own lexicons.

Possibility 3.   The shortcomings of possibilities 1 and 2 lead us to argue for a third possibility, one that represents an interaction between a universally available expectation inherent in infants, and the shaping role of the environment (here, the structure of the native language). We propose that infants across the world's languages embark upon the task of word-learning equipped with a broad, universally shared expectation, and that this expectation is itself subsequently shaped by the structure of the particular language under acquisition. Infants begin with a perceptual preference for listening to open class words, with a repertoire of accessible perceptual and conceptual categories, and with a broad expectation that novel (open class) words, independent of their grammatical form, highlight commonalities among named objects. This initial link serves (at least) three essential functions. First, with words directing attention to commonalities, this link facilitates the formation of an expanding repertoire of concepts, concepts that may not have been detected in the absence of a novel word. Second, this initial expectation supports infants' first efforts to establish symbolic reference, to form a set of stable 'word-to-world' mappings. Finally, and perhaps most radically, this initial expectation sets the stage for the evolution of the more specific expectations linking particular types of words (nouns, adjectives, verbs) to particular types of relations among objects (object categories, object properties, actions) in the native language under acquisition (Waxman, 1999b).

How might this evolution come about? Infants' early expectation (that words refer to commonalities) supports the establishment of a rudimentary lexicon. This lexicon serves as a base upon which infants (a) begin to tease apart the various grammatical forms presented in the language under acquisition, and (b) begin to detect the correlations between these emerging forms and their meaning. Recall that infants' earliest lexicons include words that refer to a range of relations, including category-based commonalities (dog), property-based commonalities (hot), and common social routines and actions (bye-bye; up). Recall also that across languages, nouns are by far the most prevalent type of word represented in the early lexicon, and that these tend to refer to salient basic-level categories of objects (e.g., dog, horse, cup). Because the pairing between nouns and object categories are the most prevalent and most consistently represented in the early lexicon, infants are likely to first tease apart the nouns (from among the other open class grammatical forms)[2] and to notice that words from this grammatical category tend to refer to object categories (as opposed to other types of commonalities, including property-based or action-based commonalities). In other words, we argue that infants' initial expectation (linking words in general) to commonalities (in general) will direct their attention to just the sorts of regularities in the input that will promote the rapid discovery of the distinct grammatical forms present in the language under acquisition, and will support the induction of more specific expectations. Infants will first tease apart the nouns and map them to categories of objects. Subsequent linkages will build upon this referential base, and will be fine-tuned as a function of experience with the specific correlations between particular grammatical forms and their associated meanings in the native language.

The Evidence: The Evolution of Infants' Word-to-World Expectations

To test these possibilities, we must identify the expectation(s) of infants on the threshold of word-learning, and observe how these are shaped in the course of acquiring their native language. In this section, I offer the evidence. I first describe a series of experiments demonstrating the precise expectations held by preschool-aged English-speaking children. I then go on to consider the origin and evolution of these expectations in infants ranging from 9 to 15 months of age.

Unifying features of the experiments

The experiments that I will describe utilize an array of methods and subject populations, but share several important features. Each is essentially an object categorization task, tailored to suit the very different behavioral repertoires of infants versus young children. In each, the goal is to observe the relation between object naming and categorization. To do so, we compare subjects' categorization of objects in "neutral" conditions (involving no novel words), with their performance when they are introduced to novel words. Because our goal is to examine an abstract linkage between particular grammatical forms and particular types of relations, we introduce novel words (e.g., *fauna*), rather than familiar words (e.g., *animal*). This insures that the words themselves carry no a priori meaning for the child. To examine the influence of grammatical form, we vary the frame in which the novel word is embedded. We use short, simple syntactic constructions that (1) are typical in infant- and child-directed speech, and (2) provide unambiguous contextual evidence that the novel word is either a count noun or an adjective. In the *Novel Noun* conditions, we introduce objects saying, for example, "This is a *blicket*." In the *Novel Adjective* conditions, we present the same word using a different frame, saying, for example, "This is a *blick-ish* one" (see Gerken & McIntosh, 1993; Waxman & Markow, 1995; Waxman & Markow, 1998 for evidence that infants are sensitive to these distinct frames). In the *No Word* control conditions, we introduce no novel words, but point out the objects, saying, for example, "Do you like this?" or "Look at this." Performance in this *No Word* control condition assesses how readily subjects form the various categories presented in our tasks (e.g., dog, animal, purple things). Performance in the *Noun* condition assesses the role of naming in this important endeavor. Performance in the *Adjective* condition permits a strong test of the specificity of the relation between form and meaning. Because both count nouns ("That is a *dog*") and adjectives ("That is *purple*") can be applied ostensibly to objects, this is an important control.

Evidence from preschool-aged children

By the time they are 3 years of age, children reveal very specific expectations linking particular types of words with their meaning. The cross-linguistic evidence reveals that these

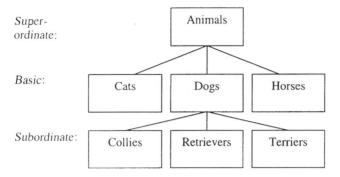

Figure 5.1 Representation of an object hierarchy

links are shaped by the structure of the native language (Waxman & Guasti, in preparation; Waxman et al., 1997). For English-speaking children, novel nouns direct attention specifically to categories of objects (e.g., dog, animal), and novel adjectives direct attention specifically to properties of objects (e.g., color, texture). These links have been documented in a highly structured object-classification task (Waxman, 1990; Waxman & Gelman, 1986). An experimenter introduced children to some "very picky" puppets, explaining that they "only want(ed) a certain kind of thing." To indicate the "kind of thing" that each puppet wanted, the experimenter displayed three typical instances of a familiar object category (e.g., a dog, a horse, a duck to indicate the category *animal*). Children were then asked to categorize additional items for the puppets.

To identify an influence of novel words on categorization, we compared performance in three conditions. In the *No Word* (control) condition, the experimenter introduced the three instances by saying, "Look at these." In the *Novel Noun* condition, children saw the same instances, but these were labeled with a count noun (e.g., "These are *dobutsus*"). In the *Novel Adjective* condition, children heard, e.g., "These are *dob-ish* ones." The only difference between these latter two conditions was the grammatical form in which the novel word was presented. We examined children's categorization at three different hierarchical levels (subordinate, basic, and superordinate) within two different natural kind hierarchies (animals and food) (see figure 5.1).

Children in all three conditions formed the basic-level categories very successfully. It was at the non-basic levels that the specific influence of novel words became apparent. In the absence of a novel word, children in the *No Word* condition had difficulty forming both subordinate- and superordinate-level categories. Novel nouns directed children's attention specifically to the category-based commonalities among objects. As a result, novel nouns facilitated the formation of superordinate-level categories, but had no effect at the subordinate level (see Markman & Hutchinson, 1984; Waxman & Gelman, 1986). Children hearing novel adjectives displayed a very different pattern: Novel adjectives directed children's attention specifically to property-based commonalities among objects (e.g., color), and therefore facilitated categorization at the subordinate, but not superordinate, level. These results, coupled with converging evidence from other paradigms (Bloom, 2000; Hall & Graham, 1999; Landau, 1994; Waxman & Hall, 1993) document clearly that preschool-aged children have the *linguistic* capacity to distinguish among the relevant grammatical forms (count noun vs. adjective), the *conceptual* or *perceptual* ability to appreciate different kinds of relations among objects (category- vs. property-based), and a tacit expectation that these linguistic and conceptual abilities are interwoven. To discover which linkages (if any) guide acquisition from the outset, and how these are shaped by experience, we must go on to consider infants on the very threshold of language acquisition.

Evidence from infants

What capacities do infants recruit at the very onset of acquisition? How do they begin to map words to the objects and events they perceive in the world? We know that by the end of their first year, infants have a remarkable ability to identify novel words, to notice perceptual and conceptual similarities among objects, and to interpret the rich social and pragmatic cues in which novel words are introduced. These major accomplishments certainly provide a foundation for infants' entry into the process of word learning. However, these accomplishments are not, in themselves, sufficient to guarantee that word-learning will proceed smoothly. What remains to be seen is whether naming has any consequences on conceptual organization. Is there a relation between naming and conceptual organization before the onset of productive language?

Prelinguistic infants: cognitive consequences of naming.   Recent research suggests that naming does have several cognitive consequences, even for infants who have not yet begun to produce words on their own. For example, by 10 months, infants devote more attention to objects that have been named than to objects that have been presented in silence (Baldwin & Markman, 1989). This confirms that even before infants begin to talk, naming directs their attention to an object. This raises two further questions: Does the increased attention stem from the salience of words or from the attention-engaging functions of auditory stimulation in general? And does naming promote attention to a named individual only, or does it exert an influence beyond the named individual?

To answer these questions, Marie Balaban and I (Balaban & Waxman, 1997) compared the effect of novel words versus tone sequences on 9-month-old infants. We used a novelty-preference task to assess infants' attention to individual objects and categories of objects. During a *familiarization* phase, infants saw a sequence of slides, each depicting a different member of a basic-level category (e.g., rabbits). To examine the influence of words, we randomly assigned infants to either a *Word* or a *Tone* condition. For infants in the *Word* condition, a naming phrase (e.g., "a rabbit!") accompanied the familiarization trials. For infants in the *Tone* condition, a sine-wave tone (matched to the naming phrase in amplitude, duration, and pause length) accompanied the familiarization trials. This familiarization phase was immediately followed by a *test* trial, in which infants in both conditions saw (a) a new member of the now-familiar category (e.g., another rabbit) and (b) an object from a novel category (e.g., a pig). Test trials were presented in silence.

We reasoned as follows: If words focus attention on commonalities among objects, then infants hearing words during familiarization should notice the commonalities among

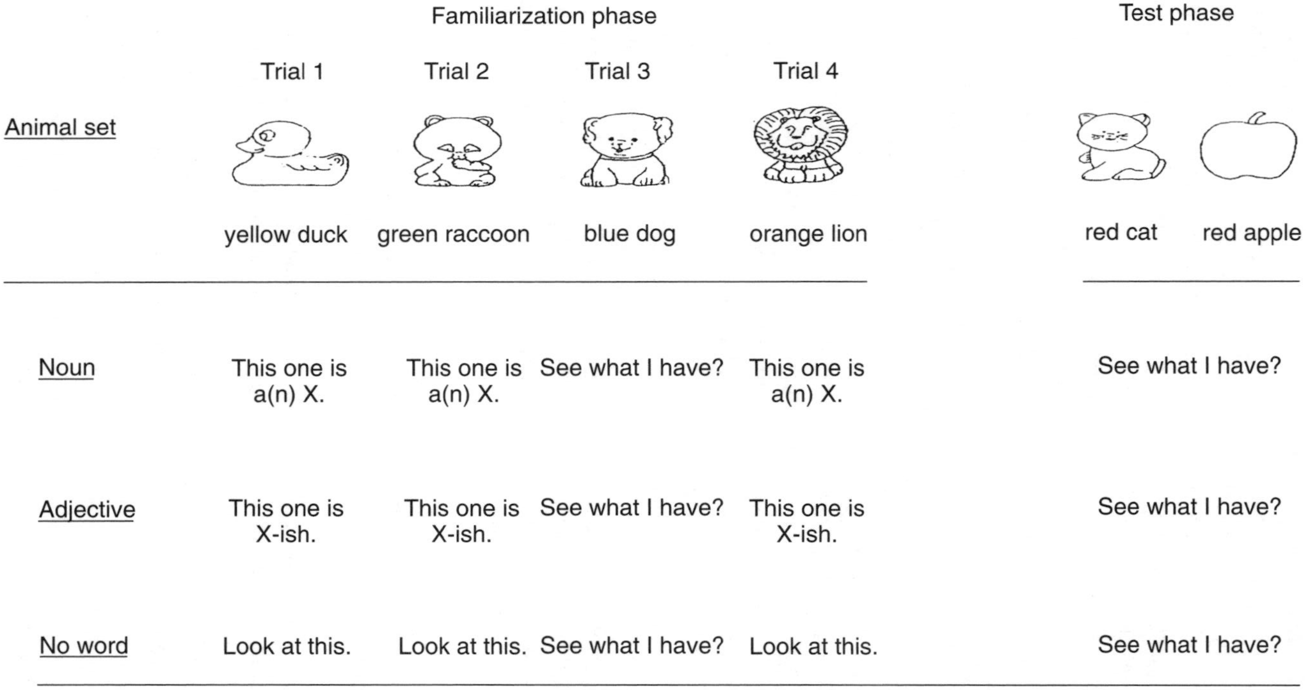

Test phase

Familiarization phase

	Trial 1	Trial 2	Trial 3	Trial 4		
Animal set						
	yellow duck	green raccoon	blue dog	orange lion	red cat	red apple
Noun	This one is a(n) X.	This one is a(n) X.	See what I have?	This one is a(n) X.		See what I have?
Adjective	This one is X-ish.	This one is X-ish.	See what I have?	This one is X-ish.		See what I have?
No word	Look at this.	Look at this.	See what I have?	Look at this.		See what I have?

Figure 5.2 A schematic presentation of introductory phrases from Waxman & Markow (1995) and an example of a single stimulus set

the familiarization objects. If this is the case, then these infants should reveal a preference for the novel test object (e.g., the pig). If this effect is specific to words, and not to auditory stimulation more generally, then infants hearing tones during familiarization should be less likely to notice these commonalities and less likely to reveal a novelty preference at test. This is precisely the pattern of results that we obtained. We can therefore conclude that for infants as young as 9 months of age, there is indeed something special about words, as opposed to a more general facilitative effect of auditory input, and that the cognitive consequence of naming extends beyond the named individual(s) to highlight commonalities among named individuals and to promote the formation of object categories.

Naming has other cognitive consequences as well. Recent evidence suggests that 10-month-olds find it difficult to keep track of the unique identities of two distinct objects (e.g., a ball and a duck), especially if these objects are presented in constant motion, with one appearing and disappearing from one side of a screen, and the other appearing and disappearing from the other side of the same screen (Xu & Carey, 1996). However, infants' difficulty tracking these distinct objects diminishes dramatically if each is labeled with a distinct name as it emerges from behind the screen.

Together, these results reveal that naming has powerful cognitive consequences, even in pre-linguistic infants. Naming distinct objects with the *same* name highlights their commonalities and promotes the formation of object categories (Balaban & Waxman, 1997). Naming distinct objects with *distinct* names (e.g., *ball, duck*) highlights their differences and promotes the process of individuation (Xu, 1999). Thus, naming supports the establishment of a repertoire of object categories and provides infants with a means of tracing the identity of individuals throughout development. These links appear before the advent of productive language.

Infants on the threshold of word learning: changing expectations of word-to-world mappings

In this section, we go on to trace the evolution of infants' expectations regarding word-to-world mappings as they cross the important developmental threshold of producing words on their own.

In one series of experiments, Dana Markow and I examined the influence of novel words on object categorization in 12- to 14-month-old infants (see Waxman & Markow, 1995 for a complete description). Once again, we used a novelty-preference task (see figure 5.2 for a sample set of stimuli and introductory phrases). During a *familiarization* phase, an experimenter offered an infant four different toys from a given category (e.g., four animals) one at a time, in random order. This was immediately followed by a *test phase*, in which the experimenter simultaneously presented both (a) a new member of the now-familiar category (e.g., another animal) and (b) an object from a novel category (e.g., a fruit). Each infant completed this task with four different sets of objects. Two involved basic-level categories (e.g., horses vs. cats); two involved more abstract superordinate-level categories (e.g., animals vs. fruit). Infants in this procedure manipulated the toys freely. Their manipulation served as the dependent measure.

To test the influence of novel words, we randomly assigned infants to one of three conditions. In all conditions, the infants heard infant-directed speech. The conditions differed only in the experimenter's comments during *familiarization*. In the *No Word* condition (control), she said, "See here?" as she introduced each object; in the *Novel Noun* condition, she said, "See the *blicket*?" In the *Novel Adjective* condition, she said, "See the *blick-ish* one?" In the test phase, infants in all conditions heard precisely the same phrase ("See what I have?").

We reasoned as follows: if infants detect the presence of the novel word, and if novel words direct infants' attention to object categories, then infants who hear novel words in conjunction with the objects presented during familiarization should be more likely than those in the *No Word* condition to form object categories. Including both a *Novel Noun* and *Novel Adjective* condition permitted us to test the specificity of infants' initial expectation. If the expectation is initially general, as we have proposed, then infants hearing either novel nouns or adjectives should be more likely than those hearing no novel words to form object categories.

For infants who had begun to produce words on their own, the data were entirely consistent with this prediction. Interestingly, the facilitative influence of novel words was most powerful on superordinate-level trials. On basic-level trials, all infants successfully formed categories. But on superordinate trials, infants in the *No Word* condition did not detect the commonalities. This difficulty is likely due to the fact that there is considerable variation among category members at superordinate levels, and as a result, the commonalities among them can be difficult to trace. However, infants who heard novel words during familiarization (either count nouns or adjectives) detected the commonalities among objects and successfully formed superordinate-level object categories.

These results reveal that infants on the threshold of producing language can reliably detect novel words presented in fluent speech, and that these novel words (both adjectives and nouns) direct infants' attention to commonalities among objects. In this way, words facilitate the acquisition of object categories. We have interpreted this finding as evidence that words serve as "invitations to form categories" and have pointed out that this invitation has several dramatic consequences. First, novel words invite infants to assemble together objects that might otherwise be perceived as disparate entities. We suggest that words promote comparison among objects, and that this process of comparison supports the discovery of other commonalities that might otherwise have gone unnoticed (Gentner & Namy, 1999; Gentner & Waxman, 1994).

Naming may also have dramatic consequences in situations in which infants have already formed groupings and noticed (some of) the commonalities among objects. For example, although infants in this series successfully formed basic-level object categories (whether or not they were introduced to novel words), their knowledge about these categories is not on a par with the knowledge of an older child or adult. Even preschool-aged children lack detailed knowledge about most categories (Gelman, 1996; Keil, 1994). Nonetheless, despite their relative lack of information, children seem to expect that members of object categories share deep, non-obvious commonalities (Gelman & Opfer, ch. 7 this volume). Indeed, children depend upon these to support inference and induction. I suspect that novel words are instrumental in motivating infants and young

| | Familiarization | | Contrast | Test | |
	Trial 1	Trial 2		Category	Property
Purple animal set	bear lion	elephant dog	red apple	purple horse vs. purple chair	purple horse vs. blue horse
Noun	These are blickets. This one is a blicket & this one is a blicket.	These are blickets. This one is a blicket & this one is a blicket.	Uh-oh, this one is not a blicket!	Can you give me the blicket?	Can you give me the blicket?
Adjective	These are blickish. This one is blickish & this one is blickish.	These are blickish. This one is blickish & this one is blickish.	Uh-oh, this one is not blickish!	Can you give me the blickish one?	Can you give me the blickish one?
No word	Look at these. Look at this one & look at this one.	Look at these. Look at this one & look at this one.	Uh-oh, look at this one!	Can you give me one?	Can you give me one?

Figure 5.3   A schematic presentation of introductory phrases from Waxman & Booth (1999) and an example of a single stimulus set

children to discover the deeper commonalities that underlie our richly structured object categories (Barsalou, 1983; Gelman, 1996; Gelman, Coley, & Gottfried, 1994; Gelman & Medin, 1993; Kalish & Gelman, 1992; Keil, 1994; Landau, 1994; Landau, Smith, & Jones, 1988; Lassaline & Murphy, 1996; Macnamara, 1994; Markman, 1989; Medin & Heit, in press). Most importantly, the results of this series of experiments documents that a link between word-learning and conceptual organization is in place early enough to guide infants in their very first efforts to establish word-to-world mappings. (See Smith, 1999, for arguments to the contrary.)

In a more recent series of experiments, our goal was to capture more precisely the scope, power, and evolution of infants' expectations in word-learning. We extend the work described in the previous section in three ways. First, we include a developmental component, comparing the performance of 11-month-old infants on the very threshold of producing words with that of 14-month-olds whose lexicons already include a modest set of entries.

Second, we expand the range of commonalities under investigation. In the previously described studies (Waxman & Markow, 1995), the only commonality among objects was category-based (e.g., four animals, all of a different color). In the next series, we ask whether infants link novel words specifically to category-based commonalities (e.g., *animal*), or whether they also link words to a wider range of groupings including, for example, property-based commonalities (e.g., *pink things, lumpy things*).[3] We also considered the conditions under which naming objects (with either a count noun or adjective) would systematically influence infants' construals of the very *same* set of objects (e.g., purple animals) either as members of an *object category* (animals) or as embodying an *object property* (purple).

A third goal of the current series is methodological. The evidence reviewed thus far regarding infants' expectations in word-learning has been based entirely on the novelty-preference task. It remains to be seen whether infants' expectations are sufficiently strong to support performance beyond this task. In the current series, we asked whether infants' expectations would influence performance in a word-extension task. Our goal here was to bridge a methodological gap between research with infants and preschoolers. From the onset of word-learning, infants advance from producing single word utterances (at approximately 9 to 12 months) to creating rich multi-word expressions (at approximately 24 months). We have proposed that in the intervening period, infants fine-tune their initially general expectation (that content words, in general, highlight commonalities among objects, in general) to develop the more specific expectations characteristic of their native language (that nouns refer to category-based commonalities, adjectives refer to property-based commonalities, etc.).

Unfortunately, however, our view of this critical transition has been clouded, at least in part, by the difficulties of accommodating the very different behavioral capacities of individuals at either end. *Novelty-preference tasks* have been successful with infants, but beyond 18 months of age infants lose interest in such tasks. *Word-extension tasks* have been successful with toddlers and preschoolers, but lack sensitivity with infants under 18 months, who have difficulty choosing systematically among objects in forced-choice tasks. To bridge this methodological gap, we developed a new method, which weds features of the novelty-preference procedure with those of the word-extension paradigms. See figure 5.3 for a schematic description of the procedure and a summary of the instructions presented in each condition.

In the *Familiarization phase*, the experimenter introduced infants in all conditions to four objects, all drawn from the *same object category* (e.g., horses or animals) and embodying the *same object property* (e.g., purple). These were presented in pairs, and infants manipulated them freely. During the *Contrast phase*, the experimenter presented a new object (e.g., a brown rolling-pin), drawn from a contrastive object category and embodying a contrastive object property. In the *Test phase*, infants were presented with one familiar object (e.g., a purple horse), and one novel object. For half of the infants in each condition (see below), this novel object was a member of a novel object category, but embodied the same property (e.g., a purple plate). This constituted a Category test. For the remaining infants, the novel object was a member of the same category as the familiarization objects, but embodied a novel property (e.g., a blue horse). This constituted a Property test. Infants were first permitted to play freely with the two test objects. Then, to assess word-extension, the experimenter removed the test objects. At this point, she introduced a target object, drawn from the familiarization set (e.g., a purple horse) and then re-presented the two test objects, asking the infant to give her one. See figure 5.3 for the instructions used in each condition. This word-extension task was presented a second time for each set of familiarization objects. This permitted us to observe the consistency of infants' responses. Infants completed this entire procedure four times, with four different sets of objects, two representing basic-level object categories and two representing superordinate level categories.

To trace the proposed developmental trajectory from an initially general expectation linking open class words (either count nouns or adjectives) to commonalities among objects (either category-based or property-based) to a more specific set of expectations, we compared the influence of novel nouns and adjectives in the performance of infants at 11 and 14 months of age. To answer this question, we present infants in all conditions with objects that are members of the *same object category* and share the *same object property* (e.g., four purple animals). We have proposed that infants begin the process of lexical acquisition with a general expectation linking words (in general) to commonalities among objects (in general). If this is the case, then for infants of 11 months, both nouns and adjectives should highlight both category-based (e.g., animal) and property-based (e.g., purple things) commonalities. We further proposed that this initial expectation is refined once the process of lexical acquisition is under way, using the early lexicon as a basis for discovering the more precise links between kinds of words and their associated meaning. If this is the case, then for more advanced learners, a more specific pattern should emerge. Different kinds of words should direct infants' attention to different aspects of the same experience: naming objects (with either a count noun or adjective) should systematically influence infants' construals of the very *same* set of objects (e.g., purple animals) either as members of an *object category* (animals) or as embodying an *object property* (purple). Based on our previous work (Waxman, 1999b; Waxman & Booth, 2000a), we expected that at 14 months, infants would have begun to distinguish count nouns (from among the other grammatical forms) and to map these specifically to category-based, but not property-based, commonalities. We expected that at this same developmental moment, infants' expectations for adjectives would still be quite general, directing their attention more broadly toward commonalities (be they category- or property-based).

The results were consistent with these predictions. At 11 months, infants hearing novel words (both nouns and adjectives) performed differently than those in the *No Word* condition. Infants extended both novel nouns and adjectives consistently to the familiar test object (e.g., the purple horse) on both Category and Property trials. This confirms that at the very onset of building a lexicon, (a) novel (open class) words direct infants' attention broadly to both category- and property-based commonalities among named objects, and (b) this link is sufficiently strong to support the extension of novel words. This outcome provides strong support for our proposal that infants on the very threshold of word-learning harbor a general expectation linking words (both nouns and adjectives) to commonalities (both category- and property-based) among objects.

We also proposed that once word-learning is underway and infants have established a modest lexicon, a more specific pattern should emerge. In support of this aspect of our proposal, we have found that by 14 months, infants begin to distinguish between novel words presented as nouns as compared to adjectives, and this distinction is recruited in word learning. Fourteen-month-old infants were more likely to extend novel nouns to the familiar object (e.g., purple horse) on Category trials (e.g., purple horse vs. purple plate) than on Property trials (e.g., purple horse vs. blue horse). This suggests that they expect nouns to refer to category-based, rather than to property-based, commonalities among objects. However, infants' expectations regarding the extension of novel adjectives were more general. Infants hearing adjectives were equally likely to select the familiar object on both types of test trials. This result has been replicated in our laboratory (Waxman, 1999b; Waxman & Booth, 2000a), using various properties (e.g., color, texture). Clearly, by 14 months, infants have begun to distinguish among the various grammatical forms and these distinctions are recruited in the service of mapping words to their meaning. As this process of refinement unfolds, infants first tease apart the nouns from among the other grammatical forms, and map them specifically to category-based commonalities. At the same time, however, infants' expectations for novel adjectives are less precise; adjectives appear to highlight the commonalities underlying object categories as well as object properties. This suggests that the more specific expectations linking adjectives to their meaning is a subsequent developmental accomplishment, one that appears to depend upon infants' prior establishment of the link between count nouns and object categories, and one that is shaped by the semantic and syntactic properties of adjectives in the language under acquisition. Thus, at 14 months, infants' expectation for count nouns is more precise than their expectations for adjectives (table 5.1).

Clearly, 14-month-olds are sensitive to (at least some of) the relevant cues (e.g., prosody, morphology, structural position within a phrase) that distinguish count nouns from adjectives. Recent work confirms that cues like these are sufficiently rich to support an emerging distinction among major grammatical forms (e.g., noun, adjective, verb) (Morgan & Demuth, 1996). The current results go one step further to reveal that these cues are detected reliably in fluent speech, that they support an emerging distinction between count nouns and adjectives, and that this distinction may be recruited in the process of word learning. Although infants' grammatical distinctions are certainly not as well honed as those of adults, and although their knowledge of categories and properties

Table 5.1   Means and standard deviations of the proportion
of word-extension test trials on which the familiar object
was chosen

	14-month-olds (Waxman & Booth, in press)		11-month-olds (current data)	
	M	SD	M	SD
NOUN				
Category	.68*	.13	.57	.24
Property	.44	.15	.55	.14
ADJECTIVE				
Category	.50	.18	.59	.24
Property	.52	.17	.58	.15
NO WORD				
Category	X	X	.46	.15
Propery	X	X	.49	.09

* p < .05 versus chance of .50.

of objects is certainly not as rich, 14-month-olds do appear to share with adults an expectation that different types of words (count nouns versus adjectives) refer to different types of relations among objects.

The Evidence in Review

The experiments described in this chapter were designed to discover what expectations, if any, infants recruit in the process of establishing their first word-to-world mappings, and how these evolve over development. We offered a developmental proposal, in which infants begin the task of word-learning equipped with a broad, initial, and universally available expectation linking novel open class words (independent of their grammatical form) to a wide range of commonalities among named objects. Infants' performance provided clear support for this aspect of the proposal. At 11 months, infants revealed a broad initial expectation, linking words (both count nouns and adjectives) to commonalities (both category- and property-based) among named objects. We have suggested that this initially general expectation, which appears before the advent of word learning, is universally available and provides the foundation for infants' early establishment of symbolic reference and lexical acquisition. It also sets the stage for the evolution of the more specific expectations, which are calibrated in accordance with the observed correlations between particular grammatical forms and their associated meanings in the language under acquisition (Waxman, 1999b; Waxman & Booth, 2000a; Waxman & Markow, 1995). Infants' performance at 14 months offered clear support for this aspect of the proposal. At this point in development, infants' expectations have indeed become more fine-tuned. They distinguish among the various grammatical forms and treat these distinctions as relevant when mapping words to their meaning. At 14 months, infants have begun to distinguish the count nouns and map them specifically to category-based, but not property-based, commonalities among objects. They have yet to acquire the specific links between adjectives and object properties that are characteristic of more mature speakers of English.

These results provide substantial support for our developmental proposal. More generally, they point to substantial continuity across development in the types of concepts we tend to form, in the influence of naming in their acquisition. I see this line of work as providing evidence that words are powerful engines for conceptual development: words advance us beyond our initial groupings, fueling the acquisition of the essential, rich relations that characterize our most powerful concepts.

Two other developmental proposals have recently been offered, and each of these is committed to a very different set of assumptions than those I have argued for in this chapter.

Entry points for categorization: acquiring global versus basic-level object categories.   One issue concerns the breadth of infants' earliest categories, and the bases upon which they are formed. My colleagues and I have argued that basic-level object categories (e.g., dog, cup) serve as an important entry point in object categorization, naming, and inductive inference (Gelman et al., 1994; Hall & Waxman, 1993; Waxman, 1999b; Waxman & Booth, in press; Waxman & Markow, 1995). There is strong evidence for the developmental primacy of basic-level object categories in cognitive and lexical development (Brown, 1958; Fenson, Cameron, & Kennedy, 1988; Mervis & Crisafi, 1982; Quinn, Eimas, & Rosenkrantz, 1993; Rosch & et al., 1976; Waxman, 1990). However, this position has been challenged. Mandler and her colleagues (Mandler, 1992; Mandler & Bauer, 1988; Mandler, Bauer, & McDonough, 1991; Mandler & McDonough, 1993; Mandler & McDonough, 1996) have argued that (1) conceptual development begins at a more abstract, global (e.g., animate vs. inanimate objects) level, (2) the basic-level groupings formed by infants and toddlers are entirely perceptually based, lacking in any conceptual grounding or inductive strength, and (3) the acquisition of global concepts *precedes* the acquisition of basic-level concepts.

Let us examine these claims in turn (see also Quinn, ch. 4 this volume). First, there is no doubt that basic-level object categories enjoy considerable perceptual support. But this does not, in itself, mean that they lack conceptual force, for perceptual and conceptual information are not mutually exclusive. In fact, we find no logical or empirical basis to the claim that perceptual and conceptual information or processes are as distinct as Mandler's theory suggests, either in infancy or in adulthood. Second, we take no issue with the possibility that both global (e.g., animate vs. inanimate objects; land vs. sea animals) and basic-level (e.g., dog vs. cow; cup vs. plate) conceptual categories are acquired early in development. We suspect that infants can, under certain circumstances, form object categories at various levels of abstraction, and that in doing so, they attend to several different kinds of perceptual and conceptual information, including an object's form, function, and type of movement (Baldwin, Markman, & Melartin, 1993; Nelson,

1995; Smith & Heise, 1992). The early acquisition of global, as well as basic, categories also ensures considerable continuity in conceptual development.

However, we strongly doubt that the acquisition of global concepts *precedes* the acquisition of basic-level concepts, with the latter being strictly derivative of the former. We also doubt that there is a frank dissociation between perceptual and conceptual factors, in which infants' basic-level object categories are entirely perceptually based, while their global categories are conceptual (Gelman & Medin, 1993; Gibson, 2000; Quinn & Eimas, 2000). These doubts are based on both logical and empirical grounds. First, the claim that global categories are conceptual, rather than perceptual, lacks empirical grounding. There are indeed perceptual cues to the distinction between animate and inanimate objects. For example, we know that infants are quite sensitive to the perceptual distinction between the types of motion displayed by animate versus inanimate objects early in development (Bertenthal, Proffitt, Kramer, & Spetner, 1987).

Second, the empirical evidence provides insufficient support for the precedence of global over basic-level concepts (see Waxman, 1998 for a full discussion). If the global-to-basic-level developmental progression were correct, then the *conceptual* commonalities among objects in our superordinate-level sets (e.g., animal vs. vehicle) should have been readily detected by infants. If this were the case, then infants in the *No Word* control conditions should have categorized at least as well on superordinate- as on basic-level sets. However, this was not the case. Despite their successful categorization on basic-level sets, infants in the No Word conditions evidenced no appreciation of the more abstract, superordinate-level categories. Infants' facility forming (or recognizing) commonalities at the basic level, as opposed to those at a more abstract global level, calls into question the global-to-basic progression. And the facilitative effect of naming that we observe on the superordinate-level sets is consistent with our claim that words serve as conceptual invitations, highlighting these more abstract object categories.

The evidence from early lexical acquisition also calls into serious question the assertion of a global-to-basic progression. Early in lexical development, words for basic-level categories are readily acquired (Gentner, 1982; Nelson, 1973; Nelson et al., 1993; Saah et al., 1996) while words for global categories are extremely rare (Fenson et al., 1994). In fact, infants' and young children's tendency to extend novel words, applied to novel objects, to other members of the same *basic*-level object category is so strong that it can override the use of syntactic form as a cue to word meaning (Au & Markman, 1987; Hall & Waxman, 1993; Hall, Waxman, & Hurwitz, 1993; see Waxman, 1998 for a review). How can the global-to-basic position be reconciled with the evidence for the central role of basic-level categories and the early acquisition of their names? On Mandler's account, infants' basic-level categories are purely perceptual. Could it be, then, that infants map their first words to perceptual, rather than to conceptual, groupings? This is unlikely. Why would abstract symbols (words) be tethered so tightly to perceptual groupings (basic-level categories, in Mandler's view), but not extended to groupings with an abstract conceptual base (global categories, in Mandler's view)? Second, even if we accepted the argument that basic-level categories are purely perceptually based, why would infants reveal such a strong talent for mapping words to only some perceptual groupings (namely, basic-level categories), to the exclusion of others (namely, perceptual properties like color and texture)? In fact, property terms like these enter the lexicon close to one year after the appearance of basic-level names, and their acquisition appears to depend upon the prior acquisition of basic-level categories and their names (Klibanoff & Waxman, 2000; Waxman & Markow, 1998).

Object categories versus object shapes.   There has also been debate concerning the types of meaning that children (and adults) associate with novel count nouns. This debate centers around whether count nouns direct word learners' attention to *categories* of objects (e.g., Gelman & Medin, 1993; Markman, 1994; Soja, Carey, & Spelke, 1991; Soja, Carey, & Spelke, 1992; Waxman, 1990; Waxman, 1994) or to *shapes* of objects (e.g., Landau, Jones, & Smith, 1992). There are several points of convergence between the noun-category and noun-shape positions. Most importantly, both document a powerful role for count nouns in object categorization. Moreover, both assume that perceptual properties play a role in our judgments of category membership and noun extension. Both assume that an object's shape and its category membership often covary, and that this is particularly true for basic-level categories (see also Gelman & Opfer, ch. 7 this volume). However, these positions also have fundamental differences, including (1) the role ascribed to development, and (2) the underlying model of word extension.

Role of development. According to the noun-shape position, infants come to the task of word learning with no a priori expectations (as in possibility 2, above). On this view, sometime after age 2, children *develop* an expectation, one that is based on their already acquired words. They infer from their own lexicons that count nouns refer to objects with the same shape (Landau et al., 1988; Landau et al., 1992; Smith, Jones, & Landau, 1992). There are two serious problems with this view. First, it cannot account for the evidence (reviewed in this chapter) that even in advance of word-learning, words have dramatic cognitive consequences, focusing infants' attention on commonalities as well as distinctions among objects (Balaban & Waxman, 1997; Waxman & Booth, in press; Xu, 1999). Second, it cannot account for the fact that shape-based similarities do not fully represent the commonalities underlying noun extension. On the contrary, if two objects look alike (say, by virtue of shape), then adults and children expect these will also share other, perhaps deeper, perhaps non-perceptual commonalities as well (Baldwin et al., 1993; Gelman, 1996; Gentner & Namy, 1999). In addition, even when objects are perceptually dissimilar (also see Gelman, 1988; Waxman & Booth, in press; as in superordinate-level sets in Waxman & Markow, 1995), if these objects share a common label, then children and adults expect that these objects also share other, perhaps deeper, non-perceptual commonalities. It is clear that for both adults and children, the extension of novel nouns rests upon more than shape-based similarities alone (Gelman & Medin, 1993; Gentner & Waxman, 1994; Soja et al., 1991; Soja et al., 1992; Waxman & Braig, 1996; Waxman & Markow, 1995). Yet the noun-shape account cannot specify how the learner moves from primarily shape-based extensions to those that capture additional, perhaps deeper, properties.

In contrast, the noun-category position ascribes a more central role to development. The central claim is that words serve as a catalyst for object categorization and for change. On this account, grouping objects together on the basis of shape can serve as one entry point (and perhaps an especially important entry point for simple artifacts in particular, see below). Naming promotes the discovery of additional, perhaps deeper, commonalities than those that might have formed the initial basis of the word's extension. Thus, the noun-category position incorporates a developmental mechanism that motivates learners to discover these powerful, additional commonalities among objects (Gelman & Medin, 1993; Gentner & Waxman, 1994; Waxman & Braig, 1996; Waxman & Markow, 1995). Another advantage is that this mechanism provides for continuity over development, with infants and adults attending to both perceptual and conceptual relations among objects in the context of word learning.

Models of word extension. The noun-shape and noun-category positions instantiate different models of word extension. The noun-shape position is essentially a univariate model. Univariate models can pit one predictor (e.g., shape) against another (e.g., texture, size, function, animacy cues). And indeed, most work on the shape bias follows just this strategy: pitting object shape, texture, and size against each another in a binary fashion. But it is clear that the interactions among these predictors are crucial. A univariate model cannot capture these interactions or the complexity underlying word meaning and its evolution.

The noun-category position takes into account multiple indices, including (but not limited to) shape. It can accommodate the fact that the relative weights associated with each predictor will vary as a function of ontological kind. For example, although shape may be weighed heavily in some categorization judgments (e.g., judgments of simple artifacts), it carries less weight in others (e.g., judgments of animate objects). This position can also accommodate the fact that shape may receive greater emphasis early in development, but its relative importance may wane as infants and young children discover the additional commonalities underlying categorization and word extension (Imai, Gentner, & Uchida, 1994). A multivariate approach articulates well with current work documenting the contribution of many perceptual and conceptual factors in object categorization, naming, and induction (Medin & Heit, in press).

In sum, the noun-category position offers a more comprehensive account. It ensures that categorization in humans is a flexible and ongoing process. We continually incorporate new, perhaps deeper, information about commonalities within our existing categories; we also admit new instances into existing categories. These evolutions are, at least in part, an effect of naming. The complexities of objects (artifacts and natural kinds) and languages in the real world require that we attend to more than shape alone if we are to develop words and categories for the objects with which we daily do commerce.

Conclusions

The goal of this chapter has been to articulate a developmental account of the powerful relation between word-learning and conceptual organization. We proposed that (1) infants begin the task of word-learning equipped with a broad, initial, and universally available expectation linking novel words (independent of their grammatical form) to a wide range of commonalities among named objects, and that (2) this initially general expectation sets the stage for the evolution of more specific expectations, calibrated in accordance with the correlations between particular grammatical forms and their associated meanings in the language under acquisition (Waxman, 1999b; Waxman & Booth, 2000a; Waxman & Markow, 1995).

This developmental account has several distinct strengths. First, it embraces both the importance of the expectations imposed by the learner, as well as the shaping role of the environment. The power of adopting this integrative approach to questions of acquisition has been recognized across disciplines. It can be seen in the elegant work of Marler (1991) on the acquisition of birdsong, of Held and Hein (1963) on the acquisition of depth perception in kittens, of Baillargeon (1993) and Spelke (1993) on the acquisition of physical knowledge about objects in human infants, and of R. Gelman (1991) on the acquisition of number concepts. Although each of these research programs considers very different domains of knowledge, they are all committed to considering carefully the relative contributions of both (a) the amount and type of information present in the environment, and (b) the structure or constraints imposed by the learner when characterizing the rapid acquisition of complex, sophisticated systems. (See Gallistel, Brown, Carey, Gelman, & Keil, 1991 for an extended discussion of this topic.)

In the case of word-learning, this interplay between factors inherent in the child and factors within the environment is essential. Infants across the world will encounter different objects, will acquire different languages, and will be provided with different types of language input and training (Cole, Gay, Glick, & Sharp, 1971; Laboratory of Comparative Human Cognition, 1983).

We have offered a proposal in which early acquisition is sufficiently constrained to permit infants to form fundamental categories of objects and to learn the words to express them, and sufficiently flexible to accommodate the systematic variations in the word-to-world mappings that occur across languages. Notice that our view of constraints on acquisition is not an argument for innate knowledge. Neither is it a polarized argument that locates the engine of acquisition solely within the mind of the child. Rather, these are constraints (Gelman & Williams, 1999) that direct the infant's attention toward precisely the sort of information and regularities in the environment that will make possible the rapid acquisition of complex systems of knowledge, including the acquisition of word-meaning and object categories. In our view, infants across the world's languages begin the process of word-learning equipped with the same, initially general expectation linking words to commonalities among named objects. At the same time, our proposal is flexible enough to account for the fact that infants naturally acquire a wide range of human languages, and that these differ in the ways in which they recruit the particular grammatical forms to convey particular types of meaning. We have suggested that the specific links between particular grammatical forms and their associated meanings are calibrated on the basis of correlations or regularities that are present in the language under acquisition. It therefore stands to reason that these more specific links would not be available at the onset of word-learning, but instead would emerge later, once the process of lexical acquisition is underway.

Notice also that our proposal is a dynamic one: We have argued that the initial expectations that we observe in infants at the outset of acquisition are not rigidly fixed, exerting a uniform influence throughout development. On the contrary, the infants' expectations regarding the specific relations between word meaning and conceptual organization themselves evolve over the course of development in accordance with the observed regularities in the language under acquisition.

Notes

1. Note, that this was, in fact, Keller's second language. She had begun to acquire English before becoming deaf and blind.
2. We suspect that infants' discovery of grammatical form is aided by cues that are perceptually available in the input. For instance, we suspect that infants will notice which words tend to be stressed or inflected, which tend to be preceded consistently by (unstressed) closed class words, which tend to occur in particular positions (initial, final) within phrases, etc. These cues, which are perceptually available in the input, are also integral cues to grammatical form.
3. This question itself hinges on there being a psychological distinction between object categories and object properties. Recent approaches in cognitive psychology distinguish object categories (sometimes known as *kinds* or *sortals*) from other types of groupings (e.g., *pink things, things to pull from a burning house*) on at least three (related) grounds: object categories (1) are richly structured, (2) capture many commonalities, including deep, non-obvious relations among properties (as opposed to isolated properties), and (3) serve as the basis for induction (Barsalou, 1983; Gelman & Medin, 1993; Kalish & Gelman, 1992; Macnamara, 1994; Medin & Heit, in press; Murphy & Medin, 1985). Although infants and children lack detailed knowledge about most object categories, they clearly expect named object categories to serve these functions (Gelman, 1996; Keil, 1994). In addition, there is now evidence for a psychological distinction between individual properties and relations among properties in infancy (Bhatt & Rovee-Collier, 1997; Younger & Cohen, 1986). We selected color and texture because these properties are perceptually salient to infants, and because these property-based commonalities typically do not underlie object categories. We suspect that an object's shape is more centrally related to category membership, particularly for simple artifacts and for animate objects (Waxman & Braig, 1996).

CHAPTER SIX

Early Memory Development

Patricia J. Bauer

The study of memory development in infancy and early childhood has been extremely active in recent years. We owe the credit for intense interest to a variety of factors, including (but not limited to) (a) development of techniques for studying memory and other cognitive functions in infants and young children who do not speak or readily engage in conversations about the past, (b) resulting changes in the way we think about the nature of mental life in the first years of life, (c) recognition that mnemonic competence is best revealed in areas of relative expertise for children, and (d) ironically, attention to the adult phenomenon of infantile amnesia.

Until not so very long ago, it was widely believed that the period of infancy was one during which the human organism was unable to participate in a type of mental act that most adults take for granted. That is, it was thought that they were unable to encode, store, and subsequently retrieve memories of specific past events. Moreover, it was thought that, although children of preschool age could remember specific episodes, their memories were poorly organized and generally unremarkable. These perspectives held sway for both conceptual and methodological reasons. In the period of infancy, from a theoretical standpoint, it was widely believed that infants lacked the capacity for mental representation of objects and events. This perspective is most closely associated with the work of Jean Piaget (1952c, 1962a). For the first 18 to 24 months of life, infants were thought to live in a "here and now" world that included physically present entities but which had no past and no future. Lacking the symbolic means to represent information not available to the senses (i.e., to *re-present* it), infants were thought unable to remember the past.

Preparation of this chapter was supported by a grant from the National Institutes of Health (HD-28425). Thanks to Tracy DeBoer for her comments on a draft of this chapter. I dedicate this work to the memory of my father, Rudolph Joseph Bauer (1927–2000).

Correspondence may be addressed to Patricia J. Bauer, Institute of Child Development, 51 East River Road, University of Minnesota, Minneapolis, Minnesota 55455-0345, USA; <pbauer@tc.umn.edu>.

Even as tenets attributed to Piagetian theory were being challenged on multiple fronts (e.g., Gelman & Baillargeon, 1983; Baillargeon, ch. 3 this volume; Gergely, ch. 2 this volume), the suggestion that infants were unable to remember the events of their lives went unexamined for want of suitable methodology. In older children and adults, memory is examined primarily through verbal report. For infants and young children, this is not a viable alternative: it is not until age 3 that children become reliable partners in conversations about the past. It was seen as more than coincidence that the age of 3 marks the end of the period of infantile amnesia (i.e., the relative paucity among adults of verbally expressible memories of specific events from the first years of life). Indeed, that the average age of earliest reportable memory among adults is 3.5 (see West & Bauer, 1999, for a review), and that age 3 to 3.5 marks the beginning of children's abilities to share past experiences verbally, "conspired" to create the impression that age 3 marked the onset of the ability to remember.

Methodological factors also contributed to the perspective that children of preschool age are poor mnemonists. In the early days of modern cognitive developmental research, young children's memories were tested using extensions of laboratory paradigms employed with adults. A common research design involved asking 3-year-olds, 5-year-olds, and 7-year-olds to study lists of word and picture stimuli and then testing their recall of them. The reliable result was that 7-year-olds behaved strategically and competently, 3-year-olds performed abysmally, and 5-year-olds performed somewhere in between (see Schneider & Bjorklund, 1998, for a review).

In this chapter I summarize some of the research that has contributed to revision of the perspectives that infants are unable to remember the past and that preschoolers are not much better. The organization of the chapter is largely chronological. Because questions of whether infants and young children are able to create, retain, and later retrieve coherent memories of specific past experiences has been the focus of much of the research attention, this type of memory (i.e., long-term memory for specific events or episodes) will be featured. As the review progresses to coverage of research in the preschool years, the focus will be on the emergence of a particular type of episodic memory, namely, autobiographical memory. Autobiographical or personal memory refers to memories of specific events or experiences in which the individual has a sense of personal involvement. They make up one's life story or personal past. Developments in early autobiographical memory are featured because it is in this domain that recent research has made some of the most striking advances (see also Gergely, ch. 2 this volume).

Memory in Early Infancy

Since the beginning of the modern era of research on infant development it has been clear that infants are able to learn and otherwise benefit from past experience and thus, evidence memory of some sort (Baillargeon, ch. 3 this volume). In fact, DeCasper and Spence (1986) suggest that even prenatal experiences later may manifest themselves in changes in behavior toward stimuli: mere hours after birth, infants distinguish between a novel story passage and one that their mothers read aloud during the last weeks of pregnancy. The data on infants' memories are derived primarily from two paradigms: visual paired comparison or habituation and mobile conjugate reinforcement. As will become apparent, one of the major questions associated with these techniques and the literatures derived from them is precisely what type of memory the paradigms measure.

Visual paired comparison or habituation

The technique of visual paired comparison was introduced by Fantz (1956). It involves exposing infants to pairs of pictures of a stimulus and then, after some period of familiarization, presenting the "familiar" picture along with a different, novel picture, and observing at what infants look. A variant of the technique, visual habituation, involves sequentially exposing infants to numerous pictures of a stimulus and then, after some criterion is reached (typically, a 50 percent decrease in looking time), introducing a novel stimulus and noting any changes in the amount of time infants spend looking. In both techniques, differential division of attention, as evidenced by looking time to novel compared with familiar stimuli, is taken as evidence of memory. Typically, after short familiarization, infants prefer to look at familiar stimuli whereas after longer periods of familiarization (or habituation), they spend more time looking at novel stimuli (see Bahrick & Pickens, 1995, for a review). The number of seconds of familiarization required to produce a novelty preference interacts with age, with younger infants (e.g., 3.5-month-olds) requiring more encoding time to produce a novelty preference, relative to older infants (e.g., 6.5-month-olds; Rose, Gottfried, Melloy-Carminar, & Bridger, 1982).

Changes in the distribution of looking time to familiar and novel stimuli typically are examined over relatively short spaces of time, with delays ranging from 0 seconds to a few minutes. However, these delays do not represent the upper limit on infant recognition memory (see Slater, 1995, for a review). For example, 5-month-olds recognize face stimuli over a delay of two weeks (Fagan, 1973). More recently, visual preference has been used to examine retention over as many as one to three months. Over such long intervals, the evidence for recognition changes, such that it is manifest as a preference for familiar stimuli. Over intermediate periods of one day to two weeks, no preference is detected (i.e., amount of looking to familiar and novel stimuli does not differ; Bahrick & Pickens, 1995). The same pattern has been observed for auditory recognition of familiar versus novel nursery rhymes (Spence, 1996). The shifting distribution of attention is taken as evidence of the differential status of mnemonic traces over time. The assumption is that on the basis of a "fresh" memory trace, infants need not spend time processing familiar stimuli and consequently, spend more time attending to novel stimuli. As the memory trace begins to fade, infants distribute their attentional resources more evenly, encoding the novel stimulus and updating their memories for the familiar stimulus. With further degradation of memory, infants devote the majority of attentional resources to reconstruction of the mnemonic trace for the once familiar stimulus (see Bahrick, Hernandez-Reif, & Pickens, 1997; Courage & Howe, 1998 for discussion). In summary, the technique of paired comparison can be used to test infants' retention of particular stimuli; retention is demonstrated over both the short and the long term; and depending upon the circumstances of testing, recognition may be evidenced through greater attention to familiar stimuli or through greater attention to novel stimuli.

Whereas attentional preference techniques measure changes in infants' responses to previously encountered stimuli, it is unclear whether they measure the same type of recognition as evidenced when, for example, adults affirm or deny that they have seen a particular stimulus before. For example, Mandler (1998) has suggested that infant recognition memory experiments actually are more analogous to adult priming studies than they are to adult recognition memory studies. She argues that the fact that the infant responds differentially to old and new stimuli indicates that information about the old stimulus has been stored, but it does not provide evidence that the infant was in any way aware of having experienced the stimulus before. That a sense of familiarity need not accompany primed responses is evidenced by the fact that adults suffering from amnesia show normal priming even as they evidence pronounced deficits in recognition memory (Warrington & Weiskrantz, 1974). Mandler acknowledges that changes in the distribution of infant attention as a result of prior exposure *may* be based on familiarity, but since such judgments are not required to produce the response (McKee & Squire, 1993), they should not be assumed. C. A. Nelson (1995, 1997) has sounded a different note of caution to interpretation of infant attentional responses. He suggested that early preference for novelty, which remains the most typical index of recognition memory, may actually be an obligatory response that is not under the organism's control. The suggestion is derived in part from findings that until about 8 months of age, infants' responses to novel stimuli are driven more by the frequency with which the stimuli are presented than by their novelty per se (see Nelson & Collins, 1991, 1992, for discussion). For both Mandler and C. A. Nelson, the question is whether infant looking time studies evidence adult-like recognition, or some more "primitive" recognitory response (see later for further discussion).

Mobile conjugate reinforcement

The second major technique that has been used to test retention in early infancy is mobile conjugate reinforcement. In this paradigm, an attractive mobile is suspended above an infant's crib or playpen. For a period of one to three minutes, researchers measure the baseline rate of infant kicking. They then "tether" the infant's leg to the mobile with a ribbon such that, as the infant kicks, the mobile moves. Over the course of a three- to nine-minute acquisition period infants learn the contingency between their own kicking and the movement of the mobile. Once the conditional response is acquired, a delay is imposed, after which the mobile again is suspended above the infant; the infant's leg is not attached to the mobile. If the post-training rate of kicking is greater than the rate of kicking in the procedurally identical baseline (i.e., before the infant experienced the contingency), then memory is inferred (see Rovee-Collier & Gerhardstein, 1997, for a description of this and related procedures).

The mobile conjugate reinforcement paradigm has been quite productive, yielding many important findings. With it, researchers have learned that infants 2 months of age remember the mobile for one to three days and that by 6 months, they remember for as many as 14 days (Hill, Borovsky, & Rovee-Collier, 1988). The length of time over which behavior toward the mobile is retained can be extended if infants are "reminded" of the mobile during the delay (Rovee-Collier, Sullivan, Enright, Lucas, & Fagen, 1980). A number of other factors also affect the length of time over which the conditioned response can be retained, including the amount of training that infants receive, the distribution of training, and the affect that they display during training (see Rovee-Collier & Gerhardstein, 1997, for a review). One of the most striking characteristics of memory as evidenced by this paradigm is its specificity. For example, 2- and 3-month-olds fail to recognize the training mobile if even a single element of it is changed. Minor changes to the fabric that lines the crib or playpen (e.g., changing the shape of the figures on the liner from squares to circles) also produces pronounced disruptions in performance (e.g., Borovsky & Rovee-Collier, 1990; Rovee-Collier, Schechter, Shyi, & Shields, 1992). Generalization from the stimulus or context associated with the learning episode to other similar stimuli occurs only as the details of the original stimulus are forgotten.

The very specificity of memory as demonstrated in the mobile conjugate reinforcement paradigm is one feature that has led to the suggestion that the type of memory measured by this technique is different from that assessed through verbal report and other paradigms used with older children and adults. Indeed, as noted by Mandler (1998), the responses observed in the conjugate reinforcement paradigm show patterns of generalization, extinction, and reinstatement that are typical of operant conditioning paradigms (e.g., Campbell, 1984). For this and other reasons (including speculation regarding the neural substrate underlying the behavior; see C. A. Nelson, 1997), rather than of explicit memory for a particular event or episode, the memory demonstrated in mobile conjugate reinforcement is thought to be reflective of implicit learning (e.g., Mandler, 1990; C. A. Nelson, 1997; Schneider & Bjorklund, 1998; Squire, Knowlton, & Musen, 1993; although see Rovee-Collier, 1997, for a different view). Because the distinction between different types of memory plays such a prominent role in conceptualization of its development, the concepts are taken up next.

Distinguishing Declarative and Non-Declarative Memory

Multiple memory systems view

Although it is not universally accepted (see, for example, Roediger, Rajaram, & Srinivas, 1990; Rovee-Collier, 1997), by both developmental and adult cognitive scientists, it is widely believed that memory is not a unitary trait but is comprised of different systems or processes, which serve distinct functions, and are characterized by fundamentally different rules of operation (e.g., Squire, 1992). The type of memory termed declarative or explicit captures most of what we think of when we refer to "memory" or "remembering" (Zola-Morgan & Squire, 1993). It involves the capacity for explicit recognition or recall of names, places, dates, events, and so on. In contrast, the type of memory termed non-declarative represents a variety of non-conscious abilities, including the capacity for learning habits and skills, priming, and some forms of classical conditioning (see Parkin, 1997, for a review). A defining feature of non-declarative memory is that the impact of experience is made evident through a change in behavior or performance, but that the experience leading to the change is not consciously accessible (Zola-Morgan & Squire, 1993). Declarative memory is characterized as fast (e.g., supporting one-trial learning), fallible (e.g., memory traces degrade, retrieval failures occur), and flexible (i.e., not tied to a specific modality or context). Non-declarative memory is characterized as slow (i.e., with the exception of priming, it results from gradual or incremental learning), reliable, and inflexible (Squire et al., 1993).

The distinction between different types of memory originally was derived from the adult cognitive and adult neuroscience literatures. As such, much of the work supporting the multiple memory systems view comes from adult humans with amnesia and from non-human primates. Some have argued that because human infants are neither brain-damaged adults nor monkeys, the distinction is not relevant to human developmental science (e.g., Rovee-Collier, 1997). However, a long tradition of comparative psychology suggests that "lessons" learned from one population can, with appropriate care, be applied to others. Another caution in application of the multiple memory systems view to human cognitive development stems from use of the construct of conscious awareness as one of the criteria to differentiate declarative and non-declarative forms of memory. As noted by C. A. Nelson (1997) and Rovee-Collier (1997), it is not clear how consciousness can be assessed in a non-verbal infant or non-human animal. As will be seen later, researchers have addressed this concern by designing tasks that bear the remaining characteristic features of declarative memory tasks and which produce behaviors that look quite different from those exhibited in non-declarative memory paradigms.

For developmental scientists, the distinction between different types of memory is vitally important because declarative and non-declarative forms of memory are thought to rely on different neural substrates that mature at different points in time. Our understanding of brain development thus provides constraints on the expectations that we have for performance and also should inform our interpretation of data. Although the story is still unfolding, it is increasingly clear that multiple areas of the brain support declarative memory, including (a) medial temporal lobe structures (including the hippocampus and perirhinal cortex), (b) the medial diencephalon, and (c) higher cortical association areas, including the prefrontal cortex and limbic/temporal association areas (Bachevalier & Mishkin, 1994). There are a number of indicators that most (*although not all*) of the medial temporal lobe and the diencephalic components of declarative memory develop early. In addition, the various brain regions implicated in support of the cluster of mnemonic behaviors that fall into the category of non-declarative (including striatum and cerebellum) seem to develop early (see C. A. Nelson, 1997, for review). In contrast, the association areas and the reciprocal connections between them and the hippocampus develop more slowly (Bachevalier, Brickson, & Hagger, 1993; Bachevalier & Mishkin, 1994). The best available evidence suggests that in the human infant, whereas it continues to develop for months to come, the entire circuit begins to coalesce near the end of the first year of life (C. A. Nelson, 1997). If this is the case, then we would expect that behaviors that either do not depend upon the declarative memory substrate (e.g., visual expectancies: see Haith & Benson, 1998, for a review) or behaviors that depend only on the medial temporal components (e.g., recall over the short term; retention of the kicking response in the mobile conjugate reinforcement paradigm) should be evident early in development and that behaviors that depend upon the full circuit should first appear near the end of the first year of life. A test of this hypothesis obviously requires a non-verbal analogue to the paradigm of choice for research on declarative memory in adults, namely, verbal report.

Deferred imitation as a non-verbal test of declarative memory

Deferred imitation originally was suggested by Jean Piaget (1952c, 1962a) as one of the hallmarks of the development of symbolic thought. Beginning in the mid 1980s, the technique was developed as a test of mnemonic ability in infants and young children throughout the first three years of life (e.g., Bauer & Shore, 1987; Meltzoff, 1985). As used in laboratories today, the technique of elicited or deferred imitation involves using props to produce a single action or a multi-step sequence of actions and then, either immediately, after a delay, or both, inviting the infant or young child to imitate.

As discussed in detail elsewhere (e.g., Bauer, 1995, 1996, 1997; Carver & Bauer, 2000; Mandler, 1990; Meltzoff, 1990b; Squire et al., 1993), the conditions of learning and later testing in deferred imitation are conducive to formation of declarative memories but not non-declarative memories, and the resulting mnemonic behaviors share characteristics of declarative memories. To summarize the argument, in deferred imitation (a) acquisition of to-be-remembered material is based on brief exposure to novel, and in some cases unusual and noncanonical, actions or sequences (e.g., Meltzoff, 1988a, 1995b); (b) there is no opportunity for practice during exposure to the material; and (c) immediate reproduction of the test material is neither necessary for nor even reliably facilitative of later reproduction (e.g., Bauer, Hertsgaard, & Wewerka, 1995; Carver & Bauer, 1999; Mandler & McDonough, 1995; Meltzoff, 1988a, 1988b, 1995b). These conditions are not conducive to procedural, sensorimotor, or implicit acquisition (Bachevelier, 1992; Mandler, 1990; Meltzoff, 1990b; Schacter & Moscovitch, 1984; Squire et al., 1993. In addition, consistent with the characterization of declarative memory as flexible, (d) performance is relatively unaffected by surface-feature manipulations that profoundly affect implicit memory tasks such as priming (e.g., Barnat, Klein, & Meltzoff, 1996; Bauer & Dow, 1994; Bauer & Fivush, 1992; Hanna & Meltzoff, 1993; Klein & Meltzoff, 1999; Lechuga, Marcos-Ruiz, & Bauer, in press). Finally, as described later, (e) memories formed in deferred imitation are verbally accessible (e.g., Bauer & Wewerka, 1995, 1997).

Ideally, the logical argument that deferred imitation is mediated by declarative memory processes would be complemented by direct evidence of the neural basis for performance on the task. McDonough, Mandler, McKee, and Squire (1995) tested adults with amnesia (in whom declarative memory processes are impaired) and control participants in a deferred imitation task using multi-step sequences. Whereas normal adults performed as expected on the task, patients with amnesia did poorly (see also Schneider, ch. 11 this volume). This finding strongly suggests that deferred imitation taps the same neural structures as those that support declarative memory in adults.

Finally, there is reason to argue that deferred imitation taps recall memory, rather than recognition. That recall processes are involved is particularly apparent in the case of temporally ordered reproduction of multi-step sequences: once the model is gone, so is information about the order in which the event unfolded. To reproduce an ordered sequence, temporal order information must be encoded during presentation of the event sequence and subsequently retrieved from a representation of the event, in the absence of ongoing perceptual support. Neither is the analogy with verbal recall undermined by the fact that the available props provide cues to recall: all recall is cued, either by an external prompt or by an internal association (Spear, 1978). Because ordered reproduction of action sequences provides particularly compelling evidence that the mechanism supporting the behavior is recall, I will pay particular attention to developments in ordered recall. Moreover, because recall of temporal order information is thought to depend upon the integrity of the frontal lobes as well as connections between the medial temporal and frontal lobes (e.g., Shimamura, Janowsky, & Squire, 1991; Yasuno et al., 1999), it provides particularly compelling evidence that the circuit supporting declarative memory is "in play."

Declarative Memory in Infancy and Very Early Childhood

Deferred imitation has been used to test infants as young as 6 months and children as old as 32 months. Because the same technique has been used across such a wide age span, we are afforded a picture of developments in recall memory from infancy throughout the period of transition to early childhood. The developmental picture that has emerged is of relatively early competence in recall over the short term, developments in long-term ordered recall near the end of the first year of life, and consolidation of the ability over the course of the second year.

Recall in the first year of life

To date, the youngest infants tested with deferred imitation of actions or action sequences are 6-month-olds. In Barr, Dowden, and Hayne (1996) infants as young as 6 months of age were tested for immediate and 24-hour delayed recall of the three-step action sequence of pulling a mitten off a puppet's hand, shaking the mitten (which, at demonstration, contained a bell), and replacing the mitten on the puppet's hand. They found that 75 percent of 6-month-olds imitated at least one action after the 24-hour delay. These data thus provide evidence of recall over the short term as early as 6 months. Interestingly, what was not apparent in Barr et al.'s data was compelling evidence of ordered recall over the delay. Specifically, whereas 75 percent of 6-month-olds produced one action after 24 hours, only 25 percent of them provided evidence of memory for more than one step of the sequence. In light of the demands of recall of temporal order on frontal structures (which, at 6 months, are relatively immature), this disparity in recall of content versus temporal order is suggestive regarding the developmental status of the entire cortico-limbic-diencephalic circuit. (See Yasuno et al., 1999, for a similar "dissociation" in an adult patient in whom the integrity of the cortico-limbic-diencephalic circuit was undermined by damage to the tissue connecting the frontal lobe and the hippocampus.)

By 9 months of age developments in ordered recall ability are readily apparent. In Carver and Bauer (1999), deferred imitation was used to test 9-month-old infants' recall of novel two-step event sequences after a five-week delay. In the sample as a whole, the infants showed evidence of recall of the individual target actions of the event sequences. Forty-five percent of the infants showed evidence of temporally ordered recall memory after the five-week delay; the remaining 55 percent of infants did not show evidence of temporally ordered recall. This distribution since has been replicated in a separate sample of 9-month-olds (Bauer, Wiebe, Waters, & Bradley, in press). What is more, Carver, Bauer, and Nelson (2000) reported an association between infant brain activity as measured by event-related potentials (ERPs) and behavioral evidence of ordered recall. Infants who subsequently evidenced ordered recall earlier had shown evidence of differential ERP responses to pictures of event sequences to which they previously had been exposed and event sequences new to them. Infants who after five weeks did not show evidence of ordered recall did not produce ERP responses indicative of recognition memory.

Although it is not yet entirely clear precisely what the individual differences in long-term ordered recall and ERP responses mean, the data are indicative of developmental differences in infants' abilities to store and/or retrieve information over extended periods of time (Carver & Bauer, 1999; Carver et al., 2000). That the differences are observed at 9 months suggests that this is an especially important period in development of long-term recall ability. This conclusion fits well with the proposed time frame for the coalescence of the declarative memory circuit (e.g., C. A. Nelson, 1995, 1997; Schacter & Moscovitch, 1984). Additional evidence of important developments at this time comes from a study of long-term memory in which different infants were enrolled at the ages of 9 months and 10 months, and tested after delays of both one and three months (different event sequences were tested at each delay). As a group, the 9-month-olds showed evidence of memory for the temporal order of the events after one month but not after three months. In contrast, as a group, the 10-month-olds showed evidence of memory for temporal order after both the one- and the three-month delay intervals (Carver & Bauer, 2000). Together with the results of Barr et al. (1996), Carver and Bauer (1999), and Carver et al. (2000), these data are consistent with the suggestion that relatively early in development, mnemonic behaviors that can be supported by medial temporal lobe structures themselves will be in evidence (e.g., recall over the short term), whereas behaviors that likely require further maturation of the neural substrate (e.g., recall of temporal order information and recall after long delay intervals) show a more protracted course of development.

If long-term ordered recall is newly emergent near the end of the first year of life, it likely undergoes significant development and consolidation over the course of the second year. The results of a recent large-scale study of remembering and forgetting during the transition from infancy to early childhood bear out this suggestion.

Recall in the second and third years of life

To date, the most comprehensive study of long-term recall memory throughout the second and into the third year of life is Bauer, Wenner, Dropik, and Wewerka (2000). A total of 360 children were enrolled at the ages of 13, 16, or 20 months. At each of three sessions, spaced one week apart, the children were exposed to the same six multi-step event sequences. The children returned for delayed recall testing after delay intervals of either one, three, six, nine, or 12 months (delay condition was a between-subjects

Table 6.1　Percentage of 13-, 16-, and 20-month-olds showing evidence of temporally ordered recall memory

Delay interval	Age at experience of to-be-remembered event sequences		
	20 months	16 months	13 months
1 month	100*	94*	78*
3 months	100*	94*	67
6 months	83*	72*	39
9 months	78*	50	44
12 months	67*	61	39

Note: Data are from Bauer, Wenner, Dropik, & Wewerka (2000). An asterisk indicates that the number of children exhibiting the pattern of ordered recall (i.e., higher level of performance on previously experienced than on new event sequences) was reliably greater than chance. Because determination of chance levels is affected both by the number of observations and by the number of tied observations, identical values will not necessarily yield identical outcomes (e.g., 13-month-old 3-month delay and 20-month-old 12-month delay).

manipulation). At the delayed recall session, the children were tested for recall of the six event sequences to which they previously had been exposed, as well as on three new events, as a within-subjects control. For all nine of the event sequences, the children first experienced a delayed-recall period during which they were prompted by the event-related props alone, after which they were provided with verbal reminders of the event sequences (see Bauer et al. (2000) for details of the procedure).

In table 6.1 are the percentages of children at each age at enrollment who, at delayed testing, evidenced temporally ordered recall. An asterisk indicates that the number of children with this pattern is greater than the number that would be expected by chance. Overall, the forgetting function is very similar to that seen in older children and even adults (Schneider & Pressley, 1997). That is, there was an initial relatively steep decline in performance, followed by a smooth, shallow declining function (see Klein & Meltzoff, 1999, for a similar forgetting function in children in this age range).

Although declines in performance as a function of delay were in evidence, for infants who had been 20 months of age at the time of exposure to the event sequences, even after 12 months, the number of children who demonstrated ordered recall was reliably greater than chance. For the children who had been 16 months of age at the time of experience of the events, the percentage of children evidencing ordered recall was reliably greater than chance in the one-, three-, and six-month delay conditions, but not in the nine- and 12-month delay conditions. Among the 13-month-olds, there was an even more rapid decline in performance across the delay conditions. After six months had elapsed, fewer than 50 percent of infants evidenced the pattern indicative of ordered recall. Beyond one month, the number of 13-month-olds who performed at higher levels on previously experienced than on new event sequences was not greater than chance. Together, the data are reflective of increasing reliability in long-term ordered recall across the second year of life. As delay interval increased, fewer and fewer children remembered the event sequences. The children "dropped out" faster the younger they were at the time of experience of the events.

In addition to evidence of increasingly reliable recall, Bauer et al. (2000) also provides evidence of increasingly *robust* memory over the course of the second year. Simply put, older children remembered more than younger children. Moreover, age-related differences in the amount remembered were particularly apparent under conditions of greater cognitive demand. For example, when the children were prompted by the event-related props alone, age differences in the amount of information retained were observed in all delay conditions. When the children were prompted by the event-related props and by the verbal reminders of the event sequences, age differences obtained only at the longer delay intervals of nine and 12 months. Thus, age effects in how much information was retained over the long term were observed (a) when the children had less support for recall (i.e., when they were prompted by event-related props alone), and (b) at longer retention intervals. Together, the data indicate that over the course of the second year of life there are increases in the reliability and the robustness of long-term recall. The changes are highly suggestive of consolidation of long-term mnemonic function over this space of time.

Determinants of young children's long-term recall

To say that there are age-related changes in the second and third years of life is not to say that the length of time for which a child has lived on the planet is the sole determinant of whether and for how long a memory will survive in an accessible format. Nor is it the case that the delays over which ordered recall is apparent in Bauer et al. (2000) are the absolute limits of time over which children of various ages can be expected to remember. Indeed, it is highly unlikely that we ever will be able to establish "growth chart" type functions for the anticipated durations of memories of children of different ages. A major reason why such functions are unlikely is because memory is multiply determined. As discussed in detail elsewhere (e.g., Bauer, 1995, 1996, 1997; Bauer et al., 2000), within the context of both laboratory studies and naturally occurring events, a number of factors have been shown to affect children's recall over both the short and the long term. First, children's ordered recall of events characterized by enabling relations (i.e., inherent constraints on the order in which the event unfolds) is better than their ordered recall of event sequences lacking enabling relations (the orders of which are arbitrary). The effect is apparent both at immediate testing (e.g., Bauer, 1992; Bauer & Thal, 1990) and after short delays (e.g., Barr & Hayne, 1996; Bauer & Hertsgaard, 1993; Mandler & McDonough, 1995). It also is apparent even after several experiences of arbitrarily ordered events in an invariant temporal order (Bauer & Travis, 1993) (see Bauer, 1992, 1995, and Bauer & Travis, 1993, for discussions of the means by which enabling relations in events may influence ordered recall). Whereas from as young as they have been tested, children demonstrate the ability to accurately recall event sequences constrained by enabling relations (e.g., Carver & Bauer, 1999; Mandler & McDonough, 1995), development of the ability to reliably reproduce arbitrarily ordered sequences is more protracted (Bauer, Hertsgaard, Dropik, & Daly, 1998; Wenner & Bauer, 1999). Even once children gain facility with arbitrarily temporal relations, the advantage associated with enabling relations remains (see van den Broek, 1997, for a review).

Second, the number and timing of experiences of events also influences children's memory. Repeated experience aids memory both in terms of (a) the amount of information that is remembered, and (b) the length of time over which events can be recalled (e.g., Bauer et al., 1995; Bauer et al., in press; Fivush & Hamond, 1989). The timing of subsequent exposures to events also affects the efficacy of repeated experience. Hudson and Sheffield (1998) found that the effects of re-experiencing events after eight weeks were more pronounced than re-experiencing the events after 15 minutes or after two weeks; the facilitating effects of a longer delay between experiences were even more pronounced when recall was tested six months later. Hudson and her colleagues also have shown that events need not be re-experienced in their entirety in order for recall to be facilitated. Simply showing children a subset of events (i.e., three of an original six experienced) facilitates memory for the entire set (Sheffield & Hudson, 1994). With age, increasingly symbolically remote experiences serve to facilitate memory: at 18 months, exposure to a videotape of another child performing activities facilitates memory for them; at 24 months, still photographs of previously experienced events facilitates memory for them; by the age of 3 years, verbal description of previously experienced events facilitates children's memories for them (Hudson, 1991, 1993; Hudson & Sheffield, 1998).

Third, although active participation in events is not necessary for later recall of them (e.g., Barr & Hayne, 1996; Bauer et al., 1995, 2000; Carver & Bauer, 1999; Meltzoff, 1995b), at least over short delay intervals, it is associated with better recall in older children (e.g., Baker-Ward, Hess, & Flannagan, 1990) as well as in younger children (e.g., Bauer et al., 1995; Meltzoff, 1990a). In contrast, over longer delays, effects of active participation seem to be less apparent: in Meltzoff (1995b), recall after two and four months was comparable for children who were and were not allowed to imitate prior to imposition of the delays. Likewise, in Bauer et al. (2000), recall after delay intervals of as many as 12 months was comparable for events that children had been and had not been allowed to imitate one time prior to imposition of the delays. Thus, over the short term, there seems to be an effect of the opportunity to imitate; over the long term, the effect may dissipate.

Fourth, in older children, cues or reminders of previously experienced events facilitate memory retrieval after a delay (e.g., Fivush, 1984; Fivush, Hudson, & Nelson, 1984; Hudson & Fivush, 1991). Verbal reminding also aids memory retrieval in children as young as 13 months at the time of experience of novel event sequences, over delay intervals of as many as 12 months (Bauer et al., 2000; see also Bauer et al., 1995). Indeed, as noted above, verbal reminding has the effect of reducing age-related differences in the amount of information that young children recall after a delay (Bauer et al., 2000). Critically, the effects of verbal reminding cannot be attributed to "suggestion" of plausible event sequences: children do not generate the target actions and sequences of events for which they have been provided a verbal label but to which they have not been exposed (Bauer et al., 1995; Bauer et al., 2000). It is only when children have seen sequences produced that they exhibit performance indicative of recall of the specific events to which they have been exposed. That memories can be triggered by verbal reminders is particularly important to recall after long periods of time: over significant delays, regardless of age, little that is not reminded is retrieved (e.g., Hudson & Fivush, 1991).

Retrieval of information about a previously experienced event also depends upon what was originally encoded about the event. As discussed by Howe (2000), this fact poses one of the greatest challenges to valid research on developmental differences in the length of time over which memory persists because of age-related differences in learning rate. Older children learn at a faster rate than younger children and as a result, after a single experience of an event, or even after a fixed number of experiences of an event, older children are likely to have more detailed and elaborated memory representations, relative to younger children. In addition, there is speculation that age-related changes in the amount remembered over the long term are related to potential age-related differences in the amount of information retained over the short term (Bauer, Van Abbema, & de Haan, 1999). Until more is known about the processes of consolidation of to-be-remembered information for long-term storage, and possible age-related differences therein, a potentially large source of variance in long-term recall ability will remain unexplored.

Transition from Nonverbal to Verbal Expression of Event Memory

Both in their ability to recall specific events after long delays and in the factors that affect long-term memory, there are continuities in mnemonic processes from infancy to early childhood and beyond. That does not mean that there are not important differences across this wide age span. One of the most striking differences between infants and pre-preschoolers and older children is the mode of expression of memory: whereas infants and pre-preschoolers demonstrate memory almost exclusively non-verbally, by 3 to 4 years of age, children evidence memory primarily verbally. At first glance, this difference between older and younger children may sound trivial: of course older children are able to provide verbal reports of their past experiences because they have command of the verbal medium. However, the difference in mode of expression of early compared with later memories persists even once language is available. It is as if events and experiences encoded without the benefit of language remain inaccessible to it. Historically, this difference has had profound implications for conclusions about the continued accessibility of very early memories. Following Nelson and Ross (1980), Pillemer and White (1989; p. 321) argue that, if young children are able to recall specific past events over long periods of time, then their "memories should not only be expressible through behavior, they also should become verbally expressible when the child has the ability to construe preverbal events in narrative form."

What evidence bears on the issue of children's ability to express their early memories verbally? It is clear that children can provide verbal reports of events experienced in the distant past (see Fivush, 1997, for a review). Indeed, it was in part this fact that provided the original impetus for research on pre- and early-verbal children's event memory. However, a striking characteristic of these early reports is the amount of work that an interviewer must do to obtain them. In Hamond and Fivush (1991), for example, fully 78 percent of the information provided by the 3- to 5-year-old participants was elicited in response to direct questions and prompts provided by the interviewer.

Evidence of the difficulty that even younger children have verbally expressing their memories of past events is apparent in Peterson and Rideout (1998). The researchers interviewed children about their memories for emergency room procedures necessitated by accidents. The accidents occurred when the children were between 13 and 35 months of age; the interviews were conducted shortly after the children's visits to the emergency room and then again six months, 12 months, and 18 or 24 months later. Children who were 18 months of age or younger at the time of their injuries were unable to provide verbal accounts of their experiences, even though, at the later interviews, they had the language ability to do so. In contrast, although they had not been able to talk about their experiences at the time, children who were injured at between 20 and 25 months were able to provide verbal reports at the six-month interview. Some of the children maintained verbal accessibility of their memories over subsequent delays between interviews. Children who were 26 months of age or older at the time of the experience were able to provide verbal reports at all of the delays. These data seem to suggest that, regardless of later verbal facility, children younger than 18 months at the time of experience are not able to talk about past events. Children slightly older are able to, but there is no assurance that verbal accessibility will be maintained.

Young children's difficulty in talking about the past stands in sharp contrast to their rapidly developing ability to talk about the "here and now." This has led to the suggestion that it is the decontextualized nature of the circumstances under which verbal reports of the past typically are elicited that makes it difficult for young children to produce them (Bauer & Wewerka, 1997). Consider that in Peterson and Rideout (1998), as in most studies of verbal expression of memory, at the time of the report, the children were not only temporally, but also spatially, separated from the to-be-recalled material. The children were provided a verbal prompt about the event but, as discussed earlier, verbal prompts alone may not be effective retrieval cues for children younger than 3 (Hudson, 1991, 1993). If it is the decontextualized nature of the activity that limits young children's ability to talk about the past, then "contextualizing" the task, by allowing children to return to the physical location of a previous experience, for example, should facilitate verbal expression of memory.

Although relevant data are not plentiful, there is evidence that with contextual support, children are able to talk about events from the distant past. For example, in Bauer, Kroupina, Schwade, Dropik, and Wewerka (1998; see also Bauer & Wewerka, 1995, 1997) we analyzed the spontaneous verbal expressions of some of the 16- and 20-month-olds who had taken part in Bauer et al. (2000). At the time of test, the children were between 22 and 32 months of age. Although the researchers did not elicit them, the children spontaneously produced verbalizations over the course of the session. Some of the verbalizations were indicative of memory for the past events. Thus, in a supportive context, even after long delays, children spontaneously expressed their memories (see Myers, Clifton, & Clarkson, 1987, for another example of verbal expression of preverbal memory, and Nelson & Ross, 1980, and Todd & Perlmutter, 1980, for examples derived from parental diary reports of early mnemonic behavior). Measures of concurrent verbal fluency accounted for 35 percent of the variance in spontaneous mnemonic expression.

Suggestively, age at the time of experience of an event may take on an increasingly important role as the interval between experience of an event and verbal expression of it increases. At 36 to 42 months of age, the children who participated in Bauer, Kroupina, et al. (1998) returned to the supportive context of the laboratory once again. This time, they were explicitly probed for verbal memories of the events. The children who had been enrolled at 16 months of age did not maintain verbally accessible memories into the fourth year of life. In contrast, the children who had been 20 months at the time of the original experience subsequently provided verbal reports about the events. What predicted verbal expression was not concurrent language ability, but previous mnemonic expression. Thus, when memory is queried in decontextualized circumstances, age or verbal fluency at the time of experience may be a major determinant of later verbal accessibility (e.g., Peterson & Rideout, 1998). In contrast, in a supportive context, concurrent verbal facility permits linguistic augmentation of event representations originally encoded without the benefit of language; previous verbal mnemonic expression aids in the long-term maintenance of verbal accessibility (Bauer, Kroupina, et al., 1998).

Preschool Years: Autobiographical Memory Development

Just as until relatively recently it was widely assumed that infants and very young children were unable to form memories of specific events that would endure and be accessible over time, so was it assumed that children of preschool age had difficulty forming and maintaining organized memories. The assumption was particularly prominent in theories designed to account for the phenomenon of infantile or childhood amnesia. Infantile amnesia is characterized by (a) a relative paucity among adults of memories of events that happened before their third or fourth birthday (e.g., Sheingold & Tenney, 1982; West & Bauer, 1999; although see Eacott & Crawley, 1998, and Usher & Neisser, 1993, for adults' reports of events from the age of 2 years), and (b) a smaller number of verbally accessible memories from the years of 3 to 7 than would be expected based on forgetting alone (e.g., Rubin, 1982). Freud referred to the relative absence among adults of recollections of unique events experienced in the first years of life as the "remarkable amnesia of childhood", "the forgetting which veils our earliest youth from us and makes us strangers to it" (1966, p. 326). A variety of explanations for the amnesia have been advanced (see Howe & Courage, 1993, for a review). Most share the perspective that over the course of development, recall processes change qualitatively. For example, in addition to his more widely known explanation of infantile amnesia, namely, that memories of early childhood exist, but are repressed (Freud, 1966), Freud also proposed that the memories created by very young children are qualitatively different from those formed later in life. Early in development, children were thought to retain traces, fragments, or images of events, but not to create coherent representations of past experiences (Freud, 1953). Freud suggested that childhood amnesia exists because adults failed to reconstruct or "translate" these fragments into a coherent narrative (see Pillemer & White, 1989, for further discussion of this and related proposals). The notion that preschoolers were poor at constructing organized memories of the past seemingly was supported by consistent findings of their relative incompetence in laboratory tasks of word and picture list recall (see Kail, 1990, for a review).

Children's autobiographical reports

Until surprisingly recently, largely absent from the scene of speculation as to the source (or sources) of infantile amnesia were any data that bore on the issues of whether *children* actually are able to form and retain accessible memories of the events that they experience. The past 20 years have been witness to a correction to this oversight in the form of a virtual explosion of research on memory of children of preschool age. Indeed, although during the preschool years of roughly 3 to 5 years of age there are developments in a number of facets of memory, including short-term and working memory, deliberate use of strategies to improve memory performance, and metamemory, or awareness of mnemonic processes (see Luciana & Nelson, 1998, and Schneider & Bjorklund, 1998, for reviews), none of these areas has captured the imagination and thus the attention of researchers to the same extent as has development of autobiographical or personal memory.

An early impetus for focus on preschool age children's memories for personally experienced events was groundbreaking research by Nelson and Gruendel (1981, 1986). Instead of asking children to learn and remember lists of words or pictures selected by researchers, they asked young children to report on their own experiences. For example, they asked children to tell "what happens" in the context of common activities such as going to a fast food restaurant or grocery shopping or making cookies. They found that children as young as 3 were able to provide brief, yet nevertheless coherent, well-organized reports about these common activities (see Fivush, 1997, for a review of children's recall of routine events). These studies literally changed the way that researchers viewed young mnemonists: rather than as a "floor effect" comparison group for older, more competent mnemonists, children as young as 3 were, for the first time, viewed as reliable informants about past events. This change in perspective opened the door for examination of questions as to the fate of children's memories for the unique experiences of their lives.

An influential study of children's autobiographical memories was Hamond and Fivush's (1991) examination of 4- and 6-year-olds' recall of a trip to DisneyWorld. At the time of the interviews, half of the children in each age group had visited the theme park six months previously and half had visited 18 months previously. The children of both ages were able to provide accounts of their experiences. Moreover, the younger and older children recalled similar amounts of information, and the amount of time that had passed since the event was not a major determinant of the amount remembered. This study made clear that even children who were as young as 2.5 years at the time of experience of a novel, personally meaningful event are able to recall it over extended periods of time.

Additional evidence of the durability of early memories comes from Fivush et al. (1984) and a follow-up study by Hudson and Fivush (1991). The investigators interviewed 15 first-graders about a specific museum trip that they had taken one year earlier. Fifty-three percent of the children were able to recall details about the event. Fully six years after the trip, the 15 children again were questioned about their memory for the event. Only one child reported remembering the trip with the aid of a generic prompt (e.g., "Can you tell me what happened when you went to the Jewish Museum?"). Impressively, 13 of the children provided accurate reports of the event when given more specific reminders (Hudson & Fivush, 1991). Moreover, the ability to remember over long delays is not restricted to children who were beyond the reaches of infantile amnesia at the time of the experience. In Fivush and Schwarzmueller (1998), 8-year-old children recalled events that they had experienced five and more years in the past. Studies such as these make abundantly clear that children of a young age are able to retain detailed, accessible memories of specific past events over long delays. They have forced revision of major theories as to the source of infantile amnesia. Rather than focusing on developments in the basic cognitive abilities of encoding, storing, and retrieving memories of specific events, current explanations of the offset of infantile amnesia focus on developments in the ability to maintain a representation of an event that distinguishes it from the myriad other events in one's life, and to integrate the event memory into a coherent life story. This perspective places particular emphasis on the functional significance of autobiographical memory and the social context in which personal stories are constructed and shared.

The social construction of autobiographical memory

The purpose of autobiographical memory is inherently social: it is in order to share past experiences that individuals create stories about personally relevant events in their lives. Because young children are not particularly accomplished story-tellers, early in development, autobiography is crafted at the knees of those more skilled at the practice. In Western culture, the more skilled partner often is a child's parent. As summarized by K. Nelson (1993), researchers have noted two different styles that mothers exhibit when they engage in memory talk with their children. Mothers who frequently engage in conversations about the past, provide rich descriptive information about previous experiences, and invite their children to "join in" on the construction of stories about the past, are said to use an *elaborative* style. In contrast, mothers who provide fewer details about past experiences and instead pose specific questions to their children (e.g., "What was the name of the restaurant where we had breakfast?"), are said to use a *repetitive* or *low elaborative* style.

Stylistic differences have been found to have implications for autobiographical memory reports. Specifically, children of mothers using the elaborative style report more about past events than children of mothers using the repetitive or low elaborative style (e.g.,

Fivush & Fromhoff, 1988; Hudson, 1990; Tessler & Nelson, 1994). Effects of maternal style typically are interpreted from a social construction perspective. Researchers in this tradition suggest that exposure to the elaborative style engenders socialization of narrative function. In addition, the elaborative style provides the young child with, in effect, a "prototype" of the narrative frame into which information about the actors, actions, intentions, and affective experiences of those involved in an event are inserted. The advent of the narrative organization allows the child to begin to construct the personal history that is the hallmark of autobiographical or personal memory (see, for example, Fivush, 1988; Hudson, 1990; Nelson, 1993 for further discussion). Consistent with this suggestion is evidence of cross-lag correlation from maternal style variables at 40 and 46 months to child verbal report variables at 58 and 70 months of age: maternal use of a more elaborative style facilitates children's independent narrative accounts (Reese, Haden, & Fivush, 1993).

Although much of the research on stylistic differences in early autobiographic contexts has been with mothers, the limited research done with fathers indicates that they too exhibit stylistic differences (Haden, Haine, & Fivush, 1997). Generally speaking, both mothers and fathers are more elaborative with their daughters than with their sons (Reese, Haden, & Fivush, 1996). What is more, both mothers and fathers become more elaborative with time and thus, as their children become more skilled in autobiography (Reese et al., 1993). Nevertheless, mothers show similar patterns with multiple children in the family (Haden, 1998). (The relevant studies with fathers simply have not been done.)

There is growing evidence that stylistic differences first documented in middle-class Western samples extend beyond American homes. As summarized in Han, Leichtman, and Wang (1998), there also are cross-cultural differences in the ways in which mothers and their children talk about the past. Korean dyads have been found to engage in talk about the past less frequently than American dyads and their conversations include fewer details than those of American dyads (Mullen & Yi, 1995; see also Choi, 1992, for comparison of Korean and Canadian mothers). The consequences of these differences may be similar to those observed within American samples: Han et al. found that American children's personal narratives were longer, more elaborate, and more detailed, relative to those of Korean and Chinese children. It is tempting to relate these findings to those observed in studies of adults' recollections of their childhoods. Mullen (1994) found that the average age of earliest reportable autobiographical memory for European Americans was six months earlier than that of Asian Americans and fully 16 months earlier than the earliest reportable autobiographical memory for Koreans living in America.

An important caveat relevant to the work on social influences on early autobiographical memory is that it is not clear whether stylistic differences affect memory per se, or whether they affect the reporting of memories. That is, it is apparent that under the tutelage of a parent who uses a more elaborative style, over time, children come to produce longer memory reports, to include more sophisticated narrative devices, and to include more evaluative comments. Each of these features contributes to a more "colorful" narrative. However, as discussed by Bauer (1993), a more detailed narrative account is not the same as a more detailed memory representation. Individuals who produce shorter, less dramatic accounts of their experiences may have memory representations every bit as detailed, integrated, and coherent as individuals who produce more dramatic ones: the difference may be in the public story, rather than in the private memory representation. What is more, it is unknown whether stylistic differences in the narrative model to which individual children are exposed have an effect on other types of personal memories, such as memories for the faces of one's preschool classmates (e.g., Newcombe & Fox, 1994).

Summary

In the past two decades the face of research on memory development in infancy and early childhood has changed substantially. Contrary to earlier suggestions that children of preschool age were poor mnemonists and to speculations that younger children and infants were no mnemonists at all, it now is clear that from early in life, the human organism stores information over the long term and that the effects of prior experience are apparent in behavior. In the first months of life, infants exhibit recognition memory for all manner of natural and artificial stimuli. Recognition memory is apparent over delays of as long as three months (e.g., Bahrick et al., 1997; Bahrick & Pickens, 1995; Courage & Howe, 1998). Whether or not the recognition memory behaviors exhibited by very young infants index the same type of memory as tapped by verbal recognition paradigms used with older children and adults (see Mandler, 1998; and C. A. Nelson, 1997 for discussion), the mnemonic feats that they perform make clear that the human organism is, from birth, exquisitely prepared to benefit from its experiences.

Elicited and deferred imitation procedures provide a means of examining questions of continuity and discontinuity in mnemonic processes from infancy through early childhood and beyond. By 6 months of age, infants demonstrate recall memory over the short term (Barr et al., 1996). By 9 months of age, they not only demonstrate retention over long delays, but a substantial number of infants also evidence ordered recall (Bauer et al., in press; Carver & Bauer, 1999). Over the course of the second and into the third years of life, there are age-related changes in the reliability and robustness of long-term ordered recall, suggesting consolidation of declarative mnemonic processes (Bauer et al., 2000). Nevertheless, because memory is multiply determined, we cannot establish "growth chart" type functions for the lengths of time over which memories will be evidenced.

A vitally important question about early memories is whether they later are verbally accessible. Although the body of relevant research is small, that which does exist suggests that when children are required to report on experiences without the benefit of contextual support for recall, verbal ability at the time of experience of an event determines whether it later will be verbally accessible (e.g., Peterson & Rideout, 1998). When children are permitted to report on experiences supported by props and a familiar context, later verbal accessibility is determined by concurrent language ability and by previous verbal mnemonic expression (Bauer, Kroupina, et al., 1998). These findings inform the question of why so few memories from early in life later are verbally accessible: rarely is the context in which an event occurred re-experienced. Because a rather restricted range of conditions effectively reinstate memories for younger children (e.g., Hudson &

Sheffield, 1998), it is uncommon for the representation of an event and newly acquired language to describe it to be available at the same time.

Once language is well instantiated, children demonstrate the ability to report on the experiences of their lives over remarkably long periods of time (e.g., Fivush & Schwarz-mueller, 1998; Hamond & Fivush, 1991). At least under some circumstances, the events survive the transition into middle childhood, thereby permitting recall of them beyond the period typically obscured by infantile amnesia. The production of autobiographical memory reports is influenced by the social context in which narrative skills are acquired (e.g., Reese et al., 1993). Moreover, there is increasing speculation that early stylistic differences have implications for adults' recollections of their childhoods, such that individuals exposed to a more elaborative style have verbally accessible memories from earlier in life, relative to individuals exposed to a less elaborative style (e.g., Mullen, 1995).

The great strides that have been made in our understanding of memory development in infancy and early childhood are to be celebrated. We can hope that, at the writing of the next edition of the *Handbook*, further advances will have been made. In particular, we may anticipate further developments in our understanding of structure/function relations between brain and behavior. One of the means for that will be increased use of non-invasive techniques, such as ERP and fMRI, to study memory and brain. Another means may be borrowed from the literature that gave rise to the distinction between declarative and non-declarative memory, namely, theoretically interesting special populations. Already there are suggestions that children whose early environmental conditions were other than expected may have suffered subtle yet important memory deficits (de Haan, Bauer, Georgieff, & Nelson, 2000). We also can anticipate advances in our understanding of individual and cultural differences in memory performance. Finally, the range of phenomena that are under investigation will widen, to include the complement of remembering, namely, forgetting.

PART II

Cognitive Development in Early Childhood

This second section of the handbook considers further development in the foundational domains of psychology and biology in early childhood. The development of principled biological knowledge is discussed by Gelman and Opfer, extending the work reported by Quinn. An overview of the development of psychological understanding (the child's acquisition of a "theory of mind") is presented by Wellman, extending the work discussed by Gergely and Meltzoff. Lillard provides an exploration of pretend play, which is core to the development of psychological understanding and also important for the development of social cognition in general. A key mechanism for cognitive development in this period, the development of symbolic representational formats other than language, is considered by DeLoache.

Gelman and Opfer focus their discussion of the development of categorical knowledge in early childhood around the animacy–inanimacy distinction. They argue that this distinction is fundamental to the development of biological knowledge, and is cross-culturally universal. The development of a core principle such as the animacy–inanimacy distinction enables young children to integrate new conceptual knowledge to existing knowledge in a causally coherent way – learning can become "explanation-based." The animacy–inanimacy principle also links to research in many of the other domains discussed in the first section of the handbook. For example, the work discussed by Meltzoff, Gergely, and Waxman concerning the probably innate propensity to attend to and interact with people is intimately related to the relatively early distinction that young children make between people (animates) and objects (inanimates). Processing of the kind of featural information discussed by Quinn must be important for deciding what is animate (e.g., "has legs" vs. "has wheels"), as must processing of the kind of dynamic information discussed by Gergely (agency, contingency of behavior, and goal-directedness of behavior). Gelman and Opfer propose that the animacy–inanimacy distinction is *the* innate organizing principle that underpins children's naive theory of biology. They demonstrate that evidence from topics as diverse as children's understanding of death and of goal-directed movement supports this view. Theoretically, they argue for a form of the "continuity" view outlined at the end of the first section. They propose that the animacy–inanimacy distinction is one of the core organizing principles that constrains the child's conceptual system and that guides biological learning and development throughout childhood. Gelman and Opfer also join Waxman in arguing that "shape" is not a crucial component of young children's ontological distinctions, although of course it is an important and salient clue to category membership.

Wellman manages to condense a vast amount of empirical work into children's development of a theory of mind into a clear summary of what children understand about the mind and when they understand it. He shows that a division between the mental (thoughts, ideas, beliefs) and the physical (substantive, objective objects) is present early in childhood, and that development chiefly consists of a gradual understanding of mental states and in particular of how they provide causes and explanations for the actions of others (note again a role for "explanation-based learning"). A basic understanding of desires and emotions is present relatively early, whereas an understanding of *representational* mental states (thoughts, beliefs, knowledge, ideas, false beliefs) develops more slowly. Wellman's thesis is in tune with that of Gergely, who suggested that infants' conscious awareness of their own emotional states and of how they are related to the actions of their caregivers develops during the first year of life. Wellman also attributes important causal roles to infants' ability to process the kind of dynamic information discussed by Gergely and by Gelman and Opfer to the development of psychological understanding (agency, contingency of behavior, and goal-directedness of behavior). Wellman then shows how social factors within families (e.g., conversations about mental states and emotions) can affect theory of mind development, underlining the critical role of individual experiences discussed also by Baillargeon in her overview of the development of physical knowledge. Wellman ends his chapter with a formal consideration of the kinds of theoretical explanations offered for the developments in psychological understanding found across communities and cultures in preschool children. These different theories and their detailed claims can appear confusingly similar, and Wellman does an elegant job of distilling each and comparing it with the others. His conclusion is that the course of theory of mind development is shaped by elements of all the major current theoretical accounts. A set of core principles available in infancy forms the basis of an extended series of developmental accomplishments that require considerable learning and that are acquired world-wide on a roughly similar trajectory.

Lillard tackles the important role of pretending in cognitive development. As she points out, pretending is an early example of the child's symbolic capacity, and also appears to play a critical role for the child in interpreting their own experience. Children across the world play pretend games, based both on the everyday actions and habits of their caretakers and on their own experiences of stories and videos and their own autobiographical happenings. Pretend play is innate, but appears to have no apparent survival value. Lillard shows that pretending actually has a very important developmental purpose, both for the development of the cognitive understanding of the minds of others (thereby extending Meltzoff's theme regarding imitation) and for the development of social cognition more generally. Pretending involves social referencing (using another person's response to a situation to guide one's own), and reading the goals and intentions of others, both skills that appear outside the domain of pretense as well. Pretending also requires children to distinguish pretend situations from real ones ("quarantining"), to engage in hypothetical reasoning, and to clarify the reality status of entities such as witches and television programmes. These skills develop more slowly, and so unsurprisingly pretending itself also develops. Pretense activities focused on objects and props begin during the second year of life, sociodramatic pretending with caretakers and peers typically emerges at around 3–4 years, and the comprehension of pretense may not initially involve a symbolic capacity. Pretense probably never disappears, rather it goes "underground." Lillard suggests that all counterfactual and hypothetical thinking involves a kind of pretense, as does the simulation of the thoughts and feelings of others when trying to understand their behaviors and actions. The very fact that the developing cognitive system spends a large amount of time in purposely thwarting reality (i.e., in making things other than what they are) at just the same time as the child is learning what reality is suggests a deep and as yet not well understood cognitive function for pretend play.

The idea discussed in Lillard's chapter that early pretending may not involve a symbolic capacity fits well with DeLoache's research on the gradual emergence of the symbolic understanding of artifacts. Human cultures create a variety of artifacts to serve symbolic functions (models, maps, pictures, religious artifacts), and young children learn gradually that these artifacts are intended to stand for or represent something other than themselves. The ability to map from a given symbolic artifact to its referent does not appear to be the key constraint in symbolic development. For DeLoache, the unique aspect of symbolic artifacts is that they have an inherently dual nature – they are both objects in their own right and something entirely different. DeLoache argues that the achievement of the "dual representation" necessary for interpreting symbols goes through a number of developmental steps in early childhood. The critical change in very young children's understanding of the symbol–referent relations in the different tasks (usually search tasks) used by DeLoache appears to depend on "representational insight." Without insight into the symbol–referent relation in a particular task, young children are relatively impervious to training in the use of symbolic media, and even very high motivation to succeed does not improve their performance. The achievement of dual representation also depends on young children's ability to maintain two active mental representations of a single entity, an ability which is known to develop during the preschool years in many domains (e.g., in the false belief task discussed by Wellman). It further depends on concrete experience of symbols, coupled with the social and cultural context in which they are presented. For example, DeLoache points out that an inherent aspect of any symbol–referent relation is the intention on the part of the creator and/or user of that relation that that artifact should symbolize that chosen referent. Aspects of this understanding must be culturally acquired. Given that much of our knowledge about the world is symbolically mediated rather than acquired via direct experience, these early developmental steps in symbolic development are of great importance for cognitive development in general.

DeLoache's recognition of the importance of individual experience for symbolic development echoes findings discussed by many other authors in the first two sections of the handbook. For example, she reports a video study with 2-year-olds in which training with video in the children's own homes was provided for a two-week period. The children then came into the laboratory and were given an experimental search task. Prior experience with video at home resulted in successful search performance for these very young children, whereas experience of themselves on video in the laboratory during a ten-minute training session prior to the experimental task did not. This study has relevance to the laboratory-based studies discussed in Gergely's chapter, in which young children apparently did not use information about themselves given via a recently-recorded video until 4 to 5 years of age. Would these older children have been able to perform the video tasks in these studies if they had had prior relevant video experience in their own homes? The central role of individual experience in so many aspects of the cognitive development of young children suggests that educators such as Maria Montessori (who stressed the important role of "doing" for learning) and theorists such as Jean Piaget (who argued that action is the source of knowledge) were tapping into something very important for young children's developing cognition.

Another important emerging theme in this second section, which has traditionally received less attention in the study of cognitive development, is the importance of the social and cultural context in which young children's individual experiences occur. The ways in which we talk to our children, the things that we talk to them about, the social contexts of the experiences that we provide for them, and the emotional contexts in which these experiences take place all play key roles in cognitive development. For example, Wellman discusses how family conversations about mental states affect the development of theory of mind, and Lillard shows how parental attitudes and parental engagement affect the frequency of pretend play. Lillard also shows that cultural contexts affect children's choice of pretend play topics. Parents and caretakers are acting, usually quite unconsciously, in ways that promote and influence cognitive change. Cognitive development is socially mediated in a surprising number of ways.

Again, the theoretical model that runs through all of the chapters is one in which certain core principles or understandings are continually enriched, revised, and reshaped through experience. The mechanism of learning is largely explanation-based (Gelman & Opfer, Wellman, Lillard), with an additional explanatory role for relational mapping (DeLoache, Lillard, Gelman & Opfer). For example, Gelman and Opfer show that young children use the animacy–inanimacy principle to integrate new conceptual knowledge to existing conceptual knowledge in an explanation-based, causally coherent way. They also show that there is a developmental role for mapping similarity on the basis of relational mechanism rather than on the basis of perceptual appearance. For example, despite their very different perceptual appearance, young children expect plants and animals to be similar with respect to properties such as healing. All three of these themes – the role of individual experience, the role of social context, and the role of core principles coupled with powerful learning mechanisms such as explanation-based learning and relational mapping – will be revisited in the final section of this handbook, which discusses theoretical approaches to the study of children's cognitive development.

CHAPTER SEVEN

Development of the Animate–Inanimate Distinction

Susan A. Gelman and John E. Opfer

Introduction: What is the Animate–Inanimate Distinction and Why is it Important?

A newborn looks longer at abstract shapes arranged in a face-like configuration than at the same shapes arranged randomly. An English-speaking 2-year-old appropriately uses word order in his sentences, so that the "doer" of an action appears before the verb. A 5-year-old ponders the potential consequences of death. In each of these cases, children are making use of an animacy distinction (the distinction between animals and other sorts of entities) to sort the world and organize it into sensible categories.

There are countless categorical distinctions available to humans: color, shape, size, texture, etc. Certainly we would not wish to devote an entire handbook chapter to children's understanding of each one. So why focus on animacy? There are two primary reasons. First, the distinction is a fundamental, foundational one. The distinction between animate and inanimate arises early in infancy (Rakison & Poulin-Dubois, in press), appears to have neurophysiological correlates (Caramazza & Shelton, 1998), is cross-culturally uniform (Atran, 1999), and is central to a broad array of more complex understandings, including causal interpretations of action (Woodward, Phillips & Spelke, 1993), attributions of mental states (Baron-Cohen, 1995), and attributions of biological processes (Carey, 1985). Indeed, a creature that was incapable of distinguishing animate from inanimate would be severely impaired. Oliver Sacks (1985) describes a real-life example of a man who could not identify things as animate or inanimate on the basis of

Support for writing this chapter was provided by NICHD Grant R01-HD36043 to the first author, and by a postdoctoral training grant to Carnegie Mellon University for the second author (NIMH 2 T32 MH19102 11).

visual perception, thus, for example, mistaking his wife for a hat (and attempting to place her head on his own).

A second reason for special interest in the animate–inanimate distinction is that it sheds light on central theoretical debates concerning the nature of cognitive development. Consider key issues such as the following: Are there innate concepts? Are cognitive systems modular? Can subtle and complex concepts emerge bottom-up on the basis of a perceptually based associative learning mechanism? How domain-general versus domain-specific is human cognition? Do children's concepts undergo qualitative reorganizations with age? At what age can children be said to have constructed a theory of psychology, or a theory of biology? All of these issues are informed by work on the animate–inanimate distinction.

Given the centrality of animacy as sketched out above, it is not surprising that there is a rich literature on children's understanding of this concept, spanning decades of scientific investigation, from numerous theoretical and methodological perspectives. The research includes non-verbal experimental methods with infants, interview studies with preschoolers, analyses of natural language, and a wide array of stimuli that manipulate both static and dynamic features that are central to the determination of animacy. In this chapter, we aim to reflect the breadth of this literature, but in a selective manner that recognizes the theoretical contexts motivating the work. We thus set forth the following central questions:

- What knowledge about animacy is present in infancy?
- What are the developmental paths by which this knowledge becomes enriched over time?
- When in development does this knowledge get recruited to build a framework theory of biology?
- How does an animacy distinction inform other aspects of cognitive development?

What Knowledge about Animacy is Present in Infancy?

Four key issues arise in studies of animacy in infancy: (a) whether and at what age infants reliably distinguish animates from inanimates; (b) what information is used to decide whether something is animate or inanimate; (c) how and whether this distinction gets recruited in infants' *conceptual* understanding of the world (as measured by, for example, emotional responses, imitation, or causal attributions); (d) by what mechanism the animacy distinction develops. For excellent reviews of these topics, see Legerstee (1992), Poulin-Dubois (1999), and Rakison and Poulin-Dubois (in press).

When in development do infants reliably distinguish animates from inanimates?

Of all the animals that infants must (eventually) differentiate from inanimate objects, the most important is the human animal – people. Humans care for infants, serve as potential models to imitate, and engage in a variety of behaviors that indicate they are motivated by psychological processes. For these reasons, most studies examining the animate–inanimate distinction in infancy have focused on the person–object distinction (see also Gergely, ch. 2 this volume; Wellman, ch. 8 this volume).

The first signs of the person–object distinction appear quite early – much earlier than the age of 8 months, as Piaget (1952c) had thought. Infants show differences in looking time by 12 weeks of age when presented with a person versus a musical mobile (Klein & Jennings, 1979), a person versus a toy monkey (Brazelton, Koslowski, & Main, 1974), a person versus a manikin (Carpenter et al., 1970), or a person versus a Raggedy Ann doll (Field, 1979b). By 2 months of age, infants smile and coo when faced with a responsive adult, but not when faced with a toy monkey (Brazelton et al., 1974; Trevarthen, 1977; cited in Legerstee et al., 1987).

One potential concern is that infants may not be distinguishing between animate and inanimate so much as they are reacting differentially to other factors, such as the item's activity or familiarity. To address this issue, Legerstee, Pomerleau, Malcuit, and Feider (1987) presented infants with both a doll and a person, manipulating both the familiarity of the item as well as its activity. Infants were studied longitudinally from 3 to 25 weeks of age. The results indicated that by age 9 weeks, the infants smiled and cooed more at the person than the doll, when familiarity and activity were controlled. Later, at 4 months, the infants also reached significantly more for the doll than the person. Thus, the communication-like acts that infants direct toward people versus other objects suggest that infants are aware of differences between people and objects as young as 2 months of age.

Does infants' person–object distinction reflect a broader animate–inanimate distinction, or does it instead reflect the special status of people? For example, Klein and Jennings's (1979) finding that 12-week-old infants distinguish a human face from a rotating musical mobile is consistent with either interpretation. Studying this question is challenging. Ideally we would wish to know whether infants smile and coo at non-human animals, as they do for people, or whether they can imitate the tongue-protrusions and mouth-openings of non-human animals (a point also noted by Rakison & Poulin-Dubois, in press).

Perhaps not surprisingly, few relevant studies have been conducted. We know that 9-month-olds do respond differently to humans versus non-human animals, at least in some contexts (e.g., Ricard & Allard, 1993). Nonetheless, such evidence does not speak to the issue of primary interest, namely, whether infants honor a principled animate–inanimate distinction. In other words, the finding that infants treat humans differently from non-human animals does not tell us whether or not they are aware of the ways in which human and non-human animals are similar to one another, and systematically different from inanimate objects. This important topic awaits further research.

What information is used to decide whether something is animate or inanimate?

Although the research cited above documents an early-emerging distinction between some sorts of animates (such as people) and some sorts of inanimates (such as mobiles), it often leaves open the question of what cues infants are attending to. Typically the experimental design does not allow one to determine precisely the basis of the distinction. As noted above, one gap in the literature concerns the extent to which the person–object distinction reflects a more general animal–object distinction. But even if this question were to be resolved, there is still the further question of what perceptual cues signal to the infant that an entity is animate.

There are two broad classes of perceptual cues that could indicate that a given entity is either animate or inanimate: *featural* aspects of the object (e.g., whether or not it has a face; the texture of its contour), and *dynamic* aspects of the object's motion (e.g., whether or not it propels itself, whether or not it moves in the direction of another entity, whether or not it moves contingent on the movements of another). Some cues are arguably a combination of featural and dynamic information (e.g., a person's gaze has both characteristic static features [e.g., shape and configuration of eyes] as well as characteristic motion properties [contingently following the gaze of another]).

Featural cues.   Among featural qualities, one of the most reliable cues that something is an animal is that it possesses a face. Indeed, faces seem to be especially compelling to infants even in their first month after birth. During this period, although infants can only discern the schematic elements of faces (i.e., two dark areas above a mouth-shaped area; Maurer, 1985), when they are shown drawings of schematic faces, infants pay more attention to them than to drawings of non-faces (Fantz et al., 1975). Indeed, neonates between 9 and 37 *minutes* old pay more attention to moving faces with a proper configuration (e.g., eyes level and above the nose) than those with scrambled configurations (Goren, Sarty, & Wu, 1975; Morton & Johnson, 1991). Moreover, eyes appear to be particularly attention-getting and critical. An attentional bias toward faces could help even young infants begin to parse the world into animals and non-animals. (See Johnson & Morton, 1991; Nelson & Ludeman, 1989, for reviews of this literature.)

Rakison and Butterworth (1998) propose that another featural quality by which infants differentiate animals from non-animals is the presence of wheels versus legs. Not only do 18-month-olds distinguish toy animals (with legs) from toy vehicles (with wheels; Mandler, Bauer, & McDonough, 1991), but also 14- and 18-month-olds violate the animal–vehicle distinction when toy animals are portrayed as having wheels rather than legs and toy vehicles are portrayed as having legs rather than wheels (Rakison & Butterworth, 1998). However, a problem with calling legs a perceptual feature is that only some legs are animate. For example, legs of a table or chair are inanimate, yet infants do not treat animals and furniture as a single group. Some inanimate legs even have feet and toes (e.g., the legs on a bathtub or statue). We suggest instead that infants are likely to be using other qualities, such as texture, contour, or material kind, to differentiate animals and inanimates.

Indeed Heise, Rivera, and Smith (cited in Smith & Heise, 1992) find that the contour of toy objects sufficiently distinguishes animals from inanimates, by 12 months of age. Likewise, Van De Walle (1997) found that 9-month-olds use information about part structure (e.g., curvilinear vs. rectilinear contours, smooth vs. angular joints) to differentiate animals from vehicles. Interestingly, results indicated that the specific presence of eyes or wheels was not used by the infants.

There may be additional cues that are difficult to assess in experimental paradigms, and to which infants may be sensitive. We speculate that texture (e.g., metal vs. fur), odor, and sounds all provide important information in the real-world differentiation of animals versus inanimates, though none of these cues are defining or absolute. Certainly even young infants show exquisite sensitivity to differences in odor (Marlier, Schall, & Soussignan, 1998) and sound (e.g., Aslin, Jusczyk, & Pisoni, 1998), including differentiating and preferring the human voice from non-linguistic stimuli such as tones (Glenn, Cunningham, & Joyce, 1981) and preferring the odor of human milk to raw cow's milk (Russell, 1976). Studies that use small-scale replicas or photos will be impoverished with respect to some of these cues.

Dynamic cues.   Some researchers have proposed that entities are classified as animate or inanimate not solely by virtue of their static features, but also by virtue of dynamic information, such as movement. Dynamic information is of particular theoretical interest because it seems to have the capacity to signal quite *abstract* conceptual information, such as agency, intentionality, or goal-directedness.

Central among such claims is the suggestion that animates can engage in self-generated and self-sustained motion, whereas inanimate objects typically cannot (Mandler, 1988a, 1992, 2000a; Premack, 1990). By 7 months of age, infants seem to appreciate that people – but not inanimate objects – can move on their own. Woodward, Phillips, and Spelke (1993) assigned 7-month-olds to one of two conditions: a person condition or an object condition. In both conditions, infants were habituated to a video-taped event. In the person condition, one person moved behind a screen and a second person emerged from the other side. In the object condition, an inanimate object moved behind a screen and a second inanimate object emerged from the other side. Infants in the *object* condition looked longer if the two inanimate objects failed to make contact before the second object moved. However, infants in the *person* condition looked longer if the two people did make contact before the second person moved. Thus, 7-month-olds seem to believe that people – but not inanimate objects – are capable of self-initiated movement. In further support of this interpretation, 9-month-olds become emotionally distressed on viewing inanimates moving on their own (Poulin-Dubois, Lepage, & Ferland, 1996).

In addition to the importance of motion per se, particular *patterns* of motion – such as walking or pursuing a goal – appear to be distinctively animate (see also Blythe, Todd, & Miller, 1999, for discussion). One method used to study the perception of walking employs "point-light displays," in which a number of luminous dots are placed on the torso and joints of a person. The person is then filmed in the dark while moving about such that these lights are the only visible stimuli. When adults view these displays, they can determine within a half-second that the moving entity is a person (Johansson, 1973). Several studies indicate that infants between 30 and 36 weeks of age perceive the difference between a person-based point-light display and an artificial display (Bertenthal et al., 1985; Fox & McDaniel, 1982). Thus, by about 8 months of age, infants can distinguish between humans and non-humans on the basis of gait. It is not yet known, however, how broad this distinction is, for adults or children. For example, do fish or snakes have distinctively biological patterns of motion as well, or do these findings apply only to the motion of quadrupeds?

A third type of dynamic cue is that of goal-directed movement, of which all living things are capable – including animals (Carey, 1999) and insentient living things such as plants, amoebae, and leaves (Bargh, 1990; Opfer & Gelman, 1998; Opfer, 2000). Some recent studies suggest that infants 9 months of age expect goal-directed agents to move *directly* toward goals (i.e., taking the most direct path of motion; Csibra et al., 1999; Gergely et al., 1995; Phillips, Wellman, & Sootsman, 2000; see also Gergely, ch. 2, and Wellman, ch. 8, this volume).

A final type of dynamic cue is *contingency* of behavior, in which the actions or behaviors of an entity are time-linked to those of another (e.g., an object that moves or vocalizes in response to a baby's movements or vocalizations) (Gergely & Watson, 1999; Johnson, Slaughter, & Carey, 1998). Watson (1972) presented 2-month-olds with both contingent caregivers and contingent mobiles over a period of two weeks, and found that the infants responded to each with an equal amount of smiling and cooing – thus treating the contingent mobiles in a "social" fashion. Watson and Ramey (1972) suggest that social responsiveness may have evolved to be elicited by contingent stimuli rather than by particular physical characteristics (such as the human face; see Gergely, ch. 2 this volume).

How the animate–inanimate distinction gets recruited in infants' conceptual understanding of the world

What meaning do infants attach to the animate–inanimate distinction? As noted earlier, some of the earliest evidence that infants distinguish people from inanimate objects comes from infants' socio-emotional reactions, including gazing, smiling, and cooing (Legerstee et al., 1987; Legerstee, 1992). Furthermore, several researchers have proposed that infants imbue animates (particularly people) with important psychological characteristics. Baron-Cohen (1995), for example, credits infants with wired-in capacities to detect intentionality and eye-direction in other humans, and posits that these capacities are crucial components to a theory of mind. Likewise, Premack and Premack (1997) propose that infants attribute psychological intent to objects that move spontaneously in a goal-directed fashion. Infants as young as 6 months also seem to expect that people but not objects pursue goals (Woodward, 1998). Older infants also seem to have different expectations for how objects and people act toward goals (Meltzoff, 1995a).

Summary: animacy in infancy

The animate–inanimate distinction is well in place by early infancy. Infants make use of both featural information (e.g., faces, contour) and dynamic information (e.g., autonomous motion, contingent motion) to determine which entities are animate versus inanimate. At the same time, no single featural or dynamic cue seems to be necessary for treating an entity as if it were an animal (e.g., Gelman, Durgin, & Kaufman, 1995; Johnson et al., 1998; Watson, 1972). The distinction is recruited in infants' conceptual understanding of the world, with respect to socio-emotional understandings, theory of mind, and predictions of actions.

What are the Developmental Paths by which this Knowledge Becomes Enriched over Time?

Although we have argued that the animate–inanimate distinction emerges in early infancy, it is far from complete at that point. How, then, does an understanding of animacy develop? We can coarsely characterize two major theoretical positions: (a) restructuring (qualitative change in children's understanding, with characteristic patterns of errors) and (b) continuity (core principles that undergo little or no change with development).

Restructuring

The classic restructuring position is Piaget's stage theory of cognitive development, which predicts radical reorganization of knowledge with age (Smith, ch. 23 this volume). The claim is that, in accordance with the developmental stages of pre-operational to concrete operational to formal operational thought, children progress through a series of five levels of animacy understanding, from fundamental confusion (a chaotic mixing of animate and inanimate), to initial but flawed distinctions (e.g., linking animacy with the capacity to move, thus yielding the belief that clouds and bicycles are alive), to the eventual adult distinction (Piaget, 1929). The Piagetian view predicts that children will display two sorts of errors until about 11 or 12 years of age: animacy errors, in which inanimate entities are imbued with life (e.g., thinking that anything that moves, including bicycles and clouds, are alive), and artificialism errors, in which all entities and events are the outcome of human intentional action (e.g., thinking that people made the rivers and mountains).

Piaget's initial work seemed to support this view. Relying on his "clinical interview" method, Piaget posed questions to children concerning which things are alive, could know, and could feel, and proposed five stages in children's understanding: (0) no understanding, (1) identifying life based on activity, (2) identifying life based on movement, (3) identifying life based on autonomous movement, and (4) correct (identifying either animals or animals and plants as alive). However, numerous scholars have noted methodological limitations of this work, including its reliance on verbal justifications, the use of anomalous questions, the scoring system, the choice of items (particularly remote or unfamiliar items), the wording of the interviews, etc. (e.g,. R. Gelman & Baillargeon, 1983; Holland & Rohrman, 1979; Massey & R. Gelman, 1988; Carey, 1985; Richards & Siegler, 1984). Studies that correct these flaws are in agreement that young children cannot be characterized as generally "animistic" at any point in development (e.g., Massey & R. Gelman, 1988, for review).

A more recent radical restructuring view has been put forth by Carey (1985, 1995), whose position differs importantly from that of Piaget. Carey suggests that children's errors result not from domain-general cognitive stage limitations, but rather from domain-specific misapplications of developing theories. In this case, Carey has argued, children misconstrue biological processes by inappropriately interpreting them within psychological framework theories (see Carey, 1985; Gopnik & Wellman, 1994, regarding naïve theories). For example, eating is understood as (psychologically) necessary in order to fulfill a person's desire for food and to assuage their hunger, rather than being understood as (biologically) necessary in order to maintain a person's physiological state.

Evidence for this position can be found in a broad array of studies showing that children have limited understanding of the body and of biological functioning (Carey, 1985; Slaughter, Jaakkola, & Carey, 1999; Au & Romo, 1999; Siegal & Peterson, 1999), in preschoolers' denial that plants are alive or can sensibly be grouped with animals (Carey, 1985; Hatano et al., 1993; Richards & Siegler, 1984; Smeets, 1973), in their inferences of biological properties that rest on similarity to humans rather than to biological similarity (Carey, 1985; Inagaki & Hatano, 1987, 1991), and in their difficulty grasping that humans are "one animal among many" (Carey, 1985; Coley, 1993; Johnson, Mervis & Boster, 1992).

This theory-revision view has four implications for the animate–inanimate distinction. First, children appear to have difficulty grasping that humans are a type of animal (Carey, 1985; Johnson, Mervis, & Boster, 1992; Coley, 1993). Second, preschoolers fail to differentiate "not alive" from a variety of related (but distinct) concepts: dead, inactive, unreal, and absent (Carey, 1985; Slaughter, Jaakkola, & Carey, 1999). Third, preschoolers have persistent difficulties explaining animate processes, such as illness and contagion (Au & Romo, 1999; Solomon & Cassimatis, 1999). Finally, preschoolers treat inanimate bodily organs as agentive (also known as vitalism; Inagaki & Hatano, 1993; Hatano & Inagaki, 1994; Miller & Bartsch, 1997; Morris, Taplin, & Gelman, 2000).

The theory of radical theory change in early childhood remains controversial. Competing data and arguments are brought to bear, both with respect to when conceptual change occurs (initial reports of radical change at around 10 years of age have been modified, placing them much younger, between 4 and 6 years of age [Carey, 1995], though others suggest that no radical changes occur; see below), and with respect to whether such changes constitute fundamental misconstruals. Below we review evidence arguing that children's understanding of the biological realm is fairly continuous from age 3 or 4 years onward.

Continuity

In contrast to a theory of restructuring, a continuity theory posits little substantive change with age. Continuity views take at least two very different forms. On the one hand, continuity may reflect simply the accretion of facts and beliefs, stored in memory. According to such a view, developmental change is best understood as resulting from the accumulation of environmental inputs. On the other hand, continuity may reflect innate organizing principles that constrain the child's conceptual system and that do not change (or, change little) with age. Here we focus on the latter type of continuity theory.

Several researchers have proposed that the animate–inanimate distinction is well entrenched and essentially unchanging from the preschool years onward. Keil has argued that certain ontological distinctions, including the animate–inanimate distinction, are firmly established and innately constrained (1979, 1995). He initially studied this issue by noting that ontological distinctions can be gauged by "category errors" – statements in which the predicate cannot sensibly be applied to the subject noun. For example, "The cow is one hour long" is a category error, because the predicate "one hour long" does not sensibly apply to "the cow." In fact, physical objects (such as cows) do not have durations (such as an hour in length); only events have durations. Category errors contrast with run-of-the-mill false statements, such as "The cow is blue." False statements are sensible but depart from reality; category errors cannot even be interpreted in a literal way.

Keil (1979) successfully trained children of different ages to make judgments of category errors (e.g., reporting that "The cow is one hour long" is silly, but "The cow is blue" is not). Of particular interest to the animate–inanimate distinction, 4-year-olds recognized the inappropriateness of applying animate predicates to artifacts (e.g., "The chair is asleep" was judged as "silly"). Thus, by preschool age, children recognize an ontological partition between animate and inanimate.

Similarly, R. Gelman has suggested that the animate–inanimate distinction is one of the "skeletal principles" children possess, that organize experience, direct attention, guide learning, and promote conceptual coherence (Gelman, 1990). Indeed, preschool children (3 and 4 years of age) display remarkably accurate knowledge about the ways in which persons differ from inanimate objects (rocks and dolls), for example with respect to actions, parts, mental states, and reciprocal actions (e.g., talking to one another) (Gelman, Spelke, & Meck, 1983). Likewise, 3- and 4-year-olds have a rudimentary grasp that animal movement is governed by an "innards principle" (movement is self-generated), whereas the movement of inanimate objects is governed by an "external-agent principle" (movement is caused by an external agent) (R. Gelman, 1990; see also section on autonomous motion, below).

In large part motivated by the theoretical divide between Carey's (1985) claims regarding conceptual reorganization versus Keil's (1979, 1989) and R. Gelman's (1990) claims of unchanging skeletal principles, the last 15 years have seen an explosion of research examining children's biological understanding, with implications for the animate–inanimate distinction. For review, see Wellman and Gelman (1998), Springer (1999), Gelman (1996). Topics of investigation include children's understanding of: life, death, movement, growth, origins, reproduction, inheritance, germs and illness, organ transplants, teleology, and goal-directed action. Many of these topics are of inherent interest even apart from the larger theoretical issues, because of the pervasiveness of these issues in everyday life, their relevance to human actions, and their practical implications for education. We provide a selective review below, focusing on those studies and results most directly relevant to the animate–inanimate distinction.

What is "alive." The distinction between living and non-living kinds does not map directly onto the distinction between animate and inanimate kinds, because plants are living but inanimate. Nonetheless, the classic question for gathering evidence on children's animism came from asking children which of a variety of entities were alive, and children's errors raise questions regarding their capacity to distinguish animate from inanimate. As noted earlier, although children do make errors on this task, it is perhaps more striking how generally accurate even preschool children are, when questioned about animals and inanimate objects (Laurendeau & Pinard, 1962; Dolgin & Behrend, 1984; Carey, 1985; Holland & Rohrman, 1979; Hatano et al., 1993; Richards & Siegler, 1984, 1986). This finding contrasts with Piaget's (1929) claim that children under 7 to 10 years initially adhered to "animism," that is, believing everything (including non-living things such as clouds and bicycles) to be alive.

Generally, 4- to 6-year-olds make very few animistic errors when items queried include rocks, dolls, household goods, and vehicles (Dolgin & Behrend, 1984; Gelman, Spelke, & Meck, 1983; Hatano et al., 1993; Looft, 1974; Richards & Siegler, 1984; Sharp et al., 1985). Tasks that include non-living natural kinds (e.g., clouds and rivers) generally elicit more animistic errors (e.g., Carey, 1985; Laurendeau & Pinard, 1962; Smeets, 1973; see Nass, 1956, for discussion of content effects); however, even with such items, preschoolers are no more likely to overattribute life than to underattribute it (Hatano et al., 1993; Smeets, 1973).

When preschoolers do err on life-judgment tasks, they are not simply guessing: preschoolers who correctly judge plants to be alive are more likely than otherwise to overextend "alive" to non-living things (saying everything is alive), and preschoolers who correctly judge non-living things to be "not alive" are more likely than otherwise to underextend "alive" to plants (saying only animals are alive), whereas older children (7-year-olds to adults) are unlikely to make either error (Berzonsky et al., 1987; Beveridge & Davies, 1983; Carey, 1985). It seems that preschoolers' two types of errors reflect the same underlying conceptual problem: a difficulty integrating plants and animals into a single *living thing* category that excludes non-living inanimates (see Wellman & Gelman, 1998, for a review).

Death.   Although at first it might seem that concepts of death should reflect the same knowledge as concepts of life (i.e., those entities that can die are precisely the same as those entities that are alive), death concepts in fact warrant separate investigation. First, children are not wholly consistent, at times reporting different responses for what is alive and what can die (e.g., Berzonsky, 1987; Keil, 1979). Second, children could accurately report which entities live and die, without understanding the necessity and permanence of death (Slaughter, Jaakkola, & Carey, 1999). For present purposes, of interest is when children grasp that all animals can (and eventually must) die, whereas inanimate objects – with the exception of plants – do not.

Nguyen and Gelman (2000) presented 4-year-olds, 6-year-olds, and adults with displays of pictures of various plants, animals, and artifacts, and asked them to point to which of these would "have to die later on" and "stay dead after they die." Even 4-year-olds maintained a firm distinction between living and non-living things, with over 90 percent accuracy in reporting that artifacts do not undergo death. Similar results were obtained by Inagaki and Hatano (1996, experiment 3) and Hatano, Siegler, Richards, Inagaki, Stavy, and Wax (1993). Although clearly children's understanding of death undergoes considerable modifications over time (e.g., Slaughter et al., 1999), the animate–inanimate distinction appears to provide a fundamental basis for judgments of which things can die.

Autonomous motion.   Although movement was one of the features that Piaget proposed children relied on *erroneously* (for example, treating bicycles and clouds as alive), others have suggested that certain qualities of movement (such as autonomous movement) might be appropriately diagnostic of whether an entity is animate or inanimate. We have discussed some of this work in the infancy portion of the chapter, above. Here we focus on research with older children.

One especially clear-cut demonstration that the animate–inanimate distinction is linked to the presence or absence of autonomous motion comes from an elegant study by Massey and R. Gelman (1988). Three- and 4-year-olds were shown photographs of unfamiliar objects, and were asked whether or not each could move itself up and down a hill. There were a variety of items, including atypical animals (e.g., insects), complex artifacts, and statues with animal-like forms and parts. The children responded accurately in most cases, honoring the animate–inanimate distinction even with machines and statues. It is particularly noteworthy that children's excellent performance here was with *unfamiliar* items that in some cases were perceptually atypical (e.g., praying mantis, echidna, figurine). Thus, preschool children appropriately recognize that animates are capable of self-generated movement, in a way that inanimates are not.

Interestingly, autonomous movement alone may not be as diagnostic as *goal-directed movement* (Opfer, 2000). Goal-directed movement is a type of autonomous movement in which the agent contingently moves toward another object, state, or location (i.e., the agent's goal). Examples include an animal pursuing prey, or a plant growing toward the sun. Opfer (2000) found that children 5–10 years of age and adults use goal-directed movement to identify novel entities as living things. In one condition, the goal-directed movement condition, 4-, 5-, 7-, and 10-year-olds and adults viewed a set of unfamiliar, rather shapeless entities (hereafter referred to as "blobs") moving toward a goal. By 5 years of age, participants tended to attribute life, biological properties, and psychological capacities to these blobs. In contrast, in a control condition, participants viewed the same blobs moving identically, but without the presence of a goal. In this condition, no age group was likely to attribute life, biological properties, or psychological capacities to the blobs.

Additionally, when asked what the blobs actually were, participants 5 years of age and older were more like to identify them as animals (such as a bug or a jellyfish) in the goal-directed movement condition than in the control condition (in which the blobs were more often identified as clouds, lava, or meteors).

Biology-specific processes.   Processes such as growth, metamorphosis, healing, reproduction, inheritance, illness, and contagion are specific to living things (see also Keil, 1994, pp. 236–237, for a list of some distinctive properties of living things). For example, animals predictably undergo increased size and complexity during maturation, but inanimate objects fail to undergo any analogous metamorphoses. At what age do children realize the domain-specificity of these processes? The answer, according to much research evidence, is that children grasp these distinctions by 4 years of age, at least with regard to prototypical living and prototypical nonliving things.

Four-year-olds understand that an individual animal can change shape, color, and size over the course of growth, yet still keep the same name and identity (Rosengren, Gelman,

Kalish, & McCormick, 1991). In contrast, artifacts do not experience such predictable changes (Rosengren et al., 1991). Four- to 6-year-olds recognize that plants and animals grow whereas artifacts do not (Inagaki & Hatano, 1996). Preschoolers recognize that growth itself comes about due to natural processes (such as sunshine and rain), and not due to artificial processes (such as human activities) (Hickling & Gelman, 1995). Springer and Keil (1991) found that children 4–7 years of age preferred natural mechanisms for color inheritance in biological kinds, versus human intentions in producing the color of an artifact. They recognize that living things (both plants and animals) are capable of healing, whereas artifacts are not (Backscheider, Shatz, & Gelman, 1993). Thus, for example, a scratch on someone's hand will spontaneously heal, whereas a scratch on a table will not. They recognize that a range of biological properties apply to animals but not inanimate objects (Gutheil, Vera, & Keil, 1998). Interestingly, at least some of this knowledge seems to be derived from general expectations rather than specific facts, so that children for example have a general expectation that animals and artifacts will have different insides, before learning the particulars of how in fact their insides differ (Simons & Keil, 1995).

Causal explanations.   Schult and Wellman (1997) and Wellman, Hickling, & Schult (1997) make the important point that when considering conceptual domains, modes of explanation are as central as type of entity, because the same entity can be construed from multiple perspectives. For example, a person can be understood as a physical object (e.g., subject to the forces of gravity), as a biological object (e.g., capable of life and death), and as a psychological object (e.g., possessing intentions, desires). With respect to the animate–inanimate distinction, the relevant point is that children need to distinguish not just between types of entities (animals vs. non-animals), but also between types of explanations (biological vs. non-biological). Furthermore, they need to learn that types of entities constrain the types of explanations (so that, for example, biological explanations cannot pertain to artifacts; see also Gutheil, Vera, & Keil, 1998).

As mentioned in an earlier section of this chapter, Gelman and Gottfried (1996) found that preschoolers provide different causal explanations for animate versus inanimate movement. Four-year-old children viewed brief videotapes in which unfamiliar animals and objects were moving, either autonomously or by means of a visible human agent. In several respects, children's causal explanations differed for the animals versus the inanimate objects. For the inanimates in the external-agent condition, children were much more likely to attribute the cause of motion to a person than to anything inside. With animals, however, the pattern was reversed. Children in the external-agent condition regularly denied that a person made the animals move. This result is striking, given that the animal was carried and that the human agent's hand was visible throughout the event. Instead, over 90 per cent of the children in each condition claimed that the animals moved by themselves. Even in the external-agent condition, children insisted that the animal itself was responsible. For inanimates, only children in the autonomous motion condition said the objects moved by themselves. The absence of an external agent led them to endorse immanent cause. Interestingly, children invoked *internal* cause for animals and for artifacts equally, but they consistently denied any *external* cause to explain the animal events, even when a human visibly carried the animal. Therefore, children maintain appropriate distinctions even when considering boundary cases, such as robots or computers (Koziol & Klahr, 2000; Van Duuren & Scaife, 1996).

Studies of natural language reveal similar domain distinctions in even younger children. Hickling (1996) conducted a natural language study, in which she examined the causal explanations that 2-, 3-, and 4-year-old children spontaneously produce when discussing entities of different types. Importantly, she found that young children honor a clear distinction between living and nonliving things, rarely using biological or psychological explanations in reference to inanimate objects. This was true even of the youngest age group (2-year-olds).

Summary

We propose that there is a potent animate–inanimate distinction by preschool age that serves readily as the center of a vast cluster of conceptual distinctions. There is a core distinction that is the seed of a naïve theory of biology. At the same time, it undergoes much change, including refinement (what is the scope of the distinction?), causal understanding (from framework to mechanistic; e.g., Au & Romo, 1999; Morris, Taplin, & Gelman, 2000), and specificity (Simons & Keil, 1995). Furthermore, the question of whether children (and adults) retain non-rational modes of thought – as well as how genuinely such convictions are held – remains for future research.

How Does an Animacy Distinction Inform Other Aspects of Cognitive Development?

As noted earlier, animacy is an *ontological* distinction (Keil, 1979). Accordingly, we should expect the animate–inanimate distinction to have ramifications for other aspects of cognitive and linguistic development. There are potentially numerous such implications, for topics that include: categorization (Barrett, Abdi, Murphy, & Gallagher, 1993; Diesendruck & Gelman, 1999; Freeman & Sera, 1996; Keil, 1995); metalinguistic judgments (Schwartz, 1980); metaphor (Gottfried, 1997); homonyms (Backscheider & Gelman, 1995); myth-making (Kelly & Keil, 1985); syntax (Lempert, 1989), theory of mind (Lillard, Zeljo, Curenton, & Kaugars, 2000), and physical reasoning (Heyman, Phillips, & Gelman, 2000). Below we focus briefly on just two areas of influence that have received sustained attention in the literature: word meanings and essentialist reasoning.

Animacy as constraint on word meanings

Not only are children *sensitive* to an animate–inanimate distinction; in addition, the animate–inanimate distinction appears to guide children's word meanings and classifications on sorting tasks. We cite just a few examples here. By 9 months of age, infants sort together different basic-level animal categories (e.g., dogs and fish) and separate birds-with-outspread-wings from airplanes (Mandler & McDonough, 1993). By 4 years of age, children treat plants and animals as alike with respect to certain properties of growth and healing, despite the extreme differences in shape between, say, a cow and a tree (Backscheider, Shatz, & Gelman, 1993; Hickling & Gelman, 1995). Conversely, children treat humans and apes as belonging to distinctly different categories, despite their greater similarity (as noted earlier; Johnson et al., 1992; Coley, 1993). Preschool children also overlook similarity in shape when making predictions about how statues versus live animals will move (Massey & R. Gelman, 1988). By age 7, children can sort objects into superordinate categories in ways that require overlooking shape (e.g., classifying a snake with other animals, or a sailboat with wheeled vehicles) (Sigel, 1953).

Nonetheless, the notion that words honor the ontological distinction between animate and inanimate has been called into question by recent studies suggesting that *shape* is a crucial component of children's semantic representations. On this view, children have a general shape bias in their interpretations of novel count nouns, such that a new word (e.g., "a dax") is assumed to refer to a set of objects that share a common shape (Imai, Gentner, & Uchida, 1994; Landau, Smith, & Jones, 1988, 1992). One interpretation of the bias is that ontological status is irrelevant, at least in naming and perhaps in conceptualization (e.g., toy bears and real bears are both "bears" because they have a common shape; Jones & Smith, 1993). In favor of this position, many studies indicate that shape is an important and salient feature for children, particularly in word-learning contexts (Baldwin, 1992).

However, a closer look at the evidence suggests that children attend to shape not because it is the basis on which words are extended, but rather because it is an indirect indicator of category membership; it correlates with and "is often . . . a good source of information about" what kind of thing an object is (Soja, Carey, & Spelke, 1992; see also Gelman & Diesendruck, 1999; Waxman, ch. 5 this volume).

When shape is disentangled from taxonomic relatedness, we find that even 2-year-olds show no tendency to use shape more than taxonomic kind (Gelman, Croft, Fu, Clausner, & Gottfried, 1996). One set of items in this study crossed shape with animacy (i.e., the children were asked whether the word "dog" applied to inanimate items of the same shape [e.g., dog-shaped chair], and animate distractors differing in shape [e.g,. chicken]). Results indicated that children were typically correct in comprehension, but when they did err, they typically overextended to items that matched the target word in both shape *and* taxonomic relatedness (e.g., "dog" was more often extended to a cow [same kind and same shape] than to a chicken [same kind only] or a dog-shaped chair [same shape only]). Also, in comprehension children were as likely to overextend based on taxonomic relatedness alone (e.g., chicken) as on shape alone (e.g., dog-shaped chair). All of these findings suggest that animacy is at least as powerful as shape in young children's semantic representations.

To summarize, animacy is a powerful factor in children's naming and classification. Shape, although argued to be a strong contender, is not the sole or even primary factor. On tasks that provide information only about perceptual dimensions (e.g., sorting of simple, novel artifacts that vary only in shape, texture, and color), shape is an especially salient dimension. However, its salience derives largely from its value as an index or predictor of other information (Medin, 1989; Soja et al., 1992; Waxman & Braig, 1996). When ontological knowledge (including information about animacy) and theoretical beliefs are available, and when they conflict with shape, children often sort and name on the basis of these other factors.

Animacy and essentialist reasoning

Our last example comes from children's "essentialist" reasoning. Essentialism is the view that categories have an underlying reality or true nature that one cannot observe directly but that gives an object its identity (Gelman & Hirschfeld, 1999; Locke, 1959; Schwartz, 1977). In other words, according to essentialism, categories are real, in several senses: they are discovered (vs. invented), they are natural (vs. artificial), they predict other properties, and they point to natural discontinuities in the world. Essentialism requires no specialized knowledge, and people may possess an "essence placeholder" without knowing what the essence is (Medin, 1989). For example, a child might believe that girls have some inner, non-obvious quality that distinguishes them from boys and that is responsible for the many observable differences in appearance and behavior between boys and girls, before ever learning about chromosomes or human physiology.

Animacy appears to be particularly relevant, in that children assert essentialism almost exclusively in the domain of animals. One powerful example can be found in children's reasoning about identity across transformations (Keil, 1989). For even preschoolers, on some tasks, identity can change from one animal kind to another, but not from an animal kind to an inanimate kind (e.g., porcupine to cactus). For older children, identity can change from one artifact kind to another, but not from one animal kind to another. In this sense, animals are construed in essentialist terms, artifacts are not.

Another indication comes from children's inductive inferences (see also Goswami, ch. 13 this volume). Children draw a richer array of inferences from animals than from artifacts (Gelman, 1988). Heyman and Gelman (2000) found that category-based inferences differ for animate versus inanimate entities, even when controlling for outward appearances of the entities. In a procedure adapted from Gelman and Markman (1986), 4-year-old participants saw line drawings of three different faces that were described as depicting either children or dolls. Participants were asked to predict whether one of the children/dolls would share properties with a child/doll who has the same novel predicate (e.g. "is zav," which is never defined for participants) but is dissimilar in appearance, or with a child/doll who has a different novel predicate but is similar in appearance. Participants tended to use the novel predicates rather than superficial resemblance to guide their inferences about people. In contrast, when the line drawings were described as depicting dolls rather than children, participants showed no such emphasis on the novel predicate information. The results suggest that children have a general assumption that unfamiliar words hold rich inductive potential when applied to people, but not when applied to dolls.

In addition to inductive inferences, category-wide generalizations in language (generics) are also more frequent for animates than inanimates. For example, mothers are more likely to say something general about squirrels (e.g., "They like to eat nuts") than something general about shoes (Gelman, Coley, Rosengren, Hartman, & Pappas, 1998), and this is true for both English- and Chinese-speaking mothers (Gelman & Tardif, 1998). Preliminary evidence suggests that children likewise honor the animate–inanimate distinction by 2 or 3 years of age (Gelman, Rodriguez, Nguyen, & Koenig, 1997).

Summary and Conclusions

Developmental data suggest that the animate–inanimate distinction is fundamental, in the sense that it emerges early in infancy, robustly, and on a variety of tasks. Indeed, the early point at which the distinction develops contradicts traditional Piagetian analyses of animism, and suggests instead that the animate–inanimate distinction may be a "skeletal principle" (in R. Gelman's [1990] terms) that organizes children's experience from quite early on. What remains an open issue is whether the distinction is a wired-in, domain-specific capacity or the result of (universally) massive exposure/experience from birth onward with faces, people, etc.

What is the basis of the distinction, at different ages? That is, what cues are used to determine whether an entity is animate or inanimate? We reviewed evidence that both featural properties (e.g., faces) and dynamic properties (e.g., autonomous motion, goal-directed action) are important, though neither alone appears to be conclusive. Interestingly, children appear to maintain a firm distinction even in the face of potentially ambiguous entities, such as computers and robots. As technology improves and robots become increasingly animal-like in appearance and capacities, it will be intriguing to examine if and/or how children interpret such entities.

CHAPTER EIGHT

Understanding the Psychological World: Developing a Theory of Mind

Henry M. Wellman

Humans are raised by parents, in familial communities constantly interacting with other people. Consequently, we develop a great many conceptions and beliefs about people, about human behavior, about social interactions, rules, and roles. Given this welter of everyday social cognition, a key question arises: are there core under-standings that are crucial to and organize this commonplace but remarkable knowledge? The claim behind the phrase "theory of mind" is that there are. In particular, for adults at least, social cognition is founded on an understanding of ourselves and others in terms of our inner mental, psychological states. Consider how Melville begins *Moby-Dick*:

> Call me Ishmael. Some years ago . . . having little or no money in my purse and nothing particular to *interest* me on shore, I *thought* I would sail about a little and see the watery part of the world . . . There is nothing surprising in this. If they but *knew* it, almost all men in their degree, some time or other, *cherish* very nearly the same *feelings* towards the ocean with me. (Melville, 1964, p. 23, italics added)

This is great literature. But understanding persons as interest-seeking, thinking, knowing, cherishing, feeling beings is not only the stuff of great literature, it is the stuff of every-day life, conversation, musing, and gossip. If such a psychological construal of persons is common yet crucial for adults, when and how does it develop? Over the last 15 years an increasingly large number of researchers worldwide have addressed this issue. Two sorts of questions have been tackled: Descriptively, what do children understand about the mind? Theoretically, what sorts of explanations best account for this developing understanding? In any scientific endeavor description and theory inextricably intertwine – theoretical commitments shape the studies conducted, and any statement of descrip-tive phenomena requires some interpretation. Still, these issues are partly separable; in this chapter I provide a developmental description of theory of mind accomplishments, followed by a consideration of theoretical explanations designed to account for the descriptive data.

Developing Understandings of Mind

Historically, research interest in children's understanding of mind goes back at least as far as Piaget's early writings (Piaget, 1929). Piaget cogently argued that mental phenomena, because they are insubstantial and nonobvious, were quite confusing for young children. Piaget focused on two separable aspects of an understanding of mind: an understanding of the nature of mental entities (e.g., thoughts, dreams) and the use of psychological reasoning to explain human actions (e.g., how intentions and desires cause and explain human acts). With respect to mental entities, Piaget claimed that young children, preschoolers, were "realists" who think of mental entities as tangible, physical ones – for example, believe that dreams are objective pictures in public view. With respect to psychological reasoning, Piaget argued that young children often incorrectly applied psychological reasoning to physical objects, and, conversely, often incorrectly applied physical reasoning to human acts.

Contemporary research has re-addressed both these issues. This renewed research interest began in the mid-1980s with investigations of children's understanding of mental states (e.g., Shatz, Wellman, & Silber 1983) as well as investigations of psychological reasoning, especially, initially, reasoning about the mistaken actions that result from false beliefs (e.g., Wimmer & Perner 1983). In general, this contemporary research shows, in contradiction to Piaget, that a mentalistic understanding of persons emerges rapidly in most children (Gergely, ch. 2 this volume). At the same time, reasoning about people mentalistically also undergoes extensive development from infancy through maturity, as early insights set the stage for further conceptions.

Piaget came to his conclusions by analyzing children's responses to open-ended questions such as, "What are dreams?" Contemporary researchers have more carefully probed children's judgments of contrasting alternatives. For example, in a typical false-belief task, a character, Jill, puts some chocolate in a drawer but then while she is away, and cannot see what happens, someone moves the chocolate to a cupboard instead. Upon Jill's return, children are asked, "Where will Jill look for her chocolate, in the drawer or in the cupboard?"

Just as in this example, the great majority of "theory of mind" research elicits children's verbal judgments, or at least, their responses to verbal questions. This raises the suspicion that children's answers may reflect general language-communicative developments (or test-taking, answer-giving strategies) rather than their understandings of mind more specifically (e.g., Astington & Jenkins, 1999). However, contemporary research with verbal judgment tasks is complemented by observational research that examines everyday conversations and actions (e.g., Bartsch & Wellman, 1995) and from tasks using less verbal (e.g., Chandler, Fritz, & Hala, 1989) and nonverbal (e.g., Call & Tomasello, 1999) methods.

Evidence concerning children's understanding of the psychological world, from these various sources, is most abundant for 3-, 4-, and 5-year-olds. I begin, therefore, with a focus on preschool children then go forward and backward to consider later and earlier developments.

Mental entities

A basic divide within our everyday conception concerns the mental–physical distinction – for example the ordinary belief that thoughts and ideas are nonmaterial, subjective, mental "things" in contrast with substantial, objective, physical objects. Thus, Piaget claimed that preschoolers fail to distinguish the mental from the physical: "The child cannot distinguish a real house, for example, from the concept or mental image or name of the house" (Piaget, 1929, p. 55).

However, it now seems abundantly clear that quite young children understand the fundamental contrast between the mental versus physical worlds. For example, what if 3-, 4-, and 5-year-old children are told about one person who has a dog versus another person who is thinking about a dog, and then asked to judge which "dog" can be seen, touched, and petted? Even 3-year-olds correctly make these judgments (Harris et al., 1991; Wellman & Estes, 1986). What if such young children are told of a thought about a raisin "in the head" versus a swallowed raisin "in the stomach"? Even 3-year-olds know that neither raisin can be seen or touched, but nonetheless one is mental ("only imagination") whereas one is physically real (Estes et al., 1989; J. K. Watson et al., 1998). Three- and 4-year-olds also distinguish thinking from doing. They see thinking as internal, private, and "just" mental, in contrast to overt, public, and physically consequential action (e.g., Flavell, Green, & Flavell, 1995; Wellman et al., 1996).

Psychological reasoning

Potentially, young children might view mental states and processes as so ethereal and nonphysical as to be completely divorced from the world of action and objects. However, for adults, mind and world causally interact – we see mental states as providing the causes and explanations for persons' actions, just as we see real-world objects and situations as providing the causes for many inner experiences. Philosophers and psychologists often characterize this everyday system of reasoning about mind, world, and behavior as a belief-desire psychology (D'Andrade, 1987; Fodor, 1987; Wellman, 1990). Such an everyday psychology provides explanations and predictions of action by appeal to what the person thinks, knows, and expects coupled with what he or she wants, intends, and hopes for. Why did Ishmael ship on the *Pequod*? Because he *wanted* money ("having little . . . in my purse") as well as the adventure of the sea ("having . . . nothing to interest me on shore") and he *thought* joining a whaler would be exciting and remunerative. More mundanely, why did Jill go to the drawer? She *wanted* her chocolate and *thought* it was in the drawer. Everyday psychological reasoning also includes reasoning about the origins of mental states (Jane wants candy because she is hungry; Ishmael has his prior experiences of the sea to inform him). That is, naïve psychology incorporates a variety of related constructs such as drives and preferences that ground one's desires, and perceptual-historical experiences that ground one's beliefs. It also includes emotional reactions that result from these desires, beliefs, preferences, and perceptions: Jill will be disappointed because the chocolate is not in the drawer; Ishmael will experience an affective journey of life-altering spiritual magnitude. As follows from this quick outline of everyday psychological reasoning, considerable research has charted children's understanding of beliefs, desires, perceptions, emotions, and how these relate to real-world actions, situations, and objects.

False belief.   One of the earliest and most frequently researched topics has been children's understanding of beliefs and particularly false beliefs. Recall the example about Jill and the chocolate. Typically, children 4- to 5-years and older accurately predict that Jill will mistakenly look for the object in the original location (Avis & Harris, 1991; Moses & Flavell, 1990; Wimmer & Perner, 1983). Such responses show, potentially, an understanding of how mind causes action yet differs from reality, because Jill's action is predicted on the basis of her representation of the world rather than the world itself. Similarly, if 4- and 5-year-olds are shown a distinctive candy box that actually contains pencils, they can correctly attribute to a naïve viewer of the box the belief that it contains candy, not pencils (Gopnik & Astington, 1988; Perner et al., 1987). Understanding false beliefs thus neatly reveals an appreciation of the difference between "contents" of the mind and contents of the world ("candy" vs. pencils) and an ability to reason about how mind influences action.

While 4- and 5-year-olds often pass false-belief tasks, younger children typically fail such tasks. In this, they say that the person's action and beliefs will correspond to what is really true (e.g., Jill will look for the chocolate in the cupboard; the other person will think that the candy box contains pencils all along). That is, they do not distinguish between the person's belief and objective reality. As detailed in a recent meta-analysis, this developmental difference from younger to older preschool children has been found when the questions are about mental states directly or when they are about behavior (what the person thinks vs. where will they look), when the target person is a story character, a videotaped character, a puppet, a child, or an adult, and even in tasks that focus on the child's own beliefs (Wellman, Cross & Watson, in press).

At about the same age that children pass false-belief tasks, in other tasks they prove able to use information about what a person perceives to predict what he or she knows or believes (Pillow, 1989; Pratt & Bryant, 1990; Wimmer, Hogrefe, & Perner, 1988) and can judge how various sources of information shape distinctive mental states (O'Neill & Gopnik, 1991; Woolley & Bruell, 1996). Similarly, by 4- and 5-years preschoolers understand various reality–appearance distinctions – that a physical object can look one way to the eyes, yet be something altogether different "in reality" (e.g., Flavell et al., 1986). Based on these accumulating findings young children have been claimed to develop from an understanding of personal connections to an understanding of mental representations (Flavell, 1988), from a situationist to a representational understanding of persons (Perner, 1991), or from a desire to a belief-desire naïve psychology (Wellman, 1990).

Before belief?   At times these developmental claims have been framed in terms of conceptions that are absent in 3-year-olds and emerge in 4-year-olds. Characterizations of this sort are inaccurate in two regards. First, the sort of understanding assessed in false-belief tasks is not abruptly discontinuous. Several studies show that, at least in some situations on at least some task variations, 3-year-olds, too, can perform correctly on false-belief tasks. For example, 3-year-olds at times perform well if they are more actively engaged in deceiving the target person (Chandler et al., 1989; Sullivan & Winner, 1993; but see Sodian, 1994), if the key features of the false-belief narrative are overlearned (Lewis et al., 1994), or if certain ways of phrasing the false-belief question are used rather than others (e.g., Lewis & Osborne, 1990; Siegal & Beattie, 1991). At the same time, even the most simplified, well-controlled tasks reveal a fundamental developmental progression: meta-analysis of more than 500 false-belief conditions with a variety of ages and procedural details shows that overwhelmingly in the age range from 2.5 to 5 years children proceed from consistently making false-belief errors to becoming significantly correct (Wellman, et al., in press).

Furthermore, it is *not* the case that young preschoolers have no understanding of mental states and that an appreciation of false belief indicates the onset of such an understanding. To the contrary, the data show that while preschool children acquire an understanding of *representational* mental states, such as thoughts, beliefs, and knowledge, over several years, nonetheless at the start of the preschool years children already evidence a subjective, psychological understanding of persons' desires and emotions. Thus, in simplified judgment tasks 2-year-olds show that they know that people may have different emotions from their own (e.g., Denham, 1986) and moreover judge that people may have different emotions about and different desires for the exact same object or event (e.g., Wellman & Woolley, 1990). Although very young preschoolers evidence such understandings of desires and emotion, the same young children consistently fail to understand beliefs and knowledge, even if tested with carefully comparable tasks (Flavell et al., 1990; Wellman & Woolley, 1990). Indeed, an understanding of desires and emotions – a person's wants and preferences – as subjective and as distinguished from overt behaviors may well be in place even earlier than 2 years. Repacholi and Gopnik (1997) had 18-month-old toddlers taste two snacks: broccoli and goldfish crackers. Then an adult, facing the child, tasted each snack saying, "Mm" and smiling to one snack, and saying, "Eww" and frowning to the other. In a *Match* condition the adult liked the crackers and disliked the broccoli, matching the child's preference. In a *Mismatch* condition she liked the broccoli instead. When the adult then held her hand halfway between the two snacks and said "I want some more, can you give me some more?" 18-month-olds overwhelmingly gave the adult more of what she, the adult, had liked. In doing so in the Mismatch condition, the children demonstrated an understanding of desires as subjective – realizing that the adult wanted broccoli, contrary to their own preference for crackers.

Conversations and explanations.   In the research reviewed thus far children make elicited predictions and judgments in tasks that guide their attention to mental states. If children's ordinary construal of persons is mentalistic, however, these conceptions should be apparent in their everyday life. Research on everyday conversations and research on children's spontaneous explanations of human actions address this concern.

Children produce such words as *happy, sad, want,* and *like* by late in the second year of life (e.g., Bretherton & Beeghly, 1982). Moreover, systematic analyses show that by

2 years, children use these terms to refer to persons' internal experiential states distinct from their external behaviors, physical features, and facial expressions. These conceptual distinctions are clearest when young children explicitly contrast desires and reality, or two individuals' different desires or preferences (e.g., "I don't like shaving cream; Daddy like shaving cream"). A variety of such contrastives – evident shortly after the second birthday – provide evidence for an early subjective, psychological rather than objective, situational understanding of desires and emotions (Bartsch & Wellman, 1995; Wellman et al., 1995). Indeed, analyses of children's everyday conversations provide further evidence of a shift in children's understanding of mental states from an early understanding of desire and emotion to a later understanding of beliefs, thoughts, and knowledge. While children use such words as *want* and *mad* to refer to desires and emotions by 24 months or so, they do not use words such as *think* and *know* to refer to thoughts and beliefs until about 3 years of age or older (Bartsch & Wellman, 1995; Brown & Dunn, 1991). This absence of references to thinking and knowing in very young preschoolers is striking considering that their parents talk to them about beliefs and thoughts as well as desires and emotions (Bartsch & Wellman, 1995).

Children's explanations also reveal the extent to which a mentalistic understanding of persons is central to their lives. If preschool children are asked to explain simple human actions (e.g., Jane is looking for her kitty, why is she doing that?), they, like adults, predominantly advance belief-desire explanations (she wants her kitty, she thinks the kitty is missing) (Bartsch & Wellman, 1989; Schult & Wellman, 1997). Children offer such psychological explanations for emotional reactions as well, to explain characters' happiness, sadness, or surprise, (Trabasso, et al., 1981; Wellman & Banerjee, 1991). These explanations are not mere fragmented attributions of this desire or that belief or yet some other emotion. Instead, in the years from 2 to 5 children use a network of mental-state constructs in concert to come to sensible, coherent psychological understandings of persons' lives, experiences, and actions (e.g., Lagattuta, Wellman & Flavell, 1997). Moreover, when presented with action scenarios, for example a picture of a boy holding a paintbrush, young children offer and prefer mental-state descriptions of the action rather than behavioral descriptions (e.g., preferring "he's thinking about painting" to "he's holding a paintbrush") (Lillard & Flavell, 1990).

Individual differences.   Thus, even as toddlers children go beyond person's external appearances and overt behavioral movements to consider the intentions, desires, and emotions that underlie and cause overt action and expression. By the time they are 4 and 5 children typically further consider persons in terms of representational mental states, such as their thoughts, imaginations, and knowledge. However, it is also clear that the developmental trajectory just described occurs amidst considerable individual differences. The age when a child correctly solves false-belief tasks, or starts to talk about persons in terms of beliefs as well as desires, or reasons easily about emotions, varies considerably within the preschool years (e.g., Dunn, Brown, Slomkowski, Tesla, & Youngblade, 1991; Astington & Jenkins, 1995; Bartsch & Wellman, 1995; Denham, 1986).

Such individual differences have allowed investigations into factors that may be influencing the achievement of early psychological understanding. Consider again, children's understanding of false beliefs. Perner, Ruffman, and Leekam (1994) reported that

3- to 5-year-old children with one or more siblings pass false-belief tasks at twice the rate of children with no siblings (see also Jenkins & Astington, 1996). Increased experience with older versus younger siblings (Ruffman, Perner, Naito, Parkin, & Clements, 1998; Youngblade & Dunn, 1995), or with older people in general (Lewis, Freeman, Kyriakidou, Maridaki-Kassotaki, & Berridge, 1996), are also associated with earlier understandings of belief and mental representation. Such findings suggest that differing social-interactive experiences shape young children's insights into persons and minds.

Individual differences in children's knowledge about mental states have also been linked to more specific social experiences such as family conversations and interactions (see also Lillard, ch. 9 this volume). Consider children's understanding of pretense and emotions. Potentially, young children's fascination with pretense could reveal an early understanding of mental states in general and of mental representation in particular (e.g., Leslie, 1987). Before their second birthday most children begin to pretend, and by 2 years they engage in various pretense actions – e.g., pretending to sleep, treating a block as a car (e.g., McCune-Nicolich, 1981). Pretending arguably provides a context for learning about mental states that are contrary to reality (see Leslie, 1987; Harris, 1991). And, for adults at least, a person's pretend actions demand explanation in terms of that person's representations of fictional situations.

By 2 or 2.5 years children show that they understand others' pretense actions as not-real (Harris & Kavanaugh, 1993). However, children at this age may understand pretense simply as distinctive overt actions (e.g., Eric is *acting as* a rabbit acts, because he's hopping up and down), devoid of a more mentalistic interpretation of these peculiar behaviors (e.g., Eric is *thinking* he is a rabbit). In fact, it is controversial how much, if any, even older 3- and 4-year-olds understand of the mental states involved in pretend actions (Lillard, ch. 9 this volume). Some investigators claim that 3-year-olds show an early mentalistic understanding of pretense (e.g., Hickling, et al., 1997; Custer, 1996) but others have claimed that this is not achieved until 4 or 5 years, well after a comparable mentalistic understanding of beliefs, imaginings, and knowledge (e.g., Lillard, 1993). Regardless of these controversies, however, children's *participation* in pretend play is associated with learning about mental states. For example, frequent engagement in certain types of pretense (Astington & Jenkins, 1995) including engagement in role-play pretense games with older siblings (Youngblade & Dunn, 1995) can predict children's false-belief understanding. Relatedly, Taylor and Carlson (1997) found that 3- and 4-year-olds with extensive fantasy experiences (e.g., imaginary playmates, frequent pretend play, several fantasy toys) are more likely to pass false-belief tasks than children with less involvement in fantasy play.

Family discourse about emotions also influences children's understanding of mental states. Although reference to emotions occurs in almost all households, these conversations vary across families in terms of frequency, content, and child versus adult participation (Dunn, Brown, & Beardsall, 1991b; Fivush, 1991; Reese, Haden, & Fivush, 1993). Differences in how families talk about feelings is predictive of children's ability to identify and understand emotions: Dunn, et al. (1991b) found that 2-year-olds in families who frequently talked about emotions, particularly the causes of emotions, then evidenced more sophisticated knowledge about emotions at 3 years; Dunn, Brown, Slomkowski, et al. (1991) reported that talk about emotions at 3 years was predictive of children's affective perspective-taking at 7 years. More broadly, early family conversations about emotion predict children's later understanding of a variety of mental states. In particular, early frequent conversations about emotion predict later understandings of belief and false belief as well (Dunn et al., 1991b; see also Bartsch & Wellman, 1995).

Cross-cultural differences and similarities. There are differences across cultures and language communities, as well as across individuals, in the timing and frequency of everyday psychological reasoning. Again false-belief understanding has been the most widely studied. Children in the US, China, Austria, Germany, Canada, UK, Australia, Turkey, and Japan, have been given appropriately simplified false-belief tasks, as have non-literate, hunter-gathering sub-Saharan Africans (Avis & Harris, 1991) and indigenous Quecha-speaking Peruvian highlanders (Vinden, 1996). Children in these differing countries and communities achieve better-than-chance false-belief performance at different average ages ranging from 4 to 6 or 7 years. However, in all countries tested so far the underlying developmental trajectory is similar in shape and in slope (going from below chance to above chance performance in these early years) (Wellman, et al., in press; see also Vinden, 1999). Indeed, even mentally handicapped Down's syndrome children come to reason about persons in terms of their beliefs and false beliefs at about 4 to 5 years of mental age (e.g., Baron-Cohen et al., 1985). British, American, Japanese, and Chinese preschoolers similarly distinguish between real, inner emotions versus apparent, displayed emotions (Gross & Harris, 1988; Gardner et al., 1988). Moreover, just as English-speaking children talk about persons' desires well before later conversations about their beliefs, so too do Beijing and Hong Kong children learning Mandarin and Cantonese (Tardif & Wellman, 2000).

In short, differences across individuals and communities in the timing and frequency of everyday psychological reasoning are important. But at the same time, during the preschool years various landmark achievements in a psychological understanding of persons commonly emerge across individuals, countries, cultures, and languages. The widespread achievement of these basic aspects of a mentalistic construal of persons raises descriptive questions about the earlier and later developments that precede and follow from these preschool achievements.

Later developments

Children's understanding of mind and of persons continues to develop in important fashions beyond the age of 4 or 5. Children's improving understanding of thinking, for example, shows considerable development. As described earlier, 3- and 4-year-olds know that thinking is an internal mental event that is different from seeing, talking, or touching an object and that the contents of one's thoughts (e.g., a thought about a dog) are not physical or tangible. Relatedly, from 3 to 5 years of age, young children grasp something of the subjectivity, and thus diversity, of thoughts. For example, if 3-year-olds do not themselves know what is in a box they are able to state that while Mary thinks a particular box has a doll in it, Bill thinks it contains a teddy bear (Wellman et al., 1996).

However, such young children seem to have little or no understanding of the constant flow of ideas and thoughts experienced in everyday life and involved in actively, consciously thinking. For example, 7-year-olds and adults assert that a person sitting quietly with a blank expression is still experiencing "some thoughts and ideas" and that it is nearly impossible to have a mind completely "empty of thoughts and ideas"; but children 5 and younger do not share these intuitions (Flavell, Green, & Flavell, 1993, 1995, 1998). Moreover, it is not until 6 to 8 years of age that children consistently judge that people are thinking when engaged in tasks such as pretending (Lillard, 1993), reading, listening, and talking (Flavell et al., 1995), tasks that patently require ideation and cognition from an adult point of view. Even when preschoolers do acknowledge that a person is having thoughts, they find it difficult to report the content of those thoughts in situations which are completely transparent to older children (e.g., a target adult looks pointedly at a glass of muddy water rather than a teddy bear, and the child need only report whether the adult is thinking about the water or thinking about the teddy bear) (Flavell et al., 1995).

Preschool children have similar difficulties in reporting their *own* thoughts (Flavell et al, 1995; Bauer, ch. 6 this volume), and young children are surprisingly unaware that thoughts sometimes take the form of "inner speech" or covert verbal talk (Flavell, Green, Flavell, & Grossman, 1997). Flavell summarizes such findings by concluding that young children conceive of thoughts as essentially isolated mental happenings, rather than embedded in Jamesian streams of consciousness (James, 1890). Because young children, unlike even 6- and 7-year-olds, are "unaware of the chain-reaction-like flashings of whole sequences of thoughts, each cognitively cueing its successor, they greatly underestimate the sheer quantity of conscious mental content that people spontaneously experience." (Flavell, et al., 1995, p. 85).

Not surprisingly, therefore, it is only beyond the preschool years that children achieve a deepening appreciation of the mind itself, as opposed to an understanding of various mental states. In particular, in middle childhood, at least for children in our literate western European society, children come to see the mind as an active constructor of knowledge (e.g., Flavell, 1988; Pillow, 1988; Wellman, 1990), and as a "homunculus," or processing center, that can be partly independent with a "mind of its own" (Flavell, Green, & Flavell, 1998; Wellman & Hickling, 1994). Similarly, school-age children go from an understanding that beliefs can be false to an understanding of beliefs and mind as "interpretive" – illustrated, for example, in a burgeoning awareness that one and the same event can be open to more than one legitimate interpretation (Carpendale & Chandler, 1996).

Finally, as revealed in a great many studies of children's developing metacognition, during the school years children achieve skill at applying an awareness of mind to the job of using one's mind (Kuhn, 1999). Thus, during the school years children get increasingly proficient at generating, using, and evaluating various strategies for accomplishing cognitive tasks – such as memory strategies, learning strategies, and comprehension strategies (see e.g., Schneider & Bjorklund, 1998; Schneider, ch. 11 this volume). Moreover, they get increasingly accurate at monitoring their own states of knowledge and ignorance – their feelings of knowing (Wellman, 1971) and their source monitoring (Johnson, et al., 1993), for example.

Earlier developments

If 2-year-olds demonstrate genuine appreciation of a person's desires, emotions, and intentions, then the developmental story very likely begins in infancy. Indeed, we know that from a very young age infants preferentially attend to faces (Banks & Salapatek, 1983; Johnson & Morton, 1991; Nelson, 1987), and after a while become visibly upset when people do not behave actively and contingently, or when they maintain a "still face" (see review by Muir & Hains, 1993). This suggests that infants develop expectations about persons. Moreover, these expectations seem to contrast with their expectations about physical objects. Even young infants will imitate the actions of persons (Meltzoff & Moore, 1983); however, they will not imitate similar activities of mechanical objects (e.g., Legerstee, 1991). From about 7 months infants appear surprised if objects begin moving without some external force causing them to, but not if people do so (Golinkoff, et al., 1984; Spelke, Phillips, & Woodward, 1995).

These distinctions and expectations are undoubtedly important, but they do not evidence a distinctively psychological construal of persons. What sorts of understandings might be crucial for conceiving of persons as psychological agents, beyond just seeing them as self-moving, animate entities? An increasing number of investigators have argued that understanding persons as *intentional* beings is central (Baldwin & Moses, 1996; Wellman, 1993; Woodward, 1998). At the least, ordinary intentional action – deliberately reaching for an apple – is not just self-propelled movement, it is goal-directed movement. Moreover, intentional actions, as *actions*, are observable to infants, yet as *intentional* such acts potentially manifest an actor's psychological states, such as his or her desire (*for* an apple).

Infant researchers consistently describe a transition in the period from 8 to 14 months in the type of social interactions infants can achieve (see Gergely, ch. 2 this volume). For example, older infants (10 to 14 months or so) begin to show success at following others' visual gaze (Butterworth, 1991; Scaife & Bruner, 1975), engage in social referencing (Feinman, 1982; Sorce et al., 1985), and comprehend words and engage in simple communicative interchanges with words and gestures (Bates et al., 1979). Several interpretations of these developments have argued that via these behaviors infants are displaying a sense of intersubjectivity (Stern, 1985; Trevarthen & Hubley, 1978), an understanding of intentionality (Bates et al., 1979), or even an implicit theory of mind (Bretherton, McNew, et al., 1981). There is unclarity and controversy about these characterizations, however, and, relatedly, controversy about whether and when infants understand persons as intentional, subjective, beings. To illustrate, consider older infants' social referencing abilities, where infants as young as 10 months glance to the parent and then subsequently behave toward a current object or situation in accord with the affect shown by the parent (Hornick et al., 1987; Sorce et al., 1985; Walden & Ogan, 1988). A rich interpretation of social referencing abilities is that infants seek emotional information from parents and interpret emotional displays as providing evidence as to the parent's internal dispositions toward the object or situation. However, alternatively, infants may just be looking to the parent to maintain proximity or receive comfort (see Baldwin & Moses, 1996), and then be influenced behaviorally by the mothers' displays of affect.

Thus, while infants attend to people, and others' acts and expressions influence the baby, it is not clear – from research on social referencing, gaze-following and the like – exactly what infants understand about the person's actions and displays. In particular, it is not clear to what extent infants understand persons as intentional actors and experiencers. To help address these ambiguities, in the last several years, investigators have turned to preferential looking methods to further examine infants' understanding. This most recent wave of infant research has focused on three related topics: understanding actions as goal-directed, understanding actions as connected to perceptions and emotions, and parsing the intentional action stream.

Infants seem to understand that intentional behaviors are more than merely self-propelled; they are goal- or object-directed. For example, Woodward (1998) habituated infants to the sight of a human hand and arm reaching to and grasping one of two toys. Then infants saw two test events in which the left-right location of the two toys was switched. In the *old path/ new object* event the arm-hand reached to the old location and thus now grasped a different toy. In the *new path/ old object* event the arm-hand grasped the same toy as in habituation, but it was now of course in the other location. If the infants perceived or encoded the habituation movement in terms of the hand and arm as connected with a particular target object, then the new path/old object event would be familiar. Results supported this interpretation: in a series of studies 5- and 9-month infants looked longer at the old path/new object event, consistent with having encoded the initial reach and grasp in terms of its object.

Beyond connecting actions and objects, do infants construe certain actions as *directed toward* their goal objects? That older infants recognize the goal-directedness of certain acts received initial confirmation in research by Gergely and colleagues (Gergely, ch. 2 this volume; Gergely, Nádasdy, Csibra, & Bíró, 1995; Csibra, Gergely, Bíró, Koós, & Brockbank, 1999). They habituated infants to animated video displays of one circle moving up to and then over a wall-like barrier, then back down from the barrier to join up with a second, smaller circle. After habituation infants saw two test events where the barrier was removed. In the *indirect* test event the first circle moved in the same path as in habituation (although the barrier no longer intervened). In the *direct* test event, now that there was no barrier the first circle moved directly in a straight line to link up with the second one (a path quite different from the indirect habituation motion). Nine- and 12-month-olds looked longer at the *indirect* test event. This suggests that infants expected the moving circle to go directly for its object and, thus, were surprised to see that circle taking the indirect route when it was no longer needed. Research by Phillips & Wellman (submitted), using a live person's actions rather than animated nonhuman shapes, corroborates this conclusion that an understanding of goal-directed action is established by 9 to 12 months.

In everyday life, if a person executes an intentional reach, then movements of the arm itself are functionally connected to the person's perceptual regard (e.g., perception is required to guide the reach to the object) and emotional expression (e.g., if the object is successfully grasped this often yields a pleasant expression, if missed a puzzled, displeased expression). Intriguingly, then, by 12 months of age infants connect an actor's action to his or her perceptual-emotional regard in some telling ways. For example, Phillips, Wellman, & Spelke (in press) showed infants a person who looked at one of two objects with an expression of interest and joy and then was shown holding an object. In the *consistent* event the actor first looked positively at one object and then held that same object (consistent with an expectation that perceptual-emotional regard connects to and thus predicts later action). But, in the *inconsistent* event the actor first looked positively at one object but then went on to hold the other object. Twelve-month-olds looked longer at the *inconsistent* event, thus, recognizing that object-directed actions are intimately connected to the person's perception and emotions.

In the research discussed thus far the actions presented to infants were prepackaged and carefully segmented in various ways – for example, infants were habituated to a single reaching behavior shown for multiple trials. In everyday behavior, however, such action segments merge more seamlessly in ongoing streams (e.g., a mother goes to the closet, gets a mop, mops the floor, rinses the mop, and so on). Baird and Baldwin (in press) created videos of such everyday streams of action and then asked adults to identify portions that were "meaningful in terms of understanding the actor's intentions." Adults showed high levels of agreement in how they conceptually parsed the physically continuous videos. Ten- to 11-month-old infants were then shown such videos. In familiarization trials infants saw a video several times. Then they saw the same video once again in two different test formats. In *intention-completing* test videos, a pause was inserted in the video at a point that adults had identified as the endpoint of an intentional-action segment. In *intention-disrupting* test videos, a similar pause was inserted but this time in the middle of, instead of at the end of, an intentional-action segment. Infants looked longer at the *intention-disrupting* test videos. Baird and Baldwin argue that infants were parsing ongoing behavior along the same sorts of intentionally meaningful boundaries that adults identified.

Even in this new wave of looking-time studies, no definitive evidence exists showing that 6- to 12-month-olds understand that people possess internal intentional states such as goals, perceptions, desires, and emotions; the available evidence can also all be interpreted as infants simply understanding a variety of overt movement regularities and facial-bodily displays. That is, infants may be evidencing an appreciation of the sorts of movement regularities that are correlated with an actor's underlying intentions, but without any awareness by the infant of such intentionality. Regardless, however, infants *have* learned about some especially informative behavioral regularities. These regularities – the directedness of acts toward objects, the connection of action to perception and emotion, and the segmentation of action into informative units – are important just because they do correspond with an adult intentional understanding of behavior. At the very least then, these early understandings set the stage for, and may even be revealing, an early developing psychological understanding of persons.

Explanatory Accounts

Several alternative explanations have been advanced to account for the burgeoning research documenting developments in children's understanding of the psychological world. These theoretical accounts split, roughly, into those that are domain-general versus those that are domain-specific.

It is increasingly accepted that cognition differs substantially in different areas or domains (Fodor, 1983; Cosmides & Tooby, 1994; Chi, 1978). Of course, the notion of a cognitive domain admits of several separable interpretations: innately given, modular abilities, such as a specialized faculty for language (e.g., Fodor, 1983); areas of knowledge with special contents and distinctive reasoning systems (e.g., Wellman & Gelman, 1992); specific learning mechanisms dedicated to certain phenomena (e.g., Baillargeon et al., 1995). There is little doubt that by 3 or 4 years children's knowledge about psychological versus physical phenomena contrasts in several ways. By that age children insist that mental and physical entities differ, that physical mechanical forces account for changes in the physical world but that a very different set of forces – beliefs and desires – account for intentional actions and experiences. However, it is possible that (1) these knowledge differences arise solely from the workings of general processes of cognition, and complementarily that developmental changes within children's theories of mind are due to quite general developmental changes, such as changes in memory capacity, abstract reasoning, etc., or (2) that they arise due to constraints, mechanisms, or innate knowledge dedicated specifically to understanding persons.

Domain-general accounts

Knowledge of the mind is conceptual knowledge, and the classic proposal is that all such knowledge arises from general processes of similarity detection and feature abstraction. Arguably, inanimate objects have certain features in common with each other and those features contrast with the features that make people similar to each other and yet dissimilar to rocks and doors – skin and bones versus metal and wood, faces versus handles and windows, biological motions versus mechanical movements. Keil, in particular, has been especially articulate as to how traditional domain-general, similarity proposals fail to account for cognitive development in such knowledge domains as theory of mind, naïve biology, or naïve physics (Keil, 1989; Keil et al., 1998). More contemporary domain-general accounts exist, however. One increasingly influential contemporary account focuses on the development of executive function.

Executive function accounts. At the time that sizable developments are occurring in children's mentalistic understanding of persons (1 to 5 years), executive function abilities are dramatically improving. "Executive functioning" encompasses several constructs and abilities including planning, response inhibition, self-regulation, and cognitive flexibility that may themselves be quite heterogeneous (Zelazo & Müller, ch. 20 this volume; Zelazo, Carter, Reznik & Frye, 1997). Not surprisingly, then, there are several possibilities for how theory of mind developments might be explained by more general executive function developments. To illustrate, consider an analysis of how advances in inhibitory control might account for advances in false-belief understanding (e.g. Carlson & Moses, in press). Task performances often require the ability to inhibit an initial or prepotent response (e.g., not to shout out a correct response but to raise your hand) or to inhibit salient thoughts (e.g., not to think about your birthday presents so as to wait more patiently for the time to open them). Ability to inhibit salient experiences and inhibit typical or prepotent responses develops markedly in the preschool years. And performance on theory of mind tasks arguably requires this sort of inhibitory control – e.g., in a false-belief task, to be correct the child must inhibit a prepotent tendency to say or point where the item really is (in the cupboard) and attend instead to the character's belief about where it is (in the drawer). Or, consider a different possible analysis, whereby executive-function-based, cognitive flexibility accounts for false-belief reasoning (Frye et al., 1995). In this analysis, responses to false-belief tasks require flexible, "embedded-rules" reasoning such as: if the focus is reality, then the item is in the cupboard, but, if the focus is the character's belief, then the item is "in the drawer."

Performance on inhibitory control tasks correlates highly with performance on false-belief tasks even when age and language ability are partialed out (Carlson & Moses, in press). Moreover, performance on several non-social embedded-rules tasks increases in parallel with performance on false-belief tasks (Frye et al., 1995). At the same time, however, executive function developments alone seem insufficient to account for important differences and developments within an understanding of mind. Return to the comparisons made earlier between children's understanding of desires versus beliefs. If, in a false-belief task children have to inhibit a prepotent consideration of what they know to be true in order to consider what the other person thinks to be true, then, similarly, in Repacholi & Gopnik's (1997) broccoli–crackers task, children have to inhibit their own prepotent preference for the crackers in order to attribute to the adult a preference for broccoli. These parallel tasks not only seem to require comparable inhibitory control, they seem to require parallel embedded rules reasoning. In the desire task: *if* the focus is my desire, crackers are the attractive object, *but, if* the focus is the other person's desire, broccoli is the attractive object. Yet children judge correctly for desires at 18 months, but only do so for beliefs at about 4 years of age. Indeed, when tasks are designed to have closely comparable demands and formats, 2- and 3-year-old children can attribute different desires to self versus others, but not different beliefs (Flavell et al., 1990; Wellman & Woolley, 1990). In short, although executive functioning skills undoubtedly impact children's understanding of mental states, executive function developments fall short of explaining theory of mind development. Apparently something more specific to an understanding of persons and minds is also crucial.

A representational-mind account.   A different sort of domain-general account was advanced by Perner (1991). Perner argued that with increasing age the child's own representational abilities develop and that it is these larger changes that are also manifest in, and account for, developments in children's understanding of persons and minds. In Perner's account, infants represent the world, but do so only in terms of developing a single model of the world that they update as the world changes. Somewhere around 1 to 1.5 years toddlers become able to deal with multiple models of the world – for example in their own problem-solving behavior they generate a model of a desired end-point as well as a model of the current state of affairs. Multiple models are sufficient, according to Perner, to engage in pretend play, to learn language, to recognize one's mirror reflection (as a model of oneself). It is only still later, however, at about 4 years, that children come to understand models themselves as *representations* of the world, and in fact come to understand representations (pictures, words, thoughts) *as* representations. An understanding of mental representations (beliefs, knowledge, false beliefs, imaginings), then, may just be part and parcel of this domain-general understanding of representations.

In line with such an account, for normally developing children an understanding of beliefs as representations and an understanding of photographs as representations emerges at about the same time. Zaitchik (1990), for example, compared children's understanding of false beliefs and false photographs. For a false-belief task: Ann puts her bear on a chair not a bed; while Ann is away the bear is moved to the bed, and the child asked, "Where will Ann think the bear is, on the bed or on the chair?" For a false-photograph task: a Polaroid camera takes a picture of a bear on a chair not a bed; while the photo is face-down developing into a clear picture, the bear is moved to the bed, and the child asked, "Where will the photo show the bear is, on the bed or the chair?" Correct performances emerge in a roughly similar fashion on both tasks from 3 to 4 to 5 years of age (Zaitchik, 1990; Slaughter, 1998).

Of course, Zaitchik's data could just be showing us that normal children learn about two separate things – physical representations versus mental representations – at a coincidentally similar time in development. A more critical test of Perner's account, therefore, has come from studies of individuals with autism (see also Baron-Cohen et al., ch. 22 this volume). As I will discuss in more detail shortly, individuals with autism have great difficulty understanding persons in terms of mental states and even high-functioning autistics typically fail false-belief tasks. Do such difficulties reflect domain-general difficulties in inference, memory, or representational reasoning, or do they reflect difficulties more specific to reasoning about *mental* states? To address this question, in two separate studies (Leekam & Perner, 1991; Leslie & Thaiss, 1992) high-functioning autistic children's performance on false-belief and false-photographs task were compared. In both studies autistics consistently failed false-belief tasks, yet they consistently passed false-photo tasks. General problems with memory, attention, and representational reasoning thus fail to account for these individuals' special and specific problems in reasoning about mental states. Data such as these lend support to more domain-specific accounts of psychological understandings.

Domain-specific accounts

In contrast to domain-general accounts, domain-specific accounts assume that our human propensities to understand people mentalistically stem from special knowledge, processes, and mechanisms that privilege and shape *social* learning and understanding. At the very least, humans as a species do seem especially prepared for and adept at social informative acquisition – learning about the world indirectly via information and affect from other persons (Baldwin & Moses, 1996). For example, regardless of how we interpret it, infants certainly do engage in social referencing – thereby coming to appraise objects and situations on the basis of someone else's reaction to them. Most obviously, perhaps, humans universally learn about the world via language – an undeniable form of social information acquisition. However, considered more closely, these sorts of social information acquisition constitute a notably *domain-general* learning propensity. For example, in school we acquire information from teachers (hence socially) about physics and chemistry not just, or even especially, about social studies. Similarly, in everyday life social information acquisition informs us about physical objects, numbers, plants, and animals as well as about people.

Is there some more precise, domain-specific learning mechanism that subserves human social cognition? Meltzoff (e.g., Meltzoff & Moore, 1998c, see also this volume) argues that such a mechanism is revealed in infants' ability to imitate others. Even newborn imitation, Meltzoff asserts, manifests an understanding of others as "like me" (and vice versa, me being like others). Consider neonates' and young infants' imitation of someone else's mouth movements. The infant can see the other's movements visually, but only feel, not see, their own mouth movements. Yet infants successfully match their movements to that of the model. Imitation thus depends on and manifests a mechanism that binds together information about internal states and external action, by fusing together information from self *and* others. More generally, according to this analysis, understanding the psychological world is made possible by a unique fusion of first-person and third-person perspectives on action and mind (e.g., Baressi & Moore, 1996). From the vantage point of such an analysis, it is far from coincidental that humans engage in early, frequent imitation, not evident in other mammals or primates (Tomasello & Call, 1997), *and* that humans engage in early, frequent construal of others in terms of mental states, not evident in other mammals or primates (Tomasello & Call, 1997; Povinelli & Prince, 1998). If understanding persons is subserved by such a mechanism, it certainly seems domain-specific – applicable to and yielding insights specific to the domain of psychological phenomena rather than the physical world of objects and physical forces.

Theorists who believe that social cognition is clearly domain-specific have staked out several contrasting characterizations of such a social cognitive domain: as a core naïve theory, as a mental module, as the manifestation of a basic human ability to simulate mental states.

Theory theories.   One account of theory of mind development takes the term "theory" in this phrase quite seriously. This theory-theory account (e.g., Gopnik & Wellman, 1994; Wellman & Gelman, 1998) claims that young children's psychological understandings are demonstrably theory-like in that unobservable constructs – such as beliefs and desires – are used to explain, predict, and understand human behavior and experience. A theory-theory account is a constructivist account (albeit a domain-specific one): the basic claim is that children achieve a coherent understanding of persons via everyday theoretical *constructs*. Developmentally, theory theory contends that an initial theory of mind is revised into later understandings because accumulating data and information lead to theory change. Thus, according to this position, the progression of observable developmental changes – from understanding of desires and emotions but not beliefs, to understanding of beliefs but still explaining behavior only in terms of other states, to only later incorporating an understanding of beliefs into psychological explanations – closely mimics a process of theory change whereby a conception of belief is first absent, and then developed only as a marginal auxiliary hypothesis, before becoming theoretically central to children's understanding (Gopnik & Wellman, 1994).

Mental modules.   In contrast, other theorists contend that "theory of mind" is a misnomer, and psychological understandings are achieved instead via the computations of an innate mental module. Mental modules, as described initially by Fodor (1983), generate representations of perceptual inputs, as in the 3D representations of spatial layout achieved by the visual system (Marr, 1982). Such perceptual modules are innately specified, their processing is mandatory and encapsulated, and thus they are essentially unrevisable – no amount of training or counter-experiences would cause us to perceive the world in terms of two dimensions rather than three. On analogy to such perceptual modules, Fodor (1992) and Leslie (1987, 1994) propose there is a distinct theory of mind module that produces representations of human activity in terms of a person's mental attitudes toward events, such as his beliefs about X, desires about X, emotions about X. As detailed especially by Leslie (1987) this module – ToMM, or the theory of mind module – enables the child to represent not just actions, but also representational states themselves (e.g., another person's belief about the world). The rapid development of person-understandings apparent in normal children, such as the acquisition of an understanding of false belief, depends on this specialized mental module "coming on line" in the preschool years.

Theories versus modules.   Both theory theory and modular perspectives provide a plausible account of certain changes in theory of mind reasoning, for example, how children might at first fail then later pass false-belief tasks (a later theory is built on an earlier one versus a mental module comes on line). However, these different accounts have gone on to generate their own additional studies and divergent findings. In particular, modular theorists initiated theory of mind research with individuals with autism. They proposed that the social and communicative deficits of autism reflect neurological impairment to the theory of mind module leading to deficits in the normally developing ability to construe persons in terms of mental states (Leslie, 1987; Baron-Cohen et al., 1985). Many studies now show impairment in reasoning about mental states in high-functioning individuals with autism who at the same time show very good reasoning about physical phenomena, such as the false-belief versus false-photograph research described earlier (see Baron-Cohen, 1995 for a review). These sorts of deficits in psychological reasoning are not apparent in control groups of subjects with Down's syndrome, general retardation, or specific language delays.

Theory theorists have focused more on charting the extended progression of conceptions that children achieve in their early years. An extended series of developmental achievements in infants', young children's, and older children's mental-state understandings – of the sort reviewed earlier – fits a theory construction perspective that expects children to achieve a progression of intermediate understandings as initial conceptions fail to adequately explain behavior and thus get revised in the face of counter-evidence. Complementarily such extended developments seem antithetical to the hypothesized activation of a single mental module. If a theory of mind module yields representations of desires, emotions, *and* beliefs, as claimed by Leslie (1987, 1994), why is childhood understanding of desires so advanced over that for beliefs?

The interplay between theoretical accounts and accumulating empirical findings has yielded revisions for both of these positions. Thus, although modular accounts based on the activation of some single theory of mind module have trouble accommodating data that reveal extended developmental changes in young children's conception of persons, a series of modules, triggered or maturing at separate points in development, might more closely fit the developmental data. Leslie (1994) and Baron-Cohen (1995) now propose a developmental sequence of three or four mental modules. In general, mental modules are part of a larger hypothesis about the mind as having a componential architecture, that is, being composed of specialized subsystems; theory of mind capacities themselves need not be subserved by a single module.

However, one implication of positing theory of mind modules is that individuals who are not impaired in the relevant modules – for example, who do not have autism – should achieve mental-state understandings on a roughly standard maturational timetable. Yet in recent studies deaf preschool children raised by hearing parents show delays and deficiencies on theory of mind tasks comparable to those of children with autism (Gale et al., 1996; Peterson & Siegal, 1995, 1997). These deaf children have not suffered the same sort of neurological damage that autistics have, as evident by the fact that deaf children raised by deaf parents do not show theory of mind delays. Findings such as these challenge accounts of theory of mind development relying solely on neurological-maturational mechanisms. So too do the data reviewed earlier on individual and cultural differences in preschool theories of mind, in that they highlight a sizable role for experience-based learnings about the mind.

On the other hand, if children are actively constructing their own theoretical accounts, why is it that so many children so regularly come to a conception of desire and emotion followed by belief and false belief in the preschool years? Conceivably, beginning with some key innately given infantile knowledge and attentional biases, coupled with children growing up in social environments universally full of thinking, feeling persons, children everywhere, guided by their elders, could achieve very similar understandings (Gopnik & Meltzoff, 1997). Nonetheless, all the way back to Piaget, it has been a deep challenge for *constructivist* accounts to articulate how experience-based constructions can yield near-universal sequences of development.

Simulation.   As described thus far, mentalistic reasoning depends on representations that function like theoretical constructs in that they allow us to interpret behavior in intentional terms by attributing to ourselves and others mental states, and thereby to predict and explain actions, understand others' minds, and so on. Even modular theorists adopt this basic sort of characterization. In contrast, simulation theory contends that ordinary reasoning about persons and minds proceeds *not* via conceptual constructs or abstract representations, but instead by way of our own first-hand experiences (Goldman, 1992; Gordon, 1986; Harris, 1991). Since we are creatures who have mental-state experiences (e.g., beliefs and desires), we certainly come to refer to such states, but our capacity to do so does not depend on developing concepts and representations. Rather, we simply experience and report our own mental experiences. Attributing such experiences to others, relatedly, requires not a series of conceptual constructs and inferences, but instead a process of simulation. To think about others' minds we project ourselves into the other person's situation, imaginatively experience what we would feel in that situation ourselves, and then attribute that (simulated) experience to the other (see also Lillard, ch. 9 this volume).

Simulation accounts also have generated novel findings. Simulation theory focuses especially on pretense and imagination as skills of young children (rather than, or more than, mental states for children to understand). For example, Harris (in press) argues that pretend play, so frequent in young children and so nonapparent in adults, never really disappears; it manifests itself throughout life in our ability to empathize and understand the lives of others. Moreover, in a series of studies he has shown that pretense and imagination underpin the ability of older children and adults to reason counter-factually and to understand and create fiction and drama.

Simulation theorists advance a developmental account of theory of mind achievements as well. Developmentally children must learn not to attribute their own states to others, but to simulate others' states from information about that person's situation. Harris (1992), for example, accounts for children's difficulty with false-belief attributions as follows. Children's simulations operate against a backdrop of two default settings, namely the mental states of the self and the real state of the world. Simulations are more or less difficult depending on how many defaults the child must override. To simulate someone else's diverse desire or belief, for instance, one must ignore one's own state and imagine the state of the other. Suppose a child does not know what is in a box but thinks it holds a doll. To simulate the belief of someone who thinks it holds a toy truck, the child must override her own belief and simulate the other's contrasting belief. An understanding of false beliefs, however, requires the child to override not only her own mental stance, but reality as well. Thus, if the child *knows* the box holds a doll and must simulate the thought of someone else who mistakenly believes it holds a truck, then the child must set aside known reality and in addition imagine that other person as having a different thought about that reality than they themselves have.

Accumulating developmental findings speak, in part, to these proposals. For example, according to Harris's proposal, attribution of desires *and* beliefs to others should be equally easy as long as only one default must be overridden, as in the example above of attributing diverse beliefs to others. False beliefs should be remarkably more difficult, because in this case two defaults must be overcome. However, as noted when discussing executive function accounts, the empirical data consistently indicate that attributing diverse desires is considerably easier than attributing diverse beliefs – a difference that challenges simulation proposals. The data from everyday conversations are also relevant. Toddlers and young preschoolers clearly refer to diverse desires at a time when they never mention diverse beliefs; and references to false beliefs appear in children's conversation at about the same time as references to diverse beliefs (Bartsch & Wellman, 1995), instead of considerably later as predicted by simulation accounts.

Explanatory accounts: the state of the art

Theoretical debates about children's understanding of the psychological world have yielded not only further illuminating research, but also more clearly articulated theories. Consider modular and simulation theorists' insistence that mentalizing cannot be anything like a theory: young children are notoriously bad at scientific reasoning and thus incapable of developing theories; moreover scientific theorizing is an enterprise of recent historical origin, restricted to only some of the world's societies, yet "theory of mind" is arguably universal. In response, theory theorists have clarified that theory of mind is (everyday) theory not science, and children are certainly not scientists. The claim here is that "theory" is a superordinate term with at least two subordinate types, namely every-day theory and scientific theory. Only some features of scientific theory help in charac-terizing the general type (theory) which in turn helps in characterizing both subtypes. The attempt, they insist, is to develop a *new* theoretical construct – everyday theory – to advance our understanding of the nature of human cognitive development.

Complementarily, consider theory theorists' contention that mental modules, à la Fodor, are "anti-developmental." That is, modules come on line (or fail to), triggered perhaps by certain experiences, but do not change or develop as a *result* of the nature and content of those experiences. Indeed, the representations they yield are mandatory and unrevisable. In response, modular theorists have clarified that "module" is a superordi-nate type admitting of at least two subtypes: Fodorian modules and what might be called developmental modules (e.g., Karmiloff-Smith, 1992). Fodor's original analysis of a certain type of perceptual module helps characterize the general type – module – and that in turn can help inspire, but not strictly define, analyses of other types of modules (Sperber, 1994). In particular, some sorts of modules, modular theorists insist, are to be seen as dynamic learning mechanisms not static computational machines (Leslie, in press). The attempt is to develop and clarify a *new* theoretical construct – modular learning mechanisms – to advance understanding of the nature of human cognitive development.

Similarly, for simulation theorists, the attempt is to articulate and clarify a potentially unique and foundational aspect of our cognition about the social world – a mechanism that allows us to see and depend on a crucial similarity between ourselves and other people as *experiential,* acting beings. In this regard, simulation proposals are closely related to Meltzoff's arguments for a special learning mechanism that produces an integration of perspective across self and other. To be clear, however, Meltzoff argues that his "like me" mechanism begins a process of theory acquisition and revision – i.e., he advocates a theory-theory position (Gopnik & Meltzoff, 1997). More generally, theory theorists and modular theorists concede that self experiences and projections are important occurrences, but contend that any simulations are conceptually framed or theory-driven. To explain others' behavior we do not simulate any and all experiential states (stomach aches, etc.) but only certain mental state categories (beliefs and desires) that are important for, are theoretically central for, explaining and understanding persons and minds.

Conclusions

Most researchers in this area now believe that elements of all three of these importantly different accounts, as well as domain-general increases in certain information-processing capacities and functions, shape the course of theory of mind development. This may seem like an imprecise, unsatisfying, "everybody is right" sort of conclusion. Instead, I believe it represents an important, indeed remarkable, consensus that theory of mind knowledge: (1) is rapidly acquired in the normal case; (2) is acquired in an extended series of developmental accomplishments; (3) encompasses several basic insights that are acquired world-wide on a roughly similar trajectory; (4) requires considerable learning and development based on an infantile set of prepared abilities to attend to and represent persons; (5) manifests an important fusion of first- and third-person perspective that allows us to use our own experiences to consider the nature of others' minds; and (6) is severely impaired in autism. Not all researchers would agree to each and every one of these points, of course. Moreover, researchers in this area remain in serious dispute about how to characterize the sort of learnings required for, and manifest in, theory of mind development. This is not surprising: how to characterize learning and development is perhaps the crucial issue facing the field of cognitive science today. Theory of mind research is a key forum for addressing this crucial issue. Developments in understanding the psychological world, therefore, are not only important to us as individuals, they are of focal importance to contemporary research on cognition.

CHAPTER NINE

Pretend Play and Cognitive Development

Angeline Lillard

Introduction

Pretending is among the most interesting of childhood's activities. As many have noted, pretending appears to be an early instance of the child's ability to use and understand symbols (Piaget, 1945/1962). Using symbols is one of the human species' major achievements; some would argue that it is the most important factor in our uniqueness among animals. Yet in contrast to other activities in which the symbolic function is central, pretend play receives relatively little attention. Language acquisition, an important aspect of which is learning to use words as symbols, is perhaps the most-studied phenomenon in child development. Theory of mind, which is in large part the study of minds as representing or symbolizing a state of the world, has become a dominant topic of study in cognitive development (Wellman, ch. 8 this volume). DeLoache's (ch. 10 this volume) studies of children's use of scale models have received much well-deserved attention, for casting light on the development of symbolic understanding. Yet pretend play is rarely even accorded a chapter in child development handbooks.

Pretending is also of interest because of its mysterious place amongst apparently innate activities. Pretending is judged to be innate in part because it is universal and emerges on a set timetable (Eibl-Eibesfeldt, 1989). The world over, babies begin to pretend when they are 18–24 months of age. This apparently occurs regardless of whether pretending is modeled for them; even in cultures in which parents discourage pretending, children still do it, suggesting a biological basis (Carlson, Taylor, & Levin, 1998; Gaskins, 1999; Haight, Wang, Fung, Williams, & Mintz, 1999; Schwartzman, 1978; Taylor & Carlson, 2000). Another criterion for innate behaviors is that they are stereotyped in appearance; this also holds for pretending, which begins with simple object substitutions that are self-directed, and evolves to complex role-play.

I am grateful to Patricia Ganea, Rebekah Richert, Lori Skibbe, Young-Joo Song, Peter Smith, David Witherington, and Jessi Witt for comments on an earlier draft of this chapter.

Yet unlike many other innate behaviors, pretend play does not serve any obvious survival function. Innate behaviors are generally phylogenetic adaptations to the environment (Eibl-Eibesfeldt, 1989). Even babbling, another innate human behavior, serves apparent developmental purposes. Human babies babble between 3 and 12 months, the world over. Accumulating evidence suggests that the selective value of this behavior is to exercise and tune vocal chords to prepare them for speaking (Levit & Utman, 1992; Locke, 1993). Babbling also serves protoconversations, because parents (at least in many cultures) tend to "talk back" with their babbling infants. Such protoconversations set infants up for understanding the back and forth nature of verbal exchange (Bruner, 1983), as well as promoting attachment and intersubjectivity (Isabella & Belsky, 1991). By comparison, pretend play's purpose is a mystery. The mystery is this: young children need to adapt to the world as it is, yet in pretend play they contrive the world to be as it is not.

Below I briefly review the history of the study of pretend play, the developmental course of pretend play, and literature on cultural universals and variations. The bulk of the chapter then reviews cognitive skills that are involved in pretend play. Focus alternates between pretending oneself and understanding pretense in others. Pretending oneself requires some understanding of pretense, for example understanding that pretending is not real. Understanding pretense in others, however, may require some skills that are not involved in pretending oneself, for example, reading others' intentions.

History of study

Parten (1932, 1933) was an early chronicler of the appearance of different forms of play in children using naturalistic sampling methods in group play situations. Fein (1981) notes that the 1920s–1930s saw a first wave of interest in pretend play, and that it was often included in the era's scholarly overviews of child development. A second wave of interest in pretense occurred in the 1940s, stimulated by personality theorists and play therapy (Fein, 1981). A third wave of interest was stimulated by Piaget's (1945/1962) writing on the emergence of pretending in his own children. Experimental methods of studying pretend play emerged as part of this movement, although Piaget himself used naturalistic observations of pretense.

Piaget designated pretending a major hallmark of the sixth stage of the sensorimotor period, along with language and deferred imitation. All three activities were seen as evidence of representational capacity (Smith, ch. 23 this volume). For Piaget, pretending is symptomatic of the child's inability to accommodate cognitive structures to the world: a mature cognitive system does not need to twist reality to its own ends. In addition, Piaget focused on pretending as an individual process; this is often read as embodying a view that the child alone invented and used symbols (Smolucha & Smolucha, 1998). Although Piaget (1945/1962, p. 4) noted that "obviously social life plays an essential role in the elaboration of concepts and of the representational schemas," his research focused on the emergence of pretending as a solitary activity. This perspective on pretending as an initially asocial activity has dominated the field, although recently many scholars take a Vygotskian perspective and consider how pretense arises during social interactions with more experienced players (Goncu, 1993; Haight & Miller, 1993; Howes, Unger, & Matheson, 1992).

During the 1970s, pretend play became a lively topic of research. Studies emerged detailing the stages of pretending, as well as how children engage in object substitutions and the application of agency to pretend entities (Fein, 1975; McCune-Nicolich, 1977; Nicolich, 1977; Watson & Fischer, 1977). The relationship between pretend play and language, another major hallmark of the symbolic capacity, was also intensively investigated (Bates, Benigni, Bretherton, Camaioni, & Volterra, 1979; Bretherton, Bates, et al., 1981). In addition, pretend play training was used to determine if it would facilitate children's performance on other cognitive tasks, such as conservation. This was done because pretending appears to involve a form of Piagetian decentration (Smith, ch. 23 this volume): the separation of symbol and referent. These training studies did not, in the end, produce definitive results, largely due to methodological problems (Rubin, Fein, & Vandenberg, 1983; Smith, 1988). As is too often the case in training studies, the control groups were generally not treated appropriately (e.g., all things equal except the pretend). Another common problem was that experimenter effects were not controlled for by use of a blind post-test experimenter. In the wake of the 1970s surge of activity, pretend play research declined until just recently, when it has received new vigor as a possible early marker of a theory of mind, as discussed by Wellman (ch. 8 this volume) and later in this chapter.

Developmental course

Many excellent detailed reviews describe the developmental course of pretend play (Fein, 1981; Nicolich, 1977; Piaget, 1945/1962; Rubin et al., 1983); a short summary is provided here. Studies of pretense have primarily involved middle-class European and Euro-American children, although there is emerging interest in cultural differences and similarities.

The earliest instances of pretending are usually noted in the second year (Fein, 1981). In one classic example, Piaget (1945/1962) described Jacquelyn at 15 months, putting a blanket under her head, blinking her eyes, laughing and saying "Nono" (Obs. 64A). This combination of activities suggested she was pretending to go to sleep on the floor, and that the blanket was serving as a symbol for her pillow; indeed, the blanket was used in this manner several times over the next few days. A dramatic increase in symbolic acts often occurs between 15 and 18 months of age (Rubin et al., 1983), and by about 24 months of age, pretending is in full swing (Bates et al., 1979; Bretherton, 1984; Dunn & Wooding, 1977; Fein, 1981; Nicolich, 1977; Tamis-LeMonda & Bornstein, 1991). One- to 2-year-olds spend 5–20 percent of their play time engaged in pretense activities (Dunn & Dale, 1984; Dunn & Wooding, 1977; Haight & Miller, 1993; Miller & Garvey, 1984). Two-year-olds not only engage in pretense themselves, but are also proficient at interpreting and responding to the pretense acts of experimenters (Harris & Kavanaugh, 1993; Walker-Andrews & Kahana-Kalman, 1999). Sociodramatic pretending with peers appears around 4 years of age, or earlier in the context of a more proficient partner such as an older sibling, or the mother (Dale, 1989; DeLoache & Plaetzer, 1985; Dunn & Dale, 1984; Fiese, 1990; Haight & Miller, 1993; Howes et al., 1992;

Kavanaugh, Whittington & Cerbone, 1983; Miller & Garvey, 1984; O'Connell & Betherton, 1984), or the father (Farver & Wimbarti, 1995). Pretense with these more accomplished partners is at a higher level than is pretense when alone. Although Piaget claimed that pretending declines in middle childhood, elementary school children still pretend in their free time (Eifermann, 1971). Some theorists maintain that pretense does not disappear, but only goes underground as it becomes socially unacceptable. Indeed, all counterfactual and hypothetical thinking may be thought of as a form of pretense (Hofstaeder, 1979), as may engaging with all forms of art (Walton, 1990).

As mentioned earlier, pretend play does appear to be universal; the developmental patterns just mentioned above have been observed in a variety of communities around the world. Haight and colleagues (Haight et al., 1999) have proposed that the universality goes beyond the fact and early appearance of pretense, to how pretense is conducted. For example, they speculate that the world over, children use objects in their pretend play, and that pretend play takes place largely in a social context. However, there are also variations across cultures in pretend play.

Cultural variation in pretense

Cultural differences in pretend play have been noted concerning the topics of children's pretense, and the frequency of different types of pretense at given ages. These differences appear to stem from the values of the adult community and ecological features (such as availability of toys). For example, Haight et al. (1999) found that American preschoolers enacted more fantasy themes than did Taiwanese children; Taiwanese children engaged in more social routine and proper conduct themes in pretense. Similarly, Farver (1999) found that Korean American preschoolers' play emphasized family roles, whereas that of European Americans emphasized danger and fantasy themes. Cultural values seem to be a likely source of these differences.

Regarding amount and ages of pretense, several studies note differences. In one study, American toddlers engaged in more pretend play than did Mexican children (Farver & Howes, 1993). Goncu and his colleagues found that American and Turkish children engaged in more pretend play than did Guatemalan and Indian children (Goncu, Tuermer, Jain, & Johnson, 1999). And Gaskins (1999) noted very few instances of pretend play among Mayan children. Regarding level of pretense, the symbolic play of Japanese 1-year-olds was more advanced than was that of their American counterparts, in a manner that was directly correspondent to the level of play of their mothers (Tamis-LeMonda, Bornstein, Cyphers, Toda, et al., 1992).

Importantly, in all these communities some pretending did occur, and the sequence and level of its occurrence was in keeping with that seen in the review studies (of mainly Euro-American and European children) mentioned in the prior section. Changes in frequency of pretense at different ages seem consistent with parental attitudes and engagement. Where pretense was frequent, adults believed it was important to development, and engaged in it themselves with children. Where it was less frequent, parental attitudes ranged from mildly accepting (it keeps the children out of the way, it is fun for them) to discouraging (the children should be working), and parents did not engage with children. Gaskins (1999) noted that when parents stopped children's pretense it was often because children were inappropriately using household objects (for example, placing fruit on and turning the wheel of a wheelbarrow as if to grind corn).

Pretense play connects with several important cognitive skills: social referencing, reading intentions, quarantine of hypothetical and real worlds, the symbolic function, and role-taking. These connections are examined in the remainder of this chapter.

Social Referencing

In the United States, at least, people pretend in front of very young children. For example, Haight and Miller (1993) found that all eight mothers they studied pretended in front of their 12-month-olds; Kavanaugh et al. (1983), in just 40 minutes of observation, noted 75 distinct pretense utterances by eight mothers playing with 12- to 15-month-olds; and Tamis-LeMonda and Bornstein (1991) found that 16 of 45 mothers pretended with 13-month-olds during a narrow 15 minutes of observation (see also Crawley & Sherrod, 1984). How are such young children to understand acts of pretense?

Knowledge about what is real could be an important cue. A person talking into a banana must be pretending it is a telephone, since we do not typically talk into bananas otherwise. But very young children lack much knowledge about what is real, making their ability to interpret acts as pretense especially puzzling. New events are witnessed every day by young babies; why shouldn't talking into bananas be yet another new real event? One might expect that young children see pretend events as symbols of known real ones right away, and yet their symbolizing abilities do not seem sufficient at such young ages (DeLoache & Smith, 1999; Tomasello, Striano & Rochat, 1999). One possibility is that social referencing abilities enable children to categorize new pretense events as pretense rather than real.

Social referencing is using another person's response to an ambiguous situation as a guide for one's own response (Campos, 1980; Feinman, 1992). In the classic experiments on social referencing, 12-month-olds chose not to venture across an illusory drop-off (the visual cliff) when their mother exhibited a negative expression, but frequently did so when she exhibited a positive one (see also Mumme, Fernald, & Herrera, 1996). In such situations, children appear to adopt the parent's emotional response to an ambiguous situation, and act accordingly. Novel pretense events may present infants with a similarly ambiguous situation: what is one to make of talking into a banana? The infant can properly respond to this novel event if she adopts the parent's emotional stance. If the child fails to adopt the adult's pretend stance towards this event (a stance one might describe as "silly"), the child could become confused by the event, and mix it with her representation of the real world (discussed later). It is quite plausible that the ability to reference adults for appropriate attitudes is a key reason for children not being generally confused by pretense acts. Indeed, the times when children do get confused by pretense may usually be ones in which "silly" signals are not given.

Although this account is speculative, some recent research supports the possibility that infants engage in social referencing when adults pretend in front of them (Lillard & Witherington, 2000). Parents were asked to have a real snack and a pretend snack (in counterbalanced orders) with their young children, each for a two-minute period. Parent behaviors were then analyzed for differences across the two scenarios. Two differences of relevance to social referencing were observed. First, during pretense episodes (relative to real ones), adults smiled more frequently, perhaps signaling the "silly" interpretation. Second, adults looked more often at their infants, and each look was of longer duration, suggesting a possible communicative function of the smiling from the adult's point of view. Hence proper conditions for social referencing were met on the part of the parent. Further analyses will focus on whether infants attended to and adopted the positive affect that the adults displayed towards their activities.

Reading Intentions

In interpreting pretense one must also read through the pretender's actions to his or her intention. For example, if a pretender is flying a pen around through the air, pretending it is an airplane, children must realize that the actor means that the pen is an airplane. The child must cognitively insert a "real" airplane into the scene, in place of the pen. Likewise, if a pretender is holding a stick at her mouth and miming eating actions, children must complete the goal, reading her behavior as "eating" even though the pretender is not actually eating. Pretense acts are instances of ellipsis: something is left out of a scene and must be filled in.

When infants learn to read goals and intentions has recently become a very exciting area of research (Carpenter, Akhtar, & Tomasello, 1998; Gergeley, ch. 2 this volume; Meltzoff, 1995a; Wellman, ch. 8 this volume; Woodward, 1998). This research suggests that by 18 months of age, or even earlier, infants may attribute intentions or goals to actors even when the intended outcomes are not achieved. For example, Carpenter, Akhtar, et al. (1998) used verbal signs to indicate that some acts were intentional (by having the actor say "There!") and others were mistakes (by having the actor say "Whoops!"). Even many 14-month-olds imitated the "There!" but not the "Whoops!" acts, thereby appearing to read which acts were intentional.

Meltzoff's (1995a) experiments go a step farther, requiring that children read the content of an intention – what an adult was trying to do – into unsuccessful attempts at achieving that content. For example, on one trial an adult was shown trying to pull apart the ends of a barbell, but not succeeding. Children were later given the barbell. Eighteen-month-olds were observed to engage in the acts that the adult had been trying to carry out: they pulled the barbell apart. Children who had not observed unsuccessful attempts did not do this; nor did children who had watched a machine "try" to pull the barbells apart.

Pretense scenarios are often like the Meltzoff one, with the cues to what is being pretended located in acts that are often not completed, and with the child needing to decipher missing content. In pretending to eat a pretend cookie (a rock), one raises the rock close to the mouth, and mimics biting and chewing behaviors, but does not actually eat the rock. The child must read through these incomplete acts to what is intended, in order to comprehend pretense acts. Some research suggests that young children are able to do this by at least 2 years of age. When shown pretend gestures (such as a hammering motion, with no object), many 18-month-olds were able to correctly select a hammer (Tomasello et al., 1999). They correctly interpreted that the experimenter's pretend intention was to hammer.

Harris and Kavanaugh (1993) also tested children's ability to read pretense intentions. For example, after watching an experimenter pour pretend tea on one of two pigs, most young 2-year-olds (but not 1-year-olds) correctly dried the one who had been "made wet." This suggests that they correctly understood that the experimenter "intended" by the pretense actions to make that pig wet. Children were probably assisted here by verbal intervention. In pretending at home, parents of 13-month-olds often accompany pretense portrayals with verbal labels that might ease the infants' task of interpretation (Kavanaugh et al., 1983).

Quarantine

A third cognitive skill involved in interpreting an event as pretense is to quarantine the pretend situation from the real one. This skill is also involved in pretending oneself; one should not confuse one's pretend imaginings with the real world (a classic symptom of schizophrenia). The separation of pretense and real has been noted by several theorists, for example, Bateson (1955/1972) pointed out that pretending is a special frame (a concept developed later by Goffman, 1974) that organizes the activities within it; in Ryle's (1949) terms, pretense episodes occur in quotes; Vygotsky (1978) noted that "The child at play operates with meanings detached from their usual objects and actions" (p. 98); and Leslie (1987) described the separation as "decoupling."

The ability to quarantine hypothetical worlds from real ones is a crucial cognitive skill. Unlike social referencing and reading intentions, which are observed in young children when they are not pretending, the ability to quarantine does not appear until later outside of pretense domains. As one example of this, young children's ability to reason hypothetically is relatively poor. However, it improves when the hypothetical premises are placed in a fantasy context (Goswami, ch. 13 this volume; see also Dias & Harris, 1988, 1990; Hawkins, Pea, Glick, & Scribner, 1984; Kuczaj, 1981; Scott, Baron-Cohen & Leslie, 1999). When told, "All pigs can fly. John is a pig," preschoolers usually cannot draw the conclusion that John can fly; but if one precedes the premises with an invocation to pretend (as in "Let's pretend that all pigs can fly") they do significantly better. Recent research shows that pretending is one of a number of means of getting children to drop reliance on what they know is real to engage in hypothetical thinking (Harris, 2000).

Pretense always involves reasoning about a hypothetical world. If children did not hold the pretense world separate from the real one, they would become confused. Pretend acts must be marked as such, as not to be taken seriously or as reflecting the real world. The developing cognitive system's ability to do this is amazing, as Leslie (1987) pointed out. Natural selection, one would think, would evolve a cognitive system that constructs models of how the world actually is; a cognitive system that misrepresents would be suboptimal. So how is it that the cognitive system, especially very young versions of it, can purposefully construct a mis-representation of the world, and reason and act upon it? One pertinent question here is the extent to which very young children actually do keep pretend and real systems separate, such that they know their "misrepresentation" is a misrepresentation.

Logic would suggest that children who are exposed to pretense must usually quarantine pretense events from real ones (Leslie, 1987). Imagine the converse, that young children saw pretense and real events as being of the same kind. If this were the case, then having viewed their mother pretending the banana is a telephone, children would later attempt to answer the banana. They would no longer have a distinct representation of bananas as bananas, because they had perceived the banana as a telephone during that previous encounter. Although I know of no systematic studies of this issue, their lack of report in the literature suggests that these sorts of confusions are rare. For the most part, children probably manage to keep pretense and real identities separate. If pretense were often confused for real, young children who pretend a lot, or who watch others pretend frequently, would be far more confused than they appear to be.

At times, however, young children do appear to mistake pretense for real. This mistake has been referred to as failing to maintain the real–pretense boundary (Scarlett & Wolf, 1979). Three types of situations in which confusion has been noted are discussed next.

Describing events or entities as pretense or real

Children have sometimes appeared confused about the reality status of pretense and real when asked to describe pictures, verbally described events, or television events. Errors occur in three circumstances, in particular. First, when the pretense entities are marginal ones about which adults intentionally deceive children (like Santa Claus or the Tooth Fairy), children sometimes claim the pretense entity is real (Clark, 1995). This is not really surprising, given the orchestrated cultural hoax involved (Santa Claus at the mall; parents, who are usually reliable sources of truth, telling the Santa myth with no visible signs of pretense; letters to Santa; and so on). Many children are seriously duped until they reach an age when the impossibility of the situation dawns on their emerging logic.

Another circumstance in which children err is when the entities that children are asked to classify as pretense or real "walk the boundary" even for adults, as do witches. Witches are often portrayed by real people and act in many ways like real people in movies and stories. Indeed, many otherwise sane-seeming adults also believe witches are real; Luhrman (1989) offers a fascinating account of witchcraft cults in modern-day London. The self-believed "witches" she studied typically had normal day jobs (often as computer programmers!). Although researchers might comfortably assert that witches should be classified as pretense (Morison & Gardner, 1978), children's reduced level of certainty may not reflect a specifically developmental cognitive deficit. (I hope no witches come get me for this!).

The third circumstance in which children do not do well in such tasks is when knowledge is squarely at issue. Sometimes the entities that children are asked to classify are ones with which they have little or no real world experience (such as a moose, portrayed cooking in a kitchen: Samuels & Taylor, 1994). To adults, this is obviously fiction, but given the preponderance of books with talking pigs who live in houses and wear clothes and otherwise behave just like humans, how are young children to know that such animals do not exist somewhere? Likewise, children have been found to be confused about the reality status of television events (such as a marriage on "The Brady Bunch": Downs, 1990), but this is probably due to not understanding television as involving acting. Anthropologist Eve Danziger (personal communication, May, 2000) described a similar case with Mopan Mayan adults in Belize. For entertainment, she was showing the cartoon film *The Jungle Book* . The adults appeared quite confused by the cartoon medium, and repeatedly asked her if it was "true." In sum, some purported cases of pretense–reality boundary breakdown involve classes of entities about which children lack knowledge, even coupled at times with deliberate attempts by adults to make the pretense seem real. These mistakes seem quite different from being mistaken about whether a parent flying a pen about with her hand is flying a pretend or a real airplane.

Scary pretense episodes

A second case in which children have appeared to think that pretense is real involves children's behavioral responses to scary pretend situations. Children occasionally appear truly frightened during scary pretense play, such as pretending to be monsters, and they have even asked to cease playing (Garvey & Berndt, 1975; Scarlett & Wolf, 1979). Consistent with these observations of relatively naturalistic play, Harris and colleagues have found that preschool children will avoid a box after having imagined it contained a scary creature (Harris, Brown, Marriott, Whittall, & Harmer, 1991; Johnson & Harris, 1994). They suggested that preschool children might do this because they sometimes believe that what they imagine can become true, in other words that entities can cross the boundary from pretend into real. Such children really do seem to believe the monster is in the box: Kavanaugh and Harris (Harris, personal communication, September, 2000) recently had pairs of children alone in the room with the box they had imagined contained a monster, and the children discussed, with apparent seriousness, the possible existence of the monster. Interestingly, there is a high degree of individual variability in this tendency, such that some children are prone to the tendency and others are not (Bourchier & Davis, 2000; Johnson & Harris, 1994).

Children's attempts to stop partaking in scary pretense episodes, or to avoid boxes about which they have pretended scary things, may not indicate that they are *generally* susceptible to pretense–reality breakdown. The scary element of the Harris and Johnson situation is probably operative. Indeed, when Woolley and Phelps (1994) had preschoolers imagine a non-scary object in a box, and later children asked to give the imagined object to a confederate experimenter, they did not go to the box for the item. Emotions are usually reliable cues to reality (Damasio, 1994; Zajonc, 1980). Physiological reactions to real and imagined scary events are similar (Lang, 1984). Children, experiencing the physiological signs of fear, might interpret their emotion as a cue to reality (see discussion in Harris, 2000). Further, children are notoriously poor at monitoring sources (Foley, Harris, & Hermann, 1994; Foley & Ratner, 1998). They may fail to note that the source of fear, and indeed of the monster in the box, is purely their own imagination. Having failed to monitor the source, children may proceed to read the feeling of fear associated with that box as emanating from a real situation. In short, pretend–real boundary problems in the case of frightening entities certainly do exist. Yet even adults are not immune to such problems: emotions from pretend events frequently color our real-world behavior and possibly even our representations. Such cases are very interesting, but may not be relevant to more everyday pretense. Next we turn to the third case: young children's ability to quarantine more everyday, nonscary pretense events.

Nonscary pretense episodes

The third type of case to consider, regarding young children's maintaining of the real–pretend boundary, is how frequently children who are engaged in everyday, nonfrightening pretense behave as though the pretense were real. One experiment suggested that even 5-year-olds might have this problem, seeming disoriented when an adult, for example, changed the status of a pretend prop in the middle of a pretend game (DiLalla & Watson, 1988). However, more tightly controlled experiments indicated that by 4 years of age children probably manage quite well to engage in pretense without being disrupted by such interventions (Golomb & Kuersten, 1996). Taylor (1999) also found that the youngest children with whom she spoke about imaginary companions (age 4) sometimes expressed concern that the experimenter was taking their imaginary friend too seriously, and would remind her, as one child did, "It's only pretend, you know." Wellman and Estes (1986) observed that even 3-year-olds were very clear in their understanding of the differences between pretend and real entities. They told children about one boy who had a cookie and another who was just pretending to have a cookie, and asked which boy could eat the cookie, touch the cookie, see the cookie, and so on. Even 3-year-olds did very well, suggesting clear understanding of the difference between pretend and real entities. In a recent review of this area, Woolley (1997) concluded that children are not fundamentally different from adults in their separation of real and pretense.

Can even younger children keep everyday pretense and real episodes separate? Harris and Kavanaugh (1993) suggest that by age 2, children can usually follow pretense episodes even when substitute objects are involved. DeLoache and Plaetzer (1985), in examining mother–child pretense play (at ages 15 through 30 months), saw clear examples of pretense–reality confusion in a quarter of the children studied. For example, when a mother asked a child to wipe up some spilled "tea" the child searched around as though looking for real tea. In our laboratory we also have witnessed signs of confusion when mothers pretend to have a snack with their 18-month-olds. It is uncertain why the confused responses occurred; DeLoache and Plaetzer's (1985) sense was that the mother's pretense was of too elaborate a nature for the child's current level. Other studies show that such ongoing pretense is rare with young children, so perhaps the pretense events that lead to confusion occur too rarely to threaten developing real-world knowledge. Closer analysis of the types of pretense adults engage in with young children, and the length of those episodes, would be helpful. Although logic would suggest that even young children generally must quarantine pretense and real, cases of confusion do exist.

The appearance–reality distinction

A special case of quarantine involves the appearance–reality distinction (Flavell, Green, & Flavell, 1986). As with hypothetical reasoning, there have been suggestions that a pretend frame improves children's ability to understand that appearances can differ from reality. In the generic, non-pretense case, Flavell and his colleagues showed children entities that were purposively deceptive, for example, candles made to look like apples and sponges made to look like rocks. After demonstrating the apparent and real identity of each object, they asked children two questions: What does it look like to your eyes right now? and What is it really and truly? They found a marked change in children's responses from 3 to 4 years of age. Whereas 4-year-olds answered like adults would, saying it looked like an apple but was truly a candle, 3-year-olds gave the same answer to both questions, usually that it looked like and truly was a candle. In other words, young children seemed unable to distinguish reality (candle) from appearance.

The researchers went on to examine whether children's ability to discriminate reality from representation would be somewhat better in the realm of pretense (Flavell, Flavell, & Green, 1987), reasoning that children's regularly pretending that one object is another should facilitate their representational understanding. For example, when a child pretends that a stick is a horse, the child has a representation that he or she maps onto some real object, namely the stick (Lillard, 1993). In such cases, it seems, children can keep reality and representation separate. To test this, in a pretense version of the standard appearance–reality paradigm, the experimenter asked, "Is she pretending that thing is a candle or pretending it's an apple?" In the appearance condition, she asked, "Right now, does that thing look like an apple or look like a candle?" In both cases, the adult was miming eating an apple. Children performed significantly better on the pretense question than on the appearance question, possibly suggesting that pretense is an area of early competence for understanding mental representation, or keeping mental events separate from real ones.

However, an alternative explanation is that children might have done well by interpreting pretense as false action, not false representation (Lillard, 1993). The experimenter was engaging in "pretend-to-eat-an-apple" actions, not actions that would really be addressed at candles, so when asked if she was pretending it was an apple or a candle, they could answer correctly simply by reading off her false behavior. This suggestion has recently been empirically supported by Sodian and Huelsken (Sodian & Huelsken, 1999, April; Sodian, Huelsken, Ebner, & Thoermer, 1998). As in other experiments (Harris & Kavanaugh, 1993; Lillard, 2000; Tomasello et al., 1999) children's quarantining of pretense and real seems dependent on the actions that go along with pretend (discussed later). This has important implications for children's understanding of symbols in pretend play, discussed in the next section.

Summary

There is good evidence that children over age 2 usually understand that pretense events are not real. Exceptions have been noted when the pretense was frightening, involved marginal characters, or was possibly at too high a level. Logic would suggest that young children must not be frequently confused as to the status of pretense events, or children who were exposed to pretense would seem much more confused about the real world than they do.

Pretense Play as Symbolic

In interpreting pretense, children must not only keep pretense separate from real, but they must also understand what real events and objects are symbolized by pretense events and objects. Pretense events and objects refer to their real counterparts, just as words refer to real-world (or abstract) entities. To what extent, when children pretend or watch others pretend, do they perceive the pretend objects and events as symbols of other, real objects and events?

Language

Language has often been held out as a parallel development to pretense, as both appear to involve use and comprehension of symbols (Bates et al., 1979; Piaget, 1945/1962; Werner & Kaplan, 1963). Language production, particularly after the "vocabulary spurt" that often occurs around 18 months, may be assisted by an understanding that words are symbols for referents (Bloom, 1993). If this is the case, then the rapid increase in productive vocabulary is linked to a more general cognitive advance: understanding that one thing (in this case, a word) can stand for another (an object, situation, aspect, etc.). If so, one would expect the production of symbols in pretense to be related to the production of words as symbols. Several studies have found this to be the case: even for children under 18 months of age (e.g., before the typical vocabulary spurt), pretense and language production are significantly correlated (Bates et al., 1979; Nicolich, 1977; Tamis-LeMonda et al., 1992).

However, the notion that either early word or pretense productions are symbolic is not uncontroversial (Huttenlocher & Higgins, 1978; Piaget, 1945/1962; Tomasello et al., 1999). The fact that correlations are observed suggests some common underlying function; exactly what that is deserves further investigation.

Gesture

Pretense comprehension is often measured by imitation: adults demonstrate pretense acts and note if children imitate those acts (Bates, Bretherton, Snyder, Shore, & Volterra,

1980; Fenson & Ramsay, 1981; Ungerer, Zelazo, Kearsley, & O'Leary, 1981). Imitation measures suggested pretense comprehension in children of 13 months (Bates et al., 1980), hence at a similar age to early pretense production. However, the assumption that such imitation implies symbolic understanding is clearly problematic: such actions might involve imitation without comprehension of what the acts and objects symbolized. Recent studies by Harris and Kavanaugh (1993) remedy the imitation problem but replace it with the language one. Children were shown a yellow block and a teddy, and told that the yellow block was teddy's sandwich. Asked to show what Teddy does with his sandwich, on 50 percent of trials children in a younger group (M = 18 months) correctly had Teddy display eating behaviors towards the block; on 75 percent of trials children in an older group (M = 28 months) did. But children might have been responding based on language rather than an underlying understanding of the symbol. Indeed, research by DeLoache (ch. 10 this volume) suggests that symbolic understanding emerges later.

Understanding what pretense acts and objects symbolize appears to develop gradually over the second year, with much scaffolding by more competent players. This scaffolding occurs in two main ways. First, as may be the case with the Harris and Kavanaugh experiment just described, language scaffolds pretense comprehension. Kavanaugh et al. (1983) found that parents of 12- to 21-month-olds initiated almost all pretense episodes by making verbal pretend attributions to objects, thereby facilitating the symbolic mapping task. Second, children may read what is symbolized from pretense gestures. This is suggested by several lines of research.

Tomasello et al. (1999) asked children to select one of four objects to put down a chute. Objects were indicated by either gesture (the gesture condition) or a replica (the symbol condition). For example, children were shown either a hammering gesture (using a fist as the head of the hammer, gesture condition) or a doll-house-sized hammer (symbol condition) and the experimenter said "Can you get me the?" (no verbal referent was provided; in the first case the gesture was enacted and in the second the toy hammer was picked up). Twenty-six-month-olds succeeded in selecting the hammer in both conditions, but 18-month olds succeeded only in the gesture condition. In a more difficult phase of the experiment, children watched the experimenter throw a wadded-up bit of paper into the air, as if it were a ball. Children were later asked to retrieve the "ball" in one of two ways. In the gesture condition, they were shown a different action one could make with a ball (pretending to roll an imaginary ball). In the symbol condition, they were shown a real ball. Only 33-month-olds (not 26-month-olds) retrieved the wadded-up paper ball, and only in the gesture condition. These results suggest that young children's understanding of pretense is guided by their ability to read gestures, not by an ability to see one object (even a replica) as a symbol for another. This is particularly interesting in light of Goldin-Meadow (1997) and her colleagues' recent work showing that new cognitive advances are revealed by children's gestures before they are revealed in other ways. There is a growing sense that activity leads cognition, an insight implicit in Montessori's notion that the hand leads the mind (P. Lillard, 1996) and in Piaget's reliance on action as the source of knowledge (Flavell, 1963).

Findings such as these suggest that comprehension of pretense may not initially involve a symbolic capacity. Children's ability to comprehend pretense symbols lags considerably behind production in both domains and behind language comprehension. If a single ability to see one object as signifying another underlies all four capacities, then pretense comprehension should not lag. Furthermore, an opposing acquisition pattern is seen in language and pretense: in language, comprehension precedes production, so at any given age children understand much more language than they can produce (Benedict, 1979); not so for pretense.

Pretend Play and Social Cognition

Recent work in the area known as theory of mind (Wellman, ch. 8 this volume) suggests there is an association between pretend play and understanding the mental states of others, such that frequent or high-level pretenders also appear to have advanced understandings of others' mental states (Astington & Jenkins, 1995; Connolly & Doyle, 1984; Dunn & Cutting, 1999; Hughes & Dunn, 1997; Lalonde & Chandler, 1995; Lillard, in press; Schwebel, Rosen, & Singer, 1999; Taylor & Carlson, 1997; Watson, 1999, April; Youngblade & Dunn, 1995). It is uncertain what the direction of effects are for this relation. One possibility is that pretense in some way might drive social understanding. One study has included a significant time dimension that suggests this may be the case: Youngblade and Dunn (1995) found that level of pretense at 33 months was related to mental state understanding seven months later. It is also possible that the reverse relation occurs, such that advanced social skills enable pretense, and it is also possible that a third underlying variable drives both pretend play and social cognition. Various means by which the two domains might be related are explored in this section.

Metarepresentation

One way in which pretend play might drive social understanding is via metarepresentation, or mentally representing mental representations (Wellman, ch. 8 this volume). Pretending involves mental states that differ from reality, and children might be aware of this fact while they are pretending. While children are engaged in pretend play, they might reflect on the fact that they are entertaining mental ideas that are distinct from reality, and this understanding could then be applied outside of pretense (Taylor & Carlson, 1997). Some studies purport to support this, whereas others do not (see review in Lillard, 2000). One problem with the early-insight-in-pretense account is that, were it true, one would expect all pretend play to be associated with precocious theory of mind task performance, since both solitary and social pretend play involve having mental representations that differ from reality. However, only social forms of pretending (including social interaction with an imaginary companion, Taylor, 1999) are consistently related, making a link via metarepresentation unlikely.

Decentration

Pretending might also assist social understanding via decentration, moving away from a single point of view to take other views into account (Piaget, 1945/1962). Pretend play seems to require this, because a child must decenter from one view of an object as what it really is, and adopt a different view of what that object is. This same skill is involved in perspective-taking. A body of research conducted in the 1970s did find that perspective-taking skills and pretend play were correlated (Rubin et al., 1983). However, as with metarepresentation, this view is diminished by the fact that social but not solitary pretend play are linked to social cognition.

Role-taking

A skill more specific to social pretense, which might promote social cognition, is role-taking. Children may become, emotionally and mentally, like the characters that they impersonate (Harris, 2000). Practice at taking the perspective of others at least outside of pretense is associated with social understanding. For example, children whose parents discipline them by asking them to imagine how something must feel to someone else are precocious at understanding of belief (Ruffman, Perner, & Parkin, 1999). One important issue is whether young children's pretending involves experiencing the feelings of the characters, or simply playing their roles. Historically, the practice of acting has been a practice of playing roles, not adopting the psychological characteristics of enacted characters. The insight that one could act by "becoming," in a psychological sense, the characters that one played, was the enormous contribution of Stanislavsky (1922/1984) to acting around the turn of the last century. Whether children naturally act in a Stanislavskian manner during sociodramatic play would be a pertinent topic of inquiry.

Social pretend play themes

Social pretense might also lead to understanding minds via the themes children adopt in play. Such themes are frequently emotional in nature, and require the discussion of mental states (Fein, 1989; Haight & Miller, 1993). Several theorists have even argued that a fundamental drive to pretend is to work out emotional issues (Bretherton, 1989; Fein, 1989). In keeping with this emphasis, children use more internal state words while pretending than not (Hughes & Dunn, 1997). In addition, children who pretend frequently use more internal state words than do children who pretend less (Howe, Petrakos, & Rinaldi, 1998). Other studies have shown that children who engage in more discussion about emotions pass theory of mind tasks earlier (Dunn, Brown, & Beardsall, 1991), so it might be simply that role-play pretense provides a context in which many such learning discussions take place. Further, in enacting emotional plots children practice event schemas related to internal states: emotions lead to actions which lead to subsequent emotions and actions (Bretherton, 1989; Nelson & Seidman, 1984; Schank & Abelson, 1977). Hence social pretend play might enable theory of mind because it involves discussion centered around emotional themes, and the practicing of emotion-driven scripts.

Negotiation

The aforementioned possibilities all concern what has been termed "in-frame" pretending: the events and discussion that go on while children are playing at being others. But when children pretend, they sometimes step out of pretense in order to negotiate turns of the plot, object identities, and so on (Giffin, 1984). Indeed, pretend play is often prefaced by several minutes of such negotiations; as children grow older, increasing proportions of play time are given over to out-of-frame negotiation. Another possible way that sociodramatic pretend play might engender social cognitive skills is by forcing children to negotiate their viewpoints and wishes with those of other players (Nelson & Seidman, 1984). Supporting this, siblings engage in more internal state talk during out-of-frame pretense negotiations than during pretense itself (Brown, Donelan-McCall, & Dunn, 1996; Howe et al., 1998) (but see Wolf, Goldfield, Beeghly, Waner, & Cardona, 1985, October, cited in Bretherton, 1989). The foregoing was particularly true of sibling pairs that frequently engaged in pretense, and such pairs also negotiated pretense at a higher level than did less frequent pretenders. Hence the cognitive skills related to understanding minds might be honed by out-of-frame pretending.

Attachment

Children who are securely attached to their parents are likely to engage in pretend play early (Howes & Rodning, 1992; Meins & Russell, 1997), and secure attachment is also associated with better theory of mind performance (Fonagy, 1996; Meins, Fernyhough, Russell, & Clark-Carter, 1997). Secure attachment is also associated with a style of parent–child discourse in which parents frequently discuss feelings and use reason, both of which are associated with theory of mind skills (Ruffman et al., 1999). According to Meins (Meins & Fernyhough, 1997) the links may come about because parents of securely attached children treat their children as mindful beings.

Older peers

Several studies have shown that children with older siblings acquire theory of mind skills relatively early (Jenkins & Astington, 1996; Lewis, Freeman, Kyriakidou, Maridaki-Kassotaki, & Berridge, 1996; Ruffman, Perner, Naito, Parkin, & Clements, 1998) (but see Dunn & Cutting, 1999), and older siblings also lead younger ones to early engagement in sociodramatic play (Dunn, 1988; Dunn & Dale, 1984). For example Youngblade and Dunn (1995) found that the older a first-born child was, the more likely it was that the second-born child would engage in pretend role-play. Even extrafamilial daily peer contacts create such effects: Fein, Moorin, and Enslein (1982) showed that children with more day-care experience engaged in a higher level of pretense than did children without.

Social competence

Social competence might also underlie both theory of mind skills and sociodramatic play. Negotiating with others about pretending requires a certain level of competence. Several studies have shown relationships between social competence and sociodramatic play (Connolly & Doyle, 1984; Howes & Matheson, 1992). For example, Black (1992) has shown that more popular children engage in more pretend play and behave in more socially competent ways during pretense. They were more likely to provide explanations about ongoing play to peers and to include the ideas of peers in their negotiations about play themes and roles. More recently, several researchers have shown relations between sociometric status and theory of mind skills (Dockett & Degotardi, 1997; Dunn & Cutting, 1999).

Personality

Another possible reason for the link between sociodramatic play and theory of mind is an underlying personality dimension, such as interest in people (Lillard, 1998). Two main styles of pretenders, dramatists and patterners, were identified by Wolf (Wolf, Rygh, & Altshuler, 1984). Dramatists frequently enacted plots involving other people, whereas the play of patterners was focused on objects and did not involve social, communicative exchanges. These styles emerged at 1 year of age and remained distinct well into the preschool years. What might underlie these different play styles is degree of interest in people, and being interested in people might in itself lead to earlier development of a theory of mind.

Summary

In sum, several studies have noted consistent respectably strong correlations between various forms of social pretend play and the cognitive skills of understanding others' minds. What underlies these correlations is unclear. There are several possible reasons for the link between social pretend play and social cognitive skills, some of which are direct and others of which involve third variables that could reasonably account for both. Future work should explore the direction and possible sources of the relations between pretend play and social cognitive skills in young children.

Conclusion

Pretending is a fascinating development in young children. Pretend play emerges early and consumes a large portion of young children's unstructured time (Haight & Miller, 1993). It involves a remarkable cognitive feat: the child's mind purposely thwarts reality, making things other than they are, at an age when the child is just learning what reality is. Pretending apparently involves several important cognitive skills, among them social referencing, plying surface behaviors for underlying intentions, quarantining of a pretend world, understanding that entities or events can refer to other ones, and understanding alternative representations of the world. Although several waves of research have made progress toward understanding these interesting relations, the puzzles loom large. Is early pretense symbolic, and when? How do children pick up on pretense when they are just beginning to understand reality? How does the cognitive system manage to quarantine pretense acts? Why do we see correlations between pretending and theory of mind? These questions call for more research, enabling our deeper understanding of a hallmark ability of the human species.

CHAPTER TEN

Early Development of the Understanding and Use of Symbolic Artifacts

Judy S. DeLoache

"a rose is a rose is a rose"

In this famous statement, Gertrude Stein emphasizes that any given rose is incontrovertibly a singular object. Ironically, this oft-quoted line also draws our attention to the fact that a rose can also be something other than a rose. For example, these flowers have traditionally served as symbols of love, death, and success. Roses are not alone; virtually any natural object can be used to stand for something other than itself. Consider the meanings we project onto rainbows, majestic peaks, and dark, dank swamps.

Artifacts can also serve as symbols; indeed, our world is replete with objects that have been specifically designed to fulfill a symbolic function. Symbolic artifacts are a ubiquitous and vital feature of modern life. This fact is well illustrated by William Ittelson's (1996) description of the wealth of pictorial media present in his breakfast room one morning:

> As I sit here at my breakfast table, my morning newspaper has **printing** on it; it has a **graph** telling me how the national budget will be spent, a **map** trying to tell me something about the weather; a table of baseball **statistics**, an engineering **drawing** with which I build a garden chair, **photographs** of distant places and people, a **caricature** expressing what the editor thinks of a political figure . . . On the wall in front of me hangs . . . a **calendar** [and above it] is a **clock**. All this and more, and I haven't even turned on the **TV** or the **computer** . . . (p. 171)

Before proceeding further, we should note that the term "symbol" has been used in many different ways in psychology, as well as in other disciplines. The word has also been used

Preparation of this chapter was supported in part by Grant HD25271 from the National Institutes of Health.

for language and certain gestures. Most of the scholars who have written about symbolization – from Peirce (1903) to Langer (1942) to Deacon (1997) – have been primarily interested in language. In addition, "symbol" is used to refer to purely internal, mental representations – the coding of experience in memory (e.g., Newell & Simon, 1972). A third use – the one of primary relevance to this chapter – is to refer to a variety of artifacts created to serve a referential function. Unlike mental representations or words, many symbolic artifacts are *iconic* representations: They bear some physical resemblance to what they stand for, whereas others have only an abstract relation to what they represent. Although some theorists prefer to reserve the term "symbol" for arbitrary, non-iconic representations (e.g., Peirce, 1903; Bruner, Olver, & Greenfield, 1966), others argue persuasively that iconicity *per se* is irrelevant to whether something serves a symbolic function (e.g., Goodman, 1976; Huttenlocher & Higgins, 1978).

I have offered this definition: *A symbol is something that someone intends to stand for or represent something other than itself* (DeLoache, 1995a). The first and foremost of the four components of the definition is *someone*. Humans are the "symbolic species" (Deacon, 1997); symbolization is the "most characteristic mental trait of mankind" that "makes [us] lords of the earth" (Langer, 1942, pp. 72 and 26). The second element – the very indefinite term *something* – is used quite deliberately in this definition to signify both that almost anything can serve as a symbol for almost anything else. The third element is *representation*. A symbol *represents*, refers to, denotes, something other than itself. As a consequence, symbols are inherently asymmetrical, even when symbol and referent resemble one another. A scale model of the Tower of London represents that structure, but the tower does not represent the model. One important source of this asymmetry is that symbol and referent typically have different action affordances: one can, for example, climb the steps of the real tower, but not the model of it.

The last, but certainly not the least, element of the definition is *intention*: one entity stands for another only if some person *intends* for it to do so. Intention is both necessary and sufficient to establish a symbolic relation (see also Lillard, ch. 9 this volume). Thus, nothing is inherently a symbol; only as a result of someone using it with the goal of denoting or referring does it become a symbol. A dozen long-stemmed red roses can simply be a beautiful sight. Or, presented by a lover to his beloved, the same roses serve as a symbol of love and devotion.

A unique aspect of symbolic objects is that they have an inherently dual or double nature (Kennedy, 1974; Potter, 1979; Sigel, 1978; Werner & Kaplan, 1963). An object, such as a picture, that is created and/or used to serve a symbolic function, is seen both as itself and something entirely different (Gregory, 1970).

> A picture, no matter how "realistic" or "representational," always presents two broad classes of visual information: (1) information that would be provided by viewing the pictured real-world scene . . . and (2) information that is unrelated to the pictured scene but comes from the real-world surface on which the picture appears . . . These two types of information can be analyzed separately by the psychologist, and they can be decoupled by the observer, but they are always encountered together. (Ittelson, 1996, pp. 175–176)

Because of the dual nature of symbolic objects, both aspects of their reality must be represented to use them. *Dual representation* must be achieved; one must think about both the concrete object itself and its abstract relation to what it stands for. As we shall see, the need for dual representation presents a substantial challenge to young children's understanding and use of symbolic objects. They tend to focus on either the conceptual referent or on the symbolic object itself, missing the relation between them (DeLoache, 1995a; Potter, 1979).

A crucial role that symbolic artifacts play in our everyday lives is as a source of information. Interaction with symbols expands our intellectual horizons in both time and space. Because of our access to books, pictures, models, maps, and other media, we can indirectly experience and learn about events, objects, and people we have never directly encountered. From an infant on her father's lap looking at a picture book of zoo animals she has never seen to an adult studying the diagrams in an instruction manual on car repair, new and useful information about the world can be acquired from a variety of symbolic artifacts. A weather map seen on television can be an excellent source of information for making travel plans. A scale model of the Rotunda designed by Thomas Jefferson can provide useful clues for understanding Palladian architecture.

Given the important informational role of symbolic artifacts and the degree to which our world knowledge is symbolically mediated rather than acquired through direct experience, the process of coming to understand and use symbols as a source of information is a vital part of early cognitive development. All children, everywhere in the world, must master the symbols and symbol systems that are important in their society. In spite of the importance of learning from symbols, we know relatively little about how children develop the ability to do so.

There is, of course, an enormous body of research on symbolic development, with by far the most work on language development. With respect to symbolic artifacts, researchers have investigated children's developing abilities to interpret and produce instances of various media. Substantial attention has been paid to pictures, both with respect to children's ability to interpret pictures and to produce them through drawing (Freeman, 1993; Robinson, Nye, & Thomas, 1994; Thomas, Nye, & Robinson, 1994), as well as children's interpretation of television (Huston & Wright, 1998). Pretend play has also been the focus of a substantial amount of research (see Lillard, ch. 9 this volume). However, other than research on maps (Liben, 1999, ch. 15 this volume; Uttal, 2000a), little attention has been paid to young children's ability to acquire information via symbols. And virtually no research has examined the emergence and very early development of children's use of symbol-mediated information. The research that is the focus of this chapter concerns very young children's ability to appreciate and exploit the relation between a symbolic artifact and some aspect of reality that it represents. Most of the research discussed concerns children's use of information from three types of symbols – scale models, pictures, and video.

Symbol-Mediated Problem-Solving

In the program of research discussed here, young children's understanding of symbolic artifacts is studied by using symbols to provide them with information to solve a problem.

If the children appreciate the relevance of the symbol, it is relatively easy to solve the problem using the symbol-mediated information. If they do not understand the relevance of the symbol to the problem at hand, they have no means of solving it.

The basic problem is retrieving a hidden object. Finding an object that they have observed being hidden is well within the competence of very young children: After watching as an attractive toy is hidden somewhere in a natural environment, children as young as 18 months of age are very successful at retrieving it, even after relatively long delays (e.g., DeLoache & Brown, 1979, 1983). In other words, even children younger than 2 years of age remember the information they receive by directly observing a hiding event and are able to use that information to guide their search for a hidden toy. The question addressed in the research described here is whether children can remember and use information that they experience *indirectly*, that is, information presented to them via a symbolic medium. The underlying question is whether children understand the relevant *symbol–referent relation*.

Scale model task

The majority of the research that I and my colleagues have conducted investigating this question has employed a scale model as the source of information about the current state of reality, that is, about the current location of a hidden object (see DeLoache, 1995a, and DeLoache, Miller, & Pierroutsakos, 1998, for reviews of this work). Typically, the model is a realistic scale model of a regular room containing miniature items of furniture corresponding to the items of furniture in the room itself. The miniature items are highly similar in surface appearance to their larger counterparts in the room, and they are in the same spatial arrangement. The children in these studies typically receive an extensive orientation in which the relation between the model and room and all the individual items contained in them is described in detail and demonstrated by the experimenter. A crucial part of the orientation is that the experimenter takes each of the miniature items of model furniture into the room and directly compares it to its larger counterpart.

On each of the retrieval trials, children watch as the experimenter hides a miniature toy ("Little Snoopy" – a toy dog – or "Little Terry" – a troll doll) somewhere in the model (behind the couch, under a chair, etc.). They are told that a larger toy ("Big Snoopy," "Big Terry") will be hidden in the corresponding place in the room itself, and they are instructed to remember where the smaller one is hidden in the model so they will know where to find the larger one in the room. After the experimenter hides the larger toy, the children are invited to find it. The only way they know where to search for the large toy in the room is if (1) they remember where the small one is in the model, and (2) they understand the relation between the model and room and between the hiding events in the two spaces.

After searching in the room, the children return to the model to find the miniature toy they had originally observed being hidden. This serves as a memory and motivation check. If the children can find the toy in the model, it indicates they remember the hiding event they observed earlier and they are motivated to find it. Thus, if they fail to retrieve the larger toy in the room, it must be for some other reason than memory or motivational problems.

Picture and video tasks

The same symbolic object-retrieval task has also been used with pictures and video. Various types of pictures have been used, ranging from highly realistic photographs of single items of furniture in the room to colored line drawings of the entire room. In the picture task, children again receive an extensive orientation to the relation between the picture or pictures and the room. On each trial, the experimenter points to the appropriate picture or to a location on a picture to communicate to the children the location of the toy in the room. In the case of video, children again receive an extensive orientation, designed to demonstrate to the child that what they see on a monitor is being filmed at the same time. They see themselves, their parent, and the room on the monitor as the experimenter talks about what they are looking at and how it is being filmed by the camera. On the retrieval trials, the child watches on the video monitor as the experimenter goes into the room and hides the toy. The child is then invited to search for it. Again, the question is whether children are able to use the relevant symbol–referent relation to solve the problem, with successful retrieval taken as evidence that the children appreciate something about the nature of that relation.

Our symbol-mediated object-retrieval tasks are thus essentially analogical reasoning problems, in which children must reason from a base to a target problem (Goswami, 1992, and ch. 13 this volume). The target problem is finding the toy that is hidden in the room. To solve it, the child has to use the base information he or she has been given via a symbol to construct a mental model of the location of the toy. The unique element is that the base information is provided via a symbolic artifact (DeLoache, Miller, & Pierroutsakos, 1998).

Advantages of the symbolic object-retrieval task

There are several advantages to this format for investigating the early development of symbolic understanding (Marzolf & DeLoache, 1997). An important one has to do with the relatively low verbal demands made by this task. Children do, of course, have to understand the simple instructions they are given, but they are not required to respond verbally. Therefore, performance in these search tasks is much less likely to be confounded with limited verbal ability, a perennial problem in research with young children.

A related advantage is that we can be reasonably confident that even very young children will encode and remember the base information. Young children generally perform more competently on memory tests that require them to retrieve a hidden object than they do in standard verbal memory tasks (Myers & Perlmutter, 1978), and their memory-based retrieval performance is very good. For example, after observing a toy being hidden somewhere in a room, 18- to 24-month-old children retrieve it over 80 percent of the time (DeLoache & Brown, 1983).

Furthermore, since the dependent variable is searching for a hidden object, children's performance is unambiguous: Either they find the toy in the first location they search, or they do not. (Our results are typically reported only in terms of children's first

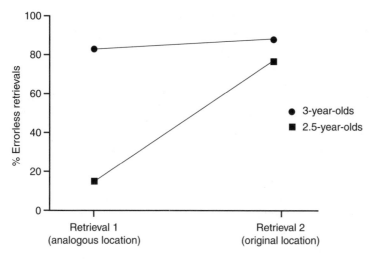

Figure 10.1   The performance of 2.5- and 3-year-old children in the standard model task. Both age groups are successful on the memory-based retrieval 2, but only the 3-year-olds succeed on the symbol-mediated retrieval 1

search.) Because very young children's behavior is often difficult to interpret, the relatively straightforward nature of the relevant response is another benefit of object-retrieval tasks.

Another beneficial feature of search tasks for studying toddlers is that these tasks are highly motivating. One of the major challenges in doing research with young children is designing tasks that will engage and hold their attention. By capitalizing on young children's natural enjoyment of searching for hidden objects, we can obtain reliable and consistent data, even from such a notoriously uncooperative age group.

Finally, object-retrieval tasks have relatively high ecological validity. Searching for objects is ubiquitous in everyday life, and children are frequently faced with the need to retrieve misplaced shoes and mittens and to locate items needed for play. Thus, this part of the task is highly familiar to young children. The only unfamiliar part is receiving the information about where to search from a symbol. The set of advantages of search tasks means that we do not have to worry that our results will be caused by something other than what we wish to study – children's understanding of symbol–referent relations. As it turns out, the simplicity of our task has revealed a wealth of complexity in young children's developing symbolic abilities.

Young Children's Performance in Symbolic Object-Retrieval Tasks

The original scale model study resulted in the pattern of results shown in figure 10.1 (DeLoache, 1987). This study was based on the *standard model task*, in which the room was a large room with basic living-room furniture, and the model contained miniature items of furniture that were in the same spatial positions and that were highly similar in appearance to those in the room. The older children in this study were 3-year-olds, and the younger ones were 2.5-year-olds. Retrieval 1 refers to finding the larger toy in the room, based on the hiding event the children had seen in the model; hence, this search is symbol-mediated. Retrieval 2 is finding the miniature toy in the model; hence, this search is based on direct experience.

As is apparent in the figure, both the older and younger children were highly successful at retrieving the miniature toy in the model. Having directly observed a hiding event, they remembered the location of the toy and successfully retrieved it. The older children, the 3-year-olds, were equally successful in the symbol-mediated retrieval. They used their memory representation of the location of the miniature toy in the model to figure out where to search for the larger toy in the room. There was no difference between their success in the retrievals based on direct versus symbol-mediated experience. In contrast, the younger children, the 2.5-year-olds, had virtually no idea where to search in the room. They failed to use their memory for where the miniature toy was in the model to infer where to find the larger toy in the room.

This pattern of results reveals a large difference in the understanding of the two age groups of the relation between the model and the room, that is, the symbol–referent relation. The difference apparent in the mean levels of performance shown in figure 10.1 is equally evident in the performance of the individual children: The great majority of 3-year-olds are successful in the retrieval task (over 75 percent correct on Retrieval 1), and the great majority of 2.5-year-olds are markedly unsuccessful. Thus, the older children clearly appreciated the symbol–referent relation and used it to succeed in the task. The younger children gave no evidence of understanding anything about the model–room relation.

This basic pattern of performance has been replicated many times, both in our lab and others (O'Sullivan, Mitchell, & Daehler, 1999; Dow & Pick, 1992; Sharon, 1999; Solomon, 1999). Across a large number of studies that have been performed using various versions of the standard scale model task, as well as other symbolic object-retrieval tasks, the performance of children of 2.0, 2.5, 3.0, and 3.5 years of age has been shown to vary dramatically as a function of age and several task factors. A consistent but complex pattern of results has emerged. Accounting for this complex pattern of performance requires consideration of the interaction of several different variables.

A Model of Young Children's Symbol Use and Understanding

A substantial amount of research using the scale model and other symbolic-retrieval tasks led to the formulation of a conceptual *Model of Symbol Understanding and Use*. The model shown in figure 10.2 is a revision of one published earlier (DeLoache, 1995a, 1995b). Note that this is not a formal path model; rather it is a heuristic representation of several factors known or hypothesized to affect young children's ability to understand and use a symbolic artifact as a source of information. Note also that the pivotal element in the model is *representational insight*. This component concerns children's insight into the existence of a symbol–referent relation in a particular task. Thus, the model represents the

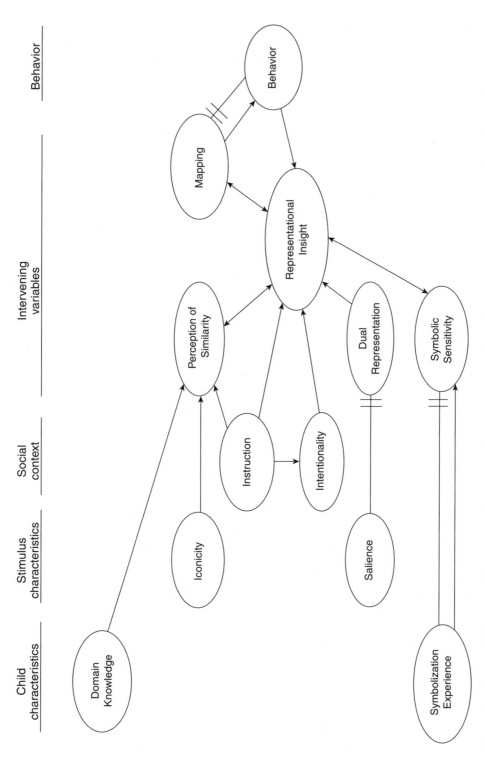

Figure 10.2 A *model* of young children's understanding and use of symbols (an earlier version appeared in DeLoache, 1995a, 1995b)

factors that combine to determine the likelihood that young children will achieve representational insight and hence be successful in a specific situation. Representational insight does *not* refer to children's ability to understand and use symbols in general. Their general symbolic ability does, as will be discussed later, influence the likelihood of achieving representational insight in any specific task. We will briefly describe the components of the model and then focus in detail on some of the evidence for each of them. We will particularly highlight some relatively recent results regarding intentionality that motivated revision of the original model.

Behavior and mapping

Starting at the end point, the *behavior* in question in this research is, of course, retrieving a hidden object, based on a mental representation of the correct location. *Mapping* is the process of constructing and using a mental representation of the current location of the toy in the room based on what was observed via the symbolic artifact (model, picture, or video image). To map from symbol to referent, children must draw on their memory representation of the location of the small toy in the model, and based on insight into the general model–room relation, infer the location of the large toy in the room. Their mental representation of that inferred location must then serve as the guide for their search behavior in the room.

The perception of similarity

Physical similarity always makes it easier to detect the relation between two entities, and it plays an important role in relational reasoning of various sorts (DeLoache, Miller, & Pierroutsakos, 1998). The more two things resemble one another, the more likely it is that one will believe they belong to the same conceptual category. In analogical reasoning problems, higher levels of surface similarity between base and target increase the likelihood that the relation between them will be detected.

The same is true for symbolic retrieval tasks. A high level of iconicity between symbol and referent facilitates reasoning between them. In the standard model task, described briefly above, there is a high level of surface similarity between model and room, including similar surface appearance (color, fabric, material) of the miniature and full-sized items of furniture. The importance of this similarity is shown by the fact that the high level of performance achieved by 3-year-olds in this task (see figure 10.1) can be seriously disrupted by decreasing the level of physical similarity between the scale model and the room. When the items of furniture in the two spaces do not look so similar, 3-year-olds perform at the same low level as 2.5-year-olds do with high similarity. With age, children become able to cope with this lower level of similarity: 3.5-year-olds are highly successful in the low-similarity task that is so difficult for 3-year-olds.

Increasing similarity has an equally strong effect in the opposite direction for 2.5-year-olds. If the larger space is only twice as large as the scale model (rather than 16 times as large as in the standard model task), 2.5-year-olds are reasonably successful, achieving a retrieval rate of around 70 percent (DeLoache, Kolstad, & Anderson, 1991; Marzolf & DeLoache, 1994).

Although iconicity has a strong effect on young children's performance in symbolic retrieval tasks, the perception of similarity between symbol and referent is not enough for success. For example, in one study, the experimenter pointed to one of the items in the model and asked 2.5-year-old children to show her one just like it in the room. The children readily matched the individual items of furniture in the model and room. However, when tested in the standard model task minutes later, they failed. Although they knew that the little couch was like the big couch, they still failed to realize that the fact that the miniature toy was hidden behind the small couch meant that the larger toy was hidden behind the large couch. Thus, appreciating the correspondence between the individual items of furniture in the two spaces is necessary, but not sufficient for success in the task.

Dual representation

Representational insight – and successful symbol use – requires *dual representation*. To use a symbolic artifact as a source of information, children must mentally represent both the concrete entity itself and, at the same time, its abstract relation to its referent. Achieving dual representation is a major challenge to young children's symbolic understanding and use. One reason, which is not at all specific to symbols, is that it is generally difficult for young children to have two active representations of a single entity (Zelazo & Frye, 1996). Specifically with respect to symbol use, the concrete features of a symbolic artifact can interfere with young children's ability to notice its relation to what it stands for. A realistic scale model like those used in our research is a highly salient, attractive, interesting object in and of itself. It affords and even invites direct physical activity – playing with the items of furniture contained in it, for example. This makes it hard for young children to treat it as standing for something other than itself. The younger the child, the more difficult it is to notice and think about both the concrete model itself and its relation to the room it stands for.

A picture or video image is much less physically salient than a model, and it has no competing affordances; there is little one can do with a two-dimensional representation other than look at it, talk about it, or think about its relation to what it represents. Thus, it should be easier to achieve dual representation with pictorial images than with real objects. This hypothesis was confirmed in a series of studies in which the experimenter pointed to a photograph of the room while telling the child, "This is where Snoopy's hiding." In every comparison, 2.5-year-olds succeeded in the various picture tasks but not in the model task (DeLoache, 1987, 1991; Marzolf & DeLoache, 1994). The superior performance by 2.5-year-old children with pictures versus real objects is strong evidence for the concept of dual representation, because such a result is counterintuitive on any other basis. Children typically perform better when real objects are used in a wide variety of cognitive tasks (such as memory or categorization tasks) than when pictures serve as stimuli.

The importance of dual representation in young children's use of symbols has received substantial empirical support from the confirmation of a series of other theoretically motivated, but similarly counterintuitive predictions. *Decreasing* the salience of a model by placing it behind a window enables 2.5-year-olds to succeed in the model task, whereas *increasing* the physical salience of a model by letting 3-year-olds play with it for several minutes before the retrieval task leads to significantly poorer performance (DeLoache, 2000). *Eliminating* the need for dual representation altogether also enhances performance: 2.5-year-olds who were led to believe that a scale model was actually a room that had been shrunk by a "shrinking machine" successfully retrieved the miniature toy based on where they had seen the larger toy being hidden in the room (DeLoache, Miller, & Rosengren, 1997).

The challenge that achieving dual representation presents for young children is not limited to symbolic retrieval tasks. For example, Tomasello and his colleagues have shown that young children can interpret gestural symbols earlier than object symbols (Tomasello, Striano, & Rochat, 1999). When an experimenter used either a symbolic gesture or a replica object to communicate which of a set of objects was the correct one, children below 2 years of age more often selected the object indicated by a gesture than the one the experimenter denoted by holding up a replica of it. Thus, the replica objects, which require dual representation were more difficult for these young children to interpret symbolically than were gestures, which do not require dual representation.

Other examples of dual representation problems come from the work of Liben and Downs (1992; Liben, ch. 15 this volume), who have documented a number of cases in which young children misinterpret the relation between a map and the space it represents. For example, when told that a red line on a highway map was a road, one child argued that it could not be because roads are not red, and another rejected the line on the basis that it was too narrow for a car. These children are responding in an overly literal way to the map, confusing its concrete and abstract nature.

Symbolic sensitivity

The only specific element in the model having to do with why children exploit symbolic artifacts more successfully with age is *symbolic sensitivity*. Adults readily assume that any novel entity they encounter may have a symbolic function, but children do not make this assumption so easily. As they gain experience with symbols, children develop a general expectation or readiness to look for and detect symbolic relations among entities. Thus, *symbolization experience* generally increases their readiness to respond to novel entities in an abstract rather than concrete mode. This view is consistent with Sigel's (1970) concept of distancing: In common is the notion that children become increasingly able to achieve psychological distance from concrete entities, enabling them to think about those entities more abstractly. Young children who are able to inspect a scale model with calm detachment rather than an overwhelming desire to get their hands on it are more likely to appreciate its relation to the room it stands for.

Support for the importance of experience in performance in the symbolic-retrieval task comes from a series of transfer studies in which children of a given age are first given experience with a task on which they can succeed – and in which they presumably achieve representational insight. When subsequently presented with a task their age group normally fails, they are now successful. For example, in one study, 3.0-year-olds successfully transferred from a high-similarity (standard) model task to a low-similarity one. In another study, 2.5-year-olds who had first performed well in a similar-scale model task later did equally well in the more difficult different-scale (standard) task (Marzolf & DeLoache, 1994). Similarly, 2.5-year-olds show substantial transfer from a picture or video to the scale model task (DeLoache, 1991; Troseth & DeLoache, 1998). (Additional transfer studies will be discussed later.)

The social context

The social context of the symbolic-retrieval task is of great importance. The nature and extent of the *instructions* that children receive about the symbol–referent relation profoundly affect their performance (DeLoache, 1989). The success of 3-year-olds depends critically on receiving very extensive instructions and demonstrations of the model–room relation. Their performance, and even that of 3.5-year-olds, is dramatically disrupted by slightly less complete instructions (such as leaving out the explicit comparison of all the individual items of furniture in the two spaces). Not until 4 years of age can children detect the model–room relation with less than the standard extensive orientation to the task, and not until 5 to 6 years are they able to figure it out with no instructions about the relation at all (DeLoache, DeMendoza, & Anderson, 1999).

Another aspect of the social context of the task is *intentionality* (a new element in the model). As discussed above, an inherent aspect of any symbol–referent relation is the intention of the creator and/or user of that relation. A hiding event in a scale model is informative about a hiding event in a different space only because someone makes it so. There is no direct causal link; it is only by virtue of the adult's intention to hide the toys in corresponding locations that the hiding event in the model has significance for the unseen event in the room. Presumably, a mature understanding of the symbol–referent relation in our symbolic object-retrieval tasks includes some recognition of the intention that establishes it.

Very young children are clearly sensitive to adult intention and use it as a guide in many ways. One clear demonstration of this is research by Meltzoff (1995a; ch. 1 this volume) in which 18-month-old infants observe an adult apparently *trying*, but failing, to do something to a toy. When children are later given the toy, they imitate what they assumed the adult wanted to do to the toy, rather than what he actually did. Children also rely on an adult's apparent intention in learning new words. For example, after hearing an adult announce her intention to "dax" a toy, children assumed that "dax" referred to an action that apparently produced an intended result but not to an action that appeared to result in the same outcome accidentally (Tomasello & Barton, 1994).

Intentionality is also important in young children's judgments about pictures. For example, Bloom and Markson (1998) reported that 3- and 4-year-old children believe that a drawing is of whatever the person who drew it intended it to be. Thus, even though someone's drawing of *X* may look at least as much like *Y*, it is a drawing of *X* if that's what the individual intended to draw. Similarly, research by Gelman and Ebeling

(1998) shows that young children regard a picture that looks like some particular entity (e.g., a bear) to be a picture *of* that entity only if it was produced intentionally, not accidentally.

In a recent series of studies, we have been examining the role of intentionality in young children's success or lack thereof in symbolic object-retrieval tasks. In some studies, we have asked whether we could improve their performance by emphasizing the intentional nature of a symbol–referent relation. In a second series, the focus is the extent to which young children assign precedence to the experimenter's intention over other aspects of the task.

Emphasizing the intentional nature of the model–room relation

We have recently tried to improve the performance of two age groups of young children by highlighting the intentional nature of the model–room relation. To do so, we modified the standard task in several ways. First, the children were given a "blind" trial in which they were told that Snoopy was hidden in the room and they should try to find him. The point was to make them realize that they had no way of knowing where the toy was. Next a "helpful" assistant to the experimenter indicated that she could help the child know how to find the toy. She then proceeded to assemble the model of the room, commenting on the similarity between the two spaces and explaining how the model would help the child know where Snoopy was hidden. On the first hiding trial, after the experimenter entered the room to hide the larger toy, the "helper" assumed a conspiratorial stance, peeking through the door as the experimenter was hiding the toy. She then hid the miniature toy in the model, telling the child this would help her know where Snoopy was hiding in the room. Finally, the child searched in the room.

A group of 3-year-old children received this assistance in the context of the low-similarity task that their age group typically fails. Their success rate of 52 percent indicates that they benefited to some degree from the "helpful" experimenter's efforts to clue them in to the model–room relation. However, a group of 2.5-year-olds, who were given the standard task that their age group typically fails, showed less benefit from the helpful assistant's conspiratorial behavior (only 31 percent). Thus, we find that emphasizing the intentional nature of the adults' actions in the task can assist 3-year-olds to appreciate the model–room relation, but, at least in this initial study, 2.5-year-olds were less receptive to the intervention.

Children's explicit awareness of the model–room relation

In another recent study, we asked whether young children's understanding of the intentional nature of the model–room relation is explicit enough to enable them to ignore irrelevant information. A group of 3.5-year-olds participated in the standard model task, with two very non-standard trials interpolated among four regular ones. On the two "accidental hiding" trials, the children watched as the experimenter hid the miniature toy in the model as usual and then went into the room to hide the larger toy. At this point, a second, "clumsy" experimenter "accidentally" kicked the model, dislodging its contents. She replaced all the furniture in the correct locations. Then, picking up the miniature toy, she said, "Hmm, I don't know where this was; I'll just put it here." She proceeded to put the toy in a different place from where the experimenter had hidden it.

The question was whether the children would realize that the "accidental" hiding was irrelevant to where the larger toy was hidden in the room. In other words, would they realize that the intention of the first experimenter determined its location, not the last hiding event that had actually taken place in the model.

The results were quite clear. The children ignored the "accidental" hiding to the extent that their retrieval performance did not suffer at all. Performance was 80 percent on the standard trials and 75 percent on the accidental trials. Thus, these children recognized the importance – and information value – of the experimenter's intentions in hiding the two toys. We are currently examining whether younger children (3-year-olds) are similarly sensitive to the intentional basis for the model–room relation.

Representational insight

As noted before, the pivotal element in the model is *representational insight*, the recognition of the existence of a symbol–referent relation. As figure 10.2 shows, mapping occurs in a particular task only if representational insight is achieved in that task. In the symbolic object-retrieval task, only if children appreciate the way that the model (or picture or video) is related to the room it stands for do they transfer their knowledge from the symbol to the referent. Although previous versions of the model showed some other factors as having a direct impact on mapping, it has become clear that successful performance is always mediated by representational insight.

The level of awareness involved in this insight can obviously be explicit knowledge of the relation that is accessible to conscious reflection and verbalizable, such as an adult or older child would have. However, it can also be some implicit form of insight that enables young children to successfully exploit the symbol–referent relation in our retrieval tasks even though they do not show evidence of awareness of that relation.

There are three aspects of children's performance in the scale model and other retrieval tasks that provide strong support for the idea that the key factor is whether or not children achieve representational insight.

The difficulty of improving performance

A second form of support for the idea that children must achieve representational insight is the great difficulty we have experienced trying to improve children's performance in our tasks. Over the years, we have tried a very large number of manipulations designed, often with great optimism and enthusiasm, to raise the performance of 2.5-year-olds in the scale model task. Although a few have succeeded (most notably the various transfer procedures), most have not. We very recently added some more unsuccessful interventions to the long list.

One was designed to highlight the idea that corresponding hiding events take place in the two spaces. In the orientation to this study, 2.5-year-olds watched two simultaneous hiding events, one in the model and one in the room. The model was positioned so the children could readily see into both it and the room. In the orientation to the task, two experimenters (one near the model and the other in the room) drew the children's attention to their hiding of the miniature and larger toys in the model and room, inviting them to look back and forth between the two events. Then the children searched – successfully – for both toys. Following this orientation, the children were given the standard model task in which they observed a hiding event in the model and then searched in the room. In spite of the orientation in which they saw the analogous hiding events taking place in the two spaces and searched successfully in both of them, the children now failed to use the hiding event they observed in the model as a guide for searching in the room.

Another unsuccessful effort was based on modeling. Strong evidence exists for imitation by toddlers and even infants (e.g., Barr & Hayne, 2000; Heimann & Meltzoff, 1996; Meltzoff, ch. 1 this volume). We thought that if 2.5-year-old children observed another person successfully performing in the model task, it might help them appreciate the basis for that person's success – especially if she explained what she was doing (Troseth, 2001). For this study, the child and an adult assistant observed the experimenter hide two miniature toys together in the same location in the model. The experimenter then hid two large toys in the corresponding location in the room. Then the child watched as the assistant retrieved one of the larger toys in the room, narrating her thought processes: "Let's see, I know Kathy hid Little Snoopy behind the couch, so that means she hid Big Snoopy behind his big couch. I'm going to look there." Next the child was given the opportunity to search for the remaining hidden toy. At this point, the child had observed the experimenter perform the original hiding event at a location in the model and the assistant search successfully at that same location in the room. Performance was 28 percent. Watching someone else use the model as a source of information clearly did not make these children aware of its relevance and usefulness. Exactly the same result occurred for a group of 2.0-year-olds in an analogous version of the video task. After watching on a monitor as the experimenter hid two toys in the room and the assistant successfully retrieved one of them, the children still failed to use the video-based information to find the remaining toy.

One other recent series of studies provided further evidence of the difficulty of improving the performance of very young children in our tasks (although in this particular case, we actually expected a negative result). This time the goal was to see if increasing children's motivation to find the hidden object would improve their retrieval performance. In a series of studies referred to in our lab as "Hide-a-Mom," the hidden object was something we could be certain any child would be extremely highly motivated to find – his or her own mother or father. To do this study, we added some hiding places to the room large enough to conceal an adult (e.g., a card table covered with a floor-length table cloth, a curtain across a corner of the room). Corresponding features were of course added to the model. On each trial, the child's parent – usually mother – hid in the room. A doll was placed in the model to show the child where Mom was waiting. The children loved the task; they were excited to search for their mothers and were filled with glee when –

typically with the experimenter's assistance – they were reunited. They did not, however, know where their mothers were; the level of correct retrievals was only 38 percent, no significant improvement over the standard level. Again, exactly the same pattern was found in a video study in which 2.0-year-olds watched on a monitor as their mother went into the room and hid herself. Thus, heightened motivation does not increase young children's use of symbol-mediated information in object-retrieval tasks.

These three recent failures to improve young children's performance (and the many that preceded them) testify to the imperviousness of young children to manipulations that any reasonable person might expect would help them. This long list of failures makes all the more remarkable the interventions that have succeeded.

Successful transfer

We have been extremely successful in improving children's performance via transfer (Marzolf & DeLoache, 1994). As described earlier, these studies show that an appreciation of one symbol–referent relation can help children recognize a more difficult one that children their age do not typically grasp, in other words, the attainment of representational insight in one task increases greatly the likelihood that they will achieve representational insight in another one.

A transfer study conducted relatively recently (Marzolf, Pascha, & DeLoache, 1996) provides further evidence that success in the model task involves an appreciation of the higher-order model–room relation. In that study, 2.5-year-old children were first given the easy similar-scale task described previously. This task was administered by two experimenters in a lab in one building using one set of toys as hidden objects. As expected, the children's performance was reasonably good (63 percent). A full week later, the same children were given the more difficult dissimilar-scale (standard) task by two different experimenters in a different lab in a different building using a second set of toys. A control group received the difficult task twice with only one day intervening. Thus, the only thing that was the same over the two sessions was the underlying structure of the tasks – using a model as a source of information about the location of a toy in a larger space. As expected, the control group performed poorly on both days (16 percent and 31 percent). The transfer group performed significantly better than the control group on the difficult task (69 percent): their success with the easy model–room relation helped them recognize a similar but more difficult relation a full week later, even with very little contextual support. Thus, these results indicate that transfer was supported by a relatively abstract representation of the relevant symbol–referent relations.

Very recently, Troseth (2000) found dramatic levels of transfer using the video task in which 2.0-year-old children typically perform relatively poorly (around 40 to 45 percent correct). In this series of studies, 2.0-year-olds were given experience with live video in their own homes before being tested in the lab. The goal was to help the children realize that what they observe on a television screen can have relevance for current reality. In our laboratory studies (Troseth & DeLoache, 1998), children have always been given experience seeing themselves, their parent(s), the experimenters, and the room on live video. However, this orientation typically lasts for only five to ten minutes. In the new study, the children's parents were asked to film them several times over a two-week period. The film was simultaneously shown live on their television set, and the parents drew the children's attention to the relation between what they were doing and what they saw on the screen. Thus, the children received extensive experience with the relation between their own and others' behavior and images they saw on television.

The children were then brought into the laboratory where they participated in the standard video task in which they watched on video as the experimenter hid the toy in the room next door. They successfully retrieved the toy 77 percent of the time, significantly more often than a control group (approximately 40 percent). Thus, experience with live video at home facilitated these children's insight into the relation between the hiding event they saw on the monitor and the unseen hiding event in the other room. Furthermore, these children were then given a second transfer test – they were tested in the standard picture study. Recall that 2.0-year-old children have been markedly unsuccessful (usually around 15 percent) in the picture task. However, the group of children who had the home video experience and who had then performed well on the video task also performed well on the picture task (60 percent correct). Their success in the picture task could have been based on their home video experience, their success in the video retrieval task, or – more likely – on both.

These and many other transfer studies we have performed using various media provide strong evidence that young children's early understanding of the correspondence between a symbolic artifact and the space it stands for involves insight into the higher-order symbol–referent relation. Once children gain representational insight into one type of symbolic relation, they readily detect another symbol–referent relation of which they would otherwise remain unaware.

Inhibitory control hypothesis

An alternative account of young children's difficulty in the basic model task has recently been ruled out. This alternative is the idea that poor inhibitory control, manifested as a strong tendency for response perseveration, causes young children to perform poorly. In the model task (and in object-retrieval tasks generally), the predominant error children make is to perseverate, that is, to return to the location where they found the toy (usually with the experimenter's assistance) on the previous trial. Across many studies and multiple labs, over half of all errors in symbolic retrieval tasks are perseverative (e.g., DeLoache, 1999; DeLoache & Burns, 1994; O'Sullivan, Mitchell, & Daehler, 1999; Sharon, 1999; Solomon, 1999).

It is possible that this high level of perseverative responding masks insight into the basic symbol–referent relation; even if children had some understanding of the model–room relation, for example, they might perform poorly because of difficulty inhibiting a prepotent (previously rewarded) response. Thus, on a given trial, the child might have a representation of the location of the toy, but fail to search there because of being drawn to repeat his or her previous response. Support for this idea comes from some studies in which performance was significantly better on the first trial than on subsequent ones (Schmitt, 1997; Sharon, 1999; Troseth & DeLoache, 1998).

The possible importance of perseveration as a cause of poor performance in the model task was evaluated in two ways. First, Sharon and DeLoache (2000) analyzed existing data from 13 separate groups of 2.5-year-olds in the standard model task. The results did not support the idea that 2.5-year-old children know more about the model–room relation than their performance reveals. Although performance on the first trial was significantly better than on the second trial, the difference was quite small, and performance subsequently improved. In addition, the level of perseveration actually decreased over trials, exactly the opposite of what one would expect if perseveration were a significant factor in children's performance. Finally, the children almost never corrected their search errors; if children have a mental representation of the correct location but cannot resist repeating their previous response, one would expect that they would go to the correct place after performing an incorrect search.

The second way the limited inhibitory control hypothesis was evaluated was by an experiment designed specifically to address this issue (Sharon & DeLoache, 2000). Following pilot work by Sharon (1999), the standard model task was modified to make it less likely children would repeat their previous response. The question was whether decreasing the level of perseverative responding would lead to an increase in correct responding; if 2.5-year-olds' typically poor performance is caused by inadequate inhibitory control, then removing the need for inhibitory control should enable them to be more successful. Accordingly, after every trial, the location that the child had just searched was modified to make it clear that it was no longer a potential hiding place, and it was left that way for the remaining trials. For example, after the child searched in the basket, it was turned over and left on its side to reveal its empty interior, and the tablecloth on the table was pulled up to show nothing was beneath it. This manipulation did, as expected, reduce the level of perseverative searching. However, there was no concomitant increase in correct responding.

A very similar study that was simultaneously designed and conducted in another lab (O'Sullivan, Mitchell, & Daehler, 1999) produced the same result. In this case, the item of furniture that had served as the hiding place on a given trial was actually removed (from both model and room). As a consequence, it was impossible to search perseveratively on subsequent trials. In spite of the impossibility of searching where they had looked before, the children still failed to search correctly.

Taken together, the results of our analysis of existing data and the two independently conducted experiments provide strong evidence that the typical poor performance of young children in the model task is not due to difficulty inhibiting a previous response. Perseveration is a consequence, not a cause, of young children's deficient performance. Thus, there is no evidence that 2.5-year-olds have representational insight into the model task but are prevented from succeeding by perseveration. Rather, the preponderance of the evidence indicates their failure is due to a lack of representational insight in the first place.

Having made the case that success in symbolic object-retrieval tasks is based on insight into the symbol–referent relation, it is important to emphasize again that this insight is not necessarily accessible or verbalizable. Even children who perform successfully in the model task have difficulty explaining what they know about the model–room relation. For example, in one study, 3-year-olds who had participated successfully in the standard model task were asked to choose which of two models of the room was better (i.e., "which one is just like Snoopy's room"). The items of furniture were either highly similar or quite dissimilar in appearance to those in the room, and they were either arranged in the same spatial organization or in a discrepant array. In spite of having exploited the model–room relation to find the toy in the retrieval task, the children chose randomly among the models. In another study, 3-year-olds were given the standard model task, except that on two trials, the toy was not in the correct location in the room; that is, it was not in the location corresponding to the hiding place of the miniature toy in the model. Although most of the children indicated that the toy should have been in that location, they could not explain how they knew it should be there.

Development in Young Children's Symbolic Functioning

The research we have reviewed here reveals that progress in young children's use of symbolic artifacts as a source of information is relatively rapid. Although 2.0-year-old children fail miserably at our basic picture task, 2.5-year-olds are very successful in it. Similarly, 2.5-year-olds generally perform extremely badly in the basic model task, whereas 3.0-year-olds perform extremely well. What accounts for the fact that children who find a task very difficult at one age find it trivially simple only six months later?

But age changes in our symbolic object-retrieval tasks are not all that must be explained. A full account must also address the fact that children of a given age who fail a task find that same task simple after experience with a related one, as well as the fact that children of a given age may be highly successful in one task but fail a *very* similar one.

Our review makes it clear that there is substantial complexity involved in the understanding and use of simple symbol–referent relations. Therefore, it should not be surprising if the developmental story is similarly complex, involving changes in numerous domains. We think this is exactly the case. It is unlikely that any one or two factors are by themselves responsible for the rapid development we have documented. Some of the likely factors appear in the model shown in figure 10.2.

One course of developmental progress has to do with the ease of achieving *dual representation*. This development is presumably facilitated by increasing inhibitory control. Although we ruled out response perseveration as a result of poor inhibitory control as a cause of young children's poor performance in the model task, it may very well be important in a different way. To achieve dual representation in the first place, a child has to inhibit responding to a symbolic artifact exclusively or primarily as an object. The more young children respond to a scale model as an interesting toy, the less likely they are to appreciate its role as a representation of something else. General inhibitory control is known to increase during the first several years (e.g., Harnishfeger & Bjorklund, 1993). This improvement is believed to be due in part to frontal lobe development, which is proceeding rapidly throughout this period (Diamond, 1990; Welsh & Pennington, 1991). Thus, basic brain development, leading to improved ability to inhibit their natural response to symbolic artifacts as objects, may underlie children's increased success in symbolic retrieval tasks with age.

The model in figure 10.2 explicitly specifies symbolic experience as an important source of development. The idea, as described earlier, is that experience with symbols would contribute to the development of symbolic sensitivity – a general readiness to assume that a novel entity may have a symbolic function, that is, that it may be used to stand for something other than itself. This increased symbolic sensitivity results in part from repeated experience achieving dual representation. Presumably, the more experience children have mentally representing the dual nature of symbolic artifacts, the easier it becomes to do so with a novel entity.

There is no question that the mostly middle-class American children who have participated in our research receive an enormous amount of exposure to a wide variety of symbolic artifacts in their early years. From very young ages, they enjoy daily picturebook interactions with their parents and others (Gelman, Coley, Rosengren, Hartman, & Pappas, 1998). Joint picturebook reading has been shown to promote vocabulary development (Whitehurst, Falco, Lonigan, Fischel, DeBaryshe, Valdez-Menchaca, & Caulfield, 1988), so it is reasonable to suppose that experience with pictures contributes to symbolic sensitivity. So might the many hours that young children spend watching television and videos.

Young children are not just consumers of ready-made symbols; 2- to 3-year-olds also begin to create symbolic mappings. Although their scribbles may not be decipherable to anyone else, evidence is accumulating that at least some of very young children's earliest artistic products do involve representational intent (Bloom & Markson, 1998). A large literature documents very young children's use of representational toys in pretend or symbolic play, as well as their increasing ability to perform object substitutions (Lillard, ch. 9 this volume). Increasing facility with drawing and pretense presumably contributes to symbolic sensitivity.

We should note that none of these experiences involves the use of symbolic artifacts to solve problems based on current reality, as is required in our symbolic retrieval tasks. To use a model, picture, or video as a source of information about reality, children have to have the cognitive flexibility to treat a familiar kind of artifact in a novel way. Part of what is involved in the development of symbolic sensitivity is increased cognitive flexibility, the ability to achieve psychological distance from something and respond to it abstractly (Sigel, 1970).

The model includes intentionality as a key element. An increasing body of research is establishing impressive levels of understanding of intention by infants and young children (Gergely, ch. 2 this volume), and such understanding expands dramatically during this period and for years to come. Paying attention to and thinking about the reasons for another person's behavior would presumably help young children figure out the basic nature of the symbolic object-retrieval task. There is no evidence, however, that success in these tasks requires full or even substantial understanding of intentionality.

Several other important aspects of early development that are likely to affect performance in symbolic retrieval tasks are not formally represented in the model. One is the large increase that takes place in the first years of life in the basic amount of information that children can mentally represent. Our symbolic object-retrieval tasks require children to represent and coordinate multiple relations. In the model task, for example, the children must use their representation of the model–room relation to infer from the relation between the miniature toy and its hiding place in the model what relation must hold between the larger toy and a location in the room. Their steadily increasing speed of information-processing and resulting increases in working memory (Kail, 1995) no doubt help young children cope with these cognitive demands. Similarly, their growing ability to represent multiple relations simultaneously would also make developmental progress possible (Case, 1992a; Halford, 1993, and ch. 25 this volume). Any symbolic-retrieval task has, at a minimum, one more relation – the relation between symbol and referent – to represent than does any task based on direct experience (Marzolf & DeLoache, 1997; Troseth & DeLoache, 2001).

In addition, between the ages of 2 and 3, children undergo extensive language development. At a minimum, their increased language skills should make it easier for them to apprehend our instructions. Young children also show substantial improvement in their ability to reason by analogy. Although even infants and toddlers can use information from a base to solve a simple target problem (Brown, 1990; Chen, 1996; Chen & Siegler, 2000a), with age they more readily gain access to analogies and are able to solve increasingly complex problems (Gentner, Ratterman, Markman, & Kotovsky, 1995; Goswami, 1992, and ch. 13 this volume). Young children's increasingly successful performance in symbolic retrieval tasks is presumably supported by more general analogical reasoning skills.

This list of factors known or assumed to contribute to the development of symbolic functioning is by no means intended to be complete; rather, it serves to emphasize that the rapid developmental improvement that occurs in our symbolic object-retrieval tasks is almost certainly attributable to several interacting and converging lines of development.

Conclusion

Children in Western societies are encountering an ever-wider variety of media and symbolic artifacts, and their exposure to these media begins at increasingly younger ages. Many parents begin picturebook interactions with young infants. Some television programming is now designed specifically for toddlers, and children begin learning numbers and letters in preschool. Computers are becoming ubiquitous, and children are being exposed to them increasingly early. Full participation in society thus requires that children begin to understand several kinds of symbolic media quite early in life.

The increasing prominence of symbolic artifacts in the lives of very young children and the importance of symbolic literacy throughout life means that it is more important than ever to increase our knowledge about the developmental processes involved in coming to understand and interpret symbols.

PART III

Topics in Cognitive Development in Childhood

This third section of the handbook is necessarily less closely themed than the first two sections. Having achieved certain core developments in understanding their psychological, biological, and physical worlds, children's cognition in relatively unrelated domains such as moral development, spatial reasoning, physics, scientific reasoning, reading, and mathematics progresses in fairly independent fashion. There are of course considerable continuities in cognitive development across these domains, for example in basic mechanisms such as the sensitivity to causal information, the accompanying drive to integrate new conceptual knowledge to existing knowledge in a causally coherent way, and the importance of understanding why things work in the way that they do – the "explanation-based" aspects of learning. Developmental accomplishments in different domains are also underpinned by the development of relatively domain-general mechanisms such as memory, causal reasoning, inductive reasoning, and deductive reasoning. Nevertheless, each domain also has its own, sometimes fairly specific, developmental mechanisms. These include phonological awareness for the development of decoding skills in reading, understanding sharing and one-to-many correspondence for the development of multiplicative reasoning in mathematics, and the distinction between morality and convention that all children make as moral development unfolds. The functioning of even these relatively specific developmental mechanisms, however, turns out to be influenced by the social, emotional, and cultural context in which learning takes place.

Memory development is one of the most-studied topics in all psychology, the field of childhood cognitive development included, and in his chapter Schneider does a remarkable job of distilling this vast literature into a clear account of what develops and when. Selecting empirical studies from as far back as 1880, he shows that general developments in memory performance are found in childhood, and that this general development appears to plateau at around the age of 11 years. The capacity of children's memory systems develops up to adolescence, the speed at which they can process information develops, and the strategies that they use for remembering develop too. All these developments are of course intimately related to each other, and Schneider discusses critical issues such as whether capacity per se really develops or whether improvement in memory strategies gives the appearance of improved capacity (a topic also addressed in Halford's chapter in the final section of this handbook). Schneider also discusses developments in different kinds of memory, such as episodic memory (the conscious recollection of events and experiences), semantic memory (our knowledge of language, rules, and concepts), procedural memory (learning our unconscious abilities such as habits and skills), working memory (the ability to hold information in or bring information to mind and operate on it) and eyewitness memory (the ability to provide accurate testimony). His broad conclusion is that development in general memory performance is affected by changes in basic capacities, in the strategies used for remembering, in metacognitive knowledge (the ability to reflect upon one's own memory and learning processes) and by children's increased knowledge in different domains. However, individual children may not show gradual change in these different aspects of memory development, but may jump from chance performance to near perfection in a given task across time, and may even discover a more efficient memory strategy but then subsequently stop using it. Schneider also notes briefly the important and under-researched role of the development of the brain in accounting for changes in memory skills, and the key role of motivation in memory and learning. He notes that the acquisition of expertise depends not just on exposure to new knowledge, but on a long-lasting process of motivated learning. Again, the social and emotional context of experience is important for childhood cognitive development.

Koslowski and Masnick also return to the roots of psychology in their chapter. They remind us that the origins of psychology were in philosophy, and demonstrate that empirical study of the development of causal reasoning has changed its paradigms as philosophical views of causal understanding have themselves changed. Causal reasoning in children was originally studied with respect to the indices of causation proposed by Hume in the eighteenth century. Hume was occupied with the event states that enable us to draw inferences about causation (e.g., that event A can only be a logically possible cause of event B if A precedes B in time). Early research into causal development treated these indices as formal principles for causal reasoning, whose development was domain-general and content-independent rather than determined by the existing state of the child's conceptual system. The early focus of research studies was therefore on whether children could reason according to the Humean indices in (typically) unfamiliar situations. More recently, the understanding that children always bring their current knowledge to bear on any new problem has led to an increased research interest in children's understanding of the mechanisms that bring about causal changes, and their developing theories or explanations for why these mechanisms operate in the ways that they do. As we saw in earlier sections of this handbook, research in areas as diverse as the acquisition of biological concepts (Gelman & Opfer) and the acquisition of a theory of mind (Wellman) have placed theoretical emphasis on the importance of causally coherent knowledge frameworks and explanation-based learning for development. Koslowski and Masnick show that children typically concern themselves first with identifying the causal agent in a given scenario, and then with issues concerning causal mechanism. Koslowski and Masnick argue that children make "inferences to the best explanation" for a given causal phenomenon depending on what they already know ("collateral information").

Access to collateral information will vary with the child's age, individual experience, with cultural practices, and with socio-historical context. This analysis again demonstrates the importance of social context in cognitive development. Koslowski and Masnick conclude that the development of causal reasoning is based on children's learning about empirical relations in the world and their knowledge of the network of collateral or background information in which these relations are embedded. Clearly, this theoretical framework has considerable overlap with those developed in earlier chapters.

In my own chapter, I show that the study of deductive and inductive reasoning in children, like the study of causal reasoning, had its roots in philosophy. Deductive reasoning studies were influenced by work in the philosophy of logic, which had focused on discovering the formal rules or principles underlying different forms of deductive reasoning such as syllogistic reasoning. These formal rules were thought to be domain-general and content-independent, and were assumed to operate in their purest form in totally unfamiliar domains. Psychologists therefore studied whether young children could use these formal rules of deduction in unfamiliar contexts, which they typically couldn't. Inductive reasoning studies were influenced by a very different branch of philosophy, concept formation and induction. Here it was taken for granted that the existing state of the child's conceptual system in a given domain would have an important effect on the child's reasoning. However, it was assumed that the basis of early induction might be different from the basis of more mature induction. Younger children were thought to be over-influenced by perceptual knowledge (reasoning was "perceptually bound"). Again, relatively unfamiliar contexts were used to assess reasoning skills, and in such situations young children indeed appeared unable to reason on the basis of relational rather than perceptual similarities until they got older. Increasing recognition of the importance of causally coherent knowledge frameworks and explanation-based learning for development meant that developmental psychologists gradually began studying children's inductive and deductive reasoning in familiar contexts and domains. With this paradigm shift, it became apparent that the basic forms of inductive and deductive reasoning were available relatively early in development. Development consisted more of knowledge accretion and the ensuing growing understanding of underlying similarities between entities at the level of causal structure for inductive reasoning, and knowledge accretion and the ensuing growing ability to recognize the logical structure of a given problem across changes in problem content or mode of presentation for deductive reasoning. Finally, social context plays a role in deductive reasoning. For example, if young children are given syllogistic reasoning problems based on unfamiliar premises using a "fantasy mode" of presentation, then they can usually reason very competently. The social context prevents the child from dismissing the premises as absurd, and deductive logic is revealed. The message for future work appears to be that more thought must be given to the social, contextual, and even emotional aspects of the situations in which we test young children's cognitive competencies.

One topic in this handbook in which social context has been accorded a central role in cognitive development is morality, as shown very clearly in Nucci's chapter on the development of moral reasoning. Historically, moral reasoning was thought to progress through a series of universal stages that transcended culture and context (e.g., Piaget, 1932; Kohlberg, 1969). Nucci makes it clear that moral concepts are not really general, and that it is very difficult to divorce moral cognition from context and culture. Although some aspects of moral cognition are probably nonarbitrary (such as issues of harm and injustice), many moral issues are matters of convention, based on contextually dependent and agreed-upon social rules. These social rules naturally vary with social context and with culture, and social structure has a big impact on how morality is experienced and thought about in everyday life. Very young children do appear to distinguish matters of convention and matters of morality, for example 3-year-olds see unprovoked harm as wrong regardless of the presence or absence of social rules. However, development along this "moral" domain entails changes in what is conceived as "fair," whereas development in the conceptually distinct domain of convention entails making sense of systems of social regulation. Different social experiences result in different rates of development in these two domains, and even apparently core moral principles such as unprovoked harm are difficult to conceptualize entirely independently of cultural and socio-historic norms. For example, doctors who fail to "scrub up" before performing an operation and therefore infect their patients would be seen as immoral today, but were not seen as immoral 100 years ago when germs and infection were not well understood. Similarly, different cultures may appear very variable in their judgments concerning moral values, but if these values are understood from within the context of that culture's beliefs about how the natural world operates (such as religious beliefs), then much of the apparent variability may disappear. Nucci ends his chapter with the challenging suggestion that morality may not be "cognitive" at all, but may rather depend on non-rational factors such as emotion and socialization. Moral issues such as unprovoked harm have intrinsic emotional content, and these emotions may form part of the initial substrate of moral development. Given that children may experience quite different emotional responses to events such as unprovoked harm from adults' behavior to them or from the affective climate within their families, the basic underpinnings of moral constructs themselves might be strongly influenced by socialization. The moral reasoning and behavior of a child who has grown up in an affectively supportive environment may thus be rather different from the moral reasoning and behavior of a child who has grown up in an aggressive and affectively unsupportive environment.

With Liben's chapter on spatial development, we return to the philosophical roots of psychology as a discipline. Should we conceptualize space as an absolute framework, one that exists even if empty? Or should space be conceptualized in relative terms, defined and changed by the positions of objects and observers within it? Clearly, both are valid in different contexts, and Liben shows how children's developing understanding of space encompasses both conceptualizations in areas as diverse as environmental space (the space we live and move about in), representational space (our referents for space, such as maps and models), and perceptual space (we see objects in space, we see space itself, we get spatial information from hearing and touch, and all this perceptual information guides our actions and understandings about where objects are in relation to ourselves). Liben shows that developments in experimental methodology, particularly for testing infants, have led to changes in our understanding of spatial development, echoing themes introduced by Bauer for memory development and by Baillargeon for the development of physical understanding. She illustrates how such work has shown that infants are remarkably aware of many spatial features of their environments, indirectly echoing Gergely's view that it is extremely unlikely that young infants are initially unable to distinguish themselves from their environments. Although young infants do tend to have a body-centered spatial perspective, this is unsurprising given their lack of independent mobility, and with motor development (crawling, climbing, walking) they develop external and proximal frames of reference and eventually external and distal frames of reference. Indeed, as they grow older, children's environments (their "home ranges") expand greatly, and children who are given more personal control over their travel through environments have relatively more spatial knowledge about these environments. This knowledge is particularly revealed through studies requiring children to *act* in space rather than to consciously reflect upon and manipulate their spatial knowledge (for example, by answering inferential questions about it). Indeed, when children's spatial knowledge is measured by action-based tasks, their knowledge of environmental space is often equivalent to that of adults. Their knowledge and understanding of representational space develops more slowly, presumably because many of the conventions of representational space (e.g., red lines on a map correspond to roads) must be learned. Liben cites DeLoache's work, discussed in part II, as evidence that a basic understanding of representational correspondences emerges quite early. She then shows how gradual mastery of spatial relations such as scale and viewing angle contribute to a deeper and more principled understanding of representational space. Almost uniquely in this volume, she also comments on sex differences. In contrast to many areas of cognitive development, there are marked and persistent sex differences in spatial development in favor of boys. Liben discusses the possible origins of these differences, arguing that a complex interplay between any proposed biological cause (X-linked recessive genes, sex hormones) and environment and social context is the most likely explanation of boys' usual superiority in spatial skills.

A central theme of the chapter on the development of intuitive physics by Wilkening and Huber is the different levels of physical knowledge revealed by action versus conscious reflection. This theme echoes the differences in spatial understanding that are revealed by experimental tasks based on action rather than inference discussed by Liben. Clearly, areas of cognition that rely more heavily on perceptual-motor skills and nonverbal learning, such as physical and spatial cognition, might need to be studied with rather different methodologies to areas of cognition that rely more heavily on language skills and verbally mediated learning. Indeed, Wilkening and Huber show that if children *and adults* are given physical problems and allowed to respond either by acting on the materials in the problem or by making judgments or choices about how the materials will behave, "better" performance (i.e., performance demonstrating an understanding of physical laws) is usually found in the action condition, where young children's performance can even be equivalent to that of adults. Another important theme in Wilkening and Huber's chapter is the early focus of the research field on assumed content-independent logical principles. As in the domains of logical and causal reasoning, traditional approaches to physical reasoning focused on uncovering when children became able to reason according to the "laws of physics." It was assumed that the purest form of these laws would be revealed in totally unfamiliar contexts, from which any collateral factors and abilities had been eliminated. Consequently, a lot of research energy was spent in searching for the logical structures underlying different stages of physical reasoning, while consistently ignoring the systematic effects of children's existing physical beliefs. In fact, many well-educated adults continue to hold physical beliefs about simple phenomena that are quite at variance with Newtonian theory. These beliefs form coherent theories which explain external reality very well in many situations, as do children's physical knowledge frameworks, and so can be quite impervious to change. As so much physical information is absorbed at a very early age via sensory-motor and perceptual processes and goal-directed action, the field of intuitive physics has now shifted to investigating how well children's physical knowledge frameworks approximate physical reality at different points in development, and under which circumstances these approximations change. Wilkening and Huber cover the development of a remarkably extensive set of physical concepts in their chapter, including time, speed, motion, force, gravity, weight, mass, volume, temperature, and density. In each area, they emphasize the need for research that links explicit understanding with motivation, perception, and action. Variability in children's intuitive physics is the norm, and cannot be eliminated by choosing the "right" methods. Rather, this variability is an intrinsic part of children's adaptive physical concepts, and should be a focus of study in its own right.

Kuhn's chapter on the development of scientific thinking also rejects the idea that there is a restricted set of "right" methods that will enable the accurate documentation of development. As she points out, scientific thinking is really a form of knowledge-seeking. To define it too narrowly as, for example, the ability to test hypotheses by the control of variables, is to miss the point that scientific thinking is an activity engaged in by everyone rather than only by scientists. Kuhn argues that any purposeful thinking that has the objective of increasing the seeker's knowledge is scientific thinking, and as such can be distinguished from scientific *understanding*, which can be broadly defined as the content of children's evolving theories within specific domains. Kuhn takes it for granted that young children develop causally coherent frameworks of knowledge in different domains in order to make sense of and organize their experience. Her interest is in the processes by which this is accomplished. Kuhn's basic premise is that scientific thinking depends on theory–evidence co-ordination. For scientific thinking to occur, the child's existing theory or understanding must be explicitly represented by the child as an object of cognition. By this definition, scientific thinking begins after the age of around 4 years, when children begin to understand that mental representations do not always duplicate external reality (see Wellman's chapter in this handbook). Kuhn argues that the requisite skills for conscious scientific thinking are the formation of a question or hypothesis, planning and conducting an investigation, analyzing the results, drawing inferences, and debating their implications. The prototypical form of scientific inquiry is a situation in which a number of variables have potential casual connections to an outcome, and the child must choose examples for investigation that will enable the identification of those that are causal and those that are non-causal. This entails the prediction and explanation of variations in outcome. As children's knowledge of the network of collateral or background information in which these variables are embedded necessarily affects the success of the inquiry process, scientific thinking, like causal, moral, and deductive reasoning, cannot be divorced from the context in which it takes place. Furthermore, social processes in the form of justifying your views and beliefs to your peers may be especially important for development. Kuhn's chapter provides an elegant description of how "explanation-based" learning at the metacognitive, reflective level might proceed. The processes whereby younger children arrive at their implicit theoretical frameworks for imposing causal coherence on the everyday world have not yet been widely investigated, but would be an obvious focus for future work.

Reading is a critical aspect of cognitive development, because in later childhood so much information about the world comes via the written word. However, it is also a somewhat unique cognitive skill, as our brains were not designed for reading. Our brains were designed to process spoken language. As Snowling shows in her chapter on reading development and dyslexia, this fundamental insight is very important for understanding the cognitive skills that underpin efficient reading acquisition. Preschool children's *phonological awareness* skills, namely their ability to reflect upon the sound patterning or phonological structure of their spoken language, is the most important precursor skill to acquiring the alphabetic principle. Although general cognitive skills such as drawing analogies and symbolic representational abilities also play a role in acquiring efficient "decoding" procedures (the accurate mapping of sequences of letters to spoken words), individual differences in such cognitive skills do not seem to play a role in dyslexia. Rather, the basic problem in dyslexia is a "phonological deficit" – a deficiency in acquiring competent phonological awareness skills. This phonological deficit is not caused by low general ability, as dyslexic children are typically very competent in other aspects of the curriculum. The impact of a phonological deficit also varies with the language that is being acquired, as children who are learning to read orthographies with consistent 1:1 mappings between letters and sounds (such as Italian and Greek) acquire efficient decoding skills very quickly, and dyslexic children in these orthographies also acquire very competent decoding skills, albeit more effortfully and slowly. A phonological deficit has more far-reaching consequences for children attempting to acquire inconsistent orthographies such as English, in which letters can make more than one sound (e.g., "a" in "cat," "ball," "garden"), and the same sound can be spelled in many ways (e.g., "hurt," "dirt," "Bert"). Dyslexic children in English rarely acquire fully efficient decoding procedures, and in addition are slow and effortful readers. For normally progressing children, once decoding is efficiently under way a whole range of higher-level cognitive processes become important for transforming the printed word into meaning. These include the ability to use surrounding contextual information to disambiguate meaning, the ability to make inferences from text that go beyond its literal meaning and the use of pragmatic cues. Indeed, some children acquire normal decoding skills but end up as poor readers because of deficiencies in these higher-level semantic component skills. Snowling ends by noting the importance of social context for reading acquisition. The cultural milieu in which reading develops in different nations is known to have a strong influence on how well children in different social classes and of different gender learn to read.

Mathematical knowledge is another critical aspect of cognitive development, necessary for much of school learning, and in particular for understanding aspects of the physical and biological sciences. In contrast to reading development, however, some researchers have suggested that there is a "mathematical brain," a cerebral substrate that is specialized for number. This brain area is thought to be nonverbal, with clear antecedents in evolutionary history. Some form of preverbal numerical abilities is even thought to be present in other species. A natural extension of this theoretical position is that human infants should have some innate knowledge about number. In their chapter on children's understanding of mathematics, however, Bryant and Nunes question this popular hypothesis. They argue instead that mathematical knowledge, like knowledge about reading, develops over time. They show that children learn a lot about the underlying logic of mathematics through their own experiences, a hypothesis first proposed by Piaget. According to their analysis, cardinal and ordinal knowledge of number – the understanding that all sets with the same number are qualitatively equivalent, and that numbers come in an ordered scale of magnitude – develops relatively slowly during the first years of life. Children can learn to count at a young age, but this is not the same thing as understanding ordinal number. In fact, a number of research studies (including some of Piaget's studies about conservation) suggest that children at first count without understanding what they are doing. They do not seem to understand that if two sets have the same number, then they must be equivalent in numerosity. Further, although children do have some understanding of one-to-one correspondence (they are quite good at sharing), they do not seem to extend this knowledge to counting. Learning about the arithmetical operations of adding, subtracting, dividing, and multiplying also develops during the first few years, with an understanding of addition developing first, at about 3 years. However, being able to add two numbers is not the same thing as additive reasoning, which requires understanding of the inverse relation between adding and subtracting. This takes a bit longer to develop, emerging at around 5 years. Similarly, sharing and an understanding of one-to-many correspondence develop relatively early, at around 4 and 5 years, but full multiplicative reasoning develops quite a bit later, and much of it requires formal teaching. Bryant and Nuñes end their chapter by stressing the importance of teaching in all areas of mathematical development. Children have to be taught our counting systems and taught how to use them. Like the alphabet, human counting systems are a cultural invention. It is unreasonable to expect each child to reinvent or intuitively understand the symbol systems that we now take for granted. Mathematics, like reading, must be taught.

The continuities and similarities between the aspects of cognitive development discussed in this section are striking. A quest for explanation and mechanism seems to underpin cognitive development in areas as diverse as moral development and intuitive physics. Children's causal focus – their drive to develop causally coherent frameworks of knowledge that make sense of and organize their experience across domains – is also notable. This "causal bias" view of the question of how knowledge develops suggests that the development of causal reasoning might in itself provide a useful model for thinking about the development of cognition. In their chapter on causal reasoning, Koslowski and Masnick suggest that children typically concern themselves first with identifying the causal agent in a given scenario. If we extend this idea across domains, we can see an obvious parallel in infants' early focus on agency and intentionality, as discussed in the chapters in the first section by Gergely, Meltzoff, and Waxman. Koslowski and Masnick suggest that children next concern themselves with issues of causal mechanism. Again, if extended across domains this tendency creates an obvious role for explanation-based learning. In earlier chapters, we have seen that a search for causal mechanism drives development in areas as diverse as theory of mind and infant physics. Although development in virtually every domain discussed in part III draws also upon some fairly specialized mechanisms, the theoretical continuity with earlier sections is clear.

Research in certain domains, notably spatial and physical reasoning, has also high-lighted the continuing importance of perception and action in cognitive development. In some domains, children "know" things in these modalities before they "know" them cognitively. Both Liben and Wilkening and Huber show that spatial and physical know-ledge is often represented first in terms of action. Children's ability to reflect upon their action-based knowledge then becomes important for cognition to develop further. The social context in which learning occurs is also once again shown to have a profound effect in shaping cognitive development in all domains. Whether the child is learning morality or reading, the behavior of surrounding adults and the emotional and cultural context of learning can have an important impact on what is learned.

Finally, many of the domains discussed in this section also show similar theoretical developments. In these domains, early research searching for universal laws of reasoning and ignoring the importance of background and collateral information in children's cog-nition has been found to be flawed. Research strategies have changed accordingly. Instead of seeking to describe cognitive change in terms of the discovery of the formal laws or rules that actually describe a given domain, research in many areas has converged instead onto a theoretical model that can be broadly described as "explanation-based." The focus of interest is not the laws themselves, but children's understanding of the mechanisms that bring about the particular changes in their environments described by these laws, and their developing theories or explanations for why these mechanisms operate in the ways that they do. Whether these theoretical changes necessitate a change in the research strategies currently used in cognitive developmental psychology is considered in the intro-duction to the final section of this handbook.

CHAPTER ELEVEN

Memory Development in Childhood

Wolfgang Schneider

In a recent review of children's memory development (Schneider & Bjorklund, 1998), it was emphasized that memory development has been one of the most-studied topics in all of cognitive development, and deservedly so. In fact, an impressive amount of scientific studies on this issue have been published within the last three decades, stimulated by a shift away from behaviorist theories to information-processing considerations. Given the extent and diversity of the memory development literature, this overview will be restricted to a discussion of major trends in the field, thereby focusing on the period between childhood and adolescence (i.e., approximately ages 5 to 15). Memory development in very young children will not be discussed because it is already addressed in a separate chapter (see Bauer, ch. 6 this volume). Before getting to the bulk of research carried out with older children and adolescents, major historical developments are briefly summarized.

Experimental studies of memory are as old as scientific psychology. When Ebbinghaus (1885) started with his classic experiments on memory and forgetting in 1879, Wundt founded the first psychological laboratory. Although this is widely known, it is not equally well known that research on memory *development* also started at about that time. Around the turn of the century, numerous studies were carried out in Europe to investigate developmental and individual differences in children's memory. There were three rather independent lines of research that contributed to this early trend. First, carefully conducted case studies of young children's development (which also included systematic observations of memory development in early childhood) received a lot of attention, leading to the scientific foundation of child psychology in Germany.

A second line of research was directly derived from memory experiments with adults. Some of these studies explored whether findings obtained for adult populations could be easily generalized to children of different ages. Other investigations were less basic in nature and were driven by educational interests. These studies tested common (mis)conceptions held at that time, for example, that children, because they practice their memory skills in school almost every day, are better at remembering verbal material than adults. Also, many of these studies examined the popular assumption that boys have a better memory than girls. As the issue of co-education was at stake in Germany around the turn of the century, this question was of high practical relevance.

The third line of research on children's memory was even more applied, focusing on children's and adults' testimonial competence. The prevailing legal attitude had been one of scepticism about the testimony of child witnesses. Nonetheless, interest in children's eyewitness memory competencies was particularly strong in Germany and France, where systematic research on this issue flourished at the start of the twentieth century (e.g., Stern, 1910; Whipple, 1909, 1911). Most studies focused on children's suggestibility, developing methodologies that are still in use in modern research on the topic.

Early Investigations of the General Course of Memory Development

Although most findings from the early period are no longer of core interest, one of the major insights concerning the "general" course of memory development stems from a large-scale study conducted in the early 1930s. Brunswik, Goldscheider, and Pilek (1932) conducted a developmental study that aimed at providing a general description of short-term and long-term memory in school-age children and adolescents. This study also differed from earlier investigations in that the issues addressed were directly derived from truly developmental theory, that is, Charlotte and Karl Bühler's doctrine of phases and stages (e.g., Bühler, 1930). A large variety of memory tasks were presented to a sample of about 700 participants, ranging from 6 to 18 years of age. Tests involved short- and long-term memory for nonsense and meaningful words, colors, and numbers as well as memory for poems. Moreover, several nonverbal memory tasks such as memory for motor actions and their correct sequence were included.

As a main result, reliable age differences were observed for most short-term memory tasks. Six- to 13-year-olds required more practice to learn nonsense syllables than words or numbers. This difference was particularly marked for the youngest children. The findings for short-term memory in the older students were not clear-cut because performance differences between the 14- and 18-year-olds were not consistently observed. Whereas older participants remembered more nonsense syllables than the 14-year-olds, no age effects were reported for the two tasks involving meaningful word materials (i.e., paired concepts and poems). Given the different developmental patterns, Brunswik and colleagues concluded that there must be different memory functions.

Undoubtedly, the study by Brunswik et al. (1932) represents a valuable contribution to memory development research. The use of relatively precise methods and various learning materials gave rise to more specific hypotheses concerning age differences in memory development. The attempt to construct a curve of the general development of immediate

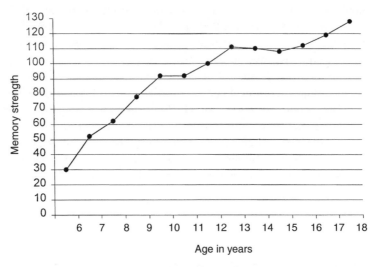

Figure 11.1   Memory development in children and adolescents. Constructed with data from Brunswik et al. (1932)

memory ("memory strength") is particularly interesting. The curve was based on scores of all participants and represented an aggregation across all measures included in the study (see figure 11.1). The outcomes were compatible with findings from other early studies in that linear and steep rises in memory performance were found from 6 to 11 years of age, and that there was a plateau in performance during pre- and early adolescence.

One obvious problem with the study was that the authors tried hard to make their findings compatible with the Bühlers' perspective. Accordingly, they claimed to have found support for their position that memory development during the early years is dominated by rote-associative processes ("mechanical learning"), whereas learning and memory predominant in older children and adults is based on the creation of meaning ("logical memory"). A closer inspection of findings revealed that the theoretical position was not entirely supported by the data: in fact, younger children required more practice to learn nonsense syllables than meaningful words, with continuous improvement in the learning of nonsense syllables up until age 18. Although subsequent reports on the Brunswik et al. study emphasized the qualitative shift from mechanical to logical memory (for instance, see Werner's comments on the findings by Brunswik et al. in the thoroughly revised third edition of his textbook which appeared in 1953), the basic assumptions by Brunswik et al. (1932) were subsequently questioned and empirically falsified by Russian and German psychologists (Rubinstein, 1973; Smirnov, 1948 (cited in Smirnov, 1973; Fechner, 1965; Weinert 1962). Thus, whereas the developmental curve regarding improvements in memory performance was in accord with many studies of the early period and also validated in subsequent investigations, the assumptions concerning qualitative shifts of memory development favored by the Bühlers and Brunswik and colleagues were not compatible with the existing database.

The Beginning of a New Era: Focus on Mechanisms of Change

How does modern research on memory development differ from the historical approaches outlined above? One of the crucial differences concerns a shift from an emphasis on describing developmental differences in memory to an emphasis on identifying the underlying mechanisms of change. Another difference concerns the theoretical framework used. Since the mid-1960s, research on memory development has been influenced strongly by theoretical models derived from information-processing and neuroscience approaches (see the reviews by Kail, 1990; Schneider & Bjorklund, 1998; Schneider & Pressley, 1997). Developmental psychologists began looking at changes in children's thinking in terms of a computer metaphor. From this perspective, memory development can be seen as reflecting either *hardware* (the capacity of memory systems and the speed at which information can be processed) or *software* (e.g., use of strategies). Developmental research was strongly influenced by multistore memory models that distinguished between a sensory register, a short-term store, and a long-term store.

Regarding the content of the long-term store, it was proposed that information can be represented in two ways. *Explicit* or *declarative* memory refers to our capacity for conscious recollection of names, places, dates, or events and comes in two types, episodic and semantic. Whereas episodic memory concerns events and experiences that can be consciously retrieved, semantic memory refers to our knowledge of language, rules, and concepts. In contrast, implicit or procedural memory represents a variety of nonconscious abilities, including the capacity for learning habits and skills, and some forms of classical conditioning.

The distinction between implicit and explicit memory is more than one of conceptual convenience. There is evidence that different areas of the brain are involved in declarative and procedural memory (Schacter, 1992), suggesting that memory is not a single phenomenon but a set of domain-specific operations that may show different patterns of developmental function.

The vast majority of studies on memory development since the mid-1960s have been carried out with older children, mainly dealing with explicit memory, that is, conscious remembering of facts and events. It was repeatedly found that particular clear improvements in declarative memory can be observed for the age range between 6 and 12 years, which roughly corresponds to the elementary school period in most countries. This finding is in accord with the results of Brunswik et al. (1932) described earlier. In order to explain these rapid increases in memory performance over time, different sources or determinants of memory development have been identified. According to most contemporary memory researchers, changes in *basic capacities, memory strategies, metacognitive knowledge,* and *domain knowledge* all contribute to developmental changes in memory performance. There is also broad agreement that some of these sources of development contribute more than others, and that some play an important role in certain periods of childhood but not in others (see Schneider & Pressley, 1997; Siegler, 1998). In the following, evidence concerning the relevance of these sources for memory development will be summarized.

Aspects of Memory Development

The role of basic capacities

One of the oldest and most controversial issues concerning children's information-processing is whether the amount of information they can actively process at one time changes with age (see also Halford, ch. 25 this volume). Age differences in the capacity of the short-term store (STS) were typically found in developmental studies that used *memory span tasks*. Such tasks require that participants must repeat, in exact order, a series of rapidly presented items such as digits or words. Age differences in memory span are very stable. In an extensive review of the literature, Dempster (1981) reported that the memory span of 2-year-olds is about two items; of 5-year-olds about four items; of 7-year-olds about five items, and of 9-year-olds about six items. The average memory span of adults is about seven items.

The robustness of these differences makes the interpretation that the actual capacity of the STS is increasing with age very attractive. Appealing as this is, however, it is too simple. Research over the past two decades has made it clear that memory span is *not* a domain-general phenomenon that is essentially identical regardless of what type of information is being remembered. Rather, how much a person knows about the stimuli he or she is remembering definitively affects memory span, with knowledge presumably having its effect by influencing speed of processing. The impact of knowledge on memory span has been demonstrated in studies assessing the memory span of child chess experts and adult chess novices for chess positions on a chessboard and for other types of items, such as digits (Chi, 1978; Schneider, Gruber, Gold, & Opwis, 1993). Although the adults outperformed the children on the digit-span task, the children excelled when tested on the chess-span task. This suggests that memory span is domain-specific, varying with the person's knowledge about the to-be-remembered material.

However, there are also indications that age differences in memory span (and increases in processing speed) are due to a presumably domain-general mechanism. One reason for the regular age-related improvements observed on most memory-span tasks is that older children typically have a larger vocabulary and know more about most domains under investigation. For instance, when age differences in task-relevant knowledge are experimentally controlled for, age differences in memory span no longer occur (cf. Dempster, 1985). It has been well established by now that speed of information-processing increases with age across a wide range of tasks (cf. Case, 1985a; Dempster, 1981; Kail & Salthouse, 1994).

A model of *working memory* that accounts for age differences in memory span primarily in terms of speed of processing has been developed by Baddeley and Hitch (Baddeley, 1986; Baddeley & Hitch, 1974; Hitch & Towse, 1995; for a recent review, see Gathercole, 1998). Tests of working memory are similar to memory span tasks in that participants must remember a series of items in exact order, but they are embedded in an additional task in which participants must transform information held in the short-term store. In general, children's performance on working-memory tasks shows the same age-related increase in their performance as their performance on memory span tasks, although the absolute level is somewhat reduced in working-memory tasks.

Working-memory models emphasize the fact that information-processing is restricted by capacity limits *and* time limits. That is, the amount of information that one can bring to mind all at once is quite limited, and this limited amount of information that is brought to mind at any one time can be kept in mind only briefly unless the person invests enormous effort in retaining the information. Accordingly, models of working memory place substantial emphasis on *speed of processing.* For instance, the working-memory model developed by Baddeley, Gathercole, Hitch, and their colleagues assumes that age differences in verbal memory span are primarily the result of age differences in a phonological subsystem called the *articulatory loop.* Verbal information is stored in the articulatory loop, and these traces decay rapidly if verbal rehearsal is not performed. Although some researchers have reported age differences in the rate at which information decays (see the review by Cowan, 1997), most researchers propose that age differences in rehearsal rate are primarily responsible for developmental differences in memory span. One factor that influences rehearsal rate is word length. Several studies on the development of working memory have reported age differences in the speed with which words can be articulated and corresponding differences in memory span and working-memory span (e.g., Hitch & Towse, 1995; Hulme, Thompson, Muir, & Lawrence, 1984).

Overall, there is converging evidence that developmental changes in memory capacity are due to significant increases in information-processing speed which are most obvious in early ages, with the rate of changes slowing thereafter. Age differences in speed of processing influence a wide range of tasks and may represent a cognitive primitive (see Kail, 1991c, 1993; Kail & Salthouse, 1994). However, considerable controversy has arisen over whether the increased speed is due to greater use of strategies, to greater familiarity with the items used, or to speed per se. Recent evidence suggests that age differences in speed of processing are primarily influenced by maturational factors. For instance, Cowan and colleagues (Cowan, Nugent, Elliott, Pnomarev, & Saults, 1999) evaluated age differences in the *span of apprehension,* which refers to the amount of information that people can attend to at a single time or the number of items that people can keep in mind at any one time. Span of apprehension can be assessed only when factors such as focused attention, knowledge about the target items, and encoding strategies can be eliminated, factors that are not eliminated on memory span or working-memory span tasks. Cowan and his colleagues reported that the average span of apprehension increased significantly with age (2.41, 3.13, and 3.56 digits for the 7-year-old, 10-year-old, and adult participants, respectively), and interpreted these differences as reflecting a true developmental difference in the capacity of the short-term store. Supporting evidence for the assumption that speed of processing per se increases with maturation comes from analyses demonstrating that the best-fitting mathematical function for describing the increase in processing speed with age is different from the one that best describes the improvements that come with practice (Kail, 1991c). Further, as noted by Siegler (1998), similar increases in processing speed can be demonstrated as much for tasks that children rarely encounter (e.g., mental rotation) as for ones they encounter daily (reading and arithmetic).

Overall, then, age differences in speed of processing are influenced by maturational and experiential factors. Maturational factors place biological limits on how quickly children can process information and retain items in their STS. However, speed of processing is also influenced by experiential factors (e.g., knowledge base), making it clear that development of basic memory abilities is a result of the dynamic interaction between biological and experiential factors that vary over time.

Effects of memory strategies

Memory strategies have been defined as mental or behavioral activities that achieve cognitive purposes and are effort-consuming, potentially conscious, and controllable (Flavell, Miller, & Miller, 1993; Pressley & Van Meter, 1993). Since the mid-1960s numerous studies have investigated the role of strategies in memory development. Strategic memory was at the center of early investigations in this area (see Harnishfeger & Bjorklund, 1990 for a historical sketch) and continues to be so today, although the topic no longer dominates the field as it once did. Research interest in strategies such as rehearsal and semantic organization was partially motivated by the crucial role of such control processes in general multistore memory models, and by John Flavell's work establishing rehearsal and organization as strategies that develop between 5 and 10 years of age.

Strategies can be executed either at the time of learning (encoding) or later on when information is accessed in long-term memory (retrieval). The example of organizational strategies will be used to illustrate the case. Typically, the development of such strategies is explored in sort-recall tasks that involve organizing pictures or words into semantic categories. Children are given a randomly ordered list of categorizable items (e.g., animals, furniture, and the like). They are then told that their task is to remember the items later on, and that they are free to do anything with the materials that may help their recall. Following a short study period, children are asked to recall as many stimuli as they can. Children's organization of items during study (sorting) and recall (clustering) has been measured using various clustering indices. For most of these measures, values close to 1 represent almost perfect organization of stimuli, whereas values close to 0 indicate random responding.

Early research by Flavell and colleagues as well as subsequent studies confirmed a specific trend in strategy development (for reviews, see Kail, 1990; Schneider & Pressley, 1997). Typically, deliberate strategies were not observed in children younger than 5 or 6 years of age. The lack of strategic behaviors in very young children was labeled *mediation deficiency*, indicating that children of a particular (preschool) age do not benefit from memory strategies, even after having been instructed how to use them. Although slightly older children such as kindergarteners and young schoolchildren also did not utilize strategies spontaneously, their problem was different. These children were shown to suffer from a *production deficiency*. That is, they failed to use (or to produce) strategies when given "neutral" instructions but could be easily trained to do so, usually with corresponding improvements in memory performance. Much research in strategy development has concerned the factors responsible for production deficiencies, the subsequent failure to transfer an acquired strategy to a new situation, and ways in which to improve children's strategy effectiveness (for reviews, see Pressley & Van Meter, 1993; Schneider & Pressley, 1997). This research demonstrated that insufficient mental capacity was partially responsible for production deficiencies in young children. Research based on dual-task procedures in which children are asked to perform two tasks, both separately and together, demonstrated that young children require much more mental effort than older ones in order to implement and execute memory strategies (cf. Guttentag, 1984). Moreover, individual differences in domain knowledge contribute to the age differences in strategy use. As noted above, rich knowledge influences the speed with which children can process domain-related information. As a consequence, less mental energy is needed to execute a strategy based on this information.

Numerous studies showed that memory strategies develop most rapidly over the elementary school years. Older children are more likely to group items on the basis of meaning and to study same-category items together, with higher levels of sorting and clustering yielding higher levels of recall (e.g., Hasselhorn, 1992). However, the ages of strategy acquisition are relative, and variable within and between strategies. Even preschoolers and kindergarten children are able to use intentional strategies, both in ecologically valid settings such as hide-and-seek tasks, and in the context of a laboratory task.

More recently, research on strategy development has focused on two interesting phenomena. First, memory researchers have observed that higher levels of organization are not always accompanied by higher levels of recall. Such *utilization deficiencies* have been shown in several studies with both preschoolers and elementary schoolchildren (for reviews, see Bjorklund & Douglas, 1997; Miller & Seier, 1994). It appears from this research that using a strategy such as organization is only a first step. Once the mechanics of the strategy are learned, children need more time before they can execute it proficiently. Although there is plenty of evidence supporting the utilization deficiency paradigm (cf. Bjorklund & Coyle, 1995; Miller, 1994, 2000), it is important to note that findings are not always consistent and seem to depend on the particular definition and on certain characteristics of the task (Schneider & Sodian, 1997; Waters, 2000). Research findings concerning utilization deficiencies with regard to organizational strategies are particularly difficult to reconcile. Whereas some researchers consistently find evidence for the deficiency in both training studies and microgenetic analyses (Bjorklund, Miller, Coyle, & Slawinski, 1997; Coyle & Bjorklund, 1997), others consistently failed to do so (Schlagmüller, 2000; Schneider & Sodian, 1997). Clearly more research is needed to clarify this interesting issue. Despite these problems, however, this new line of research on strategy development has broadened our view of strategy development. As noted by Miller (2000), one important aspect of research on utilization deficiencies is that it has rejuvenated the study of strategy development by challenging the assumption that children's behavior is driven by what works. It is not only possible that children sometimes drop an efficient strategy, but also possible that children continue to use a strategy that does not help them.

A second new line of research based on longitudinal data has also broadened our knowledge concerning strategy development. In particular, this research showed that findings based on cross-sectional studies and the analysis of group data do not tell us the whole story about individual developmental trends. Schneider and Sodian (1997; Sodian & Schneider, 1999) explored the issue of whether the impression of gradual developmental increases in strategy use and recall derived from cross-sectional studies could be confirmed by the analysis of longitudinal data. Although Schneider and Sodian confirmed earlier results on the group level, they were struck by low individual stabilities for the strategy and recall variables over time. If individual children change their relative positions in the sample considerably between measurement points (as indicated by low group stabilities), the model of gradual improvement does not seem to hold. In fact, Schneider and Sodian found that gradual, steady increases were rarely observed. Only about 8 percent of the children showed a gradual improvement in the use of organizational strategies (sorting and clustering), as suggested by the group data. In comparison, about 81 percent of the children "jumped" from chance level to near perfection between subsequent measurement points. Whereas about 8 percent were perfect from the start, another 3 percent never showed any signs of a strategy throughout the study. There was also considerable variation in the age at which children first used the strategy, and many children who used it at early measurement points lost it subsequently and "rediscovered" it at some later point. These findings thus confirm that children go from chance levels of sorting to perfection, but they do it at different points in time. The data also seem to square well with other evidence of substantial inter- and intrasubject variability in strategy use, with children using different strategies and combinations of strategies on any given memory problem (Siegler, 1996).

Taken overall, research conducted during the last three decades has convincingly shown that age-related effects in the frequency of use and quality of children's strategies play a large role in memory development between the early school years and adolescence. However, there is now an increasing realization that the use of encoding and retrieval strategies largely depends on children's strategic as well as nonstrategic knowledge. There is broad consensus that the narrow focus on developmental changes in strategy use should be replaced by an approach that takes into account the effects of various forms of knowledge on strategy execution.

The impact of metacognitive knowledge

Almost 30 years ago, John Flavell (1971) introduced the term *metamemory* to refer to knowledge about memory processes and contents. From a developmental perspective, this concept seemed well suited to explain young children's production deficiencies on a broad variety of tasks. Whereas young children do not learn much about the advantages of memory strategies, schoolchildren are regularly confronted with various memory tasks that eventually help them to discover the advantages of strategies and improve their metamemory.

Two broad categories of metacognitive knowledge have been distinguished in the literature (Flavell & Wellman, 1977). *Declarative metacognitive knowledge* refers to what children factually know about their memory. This type of knowledge is explicit and verbalizable and includes knowledge about the importance of person variables (e.g., age or IQ), task characteristics such as task difficulty, and strategy knowledge. In comparison, *procedural metacognitive knowledge* is mostly implicit (subconscious) and refers to children's self-monitoring and self-regulation activities while solving memory problems.

Empirical research exploring the development of declarative metamemory revealed that children's knowledge of facts about memory increases considerably over the primary-grade years, but is still incomplete by the end of childhood. Recent studies also showed that increases in knowledge about strategies are paralleled by the acquisition of strategies, and that metamemory–memory behavior relationships tend to be moderately strong (cf. reviews by Joyner & Kurtz-Costes, 1997; Schneider, 1999; Schneider & Pressley, 1997). Thus what children know about their memory frequently influences how they try to remember. However, although late-grade-schoolchildren know much about common strategies, there is increasing evidence that many adolescents and adults (including college students) have little or no knowledge of some more complex, important, and powerful memory strategies such as those related to the processing of text information.

The situation regarding developmental trends in procedural metacognitive knowledge is not entirely clear (cf. Schneider, 1998). Several studies explored how children use their knowledge to monitor their own memory status and regulate their memory activities. There is evidence that older children are better able to predict future performance on memory tasks than younger children, and that there are similar age trends when the task is to judge performance accuracy after the test has been taken. Also, older children seem better able to judge whether the name of an object that they currently cannot recall would be recognized later if the experimenter provided it (feeling-of-knowing judgments).

However, although monitoring skills seem to improve continuously across childhood and adolescence, it is important to note that developmental trends in self-monitoring are less pronounced than those observed for declarative metamemory. Contrary to earlier assumptions, recent research shows that even young children are well able to monitor their progress in memory tasks (cf. Butterfield, Nelson, & Peck, 1988; Schneider & Lockl, in press). It appears that the considerable developmental improvements in procedural metamemory observable in elementary schoolchildren are mainly due to an increasingly better interplay between monitoring and self-regulatory activities. That is, even though young children may be as capable of identifying memory problems as older ones, in most cases only the older children will effectively regulate their behavior in order to overcome these problems. For instance, several studies investigating children's and adolescents' allocation of study time found that even young grade-schoolchildren showed adequate monitoring in that they correctly discriminated between recalled and unrecalled items as well as between easy and difficult items (e.g., Bisanz, Vesonder, & Voss, 1978; Dufresne & Kobasigawa, 1989). However, the younger children did not use this information for subsequent learning. Only the older participants were likely to select previously unrecalled information for further study.

One of the main motivations to study metamemory has been the assumption that there are important relationships between knowing about memory and memory behaviors (cf. Brown, 1978; Flavell & Wellman, 1977; Weinert, 1986). However, early investigations did not find substantial links between the two components (Cavanaugh & Perlmutter, 1982). More recent research has shown that the relation one finds between memory and metamemory is considerably stronger than previously assumed. For example, in a meta-analysis based on about 60 studies and more than 7,000 participants, Schneider and Pressley (1989) reported a correlation of .41 between metamemory and memory behavior. The strength of relation varied as a function of type of task (e.g., organizational strategies or memory monitoring), task difficulty, when metamemory was assessed (before or after the memory task), age, and the interaction of these various factors.

A typical feature of more recent studies is that they do not limit themselves to analyses of simple intercorrelations. For instance, Schneider, Schlagmüller, and Visé (1998) constructed a comprehensive metamemory battery that was repeatedly given to a large sample of third- and fourth-grade students. Children's verbal IQ, their memory span, and their performance on a sort-recall task were also assessed. Causal modeling analyses showed that both IQ and memory capacity had a moderate effect on metamemory, which in turn had a strong direct impact on strategic behavior and a modest direct influence on recall. Moreover, metamemory had a substantial indirect effect of about .6 on recall (via strategic behavior). As a consequence, individual differences in metamemory explained a large proportion in the variance of the recall data. These findings are in accord with theoretical assumptions that emphasize a bidirectional relationship between metamemory and memory behavior (e.g., Brown, 1978; Hasselhorn, 1995). Accordingly, metamemory can influence memory behavior, which in turn leads to enhanced metamemory.

Taken together, research on the role of metamemory in memory development has created a large body of evidence supporting the utility of the concept. Mainly due to methodological improvements, more recent work on the metamemory–memory link has provided evidence for rather strong relations among metamemory, memory behavior, and memory performance (see Schneider, 1999, for a review of this literature). Despite this positive trend, developmental research on children's metacognitive knowledge is no longer the hot topic it used to be, mainly due to the fact that a related but more general line of research focusing on children's theory of mind has attracted researchers interested in cognitive development (cf. Flavell, 2000).

Effects of domain knowledge

Surprisingly, one of the most obvious sources of individual differences in memory performance, prior knowledge of task-related content, was discovered relatively recently. Since the late 1970s, however, a large number of developmental studies have demonstrated that the amount of knowledge in a particular domain such as chess, physics, or sports determines how much new information from the same domain can be stored and retrieved (see the reviews by Bjorklund, 1985; Bjorklund & Schneider, 1996; Chi & Ceci, 1987; Schneider & Bjorklund, 1998).

Prior knowledge of related content affects memory in several ways. It not only influences how much and what children recall, but also affects their execution of basic processes and strategies, their metacognitive knowledge, and their acquisition of new strategies. Rich domain knowledge can also have nonstrategic effects, that is, diminish the need for strategy activation. Interestingly, domain knowledge can serve as an explanation for other memory changes. Increasing domain knowledge improves efficiency of basic processes, acquisition and execution of strategies, and metacognitive knowledge (cf. Hasselhorn, 1995).

Evidence for the powerful effects of domain knowledge on memory performance comes from studies using the *expert–novice paradigm*. These studies compared experts and novices in a given domain (e.g., baseball, chess, or soccer) on a memory task related to that domain. From a developmental perspective, the major advantage of the expert–novice paradigm is that knowledge and chronological age are not necessarily confounded, a problem inherent in most studies addressing knowledge-base effects. Several studies demonstrated that rich domain knowledge enabled a child expert to perform much like an adult expert and better than an adult novice – thus showing a disappearance and sometimes reversal of usual developmental trends. Experts and novices not only differed with regard to quantity of knowledge but also regarding the quality of knowledge, that is, in the way their knowledge is represented in the mind. Moreover, several studies also confirmed the assumption that rich domain knowledge can compensate for low overall aptitude on domain-related memory tasks, as no differences were found between high- and low-aptitude experts on various recall and comprehension measures (for a review, see Bjorklund & Schneider, 1996). Perhaps the most robust finding in the literature on knowledge effects is that experts in an area learn faster and more when studying "new" information in their domain of expertise than do novices.

How is such a rich knowledge base acquired? The few available longitudinal studies indicate that expertise is based on a long-lasting process of motivated learning. Building up a rich knowledge base not only requires cognitive abilities but also high levels of interest and motivation. In several domains, it is the amount of practice and not so much the level of general aptitude that determines exceptional performance (see Ericsson, Krampe, & Tesch-Roemer, 1993, for a review). However, even though most available developmental studies on expertise highlight the importance of deliberate practice in developing domain-specific expertise, they do not support the assumption that individual differences in basic abilities (such as memory capacity) can be completely neglected when it comes to predicting the development of exceptional performance (cf. Schneider, 2001).

Overall, research on the effects of domain knowledge conducted during the last 25 years has convincingly shown that any explanation of memory development must reserve a large place for increasing knowledge of specific content (Siegler, 1998). Domain knowledge is a powerful determinant of memory and learning. It increases steadily from infancy to adulthood and contributes to the development of other sources of memory competencies, such as basic capacities, strategies, and metacognitive knowledge. Research on the development of domain knowledge has illustrated the fact that the sources of memory development interact in numerous ways, which sometimes makes it very difficult to disentangle the effects of specific sources from that of other influences. The importance of these interactions was highlighted in the *model of good information-processing* (Pressley, Borkowski, & Schneider, 1989; Schneider & Pressley, 1997), which emphasizes the interplay of intact neurology (basic capacities), strategic, knowledge-base, and motivational components in determining cognitive performance.

New Research Trends

Through most of the 1980s, research into deliberate, usually strategic, memory, dominated the field of memory development. However, it seems fair to state that despite the importance of deliberate, strategic memory, much of what children and adults remember is acquired without attention and often retrieved without awareness. Thus, it seems logical and straightforward that new lines of basic research on memory development have focused on *nonstrategic factors*, not only reactivating old issues such as unintentional/ implicit memory or long-term retention and forgetting, but also developing conceptual frameworks such as fuzzy-trace theory that question the importance of higher-order cognitive processes for memory development and thus challenge the strategic memory view. There is also rather new evidence on the development of visuo-spatial memory that has been ignored in previous reviews of the field. Another new exciting line of (more applied) research that has received substantial attention during the last 15 years and also represents the revival of a classic theme concerns autobiographical memory, in particular, children's eyewitness memory. In the following, the main outcomes of these new research trends will be briefly reviewed.

Implicit memory

By definition, implicit memory is "memory without awareness." Since the late 1980s and early 1990s, researchers interested in adult memory have explored differences between explicit memory, that is, conscious recollections of experiences, and implicit memory, that is, memory for some information without being consciously aware that one is remembering. One of the main outcomes of this research is that there are clear dissociations between explicit and implicit memory. For instance, some brain-damaged patients were found to be seriously impaired with explicit memory compared to normal, but did not show implicit memory impairment (for a review, see Roediger & McDermott, 1993).

Subsequently, research on implicit memory with children was carried out to assess the generalizability of these findings. Most developmental studies involved the use of fragmented pictures, perhaps a dog, that have to be identified by the participants. This is very difficult to do initially, but as more of the picture is completed, it becomes increasingly easier to identify the pictures. After a series of such picture-identification tasks has been given, children are provided with degraded pictures of both previously seen and unseen objects. The typical finding is that repetition priming is observed. That is, children identify fragmented pictures of previously seen pictures much faster than fragmented pictures of previously unseen objects (see Ausley & Guttentag, 1993).

Findings from developmental studies further indicate age-related dissociations. That is, age-related differences between younger and older children typically observed on explicit memory tests are greatly reduced with implicit memory tests (Parkin, 1993). More specifically, the perceptual priming effects seem comparable for older and younger participants. Although older children typically show better explicit memory (i.e., they recognize more pictures than the younger children), no developmental differences in implicit memory are found.

One problem with the generalizability of these findings is that most developmental studies have focused on a single type of implicit memory, that is, perceptual priming. In order to draw firm conclusions about the developmental invariance of priming, other types of implicit memory testing such as conceptual priming are needed. For instance, a conceptual measure of implicit memory provides participants with a list of category names and requires them to produce the first exemplars of the categories that come to mind. The typical finding from studies with adults is that prior presentation of a category exemplar increases the likelihood of that word being named as a category instance (Schumann-Hengsteler, 1995).

Given that these tests emphasize the semantic relationships between studied and tested items and thus require conceptually driven processing, one should expect age differences in conceptual priming. That is, older children should show more priming because the semantic categories are more meaningful to them than to younger children. However, the research situation is not clear. Some of the few studies that have examined developmental trends in conceptual priming indicate that priming is age-invariant (see Anooshian, 1997). Other researchers have argued that the unexpected finding of age-invariant conceptual priming could be due either to the rather narrow age ranges or to the predominance of familiar semantic categories in those studies (Hupbach, Mecklenbräuker, & Wippich, 1999). In fact, Hupbach et al. (1999) found reliable age differences in conceptual priming for atypical but not for typical category exemplars when performances of 4-, 6-, 8-, and 10-year-olds were compared. Accordingly, although there is substantial evidence for the age invariance of priming effects, more studies are needed to explore the generalizability of findings across different task settings.

Overall, the implicit memory results to date point to an independent memory system. It seems that the brain systems mediating perceptual and conceptual priming are fully developed early in life, which clearly contrasts to the continuous development of the explicit memory system (cf. Squire, Knowlton, & Musen, 1993). There is substantial evidence in cognitive neuroscience that perceptual and conceptual priming do not depend upon the medial-temporal and diencephalic brain structures that mediate intentional declarative memory. Although early Russian research pointed to young children's surprisingly well-developed "involuntary" memory, contemporary findings on implicit memory provide a convincing explanation for dissociations between involuntary and voluntary memory that are found throughout the life-span.

Visuo-spatial memory

The vast majority of studies on memory development have focused on verbal memory. Given that there is considerably less research concerning the development of other memory components such as children's visuo-spatial memory skills, findings from this domain are mostly ignored in contemporary reviews of the state of the art.

What do we know about developmental trends in visuo-spatial memory? First of all, it is important to note that there seem to be several visuo-spatial memory systems, and not just one. Although the inclusion of a visuo-spatial subsystem ("visuo-spatial sketchpad") in Baddeley and Hitch's (1974) working-memory model suggests that the retention of visual and spatial material is organized by the same underlying system, the empirical evidence based on studies with adults does not support this assumption (cf. Logie & Marchetti, 1991). Moreover, the findings indicate that developmental pathways for processing visual and spatial information differ considerably (for a review, see Schumann-Hengsteler, 1995). For instance, Schumann-Hengsteler (1992) used a picture-reconstruction task to disentangle memory for visual and spatial components. Children of different ages (5-, 8-, and 10-year-olds) were first shown large picture frames that contained several small pictures of familiar objects and were then asked to remember the items and their locations. There were clear-cut age effects in the ability to associate a given picture with its location (older children outperformed the younger ones). However, memory for locations, that is, memory for the original positions of the small pictures (regardless of their identity) was generally well developed and did not vary as a function of age. See Ellis, Katz, and Williams (1987) and Mandler and Robinson (1978) for additional evidence supporting the position that there are no major age differences in short-term spatial memory.

The developmental evidence for permanent (long-term) visuo-spatial memory is roughly comparable. We know from many developmental studies that very young children already possess efficient search strategies, as indicated by their performance on hide-and-seek tasks (see DeLoache, 1989; Wellman & Somerville, 1982). Moreover, even preschool children can use maps efficiently and possess relevant route knowledge, that is, represent landmarks and other significant cues in the environment when searching for target locations (Herman, Norton, & Klein, 1986). All in all, it appears that there is little development in the nature of the spatial knowledge system itself. Developmental changes in permanent visuo-spatial memory mainly reflect an increasing coordination of the knowledge system with action and with spatial markers in the world (Landau & Spelke, 1985).

The assumption that visuo-spatial memory is already well developed in young children has been supported by the everyday observation that preschoolers and kindergarteners perform well on the popular game of Concentration. The belief expressed by most lay people and many developmental psychologists that children are very good at such a task and may even outperform adults has been confirmed by one of the first scientific studies on the topic (Baker-Ward & Ornstein, 1988), which did not find significant differences between children's and adults' performance. However, there is conflicting evidence. In a series of carefully designed experiments, Schumann-Hengsteler (1995, 1996) assessed developmental differences in three task-relevant skills (i.e., picture identification, relocation of picture cards, and search strategies). In short, her findings based on four age groups (5-, 8-, 10-year-olds, and adults) revealed that the adults were actually better players than the children, who did not differ from each other. Overall, older children and adults used more efficient strategies, particularly later during the game. However, there were no age differences in picture recognition, and even the youngest children in the sample played the game rather well. Thus, even though children's visuo-spatial memory relevant for the game of Concentration may not be better than that of adults, it undoubtedly is very good.

Taken together, findings from this field indicate that there are age-related trends in visuo-spatial memory skills, the effects of which are generally small. Thus research on this topic has shown that age differences – if noticed at all – are far less pronounced than those observed for verbal memory.

Fuzzy-trace theory

An increasingly popular theory that attempts to explain memory and cognitive development without invoking conscious awareness is fuzzy-trace theory (see Brainerd & Reyna,

1993; Reyna & Brainerd, 1995). This theory provides a developmental description of the nature of memory traces and the processes that act on those traces when people perform cognitive tasks. It is a basic-process theory, eschewing concepts such as strategies or metacognitive knowledge to account for developmental changes in cognitive processing.

Brainerd and Reyna propose that memory representations exist on a continuum from literal, verbatim representations to fuzzy, gistlike traces and that multiple-memory traces exist for any event one experiences. The type of trace people will use depends on the nature of the task, the durability of the trace, and the processing preferences of the individual. Although the assumption is that people of all ages extract the gist of a message and thus build up fuzzy traces, there are developmental differences in gist extraction. That is, children of all ages extract gist, but young children are biased toward storing and retrieving verbatim traces, resulting in a "verbatim to gist shift" that occurs sometime during the early elementary school years. This implies that the memory system for processing verbatim information develops earlier than the system for processing gist. The theory also assumes that relying on fuzzy traces enables children to resist the adverse effects of interference. Thus, Brainerd and Reyna propose that age differences in cognitive processes can be attributed to age-correlated changes in the construction of memory traces, with an increasing reliance on gist-like fuzzy traces.

Although fuzzy-trace theory has been tested using various cognitive tasks, investigations using memory tasks focused on *cognitive triage*, which conceptualizes free recall as a process in which the most difficult items are recalled first, analogous to the battlefield surgical practice of treating the most difficult cases first. Brainerd, Reyna, and colleagues developed an "optimization model" which predicted that recall of a word list should begin by recalling items with relatively weak memory strength, followed by strong items, and be completed by weaker items. This model definitively is not in accord with assumptions of the traditional "strategic memory model" that would predict that recall of stronger items should precede that of weaker items.

Although further details of the model cannot be presented owing to space restrictions, it seems important to note that several experiments conducted by Brainerd, Reyna, and colleagues have directly contrasted strategic versus triage models of free recall, with most results yielding a closer fit with the triage than with the strategic model (e.g., Brainerd, 1995; Harnishfeger & Brainerd, 1994). However, the available evidence is not entirely conclusive because the materials used in most of these experiments were unrelated and thus did not stimulate the spontaneous use of memory strategies. In a recent study with second- and fourth-graders, Büttner (in press) selected both semantically related and unrelated stimuli to test the assumption that the optimization model explains recall patterns better than the traditional strategy model. Although the recall patterns found for both types of materials were compatible with the assumptions of cognitive triage, individual differences in recall of semantically related items were more closely related to the degree of semantic organization (clustering during recall) than to the amount and pattern of cognitive triage. Although it appears that cognitive triage is real, the crucial issue to be addressed in future research will be whether fuzzy-trace theory can also explain findings from other memory paradigms, thus eliminating concepts such as strategies and metacognition from the developmental study of memory.

Long-term retention and forgetting

The paucity of research since the early 1930s on long-term retention and forgetting may be due to the failure to find age differences in the early studies conducted around the turn of last century. Only recently, Brainerd, Howe, Reyna, and colleagues implemented a research program that tried to overcome certain weaknesses of the classic studies (cf. Brainerd, Reyna, Harnishfeger, & Howe, 1993; Howe & Brainerd, 1989). To do so, they replaced age-insensitive recognition measures by cued or free-recall tasks, and also avoided floor effects in forgetting by using less memorable materials and longer forgetting intervals. Finally, the "levels-of-learning" problem of earlier research (i.e., the fact that age differences in immediate levels of learning can mask age differences in subsequent amounts of forgetting) was dealt with by requiring participants of all age levels to learn the material to a perfect-recall criterion. Once accomplished, participants were tested again for the target materials using recall measures, often days and weeks later.

As a main result, Brainerd, Howe, Reyna, and colleagues found substantial developmental differences in long-term retention in that older children retained more (and thus forgot less) than younger ones. Consistent improvements in retention were documented from the early elementary school years to adolescence. Although most forgetting experiments of the type described used lists of words, several others that used stories as stimuli (e.g., Howe, 1991) yielded similar results in that forgetting was greater for the younger relative to the older children, regardless of the retention interval. Thus, the use of more sophisticated experimental paradigms indicates that long-lived assumptions concerning the developmental invariance of long-term retention and forgetting need to be revised.

It should be noted, however, that the new interpretations are restricted to the particular methodology used in this research paradigm. For example, it may be difficult to generalize findings from a paradigm that requires perfect learning to the world outside the laboratory, where perfect learning is the exception rather than the rule. The new interest in applied aspects of memory development, in particular autobiographical memory and eyewitness testimony, may provide an appropriate basis for such badly needed tests of generalizability.

The development of eyewitness memory

One form of autobiographical memory that has received substantial attention in the last decade has been eyewitness memory, a topic that – as noted above – was highly relevant to European memory researchers around the turn of the last century but was given up in subsequent decades. With children being increasingly called upon to provide testimony in legal cases, issues about how much and how accurately children remember, and the degree to which they are influenced by suggestion, has become a high-priority research interest (for recent reviews, see Bruck & Ceci, 1999; Ceci & Bruck, 1998).

Eyewitness memory represents one specific form of event memory that emphasizes the accuracy rather than the amount of information recalled about an experienced event. In most experimental studies, children witnessed events either staged at their schools, or videotaped events, or were asked to recollect some potentially traumatic experiences, such as visits to the doctor or dentist. During the interview period following the event, children were typically first questioned using general prompts, usually followed by more specific questions.

Regarding *age differences* in eyewitness memory, most investigations revealed that levels of recall to general questions are generally low, and that free recall increases with age (e.g., Cassel & Bjorklund, 1995; Poole & Lindsay, 1995). However, despite low levels of free recall, what preschoolers and kindergarteners do recall is usually accurate. Thus, despite age differences, most young children possess the cognitive capacity necessary for accurate testimony. Age differences may diminish or even disappear under certain conditions, for instance, if an event is particularly salient or personally meaningful to young children. In most studies, levels of correct recall increased when more specific cues were provided; *unfortunately* in most cases this was also accompanied by an increase in the number of inaccurate responses, which reduced overall accuracy, particularly in younger children. However, even young schoolchildren can enhance the accuracy of their testimony by screening out wrong answers when given explicit incentives for accuracy (Koriat, Goldsmith, Schneider, & Nakash-Dura, in press; Roebers & Schneider, in press). This finding indicates that young children can regulate their memory reporting to produce a more accurate record of past events when they are allowed and encouraged to screen out wrong answers (e.g., by saying "I don't know") and when they are explicitly motivated to do so.

Although eyewitness memory improves with age, differences seem most pronounced for the period between 4 and 7 years of age. Most studies that included samples of adults illustrated that elementary schoolchildren's free recall of witnessed events is comparable to that of adults (e.g., Cassel, Roebers, & Bjorklund, 1996).

An important topic in children's eyewitness memory concerns *age differences in susceptibility to suggestion.* In most suggestibility paradigms, participants witness an event and are later asked sets of misleading questions, suggesting an inaccurate "fact." Most studies that have looked for developmental differences in suggestibility have found them, with preschool children being particularly prone to suggestion, much more than schoolchildren and adults. It appears that young children's erroneous answers do not always reflect an actual change in memory representation. It is likely that some of the young children's compliance with misleading questions is related to the social demand characteristics of the situation. However, other research suggests that misleading questions actually result in changes in the underlying memory representations, with young children being more likely to make such changes than older children (Ceci & Bruck, 1998).

How long do memories of witnessed events last? Are there developmental differences in long-term recall and forgetting rates? Several studies have investigated children's memories of specific events for periods ranging from several weeks to two years. Although the results of these studies are not totally consistent, they indicate that age differences in the accuracy of recall increase with increasing delays, at least when delays are longer than one month. This finding is in accord with the experimental research on long-term retention and forgetting conducted by Brainerd, Howe, Reyna, and colleagues, and may be explained by fuzzy-trace theory. That is, given that verbatim traces, favored by young children, deteriorate more rapidly than the gist or fuzzy traces preferred by older children, greater losses of information over delays should be expected for younger as compared to older children.

Overall, the findings of recent eyewitness memory research confirm several findings of the early period, such as age differences in recall of events and the particularly large effects of misleading questions and repeated questioning on young children's memory reports. On the other hand, however, recent studies do not support the assumption held by the early eyewitness memory researchers that young children are generally unreliable witnesses. One merit of contemporary research is that conditions have been identified that increase the probability for obtaining accurate memory reports from young children. For instance, new and promising interview techniques have been developed that avoid the problems of previous interrogations and provide the conditions for optimal recall, particularly in young children.

Future Directions for Memory Development Research

Although memory development is a rather mature field, there is still much to learn, and the centrality of memory to all other aspects of cognition makes it likely that the ontogeny of memory, in one form or another, will continue to be a primary focus of cognitive development. Examples of much-studied topics that require more in-depth investigation in the years ahead include strategic memory and children's autobiographical memory. Regarding strategic memory, one fruitful area for future research concerns the occurrence of utilization deficiencies and the role of variability in children's strategy use, in particular, the relation between variability, age, and strategy effectiveness (see also Bjorklund & Douglas, 1997). Also, more should be known about strategies that develop in more naturalistic (i.e., nonschool) contexts. For instance, what roles do parents and peers play in this process? What type of memory strategies do children use when playing computer or other types of games such as the game of Concentration (e.g., Oyen & Bebko, 1996)?

As noted above, there are several under-studied areas, such as implicit memory and visuo-spatial memory, that await further research. In particular, the topic of implicit memory seems important because it addresses the significance of unconscious cognition in general. It has been proposed that implicit memory is ontogenetically and phylogenetically an earlier acquisition than explicit memory, based on more basic and primitive brain structures. Much still has to be learned about interrelations between implicit and explicit representations of information and the transition from implicit to explicit (conscious) representations of knowledge. Thus studying implicit processes becomes not only interesting in itself but also for its potential relationships with the development of explicit, conscious processes.

Many cognitive developmentalists, meanwhile, have recognized that the development of information-processing cannot be isolated from development of the brain (Johnson, 1998; Schneider & Bjorklund, 1998). As noted by van der Molen and Ridderinkhof (1998), developmental psychology has been relatively "brainless" for a long time, despite the fact that its founding father, Wilhelm Preyer, was concerned specifically with brain–behavior relations (Preyer, 1982). In the field of memory development, there is an increasing emphasis on the need for greater awareness of and interaction with neuro-science perspectives (e.g., Gathercole, 1998; Nelson, 1997). However, we still know very little about the neuropsychology of memory development, at the level of both descrip-tion and explanation.

Neuropsychological research can influence memory development research in a number of ways. For instance, recent research contrasting the deferred imitation abilities of adults with certain types of brain lesion has shed light on the nature of young children's memory. There is evidence that young children's deferred imitation abilities reflect a form of explicit memory rather than implicit memory. In a study by McDonough, Mandler, Kee, and Squire (1995), neurologically normal adults and adults suffering from amnesia (with con-firmed or suspected damage to the medial temporal lobe) were shown different action series on one day, and on the next day tested under two conditions: they were either instructed to imitate the previously seen action sequences or simply observed to see if they imitated these sequences spontaneously. In contrast to the findings reported for young children on this task, the adults with amnesia (but not the normal controls) failed to reproduce the action sequences in either condition. The results obtained by McDonough et al. (1995) suggest that the hippocampus and surrounding structures support memory for event sequences (or deferred imitation). Related research based on adults with lesions to the hippocampus has illustrated the existence of different memory systems in that these people were unable to acquire new explicit/declarative memories but were able to form new implicit/nondeclarative memories. Another line of research that already shows great promise (at least in the area of implicit memory) is to conduct par-allel memory studies with human infants and age-matched nonhuman primates, or to develop tasks with infants that are based on tasks already being used with human adults (cf. Nelson, 1997). Although it seems important for memory development researchers to become familiar with neuropsychological techniques and research findings, it is also important not to lose sight of the cognitive and behavioral levels while examining brain functions. Accordingly, biological levels of explication should not replace psychological-level theories, but be integrated with them to yield a proper perspective on memory devel-opment (Bjorklund, 1997).

On a more general level, an interesting question is whether the study of memory needs to be situated in a number of broader conceptual and research contexts, or whether future research activities should focus on more specific memory functions. The position that future research on memory development should be embedded within the context of broader topics such as comprehension, knowledge, context, and strategy has been recently proposed by Kuhn (2000a and ch. 17 this volume). The basic claim is that although memory research has contributed significantly to our understanding in each of these four areas, the study of memory development in turn needs to profit from what has been accomplished in each of those areas and to be enriched by integration with each of them. Kuhn distinguishes between two increasingly divergent branches of memory research, one connected to the topics of comprehension and knowledge and focusing on the study of "memories," and the other invoking the topics of context and strategies and referring to the study of "memorizing." She votes for an approach that connects the studies of memories and memorizing to the four broader topics described above, and that inter-prets the results within the frameworks that those topics provide.

On the other hand, there is also research indicating that the assumption of general memory concepts may oversimplify the case. For instance, several recent studies concern the issue whether the concept of verbal memory represents a domain-general skill or consists of domain-specific verbal abilities (see the review by Schneider & Bjorklund, 1998). The way to assess this question empirically is to administer different verbal memory tasks and assess the intertask correlations. Overall, numerous cross-sectional studies showed that intertask correlations were rather low, regardless of children's age, and that the low correlations were not due to reliability problems. Further confirming evidence came from recent longitudinal research (Schneider & Weinert, 1995). Here, intertask consistency was high only for very similar verbal memory tasks (e.g., parallel measures of story recall or memory span). Thus these findings are consistent with the position that there is no "unitary" verbal memory construct, and that deliberate verbal memory may be better thought of as a set of specific abilities rather than a domain-general concept. Apparently, more research is needed to explore the dimensionality of the construct and possible changes across the life-span. Needless to say, this discussion has to be generalized to areas of nonverbal memory such as visuo-spatial memory discussed above. Overall, although the field of memory development constitutes one of the oldest and most active research areas in the field of cognitive development, there are still many open issues that need to be clarified in future research.

CHAPTER TWELVE

The Development of Causal Reasoning

Barbara Koslowski and Amy Masnick

In its early years, psychology was a branch of philosophy. Issues in philosophy motivated many of the issues addressed by early psychologists. The philosophical roots of psychology continue to be evident in psychological research on causal understanding, and on causal reasoning or explanation. Furthermore, in both disciplines, approaches to causal reasoning have been bound up with approaches to scientific inquiry, and this makes sense. One of the main aims of science is to identify the causes of phenomena.

In both philosophy and psychology, as descriptions of scientific inquiry have changed, approaches to causal reasoning have followed suit. The shift over time can be seen with respect to three themes. First, early philosophical approaches argued that, ultimately, causation could be reduced to the Humean indices. The Humean view of causation (at least as interpreted by psychological researchers) is that we have no actual evidence for causation. Rather, we come to infer that event X causes event Y when the two events are characterized by what are termed "Humean" indices: X is temporally prior to Y, is contiguous with it in time and in space, and the contiguity is regular. For Hume, causation is an inference that we draw from these indices (Hume, 1973). Second, early philosophical approaches also treated the Humean indices as formal, or content-free, or content-independent. That is, the Humean indices were treated as abstract rules applicable to any content area or domain, from epidemiology to attachment. Thus, in psychology, causal understanding was operationally defined as being equivalent to understanding the Humean indices. One result was that psychologists aimed to avoid tapping the participant's pre-existing information about particular causes in a domain and tried instead to tap beliefs about causation as a set of abstract rules that could, in principle, be discerned in or applied to any domain. In many tasks, this meant that performance was stipulated to be correct if the participant could not only ignore but also override the causal information that she brought to the experimental situation. Third, because causation was

We thank Richard Boyd, Marianella Casasola, and Brad Morris for their many helpful comments.

equated with the Humean indices, there was little attention given in either philosophy or psychology to the role of mechanism, process, or theory in causal understanding. The focus was on identifying which events were prior to, contiguous with, and covaried with an effect. The focus ignored mechanism, theory, or explanation that described the process by which an event brought about an effect.

In more recent philosophy and psychology, researchers have begun to argue that causation involves more than just the Humean indices. Researchers have made this claim by noting that the Humean indices are content-bound; whether covariation indicates genuine cause or mere artifact depends on the particular events involved in the covariation. More specifically, researchers have argued that understanding the metaphysics of causation as well as understanding the psychology of causal reasoning requires taking account of the role of theory, or mechanism, or explanation. Instead of merely relying on the Humean indices to decide which event is causal, it is also important to deal with the mechanism or process that can explain how the event brings the effect about.

Reasoning about Physical Causality in Infancy

In philosophy, the early Humean approach was met with early criticisms from Kant (1781/1787). Much of the research on causal reasoning in infancy has been explicitly framed in terms of the classic epistemological debate between Hume and Kant. For Hume, causation was an inference based on information about contiguity and regularity. For Kant, the focus was on why it is that only some of the regular contiguities in the world are deemed by us to be causal. Kant proposed that causation and causal connections are not mere inferences; they exist in the world. Further, the reason that we can know about causal connections is because we hold an a priori notion of causation within which we interpret sequences of events in the world.

Researchers studying infants' understanding of physical causality have focused on mechanical causality and have operationalized causality in terms of the "launching event." In the launching event, an agent object (such as a red brick) moves across a screen and either does or does not contact a recipient object (such as a green brick). When the agent stops, the recipient, either immediately or after a delay, moves the rest of the way across the screen, following the same trajectory. When using the launching event, researchers of both a Humean and a Kantian persuasion operationally define causation as consisting of contact by the agent followed by immediate movement by the recipient, that is, in terms of spatial and temporal contiguity. In the typical procedure, infants are habituated to or familiarized with one sort of event (for example, contact/immediate movement) and tested on a different sort of event (for example, contact/delayed movement).

A note about terminology: When the launching event involves both contact and immediate movement, we will refer to the event as "causal." When the event involves either non-contact and/or delayed movement, we will refer to it as "non-causal." Our own view is that spatio-temporal contiguity does not guarantee that an event is causal. However, we will use "causal" and "non-causal" to be consistent with the literature.

Does direct launching have a special status?

Both Humeans and Kantians use the launching event to study causation but differ in their predictions. Psychologists of a Kantian persuasion expect that the contact/immediate (causal) condition should be given a "special status" and treated as qualitatively different from the other (non-causal) conditions. They also expect that there should be no significant differences among the non-causal conditions, because they are equivalently non-causal. In addition, the special status of the causal condition should come in, developmentally, as a full-blown tendency or "module" – a Kantian feature of the mind.

In contrast, Humeans expect that infants might initially process the launching event in terms of its individual temporal and spatial features and only later infer that the contact/immediate event is causal. Thus, development should consist of increasing attention to various features, rather than a full-blown causation module. Processing individual features might also lead to non-equivalence among non-causal events, as different features are accorded more or less status as causal indicators.

Two additional points are worth noting. One is that both camps (tacitly) assume that the launching event is measuring the abstract notion of causation, rather than beliefs about causation in the particular experimental situation. The other is that the launching event is typically presented as a film.

Motivated by Kantian expectations, Leslie (1984), testing 6.5- to 7-month-olds, changed two features (contact and immediacy) from habituation to test. He found that when infants were habituated to a causal event and tested on a non-causal event there was greater dishabituation than when the switch was from one non-causal event to another non-causal event. For Leslie, this suggested a causation module that enabled infants to treat causal and non-causal events differently, to treat the simultaneous occurrence of contact and immediacy, not as two distinct features, but as causation.

A problem for the module interpretation was that the switch from one non-causal event to the other non-causal event also produced dishabituation, though to a smaller extent than the causal to non-causal switch. Furthermore, when only one feature was changed from familiarization to test, the difference in dishabituation between a causal and a non-causal sequence was comparable to the difference between two non-causal sequences. Finally, infants treated a spatial gap no differently from the way they treated a temporal delay. These results suggest that the infants were attending to individual features (delay and gap), rather than treating the contact/immediate event as having a special (causal) status.

To account for these findings, Leslie proposed a "spatio-temporal continuity gradient" with the immediate launching event at one end, the delayed/non-contact event at the other end, and the other types of (non-causal) launching events in between. However, it is not clear how a model that invokes a (presumably continuous) gradient captures the notion of a (presumably non-continuous) causation module, in which the causal event is distinct from the non-causal events with the non-causal events being equivalent to one another.

Recall that, when two features changed, the causal to non-causal shift resulted in greater dishabituation than the switch from one non-causal event to another. Invoking neither a causation module nor a features approach, Haith and Benson (1998) note that, in a direct launching event, three visual transitions occur simultaneously: a moving agent becomes stationary; agent and recipient contact each other; and a stationary recipient moves. They argue that "Simultaneous transitions have a special status, independent of causality", and can produce a "synergistic effect" (p. 223).

Thus, consistent with a features approach, non-causal events are not treated as equivalent to one another. Furthermore, when causal events are treated differently from non-causal events, the difference can be explained in terms of simultaneous transitions.

Causal agency

However, a result difficult to account for with either a features or a simultaneous transitions approach is presented by Leslie & Keeble (1987). They habituated 7-month-olds to either a direct or a delayed launching event and then ran the films in reverse. Recovery was greater when the causal rather than the non-causal film was reversed. True, the direct launch sequence involved three simultaneous transitions, while the delayed sequence did not. However, the transitions also occurred when the film was reversed. Does this finding argue for the special status of causation? Yes, if the aspect of causation that one has in mind is causal agency. The Leslie and Keeble results suggest that, at least in this particular situation, the infants relied on the features of the causal event to learn which of the objects was the agent. Recovery was greater when the causal rather than the non-causal sequence was reversed because, in the causal sequence, reversal resulted in a change of agent. For the non-causal sequence, reversal produced no change in agent, because the spatio-temporal information used to identify one of the objects as the agent was missing.

Older infants also accord priority to agency. Cohen & Oakes (1993) found that 10- to 12-month-olds did notice when the causal agent in a launching event was switched, but seemed not to notice a switch in causal recipients.

Causation as developmentally full-blown versus continuous

Recall that, on the module view of causation, the module ought to come in, developmentally, as a full-blown tendency. This expectation is difficult to reconcile with the findings reported in the previous section. If the abstract notion of causation itself is a Kantian feature of the mind, and thus comes in as a full-blown module, it is difficult to explain why infants as old as 12 months are more attuned to the agents than to the recipients of a causal event.

Other research is also problematic for the full-blown module view. For example, 6- to 7-month-olds can distinguish between causal and non-causal events when the stimuli are simple computer animated rolling balls, but not when the stimuli are videotapes of moving toys (Oakes, 1994; Oakes & Cohen, 1990). However, by 10 months of age, infants do discriminate the causal from each of the non-causal events (and do not distinguish the non-causal events from each other) even with videotapes of relatively complex toys. Thus, the likelihood that infants accord special status to direct launching varies with both age and stimulus complexity. Does this mean that the "causation module" is not coming in, developmentally, as a full-blown tendency? This is difficult to answer, because it is not clear whether a full-blown tendency should come in during a single day, a week, a few months. What is clear is that these results do not pose a problem for a continuous model of the development of causal understanding.

Spatio-temporal contiguity versus transmission of force

In commenting on the launching event, Haith and Benson (1998) note that "it is worrisome when a single prototype event serves as the platform for a construct." They amplify this point in terms of simultaneous transitions, noted earlier. Another problem with the launching event concerns the transmission of force. Does the infant understand that, when a direct launch takes place with solid (as opposed to filmed) objects, the launch involves the transmission of force, or does she restrict herself to noting only that it involves contact and immediacy?

Using a variant of the launching event and actual solid objects, Kotovsky and Baillargeon (1994) found that 11-month-old infants understand that the size of an agent cylinder affects how far a recipient will be displaced (see also Baillargeon, ch. 3 this volume). Infants manipulated the cylinders prior to the experiment, making it likely that they detected weight differences. The infants' predictions suggest that they were inferring some transmission of force, with cylinders of different sizes (and thus weights) expected to transmit more or less force to the displaced recipient.

Particular instances versus abstract causation

Although infants' beliefs about causation are typically measured in a particular experimental situation, the results are often (tacitly) treated as reflecting an abstract notion of causation that infants bring to the experimental situation. The evidence does not support this treatment.

For example, 10-month-old infants do not categorize launching events in terms of causal versus non-causal. If having an abstract notion of a construct means being able to categorize instances of it, then 10-month-olds do not have an abstract notion of causation. In a similar vein, Haith and Benson (1998) note that, during the habituation phase of Oakes & Cohen's (1990) experiment, infants had no a priori preferences among: direct launching (causal), delayed launching (non causal), and no collision (non causal). Had the infants come to the experimental situation with an abstract notion of causation already in place, they presumably would have found the non-causal events more surprising (and thus interesting) than the causal event. That they did not suggests that, when infants show surprise during the test phase, it is because, during the familiarization phase, they have acquired certain expectations peculiar to the particular experiment.

In summary, the evidence is not consistent with what a causation module would predict. Infants seem initially to process the launching event in terms of the individual features of spatial and temporal contiguity, as well as in terms of agency. Infants show no evidence of coming to the experimental situation with an abstract notion of causation already in place. Rather, they learn during the familiarization phase to expect that certain sorts of sequences will occur in that particular situation. With the clarity of hindsight, one can see this as ontogenetically adaptive in an empirical, rather than a priori world (see also Baillargeon, ch. 3 this volume). If infants had the abstract belief that the contact and immediate movement in a direct launching event always signaled causation, then they would presumably treat filmed launching events as genuinely causal. However, since filmed events are *not* causal, treating them as such would conflict with reality. More to the point, a full understanding of causation must include understanding that, even with contact, a recipient will not always be launched. Launching will depend on whether the recipient is a dense cube or a porous sphere, is on a rough or a smooth track, is nailed to the track or freestanding, etc. It would be maladaptive to infer causation upon seeing a porous sphere "launch" a dense cube attached to a rough track. Despite the presence of both contact and immediate launching, it would be more accurate and adaptive to respond with skepticism than to infer causation. Thus, although one can describe indices of causation as though they were formal principles true of all situations, the indices can be usefully deployed only if situation-specific information (including information about friction, etc.) is taken into account. The distinction between the formulation of indices (or rules) and their successful deployment will be returned to in later sections. Furthermore, when infants do acquire expectations in an experimental situation, their expectations seem to include some notion of the transmission of force, or a mediating mechanism by which one object moves another. Finally, if causation is both continuous and situation-dependent, then other research not involving the launching event is also relevant to understanding how causal reasoning develops. For example, detecting contingency (Rovee-Collier, 1989) would seem to be a prerequisite to understanding causal agency.

Reasoning about Mechanical Causality in Older Children

Like the work on infancy, much of the research on older children involved reasoning about physical objects and was motivated either by Humean approaches or by criticisms of them. The earliest research assessed causal understanding by measuring children's reliance on the Humean indices in identifying causal agents. As in the infancy research, the Humean indices were (at least tacitly) treated as formal, as applicable across domains or content areas. The tacit assumption was that, when background information, including mechanism information, conflicted with the Humean indices, the latter should be given priority. Later work drew attention to the importance of background information, including information about mechanism or explanation. A controversy in the recent literature has revolved around the extent to which reliance on mechanism information either hinders, or is a legitimate feature of, causal reasoning.

Two approaches have examined the way in which Humean indices, which can be stated in a formal way, interact with background information or content. One approach focuses on causal agents; the other on causal mechanism. The distinction between agents and mechanisms is both important and slippery. It is important because, although we can often identify a causal agent, we may have little or no knowledge of the mechanism by which the agent operates. Instead, we depend on the division of cognitive labor and believe that certain events are causal because experts tell us so (Boyd, 1985, 1993). Few of us, for example, understand the mechanism by which penicillin cures bacterial infections, but we believe that it does because experts tell us that it does. One result of the division of cognitive labor is that many of us have a kind of catalog of likely causal agents (drugs, electrical switches, certain nutrients or their absence, etc.) with little or no knowledge of how the agents operate. The distinction between agent and mechanism is slippery, because as knowledge of the mechanism becomes more refined, mechanisms at one level become agents at the next. For example, treatment with penicillin can cause death, the mechanism being an allergy to molds. In turn, the allergy to molds can become the causal agent, the mechanism being that it causes the body to produce histamines, which in turn constrict the lungs, etc. Despite its slipperiness the distinction between agent and mechanism is often useful when dealing with causation at a particular level.

In the present section, we touch briefly on Humean approaches, in which the tasks consisted of identifying causal agents. We then turn to studies that examine the role of background information, including mechanism, and the way in which background information tempers assessments based on Humean indices.

Humean approaches to mechanical causality

For early researchers, understanding causation meant relying on Humean indices as formal abstractions applicable to any content area. To avoid tapping knowledge about particular causes acquired before the experiment, researchers devised tasks involving unfamiliar events, unlikely initially to be treated as causally related. If the children treated the events as causally related when the events were, for example, contiguous with each other, the children were seen as having correctly relied on the Humean index of contiguity. This led to a misleading picture of children's causal understanding, because totally unfamiliar events are difficult to come by. Thus, to perform "correctly" and treat the situation as causal, the children sometimes had not merely to ignore but actually to *override* information (including mechanism information) acquired before the experiment, because the information conflicted with the Humean index under study.

1. Temporal contiguity and regularity.   For example, Siegler (1975) and Siegler & Liebert (1974) presented 5- and 8-year-old children with tasks in which they had to decide whether a computer or a card programmer caused a light to go on. After a card was inserted into the programmer, a light went on either immediately or after a five-second delay. In some conditions, this relation held 100 percent of the time, in others only 50 percent of the time. The children were asked whether the card programmer made the light flash all the time, or some of the time. Whether the children had prior beliefs about mechanism was not considered. Indeed, in some of the tasks, children were explicitly told the experimenter did not want them "to worry about the way the wires and the electricity cause the light to go on." This was unfortunate, because children treat wires and such as a mechanism that accounts for temporal delays (see below). Although the older children were more likely than the younger ones to take covariation into account, all of the children were more inclined to base their judgments on temporal contiguity rather than covariation, perhaps because they worried about and assumed mediating wires despite directions to the contrary.

2. Temporal priority.   Research on children's beliefs about temporal priority also illustrates the tension between, on the one hand, relying exclusively on Humean indices and on the other hand, taking account of Humean information in conjunction with background information, including information about mechanism. For example, Shultz & Mendelson (1975), asking children to reason about a mechanical apparatus, found responses consistent with a belief in backward causation. They presented 3- to 11-year-olds with tasks in which event A and event B could either precede or follow an effect. For example, pulling down one of two levers to turn on a light, or dropping a marble into one side of a box to produce an effect. Each task also included a facilitatory-inhibitory covariate: for example, a blue pipe-cleaner coiled around the appropriate bar, a plastic tip on a lever, or a small toy car placed on the side of the box where the marble was dropped. The older children appeared to assume that causes preceded effects, while the 3-year-olds tended to identify an event that followed the effect as the cause. Shultz & Mendelson concluded that the youngest children's behavior reflects either a kind of recency effect or an actual "belief that causes can follow, as well as precede, effects," that is, a belief in backward causation.

In contrast, Bullock & Gelman's (1979) results are inconsistent with a belief in backward causation. They presented 3-, 4-, and 5-year-olds with an apparatus in which one marble rolled down one runway and another down a different runway. The runways appeared to disappear into a jack-in-the-box. One marble rolled down a runway before, and the other after, the jack popped up. Of the 3-, 4-, and 5-year-olds, 75 percent, 87 percent, and 100 percent, respectively, consistently chose the first event as the cause of the jack popping up. Bullock & Gelman provided even stronger evidence for the priority principle in children by pitting priority against spatial contiguity. To do this, they moved one of the runways 2 inches away from the jack-box. The children consistently selected the prior event as the cause, even when the runway in question was unconnected with the jack-box.

Why the inconsistency between the 3-year-olds in the Bullock & Gelman study and the 3-year olds in the Shultz & Mendelson study? We suggest that even 3-year-olds have already learned that toy cars, bits of plastic, and pipe-cleaners do not, when stationary, function as causes. Thus, in the Mendelson & Shultz study, the child had not only to ignore her previously acquired information (about, for example, bits of plastic); she had also to *override* it. We suspect that, for the 3-year-olds, this situation resulted in simple confusion, which in turn resulted in a reliance on the recency principle as a way of minimizing memory demands in an already confusing task. It seems unlikely that it tapped a belief in backward causation. In contrast, in the Bullock & Gelman study, it is reasonable to assume that the children had already learned that rolling objects with the density of marbles can push things. The only thing distinguishing the two rolling marbles was priority, and the children, correctly, relied on it. Additional research in which correct performance requires overriding previously acquired information will be covered in other sections below.

The role of mechanism in reasoning about mechanical causality

Researchers who have concentrated on background information about mechanism have asked two questions. One is whether children assume a mediating mechanism in causal situations. A more recent question asks whether non-Humean mechanism information is overridden by Humean contiguity when the two are in conflict.

1. Mechanisms as necessary to causation. Much of the work on children's assumptions of mechanism relies on tasks in which the mediating mechanism is either not visible (as is the case with electrical phenomena) or else is difficult to discern because the task involves a complicated apparatus. The general finding is that children do indeed assume a mediating mechanism, but they sometimes do this only after they have first concerned themselves with identifying the causal agent.

Piaget (1972) asked children to explain the working of, for example, a steam engine, a bicycle, etc. A standard explanation consisted of noting, for example, that the fire makes the wheel of a steam engine go or that the wheels of a bicycle turn when you push the pedals. Such explanations included no mention of the steam that mediated between the fire and the wheels of the steam engine, or of the cogwheel and chain that function as mediating connections in a bicycle.

In different parts of his writing, Piaget provided different accounts of what such answers reflect (Piaget, 1930/1972; Koslowski, et al., 1981). One is that they reflect a belief in action at a distance, with no mechanism mediating between cause and effect. This interpretation is most consistent with Piaget's notion of qualitative differences in development, and is typically the one attributed to Piaget (e.g., Bullock, et al., 1982).

Bullock (1979) showed 3-, 4-, and 5-year-olds the same jack-in-the-box apparatus described earlier. However, in this study, pushing a handle started two simultaneous events: a marble rolled down one runway towards a jack-in-the-box, while the phi phenomenon made it appear that a light "rolled" down the other. In the connected condition, the runways appeared to go into the jack-box; in the unconnected condition, there was a gap between the end of the runways and the jack-box. When both ball and light simultaneously reached the end of the runway, the jack popped up a second later. Participants were asked to choose which event was causal and to explain *how* the causal event made the jack come up.

In the connected condition, children as well as adults chose the rolling ball as the cause. However, with decreasing age, participants were less likely to provide mechanistic explanations. That is, the younger children identified the ball as the causal agent but were less able than older children to suggest that, for example, the ball had triggered a lever or spring to make the jack pop up.

In the unconnected condition, adults either rejected both events as plausible causes or chose the rolling light, presumably because in adults' experience, electrical phenomena often appear to act at a distance. Five-year-olds, divided in their choices, proposed mediating mechanisms for whichever causal agent they chose (for example, a pathway under the table for the balls, or that "electricity can go over" to the effect). The 4-year-olds also mentioned connections, though they were less explicit about the mechanisms. In contrast, the 3-year-olds, most of whom chose the ball as the cause, made no mention of intermediary events or connections. Further, although 90 percent of the 5-year-olds and 70 percent of the 4-year-olds commented on the spatial gap, only 20 percent of the 3-year-olds did so.

Consider the mediating mechanism proposed by those older children who chose the light as the cause. Koslowski, Spilton, and Snipper (1981) found similar explanations when preschool children predicted whether switching on a battery would make a bell ring if the electrical wire running from the battery were disconnected from the bell. Children who predicted that it would work argued, for example, that the "electric stuff" would "whoosh" through the end of the wire and hit the bell. Children who predicted that it would not work argued that the electric stuff would dribble out of the end of the wire and not be able to hit the bell. That is, both types of predictions did invoke a mediating mechanism, and attributed to it properties congruent with the prediction. This finding is analogous to one of the results in Schlottmann's (1999) study, below.

But what of the behavior of the 3-year-olds in Bullock's unconnected condition? On the surface, it is consistent with a belief in action at a distance; the 3-year-olds mention no intermediary events and seldom comment on the spatial gap. We suggest an alternative explanation: when children learn about a particular causal event, they do not treat the event as an integral unit. Rather, they concern themselves first with identifying the causal agent and only then concern themselves with the mechanism that mediates between agent and effect. That is, they echo the behavior of infants in the launching task, for whom agency is an important focus. For example, Koslowski, et al. (1981) showed 3- and 4-year-old children a task in which turning the handle attached to a driving wheel caused a second wheel to turn. After the children operated the pulley, the experimenter removed the highly visible pink rubber band that connected the two wheels and asked the children to predict whether turning the first wheel would still make the second turn. Younger children predicted, incorrectly, that the driven pulley would continue to work with the connecting band removed – a prediction consistent with a belief in action at a distance. However, the children's justifications for their predictions suggested a different interpretation. Justifications noted, for example, that "It'll still work because you can still turn this (driving pulley)" or, "It will still work, because the (driving) wheel's not broken, and not gunked up" (p. 200). Predictions that appeared to reflect a belief in action at a distance instead reflected no concern one way or another with the issue of mechanism. The experimenter was asking about mechanism, but the children were commenting on the condition of the causal agent.

Did the youngest children's indifference to mechanism reflect a *general* indifference? Such a conclusion would be difficult to reconcile with the Kotovsky and Baillargeon (1994) study, in which infants drew (appropriate) inferences about the distance to which cylinders of different sizes (and presumably different weights) could push a recipient. Another possibility is that *in this particular task*, the youngest preschoolers were showing an early indifference to causal mechanism, while they first concentrated on identifying the causal agent.

2. Mechanism versus contiguity. Although children concern themselves with mechanism (once they identify the causal agent), do they accord mechanism priority when it conflicts with contiguity? Shultz (1982) asked 3-year-olds to judge, for example, which of two tuning forks made a noise, or which of two fans blew out a candle. The children chose the causal rather than the contiguous event as the cause. Similarly, Mendelson & Shultz (1976) showed 4- to 7-year olds two marbles dropped in succession into different holes in a box followed by a bell ringing in another box. One marble consistently produced a delayed ring; the other, an inconsistent but immediate ring. When a long tube ran from the marble box to the bell box, children chose the non-contiguous but consistent marble as the cause, presumably because the mediating tube provided a rationale for the delay. Thus, in both tasks, mechanism had priority over contiguity when the two were in conflict.

However, Schlottmann (1999) argues that, when the two are in conflict, temporal contiguity has priority over mechanism. Children were told that the task was "about what happens inside." In the task, ball A was dropped into a hole in a box, there was a three-second pause, ball B was dropped into another hole in the same box and then a bell immediately rang. Children were told that one ball just falls to the floor, while the other makes the bell ring. That is, the contiguous ball was the one that rolled, so that contiguity and mechanism were congruent. Five- to 10-year-olds identified the contiguous ball B as the cause of the ring. The children then saw either a slow mechanism (which would delay the marble) or a fast mechanism placed in the box, but did not see which hole the mechanism was put under. With the fast mechanism in place, children at all ages were accurate, because predictions based on temporal contiguity were congruent with those based on the fast mechanism. However, when the slow mechanism delayed the marble, the youngest children were mostly wrong, choosing the marble that was temporally contiguous with the effect even when the slow mechanism suggested the other ball. This appears to suggest that young children accord temporal contiguity priority when it conflicts with mechanism. Note, however, that even when children were wrong, they usually assumed mechanisms congruent with a contiguity prediction, just as they assumed mechanisms congruent with their predictions of whether a disconnected battery wire would continue to ring a bell (Koslowski, et al., 1981). They suggested for example that the (slow) mechanism must have been faster *that* time, to explain why the delay between marble and bell was short.

In the initial phase of the study, children learned that contiguity and mechanism were congruent (that the contiguous ball was the one that rolled to the bell). Their predictions based on congruence were not challenged. We suggest this made it difficult for them to switch criteria from contiguity congruent with mechanism to contiguity in conflict with mechanism. We argue that the data do not demonstrate a reliance on contiguity rather than mechanism when the two are in conflict; rather, they demonstrate difficulty in switching criteria when expectations ratified in one phase of an experiment are then changed.

To summarize the sections on mechanical causality, children do not believe in backward causation; they treat causes as preceding effects. In addition, when the tasks are complex, children do not always apprehend instances of causation as integrated wholes. Instead, they concern themselves first with identifying the causal agent and then with issues concerning causal mechanism. Thus, when the experimenter asks questions about mechanism, the child might be providing answers about agent. In general, children give priority to mechanism over temporal contiguity when the two are in conflict. However, they have trouble doing this if they have been initially led to believe that contiguity and mechanism will yield congruent predictions. When this happens, rather than ignore mechanism information, they assume mechanisms congruent with the predictions that contiguity would suggest.

Reasoning about Non-Mechanical Causality

When causation is mechanical, the mechanism in question is typically some sort of physical connection (often potentially visible) that mediates between cause and effect. However, many instances of physical causality cannot be reduced to the laws of mechanics. They involve, for example, chemical reactions, historical pressure, or natural selection. The preceding section dealt with non-mechanical causation when it summarized studies that asked whether, when faced with electrical phenomena, children would assume some sort of mediating mechanism. The present section also summarizes studies of non-mechanical causation, but the aim is somewhat different, namely, to examine the interdependence of covariation and background information in general and mechanism information in particular. In addition, the research in this section is often treated as explicitly relevant to scientific reasoning, and this is not surprising given that scientific inquiry often addresses questions about non-mechanical causation (see, e.g., Zimmerman, 2000 for a review of research on scientific reasoning, as well as Kuhn, ch. 17 this volume). When viewed from the perspective of scientific reasoning, one of the controversies in this literature concerns the extent to which reliance on mechanism information either hinders, or is a legitimate feature of, causal reasoning.

The interdependence of covariation and general background information

Klahr and his colleagues have examined the Humean index of covariation. Although they did not examine the way covariation judgments are affected by mechanism information, they did demonstrate that covariation judgments are affected by other sorts of background information. They asked participants to identify the rule that governed the actions of either a robotic toy (BigTrak) or an icon in a computer microworld. In the BigTrak study (Klahr, 2000; Klahr & Dunbar, 1988), participants were taught how to use BigTrak's basic commands. Participants were then asked to determine the function of the "RPT" key. To do so, participants could use several types of prior knowledge. They could use their knowledge about the meaning of the word "repeat," which would suggest the key would lead to some repetition of previously entered commands. They could use their knowledge of programming in general to constrain the plausibility of different hypotheses. And they could use their knowledge of BigTrak's functions, which they learned through experimenting with the known commands.

That is, in order to perform the task, participants needed to rely on background information about the constraints involved in programming a robotic toy. Not only did they do so, but they also used the background information and covariation information in an interdependent way. They did not search for possible covariations at random. Rather, they used their background information about programming as a basis for generating and testing hypotheses about what sorts of covariations should obtain. In turn, the results of the tests constituted additional background information, which motivated yet additional hypotheses. In short, the Humean index of covariation, which can be stated in a formal way, interacted with background information, or content. For Klahr and his colleagues, relying on background information as well as covariation was seen as appropriate, because it was seen as analogous to sound scientific reasoning.

The interdependence of covariation and mechanism information

Koslowski and her colleagues have focused on the specific type of background information that consists of information about mechanism. For these instances of causation, the mechanism typically consists of some sort of explanation or theory (where "theory" is used very broadly) to explain *how* one event brings about another. Nevertheless, the central issue is the same. Can causal reasoning consist only of relying on the Humean indices, or must background information, including mechanism, also play a role? Just as Klahr argues for the interdependence of covariation and general background information, Koslowski argues for the interdependence of covariation and mechanism information.

Koslowski (1996) acknowledges that theoretical beliefs or commitments can definitely filter out or distort data inconsistent with the beliefs, as is the case, for example, with illusory correlations (Chapman & Chapman, 1967, 1969) and with the tendency of some jury members to rely on satisficing in drawing conclusions (Kuhn & Lao, 1996). However, she argues several points. First, the kind of causal reasoning that occurs in scientific inquiry involves plausibility assessments rather than either possibility or certainty. Scientific inquiry cannot be concerned with explanations that are merely possible, because some possible explanations (for example, that speciation resulted from a Martian invasion rather than evolution) are so implausible that taking them seriously would result in much wasted time and effort. Analogously, scientific inquiry can rarely if ever conclude that an explanation is either certainly correct or certainly false. New data that might be discovered in the future could call a seemingly certain explanation into question, while new data can also constitute evidence for explanations that might otherwise seem definitely false. Thus, the aim of science is to assess plausibility. Second, if plausibility is the aim, then sound scientific reasoning gives priority to *neither* theory *nor* evidence, but rather uses both *interdependently* in a bootstrapping fashion, with each enhancing rather than hindering the other. Concretely, this means that consistently giving evidence (covariation) priority over background information (including theory) yields conclusions that, though possible, or that give the illusion of certainty, are often quite implausible. Third, this view of science has implications for how scientific reasoning is actually measured or operationalized in research. The interdependence of theory and evidence suggests that research participants should not always be counted as engaging in flawed scientific reasoning when they fail to give priority to evidence over theory. Fourth, when the interdependence of both theory and evidence is acknowledged, then both children and adults can be seen as having certain capabilities related to sound causal reasoning. These points can be illustrated with respect to three issues.

1. Mechanism and covariation as interdependent.   Concretely, the interdependence of covariation and mechanism information means that, in scientific inquiry, mechanism guides the assessment of covariation, and covariation can help discover new mechanisms. Specifically, in scientific inquiry, theory or mechanism helps point the way to which correlations are likely to be causal rather than artifactual. For example, the correlation of ice-cream consumption and level of violent crime is unlikely to be treated as causal, but it might prompt further investigation if one learns that ingesting fats increases testosterone production. Asked to reason about analogous situations, even 11-year-olds were more likely to treat an unusual correlation as causal if they learned of a possible mechanism that might have mediated between the event and the effect. For example, if presented with evidence that red cars get better mileage than blue cars, even 11-year-olds treat the correlation as artifactual. However, they become increasingly likely to treat it as causal if they are told of a possible mechanism that might mediate between car color and gas mileage, for example, if they are told that red causes people to be alert and alert drivers are more likely to drive well, which conserves gas.

In addition, interdependence also means that implausible correlations are sometimes pursued even if no mechanism is currently known to be mediating between the two correlates, because the correlation might suggest a mechanism that has yet to be discovered. This is especially likely when the correlation is systematic and likely alternative causes have been ruled out. For example, the correlation between recently cleaned carpets and Kawasaki's syndrome was pursued (even though a possible mediating mechanism was not initially known), because likely alternative causes of the symptoms had been ruled out, and the correlation was systematically observed. Analogously, when presented with a correlation for which no mechanism is known, even 11-year-olds become increasingly likely to treat the correlation as possibly causal if the association of event and effect is systematic, and provided that likely alternative causes have been ruled out.

In short, even 11-year-olds treat mechanism and covariation in a bootstrapping way. They rely on mechanism to decide which correlations are likely to be causal; when unexpected correlations occur systematically and likely alternatives have been ruled out, they rely on the correlations to suggest possible mechanisms that have not yet been discovered. Thus, emphasizing the interdependence of covariation and mechanism in scientific inquiry has consequences for how sound scientific reasoning is operationalized. It suggests that according mechanism information or background beliefs priority over covariation information does not always constitute flawed reasoning. This approach contrasts with the approach of Kuhn, Amsel, and O'Loughlin (1988). In some of their studies, a participant who believed, for example, that type of cake (carrot versus chocolate) was causally relevant to colds (because of the mechanism of extra sugar in chocolate cake), would be shown data in which type of cake did not covary with colds. Kuhn et al. (1988) operationalized sound scientific reasoning as concluding that type of cake is not causal, that is, as giving covariation information priority over the background (mechanism) belief that type of cake is causally relevant to colds.

Even though children as young as 11 years of age treat covariation and mechanism information as interdependent, developmental differences do nevertheless occur. Adolescents have an inflated notion of the range of possible mechanisms that can operate in a situation. They treat, as reasonable, mechanisms that college students find dubious. In addition, when asked to explain a covariation that is implausible, 11-year-olds are more likely than college students to propose a mechanism that could render the covariation causal but that, to a college student, is quite dubious.

2. Confounding, indeterminacy, and the plausibility of possibly causal factors.   Mechanism information can help decide when confounding is likely to be artifactual and when it is likely, instead, to yield genuine causal indeterminacy. Imagine that, in two orphanages, wall color is confounded with quality of caregivers. Theory or mechanism would lead us to conclude that developmental differences between children in the orphanages were likely to have resulted from caregiver quality. Although it is possible that an undiscovered mechanism exists that can render wall color a cause of differences in development, it is not plausible. However, if the confounded variables had been responsive caregiving and good nutrition, one might be more likely to cite indeterminacy (at least, if restricted to citing only one cause.) In short, mechanism information enables us to distinguish a cause that is merely possible from one that is also plausible.

College students and college-bound adolescents make analogous judgments. When the two confounded factors that correlate with an effect consist of one factor that is a plausible cause (given mechanism information) and one factor that is an implausible cause (given mechanism information), then even 11-year-olds cite the plausible factor as the actual cause and tend to dismiss the implausible factor. When both confounded factors are implausible causes, participants conclude causal indeterminacy. For example, if both color and size of car covary with gas mileage, participants choose size as the causal factor; if both confounded possible causes are plausible (for example, if car make and size both covary with mileage), then even 11-year-olds treat the confounded data as causally indeterminate. They do understand that confounding is problematic. However, they rely on background information to decide when confounding is likely to yield causal indeterminacy (Koslowski, 1996).

This approach contrasts with the stance taken by Kuhn et al. (1988). In their studies, pairs of confounded variables consist of one plausible and one implausible cause. For example, color and texture of sports balls are confounded with each other and both covary with bounceability. Kuhn et al. (1988) operationalize sound scientific reasoning as concluding that (because of the confounding) the actual cause of bounceability is indeterminate.

3. Disconfirming evidence, working hypotheses, and rejection versus modification.   An important feature of scientific inquiry is the generation of working hypotheses, that is, general hypotheses that are based on some background information, but in which numerous potentially relevant variables are not specified and may not yet be known because of insufficient data. A working hypothesis might suggest that drug X controls diabetes, but might not initially specify whether the effect of the drug depends on type of diabetes, diet, or weight. If drug X were found to be ineffective for some people, one would not reject the hypothesis at the outset. Rather, one would first try to gather additional data to help modify it, that is, to specify more precisely the situations (such as Type II diabetes) in which it does, and does not, work. Rejecting a hypothesis at the outset might dismiss an approximately accurate hypothesis that simply needs refining. In short, outright rejection of a theory in the face of disconfirming data is not always warranted.

This approach contrasts with other approaches (for example, Kuhn, ch. 17 this volume; Mynatt, Doherty & Tweney, 1977) in which the correct response is operationalized to consist of rejecting rather than modifying a theory or hypothesis as soon as disconfirming data come to light (Koslowski & Maqueda, 1993).

However, a problem is that, in principle, a hypothesis can always be modified to account for disconfirming evidence. Thus, an important question is: when are modifications warranted (or scientifically legitimate) and when are they ad hoc attempts to patch up a theory that should in fact be rejected? Modification rather than rejection is more likely to be warranted if the resulting modifications are congruent with existing background information, including information about mechanism. For example, if the diabetes drug is not effective in obese people, it is reasonable to keep the hypothesis in modified form; background information tells us that fat cells release resistin, which in turn interferes with the activity of insulin. A modified hypothesis, congruent with background information, would note that drug X controls diabetes unless obesity is a problem. Note that we would be adjusting our theory to fit the data, claiming the theory "was right with respect to those instances that conformed to the covariation pattern but was wrong with respect to those instances that did not" (Kuhn et al., 1988). Thus, we would offer the sort of response that Kuhn et al. treat as flawed scientific reasoning. However, in having our modification informed by the disconfirming data, we would obtain a more refined understanding of how the drug works.

In contrast, imagine we found that the diabetes drug was ineffective for people who prefer opera to jazz, and red to blue. It would be difficult to modify the hypothesis to account for the anomalies in a way congruent with background information. There is currently no mechanism known that could mediate between music and color preferences and that could interfere with the operation of a drug for diabetes. In short, we rely on background information, including mechanism, to decide whether disconfirming evidence warrants rejection or modification of a working hypothesis. We do not always give priority to evidence (covariation) over theory (mechanism).

Conversely, disconfirming evidence can sometimes lead to the discovery of new mechanism information. If the diabetes drug is systematically ineffective for opera- rather than jazz-lovers, and if plausible alternatives to musical preference had been ruled out, the pattern to the anomalies would warrant looking for a possible factor that might be correlated with music preference and that might interfere with the drug.

In short, mechanism information influences decisions about whether to reject or modify hypotheses in light of disconfirming evidence. In turn, such evidence can lead to the discovery of additional information about mechanism. That is, when dealing with anomalies is at issue, theory and evidence are interdependent.

In fact, children do adopt a tempered approach to disconfirming data. Schauble (1990) found that children who did not reject their hypothesis at the first sign of disconfirming data did do so as such data mounted up. The children treated their hypotheses as working hypotheses, initially modifying them in response to anomalous data, but rejecting them as the disconfirming data accumulated. Asked to reason about analogous situations, college students and college-bound adolescents behave in comparable ways. When presented with disconfirming evidence, they treat modification rather than rejection as warranted when the modification is congruent with background information or when the anomalous instances have something in common, thus forming a pattern and suggesting an underlying mechanism that might later be discovered. That is, they "adjust the theory to fit the data," but do so judiciously, when the disconfirming data provide additional information about the sorts of factors that constrain the operation of the target mechanism. Mechanism informs the response to disconfirming evidence, and such evidence often enhances knowledge of mechanism.

When responding to disconfirming data, people treat theory and evidence as interdependent in another way as well. Kuhn et al. (1988) operationalized sound scientific reasoning as giving priority to evidence (covariation) over theory (beliefs including beliefs about mechanism). Within this framework, they found that people have more difficulty relinquishing a causal than a noncausal belief. Recall, also, that many of the participants in these studies explicitly verbalized beliefs about mechanism, albeit not always the correct mechanism (such as that chocolate cake is unhealthy because sugar raises blood pressure). Koslowski argued that causal beliefs consist of (at least) two components: a belief that a possible causal agent covaries with the effect and a belief that a mechanism mediates between cause and effect. When Kuhn et al. (1988) disconfirmed participants' causal beliefs, they noted only that the assumed covariation had not obtained. Thus, they called into question only the covariation component; they left intact the mechanism component of the participant's belief. In contrast, the noncausal belief included no mechanism component, so that calling the non-covariation component into question was sufficient to prompt rejection.

A preliminary study (Koslowski, 1996) suggested that, when the disconfirming evidence consisted of information about mechanism as well as covariation (rather than covariation alone) there was a greater effect for precisely the sort of (causal) theory that Kuhn et al. (1988) found to be the more resistant to disconfirmation. The results suggest that, even for adolescents, when causal beliefs include beliefs about mechanism as well as covariation (not only that candy covaries with sleeplessness, but also that the mechanism involves changing brain chemistry), disconfirming both components is important to disconfirming the belief. Beliefs about which covariations are likely to be causal do not exist in isolation; they are embedded in and evaluated with respect to beliefs about mechanism.

To summarize, people rely on background information or beliefs (including information about mechanism) to decide whether a covariation is likely to be causal; in turn, people rely on covariation information to help point the way to the discovery of additional mechanism information. Furthermore, because mechanism information helps distinguish causal from artifactual covariations, it is also useful in deciding whether confounded variables are causally indeterminate. In addition, background information, including information about mechanism, suggests that explanations should not always be rejected in the light of disconfirming evidence. Sometimes, rather than calling an explanation into question, disconfirming or anomalous information constitutes information that describes how a working hypothesis can be fine-tuned in order to become more precise. In addition, because covariation information is embedded in and judged with respect to background information, it may be that, for anomalous information to lead to the rejection of a belief, the background information as well as the belief itself must be called into question. Finally, the importance of background information in evaluating covariation suggests that covariation cannot function as a formal rule, that is, one which is independent of the content to which it is applied. Whether a relation is causal depends not only on whether covariation is present, but also on whether background information suggests that the covariation is not merely an artifact. In short, just as background information about, for example, friction and weight ought to and does inform causal reasoning in infancy, background information ought to and does inform reasoning about non-mechanical causation.

Reasoning about and Evaluating Causal Mechanisms

Return to the distinction between a causal agent and the mechanism or process by which the agent brings about an effect. Within this framework, much of the research in the preceding sections examined how people identify causal agents. Insofar as the literature examined the role of mechanism, it was to note that even children rely on mechanism information in deciding whether an event is likely to be a causal agent. Furthermore, with the exception of studies that involved, for example, electricity, the mechanisms were, for the most part, some physical connection between cause and effect.

However, for many causal phenomena, the mechanism often consists of an explanation, or theory (broadly construed) that explains how an event brings about the effect. Furthermore, just as not all events are plausible causal agents, not all explanations constitute plausible mechanisms. Thus, an important part of causal understanding consists of reasoning about and evaluating causal mechanisms or explanations. For example, an explanation for speciation based on evolution is more compelling than an explanation that treats speciation as the result of a Martian plot to mislead earthlings. Similarly, some explanations for a person's illness or death make more sense than others, as do some explanations for the fall of Rome, whether the dinosaurs were cold-blooded or warm-blooded, etc. That is, to be useful, possible mechanisms must be evaluated. Except for noting that some mechanisms are plausible and others dubious, the research described in the preceding sections did not examine how explanations are evaluated.

Some possible strategies for evaluating explanations might seem quite straightforward and as though they consist of formal rules. However, although the strategies can be couched in formal terms, they can be successfully implemented only if collateral or background information is also taken into account. For example, one might test an explanation by controlling for or ruling out alternatives – a principle that can be stated in formal terms. However, one would need to rely on background information to decide which alternatives were plausible rather than dubious and thus worth taking seriously. Similarly, one might test an explanation by generating predictions that follow from the explanation and seeing whether the predictions obtain – another principle that can be stated in formal terms. For example, if the reduced oxygen supply at high altitudes is what explains the shorter stature of mountain-dwellers, then (at least) two predictions follow. One is that mountain-dwellers who like blue and those who prefer red should have comparably short stature. The other is that mountain-dwellers who move to sea level should have children who are taller than might otherwise be expected. Clearly, we would treat the second prediction as the more informative of the two because of our background or collateral information (Koslowski & Thompson, in preparation).

Three lines of research have examined the way in which people reason about explanations. We suggest that all three lines illustrate the point that explanations are assessed, not in isolation, but in the context of a related web of collateral information, or what else we know about the world.

Evaluating responses to anomalous data

Explanations are rarely if ever perfect. Often subsequent anomalous data call an explanation into question. Thus, one way of examining how explanations are evaluated is to look at how they are affected by anomalous data. In the previous sections, when tasks involved identifying causal agents, anomalies were typically couched in a covariation framework. Thus, for the belief that type of cake caused colds, an anomaly would have been that type of cake and colds did *not* covary. However, in many situations anomalies cannot be easily seen in covariational terms. Thus, reasoning about explanations requires relying on collateral information besides covariation.

Chinn & Brewer (1998) treat anomalies as data that are (at least initially) problematic for an explanation or mechanism. For example, an anomaly to the theory of dinosaurs as cold-blooded is that their bone density is comparable to that of extant, *warm*-blooded animals. Chinn & Brewer document eight possible strategies for dealing with anomalies. The strategies include not accepting the data (by, for example, ignoring or reinterpreting it or questioning its validity); disagreeing that the data warrant a change in theory (by, for example, excluding the data from the domain of the theory); and changing the theory. Chinn & Brewer's strategies are remarkably convergent with, and can be seen as refinements of, the strategies proposed by Abelson (1959) for dealing with inconsistent beliefs: denial, bolstering, differentiation, and transcendence.

We draw attention to the fact that the strategies rely on collateral information. For example, a way of resolving the bone-density anomaly to the theory of dinosaurs as cold-blooded notes that bone density might be affected by calcium intake as well as by warm-bloodedness. That is, the resolution invokes collateral information about the properties of calcium as well as the properties of bones.

Vosniadou & Brewer (1992) provide some evidence that children rely on analogous strategies in response to data anomalous to their beliefs about the earth. There is a sense in which children exclude data from the domain of theory by noting, for example, that the earth is round, but people live on flat pieces of it (which are presumably exempt from the earth-is-round constraint). Children also change their beliefs, moving for example from their initial flat model to a pancake model in which the earth has a flat top and bottom but "rounded" sides. This accommodation preserves the child's belief in a flat earth but takes account of the adult claim that the earth is round.

Relying on metaconceptual criteria

A second approach to studying how people evaluate causal explanations asks whether we rely on various metaconceptual criteria. For example, Samarapungavan (1992) asked first-, third-, and fifth-graders, to evaluate theories from chemistry and astronomy. She found that even first-graders preferred explanations that accounted for a broad range of data, and that were logically and empirically consistent. Fifth-graders also preferred non-ad hoc theories (which, in her study, provided a single explanation for the initial as well as the subsequent anomalous observation) to ad hoc theories (which, in her study, offered one explanation for the initial observation and a different explanation for the anomalous observation). Note that, for the first- through third-graders, reliance on metaconceptual criteria was especially likely when the theories were neutral with respect to the child's prior beliefs or when the theories were consistent with the child's prior beliefs. That is, for these children, preferences were informed by content or background information and beliefs as well as by metaconceptual criteria.

In terms of the argument we have been making, we suggest that, in many cases, it is sensible to have background information inform (or even take priority over) metaconceptual criteria. In the empirical world, collateral information or prior belief tells us that, sometimes, explanations that account for a broad range of data are less accurate than those that account for a narrow range, because a single explanation might mistakenly group together data that, in fact, are explained by distinct mechanisms. For example, collateral information tells us that there may not be a single, broad explanation for two diseases that are both characterized by headache, fever, and vomiting, because each disease might have its own etiology warranting two distinct explanatory mechanisms. Analogously, collateral information also tells us that, sometimes, a theory that provides a single explanation for both an initial and an anomalous observation is not warranted, because the initial and the anomalous observations might differ in some fundamental way. That is, the fact that different theories are offered to explain an initial and an anomalous observation does not necessarily make a theory ad hoc if by "ad hoc" one means a modification that is unwarranted.

Thus, like the Humean indices, metaconceptual criteria can be articulated as a formal rule, applicable to all content areas; however, they are deployed successfully only when collateral or background information is also considered. To be sure, the participants might be relying on collateral information that is incomplete because it has not yet been discovered or is inaccurate because it has not been carefully checked. However, that argues for having increased access to collateral information that is accurate; it does not argue for consistently dismissing collateral information in favor of formal rules.

Congruence with collateral information

Another approach to how people evaluate explanations notes that explanations are plausible to the extent that they are congruent with what else we know about the world, or what we have been calling collateral information. (Murphy & Medin, 1985; Masnick, Barnett, Thompson, & Koslowski, 1998; Koslowski, Barnett, Masnick, & Thompson, in preparation). Thus, we find evolution to be a more compelling explanation for speciation than an explanation based on visiting Martians, because evolution is congruent with collateral information about population genetics and the likelihood of Martian travel. Further, as noted in the second section of this chapter, collateral information must include more than covariation information to decide which covariations to treat as causal and which alternatives are plausible enough to be controlled for. It is also crucial in deciding which predictions that follow from an explanation are informative rather than trivial (Koslowski & Thompson, in preparation). Explanations are evaluated not in isolation but in the context of collateral information (Koslowski, 1996).

However, for collateral information to be a useful construct, it must be more precisely described (Koslowski & Thompson, in preparation). Two types of collateral information include alternative explanatory mechanisms and information that fleshes out the details of the target mechanism, as population genetics fleshes out the mechanism of natural selection. Additional types include information that yields anomalous predictions and information that yields congruent predictions. Anomalies are events we infer should not obtain if the explanation is correct *and given* corollary information. For example, if two populations differ in stature, a possible explanation is that they come from different gene pools. Given what we know about genetics, then if the different gene pool explanation is accurate, we should expect little intermarriage between the two populations. If intermarriage were frequent, that would constitute an anomaly for the different gene pool explanation. Congruent events, the flipside of anomalies, are events we infer should obtain if the explanation is correct *and given* corollary information. Consider again the stature differences between mountain-dwellers and people who live at sea level. A possible explanation is that mountain-dwellers have shorter stature because of reduced oxygen supply. If this explanation is accurate, then given collateral information about oxygen and genes, we should expect that mountain-dwellers who move to sea level should have children who are taller than would otherwise be expected. Both types of inferences are empirical rather than logical, because they are not content-free but depend on facts about the way the world works, rather than on the application of principles that are formal, or content-free.

College students rely on all four types of collateral information in evaluating explanations (Masnick et al., 1998; Koslowski et al., in preparation). Do younger children also do so? The second section presented evidence that even preschoolers show a concern with mechanism in experimental tasks. Preschoolers' spontaneous comments also show a concern with mechanism, such as a 4-year-old's question, "Why do some trees keep their leaves in winter?" and the answer that he later proposed, "I know; they're put on with stronger glue (sap)" (Koslowski & Winsor, 1981). By 11 years of age, 18 of 19 participants spontaneously proposed mechanisms when asked to devise ways of finding out whether having parents stay overnight with their hospitalized children improves the children's recovery rate (Koslowski, 1996). For example, "You could have some parents stay overnight and some not, because parents might help their kids by telling the doctors if there are problems" (p. 242).

Spontaneous questions and explanations show that even preschoolers also show a concern with anomalies. Consider a 4-year-old who, told that his friend's cat had died and gone *up* to heaven, reported, "His cat couldn't have gone up to heaven, because cats have bones, bones are heavy and clouds are just water and the bones would have fallen right through those clouds." This child's collateral information about clouds and bones led him to generate an anomaly to his friend's claim (Koslowski & Winsor, 1981). Analogously, the preschoolers in Sodian, Zaitchik, and Carey's (1991) study drew inferences about which events would be anomalous to or congruent with hypotheses when they predicted that a box with a small rather than large opening would enable them to decide whether a mouse was large or small. Their inferences relied on collateral information that mice do not change their girth and that openings in the walls of boxes do not expand.

What about alternative accounts? Even third-graders consider alternatives that consist of the absence of a causal agent, noting for example that to see whether a roof on a lantern keeps the candle inside from blowing out, one would need to examine one lantern with, and one without, a roof (Bullock, 1991). At least by 11 years of age, children also spontaneously propose alternatives that invoke different causal agents, not merely the absence of the target agent. For example, in discussing whether parents staying overnight with their hospitalized children improves the children's recovery rate, 33 percent of the 11-year-olds (versus almost 90 percent of the college students) proposed alternatives such as, "You'd have to make sure doctors didn't just provide better care when parents were there."

In terms of developmental precursors of a concern with alternatives, we suggest it is the child's tendency to notice contrasts. For example, "Why is walking uphill harder than walking downhill?" or, "Why do we eat some seeds and plant others?" Alternatives are the basis for control groups; we suggest that the tendency to notice contrasts provides a basis for noticing alternatives.

Note that available collateral information can be limited by both individual differences (in age and knowledge) and by historical time period and culture or group (Hilton, in preparation; Koslowski & Thompson, in preparation). Not every child learns about the relative density of clouds and cats' bones. Similarly, during one of the plague periods of the Middle Ages, some scientists considered and ruled out the alternative hypothesis that plague was caused by poverty by noting that the wealthy and the poor died in comparable numbers. Although they considered alternative hypotheses, they lacked the relevant collateral information about how some germs are transmitted and so did not consider the alternative causal factor of proximity to rats and fleas. Analogously, it is only recently that the Tuskegee Airmen came to be known in the USA as the only group of fighter pilots who never lost a bomber during the Second World War – and that all of the Tuskegee Airmen were Black. Restricted access to this sort of information about Black achievement makes it less likely that institutionalized racism will be offered as an alternative to the hypothesis of genetic inferiority when trying to explain, for example, racial differences in IQ scores, employment, etc.

If explanations or mechanisms are embedded in and evaluated with respect to networks of collateral information, then changing a belief might require disconfirming not only the target belief, but also related beliefs that support the target belief. There is some evidence that this is true for adults (Masnick, 1999; Swiderek, 1999) with respect to fairly complex beliefs about affirmative action and capital punishment, beliefs embedded in networks of information about justice, bias, pragmatic implementation, etc. As noted in the third section of this chapter, there is also analogous evidence for this even among adolescents, when the belief involves whether eating candy causes sleeplessness and the collateral information involves mechanism information about how sugar affects the brain.

Finally, the notion that explanations are embedded in and evaluated with respect to networks of related beliefs is related to recent philosophical work on inference to the best explanation (IBE) (Harmon, 1986; Lipton, 1991). According to IBE, one reason (perhaps the most general) for accepting a hypothesis is that it provides a better explanation of the evidence than do other hypotheses. The IBE model of explanatory choice relies heavily on background or collateral information, for example, to decide which possible explanations are actually worth considering and which aspects of what else we know about the world ought to be treated as relevant to evaluating the explanations.

To summarize this section, if causal reasoning is informed by background information, including information about mechanism, then there is a premium on evaluating mechanisms or explanations to distinguish those that are plausible from those that are not. One strategy for doing this is to rely on metaconceptual criteria that are formulated as content-free (such as whether the explanation accounts for a broad rather than a narrow range of data). We argue that, just as Humean indices yield more accurate judgments when used in conjunction with background or collateral information, so do other formal criteria, such as breadth of explanation. In fact, both children and adults rely on collateral information in deciding whether to apply metaconceptual criteria when evaluating explanations. Analogously, even children rely on collateral information in responding to data that are anomalous to their beliefs. In turn, the importance of collateral information puts a premium on trying to identify the sorts of collateral information that are likely to be treated as causally relevant. Roughly, causally relevant collateral information might be thought of as a web or network of knowledge about plausible causal structures in which the mechanism is embedded and with respect to which it is evaluated. Thus, causally relevant collateral information includes information which, when used in conjunction with the explanation being evaluated, yields several possible consequences. These include plausible rival or alternative explanations, details of how the mechanism operates, congruent events that should obtain if the mechanism is accurate, and anomalous events that should not obtain if the mechanism is accurate. There is some evidence suggesting that even young children take account of such information. Furthermore, access to collateral information may vary with individuals and sociohistorical context. Finally, the fact that explanations are embedded in and buttressed by networks of collateral information might explain why beliefs that are called into question in a circumscribed way are often resistant to disconfirmation.

General Summary and Conclusions

Several themes and suggestions run through this chapter. Perhaps the most general is that causal reasoning is essentially an empirical rather than a formal activity. This theme rests on two arguments. The conceptual argument, made at several points, is that causal judgments *ought not* to be based exclusively on formal rules, because such reliance leads to mistaken judgments. The empirical argument is that, in fact, people *do not* base their causal judgments exclusively on formal rules.

Infants do not come to the experimental situation already equipped with an abstract Humean belief that contact and immediate movement in a direct launching event always signals causation. Rather, they learn (in and outside of experimental situations) to expect certain sequences in certain situations. In addition, they process causal events in terms of features that certainly include the Humean indices, but include as well information about causal agents. By not coming equipped to rely exclusively on Humean indices, infants are able to learn that causation also depends on friction, relative weights of agent and object, etc. Finally, when infants do acquire expectations in an experimental situation, their expectations seem to include some notion of the transmission of force, or a mediating mechanism by which one object moves another.

Like infants, older children reasoning about mechanical causation also often concern themselves with causal agents. In addition, they often concern themselves with mechanism to such an extent that they often assume mechanisms consistent with their predictions. With tasks that are complex, they seem to identify the causal agent first and only afterwards concern themselves with issues of mechanism.

Similarly, older children and adults who are reasoning about non-mechanical causation also do not rely exclusively on formal rules. Rather, they use formal rules and content in an interdependent or bootstrapping way, especially when the content consists of information about theory or mechanism. They use mechanism information to decide whether to treat formal indices as reflecting causation; they use formal indices to draw their attention to content (including mechanism) that has not yet been discovered. Similarly, background information helps identify situations in which confounding does and does not yield causal indeterminacy and helps distinguish situations in which anomalous evidence calls for fine-tuning rather than rejecting a mechanism.

The important role of mechanism information in causal reasoning puts a premium on distinguishing mechanisms that are plausible from those that are not, and this distinction involves relying on the collateral information in which the mechanism is embedded. Children as well as adults rely on several types of collateral information to evaluate explanations. In turn, relying on collateral information limits how accurate causal explanations can be, either because the relevant background information has yet to be discovered, or because it is not readily available in certain cultures or to certain age groups. Finally, the fact that mechanisms are embedded in networks of collateral information might explain why beliefs that are called into question in a circumscribed way are often resistant to disconfirmation.

In short, causal reasoning involves learning about empirical relations in the world. This includes learning about likely causal agents, plausible causal mechanisms, and the network of collateral or background information in which causal relations are embedded. It also involves using collateral information and formal rules in a bootstrapping fashion, using each to inform the other.

The importance of background information in causal (including scientific) reasoning has several consequences. One is that, to the extent that formal rules are useful, it is because they function as heuristics or rough rules of thumb, rather than as algorithms whose application guarantees the right answer. This, in turn, means that causal reasoning does not always yield certainty. Rather, the result of causal reasoning is a guess about plausibility. An informed guess to be sure, but a guess informed by background information that may be mistaken, unavailable, or as yet undiscovered. The lack of algorithms that yield unassailable conclusions and the importance of background information are what make causal (and scientific) reasoning often contentious and frequently a challenge. Because they put a premium on empirical discovery, they are also what make causal reasoning fun.

CHAPTER THIRTEEN

Inductive and Deductive Reasoning

Usha Goswami

In their everyday worlds, adults and children are frequently required to "go beyond the information given" and make inferences that are not deductively valid. When there are gaps in our knowledge, we have to reason by induction. Generalizing on the basis of a known example, making an inductive inference from a particular premise, or drawing an analogy are all examples of inductive reasoning at work. Inductive reasoning is ubiquitous in human thinking.[1] Deductive reasoning can also fill gaps in knowledge. In contrast to inductive reasoning, however, in a deductive reasoning problem there is only one logically valid answer. Deductive reasoning is usually measured by the ability to apply deductive logic to known information that is given. For example, if a child is given the two premises "All dogs bark" and "Rex is a dog", there is only one logical deduction. Rex is a dog, all dogs bark, therefore Rex must also bark.

One important difference between inductive and deductive reasoning is that deductive reasoning problems can be solved without (or despite) real-world knowledge. In the above example, a child can make a logical deduction about Rex barking even if "barking" is a totally unfamiliar activity. If the child had been told instead "Rex is a cat. All cats bark. Does Rex bark?", then the correct deduction would again be that Rex must also bark, even though in the real world cats do not bark (thus the logical deduction is counterfactual). Counter-factual deductions are still logically valid. In contrast, there is no logical justification of induction (Hume, 1748/1988). Nevertheless, inductive reasoning is subject to certain constraints, which are largely dependent on real-world knowledge. Many of the same constraints can be demonstrated in children and in adults. A typical inductive reasoning problem would take the form "Humans have spleens. Dogs have spleens. Do rabbits have spleens?" (see Carey, 1985). In the absence of any knowledge about spleens, it is impossible to be sure whether rabbits have spleens or not, but it seems likely that they might because humans are usually a good exemplar to use as a basis for inductive inferences to other mammals. However, if the problem had been phrased differently as follows: "Dogs have spleens. Bees have spleens. Do humans have spleens?," the induction is less intuitively compelling. Humans might be similar to dogs, but they are not that similar to bees, and so perhaps they don't have spleens. As we will see in this chapter, judgments about similarity are the most important constraints on inductive reasoning.

Recent work in developmental psychology has shown that both inductive and deductive reasoning show remarkable continuity across the lifespan. Inductive reasoning and deductive reasoning are influenced by similar factors and subject to similar heuristics and biases in both children and adults. This current view of developmental continuity stands in sharp contrast to the historical view that reasoning is age-dependent and content-independent (see Brown, 1990). Historically, it was thought that reasoning developed relatively slowly. It was thought that children gradually became increasingly efficient all-purpose learning machines, acquiring and applying general reasoning strategies irrespective of the domain in which they were reasoning. Traditionally, developmental textbooks had separate sections for "problem-solving" and "concept formation." Problem-solving was about the acquisition of logical rules, and was usually studied by seeing whether children could acquire isolated rules in completely unfamiliar situations – which they were typically bad at. Conceptual development was about the growth of real-world knowledge, and the need for transfer of learning by induction was taken for granted – after all, even toddlers could do it. The focus in conceptual development was on the extent and organization of knowledge that determined transfer. The obvious connection between the two topics was widely ignored.

More recently, it has become clear that as long as children are reasoning in familiar domains, they are capable of inductive reasoning, and that as long as they are reasoning in pragmatically acceptable scenarios, they are capable of deductive reasoning. They are not inductively "perceptually bound," as was believed for so long, able to transfer knowledge only when surface appearances suggest that transfer is appropriate. Children can go beyond surface features and transfer knowledge on the basis of relational similarity or knowledge about the kind of thing that they are dealing with, even when perceptual attributes are pitted against category membership (e.g., Gelman & Markman, 1987). For deductive reasoning, they are not bound by the "empirical bias," able only to reason about premises that they know from personal experience to be true. They can make deductive inferences about fantasy premises or about premises that are contrary to their real-world knowledge, as long as they understand that the premises should be accepted as valid for the purpose of deduction (Harris & Leevers, 2000). Broadly speaking, both inductive and deductive reasoning are constrained by the nature of the knowledge to be learned, the existing state of the conceptual system, and the context in which the new concept is first encountered. This is as true for adults as for young children.

Inductive Reasoning

Inductive reasoning in children has been studied in a variety of ways. Many studies of categorization and conceptual development involve inductive reasoning. For example, children may be told that sparrows can fly, and then asked whether eagles can fly. There are many examples of such studies in this book (see the chapters by Gelman & Opfer, Quinn, and Waxman for examples of experiments in which even infants and toddlers make inductive inferences). This aspect of induction will therefore be covered extremely briefly. Studies of "insight" are also studies of inductive reasoning. "Insight" refers to the apparently spontaneous solution of a difficult problem without the application of any conscious reasoning strategies. It was first studied in detail by the Gestalt psychologists (e.g., Maier, 1931), who focused on adults. Insight has not been studied widely in young children. Thirdly, inductive reasoning in children has been studied by investigating analogical development. Studies of analogical reasoning are widely available, and span the age range from 2 to 12 (see Goswami, 1991, 1992, 1996 for reviews). Analogical reasoning can also be described as the study of similarity-based reasoning. As we will see, all inductive reasoning in humans appears to be similarity-based. Hence analogical reasoning is a useful paradigm within which to explore the development of inductive reasoning more generally.

Inductive inferences

Inductive inferences are made surprisingly readily by very young children. For example, Gelman and Coley (1990) asked 2-year-old children questions about the properties of typical and atypical members of familiar categories such as birds. The children were shown a picture of a typical category member, such as a robin, and were asked "This is a bird. Does it live in a nest?" They were then shown other pictures of birds, such as a dodo (atypical category member) and a bluebird (typical category member). For each picture, they were asked the same question ("Does it live in a nest?"). The category label "bird" was not repeated. Gelman and Coley found that the children ascribed the relevant properties (lives in a nest) to the typical category members (bluebird) 76 percent of the time, and to the atypical category members (dodo) 42 percent of the time. Similar results for 3- and 4-year-olds were reported by Gelman and Markman (1986). Such studies show that children, like adults, make inductive inferences on the basis of *typicality*. When the premise category is very typical (a robin is a very typical bird), then children are ready to reason inductively. Further, when the premise and conclusion categories are very similar (as in robin and bluebird), inductive reasoning is promoted. This similarity effect is also found in adults.

Two other factors also appear to promote inductive reasoning in adults. These are the number of observations upon which the induction is based, and the nature of the property being projected. For example, if you are told that dogs, cats, bears, monkeys, bees, horses, and blackbirds have spleens, you should be more likely to judge that rabbits have spleens than if you are told only that dogs and bees have spleens (the sample size effect). However, if you are told that a coat "smells yucky," you are unlikely to project this property to other coats, as "smelling yucky" should be treated as an idiosyncratic property of a particular coat rather than as a general property of coats. Real-world knowledge tells you that "smelling yucky" is not an enduring property in the way that "having a spleen" is.

There is a small amount of evidence that children's inductive reasoning is subject to the same effects. Gutheil and Gelman (1997) asked children aged from 8 to 10 years to make inductions based on varying sample sizes. For example, the children were shown pictures of butterflies and told "Here is one butterfly. This butterfly has blue eyes." "Here are five other butterflies. These five butterflies have grey eyes." The experimenter then looked at another picture card that wasn't shown to the child, and said "I'm looking at another butterfly. Do you think this butterfly has blue eyes like this butterfly (single exemplar) or grey eyes like these butterflies (many exemplars)?" The children chose to project the properties of the larger sample (e.g., grey eyes) at rates significantly above chance. Nevertheless, they did not perform as consistently as adults, leading Gutheil and Gelman to conclude that young children's inductive reasoning about categories is driven by category membership (i.e., they reason that these are all butterflies, and so some could have blue eyes and others grey eyes). Information about sample size within categories (and the diversity of that sample) is not used systematically by children in the way that it is by adults.

Gelman (1988) explored the nature of the properties that children will use as a basis for inductive inferences. She examined whether preschool children (aged on average 4 years 8 months) and second-graders (aged on average 8 years) would differentiate between generalizable and non-generalizable properties in their inductive inferences. Generalizable properties were chosen to legitimately promote inferences between category members, and were deliberately unfamiliar, such as "likes to eat alfalfa" for rabbits, and "needs CO_2 to grow" for flowers. Non-generalizable properties were chosen to be familiar, as a strong test of whether the children realized that inductive inferences about these properties were non-legitimate, such as "smells yucky" for a coat, "has a little scratch" for a clock, or "has a piece of grass stuck to it" for a fish. For each item, the children were told "This brown rabbit likes to eat alfalfa. See this white rabbit? Do you think it likes to eat alfalfa, like this rabbit?" Children were also asked about other natural kinds, such as dogs ("See this dog? Do you think it likes to eat alfalfa, like this rabbit?"), and about artifacts such as telephones, to test the limits of generalization. Gelman found that all of the children were sensitive to the generalizable nature of the different properties. Even the preschoolers differentiated clearly between the generalizable properties (such as eating alfalfa) and the non-generalizable properties (such as smelling yucky). They seemed to realize that these properties were temporary or accidental, and, like adults, they took the nature of the property into account when making inductive inferences.

The related question of whether children realize that some properties are more suited to certain categories than others was explored by Kalish and Gelman (1992). They examined whether 4-year-olds distinguished between functional properties, such as what an object is used for, and dispositional properties, such as the material that an object is made of, and varied their inductive inferences accordingly. Novel combined categories, such as "glass scissors" and "fur baseball bats," were used to investigate this question. For example, the children were shown a picture of some glass scissors, and told that this was the experimenter's object. They were also given two objects of their own, a picture of metal scissors and a picture of a glass bottle. They were then asked about either the functional or dispositional properties of their objects in a random order. For the functional property the experimenter said "I use my glass scissors for *partitioning*." The child was then asked which of their objects could be used for partitioning. For the dispositional property the experimenter said "My glass scissors will get *fractured* if I put them in really cold water." The child was then asked which of their objects would get fractured in really cold water. These novel properties (partitioning, fracturing) were deliberately chosen to be unfamiliar to the children.

Kalish and Gelman found that the children recognized which categories supported inductions of which types of properties. They realized that other kinds of scissors could also be used for partitioning, and that other kinds of glass objects would break if put into really cold water. The nature of the property being projected is thus another factor that seems to affect the inductive reasoning of children as well as of adults. Although the systematic manipulation of all the factors that affect inductive reasoning in adults is currently lacking in the developmental literature (see Heit, 2000), in general inductive inferences seem to operate in very similar ways throughout development.

Insight

Another form of inductive reasoning is a sudden "insight" into how to solve an apparently intractable problem. The reasoner is conscious of no inductive inferences in reaching the solution, which seems to appear spontaneously "in mind." This form of inventive or creative reasoning was first studied by the Gestalt psychologists (e.g., Duncker, 1945; Maier, 1931), who focused their investigations on adults. Two classic "insight" problems are the following. In the "cord problem" (Maier, 1931), the participant is required to tie together the free ends of two cords that are hanging from the ceiling. It is impossible to hold the end of one cord and simultaneously reach the end of the other. The solution is to find something to act as a weight at the end of one cord, enabling it to be swung like a pendulum. It can then be caught at the end of an upswing while the stationary cord is held, and the cords can be tied together. In Maier's original work, the only weight available was a pair of pliers, which had recently been used as pliers by the participants. Many participants did not think of now using the pliers to create a pendulum. In the "matchbox" problem (Duncker, 1945), participants are required to fix a candle to a vertical surface so that it can burn properly. Various tools such as string and drawing pins (tacks) are provided to assist them. The drawing pins are in a small box. The solution is to empty the box and pin it to the vertical surface, thereby creating a horizontal shelf on which to stand the candle. Again, many participants did not think of this solution, because the box was seen only in terms of its function of containing the drawing pins.

Rather than studying how insight could be promoted, therefore, the paradigms invented by the Gestalt psychologists led to the study of how insight was impeded. Failures of "insight" were originally interpreted as showing "functional fixedness." Potential solution tools were thought to be "burdened" by their habitual use, and thereby rendered unavailable for a novel use. In fact, potential solution tools were not even recognized because of "cognitive embeddedness" – they were too embedded in their familiar context. Both functional fixedness and cognitive embeddedness can be seen as constraints that *interfere* with inductive reasoning. Brown showed that the same constraints apply to young children, and went further to demonstrate that attempts to generate inverse mechanisms can enable cognitive flexibility and promote inductive learning.

To investigate functional fixedness in young children, Brown and her colleagues used an analogy paradigm originally developed by Holyoak, Junn, and Billman (1984). The child's job was to enable a genie to move his jewels from one bottle to another without breaking them and without moving his feet, which had been glued into the first bottle by a wicked witch (Brown, 1989). Various tools were available to solve this problem, including glue, string, tape, and a sheet of paper. The solution was to use the paper to make a tube, through which the jewels could then be rolled. Children aged 5 and 9 years were tested on the genie problem in two conditions. In the Functional Fixedness condition, the children were first asked to make drawings on three sheets of paper prior to receiving the genie problem. In the Cognitive Flexibility condition, the children used the three sheets of paper to make a tent, to make a drawing, and for a communication game. Only 20 percent of the 5-year-olds and 35 percent of the 9-year-olds who had spent time making three drawings prior to the test thought of rolling the paper into a tube to help the genie. In contrast, 75 percent of the 5-year-olds and 80 percent of the 9-year-olds spontaneously generated the rolling solution in the Cognitive Flexibility condition. Brown and Kane argued that the experience of using the paper for drawing fixed its function for the former group, impeding inductive reasoning. Experimenting with a variety of uses for the paper freed it from a specific role for the Cognitive Flexibility group, making it available for other creative solutions.

Recently, German and Defeyter (2000) have produced the interesting argument that younger children might actually be *less* susceptible to functional fixedness than older children, because they have a more fluid notion of function than older children. German and Defeyter explored this possibility by giving a variant of Duncker's candle problem to children aged from 5 to 7 years. The children were introduced to Bobo, a toy bear with short legs who wanted to reach his toy down from a shelf. They were told that he couldn't jump because of his short legs, and asked to help him to reach his toy. Various tools were available, including toy blocks, a magnet, a ball and a car, all presented inside a small box. The toy blocks could be used to build a tower, but it was too short to enable Bobo to reach his toy. The solution was to empty the box and turn it over, and then to build the tower on top of it. In a control condition, the box was given to the children empty. German and Defeyter found that the 5-year-olds were equally fast at using the box as a support for the tower in the Functional Fixedness condition and the control condition, whereas the 6- and 7-year-olds were significantly slower in the Functional Fixedness condition than in the control condition. They were also significantly slower than the younger children in the experimental condition, taking on average 120 seconds to think of the box solution compared to 40 seconds for the 5-year-olds. German and Defeyter argued that younger children may be immune to functional fixedness in certain scenarios, because they have more flexible notions of object function. This interesting hypothesis requires more direct investigation. German and Defeyter suggest that one useful avenue of inquiry could be whether younger and older children differ in the flexibility with which they can set aside a newly taught function for a novel object and use it for a different purpose. Given the early focus on function demonstrated by Kalish and Gelman (1992), this could be an interesting approach.

Work by Brown and her colleagues suggests that large age differences in inventive flexibility per se might not be expected, however. In an extension of her "functional fixedness" studies, Brown applied the functional fixedness versus cognitive flexibility manipulation to the privileged domain of biology and natural kinds, where inductive reasoning is found in many forms.. She taught 4-year-old children about different mimicry defence mechanisms in real animals (Brown, 1989). Children in the Fixedness condition learned about one such defence mechanism, visual mimicry of a more dangerous animal. They learned about the capricorn beetle, which reveals wasp-like markings when attacked, the hawkmoth caterpillar, which has underside markings like a poisonous snake, and the crested rat, which can part its hair to show skunk-like markings. Children in the Flexibility group learned about three different mimicry mechanisms. They learned about the hoverfly, which makes a sound like a bee, the opossum, which can freeze and play dead when attacked, and the walkingstick insect, which can change shape to look like a twig or a leaf. Both groups were then tested for their ability to learn a novel mimicry solution, camouflage by color change.

In this test phase of the experiment, the children were told about two novel examples of mimicry. These were peppered moths, whose natural mixed white/grey colouring had been predominantly white prior to industrialization in northern England, but some of whom could be grey/black, and pocket mice, who had been predominantly light-coated rather than red-coated when they had lived in a sandy-floored forest, but who had been forced to move into a forest with reddish soil. The children were asked what had happened to the moths/mice. The correct answer was that over time the moths had evolved to be predominantly grey/black (making them less visible in the polluted air), and the mice had evolved to be predominantly red-coated (making them less visible against the reddish soil). The Fixedness group, who had learned only one mechanism of camouflage (look like something scary), were poor at inventing the new solution (color change), with only 10 percent inventing this solution. In contrast, the Flexibility group were very good, with 82 percent inventing this solution. Given that 4-year-olds are close to ceiling in this particular test of inventive flexibility (following optimal contexts of learning), it seems unlikely that older children will perform more poorly. Indeed, in related experiments (Brown, Kane, & Long, 1989) this was not the case. Close attention will have to be paid to the nature of the function to be learned, the existing state of the child's conceptual system, and the context in which the new function is first encountered if German and Defeyter's hypothesis about immunity to fixedness in younger children is to be tested adequately.

Analogical reasoning

The constraints on induction discussed in the preceding sections apply as well to analogical reasoning in children. Children's analogies are affected by the similarity of premise and conclusion categories (at the levels of both surface and relational similarity), by the number of exemplars on which the analogy is based, and by the nature of the relations in the analogy, as we will see. Analogical reasoning is also impeded by factors such as functional fixedness and cognitive embeddedness. Unsurprisingly, therefore, analogical reasoning is similar to other forms of inductive reasoning in that, as long as children are reasoning in familiar domains, they can go beyond surface features and make analogies on the basis of structural or relational similarity. This is particularly true when there is underlying similarity at a level of causal structure that is wholly or even partially understood. The standard view of analogical development has shifted from the notion that analogy is a content-independent strategy characteristic of the later stages of reasoning development (Piaget, Montangero, & Billeter, 1977), through a notion that younger children are "perceptually bound" and rely on surface similarity to solve analogies (Gentner, 1989), to the view that analogy is an early-developing form of inductive reasoning that is probably available from infancy (Goswami, 1992, 1996). Children, like adults (Chi, Feltovich, & Glaser, 1981), will be supported in making analogies when surface similarity supports relational similarity, but they are not constrained by surface similarity such that they are incapable of inductive reasoning on any other basis.

The relational similarity constraint

The hallmark of analogical reasoning is its dependence on structural or relational similarity (the "relational similarity constraint": Goswami, 1992). A striking example of this constraint in action comes from the analogy that led to Kekule's (1865) theory about the molecular structure of benzene (see Holyoak & Thagard, 1995). In a dream, Kekule had a visual image of a snake biting its own tail. This gave him the idea that the carbon atoms in benzene could be arranged in a ring. The similarity between the snake and the carbon atoms was at a purely structural/relational level – circular arrangement. Similarity of appearance can of course support an analogical mapping in scientists as well as young children, as shown by the invention of Velcro. This apparently followed the observation by Georges de Mestral that burdock burrs stuck to his dog's fur (again, see Holyoak & Thagard, 1995). The "surface similarity" in the appearance of the small hairs coating burdock burrs and the fuzz on Velcro supported the induction about "effective sticking mechanism." Given the "perceptually bound" hypothesis popular in early discussions of young children's inductive abilities (Gentner & Toupin, 1986), experiments examining analogical reasoning in young children often include controls for perceptual similarity.

Classic investigations of analogical development have hence focused on when children become able to reason according to the relational similarity constraint. Formal tests of analogical reasoning skills in children are usually based on "item analogies." In item analogies, two items A and B are presented to the child, a third item C is presented, and the child is required to generate a D term that has the same relation to C as B has to A. Successful generation of a D term requires the use of the relational similarity constraint. For example, if the child is given the items *horse is to foal as cat is to ?*, she is expected to generate the solution term "kitten." The response "dog," which is a strong associate of "cat," would be an error. Another test of understanding of the relational similarity constraint is to offer an apparently successful child alternative completion terms or "counter-suggestions" to the analogy that they have just formed. For example, a child who accepted "bird" as the completion term for the analogy *horse : foal :: cat : ?* would not be credited with understanding the relational similarity constraint.

The first developmental psychologist to study analogical reasoning, Piaget, used both of these tests. He designed a pictorial version of the item analogy task suitable for children from 5 to 13 years of age (Piaget, Montangero, & Billeter, 1977). The analogies were largely based on functional and causal relations, such as *bicycle* : *handlebars* :: *ship* : *?* and *dog* : *hair* :: *bird* : *?*. Younger children (5- to 7-year-olds) tested by Piaget offered solutions like "bird" to the *bicycle* : *ship* analogy, giving reasons such as "both birds and ships are found on the lake." Piaget concluded that younger children solved analogies on the basis of associative reasoning (see also Sternberg & Nigro, 1980). Slightly older children, aged approximately 7 to 12 years, were very susceptible to counter-suggestions from the experimenter. They were happy to accept a D term such as "pump" to complete the *ship* : *bicycle* analogy (*ship* : *ship's wheel* :: *bicycle* : *pump*). Piaget thus argued that understanding of the relational similarity constraint did not develop until early adolescence, during the formal operational period (Smith, ch. 23 this volume). This conclusion was accepted in developmental psychology for many years.

The role of relational familiarity in analogical development

One problem with Piaget's methodology, however, was that he did not check whether the younger children in his experiments understood the functional and causal relations on which his analogies were based (for example, the relation "steering mechanism" in the *bicycle* : *ship* analogy). Some of these relations may not yet have been specified in the child's conceptual system. As noted earlier, in the absence of the requisite knowledge, it is difficult to reason by induction. In such circumstances, novice learners are likely to fall back on simpler solution strategies such as associative reasoning and matching on the basis of surface similarity. Item analogies based on *unfamiliar* relations will obviously *underestimate* analogical ability.

One way to test this possibility is to design analogies based on relations that are known to be highly familiar to younger children from other cognitive developmental research. For example, relations between real-world objects such as "trains go on tracks" and "birds live in nests" are very familiar to 4- and 5-year-olds. Item analogies such as "bird is to nest as dog is to doghouse" can thus be used to examine whether even 4- to 5-year-olds (the youngest age group tested by Piaget) have the ability to reason by analogy. Such simple relations were used as a basis for analogy in a pictorial item analogy task designed by Goswami and Brown (1990). They gave children picture sequences for analogies such as the *bird* : *dog* analogy, and then presented a variety of solution options. For the *bird* : *dog* analogy, these were pictures of a *doghouse*, a *cat*, another *dog*, and a *bone* (see figure 13.1). The correct choice, which would indicate analogical ability, was the *doghouse*. The associative choice was the *bone*. Selection of the bone would be expected if younger children rely on associative reasoning to solve analogies, as Piaget and Sternberg had claimed. The other choices were a "surface similarity" match (the second dog), and a category match (the cat). The surface similarity match should be selected if young children are perceptually bound in analogical reasoning tasks.

The analogy task showed that all children tested (4-, 5-, and 9-year-olds) performed at levels significantly above chance, selecting the correct completion term 59 percent, 66 percent, and 94 percent of the time respectively. There was no evidence of responding on the basis of surface similarity. The children were also resistant to the notion that there

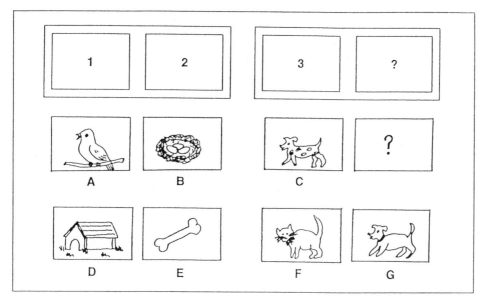

Figure 13.1   Schematic depiction of the pictorial analogy dog: doghouse :: bird : nest and the incorrect solution choices. Reprinted from U. Goswami and A. L. Brown (1990). Higher-order structure and relational reasoning: Contrasting analogical and thematic relations. *Cognition, 36,* 207–226, with permission from Excerpta Medica Inc.

could be another correct answer in the analogy task. Most of them said that only *one* answer could be correct (9 year olds: 89 percent, 4 year olds: 60 percent). Although many younger children were shy of making predictions prior to seeing the solution choices, those who were more confident showed clear analogical ability on this measure as well. For example, when 4-year-old Lucas was given the analogy *bird is to nest as dog is to ?*, he first predicted that the correct solution was *puppy*. He argued, quite logically, "Bird lays eggs in her nest [the nest in the B-term picture contained three eggs] – dog – dogs lay babies, and the babies are – umm – and the name of the babies is puppy!" Lucas had used the relation *type of offspring* to solve the analogy on the basis of the relational similarity constraint, and was quite certain that he was correct. He continued "I don't have to look [at the solution pictures] – the name of the baby is puppy!" Once he looked at the different solution options, however, he decided that the *doghouse* was the correct response. This cognitive flexibility displays a full understanding of analogy, and provides evidence of truly mental operations, thereby meeting Piaget's original criteria for the presence of "true" analogical reasoning.

However, the analogy task used by Goswami and Brown (1990) may still have underestimated analogical ability. This is because relational knowledge was not measured *independently* of analogical success. Instead, it was simply assumed that familiar relations had been selected for the analogies, leaving open the possibility that the younger children may have failed in some trials because the relations used in those particular analogies were unfamiliar to them, or because, like Lucas, they were actually reasoning about relations that were *different* from those intended by the experimenter. To explore whether even younger children could reason by analogy, Goswami and Brown (1989) designed a series of item analogies based on causal relations. Causal relations were chosen because children understand simple causal relations such as cutting, wetting, and melting by at least the age of 3 to 4 (Koslowski & Masnick, ch. 12 this volume). Children aged from 3 to 6 years were shown these relations instantiated in familiar entities, such as *chocolate is to melted chocolate as snowman is to ?*, and *playdoh is to cut playdoh as apple is to ?*. A number of different solution options were again shown to the children. Knowledge of the causal relations required to solve the analogies was measured in a control condition. In this control, the children were shown three pictures of items that had been causally transformed (e.g., cut playdoh, cut bread, cut apple), and were asked to select the causal agent responsible for the transformation from a set of pictures of possible agents (e.g., a knife, water, the sun).

The results showed that both analogical success and causal relational knowledge increased with age. The 3-year-olds solved 52 percent of the analogies and 52 percent of the control sequences, the 4-year-olds solved 89 percent of the analogies and 80 percent of the control sequences, and the 6-year-olds solved 99 percent of the analogies and 100 percent of the control sequences. There was also a significant *conditional* relationship between performance in the analogy condition and performance in the control condition, as would be expected if successful inductive reasoning depends on the existing state of the child's conceptual system. There was no evidence of matching on the basis of surface similarity. Goswami and Brown argued that analogical reasoning in children is highly dependent on relational knowledge. This raises the possibility that children younger than 3 years of age may be able to reason by analogy – as long as they have the requisite relational knowledge.

The early availability of analogy?

It is difficult to use the item analogy task with children younger than 3 years of age, because of its formal nature. For this reason, problem-solving paradigms ("problem analogies") are more useful. Children are shown a problem, A, and are also shown its solution. A different problem, B, is then presented. The measure of analogy is whether the child solves problem B by analogy to problem A.

A number of problem analogy paradigms have been used with children aged 3 years and younger. For example, Chen, Sanchez, and Campbell (1997) devised a way of giving analogies to infants as young as 10 months of age, using a procedure first developed by Brown (1989) for 1.5- to 2-year-olds. In Chen et al.'s procedure, the infants came into the laboratory and were presented with an Ernie doll that was out of their reach. The Ernie doll was also behind a barrier (a box), and had a string attached to him that was lying on a cloth. In order to bring the doll within reach, the infants needed to learn to perform a series of actions. They had to remove the barrier, pull on the cloth so that the string attached to the toy came within their grasp, and then pull on the string itself so that they could reach Ernie. Following success on the first trial, two different toy problem scenarios were presented, each using identical tools (cloths, boxes, and strings). However, each problem appeared to be different to the problems that preceded it, as the cloths, boxes, and strings were always perceptually dissimilar to those encountered before. In addition, in each problem *two* strings and *two* cloths were provided, although only one pair could be used to reach the toy.

Chen et al. tested infants aged 10 and 13 months in the Ernie paradigm. They found spontaneous analogical reasoning in the 13-month group. Most infants of this age needed their parents to model the solution to the first toy acquisition problem for them, but once the solution had been modeled they readily transferred it to the second and third problems. The younger infants (10 months) needed more salient perceptual support in order for reasoning by analogy to occur. They only showed spontaneous evidence of using analogies when the perceptual similarity between the problems was increased (for example, by using the same goal toy, such as the Ernie doll, in all three problems). This is not surprising, as the younger infants have less experience of the underlying causal structure in the different situations (e.g., box-moving, string-pulling), and so would be expected to need surface similarity cues to guide their inductions. Further examples of very young children reasoning by analogy are given in Goswami (1992, 2001).

Facilitating and impeding analogical reasoning

As noted earlier, inductive reasoning in general is broadly constrained by the nature of the knowledge to be learned, the existing state of the child's conceptual system, and the context in which the new concept is first encountered. This analysis implies that if a privileged domain such as biological knowledge is selected, for which a relatively rich conceptual system develops relatively early, and new concepts within this system are introduced in ways that facilitate cognitive flexibility, then analogical reasoning should be easy to find. Early examples of such biological analogies were given by Carey (1985), whose work was discussed briefly in the introduction. She used an inductive inference paradigm ("Dogs have spleens. Bees have spleens. Do people have spleens?"). Her data suggested that younger children base their understanding of animals on their understanding of people, projecting behavioral and psychological properties on to other animals according to how similar these animals are to human beings. Inagaki and her colleagues have termed this the "personification analogy."

Inagaki and her colleagues (Inagaki & Hatano, 1987; Inagaki & Sugiyama, 1988) then investigated in some detail how often children base their predictions about biological phenomena on analogies to people, the biological kinds best known to young children. For example, Inagaki and Sugiyama (1988) asked 4-, 5-, 8-, and 10-year-olds a range of questions about various properties of eight target objects, including "Does X breathe?", "Does X have a heart?", "Does X feel pain if we prick it with a needle?", and "Can X think?" The target objects were people, rabbits, pigeons, fish, grasshoppers, trees, tulips, and stones. Prior similarity judgments had established that the target objects differed in their similarity to people in this order, with rabbits being rated as most similar and stones being rated as least similar. The children all showed a decreasing tendency to attribute the physiological properties ("Does X breathe?") to the target objects as the perceived similarity to a person decreased. A similar pattern was found for the mental properties ("Can X think?"). Hence judgments about similarity based on the existing state of the children's conceptual systems were acting as a constraint on their analogies.

How can new concepts be introduced into biological frameworks in ways that promote analogy? This question was investigated by Brown, whose work on other factors that impede and facilitate analogies was discussed in the section above on insight (i.e., functional fixedness, cognitive flexibility). One factor that could plausibly promote analogy is the provision of multiple exemplars (given that sample size affects inductive inferences in adults and children). Accordingly, Brown and Kane (1988) designed some more animal defence mechanism analogies for 3-year-olds, comparing analogical transfer on the first analogy with transfer after three different analogies. The design depended on three pairs of biological analogies, one based on camouflage by color change, one based on camouflage by shape change, and one based on mimicry of a more dangerous animal. For example, the children were first told about the arctic fox, who changes color in winter, and the chameleon, who changes color to match his surroundings. They were then told about the walkingstick insect, which can resemble a twig or leaf, and the pipe fish, which can resemble a reed. Finally, they were told about the crested rat and the hawkmoth caterpillar (see previously). The measure of analogical reasoning was performance on the final problem pair. Children were asked "How could the hawkmoth caterpillar stop the big bird that wants to eat him?"

In this context of multiple analogies (which Brown calls the A_1A_2, B_1B_2, C_1C_2 or "learning-to-learn" paradigm), 70–80 percent of the 3-year-olds reasoned by analogy on the final problem pair (i.e., unaided solution of C_2). In contrast, successful solution of the first problem pair (i.e., solution of A_2) was around 25 percent. The provision of multiple analogies was clearly important in fostering this high level of performance, but so was the nature of the relations on which the analogies were based. In a different study, Brown and Kane gave 3-year-olds the same manipulation (three pairs of analogies in the order A_1A_2, B_1B_2, C_1C_2), but instead of setting the analogies in the biological domain, they used story scenarios with toy characters. These characters had to solve problems based on stacking real objects or pulling real objects. Although these should also be familiar relations to young children, analogical reasoning on the third problem pair was much lower in this study, at around 40 percent correct. One possibility is that the relations necessary to the analogy (stacking etc.) were not part of a causally relevant conceptual system in the same way that animal defence mechanisms were. In this sense they were quite different from the arguably less familiar but more systematically constrained relations about how biological kinds can avoid predation.

Summary

Inductive reasoning in children is facilitated by the nature of the function to be learned, the existing state of the child's conceptual system, and the context in which the new function is first encountered. Inductive reasoning is similarity-based, and factors that facilitate or impede the recognition of similarity will facilitate or impede inductive reasoning. Some kinds of knowledge (e.g., about natural kinds) are acquired very early and enable the development of a relatively sophisticated conceptual system at a young age (e.g., some children's dinosaur knowledge), and new knowledge is easily absorbed into the system, particularly in certain contexts (those promoting cognitive flexibility, such as experiencing a multitude of uses for a tool, or experiencing multiple exemplars for a new concept). For inductive reasoning, Brown (1990) has argued that the key factor in transfer of learning is a search for underlying similarity at the level of causal structure. If children have some insight into the causal mechanisms in question, then inductive inferences are difficult to impede. On this view, investigations of whether children reason inductively on the basis of perceptual attributes, lower-order relations, or higher-level causal or systematic relations are better understood as a sensitive index of their depth of understanding of a domain, rather than as an indication of their developmental status per se.

Deductive Reasoning

The very term "deduction" implies that deductive reasoning involves combining existing information by following specific mental operations. These operations can only be performed on information in logically valid ways. The simplest form of deductive reasoning is the *syllogism*. In a syllogism, the reasoner is presented with two premises that allow only one logical conclusion. An example is: "All cats bark. Rex is a cat. Does Rex bark?" Deductive reasoning has also been studied via the selection task, which can also be called a *conditional syllogism*. The selection task is based on the logical implication *If p then q*. Participants are asked to work out the minimum number of pieces of evidence that they need in order to decide whether the statement "If p then q" (i.e., if p is true, then q is true) is correct. Syllogistic reasoning and the selection task have been fairly widely used with young children, and will be discussed in some detail. Finally, the kinds of deductive reasoning discussed by Piaget will be considered briefly. A mental operation such as transitivity (A is greater than B, B is greater than C, therefore A is greater than C) is a linear syllogism. The deduction that "A is greater than C" must follow given the premises "A is greater than B" and "B is greater than C." Traditionally, deductive reasoning was thought to develop rather slowly in children. For example, Piaget thought that certain mental operations could only be applied to information by children older than around 6 to 7 years (the concrete operations, such as transitivity and class inclusion, see Smith, ch. 23 this volume). More complex mental operations (such as scientific reasoning and hypothesis-testing; see Kuhn, ch. 17 this volume) could only be applied by adolescents. Physical reasoning (Wilkening & Huber, ch. 16 this volume), and causal reasoning (Koslowski & Masnick, ch. 12 this volume) can also involve deductive logic. Because these forms of deductive reasoning, including scientific reasoning, are extensively covered in other chapters, they will not be considered here.

Syllogistic reasoning

Aristotle apparently claimed that syllogistic reasoning represented the highest achievement in human rational thought (see Mayer, 1992). Perhaps unsurprisingly given this particular premise, young children and adults from non-Westernized cultures were for a long time thought to be very poor at syllogistic reasoning. The critical test upon which this conclusion was based involved syllogisms utilizing unfamiliar information. For example, peasants from Uzbekistan (a hot, plains region of Russia) were given syllogisms such as "In the Far North, where there is snow, all bears are white. Novaya Zemla is in the Far North. What color are the bears there?" (Luria, 1977). Snow was completely unfamiliar to these villagers, who performed rather poorly on such syllogisms. However, they did well on syllogisms that were based on familiar information, such as the factors that affect the growth of cotton. The same peasants could make logical deductions from premises such as "Cotton grows well where it is hot and dry. England is cold and damp. Can cotton grow there or not?"

The tendency of adults from traditional societies to reason poorly with unfamiliar premises was labeled the "empirical bias" by Scribner (1977). She found that West African Kpelle tribespeople showed good syllogistic reasoning when given premises that they could empirically verify as being true, such as paying a house tax. However, when given premises that they could not verify as true, such as whether "Mr Smith" was a Kpelle man given that he was not a rice farmer and that all Kpelle men are rice farmers, they performed poorly or even refused to reason ("I don't know the man in person . . . I cannot answer that question"). Schooling had a remarkable effect on these adults' ability to make deductive inferences about unfamiliar premises. Scribner argued that this was because education enables participants to set empirical considerations aside, and to utilize the premises as stated, independently of their plausibility. As young children are typically relatively unschooled, the assumption that young children were incapable of syllogistic reasoning about unfamiliar premises followed quite naturally from this cross-cultural work.

For example, Hawkins, Pea, Glick, and Scribner (1984) gave 4- and 5-year-old preschoolers syllogistic reasoning problems that were either based on familiar knowledge ("bears have big teeth") or unfamiliar (incongruent) knowledge ("everything that flies has wheels"). The children did poorly with the incongruent problems, displaying an empirical bias. However, they did relatively well with fantasy premises ("Pogs wear blue boots. Tom is a pog. Does Tom wear blue boots?"). This prompted Dias and Harris (1988, 1990) to explore whether preschoolers can reason syllogistically about incongruent premises when the reasoning task is presented in a "fantasy" mode. The fantasy mode was created by telling the children that they should pretend that the experimenter was on another planet, and that everything on that planet was different from how it was in the world. For example, the experimenter would say "All cats bark. On that planet I saw that all cats bark", using a "make-believe" intonation, and would then verbally present the syllogism "All cats bark. Rex is a cat. Does Rex bark?" In these fantasy conditions, the levels of syllogistic reasoning shown by these young children approached ceiling levels. The "fantasy" effect was robust whether the premises were presented as referring to another planet, presented using a make-believe intonation, or presented using visual imagery ("make a picture in your head"). Dias and Harris concluded that young children were capable of deductive reasoning, even about counterfactual premises, as long as logical problems were presented in a context that clearly marked for the child that the situation was make-believe.

Later work by Leevers and Harris (1999, 2000) extended these findings, and showed that the "make-believe" nature of the situation was not the critical factor in determining whether children showed deductive logic or an "empirical bias." Rather, the important feature was the *pragmatic* aspects of the reasoning situation. Situations that enabled young children to set empirical considerations aside, and to utilize the premises as stated, independently of their plausibility, facilitated the application of deductive reasoning. The manipulation used by Leevers and Harris was simply to ask the children to *think* about the problems ("I want you to *think about* what things would be like if it was true . . . are you *thinking about* X?"). They then gave them counterfactual syllogisms of the type used by Dias and Harris, such as "All snow is black. Tom sees some snow. Is it black?", and "All ladybirds have stripes on their backs. Daisy sees a ladybird. Is it spotty?" Leevers and Harris found that "thinking about" the empirically incongruent premises facilitated syllogistic reasoning just as much as fantasy presentation of the same premises. They argued that the key feature for successful reasoning was whether the children *processed* the premises mentally instead of dismissing them as absurd. Once the children were able to utilize the premises as stated, they could apply deductive logic, just like unschooled adults.

Conditional syllogisms: the selection task

The selection task provides a different measure of deductive reasoning, as the task is presented in such a way that participants do not have to make a logically valid inference. Rather, they have to choose the conditions that would enable a valid inference to be made. In the selection task, the participant is usually told about a certain state of affairs, "If *p* then *q*." For example, the participant might be shown a pack of cards which all have a letter on one side and a number on the other side, and told the rule "If a card has a vowel on one side, then it has an even number on the other side" (Wason & Johnson-Laird, 1972). Four cards are then presented, showing respectively A, D, 4, 7. The participant's task is to decide the minimum number of cards that must be selected in order to validate the rule. The correct solution (A and 7, or *p* and *not-q*), is typically selected rather rarely (only five out of 128 adults selected this pair of cards in the original studies). However, it was soon discovered that this apparently massive failure in deductive logic could be reduced or eradicated by changing *pragmatic* aspects of the reasoning situation.

One of the first demonstrations of this was in an experiment that set the selection task in the context of a post office. Participants were told to imagine that they were postal workers sorting letters on a conveyor belt. They had to make sure that the post did not violate the rule "If a letter is sealed, then it has a 5p stamp on it." The pieces of evidence available were *p* (a sealed letter, shown face down), *q* (a letter with a 5p stamp, shown face up), not-*p* (an unsealed letter, shown face down), and not-*q* (a letter with a 4p stamp, shown face up). Most adult participants easily solved this version of the selection task, correctly selecting the sealed envelope and the envelope with the 4p stamp (Johnson-Laird, Legrenzi, & Sonino-Legrenzi, 1972). Following other demonstrations of successful reasoning in the selection task when presented in more familiar contexts, Wason and colleagues realized that difficulties in deductive reasoning are not usually determined by the intrinsic logical structure of the task. Rather, they are determined by the problem content or mode of presentation of the problem itself.

This conclusion about *deductive* reasoning in adults is obviously very similar to the conclusions that we reached about *inductive* reasoning in young children. If inductive reasoning is affected by problem content (is it familiar to children?) and by mode of presentation (the context in which the problem is encountered), then presumably deductive reasoning in children will be affected by the same parameters. A series of experiments utilizing "permission schemas" suggest that this is indeed the case. As pointed out by Cheng and Holyoak (1985), most selection tasks tap into permission scenarios in real life. In the post office experiment discussed above, the scenario is very similar to the permission rules that govern the actual delivery of letters, such as "If you want the lower airmail rate, the letter must be unsealed." Children encounter permission rules all the time ("If you want to stay up late, you must finish your homework and have your bath," "If you are outside school premises, you must wear your blazer and your cap"). Hence if children are given selection tasks in the context of familiar permission rules, they too should be able to reason deductively about the conditions that enable a valid test of whether the rule is being obeyed.

Harris and Nunez (1996) have shown that even 3- and 4-year-olds are sensitive to the pragmatics of permission and inhibition in the selection task. They used a story-based format to present the permission rules, and presented the different conditions via pictures, asking the children to select the picture that depicted a breach of the rule (the *p*, not-*q* picture). For example, in one study the children were told "This is a story about Sally. One day Sally wants to play outside. Her Mum says that if she plays outside, she must put her coat on." The children were then shown four pictures, a picture of Sally outside with her coat on (*p*, *q*), a picture of Sally outside without her coat on (*p*, not-*q*), a picture of Sally inside with her coat on (not-*p*, *q*), and a picture of Sally inside without her coat on (not-*p*, not-*q*). The children were asked "Show me the picture of where Sally is being naughty and not doing what her mum told her." The correct answer was Sally outside without her coat on, the combination of *p* and not-*q*.

The majority of 3- and 4-year-old children were able to choose the picture of Sally outside without her coat on. This is presumably a familiar situation for young children, who often fail to see the need to wear a coat when going outside. Hence in principle it could be solved without making a logical deduction. However, Harris and Nunez were able to demonstrate that the children were also successful with novel permission rules tapping scenarios that they had not experienced, such as "Carol's Mum says if she does some painting she should put her helmet on" and "Carol's Mum says if she rides her bicycle she should put her apron on." Harris and Nunez's paradigm may be less demanding than the traditional selection task, as the children had to select the picture that depicted the combination of *p* and not-*q* rather than independently identify *p* and not-*q*. Nevertheless, their conclusion that 3- and 4-year-old children are quite capable of identifying breaches of a permission rule seems convincing. Once again, when a deductive reasoning problem is presented within a pragmatically plausible setting, young children can reason by deduction almost as efficiently as adults.

Linear syllogisms: transitive reasoning

As noted earlier, deductive reasoning basically involves performing specific mental operations on information in logically valid ways. Piaget's theory of logical development
(Smith, ch. 23 this volume) was based on this kind of notion. He argued that, as they
get older, children become able to operate on information in increasingly logically sophisticated ways. The final stage of logical development involves a dissociation between form
and content ('formal operational reasoning'). An example of formal operational reasoning given by Piaget is analogical reasoning. As already shown, children can reason by
analogy from an early age when the analogies are based on familiar relations. In Piaget's
terms, "this notion [of formal operations] . . . also expresses the general characteristic of
formal thought – it goes beyond the framework of transformations bearing directly on
empirical reality (concrete operations) and subordinates it to a system of hypothetico-
deductive operations, i.e., operations which are *possible*" (Inhelder & Piaget, 1958,
p. 254). As shown by work with adults using syllogisms, analogies, and the selection task,
however, a total dissociation between the form and content of reasoning is seldom found
in human cognition (apart perhaps from the disciplines of mathematics and formal logic,
in which excellence is attained by rather few).

I will focus here on just one logical concept identified by Piaget, the transitive inference. This is an example of one of Piaget's "concrete operations," that set of logical concepts that describes classes of objects and their relations. I have chosen transitivity because
it is also a linear syllogism, making links between this form of deductive reasoning and
the other forms discussed in this chapter easier to formulate. Given the evidence discussed
so far, it seems possible that if a problem requiring a transitive inference is presented in
a pragmatically plausible setting, then young children too will demonstrate deductive
logic.

Transitive relations hold between any entities that can be organized into an ordinal
series. If a series of sticks can be ordered by length, such as A = 10″, B = 8″, C = 6″, D
= 4″ and E = 2″, then the transitive relations are A > B, B > C, C > D, and D > E.
Notice that logical inferences ("transitive inferences") can be made about pairs of sticks
that are not adjacent. For example, if A > B and B > C, then A > C. There is no other
logical deduction given the relations between A and B, and between B and C.

In Piaget's classic tests of transitive inference in young children, problems were presented in the following form: "If Jane is bigger than Mary, and Mary is bigger than Sarah,
who is bigger, Jane or Sarah?" The child had to mentally arrange the girls into the series
Jane > Mary > Sarah, and reply that Jane was bigger. Clearly, the memory load here is
considerable for a young child, and Piaget found that children younger than 6 or 7 years
were very poor at solving such problems. Pears and Bryant (1990) argued that there were
at least three ways of removing the memory load. One was to give the children lots of
prior experience or training with the premises, so that they learned them thoroughly
before being asked the inferential question (see Bryant & Trabasso, 1971). The second
was to provide children with symbolic aides-memoires of the premises at the time of the
inferential test (Halford, 1984). The third, which was the one tested by Pears and Bryant

themselves, was to eliminate the memory load altogether by designing a transitive inference task in which the children could see the premises at the time that they were asked the inferential question.

In Pears and Bryant (1990), the premises were pairs of coloured bricks, and the bricks were presented in little "towers" one on top of the other (e.g., red on top and blue beneath, blue on top and green beneath). In this example involving two premise pairs, logically a three-term series can be created (e.g., red on top of blue on top of green). The task was introduced as a game about building towers. All participants were 4-year-olds. The children's job was to build complete towers of bricks from single bricks of the appropriate colors, using the premise pairs as a guide. Three kinds of tower had to be constructed during the experiment: four-brick towers (involving three premises), five-brick towers (involving four premises), and six-brick towers (involving five premises). To take a five-brick tower as an example, if the little towers showed red on top and blue beneath (R_TB), blue on top and green beneath (B_TG), green on top and yellow beneath (G_TY), and yellow on top and white beneath (Y_TW), then the target tower was ($R_TB_TG_TY_TW$).

Prior to being allowed to build the target towers, the children were asked a series of inferential questions such as "Which will be the higher in the tower that you are going to build, the yellow brick or the blue one?" In order to answer these inferential questions correctly, the children had to combine the information from two premises (B_TG, G_TY) using a transitive inference. Such questions were the critical inferential questions, as they involved comparisons based on bricks that appeared *twice* in the towers and hence had two absolute values, high and low. Pears and Bryant found that the children were significantly above chance in their performance on two-thirds of the critical inferential questions. From this finding, they argued that 4-year-olds do possess the ability to make transitive inferences, at least about the continuum of space.

Young children's success in the tower-building task is reminiscent of the other demonstrations of successful deductive reasoning discussed in this chapter. When the task is set in a familiar context and children are reasoning about pragmatically plausible content, then their deductive reasoning can be as efficient as that of adults. Difficulties in deductive reasoning do not usually appear to be determined by the intrinsic logical structure of a particular task. Rather, they are determined by the problem content or mode of presentation of the problem itself.

Summary

Deductive reasoning in children is affected by the nature of the problem to be solved and the context in which the problem is first encountered. As long as deductive reasoning is tested using content that is represented in the child's existing conceptual system (e.g., permission rules about familiar activities, building towers from blocks), then young children can perform successfully in deductive reasoning tasks. The same is true of adults, who for example are impaired in reasoning about permission rules instantiating very abstract concepts (the A, D, 4, 7 study). Similarly, the context of problem presentation can impede the application of deductive logic by both children and adults. If syllogisms based on unfamiliar premises are presented to unschooled adults, or if counter-factual syllogisms are presented to children in ways that fail to signal that they should reason about the premises as given, then children and adults show poor deductive reasoning. However, if children and adults recognize that they must utilize the premises as stated, irrespective of their truth value, then deductive reasoning is successful.

Conclusion

There is considerable continuity across the lifespan in both inductive and deductive reasoning. In both children and adults, successful inductive and deductive reasoning appears to be influenced by similar factors and subject to similar constraints. Inductive reasoning in children is facilitated by the nature of the function to be learned, the existing state of the child's conceptual system, and the context in which the new function is first encountered. Deductive reasoning is facilitated by the use of familiar problem content and the use of pragmatically appropriate contexts of problem presentation. It is easy to make children perform poorly in reasoning experiments. The experimenter simply has to give them unsuitable tasks based on unfamiliar concepts. It is also possible to make adults perform poorly in reasoning experiments. However, if the intrinsic logical structure of inductive (e.g., analogy) and deductive (e.g., transitive inference) reasoning problems is accepted to be maintained in some of the ingenious paradigms reported in this chapter, then it is difficult to escape the conclusion that even very young children are capable of inductive and deductive reasoning.

This view of young children as competent reasoners is very different to the more traditional notion that reasoning becomes increasingly logical with increasing age. The traditional view was based on the false assumption that reasoning strategies are independent of context and content. Given this assumption, it seemed natural to suppose that children became increasingly efficient "domain-general" reasoners as they got older, able to apply deductive or inductive (e.g., analogy) strategies to almost anything. Now that more recent work in adult reasoning has shown that even supposedly efficient reasoners are affected by problem content and problem context, developmental views are gradually changing. Of course, it would be absurd to argue that there are no developmental differences between children and adults (or between younger and older children). There are considerable differences in many experimental paradigms with age, but these differences may not be linked to the intrinsic logical requirements of the reasoning tasks instantiated in these paradigms. Rather, they may reflect a variety of factors such as lack of knowledge about the problem content, differences in basic mental capacities such as short-term memory (see Halford, ch. 25 this volume), ineffective general learning strategies such as the use of appropriate mnemonic devices (see Schneider, ch. 11 this volume), and metacognitive difficulties (also Schneider, this volume). Accordingly, children become able to learn almost anything with appropriate effort, tuition, skill, and strategies as they get older. The important point is that while these factors all affect overall performance, they do not necessarily change basic competence.

Note

1. This argument was made most forcefully and eloquently by Ann Brown, whose elegant work on learning in children is a testimony to the power of induction. Her untimely death in 2000 was a great loss to the field, and I dedicate this chapter to her memory.

CHAPTER FOURTEEN

The Development of Moral Reasoning

Larry P. Nucci

The contemporary study of the development of moral reasoning originated with the account of Piaget (1932) subsequently extended by Kohlberg (1984). While differing in their details, both explanations held that moral reasoning progresses through a universal sequence of stages eventuating in conceptualizations of morality that transcend the particulars of culture and context. Over the past 25 years, the study of moral reasoning has largely been about challenges and responses to the basic story contained in the Piaget/Kohlberg theory. These challenges and revisions have led to a serious reworking of our notions of moral development, and have left a number of issues unresolved. This chapter will review some of those challenges, and the attendant changes they have brought to our view of moral development.

Recent work on moral development can be viewed in terms of three main interrelated issues. The first has to do with the structure of moral cognition. Questions have been raised in terms of the breadth of what should be included within the moral domain, whether morality can be defined in terms of a single developmental progression, and whether age-related changes in moral cognition constitute a stage-like sequence. The second set of questions has to do with the generality of moral concepts, and how moral cognition interacts with context and culture. Questions have been raised regarding the degree of internal consistency displayed by individuals in their moral judgments across contexts, and whether morality can be viewed as independent of cultural norms. Finally, questions have been raised regarding whether morality is a function of judgment at all, or whether it is instead the result of non-rational factors such as emotion and socialization. While theorists and researchers often address more than one of these issues in a single paradigm, this chapter will examine each of these three major sets of issues separately.

The Structure and Scope of Morality

The moral domain

For both Piaget (1932) and Kohlberg (1984), moral development moves from earlier stages, in which morality is intertwined with self-interest and social norms, to later more mature stages, in which morality as justice is differentiated from and displaces social convention as the basis for moral judgments. Piaget (1932) characterized this transition as involving two levels of moral judgment. The first level, typical of young children, was labeled heteronomous, and the second autonomous. Children in the heteronomous level were thought to base their moral judgments on unilateral respect for authority, and adherence to externally determined and fixed rules. This conventional basis for morality is replaced at the autonomous level, according to Piaget, by a moral orientation based on mutual respect and cooperation. What is moral at the autonomous level is not defined by externally imposed rules, but rather by concerns for reciprocity and fairness. In the late 1950s, Kohlberg (1958) extended Piaget's work on the development of moral judgment to include adolescents and young adults. Kohlberg maintained Piaget's basic focus on moral judgment rather than the acquisition of moral norms. He assessed moral development by asking people to solve moral problems, or dilemmas that pitted the needs of a person against a prevailing social norm or law. For example, Kohlberg's most famous dilemma involves a situation in which a man has to decide whether or not to steal a drug in order to save the life of his wife. Using this approach, Kohlberg determined that moral development was a slower process than Piaget had thought, and that morality progressed through three levels (pre-conventional, conventional, post-conventional), rather than two as Piaget had described. Each of these three levels was thought to contain two stages. According to Kohlberg's research, only at the final post-conventional level, typical of a minority of older adolescents and young adults, does morality become separated from conventions and laws, and rest fully on principles of fairness and concerns for the welfare of persons (Kohlberg, 1969). A summary of Kohlberg's stages of moral development is presented in table 14.1.

During the 1960s and early 1970s a considerable amount of evidence was generated in support of the six-stage sequence of moral development described by Kohlberg (1984). However, in the late 1960s, results from longitudinal studies began to turn up evidence that was in conflict with the assumptions of Kohlberg's stage theory. In particular, researchers uncovered that a number of young adults appeared to move from Kohlberg's stage 4 (a developmental period in which morality is defined by the laws of society) to what looked to be a less mature form of reasoning based on the immediate context and self-interest typical of children at Kohlberg's stage 2 (Kohlberg & Kramer, 1969). This apparent adolescent regression went contrary to the basic assumptions of structuralist stage theory, and posed a major challenge to the Kohlbergian account.

Kohlberg and Kramer (1969) initially explained these results as a temporary regression brought on either by the pressures of college life, or as regression "in the service of the ego" (Turiel, 1974, p. 16) that would lead to developmental progress. This assumption was buttressed by findings that their young adult subjects did not long remain at stage 2, but moved on to the next stage (5) within Kohlberg's framework (Kohlberg & Kramer, 1969). On closer examination, however, the moral reasoning of these young adults turned out not to have matched the instrumentalist thinking of stage 2 children (Turiel, 1974). Instead, the apparent regression reflected a conflation of an understanding of convention as the particular construction of a given social system with morality itself. In the thinking of these young relativists, there was no particular force to the morality of any given system of conventions, and thus no reason to favor the morality of one system over another. More importantly, no one, according to the line of reasoning employed by these subjects, had the moral right to privilege one conventional system of laws over those of another. Thus, morality had to be worked out by individuals within each situation as best as one could based upon one's reading of what was right in the context. Behind this relativism, however, there appeared to be a moral principle of mutual respect, and just reciprocity. Following this thread, researchers committed to Kohlberg's sequence felt that they had accounted for the apparent developmental discrepancy uncovered in their longitudinal studies (Turiel, 1974). This period of relativism was explained as a transition in which the conventional basis of stage 4 reasoning was replaced by post-conventional (stage 5) principled moral thought.

While the above explanations seemed to satisfy many in the Kohlberg camp (Colby, Kohlberg, Gibbs, & Lieberman, 1983), others began to explore whether in fact the distinctions between convention and moral issues of justice being made by young adults in the midst of their apparent period of relativism was particular to that period of development, or if it reflected a manifestation of conceptual frameworks from earlier ages. The latter seemed to be a likely possibility since all developmental theories presuppose that concepts do not simply appear out of nowhere, but have a developmental history. Following up on that hunch has led to one of the most fruitful lines of inquiry in the field.

Domain theory: the distinction between morality and convention.　Following his analysis of the reasoning of the relativists uncovered in Kohlberg's longitudinal work, Turiel (1975) and his colleagues began to explore whether young children also maintain a set of conceptual distinctions between morality (nonarbitrary and unavoidable features of social relations pertaining to matters of human welfare and fairness) and matters of convention (contextually dependent and agreed upon social rules). What they discovered was that very young children differentiate between matters of convention and morality employing criteria consistent with the formalist properties of these two types of social regulation (Turiel, 1978). Since then, over 60 studies have been conducted that have reported results concordant with these initial findings (for recent reviews see Helwig, Tisak, & Turiel, 1990; Smetana, 1995; Tisak, 1995; Turiel, 1998). This research has indicated that the differentiation between morality and convention emerges at very young ages (as young as age 3: Smetana & Braeges, 1990) and is maintained by individuals across cultures (for recent reviews see Nucci, 2001; Turiel, 1998). With some variations in specific findings regarding convention, the distinction between morality and convention has been reported in each of the cultures examined. Only one study (Shweder, Mahapatra, & Miller, 1987) has claimed to obtain data indicating that individuals within a non-Western culture (members of a temple village in India) make no distinction between morality and

Table 14.1 Levels of moral and conventional development in relation to Kohlberg's stages

Approximate ages	Conceptual framework		
	Moral domain	*Conventional domain*	*Kohlberg stage*
5–7 years	Recognition of prima facie obligations (e.g., not to hit and hurt others). However, beyond those basic requirements, fairness is prioritized in terms of self-interest.	Conventions are "reified" as descriptions of empirical regularities (e.g., women are supposed to wear dresses because women wear dresses and men don't).	*Stage 1* Rules are to be obeyed. One should avoid physical damage to persons and property. Inability to coordinate perspectives of self and others, thus favoring the self is seen as right.
8–10	Fairness is now coordinated with conceptions of "just" reciprocity defined primarily in terms of strict equality with some beginning concerns for equity.	Negation of the conception of conventions as empirical regularities. Exceptions to conventions (e.g., some women wear trousers) taken as evidence that conventions are arbitrary. The mere existence of a norm not a sufficient basis for compliance.	*Stage 2* Morality as instrumental exchange – "You scratch my back I'll scratch yours. Act to meet one's own interests and needs and letting others do the same. Rules followed only when in someone's interests.
10–12	Fairness seen as requiring more than strict equality. Concerns for equity (taking into account the special needs, situations, or contributions of others) are now coordinated with reciprocity in structuring moral decisions.	Concrete understanding that conventional rules maintain order (e.g., prevent people from running in the halls). Top-down conception of social authority and rules. People in charge make rules that preserve order. Rules may be changed and vary by context.	*Stage 3* Being good means living up to what is expected by people around you, and by one's role (e.g., good brother, sister). Fairness is the golden rule. One should be caring of others.
12–14	Consolidation of the relations between equity and equality in conceptions of what is fair and caring in social relations.	Conventions are now viewed as "nothing but" social expectations. The arbitrary nature of convention is viewed as undercutting the force of a rule. Acts are evaluated independent of rules.	*Stage 3B (Pseudo Stage 6)* Moral decisions based on the fairness or harmful impact of actions independent of governing rules, laws, or role expectations. Morality prioritized over convention. No evidence of a "prior to society" orientation.

Age	Social Convention	Morality
14–17	Emergence of systematic concepts of social structure. Conventions as normative and binding within a social system of fixed roles, and static hierarchical organization.	*Stage 4* Morality as codified in the laws of the governing system. Adherence to law provides an objective basis for the right. Maintaining social system basis for moral order, and equal protection from harm. Notions of equity and equality same as in Stage 3.
17–20	Negation of view that uniform norms serve to maintain social systems. Conventions are "nothing but" societal standards that have become codified through habitual use. Systems of norms are arbitrary.	*Stage 4 1/2* Morality is relative to systems of laws and norms. No system may lay claim to moral superiority. What is right is a function of what seems most right for the person in his/her situation.
Adulthood	Conventions as uniformities that are functional in coordinating social interactions. Shared knowledge of conventions among members of social groups facilitate interaction and operation of the system.	*Stage 5* "Prior to society" perspective. What is moral are values and rights that exist prior to social attachments and contracts. Such values and rights are those which any rational being would want to see reflected in a moral society.
	(Moral Domain Extrapolation) Application of conceptions of fairness and beneficence to reasoning about one's social system. Morality understood to be independent of norms of particular systems. Coordination of universal and prescriptive features of morality with incommensurate/intrinsic worth of all persons. Logical extension of moral obligations to treatment of humankind.	

Note: Stage 6 is not included because longitudinal studies (Colby et al., 1983) did not provide sufficient evidence of the existence of this stage to warrant its status as an empirically validated developmental period. Stage 6 remains as a theoretical end-point within the Kohlberg paradigm.

convention, and that result has been disputed by findings from a subsequent study (Madden, 1992). In all cases, children and adolescents have been found to treat moral issues entailing harm and injustice in much the same way. Children across cultural groups and social classes have been found to treat moral transgressions, such as unprovoked harm, as wrong regardless of the presence or absence of rules, and have viewed the wrongness of such moral transgressions as holding universally for children in other cultures or settings, and not just for their own group.

This set of results has led to a reconceptualization of the breadth and scope of what falls within the scope of moral judgment. Rather than entailing a process of gradual differentiation of morality out of convention as envisioned by Kohlberg (1969), social domain theory posits that conceptions of morality, convention, and other social concepts are structured within what Piaget (1985) referred to as partial systems or subsystems. On this account, each partial system forms an internally equilibrated structure that in certain contexts may interact with other systems requiring interdomain equilibration or coordination. These partial systems are thought to correspond to qualitatively different aspects of social interaction, and to follow discrete, identifiable courses of development (Turiel, 1978, 1979). Observational research has reported that the patterns of social interactions associated with moral events among children and between children and adults focus on features intrinsic to the acts such as the harm that is caused or the fairness or unfairness of actions. Interactions surrounding conventional events, on the other hand, focus upon aspects of the social order such as the governing rules, social expectations, wishes of authority, and elements of the social structure and hierarchy (for reviews see Smetana, 1995; Turiel, 1998).

Research on the development of reasoning within each domain has also provided evidence consistent with the notion that morality and convention are distinct developmental systems. Development within the moral domain entails shifts in the ways in which people conceptualize what it means to be fair, along with attendant changes in conceptions of the obligations that follow from moral concerns for the welfare of others (Damon, 1977, 1980; Davidson, Turiel, & Black 1983; Enright, Franklin, & Manheim, 1980; Lapsley, 1982, 1996). Development of concepts of convention follows an oscillating pattern of affirmations and negations tied to shifts in understandings of the role conventional norms play in structuring predictable patterns of conduct among members of a social group. This oscillation is indicative of the difficulty children and adolescents have in making sense of the function of these arbitrary social norms, and maps onto their efforts to understand social organization and systems of social regulation. By middle to late adolescence, children come to an understanding of social conventions as constituent elements of social systems, and as important to the coordination of social life within a particular social unit (Searle, 1969; Turiel, 1983). A summary of the levels of development of social convention along with developmental changes in the moral domain is presented in table 14.1. A more complete overview of the developmental changes in morality and social convention is available in Nucci (2001).

Further support for the structural and developmental independence of morality and social convention was provided in an experimental educational intervention (Nucci & Weber, 1991), in which students either focused the content of their group discussions around moral issues of fairness and harm to others, or matters of social convention and social organization. Findings were that at the end of the four-week instructional period the group that focused on moral issues had higher levels of moral judgment than the group that focused on matters of convention. Conversely the group that focused discussions around convention had attained higher levels of understanding in the conventional domain. This relatively short-term intervention demonstrated that differential social experiences can result in different rates of development in these two domains, and provides additional evidence that morality and convention comprise distinct conceptual and developmental systems.

Moral development and inter-domain interactions.   Work demonstrating the conceptual independence of morality and convention has focused on children's and adults' reasoning about prototypical issues. Unprovoked harm is an example of a prototypical moral issue, while addressing teachers by their titles rather than first names is an example of a prototypical conventional issue. Many everyday social judgments, however, involve overlap across domains necessitating the sorts of inter-domain equilibrations envisioned in Piaget's (1985) theory. Interactions between morality and convention are inevitable since all social interactions occur within broader contexts structured by conventions. When overlaps occur an individual's reasoning will reflect both the degree to which the individual attends to the domain-salient features of the given issue and the degree to which an individual is able to bring elements across domains into coordination or harmony. In some cases conventions merely codify, or are consistent with, morality. In other cases conventions that serve to maintain social organization are in conflict with moral concerns for what might be objectively considered fair or just. An example of such conventions is gender norms that describe roles in such a way that members of one sex are accorded privileges not given to the other. In such cases people either subordinate the issue to a single domain (viewing it either as an issue of fairness or of custom, convention, and tradition), are conflicted as to how to think about the issue, or arrive at a coordinated integration of the need for conventional organization and moral requirements of equitable and beneficent treatment of persons. What this analysis suggests is that we should anticipate considerably more variance across and within individuals' applications of moral reasoning in context than is allowed within the traditional Kohlberg system. This is in fact what the data on moral reasoning indicate (Bandura, 1991; Keller, Eckensberger, & von Rosen, 1989; Rest, Narvaez, Bebeau, & Thoma, 1999).

For example, in the process of conducting their careful and extensive research aimed at standardizing moral stage scoring, the Kohlberg group (Colby & Kohlberg, 1987; Colby et al., 1983) discovered that individuals at all points in development may respond to Kohlberg's moral dilemmas by reasoning from a perspective of either rules and authority (Type A reasoning), or justice and human welfare (Type B reasoning). In addition, individuals at all ages and levels, and not just the young adults described earlier in this chapter, may present what the Kohlberg group has referred to as a "relativistic metaethical orientation" reflecting a confounding of morality with the arbitrary nature of convention and conventional systems. Others have reported that adult tendencies to display conventional (stage 4) or post-conventional, principled (stage 5) moral reasoning is significantly associated with whether one has a conservative or liberal political ideology

(Emler, Palmer-Canton, & St. James, 1998; Emler & Stace, 1999). These latter findings lead to either the questionable assumption that people on the political left are more morally developed than people on the political right, or to an alternative interpretation that political affiliation tends to raise the salience of either moral or social organizational concerns in one's interpretation of complex social and political issues.

From the vantage point of our current understanding of the domain-related hetero-geneity in people's social cognition, such within-stage variation can be accounted for by recognizing that the Kohlberg tasks generate reasoning employing knowledge from more than one conceptual system, and that the six-stage sequence reflects an approximation of age-related typical forms of inter-domain equilibration, rather than acting as a complete description of moral reasoning in context. By looking at table 14.1, the reader can see how Kohlberg's stages capture the age-typical integrations that can occur between morality and convention. One can also see how individuals at all points in development might reason about an issue primarily in terms of one domain or the other.

Moral pluralism

Multiple conceptions of fairness.   The position offered by domain theory, that morality is distinct from convention, is challenged by some as having not gone far enough (Thorkildsen, 2000). Based on a series of studies of children's conceptions of the fairness of school practices, Thorkildsen (2000) argues that children have multiple concepts of fairness rather than a single moral framework applicable to all contexts. Her view is resonant with the particularist moral philosophy of Michael Walzer (1994), and calls into question whether one can define moral development within a single developmental system. In particular, Thorkildsen (2000; Thorkildsen & Schmall, 1997) critiques what she views as the misapplication of research on children's judgments of moral conduct to their conceptions of fair social practices. In a series of well-conceived studies she has inves-tigated children's concepts of the fairness of commonly employed school practices of instruction and testing (Thorkildsen, 1989; Thorkildsen, Nolen, & Fournier, 1994). What she discovered is that children employ somewhat different moral criteria to evaluate teaching and testing practices. Moreover, according to Thorkildsen (2000) these criteria do not readily map onto the sorts of judgments children make about distributive justice in basic interpersonal situations.

Thorkildsen's (1989; Thorkildsen & Schmall, 1997) developmental analyses reveal a basic overall pattern in which children's conceptions of fairness involve a progressive working through of notions of equality, followed by the introduction of notions of equity, and eventually a coordination of both equality and equity. In addition, Thorkildsen's work provides evidence that children attempt to integrate their disparate frameworks of the fairness of school practices into a broader theory of social justice about the educational practices that they experience. The general pattern of changes in moral reasoning presented in Thorkildsen's work is quite similar in its overall focus and pattern to the sequence of levels of development in the moral domain (Damon, 1977; Lapsley, 1982) outlined in table 14.1. Thus, one could argue from a structuralist point of view that what her work reveals is a series of isomorphic structures similar at a deep structural level to what has already been described. In other words, the question could be raised as to whether her work indicates that concepts of fairness vary, or if the manifestations of those concepts vary as a function of their application (Turiel, 1998). This remains an open question. From Thorkildsen's point of view, the strong structuralist position would be like arguing that a hawk wing and a hummingbird wing are structurally isomorphic and therefore the same at some deeper structural level (which is all well and good unless of course you are a hawk with the wings of a hummingbird). From the opposing point of view, Thorkildsen's (2000) particularism would entail a view of human cognition so situated as to disallow individuals to engage in meaningful cross-situational integrations of basic notions such as morality.

Multiple moral orientations: justice and care.   A different conception of moral pluralism is offered by Carol Gilligan (1982; Gilligan & Wiggins, 1987) who makes a distinction between a morality of justice and a morality of care. These two moral orientations according to Gilligan correspond to two different, compelling moral injunctions. The morality of justice corresponds to the injunction not to treat others unfairly, while the morality of care corresponds to the injunction not to turn away from someone in need. In her initial work, Gilligan saw these two moral orientations as strongly linked to gender, and viewed Kohlberg's moral theory as gender-biased as a result of an under-representation of females in his original research sample (Gilligan, 1982). Gilligan's (Gilligan & Wiggins, 1987) theorizing about the origins of the gender differences in morality employed the neo-Freudian characterizations of family relations offered by the feminist sociologist Nancy Chodorow (1978). The morality of care as characterized by Gilligan emphasizes inter-connectedness and presumably emerges to a greater degree in girls owing to their early connection in identity-formation with their mothers. The morality of justice, on the other hand, is said to emerge within the context of coordinating the interactions of autonomous individuals. A moral orientation based on justice was proposed as more prevalent among boys because their attachment relations with the mother, and subsequent masculine identity-formation entailed that boys separate from that relationship and individuate from the mother. For boys, this separation also heightens their awareness of the difference in power relations between themselves and the adult, and hence purportedly engenders an intense set of concerns over inequalities. Girls, however, because of their continued attachment to their mothers, are not as keenly aware of such inequalities, and are, hence, said to be less concerned with fairness as an issue.

While Gilligan's (1982) initial studies were consistent with her strong, gender-based hypotheses, further research has indicated, that moral reasoning does not follow the distinct gender lines that Gilligan originally reported. The preponderance of evidence is that both males and females reason based on justice and care. A recent meta-analysis (Jaffee & Hyde, 2000) examining more than 180 published studies revealed a small difference in the care orientation favoring women and a small difference in the justice orientation favoring men. Overall, gender accounted for less than 17 percent of the variance in effect sizes for justice and care reasoning leading the authors to conclude that the findings do not offer strong support for a linkage between moral orientation and gender.

Beyond these empirical challenges, Gilligan's claims have come under scrutiny from feminist critics who question the assumption that girls and women do not have intense experiences with and concerns for issues of justice and equality (Okin, 1996) stemming from the hierarchical, gender-based structure of most families and cultures throughout the world. Conversely, boys' involvement in cliques, team sports, and gangs would appear to foster cooperation, attachments, and solidarity. Thus, one would be hard pressed to argue for a simple divergence in social experience that would lead to the presence or absence of either concerns for justice and autonomy or inter-personal connectedness and caring in either gender (Turiel, 1998).

Finally, the dichotomy drawn by Gilligan has been challenged as overdrawn, and as parsing elements of a comprehensive conception of justice. In a response to critics, Kohlberg (Kohlberg, Levine, & Hewer, 1983) argued that Gilligan's differentiation captured two sides of the same coin. Principled morality means that one cannot be fair and uncaring, and that one cannot be caring without doing so in a way that is just. In his recent review of the field, Turiel (1998, p. 888) quotes Susan Okin saying the following:

> The best theorizing about justice, I argue, has integral to it the notions of care and empathy, of thinking of the interests and well-being of others who may be different from ourselves. It is therefore, misleading to draw a dichotomy as though they were two contrasting ethics. (Okin, 1989, p. 15)

Morality and Culture

Culture theory perspectives

The previous section on the structure of morality also raised questions regarding the relations between cultural experiences and moral development. One of the primary influences upon the ways in which people read social situations is the cultural frame in which they live. It is a truism that values differ across cultures, and that people from different cultures tend to express the values of their cultures. What is less clear is the extent to which such variations represent fundamental differences in human morality. Nor is it self-evident that such differences reflect a direct mapping between cultural norms and individual moral cognition. Culture theorists, however, have tended toward the view that individual morality is a reflection of the norms of the person's culture (Miller & Bersoff, 1995; Shweder, 1990a). Central to their position is a tendency to define cultures in ways that emphasize their internal consistency (Geertz, 1984). Cultures are said to be shared systems of values and symbols with their origins in collective activity (Geertz, 1984). Individuals, according to this view, construct their social values through a reconstruction at an individual level of the normative social constructions of their respective cultures (Shweder et al., 1987). Thus, the process of moral socialization involves the child's active construction at an individual level of an internal value system through the personal interpretation of overt and tacit social messages transmitted by the agents of the culture such as parents and other family members and elders. The structure and content of these social values is thought to be constrained by the formal properties of justice (Shweder et al., 1987). However, these formal constraints are minimal since they gain meaning only through their operation within the context of variations within sets of moral qualities corresponding to notions of rights, duties, autonomy, interdependence, and sanctity (Shweder et al., 1987; Turiel, 1998). These patterns of variation correspond to cultural types that differ in terms of their definitions of personhood and community. Some cultures are thought to operate in terms of moralities emphasizing rights and equality of persons, while others are thought to emphasize interdependence, duties, hierarchy, and respect for authority (Shweder, 1990a).

These broad classifications of cultures lead to a set of interesting predictions about the moral and social reasoning of their members. One would expect that children and adults reared in a collectivist culture would place a higher priority on social convention than would individuals reared in so-called individualist cultures such as that of the United States. That expectation is borne out in some of the cross-cultural data on children's judgments about social convention. Ijo children and adolescents in Nigeria (Hollos et al., 1986), Arab children in Israel (Nisan, 1987), and lower-class children in north-eastern Brazil (Haidt, Koller, & Dias, 1994; Nucci et al., 1996) tend to affirm the importance of customs and tradition to a greater degree than American children. Children within the more traditional cultures were less likely to view the conventional norms of their society as alterable, and more likely to generalize their conventions to other cultural settings than were American children. One probable consequence of these differences is that individuals in more traditional cultures would be more sensitive to the salience of custom and convention in contexts where convention and morality (justice, human welfare) overlap. There is some indirect evidence that this is the case. It comes from the cross-cultural work done using the Kohlberg stage sequence (Snarey, 1985). One of the striking findings of this cross-cultural work is that post-conventional reasoning (as defined within the Kohlberg framework) is almost absent from the adult population of traditional cultural groups.

Such findings, however, are not conclusive evidence that the morality of persons within collectivist or traditional cultures is markedly different from that of others. Nor does it show that individual morality is reducible to the acquisition of shared cultural norms. We have already discussed some of the contradictory evidence in the previous section. Children and adults across a wide range of cultures, including those used as evidence in support of the contentions of culture theorists, have been shown to treat moral issues of fairness and human welfare as independent of the presence of cultural norms, and as obligatory and binding for all persons (Shweder et al., 1987; Turiel, 1998). A second challenge to the assumptions of culture theory are findings indicating that (1) cultures themselves are internally heterogeneous, (2) conceptions of personal autonomy and interdependence exist side by side within members of all cultures, and (3) individuals offer active resistance and challenge to the existing norms of societies on the basis of their own independent assessment of the morality (fairness) of the conventional framework.

Culture, morality, and personal choice

Part of the evidence comes from research on a third domain of social judgments having to do with what people consider to be legitimate areas of personal discretion, and privacy

(Nucci, 1996; Nucci & Turiel, 2000). As such, these actions are not subject to considerations of right and wrong. Control over such actions permits the individual to establish a unique, bounded social identity. Thus, individuals endeavor to control areas of conduct that permit them opportunities to engage in self-expression, personal growth, selection of intimates, and zones of privacy. The view of the personal as just described is not in accord with the views of culture theorists who consider such a construct with its links to notions of individual identity and autonomy to hold only for members of so-called individualist cultures (Geertz, 1984). Recent work, however, has documented that efforts to establish a personal domain are made by children and adolescents in cultures presumed to be collectivist (Triandis, 1988), and that the reasons subjects adduce to justify their treatment of issues as personal matters center on efforts to maintain a sense of individuality, autonomy, and rights. These studies have been conducted with children and mothers in north-eastern Brazil (Lins-Dyer, 1999; Nucci, Camino, & Sapiro, 1996), adolescents and parents in Hong Kong (Yau & Smetana, 1995), adolescents in Japan (Hasebe, Nucci & Nucci, 2001), and among mainland Chinese immigrant children and mothers living in the USA (Xu, 2000). These same studies have also shown that children and adolescents, while staking claim to a set of behaviors as personal and private, also maintain the legitimacy of conventional regulation, and moral obligation. In other words, children and adolescents in purportedly collectivist cultures hold social values that are simultaneously collectivist and individualist. This evidence of heterogeneity in children's social reasoning is similar to what was uncovered in studies of the supposed dichotomy between justice and care orientations in moral judgment, and suggests that such pigeonholing of people and cultures is the result of the misreading of dimensions of social judgment as evidence of cultural or individual types.

Because what is personal sits at the edge of what is subject to collective regulation, the content of the personal domain is culturally variable, and the subject of negotiations between children and adults within families (Nucci & Smetana, 1996; Nucci & Weber, 1995). As children enter adolescence, these negotiations often take the form of family conflicts as children's claims to independence generally outstrip the readiness of parents to concede control of such decision-making to their children (Smetana, 1995). Smetana's work on adolescent–parent conflicts has identified the primary source of such conflicts as stemming from adolescents' resistance to parental control over what the adolescents view as their zones of personal choice and privacy. While the degree of conflict appears to vary across cultures, the nature and source of the conflicts appears to be the same (Smetana, 1995).

These conflicts belie the simple assertion of socialization as the ready recapitulation of the cultural status quo, and signal a more active evaluative dynamic to social development. Other evidence suggests that such a dynamic tension between the needs and claims of individuals is operating at a broader cultural level as well (Nucci & Turiel, 2000). These conflicts express not only a sense of what one ought to be able to claim as a matter of rights, but also resistance to perceived inequities in the distribution of rights and privileges as defined by the system of conventions and customs structuring the social order. Within traditional hierarchical societies, such tensions between morality and hierarchy have been less obvious to outside observers (Turiel, 1996). Recent anthropological (Geertz, 1984; Shweder et al., 1987) and cultural psychology (Triandis, 1988) accounts have tended to depict patterns of living and expressions of values that reflect the dominant ideologies and belief systems of cultures. The resulting portraits of culture, while rich in detail and oftentimes breathtaking in their ethnographic sensitivity (cf. Geertz, 1984), do not generally capture the dissident undercurrents hidden in the beliefs of individuals, or in the surreptitious practices of subordinate groups (Abu-Lughod, 1993; Spiro, 1993). As a result, the picture that emerges of traditional societies is of predominantly conflict-free commitment to tradition, custom, and respect for authority. This picture has been so compelling that the anthropologist Richard Shweder (1990a) has characterized such hierarchical cultures as having a second moral code of respect for authority and tradition in addition to the morality of justice and human welfare.

Culture, hierarchy, and values heterogeneity

As previously stated, there is no question that traditional, hierarchical systems tend to foster adherence to convention. It is a mistake, however, to assume that compliance with convention reflects a homogeneous reading of society by its members. In fact, there are marked differences in the ways in which individuals within a culture read the morality of conventional norms that assign privilege and power to classes of people. These differences in perception are systematically related to an individual's status within the social hierarchy. This set of issues has been most carefully investigated with respect to the relative power and freedom men enjoy relative to women in most of the world's cultures (Abu-Lughod, 1993; Okin, 1996; Turiel, 1998; Wainryb & Turiel, 1994). One such series of studies (Wainryb & Turiel, 1994), looked at how Arab Druze villagers thought about issues of fairness and duty with regard to gender relationships. Adolescent males and females were interviewed about decision-making about everyday types of activities, pitting husbands' or fathers' desires or wishes versus those of their wives, sons, or daughters. Scenarios included such things as choices of occupational and educational activities, household tasks, and leisure activities. Conflicts were presented in such a way that half depicted situations in which the person in the culturally defined dominant position objected to the choices or activities of a person in a subordinate position (e.g., a husband objects to his wife's decision to take a job), while the other half presented the person in a culturally defined subordinate position objecting to a dominant person's choices (e.g., a wife objects to her husband's decision to change jobs).

The results of the study with regard to the responses of the males (husbands, and fathers) are not surprising. In virtually all situations, including those in which the female objected to the behavior of the male, the male's decisions and choices were judged to be the position that should prevail. The adolescent and adult males in the study viewed it as not only the right of men to decide such things for themselves, but as both fair and as a matter of personal rights for husbands and fathers to decide such things for their wives and daughters as well. Wives and daughters were expected to comply with the wishes of husbands and fathers as a matter of tradition and duty. Within this traditional family structure the roles of women were defined as dependent upon the corollary and inverse roles of men acting within their responsibilities of husband and father. In other words, from the perspective of the Arab Druze males, the customs and conventions structuring the hierarchical relations between men and women conformed to a "moral order."

Interviews with Arab Druze females showed that they also saw daughters and wives as bound by culturally defined role obligations, and therefore thought they should not act contrary to the man's wishes. Unlike the males in the study, however, the women did not simply justify their answers in terms of obligations to the existing normative order. Instead, they often referred to the need for women to comply out of *pragmatic* concerns for the consequences that might ensue if they did not accept the men's choices. Women referred to possible consequences such as physical violence, abandonment, or divorce if they did not accept the man's wishes. Furthermore, Wainryb and Turiel (1994) reported that a large majority (78 percent) of the Druze females in their study thought that it was unfair for a husband or father to interfere with the choices of activities on the part of the wife or daughter depicted within the study scenarios.

The almost inverse responses of the Druze Arab men and women indicate that perceptions of the "morality" of hierarchical systems depend upon "where you sit" within the hierarchy (Turiel, 2000). The compliance of the women was not the simple result of commitment to a "moral code" of respect for authority and tradition (Shweder, 1990a), but also included a pragmatic response to power and the attendant potential for negative consequences. The men's sense of "right" was offset by the women's sense of injustice. The picture of oppositional points of view which emerges from this study of gender relations within the Druze Arab family sits in stark contrast with the pacific depiction of traditional culture offered up by cultural anthropology (Geertz, 1984; Shweder et al., 1987). Turiel (1996) is quick to point out, however, that it would be equally simplistic to cast traditional cultures simply in terms of oppositional perspectives maintained by persons at different points within the hierarchy. Members of a culture (such as the Arab Druze men and women we have been referring to) have many commonalties and shared values. Thus, the tensions that exist within their hierarchical family system sit within a relatively stable and enduring cultural system.

In sum, the work that has been done on culture and moral reasoning indicates that cultures, like individuals, are multifaceted and complex. The lesson to be gained from such cross-cultural research is that social structure may have considerable impact on the ways in which morality is experienced and thought about in everyday life. This is something different, however, from asserting that culture determines individual morality, or that morality is culturally divergent in some incommensurate or fundamental respect. The ways in which cultures structure the conventions and customs of society are often the accidents of history resulting from collective efforts to structure and coordinate the social interactions of a particular group of people. But, in many cases these norms are also informed by the factual assumptions people make about the world, and/or the presumed relations between humanity and the cosmos. For example, some of the norms people establish to structure male–female relations are based on factual assumptions people make about the differing nature and capacities of members of each gender. We will close this discussion of the ways in which our moral judgment is affected by cultural setting by looking at the ways in which factual assumptions may enter into the picture.

Morality, culture, and informational assumptions

Imagine a situation in which a surgeon fails to scrub up prior to engaging in an elective abdominal surgery on a patient. Most people, and we can assume the reader, would judge such an action by the surgeon to be immoral. This is because we all assume that by failing to engage in proper cleansing procedures, the doctor is likely to introduce micro-organisms into the patient and place him/her at severe risk of infection and possible death. Very few of us, however, have ever actually seen a germ or virus presumed to cause such an infection, and our certainty about the risks of the doctor's actions is based on faith that our sources of scientific information about the nature of the world are accurate. In fact, at the beginning of the previous century doctors were unaware of the existence of germs, and did not take the same precautions prior to engaging in surgery as the doctors of today. Because of this, surgeons were often themselves the cause of illness and death among their own patients. Nonetheless, we would hardly engage in the same moral condemnation of their actions as we would of the surgeon described at the beginning of this paragraph. This is because of the differences in assumptions about the facts of the world that we can attribute to the early and modern-day surgeons.

The issues raised in the above illustration may help us to account for some of the findings of apparent cultural variability in morality reported by anthropologists. As an example, let's consider the rather shocking findings reported in an anthropological study of the moral values of devout Hindus living in the Temple community of Bhubaneswar, Orisa, India (Shweder et al., 1987). In one part of this study, Shweder and his colleagues presented their subjects with descriptions of 39 different behaviors entailing breaches of their community norms and asked them to judge them in terms of their "seriousness." The act rated as the most serious breach was for the eldest son in a family to get a haircut and eat chicken the day after his father died. Rated thirty-fifth in seriousness among the 39 behaviors was a man beating his disobedient wife black and blue! Certainly, on the face of it, these data would appear to be evidence that this community of Hindus has a very different way of conceptualizing morality from what is generally considered moral in the West. Shweder and his colleagues (1987), however, provide additional information in their report, which helps to account for the ways in which the subjects in their study reasoned about these issues. As it turns out, the actions of the eldest son getting a haircut and eating chicken the day after his father's death, while morally neutral from a Western point of view, take on a different meaning within the context of the Hindu subjects' beliefs about the impact of these actions upon the father. In particular, the judgments of these subjects must be seen from within the context of their beliefs about the ways in which events in the natural world operate in relation to *unobserved entities*, such as souls and spirits of deceased ancestors. In this case, the father's soul would not receive salvation if the norm prohibiting the eating of chicken was not observed.

If we allow ourselves to role-take for a moment, and imagine that we are in the son's position, we can see how the act of eating chicken becomes a serious matter of causing grave harm to another being. We don't need to assume a new set of *moral* understandings, but rather to apply our moral conceptions of harm and fairness to this situation once the *facts* of the matter are understood. Our relation to Shweder's Hindu subjects is quite analogous to that of the twentieth-century surgeon to his nineteenth-century counterpart with respect to germ theory, and the morality of maintaining a sterile environment for surgical procedures. Now, it might be argued that knowledge derived from science has a different epistemic claim to validity than knowledge provided by religious belief. What cannot be argued, however, is that the assumptions one has about the natural world, however arrived at, have an impact on our moral evaluations of actions.

Within our own culture, for example, people hold different views about whether it is morally wrong or all right to engage in the physical punishment of children. In her research on this issue, Wainryb (1991) found that pro-corporal punishment parents held the view that this behavior was all right because it was a highly effective, educative act rather than one of unprovoked harm or abuse of the child. When such parents were presented with information that spanking is no more effective than other methods of disciplining children, significant numbers of parents shifted in their view of corporal punishment and maintained that it was not all right for parents to engage in the behavior. Conversely, when parents who maintained that it was wrong to engage in corporal punishment were presented with information that experts had found spanking to be the most efficient method to teach young children, there was a tendency for such parents to shift toward a view that corporal punishment would be all right.

Morality and Emotion

The relation between emotion and judgment

Up to this point, our discussion has focused on the structure of moral reasoning. Some have argued, however, that the emphasis on moral judgment is wrongheaded since morality is primarily a function of responses to moral emotion, and the playing out of moral habits (Wilson, 1993). Interestingly, Piaget (1981) rejected the dualism between cognition and affect inherent in such positions. As Bearison and Zimiles (1986) summarize, "for Piaget, the dichotomy between intelligence and affectivity has been artificially created by analytic abstractions to serve as an axiomatic device for the convenience of exposition, whereas in reality, neither can function without the other" (p. 4). The construction of any cognitive scheme, such as the simple means–end relationships involved in reaching and grasping a ball, don't only involve the generation of computational sub-routines (as would be employed by a computer), but also incorporate the associated affect (e.g., desire for the ball, joy at grasping it). Cognitive scientists who share Piaget's position on this issue have ascribed to affect the role of weighting various schemata that may be evoked in a problem space, thereby serving as a heuristic selection device for honing in on a plausible "right" answer when consideration of all rational possibilities would render practical decision-making impossible (Pugh, 1977). Such heuristics are not in place of reasoning, but are instead part and parcel of everyday cognition (Kahneman, Slovic, & Tversky, 1982).

Moral emotion

A question we might ask regarding the relations between emotion and the child's construction of moral understandings is whether morality is associated with particular emotions. There are at least two ways to understand this question. The first is whether there are particular kinds of emotional experience that lead to moral constructions, rather than the development of knowledge about other social-cultural rules such as conventions. The second, related question is whether certain kinds of feelings help to motivate and direct moral behavior. A good place to begin consideration of the issues raised in these questions is the work of William Arsenio (Arsenio, 1988; Arsenio & Lover, 1995). Arsenio set out to discover whether social events that involve moral forms of "right and wrong" elicit different emotions than events that have to do with conventional or personal matters. In his initial studies, Arsenio (1988) presented kindergarten, third-, and fifth-grade children with drawings depicting children engaged in actions that fit within six social or moral rule systems. Four of these rule types were within the moral domain. These were:

- active morality (interventions on behalf of victimized others such as stopping a child from hitting another child),
- distributive justice (distributing group-earned resources such as dividing up the money earned by a group of children working together to clean someone's yard),
- prosocial morality (engaging in helpful behavior toward another such as carrying the groceries for an aged person), and
- inhibitive morality (actions which one should refrain from engaging in; acts which cause harm or unfairness to others such as stealing another child's toy).

The remaining two rule types were violations of conventions such as wearing inappropriate attire to school, and engaging in behavior that the child might consider personal, but which an adult authority wishes to regulate (e.g., a child writes something in a notebook at recess and the teacher requires the child to reveal what was written).

Children were asked to indicate how three actors in each of the scenarios would feel. These three were the child engaged in the action, the person who was the recipient of the action, and a third-person observer. The drawings depicting each of the scenarios presented the characters with neutral facial expressions so that the children would have to infer what the characters felt from their own personal experiences and understandings of these situations, rather than by reading the facial expressions of characters shown in the drawings.

Findings were that with respect to violations of convention, children judged that the child violating a convention would be neither happy nor sad about it and would experience essentially neutral affect. They also expected neutral affect from a third-person observer, and thought they (the child subjects) would themselves have neutral affect if they were to observe the situation. On the other hand they expected the adult governing the convention (teacher) to be upset about the violation and to experience some degree of negative affect. In terms of personal issues, the children expected the governing adult, and the third-person observer, to have relatively neutral affect, but expected the main actor in the personal scenarios to experience negative affect such as anger or sadness at having his/her personal forms of conduct controlled by an adult authority. This latter reaction is consistent with children's and adolescents' views that the personal domain constitutes a zone which it is illegitimate for adults to intercede in or regulate.

With respect to the four moral scenarios, the results were as follows. In the case of inhibitive morality, children judged all parties, including themselves, to experience considerable negative affect (sadness, anger, fear) in the face of such events with the exception of the perpetrator of the act, who was judged to experience positive affect (happiness) with his/her behavior. This "happy victimizer" effect is something which will be discussed in greater detail below. In contrast with the findings regarding inhibitive morality, they expected all parties involved to experience positive affect (happiness) in response to acts that entailed distributive justice or prosocial conduct. Not only were the recipients of such actions thought to be happy, but so were the actors themselves.

In the second part of the study, Arsenio (1988) investigated whether children would use emotional information conveyed by drawings of people's expressions to make inferences about what sort of interaction produced the depicted emotions. Specifically, children were presented with drawings of individual characters displaying various emotional expressions. These were based on emotions that the children had attributed to the actors in various situations depicted in the first part of the study. They were then presented with two storyboards in which the actors had neutral expressions. One storyboard depicted a scenario consistent with the emotions shown in the individual character drawings, the other did not. Children were shown the two storyboards and asked which depicted the scenario most likely to have produced the emotions displayed by the characters shown in the individual drawings. Findings were that children, including preschoolers, accurately matched the emotional displays of the actors with the scenario most likely to have produced the depicted emotions.

As Arsenio's work demonstrates, children associate different feelings with different domains of social events. Issues of social convention generally elicit "cool" affect on the part of children who expect both compliance and violations of conventional norms to elicit neutral affect from other children. To the extent that emotion is generated by convention, children see it as emerging on the part of adults who might become upset at the violation of such norms. Thus, it would appear that children do not experience the conventions of society as containing much in the way of intrinsic emotional content. However, as Shweder's work in India (Shweder et al., 1987) and our work in Brazil (Nucci et al., 1996) has shown, children may well experience "hot" emotion such as anger in the context of violations of conventions emanating from adults responding to transgressions of importantly held cultural norms.

Issues of morality, however, are viewed by children as rife with emotional content. All parties to moral interactions, not just the guardians of the social order, as with convention, are thought by children to experience identifiable emotional responses to moral events. This is the case whether the moral behavior is positive or negative in impact. In Arsenio's (1988) study, children described the participants in distributive justice situations as experiencing happiness – or a sense of satisfaction that things turned out fairly. They likewise attributed positive emotions to all participants in prosocial moral situations. In contrast, moral transgressions entailing violations of inhibitive morality were seen by children as arousing feelings of anger, sadness, and fear in victims and bystanders alike. Only the perpetrators were viewed by young children as having positive feelings in the context of moral transgressions.

Morality, then, is an area of human conduct associated with "hot" affect. In addition to the emotions identified in Arsenio's work (Arsenio & Lover, 1995), prosocial morality has been associated with feelings of care (Gilligan, 1982), and empathy (Eisenberg, 1986; Hoffman, 1981). Inhibitive morality has been associated with shame and guilt (Ferguson, Stegge, & Damhuis (1991), and disgust (Haidt et al., 1994). And the victims of moral transgression are said to respond not simply with anger, but outrage.

As Arsenio explains, "emotions appear to be routinely stored as a part of our basic cognitive and social-cognitive representations" (Arsenio & Lover, 1995, p. 90). Not all social events elicit similar emotions. Children extract different affect–event links depending on the particular nature of the acts. Repeated experience with events with similar emotional outcomes allows children to form generalized scripts. The automatic reactions to familiar events, or events of similar type, result from the affective triggering of these scripts or habits. Thus, we begin to see how the basic connections between affect and cognition play out in the domain of morality.

Arsenio (Arsenio & Lover, 1995) adds an additional step to the processes of moral knowledge formation. He states:

> Children coordinate their knowledge of sociomoral affect to form more general sociomoral principles. For example, commonalties in the expected emotional outcomes of being a target of theft, a target of undeserved aggression, and a target of verbal abuse might all be combined to form a concept of unfair victimization. (Arsenio & Lover, 1995, p. 91)

As mentioned earlier in this chapter, there is considerable evidence that children experience qualitatively different forms of interaction in the context of moral and non-moral social events. For Arsenio, the most important feature of moral interactions is their affective content. In Arsenio's view, sociomoral affect provides the raw data from which more general abstract principles are formed using a variety of cognitive abilities. The cross-cultural consensus that we observe in the meaning of moral acts may be accounted for, according to Arsenio, by the basic similarities in meanings people attribute to the emotions that accompany moral events.

Moral development and emotion

The work of Arsenio and others has provided a plausible portrait of the developmental connections between morality and affect. Beginning in infancy we initiate the process of constructing the schemata that form our social and moral values. Incorporated within those schemata are the emotions associated with particular event types, including the affect associated with adult reactions to children's compliance with or violation of social norms (Hoffman, 1983; Kochanska, 1993; Zahn-Waxler, Radke-Yarrow, & King, 1979). The development of these early social and moral schemata forms the substrate of our moral habits, and in the view of some researchers, the beginnings of our moral character (Kochanska, 1993). Variations in the nature of these interactions stemming from such things as differences in children's temperament (Kochanska, 1993), the degree of anger displayed by adults in reaction to children's transgressions, or warmth in reaction to children's prosocial conduct (Emde, Biringen, Clyman, & Openheim, 1991), and the overall affective climate of the household (Katz & Gottman, 1991; Zahn-Waxler & Kochanska, 1990) appear to impact the ways in which young children construct the basic underpinnings of their concepts of how to react within interpersonal situations.

The basic social action schemata developed in infancy are incorporated within the construction of the overall conceptions of moral and social norms that we observe in preschool children. Thus, the affective content associated with the construction of particular moral action schemes (e.g., hitting hurts and makes one sad or angry) becomes integrated within the overall conceptual framework guiding the child's morality. As the child develops, the meaning and relations among those affective components is altered as the child attempts to coordinate or bring into balance the competing needs, desires, and deserts of individuals and groups impacted by the child's moral judgments and actions. This is an interactive process wherein the child's moral understandings alter the meaning or salience attributed to affectively laden events, and the child's emotional experiences impact the child's constructions of moral positions.

This developmental process can be seen in the results of recent research on what has been referred to as the "happy victimizer" phenomenon (Barden, Zelko, Duncan, & Masters, 1980; Nunner-Winkler & Sodian, 1988). This is also one of the more interesting contexts within which to observe both common threads and disruptions in the relations between children's emotional development and their morality. The happy victimizer phenomenon refers to the tendency of preschool-aged children to attribute positive emotions to the perpetrator of moral transgressions. In the Nunner-Winkler and Sodian (1988) study, children between 4 and 8 years of age were presented drawings depicting a scenario in which a child is shown deliberating over whether or not to steal candy from another child's coat which is hanging unattended in the cloakroom. In one version of the scenario, the child resists the temptation and does not steal. In the other version, the child steals some candy. Subjects in the study were asked to indicate how the protagonist in each situation would feel, and why. There were no effects of the sex of the subjects in terms of children's answers. All of the children included in the research indicated that they thought it was not right to steal the candy. Nonetheless, 74 percent of the 4-year-olds, and 40 percent of the 6-year-olds expected the protagonist in the story to feel "good" or "happy" about having stolen the candy. In contrast, 90 percent of the 8-year-olds expected the (thief) protagonist to feel "sad," "bad," "not good," or "not happy" having committed the theft. With regard to the scenario depicting the child who resisted temptation to steal the candy, the majority (67 percent) of the younger children thought that the protagonist would experience negative emotions, while a minority (41 percent) of the 8-year-olds thought that the child resisting the temptation to steal would have negative feelings about having done so. Few children at these ages in either situation reported that the protagonist would have mixed feelings.

The younger children explained their reasoning by focusing on the outcome. The child in the story would be "happy that he got the candy," or "sorry because he didn't take the candy, and now he doesn't have any." The 8-year-olds, on the other hand, tended to focus more on the moral consequences of the act. The child "would be sad because he had stolen his friend's candy"; "she was nasty to do that"; "because he is a thief and he shouldn't do that," or "He would be happy with himself for not taking the candy, and being good," "She would be sad at having thought about taking her friend's candy." These age-related patterns of emotion attributions and justifications held up for situations depicting the victimizer engaged in actions that had no direct benefit to the protagonist (i.e., teasing another child), and to actions in which the victimizer physically harmed another child. In all cases, the majority of 4-year-olds expected the victimizer to be pleased with the outcome of their hurtful behavior, while the majority of 8-year-olds expected the victimizer to experience remorse, sadness, or other negative feelings in response to transgressions.

Finally, Nunner-Winkler and Sodian (1988) reported on children's judgments of who they thought was worse, a child who appeared happy or one who appeared sad with what s/he had done. Findings were that 90 percent of the 8-year-olds thought that the child who appeared happy with the acts of victimization was worse than the child who appeared sorry for the action. A majority of 4-year-olds, on the other hand, judged both children to be about equally bad.

These findings are interesting in light of consistent reports that young children judge actions of moral harm to be wrong. The complexity of the findings with young children is inconsistent with simple accounts of morality as emerging from an inherited moral sense of right and wrong (Wilson, 1993). Subsequent work in this area has indicated that there is a developmental progression in children's abilities to coordinate the mixed feelings that acts of victimization generate, and to bring these mixed feelings together with their moral understandings of the actions. The well-reported finding that children, some even as old as 11, expect the victimizer to feel happy, has to be placed along side the fact that children as young as 4 know and express that the victims of such actions suffer, and experience negative emotions. Moreover, a study by Arsenio and Kramer (1992) reported that children do not view victimizers as atypical children, or bullies; rather, they expect that positive emotions are experienced through obtaining one's desired goals through immoral acts.

As children get older they understand that one can maintain more than one emotion in response to a given event. The work of Harter and Buddin (1987) has demonstrated that children do not understand mixed emotions (that one can maintain opposite feelings) until about age 11. Arsenio and Kramer (1992) found that this developmental pattern matched children's tendency to attribute mixed emotions to the victimizer in moral situations. According to Arsenio (Arsenio & Lover, 1995) what seems to occur is a gradual coordination of the knowledge that children have of the victim's suffering with their assumptions of positive emotion that would come from the victimizer's goal attainment. A part of that development is the modulation of positive feelings children might have as they contemplate engaging in immoral actions. As children progress through the normal course of development, they begin to weigh the positive feelings that come from maintaining positive peer relations against the gains that they might achieve through victimization. Their developing sense of justice integrates this balancing of emotional gains and losses to form a moral position rejecting victimization as a positive course. Thus, the interplay between changes in how children think of persons and their feelings, along with developing understandings of reciprocity, equity, and human welfare leads to shifts in the ways in which affect guides moral behavior.

Morality, emotion, and the "problem of will"

The juxtaposition between the suffering caused by one's victimization and the positive feelings that result in gains to oneself provides opposing motivations for one's actions. Piaget (1962b) was aware of these affective conflicts, which he referred to as the "problem of will." Coordinating these affective opposites was viewed by Piaget as analogous to intellectual decentration. For Piaget (1962b), an act of will requires the subordination of desire to what is necessary as determined by coordinated reversible values. While Piaget never directly addressed the issue, his notion of will may be seen as placing what is rationally understood to be morally necessary as superordinate to one's personal desires in a given context. To be moral then, is to do what is right, even when it is counter to one's immediate desire. We are obligated to act morally even toward those for whom we don't have an affective connection.

For the child growing up in an affectively supportive environment, the construction of moral reversibility (fairness) is supported by the experience of "goodwill" that comes from acts of fair reciprocity. Moreover, this "goodwill" complements the positive feelings and happiness that children experience when engaged in acts of prosocial conduct (Eisenberg, 1986). In contrast with this positive picture, Arsenio (Arsenio & Lover, 1995) uses evidence from studies of aggressive children to suggest that some children's early experiences are ones which establish a pattern of "ill will" in which long-term patterns of victimization and peer rejection distort the construction of moral reciprocity such that the child feels "entitled" to act aggressively toward others. Aggressive children are found to be outliers in most of the studies of children's concepts of victimization in that aggressive children are more likely to attribute positive emotions to the victimizer, and to do so at later ages than non-aggressive children.

The deviations that we see in aggressive children's moral judgments and actions point to the importance of gaining greater understanding of the role of affect in children's moral development. At a more general level, the developmental work on children's affective development has demonstrated the process by which normal affective experiences are integrated into the child's moral constructions. Morality is not simply guided by "feelings" as the emotivist philosophers (Moore, 1903) would have it. Nor is it cold-blooded rationality as depicted in some misreadings of cognitive accounts of morality (e.g., MacIntyre, 1984). Our feelings are an integral part of the very schemes that constitute the whole of our so-called moral habits. Our moral reasoning and processes of reflection are in reciprocal relation with the schemes that generate our moral behaviors.

Conclusion

The picture that emerges from our current understanding of the development of moral reasoning is both more clear and more complex than the one we once held. What has become clarified is that the domain of morality constitutes a basic knowledge system for regulating social interactions around issues of fairness and human welfare. This basic knowledge system stems from patterns of social interaction that are inherent to social relations, and appear to have connection to a common set of affective experiences. Social judgments that involve a moral component, however, are more variable and heterogeneous than we once supposed. This is because morality is but one component involved in the generation of social judgments in context. Such contextual social judgments entail the application of multiple knowledge systems that may be coordinated in a variety of ways. Part of what enters into such variation are the factual assumptions, customs, and social conventions of the person's culture and society. These factors, however, are themselves reflections of systematic and basic elements of social life. What is more, the relation between cultural values and norms, and those of the individual are reciprocal and interactive rather than unidirectional. The process of moral development involves the progressive generation of regulatory structures of justice and human welfare. These non-arbitrary aspects of morality form part of the dynamic tension that exists both within individuals and social systems inasmuch as each must balance and trade off the needs of persons and the requirements of social structure and organization. What this means for future research on moral development is that we must look not only at the progression of transformations within the moral domain, but also at the ways in which children and adolescents coordinate morality with other social knowledge systems in generating judgments in context.

CHAPTER FIFTEEN

Spatial Development in Childhood: Where Are We Now?

Lynn S. Liben

Space is everywhere. Indeed, just as Monsieur Jourdain of Molière's *Bourgeois Gentil-homme* was shocked to discover that he had been using prose all his life, we may be equally stunned to realize how pervasively we use space in our mental, physical, and even our social lives.

There is "ecological" space: we live in and move about our spatial worlds. We do so to find food (whether hunting in a forest or driving to the grocery store or walking into the kitchen of our suburban home), to rear our young, to work. There is "outer" space: we see a world beyond the one that we can reach using the motor apparatus of our species. Planets, moons, and stars have been providing guides for navigation and agri-culture long before we developed the optical apparatus to study them or the space ships to visit them. There is "perceptual" space: we see objects *in* space, we see space itself, and these perceptions guide our actions. We make judgments about where objects are in rela-tion to our bodies and thus where to search for them or how to reach them; we decide where to look for our missing keys, whether to venture out on a ledge, whether to stretch up for a dish or to get a ladder. There is "imaginal" space: we move things about in our heads: We picture how our favorite sculpture would look on the bookshelf just a few inches to the left (translation), if turned by 45° (rotation); or if placed on a higher shelf (changing our viewing angle and viewing distance). There is "representational" space: we create and interpret marks on surfaces or three-dimensional models as standing for ref-erent spaces and of objects within them (a London underground map, an architect's scale model of a new mall; a Landsat image of Earth; a map of the library or campus). There is "personal" space: we define a spatial bubble around us and others, and cross its bound-aries differently depending upon the category of relationship (colleague? lover? perhaps both?) and the culture in which we have been raised.

Any one of these spaces would require an entire book to describe relevant con-cepts and research, and a companion volume to describe their development. Although this review is thus necessarily selective, it should provide adequate background (and,

I hope, motivation) for further reading. I begin by describing some early work in both philosophy and psychology, then review empirical work on spatial development, discuss approaches for identifying causes of spatial development, and end by commenting upon the continuing themes of our scholarship on spatial development.

Philosophical and Psychological Origins of Space

Philosophical origins

The concept of "space" has long been important in philosophical thought. Plato conceptualized space as an absolute framework used to locate something within it, a framework that exists even if empty. Such a framework is thus independent of an observer's own location, and although locations may be related to one another, they may also be specified independently of one another by their relation to the framework itself. Illustrative is a Cartesian coordinate system that establishes a point of origin and a set of horizontal and vertical coordinates. In contrast, Leibniz and Kant conceptualized space in relative terms, defining relationships among objects. Under this conceptualization, "empty space" has no meaning. Space itself is defined by and changed by the positions of objects and observers within it. Other important conceptual distinctions include environmental place versus abstract space, physical versus psychological space, spatial action versus thought, and Euclidean versus non-Euclidean space (see Cassirer, 1950; Eliot, 1987; Jammer, 1954; Liben, 1981; O'Keefe & Nadel, 1978).

Psychological origins

The origin of the psychological study of space is usually traced to the psychometric testing movement of the early twentieth century. Its goals were not so much scholarly ones aimed at understanding the etiology of individual differences, nor educational ones aimed at finding ways to reduce differences through interventions, but rather practical ones rooted in social Darwinism and eugenics. Testing in the United States was aimed at deciding who should be allowed to immigrate, be assigned to various vocational or educational paths, institutionalized, or accepted into the armed forces (Eliot, 1987). Of particular relevance here is the fact that virtually all intelligence tests and theories have some spatial component (for an overview, see Sternberg, 1994).

Spatial abilities tests have been especially important for assessing individuals across differing levels of verbal skills. Spatial measures for infants use action-based tasks. For example, in the Bayley Scales of Mental and Motor Development (Bayley, 1993), the child is encouraged to imitate the tester's action of placing an object inside a cup. The infant's success is taken as demonstrating an ability to relate objects in space, here the notion of containment. Spatial measures for older children typically use representational tasks. For example, the Spatial Relations Test of the Primary Mental Abilities

Test (Thurstone, 1962) asks respondents to discriminate rotations from mirror images of letter-like designs.

The psychometric tradition has provided several important legacies. First, this work has established that there are reliable and relatively stable differences in spatial performance among individuals within any single group (e.g., children in the same school grade). Second, the data have revealed reliable differences in spatial performance between *groups* of individuals. The group differences of greatest concern here are, of course, those tied to chronological age, and the bulk of this chapter is devoted to trying to detail and explain these age-linked differences. However, a group difference that has attracted almost as much (or perhaps even more) attention in developmental psychology is related to sex: boys and men repeatedly (and often dramatically) outperform girls and women on a range of spatial tasks (e.g., Linn & Petersen, 1985). All three of these factors – individual differences, age-linked differences, and sex-linked differences – have been useful in trying to identify the factors that facilitate spatial development, a topic to which I return later.

Empirical Work on Spatial Development

Organizing the empirical space

Organizing and characterizing any empirical literature is one of those scholarly pursuits for which there is no single right answer. One might organize the empirical work on spatial development by age, by theory, by task, by history, or – as here – by "types" of spaces. This latter scheme is useful largely because types of spaces have intuitive meaning even for readers who may be exploring the scholarly domain of space for the first time. However, the divisions should not be taken too literally: there are fuzzy boundaries between types of spaces, and development in one necessarily affects development in another. Below I highlight major empirical methods and findings for three types of spaces that have been particularly important within developmental psychology: perceptual, environmental, and representational space.

Perceptual space

Terms whose meaning appears to be transparent are surprisingly difficult to define, and the term "perceptual space" is no exception. Roughly, the term refers to those aspects of our spatial world that are currently available to, and processed by, our senses. Here as in most scholarship on space, the focus is on vision, but auditory spaces, tactile spaces, and olfactory spaces are likewise important in our perceptual and conceptual spatial worlds. Indeed, one of the continuing controversies in developmental psychology is whether infants must unify these various spaces as an outcome of extended interactions with the environment or if instead babies enter the world with these spaces already well coordinated.

Even within the more restricted domain of visual space, the definition remains challenging. What does it mean to say that some aspects of our spatial world are "available to" our visual senses? Is this meant to imply that all necessary visual information is *in* the external environment (the stance taken by perceptual-ecological psychologist J. Gibson, 1979)? Does the phrase "and processed by our senses" mean that our *sensory* apparatus is separate from our higher-order *cognitive* apparatus? Some theorists would argue in the affirmative, proposing that sensory stimuli are first registered using low-level, automatic processes (see Marr, 1982), whereas others would argue instead that input is virtually never cognitively innocent, and that even perceptions as simple as seeing the orientation and length of lines are influenced by cognitive structures (see Piaget, 1969; Piaget & Inhelder, 1956). Empirical work on the development of perceptual space has largely focused on how soon individuals can perceive spatial qualities of their worlds.

Historically, infants were thought to be oblivious to their perceptual spatial worlds. Almost every introductory textbook in developmental psychology quotes William James's description of the infant's world as a "blooming, buzzing confusion" (James, 1890, p. 462). Early generalizations of this kind stemmed from the fact that researchers had not yet developed sensitive methodologies for testing infants. Consider, for example, what happens if one must rely upon an infant's grabbing an object as an indication that the infant has perceived the object's location in three-dimensional space. A failure to grasp something might indicate a failure to know where the object is to be found in space, but alternatively it might simply indicate that the infant does not yet have the motor skills needed for grasping. During the last several decades, new methodologies for testing infants have been developed (for further detail, see Bertenthal & Clifton, 1998; Kellman & Arterberry, 1998; Kellman & Banks, 1998; and Quinn, ch. 4, and Baillargeon, ch. 3, this volume). These more sensitive methodologies have led to the conclusion that many spatial relations are perceived very early in infancy.

What aspects of the spatial world *do* infants perceive? Among the candidates are depth, distance, size, and shape. The classic study of infants' depth perception was conducted by E. Gibson and Walk (1960). Young infants were placed on one side of a raised platform, and urged by a parent to cross to the other side, despite the fact that it would mean crawling beyond what appeared to be a precipice. (In actuality the surface was covered with plastic so that babies could not really fall.) Gibson and Walk reported that by 6 months, most babies would not cross the "cliff" edge. Subsequent empirical work has suggested that the infant's wariness is closely linked to the emerging ability to self-locomote (e.g., Campos, Hiatt, Ramsay, Henderson, & Svejda, 1978), although there are complex interactions with certain experiences (e.g., using an infant walker, see Spelke & Newport, 1998).

Infants' abilities to perceive distance have been studied by examining responses to looming objects. Even infants as young as 1 or 2 months of age show startle responses to an expanding optical array that is like what would be experienced from a rapidly approaching object (e.g., Ball & Tronick, 1971). A related issue is the infant's ability to display "shape and size constancy," which is the ability to perceive the actual size and shape of objects despite changes in the size and shape of the retinal image that occur when vantage point changes. To illustrate, Caron, Caron, and Carlson (1979) repeatedly showed 3-month-old infants either rectangular or trapezoidal solids at different angle tilts until the infants became bored (indexed by short looking times). After reaching this state of "habituation," infants were shown either the shape they had seen during habituation trials, or, alternatively, the other (novel) object. Both objects were positioned so that the retinal images would be different from those experienced during habituation trials. Infants became attentive again (i.e., dishabituated or looked longer) only when the novel shape was shown. In later studies using slightly different paradigms, Slater and his colleagues (e.g., Slater, Mattock, & Brown, 1990; Slater & Morrison, 1985) have demonstrated that even neonates are able to perceive information about the size and shapes of objects apart from the particular image they make on the retina itself.

Another line of research has examined young children's ability to reach objects in space, important because reaching requires calculation about the distance between self and object. These calculations can be complex in situations in which the target is moving. Illustrative is research by Ronnqvist and von Hofsen (1994) who placed 2-day-old infants in an infant seat and had objects move quickly past them. Even though the infants were unable to grab the objects successfully, they made sweeping motions towards them in synchrony with the objects' trajectories. Again, these data add to the generalization that very young infants are able to perceive various kinds of spatial information before they can act upon that space successfully. Researchers continue to develop increasingly clever methodologies that reveal younger and younger infants' abilities to perceive qualities of their spatial environments (see e.g. Bertenthal & Clifton, 1998; Kellman & Arterberry, 1998; Kellman & Banks, 1998).

Taken together, a wealth of empirical research employing diverse tasks suggests that infants are remarkably aware of many spatial features of their environments (see also Baillargeon, ch. 3 this volume). Although details remain to be discovered, there is little question that the infant's spatial world is not the "blooming, buzzing confusion" suggested by William James over a century ago.

Ecological space

Extending outward in physical distance from the individual's perceptual space is "ecological" or "environmental" space. This is the type of space that cannot be seen from a single vantage point, but is instead encountered in pieces as we go about living our daily lives. The focus here, typically studied under the rubric of "environmental psychology" (e.g., Stokols & Altman, 1987), is thus on large-scale, navigable space (as contrasted with "body space" or "vision/grasping space"). The empirical work on the development of ecological space has addressed questions such as: What are the spaces that children encounter? What information about these spaces do children extract from their encounters? How is this information organized? How do children use the resulting mental representations to navigate through or extract other kinds of information about these environments?

It is obvious that the "what" of environmental space changes radically with ontogenetic development. Newborn infants can control only their gaze, and even then, can do so within only a limited focal range. Bit by bit, they master movement (head-lifting, head-turning, body-turning, sitting, crawling, walking) and develop into children, adolescents, and adults who have far more diverse means of locomotion (biking, driving, flying). With each new means of locomotion – in interaction with a host of cognitive and social factors – individuals' ecological worlds expand.

Environmental knowledge

One line of research has been aimed at describing children's environments (e.g., Poag, Goodnight, & Cohen, 1985) and at documenting children's "free range" or "home range," that is, the area to which children have independent access. This range is larger for boys than girls, for older than for younger children, and for those living in safer neighborhoods and historical times than for those living in more dangerous ones (Ottosson, 1987; Spencer, Blades, & Morsely, 1989). Developmental environmental psychologists have shown that free range and environmental knowledge are correlated (see e.g. Hart, 1981). Children who have greater personal control over travel through environments (e.g., traveling by foot or bike rather than being driven by an adult in car or bus) have relatively more knowledge about those environments (Hart & Berzok, 1982; Spencer & Darvizeh, 1981; Ottosson, 1987). Another line of research has been aimed at studying the microgenetic changes toward more and better-integrated environmental knowledge that emerge from repeated exposure to the same environment (as in moving to a new neighborhood, see Wapner, Kaplan, & Ciottone, 1981).

A common means of assessing environmental knowledge has been to ask respondents to create some kind of external representation of the target environment such as sketch maps or three-dimensional models. Investigators (e.g., Gerber, 1981, 1984; see reviews in Liben, Patterson, & Newcombe, 1981; Ottosson, 1987; Spencer et al., 1989) have reported that in making such representations, young children typically fail to apply a consistent scale, use inconsistent viewing perspectives (e.g., showing some objects from overhead and others from an eye-level viewing angle), and distort relationships among neighborhoods (e.g., school, home, and town) even while showing reasonably accurate spatial relationships within each individual one. Another common method has been to ask respondents to point to various locations in the environment. By having children point to the same target location (e.g., the front door to their school) from three different sighting locations (e.g., their own desk, the entrance to the cafeteria, and the principal's office), a "triangulation" method can be used to infer respondents' beliefs about the relative location of targets. In an early use of this method with first-graders, fifth-graders, and adults, Hardwick, McIntyre, and Pick (1976) found that performance improved with age, particularly when sightings were taken from three different *actual* (rather than *imagined*) locations. Importantly, however, even among the older children, the three sightings converged at one location only about half the time.

One problem in interpreting data from studies using these kinds of measures is that performance reflects not only what children know about the environment, but also their ability to perform the specific task. That is, to the degree that the task requires the child to create some *externalization* of what is known about the space, any errors or omissions may be due to children's difficulty in accessing and manipulating existing knowledge to make their responses, rather than lacuna in the knowledge base itself. Based on this reasoning, some investigators have thus argued that children's knowledge of environmental space should be tested by asking children to *act* in space rather than to create a representation of it or to answer inferential questions about it (see e.g. Cornell & Hay, 1984; Siegel, 1981; Spencer & Darvizeh, 1981).

Findings from some studies support the proposition that children may have more sophisticated and well-integrated knowledge of their environments than might be inferred on the basis of their environmental representations. For example, Spencer and Darvizeh (1981) reported that at least some 3-year-old children who were taken on a single novel walk through an urban environment were able to lead an adult back along the same route. More recent work by Cornell and colleagues (e.g., Cornell, Heth, & Broda, 1989; Cornell, Heth, & Rowat, 1992; see also Allen, 1999) demonstrates that children's environmental knowledge can be enhanced from some relatively simple interventions such as suggesting to children that they "look back" as they travel, or by pointing out landmarks that can serve as useful choice points for a return journey. Interestingly, however, the success of such interventions interacts markedly with age, typically having salutary effects on performance for those in late, but not early childhood (see Cornell et al., 1989, 1992). Furthermore, there is evidence that children's difficulties in creating representations of familiar places cannot be explained entirely by the use of representational measures. For example, when asked to show the normal arrangement of their classroom furniture, some preschool children perform dismally not only when asked to place model furniture in a scale model (Siegler & Schadler, 1977), but also when asked to return real furniture to its normal location (Liben, Moore, & Golbeck, 1982).

In short, there is still considerable uncertainty about how to characterize the child's environmental knowledge. As I have argued in detail elsewhere (Liben, 1981, 1988, 2001a), part of the continuing uncertainty stems from insufficient clarity about what construct we are studying. Are we interested in what information about the environment children have stored in their heads, irrespective of the format in which it resides (what I have called *spatial storage*), or are we concerned with the environmental information the child can consciously reflect upon and manipulate (what I have called *spatial thought*)?

Measuring spatial thought

Contributing to the confusion between these two possibilities is the popularity of the term *cognitive map* (Downs & Stea, 1977) to refer to environmental knowledge. As discussed in writings on both adult and child spatial cognition (see Downs, 1981; Downs & Siegel, 1981; Liben, 2001a; Spencer et al., 1989), there is a tendency to turn the *metaphorical* concept of the "cognitive map" into the assumption that people are carrying around cartographic maps in their heads. Although it is undoubtedly the case that sometimes people do consult map-like mental images when making judgments about spatial environments, it is also the case that people may draw upon pieces of spatial knowledge that are not combined into map-like configurations. For example, I may know the angle and distance from my home to my school and from my home to the public library. Furthermore, these individual pieces of information – when combined – specify the angular and distance relation between school and library. But this need not mean that *I* have cognitive access to the relation between school and library. Thus, even when we –

as researchers – produce map-like models of children's stored environmental knowledge, we cannot assume that similar map-like models are also in the child's head. Furthermore, even if it is the *child* who produces a map-like (or other) representation of environmental relationships, the data may show something about how the child has extracted or used or combined stored environmental information *for the particular task*, rather than how the child had been thinking about the environment in the first place.

A paradigm developed by Kosslyn, Pick, and Fariello (1974) is useful for illustrating this distinction. Their paradigm also bears on another question that has been central in the study of spatial development: does physical experience in an environment affect the way that the environment is mentally represented? If so, do these effects differ with age?

Kosslyn et al. (1974) placed ten objects in a square room that had been divided into quadrants by an opaque barrier (preventing both travel and vision), and a transparent barrier (preventing only travel). Critical object pairs were separated by either 3′ or 5′ and fell either within a single quadrant or on either side of a barrier. Children (5 years) and adults first learned to go from a home position to put each individual object in its correct location. After learning all objects' locations to criterion, respondents were taken to a test location, given one object, and asked which of the remaining nine had been closest in the room, which next closest, and so on, until all were ranked. Another object was then selected as the referent, and the child was asked to rank the distances of the other nine items. This cycle was repeated until each object had served once as the initial referent. From the resulting data, Kosslyn et al. (1974) concluded that whereas physical movement was important for children, only visual integration mattered for adults. That is, relative to object pairs falling *within* a single quadrant, both children and adults exaggerated distances between pairs that had been separated by opaque barriers, but only children also exaggerated distances between objects separated by transparent barriers.

One line of subsequent work has been aimed at evaluating the role of the dependent measure used to externalize knowledge of locations. Newcombe and Liben (1982) replicated the procedures used by Kosslyn et al. (1974) except that only half the participants were given the original rank-ordering task. The remaining respondents were asked to judge distances separating critical object pairs directly: the referent object was placed on the floor, and the experimenter moved a second object away until the respondent said that the two objects were as far apart as they had been in the room. Importantly, the data from the two measures led to strikingly different conclusions about what participants "knew" about the layout of objects in space. Data from the rank-ordering task replicated those of Kosslyn et al. (1974), apparently supporting the conclusion that direct action was important for children's, but not adults', environmental knowledge. However, data from the distance-estimation task revealed similar response patterns by both children and adults: distances were exaggerated only when objects were separated by opaque barriers. Which measure reveals what is "really" known about the spatial layout?

Egocentric and allocentric codes

A second line of work has been aimed at exploring the role of physical action in space. Whereas Kosslyn et al. (1974) were interested in the role of *any* movement between locations, other investigators have focused on the impact of *direction* of movement. Of particular interest has been whether children would define locations in terms of their own bodies, or in terms of the surrounding environment. This question has long been studied in animal research. In a now classic study by Tolman, Ritchie, and Kalish (1946), rats were placed at the starting point of a maze, and learned to make a series of turns to reach a goal box containing food. The initial alley was then blocked. Would rats enter a nearby alley, or instead execute a more dissimilar motor response and choose an alley that was oriented directly toward the goal box? Rats did the latter, demonstrating "place learning," and leading Tolman (1948) to suggest that rats relied on a "cognitive map" rather than a motor sequence (or "response learning"). Are infants as clever?

One reason that researchers thought that they might *not* be comes from Piagetian theory. Specifically, Piaget (1954) suggested that as part of infants' general inability to differentiate their own bodily actions from the surrounding world, space would be encoded in terms of the child's own body. Thus, for infants, spatial locations were thought to be identified in relation to a frame of reference that is *egocentric* (i.e., with the self used as the reference point). Once infants were able to differentiate self from space and thus appreciate space as a container of both themselves and other objects, they could identify spatial locations with reference to a frame of reference that is *allocentric* or external.

Empirical paradigms used to test infants' egocentric versus allocentric environmental actions are much like those used with animals, except that rewards are typically interesting events or objects rather than food. In one illustrative paradigm, developed by Acredolo (1978; Acredolo & Evans, 1980), infants were placed in an infant seat in the middle of a room. The walls to their right and left contained two identical windows. Immediately after a buzzer sounded, a smiling, talking person appeared in the window to the infant's right. After a number of trials, the buzzer's sound led infants to look immediately at the right window in anticipation of the interesting event. To test whether each infant had learned the event's location in relation to *body* space or in relation to *room* space, the baby was moved to the other side of the room. Of interest was which way the infant would look in anticipation of the interesting event when the buzzer was sounded. When the windows were physically identical, 6-, 9-, and 11-month-old infants responded egocentrically, that is, they still turned to their right (now the incorrect window). When the correct window was marked by a relatively minor "landmark" (a star over the window), the oldest infants increased their room-based (i.e., correct) responding. When the window was marked by extremely salient cues (flashing lights and stripes), only a few infants responded egocentrically. However, whereas most infants in the two older groups looked immediately to the correct window, those in the youngest group tended to look back and forth at both, seemingly torn between egocentric and allocentric solutions.

A second common paradigm used to test the role of action-based versus environment-based encoding is the search task in which an interesting object is hidden in one of multiple containers (Bremner, 1978; Bremner & Bryant, 1977). Between the time that the object is hidden and the child is permitted to look for it, the child is moved to a new position. As in the room-size spaces, if children have encoded location with respect to their own bodily position, they should search in the incorrect location; if they use an allocentric frame of reference or update their own position, they should search correctly. Findings from this search paradigm are similar to those from the anticipation paradigm discussed above. That is, infants have difficulty finding the allocentrically defined locations when the containers are identical. Relatively modest cues that differentiate locations (e.g., painting the sides of the table different colors) have little effect, but highly salient cues (e.g., using different-colored cloths to hide objects) are powerful, leading even 9-month-old infants to search in the correct container.

Both these paradigms have been used in many subsequent studies with infants (see e.g. reviews by Acredolo, 1981; Bremner, 1993; Newcombe & Huttenlocher, 2000; Pick & Lockman, 1981; Wellman, Cross, & Bartsch, 1997), varying such factors as whether children moved actively or passively, different qualities of spaces, familiarity with test spaces, amount of experience with the event in the initial location, delay times, and other stimulus and condition variables.

In summary, there is an extensive empirical literature addressed to children's developing knowledge of the environments in which they move, and of their own spatial relation to them. By and large, the data show that young infants do have considerable difficulty in overcoming their body-centered perspectives, and that they gradually come to rely more heavily on external landmarks and then on distal frames of reference. However, which frame of reference is used at any given time is affected not only by the age of the child, but also by characteristics of the environment (e.g., whether right and left choices are symmetrical or contain differentiating features) and by the nature of the task. How do children come to understand and use knowledge about environments that comes not from actual experience in the space itself, but rather from *representations* of environments? Developmental research on this topic is reviewed next.

Representational Space

When trying to navigate through or learn the layout of a new space, a common strategy is to consult some *spatial product* (Liben, 1981), that is, an external (not mental) representation that carries information about a referent space. Not all spatial products are themselves inherently spatial (for example, linguistic descriptions of locations). Given the current focus, here I consider only those spatial products that do carry information about the spatial referent via their own spatial properties. (More detailed discussions of categories of and distinctions among spatial products may be found in Liben, 1981, 1999; Liben & Downs, 1992.) Empirical work using external spatial representations with infants and older children has taken somewhat different forms, and thus each is described in turn.

Infancy

In infancy, research on external spatial representations has largely been directed to asking some very basic questions about pictorial interpretation. Much of this work has addressed the question of whether, and if so when, infants become sensitive to specific spatial qualities (e.g., relative distance of two objects) depicted in pictures. Results from studies using a range of methodologies converge on the conclusion that infants' sensitivity to pictorial depth cues (e.g., perspective, size, interposition, shading) emerges between about 5 and 7 months (see review by Kellman, 1995). Contemporary research is directed to investigating the reasons for this timing (e.g., locomotor experience, brain maturation, exposure to visual stimuli), and to identifying precisely which features of pictorial stimuli infants use in their discriminations (e.g., Bhatt & Bertin, 2001; Kellman & Banks, 1998). Some recent work (Quinn, in press-b) has also been directed to studying the emergence of more general spatial concepts such as "above" and "below."

Another question addressed in research on infants' processing of external representations is whether babies take meaning from representations that is similar to the meaning that they take from objects themselves. There is considerable evidence that young infants can respond quite early to the referential content of representations. For example, DeLoache, Strauss, and Maynard (1979) showed that 5-month-old infants who had been habituated to some three-dimensional object (e.g., a stuffed animal) did not dishabituate when shown a photograph of the same animal, but did dishabituate when shown a novel animal irrespective of whether it was an object or picture. There are also observations suggesting that infants may extract meaning from representations because they think that they are actually looking at the referents. For example, there are informal reports of infants attempting to lift patterns off fabric or paper (Liben & Downs, 1992; Ninio & Bruner, 1978) and more formal reports of infants grasping at photographed objects (DeLoache, Pierroutsakos, Uttal, Rosengren, & Gottlieb, 1998). Interestingly, infants adjust their grasping movements in ways that suggest that they have extracted spatial (shape) features of the objects from those pictures. As suggested earlier (Liben, 1999), however, it is unclear whether such behaviors represent a failure to differentiate between picture and object, or instead reflect the infants' attempts to explore the similarities and differences of representational and physical objects.

Perhaps as interesting as the research that has been done with infants is the research that has *not* been done. For example, to my knowledge, there is no work that has attempted to introduce infants to new environments (e.g., a day-care center) through representations (e.g., photographs), and test whether these infants appear to be more familiar with or comfortable in the new space than infants who did not have this experience. Or, to take another example, although there has been a test (Rieser, Doxsey, McCarrell, & Brooks, 1982) of whether infants can use an overhead view of a space to acquire information about how to reach a "goal" (the baby's mother), the aerial view was provided by holding the baby up over the actual space, not by showing a representation of it. And as a final illustration, although there has been recent research that tests infants' ability to encode the specific location at which an object has been buried in a small sandbox (Newcombe, Huttenlocher, & Learmonth, 1999), there have not yet been tests of whether infants can use information about location from a small space to learn something about an analogous location in a larger space. Such questions have been addressed in research on older children, as reviewed next.

Toddlerhood and beyond

As just suggested, the research on external spatial representations with older children has included many studies testing whether children can take information presented in a representation and apply it in some way to a referent space. In any place representation, two kinds of relations between referent space and their representational space are critical: *representational correspondences* and *geometric correspondences* (Liben & Downs, 1989).

Representational correspondences.   Representational correspondences refer to the links between "things" (or parts of things) in the referent space and the symbols used to stand for those things in the representation (see DeLoache, ch. 10 this volume). Representations are necessarily selective about *what* is symbolized. For example, a city map might include representations of major streets and public structures, but not minor streets or residential apartment buildings. Representational symbols may take endless forms. Buildings might be shown by circles or squares or stars, and may be further distinguished so that, for example, educational buildings are shown in blue, governmental offices in green, and tourist attractions in purple. Different representational media (e.g., drawings, maps, photographs, architectural blueprints) have different levels of detail and different conventions, and part of the child's developmental challenge is coming to recognize these differences and the purposes that they serve (see Liben, 1999).

There is considerable evidence that an elementary understanding of the basic "stand for" relationship between representations (such as scale models or maps) and their referents (e.g., objects in a room) emerges quite early. On the basis of an extensive program of research, DeLoache (ch. 10 this volume) places the emergence of basic "representational insight" at roughly 2.5 to 3 years of age. But even after children have come to understand the basic idea that one thing can be used to stand for another, and thus to appreciate representational correspondences, there is still much to learn. Some particularly charming demonstrations of the gradual nature of mastery comes from an interview study of 3- to 6-year-old children who were shown various kinds of place representations (Liben & Downs, 1989, 1991). Even the youngest children were generally good at recognizing that these representations showed environments. For example, when shown a small scale, black-and-white aerial photograph of Chicago, many spontaneously identified it as "a city" or "buildings and roads." At the same time, however, some made fairly significant errors with respect to the kind of place, as for example suggesting it showed "the United States," "Africa," and "the whole world." With more abstract representations, some preschoolers even failed to understand the referent was a place, as when a tourist map of Washington DC was identified as "a cage" and "a space ship."

Preschoolers more commonly have difficulty distinguishing between characteristics of the representation that imply something about the referent versus those that are simply qualities of the symbol (or "attribute differentiation," see Liben, 1999, 2001a). Illustrative are preschoolers' interpretations that a red line on a road map meant that the road, itself, is red or that the yellow areas of the map (indicating cities) show "eggs" or "firecrackers." These two are examples in which the child inappropriately extended a feature of the representation (color) to the referent, but the reverse occurred as well, as when a child denied that an area of a black-and-white aerial city photograph could be grass because "grass is green" or when another denied that a small rectangular shape could be the building in which his father works because "his building is *huge* . . . It's as big as this whole map!" The latter example also illustrates misunderstanding of the scale relation between the representation and the referent space, and thus provides a segue into the second category of linkages – geometric correspondences – which is even more relevant to our focus on spatial development.

Geometric correspondences.   Geometric correspondences concern the spatial relations between space and representation, and include *scale* or the ratio between the size of the referent space and the representation; *viewing azimuth* or the direction from which the space is viewed, as in viewing a town from the east; and *viewing angle* or the vantage point along the vertical dimension, as in viewing a space from directly overhead (Downs, 1981). One particularly useful approach for studying the developmental mastery of representational scale, azimuth, and angle is Piagetian theory. In brief, Piaget and Inhelder (1956) proposed that even preschool children can conceptualize space in topological terms (e.g., ideas such as "next to" and "on" and "near") which permit the child to represent spatial relations in configurational terms (e.g., that the library is next to the grocery store). During early and middle childhood, projective and Euclidean conceptual systems emerge. Projective concepts allow the child to represent space in relation to point of view (e.g., as I approach the front of the library, the store is to my right, but as I leave the library, the store is to my left; as I look at a round table from directly above, the top appears circular, but as I view it from an oblique angle, it looks elliptical). Euclidean concepts allow the child to represent space in relation to stable, abstract, overarching systems (e.g., the library and store are twice as close to one another as are the store and the school; the flagpole is located at the intersection of particular coordinates).

Before describing some of the empirical work that can be interpreted using topological, projective, and Euclidean language, it is important to point out that there is controversy about whether or not this theoretical approach is a good one. Those working from a nativist perspective have suggested that Euclidean concepts are given in human biology and are present if not from birth, then soon thereafter, perhaps even without visual experience (see e.g. Landau, Gleitman, & Spelke, 1981; Mandler, 1988b; Spelke & Newport, 1998). Others have offered alternative narratives of the developmental course (see for example the discussion of the developmental course of "hierarchical spatial coding" proposed by Newcombe & Huttenlocher, 2000). Even Piaget himself later replaced the topological, projective, and Euclidean developmental conceptualization with a sequence of intra-, inter-, and transfigural relations (Piaget & Garcia, 1989). Thus, although the empirical review that follows often alludes to topological, projective, and Euclidean concepts, it should be clear that this is meant to offer a useful, but not a unique way to conceptualize developmental phenomena.

Importantly, many studies that at first glance appear to be investigations of children's abilities to understand *spatial* representations (i.e., geometric correspondences), actually tap children's understanding of *symbols* (i.e., representational correspondences). As discussed in more detail elsewhere (see Blades & Spencer, 1994; Liben, 1997, 2001a; Liben & Yekel, 1996), this condition occurs when (a) the links between referents and representations are unique, and (b) "correct" locations are defined by an object as a whole. Illustrative is the search task used by DeLoache (1987) in which a child is shown a location on a scale model of a room and asked to find the analogous location in the referent room. Because representation–referent links are unique (e.g., the only big blue couch is represented by the only miniature blue couch, the only big table by the only miniature table, and so on), and because the "correct" location is defined by the complete object (e.g., anywhere under the couch), the child can identify analogous locations simply by identifying the referent of the representation. To test the child's understanding of geometric correspondences, it is necessary to force the child to discriminate among *spatial* features. For example, the child might be asked to select a particular desk in a room from among many shown in the representation (e.g., one of many identical miniature desks in a model, or one of several identical rectangular symbols on a map). To solve such a task, the child would need to draw upon topological concepts (e.g., "the desk next to the door"), projective concepts (e.g., "the desk immediately to my right when I enter the room"), or Euclidean concepts (e.g., "the desk at the intersection of two imaginary lines extrapolated out from particular points on two walls").

When tasks of the latter kind are employed, data reveal a far more extended developmental course. Blades (1991), for example, conducted a search study using two identical model rooms. The two models were the same size, thus obviating the need for the child to understand scale change. However, the models contained not only distinct hiding-places (one wardrobe and one bed), but also a pair of identical hiding-places (two chairs of the same shape, size, and color). When an object was hidden under a distinct piece of furniture, 3-year-old children succeeded at finding its counterpart even when the second model was rotated ("misaligned"). In contrast, when an object was hidden under one of the chairs, only the 5-year-old children were consistently successful. Similar findings have been reported in studies in which the two spaces differed in size and format. In one such study (Bluestein & Acredolo, 1979), a room contained four similar green boxes in each corner. A toy elephant was hidden in one of the boxes. The child was shown where the elephant was hidden by an elephant sticker placed on the appropriate symbols on a map of the room. When the map and room were aligned, the elephant was found successfully by most children age 4 and 5 years, and even by about half of those aged 3. When the map was misaligned, however, it was only in the oldest group that most children succeeded (80–90 percent). Among the 3- and 4-year-old children, performance was extremely poor (close to 0 percent and 20 percent correct, respectively).

Even by an age at which children are successful in using aligned maps of very simple laboratory spaces, they continue to be challenged by maps of ecologically rich environments. This is particularly true if the symbols used to represent objects are spatially motivated (e.g., depicting geometric shapes of furniture from directly overhead) rather than semantically motivated (e.g., depicting furniture with content-related symbols such as pictures of paint brushes for an art area). An illustrative study was conducted with 3- to 6-year-old preschool children using a map of their highly familiar classroom (Liben & Yekel, 1996). Objects (e.g., a teddy bear and lunch box) were first placed in the room. Each child was asked to point to a particular object, and then to place a sticker on a classroom map to show its location. Two maps were used. In one, a plan view map, the furniture was depicted from directly overhead, so that symbols were simple geometric forms (e.g., a rectangle for a bookcase; a circle for a round table). In the other, an oblique perspective map, the furniture was shown with perspective line drawings so that symbols were more pictorial or iconic. Map order was counterbalanced so that some children worked with the plan map first, and others began with the oblique map. Overall, performance was better on the oblique than the plan map, with performance on the latter being quite poor. Young children had difficulty interpreting abstract geometric shapes as furniture symbols, and in using other kinds of spatial information to discriminate among similar symbols. The data also revealed a striking order effect. Children who were given the oblique map first performed significantly better. Working with the more comprehensible oblique map seemed to help children "crack the code" of the more difficult plan map. Even when children understand the general nature of the geometric correspondences between the referent space and the representation, however, they continue to be challenged to understand their specific spatial qualities. Illustrations of the gradual nature of understanding metrics, viewing angles, and viewing azimuths of representations are provided below.

Understanding metrics. Results from the study by Liben and Yekel (1996) revealed not only the order effect described above, but also a significant effect of location type. In particular, correct responses were generally limited to target locations that could be identified by some topological or landmark cue (e.g., the teddy bear "on" the toy stove, or the lunch box "next to" the piano). When the placement of an object was in an expanse of undifferentiated area (i.e., somewhere in an open region of the floor), performance was significantly worse. This difference is consistent with the theoretical notion discussed earlier that Euclidean or metric understanding is a relatively late achievement. Findings reported by Uttal (1996) are also indicative of young children's difficulty with metrics. He first taught 4- to 6-year-old children the locations of toys in a room by using a plan map. Once the locations had been learned on the map, children were asked to place the real toys in the real room. Although children were quite good at reproducing the configural relations among the toys, they were not good at scaling up the configuration accurately, sometimes simply clustering the configuration of toys in a corner of the room. These data are consistent with the idea that children have particular difficulty with spatial tasks that draw upon an understanding of metrics.

Another indication of young children's difficulty in understanding the scale relations between representations and the referent space comes from their spontaneous identifications when looking at place representations. For example, many preschool children who correctly identified the overall referent of an aerial photograph of Chicago as a place (e.g., "a city") and had correctly identified components of the image (e.g., buildings) went on to identify other portions of the image in ways that were completely inconsistent with scale. Examples are children who saw "fish" (actually boats), a "snake" (a river), or "rope" (a street; see Liben & Downs, 1991). Similarly, Spencer, Harrison, and Darvizeh (1980) reported that 3- and 4-year-olds who just identified the sea on an aerial photograph went on to identify the neighboring hills as "pebbles." Scale errors have been found on other kinds of place representations as when preschoolers reject a line as showing a road because it is "too skinny" for two cars (Liben & Downs, 1991).

Understanding viewing angle. The preceding discussion has focused primarily on research relevant to developing understanding of one of the three categories of geometric correspondence – scale. There are also empirical data bearing on children's developing understanding of viewing angle, that is, the direction along the vertical dimension from which a space is viewed or depicted. Viewing angles range from directly overhead (referred to as nadir, orthogonal, or vertical views, or 90°) to eye-level views like those encountered as one walks around through the environment (referred to as elevation views, 0°). Those falling between these two extremes (for example, 30° or 45°) are referred to as oblique viewing angles.

Evidence that young children have difficulty understanding viewing angle comes from a study in which children were shown a vertical photograph of a city and asked where they thought the camera had been (Liben & Downs, 1991). Only two of 30 preschool children described an overhead position (although of course their difficulty could be in communication rather than comprehension). When asked to produce overhead views of their own classroom or school (see Liben & Downs, 1994), many first- and second-grade children produced elevation rather than plan views. Even when given an aerial photograph from which to work, some children produced generic elevation views of a city rather than a nadir view. Data from a selection task demonstrate that it is not simply the production process of drawing that is difficult: given six alternative drawings of an orthogonal view of their school building, correct selections were made by only about 25 percent of first- and second-grade children. Similar kinds of difficulties have been reported by Gerber (1981, 1984).

Children's spontaneous interpretations of representations also suggest that children misinterpret orthogonal views as if they were elevation views: preschool children identified trains lined up in parallel as "bookshelves," a triangular-shaped parking area as a "hill" (Liben & Downs, 1991) and tennis courts as "doors" (Spencer et al., 1980). These interpretations would make sense *if* one were seeing these shapes from straight ahead rather than from straight down. Finally, another line of evidence for the view that young children have particular difficulty understanding a viewing angle that is not experienced directly comes from research showing that children perform better in identifying and using oblique rather than nadir representations, both photographic (Blades, Hetherington, Spencer, & Sowden, 1997; Liben, Dunphy-Lelli, & Szechter, 2001) and cartographic (Liben & Yekel, 1996).

Understanding viewing azimuth. The last of the three geometric correspondences – viewing azimuth – is undoubtedly the one that has attracted the most attention within developmental psychology. Some of the relevant work has been alluded to earlier. For example, in the course of the earlier discussion of the child's difficulty in finding the referent of a non-unique symbol, it was noted that such tasks are particularly difficult when the representation and the referent space are "misaligned." Data from these investigations, as well as the huge research literature on various kinds of perspective-taking tasks (see e.g. Laurendeau & Pinard, 1970; Newcombe, 1989; Weatherford, 1985) have established beyond doubt that understanding the relation between depicted viewing angle and the referent space is difficult for preschool children.

But there is also ample evidence that misalignment continues to challenge individuals well beyond the preschool years. For example, Presson (1982) showed that kindergarten and second-grade children were virtually always able to go correctly to one of four identical containers in a room after seeing the location indicated on one of four identical symbols on a map. However, success rates dropped to about 30 percent and 52 percent, respectively when the map was misaligned by 180° with the space. Similarly, Liben and Downs (1993) asked children to place arrows on classroom maps to show where someone was standing, and which direction he was pointing. When the map and room were aligned, children performed extremely well by second grade; when, however, map and room were unaligned (180° rotation), children continued to err well into fourth grade. There is evidence that even adults find it difficult to understand the relation between representations and spaces when the map and space are unaligned. The classic demonstration of this difficulty comes from research by Levine on "You Are Here" (YAH) maps such as those found in airports, shopping malls, and the back of hotel room doors. For example, Levine, Marchon, and Hanley (1984) found that college students who consulted a floor plan of a university library took longer to study the map and were less likely to reach the target when the map was rotated 180° than when it was aligned with the space.

As might be inferred from the examples given above, the spatial representations used in research by developmental psychologists commonly depict quite small, simply furnished laboratory spaces or familiar rooms, whereas those used by environmental psychologists and geographers tend to be of larger spaces such as cities, large regions, and countries. Increasingly, interdisciplinary research has been combining the methods of psychology with the representations of earth science (see e.g. Golledge, 1999; Liben, 2001a; Uttal, 2000b). Research using such representations is of interest not simply because it challenges users' understanding of scale. It also allows us to study how children acquire knowledge of environments that have not been experienced directly, and how children come to recognize patterns of distributions on thematic maps (e.g., weather or population maps). Furthermore, spatial representations of large portions of the Earth's surface (such as continents) permit us to study children's understanding of how the surface of a three-dimensional sphere may be projected on to a two-dimensional plane (see Liben, 2001a, 2001b; Liben & Downs, 1991).

As we move out from our navigable environments even further (leaving "environmental" and entering "outer" space), there are some additional challenges. For example, we must reconcile the flatness of the land beneath our feet with the curvature of Earth; our bodily sense of stability with the notion of Earth's orbit and rotation; our visual experience of the sun "rising" and "setting" with the notion that it is actually Earth that is moving; our own sense of gravitational upright with an appreciation of the gravitational upright of someone on the opposite side of the globe; and so on. Research by Vosniadou and Brewer (1992) has provided dramatic evidence that children harbor fundamental confusions about these issues, even though they are perfectly capable of responding correctly to questions that draw upon the factual information that they have been taught directly (e.g., that the Earth is round). In short, long after children have come to be able to interpret spatial representations, their bodily experiences may continue to challenge their full interpretation of those representations.

Conclusions

In prior sections of this empirical review I highlighted major questions, methodologies, and findings in the domain of spatial development. In closing, I reassemble the disparate empirical findings to provide some integrative generalizations about spatial development. Like any generalizations, they have exceptions, there are fuzzy boundaries, and not everyone would endorse them. Thus, they are offered as guides, not as universally accepted truths.

First, development may be characterized as shifting from action to representation, from perception to cognition. Within Piagetian theory, this point is developed as the distinction between the child's ability to act, practically, in space (e.g., to avoid barriers, to find alternative pathways in movement; to reach and hold objects) and the child's ability to think about space using some kind of representational means (e.g., imagery, drawing, language). Similar kinds of distinctions have been drawn by others as well (see Presson & Somerville, 1985).

Second, individuals' representations of their own place in space may be characterized as shifting from reliance on bodily referents toward reliance upon external but proximal referents (such as a piece of furniture in a room), followed, in turn, by reliance on external and distal referents (such as the orientation of the room within the building, the building in relation to the town, and perhaps the town in relation to a celestial body).

Third, and paralleling the second, individuals' representations and cognition about large, external spaces also seem to expand from local places (e.g., representing a cluster of proximal places as in a neighborhood), to linear relations (e.g., knowing a sequence of buildings or streets that will be encountered along a route), to configural relations (e.g., knowing the overarching pattern of relations among places, irrespective of any particular starting position or path). The latter is not simply using some external framework to identify one's *own* location in the spatial world (e.g., from standing in a certain position, pointing east), but rather it is conceptualizing locations in relation to one another, irrespective of one's own place in that space. This developmental sequence was described by Siegel and White (1975) as the shift from landmark to route to configural knowledge, but is also much like that offered by Shemyakin (1962), and still earlier by Freeman (1916). It appears that even as we continue to acquire new empirical data, we can still organize those data by reference to basic developmental sequences that were described long ago.

Causal Explanations of Spatial Development

At least at some general level, all intact individuals appear to display the kinds of spatial achievements described in the preceding section, and thus part of the goal of developmental psychology is to find explanations for why these normative achievements take place. At the same time, however, and as discussed earlier in the course of reviewing psychometric research on spatial abilities, there are also dramatic variations among individuals and between groups of individuals. There are variations in how quickly children move through developmental sequences, in the skill levels demonstrated on any particular spatial task, and perhaps even in whether the most sophisticated levels of achievement are ever reached.

Both of these observations – one highlighting normative progress and the other highlighting differential progress and achievements – are useful for illuminating causes of spatial development. The first leads us to take the *normative developing child* as the starting point. Here we begin with what is known about ontogenetic development, in general, and ask how this development may shape and facilitate spatial development, in particular. For example, how does physical maturation of the visual system affect how children see and interpret space? How does the shift from being a creature whose movement through the environment is entirely dependent upon others to one whose movement is independently planned and executed affect how space is encountered, thought about, and used? How might children's developing logical skills affect spatial behaviors and thought? For example, is there a parallel between the developmental change in children's ability to categorize objects along unitary and later multiple dimensions (e.g., color and then color *and* shape) and children's ability to use single and then multiple spatial reference frames (e.g., the child's own body and later the body *plus* external landmarks and distal referents)? An extended discussion of research that examines spatial development in relation to more general ontogenetic development in the physical, social, cognitive, and experiential realms may be found in Liben (1991a).

The second approach takes *individual and group differences* as its starting point. Here we begin by having identified – perhaps unexpectedly – differences among individuals or between groups of individuals. We then try to find other factors that vary along similar lines and test whether these factors cause and affect spatial development. To take an example focused on individual differences, one might find that a handful of children within the same classroom have unusually good mental rotation skills, and discover that all of these children spend an atypical amount of time building model airplanes outside of class. Of course, this correlation, alone, cannot support the conclusion that model-building enhances mental rotation. It is just as likely that children who have good mental rotation skills find greater pleasure in building models, and hence spend more time doing so. Thus, to test the efficacy of model-building, one would need to provide model-building activities to randomly selected children, and test whether their mental rotation skills improved relative to those of a control group. A significant effect would add credence to the hypothesized causal relation, but even these data would demonstrate only that model-building *can* have an effect, not that it actually *does so* in the natural environment of the developing child.

As noted earlier, one of the richest sources of hypothesized causal factors for spatial development comes from a group rather than an individual difference, namely the consistent finding that boys and men typically outperform girls and women on a wide range of spatial tasks (for reviews see Linn & Petersen, 1985; McGee, 1979; Newcombe, 1982; Voyer, Voyer, & Bryden, 1995). Attempts to explain this difference have included all the classic explanations of developmental change more generally, that is, biological (nature), experiential (nurture), and interactive (nature-nurture) mechanisms. Entire chapters and indeed books have been devoted to research attempting to explain these sex differences, and thus again only a flavor of the extant work can be included here.

The role of nurture has been emphasized by many people, both those who conduct academic research and those who are interested in educational and social policy. The most extreme position is probably that taken by Bem (1983, 1993), who has argued that all sex differences save those connected with biological reproduction per se are the consequence of societal experience, and are created simply by differentiating boys and girls (e.g., having them line up separately to go to recess, or dressing them differently). A more common position is that the explanation lies in the different life experiences of boys and girls. Several investigators have reported correlational data consistent with the hypothesis that exposure to different toys, leisure activities, and educational curricula lead spatial skills to be enhanced differentially in males and females (e.g., Connor & Serbin, 1977; Newcombe & Bandura, 1983; Newcombe, Bandura, & Taylor, 1983; Serbin & Connor, 1979; Serbin, Zelkowitz, Doyle, Gold, & Wheaton, 1990; Signorella, Jamison, & Krupa, 1989). Experimental studies have explored the effects of spatial training, curriculum interventions, and even simple practice. Results have typically shown enhancement of females' performance, but commonly that some sex difference remains even after the intervention (see Baenninger & Newcombe, 1989).

Other investigators have explored a variety of biological explanations of the observed sex differences in spatial skills. Some investigators have reported data consistent with the suggestion that strong spatial skills are controlled by an X-linked recessive gene, thereby favoring males (Bock & Kolakowski, 1973; Thomas, 1983; Vandenberg & Kuse, 1979), although there is not universal support for this position (see Allen, Wittig, & Butler, 1981). Evolutionary psychologists (e.g., Silverman & Eals, 1992) suggest that inheritance patterns favoring high spatial skills in males can be accounted for by natural selection. For those who hunt (men), there is survival value for spatial skills that aid in navigation and the calculation of angle and distance needed to shoot prey. For those who stay home to tend to their children and nearby fields (women), there is adaptive value in being sensitive to proximal, detailed environmental cues that aid in detection of opportunities for foraging or of an intruder in the home.

Another major category of research directed to biological mechanisms in spatial development is that concerned with the effects of sex hormones on the developing child. One hypothesis is that spatial abilities are affected by the effects of testosterone. A number of complex hypotheses have been offered concerning what levels of testosterone may be best for spatial skills (see e.g. Hines, 2000; Kimura, 1999; Liben et al., 2002). There is fairly high consensus from this literature that prenatal exposure to differential levels of sex hormones are associated with different later spatial performance (e.g., Kimura, 1999). Among the most compelling data are findings showing that girls who were exposed prenatally to atypically high levels of testosterone due to congenital adrenal hyperplasia (CAH) have better spatial skills than their non-CAH sisters (Resnick, Berenbaum, Gottesman, & Bouchard, 1986). Spatial performance may be affected by sex hormones at later ages as well, although the evidence for hormonal effects on spatial skills at puberty is mixed (e.g., Davison & Sussman, in press; Liben et al., 2002; Newcombe & Bandura, 1983; Newcombe, Dubas, & Baenninger, 1989; Waber, 1977).

Although most investigators generally focus their own work on either biological or environmental mechanisms, virtually all at least acknowledge that the other mechanism also plays an important role. Increasingly, researchers are trying to study empirically the kinds of interactions between nature and nurture that most people believe in at the theoretical level. For example, Casey (1996) has offered a "bent twig" hypothesis in which she is exploring how initially small, biologically given differences may lead children to have different kinds of experiences and to take different lessons from the "same" experiences. Research of this kind is important if we are to go beyond the rhetoric of nature–nurture interactions in our explanations of spatial development.

Concluding Comments

The quantity, quality, and diversity of research reviewed in this chapter are testimony to the richness of the questions addressed in the study of spatial development. The issues range from those focused on the nearby and visually available spatial world to those that concern distant and invisible spaces. (How do infants perceive the relative position of two objects in space? How do we understand the movement of the Earth and sun?) They concern the entire lifespan. (How do infants perceive and move through their spatial worlds? How do elderly people negotiate their neighborhoods, and adapt to new spaces when they must relocate?) They address action and representation. (How do infants know where to reach for objects? How do children use maps to navigate through environments or learn about distant lands?)

The theoretical and empirical controversies that continue to attract attention are largely concerned with whether some particular skill or concept is given as part of our species-level endowment, and with how early a particular skill or concept is present. An especially common approach has been for developmental psychologists to find ways to strip down tasks in an attempt to determine whether – given the right circumstances – ever younger children or infants can demonstrate some milestone that had initially been reported (typically by Piaget) to emerge later.

A particularly dramatic example is research related to the construction of a Euclidean conceptual system that entails an understanding of distance and angle. When Piaget initially suggested that spatial representation and thinking might be modeled in Euclidean terms, he placed its emergence during middle to late childhood (Piaget & Inhelder, 1956). Perhaps not surprisingly given the increasingly nativist *Zeitgeist* in developmental psychology, some investigators have since argued that these concepts emerge far earlier and perhaps even by innate mechanisms. For example, Landau et al. (1981) suggested that – based on a young blind child's ability to go from a starting position to a target by using an inferential route – preschoolers (even without the benefit of sight) can calculate distance and angles, and that Euclidean concepts are innate. While this particular conclusion has been both criticized (e.g., Liben, 1988; Millar, 1994; Morrongiello, Timney, Humphrey, Anderson, & Skory, 1995) and supported (Mandler, 1988b; Spelke & Newport, 1998), even those who reject a radically nativist position report evidence of early metric representation. For example, Newcombe and Huttenlocher (2000) report a series of studies with their colleagues (e.g., Huttenlocher, Newcombe, & Sandberg, 1994; Huttenlocher, Newcombe, & Vasilyeva, 1999) using the "continuous space" of a sandbox in which objects are buried. Infants appear surprised (look longer) when objects reappear from a location different from the one at which the object was buried, toddlers dig in the correct location to uncover the buried object, and many 3-year-old children find a buried object by using the location of a dot in a paper rectangle as their guide. Taken together, these findings led Newcombe and Huttenlocher to conclude that even very young children encode space metrically.

Would this demonstration satisfy Piaget that these children had a Euclidean conceptual system? Piaget would probably argue that the child's solution would be better understood as a perceptual rather than a conceptual one, that is, one based on "eyeballing" rather than on understanding the need for measurement from more than one axis (see Piaget, Inhelder, & Szeminska, 1960). Piaget might also object to the imprecision of the children's identification of the "correct" locations, and to the highly constrained nature of the "continuous space" which is neatly bounded by borders that amount to ready-made Cartesian axes. Although a full discussion of these alternative positions is beyond the scope of this chapter, the example is adequate to make three general points.

First, developmental psychologists will undoubtedly continue to argue about what skills and concepts are given in our species-level biology, and about the earliest point at which they may be demonstrated. Second, these issues cannot be resolved simply by empirical work. Even when we can agree about the empirical data themselves, their interpretation is highly dependent upon our theory-based definitions (see e.g. Overton, 1998). But third, and perhaps most importantly for an introduction to spatial development, even if our empirical work does *not* allow us to agree about when and why skills initially appear, it *does* allow us to identify the sequence of accomplishments, and to identify the conditions under which higher-level functioning is more or less likely to occur. These scholarly achievements are important ones as we continue to develop our theories, and as we continue to try to build educational programs to enhance spatial skills and concepts (see e.g. Liben & Downs, 2001; Uttal, 2000b).

I end this empirical review as I began by noting again the impossibility of even touching upon all topics and paradigms within a single chapter, much less discussing each in detail. Among the topics that readers may wish to pursue (and suggested references) are: the neurological foundations of spatial development (Nadel, 1990; Stiles-Davis, Kritchevsky, & Bellugi, 1988; Potegal, 1982); the role of vision in spatial development (Rieser, 1990); developmental susceptibility to spatial illusions (Pollack, 1969), development of mental rotation skills (Kail, 1991b); a propositional approach to spatial representation (Olson & Bialystok, 1983); the development of concepts of horizontality, verticality, and diagonality (Liben, 1991b; Olson, 1970; Thomas & Turner, 1991); the development of spatial representation in art (Hagen, 1985); the language of space (Bowerman, 1996a; Landau & Jackendoff, 1993); logical search and route-planning (Wellman, 1985); spatial thinking and problem-solving in the cultural context (Gauvain, 1993); personal or social space (Goodnight & Cohen, 1985); the implications of spatial development for other cognitive domains such as problem-solving (Gattis, 2001); and the role of spatial thinking in education (Liben & Downs, 2001). Even this list is not exhaustive, but it does help to remind us again of why Molière's Monsieur Jourdain might have been even more awed if had he stopped to reflect upon his use of space rather than his use of prose. Space is, indeed, everywhere, including in the scholarly domain of cognitive development.

CHAPTER SIXTEEN

Children's Intuitive Physics

Friedrich Wilkening and Susanne Huber

Children in all cultures have some knowledge about the physical world, generally long before they get formal instruction about physics in school. These early commonsense concepts of, say, time, speed, mass, force, and temperature are of course interesting phenomena in themselves, not only because appropriate knowledge in each of these elementary domains has a high survival value. In addition, there has been another important reason for studying children's intuitive physics. For a long time, it has been considered the *via regia* to the investigation of cognitive development in general, an idea going back to the seminal work of Piaget (1929). His goal of a genetic epistemology led quite naturally to his predominant interest in the development of children's physical knowledge. With his numerous fascinating discoveries of children's understanding of the physical world, Piaget not only opened this field to developmental research, but also motivated subsequent generations of scholars to study the questions raised by him in greater detail. In recent decades, the interest in researching children's intuitive physics appears to have increased even further. The field continues to be recognized as a "foundational domain" in the study of general issues of knowledge acquisition (Wellman & Gelman, 1998).

Intuitive physics is also a rich field, with something to offer nearly every branch of psychology (Anderson & Wilkening, 1991). It includes blends of perception, cognition, and goal-directed action. It is biologically natural, our perceptual-motor skills (and perhaps some of our more cognitive capabilities, too) being the result of a long evolutionary history. Intuitive physics is ecologically basic, with our ever-present environment having the potential of both confronting us with natural tasks of variable difficulty and of providing permanent feedback, usually in precise and strict terms. It is therefore a prime field for learning. And a question of special interest for educational psychology is how – if ever – our commonsense knowledge can be translated into the concepts of textbook physics. Furthermore, much of intuitive physics can be studied via nonverbal tasks, which is of great advantage for comparisons across ages and across cultures. This feature also allows the joint study of nonverbal behavior and conscious reflection, and thus comparisons of different levels or forms of knowledge, implicit and explicit.

For a long time, this richness of the field of intuitive physics was not fully acknowledged. Piagetian theory, which guided the research until at least the 1970s, took quite a narrow look at children's intuitive physics. The main reasons for this were Piaget's focus on logical structures and his isomorphism assumption. His postulate was that cognitive development follows a sequence of stages, the final stage of knowledge being isomorphic to the laws of physics, that is, to idealized physical reality. The developmentally less advanced stages were construed as being deficient in one way or another, each stage emerging with logical necessity out of the earlier one.

Associated with these ideas was a research tactic that dominated the field far into the post-Piagetian era. Development of children's knowledge about the physical world was studied by reference to a presumed adult conceptual structure that was thought to mirror the laws of physics. The less mature knowledge structures in the earlier stages, it was held, ought to be revealed in their pure form. Accordingly, the ideal of developmental research was seen as eliminating all kinds of collateral factors and abilities, that is, those not being relevant from a logical point of view but which might help to solve the diagnostic task. It should be noted that this strategy became even more characteristic of many of those who set out to criticize Piaget than it had been of his own methodology. This chapter will show that this traditional approach largely misled developmental inquiry and failed to capture vital facets of children's intuitive physics.

Interest in the field was renewed and a new look appeared in the early 1980s. Most influential was McCloskey's (1983) *Scientific American* paper titled "Intuitive Physics," which – besides popularizing the term for a broad scientific community – pointed to the fact that many well-educated adults hold beliefs about simple phenomena of motion that are astonishingly at variance with physically correct Newtonian theory. The beliefs of these adults were not just local misconceptions but formed a coherent theory, in this case a theory of motion that was held in the Middle Ages. Other similar naïve, commonsense, or folk theories were soon found in other domains (e.g., Carey, 1985). A common characteristic of the beliefs entrenched in these theories is that they provide, under certain circumstances, good approximations of external reality. The knowledge represented in these theories, however, is generally not isomorphic to physical laws, as had been postulated by Piaget for the final stage of cognitive development. Moreover, these naïve theories appeared to be highly domain-specific, even within the field of intuitive physics (see also Baillargeon, ch. 3 this volume).

For cognitive-developmental research, this new way of looking at intuitive physics had the effect that conceiving of it mainly as a research instrument for studying the more fundamental and general questions of knowledge acquisition – a view that was typical for Piagetian genetic epistemology – lost its importance. Researchers regained interest in intuitive physics in itself, focusing on issues that in traditional developmental theory would have been devalued as surface phenomena.

Among these new issues of research were questions of learning (Anderson, 1983), of intra- and inter-individual variability (Siegler, 1995), and of children's adaptive capabilities in tasks involving intuitive physics and emphasizing goal-directed action (Anderson & Wilkening, 1991). Probably most remarkably, the past decade has seen a revival of the study of the perceptual-motor aspects of intuitive physics – with children who, according to the traditional view, are far beyond the so-called sensorimotor stage. Since the early work of Krist, Fieberg, and Wilkening (1993) in this field, several recent studies have found interesting interrelations and also dissociations of sensorimotor, perceptual, and cognitive components of children's physical knowledge. The focus in these studies shifted away from merely diagnosing the correctness or incorrectness of the responses to investigating how well they are approximated to physical reality, and under which circumstances these approximations change. It seems, thus, that the richness of the field of intuitive physics has been rediscovered in recent years and has become more and more represented in contemporary research.

In the following sections of this chapter, we will attempt to give an account of the progress the field has seen during the past two decades or so. We will do this separately for each of the various domains – time, speed, force, mass, and so on – focusing on those that have received the greatest attention in recent research. The headings of these sections will, accordingly, read like chapters of an elementary physics textbook; the content, it should be noted, is of course about psychology. In a final section, we will try to integrate the findings under common themes of cognitive development and also point to questions that are still unanswered. As to the age dimension, the chapter will focus on children from preschool age onward. Findings obtained with adults will sometimes be mentioned, but mainly as a standard of reference. And infancy will be largely excluded, because a separate chapter is devoted to this extremely interesting and rapidly expanding field (Baillargeon, ch. 3 this volume).

Time and Speed

From a psychological point of view, time has many facets. In the developmental literature, three aspects have received most attention: conventional time, psychological time, and physical time (see Friedman, 1990). The first is concerned with children's grasping of the calendar system and of the more or less arbitrary partitioning of time in units such as seconds, hours, weeks, and years. The second aspect focuses on people's subjective representations (and estimations) of durations, i.e., intervals of time, an aspect that can include, for example, questions about children's particular problems with waiting. The third aspect inquires into children's understanding of the functional relationships that, according to Newtonian physics, exist between time, speed, and distance. Of special interest in the latter context have been issues about children's "concepts" of time, particularly the question when and how they come to understand that time is different from both speed and distance and, at the same time, can be defined in terms of these entities. This third aspect, physical time, has been studied most intensively in cognitive-developmental research and is, of course, the aspect of time we will concentrate upon in a treatment of children's intuitive physics. This will lead naturally to the domain of speed.

As reported by Piaget, the impetus for this line of research came from a question Albert Einstein had posed him in the 1920s: when we look at children, which concept develops first, time or speed? Piaget's answer, published in two books about twenty years later

(Piaget, 1946a, 1946b), was somewhat surprising and proved to be more complex than he had originally anticipated: the acquisition of the concepts of time and speed was found to undergo a lengthy developmental progression, and when one of the two concepts develops first, if at all, it seemed to be, not time. This finding was counter-intuitive because, according to Newtonian theory (and Kantian philosophy), one would have expected that time as a basic entity would be grapsed first, and that an understanding of speed, an entity that can be conceptualized as derived from time (and distance), would appear later in the course of development.

Traditional studies of time and speed

The evidence for Piaget's conclusions came from his *choice* tasks. In the prototypical task, two trains moved on parallel tracks at the same or different speeds, covering the same or different distances. Children between 4 and 11 years of age were asked which train traveled for the longer time, at the higher speed, or for the greater distance; or whether the two durations, speeds, or distances, respectively, had been the same. The general finding was that correct answers for speed (and also for distance) were given at an earlier age than those for time. For Piaget, the data from these and similar studies suggested that speed and distance are the primitive concepts and that the concept of time is derived from them.

Virtually all of the early follow-up studies kept the task format introduced by Piaget and more or less supported his conclusions concerning the developmental sequence of the concepts of time and speed (e.g., Acredolo & Schmid, 1981; Crépault, 1979; Montangero, 1979; Richards, 1982; Weinreb & Brainerd, 1975). Most notable is the often cited work of Siegler and Richards (1979), a first attempt to apply Siegler's rule-assessment methodology in this domain of intuitive physics. After having systematized Piaget's task format and eliminated some of the methodological shortcomings in his approach, these authors still found the same developmental sequence: the concept of speed was again said to be mastered in advance of that of time, the major difference to Piaget's conclusions being that the age of mastery was set even higher than in the original studies: "somewhere between 11 years and adulthood" (Siegler & Richards, 1979, p. 297).

The finding of such a late mastery of the concept of time can be seen as challenged by results from studies by Levin (1977, 1982). She showed that even young children have the capacity for comparing durations, if they are not confused by interfering cues. In the original Piagetian task, the child could attend to time, speed, and/or distance cues. If he or she attempted to judge and compare the durations solely on the basis of the starting and stopping times, which is not only a logical possibility but a sensible information-processing strategy, speed and distance cues would not have been necessary to arrive at a correct decision and therefore would have been distracting rather than useful. Presenting time problems without movement cues, which was done for example via sleeping times of dolls, or presenting time information in rotational instead of linear movements, Levin found that children's capability to judge time detoriates with the number of interfering cues. This seems to be true for relevant cues such as speed and distance, as well as for irrelevant ones such as the intensity of a light in judging the duration of its burning (Levin, 1982).

New approaches to studying time and speed

A quite different approach to studying children's time and speed judgments, and their knowledge about time–speed–distance interrelations, was developed by Wilkening (1981, 1982). Rather than using the choice task, which tends to confound the relevant variables and asks for qualitative judgments only, he presented information on two of the dimensions in the time-speed-distance triad separately and asked the children to infer the quantitative value of the third. In one of the tasks, for example, children made judgments about how far an animal would have fled from a barking dog for various levels of time (how long the dog barked) and speed (fleetness of the animal, e.g., turtle, guinea pig, cat). Information integration theory and functional measurement (Anderson, 1996) served as the theoretical and methodological framework.

In these studies, children as young as 5 years of age were found to integrate the relevant information according to algebraic rules. Whereas 10-year-olds – as well as adults – combined the information in agreement with the normative multiplicative or ratio rules, 5-year-olds' judgments followed an additive rule if the initial possibility of an eye-movement strategy was eliminated (or a subtractive rule for distance and speed integration, as if Time = Distance – Speed). Although the additive and subtractive integration rules are wrong from a normative point of view, the results reveal a quantitative, functional understanding of time and speed even at 5 years of age, in sharp contrast to Piagetian theory and the conclusions drawn by others in the follow-up work using the Piagetian choice task.

The contrast comes out clearly if one considers the implications of an algebraic rule for information integration. First, an additive rule – even more than a multiplicative rule – suggests that dimensions from which the information is integrated are conceptualized as separate variables, independent from each other. Five-year-olds, thus, appear to see time and speed as different entities and do not confound them. Second, time and speed are obviously grasped as entities that have a metric, at an age which is far below the so-called stage of formal operations. If the children did not have a subjective metric for each of the concepts, an algebraic rule could not have been obtained. Third, concepts of time and speed were found to be interrelated in a sensible way even in 5-year-olds. Although this interrelation was sensible in both a practical and a formal sense, the conceptual structure concerning the time-speed-distance triad was not a perfectly reversible one. Taking all this together, the integration rules revealed a knowledge system that appears to be fundamentally different from that envisaged in the Piagetian and post-Piagetian studies.

It is interesting to note that in recent connectionist simulations of children's acquisition of concepts of time, speed, and distance, rules and networks emerged that were consistent with those that had been found in Wilkening's information integration studies (Buckingham & Shultz, 2000). Of course, the data from connectionist modeling cannot be taken as a proof of the integration rules. However, the simulation data are no less compelling than the results from other recent experiments that tried to expand upon the traditional choice paradigm and/or to somehow combine it with the information integration approach (Acredolo, 1989; Matsuda, 1994, 1996; Zhou, Peverly, Boehm, & Chongde,

2000). Rather than elucidating the acquisition of concepts of time and speed, the results from these studies further obscured the problem. All these attempts to elaborate on the choice method did not lead to a convergence of the conclusions – contrary to what the authors had expected – but made the data even harder to interpret, particularly the discrepancies between the findings of the various studies employing the choice method. As Zhou et al. (2000) rightly acknowledge, a serious limitation of the choice format in these tasks is that it is not suited to what they are designed to assess: the integration of concepts. As a consequence, children's knowledge can be misrepresented in one way or another.

Concepts of time and speed in different contexts

Although, in the early information integration experiments, children from 5 years on were found to have virtually perfect function knowledge about time–speed–distance interrelations, this does not mean that they can apply it in all contexts. The same, incidentally, seems to be true of adults. Under some circumstances, even in tasks that are quite simple from a formal point of view, both children and adults give judgments that are wrong in an amazing way. This was shown in recent experiments by Wilkening and Martin (in press) and by Huber, Krist, and Wilkening (in press). These studies addressed concepts referring to issues of time-saving and speed-averaging. The basic problem of interest here can be exemplified as follows: If drivers of two cars travel the same distance, one with a constant speed of 100 km/h over the whole distance and the other with a (constant) lower speed for the first half of the distance – say 75 km/h, how fast does the second driver have to be for the second half to compensate for the time loss experienced in the first half and so arrive at the same time as the first one? The correct answer, by the way, is 150 km/h, not 125 km/h which appears to be the standard response even in adults.

In the experiment by Wilkening & Martin, this problem was presented in the following task: two toy cars traveled on parallel tracks, one always at the same speed over the whole track, the other starting at one of three lower speeds. Exactly half-way along the track, the first car went into a tunnel that hid it from view for the second half of the distance. For each of the lower speeds of the second car, the question was how fast it had to travel to catch up exactly with the other car at the end of the track. The child was told that the second car could change its speed either half-way along the track (nonlinear condition), or when the first car entered the tunnel, that is, when half of the total time had elapsed (linear condition). Children could give their responses either on a quasi-numerical, graphic rating scale (judgment condition), or by actually pushing the second car (action condition) and thus producing the speeds, which could be recorded by photometers.

In the judgment part of the nonlinear condition, the same misconception appeared at all ages, from 6-year-olds to adults: instead of grading the required speeds in a nonlinear fashion, these participants gave "linear" responses by just adding the speed differences – as in the numerical example above. This would have been correct in the linear condition when the speed could be changed in the middle of time, but not of distance. In this condition, virtually all children and adults gave the same linear responses as in the nonlinear condition. They were obviously unable to differentiate between two situations which, particularly when speed differences become remarkable, require very different judgments. Interestingly, this differentiation was found to emerge in the *actions* of children around 10 years of age and was clearly there in adulthood, the produced speeds being in correspondence with physical laws, linear in the linear condition and nonlinear in the nonlinear condition. The same children, it should be noted, adhered to a linear rule in the nonlinear condition when judgments were asked for – a result indicating that children's knowledge in this domain may be dissociated.

This was corroborated in the follow-up study by Huber et al., which implemented the Wilkening and Martin task in a virtual environment, with respect to both the visual and haptic sense, and at the same time reduced the imagery demands. Even more 10-year-olds acted according to physical laws, as could be seen from their speed productions, while still adhering to the wrong linear rule in their judgments. Many adults, on the other hand, now also judged according to physical laws, as had been found to hold for their actions. In other words, by varying the task while keeping their logical structure, the knowledge dissociation was found to decrease in adults and to increase in children. Instead of asking which of the tasks is the more adequate to assess children's "real" knowledge, the phenomenon of knowledge dissociation may be worth studying in itself. It does not seem to be peculiar to children's concepts of time and speed. This will become evident in the next section.

Trajectories of Moving Objects and the Straight Throw

How do objects behave once set in motion? What kind of path do they take, and what changes in speed occur under the influence of different forces? Of particular interest are two forces, as well as their interaction: the force originally exerted on the object to set it in motion, and the force of gravity. Although the physical principles governing such motions have been well known since Newton, many adults still seem to believe that objects behave otherwise. This was discovered by McCloskey and his associates in a series of pioneering experiments (see McCloskey, 1983), studies which laid the ground for attempts to investigate the adult misconceptions from a developmental point of view.

The straight-down belief

One of the most striking misconceptions found by McCloskey – and certainly the most extensively studied – is the so-called straight-down belief. Most children, and even about half of well-educated adults, predict that an object dropped from a moving carrier – from a running person or from an airplane – will fall in a straight vertical path and land directly beneath the point of release. Based on these observations and findings in similar tasks, McCloskey offered an interesting interpretation of children's and adults' misconceptions. They are consistent with a pre-Newtonian, medieval theory of motion: the impetus theory. According to this theory, each motion must have a cause. In the case of a thrown ball, the cause is the force (impetus) that the thrower implants into it, which steadily diminishes until the ball falls down. In the case of an object's "passive" release from a moving carrier, there is no longer a force acting horizontally on the object, so according to the impetus theory, it will fall straight down, by the shortest path.

Would the same children who adhere to the straight-down belief (and presumably to the impetus theory) in the moving-carrier task predict that a ball pushed from a table – with more or less speed – will fall straight down from the edge of the table to the floor? Intuitively, the two situations may seem quite different, a view that would be in line with the medieval impetus theory. According to Newtonian physics, however, the two situations are formally equivalent. How are these problems represented and conceptualized in children's intuitive physics?

A first attempt to investigate this question was made in a study by Kaiser, Proffitt, & McCloskey (1985). They asked children from preschool to sixth grade to predict where a ball would land if it (a) rolled off a table, or (b) dropped from a toy train traveling at the same speed as the rolling speed of the ball on the table and at the same height above the floor. In the first task, the percentage of children who correctly predicted that the ball would continue to move forward (for a while) increased continuously with age. In the second task, by contrast, there was no age trend: the great majority of children predicted that the ball would fall straight down.

In their interpretation of these data, Kaiser et al. conjectured that the straight-down belief, corresponding with the impetus theory, is a developmentally basic one. As children get older, they revise this belief only in the light of perceptual counter-evidence. In everyday life, they get many opportunities to accumulate experiences about how moving objects fall from the edge of a surface. However, such perceptual evidence is usually lacking in the case of objects falling from moving carriers. And even if children do have the chance to perceive such events, a visual illusion is normally involved: The falling object is seen as taking a straight-down path – or even a backward path if there is an air drag. This is because the moving carrier (and not the landing ground) is taken as the frame of reference for the perception. If this frame is used, of course, the falling object does not continue its forward movement. Following this line of reasoning, Kaiser et al. concluded that the straight-down belief for carried objects cannot be overcome via perceptual experience but only via formal instruction in physics.

Children's actions and the straight-down belief

All these considerations refer to children's judgments concerning hypothetical, imagined events. What can we say about children's actions? Watching children when they are throwing balls, stones, and sticks, or when they are trying to bring about or prevent collisions of moving objects, one may get the impression that they are quite proficient in this domain. Are their beliefs as expressed in their judgments reflected in their actions, and vice versa? Further questions are: Do children's beliefs guide their actions? Are their beliefs derived from their actions, or do judgments and actions represent forms of knowledge that are inseparable?

These questions were addressed in a study by Krist, Fieberg, and Wilkening (1993), which laid the ground for a series of follow-up experiments by Krist and his colleagues. Of particular interest was children's knowledge about the role of two factors influencing an object's movement in the so-called straight throw: the (horizontal) target distance and the (vertical) height of release. To this end, children from 5 years on had to determine the speed a tennis ball should have on a horizontal platform to hit a target on the ground. Height of the platform and target distance were each varied by three levels and factorially combined. For each height-distance combination, the speed of the ball could either (a) be judged on a graphic rating scale or (b) be produced by actually pushing the ball.

According to the laws of physics, speed in this situation is a direct function of distance (the farther, the faster), and an inverse function of height (the higher, the slower). Moreover, distance and height interact according to a multiplicative rule in determining the launch speed. All these principles were mirrored in the patterns of the speed productions, that is, in children's actions, with virtually no age trend from the youngest children investigated up to adults. The judgment condition, however, yielded a very different picture: The 5-year-olds now failed to integrate the relevant dimensions, and many 10-year-olds (and even several adults) showed striking misconceptions. Judging from their judgments, most of these children seemed to hold an inverse-height belief: that the ball should fall faster the higher the level of release. It should be noted that all of the participants with this pattern of incorrect judgment had produced the perfect pattern in their actions, no matter which condition was presented first. An additional experiment, in which throw feedback was eliminated, secured that the speed gradations, both in judgments and in actions, were not learned ad hoc in the experiment but reflected pre-existing knowledge.

Follow-up work has provided interesting additional information. On the action side, children's intuitive physics regarding the straight throw seems to be highly effector-specific. For instance, young children did not exhibit the perfect speed-production patterns when the ball had to be kicked (by foot and leg), rather than pushed (by hand and arm), or when the ball had to be set in motion via a simple shooting apparatus (Krist, Loskill, & Schwarz, 1996). As to the judgment side, children's predictions for the case of the upward throw were found to be no less deficient than those for the straight throw. For release angles below 45°, many children up to 12 years of age were found to hold the following false belief: the smaller the angle, the farther the ball will go – apparently not knowing that the reverse is true, with 45° being the optimum for achieving maximal horizontal distance with the upward throw (Krist, 1992).

Action versus judgment

In a recent in-depth developmental analysis of the straight-down belief in action and judgment, Krist (2001) found that, in contrast to the earlier conjectures by Kaiser et al., many children are able to revise the misconception, without formal instruction, between 8 and 12 years of age. Moreover, the data of these experiments suggest that the straight-down belief is not rooted in a perceptual illusion, which could be demonstrated by ingenious variations of the task. And most interestingly, the experiments provided clear converging evidence for an early assumption put forward by McCloskey and his associates: that people use their naïve beliefs to plan their actions. This was now shown to be true even of children. When asked to hit a target on the floor by dropping a ball while moving, those children who held the straight-down belief in a judgment condition dropped the ball significantly later (above the target) than those who exhibited correct judgmental knowledge; they seemed to realize that the ball should clearly be released before being exactly above the target.

It would be a misinterpretation of Krist's findings to say that, by 12 years of age, children have a full-fledged understanding of the inertia of moving objects. The knowledge of even the oldest children in his study seemed to be fragile, and to have developed in a slow and piecemeal fashion. These conclusions are reminiscent of those drawn by Kim and Spelke (1999), who studied the development of the understanding of gravity and inertia on object motion at much younger ages, from 7-month-old infants to 6 year-old children. Of particular interest in the present context are the changes in understanding beyond infancy. In the final experiment in the Kim and Spelke study, children had to predict where a ball would land if rolled off a slightly downward slanted ramp. Three possible landing locations were shown: one consistent with the straight-down belief, one corresponding to the correct parabolic path, and one that would result if there were no gravity. Children had to choose one of the three possibilities for their judgments. Whereas children up to 4 years of age predicted that the ball would land in the straight-down location, 6-year-olds consistently judged that the ball would land in the location prescribed by a parabolic path. The younger children seemed to be sensitive to gravity only. The 6-year-olds, by contrast, who expected the ball to move both downward and forward, appeared to be sensitive to both gravity and inertia. However, if children were given the opportunity to view the three fully visible motions and had to judge their "naturalness," even the 3- and 4-year-olds reliably chose the parabolic path as the normal one, now showing a sensitivity to both gravity and inertia which, in the prediction task, did not appear before 6 years of age. The developmental patterns observed in the different tasks thus provide further evidence for a dissociation in children's performance, in this study even in the case of judgments only (Kim & Spelke, 1999).

Considered together, the findings by Krist and his associates and by Kim and Spelke allow two general conclusions. First, children's developing understanding of object motion is a complex, multifaceted process. It has now repeatedly been shown that some aspects of knowledge may be expressed in – and are revealed by – a particular task but not another, without either of them necessarily being the more adequate or sensitive for diagnosing the "true" concept in question. Second, following from the above, children's knowledge about object motion reveals itself and can be studied in a broad array of contexts (Kim & Spelke, 1999, p. 361).

A further compelling example is provided by the experiments of Hood (1995). He studied young children's understanding of object motion by contrasting aspects of gravity and solidity. Children from 2 to 4 years of age were asked to find a ball that was dropped down one of three opaque tubes that could be interwoven. Most of the children searched in the wrong location: beneath the point where the ball was dropped, not at the lower exit of the tube into which the ball was dropped. For these children, gravity obviously outperformed solidity. Hood termed this a "gravity error," which can be seen as another instance of the strength of the straight-down belief. However, when transparent tubes were used and thus the children could see the trajectory of the ball, even the youngest children tested, 2-year-olds, searched at the correct location, now acknowledging the solidity aspect and having overcome the gravity error. Amazingly, these children were unable to transfer these experiences to the case of opaque tubes, ones without visible object motion. This again illustrates the context-specificity and the piecemeal fashion of the development of intuitive understanding in this domain.

Force and Weight

In terms of physics, the last section addressed two different concepts of mass, with mass having the same numerical value in both. One concept is related to the fact that mass is inertial, which means that a change in an object's velocity needs some force to act against the inertia of mass. The second concept deals with the fact that mass has a weight due to gravitation (under constant gravitational conditions the weight of an object is directly proportional to its mass). When we studied children's understanding of translatory movements, which was the main topic of the last section, both concepts of mass were relevant – although this was not explicitly mentioned there. When we studied children's understanding of time–speed–distance relationships in the first section, we considered simple kinetics; no change in velocity took place and, accordingly, neither force nor weight played a significant role. In this third section, we will focus on force and weight explicitly, and we will start with tasks dealing with phenomena in which one aspect of mass plays the dominant role: the weight of an object due to gravitational force.

The balance-scale task

In this domain, the instrument most extensively used has clearly been the balance scale, originally designed by Inhelder and Piaget (1958) as a means of studying formal operational reasoning. Since then, the balance-scale task has developed into a paradigm per se, a sort of *drosophila* in research on children's intuitive physics, if not on cognitive development in general. The task exists in several variations and has been studied across all ages: in infants (Case, 1985a), pre-schoolers (Siegler, 1978), schoolchildren (Amsel, Goodman, Savoie, & Clark, 1996; Ferretti & Butterfield, 1986), and adults (Hardiman, Pollatsek, & Well, 1986). It has been used to gather evidence for a variety of theories in accounting for developmental data: Piagetian (Inhelder & Piaget, 1958; Karmiloff-Smith & Inhelder, 1974), neo-Piagetian (Case, 1985a; Marini, 1992) cultural-contextualist (Tudge, 1992; Weir & Seacrest, 2000), symbolic information-processing (Klahr & Siegler, 1978; Langley, 1987; Newell, 1990), information integration (Surber & Gzesh, 1984; Wilkening & Anderson, 1982, 1991), and connectionist (McClelland, 1995) and psychometric approaches (Jansen & van der Maas, 1997; Wilson, 1989). It has also been used to examine a large range of issues on factors that may determine rule use (Amsel,

Goodman, Savoie, & Clark, 1996; Ferretti, Butterfield, Cahn, & Kerkman, 1985; Tudge, 1992; Wilkening & Anderson 1982, 1991).

Siegler's (1976) account of children's reasoning about the balance-scale problem, which entered into many textbooks and served as a point of reference for a vast amount of follow-up research in various fields of cognitive development, has certainly been the most influential in the past two decades. He used a very common version of the task, called here the "choice" task. Different or the same numbers of weights are placed on each side of a horizontal, two-arm balance beam. The weights are at different or the same distances from the fulcrum. The child is asked to predict which side will go down if the beam, which initially is presented as being fixed, were left free.

A rule-assessment methodology based on choice tasks

In an attempt to systematize the notions put forward by Piaget, Siegler postulated that children, in the course of development, use four different rules in solving the balance-scale problem, each rule representing a different level of knowledge. Each rule is based on binary decisions, and the rules are usually represented as binary decision trees, resembling simple computer programs. To diagnose the rule a child uses in solving the task and, at the same time, to diagnose his or her pre-existing knowledge, Siegler developed a relatively sophisticated procedure, the so-called rule-assessment methodology. This requires the presentation of a carefully selected series of problems, with different combinations of weights on the balance beam and distances from the fulcrum, so that the different rules yield unique performance patterns that can be attributed to the operation of one of the four rules.

From the data in these tasks, Siegler (1976) concluded that children, in the course of development, progress through a sequence of rules, these rules being hierarchically ordered in a quite simple way. In accordance with Piaget, the physically correct, normative rule was postulated as the end-point of development. For the balance scale, this rule predicts that the side with larger momentum of force (torque) will go down, the momentum of force resulting from a multiplication of units of weight and distance on each side. Most children were found to use other, simpler rules. The majority of 4- and 5-year-olds typically based their predictions on weights only (Rule I), always ignoring distances and thus the momentum of force. By the age of 9 years, most children were found to use Rule II, beginning to consider distance, but only in those special cases in which the weight on both sides of the fulcrum were the same. By the age of 13 years, most children were found to use Rule III, now considering both weight and distance in all possible cases, but apparently not knowing how to integrate the information in "conflict" problems, problems in which one side has more weight, but in which the weight on the other side has a greater distance from the fulcrum. The normative solution (Rule IV) was assessed quite rarely in Siegler's studies, even up to late adolescence.

Because each of the developmentally "lower" rules is included in the decision-tree representation of the one above, the question of rule-learning has aroused particular interest in this approach (Siegler, 1976, 1978; Siegler & Chen, 1998). In a series of training studies, the more recent using the microgenetic method, Siegler and his co-workers showed that young children can learn higher rules when four components of the learning process are mastered: noticing potential explanatory variables, formulating predictive rules, applying the rules to new problems, and maintaining them under less supportive conditions. The first component in particular, that is, the noticing and encoding of relevant variables, appears to be the major problem for young children in these kinds of tasks. However, as found by Siegler (1976) in his early research, an extensive weight-encoding training may help children as young as 3 years of age to learn at least his Rule I.

Amsel et al. (1996) took this research one step further, by investigating children's reasoning about causal and non-causal influences on the behavior of the balance scale – and on levers in general. In addition to the well-investigated causal factors – weight and distance from the fulcrum – non-causal factors were varied, for example the color of the weights and/or their orientation, and whether they were standing on the beam or hanging from it. The results of these studies suggest that there are separate processes underlying children's ability to identify causal influences and to dismiss non-causal ones. These processes, however, were found to be dependent on the kinds of features involved. In the course of development, children appear to pay attention primarily to salient physical features – causal and non-causal – such as the weight and color of the objects, and only thereafter consider spatial features, again both causal and non-causal, such as distance from the fulcrum and the particular orientation or mounting of the objects. Based on these results, Amsel et al. concluded that children's theory revision occurs in a piecemeal fashion. More generally and more importantly, we believe, these data also show that the selection of cues that a child considers to be relevant does not necessarily follow principles that could be derived from logic or the normative laws of physics, as held in traditional views.

Alternative rule-assessment methodologies

The overwhelming majority of the balance-scale research employed the choice paradigm: For different weight-distance combinations on both sides of the fulcrum, the child had to predict which side would go down – or if the scale would stay in balance. Wilkening & Anderson (1991) varied this approach by not only asking the choice question but by also asking the child, after he or she had said that one side would go down, to adjust the weight and/or distance on one side so that the scale would come into balance. These production responses, embedded in an alternative rule-assessment methodology, yielded quite different results than those to be expected if Siegler's rule sequence were a true account of children's knowledge in this domain. Most importantly, many children were found to integrate the relevant information, weight and distance, according to a non-normative adding-type of rule. These children showed integration according to Wilkening and Anderson's alternative rule assessment methodology, whereas according to Siegler's choice response rule methodology they should not have. Indeed, for virtually all of the same children, one of Siegler's rules had been assessed on the basis of their initial predictions (choice responses) and analyzed as prescribed by Siegler's criteria. These rules turned out to describe a very different kind of knowledge. For example, Rule III, which was the predominant one in this context, would imply that the children who were found to follow an adding rule in the non-choice production task should have no idea how to integrate weight-distance information, and thus should just be guessing in all conflict situations. These discrepant findings point to serious problems of knowledge representation, which had been raised earlier by Wilkening and Anderson (1982) and which we will take up again at the end of this chapter.

Force and weight concepts in other paradigms

Tasks related to the balance-scale problem have been studied by Pauen (1996). Her experiments investigated children's knowledge of the addition of force vectors. In a king-on-the-ice game, two unequal forces were pulling at the target object, a toy king fixated to the center of a circular platform. The forces were weights positioned on small plates that hung from two cords, thereby pulling the target towards the edge of the platform. Children were asked to predict in which direction the target would be moving if released. The vast majority of first- to third-graders, and almost half of fourth-graders, erroneously predicted that the object would always be pulled straight in the direction of the stronger force (one-force-only rule), in contrast to the correct integration rule, which requires not only the consideration of which force is the stronger, but the taking into account of both forces and the integration of the quantities and directions of the force vectors. The correct resulting direction is given by the vector addition of the two force vectors.

  Verbal reports of the children gave hints of their use of analogical reasoning, which happened to be misleading in this case: Many children appeared to employ their already existing knowledge about the behavior of balance scales to derive the answers for the vector-addition problem. This assumption was corroborated in a follow-up experiment (Pauen & Wilkening, 1997). Children who were about to overcome their false beliefs in the original task were presented with two different types of balance scales and trained to use either the one-force-only rule or the correct rule, depending on the kind of balance scale. One of them was of the common all or nothing kind, in which the difference of the momentum of force between both sides of the fulcrum is irrelevant to the balance beam's behavior and thus the stronger-force-only rule provides a perfect prediction. The other type, in contrast, had an uncommon swing suspension of the beam, so that the degree of its tilt depended on the difference of the momentum of force. Only this type of balance scale provides a correct analogy for the force-interaction problem in Pauen's original task. The training had a clear effect: the majority of children who were trained on the swing-suspension balance beam integrated the relevant forces in the vector-addition problem almost perfectly, whereas all of the children who were trained on the usual all or nothing balance scale adhered to the one-force-only rule. It appears, thus, that at least some misconceptions about the interaction of forces may have their roots in false analogies.

  In closing this discussion of children's intuitive physics of force and weight, the fact that research in this domain has strongly focused on explicit knowledge deserves mention. A notable exception is the early study by Karmiloff-Smith and Inhelder (1974), who investigated children's implicit knowledge when balancing weight-symmetric and weight-asymmetric objects. They found that 4- and 8-year-olds performed better on this action task than 6-year-olds, whose performance seemed to be derived from their naïve theory that all objects balance at their geometric center. The 4-year-olds, in contrast, performed the task by relying on proprioceptive feedback, and were thus successful. The 8-year-olds, on the other hand, appeared to have abandoned the naïve geometric-center rule guiding the 6-year-olds' behavior in favor of an explicit consideration of the weight distributions. Only when asked to close their eyes, which prevented the implementation of the naïve geometric-center rule in a simple way, did 6-year-olds attain the same level of behavioral mastery as the younger children. It appears that in this domain, too, children's intuitive physics is a non-trivial blend of sensorimotor action and operational thought, to use Piagetian terms.

Matter, Mass, Weight, Volume, and Density

We now turn from dynamic and kinetic aspects to more static phenomena of the physical environment: to the fundamental domain of matter, the stuff from which our world is built. On principle, this includes all states of aggregation – solids, liquids, and gases. In the physicist's framework, matter is defined on two levels: on the macroscopic level by its mass, volume, and density, and on the microscopic level by its atomic nature. Because the microscopic level is normally not accessible in people's everyday life, we will focus here on the mascroscopic level, which is a vital part of children's intuitive physics from their early months on. This includes contacts with different kinds of material, varying in density. In physics, density is defined quite simply: the ratio of mass to volume. People's ordinary understanding of this relation, however, seems to be complicated by their difficulties in grasping how physical transformations, such as heating, deformation, and pressure, affect each quantity. As textbook physics tells us, volume and density can change under these transformations but the mass (or the weight) remains constant. To what extent are these principles and concepts reflected in our intuitive physics, and how did they develop?

Transformations and invariances of matter and weight

To study these questions, children have often been asked about matter, weight, and related quantities before and after certain transformations of stimuli (Andersson, 1990; Driver, 1985; Galili & Bar, 1997; Piaget, 1974). Do children know that a transformation of form, without applying pressure, does not change any of these quantities? Do they know that increases of heat and pressure lead to an increase and decrease of volume and a decrease and increase of density, respectively, but do not affect mass? Another important aspect necessary for a proper understanding in this domain is the difference of extensive and intensive quantities. Mass and volume are extensive quantities; changes in the amount of matter lead to clear-cut changes in these quantities, generally according to principles of addition. Density, in contrast, is an intensive quantity; it does not change if the amount of matter is changed.

Many psychologists and educators have noted that the relation of mass, volume, and density is extremely difficult for children to understand – and therefore very difficult to teach them (see Smith, Snir, & Grosslight, 1992). Questions of interest have been why this should be so, and how learning procedures may facilitate the understanding of these relations.

As to children's concepts of matter, it appears that their knowledge system, although highly adapted to their everyday needs, differs substantially from the definitional system of physics. For instance, preschool children do differentiate between physical objects on one side and dreams or wishes on the other, but they seem to do so on an axis of reality instead of a material-immaterial axis (Estes, Wellman, & Woolley, 1989). Between 4 and 11 years of age, almost all children who categorize solids, liquids, and gases as matter also say that electricity, temperature, light, echo, or shadow are of material kind (Carey, 1991; DeVries, 1986; Piaget, 1960a). Whereas matter has the status of a characteristic feature in differentiating material kinds, this is untrue of both mass and weight. Of course, objects of different material kind can have the same weight, just as objects of the same material kind can have different weights.

Children's concept of weight has been studied mainly in conservation tasks (Driver, 1985; Galili & Bar, 1997; Piaget & Szeminska, 1939; Smedslund, 1961; Stavy & Stachel, 1985). Much data suggests that younger children have a concept of weight that is highly influenced by the felt weight of an object. For instance, more than half of 4-year-olds, and half of 6-year-olds, have been found to judge that a small rice corn or even a sizable piece of styrofoam weighs nothing (Smith, Carey, & Wiser, 1985). Only at around 9 years of age, according to these authors, do children develop a concept of weight that is less dependent on their personal sensations. They then begin to relate weight to the amount of matter, and to realize that neither matter nor weight ever disappear if an object is divided into smaller and smaller pieces. At around the same age they develop the analogous insight for the case of transparent gases, if water is transformed into vapor, for instance (Carey, 1991). It appears, thus, that weight is not a simple concept for children to grasp. They seem to start out with diverse concepts of weight, and it takes them a long time to integrate them into one, coherent concept that can finally, though it doesn't always, become isomorphic to the concept of weight held in physics.

Density: different from weight?

Conceptualizing density appears to be even more difficult for children. This has been found in a large variety of studies, including tasks on sorting objects according to material kind, judging effects of thermal expansion, and predicting the floating or sinking of objects. A general conclusion has been that children's problems are due to an undifferentiated weight-density concept (Hewson, 1986; Piaget & Inhelder, 1974; Smith, Carey, & Wiser, 1985; Smith, Snir, & Grosslight, 1992). It has also been suggested that the concept of density is difficult because it requires, in a more general sense, the understanding of ratio and proportionality which, according to the Piagetian view, is not fully developed before children enter the stage of formal-operational reasoning. Of course, these two hypotheses need not be mutually exclusive. We will first look at studies focusing on the former hypothesis and come back to the latter one in the following section.

In a series of experiments, including both verbal and nonverbal tasks, Smith, Carey, and Wiser (1985) investigated children's distinctions of weight and size as well as of weight and material type (or density). They asked children to compare the weight, the size, or the material of objects, and to respond verbally or nonverbally. In the nonverbal tasks, children had to sort the objects into steel and aluminum families, for instance (density being the relevant factor), make a sponge bridge collapse (weight being the relevant factor), or judge whether a piece of matter would fit into a box (size being the relevant factor). Children as young as 3 years of age did not have any problems in differentiating between size and weight, but they were unable to discriminate between weight and density, which was found to remain a major difficulty for much older children, up to middle-school age. They frequently made errors, with intrusions of weight into the density task (i.e., sorting large aluminum objects into the steel family because they were heavy) and vice versa.

Flotation and buoyancy

In the search for alternative nonverbal tasks suitable for investigating weight–density differentiation, phenomena of flotation and buoyancy came into focus – buoyancy being the more general concept because it relates to both the floating and sinking of a solid object in a liquid with a given density. If the density of a solid is less than the density of the liquid, the object will float, and the object will sink if its density is greater than that of the liquid.

The studies by Halford, Brown, and McThompson (1986) and Smith et al. (1992) deserve special mention in this context. Children between 8 and 13 years of age had to judge whether cubes of different size and weight would sink or float. Most of these children had a clear tendency to focus on weight and to disregard density as the primary relevant variable. Kohn (1993) devised a flotation prediction task capable of finding earlier forms of understanding of density. Preschool children, as well as adults, made floating/sinking predictions concerning a set of objects with systematic variations in density, weight, and volume. From the age of 4 years onward a rudimentary understanding in this domain seemed to emerge: children's judgments of the floating or sinking behavior of objects with densities much above or much below that of water were more accurate than for objects with densities relatively close to that of water. However, irrelevant weight and volume information still interfered in systematic ways. The children at even younger ages, in comparison, gave very inconsistent responses, indicating that they did not have any idea about density as a factor relevant to an object's floating or sinking.

Penner & Klahr (1996) tested 10-, 12-, and 14-year-old children's knowledge about a more specific aspect: the sinking time of various objects. These authors were particularly interested in the question of if and how children use self-designed experimental strategies to test and revise their a priori beliefs. Most children initially held the belief that weight alone determines which one of two objects will sink faster. After having experimented, however, all children came to realize that other factors such as object shape and material also had an effect on the sinking speed. The main difference between the age groups appeared to be not their a priori knowledge but, rather, their belief that experimentation can help to identify the relevant factors and the corresponding effects – which is not a trivial task in this micro-domain. This belief was typically held by the older children and virtually absent at younger ages.

Piaget's early studies, having laid the ground for the research in this field, had been mainly concerned with children's qualitative explanations of flotation-related phenomena. He asked children to make predictions and give explanations of if and why everyday objects such as boats would float or sink (Piaget, 1960a). Children started out by mentioning animistic principles ("the boat floats because a hidden force lifts it up"). These explanations were characteristic of 5-year-olds and could still be observed in some 8-year-olds. Reference to objective concepts of physics ("they are light," "they are full of air"), however inappropriate, did not appear before the age of 9 years, and the role of relative density seemed to be understood only beyond that age. Several follow-up studies, also relying on children's explanations and verbal reports, largely supported Piaget's findings (Dentici, Grossi, Borghi, DeAmbrosis, & Massara 1984; Klewitz, 1989; Laurendeau & Pinard, 1962).

A novel approach to studying children's intuitive physics of flotation was used by Janke (1995) by applying principles of functional measurement. As in the previous studies, children were presented with objects varying in volume and weight. However, instead of asking for verbal explanations and for binary choices as to whether the objects would float or sink, children had to give fine-graded quantitative ratings. These were judgments about the maximum load that boats differing in volume and weight could carry. Although the integration of the relevant variables was found to improve with age, in children between the ages of 8 and 12 there was still a strong tendency to overvalue the role of weight. However, this misconception largely disappeared in a task in which the unloaded boats were presented floating on water (with different amounts of dip) and thus the effects of both volume and weight were perceptually accessible. Thus it appears that children's concepts of flotation and buoyancy do not develop in an all-or-none fashion. In this micro-domain, in particular, a complete understanding seems to take a long time to develop (see also Esterly & Barbu, 1999). This is one reason why it is especially suited for studies on learning and belief revision (Penner & Klahr, 1996), with many possibilities for future research.

Density, temperature, sweetness, and other intensive quantities

Why do children fail to understand the concept of density? Do they have specific problems with this particular concept, or do they have similar problems with other intensive quantities, perhaps due to a general lack of the ability to perform the logical operations necessary for proportional thinking? As already said, intensive quantities may be conceived as involving proportions. The sweetness of a drink, for example, may be judged by comparing the amount of water with the amount of sugar dissolved in it, according to principles of proportionality and ratio rules. However, as data from several studies suggest, children appear to have considerable difficulties attaining a deep understanding of these principles, sometimes even up to adolescence (Hart, 1988; Karplus, Pulos, & Stage, 1983).

Several micro-domains studied by various researchers are of interest in the present context: sugar or acid concentrations in water; viscosity; color brightness; and temperature (Jäger & Wilkening, 2001; Moore, Dixon, & Haines, 1991; Reed & Evans, 1987; Stavy, Strauss, Orpaz, & Carmi, 1982; Strauss & Stavy, 1982). These are all instances of intensive quantities: their values remain unchanged under the variation of matter, which is an extensive quantity.

In the pioneering studies by Sidney Strauss and his colleagues, for example, children were asked about the sweetness of a mixture contained in two glasses, which were filled with water, and then had the same or different numbers of pieces of sugar dissolved in them. In an analogous task on temperature mixture, the number of pieces of sugar was replaced by the number of candles heating the water, and the child was asked about the resulting temperature. These authors found that children younger than 5 years of age arrived at (qualitatively) correct answers by relying on their experience-based intuitive understanding of intensive quantities. Children between 6 and 10 years of age, in contrast, typically tried to apply quantitative rules, but chose the incorrect one, which led to a drop in their performance. Most of the children predicted that the mixture would become sweeter or warmer, respectively, than the sweetest or warmest of the two initial components. Children seemed to add the values of one extensive quantity (amount of sugar or number of candles) without taking into account that the other extensive quantity (water) also increased. The correct answer reappeared in children from about 10 years on who, as concluded by the authors, understood the role of both relevant extensive quantities and were able to integrate them. For Strauss and his colleagues, these findings were of a more general theoretical importance, beyond speaking of children's intuitive physics of intensive quantities. This field appeared to be well suited to demonstrate phenomena of U-shaped behavioral growth in cognitive development (Strauss, 1982).

Colleen Moore and her colleagues (Ahl, Moore, & Dixon, 1992; Dixon & Moore, 1996; Moore, Dixon, & Haines, 1991) were particularly interested in the development of function knowledge in tasks involving intensive quantities. They investigated children's understanding of temperature mixture so as to study their self-initiated generation of mathematical strategies. A general conclusion from these studies was that children up to the age of 8 years tend to understand the domain quite poorly, and even fifth- and eighth-graders were far from showing a perfect understanding. Such an understanding would require the grasp of different principles, as has been pointed out by detailed task-analyses in these studies. Children appear to have difficulties even with the seemingly simplest of these, the Range principle, stating that the value of the mixture of intensive quantities must always fall between those of the two initial components, or at least cannot lie above or below either of them.

All these studies have presented the intensive quantities in some symbolized form. Temperature and sweetness, for example, were not perceivable, in contrast to the extensive quantity of the stimuli, volume in these cases. Therefore, Jäger and Wilkening (2001) speculated that children's errors might result from their difficulties with inferring the intensive quantity, and that these might disappear when the intensities are directly visible.

For this reason, color intensity was used as a variable. Surprisingly, this study replicated previous findings in important respects. For instance, children predicted that a mixture of two liquids, one light red and the other a red of a middle intensity, would become darker than the darkest initial component. Even half of the children in the 10-year-old group gave these "additive" responses. Besides putting into question the hypothesis that children's problems in the previous studies were due to the fact that the intensive quantities were not accessible to perception, the results found by Jäger and Wilkening indicate that children's problems in this domain cannot simply be attributed to their inability to take both relevant extensive quantities (e.g., sugar and water) into account and to integrate them appropriately. The problem seems to be a different one: lacking a specific rule for these quantities, children seem to resort to a sort of general-purpose adding rule – a rule that (already) at young ages has proven its worth in the case of extensive quantities. An *extensitivity bias* (Jäger & Wilkening, 2001) seems thus to operate in children's concepts of intensive quantities. Interestingly enough, the authors found in additional experiments of the same study that this bias tends to disappear, rather than increase, if the tasks become more complex, particularly if the volume is varied and thus the extensive quantity becomes more salient. These counterintuitive results raise interesting new questions, and the complication strategy may be a promising approach with which to address them.

Although young children seem to have a strong bias in favor of additive rules – and of transferring them to the inappropriate case of intensive quantities – exceptions have been observed, not only in the experiments just cited but also in a recent study by Dixon and Tuccillo (2001). They asked children and college students to predict what would happen when quantities of a substance were combined. Two of these questions were about familiar properties: weight and sweetness. The third question was about a fictitious property, the "hemriness" of the resulting matter, which could be liquids (drinks) or eatable solids. Would children be more likely to conceptualize the fictitious property as an extensive or an intensive one, after having answered the weight and sweetness questions? That is, would the hemriness of the two initial components be added or averaged? Although there was a clear developmental shift from adding to averaging in this study, the adding rule was not always used as the default. Even some of the youngest children tested, 10-year-olds, were transferring principles from their averaging model, the appropriate one for sweetness, to make judgments about the fictitious property. These results suggest that the extensitivity bias discussed by Jäger and Wilkening is not so strong that it cannot be overcome in middle-school age, at least in some domains. Nevertheless, there is still much converging evidence that children up to the age of about 10 years have special difficulties with understanding the principles governing intensive quantities such as sweetness, in contrast to extensive quantities such as heaviness.

Conclusions

As a result of a change of emphasis in studying children's intuitive physics, the field has become much richer than originally anticipated. In the traditional view, founded by

Piaget, children's knowledge of the physical world was of relatively little interest per se. Physical knowledge was studied because it promised to be the *via regia* to the uncovering of cognitive structures and their development. The physical world seemed to have a heuristic advantage: it has a logical structure, much more – so was the belief – than the social and mental world, and the child was thought to be able to internalize this structure through active explorations in everyday life. Many laws of elementary physics can be expressed via simple algebraic rules that are structurally identical. This feature made the field attractive for stage theorists. In a strict domain-general stage theory of cognitive development, it would suffice to determine for each stage the nature of *one* concept, say time. According to the theory, all other concepts for which the physical law was structurally isomorphic would then have to be the same.

It is well known that this is not what was found over decades of intensive research. The concepts that were assessed in many studies were more or less advanced between and within different domains. Further, they often proved to be highly task-dependent. The latter was seen more as a methodological embarrassment than as a natural fact. It was still assumed that it should be possible to find the pure concepts in tasks uncontaminated by demands that were not related to the logical structure in question. As a consequence, research in intuitive physics was essentially dominated by side issues of methodology. This traditional view, based on studying children's intuitive physics as a means of attaining the higher goal of revealing cognitive structures, inevitably led to a narrowing of the field.

The new look as presented in this chapter opens the field and makes it interesting for more branches within psychology and beyond. Variability in children's intuitive physics is now seen as the norm. It is no longer regarded as something that should not be there and that can be eliminated by choosing the right methods. In virtually every domain discussed here, ranging from time and speed over force and buoyancy to temperature and color intensity, children's concepts were found to be highly adaptive. Sensorimotor skills, concrete and formal operations (to use Piagetian terminology) often go hand in hand. In other instances, remarkable knowledge dissociations have been found. In these cases it seems as if the more explicit levels do not know what the more implicit levels know – and vice versa. This variability should be taken as natural, since goals are ever-changing, and since the goals determine which kind of previous knowledge is selected and integrated. Moreover, children's goals appear to change in the course of development, as recently discussed by Sophian (1997) in relation to numerical concepts. If this is true, it seems to be at least as relevant for physical concepts. The data presented in this chapter can be best interpreted if such motivational dynamics and the adaptive capabilities of children are taken into account.

Intuitive physics should no longer be viewed only as a sub-field of cognitive psychology. Formal-symbolic components of thought are generally interwoven with motivation, perception, and action. This so-called embodied knowledge plays a vital role at all ages. Triggered by children's goals, concepts typically begin as parts of various abilities, from which they may never become entirely distinct (Anderson, 1996). Intuitive physics does not develop from diffuse to lucid – or vice versa. It remains manifold over the whole lifespan, between and within single domains.

These conclusions necessarily lead to a new research strategy. It seems obsolete – and would seriously mislead the direction of inquiry – to look for entities that are probably not there: pure, naked concepts of intuitive physics operative in a context-free world. The findings discussed in the present chapter show that the attempts to construct the one and only "ideal" task for such an endeavor have been misplaced. What is needed instead is a stronger focus on performance in different contexts and, accordingly, the use of batteries of tasks varying in content, varying in information-processing demands, varying in their relative demands on cognition and action, and varying in their motivational appeal. Only such task batteries can do justice to the wide range of children's possible goals. Such a research strategy, to be sure, requires much more work than originally envisaged. However, it opens a "horn of plenty" for future research. And if this research strategy proves necessary for getting an adequate account of children's intuitive physics from the point of view of basic research, it will be all the more necessary for attempts to derive consequences for education from that basic knowledge.

CHAPTER SEVENTEEN

What is Scientific Thinking and How Does It Develop?

Deanna Kuhn

What does it mean to think scientifically? We might label a preschooler's curiosity, a high school student's answer on a physics exam, and scientists' progress in mapping the human genome as instances of scientific thinking. But if we are willing to classify such disparate phenomena under a single heading, it becomes essential that we specify what it is that they have in common. Alternatively, we might define scientific thinking narrowly, as a specific reasoning strategy (such as the control of variables strategy that has dominated research on the development of scientific thinking), or as the thinking characteristic of a narrow population (scientific thinking is what scientists do). But to do so is to vastly limit the interest and significance the phenomenon holds. This chapter begins, then, with an attempt to define scientific thinking in an inclusive way that encompasses not only the preceding examples, but numerous other instances of thinking, including many not typically associated with science.

What is scientific thinking?

Scientific thinking as knowledge-seeking

Is scientific thinking of any relevance outside of science? In this chapter I answer this question with an emphatic *yes* and characterize scientific thinking as a human activity engaged in by most people, rather than a rarefied few. As such, it connects to other forms of thinking studied by psychologists, such as inference and problem-solving (Goswami, ch. 13 this volume). In particular, I highlight its connection to argumentive thinking (Kuhn, 1991) and characterize its goals and purposes as more closely aligned with argument than with experimentation (Kuhn, 1993; Lehrer, Schauble, & Petrosino, 2001). Scientific thinking is frequently social in nature, rather than a phenomenon that only occurs inside people's heads. A group of people may rely jointly on scientific thinking in pursuing their goals.

To fully understand scientific thinking, it must be situated in a developmental framework, with a goal of identifying both its origins and endpoints. These endpoints are more general than the practices and standards of professional science. The most skilled, highly developed thinking that we identify here is essential to science, but not specific to it.

The definition of scientific thinking adopted in this chapter is *knowledge-seeking*. This definition encompasses any instance of purposeful thinking that has the objective of enhancing the seeker's knowledge. One consequence that follows from this definition is that scientific thinking is something people *do*, not something they *have*. The latter we will refer to as *scientific understanding*. When conditions are favorable, the process of scientific thinking may lead to scientific understanding as its product. Indeed, it is the desire for scientific understanding – for explanation – that drives the process of scientific thinking.

Scientific thinking and scientific understanding

The distinction between scientific thinking and scientific understanding is an important one, since there has arisen in recent years an extensive literature on children's developing understandings in the domains of physics, biology, and psychology (see Wellman & Gelman, 1998, for review). From their earliest years, children construct implicit theories that enable them to make sense of and organize their experience. These early theories are usually incorrect, as well as incomplete. In a process that has come to be referred to as *conceptual change*, these theories are revised as new evidence is encountered bearing on them. Knowledge acquisition, then, is not the accumulation of isolated bits of knowledge, but, rather, this process of conceptual change.

In contrast to the sizable body of knowledge that has accrued regarding the content of children's evolving theories within specific domains, relatively little is known about the process by means of which theory revision is accomplished. It is this process that is the concern of the present chapter. How is theory revision possible, is there a single process by means of which it occurs, and where does scientific thinking come into this picture? From an applied, educational perspective, as well as a theoretical one, the process of theory revision assumes particular significance. Enhanced understandings of scientific phenomena are certainly a goal of science education. But it is the *capacity to advance these understandings* that is reflected in scientific thinking and is at least as important as an educational goal.

On the grounds that there is no clear dividing line between informal and formal theories (Kuhn & Pearsall, 2000), we refer here to any cognitive representation of the way things are, no matter how simple, implicit, or fragmentary, as a theory, rather than reserve the latter term for theories meeting various formal criteria that might be invoked (Brewer & Samarapungavan, 1991; Wellman & Gelman, 1998). We can claim, then, that in the early years of life, theories and theory revision are common, as children seek to make sense of a widening array of experience. This early theory revision shares two important attributes with scientific thinking. First, both involve the coordination of theory and evidence – a characterization of scientific thinking common to most current accounts of it (Klahr, 2000; Klahr, Fay, & Dunbar, 1993; Klahr & Simon, 1999; Koslowski, 1996; Kuhn, 1989; Kuhn, Amsel, & O'Loughlin, 1988; Schauble, 1990, 1996; Lehrer et al., 2001; Zimmerman, 2000). Second, both can lead to enhanced understanding. There is one important difference, however, between the two. Unlike scientific thinking, early theory revision occurs implicitly and effortlessly, without conscious awareness or intent. Young children think *with* their theories, rather than about them. In the course of so doing they may revise these theories, but they are not aware that they are doing so.

The modern view of scientific thinking as theory–evidence coordination, note, can be contrasted to the pioneering work on scientific thinking by Inhelder and Piaget (1958). Despite the centrality of meaning-making in much of Piaget's writing, in this work Inhelder and Piaget conceptualized scientific reasoning strategies largely as logic-driven devices to be applied outside of any context of understanding of the phenomena being investigated. In the modern view, in contrast, theories are integral to knowledge-seeking at every phase of the process, a view consonant with modern philosophy of science (Kitcher, 1993).

Knowledge-seeking as the intentional coordination of theory and evidence

It is the intention to seek knowledge that transforms implicit theory revision into scientific thinking. Theory revision becomes something one *does*, rather than something that happens to one outside of conscious awareness. To seek knowledge is to acknowledge that one's existing knowledge is incomplete, possibly incorrect – that there is something new to know. The process of theory–evidence coordination accordingly becomes explicit and intentional. Newly available evidence is examined with regard to its implications for a theory, with awareness that the theory is susceptible to revision.

The coordination of theory and evidence that is entailed in scientific thinking may yield either of two broad categories of outcomes – congruence or discrepancy. In the first case, the new evidence that is encountered is entirely compatible with existing theories, and no new understanding results. A new instance is simply absorbed into existing understanding. In the second, more interesting case, some discrepancy between theory and evidence exists and relations between the two need to be constructed. It is possible that the discrepancy will go unrecognized, because the theory, the new evidence, or both have not been adequately represented in a manner that allows relations between them to be constructed. In this case, a likely outcome is that the evidence is ignored or distorted to allow assimilation to existing theoretical understanding. If we decide to include this as a case of scientific thinking at all, it can only be labeled as faulty scientific thinking, since one's existing understandings have been exposed to no test. No knowledge-seeking occurs, nor is the possibility of new knowledge even allowed.

Alternatively, a mental representation of discrepant evidence may be formed – a representation distinct from the theory – and its implications for the theory identified. Such cases may vary vastly in the complexity of thinking involved, but they have in common encoding and representation of the evidence distinct from the theory, which is also explicitly represented as an object of cognition, and contemplation of its implications for the theory. It is important to note that the outcome of this process remains open. It is not necessary that the theory be revised in light of the evidence, nor certainly that theory be ignored in favor of evidence, which is a misunderstanding of what is meant by theory–evidence coordination. The criterion is only that the evidence be represented in its own right and its implications for the theory contemplated. Skilled scientific thinking always entails the coordination of theories and evidence, but coordination cannot occur unless the two are encoded and represented as distinguishable entities.

In sum, then, these six criteria for genuine scientific thinking as a process (in contrast to scientific understanding as a knowledge state) can be stipulated:

1   One's existing understanding (theory) is represented as an object of cognition.
2   An intention exists to examine and potentially advance this understanding.
3   The theory's possible falsehood and susceptibility to revision is recognized.
4   Evidence as a source of potential support (or non-support) for a theory is recognized.
5   Evidence is encoded and represented distinct from the theory.
6   Implications of the evidence for the theory are identified (relations between the two are constructed).

We turn now to tracing the developmental origins of these capacities and then go on to examine them in their more sophisticated forms. Note that none of the six criteria listed above restricts scientific thinking to traditional scientific content. We are tracing, then, the development of a broad way of thinking and acquiring knowledge about the world, rather than an ability to reason about "scientific" phenomena narrowly conceived.

Developmental Origins of Scientific Thinking

A now sizable literature on children's theory of mind (Flavell, 1999; Wellman, 1988, and ch. 8 this volume) affords insight into the origins of scientific thinking because it identifies the earliest forms of a child's thinking about thinking. Thinking about thinking is not delayed until adolescence, as Inhelder and Piaget's (1958) account of formal operations implied. Rather, it is identifiable in the early forms of awareness preschool children display regarding their own and others' thinking. By age 3, they show some awareness of their own thinking processes and distinguish thinking about an object from perceiving it (Flavell, Green, & Flavell, 1995). They also begin to use mental-state concepts such as desire and intention in describing their own and others' behavior.

Differentiating assertions from evidence

Not until about age 4, however, does a child understand that mental representations, as products of the human mind, do not necessarily duplicate external reality. Before children achieve this concept of false belief, they show unwillingness to attribute to another person a belief that they themselves know to be false (Perner, 1991). Children of this young age hold a naïve epistemological theory of beliefs as mental copies of reality (Kuhn, Cheney, & Weinstock, in press). Mental representations are confined to a single reality defined by what the individual takes to be true. The world is thus a simple one of objects and events that we can characterize for ourselves and others. There are no inaccurate renderings of events.

At this level of mental development, the evaluation of falsifiable claims that is central to science cannot occur. The early theory-of-mind achievement around age 4 – in which assertions come to be understood as generating from human minds and are recognized as potentially discrepant from an external reality to which they can be compared – is thus a milestone of foundational status in the development of scientific thinking. Assertions become susceptible to evaluation vis-à-vis the reality from which they are now distinguished. The complexity of claims that a 4-year-old is able to evaluate as potentially false is extremely limited. A child of this age is capable of little more, really, than determining whether a claim regarding some physical state of affairs does or does not correspond to a reality the child can directly observe. Yet, this differentiation of assertion and evidence sets the stage for the coordinations between more complex theoretical claims and forms of evidence that are more readily recognizable as scientific thinking.

A related development during this preschool period is the ability to recognize indeterminacy, that is, to recognize situations in which two or more alternative reality states are possible and it is not known which is true, and to discriminate these indeterminate situations from determinate ones. Fay and Klahr (1996), and before them Pieraut-Le Bonniec, 1980), report development in this respect beginning in early childhood (but continuing through adolescence), as do Sodian, Zaitchik, and Carey (1991). Sodian et al. found that, by age 7, children were able to choose a determinate over an indeterminate test to find out if a mouse was large or small by placing food in a box overnight. The indeterminate option was a box with a large opening (able to accommodate a large or small mouse) and the determinate option a box with a small opening (big enough for only the small mouse). In choosing the latter, 7-year-olds also show some rudimentary skill in investigative strategy, an aspect of inquiry we discuss at length later.

An early competency that is less compelling as an origin of scientific thinking is identification of correspondences between theory and data (Ruffman, Perner, Olson, & Doherty, 1993). Connecting the two does not imply their differentiation, as Ruffman et al. claim, based on findings that 5–7-year-olds make inferences from evidence (e.g., dolls who choose red food over green food) to theory (the dolls prefer red food to green), and vice versa. Instead, theory and evidence fit together into a coherent depiction of a state of affairs. In neither the Ruffman et al. nor the Sodian et al. studies, however, is there reason to assume that the child recognizes the differing epistemological status of theory and evidence. (See Kuhn & Pearsall, 2000, for further discussion of these studies.)

Identifying evidence as a source of knowledge

Once assertions are differentiated from evidence that bears on their truth value, it becomes possible for evidence to be appreciated as a source of support for a theory and for relations between evidence and theory to be constructed. To appreciate the epistemolog-ical status of evidence, one must be sensitive to the issue of how one knows – to the sources of one's knowledge. Several researchers have reported increasing sensitivity to the sources of knowledge during the preschool years, for example in distinguishing imagining from perceiving (Woolley & Bruell, 1996), seeing from being told (Gopnik & Graf, 1988), and something just learned from something known for a long time (Taylor, Esbensen, & Bennett, 1994).

In a study of 4–6-year-olds, Pearsall and I (Kuhn & Pearsall, 2000) investigated specif-ically whether children of this age were sensitive to evidence as a source of knowledge to support the truth of a claim, distinguishable from theory that enhances plausibility of the claim. Participants were shown a sequence of pictures in which, for example, two runners compete in a race. Certain cues suggest a theory as to why one will win; for example, one has fancy running shoes and the other does not. The final picture in the sequence provides evidence of the outcome – one runner holds a trophy and exhibits a wide grin. When asked to indicate the outcome and to justify this knowledge, 4-year-olds show a fragile distinction between the two kinds of justification – "How do you know?" and "Why is it so?" – in other words, the evidence for the claim (the outcome cue in this case) versus an explanation for it (the initial theory-generating cue). Rather, the two merge into a single representation of what happened, and the child tends to choose as evidence of what happened the cue having greater explanatory value as to why it happened. Thus, children often answered the "How do you know [he won]?" question, not with evidence ("He's holding the trophy") but with a theory of why this state of affairs makes sense ("Because he has fast sneakers"). A follow-up probe, "How can you be sure this is what happened?" elicited a shift from theory-based to evidence-based responses in some cases, but, even with this prompt, 4-year-olds gave evidence-based responses on average to less than a third of the items. At age 6, confu-sions between theory and evidence still occurred, but children of this age were correct a majority of the time. A group of adults, in contrast, made no errors.

Development of theory–evidence coordination skill as a continuing process

By the end of the preschool years, when children have begun to show an appreciation of the role of evidence in supporting a falsifiable claim, do they confront further challenges in coordinating theories and evidence? The research on older children and adolescents that we turn to now contains substantial evidence of difficulties in this respect, with degree of difficulty influenced by the number and level of complexity of the theoretical alterna-tives, as well as complexity of the evidence. Thus, as Klahr (2000) similarly concludes, coordination of theory and evidence is not a discrete skill that emerges at a single point in cognitive development. Rather, it must be achieved at successively greater levels of com-plexity, over an extended period of development. This is especially so if it is to keep pace with increasingly complex models of scientific understanding that are encountered with increasing age. In evaluating such models, requisite skills are invoked: What data support or contradict this piece of the model? How can we test whether particular segments of the model are correct? In such contexts, even able adults' limitations in coordinating theory and evidence become evident. The range and variability in the scientific thinking skills of adults is in fact striking (Kuhn et al., 1988, 1995).

Coordination of Theory and Evidence in the Early School Years

Preschool children, we noted, are able to coordinate a simple event claim and evidence regarding its truth, e.g., they can verify whether the claim that candy is in the pencil box is true or false. More complex claims, however, which begin to assume greater similarity to genuine theories, cause difficulty among school-age children. One such form of rudimentary theory is the imposition of a categorization scheme on a set of instances. Categorization constitutes a theory, in stipulating that some instances are identical to others but different from a third set with respect to some defining attribute(s). Lehrer and Romberg (1996) describe the conceptual obstacles young school-age children encounter in representing theory and data as they engage in such seemingly simple tasks as categorizing classmates' favorite activities and representing their findings.

If children are asked to first formulate the theory and then evaluate it against data, their difficulties become even more pronounced. In an interesting study of elementary forms of theory–evidence coordination, Lehrer and Schauble (2000) asked kindergarten through fifth-graders to examine a set of drawings done by other children in grades K, 1, 3, and 5, with the artists' grades not identified. The children's task was first to sort the drawings into piles according to what they believed the artists' grade in school to be. The second task was to label these categories in terms of a set of attributes that defined them, i.e., to identify the respects in which drawings in each category were similar and differed from those in other categories. In performing the second task, children were allowed to revise their sortings if they wished, and upon completion they were asked to "check" the sorted pictures against the category criteria they had developed. The sorted drawings thus constituted the data on which children were asked to impose a theory.

Lehrer and Schauble report substantial development during this elementary-school age range in the success with which children carry out this task of coordinating theory and evidence. Among younger children, sorting is treated as an empirical task of organizing and displaying data which have been categorized based on properties that can be directly observed and known and do not need to be articulated. Theory development (defining the sorted piles by their features) is a separate task that may be undertaken, but it is not connected to the empirical sorting task. Such feature identifications are treated as "after-the-fact descriptions of pictures already assigned to a category by other means" (p. 60), rather than as criteria for sorting the pictures. When asked to check sorted pictures against the category attributes they had identified, younger children did not appear to consider whether a picture's placement violated a category definition, they ignored mismatches, and they made few changes.

By fourth grade, in contrast, children were better able to coordinate the two tasks. They regarded the features not as after-the-fact descriptions but as criteria a picture must meet to be included in a category. They were able to make adjustments to the data once the theoretical criteria were formulated, going back and forth between the sorting and the category-definition tasks as needed.

The task Lehrer and Schauble pose differs in two ways from the more typical scientific thinking task that we turn to in the next section. First, the theories that Lehrer and Schauble ask children to coordinate with data are first-order theories. First-order theorizing is performed on objects or events, indicating how they are related to one another (typically, by classifying them into categories). Second-order theorizing is performed on the products of first-order theorizing. In general, second-order theories stipulate how the categories (of objects or events) that constitute first-order theories are related to one another. Most often, the relations of interest are causal, e.g., between event categories such as clouds and rain or attribute categories such as wealth and happiness. Causal relations are of course fundamental to full-fledged scientific theories.

Second, Lehrer and Schauble do not engage their young participants in the entire cycle of authentic scientific investigation: formation of a question or hypothesis, planning and conducting an investigation, analyzing the results, drawing inferences, and debating their implications within a scientific community. Instead, Lehrer and Schauble's purpose was to explore how young children cope with highly constrained forms of theory–evidence coordination. We turn now to this coordination process in its more typical, more complex forms.

Phases of Scientific Thinking: Inquiry, Analysis, Inference, and Argument

As Klahr (2000) notes, very few studies of scientific thinking encompass the entire cycle of scientific investigation, a cycle I characterize here as consisting of four major phases: inquiry, analysis, inference, and argument. A number of researchers have confined their studies to only a portion of the cycle, most often the evaluation of evidence (Amsel & Brock, 1996; Klaczynski, 2000; Koslowski, 1996), a research design that links the study of scientific reasoning to research on inductive causal inference (Lien & Cheng, 2000). Of studies in which participants acquire their own data, most, following the lead of Inhelder and Piaget (1958), have focused their attention on the control of variables strategy (in which a focal variable is manipulated to assess its effect, while all other variables are held constant), as an isolated cognitive strategy divorced from a context of the theoretical meaning of the phenomena being investigated or the goals of the investigations conducted. In the remainder of this chapter, as well as focusing on research that examines strategies in a context of theoretical understanding, we focus on more recent studies that encompass the entire cycle of inquiry, analysis, inference, and argument. These studies offer a picture of how the strategies associated with each phase of scientific investigation are situated within a context of all the others and how they influence one another.

The microgenetic method

We also focus in this chapter on *microgenetic* research (Kuhn, 1995; Siegler & Crowley, 1991), that is, studies in which an individual engages in the same essential task over multiple sessions, allowing the researcher to observe a dynamic process of change in the strategies that are applied to the task. Participants in microgenetic studies are observed in the process of acquiring new knowledge over time. Knowledge acquisition is best conceptualized as a process of theory–evidence coordination, rather than an accumulation of facts (Kuhn, 2000b). A major finding from microgenetic research has been that an individual applies a range of alternative strategies in knowledge-acquisition tasks. The selection of strategies chosen for application evolves over time, toward more frequent use of more developmentally advanced strategies. The theory–evidence coordination process of concern to us here, then, while itself dynamic, is likely to undergo modifications in its own nature as it is applied over time. Microgenetic change can thus be observed at two levels: Knowledge (or understanding) changes, but so do the strategies by means of which this knowledge is acquired. Indeed, the latter is a primary thesis of this chapter: the process of theory–evidence coordination shows developmental change. The microgenetic method offers insight into how this change occurs.

The microgenetic studies by Klahr and his associates (Klahr, 2000; Klahr, Fay, & Dunbar, 1993) have followed children and adults asked to conduct investigations of the function of a particular key in controlling the behavior of an electronic robot toy, or, in another version, the behavior of a dancer who performs various movements in a computer simulation. To do this, individuals need to coordinate hypotheses about this function with data they generate, or, in Klahr's (2000) terminology, to coordinate searches of an hypothesis space and an experiment space. Consistent with the findings reported in this chapter, Klahr and his associates find younger children less able to meet this challenge than are older children or adults.

My own microgenetic studies (Kuhn & Phelps, 1982; Kuhn, Schauble, & Garcia-Mila, 1992; Kuhn, Garcia-Mila, Zohar, & Andersen, 1995; Kuhn, Black, Keselman, & Kaplan, 2000), as well as studies by Schauble (1990, 1996) and Penner and Klahr (1996) address what we have regarded as a prototypical form of scientific inquiry – the situation in which a number of variables have potential causal connections to an outcome and the investigative task is to choose instances for examination and on this basis to identify causal and noncausal variables, with the goals of predicting and explaining variations in outcome. Examined here in their simplest, most generic form, these are common objectives of professional scientists engaged in authentic scientific inquiry.

Following our initial assessment of their own theories regarding the presence and direction of causal effects and the mechanisms underlying them, participants in our studies engage in repeated investigative cycles (within a session and across multiple sessions) in which they identify a question, select instances for examination, analyze and make comparisons, and draw conclusions. They also make predictions regarding outcomes and justify these predictions, allowing us to compare implicit causal theories regarding effects of the variables with the earlier voiced explicit theories regarding these effects. We have conducted these studies in a variety of physical and social domains involving, for example, the speed of cars traveling around a computerized racetrack, the speed of toy boats traveling down a makeshift canal, the variables influencing the popularity of children's TV programs, the variables affecting children's school achievement, the variables affecting a teacher-aide's performance in the classroom, and, most recently, the variables influencing several kinds of natural disasters – floods, earthquakes, and avalanches.

The illustrations in this chapter are drawn from pre-adolescent boys' investigations of a single domain (earthquakes), to facilitate comparison and to highlight differences in performance. The earthquake problem (designed by Vaughn, 2000) is presented as a computer simulation in which five dichotomous features have potential causal effects on the risk of earthquake (portrayed on a "risk meter" with four gradations from lowest to highest risk). Two of the features – type of bedrock (igneous or sedimentary) and speed of S waves (slow or fast) – in fact have no effect on outcome, while the other three – water quality (good or poor), radon gas levels (light or heavy), and snake activity (high or low) – have simple additive effects.

The inquiry phase

We begin with an excerpt from the investigations of 10-year-old Brad, who does not see the goal of the task as analysis. In identifying the second instance he wishes to examine, he commented:

> Last time, the [sedimentary] rock was like white. This one [igneous] is sort of like not. It looks like it's going to just blow up any second. This [sedimentary] one looks like it's okay. [So which one do you want to choose to investigate?] Sedimentary. [Why?] Because last time I chose sedimentary as well and it seemed to work out pretty good. The igneous looks like it's about to explode any second.

Brad's primary objective, it appears, is to achieve a "good" outcome, rather than to understand the role of the different features in producing different kinds of outcomes. Another approach common among students of Brad's age is to have no other goal than to "experiment," to "try different stuff and see what happens," with no particular intention or organization shaping their investigations. These students, we find, rarely go on to make any informative comparisons in the analysis phase.

The *inquiry* phase of scientific investigation (figure 17.1) is a crucial one in which the goals of the activity are formulated, the questions to be asked identified, and the remaining phases thereby shaped (see left side of figure 17.1, which lists the tasks that characterize the inquiry phase). The ovals in the upper center of figure 17.1 portray the meta-task and metastrategic knowledge associated with this phase.

The most fundamental challenge of the inquiry phase is to recognize that the database I have the opportunity to access yields information that bears on the theories I hold – a recognition that eludes many young investigators. The issue is not how heavily such data are weighed relative to pre-existing theories, but simply to recognize that these data stand independently of and *speak to* a claim being made. Once the relevance of the data in this respect is recognized, questions can be formulated of a form that is productive in connecting data and theory.

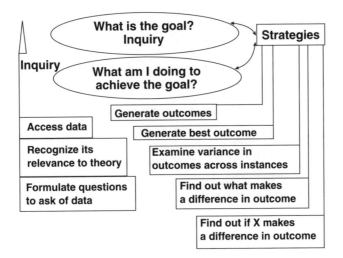

Figure 17.1   The inquiry phase

The various strategies that can be observed in response to the tasks of the inquiry phase are portrayed on the right side of figure 17.1. Here (in contrast to the left side of figure 17.1, where objectives are compatible), there appears a set of competing strategies which overlap in their usage and are of varying degrees of adequacy (with more adequate strategies appearing further down in the figure). At the lowest level, a strategy for some individuals (or for a particular individual some of the time) may be the simple one of activity, i.e., choosing instances and generating outcomes. Later, after the phenomenon has been observed a number of times, the dominant strategy may become one of producing the most desirable or interesting outcome, as Brad illustrates. The major developmental shift is one from strategies of activity to genuine inquiry, which in its most rudimentary appearance takes the form of "What is making a difference?" or "What will enable me to predict outcomes?" In more advanced forms, inquiry becomes focused on the specific features in terms of which there is variability, and, ultimately, on the effect of a specific feature, "Does X make a difference?"

Analysis and inference phases

The *analysis* phase of scientific inquiry is depicted in figure 17.2. To engage in productive analysis (left side of figure 17.2), some segment of the database must be accessed, attended to, processed, and represented as such, i.e., as evidence to which one's theory can be related, and these data must be operated on (through comparison and pattern detection), in order to reach the third phase, which yields the product of these operations – *inference*. The strategies that can be observed being applied to this task reflect the struggle to coordinate theories and evidence. As seen on the right side of figure 17.2, theory predominates in the lower-level strategies, and only with the gradually more advanced strategies does evidence acquire the power to influence theory.

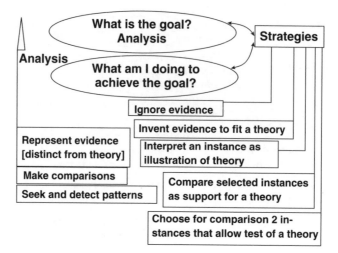

Figure 17.2   The analysis phase

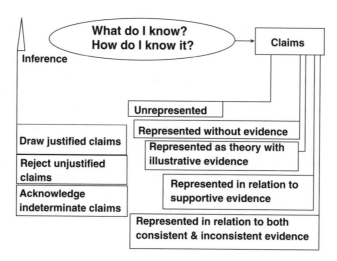

Figure 17.3   The inference phase

In moving from the analysis to the *inference* phase, we move from procedural strategies to declarative claims. As shown on the left side of figure 17.3, the inference phase involves inhibiting claims that are not justified, as well as making those that are. The inferential processes that may be applied to this task (right side of figure 17.3) range in adequacy from no processing of the evidence and no conscious awareness of one's theories (so-called "theories in action") to the skilled coordination of theory and evidence, which entails understanding the implications of evidence as supporting or disconfirming one's theories.

In contrast to Brad, 11-year-old Tom exhibits a more advanced level of investigation in which he sets out to identify effects of individual features. Two characteristics, however, limit the effectiveness of Tom's investigations. First, he believes he can find out the effects of all features at one time and hence does not focus his inquiry on any particular feature. Second, his investigations are theory-dominated to the undesirable extent that the evidence he generates he does not mentally represent in a form that is distinct from his theories.

In response to the first instance he chose to examine, Tom noted the outcome of highest risk level, but, contrary to Brad, he regarded this result favorably and commented:

> I'm feeling really good about this. [Why?] Like I said before on everything. The water quality being poor. Obviously the earthquake would contaminate the water in some way. The S-waves would go fast because logically thinking even big earthquakes happen pretty quickly. Gas, I figured it'd be kind of hard to breathe in an earthquake. Like I said before about the snakes, in the '86 earthquake, dogs started howling before it happened.

Tom, then, appeared quite ready to interpret multiple variables as causally implicated in an outcome, based on a single co-occurrence of one level of the variable and an outcome. We have referred to the mental model of causality underlying this stance as a *co-occurrence* model (Kuhn et al., 2000). Typically, the single-instance inferences deriving from this model are theory-laden in the sense that the empirical observation is seen not so much as a test of, or even evidence bearing on, the theory, as it is simply an "illustration" of the theory in operation. Tom is "feeling good" because his theories have, from his perspective, withstood the test of empirical verification. In reality, of course, they have not been tested at all.

In choosing a second instance to observe, Tom used a strategy that is also common:

> I'm going to do everything the opposite of what I did before. [Why?] Because I want to see if there's risk or no risk involved.

Tom went on to declare, however, "Actually, I'm going to mix it up kind of," and after several alternations back and forth he ended up changing bedrock from igneous (chosen for the first instance he examined) to sedimentary, water quality from poor to good, and S-wave rate from fast to slow. Gas levels he left unchanged at heavy, and snake activity unchanged at high.

Tom then observed the outcome fall to medium-high risk and made this interpretation:

> Bedrock makes no difference. No actually it makes a difference. Snake activity makes a difference. And water quality . . . hmm, yeah it brought it down. That was probably half the reason that lowered [the risk] down, with the bedrock and the S-wave. Bedrock made a difference I think because it lowered it down because . . . well, it [sedimentary rock] seemed less threatening, so I figured it lowered it down. Snake activity, like I said before, animals act up before disasters happen.

Note the predominant role that theory plays in Tom's implicating bedrock as affecting the outcome. Snake activity, note, Tom implicated as causal even though it remained at an unchanged high level in both of the instances he had observed up to this point. The interviewer probed Tom about this feature:

> [Suppose someone disagreed and said that snake activity makes no difference. What would you tell them? Could you tell them that you found out here that it did make a difference?] Well, if you did it low, probably everything's normal because the snakes wouldn't be acting up in some odd way.

Thus, Tom's claim rests on evidence (regarding low snake activity) that he does not in fact have. Tom and the interviewer go on to have a similar exchange regarding gas level, which also has remained at the same (heavy) level across the two instances, and this time, Tom does not even make reference to evidence:

> The gas makes a difference because the heavier it is, the harder it would be to breathe. [Suppose someone disagreed and said that gas level makes no difference. How could you show them that you're right? Did you see anything here that shows you that it does make a difference?] Well, I think it makes a difference because . . . let me summarize this up. When it's heavy there are more things in the air to clog up your lungs.

Finally, based on the two instances available, Tom again implicated water quality, which has covaried with outcome, as causal. He changed his mind about S-wave rates, however, which also covaried with outcome, now claiming this feature to be noncausal:

> Water quality makes a big difference. If it's good it wouldn't be contaminated by an earthquake, which also brought [risk] down. And the S-waves, they're going slowly, always moving. So they don't really make a difference.

These excerpts from Tom's investigative activity suggest that when data are not represented in their own right distinct from theory, the potential for scientific analysis remains limited. It should be emphasized again, however, that the scientific thinking tasks described here are *not* ones that ask individuals to cast aside their own beliefs about the world in favor of some arbitrary new information. Rather, they assess the ability to access and represent new evidence and to appreciate the relation it bears to different theoretical claims. Skilled scientific thinking always entails the coordination of theories and evidence, and this coordination requires that the two be clearly distinguished. Someone could say, "This is what this evidence implies for these theories, although other sources of support I have for some of these theories lead me to maintain belief in them in the face of your disconfirming evidence." This individual would do perfectly well in our tasks. More troubling are those whose beliefs *are* influenced by the evidence but who remain metacognitively unaware that this has happened and, more broadly, of why they claim what they do.

Mental models of causality and their implications for scientific investigation

Mark, also age 11, does better than Tom in representing data separately from his theories and drawing on these data as a basis for his inferences. In other respects, however, his approach is like Tom's. Mark implicates features as causal based on a single co-occurrence of variable level and outcome. In choosing an instance for observation, he intends "to try to find out about everything," and in choosing a second instance, he decides to "do the opposite of each one." Mark saw risk level drop (from instance 1 to 2) from medium-high to low risk. In interpreting the second outcome, he implicated four of the five varying features as causal (with the justification that they covaried with outcome) and yet dismissed the fifth (for which evidence was identical) on the basis of his theory that it didn't matter.

The performance of both Mark and Tom is consistent with the interpretation of their causal analysis and inference as based on the co-occurrence mental model. Both boys falsely include as causal a variable that either co-occurs with outcome in a single instance or covaries with outcome over two instances. Mark also shows an even more interesting inferential error, which (following Inhelder & Piaget, 1958) we have called *false exclusion* (in contrast to the *false inclusion* errors just noted). In choosing a third instance for examination, Mark changed some features and left others the same and observed a low-risk outcome. Following causal inferences for several features, Mark made two noncausal inferences, using false exclusion to justify each. Water quality, he said, made no difference because.

> before [instance 1] it was good and had medium-high risk. This time it's good and has low risk. [What does that tell you?] It probably doesn't matter.

The implication is that another feature has produced variation showing that feature's causal power in affecting the outcome, and the feature in question can therefore be discounted. Mark's inference regarding snake activity was identical in form. Both of these features, note, he had earlier implicated as causal, illustrating the vacillation in claims that our microgenetic studies have shown to be common.

Both false exclusion and false inclusion are consistent with the co-occurrence mental model. The co-occurrence of a level of one variable and an outcome is sufficient to explain that outcome. The potential causal influence of a second variable, therefore, need not be treated as additive. Instead, the second variable can be invoked as a different explanation for a later outcome, or the second variable can be discounted because the first feature explains the outcome (false exclusion, if the discounted variable has not been varied). Accordingly, then, the co-occurrence mental model treats causal influences as neither consistent nor additive.

Computing the consistent effects of multiple variables on an outcome rests on a different, more advanced model of causality. Identification of an individual effect ("Does X make a difference?") is only one step in explaining the causal structure of a domain. The broader task is to identify the effect of each of the varying features, and then – a part of the task that has received little attention – consider their additive (or possibly interactive) effects on outcome. Taking into account all such effects is of course the only way to achieve the goal of accurate prediction of outcomes. Doing so requires that a different mental model of causality replace the co-occurrence model, one in which multiple causes operate individually in a consistent fashion, simultaneously and additively producing an outcome. (Interactive effects require a further level of understanding.)

In our research, we have observed an association between the goal of identifying effects of individual features and use of controlled comparison as an analysis strategy (Kuhn et al., 2000). Arguably this is so because both rest on the mature mental model of causality in which multiple individual variables additively influence an outcome. In the absence of this model, one's task goal is unlikely to be identification of the effect of each of the individual variables. Accordingly, neither attribute of the controlled comparison strategy will be compelling. The "comparison" attribute is not compelling, given it entails comparing the outcomes associated with different levels of an individual variable for the purpose of assessing the effect of that variable. And the "controlled" attribute is even less compelling, since it is the individual effects of other variables that need to be controlled.

The immature mental model of causality underlying Tom's and Mark's performance, then, limits adoption of either the goals or strategies that make for effective scientific investigation. Unsurprisingly, neither Mark's nor Tom's investigations led to judgments of any greater than chance correctness. Mark, for example, concluded (after examining four instances) that all features except water quality are causal. He was thus wrong about three of the five features. Moreover, when asked how sure he was that he had found out which features were and weren't making a difference, on a 1–10 scale, Mark rated his certainty as "9."

The performance of 12-year-old Robbie can be contrasted to that of Tom and Mark. Robbie's approach initially does not look that different. He chose as the second instance "the opposite of what I did last time." When asked for his inferences, however, he initially implicated S-wave rates, but then said: "Well, I should . . . I can do a test to find out actually." Robbie then said: "I am going to keep everything the same as last time and just change the igneous to sedimentary to see if it alters the thing." In response to the interviewer's question, "Why are you keeping the others the same?" Robbie responded:

> If you alter one thing and it's different, that means it has to be the difference. So the type of bedrock does not make a difference. [How do you know?] Because it [the outcome] didn't change. If it had changed, it would mean that it mattered.

Robbie proceeded in an identical manner to assess effects of the remaining features and was able to explain his strategy explicitly:

> I'm doing the same thing as last time. I'll keep everything the same except for gas level, which I am changing to the opposite, light.

After satisfying himself that he had discovered which features did or did not make a difference, Robbie went on to the next segment of the activity, in which he is asked to make predictions about outcomes and then to indicate (as an assessment of implicit causal judgments) which features had influenced the prediction. For each of his predictions, Robbie implicated the same three features. The interviewer asked, "Would it always be these three for every prediction, or would it be different for some predictions?", to which Robbie replied: "It would always be these three for all predictions, because [the other two] didn't matter. It was only these three that actually mattered."

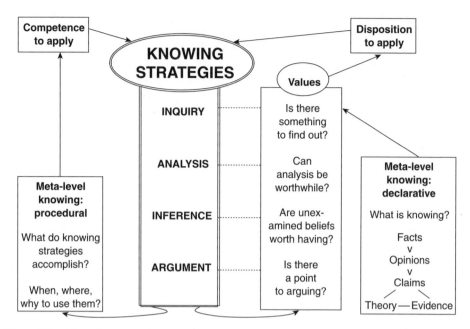

Figure 17.4 The role of meta-level operators in scientific thinking. From D. Kuhn (in press). How do people know? *Psychological Science*

With this awareness of what and how he knows, Robbie would be well equipped to defend his claims in discussion with others. This is an important achievement, since a final *argument* phase of scientific thinking consists of debate of the claims that are the product of the earlier phases, in a framework of alternatives and evidence (see figure 17.4). As is the case for the other phases, a range of strategies can be identified, strategies that an individual draws on with varying degrees of probability. Given sustained exercise, these argumentive strategies undergo development (Kuhn, 1991; Kuhn, Shaw, & Felton, 1997; Felton & Kuhn, in press). The products of the argumentive process are revised and strengthened *claims*, strengthened in the sense of being better supported as an outcome of the argumentive process.

The progression from absence of an analysis goal on the part of 10-year-old Brad to 12-year-old Robbie's explicit awareness of the effective analysis strategies he used should not be taken as implying an orderly age-related progression in the development of scientific thinking skills. To the contrary, the norm is wide inter-individual variability. As often as 12-year-olds like Robbie, we see children of similar age like Maria and even adults like Carmen, reported in our earlier research (Kuhn et al., 1995), who over seven or eight weekly sessions examine a database that in fact provides no support for a theory – for example that the presence of music increases the popularity of a TV program – and yet maintain to the end not just the correctness of their theory, but, more importantly, that the data they have examined *shows* that it is correct.

Such examples extend scientific thinking beyond traditional science and into the realm of the everyday thinking people use to justify their beliefs. In these realms, people typically hold entrenched beliefs, supported by contextually rich representations and sometimes significant affect. This richness may facilitate thinking about such topics, but it may also make it more difficult to think well about them. This was the finding of a comparison of inquiry processes in social science vs. physical science domains (Kuhn et al., 1995). Thus, while it would be hard to contest that "valid experimentation strategies support the development of more accurate and complete knowledge" (Schauble, 1996, p. 118), it is less clear that rich knowledge necessarily enhances the selection of valid experimentation strategies.

The Role of Meta-Level Processes in Scientific Thinking

Fully as important as the inter-individual variability portrayed by the preceding examples is the intra-individual variability that microgenetic studies have found to be the norm: Individuals typically have available a range of different strategies of differing levels of advancement and effectiveness (Kuhn, 1995; Siegler, 1996). Development consists of shifts in the frequencies with which different strategies are chosen for application. To explain development, we therefore need to turn to a meta-level of functioning (Kuhn, 2000b) – the level at which strategies are selected and their use monitored. The meta-level involves knowing about knowing. Strong meta-level processes afford Robbie the certainty that he has drawn correct conclusions, while insufficiently developed meta-level processes are implicated in Tom and Mark's false certainty that their inferences are correct.

Figure 17.4 places the strategies and phases of knowledge-seeking in the context of meta-level processes that regulate them. On the left side is the *procedural* meta-level that selects knowledge-seeking strategies to apply, in relation to task goals, and manages and monitors their application. Feedback from this application is directed back to the meta-level. This feedback leads to enhanced awareness of the task goal and the extent to which it is being met by different strategies, as well as enhanced awareness of the strategies themselves (in particular, increased recognition of the power and the limitations associated with each). These enhancements at the meta-level lead to revised strategy selection and hence changes in the distribution of strategies observed at the performance level. In a continuous process, this modified usage in turn feeds back to enhanced understanding at the meta-level, eventually getting the individual to the performance goal of consistent use of the more powerful strategies (Kuhn, 2000b).

A notable feature of this model is that it accounts for the common finding that efforts to induce change directly at the performance level have only limited success, reflected in failures to transfer outside a specific context. As the figure 17.4 model would predict, if nothing has been done to influence the meta-level, new behavior will quickly disappear once the instructional context is withdrawn and individuals resume meta-level management of their own behavior. This limitation applies to many of the studies that have undertaken to improve scientific thinking simply by teaching strategies ("do this"), and, if meta-level understanding is addressed at all, by assessing children's knowledge that this is what they should do. The meta-level understanding that is critical, in contrast, is *why* this is what to do and why other strategies are less effective or wrong. In one of the most meticulously designed training studies, for example, Chen and Klahr (1999) explained to second- to fourth-graders that some (confounded) comparisons were bad comparisons while other (unconfounded) comparisons were good comparisons because just one feature changed. In post-tests in new contexts, many children were able to choose a good comparison over a bad one and to justify it as good because only one feature changed. Indicative of their fragile meta-level knowledge, however, was the continued mixture of correct and incorrect strategies shown by a majority of children in conducting their own investigations.

The right side of figure 17.4 depicts *declarative* meta-level understanding regarding what it means to know something. Epistemological understanding regarding knowledge and knowing is a crucial underpinning of scientific thinking. What is science and scientific knowledge? Most children bring an *absolutist* understanding to their study of science (Hofer & Pintrich, 1997; Kuhn, Cheney, & Weinstock, in press; Smith, Maclin, Houghton, & Hennessey, 2000): Scientific knowledge is an accumulating set of certain facts. By adolescence, most have made the radical shift to a *multiplist* epistemology. The discovery that even experts disagree leads to an awareness of the uncertain, subjective nature of knowing. This awareness initially assumes such proportions, however, that it overpowers any objective standard that could serve as a basis for evaluating conflicting claims. Because claims are subjective opinions freely chosen by their holders and everyone has a right to their opinion, all opinions are equally right. By adulthood, many, though by no means all, people have reintegrated the objective dimension of knowing and espouse the *evaluativist* understanding that some claims are superior to others to the extent they are better supported by argument and evidence. It is only at this level that the coordination of theories and evidence that marks authentic science is fully understood. If facts can be readily ascertained with certainty, as the absolutist understands, or if any claim is as valid as any other, as the multiplist understands, scientific inquiry remains a shallow, marginally relevant enterprise.

Values are the final component that figures importantly in figure 17.4. Epistemic understanding informs intellectual values with respect to each of the four knowledge-seeking phases, and values in turn affect disposition to action. Meta-level procedural knowing is necessary if one is to be able to apply knowing strategies effectively, but it is the intellectual values depicted in figure 17.4 that determine whether one regards knowledge-seeking as worthwhile and is therefore disposed to engage in it. Our earlier definition of scientific thinking as knowledge-seeking thus accords values a central place in conceptions of scientific thinking.

Scientific Thinking as a Social Process

Meta-level understanding is a crucial part of what needs to develop in scientific thinking. Fortunately, like performance, it shows improvement over time, when thinking is exercised, and correspondences are apparent in the improvements that occur at the two levels (Kuhn & Pearsall, 1998). Returning scientific thinking to its real-life social context is one approach to strengthening the meta-level components of scientific thinking. When students find themselves having to justify claims and strategies to one another, normally implicit meta-level cognitive processes become externalized, making them more available. Social scaffolding, then, may assist a less-able collaborator to monitor and manage strategic operations in a way that he or she cannot yet do alone, as in this example from two girls working on the problem of what variables affect the speed that model boats travel down an improvised canal (Kuhn, 2000b):

S. We found out about the weight.
N. No, about the boat size, that's all.
S. Oh, the boat size.
N. Just talk about the boat size.

Peer collaboration can be highly variable, however, in its form and effects. The interchange in box 17.1 (which occurs just after a second instance of evidence has been observed), comes from a single segment of a session with the earthquake problem in which 10-year-old Brad is working together with 11-year-old Tod (Kuhn, unpublished). In discussing the gas-level feature, Tod supports and strengthens Brad's theory-based claim by drawing on evidence. With respect to the snake-activity and water-quality features, the boys disagree and we see Tod vacillate between endorsement and rejection of Brad's incorrect inference strategies. In one case, Tod ends up succumbing to Brad's inferior reasoning. In the other, he does not and the disagreement stands. It is clear, nonetheless, that both boys' scientific thinking has been exercised by the exchange.

Box 17.1   Excerpt of discussion of Brad and Tod in the earthquake problem

GAS LEVEL
B [Brad]. Gas level makes a difference because if an earthquake is coming the level of oxygen
        would decrease I think because the earthquake is taking up all the oxygen.
T [Tod]. Can I say something? We also know that by trial and error. Last time we had
        heavy gas and got low-medium risk. Since we changed the gas to low, we found
        out gas did make a difference.

SNAKE ACTIVITY
T. Brad, before you move on, how do you know snake activity makes a difference?
B. It makes no difference.
T. Okay, okay.
I. [Interviewer]. Well, let's talk about this a minute. One of you says it makes a difference,
        the other that it doesn't. Did you find that out, Brad, by looking at these cases?
B. Yes.
I. How did you know?
B. Well, last time I kept snake activity the same and I only changed two things, and I believe
        those were the ones that made a difference. Now I'm just gonna keep snake activity the
        same, because it does not make any difference.

I. Tod, do you disagree?

T. No. I was asking him the same question; how did he know?

I. Well, he's told you how he knows; what do you think of his answer?

T. I think it's correct, because he just made some changes [itemizes] . . . and all those changes made it go to low. But if he'd changed snake activity, it may have made a difference and it may have not.

I. But he didn't change snake activity.

T. Right, he didn't and that's why he said that snake activity didn't make a difference.

I. So, do we know then that snake activity makes no difference?

B. No, not positively, but it's a good estimate.

T. If we changed it to heavy next time, and keep all of these [other features the same], we may find out if it makes a difference.

I. But I thought before you were both telling me you'd already found out it does not.

B. That's my good estimate.

T. I agree. But just to make sure, change it to heavy. If risk went back to low, we'd know it would make a difference.

I. And what do we know now about snake activity?

T. We are pretty sure it makes no difference.

I. Why is that?

T. Because he made changes in everything else and he kept snake activity the same and it went to the lowest.

WATER QUALITY

B. Water quality made a difference because last time I kept it good. I think it made a difference because the water would be sinking down if there was an earthquake coming.

I. Do the records show whether it made a difference?

B. Yes. Because last time it was good and this time it was good too. I think it should be good because I got the lowest risk and last time I got medium-low risk. I changed two [others] and it got me down to the lowest risk. So I think the water quality should be good.

I. And how do you know water quality makes a difference?

B. Because last time it was good and this time it was good and [both times] we got the lowest risk.

I. Tod, what do you think?

T. Last time it was good and this time good. I say it wouldn't really make a difference. They were both the same and how would you see that it made a difference if they were both the same, if they were both good?

I. Brad, what do you think?

B. It makes a difference, because I kept it good and I got a medium-low risk; this time I got a [even] lower risk.

I. So what does that tell you again?

B. Two of my answers were wrong last time. And I think I changed them to the right answers this time.

I. And so does water quality make a difference?

B. It makes a difference.

I. Tod, what do you think?

T. We don't know if it does.

The excerpt in box 17.1 brings the individual reasoning strategies examined earlier into a more appropriate and richer context of social discourse or argument. A number of authors have addressed scientific thinking as a form of discourse (Hatano & Inagaki, 1991; Herrenkohl & Guerra, 1998). This is of course the richest and most authentic context in which to examine scientific thinking, as long as the mistake is not made of regarding these discourse forms as exclusive to science. Scientific discourse asks, most importantly, "How do you know?" or "What is the support for your statement?". When children participate in discourse that poses these questions, they acquire the skills and values that lead them to pose the same questions to themselves (Olson & Astington, 1993). Although central to science, this critical development extends far beyond the borders of traditional scientific disciplines.

Educating Scientific Thinking and Thinkers

Science education does not necessarily involve scientific thinking. In the kinds of learning experiences that are commonplace in much of science education, information may be presented, or a phenomenon demonstrated, with the questions the new information is intended to answer either left unclear or externally imposed. Students may, in such cases, respond in routinized ways that avoid scientific thinking entirely.

Researchers in science education of course strive to design the sorts of educational activities that are likely to stimulate and develop scientific thinking. Increasing interest in inquiry learning is apparent in educational literature in recent years (Kuhn et al., 2000). Its practice assumes a wide variety of forms and is usually embedded in a curriculum having many content goals regarding what students need to learn about the phenomena being investigated. Still, science educators also hope that inquiry activities will promote the kinds of process skills that have been the subject of the present chapter.

Methodologically, science educators face the challenge of working with an entire classroom of children. Rarely do they have the luxury of following the thinking of individual students across a sustained period, in a way that would document the detailed kinds of scientific thinking they are doing. We need to know what students are doing, cognitively, when they engage in inquiry learning and how this thinking evolves with exercise. This knowledge is the foundation needed to support the development of sound, well-justified inquiry teaching practices.

Much educational practice in preschool and early elementary years rests on the idea of young children's "natural curiosity." Practices that encourage children to ask questions, to observe, and to express their ideas in response to teachers' questions have been accepted as sufficient components to define good "constructivist" teaching practice. It becomes clear, however, by the middle elementary school years, that these practices do not by themselves constitute an adequate instructional model. Palincsar and Magnusson (in press) note "the impossibility that children will come to meaningful understandings of the nature of scientific thinking simply through the process of interacting with materials and phenomena." Video-based teacher-training material of a constructivist bent commonly features a teacher asking a bright-eyed, appealing youngster, "What do you think,

Tommy?" making a minimal acknowledgment ("Okay, good"), and then turning to the next child with the same query. The richness of inquiry teaching and learning depends on the teacher's *doing something* with that child's response, in a way that leaves the child with a richer, more elaborated conceptual representation than the child had previously. Such conceptual representations encompass far more than specific content, extending, for example, to understandings of what kinds of questions are worth asking and why. To develop these instructional skills, teachers need to understand what the child is bringing to the instructional situation and exactly what kinds of process skills are in the process of developing (Lehrer et al., 2001).

As highlighted here through the emphasis on meta-level understanding, most import-ant for teachers to convey to children about science is not the *what* or the *how* but the *why*, including ultimately, why inquiry and analysis are worth the effort they entail. These values, as shown in figure 17.4, are supported by epistemological understanding of what scientific knowing entails. It is here that the variance emerges with respect to whether learned skills will be used. If we can clearly identify what the cognitive skills are and how they develop, we are in the best position to learn how to promote understanding of their value. Thus, science educators need to base their efforts on a sound understanding of the entire complex of skills and meta-skills that have the potential to develop during the child-hood and adolescent years. Educators who are informed developmentalists stand to bring the strengths of both traditions to the challenge that science education poses.

CHAPTER EIGHTEEN

Reading Development and Dyslexia

Margaret J. Snowling

In most societies children begin formal reading instruction before they are 7 years old. However, learning to read is not a trivial task. At what is usually considered the basic level, it involves learning how the symbols of printed words are related to the linguistic features of spoken words, mappings that vary considerably in their consistency across languages. Since the goal of reading is understanding, reading also involves a range of higher-level cognitive processes that are used in the transformation of print into ideas. These include, word- and sentence-level comprehension processes and strategies for text integration.

The complexities of the process of reading acquisition pose a challenge to the developing child. Reading sub-skills draw upon a variety of different cognitive processes and, as we shall see, children come to the task of reading varying in the prerequisite skills. Children's reading skills are shaped by the language they are learning and how they are taught, as well as by their motivation to read. The corollary of this is that children experience reading difficulties for different reasons, and at different times in their development.

This chapter begins by reviewing the role of cognitive skills in the process of learning to read before proceeding to consider individual differences in reading within a developmental framework.

The Development of Reading

Stage models of reading

From a remarkably young age, children begin to "read" the print they see around them, for example, the names of local stores and advertising hoardings. However, such print

This chapter was prepared with the support of Wellcome grant 048147.

recognition depends heavily upon the context in which it is usually seen (Masonheimer, Drum, & Ehri, 1984) and the cues that are used are not at all conventional (Gough & Hillinger, 1980). Reading is usually considered "proper" from the time at which the child uses features inherent in the words themselves as retrieval cues for their pronunciation.

Stage models of reading development were at the height of their popularity in the 1980s and were used to describe the child's progress from the beginnings of reading to the stage characterized by automaticity of word recognition (e.g. Ehri, 1985; Frith, 1985; Marsh, Friedman, Welch, & Desberg, 1981). There was considerable common ground among these different models. All considered the child as starting out with a visual approach to reading. At this early point in development, often referred to as the logographic stage, the child appears to be attaching a label (the word's name) to its overall word shape, as though it were a Chinese "logogram." Seymour and Elder (1986) studied the mistakes that children made in their reading at this first stage. Reading errors came predominantly from the set of words that had been taught to the children and there was a tendency for them to preserve word length, suggesting they were relying on word form. One child read *policeman* as "children" saying, "I know it's that one because it is a long one." There was also confusion between words with salient features in common. One child read *smaller* as "yellow" and another read *stop* as "lost" because it shared the cluster "*st*." In addition, some of the children's reading errors were semantic, for example, *room* was read as "house" and *big* was read as "cat" (having first been mistaken for *dog* because of the *b/d* confusion).

Visual reading strategies provide an adequate means for recognizing printed words when a child's sight vocabulary is small. However, as more words begin to be recognized, visually similar words, such as *orange* and *organ, champion* and *campaign,* begin to create confusion, as do words that differ only in their grammatical ending or affix, e.g. *excited – excitement.* In addition, a visual reading system is not conducive to spelling. Spelling, in contrast to reading, needs to proceed using full rather than partial information, especially in English because of its inconsistent spelling patterns.

Children next enter an alphabetic stage where they begin to read using phonological strategies. These strategies enable children to read words they have not seen before. Primitive alphabetic strategies involve using letter–sound correspondences, (sometimes described as "rules"), to decipher print. Later children begin to rely more directly on orthographic patterns for reading and spelling, and they begin to use lexical analogies in reading. For example, they may read THEPHERD by analogy with "shepherd" rather than be using letter-sound rules (Marsh, Friedman, Welsh, & Desberg, 1981). These advances depend upon the development of a specialized system of alphabetic mappings, including those between letter strings and morphemes, e.g., -tion, -ment.

Stage models of reading, though descriptive, suffered from a number of limitations. First, in common with other models of this type, the mechanisms involved in the transitions between stages were unclear. In particular, the early models did not emphasize the importance of "phonological awareness" to reading development. Phonological awareness refers to the ability to reflect upon and analyze the sound structure of spoken words. Typically, children are not aware of this level of language before the close of the preschool period. Their awareness first emerges as an ability to manipulate large phonological units of words, such as syllables, at around the ages of 4 or 5. Later they become aware of sub-syllabic units, such as onsets and rimes. The onset of a syllable is the first phoneme or cluster of phonemes, while the rime comprises the vowel and the succeeding consonant or consonants (the coda). Thus, in a word like *crisp*, the onset is *cr* and the rime is *isp*; in *toast*, the onset is *t* and the rime is *oast*. Onset and rime units are more salient to a young child than the smallest segments of words, phonemes. It follows that the development of phonemic awareness is a relatively late acquisition, and may be accomplished only by readers of alphabetic orthographies (Read et al., 1986).

A second shortcoming of stage theories was that they proposed an ordered sequence of stages or phases. This universal sequence was challenged by findings showing that the course of reading development is not the same for all children. In fact, the reading strategies that children use depend not only upon the teaching they receive (Thompson & Johnston, 2000) but also, as we shall see, the language in which they are learning.

A modified stage model that allows for individual variation in development was proposed by Seymour (1990). In this "dual foundation model," the orthographic system of fluent reading is seen as the merger of two earlier systems, a logographic system and an alphabetic system, rather than as an independent stage in a developmental sequence from logographic to orthographic through alphabetic (cf. Frith, 1985). Seymour's model makes explicit that children need to have access to structures in a logographic lexicon with links to semantics. He thus acknowledges the role of meaning as a foundation for the development of automatic word recognition, a process not often acknowledged in stage models. In addition, the child needs to be able to reflect on the structure of spoken words (phonological awareness) and to have knowledge of alphabetic letter–sound correspondences to develop complete orthographic representations. Individual differences in reading development can be considered to reflect processing preferences that affect the establishment of these foundation systems to differing degrees.

Children's hypotheses about print

It will be clear from our preceding discussion that reading is a new venture for most children as they start school. Perhaps it is not surprising, therefore, that children soon set up hypotheses about how print represents language. According to Byrne (1998), the reason that young children begin reading by making visual errors is that they confront the task of reading with an incorrect hypothesis. Instead of realizing that, in an alphabetic system, the relationship between the printed and spoken forms of words is at the level of the phoneme – the smallest unit of speech, they consider the mappings to be at the level of the morpheme – the smallest unit of meaning.

In a set of experiments demonstrating this phenomenon, Byrne (1996) first taught young non-readers the relationships between the printed and spoken forms of pairs of words, such as *hat–hats* and *small–smaller*. Following training to criterion, the children were asked to distinguish new pairs of words analogous to the trained pairs, e.g. *cat–cats* and *mean–meaner*. Although most children could do this accurately, the basis of their success was unclear because the critical letters in the examples mapped to both the morphemes and the phonemes of the words. Thus, the *s* in *cats* represents both the plural morpheme and the phoneme /s/; the *er* in *meaner* represents both the comparative (the morpheme) and the "schwa" phoneme ("er").

In a second transfer test, the children had to distinguish between members of two further pairs of words, but this time success was only possible if performance was based on the phonological representations of the letters. The word pairs were *pur–purs* (phonetic versions of purr–purse) and *corn–corner*. This time the majority of children failed, because they had focused on the meaning function of the letter and had not abstracted the basic mapping unit fundamental to the alphabetic principle, that is, the phoneme. Byrne (1998) proposed that children must abandon this morphological hypothesis if they are to become successful decoders. To do so requires both awareness of phonemes (phoneme identity) and knowledge of the letters representing the phonemes.

The fundamental importance of children's concepts about print were also discussed by Stuart and Coltheart (1988) and Goswami and Bryant (1990) who suggested that children set up hypotheses about print on the basis of their phonological awareness. According to Stuart and Coltheart (1988), children who are aware of the initial and final sounds of spoken words use this knowledge to predict how that word will look in print. Their theory argues then that phonemes play a driving role in the development of children's reading strategies (Stuart, Masterson, Dixon, & Quinlan, 1999). An alternative idea was pursued by Goswami and Bryant (1990), who proposed that it was children's awareness of the rhyming relationships between spoken words (e.g., *goat, coat, moat*) that directed their attention to how the rhyming portions of such words are represented in print (e.g., *-oat*). The proposal builds on the theory that the syllables of spoken words are organized hierarchically with an intermediate level of onset and rime between the syllable and the phoneme (Treiman & Breaux, 1982).

Goswami (1988) showed that young children can use lexical analogies to read words that share orthographic rimes. In these experiments, children were first taught a cue word such as *beak*, and then told that this word would provide them with a clue for reading some new words. Next, they were presented with words that either shared the rime unit (*peak*), the onset and vowel sequence (*bean*) or all of the letters but in a different order (*bake*). Beginning readers as young as 5 years could use analogies to solve this task; having learned *beak* the children could transfer their knowledge to read words sharing the same rime, e.g. *peak, weak*. Seven-year-olds, but not younger children, were also able to use beginning-analogies; they could read *bean* having been taught *beak*, but the benefit was not as great as for end-analogies (Goswami & Mead, 1992).

The work of Goswami and her colleagues showed that children could be encouraged to use lexical analogies at a much younger age than suggested by stage theorists. However, the paradigm used in these experiments overestimates children's natural tendency to use analogies (Bowey, 1996; Savage, 1997) and a number of studies have suggested that children prefer to use letter–sound correspondences when not presented with explicit direction to do otherwise (Brown & Deavers, 1999). Perhaps the important point to be made is that children can be encouraged to harness implicit knowledge about the onset-rime structure of words as a strategy in learning to read (Goswami & East, 2000). Whether it is advantageous for them to do so is an empirical question.

The development of word recognition: beyond decoding

To become fluent readers, children must move beyond the alphabetic phase. Recognizing the importance of the alphabetic principle as a "self-teaching device," Share (1995) emphasized that "every successful decoding encounter with an unfamiliar word provides an opportunity to acquire word-specific orthographic information that is critical to the development of skilled word recognition" (see also Share, 1999). Although the term "decoding" is used loosely in the reading literature to refer either to basic single-word reading skills or more specifically to the translation of letter strings to phonological codes, Share (1999) uses the term to refer to the child's ability to decipher a novel word by whatever means. Indeed, he pointed out that phonological decoding in and of itself is insufficient. The learner also needs to be able to use contextual information to disambiguate partial decoding attempts so that, on an item-by-item basis, they can establish orthographic representations (Nation & Snowling, 1998a). As the child develops more orthographic knowledge, the phonological decoding mechanism itself becomes increasingly "lexicalized," taking it beyond its basic function of translating letters into sounds, for use in deciphering words containing a wide range of spelling patterns.

Ehri (1992) also views the child's increasing reading proficiency as the product of general experience with the orthographic system. In Ehri's model of "sight word" acquisition (Ehri, 1995), young beginning readers use their knowledge of letter names to retrieve the pronunciations of words stored in memory representations. Through this process of "phonetic cue reading," they begin to forge connections between the spellings and the sounds of spoken words. These connections can be thought of as primitive orthographic representations. The transition to accurate and automatic word recognition is gradual and quantitative until eventually the child's orthographic lexicon is fully specified, with mappings between the letters in printed words and the phonemes in spoken words.

Finally, the role of environmental factors in determining children's reading achievement should not be forgotten. Recent evidence suggests that social class accounts for substantial amounts of variance in the growth of reading skills between grades 1 and 4, even when the effects of intelligence and phonological skills in kindergarten are accounted for (Hecht, Burgess, Torgesen, Wagner, & Rashotte, 2000). Furthermore, reading practice is particularly important for ensuring progress in an opaque reading system such as English because many of its words cannot be decoded using spelling-sound rules. Tests of *print exposure* in which readers have to detect real from fictitious names of authors and titles of books provide a metric for reading practice. Importantly, print exposure accounts for variations in reading skills, even when the effects of phonological awareness, an excellent correlate of decoding skill, are controlled (Cunningham & Stanovich, 1991).

Learning to spell

Although there is a very large body of empirical evidence on learning to read, the development of spelling has attracted much less investigation. Stage models of spelling describe the child's progress from a stage when they use random letter strings to represent words in writing to one where they use partial attempts to represent the phonetic structure of the words (Gentry, 1982). A particularly interesting phenomenon sometimes observed during this period is that of "invented spelling" (Bissex, 1980; Read, 1971). Invented spelling is the term used to describe the attempts, usually of non-readers, to capture in their writing the salient phonetic features of target words. In so doing, they use a mixture of letter names and their sounds. Classic invented spellings include CHAN for "train," RM for "arm," EFNCH for 'adventure'.

Although invented spellings tend to be idiosyncratic, they highlight the child's motivation to transcribe the spoken forms of words, albeit with limited phonemic awareness and knowledge of orthographic conventions. Indeed, Treiman (1993) has shown that children's spelling errors initially reflect their immature segmentation strategies. It is common, for example, for children to reduce consonant clusters at the beginnings of words (e.g. pl → p; sp → s) or to simplify nasal clusters at the ends (-nk → -k) (Treiman et al., 1995).

A key issue in the development of spelling is the extent to which spelling depends upon reading skill (Caravolas, Hulme, & Snowling, in press; Ehri, 1997). The inconsistencies of English spelling, together with its many irregularities (e.g., yacht, colonel), provide prima facie evidence that accurate spelling cannot be accomplished on the basis of phonological analysis alone. Children must also be aware of the morphological structure of words. Nunes, Bryant, and Bindman (1997) showed that English children learn to represent the regular past-tense ending of verbs (-*ed*) at a stage in their development when they are still spelling phonetically. Morphological boundaries can also give information about phonological inconsistencies: in American English, medial /t/ phonemes are typically flapped so that phonetically they are articulated [d]. Treiman et al. (1995) showed that children were more likely to write the medial sound in such words correctly as *t* if it marked a morpheme boundary (as in *dirty*) than if it did not (as in *attic*) when it would be transcribed as *d.*

Several studies have focused on the interrelationship between reading, spelling, and phonological skills during the early school years. Cataldo & Ellis (1988; Ellis & Cataldo, 1990) followed the development of reading, spelling, and phonological awareness during the first three years of school. Explicit phonemic awareness predicted spelling at all three points in time, its influence gradually increasing. Spelling also exerted an important influence over early reading in years 1 and 2 while reading had only a small effect on spelling in this time phase.

Burns and Richgels (1989) also considered reading to have less influence over early spelling than phonological skill. In this study, young children who used invented spelling were compared with their peers who did not. Although only 44 percent of the "semi-phonetic" spellers could read, they were superior to the non-spellers in knowledge of letter sounds (but not letter names) as well as in phoneme segmentation skills. Thus, it seems that word reading is related to but independent of word-writing at this early stage in development (see also Bryant & Bradley, 1980; Caravolas et al., in press), and there is a reciprocal relationship between reading and spelling in the early years of schooling.

Predictors of Reading Achievement

Longitudinal studies of learning to read and spell

Longitudinal studies of children's literacy have investigated the cognitive skills that underpin reading and spelling development. Bradley and Bryant (1983) conducted one of the
most influential of these studies to examine the relationship between early phonological
skills and later reading achievement in some 400 children from 4 to 8 years. At the beginning of the study, each child was administered three phonological tasks. In two of these,
the child had to decide which was the odd one out of sequences of three rhyming words
(rime oddity; e.g., sun, *rub*, gun; pot, lot, *bit*) and a further task required the child to
detect the word that started with a different sound (alliteration oddity; see, sock, *hat*).
There was a strong relationship between the children's phonological awareness assessed
on these tasks at 4 years and their reading and spelling skills at 8, even when the substantial effects of IQ, memory, and social class were controlled. Moreover, the relationship between phonological awareness and literacy development was specific – individual
differences in phonological awareness at 4 years did not predict mathematical performance at 6, so it was not simply a predictor of general academic achievement.

At around the same time, Lundberg and colleagues (Lundberg, Olofsson, & Wall,
1980) reported some of the first evidence of the universality of these findings from a cross-
linguistic perspective. One of the interesting features of the work of Lundberg's group is
that it was carried out in Denmark where, at the time, reading instruction did not begin
until the age of 7 years. It was therefore possible to assess phonological awareness in individuals who were cognitively mature but (unlike British or American preschoolers) had
not yet begun to read. The strong relationship between phonological awareness prior to
literacy instruction and later reading achievement was replicated in this study and has
been confirmed by a large number of studies since (Byrne & Fielding-Barnsley, 1989;
Ellis & Large, 1987; Muter et al., 1998; Share et al., 1984; Stanovich, Cunningham, &
Cramer, 1984; Tunmer & Nesdale, 1985).

However, it needs to be borne in mind that the relationship between phonological
skills and reading development is not unidirectional (Morais, 1991). Rather, reading plays
a reciprocal role in promoting phonological awareness (Cataldo & Ellis, 1988; Perfetti,
Beck, Bell, & Hughes, 1987). Moreover, the orthography in which a child learns has an
influence on the development of their phonological awareness (Harris & Hatano, 1999).

Levels of phonological awareness and reading development

Since the strong relationship between phonological skills and learning to read has been
established, researchers have turned their attention to the more specific question of which
phonological abilities are causally related to the development of word recognition (e.g.,
Wagner, Torgesen, Laughon, Simmons, & Rashotte, 1993). It will be recalled that spoken
syllables can be segmented at the level of the onset-rime (large units) or at the level of
the phoneme (small units). Moreover, Goswami & Bryant (1990) proposed that rhyming

skills were the precursors of reading development (in children learning English). In other words, they favored the view that the first links that English children make in learning to read are between large units (onsets and rimes) and letters; the development of links between phonemes and graphemes was a second step.

In line with the view that phonological awareness comprises two component skills, Muter, Hulme, Snowling, and Taylor (1998) found that two independent factors accounted for young children's performance on phonological awareness tasks. The first factor, *segmentation*, carried high loadings from performance on syllable and phoneme tasks, while performance in rhyme-detection and rhyme-production tasks loaded on a second factor, *rhyme*. Muter at al. (1998) went on to investigate the contribution of segmentation and rhyme skills to reading development. Here their findings departed from the predictions of Goswami and Bryant's theory. Muter at al. (1998) found that segmentation was a better predictor of reading performance than rhyme in the group of children they studied, both concurrently and longitudinally (Muter & Snowling, 1998). However, at 6 years, the children's ability to use lexical analogies in reading was related to their rhyming skills (Muter, Snowling, & Taylor, 1994). Thus, rhyming skills may be important at a stage in development when a child's reading skills are more fully developed and they can benefit from redundancies in the English orthography at the level of the rime (Bowey & Underwood, 1996; Coltheart & Leahy, 1992; Duncan, Seymour, & Hill, 1997; Laxon, Masterson, & Coltheart, 1991).

Language skills and learning to read

The strength of the evidence relating phonological skills to learning to read is such that it is hard to argue against its central role in reading development. However, it is important to be clear of the limitations of the view. The important point is that phonological skills predict reading through decoding ability – specifically, children's ability to process speech sounds is related to their ability to pronounce unfamiliar printed words. While decoding skills allow the child to decipher words such as *roundabout* or nonwords like *pimrugear*, they do not yield a correct pronunciation of exception words such as *colonel* or *Leicester*. Furthermore, decoding skills do not allow the accurate reading of ambiguous words such as the word BOW in the sentence "The magician took a *bow*." Neither do they help with the understanding of sentences such as "The horse raced past the barn fell."

Thus, there is more to reading than decoding. Although it is now many years since Gough and Tunmer (1986) proposed that reading was the product of decoding and linguistic comprehension, most developmental models of reading do not recognize this fact. Arguably, by focusing exclusively on the role of phonological skills, a great deal of reading research has relegated the influence of other language factors to that of nuisance variables, usually removing their effects statistically by controlling for IQ. Yet, as many a teacher will observe, beginning readers are influenced by the non-phonological attributes of words. For example, they often read concrete words, such as *sun* and *frog* more accurately than words that are equally easy from a decoding point of view, such as *him* or *from*, probably because the latter words are abstract, making them difficult to remember.

Indeed, Laing and Hulme (1999) showed that beginning readers found learning to read acronyms for words easier if their referents were spoken words of high rather than of low imageability. In similar vein, Nation & Snowling (1998b) demonstrated the important influence of children's semantic skills on their ability to read exception words that are difficult to decode, and on their use of context to support decoding processes (Nation & Snowling, 1998b).

Connectionist models of learning to read

In recent years, connectionist models of reading have had a major influence on theories of learning to read (e.g., Harm & Seidenberg, 1998). The essential feature of these models is that representations of words are distributed across many simple processing elements in input and output systems (see Thomas & Karmiloff-Smith, ch. 26 this volume). In these models, the input system is a set of orthographic units coding the letters and letter strings of printed words and the output system is a set of phonological units coding the phonological features of word pronunciations. Patterns of activation across these input and output units gradually become associated with each other as a function of learning, just as during reading acquisition children gradually learn the associations between letter strings in written inputs and sequences of phonemes in spoken outputs. Furthermore, children, like adults, are sensitive to the quasi-regularity of English spelling (Treiman et al., 1995). As a consequence, they learn to read regular words more easily than exception words because the sequences of letters in regular words (coded across the input units) co-occur with the same sequences of phonemes (coded across the output units) more frequently than the two are associated in the case of irregular or exception words. By comparison, languages such as German or Italian are much more consistent in their mappings from spelling to sound. Not surprisingly, children find learning to read in these languages easier than in English (Cossu, 1999; Wimmer, 1996).

Arguably, the most influential connectionist framework for understanding reading has been that proposed by Seidenberg and McClelland (1989; see figure 18.1). This "triangle" model contained sets of representations dealing with orthographic, phonological, and semantic information, interconnected by sets of hidden units that capture the model's learning resource. The part of the model first implemented (referred to here as SM89) was a network with orthographic input and phonological output units connected by a set of intermediate or "hidden" units (the phonological pathway). Learning in the model used an algorithm called *backpropagation* which is essentially a mathematical procedure that is used to adjust the links between outputs and inputs to produce the correct response to each input. It should not be assumed that backpropagation involves processes similar to those used in the brain during learning. It simply provides a mechanism whereby the model can learn to abstract the relationships that exist between input and output representations in the computer model's simulation of reading.

After training on a corpus of English single-syllable words using this learning procedure, SM89 simulated several aspects of human word recognition. An important feature for present purposes was that, at the end of training, the model could generalize knowledge embodied in the connections to words it had not been explicitly taught to read.

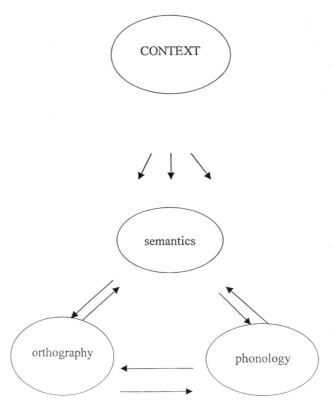

Figure 18.1 The Seidenberg & McClelland (1989) framework of reading. From *Psychological Review 1989, 96,* 523–568, p. 526. Copyright © 1989 by the American Psychological Association. Reprinted with permission

This is particularly relevant for the development of the reading system because a crucial "self-teaching device," analogous to a "lexicalized" decoding system (Share, 1995) is inherent in the architecture of the models. However, among the model's critics were Besner, Twilley, McCann, and Seergobin (1990), who pointed out that SM89 produced correct pronunciations for many fewer nonwords than would be typical of normal adult performance. Thus, it could read words well, but its nonword reading was poor.

A "second-generation" model within the same general framework was proposed by Plaut, McClelland, Seidenberg, and Patterson (1996). Essentially, Plaut et al. (1996) adopted forms of representation in their new model that contained phonemes and graphemes as entities and thereby overcame problems that had limited the ability of SM89 to read novel letter strings. When tested on nonword reading, the Plaut et al. (1996) model outperformed SM89, with performance approximating that of adult readers. Just as children learn to read most effectively when they come to the task with well-specified phonological representations (Snowling & Hulme, 1994), generalization within the connectionist architecture was better when training began with well-structured input and output representations (see also Harm & Seidenberg, 1998).

However, in common with the developmental models discussed above, another limitation of the SM89 model was that it did not deal with meaning. Plaut, McClelland, Seidenberg, and Patterson (1996) attempted to improve its simulation of reading by implementing a semantic pathway. In addition to the phonological pathway of connections between orthography and phonology, the Plaut et al. model contained a semantic pathway mapping orthography to phonology via semantic representations. Although there has been some limited success in modeling semantic representations that encode word meanings as sets of semantic features, Plaut et al.'s semantic units did not attempt to do this. Rather, the simulation involved training a network in which a semantic pathway provided additional boost to input to the phoneme units. An effect of combining semantic and phonological influences in the model was to increase the rate of learning, particularly of exception words. In the later stages of training, Plaut et al. (1996) showed that the two pathways became highly specialized, so that the semantic pathway began to deal primarily with the pronunciation of exception words while the phonological pathway continued to be involved in the pronunciation of words (and nonwords) with consistent pronunciations. This model provides a good framework for considering both the interaction of phonological and semantic skills during the course of reading development (Snowling, 1998) and individual differences in reading and its disorders (Plaut, 1997).

Individual Differences in Reading

Deficits of word recognition and decoding: dyslexia

Although in a minority of cases, problems of word identification (surface dyslexia) can be dissociated from problems of phonological decoding (phonological dyslexia), the majority of children with specific reading difficulties have phonological difficulties (Manis et al., 1996; Vellutino & Scanlon, 1991). Within the connectionist framework outlined above, dyslexic children come to the task of learning to read with poorly specified phonological representations. In the first place, this results in delayed reading development (Gallagher, Frith, & Snowling, 2000). In the longer term, problems with the generalization of word-specific lexical knowledge is marked by deficits in nonword reading (Rack et al., 1992) although both exception word reading (Metsala, Stanovich & Brown, 1997) and reading comprehension (Frith & Snowling 1983) are usually commensurate with overall reading ability.

While the role of visual problems in dyslexia continues to be debated (Talcott & Stein, 1999; Willows et al., 1993), the majority of studies point to phonological deficits in dyslexic children (Stanovich, 1994). The most consistently reported difficulties are problems of phonological awareness (Swan & Goswami, 1997) and limitations of verbal short-term memory (Brady, 1997). However, dyslexic children also have difficulties with verbal learning (Mayringer & Wimmer, 2000; Vellutino et al., 1995) and with the retrieval of phonological information from long-term memory for the purpose of naming (Bowers & Wolf, 1993; Swan & Goswami, 1997; Wolf, 1997). It is possible that these problems stem from more basic deficits in speech perception (Reed, 1989), or speech production (Snowling, Goulandris, Bowlby, & Howell, 1986), and a number of current theories suggest that dyslexic children have difficulties first in establishing, and later in accessing, adequate phonological representations (Fowler, 1991; Hulme & Snowling, 1992; Swan & Goswami, 1997).

The strength of the evidence pointing to the phonological deficits associated with dyslexia led to the proposal that dyslexia should be defined as a "core" phonological deficit. Within the *phonological core-variable difference* model of dyslexia (Stanovich & Siegel, 1994), poor phonology is related to poor reading performance, irrespective of IQ. Skills close to the "core" of dyslexia include phonological awareness; all poor readers will tend to differ from normal readers in these skills. Children with specific reading difficulties differ from generally poor readers in skills farther from the core, notably in their performance on working memory and listening comprehension tasks.

An important advantage of the phonological deficit definition of dyslexia is that it makes sense in terms of what is known about the normal acquisition of reading. A second advantage is that it accounts well for the different manifestations of dyslexia seen across the life-span. While reading problems tend to be the key behavioral symptom of dyslexia in the early school years, many adults with a childhood history of dyslexia are fluent readers though few overcome their spelling problems. A number of recent studies have shown that adult dyslexics have difficulty decoding words they have not seen before (i.e. nonwords) and have difficulties with phonological awareness, speeded naming, and verbal short-term memory tasks (Bruck, 1990, 1992; Pennington, van Orden, Smith, Green, & Haith, 1990; Snowling, Nation, Moxham, Gallagher, & Frith, 1997).

At the other end of the age spectrum, there are now a number of family studies of dyslexia investigating differences between children from dyslexic and non-dyslexic families before they learn to read. Scarborough (1990) followed the development of children of 2 to 7 years who were "at risk" of dyslexia by virtue of having one dyslexic parent. When the children were 7 and their reading skills could be assessed, it was possible to compare retrospectively the preschool data of children who went on to become dyslexic with children who did not develop reading difficulties. An important difference between the groups was in their early language skills. Although the dyslexic children used as large a range of vocabulary as their non-dyslexic peers at 2.5 years, they made more speech errors and used simpler sentence structures. At 3 years, the dyslexic children had more difficulty with object-naming, and at 5 their difficulties extended to problems with phonological awareness. Their emerging literacy skills were also poorer; they were less familiar with the letters of the alphabet and worse at matching pictures with print.

Similar results were reported by Byrne et al. (1997), who found that problems of phonological awareness, together with limitations of letter knowledge, presaged reading difficulties in high-risk children at 55 months (see also Lefly and Pennington, 1996). Gallagher et al. (2000) reported converging findings from a study in which at risk children were worse at repeating novel words at 45 months, especially those with phonological structures comprising late-acquired forms. In addition, their knowledge of nursery rhymes, a test known to predict reading achievement, was poorer and they already knew fewer letters.

Thus, there are strong reasons to suggest that children at risk of dyslexia are delayed in their phonological development. A reasonable hypothesis is that these children come to the task of learning to read with poorly specified phonological representations. According to this view, poor phonology compromises literacy development by placing limitations on children's ability to form the mappings between letter strings and the phonological units that are critical for learning to read.

Reading comprehension impairments

In contrast to dyslexic children who have phonological deficits, children with specific difficulties in reading comprehension have good phonology and decode well but have problems understanding what they read (Stothard & Hulme, 1995; Yuill & Oakhill, 1991). More specifically, they have difficulty making inferences that go beyond the literal meaning of the sentences they read (Cain et al., 2000a).

A number of studies now show that children with reading comprehension impairments have poorer vocabulary knowledge than their peers (Nation & Snowling, 1999), poorer syntactic skills (Nation, Marshall, & Snowling 2000; Stothard & Hulme 1995), and limited verbal working memory resources (Cain et al., 2000b; Nation et al., 1999). In the longer term, they have particular difficulty reading exception words that require semantic processing (e.g. *chrome, aunt*) (Nation & Snowling, 1998a), and difficulty using context to support their reading (Nation & Snowling, 1998b).

Taken together, these findings provide converging evidence for a reciprocal interaction of component reading skills during development. Poor comprehenders begin to read normally and develop good decoding skills. However, during the middle-school years when the vocabulary encountered in print increases, poor comprehension skills appear to compromise the development of word recognition for these children. In line with this hypothesis, Snowling, Bishop, and Stothard (2000) found that children with specific language impairment who showed specific difficulties with reading comprehension at the age of 8 had general reading problems encompassing poor word recognition, decoding, and reading comprehension skills at school-leaving age. Thus, just as sources of activation from phonological and semantic representations are pooled in connectionist models of reading, reading development can be viewed as the outcome of the interaction of the child's phonological, syntactic, and semantic skills with the printed words they encounter.

Reading Development in Different Languages

Languages differ in the regularity or transparency of their orthographies and therefore in the task they pose to children learning to read (Harris & Hatano, 1999). German and Italian are two of the more transparent European orthographies, and in these languages letters generally correspond to single phonemes. The same is true for Greek, though the script is different. In contrast, the English writing system is much more opaque and, very frequently, a grapheme may correspond to more than one phoneme. For example, the grapheme *e* may correspond to /E/ as in "bed," to /i/ as in "eve," and to "schwa" as in "believe." In particular, there are many inconsistencies in the way in which vowels are represented in English.

Although rather few studies have made direct comparisons between readers of different orthographies using the same stimuli, there is now substantial evidence that normally developing children learn to read and spell more quickly in transparent writing systems than in opaque systems such as English.

Cross-linguistic studies of reading development

One of the first studies to demonstrate differences between children learning to read in opaque and transparent orthographies was conducted by Oney & Goldman (1984), who compared the reading skills of children learning to read in English (American) and Turkish. Turkish is a transparent orthography containing consistent letter–sound correspondences and therefore provides an interesting comparison with the opaque orthography of English. These researchers investigated nonword- as well as word reading. While words can be read from memory by directly accessing orthographic representations, nonword reading provides a relatively pure test of decoding ability. Oney and Goldman (1984) reported that decoding accuracy, as well as speed, was more efficient among the Turkish than the English readers.

Wimmer & Goswami (1994) used a similar technique to investigate the influence of orthographic consistency on reading development in English- and German-speaking children. In this study, children were asked to read numerals (1, 3, 5), number words (ten, seven), and nonwords derived from the number words by changing the onset of the syllable (e.g., sen, feven). There were no group differences in the time or accuracy with which numerals and number words could be read, but there was a group difference in nonword reading: German children, who had learned the transparent language, made fewer errors and registered faster reading times (see also Frith, Wimmer, & Landerl, 1998, who noted that English children have particular difficulty reading vowels that are represented inconsistently in the English orthography).

Nonword reading has often been used to explore the development of orthographic representations in children learning different languages. In English, it is easier for children to read nonwords that share rime units with many other words (e.g., dake) than nonwords that have unfamiliar orthographic rimes (e.g., daik) (Treiman, Goswami, & Bruck, 1990). Goswami and colleagues used this technique to examine the salience of rime and phoneme units in readers of French and an adapted version of it to investigate readers of Greek (see Goswami, 1999, for a review).

The findings of these studies showed that the salience of rime units varied with the transparency of the language. Readers of English and French both showed an advantage in terms of speed and accuracy for nonwords that contained familiar rime units, the advantage being greater for English, the more opaque of the two languages. The same advantage was not demonstrated by readers of Greek. These data suggest that orthographic sequences that correspond to rimes are salient units of the orthographic representations created in opaque languages, but orthographic rimes are of no benefit to readers of regular languages, such as Greek.

Cross-linguistic studies of phonological awareness

Cross-linguistic studies also suggest that the nature of the orthography affects the development of phonological awareness. Thus, awareness of the phonemic segments of words develops more quickly in transparent languages (e.g. Cossu, Shankweiler, Liberman, Katz, & Tola, 1988). Arguably, this might be because the rapid development of decoding skill has a reciprocal influence on metalinguistic awareness of word structure (Harm & Seidenberg, 1998).

Strong evidence for this possibility comes from research investigating the phonological awareness of children learning to read Chinese (see Hanley et al., 1999, for a review). The Chinese writing system differs from an alphabetic system in that it contains a large number of different visual symbols or characters that represent units of meaning (morphemes) rather than phonemes as in an alphabet. However, it is important to bear in mind that these morphemes map on to syllables; in addition, characters contain a phonetic element that aids pronunciation. It is therefore incorrect to assume, as is sometimes implied, that Chinese can be read without access to phonology. Indeed, while visual skills play a more important role in learning to read in Chinese than in English, phonological skills also turn out to be good predictors of reading achievement (Ho & Bryant, 1997).

The majority of Chinese characters contain a phonetic component and a radical component and are known as phonetic compounds. The task of learning to read is a considerable feat for Chinese children, who must learn literally hundreds of these characters. Possibly for this reason, children in mainland China and Taiwan are introduced to reading using an alphabetic script before they embark on character-learning. In China they learn a script called Pinyin, which uses Roman letters, and in Taiwan they learn Zhu-Yin-Fu-Hao which consists of characters more like those they will go on to learn in Chinese proper.

Most children master these alphabetic systems quite quickly. School books are printed so that new Chinese characters are always accompanied by their representation in Pinyin or Zhu-Yin-Fu-Hao that the child can use to decode the new character. The fact that these children learn both an alphabetic and a logographic system, whereas children in Hong Kong are not taught an alphabetic system, provides a natural experiment to investigate the influence of learning to read on the development of phonological awareness.

Read, Zhang, Nie, and Ding (1986), in a classic study, showed that adults who were literate only in Chinese characters were unable to add or delete phonemes from spoken words, whereas those who had learned to read via Pinyin were able to do so. Converging evidence was provided more recently by Huang and Hanley (1995), who showed that Taiwanese children who had learned Zhu-Yin-Fu-Hao performed better on phoneme-deletion tasks than children from Hong Kong who had been taught neither Pinyin nor Zhu-Yin-Fu-Hao.

These findings demonstrate the reciprocal influence of alphabetic experience on the development of phonological awareness. A quite separate influence, worthy of consideration, is that the phonological structure of spoken language also influences the child's developing awareness of its segmental structure. In the Czech language, it is common for words to begin with complex consonant clusters and they are therefore highly familiar to children. It is reasonable to expect, therefore, that Czech-speaking children will find it easier to segment consonant clusters than English-speaking children, who typically find this difficult. Caravolas & Bruck (1993) compared Czech- and English-speaking (Canadian) children's phonological awareness and spelling ability. Consistent with the hypothesis, Czech children could isolate phonemes from onset clusters more easily than the English-speaking children and, in spelling, they made fewer errors on consonant clusters.

Durgunoglu and Oney (1999), working with Turkish children, also proposed that familiarity with phonological structures influences the salience of segments at the level of phonological representation. Turkish is a language with a small number of syllable structures, some 50 percent being CV in form. In addition, the pronunciation of vowels is highly context-sensitive (vowel harmony) and, because vowels change when morphemes are added to words, children have a lot of experience of phoneme changes within words. Furthermore, because of vowel harmony, inflections at the ends of words have a variable structure that might be expected to highlight final phonemes. These characteristics of Turkish phonology led the investigators to hypothesize that Turkish children would be better at syllable segmentation than American children (see Bruck, Genesee, & Caravolas, 1997, for a similar argument with respect to French/English) and more advanced in phoneme segmentation, especially in deleting final phonemes. Data from the children's performance on parallel tests of syllable- and phoneme-tapping, and initial and final phoneme deletion confirmed these predictions. Turkish kindergarten children performed better than English speakers in both syllable and phoneme segmentation and, strikingly, even though they had poorer letter knowledge, they found it easier to delete final phonemes from nonword syllables.

As a result of these cross-linguistic differences in the development of reading and phonological awareness, the sensitivity of phonological abilities as predictors of reading development varies across different languages. While performance on a rime oddity task is a good predictor of learning to read in English (Bradley & Bryant, 1983), Wimmer, Landerl, & Schneider (1994) found that kindergarten performance on a rime oddity task was a poor predictor of subsequent reading achievement in German readers at the end of grade 1. De Jong and van der Leij (1999) reported similar findings from the regular Dutch orthography. In this study, phonological awareness was not a good predictor of early reading development among Dutch children, whereas letter knowledge and rapid naming ability accounted for unique variance in reading ability, as measured by performance on a task-speeded reading task.

Dyslexia in different languages

The relative difficulty of learning to read in different languages has consequences for our understanding of dyslexia. Specifically, the core phonological deficits of dyslexia are harder to detect in children who have learned to read in a regular orthography where phonological awareness is not a sensitive predictor of reading skill. In these languages, difficulties can be identified most clearly on tasks that require implicit phonological processing, such as verbal short-term memory, rapid naming and visual-verbal paired associate learning tasks (Wimmer, Mayringer, & Landerl, 1998).

The reading and spelling symptoms of dyslexia are also different in regular orthographies as compared to English, and in particular, nonword reading is not difficult for such children, although it may be slow (Nikolopoulos, 1999). Wimmer and his colleagues have conducted studies showing that German-speaking dyslexic children can read long, unfamiliar words and also nonwords as well as their peers (Frith, Wimmer, & Landerl, 1998). However, the fluency of their reading is affected; they read single words more slowly than controls, and sometimes reading comprehension difficulties follow as the consequence of a "bottleneck" in the reading process (Wimmer, Mayringer, & Landerl, 1998). Studies of this type remind us that, although the main symptom of dyslexia is often a reading problem, the reading deficit is more properly considered as one of several possible behavioral manifestations of an underlying cognitive deficit (Frith, 1997).

A final caveat is that the interpretation of cross-linguistic evidence should proceed mindful of the influence of different teaching practices in different language communities. In languages in which the writing system is very regular, there are substantial benefits from teaching children to read using a phonic approach (e.g. in German). Hence it is not unreasonable to think that there may be environmental factors contributing to the superiority in decoding of children learning such languages. As Lundberg (1999) argues, the cultural milieu in which reading develops in different nations has a potent influence on how well children of different genders and in different social classes learn to read.

Conclusions

In recent years, a huge number of studies have documented the development of reading and spelling skills of children as they become literate in diverse languages and cultures. By necessity, this chapter has been selective in the research it has reviewed. Broadly it has highlighted limitations of stage theories of reading as universal models of literacy development. Importantly, learning to read in alphabetic orthographies depends critically upon phonological skills that, in turn, play a reciprocal role in reading and spelling development. Such skills develop more quickly in readers of orthographies in which the relationships between letters and sounds are highly consistent than in opaque writing systems such as English. However, there is more to reading than phonology, and language skills outside of the phonological module are important for the development of automatic word recognition and exception word reading in English.

The influence of computational models of reading on the understanding of basic literacy processes provide a useful framework for considering individual differences in reading development and disorders. Two groups of poor readers were described, dyslexic readers who have core deficits in phonological processes, and poor comprehenders, whose primary deficits are in semantic skills. The contrasting profiles of these children and their different developmental trajectories reinforce the view that there is a reciprocal interaction between language and literacy skills. Moreover, children's encounters with print, at home and at school, bootstrap their literacy development so that the behavioral mani-festations of reading difficulties differ among children in interaction with the language they are learning.

CHAPTER NINETEEN

Children's Understanding of Mathematics

Peter Bryant and Terezinha Nuñes

Mathematics poses an interesting, and a rewarding, set of questions to developmental psychologists. The crux of the psychological problem is the variety of forms that mathematical knowledge takes. Many mathematical concepts are so sophisticated, complex, and abstract that they require a lifetime's learning and much formal teaching, which means that they are completely outside the experience of the vast majority of people. Yet that same vast majority of people depends heavily on mathematical knowledge in their every day life. They have to deal with money, to calculate distances to work, to work out times, and to think about speeds, and if they do not manage these calculations well their life will be harder for them as a result, and a lot less predictable.

Not only do the forms of mathematical knowledge vary, but so also do the ways in which people acquire them. Certainly formal teaching is essential for some kinds of knowledge, such as trigonometry. But it is quite likely that, as Piaget (1952b, 1953a) claimed, children also learn a lot of the underlying logic of mathematics through their own informal experiences within their normal social and physical environments. There can be little doubt that, as well as this, people often acquire mathematical techniques either by imitating other people's solutions or by learning informally from them. Lately too, many psychologists have given their enthusiastic support to the idea that people are born with the understanding of some basic mathematical ideas, such as the concept of number and of addition and subtraction, but this as we shall see is a controversial hypothesis, and a questionable one too.

This mix of formal and informal knowledge is not unique to mathematics. For example, people can learn to talk grammatically, and even to wince whenever they hear others breaking the rules of conventional grammar, without ever having been through a single formal grammar lesson. Yet these are the rules which linguists study for themselves, and teach to their students, to a very high level of sophistication. But in this case, and in most others, the knowledge that all speakers share and acquire informally is usually deeply implicit. Most people who speak grammatically have no conscious idea of the rules they obey so well. In mathematics, on the other hand, informal knowledge is usually quite explicit. It has to be explicit, because people must often justify their mathematical solutions. They have to be able to say why the change that they have been given in a financial transaction, such as buying beer, is the right amount; they have to be able to point out not only that other people have calculated the cost of something wrongly, but also where they went wrong. Mathematics is a part of our daily discourse: we have to be explicitly aware of mathematical rules in order to be able to talk about them.

How then do children acquire these essential skills, and what barriers do they have to surmount to do so? This chapter will deal first with their ideas about number and counting, and then with how they learn to use numbers in order to calculate answers, to solve problems, and to measure.

Number and Counting

Children learn about number early in life, and yet even the most basic principles of number are highly abstract, and quite sophisticated. In order to recognize and distinguish numbers, children have to be able to transcend perceptual information. They must understand that two sets of objects can have the same number despite looking completely different (three cups arranged in a straight line, three saucers arranged in a triangle) and that the same set of objects stays numerically the same despite changes in its perceptual appearance (a flock of birds perched on a telephone line and then taking flight). Thus children must learn that all sets with the same number are qualitatively equivalent, and this is called cardinal number. They must also learn about ordinal number, which means realizing that numbers come in an ordered scale of magnitude, so that 2 is more than 1 and 3 more than 2.

On top of all this children have to learn to count, and this brings extra problems. Counting systems vary across languages and across cultures (Saxe, 1979), but nowadays most counting systems have adopted the decimal structure (Nuñes & Bryant, 1996). This, of course, is a human invention, which is effective and powerful, but often difficult for young children at first. Some of these difficulties are linguistic. Words like "eleven" and " thirteen" are not transparent: they do not make it explicitly clear that they stand for 10 + 1 and 10 + 3. "Quatre-vingt-dix," the French word for 90, is hardly better, and German children have to contend with the fact that the numbers between 20 and 99 start with the larger unit when written, but with the smaller unit when spoken.

Children, therefore, have a lot to learn about number and counting, and there are pitfalls on the way. But some psychologists have suggested that children have the help of a formidable weapon to see them through this learning – an innate understanding of number. The evidence for this idea comes mainly from work with babies, to which we should now turn.

Infants' knowledge of number: does it exist?

Discriminating numbers.   Since we are all aware that mathematical thinking is one of man's highest intellectual achievements, many of us find it hard to sympathize with the idea that some of this reasoning may be with us at birth. Yet this idea was proposed in the 1980s by Rochel Gelman (Gelman & Gallistel, 1978; Gelman & Meck, 1983; Gelman, Meck, & Merkin, 1986) and in more recent years it has been taken up by such notable figures as Dehaene (1997) and Butterworth (1999).

Gelman's attack was a two-pronged one. The first prong was a series of experiments on babies. These were done mainly by her student and colleague Prentice Starkey, who used the technique of habituation (Starkey & Cooper, 1980; Starkey, Spelke, & Gelman, 1990). Habituation experiments exploit the fact that babies seem more interested in novel objects and events than in familiar ones. When Starkey started his research, the technique had been used mainly in studies of babies' perceptual skills.

The rationale in these perceptual studies was simple and straightforward. Babies show more interest in novel than in familiar objects and events. So if they discriminate two things, one if which is familiar to them and the other not, they should attend more to the less familiar of the two. Thus making one stimulus more familiar than another is a convenient way of testing whether babies can discriminate two stimuli.

Starkey and Cooper (1980) applied this test to a cognitive question. They set up an experiment to see if 4-month-old babies can discriminate numbers of objects. Their study followed the traditional habituation study design, which consists of two phases (figure 19.1). In the first phase the babies were shown, over series of trials, a certain number of dots. In each trial the baby saw the same number of dots, but the perceptual arrangement of the dots (bunched up or spread out) varied from trial to trial. The actual numbers of dots that the babies were shown also varied. Some were shown small numbers – either two or three dots – and others larger numbers – either four or six dots. By the end of this first phase the babies' attention to the number displays had usually flagged, and the point of the second phase was to see if their interest could be revived by a change in the number of dots. In this phase, all the babies were shown a new number of dots. Those who had been shown one of the two small numbers in phase one (two or three dots) now saw displays with the other of those two numbers. Similarly the babies in the large number group who had seen four dots in the habituation phase were presented with six dots in the post-habituation phase, and vice versa.

Starkey and Cooper found definite signs of a discrimination in the babies in the small number group. There was a clear jump in the amount of time that they spent looking at the displays when the new number of dots was introduced. They clearly recognized a change, and Starkey and Cooper argued that this meant that babies do have a clear understanding of the number continuum, which they can apply at first only to small numbers but extend to larger numbers as they grow older and their cognitive powers increase.

These two results – successful discrimination with small number displays, unsuccessful discrimination with large number displays – have been repeated many times. They apply to neonates as well as to older babies (Antell & Keating, 1983), and the same pattern even emerged in a study in which the objects in the displays were in constant movement

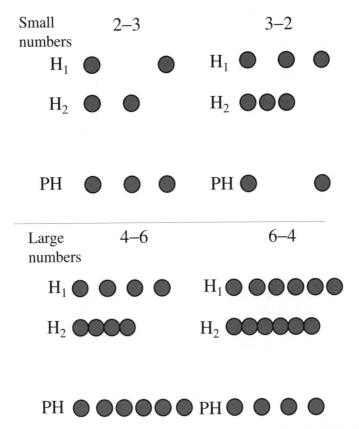

Figure 19.1 The kinds of displays used in Starkey and Cooper's (1980) study. H displays were presented in the habituation period of the experiment, and PH displays were presented in the post-habituation period. In the habituation period the babies saw the H_1 display on some trials, and the H_2 display on others

while the babies saw them (van Loosbroek & Smitsman, 1990). Their significance, however, has been questioned.

The issue is whether the experiments are about number. One team of researchers (Clearfield & Mix, 1999; Mix, Levine, & Huttenlocher, 1997; Mix, Levine, & Huttenlocher, 2001) claim that in all these studies the babies were making discriminations of continuous, not of discontinuous, quantity. They were recognizing changes not in how many objects they were being shown, but in the total amount of stuff in the displays. In none of the experiments cited so far were any precautions taken against the possibility of discriminations based on total quantity rather than on the number of objects.

The clearest evidence for this alternative hypothesis came from a study by Clearfield and Mix (1999). Their design was close to Starkey and Cooper's, except that they varied the size of the objects that each child saw in the two phases. Some children saw relatively small objects in the habituation phase and larger ones in the post-habituation phase, others vice versa.

In each of these cases the children were divided into two groups. One group of babies saw the same number of objects in the habituation phase and in the post-habituation phase, but the size, or rather the total amount of contour (for this was the continuum that the authors chose to vary), was changed from one phase to the other. For example some of the babies in this group saw three smaller shapes in the habituation phase and three larger ones in the post-habituation phase, while other babies saw two relatively large shapes first and two smaller ones later.

In contrast the total amount of contour in the objects that the other babies saw stayed the same throughout both the experimental phases, but the actual number of objects changed. Thus a child in this group would see two relatively large objects to start off with and three smaller ones in the second phase, or three relatively small ones in phase 1 and two larger ones in phase 2.

This experiment produced one negative and one positive result. When the amount of counters stayed the same and the number varied the babies showed no sign of revived interest in the second phase. However, when the number of items stayed the same, but the size and therefore the amount of contour changed from phase to phase, the babies did show definite signs of increased interest following that change. Thus the babies responded not to the number of items, but to the overall quantity of stuff presented to them in each trial. Quantity, it seems, is important to them, but not number.

Ordering numbers.   Numbers make up an ordinal scale, and naturally people have asked not just whether babies discriminate numbers but also whether they realize that a number comes in a particular place on that scale, and is therefore larger than some, and smaller than other, numbers. It is an interesting fact that, although much has been said in favor of a built in "number sense," no one has produced any evidence that there is any innate knowledge of ordinal number.

However, there is some work on the subject with infants in their second year. Strauss and Curtis (1981) made the claim that they had shown some sensitivity to number relations in a training experiment with 16–18-month-old infants, but their results were inconsistent and therefore unconvincing. For example they were successful when they trained children to respond to "less than" relations but not to "more than" relations. The results of two studies by Cooper (1984) were clearer. He worked with 10–12-month-old and 14–16-month-old babies, using the habituation technique. On each trial in the habituation phase he showed children two sets of objects in succession, one larger than the other. Half the babies were regularly given the smaller followed by the larger set, and half received the larger set first. In the second phase of the experiment he showed them pairs of number sets in the same way, some of which involved numbers that had not been used in the first phase of the experiments. In this phase he also included sequences in which the two numbers were equal (e.g., two objects followed by two objects).

Cooper reported that the babies in the younger group showed no sign of distinguishing the less/more sequences. Whatever kind of sequence they saw in the first phase, they looked equally as long at smaller followed by larger number sequences as at larger followed by smaller number sequences. However, the children in this age group did look longer at the "equal" sequences in the second phase than at the unequal ones. Cooper concluded that they could tell whether two sets have the same number or not, but, even when they know that the numbers are different, they are insensitive to which is the more and which the less numerous.

The older infants, however, did make the discrimination between the two kinds of unequal sequences. If they were originally shown smaller followed by larger sequences, they attended more to the larger followed by smaller sequences in the second phase, and vice versa.

Putting these results together, Cooper claimed that he had shown a marked developmental change at around the beginning of the second year. At that age, children become aware of number relations. This is an impressive claim, but the study is only skimpily reported (no numerical results are presented in Cooper's chapter on numerical understanding), and it needs to be repeated and extended. In fact, as we shall see, Cooper's work begs a crucial question in the study of the understanding of ordinality. We need to know, not just how children realize which is the larger of two numbers, but also how they cope with a series of numbers where at least one of the numbers is both larger than some and smaller than others.

Principles before skills: one hypothesis about innate arithmetical skills

Gelman was a colleague and a co-author in some of Starkey's work with babies, and this work and other research that appeared to show some understanding of number in babies played an important part in her own hypothesis of an innate understanding of number. However, most of the work that she herself did in support of her hypothesis was with older children and involved different procedures and some extremely interesting ideas.

Gelman and her colleagues started from the position that any number system, to be a viable number system, must have five characteristics. They called these universal characteristics "principles," and they argued that it was possible that an understanding of these principles could be built in as an innate structure of the human mind. There is, it should be noted, some similarity between this approach and Chomsky's (1986) to the significance of universals in grammar. Chomsky and Gelman both make the same point: where there are universal features in a system that the child must learn about, there may also be innate mechanisms that are specifically tuned to these universals.

These five principles were first set out in a book by Gelman and Gallistel (1978). The first three were "how to count" principles. We can consider first the *one-to-one principle*. This is that one must count all the objects in a set once and once only: each one must be given just one number tag. For Gelman and her colleagues the one-to-one principle is about how to count one set of objects. Another "how to count" principle is the *stable order principle*, which means that we must produce the number words in a certain order, and in the same set order each time. The final "how to count" principle is the *cardinal principle*. In Gelman's terms the cardinal principle is that the last number counted represents the value of the set.

The other two principles were the *abstraction principle* and the *order irrelevance principle*. The first of these states that the number in a set is quite independent of any of the qualities of the members in that set: the rules for counting a heterogeneous set of objects are the same as for counting a homogeneous one. The order irrelevance principle is that the order in which members of a set are counted makes no difference, and anyone who counts a set, for example, from left to right, will come to the same answer as someone else who counts it from right to left.

One point that should be made straightaway about these five principles is that they are right as far as they go, but that they do not go far enough. Gelman and Gallistel are right to say that each of the five principles is essential to any counting system. A system in which one did not have to obey, say, the one-to-one principle would not be a counting system at all. One could not use it to find out the number of a set or to compare two different sets reliably. However, the understanding of number involves more than this, and in particular it involves understanding the relation between different number sets, which is not touched on at all in Gelman and Gallistel's research.

Having restricted their requirements to the process of counting a single set, Gelman and Gallistel, not surprisingly, set out to find out how well children do count a set of objects. They gave children, aged between 2 and 5 years, sets that varied in number from 2 to 19 and simply asked these children to count them, recording all the while how they set about doing it. Thus they recorded whether the children always produced number words in the same order whenever they counted and always counted each object once, and also whether they seemed to recognize that the last number counted signified the number of the set.

The main pattern of the results of this study was a difference in set size. The older children did better than the younger ones, as one would expect, but at all age levels the children seemed to respect Gelman and Gallistel's principles with small number sets, although they very often failed to do so when the number in the sets was greater. The experimenters couched their explanation of these results in terms of "principles-before-skills." They reasoned that children must understand counting principles if they consistently respect them with the smaller sets. Their mistakes with the larger sets, therefore, were due not to a failure in understanding, but to difficulties in carrying out the right procedures in increasingly difficult circumstances. One-to-one counting should be harder, for example, with large sets than with small ones because one is more likely to forget which items have already been counted and which remain to be counted with a large than a small set. So Gelman and Gallistel claimed that children start with the right principles, but only gradually acquire the skills to apply them effectively.

In another set of studies Gelman and her colleagues, Meck and Merkin (Gelman & Meck, 1983: Gelman, Meck, & Merkin, 1986) asked preschool children to make judgments about a puppet which they saw counting: this puppet occasionally violated the one-to-one principle and the cardinal principle, and the aim of these experiments was to see whether the children could spot these violations. By and large the results of these studies supported Gelman's contention that, long before they go to school and are taught mathematics formally, children do have some understanding of the three "how to count" principles as these were set out in her model.

These studies demonstrate that quite young children do have some knowledge about how to count, but this does not mean that the children know about number. The big gap in this research, as we have seen, is that it ignores the understanding of relations between sets. Gelman and Gallistel's criterion for the cardinal principle (the last number counted) is adequate for the counting of one set of objects, but cardinality is also about the relations between sets. Cardinality refers to the fact that any set of objects of a particular number is the same in quantity as any other set with that same number. Equal number sets, furthermore, are in one-to-one correspondence. For each item in one set there is an equivalent item in the other. Gelman and Gallistel's scheme, even though it included principles called the cardinal principle and the one-to one principle, does not cater either for cardinality or one-to-one correspondence, and yet these are also essential features of every possible counting system.

Gelman's scheme leaves out ordinal relations too. The nearest that her data get to these is in the use of what she calls the stable order principle – the use of count words in the same order on different occasions. This, too, is an essential feature of any workable counting system, but it has nothing to do with the understanding that successive numbers represent an ascending quantitative scale – that 3 is more than 2 and 2 more than 1.

It is true to say that Gelman did not ever make the claim that preschool children understand ordinal relations, or even cardinality or the one-to-one principle in the sense that we have given it, but the fact is that a child who does not understand these principles must have a most imperfect understanding of number.

The case for an effective, innate number sense is therefore very weak. The research on the possibility of an intact mechanism for detecting and recognizing numbers in very young babies is inconsistent and questionable at some points, and the evidence from work with preschool children that is said to support the principles-before-skills hypothesis is remarkably limited. There is certainly no need to turn away from alternative hypotheses that children must in some way learn the concepts of mathematics.

Logic in the understanding of number

The suggestion that we are going to make is that the best starting point for looking at children learning about number is the work of Piaget (1952b). This may come as a surprise because of the criticism heaped on much of his work in recent years, but, when it comes to the understanding of number at least, Piaget's theory still provides a more coherent explanation than any other of children's solutions to mathematical problems.

Piaget's is a theory of learning, and the most exciting part of the theory is the story that it tells about the steps that children take in order to conquer the complexities of mathematics. But a theory that states that children have to learn mathematical rules must start with the assumption that they do not know these rules in the first place. It is this negative part of Piaget's theory which has attracted the most intense criticism, while the positive side has received little attention.

We can start with the negative side, and take Piaget's unambiguous answer to the question: do young children understand what they are doing when they count? For him, young children's counting was a clear instance of children using words without understanding what they mean. They learn the number sequence, he claimed, and they even learn how to apply it to objects and to actions, and yet for many years they do not have the slightest idea of what the sequence means.

Piaget argued that children must understand both the cardinal and the ordinal properties of number in order to grasp the meaning of number words. The cardinal properties of number concern absolute amounts, as we have seen: two or more different sets of objects which have the same number are equal in amount and for every member of each set there will be an equivalent member in the other set. The ordinal properties are about relations between different numbers. Children have to understand that the order of numbers in the number sequence is an order of increasing magnitude.

Piaget reached his striking conclusion that at first children count without understanding counting because of evidence that at this age they understand neither cardinal nor ordinal number. His main empirical justification came from the results of his well-known conservation, transitivity, and seriation experiments. The conservation experiments convinced him that children do not understand one-to-one correspondence in the preschool years and therefore have no grasp of cardinality. The seriation and transitivity experiments provided the basis for Piaget's claim that children cannot deal with a series of relations: they are perfectly capable of understanding that A is more than B at one time and at another that B is more than C, but they cannot, according to Piaget, coordinate these two pieces of information to reach the conclusion that A is more than C and this means that they are unable to understand the number sequence as a sequence of ascending magnitude.

Of these two claims the first (failure in cardinality) is easier to assess than the second (failure in ordinality), at any rate as far as children's counting is concerned. This is because Piaget's work on children's understanding of seriation and of transitivity was only done with continuous quantities and so the children did not have to count to solve these problems. On the other hand some of Piaget's work on conservation, and particularly the work that he did together with his colleague Pierre Greco, was directly concerned with children's use and understanding of number words.

In a well-known experiment Greco (1962) gave children of 4 to 8 years three different versions of the conservation of number task. One of these tasks was the traditional conservation problem, in which children saw two identical-looking sets, judged correctly that the two sets were equal in number, then saw the appearance of one of the sets being altered, and were asked once again to compare the quantity of the two sets. The second task took roughly the same form except that after the transformation the children were required to count one of the sets and were then asked to infer the number of the second set. In the third task the children were required to count both sets after the transformation and then were asked whether they were equal in quantity.

Two of the results are important here. Most children younger than 6 years failed all three tasks: the point to grasp about these children is that in the third task they counted both sets in the final part of the task, arrived at the same number, and yet still said that the more spread-out of the two sets had more objects in it than the other one did. They judged that one set with "eight" objects in it was more numerous than another set, also with "eight" objects, and that meant, according to Piaget and to Greco, that they really could not know what the word "eight" means.

The second important result was that slightly older children tended to get the first task (the traditional conservation problem) wrong and yet were right in the second task in which they counted one set and then were asked to infer the number of objects in the second set. These children therefore judged that spreading out a set of objects alters its quantity (their mistaken judgment in the traditional task) but not its number in the sense of the number one would reach if one were to count the set.

Piaget and Greco's explanation of these results took the form of a distinction between "quantité" (in this case, numerosity) and "quotité" (in this case, number words). They argued that many children realize that two sets of objects have the same number, in the sense that counting each one leads to the same number word, and yet think that there are more objects in the more spread out set. These children grasped the fact that the number words (quotité) stayed the same despite the perceptual transformation of one of the sets, and yet did not realize that the numerosity (quantité) was also quite unchanged by this irrelevant, perceptual change.

The Greco experiment was about number comparisons between sets, the aspect of number that Gelman conspicuously ignored, and it is notable that virtually all the evidence that we have on children making number comparisons seems to conflict with her optimistic picture of young children's numerical understanding. There is, for example, some striking evidence that young children who count quite proficiently still do not know how to use numbers to compare two different sets. Both Michie (1984) and Saxe (1979) found a marked reluctance in young children, whom they asked to compare two sets of objects quantitatively, to count the two sets. They could have counted them and it would have been the right thing to do, but they did not.

Their reluctance to use number as a comparative measure was demonstrated even more clearly in an experiment by Sophian (1988) in which she asked 3- and 4-year-old children to judge whether a puppet who counted was doing the right thing. The puppet was given two sets of objects and was told in some trials to compare the two sets and in others to find out how many objects there were altogether. So, in the first kind of trial the right thing to do was to count the two sets separately while in the second it was to count them together. Sometimes the puppet got it right but at other times it mistakenly counted all the objects together when it was asked to compare the two sets and counted them separately when it was asked how many objects there were altogether.

The results of this experiment were largely negative. The younger children did particularly badly (below chance) in the trials in which the puppet was asked to compare two different sets. They simply preferred to count all the items as one set, and thus they clearly had no idea that one must count two rows separately in order to compare them. This suggests that they have not yet grasped the cardinal properties of the numbers that they are counting.

Thus research on comparisons of numbers suggests that these pose great difficulties for young children. Similar difficulties can even be found in tasks where they have to count single quantities. Several studies (Frye, Braisby, Lowe, Maroudas, & and Nicholls, 1989; Wynn, 1990) have shown that when children are asked to give someone a certain number of objects ("Give me five bricks") they often fail to count and simply grab a handful of objects and the number that they hand over is for the most part wrong. Thus, even when they only have to count a single set, young children do not seem to understand the significance of counting. They may realize, when they count, that the last number is the important one, but the fact that they do not seem to know very well when to count suggests that they have not grasped why it is important. They have not understood the cardinal properties of the number words that they know so well. Their performance fits the Piagetian picture of children knowing the number words (quotité) without understanding numerosity (quantité).

Another look at one-to-one correspondence

Piaget argued that young children do not understand one-to-one correspondence. He based this conclusion mainly on the results of his well-known and controversial conservation task. The main purpose of the conservation experiments was to test children's understanding of the invariance of quantity, a question about which there is a great deal of controversy (Donaldson, 1978, 1982; Light, Buckingham, & Robbins, 1979; McGarrigle & Donaldson, 1974). Nevertheless the experiments also produced evidence to support Piaget's claim about one-to-one correspondence, at any rate when the correspondences were spatially defined.

When two sets of objects are put side by side it is quite easy to see whether each item has its pair in the other set. Of course these spatial comparisons are much easier with some spatial arrangements than they are with others. It is easier to compare two ranks of soldiers in this way than two football teams in action on a football ground. Yet there is evidence that 6-year-old children seem unable to use one-to-one correspondence even with displays where it should be very easy to do so. Piaget, for example, showed children a row of objects and asked them to lay out another row with the same number. The younger children plainly did not pair the items and usually equated the rows in terms of their length rather than their number. Piaget and Inhelder themselves (1966), and also Cowan and Daniels (1989), have shown that children often fail to use one-to-one correspondence to compare the number of items in two straight rows of counters laid side by side, even when the individual counters in each set are themselves connected by straight lines. Even this obvious cue for one-to-one correspondence makes little difference to the children's comparisons, which, not surprisingly, are frequently wrong.

It would be easy to decide from results such as these that young children have no understanding at all of one-to-one correspondence, but there is at least one good reason for not rushing to this negative conclusion. It is that children often share, and sharing is an activity that on the face of it seems to depend on one-to-one correspondence. Three quite separate studies (Desforges & Desforges, 1980; Frydman & Bryant, 1988; Miller, 1984) have shown that children as young as 4 years share out numbers of things equally between two or more recipients rather successfully, and they usually do so on a repetitive "one for A, one for B" basis. This looks like a temporal form of one-to-one correspondence.

If that is so, we have to ask the same question that we asked with counting. We have shown that children often count without understanding counting. Perhaps they also share on a one-to-one basis without any idea why this is the right thing to do. Sharing, like counting, is a common activity which young children must witness quite often and may very well imitate. They may know that sharing in a one-to-one way is the right thing to do in certain circumstances, and yet have no clear idea about how it works.

Sharing singles and doubles

A   B

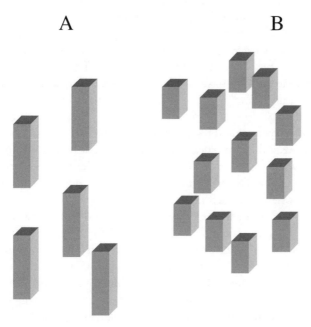

"Give singles to A and doubles to B, but make sure that A and B have the same amount."

Figure 19.2   The singles and double condition in Frydman and Bryant's (1988) sharing experiment

Olivier Frydman and I tried to find out more about children's understanding of sharing with a task in which children who share without understanding one-to-one correspondence would behave in one way, and children who understand the basis of one-to-one sharing would respond quite differently. We gave the children "chocolates" which were either single or double chocolates (figure 19.2): in fact these were plastic Unifix bricks, all of the same color, which could be stuck together. We asked the children to share the chocolates out to two recipients, so that each recipient ended up with the same total amount. But we also told the children that one of the recipients only accepted doubles and the other only singles. So the child's problem was to work out that for every double that he gave one recipient, he now had to give two singles to the other one. We reasoned that a child who had shared on a one-to-one basis in a rote fashion would not be able to make this adjustment, whereas a child who understood the basis for one-to-one sharing would see the reason for changing to a one (double) for A, two (singles) for B pattern.

This study produced a sharp developmental difference. Most of the 4-year-old children did not make the adjustment, and in fact the majority ended up giving the recipient who accepted doubles twice as many chocolates in all as the recipient who accepted singles. This was because these children continued sharing in a one-to-one manner, which meant that for every single that they gave one recipient they handed out a double to the other. In contrast most of the 5-year-olds did manage to make the necessary adjustment. These children usually gave the double to one recipient and then immediately two singles to the other, and so on. The reason for the difference between the two age groups is unclear to us, but at the very least the study establishes that 5-year-old children have a clear and flexible understanding of the mathematical basis of one-to-one sharing. They know why they do it.

What about the 4-year-olds? They had certainly hit a barrier in our new version of the sharing task, but we still had no idea how formidable that barrier was for them. So, in a later study we devised a new version of the singles/doubles task in which we introduced bricks of different colors. Our aim was to use color cues to emphasize one-to-one correspondence. In this new task each double consisted of a yellow and a blue brick joined together (figure 19.3), and half the singles were blue and half yellow. This was the only change, and yet it had a dramatic effect. Nearly all the 4-year-old children solved the problem, and they did so because they could now see how to use one-to-one correspondence to solve the problem. The typical pattern of sharing was to give a double (consisting of course of one yellow and one blue brick) to one recipient and then to give a yellow and a blue single to the other one. They adapted the one-to-one strategy successfully when the one-to-one cues were emphasized. They also learned a great deal from this experience, because when later on we gave the same children the single/doubles task with bricks of one color only (as in the original experiment) these children did extremely well. They had surmounted the barrier that we identified in the first study, and we conclude from this that even 4-year-old children have a basic understanding of the reason why one-to-one sharing leads to equal quantities. It follows that they do have a respectable grasp of one-to-one correspondence and therefore a basis for understanding the cardinal properties of number.

But do they extend this understanding to number words? We looked at this question in another study. In this we took a group of 4-year-old children who could share quite well, and we asked them to share out some "sweets" (again Unifix bricks) between two recipients. When this was done we counted out aloud the number of sweets that the child had given to one recipient, and then asked him or her how many had been given to the other recipient. None of the children straightaway made the correct inference that the other recipient had the same number of sweets even though they had meticulously shared the sweets out on a one-to-one basis: instead all of them tried to count the second lot of sweets. We stopped them doing so, and asked the question again. But even then less than half the children made the correct inference about the second recipient's sweets.

Thus many 4-year-old children fail to extend their considerable understanding of sharing to counting. We conclude from this that young children do grasp the cardinality of number and yet do not at first apply this understanding to number words. Here, it could be said, is an example of understanding numerosity (quantité) without knowing how to put this understanding into words (quotité). The children do have

Intervention: sharing singles and doubles

Experimental group's task

A   B

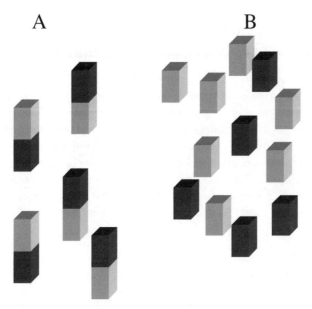

"Give singles to A and doubles to B, but make sure that A and B have the same amount."

Figure 19.3 The material given to the experimental group in the intervention experiment on sharing singles and doubles

quite a good grasp of one-to-one correspondence, but do not apply this knowledge to number words.

Conclusions about the beginnings of the understanding of number

The case for effective innate structures especially tuned to mathematical rules is not at all good. Much of the evidence produced to show that babies understand number is either unreliable or ambiguous. The mistakes that preschool children subsequently make in simple number tasks cannot be dismissed as mere procedural errors, as Gelman and her colleagues tried to do. Tasks in which these children have to compare separate quantities show genuine gaps in the young children's understanding of some basic and essential number concepts. They do not see counting as a way to measure the relative quantities of two different sets, and they are happy to assert that two sets with the same number are different in quantity. Even when they know that two sets are equal in quantity and they also know the number of items in one set, they often fail to infer the number of items in the uncounted set. They plainly have a lot to learn. How then do they learn it?

Learning about Arithmetical Operations: Additive Reasoning

So far we have dealt with number on its own. Now we must turn to the operations that children perform on numbers. There are four of these, but we have good grounds for dividing them into two broad categories and two forms of reasoning, additive and multiplicative reasoning. Additive reasoning includes addition and subtraction, which are inverse operations. Multiplication and division are the two operations which come under the heading of multiplicative reasoning, and these two operations are also the inverse of each other. There is evidence too, as we shall see, that additive reasoning comes more easily to children and generally earlier than multiplicative reasoning does.

Adding and taking away

Additive reasoning may come early, but just how early it comes is now a matter of strong contention. In 1992 Wynn, an American psychologist, made the striking claim that she had shown that babies as young as 6 months old add and subtract, and thereby started a controversy which still rages today (see also Wynn, 1998).

Wynn's ingenious studies were based on the assumption that babies pay a great deal of attention to events that take them by surprise. She argued that if babies can add and subtract they should be surprised, and their attention should be caught, by additions and subtractions that apparently end in the wrong result. Wynn therefore enacted additions and subtractions, which sometimes led to the correct and sometimes to the incorrect outcome. The addition was always 1 + 1, which she enacted by putting a Mickey Mouse on a platform in front of the child, then raising a screen between this toy and the child so that the toy was now out of sight, and finally ostentatiously placing another Mickey Mouse behind the screen, so that there were now two of these toys but both hidden from the child. At this point she lowered the screen, and the child could see how many Mickey Mouse toys there were on the platform. On half the trials two toys were there, but on the other half, by trickery on the part of the experimenter, only one toy was left.

The subtraction trials took much the same form. Wynn started these by showing the child two Mickey Mouse toys on the platform and continued by blocking the child's view of these toys with the screen: then, in full view of the child, she put her hand behind the screen and removed one of the two toys. Finally the screen was lowered, revealing one

Mickey Mouse toy on some trials, and on other trials, again by the experimenter's artifice, two of them.

Thus the additions and subtractions that Wynn enacted sometimes led to the correct outcome (1 + 1 = 2, 2 − 1 = 1) and sometimes not (1 + 1 = 1, 2 − 1 = 2). Wynn argued that any baby who can add 1 to 1, or subtract 1 from 2, should be surprised, and should look long and hard, at the two incorrect outcomes.

Her results supported this idea. The babies did indeed look longer at the wrong outcomes than at the right ones, and Wynn concluded that this meant that they had done the necessary adding and subtracting. But the differences in mean looking time at the two outcomes was relatively slight, being always less than four seconds, and Wynn's design did not exclude an alternative explanation for this difference. The problem was that the incorrect outcome was always the same as the starting point in each problem (1 in the addition and 2 in the subtraction problems). Perhaps the babies had expected a change – any change – as a result of the addition or subtraction, and were simply surprised to see the status quo.

To rule this alternative out Wynn carried out another study, this time just with the 1 + 1 addition. Again she compared the babies' looking time to the correct and incorrect outcomes, but this time the incorrect outcome was 3. Thus both outcomes, correct and incorrect, were different from the starting point. She found that the babies did indeed look longer at the new incorrect outcome (1 + 1 = 3) than at the correct one, and argued that the babies had therefore added.

These results are arresting, but there are still reasons for doubt about the conclusions that Wynn drew from them. One such reason is that Wynn apparently did not carry out the same further test with subtraction. She could for example, have given babies trials in which 3 − 1 led to the incorrect outcome of 1, but she did not. So one cannot be sure that babies have any understanding of subtraction (Bryant, 1992). Another problem is that the babies' greater interest in the 1 + 1 = 3 than in the 1 + 1 = 2 outcome could simply be due to them being more interested in the larger number of toys, or just taking more time to process three than two objects. So the apparently crucial result of the second study could be spurious, and again the acid test would be to introduce the 3 − 1 = 1 outcome. If babies look more at that than at the correct outcome of 3 − 1 = 2, one could dismiss the idea of the influence of numerosity, because here the incorrect outcome is less numerous than the correct one.

This was the starting point for an experiment by Wakeley, Rivera, and Langer (2000a, 2000b) that introduced the 3 − 1 = 1 and 3 − 1 = 2 events, and also repeated all four conditions of Wynn's first study. These experimenters found no significant difference in looking time at the 3 − 1 = 1 and the 3 − 1 = 2 outcomes, and they also failed to repeat the differences in the attention that babies spent on trials with correct and trials with incorrect outcomes that Wynn reported in her first study. This double failure is a serious blow for Wynn's hypothesis of an innate understanding of addition and subtraction. Even though some studies have repeated Wynn's original results (Wynn, 2000), others have not, and it is hard at the moment for an impartial observer to conclude anything much, except that there is a need for extreme caution. Babies may add and subtract, but, then again, they may not.

Preschool children: adding, counting all, counting on

Whatever the final outcome of the argument about babies, there is clear evidence that children are able to perform simple additions and subtractions with concrete objects long before they go to school (Hughes, 1981, 1986), and probably by the age of 3 years or so (Huttenlocher, Levine, & Jordan, 1994). There are some interesting details here, in particular Hughes's observation of a large discrepancy between the times when young children work out the results of an addition and subtraction of concrete objects (2 + 2 toys), even imagined objects, and when they can do the same calculations as abstract sums with no concrete context at all (just 2 + 2). As with sharing, so too with adding, it seems that children have great difficulty in translating a basic, effective mathematical procedure into the conventional counting system.

There is more to additive reasoning, however, than just making a calculation, and here again we must turn to Piaget (1954; Piaget & Inhelder, 1974). He and his colleagues provided the best conceptual framework for studying children's additive reasoning that exists. He argued that children do not understand the nature of additive reasoning until they have grasped the inverse relations between adding and subtracting. It is not enough, he claimed, for them to know, or to be able to work out, that $4 + 3 = 7$ and that $7 - 4 = 3$. They must also understand why each of these two sums automatically follows from the other. They must realize how one operation cancels out the other.

He went further, for he also claimed that children's understanding of number itself depends on this knowledge. Here he invoked the notion of the additive composition of number, which is an extraordinarily useful and important, but very underrated, idea in the study of children's mathematics. It means that numbers consist, or are made up, of other numbers. So 7 is made up of 4 and 3 or 5 and 2, and it follows that if you subtract 3 from 7 you will be left with 4. Thus Piaget (1952b, 2001) argued that children's understanding of the inverse relations between adding and subtracting will revolutionize their thinking about the nature of number itself.

Piaget's interest in inversion is of course directly connected to the stress that he laid on "reversibility" in his theory of cognitive development. It is curious that Piaget and his colleagues did very little empirical research on this stimulating idea, but others have. The main evidence about it comes from three rather different types of experiment – one is the study of children's use of counting to solve simple addition problems, another is research on word problems, and the final one involves direct experiments on the study of inversion.

Counting and adding

Most adults use their well-rehearsed knowledge of simple facts to solve addition and subtraction problems. We all know that $4 + 3 = 7$ and we can use this knowledge without actually having to go through the process of adding three units to four. It takes some time before young children have this sort of knowledge at their fingertips, and so they actually have to add when they are asked to do so. The way that they do so changes, as they grow older, and the change is directly relevant to the question of the additive composition of number.

The change is captured in a task where children are first given a set of objects and are told its number; then another set is added and again the children are told its number. The question that they are asked is how many there are now – how many altogether? The sharp developmental difference in children's reaction to this question (Fuson, 1988) is simple to tell. Younger children tend to count all the items: children who are older, but not yet old enough to use the number facts easily, will start by taking the number of one of the sets, and counting on, by the number of the second set, to the total. Thus, if they are dealing with a set of four and a set of three, the younger children will simply count first one set (1–2–3–4) and then the other (5–6–7) whereas the older children will, more economically, start where the first set leaves off (5–6–7).

The success of the older children in finding an economic, and usually quite untaught, strategy suggests that they have begun to realize that the total number is made up of different component numbers, and that the difference between one component (4) and the total is the other component (3).

Word problems: missing addends and subtrahends

Word problems are sums that are couched in fictional, concrete events. Some time ago, Vergnaud (1982), a French psychologist, showed that children who easily solve a direct addition word problem (Tom had five apples, and Bill gave him three more: how many does he have now?) are nevertheless in great difficulty when they face the same sum as a "missing subtrahend" problem (Bob had some apples: Bill ate five of them. There were three apples left. How many did Bob have to start off with?). Why is one so much more difficult than the other?

The main difficulty, as Nuñes and Bryant (1996) have shown, is in transforming a story that on the surface is about subtraction (Bob took and ate some apples) into an addition problem. Nuñes and Bryant showed this by giving children calculators to help them solve the problem: most children who failed to find the right solution actually performed the wrong operation (addition when it should have been subtraction and vice versa) on the calculator.

Children who make this mistake do so because they apparently cannot move quickly from information about addition to subtracting, and vice versa. To solve the missing subtrahend problem that we have just described, you must know that if $a - b = c$, then $c + b = a$: you must understand inversion.

Experiments on inversion

$254 + 178 - 178$ is an easy sum to do because one can solve it by canceling the addition with the subtraction. Children who do not grasp the inverse relation between adding and subtracting should not, however, find it easy or easier than any other similar adding and subtracting problem. Yet there is evidence that even children as young as 5 do find a + b − b problems easier than standard adding and subtracting problems, and therefore seem to be taking advantage of inversion (Bisanz & Lefevre, 1992; Bryant, Christie, & Rendu, 1999; Siegler & Stern, 1998; Stern, 1993).

Their use of inversion seems to be genuine. One potential problem is that children could solve the inversion problems just on the basis of identity rather than in a quantitative sense. If you get a shirt muddy and then the mud is washed off, the shirt is as clean as before. One change is canceled out by the other, but to work this out is not to make a quantitative judgment. Bryant et al. (1999), however, produced evidence that the children were making genuinely quantitative judgments. We gave children a + b − b and a − b + b as well as control (a + a − b and a − b + a) problems with concrete material under two conditions (figure 19.4). In one (identity) the same bricks were added and then taken away, or taken away and then added. In the other (non-identity) the same amount of bricks were added and then subtracted or vice versa in the inversion problems, but they were different bricks. Bricks were added to one end of the tower and subtracted from the other. Thus the use of inversion here would have nothing to do with identity: it had to be quantitative. We found that even 5-year-old children were, to some extent, able to take advantage of inversion in the non-identity condition, and therefore were making a genuinely quantitative judgment about inversion (though it has to be said that they did better in the identity inversion condition).

These last results do not fit well with Piaget's idea that young children fail to grasp the inversion principle, and yet the other work – on counting all and counting on, and on the missing addend/subtrahend problems – certainly does support, and is explained well by, that idea. Can these two sets of results be reconciled?

The solution, it seems to me, is to make a distinction between understanding a principle and using it to solve problems. It looks as though even 5-year-old children do have some understanding, in a quantitative sense, of the way in which an addition cancels out a subtraction, but have not used this knowledge yet to work out the additive composition of number. The understanding of inversion is, as Piaget pointed out, absolutely necessary for grasping additive composition, but it seems that it is not immediately sufficient. It takes time for children to work out the implications of inversion.

Additive composition and the decimal system

It is easy to see that an understanding of the decimal system must be heavily dependent on a good understanding of the additive composition of number. This link is essential, because the whole system depends on our knowing that 12 is composed of 10 and 2, and that 53 is composed of five 10s and a 3. So, it is not surprising, given the results that we have already presented, that 5- and 6-year-old children often do have difficulty in constructing numbers by combining 10s and units.

One task that shows this difficulty is the Shop Task, described in Nuñes and Bryant (1996). In this the children are given money and are charged for items that they want to buy in a shop set up by the experimenters. In some trials they need to pay in one denomination only – just in single pence or just in 10p coins. In other trials they must mix denominations – 10ps and pence to reach the right price. These mixed trials are the

Inversion: Concrete – identical

$9 + 5 - 5$

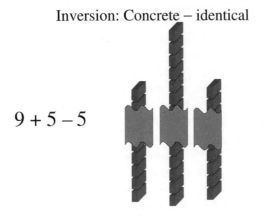

Inversion: Concrete – different

$9 + 5 - 5$

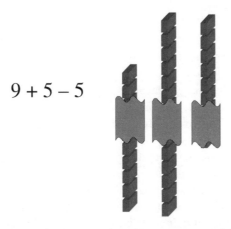

Figure 19.4   The two kinds of inversion task with concrete material. In the identical task the same items are added to and subtracted from the tower. In the different task different items are added and subtracted. The tower is partially covered by a cloth to prevent the children solving the problem by counting

hardest for 5- and 6-year-old children. It is possible that their difficulty in the mixed denomination trials is really a difficulty in additive composition of number. They do not see clearly enough that the number 19 can be decomposed into a ten and a nine.

There is another explanation, which is that their difficulty with the decimal system is a linguistic one, and the evidence for that comes from a series of studies that show that children in Asian countries are better at composing quantities by combining tens and units than children from European countries (Miura, Kim, Chang, & Okamoto, 1988; Miura, Okamoto, Kim, Chang, Steere, & Fayol, 1994). In Chinese and Japanese (the Asian countries represented in these studies) the teen and decade words are more transparent than in European languages. They do not have words like "eleven" "twelve" "thirteen": they say the equivalent of "ten-one" "ten-two" "ten-three."

There are two points to be made here. One is that the Asian superiority may not be due to linguistic differences (Towse & Saxton, 1997). There is plenty of evidence that children from the countries represented in these studies do better in mathematics generally than children from the West, and thus they may very well have understood the additive composition of number well before their Western peers. This, and not the linguistic variable, could be the reason for the differences between Asian and Western children in the effective use of the decimal system.

One final point that should be made about the understanding of the additive composition of number is that it must involve some agility in thinking about the relationships between parts and wholes. The child must eventually be able to think of the total, e.g. 7, and its component parts, 4 + 3, simultaneously. We cannot take this level of thinking for granted.

Multiplicative Reasoning

Multiplication and proportions

With multiplication and division we encounter difficulties that last throughout many children's school life (Hart, 1981), and that is not surprising because, as Piaget pointed out, multiplicative problems are inherently more complex than additive ones. If you add 5 to 17 and to 23 and 41, the ensuing change is the same with each addition: in each case there is an increase of 5. But if you multiply 17, 23, and 41 by 5 the change depends not just on the size of the multiplier but also of the multiplicand: the change will be greater when 42 is multiplied by 5 than when 17 is multiplied by 5. So multiplicative thinking requires the child to think about the interaction between two variables, and there is no doubt that this causes even quite old children and probably many adults as well a great deal of difficulty.

Inhelder and Piaget (1958) certainly showed this with children in a series of problems in which two variables covary multiplicatively. Their tasks were about the understanding of proportions, mostly in scientific demonstrations, such as their tests of children's understanding of equilibrium and of probability. A good example is their well-known study of the balance scale (see Wilkening & Huber, ch. 16 this volume). The balance scale has two longish arms and weights can be placed at various points along these arms. The child has to work out how to keep the scale in equilibrium, and therefore has to discover the multiplicative relation between the two relevant variables, the amount of each weight, and its distance from the center.

It could be argued that the context of these problems was unfamiliar and offputting, but the same difficulties have been documented too by other experimenters with problems that use mundane everyday material. Karplus, Pulos, and Stage (1983), for example, gave 12- and 14-year-old children a task in which there were two characters, Mr Short and Mr Tall. Karplus et al. then measured the height of these two characters with buttons.

Mr Short measured four buttons in height and Mr Tall six buttons. Having shown the children this, the experimenters then measured Mr Short's height with paperclips, and showed that he was six paperclips high. The figure that the children then had to work out was Mr Tall's height in paperclips. Karplus and his colleagues found some persistent difficulties among their teenage participants. Many of them made a mistake that is known as the "additive error." They argued that Mr Tall was eight paperclips high. Presumably these children added two, because they assumed that since there was a difference of two buttons between Mr Short and Mr Tall when the pair were measured in buttons, there would be the same difference when they were measured in paperclips.

Faced with errors as stubborn as this, one could quite reasonably conclude that proportional reasoning comes very late indeed to most children, but it is not as simple as that. There are often different ways to solve the same proportional problems, and there is evidence that that some of these ways come more easily to children than others. Piaget (1965) himself demonstrated that 5- to 6-year-old children can solve proportional problems on the basis of one-to-many correspondence: for example, he showed that they could work out how many flowers could go in a certain number of vases when each vase took two flowers. One-to-many correspondences are in effect ratios, and the intriguing possibility here is that children first solve proportional problems on the basis of ratios and in other ways later.

The main other way would be to use functions. The distinction between ratios and functions is neatly captured in a well-known study by Hart (1984) on 13- to 15 year-old-children's reactions to her onion soup problem. This takes the form of a recipe in which the quantities are enough to feed eight people (8 onions, 2 pints of water, 4 chicken soup cubes, 2 dessertspoons of butter, $\frac{1}{2}$ pint of cream). Hart asked the children to work out what quantities would be right for four people, and for six people.

There are two ways to solve this problem. One is to work out functions, which would mean dividing the number of onions etc. by the number of consumers and thus working out that one needs one onion and $\frac{1}{4}$ pint of water per person, and then multiplying these functions by 4 for the four-person, and by 6 for the six-person, recipe. This is called the *functional solution*. The second way to solve the problem is called the *scalar solution*. This means working out a new ratio by multiplying or dividing each figure in the original ratio by the same amount. You solve the onion soup problems by noting that the new recipe (for four people) is for half the number of people in the original recipe: so you halve the quantity of each of the ingredients. Notice that the scalar solution is much easier for the four-person recipe, where one just has to halve, than for the six-person recipe, which involves a more complex arithmetical relation. Hart found that most children adopted the scalar solution for both problems, and that this solution worked much better with the four- than with the six-person recipe.

The children's preference for the scalar solution was quite striking, because they stuck to it even when the arithmetic that they had to do was difficult and hazardous. Some later work in Brazil by Nuñes, Schliemann, and Carraher (1993) confirms this strong preference. They gave secondary school children a series of problems about the proportion of unprocessed to processed seafood. In half of the problems the arithmetic required for the scalar solution was easier than for the functional solution. In the other half it was the other way round: in arithmetical terms the functional solution was easier than the

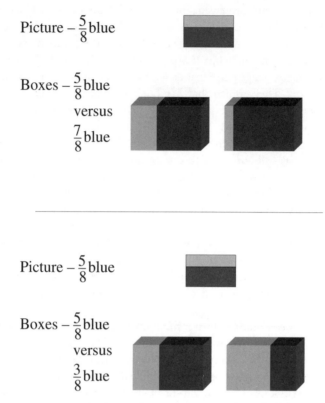

Picture – $\frac{5}{8}$ blue

Boxes – $\frac{5}{8}$ blue

versus

$\frac{7}{8}$ blue

Picture – $\frac{5}{8}$ blue

Boxes – $\frac{5}{8}$ blue

versus

$\frac{3}{8}$ blue

Figure 19.5   The material used in two conditions in Spinillo and Bryant's (1991) experiment on proportional reasoning. The top condition in which both boxes have more blue than white is more difficult than the bottom condition in which there is more blue than white in one box, and less blue than white in the other

scalar one. These children did extremely well when the scalar solution was easy to calculate, and rather badly when it posed difficult arithmetic problems for them. Their rate of success, therefore, depended entirely on the ease of the scalar solution. They did not turn to the functional solution even when it posed no arithmetical difficulty at all.

The suggestion that children are at ease with ratios is supported by research on an entirely different kind of task, in which children have to distinguish figures on the basis of the relationship between their component parts. Spinillo and Bryant (1991, 1999) showed children two open rectangular boxes, each packed full with a large number of small blue and white bricks (figure 19.5). These bricks were arranged in two sections, blue and white, and sometimes the dividing-line between the sections was horizontal and sometimes vertical. We also showed children a much smaller picture of one of the boxes and the children's task was to say which of the two boxes was represented in the picture. In the crucial condition, the perceptual arrangement in the picture was different from the arrangement in the boxes. If the division in the boxes was vertical, it was horizontal in the picture, and vice versa. We told the children that the bricks in the box represented in the picture were still the same, but they had been rearranged since the picture was made. The point here was that the only way that the children could solve the problem in this condition was on the basis of the proportion of the blue and white areas in each box.

Again, however, there are two possible ways of solving the problem. One is to compare the two parts (e.g. more white than blue or white equal to blue) and the other is to work out the relation between each part and the whole (5/8 of the box is blue and 3/8 white). The first strategy is easy when the two sections are equal in one box and unequal in the other, or when the relationship between the blue and white sections is different in the two boxes (in one box more blue than white, in the other more white than blue). This latter example should be easy, because the child can judge that there is more blue than white in one box, and more white than blue in the other, and then see which of these two blue–white relationships holds for the picture.

But what if the simple blue–white relationship (more than, less than) is the same in both boxes even though the blue–white proportion differs? Suppose, for example, that 1/8 of one box is blue and 7/8 white, while 3/8 of the other box is blue and 5/8 white. Here there is more white than blue in both boxes, and so the simple "part–part" relationship is the same in both boxes.

We found that the younger children depended predominantly on the simple part–part relationship. When these were different (equal blue and white in one box, unequal in the other, or more blue than white in one box and more white than blue in the other) the children did well. However, when there was more white than blue in both boxes, as in the example just given, or more blue than white in both, the children in all age groups, but particularly in the younger groups, made many more mistakes. So the children relied on simple part–part relations and, since ratios are also part–part relations, it is highly likely that there is a connection between this result and the evidence produced by Hart and by Nuñes et al. that children prefer to work with ratios rather than with functions.

We can suggest, therefore, a simple, but tentative hypothesis (see Nuñes & Bryant, 1996 for a more detailed account of this hypothesis). It is that the starting point for children's reasoning about multiplication is one-to-many correspondence, which leads to an understanding of ratio and also to a sensitivity to part–part relations. Eventually this provides the basis for their learning about functions and therefore about part–whole relations.

Division

So far we have only discussed multiplication and proportion. We now must consider whether children's understanding of division can be analyzed in the same way. In fact, there are relatively few studies of children and division, but the data that we have suggest a different origin for the understanding of division.

This is sharing, which we have mentioned already in the context of one-to-one correspondence. Children share at quite a young age (Desforges & Desforges, 1980; Frydman & Bryant, 1988; Miller, 1984) which means that in practical terms they divide, for that is what sharing equal portions to different recipients amounts to. However, there is a

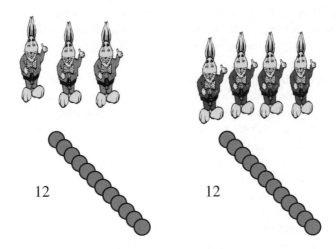

"Will each rabbit in A get the same as each one in B, or will the rabbits in one group get more than those in the other?"

Figure 19.6 The different condition in the Correa, Nunes, and Bryant (1998) division task. The same quantity is shared out among the two groups, but one group is less numerous than the other

crucial difference in the intellectual demands made by sharing and by division. When sharing, one only needs to ensure that everyone receives an equal portion. How much that portion (the quotient) is and how it is affected by the number of recipients (the divisor) is not essential information, because one can in principle share without knowing anything about either the quotient or the divisor. Fairness is all.

The relation between divisor and quotient is an inverse one: the more recipients there are the smaller is the portion that each recipient gets. We (Correa, Nuñes, & Bryant, 1998) have shown that young children who share perfectly well are nevertheless very unclear about this inverse relation. We tested this understanding by showing each child two groups of toy rabbits, and explaining that we were going to share out a certain quantity of sets – always the same quantity for each group – among the rabbits in the two groups (figure 19.6). When we had done this, we asked the children whether the individual rabbits in one group had been given the same amount as the rabbits in the other group. In some trials the number of rabbits in the two groups was the same, which meant that the portions shared out were the same for both groups. In other trials, there were more rabbits in one group than in the other, and our main question was whether children would understand that the rabbits in the larger group would get a smaller portion than those in the smaller group – the inverse divisor–quotient relationship.

Most of the children in the 5-year group and many in the 6- and 7-year groups seemed unaware of this relation. They all did well when the size of the two groups of rabbits was the same, but rather badly when it was different. In this more difficult condition the younger children tended still to say that the rabbits in each group would get the same amounts. They did not understand that the size of the divisor makes a difference. In contrast, when the older children erred in this condition, they tended to say that the rabbits in the larger group would each get more than the rabbits in the smaller group: so these children realized that the divisor made a difference, but still had not grasped the inverse relationship.

This developmental pattern is robust. It was repeated in several experiments by Correa, and independently by Sophian, Garyantes, and Chang (1997). The reason for it, we argue, is that the origins of children's understanding of division lie in their experience of sharing, and that though sharing leads them to grasp some aspects of division, it does not in any way depend on knowledge about the inverse divisor–quotient relationship.

This argument is strengthened by some research by Squire and Bryant (in press: 2002; see also Bryant & Squire, 2001). We looked at 5- to 7-year-old children's reactions to concrete representations of division. We gave them problems in which we started with a quantity of objects, (e.g., twelve sweets) to be divided among a certain number of recipients (say three dolls, see figure 19.7). Then we formed the objects into groups. We did this in two ways.

One way (number of recipients equals the number of groups) was to put the objects into as many groups as there were recipients: thus in the example of the twelve sweets to be shared between three dolls, we arranged the sweets in this condition into three groups of four sweets. The other way of grouping them (number of recipients equals number of objects within each group) was to arrange them so that each group of objects was equal in number to the number of recipients. So, in the example that we have been using, there would be four groups of three sweets in this condition, as figure 19.7 shows. Note that in the first condition the number of groups equals the divisor and the number of objects within groups equals the quotient. In the other condition these relationships are reversed, and the number of groups equals the quotient while the number of objects within each group equals the divisor.

The children's task was to tell us the quotient. Since they already knew the divisor (the number of recipients) both kinds of grouping could help. If the number of recipients equals the number of groups, the quotient must be the number of objects within each group. If the number of recipients equals the number of objects within each group, then the number of groups equals the quotient. Mathematically the two conditions are equivalent, and there is no reason in principle why one should be harder than the other.

In practice, however, there was a big and consistent difference between the two conditions. When the number of recipients was the same as the number of groups, the children did quite well. But they made many more mistakes when the number of recipients equalled the number of objects within each group. This was a much harder task for them. What is the reason for this difference? Our view is that the origins of children's understanding of division is the best explanation for the difference.

Our hypothesis is that sharing is the basis for children's first ideas about division. This hypothesis accounts for the results of the Squire and Bryant studies. The more

The number of recipients equals the number of groups

The number of recipients equals the number of items in each group

Figure 19.7   An example of the two conditions in the Squire and Bryant (in press: 2002) studies

successful condition (number of recipients equals the number of groups) reflects the procedure of sharing quite well because, when one shares, one allocates one portion to each recipient (his/her share), and therefore the number of portions is the same as the number of recipients. The other condition, in which the number of portions is not the same as the number of recipients, does not reflect what happens in sharing at all.

In different ways, therefore, the studies by Correa et al. and by Squire and Bryant point to the hypothesis that children begin by basing division on sharing and only later come to learn about the relationships between the three crucial variables of the dividend, the divisor and the quotient. When they eventually learn about the divisor–quotient relationship, they probably do so as a result of formal teaching.

Conclusions

This mention of teaching takes us back to the question that we started with: where does children's mathematical knowledge come from? The research reviewed in this chapter suggests that there are three bases to children's mathematical knowledge.

One is logic and logical development. Additive and multiplicative reasoning both depend on the use of logic, and it is clear that, as Piaget originally suggested, children do not at first apply some basic logical principles to the solution of mathematical problems. It takes them quite a time to understand the additive composition of number, for example, and to apply the inversion principle when they are dealing with additive problems. We cannot take these and other basic logical principles for granted. They are a source of genuine difficulty for children, and the idea that they come as an innate and universal gift is misguided and actually harmful, for it distracts us from giving help to children where they need it.

The second is the teaching of conventional systems. Counting systems are based partly on logic and partly on human invention. The decimal system is an invention and, linguistically, it varies from culture to culture. Inventions, by and large, have to be taught, either formally or informally. One cannot expect children to reinvent them. Children certainly have to be taught their counting systems, and how to use them. Some of the evidence that we have presented shows that children learn to count before they really know what counting means and before they apply the logic of one-to-one correspondence to number words. It is as though they have to learn, and to become used to, number words for quite a while before they can connect them with their existing mathematical knowledge.

The third factor is meaning. The evidence suggests that children learn most about mathematics on the basis of experiences with situations and actions that mean something to them. These meaningful situations affect and sometimes restrict what they learn at first. We have seen this with multiplicative reasoning. Children's ideas of multiplication seem to be based on their understanding of one-to-many correspondence, and this almost certainly accounts for the fact that they understand ratios before fractions, and adopt scalar before functional reasoning. The origins of their understanding of division seem to be in their experiences of sharing, which certainly affect the shape of their knowledge about this mathematical operation. Even before they go to school they are quite sophisticated at dividing quantities into equal shares, but have hardly any grasp of the inverse divisor–quotient relationship.

The importance of meaning in mathematical learning is most dramatically illustrated by the work of Nuñes, Schliemann, and Carraher (1993) on street mathematics. They showed that children who work in the informal economy in Brazil are able to make quite complex calculations when buying and selling in the most flexible ways. These calculations often involve combinations of different arithmetical operations and also quite sophisticated manoeuvres like decomposing numbers in order to perform complex additions and subtractions. Yet these same children make very little headway with the algorithms and procedures that they are taught at school, which mean little to them and which they do not really understand. Their mathematical world is determined by meaning. At a time when there is renewed pressure to concentrate mathematical teaching on drills and on facts, we should remember that children learn best when they understand the meaning of what they are taught.

PART IV

Topics in Atypical Cognitive Development

There are many aspects of atypical development, and it was very difficult to decide which topics to include in this handbook. One potential approach was to include a chapter on each neurodevelopmental disorder that is relatively common in childhood, for example dyslexia, autistic spectrum disorders, developmental coordination disorders, specific language impairment (SLI), and attention-deficit-hyperactivity disorders (ADHD). Another approach was to consider different theoretical approaches to neurodevelopmental disorder, for example brain-based approaches versus environmental theories. Yet a third possible approach was to analyze impairment from the perspective of normal cognitive development, considering for example the behavioral consequences of atypical language development, atypical memory development, or atypical perceptual and motor development. As this handbook focuses on cognitive development rather than cognitive disorders, I finally chose a hybrid of these three possibilities. The first chapter on atypical development (by Zelazo and Müller) takes a theoretical approach to atypical development, considering the probable developmental consequences of deficits in executive function and whether such deficits can provide a theoretical account of autism and ADHD. The second chapter (by Dodd and Crosbie) considers the impact of atypical language development on cognition, and asks important theoretical questions about the nature of the causal relationship between the two. The third chapter (by Baron-Cohen et al.) takes a single disorder (autism) and develops a specific theory to account for its neurodevelopmental profile. As will become clear, there is overlap in all these approaches. Other chapters relevant to this section in the handbook include the theoretical account of autism developed by Gergely (part I), the chapter on modeling atypical development by Thomas and Karmiloff-Smith (part V), and the chapter on reading development and dyslexia by Snowling (part III).

Zelazo and Müller define executive function as the psychological processes involved in the conscious control of thought and action. Executive function is thought to emerge around the end of the first year, with important developmental changes between the ages of 2 and 5. It continues to develop into adolescence and early adulthood. Unusually in cognitive development, research into the development of executive function has been strongly influenced by research on brain maturation, with two areas (orbito frontal cortex and dorsolateral prefrontal cortex) thought to be responsible for affective or "hot" and cognitive or "cool" aspects of executive function, respectively. Zelazo and Müller's view is that the outcome of executive function is deliberate problem-solving. Functionally distinct phases of problem-solving probably reflect distinct (although interactive) functional neural sub-systems, and therefore deficits in one of these sub-systems may lead to different patterns of behavior or disorder from deficits in another. Zelazo and Müller argue that important aspects of autism can be understood in terms of a primary deficit in the affective ("hot") aspects of executive function, whereas important aspects of ADHD can be understood in terms of a primary deficit in the cognitive ("cool") aspects. As they show, there has been an explosion of recent developmental work in executive function. It can be difficult for a non-specialist to keep in mind what all the different executive function tasks are and which aspects of executive function they are thought to measure. As well as providing an exceptionally clear overview of this wealth of research, Zelazo and Müller are to be congratulated on providing a very helpful table of the different executive function tasks and a theoretical analysis of what they can tell us about development. Their Cognitive Complexity and Control theory, which models the development of executive function in terms of the complexity of the cognitive processes that children need to use to construct plans to solve different types of problem, has remarkable theoretical overlap with some of the information-processing theories of cognitive development described by Halford in part V. Similarly, their emphasis on conscious knowledge for the development of executive function (required for the explicit selection of appropriate problem-solving strategies) echoes Kuhn's emphasis on the role of metacognition in scientific thinking.

In their chapter on atypical language development, Dodd and Crosbie point out that language and cognition are very difficult to separate after the early years. As most of our non-linguistic knowledge is brought to consciousness via language, and as much of our knowledge about the world is acquired linguistically after the earliest years, it is very difficult to map between linguistic and non-linguistic knowledge when one or the other system is impaired in children. Dodd and Crosbie thus pose two general theoretical questions: is language disorder in otherwise apparently normal children associated with cognitive deficits, and do children with cognitive deficits necessarily have language disorders? The answers to both questions turn out to be complex. Language disorders (which occur in about 15 percent of children) usually do have accompanying cognitive deficits. However, the developmental picture is complicated by the fact that most children diagnosed with specific language impairment (SLI) receive intensive speech and language therapy. Their linguistic profiles are hence very unstable over time, and so their patterns of impairment on linguistic versus cognitive tasks are continually changing. Intensive therapy is of course very good for their overall language development, but it can complicate attempts to understand what is linguistic and what is cognitive in any impairments that may be found in such children at different points in time. Similarly, children with cognitive disorders usually have some linguistic problems, although these problems can be very specific and not generally disabling. Usually, the clinical picture is one of poor language skills and poor cognitive skills occurring together, but some children have surprisingly good language skills despite fairly disabling cognitive problems. For example, children with Down's syndrome typically have very poor communication skills, with quite unintelligible speech and protracted phonological problems. Their phonological and syntactic abilities often appear more impaired than their cognitive problems would seem to warrant. Yet other children with Down's syndrome can have spared language abilities, and children with very severe cognitive impairments because of factors such as perinatal brain damage can develop into adults who speak 16 different languages! Although extremely rare, these individual cases suggest a degree of modularity in language functions. Nevertheless, there seems to be considerable overlap with the cognitive system. This overlap is shown in one apparently universal feature of children with SLI, which is later problems in literacy acquisition. Such problems would be expected given the importance of linguistic skills for reading acquisition (documented in Snowling's chapter in part III).

Baron-Cohen and his colleagues focus on autistic spectrum conditions in their chapter, conditions which frequently show disordered language development. Their focus is on the cognitive causes of the "triad" of impairments that are used to diagnose autism: atypical social development, atypical language, and repetitive behavior/obsessive interests. As they point out, the clinical picture in autistic spectrum conditions is complicated by the high degree of learning difficulties and language delay found in these populations. In their theoretical analysis, therefore, they concentrate on children with autistic spectrum disorders who are "high functioning," having IQs of 100 or above. Baron-Cohen's theory of the key cognitive impairment in autism is based on a deficit in *empathizing*. He defines empathizing as those abilities that enable us to make sense of the behavior of another agent, predict what they might do next and how they might feel, and adjust our own behavior accordingly. Clearly, the roots of such behavior must lie in a number of domains, including the development of an understanding of self and agency (Meltzoff, Gergely, part I), the development of a theory of mind (Wellman, part II), and the development of pretend play (discussed by Lillard in part II as enabling the simulation of the thoughts and feelings of others when trying to understand their behaviors and actions). Baron-Cohen and his colleagues suggest that individuals with autism and Asperger's syndrome have difficulty in understanding and responding to other people's minds. This difficulty explains their problems in social communication and language development. There is a large amount of empirical evidence for the view that "theory of mind" skills are impaired in autism, consistent with this claim. At the same time, Baron-Cohen suggests that autistic children have superior *systemizing* skills. Systemizing is hypothesized to be a separate cognitive process, important for understanding how physical rather than psychological systems operate. The roots of systemizing lie in the development of physical knowledge (see Baillargeon, part I, and Wilkening & Huber, part III), the development of causal and logical reasoning (see Koslowski & Masnick, part III, and Goswami, part III) and the development of scientific thinking (see Kuhn, part III). It also involves executive function (Zelazo & Müller, part IV). Consistent with this theoretical view, autistic children perform better than expected in pencil-and-paper tests of physics knowledge and show intense interest in mechanical systems. They are also more likely to have parents who are engineers. Baron-Cohen goes on to argue that, given that males are more likely to excel in subjects such as engineering, autism may be an extreme form of the "male brain." It remains to be demonstrated how superior systemizing develops in terms of the component skills that must underlie this relatively high-level cognitive ability. Whereas many of the component skills required to develop a theory of mind are known to be impaired in autism, it has yet to be shown that the component skills required to develop systemizing are precocious or exceptionally strong in autism.

These three chapters demonstrate that a variety of theoretical approaches can be very fruitful in enhancing our understanding of atypical cognitive development. Nevertheless, they also illustrate the importance of rooting such theories in a comprehensive understanding of normative development. For example, as shown by Zelazo and Müller, it is important to understand the systematic changes in executive function in the preschool years and beyond if it is to be argued that an adolescent with ADHD has an executive function deficit. Similarly, it is important to know the typical linguistic and cognitive milestones in early childhood if it is to be argued that an adolescent with Down's syndrome and a verbal age of 6 years has impaired cognition. Theory development in neurodevelopmental disorders can also be based on assumed deficits in higher-level cognitive processes, as shown in Baron-Cohen's chapter. He and his colleagues demonstrate how a detailed knowledge of typical patterns of cognitive development in the lower-order skills assumed to contribute to such higher-level processes as theory of mind provide us with critical tools for testing and refining more overarching theories about underlying deficits such as those of empathizing. These perspectives on atypical development also raise the possibility that atypical children might have cognitive strengths as well as weaknesses. In certain domains or cognitive tasks, atypically developing children could actually show better performance than typically developing children. Nevertheless, it is important to bear in mind that even where behavior appears normal in a given developmental disorder, atypical cognitive processes may underlie it. This is particularly well illustrated in the next section, in the discussion of Williams syndrome by Thomas and Karmiloff-Smith.

CHAPTER TWENTY

Executive Function in Typical and Atypical Development

Philip David Zelazo and Ulrich Müller

Introduction

Executive function (EF) is an ill-defined but important construct that refers generally to the psychological processes involved in the conscious control of thought and action. Although EF has long been studied from a neuropsychological perspective, with researchers seeking to map function onto neurological structure, it is now the focus of intensive research from a variety of other perspectives, including the perspectives of developmental psychology and developmental psychopathology. Developmental research on EF has revealed that: (a) EF first emerges early in development, probably around the end of the first year of life; (b) EF develops across a wide range of ages, with important changes occurring between about 2 and 5 years of age, adult-level performance on many standard tests of EF being reached at about 12 years of age, and performance on some measures continuing to change into adulthood; (c) failures of EF occur in different situations at different ages, and these situations can be ordered according to the complexity of the inferences required; (d) although EF can be understood in fairly domain-general terms, a distinction can be made between the development of relatively "hot" affective aspects of EF associated with orbitofrontal cortex (OFC) and the development of more purely cognitive, "cool" aspects associated with dorsolateral prefrontal cortex (DL-PFC; cf. Metcalfe & Mischel, 1999); (e) EF difficulties may be a common consequence of many different perturbations of the epigenetic process; and (f) different developmental disorders may involve impairments in different aspects of EF.

We would like to thank Keith Happaney and Sophie Jacques for helpful comments on an earlier draft of this chapter. Please address correspondence to Philip David Zelazo, Department of Psychology, University of Toronto, 100 St. George St., Toronto, Ontario, Canada, M5S 3G3. Email <zelazo@psych.utoronto.ca>.

In the following sections, we will first address definitional issues surrounding the construct of EF, and then consider research on prefrontal cortex (PFC) and its development. Although EF can be studied in purely functional terms, consideration of concomitant neurological systems provides an important source of constraints on functional models of EF. Our review of research on the development of EF in typically developing children will proceed according to the problem-solving (PS) framework introduced by Zelazo, Carter, Reznick, and Frye (1997). In light of this review, we will then consider the role of EF in two psychiatric conditions with childhood onset, autism and attention deficit hyperactivity disorder (ADHD), which we believe illustrate the utility of the distinction between hot and cool EF. Finally, we will conclude with several generalizations about the development of EF, including recommendations for future research.

Definitional Issues

Historically, the construct of EF has been derived from analysis of the consequences of PFC damage. These consequences are numerous and diverse, and are often described as a list of partially overlapping deficits – deficits that have family resemblance structure. Wise, Murray, and Gerfen (1996, p. 325) provide one such list:

> Lesions of PF in humans yield a constellation of neuropsychological deficits that have been described variously as difficulties with planning, concept formation, abstract thinking, decision-making, cognitive flexibility, use of feedback, temporal ordering of events, fluid or general intelligence, and monitoring one's own actions . . .

The construct of EF is intended to capture the psychological abilities whose impairment is presumed to underlie these manifest deficits, but again, researchers often rely on what amounts to a list: the ability to plan, the ability to form concepts, etc. After reviewing several such lists, Tranel, Anderson, and Benton (1994, p. 130) attempted "to distil a fairly cohesive notion of what is meant by the term executive functions," and suggested that EF corresponds to the following: planning, decision-making, judgment, and self-perception.

An alternative approach to the characterization of EF is to emphasize just one aspect of EF, such as inhibitory control, and attempt to explain various behavioral deficits in terms of this aspect (e.g., Carlson, Moses, & Hix, 1998; Dempster, 1992). Generally, however, and as we discuss later, these aspects of EF are too simple to provide an adequate characterization of the complex strategic and metacognitive processes involved in EF.

Another alternative is to treat EF as a higher-order cognitive mechanism or ability. Denckla and Reiss (1997, p. 283), for example, follow an influential line of authors (e.g., Baddeley, 1996; Norman & Shallice, 1986) when they suggest that *"Executive function* refers to a cognitive module consisting of effector output elements involving inhibition, working memory, and organizational strategies necessary to prepare a response." Unfortunately, this approach essentially invokes a homunculus and leaves unanswered questions about how EF is accomplished and about functional relations among aspects of EF such as planning and self-perception.

Luria's (e.g., 1973) approach to neurological systems suggests a way to capture the diversity of the processes attributed to EF without simply listing them and without hypostasizing homuncular abilities. For Luria, PFC and other neurological systems consist of *interactive functional systems* that involve the integration of subsystems. Subsystems have specific roles to play, but cannot be considered outside of the larger systems of which they are a part. Zelazo et al. (1997) took seriously Luria's suggestion that EF is a function, and not a mechanism or cognitive structure. Functions are essentially behavioral constructs defined in terms of their outcome – what they accomplish. In the case of EF, the outcome is deliberate PS. To a large extent, the task of characterizing a complex function such as EF is a matter of describing its hierarchical structure, characterizing its subfunctions, and organizing these subfunctions around their constant common outcome. In the case of EF, functionally distinct phases of PS can be organized around the constant outcome of solving a problem, and we can attempt to show how these phases contribute to that outcome. Figure 20.1 presents a familiar looking flowchart.

For example, consider the Wisconsin Card Sorting Test (WCST; Grant & Berg, 1948; see table 20.1), widely regarded as "the prototypical EF task in neuropsychology" (Pennington & Ozonoff, 1996, p. 55). The WCST taps numerous aspects of EF, and, as a result, the origin of errors on this task is difficult to determine (e.g., see Delis, Squire, Bihrle, & Massman, 1992). To perform correctly on the WCST, one must first construct a representation of the problem space, which includes identifying the relevant dimensions. Then, one must choose a promising plan – for example, sorting according to shape. After selecting a plan, one must (a) keep the plan in mind long enough for it to guide one's thought or action, and (b) actually carry out the prescribed behavior. Keeping a plan in mind to control behavior is referred to as *intending*; translating a plan into action is *rule use*. Finally, after acting, one must evaluate one's behavior, which includes both error detection and error correction.

According to the PS framework, inflexibility can occur at each phase so there are several possible explanations of perseverative performance on the WCST – and on global EF tasks more generally. For example, perseveration could occur after a rule change in the WCST either because a new plan was not formed (one type of *representational inflexibility*; Zelazo, Reznick, & Piñon, 1995) or because the plan was formed but not carried out (an example of *lack of response control*; Zelazo et al., 1995). As a descriptive framework, the delineation of PS phases does not *explain* EF, but it does allow us to ask more precisely when in the process of PS performance breaks down. In addition, the framework accomplishes the following: (a) it clarifies the way in which diverse aspects of EF work together to fulfill the higher-order function of PS; (b) it avoids conceptualizing EF as a homuncular ability (e.g., as a Central Executive: Baddeley, 1996); (c) it suggests relatively well-defined measures of EF (e.g., measures of rule use for which problem representation, planning, and evaluation are not required); (d) it allows us to capture key aspects of EF, including goal selection, conceptual fluency, and planning in novel situations (e.g., Tranel et al., 1994), that occur even in situations that do *not* demand resistance to interference; and (e) it permits the formulation of specific hypotheses regarding the role of basic cognitive processes (e.g., attention-switching, procedural memory, response inhibition) in different aspects of EF.

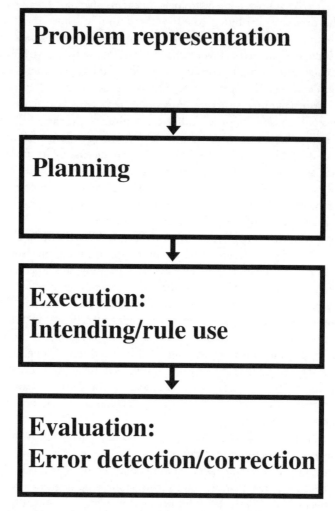

Figure 20.1 A problem-solving framework for understanding EF as a functional construct. Reprinted from P. D. Zelazo, A. Carter, J. S. Reznick, and D. Frye (1997). Early development of executive function: A problem-solving framework. *Review of General Psychology, 1,* 198–226. Copyright © 1997 by the Educational Publishing Foundation. Reprinted with permission

Structure–Function Mapping

Although EF can be studied in purely functional terms, consideration of concomitant neurological systems provides an important source of constraints on functional models of EF. Accordingly, before reviewing behavioral evidence regarding typical and atypical development of EF, we will describe briefly the results of recent research on PFC and its development. As a caveat, it should be noted that although EF has traditionally been linked to PFC, it clearly depends on the integrity of other brain regions as well (e.g., the

Table 20.1   Selected measures of EF in children

A-not-B. Based on Piaget's work with infants. An object is conspicuously hidden at one location, location A, and an infant (or child) is allowed to retrieve it. Then the object is hidden at another location, location B, and the infant is allowed to search for it. Infants often persist in searching at location A (the A-not-B error). The key dependent measures are performance on the first B trial and number of post-switch perseverative errors at B prior to success on a B trial (error run). The A-not-B task has been used in infants and preschoolers.

Children's Gambling Task. From Kerr and Zelazo (2001), based on Bechara et al. (1994). This task consists of two decks of cards that, when turned, display a number of happy and sad faces. Happy faces indicate number of candies won; sad faces indicate candies lost. One deck is disadvantageous, the other advantageous. Children are told to win as much as possible before the end of the "game" (i.e., after 50 card selections, unbeknown to the child). The first 25 trials allowed children to sample from both decks; the last 25 trials are considered diagnostic of affective decision-making. The key dependent variable is the proportion of disadvantageous choices during trials 26–50. The task has been used with preschoolers but can be used with school-age children, too.

Day-Night Stroop. From Gerstadt, Hong, and Diamond (1994). Children are instructed to say the word "day" when shown a line drawing of the moon and stars, and "night" when shown a line drawing of the sun. The key dependent measure is the number of correct responses in the experimental condition. The Day-Night Stroop has been used in preschool and school-age children.

Delayed Response. Based on Hunter (e.g., 1917). In one version, an object is placed under one of two or more identical stimuli (e.g., cups). A delay is then imposed during which the stimuli are hidden by an opaque screen. After the delay, the screen is raised and the infant or child is allowed to obtain the stimulus. The primary dependent measure is the number of correct responses. Delayed response has been used with infants and children.

Dimensional Change Card Sort (DCCS). From Frye et al. (1995, Exp. 2). Children are presented with cards depicting colored shapes that can be sorted differently, depending on whether one sorts them by color or by shape. Children are first told to sort by one dimension (e.g., color), and then told to sort by the other dimension (e.g., shape). The key dependent measure is number correct on the post-switch phase. The Dimensional Change Card Sort has been used with 3- to 5-year-old children, although versions have also been used with school-age children and adults.

False Belief Task. From Wimmer and Perner (1983). In one version, children are told a story in which a person hides a desired object at location A. Without the person's knowledge, the object is transferred to location B. The key dependent measure is whether children can correctly predict where the person will search for the object. The false belief task has been used mainly with 3- to 5-year-old children.

Flexible Item Selection Task (FIST). From Jacques and Zelazo (in press), based on Feldman and Drasgow (1951). Children are shown a set of three cards and required first to select two cards that match each other on one dimension, and then to select a different pair of cards that match each other on another dimension. The primary dependent measure is number-correct on the second selection. The Flexible Item Selection Task has been used with 3- to 5-year-old children, although more difficult versions could be used with older children.

Go-NoGo Task. Based on work by Luria (e.g., Luria, 1966). In a commonly used version of the Go-NoGo task, children are required to display a simple motor response to one cue, the Go stimulus, while refraining from responding to another stimulus, the NoGo stimulus. Scoring is based on reaction time, errors of commission (i.e., incorrectly responding to a NoGo

Table 20.1　*Continued.*

stimulus), and errors of omission (not responding to a Go stimulus). The Go-NoGo task has been used mainly with school-age children.

Handgame. Based on work by Luria (see Hughes, 1998b). Children first must imitate a pair of hand actions by the experimenter. Then, in the conflict condition, children must make the opposite responses (e.g., make a fist when the experimenter points a finger and point a finger when the experimenter makes a fist). The dependent measure is the number of errors in the conflict condition. The handgame has been used with preschoolers.

Object Reversal. Based on Overman et al. (1997). On each trial, children are presented with the same two objects and rewarded for reaching to one of them. After a certain number of trials, children are rewarded for reaching to the other object (i.e., the reward contingencies are reversed). The primary dependent variable is the number of trials needed to learn the reversal. The task has been used with young preschoolers, but could be used with infants and school-age children.

Self-Ordered Pointing. See Archibald and Kerns (1999). Children are presented with drawings of objects arranged in a matrix. The same objects are presented on each trial, but they appear in different locations. Participants are instructed to point to a different picture on each trial. The key dependent measure is the number of errors. Self-Ordered Pointing has been used with preschoolers and school-age children.

Stop-Signal Task. From Logan (1994). Children are presented via a computer with a series of stimuli and told to press one of two keys (e.g., X or O) depending on whether an X or an O appears on the screen, unless a tone (the stop signal) sounds (about 25 percent of all trials), in which case children should not press either key. Dependent measures are accuracy (correctly pressing a key), probability of stopping, and reaction time. The Stop-Signal Task is typically used with school-age children.

Stroop Test. From Stroop (1935). In the experimental condition, children are presented with color words (e.g., red) printed in nonmatching colored ink (e.g., blue ink), and required to name the color of the ink. The key dependent measure is the number of correct responses. The Stroop Test has been used with literate school-age children.

Tower of Hanoi. Based on a popular nineteenth-century puzzle, the task consists of *n* disks of graduated size placed in a particular configuration across three pegs of the same size. Children must transfer the disks from a starting position to a specified goal state, observing a number of arbitrary rules. Problems differ in difficulty, which varies with the number of moves required for solution and the type of problem (e.g., tower-ending or flat-ending). The key dependent measure is the number of moves to solution. The task has been used with preschoolers and school-age children.

Tower of London. From Shallice (1982), based on the Tower of Hanoi. This tower task uses colored balls that must be moved on three pegs of graduated sizes. Children are presented with an initial arrangement of balls and with a target tower, and they are asked to describe how they would alter their initial arrangement so that it corresponds to the target tower. The task has been used with preschoolers and school-age children.

Windows Task. From Russell, Mauthner, Sharpe, and Tidswell (1991). Children are presented with two boxes that have windows on them. The windows face the child and reveal the contents of the boxes. On each trial, one of the boxes is baited, and the child is instructed to tell the experimenter (who cannot see the content of the boxes) where to look. The experimenter searches where instructed by the child and the child receives the contents of the other box. The key dependent measure is the number of trials on which the child directs the experimenter to the baited box (hence failing to receive the bait). The windows task has been used with 3- to 4-year-old children.

Table 20.1   *Continued.*

Wisconsin Card Sorting Test (WCST). Based on Grant and Berg (1948). Children are presented with stimulus cards that differ on various dimensions, and then children are shown individual cards that match different stimulus cards on different dimensions. Children must determine the rule according to which each card must be sorted, and the experimenter informs the child after each card whether the sorting is right or wrong. After a certain number of consecutive correct responses, the target dimension is shifted, and the child must discover this new sorting principle. The key dependent measures are perseverative errors and number of categories achieved. The Wisconsin Card Sorting Test has been used with children older than about 6 years.

limbic system). Indeed, although the terms are often used interchangeably, EF is *not* synonymous with PFC function: whereas some patients with PFC damage do not show impairments in EF (e.g., Shallice & Burgess, 1991), some patients with damage outside of PFC do (e.g., Anderson, Damasio, Jones, & Tranel, 1991). More generally, despite current interest in modular processes in the brain, which may (but need not) encourage researchers to adopt a localizationalist approach, there are good reasons to reject this approach in the case of complex functions such as EF (Goldberg, 1995; Luria, 1966; Stuss & Benson, 1986).

Prefrontal cortex

PFC is the region of cerebral cortex anterior to premotor cortex and the supplementary motor area (and, according to some authors, excluding the anterior cingulate gyrus; Fuster, 1989; Stuss & Benson, 1986). In human beings, this region comprises between a quarter and a third of the cortex (Fuster, 1989). Although this proportion was long thought to be large relative to other species, more recent evidence suggests that it is not (e.g., H. Damasio, 1996). In general, the patterns of reciprocal connectivity between PFC and other, more subcortical and posterior brain regions make PFC uniquely suited for the integration (or association) of information and the regulation of emotion, thought, and action.

Over the years, different authors have provided very different accounts of PFC function, perhaps emphasizing consequences of damage to different parts of PFC. PFC comprises several distinct areas, but for the present purpose these can be grouped into two broad regions, DL-PFC and OFC, on the basis of neuroanatomical connections and the relative importance of different neurotransmitter systems. Whereas damage to DL-PFC is commonly associated with "classic" EF deficits, which involve what we would characterize as impaired PS in relatively cool contexts, damage to OFC (as in the case of Phineas Gage) often produces inappropriate social and emotional behavior, which we would characterize as hot EF.

Dorsolateral prefrontal cortex.   DL-PFC comprises the lateral portions of Brodmann's areas 9, 10, 11, and 12; areas 45 and 46; and the superior part of area 47 (cf. H. Damasio, 1996; Gazzaniga, Irvy, & Mangun, 1998) – regions that mainly receive their blood supply from the middle cerebral artery (H. Damasio, 1996; Stuss & Benson, 1986). In addition to its connections with OFC, DL-PFC is connected to a variety of brain areas that would allow it to play an important role in the integration of sensory and mnemonic information and the regulation of intellectual function and action. These include: the thalamus, parts of the basal ganglia (the dorsal caudate nucleus), the hippocampus, and primary and secondary association areas of neocortex, including posterior temporal, parietal, and occipital areas (e.g., Fuster, 1989). With respect to neurotransmitter systems, there is evidence that dopamine plays a particularly important role in DL-PFC (Robbins, 2000, for a review).

Orbitofrontal cortex.   OFC, as broadly defined here, consists of both orbital (ventral) and medial regions of PFC, including the medial portions of Brodmann's areas 9, 10, 11, and 12; areas 13 and 25; and the inferior portion of area 47 (H. Damasio, 1996; Gazzaniga et al., 1998). The medial regions receive their blood supply from the anterior cerebral artery (H. Damasio, 1996; Stuss & Benson, 1986). Unlike DL-PFC, OFC is part of a fronto-striatal circuit that has strong connections to the amygdala and other parts of the limbic system. Hence, OFC is well suited for the integration of affective and nonaffective information, and for the regulation of appetitive/motivated behavior.

Development of PFC.   An early, influential idea held that PFC was not functional during childhood. The origin of this idea can perhaps be traced to Luria (1973, p. 87), who estimated that PFC did not "become finally prepared for action" until about 4 to 7 years of age. Golden (1981, p. 292) took this suggestion a step further, proposing that PFC was not functional at all until about 12 to 15 years of age, and noting that PFC development was often incomplete until age 24 years. The first part of this proposal has now been convincingly refuted: behavioral and comparative data (e.g., Diamond & Goldman-Rakic, 1989), imaging data (e.g., Bell & Fox, 1992), and case studies of children with brain lesions (Eslinger, Biddle, & Grattan, 1997) and closed head injuries (Scheibel & Levin, 1997) all indicate some PFC function as early as the end of infancy. For example, Diamond and Goldman-Rakic (1989) showed that in monkeys, performance on the A-not-B task (see table 20.1) depends on intact DL-PFC, which suggests that 12-month-old human infants who succeed on the task rely on DL-PFC. Further support for this suggestion comes from Bell and Fox (1992), who measured electroencephalographic (EEG) activity longitudinally in infants between 7 and 12 months of age, and found a correlation between performance on A-not-B (being able to tolerate longer delays), on the one hand, and frontal EEG power and frontal/parietal EEG coherence on the other. As a final example, contrary to the notion that childhood lesions of PFC are symptomless ("silent"), several studies indicate that PFC damage does indeed produce symptoms in children, whether assessed retrospectively or by direct testing during childhood (e.g., Eslinger et al., 1997).

At the same time, however, there is some support for Golden's (1981) suggestion regarding silent lesions of PFC: Eslinger et al. (1997) reviewed several case studies of early PFC damage and found that the immediate consequences of PFC lesions in children are often less noticeable than the consequences of comparable lesions in adults. Moreover, behavioral impairments may appear later in development, when late-developing functions would normally emerge (cf. Goldman & Alexander, 1977), although it is unclear to what extent these impairments are secondary consequences of a disrupted epigenetic process.

The fact that identical lesions can have different consequences at different ages (e.g., Kolb et al., 1998; Stiles, 1998) underscores the need for a developmental approach to the problem of mapping function to neurological structure.

Indeed, it is clear that both PFC and PFC function follow an extremely protracted developmental course. Relevant measures include (but are not limited to) the following: (a) *head circumference* (e.g., Epstein, 1986), which shows peak growth rates at 7, 12, and 15 years; (b) *myelination* (e.g., Yakovlev & Lecours, 1967), which starts postnatally in PFC and continues into adulthood; (c) *interhemispheric connectivity*, which shows peak growth rates between 3 and 6 years, as indicated by structural imaging of anterior regions of the corpus callosum (Thompson, Giedd, Woods, et al., 2000); (d) *synaptic density* (in layer III of the middle frontal gyrus), which reaches a peak at about 1 year of age that is considerably higher than the adult level, remains high until about age 7 years, and then declines until about age 16, when the adult level is finally attained (e.g., Huttenlocher, 1990); and (e) *metabolic and electrical activity* (e.g., Thatcher, 1992), which show age-related changes in PFC that continue well into adolescence and are correlated with changes in performance on cognitive tasks.

Developmental theories of EF

Theories of EF and its development have generally paralleled theories of PFC function, and they have typically emphasized cool EF to the exclusion of hot EF, while failing to note the difference. Many early efforts to explain age-related changes in EF relied on the construct of inhibition (e.g., Luria, 1966), and this approach has remained popular (e.g., Carlson, Moses, & Hix, 1998; Dempster, 1992; see the special issue of *Brain and Cognition*, 1996, v. 30). Reconceptualizing EF as inhibitory control has some prima facie appeal because failures of EF are often manifested as perseverative errors. Perseveration implies that behavior is emitted that should have been inhibited, so perseveration seems to implicate inhibition by definition. However, to the extent that inhibition accounts make a substantive, empirical claim, the claim must be that individuals with EF deficits *try* to suppress interfering response tendencies but cannot do so because of an immature or inefficient inhibition mechanism.

One limitation of inhibition explanations is their inability to support predictions regarding the specific situations that will pose problems for children at different ages. For example, 3-year-olds perseverate in certain card-sorting tasks, such as the Dimensional Change Card Sort (see table 20.1; Frye, Zelazo, & Palfai, 1995), but not in the A-not-B task, where 9-month-old infants will search perseveratively despite seeing an object hidden at a new location. Although it is possible to claim that card-sorting requires *more* inhibition than A-not-B, this claim would seem to be inevitably post hoc.

A second limitation of inhibition accounts is that they are too simple to capture the full range of phenomena that are covered by the term EF, including planning in tasks with minimal inhibitory demands (Tower of London vs. Tower of Hanoi; see table 20.1), concept generation on fluency tasks, action monitoring, and source monitoring and other aspects of episodic retrieval. EF is *often* measured using an interference paradigm, but it need not be (see Zelazo et al., 1997, for discussion). Moreover, the construct of inhibition fails to address how one decides what is to be inhibited. Hence, as a function, inhibition must be secondary to the initial phases of PS, including problem representation and planning.

In contrast to inhibition accounts, a number of researchers have attributed changes in EF to changes in actual or functional capacity of working memory (e.g., Case, 1985b; Roberts & Pennington, 1996). This approach probably has its origin in early work by Jacobson (1936), who demonstrated that PFC-lesioned monkeys showed impairments on a version of Hunter's (e.g., 1917) delayed-response task (see table 20.1). Consistent with this approach, developmental studies using delayed-response tasks (e.g., Hunter, 1917), span tasks (e.g., the counting span task; Case, 1985b), and Self-Ordered Pointing (see table 20.1; Archibald & Kerns, 1999) have shown that there are regular age-related increases in working memory throughout childhood (see Gathercole, 1998). These increases could affect children's EF at any of the PS phases, but they would seem to be particularly important for planning and execution (especially, the intending phase of execution).

A third approach to the development of EF has been to suggest that EF involves both working memory and inhibition (e.g., Diamond, 1991). Although this proposal is somewhat more complex than accounts that rely on either working memory or inhibition alone, it is still fairly simple. As such, it remains unclear whether it can account for the full range of EF phenomena (see Stuss, Eskes, & Foster, 1994).

In contrast to these approaches, Zelazo and Frye have described a more complex, hierarchical account of EF. According to the Cognitive Complexity and Control theory (e.g., Frye et al., 1995; Zelazo & Frye, 1997), children's plans are assumed to correspond literally to rules, formulated in potentially silent self-directed speech, as when we tell ourselves, "If I see a mailbox, then I need to mail this letter." Over the course of the preschool period, there are several age-related increases in the complexity of children's rule systems that can be observed in card-sorting, social understanding, physical causality, morality, and other areas (see Zelazo & Frye, 1997, for review). On this theory, complexity is measured by the number of levels of embedding in these rule systems. For example, unlike 2.5-year-olds, 3-year-olds readily integrate two rules (e.g., "If red then here; if blue then there") into a single rule system (Zelazo & Reznick, 1991). However, 3-year-olds have difficulty representing a higher-order rule that allows them to switch flexibly between incompatible pairs of rules (e.g., "If sorting by color, then if red then here, if blue then there. If sorting by shape, then if car then here, if flower then there").

The importance of complexity has been recognized in the developmental literature (see e.g. Halford, ch. 25 this volume), and it is also starting to be appreciated in the neuroscience literature (Dias, Robbins, & Roberts, 1996; Stuss et al., 1999; Wise et al., 1996). For example, Halford et al. (1998b) also suggest that the systematic construction of increasingly complex relations among items is a major dimension of cognitive development.

Zelazo has further emphasized the way in which age-related changes in conscious reflection (modeled as re-entrant signalling of information; cf. Edelman, 1989) permit the increases in rule complexity identified by Cognitive Complexity and Control theory, which in turn allow children to exercise increased control over their thought and action. According to the Levels of Consciousness Model (e.g., Zelazo, 1999), dissociations between knowledge and the ability to use that knowledge occur (under conditions of interference) until incompatible pieces of knowledge are integrated into a single, more complex rule system via another degree of reflection. In the absence of integration, the particular piece of conscious knowledge that controls behavior is determined by relatively local associations.

EF in Typical Development

Corresponding to the distinction between DL-PFC and OFC function, EF comprises both hot and cool aspects. Both types of EF are best understood in terms of the PS framework, but they differ in the extent to which they involve the regulation of affect and motivation (i.e., basic limbic system functions, which Stuss & Alexander, 2000, refer to as the "four F's": feeding, fleeing, fighting, and sexual activity). Whereas cool EF is more likely to be elicited by relatively abstract, decontextualized problems, hot EF is required for problems that are characterized by high affective involvement or demand flexible appraisals of the affective significance of stimuli. This characterization of hot EF is consistent with recent proposals regarding the function of OFC. For example, on the basis of evidence that OFC is required for successful performance on simple tests of object reversal (see table 20.1) and extinction in OFC-lesioned monkeys and patients with OFC damage, Rolls (e.g., Rolls, Hornak, Wade, & McGrath, 1994) suggests that OFC is required for the flexible representation of the reinforcement value of stimuli.

A similar theory has been proposed by Damasio (e.g., 1994). According to this *somatic marker theory*, OFC is required for processing learned associations between affective reactions and specific scenarios, and it further holds that this processing plays a crucial but often overlooked role in decision-making. Support for this proposal comes from a number of studies by Bechara and colleagues (e.g., 1994; see also Bechara, Damasio, & Damasio, 2000), who developed a gambling task sensitive to OFC (more specifically ventromedial) damage. Bechara et al. (1994) found that patients with OFC damage were more likely than healthy controls to make disadvantageous choices.

Examples of affective problems include many social situations, but the social vs. nonsocial distinction fails to capture the difference between hot and cool EF. For one thing, even abstract problems such as the WCST are often administered by another person, whereas canonical measures of hot EF such as object reversal (Rolls et al., 1994) or gambling (Bechara et al., 1994) need not be. Indeed, the inadequacy of the social vs. nonsocial distinction can be seen even in Damasio's (1994) attempt to defend it: Damasio writes, "Thus the bioregulatory and social domain seem to have an affinity for the systems in the ventromedial sector, while systems in the dorsolateral region appear to align themselves with domains which subsume knowledge of the external world (entities such as objects and people, their actions in space–time; language; mathematics; music)" (p. 183). But of course, people and their actions in space–time are clearly social!

In contrast, the distinction between two types of PS that put differential demands on affect and motivation makes considerable sense from a neuroanatomical point of view, and it is supported by task analyses. First, OFC has close connections with the limbic system, whereas these connections are less direct in the case of DL-PFC (indeed, they are partly mediated by OFC). Second, measures of OFC such as extinction, object reversal, and gambling, are not (necessarily) social, but they do require revising one's appraisal of the affective significance of stimuli. In all cases, one must learn to avoid or ignore something that previously elicited (appetitive) approach.

When thinking about the development of hot and cool EF, it will be important to consider that measures of these functions need to be arranged according to developmental level. An important determinant of developmental level seems to be task complexity, or more appropriately, the complexity of the cognitive processes that a task requires. This dimension may be orthogonal to the hot–cool dimension, although characterizing the relation between these dimensions remains an important question for research. In any case, from this perspective, a task such as object reversal is a relatively simple measure of hot EF, whereas gambling is relatively complex. Similarly, delayed response is a relatively simple measure of cool EF, whereas the WCST is relatively complex.

Finally, it should be kept in mind that both OFC and DL-PFC are parts of a single coordinated system, and in the normal case they work together – even in a single situation. Thus, as Damasio (e.g., 1994) suggests, decision-making is normally biased in an adaptive fashion by physiological reactions that predict rewards and punishments. Conversely, it seems likely that a successful approach to solving some affective problems is to reconceptualize the problem in relatively neutral, decontextualized terms, and try to solve it using cool EF. For these reasons, it is probably impossible to design a task that is a pure measure of hot or cool EF, although it is clearly possible to design tasks that emphasize one or the other.

Most developmental research on EF has focused on cool EF, often using global neuropsychological tests that are either taken directly from the adult literature or adapted from adult tasks. For example, several studies have used the WCST (Heaton, 1981), which provides an index of cool EF that spans all four phases of PS. Chelune and Baer (1986) documented a linear increase in performance on the WCST between the ages of 6 and 10 years, with 6-year-olds performing at the level of adult patients with PFC damage and 10-year-olds performing like healthy adults. This pattern was obtained for the three variables assessed: number of perseverative errors, number of categories achieved, and failures to maintain set. Several other studies (e.g., Levin et al., 1991; Welsh, Pennington, & Grossier, 1991) also used the WCST with typically developing children (often in comparison with clinical samples), and these studies generally replicated Chelune and Baer's (1986) results.

It is only recently that researchers have become interested in the development of hot EF, and most of the measures employed are best considered global. For example, Overman and his colleagues (e.g., Overman, Bachevalier, Schuhmann, & McDonough-Ryan, 1997) studied object reversal in infants and young children between 15 and 54 months, and they found considerable development within this age range. As noted, object reversal is an example of hot EF because it requires one to revise one's assessment of whether an object should be approached or avoided.

To assess hot EF in somewhat older children, Kerr and Zelazo (2001) created a simplified Children's Gambling Task (see table 20.1) based on Bechara et al. (1994). The first 25 trials allowed children to sample from both decks; the last 25 trials were considered diagnostic of affective decision-making. Kerr and Zelazo (2001) found that during the last 25 trials, 3-year-olds made more disadvantageous choices (65.4 percent) than 4-year-olds (40.7 percent), and 3-year-olds made more such choices than would be expected by chance, whereas 4-year-olds made fewer. These results indicate that hot EF develops over the preschool period: 3-year-olds, but not 4-year-olds, perform like OFC patients insofar as they reliably make disadvantageous choices. However, the basis of 3-year-olds' performance remains unclear. What is it that changes between 3 and 4 years of age that allows children to choose advantageously despite the meretricious allure of the disadvantageous deck? Future work will need to address this question.

Somewhat more in line with the current componential approach to EF, a number of studies explored the development of EF by devising comprehensive neuropsychological batteries for children, and using factor analysis to determine which tasks are correlated with one another. As can be seen in table 20.2, these studies generally reveal three or four factors, a result that has been taken to support the suggestion that there are dissociable dimensions of EF, consistent with efforts to "fractionate" EF based on lesion studies in nonhuman animals (Robbins, 1996). However, the results of this research are potentially misleading: providing labels for factors may lead to the impression that researchers understand the cognitive processes underlying performance on various tasks, but this is rarely the case. Note that the same tasks are often clustered with different tasks, and characterized by different labels. Thus, for example, the WCST is considered part of a "Perseveration/Disinhibition" factor by Levin et al. (1991) and part of a "Set Shifting or Cognitive Flexibility" factor by Pennington (1997). In the absence of an understanding of underlying cognitive processes, it is unclear whether this approach can tell us anything at all about the structure of EF. For example, does cognitive flexibility rely on inhibitory control or is inhibition an outgrowth of flexibility? It is also impossible to determine the extent to which correlations among tasks are due to shared method variance, or influenced by differential sensitivity to individual differences at different ages. Nonetheless, this approach can provide an empirical characterization of correlations among tasks, as opposed to processes, and it can be used to generate hypotheses about EF processes that can then be tested experimentally.

EF according to the PS framework

We now turn to the PS framework, where EF is understood to proceed from problem representation to planning to execution to evaluation, and inflexibility can occur at each of these phases. For each PS phase, we first discuss relatively cool measures of EF and then consider hot measures. Although we made an effort to restrict this review to measures that are reasonably well focused on only one of the four phases (e.g., measures of planning that do not require plans to be executed), disagreement about how best to describe particular tasks is likely to remain. Due to space limitations, this review is necessarily selective; for more detailed reviews, the reader is referred to Zelazo et al. (1997), which focuses on preschoolers, and Zelazo and Jacques (1996), which focuses on rule use.

Problem representation. In the Gestalt tradition, problem representation was often assessed using insight problems, which require flexible restructuring of the problem

Table 20.2   Factors (and tasks) emerging from selected factor analytic studies of EF in children

Study, N, ages (in years), factors (and tasks)

Levin et al. (1991), N = 52, ages = 7 to 15
1.   Semantic Association/Concept formation (CVLT-Children's version, Word Fluency, Design Fluency, 20 Questions)
2.   Perseveration/Disinhibition (WCST, Go-No Go, Design Fluency)
3.   Planning/Strategy (Tower of London, Word Fluency, 20 Questions)

Welsh, Pennington, and Grossier (1991), N = 52[a], ages = 8 to 12; adult
1.   Fluid & Speeded Response (Visual Search, Verbal Fluency, Motor Sequencing, Recognition Task)
2.   Hypothesis Testing & Impulse Control (WCST, MFFT)
3.   Planning (ToH)

Hughes (1998b), N = 45[b], ages = 3,3 to 4,7
PCE Analysis (effects of age and verbal ability regressed out):
1.   Attentional Flexibility (Set-Shifting, Pattern-Making)
2.   Inhibitory control (Detour-Reaching, Handgame[d])
3.   Working Memory (Auditory Sequencing)

2nd PCE Analysis (effects of nonverbal ability, verbal ability and age regressed out):
1.   Attentional Flexibility (Set-Shifting, Pattern-Making, Visual Search, Auditory Sequencing)
2.   Inhibitory control (Handgame)
3.   Working Memory (Detour-Reaching, Visual Search, Auditory Sequencing)

Espy et al. (1999), N = 82[c], ages = 1,11 to 5,6
1.   Factor 1 (AB, Delayed Alternation)
2.   Factor 2 (Color Reversal)
3.   Factor 3 (AB, Self-Control1, Self-Control2)
4.   Factor 4 (Spatial Reversal)

Carlson and Moses (in press), N = 107, ages = 3,3 to 4,11
1.   Conflict (Day-Night Stroop[d], Grass/Snow, Spatial Conflict, Bear/Dragon, DCCS, Whisper)
2.   Delay (Pinball, Gift Delay, Tower Building, KRISP)

Pennington (1997), N = 537, mean age = 10.95
1.   Motor Inhibition (CPT-AX, Stopping Task)
2.   Set Shifting or Cognitive Flexibility (WCST, CNT, Stroop Test, Raven's Matrices)
3.   Verbal Working Memory (Sentence Span, Counting Span, Digit Span)

AB = A-not-B task; CNT = Contingency Naming Task; CPT-AX = Continuous Performance Task, contingent version; CVLT = California Verbal Learning Test; DCCS = Dimensional Change Card Sort; KRISP = Kansas Reflection-Impulsivity Scale for Preschoolers; MFFT = Matching Familiar Figures Test; ToH = Tower of Hanoi; WCST = Wisconsin Card Sorting Test.

[a] Factor analysis was done on subjects 8 years old and older (n = 52). However, the age range for the entire subject population was 3 years to adulthood (n = 110).
[b] Factor analysis was done on a subsample of the population (n = 45). However, the total N (for the entire subject population) = 50.
[c] Factor analysis was done on a subsample of the population (n = 82). However, the total N (for the entire subject population) = 117.
[d] See table 20.1.

representation (e.g., Duncker, 1945; see Goswami, ch. 13 this volume). Unfortunately, very few studies have used this approach with children, and indeed, to date there have been very few developmental studies of cool problem representation. One exception is a study by Jacques and Zelazo (2001), who measured problem representation in preschoolers using the Flexible Item Selection Task (see table 20.1), a measure of EF adapted from Feldman and Drasgow's (1951) Visual-Verbal Test. On each trial of the Flexible Item Selection Task, children are shown a three-card set (e.g., a purple fish, a pink fish, and a pink telephone) and required to select two cards that match each other on one dimension (e.g., shape: the purple *fish* and the pink *fish*), and then select a different pair of cards that match each other on a different dimension (e.g., color: the *pink* fish and the *pink* telephone). Successful performance thus requires selecting one of the cards (referred to as the *test* item) on both selections, according to different dimensions. On the first selection, 3-year-olds were significantly worse than both 4- and 5-year-olds, who did not differ. On the second selection, 4-year-olds were worse than 5-year-olds, suggesting that although they understood the basic task instructions and could select the first pair correctly, they had trouble re-representing the test item in a different way (i.e., according to a different dimension).

Hot measures of problem representation include most tests of theory of mind, which require flexible problem representation insofar as children are required to represent something from multiple points of view. Moreover, theory of mind has been linked to OFC through lesion studies and imaging studies with adults (Frith & Frith, 2000). The exact role of affect and motivation in reasoning about self and other remains to be determined, but it is obvious that inter- and intrapersonal perspective-taking involves the flexible evaluation of the significance (or meaning) of a situation.

To date, the large majority of research on theory of mind has been conducted in 3- to 5-year-old children (see Wellman, ch. 8 this volume), although the development of theory of mind clearly continues beyond age 5 years. Among the most widely used preschool-age measures of theory of mind are those assessing strategic deception (e.g., Russell, Mauthner, Sharpe, & Tidswell, 1991) and understanding of false belief (see table 20.1; e.g., Wimmer & Perner, 1983). Although most 4- and 5-year-olds perform well on these measures, 3-year-olds often respond incorrectly, suggesting a developmental advance in hot problem representation during the preschool years.

Planning. The best studies of planning, for our purpose, are those in which efforts have been made to develop tasks that are relatively pure measures of planning in order to minimize difficulties that may be attributed to other phases of PS such as execution (e.g., Klahr & Robinson, 1981). For the most part, these studies employ well-defined problems such as the Tower of Hanoi and its variants, and require children to describe their plans without actually executing them.

Early work by Piaget (1976) using execution versions of the Tower of Hanoi revealed poor performance even among school-age children, and subsequent research focusing on planning has confirmed that performance on tower tasks follows a protracted developmental course. For example, Klahr and Robinson (1981) modified the original Tower of Hanoi by employing upside-down cans instead of disks, thereby inverting one of the arbitrary rules to "don't put a smaller can on top of a larger one," and embodying it as an inviolable task constraint. These authors also required children simply to *describe* their plans. Using their modified version, Klahr and Robinson (1981) found that 4-year-olds typically did well on two- and three-move problems, whereas 5-year-olds usually did well on four-move problems, and 6-year-olds did well on six-move problems. Thus, clear age differences emerged in the length of the problems that children could pass. Analysis of children's pass/fail patterns in different versions of the task indicates that there are corresponding changes in problem analysis and depth of search (i.e., the number of anticipated moves that must be remembered). More recent work employing the Tower of London has extended these results. For example, Luciana and Nelson (1998) found that on four- and five-move problems, even 8-year-old children (the oldest group of children included) performed significantly worse than adults.

Brooks, Frye, and Samuels (1996) examined planning in the hot EF context of strategic deception. These authors reasoned that 3-year-olds who perform poorly on measures of strategic deception (e.g., Russell et al., 1991) might have difficulty selecting an appropriate plan, or they might have difficulty executing a plan when it is appropriate to do so. To distinguish between these possibilities, the authors showed children demonstrations of two already formulated plans, one deceptive and one not, and asked children to select the one that would trick another person. Four-year-olds chose the deceptive plan, whereas 3-year-olds did not. These results suggest that there are pronounced changes in preschoolers' planning in the hot realm.

Execution.   Following Luria's seminal work on children's rule use (see Zelazo & Jacques, 1996, for review), Zelazo and Reznick (1991) investigated rule use in 2.5- to 3-year-olds using a card sort in which children were presented with a pair of ad hoc rules (e.g, "If it's something found inside the house, then put it here. If it's something found outside the house, then put it there") and then asked them to use these rules to separate ten test cards. Two-and-a-half-year-olds failed to use the rules despite possessing knowledge about the cards, whereas 3-year-olds performed well. Subsequent research (Zelazo et al., 1995) found that 2.5-year-olds had difficulty even when they were provided with considerable aids and incentives. Analyses of children's errors revealed a tendency to repeat responses: when they erred, it usually involved putting a card into the box in which they had put a card on the previous trial. These results resemble those described by Luria for the one-light task in that 2.5-year-olds seemed to understand the task and the rules, and actually *started* to use the rules, but were susceptible to perseverative errors.

Three- to 5-year-olds' rule use has been assessed using the Dimensional Change Card Sort, which puts two pairs of rules into opposition. Frye et al. (1995, Exp. 2) presented children with colored shapes that would be sorted differently if one were sorting by color or by shape. Children were first required to sort the cards by one dimension (e.g., color), and then the other (e.g., shape). Three-year-olds were able to employ the first set of rules that they were given. However, in contrast to 5-year-olds, they often failed to switch between rule pairs. Despite being told to switch and told the new rules on each trial, they systematically perseverated on the pre-switch rules during the post-switch phase.

Subsequent studies have revealed that these age-related changes on the Dimensional Change Card Sort are robust and occur in a wide range of situations with a wide variety of task materials (e.g., Bialystok, 1999; Carlson & Moses, 2001; Kirkham, Cruess, &

Diamond, in press; Munakata & Yerys, 2001). Zelazo and Frye (1997) have interpreted these results as evidence that 3-year-olds have difficulty integrating incompatible pairs of rules into a single system of rules via a higher-order rule. Support for this interpretation comes from the finding that 3-year-olds demonstrate knowledge of the post-switch rules, even though they fail to use them (Zelazo et al., 1996, Exp. 4), and show predicted patterns of success and failure across different versions of the task (see Zelazo & Frye, 1997, for a review).

Rule use has also been studied fairly extensively in the context of hot EF. One classic paradigm is delay of gratification, which has been assessed using delay tasks and choice tasks (e.g., Mischel, Ebbesen, & Zeiss, 1972). Early studies generally failed to find age differences within the preschool range, but did find differences within the school-age years (Mischel et al., 1989, for review). Moreover, this research has identified a number of attentional and cognitive factors that contribute to the length of time that children elect to wait. For example, thinking about the abstract, non-arousing qualities of the preferred reward, instead of its concrete, arousing qualities positively influences children's ability to delay gratification. These findings suggest that one way to succeed on this task might be to convert it from a hot EF task into a cool EF task, underscoring the close relation between these two aspects of EF.

Two recent studies have examined delay of gratification in younger children using a modified choice task (Moore et al., 1998; Thompson et al., 1997). Thompson et al. (1997) found that two aspects of future-oriented hot cognition show similar developmental trajectories. Specifically, when given the option to choose between a small reward now or a larger reward later (prudence) and between a reward for self now or a reward for self and other later (altruism), 4- to 5-year-old children demonstrated significantly more prudence and altruism than 3-year-old children, and for the 3-year-olds, there was a correlation between prudence and altruism when age was partialled out. In addition to replicating these results, Moore et al. (1998) found that prudence and altruism were related to performance on measures of theory of mind.

Evaluation.   Evaluation involves both error detection and error correction, and research with normal adults and patients (e.g., Konow & Pribram, 1970) underscores the importance of this distinction. In some situations, children's ability to detect errors seems to develop in advance of their ability to correct them (e.g., Gelman & Meck, 1983). For example, using a relatively cool measure of evaluation, Bullock and Lütkenhaus (1988) found that 18- and 24-month-old children could reliably distinguish between correctly and incorrectly built towers, even when they themselves failed to build the towers correctly. Moreover, even 17-month-olds gave evidence of monitoring their own performance qualitatively (e.g., by showing care about aligning blocks on a tower). However, it was not until 26 months that children consistently monitored their progress toward a goal (e.g., creating a tower identical to a model).

As opposed to the dissociation found in toddlers, Jacques, Zelazo, Kirkham, and Semcesen (1999) found that cool error detection and correction were more closely linked in preschool-age children. In this study, children were asked to evaluate the sorting of a puppet on the Dimensional Change Card Sort. Thus, the response execution requirement was removed from the task altogether. When 3-year-olds watched the puppet perseverate, they judged the puppet to be correct. When they saw the puppet sort correctly, they judged the puppet to be wrong. Moreover, children's judgments of the puppet were highly correlated with their own performance on the Dimensional Change Card Sort.

Finally, Gladstone (1969) examined both error detection and error correction in the context of extinction, which can be considered a measure of hot EF (see Rolls et al., 1994). More specifically, he looked at rate of extinction on an operant task in which to-be-retrieved rewards were visible. After a certain amount of responding, it could be seen that the reward supply had been exhausted. Nonetheless, children below 3.5 years kept repeating their responses. Older children produced fewer responses during this extinction phase, with the oldest children (around 4.5 years) immediately ceasing to respond when it became apparent that the reward dispenser was empty. Gladstone argued that the younger children recognized the illogic of their extinction behavior, and were able to detect their errors, but had difficulty using this information to control their behavior. However, interpretation of children's performance remains unclear and future work might usefully investigate the relation between error detection and error correction in a variety of hot and cool contexts.

Summary. Evidence from diverse studies suggests that there are systematic changes during the preschool years and beyond in all phases of EF identified by the functional PS model. Indeed, it seems likely that the various phases of PS develop together. For example, rule use in execution is likely facilitated by the evaluation of outcomes, which can then prompt reflection, leading to better problem representation and planning. In this way, intelligent activity can be reflected back into earlier phases of PS, where it can come to precede execution and contribute to the development of EF as a whole.

Consistent with the Cognitive Complexity and Control theory of the development of EF, these changes in EF can be characterized in terms of the complexity of the problems that children can solve. For example, research on rule use has revealed that by 3 years of age, children can represent and employ a pair of arbitrary rules for sorting cards, but they are likely to perseverate if they are required to shift from one set of rules to an incompatible pair, or if they are required to use a pair of rules that conflicts with their a priori biases (i.e., their default rules). Nonetheless, it should be noted that there seem to be other influences on performance in addition to complexity, including perhaps, degree of affective involvement (Morton, Trehub, & Zelazo, 2000). This would suggest that when complexity is controlled, hot EF tasks may be more difficult than cool EF tasks. For example, Gladstone (1976) failed to find a difference between 3- and 4-year-olds on his measure of extinction when blocks were used as a reward, whereas such differences were clearly evident when rewards consisted of candy, gum, and small toys. The use of highly appealing rewards may have increased the extent to which the task was a measure of hot EF, and consequently increased task difficulty.

One way in which the general issue of hot vs. cool EF has been addressed is in the context of the relation between cool EF and theory of mind. Well-documented changes in children's hot EF as measured by tests of theory of mind (Astington, 1993) co-occur with changes in cool EF as measured by various tasks, including the Dimensional Change Card Sort (e.g., Frye et al., 1995) and the windows task (see table 20.1; Russell et al.,

1991). Further, a longitudinal study by Hughes (1998a) found that cool EF tasks at time 1 predicted performance on theory of mind tasks at time 2, even after age, verbal ability, and theory of mind scores at time 1 were taken into account.

The presence of a strong relation between cool EF and theory of mind is inconsistent with several theories of theory of mind (e.g., the "theory theory," which predicts that individual children's development in one domain will be independent from their development in another, and it would not be predicted by the view that theory of mind is a domain-specific module; e.g., Baron-Cohen, 1997). Nonetheless, several theoretical possibilities remain (see e.g. Perner & Lang, 1999, for discussion). From the present perspective, however, the question about how to interpret the relation between cool EF and theory of mind can be rephrased as one regarding the relation in development between hot and cool EF.

EF in Atypical Development

Several researchers have explored the possibility that childhood disorders such as autism and ADHD can be understood in terms of deficits of EF and attributed to PFC dysfunction (e.g., Barkley, Grodzinsky, & DuPaul, 1992). As Pennington and Ozonoff (1996) note, however, there are several problems with this view. Perhaps the most important is the discriminant validity problem of how the same neurocognitive dysfunction could produce different childhood disorders. Whereas EF is so broadly defined, each disorder has a unique profile of symptomatology. If an EF deficit is the primary deficit in different childhood disorders, then the deficit should be universal to the disorder, and necessary and sufficient to cause it.

One way to interpret the universality of EF deficits in several different clinical groups is to suggest that these groups may perform poorly on global EF tasks (e.g., the WCST) for different reasons (Pennington & Ozonoff, 1996). For example, different clinical populations may perform poorly on different aspects of EF (i.e., either hot/cool aspects of EF or different aspects identified by the PS framework). Another possibility is that EF deficits are a common outcome of many different perturbations of the epigenetic process, rather than a cause (Zelazo, Burack, et al., in press). That is, EF deficits may be secondary rather than primary. However, attempts to address the primacy of deficits in EF in atypical populations have generally been hampered by the lack of a metric for making cross-task comparisons. Thus, demonstrations of differences in performance across tasks are often inadequate because the tasks being compared vary in complexity. For example, Baron-Cohen (1997) argued against the role of EF in autism on the grounds that children with autism do not show impairments on the A-not-B search task. However, this task is typically passed by normally developing 12-month-olds (prior to the age at which autism can be diagnosed). What is needed is a way to equate complexity in tasks designed to assess different types of deficit (Zelazo, Burack, et al., in press). The Cognitive Complexity and Control theory provides one potential solution to this problem (see also Halford et al., 1998b).

In what follows we provide a selective review of two disorders with childhood onset for which an abundance of empirical evidence regarding EF exists, and which arguably illustrate the utility of the distinction between hot and cool EF. Thus, we tentatively propose that autism is *primarily* a disorder of hot EF and that cool EF impairments in autism are a secondary developmental consequence of impaired hot EF. On this hypothesis, neurodevelopmental damage to OFC or associated subcortical systems has cascading consequences for the development of DL-PFC. OFC typically develops earlier than DL-PFC and comes to be regulated by it; impairments in OFC will prevent this hierarchical self-organization of PFC function.

In contrast, ADHD can be seen primarily as a disorder of cool EF, with major symptoms resulting from a failure to use abstract, higher-order goals (including representations of context) to regulate attention and behavior. For example, appreciation of the goals inherent in the context of a classroom normally serves to inhibit distractibility and impulsive behavior. However, children with ADHD may fail to formulate and use these higher-order representations. Given the hierarchical relation between OFC and DL-PFC, neurodevelopmental damage to DL-PFC will have relatively moderate consequences for OFC, sparing the very basic affective functions that are impaired in autism. Consistent with this suggestion, there is evidence that dopamine, strongly linked to DL-PFC, plays an important role in ADHD, unlike in autism (which may be more closely linked to the seratonergic system).

It should be noted, however, that in the case of both autism and ADHD, EF must be considered developmentally. That is, even if people with autism are impaired in both hot and cool EF due to OFC damage, one must consider performance on measures of hot and cool EF in terms of complexity and relative to an individual's developmental level.

Finally, in addition to the disorders reviewed here, EF deficits have been discussed for several other disorders such as conduct disorder (e.g. Pennington & Ozonoff, 1996) and early-treated PKU (e.g., Diamond et al., 1997), among others. The sheer abundance of psychiatric conditions for which EF has been implicated underscores the severity of the discriminant validity problem and favors the suggestion that EF deficits may be a common outcome of various neurodevelopmental disorders (Zelazo, Burack, et al., in press).

Autism

Autism is a pervasive developmental disorder that afflicts about five children in 10,000 (DSM-IV-TR; American Psychiatric Association, 2000, p. 73), mostly boys (the ratio is about 5:1). Although it is presumed to be a genetic disorder (Bailey, Phillipps, & Rutter, 1996), it is currently defined behaviorally on the basis of three main sets of characteristics: social abnormalities, language abnormalities, and restricted and stereotyped patterns of behavior (see Baron-Cohen et al., ch. 22 this volume). The severity of symptoms varies widely, ranging from severe social remoteness and mutism to much milder impairments (Wing, 1988). About 75 percent of people with autism are mentally retarded and mental retardation is strongly associated with long-term outcome (Bailey et al., 1996).

An early PFC account of autism was put forward by Prior (1979), and recent neuro-imaging results provide some support for this approach (e.g., Zilbovicius et al., 1995). In addition, the identification of EF deficits in individuals with autism has been an extremely active research topic over the last decade (see Pennington & Ozonoff, 1996; see also Russell, 1997a). The large majority of these studies have found that individuals with autism perform worse than controls (often children with learning disabilities or mental retardation) matched for verbal and/or nonverbal IQ, although most of these studies have either conflated hot and cool EF or considered EF to be synonymous with cool EF. Pennington and Ozonoff (1996) examined group differences across a number of studies and EF tasks, and found that the average effect size was $d = 0.98$, indicating that performance in children with autism was about one standard deviation below the per-formance of controls. The EF task that best discriminated between children with autism and controls was the Tower of Hanoi, which had an average effect size of $d = 2.07$. Perseverative errors on the WCST had an effect size of $d = 1.06$.

Interpretation of these findings is complicated by the fact that many of the measures used are global EF tasks, making it difficult to specify precisely the psychological func-tions they assess, let alone the basic cognitive processes that underlie those functions. However, some leverage can be gained by considering EF tasks on which children with autism do *not* show impairments relative to controls. For example, Ozonoff, Strayer, McMahon, and Filloux (1994) showed that children with autism were not impaired when they had to respond to a neutral cue (a Go stimulus) and inhibit responding to a neutral stimulus (NoGo stimulus; see table 20.1). However, compared to controls, children with autism were moderately impaired when the Go and NoGo response designations were reversed, and they experienced greatest difficulties when the task required a frequent shifting from one response pattern to another, placing high demands on flexibility. As Courchesne and colleagues (e.g., Allen & Courchesne, 2001) have suggested, difficulty with attentional flexibility may account for the atypical social development of individu-als with autism, because social interactions generally require rapid shifts of attention. By contrast, however, children with autism have been found to be relatively unimpaired on the Stroop Test (see table 20.1; e.g., Ozonoff & Jensen, 1999), and the Stop-Signal Task (see table 20.1; Ozonoff & Strayer, 1997).

One interpretation of these findings is that individuals with autism show deficits in set shifting and planning, but not inhibition (Pennington & Ozonoff, 1996). However, this interpretation is problematic because it fails to take into account children's develop-mental level. For example, the Stop-Signal Task used by Ozonoff and Strayer (1997) involved the coordination of two pairs of rules (i.e., rules for pressing the appropriate keys in the absence of the stop signal and rules for refraining from pressing either key in the presence of the stop signal). Consequently, it is perhaps not surprising that high-functioning adolescents with autism were relatively unimpaired, because the coordination of two setting conditions is mastered by about 4 years of age in typically developing children (Zelazo & Jacques, 1996). In other studies, children with autism at different developmental levels do show perseveration. For example, Turner (1997) has found perseveration in a two-choice response task in which children with autism had to guess where the next target would appear (target locations were determined randomly). Thus, rather than characterizing autistic children as being impaired or unimpaired in inhibition per se, it may be more useful to analyze the level of complexity of a task relative to children's developmental level. High-functioning children with autism with mental ages in the preschool or school-age range are unlikely to show inflexibility on relatively simple measures of EF; more complex measures may be more sensitive to their EF impairments.

EF approaches to autism compete with approaches that consider social understanding and theory of mind to be an encapsulated module and autism to be a modular deficit in theory of mind (e.g., Baron-Cohen, 1997). Although the topic remains controversial, there is now a great deal of empirical evidence suggesting that cool EF tasks are better than theory of mind tasks at discriminating between children with autism and typically developing children, and that cool EF deficits are strongly correlated with impairments in theory of mind in individuals with autism, as in typically developing individuals (e.g., Ozonoff, Pennington, & Rogers, 1991; Zelazo, Jacques, Burack, & Frye, in press). For example, Zelazo, Jacques, et al. (in press) found that in mildly impaired individuals with autism with a mean MA around 6 years, performance on several measures of theory of mind was highly related to performance on the Dimensional Change Card Sort, even with mental age partialled out. One possibility is that cool EF demands (and not the mentalizing demands per se) account for performance on theory of mind tasks. However, from the current perspective, theory of mind can be considered a relatively complex measure of hot EF, and so the conclusion to be drawn is that autism involves related impairments in both hot and cool EF. This finding is consistent with our proposal that a primary deficit in hot EF leads to associated impairments in cool EF. In a related proposal, Dawson et al. (1998) suggest that early-emerging symptoms of autism reflect core affective and social impairments that can be linked to the dysfunction of the limbic system, particularly of the amygdala and hippocampus. The early dysfunction of the limbic system may then have downstream consequences for higher cortical prefrontal functions and may disrupt the development of higher cortical functions, including OFC (Dawson et al., 1998), which we are suggesting would necessarily lead to disruption of DL-PFC, too.

ADHD

ADHD is an externalizing disorder with three cardinal symptoms: hyperactivity, impulsivity, and distractibility (DSM-IV-TR; American Psychiatric Association, 2000, p. 90). According to recent estimates, ADHD affects about 3 percent to 7 percent of children, with boy:girl ratios ranging from 2:1 to 9:1. Between 40 percent and 90 percent of children with ADHD qualify for a comorbid diagnosis of conduct disorder and oppositional defiant disorder (Tannock, 1998).

Numerous neurobiological theories of ADHD have linked ADHD to PFC (e.g., Barkley, 1997). Structural neuroimaging studies have shown that right PFC is smaller in children with ADHD than in healthy controls (e.g., Filipek, Semrud-Clikeman, Steingard, et al., 1997), and PFC abnormalities in children with ADHD have been linked to performance on several measures of cool EF (e.g., Semrud-Clikeman, Steingard, Filipek, et al., 2000). Moreover, functional neuroimaging with children with ADHD reveals decreased metabolic activity in PFC, and sometimes *increased* subcortical activity, suggesting that the cool EF deficit associated with ADHD may be caused by functional hypofrontality (e.g., Rubia et al., 2000), which in turn may be caused by structural and/or biochemical changes in PFC, such as delayed myelination (Sieg, Gaffney, Preston, & Hellings, 1995) or dopamine deficiencies (e.g., Pennington & Ozonoff, 1996). Dopamine is implicated in ADHD mainly because stimulant medication affecting the dopaminergic system leads to behavioral and cognitive improvements in children with ADHD (e.g., Kempton et al., 1999). As noted, there is evidence that dopamine plays a particularly important role in DL-PFC (Robbins, 2000, for a review).

As with autism, most studies of EF in ADHD have either conflated hot and cool EF or considered EF to be synonymous with cool EF. In their review of this literature, Pennington and Ozonoff (1996) concluded that the vast majority (about 75 percent) of empirical studies examining EF in children with ADHD found evidence of impairment, whereas only 35 percent of the non-EF measures revealed significant differences between children with ADHD and controls. The average effect sizes were strongest for the Tower of Hanoi ($d = 1.08$), errors in the Matching Familiar Figures Test ($d = 0.87$), time in the Trail-Making Test, Form B ($d = 0.75$), and time in the Stroop ($d = 0.69$; Pennington & Ozonoff, 1996). The authors also considered a set of tasks (including Go-NoGo, the Stop-Signal Task, the Anti-saccade Task, a conflict motor task, and the inhibition component of the Neuropsychological Assessment Battery) that they referred to as motor inhibition tasks. The effect size associated with these tasks collectively was $d = 0.85$, which is considered large (Cohen, 1988).

In contrast, there were no significant differences between ADHD and controls on verbal memory tasks and verbal tasks in general, and findings with visuo-spatial measures and the WCST were inconsistent (Pennington & Ozonoff, 1996). However, it should be noted that children with ADHD have been found to make more sequential memory errors (Gorenstein, Mammato, & Sandy, 1989) and do poorly in Self-Ordered Pointing tasks (Shue & Douglas, 1992). Moreover, studies that did not find differences between ADHD subjects and controls on the WCST used mainly adolescent subjects, suggesting that group differences between ADHD subjects and controls on the WCST vary as a function of age (Barkley et al., 1992). Finally, there is some empirical evidence that children with ADHD are more likely to lose set in the WCST than to make perseverative errors (Semrud-Clikeman et al., 2000), indicative of a difficulty keeping higher-order goals in mind.

Thus, in contrast to children with autism, children with ADHD appear more likely to exhibit difficulties on relatively simple measures of cool EF, such as the Stop-Signal Task (Osterlaan, Logan, & Sergeant, 1998). One possible interpretation is that unlike those with autism, children with ADHD have impaired inhibition (Pennington & Ozonoff, 1996). Indeed, Barkley (1997) has suggested that response inhibition is the essential impairment in ADHD. Alternatively, however, the response inhibition difficulties exhibited by children with ADHD may be due to difficulty formulating and maintaining relatively abstract goal representations that serve hierarchically to inhibit lower-order functions. On our account this difficulty might be attributed to deficits in cool EF despite relatively (though not completely) intact hot EF (and keeping in mind that hot and cool EF interact in most situations).

Conclusion

The construct of EF has long been recognized to be an important but ill-defined construct. In this chapter we have presented a PS framework for understanding EF that we believe provides a better account of EF than simpler constructs such as inhibition, and also avoids reifying homuncular constructs – e.g., a Central Executive (Baddeley, 1996), or a Supervisory Attentional System (Norman & Shallice, 1986). Although EF can be understood in fairly domain-general terms, a distinction can be made between the development of relatively hot affective aspects of EF associated with OFC and the development of more purely cognitive, cool aspects associated with DL-PFC. Models of EF have traditionally been based on cool cognition, and thus a major question for future research concerns the role of hot cognition in EF, the development of hot cognition, and its relation to cool cognition, which echoes old questions concerning the relation between cognition and affect (e.g., Damasio, 1994).

Developmental research on both hot and cool EF has revealed that EF first emerges early in development, probably around the end of the first year of life, but also that it continues to develop across a wide range of ages, with adult-level performance on many standard tests of EF being reached at about 12 years of age, and performance on some measures continuing to change into adulthood. This developmental course runs parallel to the protracted growth of PFC. Moreover, failures of EF occur in different situations at different ages, and these situations can be ordered according to the complexity of the inferences required (Zelazo & Frye, 1997). Work on PFC is also beginning to take account of the role of complexity (e.g., Stuss et al., 1999). Future work should also explore the role of conscious reflection as a process whereby more complex plans can be formulated (Zelazo, 1999).

From this perspective, age-related increases in complexity can be understood in terms of the hierarchical organization of the neurological concomitants of EF, and given this organization, PFC lesions in development will have predictable consequences. As Vygotsky (1997, p. 144) put it: "What functionally suffers most is the next higher center relative to the damaged area and what suffers relatively less is the next lower center." Naturally, the challenge from a psychological point of view is to describe the hierarchical organization of the function of EF in terms of both underlying cognitive processes and corresponding brain systems.

Finally, EF difficulties may be a common consequence of many different perturbations of the epigenetic process (including many different types of developmental disorder), and different developmental disorders may involve impairments in different aspects of EF. In this chapter, we have proposed that autism and ADHD may correspond to two different types of EF disorder. Whereas autism may be primarily a disorder of hot EF with secondary impairments in cool EF, ADHD may be mainly a disorder of cool EF. Future work on EF from a developmental psychopathological perspective might explore the developmental relations between hot and cool EF in typical and atypical development and show more precisely how these types of EF are related to different regions of PFC and different neurotransmitter systems.

CHAPTER TWENTY-ONE

Language and Cognition: Evidence from Disordered Language

Barbara Dodd and Sharon Crosbie

Introduction

This chapter explores the relationship between children's language development and cognitive ability from the perspective of communication disorder. Around 15 percent of children fail to acquire language milestones appropriately. Their speech may be difficult to understand because they mispronounce many words. They may not understand others' speech, be able to construct complex sentences, or find the words they need to express ideas. Their use of language may be socially inappropriate. Phonological (speech sound system), syntactic (structuring sentences), semantic (meaning), and pragmatic (language use) functions may be impaired singly or in combination, and a deficit in one function often has implications for other functions. The causes of developmental communication disorders are various: environmental, physiological, or psychological, although the greatest proportion of children have difficulties for which there is no known etiology.

Cognition involves knowledge of a non-linguistic nature. Cognitive structures exist that abstract organizational patterns such as spatially, causally, and temporally ordered information. Theories of both language and cognition (Chomsky, 1986, Piaget, 1952c, Vygotsky, 1962) have arisen from the study of normally developing children (see Waxman, ch. 5 this volume). Interpretation of evidence from people with a communication disorder or a cognitive impairment is complicated. Mapping between linguistic and non-linguistic knowledge is not easily apparent when either one or both systems are impaired.

One way of answering the general question "How does research on communication disorders in children inform the debate concerning the relationship between language and cognition?" is to identify more definite issues. Two specific questions seem crucial:

Is language disorder in otherwise normal children associated with cognitive deficits? The first section of this chapter reviews the evidence on language disorder in otherwise "normal" children. The data indicate that aspects of cognition are not always intact, although questions remain about the nature of the relationship.

Are children with cognitive deficits always language-disordered? The second section presents evidence showing that impaired cognition is associated with very different profiles of severity and type of language impairment.

Language Disorders in the Absence of Cognitive or Sensory Deficits

Specific language impairment (SLI) is a diagnosis that describes children who fail to acquire normal language functions in the absence of any obvious cognitive or sensory deficits (Aram, Morris, & Hall, 1993; Bishop, 1997; Stark & Tallal, 1981). By definition these children appear to support the argument that language is modular (e.g., Smith & Tsimpli, 1995) and not a prerequisite for the development of cognition. However, investigation of children labeled as having SLI suggests that their cognitive functions differ from those of their non-impaired peers.

Exploring the label: SLI

Diagnosis of SLI is based on exclusion criteria. Neurological, sensory, behavioral, and emotional causality must be ruled out before comparing the child's verbal and nonverbal functioning. A range of standardized assessments are used (see table 21.1). Language test scores are compared (in terms of age equivalent scores or standard deviation cut-off points, e.g. 2SDs below the mean) to estimates of nonverbal performance. If there is a mismatch between verbal and nonverbal performance, particularly when nonverbal performance falls within the normal range, a diagnosis of SLI is made.

Consequently children with SLI are not a homogeneous group (Bishop, 1997). Recognition of this variation has resulted in attempts to develop logical and clinically relevant classification systems. Traditional taxonomies of SLI (American Psychiatric Association, 1994) make a distinction between receptive (comprehension) and expressive subgroups. This approach has been criticized by Bishop (1997) because it uses statistical cut-offs to identify language impairment, making the boundary between receptive and expressive subtypes artificial. For example, most children with SLI have receptive difficulties when assessed using appropriate language tests (see table 21.1).

More detailed linguistically based classification systems (Aram & Nation, 1975; Bishop & Rosenbloom, 1987; Rapin, 1996) have greater relevance but await validation. Rapin and Allen (1983) proposed six syndromes of developmental-language disorder, but so far only two subtypes of SLI have been statistically identified (Rapin, 1996). One group of children has a higher IQ and predominantly expressive deficits and a second group of children has a lower IQ (though still within normal limits) and receptive and expressive

Table 21.1   Examples of assessments/procedures used to establish a diagnosis of SLI

Test	Description
Reynell Developmental Language Scales III (Edwards et al., 1997)	A general language assessment (children aged 1;6–7;0). Assesses understanding of spoken language, vocabulary, and connected speech.
Clinical Evaluation of Language Fundamentals-3 UK (Semel, Wiig, & Secord, 1995)	A general language assessment (people aged 6;0–21;11); norm-referenced, six subtests that assess: word meaning, word and sentence structure, ability to recall and retrieve spoken language.
British Picture Vocabulary Scale III (Dunn, Dunn, Whetton, & Burley, 1997)	A norm-referenced test of receptive vocabulary (people aged 3;0–15;8).
Boehm Basic Concepts – Preschool (Boehm, 1986)	Assesses 26 basic concepts (children aged 3–5;0) including: size, direction, position in space, quantity, and time.
Test of Reception of Grammar (Bishop, D., 1989)	A norm-referenced comprehension test of grammar where the child is asked to point to a picture that matches a spoken sentence (children aged 4–12;0).
German Test of Word-Finding (German, 1989)	A norm-referenced test assessing word naming across a variety of conditions.
Test of Pragmatic Language (Phelps-Terasaki & Phelps-Gunn, 2000)	A norm-referenced test that assesses a range of social language skills including non-verbal language, topic maintenance, audience awareness, use of speech acts.
Language sample analyses	Analyses of spontaneous language e.g. LARSP (Crystal, 1979), MLU (Brown, 1973), TTR (Templin, 1957).
Systematic analysis of phonology	Word-elicitation tasks that examine speech sounds, consistency of production, and speech error patterns.
Test of Nonverbal Intelligence- 3 (Brown, Sherbenou, & Johnsen, 1997)	A norm-referenced, nonverbal, language-free test that estimates intellectual ability by evaluating an individual's ability to solve abstract figural problems.
Raven's Progressive Matrices (Raven, Raven, & Court, 1998)	A norm-referenced, nonverbal test that measures deductive ability.
British Ability Scales (Elliot, 1983)	Assesses a wide range of abilities including memory for sounds and pictures, interpretation of information to make a decision, speed of information processing, vocabulary, and receptive language.

Table 21.2 Description of Rapin and Allen's subgroups (adapted from Rapin, 1996)

Disorder	Subgroup
Mixed expressive and receptive	• *Verbal auditory agnosia:* Severe receptive and expressive language deficit. Speech absent or limited with disordered phonology. • *Phonologic/syntactic deficit disorder:* Receptive language equal to, or better than, expressive output that is characterized by ungrammatical utterances, impaired phonology, and a limited vocabulary.
Expressive	• *Verbal dyspraxia:* Receptive language is better than expressive language. Expressive language is limited and characterized by severely impaired phonology (not dysarthria – muscle weakness). • *Speech programming deficit disorder:* Receptive language adequate. Expressive language fluent but phonology impaired so speech is difficult to understand.
Higher-order processing	• *Lexical deficit disorder:* Receptive language difficulties in conversation. Expressive output is characterized by severe word-finding problems, simplified syntax and formulation difficulties in discourse. • *Semantic-pragmatic deficit disorder:* Receptive difficulties in conversation. Expressive language is fluent with intact phonology and syntax. However the content may be bizarre. Inadequate conversational skills.

language deficits. Clinical taxonomies differentiate these broad subtypes into sub-classifications. Rapin and Allen's clinically defined subgroups are described in table 21.2 (Rapin, 1996).

Conti-Ramsden, Crutchley, and Botting (1997) studied the characteristics of a large national cohort of 7-year-old children attending language units in England. They used a battery of standardized tests and teacher opinion to examine the extent to which psychometric tests differentiated clusters of children with SLI. They compared their data with that of Rapin and Allen (1987) and identified similar, distinct subgroups. Conti-Ramsden and Botting (1999) reassessed the children in the cohort one year later addressing two important issues: the stability of the subgroups and stability of the children's classification. The same profiles of language difficulties described in the original study remained, but individual children (45 percent of the sample) moved across subgroups primarily because of changes in the children's vocabulary or phonology. Longitudinal studies are useful as they provide information about the stability of the disorder. However, the results need to be interpreted in light of the fact that the children were receiving intensive speech and language therapy that might have altered their profile of abilities.

The use of standardized tests to collect data to establish subgroups is problematic because it limits the type of data available for analysis. Dunn, Flax, Sliwinski, and Aram

(1996) suggest that standardized assessments are more restrictive and less sensitive to language disorder than clinical judgment. One cluster identified by Conti-Ramsden, Crutchley, and Botting (1997) illustrates this point. The children were attending a language unit and receiving intensive speech and language therapy input. They were judged to have a language disorder as their primary problem and had difficulty coping in mainstream schools even with support. Yet they performed well on all of the standardized assessments (>40th percentile, where 29–71 reflects the average range) except the British Ability Scales word-reading task. Conti-Ramsden & Botting (1999) concluded that this group of children should not be considered as language-impaired because their profiles on standardized assessments appear normal. To address this issue, Dunn et al. (1996) suggested that information gathered from spontaneous language samples (utterance length and the number that contain grammatical errors, e.g. error in word order, tense markers) can reconcile the mismatch between the children who are clinically identified as having SLI and those identified by psychometric testing. They argued that a classification approach that relies solely on standardized tests fails to identify the underlying processes responsible for children's language profiles and how they use their language skills.

Despite the lack of empirically validated subgroups, it is nevertheless evident that SLI is not a unitary condition and that distinct profiles of difficulties exist (Bishop, 1997; Conti-Ramsden et al., 1997; Rapin & Allen, 1983). SLI has also been shown to be dynamic, with individuals' strengths and weaknesses changing over time. Bishop (1997) concludes that research assuming that children with SLI are a unitary group will lead to conflicting findings and different conclusions about what impaired mental processes underlie SLI.

Theories of underlying impairment

Three main theories have been put forward to account for SLI: a specific linguistic deficit, limitations in general processing capacity, and an information-processing deficit.

Specific linguistic deficit.   The hypothesis that SLI is the result of a specific linguistic deficit stems from Chomsky's theory that language is innate. Children with SLI are thought to have impaired innate knowledge. There are a number of versions of the specific-linguistic theory, each detailing a specific deficit in linguistic knowledge (see Leonard, 1998). For example, the functional category deficit theory (Leonard, 1995) proposes that children with SLI have difficulty acquiring functional categories (e.g., determiners – *a, the*). In contrast Rice, Wexler, and Cleave (1995) propose a particular difficulty with finite forms (e.g., copulas – verbs linking subject and predicate – *be*, auxiliaries; verbs that express time, aspect, mood – *do, has*).

A relatively more general deficit in linguistic knowledge has been proposed by Gopnik (1990) who described the case of a bilingual dysphasic boy. Spontaneous language samples collected over an 18-month period indicated errors for a wide range of features (number, person, tense, aspect, and gender). Nevertheless, the boy demonstrated an understanding of the rules constraining thematic relations in simple sentences. Gopnik concluded that the profile of ability was consistent with a feature-deficit hypothesis (feature blindness) that was reflected by the child's impaired ability to formulate grammatical rules. An alternative account argues that children with SLI have a restricted range of contexts in which they can apply grammatical rules (see Leonard, 1998). Other specific-linguistic accounts focus on structural deficits. For example, Van der Lely (1994) suggests that children with SLI have a representational deficit for dependent relationships.

Leonard (1998) raises two problems for specific-linguistic accounts of SLI. The predictions made are only applicable to a limited number of languages, yet SLI exists in all languages so far studied. The second problem is that the language symptoms identified may be due to a non-linguistic impairment. For example, difficulty formulating grammatical rules may reflect a more general rule abstraction deficit. It is also difficult for specific-linguistic theories to account for the dynamic nature of SLI. Accounts that fail to acknowledge the non-linguistic difficulties of children with SLI might be misleading.

Limitations in general processing capacity.   The limited-processing account stemmed from evidence that children with SLI process information more slowly than their peers (Johnston & Ellis-Weismer, 1983; Kail, 1994; Tallal & Piercy, 1973). Lahey and Edwards (1996) compared the performance of 66 children with SLI to those without SLI on three tasks designed to stress different types of processing. The tasks were naming pictures with the signal to respond presented at various delay intervals, primed naming, and vocal responding to non-linguistic stimuli. They divided the children with SLI into two groups: one with a receptive and expressive impairment, one with only expressive deficits. The children with receptive/expressive language disorder were slower on naming tasks and responding to non-linguistic stimuli then their peers. However, those children with expressive-only language deficits were not significantly slower than their peers, suggesting differences between children with different profiles of SLI. In contrast, Windsor and Hwang (1999) reported generally slow performance for all children with SLI across a range of language tasks, compared to their age-matched peers. Their "expressive" subgroup also had reading difficulties. These contradictory findings highlight the need for specific description of subject group characteristics in order to associate underlying deficits with particular language profiles.

Information-processing deficits

(*i*)   *Temporal processing deficits.* The two main information-processing accounts for SLI are temporal processing deficits and an auditory storage deficit. A large body of work suggests that SLI is the result of an impaired ability to respond to rapidly presented auditory information. Tallal and her colleagues' early work (e.g., Tallal, 1976; Tallal & Piercy, 1975) reported that children with SLI had a selective auditory impairment. These children found it difficult to distinguish auditory stimuli if the critical identifying information was brief or if the stimuli were presented in rapid sequence, interfering with the perception of phonological structure. A later, larger, study (Tallal, Stark, Kallman, & Mellitis, 1981) failed to replicate the initial auditory specific findings. While manipulating the time between stimuli did improve the ability to distinguish tones, children with SLI also differed from controls on visual stimuli and serial memory. The authors attributed these findings to the effects of age on performance as they found that the younger children (5–6 years) were impaired in processing rapidly presented information regardless of modality. Older children (7–8 years) were impaired only in processing rapidly presented auditory information.

Some researchers question whether the deficit observed is one of temporal processing or poor discrimination of visual and auditory brief/rapid stimuli. Other researchers have questioned whether the children's performance reflects a deficit in their ability to categorize acoustic information phonetically or impaired memory processes. A careful longitudinal study by Bishop, Carlyon, Deeks, and Bishop (1999) assessed a range of auditory abilities including thresholds for detection of a brief backward masked tone, detection of frequency modulation and pitch discrimination using temporal cues. Further they reported that controls performed poorly on the auditory tasks. No evidence was found to support an auditory temporal processing impairment as a causal factor in SLI.

(*ii*) *Phonological storage deficit.* Gathercole and Baddeley (1990a) propose that the phonological component of working memory may be disordered in children with language impairments. Working memory refers to the system that temporarily stores information required for complex cognitive tasks. According to Baddeley and Hitch's working memory model (see Baddeley, 1992) there are three components: a visuo-spatial sketch pad, central executive, and phonological loop. Baddeley defines the phonological loop as the "simplest and most extensively investigated component of working memory" (1992, p. 558). It is comprised of two components: a phonological store that can hold speech information for one to two seconds and an articulatory control mechanism. The function of the phonological loop is to hold information in the phonological store by subvocal repetition.

The phonological component of working memory has been linked to the setting up of phonological representations (Gathercole & Baddeley, 1990a) and vocabulary acquisition (Gathercole & Baddeley, 1989). Gathercole and Baddeley (1990b) compared six children with language disorder with control groups, matched for verbal and nonverbal abilities, on a range of memory tasks. Children with SLI had significantly impaired phonological memory that could not be attributed to auditory perceptual processes, articulation rate, failure to encode material phonologically or failure to use subvocal rehearsal. It was concluded that the impairment arose from a deficit in phonological storage.

In contrast, Joanisse and Seidenberg (1998) present evidence that the linguistic impairments in SLI could stem from basic information-processing deficits in phonology that also interfere with memory. They suggest that phonology is the link between perceptual deficits and impaired language abilities. Similarly, Elbro's (1998) studies of dyslexic readers led to the proposal that the distinctness of the stored phonological representation underlies poor performance on a range of tasks including phonological awareness and phonological memory (see Snowling, ch. 18 this volume). Elbro (1998, p. 149) defines distinctness as "the magnitude of the difference between a representation and its neighbors."

Since it is not possible to review research on different subgroups of SLI the remainder of this section will focus on children with phonological disorders. This subgroup is important to discuss in detail because:

- children with phonological impairment constitute 70 percent of all referrals to speech and language therapy (Weiss, Gordon, & Lillywhite, 1987);
- phonology has been studied from a psycholinguistic perspective to identify mechanisms underlying disorder (Dodd, 1995; Stackhouse & Wells, 1997);
- change in a child's phonology was one of two factors linked to individual children moving across subgroups of SLI (Conti-Ramsden & Botting, 1999);
- it is posited as a link between information-processing deficits and linguistic impairments (Joanisse & Seidenberg, 1998).

Phonological disorders

Children with phonological disorders make errors of pronunciation that makes their speech difficult to understand. To produce a spoken word a child uses a stored representation to assemble a phonological plan that is constrained by their understanding of the phonological system. This plan drives phonetic planning and articulatory execution (Chiat, 2000). Different deficits in this speech processing chain can underlie speech difficulties. Consequently, children with phonological disorder are not a homogeneous group. They differ in severity, type of surface error pattern, suspected causal and maintenance factors, and their response to different intervention approaches.

More than half the children with phonological difficulties have delayed development, i.e. they follow the normal course of acquisition but at a slower rate. No deficit in the speech-processing chain has yet been identified for this group. There is some evidence (Renfrew & Geary, 1973; Zhu Hua & Dodd, 2000) that spontaneous recovery can occur, and that a child with normal age-appropriate developmental errors at one assessment may warrant classification as delayed at a later assessment.

In contrast children with phonological disorder (as opposed to delay) make errors in pronunciation that deviate from the normal developmental path. Their surface error patterns are atypical of normal development (e.g., marking all initial consonants as [h]), they are less likely to recover spontaneously (Dodd, Zhu Hua, & Shatford, 2000) and are at risk of later difficulties in the acquisition of literacy (Dodd, Gillon, Oerlemans, Russell, Syrmis, & Wilson, 1995). They are, by definition, within normal limits on nonverbal cognitive assessments (e.g., TONI) at diagnosis and have intact comprehension. They may perform poorly on measures of expressive language because of their phonological disorder. For example, many delete word-final consonants, precluding the marking of tense, plurality, and possession. To maximize their intelligibility they may also produce short utterances, leading to short mean length of utterance measures and low scores on sentence complexity.

Underlying deficits

Two main areas of deficit have been identified to account for phonological impairment: peripheral deficits in auditory and motor skills, and a cognitive-linguistic impairment in rule abstraction.

Peripheral deficits.   Recent research has attempted to identify the types of deficits that might underlie phonological disorder using a psycholinguistic approach (Dodd, 1995; Hewlett, Gibbon, & Hardcastle, 1998; Stackhouse & Wells, 1997). Oro-motor skills have been the focus of considerable research, indicating that some children's difficulties in producing intelligible speech can be accounted for in terms of precision of articulatory movement (Gibbon, Dent, & Hardcastle, 1993). Listeners cannot hear differences between phonemes despite the fact that measurement of articulatory movement, using a palate prosthesis that records contact patterns of the tongue, indicates that they consistently mark differences between phonemes. For example a listener might perceive /r/ as /w/, yet the child's production patterns for /r/ and /w/ are distinct. Other research suggests that phonological disorder is associated with deficits at the input end of the speech-processing chain. Impaired auditory processing skills have been hypothesized to underlie both speech and language disorders (Tallal, 1976) However, Bishop (1997) points out that it is difficult to determine whether poor performance on auditory processing tasks is causative, or reflects correlative or consequent symptoms. Explanations that rely on impaired functioning of peripheral oro-motor or auditory processing mechanisms probably account for some speech-disordered children's difficulties. However, it does not seem plausible that children presenting with markedly different speech profiles should always have either a specific peripheral auditory or oro-motor deficit, given the complexity of the phonological aspect of language.

Cognitive-linguistic impairment in rule abstraction.   Many children's speech difficulty may lie in understanding the nature of the phonological system to be acquired. Pinker (1994, p. 480) defines phonology as:

> The component of grammar that determines the sound pattern of the language, including its inventory of phonemes, how they may be combined to form natural-sounding words, how the phonemes may be adjusted depending on their neighbours, and patterns of intonation, timing and stress.

Each language's phonology is constrained in a specific way. For example, in English words cannot begin with the velar nasal /ng/, although Cantonese words can. Phonological development involves acquisition of knowledge about these constraints and their implementation in word production. An impaired ability to derive and use the constraints or rules of the phonology to plan spoken output would result in atypical speech errors.

(*i*) *The link between spoken and written phonology.* Many children who have a phonological disorder in the preschool years later have difficulties acquiring literacy. Therefore, accounts of the deficit of phonological disorder must link disorders of both spoken and written phonology. Dodd et al. (1995) compared groups of phonologically delayed, disordered children and matched control groups' ability to read and spell using standardized tests. Children with *delayed* phonological development did not differ from age-matched controls in their ability to spell real words (South Australian Spelling Test; Westwood, 1979) or comprehend text. However, their reading accuracy was poor because they mispronounced words (Neale Analysis of Reading Ability; Neale, 1988). In contrast, children with *disordered* phonology differed from the control group on all reading and spelling measures. This pattern of performance suggests a difficulty in abstracting the constraints of spoken and written phonology.

In another experiment (Dodd & Cockerill, 1985) the ability of phonologically disordered children and reading-age-matched controls to spell three types of words was compared: words with a strict one-to-one phoneme-grapheme correspondence (e.g., rent, trips); rare spellings that have to be learned since they cannot be generated by phoneme-grapheme conversion rules alone (e.g., yacht, ocean); and rule-governed words that require the operation of spelling rules to generate correct spelling (e.g., bake, buzz). The results indicated that while the phonologically disordered children could learn the spelling of rare orthographic patterns and had mastered simple one-to-one phoneme–grapheme rules, they had difficulty with more complex relationships between sound and orthography e.g. final *e* lengthens the preceding vowel, /k/ after a short vowel is represented as *ck*. Other research, showing that poor readers with no concurrent speech difficulties make more errors when imitating unfamiliar polysyllabic words (Snowling, 1987) provides further evidence that a single deficit might underlie difficulties in speaking, spelling, and reading. That deficit, in turn, may reflect a more general impairment in using rules to aid the learning process.

Savage (1982) demonstrated that poor readers' performance was inferior to age-matched good readers when they were required to learn artificial symbol–word correspondences which varied in terms of consistency and rule application (e.g., recognizing the symbol ⧈ as representing the word "boy"). Poor readers showed particular difficulty when learning involved the use of an inconsistent rule. These results were sustained even when differences in reading experience were ruled out (Manis & Morrison, 1985). All the research studies discussed, however, have involved linguistic processing. Could the deficit affect non-linguistic behavior?

(ii) Rule abstraction: general or specific? The ability to abstract rules is a cognitive one involving pattern recognition. While an impaired ability to abstract rules would be particularly apparent during language acquisition because linguistic systems are highly rule-governed, a more pervasive impairment may exist. To test this hypothesis an experiment investigated subjects' performance on a non-linguistic rule-governed task (Dodd & Gillon, 1997). There were three groups of subjects: poor readers; chronological-age-matched normal readers (to control for cognitive knowledge and experience); and reading-age-matched average readers (to control for the possibility that experience in grapheme–phoneme rule conversion may generally enhance a child's ability to abstract rules).

All subjects attended mainstream primary schools. The "poor readers" were identified as having specific reading disability in the absence of: neurological disorder; emotional or behavioral disorder; sensory impairment; previously diagnosed language comprehension difficulties; inadequate educational opportunities; or below-average intellectual ability. Thus, all children included in the experimental group had unexpected reading difficulties in view of their other abilities.

The Neale Analysis of Reading Ability Revised (Neale, 1988) was used to obtain measures of students' reading accuracy and comprehension. The experimental subjects' reading accuracy performance was at least two years below that appropriate for their chronological age. Control subjects' performance was between three months below and 12 months above the level appropriate for their chronological age. All students performed within the average or above-average range on the Test of Nonverbal Intelligence. There were 15 subjects in each group. The poor readers had significant phonological-processing deficits as evidenced by poor performance on phoneme-segmentation tasks (identifying individual speech sounds in a word, e.g., sh-ar-k). They also showed phoneme–grapheme conversion rule difficulties as indicated by poor performance on a non-word-reading task. The CA control group were drawn from the same classes as the poor readers. The examiner was unaware of who the good and poor readers were when administering the experimental task.

The rule/nonrule-governed learning task from the Muma Assessment Program (MAP) (Muma & Muma, 1979) was used. This is a descriptive assessment procedure that examines children's ability to extract rules and assesses their flexibility in shifting from one rule orientation to another. Cards from a pack of 50 were shown to the subject one at a time. Each card had two pictures of the same common object (e.g., apple). The pictures of the objects differed according to size and color (e.g., one big red apple and one small blue apple). The subject was instructed to guess which one of the two pictures the examiner was thinking of and to point to that picture. The examiner indicated yes or no depending on whether the choice was correct or incorrect. The cards were presented as fast as possible and the subject was only allowed one choice per card. Initially, the examiner was thinking of all the red objects (referred to as the initial set of items). After the subject had responded correctly on eight consecutive cards the examiner's choice changed to selecting all the blue objects (referred to as the reversal shift). Following eight consecutive correct responses the examiner changed to selecting all the big objects (termed non-reversal shift). The task was not interrupted when changes were made from one shift to another.

The number of trials (cards) it took to gain eight consecutive correct responses was recorded for each subject for each of the three conditions (initial, reversal, and non-reversal). Some subjects took a great number of trials (e.g., 169) to demonstrate rule-learning. The results, shown in figure 21.1, indicated that the poor readers took more trials to extract the rule governing the nonreversal set.

The results suggest that poor readers' difficulty in abstracting rules was not restricted to linguistic tasks. Rather, they seem to have particular difficulty with rule flexibility in general. Rule use has been linked to a child's conscious representation and executive function (see Zelazo and Müller, ch. 20 this volume). While shifting from one salient aspect to another within the same category (e.g., color: from red to blue) provided no difficulty, they were less able than the two control groups to switch categories of salience (e.g., from color to size). These findings suggest that the nature of some poor readers' rule abstraction impairment may be a lack of flexibility in the application of rules which are either irregular or complex.

The results are consistent with those of Connell and Stone (1994), who assessed children with SLI. Their results indicated that children with SLI were able to induce novel rule-governed relationships but had difficulty making the mental shift when problems

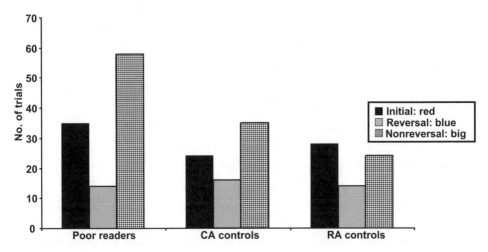

Figure 21.1 Rule-learning task

changed. They hypothesized that children with SLI experience difficulties extracting nonverbal rules that may reflect difficulties with "flexible reconceptualization." However, when Kiernan, Snow, Swisher, and Vance (1997) directly assessed this using the Muma & Muma (1979) task, the performance of children with SLI did not differ from that of their peers. The difference in findings may reflect differences in subject selection.

Is language disorder in otherwise normal children associated with cognitive deficits?

Evidence from children with phonological disorder suggests that a specific cognitive deficit affects their language acquisition. Difficulty in pattern recognition has consequences for both written and spoken phonology. Research on other clinically recognized subgroups of SLI (see Rapin, 1996) is obscured by two important methodological issues. One concerns the need for research studies to examine well-defined groups of subjects. The assumption that SLI is a unitary disorder is dangerous because it leads to conflicting evidence about the nature of associated impairments. The relationship between linguistic and cognitive impairments cannot be determined until statistically validated subgroups of SLI have been identified and investigated.

The second related issue concerns the assessment instruments that are used to define groups of SLI. Current standardized assessments constrain rather than illuminate the nature of SLI. Bishop (1997, p. 37) concludes that

> Basic research on psycholinguistic processes should be used not only to discover the basis of SLI but also to explore the range of variation in cognitive deficits, and how this relates to language profile. Once we understand what it is about language that can give children

particular difficulty, we can devise better ways of indexing underlying problems, and it is these indices, rather than current assessment tools, that have the best chance of providing us with a meaningful classificatory framework.

Perhaps examination of the language abilities of well-defined groups of children with cognitive difficulties might provide better evidence of the relationship between language and cognition.

Language in Populations with Impaired Cognition

Up until the 1970s research suggested that cognitive impairment was inevitably associated with language delays and disorders. It was assumed that the severity of the cognitive impairment predicted language attainment across the board. More recent investigations have led to three qualifications of that assumption:

- specific causes of cognitive impairment are associated with different profiles of language disability;
- specific aspects of language are differently affected within one causal category of cognitive impairment;
- some individuals who are cognitively impaired have spared language function.

These issues are illustrated by the discussion of three populations.

Down's syndrome

Nearly all cases of Down's syndrome (DS) result from all living cells of an embryo receiving, from conception, three chromosomes 21 (standard trisomy 21). There is about one infant with Down's syndrome in every thousand live births, with as many as 60 percent having a life expectancy beyond the age of 50 years (Baird & Sadovnik, 1988). Associated physiological factors include: hearing loss; visual impairment; cranio-facial abnormalities (e.g., wide pharynx); upper respiratory tract infections; hypotonia (low muscle tone); and heart defects. Down's syndrome is characterized by intellectual impairment: people with DS constitute about 30 percent of the moderate to severe intellectually impaired population. While these people do not differ from other cognitively impaired populations (matched for chronological age and IQ) on most behavioral measures, it is often claimed that their linguistic abilities are more impaired.

Nature of communication disorder in DS.   Reviews by both Fowler (1990) and Kernan (1990) report that people with DS show a consistent disadvantage for language tasks in studies comparing their performance with people from other etiological categories of cognitive impairment. The language measures used included comprehension of complex sentences (Kernan, 1990), mean length of utterance, sentence complexity, use of articles, verb inflections, and pronouns (Rondal & Lambert, 1983). Rondal and Edwards (1997) concluded that "some persistent speech and language differences may indeed exist between DS and non-DS mentally retarded persons" (p. 84). However, it is speech ability that most clearly differentiates DS from other etiological categories of cognitive impairment.

The speech of children with DS is often unintelligible. While their babbling patterns are similar to those of normally developing infants and the phonemes acquired are appropriate, the order of their emergence does not follow the typical order of acquisition. Some authors report that their errors are of the same type observed in the phonological development of intellectually average children, but that it is delayed. Other research suggests that when compared with the speech of children matched for intellectual disability who do not have DS, a greater degree of disability is revealed. Phonological development is slow and difficult, and follows a different course of development from that reported for children developing typically. While delayed phonological acquisition typifies the speech of children who are intellectually disabled but do not have DS, children with DS have a specific difficulty and are prone to inconsistent pronunciation of the same words. When children are asked to name the same pictures on a naming task on three separate occasions in a 45-minute session more than 60 percent of the words are pronounced differently (e.g., umbrella produced as [ʌnbE, ʌnbEdʌ, and ʌmbEjʌ]) ("unbeh," "ubeda," "umbeya") (Dodd & Thompson, in press).

Factors underlying the speech difficulties of children with Down's syndrome. Probably no single causal factor can account for their high level of unintelligibility. Contributing causal factors include cranio-facial anatomical abnormalities, fluctuating hearing loss, and hypotonia of the oral musculature. However, these factors fail to explain two important characteristics: first, children with DS make fewer errors in imitation than in spontaneous production of the same words (Lenneberg, 1967), and second, their inconsistency of production (Borghi, 1990). Miller (1988) proposed two alternative accounts of his finding that language production lags behind language comprehension and cognition in children with DS: motor control deficits and specific modular cognitive deficits. Another causal hypothesis is *incomplete phonological representations of words at the lexical level.* Children with DS may be unable to establish fully phonologically specified lexical representations for words because they are prone to fluctuating hearing loss or because of a phonological short-term memory deficit (Hulme & Mackenzie, 1992). If their mental representations of words are not fully specified, the range of consonant phonemes produced would vary. Finally, *the language learning environment* may be influential. Parents seek meaning in their children's speech attempts. Often what children mean is clear in context and parents understand what is meant rather than the words. If children pronounce words inconsistently and are understood, they would fail to learn that consistency of word production is essential for intelligibility. Dodd, McCormack, and Woodyatt (1994) found that training parents to encourage consistency of word production enhanced intelligibility.

Research suggests that children with DS have difficulty acquiring the formal structure of language. Their ability to master the phonological and syntactic constraints of language would appear to be more impaired than their cognitive impairment warrants. In contrast, their use of language is reported to be less impaired. Children with DS are reported to use one-word utterances to request interesting objects in the same way as normally developing children matched for Piagetian stage (Greenwald & Leonard, 1979), and Rondal and Edwards's (1997) review concluded that the variety of speech acts (questions, assertions, suggestions, commands) is appropriate for their cognitive level. Rondal and Edwards (1997) argue that the language profile of children with DS reflects relative strengths in thematic semantic and pragmatic measures and relative weaknesses in phonetic-phonological, morphosyntactic, discursive, and lexical aspects. Children with Williams syndrome present a very different profile.

Williams syndrome

Williams syndrome (WS) is a rare congenital metabolic disorder of genetic origin (see also Thomas & Karmiloff-Smith, ch. 26 this volume). It occurs in one in 25,000 live births. Associated physiological factors include cardiovascular defects, hypercalcemia (high levels of calcium in the blood), hyperacusis (sensitive hearing, but no hearing loss), gastrointestinal abnormalities, visual strabismus and motor difficulties (strength, balance, motor planning). Intellectual impairment is predominantly in the moderate to mild range (40–70 IQ), and they are reported to have difficulties with number, problem-solving and spatial cognition (see Stevens & Karmiloff-Smith, 1997). Behavioral characteristics include hyperactivity and short attention span. What is remarkable about adolescents with WS is their *relatively* intact linguistic functioning despite serious deficits in cognitive abilities. Bellugi, Lai, and Wang (1997) report that the spontaneous language of the 30 adolescents in their study was "syntactically impeccable" and that grammatically complex sentences were produced.

When asked to tell a story from sequenced pictures, adolescents with WS produced coherent, complex narratives, using extensive affective prosody, in comparison to matched subjects with DS (Reilly, Klima, & Bellugi, 1991). Their phonological and morphosyntactic abilities are spared in relation to their level of cognitive impairment (Rondal & Edwards, 1997). Although Karmiloff-Smith et al. (1997) found that the performance of people with WS (8;4 to 34 years; nonverbal age equivalent scores: 3:6 to 9:0) on a standard test of receptive morphosyntactic and expressive gender marking in French was not intact, they concluded that it was impressive given the subjects' cognitive deficits. One characteristic of their language is their lexical and semantic abilities.

Tests of vocabulary indicate that, once past early childhood, people with WS have vocabulary scores that better reflect their chronological age than their cognitive status (see Stevens & Karmiloff-Smith, 1997). On a measure of semantic fluency, where subjects are asked to say as many same-category nouns (e.g., animals) as possible in a specified time, the adolescents with WS performed better than CA- and IQ-matched subjects with DS (Bellugi et al., 1990), some of the subjects performing within normal limits. Rondal and Edwards (1997, p. 60) noted that "Consistent with their observed tendency to produce unusual words in spontaneous speech, WS subjects frequently produced not just typical category members (e.g., cat, dog, or horse, for animals), as did the DS subjects, but also low-frequency, non-prototypical lexical category members (e.g., brontosaurus, sea lion, sabre-toothed tiger).

However, there are two sources of evidence that the relatively intact lexical abilities of people with WS may not reflect a "spared" linguistic ability despite a cognitive impairment (for further evidence see Thomas & Karmiloff-Smith, ch. 26 this volume). Younger children with WS evidence delays in both expressive language and comprehension. Kelley's (1990) case study of a 4;8 boy with WS found marked delays in receptive and expressive vocabulary, verbal comprehension, mean length of utterance, and morphosyntax. Similarly, 20 of 23 children aged between 7 and 12 years studied by Arnold, Yule, and Martin (1985) performed at levels appropriate for 5 to 6-year-old children on expressive and comprehension measures of the Reynell Developmental Language Scales. Bellugi, Lai, and Wang (1997) compared preschool children with WS and DS using a parental report rating scale. The results indicated similar patterns of language development, with both groups showing marked receptive and expressive delays.

Other studies raise doubts about the nature of lexical skills in people with WS. Stevens and Karmiloff-Smith (1997) argued from studies of new word learning that lexical storage in WS is aberrant, and Jarrold, Baddeley, and Hewes (1998) claimed that findings from group studies might be attributed to some individuals having a large discrepancy between verbal and nonverbal abilities. Nevertheless, the performance of people with WS in a semantic priming task (Tyler, Karmiloff-Smith, Voice, Stevens, Grant, Udwin, Davies, & Howlin, 1997) found no differences from normal controls. Further, Grant, Karmiloff-Smith, Berthoud, and Cristophe (1996) concluded that the lexical abilities of people with WS are not the result of mimicry of auditory input, since they had difficulty imitating phonotactically unfamiliar words.

One aspect of the communication abilities of people with WS has been reported to be disordered. Rondal and Edwards (1997) summarized reports suggesting that they were hyperverbal, socially inappropriate, and had difficulties with conversational discourse (e.g., topic introduction and maintenance). Despite relative strengths in expressive phonology, syntax, and semantics, use of language by people with WS seems comparatively poor and their comprehension of morphosyntax (e.g., tense) has been questioned.

Savants

The review of the language skills of people with Down's syndrome and Williams syndrome demonstrates that cognitive impairment affects language skills differentially. Specific syndromes are associated with typical profiles of ability, both in terms of the severity of the deficits and the aspects of language functioning that are most likely to be impaired. It is also true that within moderately and severely cognitively impaired populations there are individuals (savants) whose language abilities are spared. The term "savant" refers to exceptional people who, despite cognitive impairment, demonstrate remarkable ability in one particular domain, e.g. music, mathematics, art, or language. Rondal and Edwards (1997) summarize data on a dozen cases where language abilities were exceptional in comparison to IQ, Piagetian stage, and cause of cognitive impairment (e.g., Bellugi, Marks,

Bihrle, & Ssabo, 1988; Cromer, 1991; Yamada, 1990). Two examples of exceptional language development despite cognitive impairment are now briefly reviewed.

Françoise.   Rondal (1994a, 1994b) reported a detailed case study of a 32-year-old Frenchwoman with Down's syndrome (trisomy 21). On the Wechsler Adult Intelligence Scale (WAIS) Françoise had a verbal IQ of 70, and a nonverbal IQ of 64. She had difficulty with spatial subtests, arithmetic, and memory for numbers. On the Epreuves Différentielles d'Efficience Intellectuelle (Perron-Borelli & Misès, 1974), an intelligence test consisting of eight verbal and nonverbal subtests, Françoise achieved a verbal mental age of 9 years 10 months and a nonverbal mental age of 5 years 8 months. In terms of Piagetian criteria she was at the late pre-operative to early operative stage. In terms of her nonverbal intellectual functioning, Françoise's performance is typical of adults with Down's syndrome.

In contrast her spontaneous spoken language was remarkable. Françoise's speech was fluent, with appropriate intonation, and her pronunciation was error-free. Her mean length of utterance was 12.24 morphemes. Syntactically, Françoise produced complete sentences with correct word order. She made no errors in the construction of declarative, interrogative, imperative, emphatic, or exclamatory sentences either affirmatively or negatively. Complex constructions, such as embedded clauses and passive voice, were used appropriately, articles were marked for number, gender, and for contrast between specific and non-specific reference. Extensive analyses of her spontaneous spoken language revealed Françoise's mastery of expressive syntax (see Rondal, 1994a, 1994b).

Psycholinguistic tasks assessing comprehension of complex grammatical constructions revealed Françoise's ability to be near normal. Her performance on standardized vocabulary tests was at the lower end of the normal range. Assessment of Françoise's language functioning appeared to have only two limitations. She made occasional lexical errors in locutions (e.g., *y a* for *il y a*), adverbial derivations, and expressions. More importantly, Françoise's conversational speech showed difficulties with discourse organization. For example, although she used a range of conjunctive forms (e.g., *et, alors, mais, donc*) at the beginning of utterances, these forms did not establish relationships between utterances. Rondal and Edwards (1997, p. 94) interpreted this, and other phenomena, such as the repeated use of stereotyped expressions and the alternate introduction of two ideas, as an indication that "although discourse taken at the level of the speech turn . . . is coherent, the larger text lacks cohesion."

While careful analyses and extensive testing revealed some limitations in Françoise's language-functioning, they fail to detract from the major finding. Despite moderate cognitive impairments due to Down's syndrome, which is typically associated with poor language skills, Françoise had mastered her native language.

The second case study is remarkable because its subject is multilingual.

Christopher.   Christopher's remarkable linguistic skills were first described by O'Connor and Hermelin (1991), when he was 29 years old. Although he had a nonverbal IQ of 67, Christopher demonstrated the ability to translate into English from German, French, and Spanish. His morphosyntactic comprehension was adequate in all four languages and standardized vocabulary tests revealed above-average performance in English, German,

Table 21.3   Christopher's diagnostic and psychometric profile

Investigation	Age	Finding
Neurological investigation		
EEG	13	frontal lobe slow waves
Inter-cranial pressure	14	no abnormality
Neurological assessment	15	hydrocephalic brain damage; apraxia
MRI	31	moderate cerebral atrophy with wide sulci over both hemispheres; hypoplastic cerebellar vermis
Nonverbal assessment		
Ravens Matrices	–	75, 76
Performance WISC-R	–	42, 67, 52
Draw a Man Test	14	40
Conservation of number	30+	failure to conserve
Theory of mind testing		
Sally-Anne Test	30+	Failure to impute appropriate beliefs to others
Smarties Test	30+	Appropriate performance
Verbal assessment		
Verbal WISC-R	–	89, 102, 98
PPVT (vocabulary)	29	English 121; French 114; German 110; Spanish 89
Reading comprehension	30+	Maximum score
Gollin Figures (partial representations)	30+	Words (score comparable to UG controls) Objects – poor performance

and French, and Spanish. Subsequently, Smith and Tsimpli's (1995) book presented detailed descriptions of Christopher's linguistic and cognitive abilities. One of their major concerns was to understand the extent to which Christopher could use his formal linguistic knowledge to communicate effectively. The following summary is drawn from Smith and Tsimpli (1995).

Christopher, born in 1962, cannot live independently. He has difficulty finding his way around and his gross and fine motor skills are poor. Perinatal brain damage was diagnosed at 6 weeks of age, and Christopher's developmental milestones were delayed. He was considered to be cognitively impaired and attended special schools, eventually being transferred to a school for physically handicapped children. His main interests at home and at school were foreign languages. Table 21.3 provides a summary of case-history details and psychometric assessment results.

Christopher performed within normal limits on verbal assessments, and well below the normal range on most nonverbal tests. Neurological investigations do not explain his performance. Smith and Tsimpli (1995, p. 4) concluded: "Although it is gradually becoming possible to account for certain pathologies in neuroanatomical terms, we are still far from being able to explain Christopher's (or any other subject's) enhanced performance in such a way."

After extensive testing of Christopher's linguistic abilities in English, Smith and Tsimpli (1995) concluded that "his knowledge of his first language is essentially perfect" (p. 43). Assessment included asking for judgments concerning sentence "goodness" and the correction of "bad" sentences (e.g., stimulus: *Who did you say Mary met at John's party?*; correction: *Whom did you say Mary met at John's party?*). Christopher demonstrated competence across a broad range of grammatical structures (e.g., declaratives, passives, negatives, interrogatives, involving variations in agreement and word order). Similar tasks established that his lexical and semantic skills were exceptional given his cognitive deficit. Although he demonstrated adequate performance on tests of pragmatic skills (e.g., discourse, inferencing), he was unable to understand jokes or handle irony and metaphor. This deficit reflected Christopher's difficulty with second-order representation (i.e., understanding a propositional form interpretatively rather than descriptively, as in "No man is an island"). Smith and Tsimpli interpreted this finding as an indication that despite intact grammar, Christopher's understanding of his first language is limited by his cognitive abilities.

Christopher has varying degrees of knowledge (from elementary to fluent production and comprehension) of 16 languages: Danish, Dutch, Finnish, French, German, modern Greek, Hindi, Italian, Norwegian, Polish, Portuguese, Russian, Spanish, Swedish, Turkish, and Welsh. These languages represent a wide range of language families (Indo-European, Uralic, and Altaic) and include different word orders (subject–object–verb; subject–verb–object) and different scripts (Cyrillic, Greek, Devanagari). Smith and Tsimpli (1995) assessed Christopher's linguistic knowledge of modern Greek, French, Spanish, and Italian, those second languages in which he is most competent. His lexical and morphological skills were shown to be better than his syntactic ability. The grammar of his first language influenced judgments of the grammatical soundness of sentences in other languages and his use of syntax in other languages was limited. In contrast, Christopher's acquisition of lexical and morphological information is exceptional: "He manifests an attention bordering on obsession with the orthographic form of words and their morphological make-up . . . identifying appropriate features of their number, case, gender and agreement system" (Smith and Tsimpli, 1995, p. 82). A variety of assessment tasks were used, including translation from written text into English. However, translation was not a fair reflection of Christopher's linguistic knowledge, since he treated translation as a linguistic exercise. His translation appeared to be on a word-for-word basis, so that he failed to integrate his lexical knowledge appropriately in sentence structure. For example, he failed to distinguish *savoir* and *connaître* ("to know" a fact and person respectively), despite evidence that he had knowledge of the two words and how they should be used in context.

Smith and Tsimpli (1995) concluded that Christopher's profile of abilities in his first and second languages provides evidence for the modularity of language functions. While he was able to master lexical and morphological aspects of some of his second languages, his syntax was always flawed. Evidence that his ability to communicate in any language was atypical of non-intellectually impaired people, despite encyclopaedic knowledge, was provided by his difficulty with second-order representations (e.g., jokes, metaphors). This deficit, which was argued to underlie Christopher's poor performance on the theory of mind "Sally-Anne" task, was interpreted as an indication that the language module intersects with the central cognitive system.

*Do children with cognitive deficits show similar symptoms
of language disorder?*

The profile of language strengths and weaknesses for the two syndromes described (DS and WS) differ markedly. While people with DS have difficulty with the formal structure of language (phonology and syntax) their use of language to communicate is comparatively good, people with WS show greater strengths in the formal aspects of language but their use of language is comparatively poor. The cases of the exceptional language abilities of Françoise and Christopher reveal that intellectual impairment does not always preclude the acquisition of formal aspects of one or more languages, although the pragmatic use of language seems vulnerable to cognitive deficits. Three important conclusions can be drawn from the evidence examined. Psychometric measures fail to predict language abilities (Rondal & Edwards, 1997). The profile of language abilities of people with different syndromes varies. Despite the fact that there are profiles of ability associated with particular syndromes, individuals within the same diagnostic group may show very different levels of linguistic ability.

Conclusion

The evidence reviewed in this chapter reveals the potential of research on language disorder to inform the debate on the relationship between language and cognition. However, that potential has not yet been realized. Standardized assessment tools are descriptive rather than explanatory. Consequently research focuses on identifying strengths and weaknesses rather than investigating the mental processes that underlie language performance. Further, the populations discussed in this chapter, particularly children with SLI, are heterogeneous populations. The search for one underlying deficit that accounts for language impairment obscures identification of specific linguistic and cognitive skills.

Current research is pursuing two explanatory paths to investigate speech and language differences between individuals, with and without diagnosed cognitive impairments. One approach is investigating pathological factors (brain anatomy and physiology, genetics) to identify correlates of neuropsychological development (e.g., Bellugi, Lai, & Wang, 1997). A different approach strives to account for behavior in terms of how the mind is structured (e.g., Anderson, 1992; Smith & Tsimpli, 1995).

There is, however, one reservation about the use of evidence from impaired populations for understanding the "normal" development of language and cognition. Stevens and Karmiloff-Smith (1997, p. 758) caution that "equivalent behavioral outcomes (e.g., in vocabulary scores, syntactic performance, etc.) can stem from different brain structures and processes." Another important barrier to our understanding of the nature of the relationship between impaired cognition and language arises from the way both abilities are measured. There is a tendency for specific aspects of language (e.g., vocabulary *or* syntax *or* comprehension) to be thought generally representative of language ability. Similarly, cognition can be measured by assessments that include a range of abilities or a relatively specific ability. These two issues constrain the interpretation of evidence from the populations discussed.

Nevertheless, the research reviewed in this chapter on the relationship between language and cognition from the perspective of impaired language and impaired cognition allows some tentative conclusions. People with impaired cognition provide evidence that language is modular, at least to the extent that different aspects of language can be impaired differentially. Specific language impairment is associated with cognitive deficits, although the nature of the relationship – causal, consequent, or correlative – awaits clarification (Bishop, 1997). We have argued that there is no one cause of SLI nor one language profile associated with cognitive impairment. Perhaps it is also profitless to seek one explanatory relationship between language and cognition that remains static throughout an individual's lifespan.

CHAPTER TWENTY-TWO

The Exact Mind: Empathizing and Systemizing in Autism Spectrum Conditions

Simon Baron-Cohen, Sally Wheelwright, John Lawson, Rick Griffin, and Jacqueline Hill

Autism Spectrum Conditions: Historical and Diagnostic Issues

Cognitive developmentalists have had a long-standing interest in neurodevelopmental conditions, such as autism. This is not only out of a desire to understand the causes of such atypical development, in order to advance medical science and develop interventions; it is also because studying the processes that cause atypicality can sometimes throw light on typical development. It is this two-way influence that characterizes the field of developmental psychopathology. In this chapter we focus on autism. We bring out this interaction between what we now understand about autistic cognition, and how this has helped us understand "normality."

Autism is diagnosed when a child or adult has abnormalities in a "triad" of behavioral domains: social development, communication, and repetitive behavior/obsessive interests (APA, 1994; ICD-10, 1994). In the 1960s and 1970s, many of the children with autism who were studied by cognitive developmentalists also had comorbid learning difficulties (i.e. below average intelligence) and language delay (Frith, 1970; Hermelin & O'Connor, 1970; Wing, 1976). An average IQ of 60 was not uncommon in samples studied during that period. In the 1980s, cognitive developmentalists began to focus more on what was then called "high-functioning autism" (Baron-Cohen, Leslie, & Frith, 1985,

Simon Baron-Cohen, Jacqueline Hill, and Rick Griffin were supported by the MRC during the period of this work. Sally Wheelwright was supported by the McDonnell-Pew Trust. John Lawson was supported by the Isaac Newton Trust. We are also grateful for support from the Shirley Foundation. Parts of this chapter are reprinted from Baron-Cohen, Wheelwright, Scahill, Lawson, and Spong (in press).

1986). In reality such children might be better described as "medium functioning," as although they had IQs within the average range, this simply meant their IQ fell within two standard deviations (sds) from the population mean of 100. Since 1 sd is 15 points, this means that anyone with an IQ above 70 would still have been included in this band. An IQ of 71 is by statistical definition average, but is hardly high-functioning.

By the 1990s, interest had shifted to studying the truly high-functioning strata of the autistic spectrum: those whose IQs were close to 100 or above. This would have included those with "superior IQ," i.e., those whose IQ was higher than 2 sds above the population mean (Baron-Cohen, Jolliffe, Mortimore, & Robertson, 1997; Frith, 1991; Jolliffe & Baron-Cohen, 1997; Klin, Volkmar, Sparrow, Cicchetti, & Rourke, 1995; Szatmari, Tuff, Finlayson, & Bartolucci, 1990). Since we know that IQ is a strong predictor of outcome (Rutter, 1978), it is important to take these "background variables" into account.

Asperger syndrome (AS) was first described by Asperger (Asperger, 1944). The descriptions of the children he documented overlapped considerably with the accounts of childhood autism (Kanner, 1943). Little was published on AS in English until relatively recently (Frith, 1991; Wing, 1981). Current diagnostic practice recognizes people with AS as meeting the same criteria as for high-functioning autism (HFA), but with no history of language delay, and with no cognitive delay. In concrete terms, this means that as a toddler, the individual was speaking on time (i.e., single words by age 2, and/or phrase speech by age 3) and had a mental age in line with their chronological age (i.e., an IQ in the normal range). Although some studies have claimed a distinction between AS and HFA (Klin et al., 1995), the majority of studies have not demonstrated many, if any, significant differences between these.

This background of autism and intelligence is important because it reveals that over the last 40 years there has been a major shift in research strategy. When studying the cognitive development of autism, one strategy (and one we will focus on here) is to identify the deficits or talents that are specific to this truly high-functioning group. In this way, we can be sure that no coincidental causal factors (such as mental age) are creeping in.

Cognitive Developmental Theories of Autism

In this section we briefly summarize some of the main cognitive developmental theories of autism, including some new directions of these.

The mindblindness theory

The mindblindness theory of autism (Baron-Cohen, 1995) proposed that in autism spectrum conditions, there are deficits in the normal process of empathizing, relative to mental age. These deficits can occur by degrees. Here we use the term "empathizing" to encompass "theory of mind," "mind-reading," and taking the "intentional stance" (Dennett, 1987).

Empathizing involves two major elements: (a) the ability to attribute mental states to oneself and others, as a natural way to understand agents (Baron-Cohen, 1994; Leslie, 1994; Premack, 1990); (b) having an emotional reaction that is appropriate to the other person's mental state. In this sense, it includes what is normally meant by the term "theory of mind" (the attributional component) but it goes beyond this, to also include having some affective reaction (such as sympathy).

The first of these, the mental state attribution component, has been widely discussed as being an evolved ability, given that in this universe there are entities that have intentionality (Brentano, 1874/1970). The mental state attribution component is effectively judging if this is the sort of entity that might possess intentionality. Intentionality is defined as the capacity of something to refer or point to things other than itself. A rock cannot point to anything. It just is. In contrast, a mouse can "look" at a piece of cheese, it can "want" the piece of cheese, and it can "think" that this is a piece of cheese, etc. Essentially, agents have intentionality, whereas non-agents do not. This means that when we observe agents and non-agents move, we construe their motion as having different causes (Csibra, Gergely, Bíró, Koós, & Brockbanck, 1999; Gelman & Hirschfield, 1994). Agents can move by self-propulsion, which we naturally interpret as driven by their goals and desires, while non-agents can reliably be expected not to move unless acted upon by another object (e.g., following a collision).

The second of these, the affective reaction component, is closer to what we ordinarily refer to by the English word "empathy." Thus, we not only attribute a mental state to the agent in front of us (e.g., the man "thinks" the cake is made of soft, creamy chocolate), but we also anticipate his emotional state (the man will be disappointed when he bites into it and discovers it is hard and stale), and we react to his emotional state with an appropriate emotion ourselves (we feel sorry for him).

Empathizing thus essentially allows us to make sense of the behavior of another agent we are observing, predict what they might do next, and how they might feel, and it allows us to feel connected to another agent's experience, and respond appropriately to them.

The normal development of empathizing.   Empathizing develops from human infancy (Johnson, 2000). In the infancy period, it includes

- being able to judge if something is an agent or not (Premack, 1990);
- being able to judge if another agent is looking at you or not (Baron-Cohen, 1994);
- being able to judge if an agent is expressing a basic emotion (Ekman, 1992), and if so, what type;
- engaging in shared attention, for example by following gaze or pointing gestures (Mundy & Crowson, 1997; Scaife, & Bruner, 1975; Tomasello, 1988);
- showing concern or basic empathy for another's distress, or responding appropriately to another's basic emotional state (Yirmiya, Sigman, Kasari, & Mundy, 1992);
- being able to judge an agent's goal or basic intention (Premack, 1990).

Empathizing can be identified and studied from at least 12 months of age (Baron-Cohen, 1994; Premack, 1990). Thus, infants show dishabituation to actions of "agents" who appear to violate goal-directedness (Gergely, Nádasdy, Gergely, & Bíró, 1995; Rochat, Morgan, & Carpenter, 1997). They also expect agents to "emote" (express emotion), and expect this to be consistent across modalities (between face and voice) (Walker, 1982). They are also highly sensitive to where another person is looking, and by 14 months will strive to establish joint attention (Butterworth, 1991; Hood, Willen, & Driver, 1997; Scaife & Bruner, 1975). By 14 months they also start to produce and understand pretense (Bates, Benigni, Bretherton, Camaioni, & Volterra, 1979; Leslie, 1987). By 18 months they begin to show concern at the distress of others (Yirmiya et al., 1992). By 2 years old they begin to use mental state words in their speech (Wellman & Bartsch, 1988).

Empathizing of course develops beyond early childhood, and continues to develop throughout the lifespan. These later developments include:

- attribution of the range of mental states to oneself and others, including pretense, deception, belief (Leslie & Keeble, 1987);
- recognizing and responding appropriately to complex emotions, not just basic ones (Harris, Johnson, Hutton, Andrews, & Cooke, 1989);
- linking mental states to action, including language, and therefore understanding and producing pragmatically appropriate language (Tager-Flusberg, 1993);
- making sense of others' behavior, predicting it, and even manipulating it (Whiten, 1991);
- judging what is appropriate in different social contexts, based on what others will think of our own behavior;
- communicating an empathic understanding of another mind.

Thus, by 3 years old, children can understand relationships between mental states such as seeing leads to knowing (Pratt & Bryant, 1990). By 4 years old they can understand that people can hold false beliefs (Wimmer & Perner, 1983). By 5–6 years old they can understand that people can hold beliefs about beliefs (Perner & Wimmer, 1985). By 7 years old they begin to understand what not to say in order to avoid offending others (Baron-Cohen, O'Riordan, Stone, Jones, & Plaisted, 1999). With age, mental state attribution becomes increasingly more complex (Baron-Cohen, Jolliffe, Mortimore, & Robertson, 1997; Happé, 1993). The little cross-cultural evidence that exists suggests a similar picture in very different cultures (Avis & Harris, 1991).

These developmental data have been interpreted in terms of an innate module being part of the infant cognitive architecture. This has been dubbed a theory of mind mechanism (ToMM) (Leslie, 1994). But as we have suggested, empathizing also encompasses all of the skills that are involved in normal reciprocal social relationships (including intimate ones) and in sensitive communication. Empathizing is a focused and narrowly defined domain, namely, *understanding and responding to people's minds.* Deficits in empathizing are referred to as degrees of mindblindness.

Empathizing in autism spectrum conditions.   Since the first test of mindblindness in children with autism (Baron-Cohen, Leslie, & Frith, 1985), there have been more than 30 experimental tests. The vast majority of these have revealed profound impairments in the development of empathizing ability. These are reviewed elsewhere (Baron-Cohen, 1995; Baron-Cohen, Tager-Flusberg, & Cohen, 1993), but include deficits in the following:

- joint attention (Baron-Cohen, 1989c);
- use of mental state terms in language (Tager-Flusberg, 1993);
- production and comprehension of pretense (Baron-Cohen, 1987a; Wing & Gould, 1979);

- understanding that "seeing leads to knowing" (Baron-Cohen & Goodhart, 1994; Leslie & Frith, 1988);
- distinguishing mental from physical entities (Baron-Cohen, 1989a; Ozonoff, Pennington, & Rogers, 1990);
- making the appearance–reality distinction (Baron-Cohen, 1989a);
- understanding false belief (Baron-Cohen, Leslie, & Frith, 1985);
- understanding beliefs about beliefs (Baron-Cohen, 1989b);
- understanding complex emotions (Baron-Cohen, 1991);
- showing concern at another's pain (Yirmiya et al., 1992).

Some children and adults with AS only show their empathizing deficits on age-appropriate adult tests (Baron-Cohen, Jolliffe, Mortimore, & Robertson, 1997; Baron-Cohen, Wheelwright, & Hill, 2001; Baron-Cohen, Wheelwright, & Jolliffe, 1997). This deficit in their empathizing is thought to underlie the difficulties such children have in social and communicative development (Baron-Cohen, 1988; Tager-Flusberg, 1993), and the development of imagination (Baron-Cohen, 1987b; Leslie, 1987).

The empathizing-systemizing theory

As was explained earlier, we have defined empathizing so as to include both the recognition of mental states and the appropriate emotional response to these. A deficit in empathizing might account for the social and communication abnormalities that are diagnostic of autism, but such a deficit has little if anything to contribute to our understanding of the third domain of abnormality in the triad: the repetitive behavior and obsessions. For this reason, our view of autism is now broader, and suggests that, alongside empathizing deficits, a different process is *intact or even superior*. This is what we call *systemizing*.

What is systemizing?   Whereas we think of empathizing as the drive to identify and respond to agents' mental states, in order to understand and predict the behavior of that agent, we think of systemizing as the drive to analyze and build systems in order to understand and predict the behavior of non-agentive events. Systems are all around us in our environment, and fall into at least four classes: technical systems (such as machines and tools); natural systems (such as biological and geographical phenomena); abstract systems (such as mathematics or computer programs); and even social systems (such as profits and losses in a business, or a football league table). The way we make sense of any of these systems is not in terms of mental states, but more in terms of underlying rules and regularities. So systemizing involves an initial analysis of the system down to its lowest level of detail in order to identify potentially relevant parameters that may play a causal role in the behavior of the system. These parameters are then systematically observed or manipulated, one by one, and their effects on the whole system are noted. To put it succinctly, systemizing entails an analysis of input–output relationships. Once all the inputs are known, the output of the system becomes totally predictable.

Let's take a closer look at the normal development of our understanding of just one of these classes of systems, the mechanical. We can then look at whether the level of understanding of these in autism is intact or even superior, as predicted by the empathizing-systemizing theory. In the cognitive developmental literature, children's everyday understanding of systems in the physical world has been studied under the heading of "intuitive" physics (see Wilkening & Huber, ch. 16 this volume).

The normal development of intuitive physics. Intuitive physics involves both low-level perception of physical causality and higher-level understanding of physical causality.

Low-level here refers broadly to skills present in human infancy, such as the perception of physical causality and expectations concerning the motion and properties of physical objects. Intuitive physics early in human ontogeny can be revealed through the infant's sensitivity to apparent violations of the laws of physics (Baillargeon, ch. 3 this volume). Thus, infants show dishabituation to the unexpected events of larger objects going into smaller ones, objects being unsupported, two objects occupying the same space, one object passing through another, or one inanimate object moving without being touched by another (Baillargeon, Kotovsky, & Needham, 1995; Leslie & Keeble, 1987; Spelke, Phillips, & Woodward, 1995). With age, children's understanding of mechanics grows (Karmiloff-Smith, 1992).

Higher-level here refers to skills present from early childhood and which continue to develop throughout the lifespan. These include concepts relating to mechanics. For example, by middle childhood, children are becoming much more logical in how they work out how to balance a block on a fulcrum (Karmiloff-Smith, 1992). Again, succeeding in tasks such as these requires systemizing, because the child needs to analyze carefully what is causing what. If the block has a uniform weight along its length, then placing the fulcrum in the exact center of the block will cause it to balance. Moving it one centimeter to the right or left will cause the block to fall. If the block has a hidden weight at one end, then the fulcrum will have to be placed at this end, since a different underlying rule is now governing the system's behavior. These rules are not given, but need to be extracted or inferred from the workings of the individual parameters in the system. Observation and manipulation of these will lead to the rules being revealed. In this case, the rule now becomes this: "A block with a heavier weight at one end will only balance if this end of the block is placed closer to the fulcrum."

Intuitive physics is just one example of systemizing. It might be thought we have defined systemizing broadly. However, we suggest that as a domain it is focused and narrowly defined, namely, *understanding input–output relationships.*

Systemizing in autism spectrum conditions. Are people with autism intact or even superior at systemizing? First, there is no shortage of clinical descriptions of children with autism being fascinated by machines (the paragon of non-intentional systems). One of the earliest clinical accounts was by Bettelheim (Bettelheim, 1968) who describes the case of "Joey, the mechanical boy." This child with autism was obsessed with drawing pictures of machines (both real and fictitious), and with explaining his own behavior and that of others in purely mechanical terms. On the face of it, this would suggest he had a well-developed intuitive physics.

The clinical literature reveals hundreds of cases of children obsessed by machines. Parents' accounts (Hart, 1989; Lovell, 1978; Park, 1967) are a rich source of such descriptions.

Indeed, it is hard to find a clinical account of autism that does *not* involve the child being obsessed by some machine or another. Typical examples include extreme fascinations with electricity pylons, burglar alarms, vacuum cleaners, washing machines, video players, trains, planes, and clocks. Sometimes the machine that is the object of the child's obsession is quite simple (e.g., the workings of drainpipes, or the design of windows). Our survey of obsessions in children with autism substantiated this clinical observation that their preoccupations tend to cluster in the area of physical systems (Baron-Cohen & Wheelwright, 1999).

Of course, a fascination with machines need not necessarily imply that the child *understands* the machine, but in fact most of these anecdotes also reveal that children with autism have a precocious understanding too. The child (with enough language, such as is seen in children with AS) may be described as holding forth, like a "little professor," on their favorite subject or area of expertise, often failing to detect that their listener may have long since become bored with hearing more on the subject. The child's apparently precocious mechanical understanding, while they are relatively oblivious to their listener's level of interest, suggests that their systemizing might be outstripping their empathizing skills in development. The anecdotal evidence includes not just an obsession with machines (technical systems), but with other kinds of systems. Examples of their interest in natural systems include obsessions with the weather (meteorology), the formation of mountains (geography), motion of the planets (astronomy), and the classification of lizards (taxonomy).

Clinical/anecdotal evidence must, however, be left to one side, as this may not prove anything. More convincing is that experimental studies converge on the same conclusion: children with autism not only have an intact intuitive physics, they have accelerated or superior development in this domain (relative to their empathizing and relative to their mental age, both verbal and nonverbal).

First, using a picture-sequencing paradigm, children with autism performed significantly better than mental age (MA)-matched controls in sequencing physical-causal stories (Baron-Cohen, Leslie, & Frith, 1986). The children with autism also produced more physical-causal justifications in their verbal accounts of the picture sequences they made, compared to intentional accounts.

Second, two studies found children with autism showed good understanding of a camera (Leekam & Perner, 1991; Leslie & Thaiss, 1992). In these studies, the child is shown a scene where an object is located in one position (A). The child is encouraged to take a photo of this scene, using a Polaroid camera. While the experimenter and the child are waiting for the photo to develop, the scene is changed: the object is now moved to a new position (B). The experimenter then turns to the child and asks where in the photo the object will be. These studies found that children with autism could accurately infer what would be depicted in a photograph, even though the photograph was at odds with the current visual scene. Again, this contrasted with their poor performance on false belief tests.

These "false photo" tasks (Zaitchik, 1990) closely parallel the structure of the false belief task. The key difference is that in the (folk psychological) false belief test, a *person* sees the scene, and then the object is moved from A to B while that person is absent. Hence the person holds a belief that is at odds with the current visual scene. In the false photo task a *camera* records the scene, and then the object is moved from A to B while the camera is not in use. Hence the camera contains a picture that is at odds with the current visual scene. The pattern of results by the children with autism on these two tests was interpreted as showing that while their understanding of mental representations was impaired, their understanding of physical representations was not. This pattern has been found in other domains (Charman & Baron-Cohen, 1992, 1995). But the false photo test is also evidence of their intuitive physics (one example of systemizing) outstripping their empathizing, and being superior to MA-matched controls.

In the only direct test of intuitive physics in children with AS, Baron-Cohen, Wheelwright, Scahill, Lawson, and Spong (in press) presented the test to such children, and compared them to controls. Results showed the children with AS to be functioning at a superior level relative even to children with a higher chronological age. On this test, children were presented with 20 examples of mechanical physics questions (an example is shown in figure 22.1), each one using a forced choice format. Whereas older, normally developing teenagers (age 12–16) were scoring on average about 10 out of 20 correct, a sample of children with AS (age 8–12) scored on average 16 out of 20 correct.

Family studies of empathizing and systemizing.   Family studies add to this picture. Parents of children with Asperger syndrome also show mild but significant deficits on an adult mindreading task (the adult version of the "Reading the Mind in the Eyes" task). This mirrors the deficit in empathizing seen in patients with autism or AS (Baron-Cohen & Hammer, 1997b; Baron-Cohen, Wheelwright, & Hill, 2001). This familial resemblance at the cognitive level is assumed to reflect genetic factors, since autism and AS appear to have a strong heritable component (Bailey et al., 1995; Bolton et al., 1994; Folstein & Rutter, 1977; Le Couteur et al., 1996).

One should also expect parents of children with autism or AS to be over-represented in occupations in which possession of superior systemizing is an advantage, while a deficit in empathizing would not necessarily be a disadvantage. A clear occupation for such a cognitive profile is engineering. A recent study of 1,000 families found that fathers and grandfathers (patri- and matrilineal) of children with autism or AS were more than twice as likely to work in the field of engineering, compared to fathers and grandfathers of children with other disabilities (Baron-Cohen, Wheelwright, Stott, Bolton, & Goodyer, 1997). Indeed, 28.4 percent of children with autism or AS had at least one relative (father and/or grandfather) who was an engineer. Related evidence comes from a survey of students at Cambridge University, studying either sciences (physics, engineering, or maths) or humanities (English or French literature). When asked about family history of a range of psychiatric conditions (schizophrenia, anorexia, autism, Down's syndrome, or manic depression), the students in the science group showed a sixfold increase in the rate of autism in their families, and this was specific to autism (Baron-Cohen, Bolton, Wheelwright, Short, Mead, Smith, & Scahill, 1998).

We take seriously the notion that this profile in AS (impaired empathizing, together with superior systemizing) might be partly the result of a genetic liability. This is because AS appears to be heritable (Gillberg, 1991), and because there is every reason to expect that individuals with such a cognitive profile could have been selected for in hominid

This section aims to find out whether you can easily understand how things work and function.

Each question has a diagram by it, from which the answer can be worked out. After each question there is a choice of answers. Only one is correct. When you think you have found the correct answer, please indicate your choice by putting a circle around it. An example is shown below.

Example

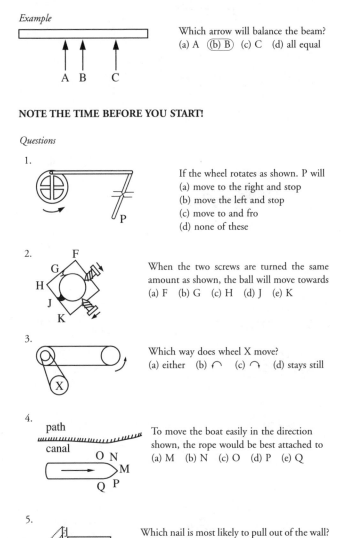

Which arrow will balance the beam?

(a) A   (b) B   (c) C   (d) all equal

NOTE THE TIME BEFORE YOU START!

Questions

1.

If the wheel rotates as shown. P will
(a) move to the right and stop
(b) move the left and stop
(c) move to and fro
(d) none of these

2.

When the two screws are turned the same amount as shown, the ball will move towards
(a) F   (b) G   (c) H   (d) J   (e) K

3.

Which way does wheel X move?
(a) either   (b) ⌒   (c) ⌒   (d) stays still

4.

To move the boat easily in the direction shown, the rope would be best attached to
(a) M   (b) N   (c) O   (d) P   (e) Q

5.

Which nail is most likely to pull out of the wall?
(a) A   (b) B   (c) C   (d) all equally likely

Figure 22.1   The intuitive physics test: example items

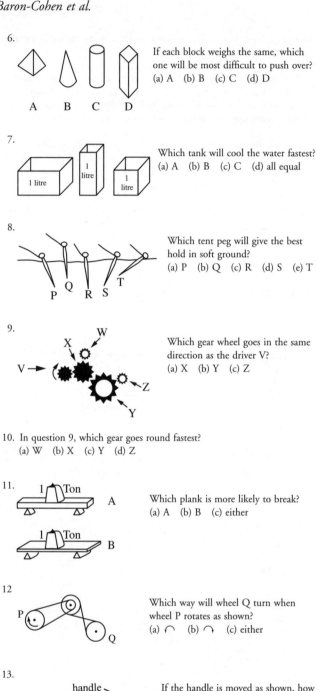

6.

If each block weighs the same, which one will be most difficult to push over?
(a) A   (b) B   (c) C   (d) D

A   B   C   D

7.

Which tank will cool the water fastest?
(a) A   (b) B   (c) C   (d) all equal

1 litre   1 litre   1 litre

8.

Which tent peg will give the best hold in soft ground?
(a) P   (b) Q   (c) R   (d) S   (e) T

P   Q   R   S   T

9.

Which gear wheel goes in the same direction as the driver V?
(a) X   (b) Y   (c) Z

X   W   V   Z   Y

10. In question 9, which gear goes round fastest?
(a) W   (b) X   (c) Y   (d) Z

11.

1 Ton   A

Which plank is more likely to break?
(a) A   (b) B   (c) either

1 Ton   B

12

Which way will wheel Q turn when wheel P rotates as shown?
(a) ⌢   (b) ⌢   (c) either

P   Q

13.

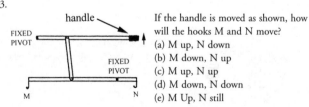

handle

FIXED PIVOT

FIXED PIVOT

M   N

If the handle is moved as shown, how will the hooks M and N move?
(a) M up, N down
(b) M down, N up
(c) M up, N up
(d) M down, N down
(e) M Up, N still

Figure 22.1   *Continued.*

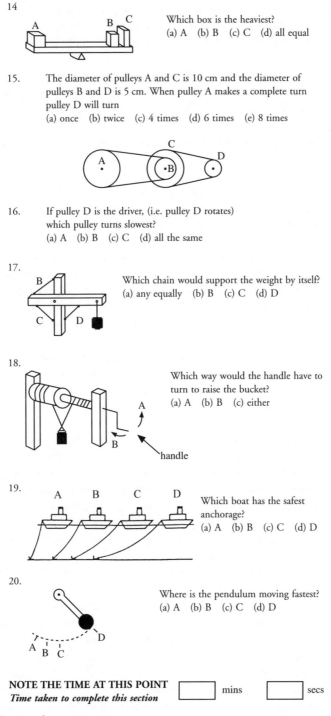

14

Which box is the heaviest?
(a) A   (b) B   (c) C   (d) all equal

15.   The diameter of pulleys A and C is 10 cm and the diameter of pulleys B and D is 5 cm. When pulley A makes a complete turn pulley D will turn
(a) once   (b) twice   (c) 4 times   (d) 6 times   (e) 8 times

16.   If pulley D is the driver, (i.e. pulley D rotates) which pulley turns slowest?
(a) A   (b) B   (c) C   (d) all the same

17.   Which chain would support the weight by itself?
(a) any equally   (b) B   (c) C   (d) D

18.   Which way would the handle have to turn to raise the bucket?
(a) A   (b) B   (c) either

19.   Which boat has the safest anchorage?
(a) A   (b) B   (c) C   (d) D

20.   Where is the pendulum moving fastest?
(a) A   (b) B   (c) C   (d) D

NOTE THE TIME AT THIS POINT
Time taken to complete this section   [   ] mins   [   ] secs

Figure 22.1   *Continued.*

evolution. Good systemizing would have conferred important advantages to an individual's inclusive fitness (e.g., tool use, hunting skills, construction skills, and even business sense), even if that individual's empathizing skills were less proficient.

Plotting empathizing and systemizing.   If empathizing and systemizing are independent dimensions, it is possible to plot on orthogonal axes possible scores from possible tests assessing these two abilities. Figure 22.2 provides a visual representation of this model of the relationship between empathizing and systemizing. It suggests appropriate labels for different possible patterns of scores. The axes show number of standard deviations from the mean. The scale of the diagram is less important than the principle underlying it.

We have used the terms *Balanced Brain, Brain Type E* (empathizing), *Brain Type S* (systemizing), to describe the three basic brain types that are generated from this model. These all fall within 2 sds from the mean on both dimensions. We have also shown on the graph the *extremes* of brain types S and E. The terms describe the discrepancy between the empathizing score and the systemizing score. In the Balanced Brain, there is no difference between scores (i.e., E = S). In Brain Type E, empathizing is 1 or 2 sds higher than systemizing (i.e., E > S). In the Extreme Brain Type E, this discrepancy is greater than 2 sds (i.e., E ≫ S). In Brain Type S, systemizing is 1 or 2 sds higher than empathizing (i.e., S > E). For the Extreme Brain Type S, this discrepancy is greater than 2 sds (i.e., S ≫ E).

It is worth underlining the fact that the key point is the discrepancy between the scores rather than the absolute scores themselves. For example, someone could score 2 sds above the mean on empathizing (a very high score), but if they scored 3 sds above the mean on systemizing, they would be described as having Brain Type S. Thus, the key issue is possible asymmetries of ability.

If empathizing and systemizing are truly independent, then it should be possible to find individuals in every square within the diagram (no correlation). If there is some trade-off between abilities in empathizing and systemizing, then the majority of individuals should have results which fit into the top left quadrant or bottom right quadrant of the diagram (negative correlation). If empathizing and systemizing abilities are subserved by the same underlying system, then the majority of individuals should have results which fit into the top right quadrant or bottom left quadrant (positive correlation). It is important to clarify that we conceptualize both empathizing and systemizing as varying with mental age. Therefore, standardized norms will need to be obtained for each level of MA.

Evidence from sex difference research (Kimura, 1992) suggests that Brain Type S is more commonly found in males, while Brain Type E is more frequent in females. For this reason we can also use the terminology *Female Brain Type* and *Male Brain Type* as synonyms for Brain Types E and S, respectively. This claim is also being tested as part of ongoing work, using a wider variety of tests and assessments. One result which is consistent with this model is that human neonates, 1 day old, show a sex difference: female babies look longer at a human face than at a mechanical mobile, while male babies show the opposite pattern of preference (Connellan, Baron-Cohen, Wheelwright, Ba'tki, & Ahluwalia, 2001).

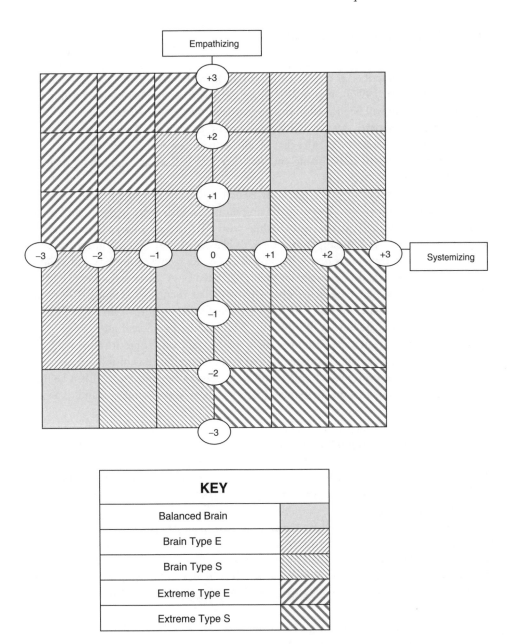

Figure 22.2 Empathizing-systemizing dimensions

The Extreme Male Brain (EMB) theory

Autism has been described as the extreme form of the male brain (Asperger, 1944; Baron-Cohen & Hammer, 1997a). Figure 22.3 illustrates where we predict the vast majority of people with autism will be located in this empathizing-systemizing (MA-matched) framework. Although this area overlaps with the Extreme Brain Type S, they are not exactly the same. This is because we predict that people with autism will always score more than 1 sd below the mean on empathizing and also that they will always score more than 1 sd above the mean on systemizing.

There are a number of other pieces of evidence that are consistent with the EMB theory of autism. First, regarding empathizing measures, girls score higher than boys on a test of understanding *faux pas,* and children with AS score even lower than unaffected boys (Baron-Cohen, O'Riordan, Stone, Jones, & Plaisted, 1999). Second, girls make more eye-contact than boys (Lutchmaya, Baron-Cohen, & Raggett, submitted) and children with autism make even less eye contact than unaffected boys (Swettenham et al., 1998). Third, girls tend to pass false belief tests slightly earlier than boys (Happé, 1995), and children with autism are even later to pass false belief tests. Finally, women score slightly higher than men on the test of "Reading the Mind in the Eyes," and adults with AS or high-functioning autism score even lower than unaffected men. There are also established sex differences in systemizing, boys tending to score higher on tests of folk physics, map use, and mental rotation, for example (Kimura, 1999), and people with autism being at least intact if not superior on these tasks (Baron-Cohen, Wheelwright, Scahill, Lawson, & Spong, in press).

This model of the independence of empathizing and systemizing also predicts the existence of very high-functioning individuals with AS, who may be extreme high achievers in domains such as mathematics and physics – equivalent to Nobel prizewinners even – but who have deficits in folk psychology. Our recent case studies are beginning to identify such very high-functioning individuals (Baron-Cohen, Wheelwright, Stone, & Rutherford, 1999).

Figure 22.3 also illustrates where the contrast case to autism is located. This area is the exact opposite of the predicted autism area, overlapping with the Extreme Brain Type E, but not matching it exactly. Some people have speculated as to whether people with Williams syndrome might have Extreme Brain Type E (Karmiloff-Smith, Grant, Bellugi, & Baron-Cohen, 1995), though this is debated (Tager-Flusberg, Boshart, & Baron-Cohen, 1998).

Note that in the same way that autism can be considered from the perspective of either difficulties (empathizing) or strengths (systemizing), so with the contrast case. In the latter case, the difficulties are predicted to be in systemizing (we could think of this as system-blindness) while the strengths are remarkable empathy. Such a case is predicted by this model but has not yet been documented. Our ongoing work is testing for such cases. We do not yet know if the Extreme Female Brain is even a risk factor for pathology, as the Extreme Male Brain can be. Being system-blind in most cultures may not be a disability, as there is always the option of getting someone else to do your systemizing for you (e.g. phoning your car mechanic or your plumber). And societies tend to be more

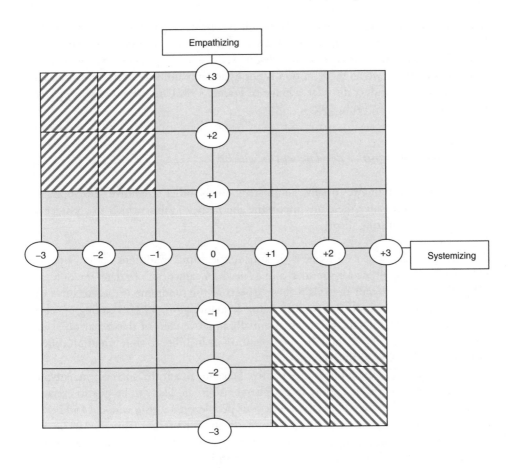

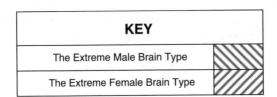

Axes show standard deviations from the mean

Figure 22.3 The extreme male and female brain types

tolerant of system-blindness than mind-blindness. Being hyper-empathic is unlikely to be maladaptive. Hyper-empathy cannot correspond to over-attribution of mental states since this would lead to inaccurate empathizing (e.g., assuming hostility where no hostile intent was present), which by definition is not hyper-empathizing. Such distortions have been reported in conduct disorder (Dodge & Frame, 1982) and paranoid schizophrenia (Corcoran, Mercer, & Frith, 1995).

Other models of cognitive development in autism

In this final section we briefly summarize some other cognitive developmental theories of autism, since these are important alternatives against which to consider the empathizing-systemizing theory.

Executive function theory.   People with autism spectrum conditions show "repetitive behavior," a strong desire for routines, and a "need for sameness." To date, the only cognitive account to attempt to explain these aspects of the syndrome is the executive dysfunction theory (Ozonoff, Rogers, Farnham, & Pennington, 1994; Pennington et al., 1997; Russell, 1997b). This paints an essentially negative view of this behavior, assuming that it is a form of "frontal lobe" perseveration or inability to shift attention (but see Zelazo & Müller, ch. 20 this volume).

We recognize that some forms of repetitive behavior in autism, such as "stereotypies" (e.g., twiddling the fingers rapidly in peripheral vision) are likely to be due to executive deficits. Moreover, we recognize that as one tests people with autism who have additional learning disabilities, executive deficits are more likely to be found (Russell, 1997a). But the fact that it is possible for people with AS to exist who have no demonstrable executive dysfunction while still having deficits in empathizing and talents in systemizing suggests that executive dysfunction cannot be a core feature of autism spectrum conditions.

The executive account has also traditionally ignored the *content* of "repetitive behavior." The empathizing-systemizing theory in contrast draws attention to the fact that much repetitive behavior involves the child's "obsessional" or strong interests with mechanical systems (such as light switches or water faucets) or other systems that can be understood in terms of rules and regularities. Rather than these behaviors being a sign of executive dysfunction, they may reflect the child's intact or even superior development of their folk physics. The child's obsession with machines and systems, and what is often described as their "need for sameness" in attempting to hold the environment constant, might be signs that the child is a superior systemizer. The child might be conducting mini-experiments in his or her surroundings, in an attempt to identify physical-causal or other systematic principles underlying events. Certainly, our recent study of obsessions suggests that they are not random with respect to content (which would be predicted by the content-free executive dysfunction theory), but that they tend to cluster in the domain of systemizing (Baron-Cohen & Wheelwright, 1999).

Central coherence (CC) theory.   It could be argued that good systemizing skills are simply an expression of an anomaly previously documented, namely "weak" central coherence

(Frith, 1989; Happé, 1996). Weak central coherence refers to the individual's preference for local detail over global processing. This has been demonstrated in terms of an autistic superiority on the Embedded Figures Task (EFT) and the Block Design Subtest (Jolliffe & Baron-Cohen, 1997; Shah & Frith, 1983, 1993). It has also been demonstrated in terms of an autistic deficit in integrating fragments of objects and integrating sentences within a paragraph (Jolliffe & Baron-Cohen, 2001; Jolliffe & Baron-Cohen, in press). The faster and more accurate performance on the EFT and Block Design Test have been interpreted as evidence of good segmentation skills, and superior attention to detail. The latter has also been demonstrated on visual search tasks (Plaisted, O'Riordan, & Baron-Cohen, 1998a, 1998b).

Our view of systemizing certainly embraces aspects of the central coherence theory. For example, systemizing requires as a first stage an excellent attention to detail, identifying parameters that may then be tested for their role in the behavior of the system under examination. So, both the E-S theory and the CC theory predict excellent attention to detail. However, the E-S and CC theories also make opposite predictions when it comes to an individual with autism being able to understand a whole system. The E-S theory predicts that a person with autism, faced with a new system to learn, will learn it faster than someone without autism, so long as there are underlying rules and regularities that can be discovered. Moreover, they will readily grasp that a change of one parameter in one part of the system may have distant effects on another part of the system. Thus, if the task is a constructional one (building a model plane, for example), they will be able to grasp that changing the thickness of the wings may cause the plane to land at a steeper angle. This kind of reasoning clearly involves good central coherence of the system. What is being understood is the *relationship* between one parameter and one distal outcome. In contrast, the CC theory should predict that individuals with autism should fail to understand whole (global) systems or the relationships between parts of a system. This has not yet been tested.

Final Thoughts

Superior systemizing depends on exactness in information-processing. Systemizing does not entail a search for approximate answers to questions. Systemizing is searching for the exact answer. We surmise that the systemizing mechanism is an exactness mechanism. By this we mean that it is only concerned with absolute facts of the most well-specified kind. Good systemizing means that excellent detail is being detected. The benefit of this is that all potentially important input is being considered, and harnessed to the aim of predicting output.

A man with AS whom we met recently told us that he thought the question "Where do you live?" was not a good question. "What information are they after?" he asked. "Do they want to know which country I live in, or which county I live in, or which city I live in, or which neighborhood, or which street, or which house?" For him, a better question would have been "Which city do you live in?" since that could only have one correct answer. Questions which could have multiple answers are unanswerable via systemizing, as they cannot be resolved. When this same man with AS was asked "When did you leave home this morning?," he could only answer "At 7.06 a.m." It would have been incorrect to say "At about 7 a.m." when he knew the correct answer was "7.06 a.m." When he was asked where he sat in the plane last year, he did not answer "Near the front" but instead answered "In seat 14B."

This exactness is seen in the speech of people with autism or AS. Their speech is described as pedantic (Tager-Flusberg, 1993). This can lead them to include far more detail in their answers than is needed for adequate communication. Here we see the interaction of an empathizing deficit (failing to appreciate what the other person needs to know) and a systemizing property (exactness). Their memories are described as astonishingly detailed, so that, for example, many adults with AS can recall not only the date they visited a place many years earlier, but an enormous amount of detail about the visit which most people would find not only irrelevant but astonishing. If one asks people with AS about their obsessional interests, typically one uncovers the fact that the person has a collection of objects (e.g. CDs, videos, or even something unusual, such as coffee mugs). The collection typically has hundreds of items, each of which can be recalled in precise detail, and they may be stored in a very precise order. The adults with AS we have met in our clinic have all worked in occupations in which they could use their very precise mind in domains which are factual, rule-based, and in which patterns can be identified. Science, engineering, maths, and physics may be clear examples of these, but by no means define the limits of such domains. Linguistics is another one, as is history or law.

One of the disadvantages of having your exactness mechanism too highly tuned is that you cannot answer questions to which an exact answer is unavailable. It also takes longer to select an answer from the range of possible answers, since this involves a search of detail. Lastly, it means that you are overloaded with detail and, where there are no systematic laws to be uncovered, you could instead be left submerged by data. Textual comprehension, and estimation, are examples of skills that would be expected to suffer, since here good systemizing would not help. We speculate that this highly tuned exactness mechanism could even affect one's empathizing skills, in that in this domain, answers are never exact ("What was John intending? He *probably* meant x").

In summary, this chapter has reviewed both the early mindblindness theory of autism and the more recent extensions of this: the empathizing-systemizing theory and the extreme male brain theory of autism. The first of these extensions addresses a problem that the early theory had, namely, needing to also account for the obsessional features of autism. The second of these may help explain the marked sex ratio in autism and throw light on the biological basis of autism (Lutchmaya et al., submitted). Both of these extensions lead to new predictions when contrasted with other cognitive developmental theories of this condition, and illustrate some of the progress that is being made in this part of the field of developmental psychopathology.

PART V

Models of Cognitive Development

The final section of this handbook presents a variety of theoretical models for making sense of cognitive development. Cognitive developmental psychology is rich in data, but relatively sparse in theories. We need productive explanatory frameworks to make sense of our data, frameworks that can guide future research and inform educators and clinicians who work with young children. Most educators and clinicians still rely on two extremely influential theoretical frameworks proposed in the last century, those of Piaget and Vygotsky. Both created detailed theoretical models that guided – and continue to guide – much cognitive-developmental research. Outlines of these two theories are presented in the chapters by Smith and by Rowe and Wertsch. However, modern cognitive developmental psychology has found limitations in each of these frameworks, and has sought new models of cognitive development in information-processing frameworks and connectionist models. These newer theories are discussed in the chapters by Halford and by Thomas and Karmiloff-Smith. The key topic of individual differences is also not really addressed by most existing theoretical accounts of what develops in children's cognition, as made clear in the final chapter in the handbook by Sternberg.

Smith's chapter on Piaget's model presents a philosophically oriented overview of Piagetian theory. Smith uses the analogy of a grand building scheme to describe Piaget's construction of his extremely comprehensive theory of cognitive development. He argues that the Grand Tower drawing the whole entity together was never actually built. Instead, cognitive developmental psychology has been left with a series of small and fine buildings addressing different aspects of Piaget's overarching question of how knowledge develops. Smith discusses Piaget's conception of the formation of knowledge in terms of equilibration, the mechanism for complex learning said to be the *tertium quid* drawing together nature and nurture in forming a cognitive system. Equilibration is the central construct in Piaget's theory, and enables a child to progress through three levels of knowing or of mental organization, broadly those of infancy (based on action), childhood (based on representational thought), and adolescence (based on formal understanding). Smith then fleshes out the stage criteria proposed for the different developmental levels of knowing, emphasizing their fluid nature and the fact that the levels are levels of knowledge, not levels of the child. The stage criteria are not age-related, although there are indicative ages at which they occur. As a developmental mechanism, equilibration is a kind of self-organizing process which takes into account the actual activities of children within their culture and social context. In this interpretation, equilibration becomes a constructivist account of knowledge acquisition, rooted in action, not in language or representation. For example, children discover via their actions on objects that 2 and 2 "make" 4 (a causal fact), and later discover that the meaning of "2 + 2" "implies" "4" (a normative fact). Smith argues that this advance from the causal to the logical was considered by Piaget to be the paradigm case of cognitive development. A comprehensive model of the development of knowledge thus requires a joint focus on causal facts (a child's understanding of what makes something happen in either the physical or social world, the typical focus of cognitive developmental psychology) and normative facts (a child's understanding of an individual's, group's or culture's use of a norm, not typically studied in cognitive developmental psychology). Equilibration is an explanatory construct which combines both. Smith's emphasis on the role that normative facts as well as causal facts play in equilibration implies that Piaget's model specifically requires that social interaction and social context make an indispensable contribution to the development of cognition.

Vygotsky has classically been seen as the developmental theorist most concerned with the role of social context and culture in children's cognition, as shown in Rowe and Wertsch's chapter on Vygotsky's model of cognitive development. He is also the theorist usually referred to for the view that language is central to cognitive development. Like Smith on Piaget, however, Rowe and Wertsch argue that Vygotsky's notion of developmental psychology was much broader and more philosophically based than is usually assumed in contemporary writing. The core idea of Vygotsky's model was that an understanding of how knowledge develops requires an understanding of the social and historical origins of knowledge and of changes in knowledge. Vygotsky argued that human knowledge originates in socially meaningful activity and is shaped by language. Processes that originate in the social world are then transferred to the inner "mental" world, and shape the development of higher cognitive processes such as problem-solving. By participating in social interaction, children appropriate linguistically mediated problem-solving, thinking, and regulatory techniques first for external social activity and then for internal mental activity. The origins of human mental function lie in direct reactions to environmental stimuli (these reactions being necessarily constrained by biology) and in cultural development – the mastery of symbolic or artificial stimuli ("signs"). "Sign" systems are used to organize one's own and others' behaviors, and the most important of these is language, which underlies abstract, categorical thinking. For example, memory development combines both the retention of actual experiences as episodic traces and the recoding of these experiences into verbally mediated, accessible "memories," perhaps supplemented by the use of sign-based mnemonic devices such as writing. The latter use of "signs" extends the operation of memory beyond the biological dimensions of the human nervous system and is unique to human beings. Part of the development of children's thinking requires "apprenticeship" into such culturally specific cognitive and social practices. The difference between a child's individual performance and their performance when guided by experts is metaphorically described by Vygotsky's "zone of proximal development." This notion of an enhanced level of mental functioning when an apprentice is guided by an expert has been very influential in education and in the study of learning disability. Rowe and Wertsch show that cognitive development does not happen just in the head of the child, but is a process of learning to operate with physical, symbolic, and cognitive tools in ways that themselves change cognitive processes. Rowe and Wertsch's formulation of Vygotsky's model has interesting similarities with Smith's formulation of Piaget's model, and these formulations seem quite contemporary, an issue that will be returned to below.

One metaphor for cognition that was not available at the time that either Piaget or Vygotsky were creating the major part of their theories was the computer metaphor. The idea that the brain was like a computer, able to take certain inputs, convert them into representations, and use these representations to compute certain outputs, led to new theoretical models for cognitive development called information-processing models. As Halford shows in his chapter, information-processing models of cognitive development have been the major theoretical alternative to Piaget's and Vygotsky's models over the last thirty years. They are currently still the major theoretical alternative to these models, in their new form as connectionist models. Information-processing models began with "neo-Piagetian" theories. The goal of these theories was to explain the data collected by Piaget and by those working within a Piagetian framework in terms of the growth of information-processing abilities such as memory capacity and the ability to coordinate different inputs (such as the different dimensions of a stimulus). Halford shows that all major information-processing theories are based on these two fundamental components, the child's assumed available memory storage and the level of complexity at which the child is assumed to be capable of processing information. As he notes, it is difficult to distinguish these empirically, as cognitive development could either be due to the child making better use of available storage capacity with age (via increased processing efficiency or expertise), or to storage capacity itself increasing with age. Halford concludes that a lot of "what develops" is accounted for by increased efficiency in the way that available capacity is utilized. He then shows that the most productive way of modeling this increased efficiency is via analyses of the complexity of the information that must be processed in a certain cognitive task, for example in terms of goal hierarchy (Case), cognitive skills (Fischer) or relational complexity (Halford). Halford illustrates the difficulties inherent in attempting to arrive at objective analyses of conceptual complexity, and concludes that the way forward is to analyze the complexity of cognitive tasks in terms of the number of variables that must be instantiated in parallel in a cognitive representation of that task. This metric for cognitive complexity is the basis of Halford's own "structure-mapping" information-processing theory of cognitive development, based on relational complexity. He illustrates how he has been able to instantiate relational complexity theory as a computational model that captures structural properties of higher cognition by the representation and processing of relations. Halford ends by arguing that the future challenge for information-processing theorists is to develop models that are related more explicitly to what we know about learning mechanisms from neuroscience and biological approaches.

Thomas and Karmiloff-Smith's chapter on the computational modeling of cognitive development shows that this challenge is already being partially achieved. In turn, they show how learning mechanisms can be understood in more detail by connectionist modeling. Current connectionist models are loosely based on principles of neural information-processing. They are intended to employ the same *style* of computation as the brain rather than to model exactly what is understood about neural circuits and the computational primitives (i.e., representations) that they extract from environmental input. Connectionist models are essentially learning systems, and so the ways in which they develop internal representations from particular training environments can help us to understand the ways in which children might acquire certain cognitive competencies. Modeling decisions that may be important in building an efficient connectionist system can also help us to understand any constraints on learning that might need to operate if children are to make the best use of the knowledge available in their learning environments. Such modeling decisions can also give insights into possible causes of atypical development. Thomas and Karmiloff-Smith give a particularly clear introduction to the general properties of connectionist models, and then discuss specific models of particular cognitive tasks such as the balance scale task, seriation, and conservation. They show how the modeler must make a series of design decisions when constructing a connectionist network, including the initial state of "knowledge" of the network, the nature of its input and output representations, the patterns of connectivity that it can form, and the learning algorithms that it will use. These initial computational constraints can be seen as corresponding to some of the innate core principles or biases for learning postulated by infancy researchers such as Baillargeon and Waxman. Thomas and Karmiloff-Smith then show that if a system has different or atypical initial computational constraints, atypical development will ensue. This principle enables the modeling of neurodevelopmental disorders. By changing different computational constraints independently (e.g., changing only the learning algorithm, or changing only the input representations), different developmental trajectories and outcomes can be reproduced. Thomas and Karmiloff-Smith discuss connectionist models of dyslexia, SLI, autism, and Williams syndrome. They show how the behavioral deficits characteristic of a certain disorder (e.g., Williams syndrome) can be reproduced by some alterations to the initial modeling constraints and not by others. They also show that more than one kind of alteration can lead to the same behavioral outcome. They finish with a brief discussion of how connectionist modeling is beginning to address the question of individual differences, and of how it might one day be able to address the active input of the child in selecting her own learning environments for cognitive development.

A difficulty common to all the theoretical models of cognitive development discussed in this section is how to conceptualize individual differences. Although it is possible to derive predictions concerning individual differences from all of the theories, no theory has taken individual difference data as its foundation. Rather, all theories have been based on data from the behavior of groups. Sternberg's chapter gives an overview of individual differences in cognitive development. He focuses on two paradigms for understanding individual differences, the psychometric paradigm and the systems paradigm. The psychometric paradigm has been an important one in psychology, leading to the development of standardized tests for the measurement of individual differences in cognitive development or in intelligence. The basic notions derived from psychometric theory (e.g., of verbal vs. non-verbal intelligence) still govern test construction today. It is also still assumed that there is a general factor "g" underlying all individual differences in cognitive abilities, which may relate to processing speed. In addition, variations in children's knowledge about and control of their own cognitive processing (metacognition and comprehension monitoring), also recognized in early psychometric work, are today seen as major factors in learning disabilities. Systems paradigms of individual differences are more recent, and are based on the idea of multiple intelligences. For example, researchers discuss "emotional" intelligence (the ability to understand and regulate one's emotions), "social" intelligence (the ability to interact effectively with other people), and "practical" intelligence (the ability to function effectively in everyday life). Sternberg's own theory of intelligence, the triarchic theory, is a systems theory, based on three types of ability (analytical, creative, and practical). Clearly, it is not simple to relate these theories to Piagetian or Vygotskyian models of cognitive development. Theories of individual differences begin with certain assumptions about "what develops" (e.g., vocabulary) and then measure individual differences in development and examine whether they are environmentally or genetically caused. Theories of cognitive development are trying to explain why development pursues its observed course. Their focus is on understanding the causes of development rather than on cataloguing differences in development. At present, related fields such as educational and clinical psychology rely heavily on individual difference theories of cognitive development and are relatively uninfluenced by more causal theories. For example, the impact of different genetic syndromes on cognitive development is measured clinically by a set of standardized verbal and non-verbal tests, rather than by for example measuring the zone of proximal development. It is obvious that both types of theory are necessary for a complete description of childhood cognitive development. Better theory integration in this area would be very valuable.

Is it possible to end this final commentary concerning models of cognitive development with a new theoretical framework for cognitive developmental psychology in the twenty-first century? An emergent newer framework, an "explanation-based/causal bias" learning framework, can be discerned in many of the chapters in this handbook. This newer framework accepts Piaget's idea that knowledge is rooted in action and experience, but rejects the related ideas that representations and language play quite peripheral roles in cognitive development. It also rejects the traditional Piagetian notion that cognitive development consists of the stage-like emergence of content-independent logical structures. The newer framework accepts Vygotsky's emphasis on the importance of language and social context for learning and his recognition of the key role of the actions of parents, caregivers, and teachers in shaping cognition. It draws from connectionist approaches in acknowledging the importance of incremental and context-dependent piecemeal learning for the child's development of causally coherent frameworks of knowledge that make sense of and organize their experience, and it draws from information-processing approaches in terms of the nature of the range of higher-order cognitive processes that are postulated to organize these experiences. This emergent theoretical framework is based on the notion that the infant begins the process of knowledge acquisition with a set of core principles that guide and constrain future cognitive development. These core principles are either innate, or are given by simple perceptual information such as a sensitivity to contingency.

Powerful learning mechanisms such as the ability to absorb statistical information from the environment, the ability to make relational mappings within and across domains, and explanation-based learning then ensure that more and more knowledge is acquired via concrete experience. This knowledge acquisition is guided by the core constraints, and also by the ways in which surrounding adults behave – the social, emotional, and cultural contexts within which learning takes place. The child's growing knowledge in any given domain can be described by a coherent causal framework that develops from an early bias to learn about causal relations and to acquire causal explanations. These developing causal frameworks are then reshaped and reorganized with further concrete experience.

Such a theoretical framework changes the research base for cognitive developmental psychology. Within this new, "explanation-based learning" model of cognitive development, it becomes important to describe the child's knowledge frameworks accurately, to discover the factors that drive change in a child's explanatory frameworks, and to understand how these factors depend on or are modified by social and emotional experience. At any given point in a child's development, in any particular domain, these explanatory frameworks can be examined in terms of how closely they approximate the physical reality of that child's social and cultural world, and how these approximations change under particular circumstances. Interestingly, this "new" theoretical framework for cognitive developmental psychology seems curiously reminiscent of a hybrid of key aspects of the new interpretations given to Piagetian and Vygotskyian theory by the authors of the opening chapters in this final section. Children's cognitive development depends on a developing understanding of what makes something happen in the physical or social world, a developing understanding that derives from socially meaningful activity, that is representational from the outset, and that is shaped by language. Children, the universal novices, are apprenticed to the "expert" adults around them, and learn from them to operate with the physical, symbolic, and cognitive tools of their culture. Developing understanding depends on powerful learning mechanisms. Coupled with developing information-processing abilities for making increasingly efficient use of available memory capacity, these mechanisms enable the cognitive system to strive for coherence and equilibrium in a self-organizing fashion. Paradoxically, this analysis suggests that at the meta-level our new theoretical approaches to understanding cognitive development, namely connectionist and information-processing approaches, are neo-Piagetian and neo-Vygotskian in more ways than might immediately be apparent. Both connectionism and information-processing, however, offer new ways forward in terms of characterizing the learning mechanisms that have been described as causally biased, explanation-based, self-organizing and striving for equilibrium.

CHAPTER TWENTY-THREE

Piaget's Model

Leslie Smith

Jean Piaget

Piaget (1896–1980) was born in Neuchâtel where he gained his Ph.D. in biology in 1918. This year marked a turning-point. His first book *Recherche* (*Search*) led to his "psychological turn," in Zurich with Bleuler, in Paris with Simon, and in Geneva with Claparède. He held chairs at Neuchâtel in 1925, at Geneva in 1929 until his retirement, and at the Sorbonne from 1952. Piaget gained his first honorary degree from Harvard in 1936, an APA Distinguished Scientist award in 1969, and the Erasmus Prize in 1972. He was director of UNESCO's International Bureau of Education during 1929–67, and the founding director of his international center from 1955 until his death.[1]

Piaget's work commanded massive international attention throughout the last century – "the most criticized author in the history of psychology, and I came through alive" was how he put it (in Smith, 1996, p. vi). Beilin (1992) was nearer the mark in comparing Piaget's contribution to that of Shakespeare to English. Other developmentalists are not sure about their legacy as "heirs to the house that Jean built" (Scholnick, 1999). A different analogy is to view Piaget's project as the construction of a Grand Tower (Smith, 1993, p. vi). This project was not completed due to disputes in a tower of Babel and, instead, we have many fine small buildings – but no Grand Tower. What, then, should we do in the twenty-first century with the master plan, Piaget's[2] (1918, p. 148) "research program"? The open question is the extent to which its principles can be preserved in the redesign of the project. After all, its origin is plain to see as the problem of knowledge in philosophy. Piaget's brilliant advance was equally plain in his first book. Kant had asked a normative question, "How is knowledge possible?" Piaget converted this into an empirical counterpart: "How does knowledge develop?" This is a massive problem-shift. It secures a bridgehead between epistemology and psychology. And it generalizes nicely to other norms and facts. In this context, "Piaget's theory" is the best available theory.[3] At any rate, that's my view, and what follows is its rationale.

Nature, Nurture, or Tertium Quid?

A classic problem in psychology concerns the contributions of nature and nurture to intellectual development. Vygotsky (1994, p. 57) characterized these as the two "lines of development," heredity and culture, whose interaction merited a better characterization (see also Rowe & Wertsch, ch. 24 this volume). But two is two, two lines with a subtle interaction still to be clarified (Moll, 1994). Piaget (1918) never accepted this view. His stance required a further factor which acts between the "two lines." This is Piaget's (1923) *tertium quid* or third alternative.

One argument is biological. "Amoeba, sponges, fish, and mammals transmit all their characteristics (and this is) a truly hereditary transmission; but they also transmit quite equally the most general properties of life in virtue of organization, and that is not transmission in the same sense. [This is because] at every step of hereditary transmission, a *living* organization is present as the necessary condition of particular transmissions since it determines the *activities* arising in that transmission" (Piaget, 1971, p. 323*).[4] This argument is based on a distinction between particular properties of an organism and general properties of organization. Particular properties of an organism (e.g., eye color) are due to hereditary transmission. General properties of organization (e.g., classification abilities) are due to something else as well. Firstly, classification is a property of an organism's activities, not an organism. Classifying a pack of fifty-two playing-cards may be dependent on visual search and motor coordination, but it is an agent – not the eye or hand – who does this. Secondly, classification is due to an organization which can be manifest in different ways (e.g., cards in two colors or four suits). This is not a biological difference. Thirdly, organizing principles behind any classification may themselves change, and change for the better, even resulting in a true classification. The equality (e.g., cards in two colors = cards in four suits) is a true equality. But truth is not a biological property. The advance from a (correct) classification to true knowledge is a major advance, which goes beyond biology. So the insufficiency of heredity is one reason for Piaget's *tertium quid* (cf. Goodwin, 1982; Messerly, 1996).

Piaget's social argument is a thought experiment, also discussed by Vygotsky. Imagine a society of exact contemporaries whose members are the same age (for example, children aged 7 years). This society has neither a traditional culture nor generational legacies from the past, still less older members. What would intellectual development be like in such a society? Vygotsky (1994, p. 351) ruled out intellectual progress, because of the absence of cultural tools and more advanced members to guide social participation. Piaget (1995a, p. 57) agreed that children would be deprived of "the essential instrument of transmission." In normal development, later generations gain benefits in that "ideas which have been painfully 'invented' by the greatest geniuses become, not merely accessible, but even easy and obvious, to schoolchildren" (p. 37). Even so, Piaget did not rule out development altogether. Although such a society would be disadvantageous, it would have compensations. One is the elimination of adult constraints (p. 149). Social rules are typ-ically interpreted as directives which lay down "this is how we do it, so this is how it ought to be done." This is "normative pressure" (von Wright, 1983, p. 55). Such pressure would be reduced for these children, who would still have the task of devising their own social rules and of creating better ones. Crucially, this society would still pose an equivalent version of the same (normative) problem for children. That problem is the reconciliation of *son moi et al loi*, the self and normative law (1995a, p. 241). This problem is general. Rules and practices in all domains and contexts have normative properties whose under-standing is central to intellectual development (see Nucci, ch. 14 this volume).

The upshot is that, in Piaget's model, factors in nature and nurture make a necessary, but insufficient contribution to intellectual development. This conclusion has indepen-dent support (Richardson, 1998; Wachs, 2000). Second, there is a third factor which is activated interdependently with the other two factors.[5] This is equilibration. This is the central construct (1918, p. 46; 1923, p. 57; 1950b, p. 36; 1970, p. 120; 1971, p. 355; 1985, p. 3; 1995a, p. 138).

Developmental Sequences

Three developmental levels

In Piaget's (1970) model, knowledge arises through a subject's (agent's) actions on objects, i.e. an *S–O* relation. The basic point running through the several formulations in box 23.1 is the construction of objects. Three levels in the sequence correspond to infancy, childhood, and adolescence.[6] One level occurs during infancy as practical intelligence. Its completion is the construction of actual objects, i.e., objects in the actual world. A second is representational thought which occurs during childhood as the construction of abstract objects applied to contexts in the actual world. This level subdivides as preparation (preoperational) and completion (concrete operations, i.e., operations on actual objects). The third is formal understanding, occurring during adolescence as the construction of abstract objects whose contextualization is not restricted to the actual world which is merely one part of reality. This level too has a comparable subdivision of early and mature forms of formal operations.

Box 23.1   Criteria of developmental periods or stages

• *Criteria of developmental stages or periods*

1   A distinct chronology in the sense of a constant order of succession. The average age for the appearance of a stage may vary greatly from one physical or social environment to another.

2   The equivalent of an integration in the transition from a lower stage to a higher one.

Continued.

---

3   In any stage, it should be possible to distinguish an aspect of achievement with respect to the stages going before and also an aspect of preparation with respect to the stages coming after. Naturally it is possible for both achievement and preparation to be promoted or hampered by favorable or unfavorable external situations.

4   All the preparations leading to a stage and all the achievements characterizing this stage (are due) to the existence of a general (or total) structure.

5   (Successive stages form) a series of equilibrium levels, the fields of which would be always more and more extensive and the mobility always greater, but whose increasing stability would depend precisely on the degree of integration and of structuration.

Source: Piaget (1960b, pp. 13–14).

- *Three periods of mental development*
   Practical intelligence: indicative ages: preparation 0–7 to 9 months; achievement 9–18 months
   Representational thought: indicative ages: preparation 1.5–2 years to 7–8 years; achievement 8–11 years
   Formal understanding: indicative ages: preparation 11–13 years; achievement 15–20 years

Source: Piaget (1970, p. 110, 1972b).

- *Three periods of social development*
   "In individual mental development, which is a progressive equilibration and therefore does not involve the essential duality between diachronic and synchronic factors, the transition from causality to implication involves three basic steps having distinct proportions of these two forms of relationship: rhythms, regulations and groupings."

   Social rules, values, and signs are meaningfully interpreted (assimilated) as
   rhythms: social activities and routines
   regulations: social interaction and practices
   groupings: social structures.

Source: Piaget (1995a, pp. 45, 56).

- *Three periods in the development of modal knowledge of necessity and possibility*
   "The first is one of nondifferentiation: reality includes many pseudonecessities, whereas possibility consists in simple, direct extensions of actual realities.

   The second period (coinciding with the formation of *groupings* and *concrete* operations) is one of differentiation of the three modalities: possibilities unfold into families of co-possibilities; necessity transcends the local coordinations, generating operational compositions determining the necessary forms; and reality consists in concrete contents.

   The third period, finally, is one of integration of the three modalities within a total system so that reality appears to the subject as a set of actualizations among others that are possible. But it is simultaneously subordinated to systems of necessary connections."

Source: Piaget (1987b, pp. 4–5)

Piaget used the terms *level, stage,* and *period* interchangeably. Equally variable was the number of levels – sometimes three (1970), sometimes five (1950c). This inconsistency is more apparent than real. An analogy – regarding a developmental level as a contour line on a map – may help. Contours chart the shape, slope, and height of a mountain. Their ordering is exact: fine-grained contours map on to large-scale contours; contours are not invalidated in virtue of their insensitivity to other properties of mountains (geology, landscape, climate). This analogy has a weakness. It breaks down in that mountains have a determinate height, in contrast to the development of knowledge which is open (non-determinable). It also has two specific strengths. One is that maps do not determine routes on mountains, but they do chart the levels of any route. In the same way, a model of complex learning (equilibration) does not determine developmental pathways. The other strength is that contours are properties of mountains, not mountaineers. Reinhold Messner has climbed all fourteen 8,000 m Himalayan peaks, but this feat does not preclude him from taking a stroll at sea level through the streets of Venice. In a similar way, developmental levels are levels of knowledge, not levels of knowers. Infant-level behavior in an adult is not a contradiction in Piaget's model.

Three developmental levels – but levels of what? There is an answer in epistemology. Epistemology is the theory of knowledge. A central problem is "What exactly is knowledge?" This problem is normative and non-empirical. And it is still under dispute. Even so, one condition of knowledge has never been challenged, in that knowledge entails the truth of what is known (Moser, 1995). No truth means no knowledge, and so no development of knowledge. Piaget realized that this normative problem had an empirical counterpart: "How does knowledge develop?" This amounts to a productive problem-shift, the conversion of a normative into an empirical problem. This problem is central to Piaget's (1950b) developmental epistemology, one of whose questions is how true knowledge develops during childhood (1923, p. 57; 1995a, p. 184). So the short answer is: three levels of knowing in the development of knowledge.

Formation of knowledge

In this model, knowing is a process whose outcome is the formation of knowledge. Two processes were identified by Piaget (1967, p. 6): access and constitution. Access is a causal process to be investigated through causal facts. This type of investigation is well known in psychology. Constitution is a normative process directed on coherence, closure, and necessity, normative because these are normative properties. The series of natural numbers is coherent: each number is unique and compatible with the others. It is closed: operations on numbers generate numbers. Numerical truths are all necessities: $7 + 5 = 12$ is, and has to be, true. In Piaget's model, the normative constitution of knowledge was investigated by reference to normative facts. This distinction is revisited in my fourth section below. Right now, it is introduced through examples in box 23.2. Notice that both causal and normative facts are empirical. Access and constitution are concurrent, leading to partial but progressive advance over time. Isaacs (1951) aptly summarized Piaget's model as a "psychology of normative facts."

Box 23.2   Causal facts and normative facts

- *Reasoning about relations*

    Causal facts. Children use language in their cognitive performance. Is their linguistic use of *bigger/smaller* a cause of cognitive performance in placing a new stick in a series of big-small sticks? Or is it the other way round? In his review of training studies of seriation, Bryant (2001) argued for the linguistic hypothesis as an interpretation of the evidence.

    Normative facts. Children's social knowledge of family relationships changes with age. What also changes is their understanding of the (normative) aspects of these relations. If Alan and George are brothers whose sister is Nicola, the relation *brother of* has three properties. (i) *irreflexive*: Alan can't be his own brother; (ii) *symmetrical*: if George is Alan's brother, Alan is George's brother; (iii) *transitive*: if Nicola is George's sister and George is Alan's brother, Nicola is Alan's sister. Alan knows the names of his brother and sister, implicitly accepting (i). But his qualifications over (ii) and (iii) verge on denials (Piaget, 1992, p. 97*):

Does George have a brother?	No
Are you George's brother?	A bit. not really
What is necessary to be someone's brother?	You have to love him
Does your sister have a brother?	Yes, George
And you, are you Nicola's brother?	A bit, not much

This amounts to an incomplete understanding of the (normative) properties of the relation *brother of*. Yet these properties, or their inverses, are true of all relations (Lemmon, 1966; Piaget, 1949).

- *Reasoning about classes*

    Causal facts. Classification is a foundational ability, present in infancy. Classification in terms of class logic is an advance during childhood. Is this development due to equilibration, manifest as the interiorization of action into operations? Or is it due to observational marking as a cue to a superordinate class? Chapman and McBride (1992) presented evidence in line with the cue-marking hypothesis.

    Normative facts. Geneva is a French-speaking, international city and canton (county) situated to the east of France, so Swiss children have ample experience of citizens and foreigners. Their normative understanding of the vicariant classification (own – other nation) was investigated thus (Piaget, 1995a, pp. 251, 264):

What is Switzerland?	It's a country
And Geneva?	It's a city
Where is Geneva?	In Switzerland
Are you Swiss?	Yes
And are you Genevan?	Oh no, I'm already Swiss . . .
What is your nationality?	I'm Swiss
Are you a foreigner in Swizerland?	No, I'm Swiss
And if you go to France?	I remain Swiss, the same as before
And a Frenchman who stays in France	It's the same as before, he remains a foreigner

Although the class *Genevan* is included in the class *Swiss*, this was denied by Claude, who believed instead that these classes are exclusive: you can't be both. Claude does understand class membership, shown in his answer to the first three questions, but had misconceptions about class inclusion. Russell (1964) pointed out that it is major fallacy to confuse the (normative) relations of membership and inclusion in class logic. Ivan realized that the distinction between *own-other* nation is exclusive, but this amounted to a "false absolute." this is to miss the normative requirement of class logic that exhaustive dichotomies of the universal class are equivalent (Boole, 1958; Piaget, 1949).

Access alone is not enough. First, actions have both factual and normative properties. "Action necessarily deforms the ideal in virtue of its mixture of fact and norm" (1918, p. 116). An action can be causally successful and normatively unsound.

Presented with a box-shaped figure whose five visible sides are white, one child argued that the back was also white *because the box is all white and so the back can't be another color.* This *response* is successful in that this child has given an answer to a question in this causal context. Yet there are three (normative) fallacies in this child's *reasoning.* (i) Is there a sixth side at all? (ii) If there is, is it white? (iii) If it is, does it have to be white? (Piaget, 1987a, p. 31).

Action is based on an assimilation which is the capacity to search for knowledge, but this "search for coherence" never guarantees success (1985, pp. 6, 13). Error (false belief) is always a possible outcome, not merely true knowledge. Indeed, a central developmental problem is the advance from causal fact to logical norm (1995a, p. 51). This leads to the second reason. Knowledge falls into systems with internal properties, such as consistency, closure, and necessity (1986, pp. 302–3). Thus knowledge requires organization. Otherwise questionable reasoning can be manifest. Mental organization may well change over time in any of three ways. And this can be a change resulting in a better organization.

From level 1 to level 3

There are reckoned to be two major advances. One is from success to understanding. Infant activity is confined to "success or practical adaptation, whereas the function of verbal or conceptual thought is to know and state truths" (1954, p. 360; 1952c, p. 240). An activity is successful if the agent's goals are met. But goals are intentional in virtue of the beliefs and desires, intentions and values, within the agent's "horizon of intentionality" (von Wright, 1983). This "horizon" is augmented, in Piaget's model, on the basis of the functioning of its own elements, resulting in "better" levels of organization within any "horizon." The second advance is from representational to formal understanding. This requires actions to be directed less on particular contexts and more on systems with infinite implications. This advance runs from the "causal to the logical" (1995a, p. 51). It is generative of acts of judgment. "To judge is . . . to assimilate; that is to say, to incorporate new content into a prior structure in an antecedently elaborated system of implications" (1952c, p. 410*). An act of judgment is the acknowledgment of the truth of what is known (Smith, 1999b, 1999c). Any act has causes for psychological investigation. Any judgment is based on reasons for epistemological investigation. To develop intellectually is to improve normative control over judgments made under causal conditions. In general, "all knowledge can be considered as being relative to a given previous state of lesser knowledge and also as being capable of constituting just such a previous state in relation to some more advanced knowledge" (1950b, p. 13). The proposal is that all knowledge has bi-directional relations with linkages to both origins and successors. Knowledge never emerges *ex nihilo*, from nothing (Inhelder & Piaget, 1964, p. 285). Nor does knowledge converge on a limit, *a priori ad quem* (1972b).

Criteria of Developmental Levels or Stages

Piaget (1960b) stated five stage criteria of his three developmental levels. These criteria deserve individual comment with the proviso that they are jointly – not severally – applicable (see box 23.1). A pseudo-criterion should also be noticed first.

A pseudo-criterion

Chronological age is *not* a criterion. Agreed: age references were included in Piaget's empirical reports. Variability in age was specifically covered by criterion 1. But ages were indicators, not criteria. Men who wear dresses have not on that account changed their sex, even though wearing a dress is an indicator of the female sex. Similarly, evidence that *preschoolers* can operate at one level, when Piaget's evidence was based on youngsters in *mid-childhood,* misses the point. A (normative) criterion and an (empirical) indicator are not the same thing (Smith, 1993, sect. 18). An indicator has relative utility: it is more or less useful in sample selection. A criterion has dichotomous validity: anything that satisfies criterion *C* is, and has to be, a *C*; anything that does not satisfy it is not, and could not be, a *C*.

Constancy in order of levels

One criterion is constancy in order of levels. This criterion is reliable (Müller et al., 1998, 1999; Shayer et al., 1988). Ordering can itself be interpreted as novel construction or "the creation of new objects" (Inhelder & Piaget, 1980, p. 21*). There are two main classes of objects. One comprises *actual objects,* familiar objects in the actual world – such as tables, clocks, and people – with their spatio-temporal and all manner of other properties. But these are not the only objects. Reality comprises *abstract objects* as well, such as number or society in their infinite complexity in virtue of subtle properties.

- *construction of actual objects.* Object permanence (conservation) is a prerequisite of further advance to objectivity. Without this experience would be "less even than a dream" (Kant, 1933). This is why Piaget demarcated tableaux and objects during infancy (Smith, 1998). This is no easy matter: young infants do not search for unobserved objects at all, or search selectively, making the A-not-B (stage IV) error (Piaget, 1952c, 1954; cf. Moore & Meltzoff, 1999).
- *construction of properties of actual objects.* Properties are abstract objects. A pack of cards is one pack and fifty-two cards, so these incompatible properties (1, 52) are not reducible to one actual object (Smith, 1999a). Number conservation is a paradigm case because the non-conservation of number is blind to this incompatibility (Piaget, 1952b; cf. Bryant, 1997).
- *construction of systems of properties.* These require conservation and novelty, conservation as a secure grasp on the past and novelty as a bridgehead to advance. Proportionality is a paradigm case whereby a new relation is imposed on available (conserved) relations (Inhelder & Piaget, 1958; cf. Bond, 1997). Analogical reasoning, which is non-quantitative, is a precursor during childhood (Piaget, 1986, 2001; cf. Goswami, 1992).

Integration of prior levels of knowing conserved

Integration amounts to convergence through advance, i.e., nothing is taken away even though something is added. Thus formal operations require concrete operations. This dependency should be respected in task design. It has been argued that this criterion has been disregarded in the selection task applied to formal operations (Adey & Shayer, 1994; Bond, 2001; Smith, 1993, p. 117).

Bi-directionality: current knowing from previous knowing to novel knowing

Preparation is the principal feature of preoperational thought whose successful completion is concrete operations, which in turn are preparatory to early formal operations. The implication is that task design should have a bi-directional focus both on what preceded and what could succeed any epistemic action. Inhelder's (2001) tasks are exemplary in this regard, covering both phases of both concrete and formal operations.

Formal model

Piaget (1953b) denied that all human thought can be formalized. But he also regarded logic as the formal science of truth (Piaget, 1949, p. 4; 1971, p. 35).[7] Piaget formalized his structures in three ways: by means of group theory (Piaget, 1949, 1950c), then through category theory (Piaget, 1992, 1977), and finally through entailment logic (Piaget & Garcia, 1991). There is an outstanding question here about operationalization. Developmental order (criterion 1) is well defined through these formalizations.

Developmental research has tended to focus on Piagetian tasks as the basis of its evaluations. How, then, is formalization linked to tasks? The answer is not clear. This means
that methodological gains in experimental design may have a theoretical cost, amount-
ing neither to a verification nor falsification of constructivism (Vonèche, 2001). And this
leads to criterion [5].

Equilibration

The final criterion is equilibration. So much is implied by Piaget's *tertium quid*. If there
are developmental levels, some mechanism of advance is required. Equilibration purports
to be such a mechanism. Commentators have repeatedly interpreted research evidence
as a compelling refutation of Piaget's stage theory (Case, 1999; Flavell, Miller, & Miller,
1993). In its own terms, this interpretation is compelling. The trouble is that "its terms"
have two massive limitations. One is a false negative: equilibration is typically denied
a place in these interpretations of the evidence. This means that a *tertium quid* commitment has been given up. The other is a false positive: alternative interpretations
are on offer as interactions between the "two lines." This results in the same non-
commitment.

   In short, three developmental levels defined by five criteria through two main advances
in the development of knowledge. The outstanding problem concerns equilibration as a
developmental mechanism.

Developmental Mechanisms

Equilibration as a developmental mechanism – well then, three questions arise:

- Is there a testable model of equilibration? Bryant (2001) has elegantly reckoned that
  there isn't a discernible way to test Piaget's model, and this view has long been standard (Flavell, 1963, p. 244).
- Is there a formal (theoretical) model of equilibration? This has been insightfully denied
  by Klahr (1999) in what is, once again, the standard view (Boden, 1979).
- Does the absence of a (testable, formal) model mean that equilibration is thereby a
  construct well past its "best by" date? The answer is the same – "No."

This last answer has several lines of independent support:

Equilibration: neither a testable nor a formal but an intelligible model

1   Piaget's construct has been persistently misrepresented in developmental psychology
    and elsewhere (Lourenço & Machado, 1996). Thus the demarcation between what
    is being rejected and what is being missed has been eroded.

2 Plato long ago stated a problem which is the construction of (atemporal) necessary knowledge through (temporal) equilibration, and it is this problem which is central to Piaget's research program, the implications of which have not been systematically worked through in developmental theory and research (Smith, 1999d).

3 A complementary problem arose in Inhelder's (2001) work as the construction of (temporal) procedures from atemporal structures of action. This is a productive problem-shift which continues to be underexploited (Vonèche, 2001).

4 Piaget's construct has a family resemblance to models of systemic organization in the life sciences, which in any case should not be understood on the basis of non-organismic models in the physical sciences (Chapman, 1992).

5 Piaget's construct has the potential to be assigned a causal interpretation in terms of self-organizing processes (Molenaar & Raiijmakers, 2000). The model matches the criteria of adequacy of equations which underpin explanatory theories in science.

6 A central problem in the life sciences is the problem of emergence. This problem has to be confronted by any adequate model of development. Key aspects of Piaget's construct are invoked in interactivist perspective applied to emergence (Bickhard, 2002).

7 All interactions are value-laden, which leads to the problem of normative exchange which is assigned a distinctive interpretation in Piaget's construct (Mays, 2000).

8 Piaget's construct straddles both causal and normative domains (Brown, 1996, 2001). This is a strong point both in itself and in virtue of the total absence of any alternative model which combines both.

9 Comparable problems occur in both individual and social interactions (Müller & Carpendale, 2000) and Piaget's construct has the potential to present a unitary account of both.

10 The link between developmental change and the nature of knowledge was central to Piaget's corpus of research and theory, and its systematic re-evaluation has yet to be done (Beilin & Fireman, 2000).

In short, despite two major deficiencies, Piaget's construct is stated to have a degree of intelligibility and fitness of purpose. What now follows are some principles which could serve in a better representation of this construct. Five principles from Piaget's (1918) model are shown in box 23.3. Five epistemological principles which fit Piaget's work are show in box 23.4. Both sets are now reviewed.

Five Principles in Piaget's Model

Five early principles are shown in box 23.3. Each is now reviewed through later work.

Action, organization, and identity

Assimilation is a property of action. This notion was specifically invoked with its complementary, initially regarded as imitation (1928), and later changed to accommodation (1952c). What remained the same was a functional role in the intelligent search for

---

Box 23.3   Five principles in Recherche

- *action, organization, and identity.* Life is nothing but assimilation, the source of all organization . . . the action of assimilation and that of undergoing the influence of context, or bring open to variation, or "imitating exterior factors" are two actions inversely related to each other. The better I assimilate, the more I remain self-identical. On the other hand, the more I vary, the less I am coherent, the less is my assimilating capacity and personality (p. 155).
- *action as the basis of knowledge.* Reason is a faculty born from action (p. 50).
- *actions as normative facts.* Action necessarily deforms the ideal in virtue of its mixture of fact and norm (*droit*) (p. 116).
- *normative facts as disequilibrium or equilibrium.* Fact is a form of equilibrium – or disequilibrium – and the ideal is another equilibrium, as real in a sense as the first, but often invoked rather than realized: the ideal is a limiting case, as the mathematicians say, or rather the full equilibrium onto which false or unstable equilibria of reality converge (p. 46).
- *processes of equilibration*
    (i)   All organization tends toward its own conservation (with two manifestations which are) equilibrium between an autonomous whole and its parts.
    (ii) Only holistic equilibrium is the outcome of the form of that organization, while partial equilibrium is a compromise between holistic equilibrium and the subsequent action of the ambient context.
    (iii) All possible equilibria are nothing but combinations of these two types.
    (iv) All equilibria in living beings tend toward holistic equilibrium (pp. 156–7).

Source: Piaget (1918).

---

knowledge. This search is a search for coherence in the conferral of meaning on the objects encountered in action (1985, pp. 13, 16). This search results in degrees of organization, present to some degree at all levels of development (2001). What changes is the extent of this logic. Any level of organization amounts to "one" construction (assimilation) of the world. Any construction has its own identity: it is what it is at the level of that person's point of view. But it is inherently vulnerable to qualification or even disqualification in virtue of the complementary, and concurrent, process which is accommodation to new content. The problem is how to fit "new" content to "one" available structure. As Piaget and Voyat (1968, p. 2) presciently remarked, "out of all the logical principles, the principle of identity is perhaps the one which remains the least self-identical throughout its development." Actions are consecutive throughout a person's life, such that each new action can preserve the organization of a predecessor or can replace it, wholly or in part.

Action as the basis of knowledge

This principle places the origin of knowledge in action on objects (1970, p. 104; 1971, pp. 6–8; 1995a, pp. 70–1). There are two points here. First, practical intelligence is based on infants' activities, which are the basis of all further development. Actions are actions on objects, and two main classes of (actual, abstract) objects were identified under Piaget's stage criterion. Second, representational and formal thought are based on actions or operations on abstract objects contextualized on actual objects initially and then contextualized independently at higher levels. These operations are what a person knows how to do in relation to these objects. In this model, what matters is not what (knowledge, concepts) anyone has but rather what is done with them. This point is captured in Piaget's claims about the regulation of action: "we speak of regulation when the results of an action, *A*, modify the repetition of that action *A*. Regulation can therefore take the form either of correcting *A* (negative feedback) or of reinforcing it (positive feedback)" (1985, p. 16). The requirement for the presence of at least two actions has consequences for the extent of the "gap" between them. This "gap" was officially recognized by Piaget (1941, pp. 268–70) as horizontal (within-level) décalage which occurs in four forms: identity, vicariance, correspondence, analogy. Vertical (between-level) décalage occurs through the three levels in box 23.1.

Piaget's position fits Goethe's famous dictum *Im Anfang war die Tat.*[8] This dictum rules out a basis of knowledge in language. Piaget's position can be clarified through a parallel with Frege, both of whom had the same view of logic as the formal science of truth (Smith, 1999b). As the architect of modern logic, Frege (1972, p. 106) aimed "to break the power of the word over the human mind." Piaget was likely to have learned about Frege's work while still at school, and had a similarly cautious view about language (Smith, 1999a). But Frege had a realist view of the abstract objects of logic in contrast to Piaget's constructivism, which located logic in the general coordination of actions. "Each new action exactly by realizing one of the possibilities generated by previous actions itself opens up a whole web of not previously conceivable possibilities. It is there, in the relation of causal reality with the possibilities opened by it where these possibilities are tied together by a link of virtuality which is ever nearer to logical implication, that is to be found the solution to the central problem of atemporal norms and actual development" (1950b, p. 34). In this model, actions have causal and normative properties and each new action has the capacity to link back to the structure of previous actions or to generate new possibilities for better levels of organization in the structuration of the world.

Action as normative fact

Any action combines causal and normative properties in that although "2 does not 'make' 4, its meaning 'implies' that $2 + 2 = 4$" (1971, p. 49). A model of causal facts could not explain this distinction. Causality (making something happen) is not entailment (implication). An abstract number such as 2 could not be part of a causal interaction on actual objects. An arithmetical truth could not have its basis in the causality of human action, which is just as capable of leading to error as to truth. It is for these reasons that normative facts are in the reckoning. Normative facts are:

> facts in experience permitting the observation that subject such-and-such considers him- or herself to be obligated by a norm, irrespective of its validity from the observer's point of view (1950b, p. 30)

> imperative rules whose origin is in social interactions of all kinds, and which act causally, in their turn, in the context of individual interactions. (1995a, p. 69)

There are three claims here with a fourth to be added. One is that normative facts are modal with an obligatory or necessary character. Second, normative facts are inter-subjective by virtue of their dual instantiation in both social and individual contexts. Third, development occurs as the reciprocal interplay between access to and the consti-tution of knowledge, between empirical opening and normative closure.[9] Fourth, nor-mative facts themselves evolve during ontogenesis as too in the history of science (1995a, p. 166).

A model of normative facts requires a model of causal facts since the knowledge gained by humans is in fact always mediated by actions, which always have a causal component. But this is not enough, necessary but not sufficient. Knowledge has a normative compo-nent bound by relations of meaning and entailment. This difference is fundamental in developmental epistemology.

> A norm is an obligation, and no obligation can be derived from an observation. That is clear. Even so, whilst consciousness embodies . . . or applies norms and therefore is not speaking in the language of facts but rather of *normative truth*, the developmentalist who is confined to facts of experience open to control for each observes, without taking sides for or against, *that norm's influence on the consciousness which instantiates it*. From this point of view, any norm is also a fact. (1950b, pp. 29–30; my emphasis)

A fact (what is the case) never entails a norm or value (what ought to or should be the case). This is "Hume's rule" (von Wright, 1983). This distinction was accepted by Piaget, whose study of normative facts does not breach "Hume's rule" just because normative facts are facts (1995a, p. 124). Such facts have a constitutive property in that a norm is internal to a normative fact (e.g., a 1-meter ruler made of wood). Third, it is an open question whether an agent recognizes the norm which is implicit in any action. This means that the investigation of normative facts centers on how a specific norm is in fact used by a specific knower. Is it ignored altogether (Freudian denial)? Is it converted into a (Vygotskian) pseudo-concept? Is it a fully recognized (Piagetian) operation? There are many levels here, as attested by these three sages.

This distinction runs into two objections. The first objection is that the causal–normative distinction is irrelevant to psychology. In psychology, Piaget's model gets half-marks since it deals with facts – but sticks to causal facts and leaves the norms out. The counter-objection is that this misses the point. First, the disjunction "causes or norms" does *not* turn on whether causes are empirical, and norms not so. Causal *facts* and normative *facts* are both empirical. Second, the explanation of causal facts is sufficient in psychology directed on the study of *people* in causal settings. But psychology alone is not enough with regard to the development of *knowledge*. Causal facts are insufficient here because knowledge has normative properties. If these properties are left out, there is no way to secure fundamental distinctions. Here are two examples in which (normative) distinctions are lost in causal studies exclusively directed on "correct responses."

- *epistemic fallacy: belief does not entail knowledge.* Although falsehoods can be believed, only truths can be known (Sosa, 1995). It follows that mere belief never amounts to knowledge: the belief might be false. Nor is true belief the same as knowledge, otherwise the distinction between belief and knowledge would collapse. How is this fallacy avoided in a causal study directed on "correct responses" which may amount to true belief without knowledge?
- *modal fallacy: truth does not entail necessity.* True knowledge and necessary knowledge are not the same thing (von Wright, 1983). Any (empirical) truth could have been otherwise; yet any necessity could not be other than it is. It follows that true knowledge never amounts to necessary knowledge, unless some further normative condition is met. How is this fallacy avoided in a causal study directed on "correct responses" which may amount to true knowledge without necessity?

The second objection concerns the relative priority of causal and normative facts. In Piaget's empirical studies, causal facts are introduced in task design through instantiation. But instantiation is not systematic investigation. In consequence, causal facts were assigned too low a status in relation to normative facts. There are two replies to this objection. One is to agree with it. Indeed, Piaget (1952b, p. 149) said as much himself, declaring a lack of interest in the experimental manipulation of causal facts. But this concession to the effectiveness of the empirical critique of Piaget's work is severely limited. An approach which is "exclusively psychological and insufficiently epistemological" (Piaget, 1963) won't do. Yet such has been the preoccupation in psychology (causal facts) without enough regard for developmental epistemology (normative facts). The implication is clear: a dual preoccupation is required. Otherwise, this second objection reduces to the first, already rejected, objection.

Normative facts as disequilibrium or equilibrium

Piaget (1980, p. xv) identified three varieties of disequilibrium: (a) instability if the same action is coupled with different results; (b) non-compensation if contrary actions are not self-canceling, and so generate an intermediary; (c) incomplete inference if action-coordination precludes necessity. These three varieties can be exemplified in number conservation (1952b, pp. 43–5). Asked to place just enough glasses to match six bottles in line on a table, Bon laid out 12 glasses from the nearby tray, i.e. the same action (laying a table) has different results ($6 = 12$). Gal succeeded in placing six glasses next to the six bottles, but then declared that there were more bottles, when the glasses were bunched together, and more glasses, when the bottles were bunched together, i.e., two lines are attributed both equal and unequal numerical properties ($6 < 6 = 6 > 6$). Mül counted correctly the six bottles and six glasses, but then denied this number-identity, i.e., the denial precludes the necessity of the numerical identity ($6 = 6 = 6$). Disequilibrium does not amount to contradiction within a train of thought, but occurs in the self-regulation of action (Piaget, 1980, p. xiv). This is a principal reason why access to a higher level of equlibrium is required to overcome disequilibrium at a lower level. It follows that metacogniton or hypercognition (Demetriou, 1998) is an integral feature of Piaget's construct.

Processes of equilibration

Due to the lack of a testable or formal model, the temptation to interpret equilibration by analogy is almost irresistible. Piaget invoked mathematical and physical analogies, and also noticed their limitations. Thus his distinction between *ideal equilibrium*, which is not in fact attained, and *real disequilibria*, which are all that is left to humans in causal settings, was sometimes interpreted by reference to the notion of a mathematical limit, i.e., truth (ideal equilibrium) is a limit toward which any actual disequilibrium converges. Although Piaget (1918, p. 46; cf. Chapman, 1988) did use a mathematical analogy, it simply postpones the epistemological problem. Convergence on a limit is lawful in mathematics, but is problematic in this model just because the analogy begs the question about whether and to what extent equilibration is lawful. Analogies based on the physical sciences break down, and were officially stated by Piaget (1985, p. 61) to be misleading. A physical explanation of the transformation in a glacier from ice to water through an equilibrial line is inconclusive when applied to the development of knowledge. Water is not a development of ice; yet *savoir* (knowing that) is reckoned to develop from *savoir-faire* (knowing how) in Piaget's model. Even so, analogies can clarify – though not clinch – a point. Thus my analogy served to clarify developmental levels as contour lines.

Operationalizations of Equilibration

There have been two operationalizations of equilibration. One was based on probabilistic processes (1968). This model is patently defective since implication is logically necessary, and so is not the same thing as stochastic likelihood. It follows that this model could not explain the advance from the causal to the logical. Piaget (1985) later offered a second account.[10] This account raises questions. First, is it consistent? The account is a retrospective account used by Piaget in the reanalysis of his own studies. Its main conclusion is that, however diverse the ends of action and thought, "the subject seeks to avoid incoherence and for that reason always tends toward certain forms of equilibrium. [This] is never achieved except in terms of provisional levels . . . [such that] in every area disequilibrium plays a functional role of first importance because it necessitates re-equilibrations" (1985, p. 139). This conclusion is congruent with the principles set out sixty years earlier by Piaget (1918). But its systematic evaluation is required. The advice given earlier by Beilin and Fireman (2000) is well taken, but beyond the scope of this chapter. Second, is the later account complete? Here are two reasons why it isn't. One is that a model of value exchange was also set out by Piaget (1995a). This account too requires interpretation and evaluation in the context of the 1975 account (Müller & Carpendale, 2000).

Another is that it has been complemented by another in Piaget and Garcia's (1989) intra-inter-trans triad as a distinct process working interdependently with equilibration. This is an effective contribution to the proliferation of interpretations! What is required is a comprehensive and critical analysis of these models, taken together. This is beyond the scope of this chapter, which now takes an epistemological detour.

Five epistemological principles: AEIOU mnemonic

The detour is Piaget's critique of Kant's epistemology. Kant (1933, B20) gave a famously affirmative answer to the question "How is knowledge possible?" Notice that this question is normative. Piaget sided with Kant by regarding human knowledge as objective. A comparable position is assumed in recent perspectives on constructivism (Chandler, 1997). But Piaget (1950b, p. 12) also criticized Kant in view of the incomplete answer given to Piaget's counterpart question "How does knowledge develop?" Notice that this question is empirical, and it points to psychology, which is the empirical science of the human mind. This counterpart question is central to Piaget's developmental epistemology. Piaget (1950b) realized that its answer required psychology to be augmented. Causal facts would be in the reckoning, but along with "other facts" for empirical investigation. These are normative facts. This amounts to a productive problem-shift. What Piaget wanted to know is how normative facts develop during children's development in line with his "research program" (1918, p. 148). Five normative principles (see box 23.4) are now reviewed, followed by an example.

Box 23.4   An epistemological quintet under an AEIOU mnemonic

Mary is asked the question $\boxed{2 + 2 = ?}$ to which her reply is $\boxed{2 + 2 = 4}$.

This is a correct response. But does it have – as well – any epistemological properties?

- *autonomy.* This equality holds in virtue of laws internal to the system of natural numbers in that 2 is a normative, not a causal, property of 4. This equality may have been compliantly accepted or accepted through reasoned assent (Piaget, 1971, p. 49).
- *equality (necessity).* This equality is a necessary, not empirical, truth. There are no exceptions, because it could not be otherwise (Piaget, 1986, p. 312). Some human knowledge is necessary knowledge.
- *intersubjectivity.* This equality is one and the same equality open to all, and so has the potential to be common ground between different thinkers (Piaget, 1995a, p. 94).
- *objectivity.* This is a true equality, and so is not false. This difference is inherent in knowledge in that only truths can be known (Piaget, 1971, p. 35).
- *universality.* This equality is always the case, and as such is one basis for mathematical generalizations such as the equivalence of addition and multiplication, $x + x = 2x$ (Piaget, 1968).

Source: Smith (1999b, 1999c).

Autonomy. Self-indulgent thinking and autonomy are not the same thing (1998, pp. 165, 213, 259). Rather, autonomy is the reconciliation which is required when "the ego's interests conflict with the norms of truth" (1998, p. 124), the self with normative rule (1995, p. 241). Each individual should be a free agent without free license. This is a commitment not to the individualism of the solitary knower, but to the *invidualization of knowledge* whereby "each individual is led to think and rethink the system of collective notions" (1995a, p. 76). Teaching is a case in point. Piaget (1995a, 1995b, 1998) accepted that teaching can be efficacious in new learning, an admission denied by Bryant (1995). Equally, teaching can amount to "normative pressure" (von Wright, 1983), which results in heteronomous thinking ("this is how we do it, so this is how you ought to do it"). At issue in Piaget's model is how the latter is converted into autonomous (spontaneous) thought.

Entailment/equality. Necessity is constituted through relations of entailment and equality (Marcus, 1993). They are central to necessary knowledge. Since necessity along with possibility are modal concepts, they are central to modal understanding. A paradigm example is the development of necessary knowledge. Evidently, Piaget stated this to be central to his work for half a century (Smith, 1999d).[11] This is not a surprise. Necessary knowledge continues to be central to epistemology. It is one thing to use an arithmetical rule correctly; it is something else again to recognize that an answer "had to be so, and could not be otherwise" (Smith, 1993, p. 63).

Intersubjectivity. The concept of intersubjectivity is variously used in reference to social interaction or to shared culture. Neither means the same as self-identical thought. Representational thinking is subjective – to each his or her own. Grasping the thought which is the Pythagorean theorem is intersubjective. This is because two thinkers can have in mind "the same thing." This common ground is the intersubjectivity of thought. How else could different acts of representation be about "the same thing" (Smith, 1999b, 1999c)? At issue in Piaget's model is the conversion of representational thinking into intersubjective thought. In Piaget's model, the use of logical structures secured intersubjective conversion in virtue of "a general logic, both collective and individual, which characterizes the form of equilibrium common to both social and individual actions" (1995a, p. 94).

Objectivity. Psychology is indifferent to the fundamental distinction between truth and falsity. This is because there can be a good psychological explanation of human error (perceptual illusion, "false" memory). It follows that not every property of thought can be explained by psychology (Smith, 1999b). Truth is one such property. It is for this reason that Piaget (1928, p. 239) insisted on a clear demarcation between logical and psychological properties. This led to the problem of the origin of "true knowledge" in the human mind (1995a, p. 184) through acts of judgment directed on the recognition of the truth of what is known (1952c, p. 240).

Universality. The term *universality* can be understood in two different ways in psychology, one about the transfer of knowledge, the other about the universalizability of knowledge. The former is a standard problem in psychology about individual, contextual, and cultural differences in knowledge-domains. Thus some children do not transfer their school knowledge of arithmetic in applied contexts, while other children do not transfer their street arithmetic to the classroom (Bryant, 1995). Successful transfer depends on multiple achievements. What Piaget (1918, p. 46) wanted to know was something else, namely how anyone can universalize their knowledge, given that its origin is always in particular domains, contexts, and cultures. How does the universalization of knowledge occur from "in this context, all the daisies are flowers" to "all daisies are flowers," from "in our culture, $6 = 6$" to "it is always the case that $6 = 6$" (2001, ch. 6)?

Case study: children's reasoning by mathematical induction

The AEIOU quintet can be illustrated through an empirical study of children's reasoning by mathematical induction. The study is reviewed in box 23.5.

An extract from John's reasoning is instructive. John (aged 7 years) had added an equal number of plastic counters to two containers, one containing one at the outset (*A*), and the other empty (*B*). The interview included repeated questioning about serial addition to *A* and *B*, including:

> Interviewer. How about if you put a great number in that one and a great number in that one? Would there be the same in each or more there or more there?
> John. That would be right up to the cover in the sky and that would be right up to God, so then they would still have to be more.

This is a superb example of analogical reasoning. After I confessed my ignorance, John explained his analogy. God is in heaven and the number in *B* is so big that it reaches God. But the number in *A* is bigger, so it would go up to the cover over heaven. This reasoning also has five epistemological properties:

- *autonomous*. John's reasoning was his own. It was a free mental act which was "spontaneous thought." This is the highest type of response in Piaget's (1929) categorization of responses in contrast to "provoked" responses in receptive understanding (1952b).

Box 23.5   Children's reasoning by mathematical induction

Reasoning by mathematical induction is a standard form of argument in mathematics and defined by Poincaré thus: if it is proved that a property is true of the number 1, and that it is true of $n + 1$ provided it is true of n, it is true of all whole numbers. This definition includes two criteria, one about a base property, and the other its generalization (recurrence) in the number series. Frege and Russell accepted this definition, but argued that this reasoning was entirely logical in contradistinction to Poincaré's view, who reckoned that such reasoning was partly logical and partly based on intuition.

In their study of children's reasoning by mathematical induction, Inhelder and Piaget (1963) sided with Poincaré. They drew two conclusions:

Continued.

- children can reason by mathematical induction
- their reasoning is modal: if the induction is true, it is necessarily so.

Their first conclusion was that children can successfully make a primitive form of this form of inference. This claim has gone largely unremarked. Their second conclusion was that children can understand the necessity of this inference. Necessary knowledge is modal knowledge which is reckoned to be under development in adolescence (Morris & Sloutsky, 1998; Moshman, 1998). Even so, the contrary view has also been stated that modal reasoning is under development during childhood (Piaget, 1986; Smith, 1999d).

Inhelder and Piaget's study was recently replicated. One hundred children aged 5–7 years in school years 1 and 2 took part in the study and were individually interviewed twice. In the first interview (equal addition to equals), the children could see that two containers *A* and *B* were empty. In the second interview (equal addition to unequals), the children could see that *A* contained one counter but that *B* was empty. The children then repeatedly made equal additions to each box in three different contexts (open to observation; not open to observation; hypothetical addition, including generalized inference). The children were also asked modal questions about the necessity of their inferences. In each case, they were also invited to make a response and then to give reasons for it. There were three main findings:

- *base criterion.* Children in both school years drew correct conclusions about the number in the containers. Across the three contexts in study I, 85 percent of the responses made by children in Year 1 were correct, which increased to 95 percent in the Year 2 children. The majority of these responses were justified.
- *generalization criterion.* The children in both school years made a generalized inference. They did so by detecting the ambiguity of *adding a great number.* Just over one-third of the Year 1 children made a correct response over the two studies, and this increased to two-fifths for the Year 2 children. The companion question about *adding any number* was correctly answered by almost three-fifths of the Year 1 children over the two studies, and by almost nine-tenths of the Year 2 children. The majority of these responses were justified.
- *modal criterion.* There was an asymmetry about the children's modal reasoning. About two-fifths of the responses made by the Year 1 children were correct, and this increased (5 percent) for the Year 2 children. Only a minority (10 percent) of these modally correct responses were combined with a modal reason. Yet twice as many (20 percent) of the modally incorrect responses were justified by modal reasons. These included pseudo-modal reasoning (*that won't be fair on that one*); modality of action (*because you can do what number you want to*); modality of thought (*because if you had them all on your desk and your mother shouted, and then you just stood up and knocked them all off, some could have landed in the bin*).

The first two findings amount to good evidence for Inhelder & Piaget's first conclusion. The third finding is partial evidence for their second conclusion. A possible mechanism of reasoning by mathematical induction is through iterative action which undergoes development during childhood.

Source: Smith (in press).

- *entailment.* John's conclusion concerned "what has to be." All mathematical truths are necessities, as too are all logical deductions (Smith, 1997a).
- *intersubjective.* John's reasoning was a valid argument. This amounts to *his version* of Euclid's axiom (*if equals are added to unequals, the wholes are unequal*). This axiom is not in the Mathematics National Curriculum at KS1 (DfEE, 2000).
- *objective.* John's answer was correct. The difference in correct responses between the children in school years 1 and 2 was significant ($\chi^2 = 28.657$, df. (1), $p < .000$).
- *universal.* Over the whole interview, John correctly answered two criterial questions relevant to mathematical induction. This amounted to the universalization of knowledge.

This example secures four points about Piaget's (1918) research program. One concerns its ontology, or the intrinsic properties of the phenomena to be investigated. This includes normative facts, manifest as the use made by particular individuals of general principles, such as the AEIOU epistemological quintet. A second concerns its methodology. The method used here was Piaget's critical method (Smith, 1993, p. 58). The use of normative principles has to be shown – by the user, not just the investigator in task design. A third concerns development. What requires systematic investigation is development in the use of these epistemological norms, and others like them. This huge undertaking has still to be carried through. The fourth concerns equilibration. A model which is exclusively causal or exclusively normative could not in principle account for the development of knowledge. Equilibration is a construct which combines both. Although this construct is currently neither testable nor formal, it has an intelligible function at work "between the two lines" of heredity and culture. The mechanism is *actual* reasoning with the potential to recast *past* reasoning in a *present* context for *future* reconstruction.

Implications

My argument has three implications, one about causal and normative facts, another about acts of judgment, and a third about empirical methods.

Causal facts and normative facts

One implication concerns causal facts and normative facts. Under this interpretation, a model of the development of knowledge requires a joint focus on both causal facts and normative facts. This does not rule out the exclusive study of causal facts in human development. But it does rule out the exclusive evaluation of a joint model through such a study. Knowledge has normative properties to which psychology with a focus on causal properties alone is officially blind. A valid psychology of "false" memory is spectacularly insufficient in an account of true knowledge. The normative facts in Piaget's model were epistemological. Equilibration as its central construct was envisaged to be both causal and normative. Crucially, a study with a joint focus would contribute to an empirical account.

There are three ways in which future study could move ahead. One is to revisit the (epistemological) norms used by Piaget with parity of focus on both causal and normative aspects. This route would avoid two deviations, the overvaluation of normative facts and the overvaluation of causal facts. Another is to augment the present stock with other epistemological norms. A notable case in point is a deontic logic of action (von Wright, 1983). A third is to generalize the axiological framework by reference to other values in all domains, and not merely scientific values (Brown, 1996, 2001).[12] The importance of this general problem continues to be acknowledged: "how is it possible that creatures like ourselves, supplied with the *contingent capacities* of a biological species whose very existence appears to be radically accidental, should have access to *universally valid methods of objective thought?*" (Nagel, 1997, p. 4; my emphasis).

Acts of judgment

A second implication concerns acts of judgment in which something is recognized as true, realized to be true, acknowledged to be true. Any such act has inclusive properties which are both causal and normative. An *act* (action, operation) is performed in causal settings and mediation through action is the basis of all knowledge gained by humans. A *judgment* has normative and meaningful implications which are central to the development of all knowledge. There is a difference between evidence about:

- an act displayed on a task designed to be compatible with a particular norm; and
- a judgment due to the use by an individual of a particular norm.

An individual may be one person, a group of collaborating individuals, or a social institution. There are all the intermediaries between a (correct) response in line with truth and a judgment in which some reason is given for the truth of any response. This point generalizes to other normative principles in the AEIOU quintet and elsewhere. The only way in which this distinction can be drawn is by reasoning with due attention to reasons which amount to good reason (Smith, 1993, sect. 13; 1997a, p. 233; 1999d, p. 25). Such reasoning would include some combination of conservation and novelty, the best of them used in the present for the development of future knowledge. The empirical question of how normative control due to any agent changes through actions over time is an open question.

Empirical methods

A third implication concerns empirical methods. An experimental method is used to generalize causal regularities from a sample to a population. A critical method is used to demonstrate that a (general) reasoning pattern is instantiated in a sample. These are distinct methods with distinct functions. Central to a critical method is an ontology (phenomena, problems) in which reasoning is on display as used by the reasoner, and not merely by the investigator. Evidence from a critical method could be useful on three fronts: (a) the respects in which children understand one and the same principle on a task standardized by an adult; (b) how well or badly reasons fit responses in human reasoning; and (c) the range of novel thinking (cf. John's superb analogy about the cover over heaven). A further feature of this method is its convergence with the standard analysis of knowledge in terms of true belief which is justified by the knower (Smith, 1999e).

In short, my argument is that the Grand Tower project can be continued through these three implications.

Notes

1. See also autobiography (Piaget, 1952a, 1972b); biography (Barrelet & Perret-Clermont, 1996; Smith, 1997b; Vidal, 1994); websites: <www.piaget.org> and <www.unige.ch/piaget>.
2. Unless otherwise indicated, all references are to Piaget's work.
3. Piaget (1970) disowned the attribution "Piaget's theory."
4. * indicates my amended translation.
5. Interdependently with, not independently of. Equilibration operates "between the two lines."
6. This common-sense distinction is captured in Piaget's "stage theory."
7. This is the standard view of logic (Frege, 1979, p. 128; von Wright, 1983, p. 130).
8. "In the beginning was the deed" (*Faust*), the contrary of which is "In the beginning was the word" (John 1: 1).
9. *Ouvertures et fermetures* (in Smith, 1993, p. 171).
10. The earlier translation (Piaget, 1978) is radically defective, and it has been retranslated (Piaget, 1985).
11. Examples covering fifty years are in Smith (1999d). For example: "the emergence of logical necessity constitutes the central problem in the psychogenesis of logical structures" (Piaget, 1967, p. 391).
12. The irony here is that the starting-point in *Recherche* was the clash between science and faith, how objectivity in science and truth arrived at through faith can be reconciled (1918, p. 21).

CHAPTER TWENTY-FOUR

Vygotsky's Model of Cognitive Development

Shawn M. Rowe and James V. Wertsch

Lev Semënovich Vygotsky was born in Byelorussia in 1896 and spent the most important period of his professional life working in research and educational institutes in
Moscow, where he died of tuberculosis in 1934. During his short life he participated in
intellectual debates and wrote about topics in philosophy, psychology, semiotics, peda-
gogy, and literary analysis. His total oeuvre amounts to something on the order of ten
volumes, and his ideas have spawned a massive new round of response during the late
Soviet and post-Soviet years, including intellectual biographies (e.g., van der Veer &
Valsiner, 1991; Vygodskaya & Lifanova, 1996).

It is possible to understand the contributions of Vygotsky to contemporary psychology in terms of three general themes that we see running throughout his writings. To one
degree or another these themes also characterize the writings of researchers influenced
by Vygotsky, researchers who have developed ideas about "cultural-historical," "sociogenetic," and "sociocultural" approaches to psychology, and they characterize much of
the writing on "activity theory" as well. These themes can be stated as follows:

- Cognition must be understood developmentally (i.e., genetically) in terms of its
  genesis and subsequent development at individual and cultural levels of analysis.
- Cognition is "mediated" by semiotic mechanisms, the most powerful of which is
  language.
- Certain cognitive processes (such as voluntary memory, problem-solving, self-
  regulation, etc.) have their origins in social activity and interaction.

These three themes cannot be easily disentangled, as descriptions of one necessarily
involve reference to the other two. The core idea of Vygotsky's work is that understanding

Partial support for the preparation of this chapter was provided by a grant to the second author
from the Spencer Foundation. The statements made and the views expressed are solely the responsibility of the authors.

individual human psychological phenomena requires understanding the social and historical origins and transformations of those phenomena. For Vygotsky, human behavior is unique in the combination of its historical and social characteristics. According to Shweder (1990b, p. 1), cultural psychology assumes that "cultural traditions and social practices regulate, express, transform, and permute the human psyche." Study of the "I" is, thus, abandoned in favor of study of the social, cultural, and historically situated ways by which "we" create "I's."

Instead of focusing on how individual psychological processes are made manifest in social expression, Vygotsky focused on how social expressions become manifest in individual psychological processes. Vygotsky's student A. R. Luria provides an elegant synopsis of the basic premises:

> In order to explain the highly complex forms of human consciousness one must go beyond the human organism. One must seek the origins of conscious activity and "categorical" behavior not in the recesses of the human brain or in the depths of the spirit, but in the external conditions of life. Above all this means that one must seek these origins in the external processes of social life, in the social and historical forms of human existence. (1982, p. 25)

Although such an approach does emphasize the social world, social interactions, and intermental activity, it does not amount to some form of social reductionism. Society is privileged as the source of the cultural heritage within which mind is formed. But the individual functioning human being is by no means removed as an actor in that development. From this point of view, the task of psychology is interpreted not as the modeling of the inner mechanisms of the mind, but as the study of the interrelationships of individuals and their social contexts and the appropriation and transformation of those interrelationships for cognitive functioning by individuals. Like G. H. Mead (1955), Vygotsky postulated that uniquely human psychological processes ("higher mental processes") must be studied as they originate and develop in social activity. The approach that has developed from Vygotsky's work can be characterized as the *developmental analysis* of how processes that originate in *social action* shaped by *semiotic mediation* (primarily language) are *transferred to the individual plane* and shape *higher mental processes*. In what follows, we will first outline Vygotsky's perspective on each of these themes individually. We will then take up some of the ways contemporary researchers have addressed the shortcomings of Vygotsky's work and conclude with some of the implications of Vygotsky's work for contemporary psychology.

Vygotsky's "Genetic Analysis"

Like Piaget, Vygotsky was concerned with the ways in which cognition developed over time. Specifically, Vygotsky argued against attempts to understand cognition in the child or adult that ignored either the *origins* or the *developmental transformations* of the forms and tools of cognition. The term "genetic" is often used in this sense instead of historical or developmental to stress the focus on the origins of children's cognition as well as its development over time. Vygotsky contrasted the genetic method he and his colleagues pioneered with what he called the "phenotypic" method that took a synchronic approach to psychological study – an approach that studies psychological phenomena in their current manifestations without regard to their history:

> Following Lewin, we can apply [the] distinction between phenotypic (descriptive) and geno-typic (explanatory) viewpoints to psychology. By a developmental study of a problem, I mean the disclosure of its genesis, its causal dynamic basis. By phenotypic I mean the analysis that begins directly with an object's current features and manifestations. (Vygotsky, 1978, p. 62)

Researchers applying a Vygotskian approach regard such phenotypic studies as valuable for their descriptive power, but insist on the explanatory power of a genetic (or histori-cal) approach.

Thus, Vygotsky insisted on a genetic, or developmental, approach for two reasons: first, he argued that human mental functioning is a product of developmental trans-formations and any attempt to understand this product in temporal isolation is likely to miss essential aspects of its organization. The fundamental transformations involved in development provide the key to understanding human action, especially language use and concept development. He gave particular importance to the interaction of two lines of development in this process: the "natural" and the "cultural," and in ontogenesis he viewed the qualitative transformation of mental functioning that results from this inter-action as key (Vygotsky, 1978, 1981b). From Vygotsky's point of view, natural develop-ment is largely driven by biological development and direct reactions to environmental stimuli, whereas cultural development is largely driven by the mastery of symbolic or arti-ficial stimuli. Memory is a useful area for exploring the difference. What Vygotsky called "natural memory," for example, "is characterized by the nonmediated impression of mate-rials, by the retention of actual experiences as the bases of mnemonic (memory) traces" (1978, p. 38). However, with the introduction of mnemonic devices such as the tying of knots, the notching of sticks, or even writing, cultural forms of memory are introduced. Cultural tools and strategies for remembering do not necessarily supplant natural forms. Rather the two lines of development coexist and continue to develop throughout the life-span of the individual. For Vygotsky the most important difference between the two lines of development is the role of signs in mediating the link between stimulus and response in cultural forms of cognition such as memory:

> Even such comparatively simple operations as tying a knot or marking a stick as a reminder change the psychological structure of the memory process. They extend the operation of memory beyond the biological dimensions of the human nervous system and permit it to incorporate artificial, or self-generated, stimuli, which we call *signs*. This merger, unique to human beings, signifies an entirely new form of behavior. The essential difference between it and the elementary functions is to be found in the structure of the stimulus-response rela-tions of each. The central characteristic of elementary functions is that they are totally and directly determined by stimulation from the environment. For higher functions, the central feature is self-generated stimulation, that is, the creation and use of artificial stimuli which become the immediate causes of behavior. (1978, p. 39)

There are two potentially problematic claims in the preceding quotation, namely that sign use is unique to human beings and the characterization of mediated cognitive activity as of a "higher" type than natural memory. But we introduce both of these claims here because they were important parts of Vygotsky's positioning of his work within the traditions of psychology in which he worked. Specifically, Vygotsky viewed any attempt to reduce all mental functions to amalgamations of lower-order, biologically driven stimulus-response patterns as being misguided. The development of intention, for instance, is not to be seen as growing out of an iterative process of stimulus-response mechanisms, but as a qualitatively different type of phenomenon grounded in social processes. These claims were part of his effort to avoid the traps of the associationist psychological approaches that sought to explain conscious, intentional action, and other aspects of human mental functioning, in reductionist terms.

The psychology of associationism sought to explain human psychology in terms of the direct associations in the brain between various stimuli and responses. What Vygotsky knew as associationism transformed into early forms of behaviorism associated with Watson, then later in the Soviet Union most closely with Pavlov and in the United States most closely with Skinner. Vygotsky argued, as noted above, that human cognition could often be described, but not explained, by reducing psychological functioning to simple stimulus-response mechanisms. Yet, he also argued against nativist or rationalist psychologies that sought the origins of human psychology in the human spirit or soul, outside the bounds of experimental science.

Avoiding what he interpreted as the twin dead ends of empiricist/associationistic approaches, on the one hand, and rationalist/nativist accounts on the other, Vygotsky developed what some (see Newman & Holzman, 1993 for instance) consider to be a Marxist psychology, which stresses the historical development of material phenomena. Although Vygotsky's commitment to a Marxist psychology may be subject to debate, the material and historically developing nature of human consciousness was central in his account:

> Once we acknowledge the historical character of verbal thought, we must consider it subject of all the premises of historical materialism, which are valid for any historical phenomenon in human society. It is only to be expected that on this level the development of behavior will be governed essentially by the general laws of the historical development of human society. (Vygotsky, 1986, p. 95)

The analysis of genetic domains

Like other major developmental theorists of his day (e.g., Werner, 1948), Vygotsky did not view genetic analysis as applying only to ontogenesis, and although much of his empirical study focused on children, he by no means assumed that genetic analysis could be equated with child psychology. Instead, it applies to several, qualitatively distinct "genetic domains" (Wertsch, 1985). For these reasons, his notion of developmental psychology was much broader than what is often assumed in contemporary writings. Specifically, his account of genetic analysis assumed that it can – and indeed must – be carried out in several domains as outlined in table 24.1.

In the analysis of phylogenesis, developmental studies concern an entire species as it evolves over time. Paleontological studies of the structure of the larynx in human

Table 24.1   The analysis of genetic domains

Analysis of phylogenesis	The study of the development of species via evolutionary processes.
Analysis of sociocultural history	The study of the historical development of culture via transformations in processes of mediation.
Analysis of ontogenesis	The study of the development of the individual via a combination of natural and cultural processes.
Analysis of microgenesis	The study of the development of a particular psychological act or across a learning session via natural and cultural processes.

ancestors, for instance, are part of a phylogenetic analysis of the natural line of development that paved the way for language use among humans. The analysis of sociocultural history focuses on the development of specific culturally determined patterns of interaction that constitute the cultural resources or what Wertsch (1998) calls "cultural tools" or "mediational means" passed on from one generation to the next becoming part of the cultural toolkit (Bruner, 1990). These include the development of specific interactive practices in various social settings: schools or workplaces, for instance. The analysis of ontogenesis focuses on the development of the individual over time and has been the topic of most studies in developmental psychology for the past several decades. It is important to note, however, that from a sociocultural point of view, ontogenesis is not simply the study of children developing into adults, but in addition the study of the developmental transformation of human mental functioning across the lifespan of individuals. Finally, microgenetic analysis focuses on one of two sorts of genetic transformations. One kind of microgenetic analysis studies the moment-by-moment (sometimes millisecond-by-millisecond) transformations involved in carrying out a particular act, and a second kind examines development as it occurs in a single problem-solving or learning session.

Cross-cultural versus cross-historical analysis

Vygotsky's approach to genetic analysis steadfastly maintains a focus on development, even where researchers would today often talk about differences that are not envisioned as stages in some kind of evolution. In the early 1930s Vygotsky and Luria carried out several classic comparative studies of abstract reasoning working with non-literate and newly literate adults in regions of Uzbekistan undergoing collectivization under soviet rule (see also Goswami, ch. 13 this volume). Their studies focused on comparing the ways in which non-literate women and men living in remote areas and men and women with some schooling and literacy training categorized abstract shapes and everyday objects (reported in Luria, 1979, see especially pp. 58–80). Vygotsky and Luria interpreted differences between Uzbek and Russian performance as reflecting different stages in a grand developmental hierarchy. For them, this was what might be termed a "cross-historical," rather than a cross-cultural, study since they interpreted differences in the groups' performance as reflecting a difference within human society at various stages in its evolution. The findings from these studies and the methods Luria (1979) used to generate them continue to provide inspiration for empirical research today. For example, work on the development of children's thinking through apprenticeship into culturally specific cognitive and social practices (Rogoff, 1981) and Scribner and Cole's work on the effects of schooling and literacy on the mathematical and logical reasoning of adults in communities in Africa and the United States (1981), as well as other work over the last three decades on cross-cultural comparisons of the psychological effects of literacy and schooling (Cazden, 1988; Scribner, 1977; Wertsch, Hagstrom, & Kikas, 1995), stems from the ideas and methods of Vygotsky and Luria.

Contemporary modes of *interpreting* such empirical findings, however, are quite different from what Vygotsky and Luria used. While accepting genetic analysis as a valuable technique in domains such as sociocultural history and ontogenesis, investigators today are likely to reject Vygotsky's assumption that cross-cultural differences can somehow be reduced to cross-historical differences. At least since the work of Franz Boas (1966) and Edward Sapir (1921), this assumption has been highly suspect in disciplines such as cultural anthropology in the USA and Europe. Specifically, any tendency to view cultural differences as differences in historical evolution is likely to lead to charges of Eurocentricism since it is virtually always the case that the perspective used to do the comparing turns out to be at the top of the developmental hierarchy. Even with this caveat, however, Vygotsky's ideas have had a powerful impact on cross-cultural comparisons of cognition and other forms of mental functioning (cf. Cole, 1996; Shweder, 1990b).

The Mediated Nature of Cognition

For Vygotsky and sociocultural approaches to cognition in general, the key to development is that social interactions are mediated by semiotic systems, most importantly language. His emphasis was on how forms of semiosis that shape human communication are appropriated by the child in the development of cognitive processes on the individual plane. Vygotsky made increasingly strong claims toward the end of his career (Minick, 1987) to the effect that an understanding of language and other such tools provides the foundation for the rest of his approach. Under the general heading of psychological tools he included "language; various systems for counting; mnemonic techniques; algebraic symbol systems; works of art; writing; schemes, diagrams, maps, and mechanical drawings; [and] all sorts of conventional signs" (1981a, p. 137). Researchers such as John-Steiner (1985) have explored the role of a variety of symbol systems including drawing, gesture, music, or diagrams in the development of cognition. Vygotsky himself paid special attention to "signs," however, which are used to organize one's own or others' behaviors, and the most important sign system in his account was human language.

Semiotic mediation and agency

Vygotsky assigned the notion of semiotic mediation such a fundamental role in his theoretical framework that it has a kind of "analytic primacy" (Wertsch, 1991) relative to the other themes that organize his writings. For example, his account of development is grounded in claims about psychological tools in that the appearance and use of these tools underlie the definition of the genetic domains outlined above and the transformations that are indicative of development. Vygotsky's emphasis on language as a psychological tool is evident in the writings of his followers as well. For example, Luria (1982) argued that just as mastery of a physical tool transforms human physical activity, mastery of the symbolic tool transforms human mental activity:

> Language, in the course of social history, became the decisive instrument which helped humans transcend the boundaries of sensory experience, to assign symbols, and to formulate certain generalizations or categories. Thus, if humans had not possessed the capacity for labor and had not had language, they would not have developed abstract, "categorical" thinking. (p. 27)

This assignment of analytic primacy is also evident in the notion of agency inherent in Vygotsky's theoretical approach. Instead of assuming that agency can be predicated of the isolated individual as is usually the case in psychology, Vygotsky's ideas suggest that we must assign agency to the "individual-operating-with-mediational-means" (Wertsch, 1991; Wertsch, Tulviste, & Hagstrom, 1993). That is, we must conceive of development as not simply something that happens in the head of the child, but a process of learning to operate with physical, symbolic, and cognitive tools such that children's cognitive processes undergo qualitative changes. The key to development is neither in the child alone, nor in the tools made available to the child as part of particular cultural practices, but in the interaction between child and tools in activity. Among other things, such an approach to agency emphasizes that mediational means always "afford" as well as "constrain" forms of human action in specific ways (Wertsch, 1998; Wertsch, del Río, & Alvarez, 1995), hence calling into question assumptions grounded in the "unencumbered image of the self" and "atomism" (Taylor, 1985) that have guided so much of contemporary research in psychology.

Mediational means changing activity

An essential aspect of Vygotsky's treatment of mediational means is that their incorporation into human action (including mental functioning) does not simply make this action easier or more efficient in some quantitative sense. Instead, their incorporation inevitably results in a qualitative transformation. In his view,

> by being included in the process of behavior, the psychological tool [sign] alters the entire flow and structure of mental functions. It does this by determining the structure of a new

instrumental act, just as a technical tool alters the process of a natural adaptation by determining the form of labor operations. (Vygotsky, 1981a, p. 137)

For example, in the "forbidden colors game" (Vygotsky, 1978), Vygotsky and his colleagues examined how the developing child learns to use mediational means as regulatory mechanisms for activities such as memory, and how the activity is subsequently changed by the use of such tools. Children and adults were asked a series of 14–18 questions, seven of which required the subjects to answer with a color. However, subjects were forbidden to use two color terms, "green" and "yellow" for instance, in their answers and were instructed that to win the game they must avoid forbidden color terms and must not repeat any other color term. Colored cards were provided to the subjects to use in any way they wished.

Young children tended not to use the colored cards at all in playing the game and often "lost," both because they used the forbidden color terms and because they used other color terms more than once in their answers. When prompted by the researcher to use the cards to help them win, young children often performed worse than they did without the cards. Conversely, older children used the cards as psychological tools in a variety of ways – to eliminate colors, to remind them of which color terms they had already used, or as a "pool" of potentially correct answers from which they could choose. Vygotsky argued that the task of memory in these differing cases was changed by the use of the colored cards from one of recall to one of thinking (Vygotsky, 1978, p. 51).

In a related sense, Vygotsky and his colleagues noted that while children might appear to use cultural tools in ways similar to adults, very often that use itself traveled along a developmental path toward adult-like usage. Their studies of concept development provide some of the clearest illustrations. In perhaps their most famous series of experiments Vygotsky and his colleagues used a block-sorting task designed to explore concept development. Concepts were operationalized in these studies as word meaning. A collection of blocks of different sizes, shapes, and colors was laid out on a table between the experimenter and the subject. The experimenter selected one block from the collection and turned it over to show the subject a nonsense word, such as "mur" written on the bottom.

> The subject was asked to set aside all of the figures on which he or she predicted the same word would be written. After each set of selections by the subject, the experimenter provided feedback by turning over a figure that had not been selected. This new figure either had the same word written on it as the one revealed at the beginning of the task and was different from it in some features and similar in others, or it was a figure with a different sign that was similar in some respects and different in others from the one turned over earlier. (Vygotsky, 1934b, p. 113)

The important aspect of the experiment is less the final collection of blocks the subject chooses but the order in which the blocks are chosen. They identified three distinct levels of operations subjects used to choose series of blocks. Young children chose blocks in what the researchers described as "unorganized heaps" where a selection criterion was not obvious to the observer. Older children used various types of "thinking in complexes" to choose objects. In these cases, objects were grouped according to some objective criterion in the object, but not some overriding category that might correspond to the meaning of the nonsense word presented at the beginning of the task. Thus, a child might move from one object to the other in making his or her choices guided by some aspect of the object just chosen. A tall yellow cylinder might be followed by a yellow circle that might be followed by a red circle that might be followed by a red cube followed by a blue cube. Only at later stages do children use what the researchers called "genuine concepts" that seek to organize blocks according to some overarching criterion corresponding to adult-like word meaning.

Limits to Vygotsky's approach to mediational means: constraints and power

Such studies by Vygotsky and his colleagues reveal that they tended to view language and other mediational means as always working in favor of more advanced human functioning, as inevitably leading to more sophisticated performance. Subsequent researchers have challenged Vygotsky's relatively uncritical stance toward mediational means in two ways: they have explored the ways in which mediational means constrain as well as facilitate action, and they have focused attention on the inequitable social value attached to mediational means. The sort of challenges we have in mind suggest that language and other mediational means may shape activity in negative, as well as positive ways, often because they emerge or are privileged for reasons other than facilitating the action in which they are eventually embedded.

The study of the forces that give rise to cultural tools has not usually been the main focus of analyses of mediated action, especially as it regards childhood development, but there are a few general points that can nevertheless be made. Perhaps the most interesting claim to explore in this connection is that many of the cultural tools employed in mediated action were not designed for the role they have come to play. An illustration of this can be found in the keyboards used to type in English. (For a detailed case study of this example, see Norman, 1988). Almost all users of such keyboards use the so-called QWERTY version, named after the fact that these letters are located at the upper left-hand portion of the array. Unless otherwise informed, most users of this keyboard assume that it was designed to facilitate their typing. As Wertsch (1991) has noted, however, just the opposite is the case from today's perspective. The QWERTY keyboard was designed in an era of mechanical typewriters when the biggest impediment to efficient typing was having two or more keys jam. As a result, the designers of the QWERTY keyboard specifically devised it to slow typists down.

With the appearance of electric typewriters and word processors, there is obviously no such need to slow typists down. Nevertheless, the vast majority of individuals who type in English continue to use the QWERTY keyboard, something that is made all the more striking by the fact that there is a readily available alternative keyboard design that is superior for most typists in terms of speed and accuracy. For example, the "Dvorak" keyboard is relatively easy to master, and most computer keyboards can easily be converted to its configuration.

The fact that the vast majority of individuals typing in English continue to use the QWERTY keyboard speaks to the power of historical, economic, and other forces in shaping the cultural tools we employ. It also speaks to the tendency to use whatever psychological tools are handed to us in an uncritical way. This suggests that many cultural tools may not be designed, or may not have evolved, to facilitate the forms of mediated action in which they are currently employed. The particular case of the QWERTY keyboard is sometimes viewed as an isolated illustration of how technological and economic forces can go wrong. As authors such as Norman (1993) have argued, however, institutional, cultural, and historical forces often result in technology that is far from ideally designed from the perspective of the user, and this raises the question of whether similar issues might not be involved for all sorts of mediational means.

The history of natural language, the premier psychological tool, presents an intriguing set of problems from this perspective. For the most part, language is not consciously planned or designed, a point that makes it somewhat different from the QWERTY keyboard example. However, many of the lessons of this illustration apply to language as well. For example, literacy and its impact on social and individual action raise several interesting questions. Literacy skills acquired in formal educational settings are associated with a specific set of cognitive skills (see Snowling, ch. 18 this volume), and the kind of language use required in formal literacy training is related to a willingness and ability to engage in tasks such as abstract reasoning.

However, it is generally accepted that literacy did not emerge as part of an effort to facilitate skills such as those required in syllogistic or other abstract reasoning tasks. Instead, literacy emerged in response to needs such as keeping records and conducting communication about commercial transactions (Olson, 1994). Furthermore, specific writing systems have often emerged when speakers of one language have borrowed the script used for another. Such facts serve to reinforce the claim that many cultural tools arise in response to forces that have little to do with the range of functions they are eventually required to serve.

In this context it is useful to reflect on the observation that changes in mediational means often reflect social, political, and cultural processes rather than a concern with cognitive functioning in some neutral sense. As an example of this, consider the decision of the National Geographic Society in 1988 to abandon its world map projection adopted in 1922 for its current Robinson Projection. Neither map is more accurate than the other in any absolute sense. Instead, the two representational tools were developed to serve different purposes, the result being that they have different psychological, social, and cultural affordances and constraints. The society's Van der Grinten projection was chosen in 1922 to avoid the "extreme exaggeration" of the sizes of continents in the northern hemisphere of the Mercator projection that had been in the standard for many years. While the Mercator map allows a navigator to plot the true compass direction between any two points on the globe accurately by drawing a straight line, the shapes and relative sizes of the continents and coastlines are greatly distorted, especially near the two poles. The map chosen in 1922 reduces this distortion, somewhat, but still represents Russia and Canada as more than twice as big as they are on the globe. The Robinson projection chosen in 1988 shrinks this distortion and gives an even "truer" picture of the relative sizes of Africa and South America with relation to Europe and North America. One of the main reasons for the National Geographic Society to change its projection was that it made it possible to be more graphic and dramatic in its representation of differences in such things as energy consumption and population between the world's relatively small but wealthy and large but poor nations.

As this example suggests, mediational means are often not simply neutral cognitive instruments. Instead, they introduce moral and political dimensions into mental functioning and its socialization. Indeed, the distribution of psychological tools is often part of larger sociocultural debates and social differentiation. An illustration of this can be found in debates in the USA surrounding the efficacy of Spanish or African American Vernacular as classroom instructional languages. These debates provide stark reminders that all mediational means are not equally valued in a society. Neither are they made equally available. This fact of course also applies to the distribution and use of more physical cultural tools such as computers in modern societies. The "digital divide" in the USA means that computers may be widespread in many well-funded public and private schools, and all but absent from working-class, city, or rural schools.

In this sense, mediational means themselves are implicated in the reproduction of social hierarchies. Many psychologists may consider these issues to be outside the boundaries of psychology proper and the study of childhood cognitive development in particular. But to the extent that sociocultural psychology is concerned with the intersection of the development of human mental functioning and the institutional, historical, and cultural contexts in which it occurs, it must take account of the social and political aspects of mediational means. As scholars such as Duncan (1996), Gee (1999), Linell (1998), and Scollon (1998) suggest, those working within a Vygotskian tradition must critically appraise the function of mediational means and access to the shared activities they both constitute and in which they are appropriated by individuals.

The implications for the study of childhood development of the idea that cultural tools both afford and constrain activity and that they are not neutral cognitive instruments but elements of larger discourses that structure society may not be immediately obvious. The most important point to make here is that mastery of certain cultural tools may be held up as a sign of development itself (as it is in schooling), but the cultural tools in question may not always be the best ones for the activity – in fact, they may be held up as best only because they are associated with a particularly powerful group in society – usually the ruling elite. The most engaging work to date in this area has been in studies of differences between school-based and home-based literacy practices. Cazden (1988) has examined the psychological effects of teachers' insistence on particular storytelling forms associated with white, middle-class US literacy practices on the school performance of African American students. Work such as Heath's (1983) points to the positive developmental effects of acknowledging the limitations of school-based literacy practices and drawing on children's home-based literacy practices. The point is that to hold traditional school-based literacy practices up as paragons of cultural tool use and as stages one must pass in "normal" development is to ignore their own history, purposes, and constraints.

Social Origins of Individual Mental Functioning

In seeking to avoid the pitfalls both of rationalist and empiricist approaches to human mental functioning, Vygotsky outlined an account that began with action, namely *mediated action* (Wertsch, 1991, 1998; Zinchenko, 1985). That is, action that is mediated by culturally provided sign systems that are mastered by the child as part of socially meaningful activity. Rogoff for instance argues that for Vygotsky, "children's cognitive development had to be understood as taking place through their interaction with other members of the society who are more conversant with the society's intellectual practices and tools (especially language) for mediating intellectual activity" (Rogoff, 1995, p. 141). Furthermore, the origins of this action are social, and in this connection, those working from a sociocultural approach seek the developmental precursors of individual mental functioning in social processes. Perhaps the most general statement of this third theme in Vygotsky's writings can be found in his "general genetic law of cultural development":

> Any function in children's development appears twice, or on two planes. First it appears on the social plane and then on the psychological plane. First it appears between people as an interpsychological category and then within the individual child as an intrapsychological category . . . but it goes without saying that internalization transforms the process itself and changes its structure and function. Social relations or relations among people genetically [that is, historically, in time] underlie all higher functions and their relationships. (1981b, p. 163)

In this view, human mental functioning originates in inter-individual activities and only gradually develops into intramental processes. The very definition of "mind" is expanded such that its origins can be traced to activities between people, and the structural and functional organization of mind on the intermental plane provides the foundation for intramental functioning.

Vygotsky's general genetic law of cultural development underlies several aspects of his account of human mental functioning. For example, his research on what Piaget had called egocentric speech convinced him that the origins of children's problem-solving and concept development lay not in interaction with the physical environment, but in their participation in social processes. By participating in social interaction, children appropriate certain linguistically mediated problem-solving, thinking, and regulatory techniques first for external, social activity, then for individual cognitive activity as well (Leont'ev, 1981). In Kozulin's words, "Development is therefore not an unfolding or maturation of pre-existing 'ideas'; on the contrary, it is the formation of such ideas – out of what originally was not an idea – in the course of socially meaningful activity" (1990, p. 114).

Egocentric speech

Vygotsky's most important and well-known work in this area is perhaps his re-examination of Piaget's account of the function of egocentric speech in childhood. Whereas Piaget had conceived of egocentric speech as having no function and disappearing as the child became able to take the point of view of others, Vygotsky argued that egocentric speech served important planning and regulatory functions in children's activity and that it derived from social speech (the intermental plane) and gradually transformed into inner speech – that is planning and regulation of activity on the intramental plane. Specifically, Vygotsky and his colleagues hypothesized that if the function of egocentric speech was planning, a child would engage in more egocentric speech when presented with a difficulty in the process of an activity. Research designed to measure children's egocentric speech use in relatively simple activities into which the researchers introduced difficulties was carried out in the 1920s. This research, in fact, demonstrated that "the coefficient of a child's egocentric speech, calculated only for those points of increased difficulty, rose quickly to almost twice the normal coefficient established by Piaget and the coefficient calculated for these same children in situations devoid of difficulty" (1934a, p. 38). These findings were corroborated by Kohlberg, Yaeger, and Hjertholm (1968).

Secondly, Vygotsky and his colleagues designed a series of experiments to test their hypothesis that egocentric speech represented a transitional stage in the development of what they called inner speech – that is, intramental linguistically mediated cognition. They reasoned that early egocentric speech should be related in function and form to social speech for others, while later egocentric speech should be related in function and form to inner speech for oneself. They thus posited the development of a functional difference between inner and external speech realized through the mechanism of egocentric speech (Wertsch, 1985, p. 117). In these studies, children whose base-line coefficient of egocentric speech had already been established were placed in situations where the functions and forms of social speech for others were made impossible. In the first, children were introduced into groups of other children who spoke a different language than the subject; in the second, children were included in groups of children they did not know, or working at a table alone; in the third, noise levels were sustained that precluded the children's conversation. In all three cases, egocentric speech disappeared in the absence of the possibility of social interaction. The social situation in effect provided a context where planning and self-regulation through speech developed. They argued that, "although the child's egocentric speech is already becoming distinguished in function and structure, it is not definitely separated from social speech, in whose depths it is all the while developing and maturing" (Vygotksy, 1934a, p. 291). Moreover, structural analyses of this egocentric speech indicated that instead of coming to approximate social speech for others (that is, becoming more intelligible from an adult perspective) as one would expect if egocentric speech simply reflected the egocentric perspective of the child, it in fact, became less intelligible with age, actually reflecting the structure of inner speech for oneself (Vygotsky, 1934a, p. 283). Later research by Goudena (1982, 1983; Goudena & Leenders, 1980) and Kohlberg, Yaeger, and Hjertholm (1968) supports, refines, and extends Vygotsky's earlier findings.

Social participation and the general genetic law of cultural development

An essential part of Vygotsky's formulation of the intermental and intramental planes is that he viewed them as being inherently related. Indeed the boundaries between social and individual functioning are quite permeable in his account, and his concern was with ongoing transformations between intermental and intramental processes rather than with any sharp distinctions that can be drawn. From this perspective an element of sociality characterizes even the most private and internal forms of mental functioning.

> [Higher mental functions'] composition, genetic structure, and means of action – in a word, their whole nature – is social. Even when we turn to [internal] mental processes, their nature remains quasi-social. In their own private sphere, human beings retain the functions of social interaction. (Vygotsky, 1981b, p. 164)

This statement does not assume that higher mental functioning in the individual is a direct and simple copy of socially organized processes; the point Vygotsky made in his formulation of the general genetic law of cultural development about transformations in internalization warns against any such view. Furthermore, it does not assume that nothing of interest goes on in the mind or brain of the individual when participating in intermental functioning. Instead, it simply posits a close connection, grounded in genetic transformations, between the specific strategies and processes of intermental and intramental functioning.

In thinking about the issue of social origins of individual mental functioning as outlined by Vygotsky in his general genetic law of cultural development, it becomes crucial to consider how the transition from intermental to intramental functioning is envisioned. As suggested by Vygotsky, development should not be understood as simply the internalizing for private uses of what were originally social forms of behavior. In fact, Cazden (1988) warns against a "mechanical conception of the process of internalization whereby overt social interaction (speaking and listening) becomes transformed into covert mental processes (thinking)" (p. 108). Instead, during learning activity, a transfer of competence – or the transfer of strategic responsibility (Wertsch, 1979, p. 12) – from expert to novice occurs. In the process, both the learner and the activity are transformed (Cole, 1985; Vygotsky, 1978). In order for this transfer and transformation to take place, both the learner (novice) and the teacher (expert) must be active partners in the dialogue surrounding an intersubjectively agreed upon task.

This focus on active participation on the part of child as well as caregiver or more expert peer has been a major theme in the writings of Rogoff (1990) on "guided participation." From this perspective it is as the essential to recognize and understand the contributions made by the learner as it is to recognize those made by the teacher. This amounts to a corrective to what some view as the sort of cultural transmission model inherent in Vygotsky's view, a model in which the learner is taken to have little active role. Instead of a passive recipient of input or a hypothesis-generating algorithm, children (or adult novices for that matter) are taken to be active participants in the co-construction of conversation, activity, and thus development. Strategic responsibility for the task is gradually transferred to them, and through activity, they transfer strategies for organizing and monitoring problem-solving from the intermental to the intramental plane. On the way, the practice itself undergoes qualitative changes. As Rogoff notes, however, the tendency is often to ignore the mutual direction of influence, focusing solely on the development of the child as a recipient of cultural transmission:

Without an understanding of such mutually constituting processes, a sociocultural approach is at times assimilated to other approaches that examine only part of the package. For example, it is incomplete to focus only on the relationship of individual development and social interaction without concern for the cultural activity in which personal and inter-personal actions take place. And it is incomplete to assume that development occurs in one plane and not in others (e.g., that children develop but that their partners or their cultural communities do not) or that influence can be ascribed in one direction or another or that relative contributions can be counted (e.g., parent to child, child to parent, culture to individual). (Rogoff, 1995, p. 141)

The zone of proximal development

The manifestation of the general genetic law of cultural development that has received the most attention in the West is the "zone of proximal development" (e.g., Rogoff & Wertsch, 1984). In many cases Vygotsky's comments about this zone are extracted from the more general context of his argument, and as a result it is difficult to remember that it is just one way in which he played out the implications of the general theme about the social origins of individual mental functioning. In fact, he developed the notion of the zone of proximal development fairly briefly on only a couple of occasions in his exten-sive writings. Specifically, he used it to argue against educators' use of IQ testing or academic performance to gauge development, an argument that seems to have new significance in the United States given the current political and social stress on academic testing.

The zone of proximal development, then, is a metaphorical description of the differ-ence between individual performance and performance that is guided by experts. The zone of proximal development is the distance between the performance level of an appren-tice operating independently on the intramental plane and the level of intermental func-tioning involving an apprentice and an expert. In Vygotsky's own words, "It is the distance between the actual developmental level as determined by independent problem-solving and the level of potential development as determined through problem-solving under adult guidance or in collaboration with more capable peers" (1978, p. 86).

The ZPD as it is usually called has provided the foundation for a great deal of research including the analysis of adult–child interaction and instruction (Rogoff & Wertsch, 1984; Wertsch, 1985), interaction and learning of children with disabilities (Brown & Ferrara, 1985), and the processes of second language acquisition (Adair-Hauk & Donato, 1994). But many writers have found it necessary to expand Vygotsky's original formula-tion. Rogoff's "guided participation" (1990) stresses the face-to-face and culturally medi-ated nature of activity described by the term ZPD. Cole (1985) focuses on the mutual influence of child on culture and culture on child as part of the activity described by the notion of ZPD. Wertsch (1979) examines the importance of children and caregivers reaching intersubjective agreement on definitions of situation as an important part of the transfer of competence that occurs as part of activity that is described by ZPD. And Valsiner (1998) explores both the limits and possibilities of the concept of the ZPD for understanding microgenetic development of activity but also ontogenesis. Despite (or perhaps because of) its metaphorical nature the ZPD remains the most commented upon aspect of Vygotsky's work, especially in introductory psychology and teacher preparation texts and that aspect of a sociocultural approach to cognition that is most often assimilated to other approaches that do not take a genetic or mediated view of cognition.

Distributed cognition

Vygotsky's discussion of intermental processes has also played a role in the recent formulation of ideas about "socially shared cognition" (Resnick, Levine, & Teasley, 1991), "distributed cognition" (Salomon, 1993; Cole & Engeström, 1993), "collective memory" (Middleton & Edwards, 1990), and other topics. In several of these cases the discussion does not posit a transition from the social to the individual plane that Vygotsky outlines in the general genetic law of cultural development. Instead of speaking of social *origins*, with the assumption that the primary role of intermental functioning is to give rise to intramental functioning, investigators of socially shared cognition are often concerned with human cognitive activity that *remains* on the intermental plane. This is now widely recognized in studies of workplace activities, and it has taken on new importance in educational settings as well, with the rise of practices such as "reciprocal teaching" (Palincsar & Brown, 1984) and "communities of learners" (Brown & Campione, 1990; Lave & Wegner, 1991), which focus on the processes by which novices become expert users of the cultural tools and mediational means of a particular social group, whether it be a family, a classroom, a workplace, or other cultural institution.

In analyzing these processes investigators such as Rogoff (1997) have begun to raise interesting questions about how to understand and assess intermental functioning in its own right, i.e., independently of how it may give rise to intramental functioning. This brings with it some interesting new assumptions about how the expression "cognitive development" is to be used. In contrast to the usual assumptions grounded in "methodological individualism" (Lukes, 1977; Wertsch, 1991), the point is that intermental functioning itself may be examined from the perspective of development. From this perspective, it is appropriate to examine the development of cognition *of a group* and not just of the individuals in it. Some dyads and larger groups such as institutions and even entire societies seem to function differently and perhaps at more advanced levels than others. Differences in how "institutions think" (Douglas, 1986) or "societies remember" (Connerton, 1989) have long been recognized by anthropologists, sociologists, and other scholars, but such expressions, let alone the conceptual framework behind them, are quite alien to most studies of cognitive development.

This raises a host of important questions requiring conceptual frameworks that will be quite different from those we currently employ. What does it mean for a group – as a group – to develop cognitively? How can we formulate the processes involved such that they can be studied in some kind of principled way? How would we go about assessing the relative levels of development of groups? And finally, how would we avoid the social, political, and ideological specter of Eurocentrism often at the base of such cross-cultural comparisons?

Conclusion

Our overview of Vygotsky's model of cognitive development has focused on three basic themes that run throughout his writings and the work of those following in what has been variously called a sociocultural, sociohistorical, sociogenetic, or cultural-historical psychology. The first of these is the supposition that genetic, or developmental, analysis must provide the foundation for understanding human mental functioning. For Vygotsky, genetic analysis was not simply one among many modes of inquiry; it was the most important and fundamental one. Furthermore, this vision of developmental analysis did not apply only to ontogenesis, but to several interrelated genetic domains.

A second theme that runs throughout Vygotsky's writings concerned the mediated nature of human mental functioning. Instead of viewing cognition as a process that occurs "within the skin" (Wertsch, 1998), his approach posits that human mental functioning is typically distributed between active agents, on the one hand, and cultural tools, on the other. This basic insight brings with it a range of conceptual implications that are still to be fully explored. Among other things, it leads us to introduce cultural and political questions into the study of cognition by asking where the cultural tools that shape cognition come from and whether they are distributed in equal or unequal ways in the contemporary world.

The third theme we discussed in Vygotsky's writings concerns the social origins of individual mental functioning. This constitutes a second sense in which Vygotsky viewed mind as extending beyond the skin and as being distributed. His claims about how higher mental processes appear first on the intermental, and then on the intramental planes of functioning underlay many other aspects of his thinking, including his claims about the zone of proximal development.

Although Vygotsky died almost seven decades ago, many of his ideas have come to have a powerful impact on discussions of cognitive development only over the past few decades in the West. This impact has grown dramatically as contemporary researchers continue to employ his theoretical claims to formulate new empirical studies. And there is every reason to expect this trend to continue as we focus on how cognitive development occurs in complex sociocultural settings.

CHAPTER TWENTY-FIVE

Information-Processing Models of Cognitive Development

Graeme S. Halford

Information-processing models have played a significant role in cognitive development research for the past 30 years, and activity is continuing to accelerate. These models are demanding, both on the theorist and the user, but they help us to understand the data of cognitive development, to gain new insights, and to frame new and useful questions. They also bring new concepts into the field from the related areas, including cognitive psychology, cognitive science, and neuroscience. These concepts are not simply "transplants" from adult to child research, but tend to provide new ways of analyzing and understanding the processes of cognitive development.

There have been many different kinds of information-processing theories of cognitive development, but the neo-Piagetian models have been a dominant early approach. These sought to explain the course of cognitive development, as observed by Piaget and his collaborators, in terms of the growth of information-processing abilities of some sort. We will consider models in this category first.

Neo-Piagetian Models

Several models have been developed in parallel in this field, often with considerable interaction between the theorists. Furthermore there has been considerable common ground, due to efforts by Case (1985a), Fischer (1980), Halford and Wilson (1980), McLaughlin (1963) and Pascual-Leone (1970), who all sought to redefine the major cognitive developmental stages observed by Piaget.

McLaughlin

The model of McLaughlin (1963), although not the first information-processing theory in the field, can probably be regarded as beginning the modern era of models in this category. McLaughlin proposed that Piagetian stage was determined by the number of concepts that could be considered simultaneously. Piaget's sensorimotor, preoperational, concrete operational, and formal operational stages required $2^0 = 1$, $2^1 = 2$, $2^2 = 4$ and $2^3 = 8$ concepts to be considered simultaneously. To illustrate, consider a set of objects with two attributes, shape (triangle, non-triangle) and color (red, non-red). This defines four possible categories: red triangle, red non-triangle, non-red triangle, and non-red non-triangle. Thus two binary valued attributes yield four categories, or $2^2 = 4$. Now consider a set of objects with three attributes, shape (triangle, non-triangle) and color (red, non-red) and size (large, non-large). Now there are eight possible categories of objects: large red triangle, large red non-triangle . . . non-large non-red non-triangle. Thus three binary valued attributes yield $2^3 = 8$ categories.

McLaughlin proposed that the number of categories that a child could consider simultaneously was determined by memory span. A child with a span of 2 could consider $2^1 = 2$ concepts, and this would put the child at the preoperational stage. A child with a span of 3 or 4 could consider, $2^2 = 4$ concepts, and would be in the concrete operational stage. A child with a span of 5 to 8 could consider $2^3 = 8$ concepts, and would be in the formal operational stage. McLaughlin pointed to a correspondence between the development of span and the progression through Piaget's stages of cognitive development.

However, McLaughlin did not apply the theory to analyze or predict performance on any specific cognitive tasks, and I am not aware of any experiments that specifically tested the model, or of any theories that specifically utilized this idea. A possible reason is that subsequent memory research made it more difficult to maintain the proposition that short-term memory span reflects the number of concepts considered simultaneously (Baddeley, 1990). Also it has not been entirely clear how to utilize McLaughlin's idea to analyze cognitive developmental tasks. For example, it would be hard to define the number of categories in the class inclusion, or transitive tasks, using his scheme. Nevertheless, McLaughlin's suggestion inspired a lot of thought by subsequent cognitive developmentalists, including myself. Interestingly, Feldman (2000) has shown that complexity of concept learning can be defined by the length of the shortest Boolean expression that is equivalent to the concept, an idea that is broadly consistent with McLaughlin's. Feldman's formulation applies to experimental concept learning (Shepard, Hovland, & Jenkins, 1961) whereas McLaughlin's theory applies to cognitive development, but there is enough common ground here to suggest that this approach to the analysis of complexity might not yet have run its full course.

Pascual-Leone

The model of Pascual-Leone (1970) was, however, empirically tested. He proposed that children's cognitive functioning was governed by central-computing space, or *M*-space, that corresponded to the number of separate schemes that they could coordinate. The value of M was $a + 1$ at age 3 and increased by 1 every two years, reaching a value of $a + 7$ at age 15, where a is a parameter that represents the processing space required for instructions and for the general task situation, and which is constant over age. To illustrate, Pascual-Leone proposed that a child for whom $M = a + 2$ would be in the last substage of Piaget's preoperational stage, and would on average be 5 to 6 years old.

Pascual-Leone developed the compound stimulus visual information (CSVI) task to assess M-space. The stimuli varied over eight dimensions, such as shape, color, size, whether the figure was closed or open, whether there was a circle in the center, and so on. Children were trained to produce a specific response for the positive attribute on each dimension (e.g. raise hand if the shape was square, clap hands if color was red, etc.). Testing consisted of presenting stimuli varying from five attributes (for 5-year-olds) to eight attributes (for 11-year-olds) and determining the number of responses given out of the total for the stimulus (e.g. given a stimulus with five positive attributes, a child might give four of the five responses they had been trained to give for that set of attributes). The number of active schemes was then estimated using the Bose–Einstein occupancy model. A good fit to the expected age norms was obtained. This method was criticized by Trabasso and Foellinger (1978) on the grounds that the estimated value of M-space was influenced by the number of responses required, and the increase with age was an artifact due to this factor (recall that the number of responses required increased with age in Pascual-Leone's method). However, see replies by Pascual-Leone (1978) and Pascual-Leone and Sparkman (1980).

Pascual-Leone then demonstrated that the M-space demands of some well-known cognitive developmental tasks predicted the ages at which they were attained. Tasks were analyzed according to the number of schemes that needed to be coordinated, and each scheme was assumed to require one unit of M-space. For example, Pascual-Leone and Smith (1969) analyzed class inclusion as requiring an M-space of 3, because it is a union of two classes, A and A' that are included in B (e.g., apples and bananas are included in fruit). It therefore requires coordination of a scheme for each of these classes, in addition to the schemes representing instructions and task situation that are assumed to be constant. The requirement to coordinate three schemes is consistent with attainment of class inclusion at approximately age 7, when M-space reaches three schemes.

Pascual-Leone's achievement can be seen as historic in that his theory was the first to give rise to a program of empirical research into information-processing capacity as an explanation for cognitive development. It was taken up by other researchers. For example, Case (1977) analyzed conservation (Piaget, 1950a) as requiring three schemes. Then Lawson (1976) and Case (1977) showed that the proportion of children showing conservation increased as M-space increased from 1 to 3, consistent with the analysis. Further tests were also developed to assess M-space, such as the digit-placement task (Case, 1972). Numbers are presented in ascending order, and when the final number is presented, children have to say where it belongs in the sequence (e.g., if 3, 8, 12 were presented followed by 6, children should say 6 belongs between 3 and 8). A stochastic model was used to predict error distributions for participants with a given M-space. Data for 6-, 8-, and 10-year-olds yielded a good fit to the values for M-space derived from Pascual-Leone's model.

Other new tests continued to be developed. Case and Kurland (1979) used the digit-placement test, the Cucui test, and the counting-span test. In the Cucui test children are shown a comical figure with colored body parts, and are asked to recall which parts were colored. In the counting-span task children count the number of colored dots on a succession of cards and are asked to recall how many were on each card. Counting span was the number of cards for which the correct number of dots was recalled. Pascual-Leone and Baillargeon (1994) describe a figural intersection test, in which a number of geometric shapes are superimposed, and the participant's task is to indicate the region where they intersect. The number of intersecting figures corresponds to the value of *M*-space required for the task. All of these tasks require a combination of memory storage, together with processing of the information. By contrast, memory-span tasks emphasize recall. For example, if a participant is presented with the digit string 483752 they are expected to recall all digits correctly, usually in the same order as they were presented. The *M*-space measures place more emphasis on processing the input. Thus the digit-placement task requires children to remember the digits presented and then to process relations between digits to determine that, for example, 6 fits between 3 and 8. The counting-span task requires children to first count the dots on a card as it is presented, and then to remember the number of dots on each card in the sequence.

One of the most difficult questions concerning measures such as *M*-space is whether they genuinely measure processing capacity, or whether the correlations they yield are due to some other kind of cognitive competence. The positive empirical findings must be judged against the positive manifold, which means that all cognitive tasks tend to correlate at a value of $r \cong .30$. The easy-to-hard paradigm (Hunt & Lansman, 1982) provides a methodology for determining whether a particular cognitive performance is capacity limited. The paradigm is very difficult to apply, but the possibility of using it to resolve the capacity issue in cognitive development was explored by Halford (1993). Foley and Berch (1997) applied the easy-to-hard paradigm to the digit-placement task, and found evidence that it was indeed capacity-limited. Thus there is positive evidence that at least one *M*-space task is a genuine measure of processing capacity.

The conception which Pascual-Leone introduced in 1970 has resulted in a repertoire of techniques for assessing children's processing capacity, and research related to the paradigm continues at the present time. A number of detailed comparisons have been made between Baddeley's (1990) working memory model and Pascual-Leone's *M*-space (Baddeley & Hitch, 2000; de Ribaupierre & Bailleux, 1994, 2000; Kemps, de Rammelaere, & Desmet, 2000). See also reply by Pascual-Leone (2000). This comparison brings two very different paradigms into direct contact and raises immensely complex issues, on which I have commented elsewhere (Halford, 1993), but it is impossible to summarize them here. The most confident prediction I can make is that the competition between working-memory paradigms is likely to yield a productive controversy.

Case

The most influential neo-Piagetian theory of cognitive development to date is almost certainly that of Case[1] (1978, 1985a, 1992a, 1992b; Case et al., 1996). Case (1985a) proposed that children's cognitive processes develop because they make better use of the available capacity. Specifically, Case proposed that total processing space (TPS) could be flexibly allocated to operating space (OS) or short-term storage space (STSS), i.e.

$$TPS = OS + STSS$$

Total processing space was held to be constant over age, after infancy. Demands for operating space declined with age because of increased processing efficiency, thereby making more of the TPS available as short-term storage space. The increase in short-term memory span with age was attributed to more efficient processing, which also became the main factor responsible for cognitive development, according to the model. Case's empirical methods are well illustrated by Case, Kurland, and Goldberg (1982), who also provided some of the most striking data supporting the model. They operationalized operating space by measures of processing speed. That is, those participants who processed faster were assumed to be more efficient, and to require less operating space. Consequently it was predicted that participants who processed faster would show superior recall, because they used less operating space, leaving more for short-term storage space. This was first tested for children between 3 and 6 years of age. STSS was assessed by measuring the children's short-term memory span for common, single-syllable words. OS was assessed by measuring children's speed of repetition of the same words. As expected, span was greater for 6-year-olds (4.49 words) than for 3-year-olds (2.95 words). Repetition speed varied in similar fashion over age, and when span was expressed as a function of speed an approximately linear function was obtained.

This finding was an application of the word-length effect discovered by Baddeley, Thomson, and Buchanan (1975) who showed that longer words, which took longer to rehearse, resulted in shorter spans. In effect, short-term memory span is approximately equivalent to the number of items we can rehearse in two seconds. This research led to the theory of the phonological loop (Baddeley, 1990) in which information is held in an acoustic form for up to two seconds, and is renewed by rehearsal. Case et al. (1982) showed that this theory could account for the growth of span with age. In terms of the assumptions of the theory, this would imply that the age-related increase in span might be due to increased operating efficiency, rather than increased overall capacity. However, the correlational data obtained from this experiment were reinforced by a subsequent experiment in which processing speed of adults was manipulated by having them rehearse nonsense words. This reduced their rehearsal rate to the same level as 6-year-olds. The striking finding was that the span of adults was also reduced to that of 6-year-olds, and the adult data fitted the same linear function between span and rehearsal rate obtained for children. Thus the growth of span could be explained by increased processing efficiency, measured by processing speed, which reduced the demand for OS, leaving more STSS available for the span task. In two further experiments Case et al. (1982) showed that the same relationships held for the counting-span task. The speed with which cards could be counted, a measuring of operating efficiency, was a good predictor of counting span, which was taken as a measure of *M*-space or processing capacity, as noted earlier in connection with the work of Pascual-Leone.

The finding that if adults' rehearsal rate was reduced to that of 6-year-olds by using unfamiliar materials, their short-term memory spans for the same materials were correspondingly reduced to those of 6-year-olds, appeared to offer a straightforward and elegant solution to the problem of whether processing capacity increased with age. As adults rehearsed faster than children because of greater familiarity with the materials, they had more of their capacity available for storage. This was essentially consistent with the claim by Chi (1978) that memory performance reflected familiarity or expertise rather than capacity. Chi measured recall of 10-year-olds and adults for digit strings and for chess positions. With digits, the usual finding that adults' recall was superior was obtained. However, the children in the sample had much greater knowledge of chess than the adults, and their recall of chess pieces on a board was superior to that of the adults (see also Schneider, ch. 11 this volume). This finding, like that of Case et al. (1982) was taken to indicate that memory capacity was not responsible for increases in span with age. Note, however, that, while both studies demonstrate an effect of variables other than capacity, processing speed in the Case et al. study, and domain knowledge in Chi's study, neither study actually assesses capacity. Chi's (1978) finding provides no direct evidence that capacity is constant over age, and it does not rule out an increase in capacity with age. It is logically consistent with the hypothesis that capacity increases, but in this case the effect of knowledge was sufficient to mask the increase. This is what more recent evidence indicates (Cowan, 2001; Halford, Andrews, & Bowden, 1998; Quartz & Sejnowski, 1997).

The link between development of rehearsal rate and memory span is consistent with Baddeley, Thomson, and Buchanan (1975), but the theory that processing space is a single resource that can be flexibly allocated to processing or storage is hard to reconcile with findings from working memory research. Baddeley and Hitch (1974), Klapp, Marshburn, and Lester (1983), and Halford, Maybery, O'Hare, and Grant (1994) found that a concurrent short-term memory load does not interfere with reasoning as would be expected according to Case's position. In the Halford, Maybery, et al. (1994) study, children were given a memory preload, comprised of a string of digits, then given a cognitive task to perform, then asked to recall the preload. Note that this procedure separates the processing and storage demands that are combined in many working memory measures, as noted earlier. That is, instead of producing a single measure reflecting combined effects of processing and storage, processing is measured by performance on the cognitive task, and memory storage is measured separately by recall of the digit preload. The difficulty of the cognitive task was manipulated independently of the concurrent memory storage task. For example, in one experiment the easy cognitive task was reading numbers while the difficult version was subtracting numbers. In another experiment easy and hard tasks were two different versions of the N-term series (transitive inference) problem. If there is a single capacity that can be flexibly allocated to storage and processing, you would expect that a more difficult cognitive task would reduce the number of digits that could be recalled, because the more difficult task would make bigger demands on OS, leaving less STSS for the digits. However very little evidence of this effect emerged. Furthermore, it would be expected that older participants, whose operating efficiency would be greater, would show smaller losses from short-term memory. However, while age was related to processing speed and to span, it was not related to rate of loss from short-term storage.

These findings are broadly consistent with more recent evidence that working memory has many components, and is not a single resource (Cowan, 2001; Schneider & Detweiler, 1987; Schneider, ch. 11 this volume).

Another aspect of Case's early work has withstood the test of time. This is the insight that cognitive development depends heavily on learning to use the available capacity more efficiently. Processing capacity is limited in both children and adults (Cowan, 2001; Halford, Andrews, et al., 1998; Luck & Vogel, 1997) and therefore cognitive processes require strategies that utilize the limited capacity effectively. The postulate that total processing capacity remains constant over age is no longer tenable, but it is true that increased efficiency in the way capacity is utilized accounts for a lot of what develops. The historic contribution from this phase of Case's work may be that he was the first to realize the importance of processing efficiency in cognitive development, and to build this principle into a systematic theory.

Case's postulate that TPS is constant did not imply that processing capacity was constant in all respects. Case (1992b) reviewed evidence that the frontal cortex continues to develop for at least two decades after birth, and EEG coherence between frontal and posterior lobes also increases. He then drew attention to correspondence between growth of EEG coherence and development of working memory over ages 4 to 10 years. He also proposed that progression through the four substages reflected patterns of increasing EEG coherence over the same age range. This work arguably marks the beginning of attempts to base systematic cognitive development theory on neuroscience data.

In his later work Case (1992a, 1992b; Case et al. 1996) developed the concept of central conceptual structures, defined as "an internal network of concepts and conceptual relations that plays a central role in permitting children to think about a wide range of situations at a new epistemic level, and to develop a new set of control structures for dealing with them" (Case, 1992a, p. 130). Development of central conceptual structures passes through the sequence of four major neo-Piagetian stages:

- The *sensorimotor* stage is concerned with coordination between actions and reactions, or between actions and effects, for example when pushing a lever on a piece of apparatus sets it vibrating, producing an interesting sight or sound.
- The *interrelational* stage is concerned with relations, such as one end of a beam moving down while the other moves up. At more advanced levels, coordination between relations occurs, so placing a heavier weight on one end of a beam and a lighter weight on the other is linked to one end of the beam going down while the other end goes up.
- The *dimensional* stage is concerned with dimensional units, such as numbers, weights, or distances. Thus the child has progressed from relations between objects or events to thinking about relations between dimensional units such as number of weights, or between distances.
- The *vectorial* (or abstract dimensional) stage, in which dimensional structures are coordinated to produce abstract systems of dimensions, for example when ratios of weights and distances are converted to new ratios having a common term.

Each major stage is divided into substages 1–3 that represent increasing structural complexity within the major stage. The same kind of progression occurs in each major stage, and we will illustrate it for the dimensional stage, using children's understanding of the balance beam. This is an apparatus with a horizontal beam on which weights can be placed on either side at varying distances from the fulcrum. The beam balances when the product of weight and distance on the left equals the product of weight and distance on the right. The example used here comes from Case (1992a, ch. 2). The substages are:

The *preliminary* substage that represents the transition from one major stage to another. The transition from the relational to the dimensional stage would occur at about 4 years of age. At this substage the child has a single goal:

1   to determine which side of the balance would go down. The strategy is to simply look at the balance beam to determine which side looks heavier.

The *unifocal* substage in which there is a hierarchy of two nested goals:

1   to predict which side of the beam will go down;
2   a subgoal to determine which side has the larger number of units (larger number of weights).

The *bifocal* substage in which there are three nested goals:

1   to predict which side of the beam will go down;
2   a subgoal to determine which side has the larger number of units;
3   a further subgoal to determine which side has weights at a greater distance.

The *elaborated coordination* substage in which:

1   the goal is to predict which side of the beam will go down;
2   a subgoal to determine whether weight or distance has the greater effect;
3   a further subgoal to determine the relative number of weights on each side;
4   a further subgoal to determine relative distance on each side.

Increased complexity means more nested goals within the hierarchy. This goal hierarchy is used to develop a control structure for dealing with the task.

The number of goals children can maintain, and hence the complexity of the problems they can solve, is determined by the size of STSS. As STSS increases from 1 to 4, due to both maturation and experience, the child progresses from the preliminary to the elaborated coordination substage. This progression occurs within each of the major stages. Thus working memory growth occurs recursively within each major stage, and is specific to the content of that stage. Notice that this also means that the short-term storage load is reset to 1 when the child progresses to the next major stage, so a task that imposed a load of 4 at the elaborated coordination substage of the relational stage would impose a load of 1 at substage 1 of the relational stage. The transition from one stage to another is achieved by coordinating two existing structures into a higher-order structure.

To summarize, Case's model is based on a hierarchy of goals or objectives which interact with the problem situation to produce a control structure or strategy. Complexity is based on the number of levels of embedding of the goal hierarchy, the most complex having four levels, and the least complex having one. Case proposed that the number of goals that children can maintain is determined by their short-term memory for the particular class of operations. The higher substages impose larger memory loads because they have more complex goal hierarchies. However, the metric is not general to all tasks, but is specific to performance within one of the major stages.

Case (1992a; Case et al., 1996) applied the theory to a wide range of domains, including scientific and mathematical knowledge, spatial and musical reasoning, understanding narrative and social roles, and motor development. Performances in each domain were classified into one of the four substages on the basis of both scores and verbal justifications. The majority of children were classified at the same substage in each content domain. Of those that were not, the majority differed by only one level. There was also positive transfer of training between domains. These findings were interpreted as showing that central conceptual structures have some degree of domain generality. Case et al. (1996) showed that training on one central conceptual structure produced across-domain transfer. Kindergarten children were trained on the central conceptual structure for representing number. This includes knowledge that numbers 1, 2 . . . 5 etc. are ordered, that each number is assigned to one and only one object, that each number is mapped to a set of appropriate size, and so on. Training improved number knowledge relative to control groups and there was transfer to other domains such as the balance beam, understanding a birthday party, time-telling, and distributive justice. The finding suggests that central conceptual structures apply to more than one domain. However, Case did not propose that they were universal, but adopted a position that was intermediate between logical rules of universal validity and modular or domain-specific processes. Central conceptual structures are regarded as applicable to a wide range of contents, but not to all.

Fischer

The theory of Fischer (1980; Fischer & Rose, 1996) was based on cognitive skill theory, where skill refers to control over sources of variation in a person's own behavior. There are four major stages or tiers, the reflex, sensorimotor, representational, and abstract. Within each tier there is a recurring cycle of four levels, the set, mapping (of sets), system (composition of mappings), and system of systems. As with Case's theory, the highest level of one tier is shared with the lowest level of the next, and represents a transition between tiers.

A set is a source of variation over which some cognitive process exercises control: "In an action, the person can control the relevant variations in the behaviors on things. An infant who can consistently grasp a rattle has a set for grasping that rattle" (Fischer, 1980, p. 481). In more conventional terms, a set is really a variable, but it implies correspondences between events or objects and actions: "The thing is always included with the behavior in the definition of a set" (Fischer, 1980, p. 481).

A set is the lowest level of structure within a tier. A single sensorimotor set would typically develop around 15 to 17 weeks of age. The next level is a mapping between sets.

A sensorimotor mapping would typically develop at 7 to 8 months. An example would be coordination of looking at an object in order to grasp it. The next level is a system, which is really a coordination of two mappings. An example would be when a child drops a piece of bread and watches it fall, then breaks off a crumb and watches it fall. There is a mapping between dropping and watching the piece of bread and another between dropping and watching the crumb. By varying one set, the dropping, and observing the result, seeing the bread fall, the child develops a concept of means–end links. The next level is a system of sensorimotor systems, and is a mapping between two systems from the previous level. However, it is also the first level of the representational tier, and is a single representational set.

Fischer (1980) illustrates the levels of the representational tier with a spring-and-cord gadget, in which a weight hangs from a cord that passes around a pulley to a coil spring that is attached to a vertical surface. As extra weight is added the spring stretches and the string moves around the pulley so that the horizontal part of the cord becomes shorter and the vertical part becomes longer, though the overall length of the cord is of course constant, which is a form of conservation of length (Piaget, 1950a). A 4- to 5-year-old child who had experience with the gadget could use size of the weight to control the length of the spring. This is mapping one set (variable) weight, onto the other, spring length. The child might also make mappings between horizontal to vertical length of cord, or between any two of the four sets: weight, vertical and horizontal cord length, and spring length. However, understanding is disjointed because each of these mappings exists independently, and there is no integration such as recognizing that the horizontal and vertical lengths of cord are segments of one cord of constant length. A representational system is formed by relating two representational mappings. An example would be a mapping between the horizontal and vertical lengths of cord with one weight, and another mapping between the horizontal and vertical lengths with a different weight. Relating these mappings shows how the horizontal length decreases as the vertical length increases, and vice versa, which in turn leads to recognition that changes in the lengths compensate each other, leading to the idea that the total length of the string is conserved. Thus the subtle and important concept of conservation emerges from the coordination of lower level structures. The next level is a system of representational systems, which is a single abstract set. Development then proceeds through the remaining three levels of the abstract tier, the abstract mapping, abstract system, and the system of abstract systems, which is identified with principles.

Complexity increases within a tier in a manner that bears a striking correspondence to McLaughlin's (1963) complexity scale. The four levels within a tier comprise a set, then a mapping between two sets, then a system which is a mapping between two mappings of sets and is equivalent to four sets, then a mapping between two systems, which comprises eight sets (see e.g., Fischer, 1980, figure 2, p. 490). This corresponds to McLaughlin's (1963) four levels defined as $2^0 = 1$, $2^1 = 2$, $2^2 = 4$ and $2^3 = 8$ concepts considered simultaneously. This again illustrates the underlying common ground between different information-processing theories of cognitive development.

Fischer also has an extensive consideration of transformation rules for creating the transition from one level to another. The first rule is intercoordination, which is a process of combining skills at one level to produce a skill at the next level. An example would be the two mappings between horizontal and vertical lengths of cord under different weights, as mentioned earlier. The mappings are intercoordinated to create a system, and recognition of the compensating changes between horizontal and vertical lengths emerges from the intercoordination. The other rules are compounding, focusing, substitution, and differentiation.

Fischer's (1980) formulation has been retained in essence in his later work, but there have been two major developments of the model. One has been to link the model to dynamic growth functions (van der Maas & Molenaar, 1992; van Geert, 1993) while the other has been to link it to spurts in brain growth (Fischer & Bidell, 1998; Fischer & Rose, 1996; Thatcher, 1994). I will try to indicate briefly how Fischer's theory has developed along these lines. Firstly, it is proposed that the major reorganizations between levels, as outlined above, correspond to growth spurts or other discontinuities in brain growth. Furthermore, these dynamic changes can occur concurrently in many independent systems, which might be localized in different regions of the brain. It is also proposed that each new level is marked by a new behavioral control system, which is supported by a new kind of neural network (Fischer & Rose, 1996). They also argue that the recurring cycles of development that are postulated to occur in each tier are supported by observations of brain growth.

The implications of the recent developments of Fischer's theory are profound and sophisticated. They offer a resolution of the anomaly, crucial to understanding development, that there is both variability and consistency in cognitive development. Dynamic systems produce variability from a relatively small set of common processes. The application of dynamic systems theory to the database provided by cognitive developmental stage theory is one of the greatest achievements of Fischer and his colleagues.

Attempts at synthesis

Attempts have been made to synthesize the neo-Piagetian theories (Chapman, 1987, 1990; Chapman & Lindenberger, 1989; Demetriou, Doise, & van Lieshout, 1998; Demetriou, Efklides, & Platsidou, 1993). Chapman's approach was arguably more directly based on information-processing concepts. He postulated that "the total capacity requirement of a given form of reasoning is equal to the number of operatory variables that are assigned values simultaneously in employing that form of reasoning in a particular task" (Chapman & Lindenberger, 1989, p. 238).

We will consider his analysis of class inclusion. A concrete example might comprise a set of beads, some red (A) and some blue (A'), all of which are wooden (B). Therefore A and A' are included in B (A $\cup$ A' = B). The child is asked to decide whether there are more red than wooden beads. Solving the problem entails assigning values to the class variables, A, A', and B, that is recognizing that A = red beads, A' = blue beads and B = wooden beads, which is a form of variable binding. Chapman and Lindenberger refer to this as the coordination of intension (the defining properties of the class) and extension (objects belonging to the class).

Chapman (1987) analyzed tasks in terms of the number of schemes required for solution: "One of the main hypotheses generated by the proposed model is that the notion of attentional capacity can be explicated in terms of the number of representational schemes coordinated by an inferential scheme" (Chapman, 1987, p. 310). However, he interpreted schemes in a way that was very like variables: "A further property of representational schemes is that they can be generalized beyond their immediate context and embedded in more abstract schemes without losing their identity" (1987, p. 309).

Chapman was very much aware of the inherent difficulties in objective analyses of complexity. After a penetrating review of the neo-Piagetian theories of Case, Pascual-Leone, and Halford, he commented: "In summary, neo-Piagetian theorists have not yet developed a method of task analysis (a) that is sufficiently rigorous to result in unambiguous predictions and (b) that can be applied with equal facility to both cognitive tasks and measurement tasks" (Chapman, 1990, p. 273).

In his later work, Chapman was more explicit in analyzing complexity in terms of variables. Perhaps therefore one of the most important achievements of Chapman and his collaborators was to have realized that the best way to analyze complexity of cognitive tasks is to determine the number of variables that have to be instantiated in parallel. Variables can be analyzed more objectively than schemes. The concept of scheme is so flexible that it may be difficult for independent observers to agree on the number of schemes required for a task.

Processing Speed

Evidence for a global processing speed factor that increases with development was provided by Kail (1986, 1988a, 1991a; Kail & Park, 1992; see also Schneider, ch. 11 this volume). The methodology was based on measuring changes in processing speed with age across a number of rather different tasks, and is well illustrated by Kail (1988a). Children were tested on a memory search task in which they studied a set of one, three, or five digits, then a single-digit probe was presented and children had to decide whether it had been in the study set. Visual search was similar, except that the study set was a single digit, and children had to determine whether this digit appeared in a probe set of one to five digits. Processing speed can be measured in both tasks by the slope of the function relating probe set size to response time. Other tasks used included mental rotation, in which children had to judge whether a pair of letters presented in different orientations were identical or were mirror images, and a mental addition task in which children had to determine the correctness of sums such as $3 + 8 = 10$. There was also an analogical reasoning task with two 3×3 matrices. Children had to determine whether the geometric figures in the cells changed according to the same rule in both matrices. It was found that the change in processing speed over the age range 8 to 22 years was very similar across all task domains, and was best fitted by an exponential function that was common to the tasks. This led Kail to propose that changes in processing speed over age reflected processing capacity rather than learning.

While these findings offer some of the strongest evidence for growth of processing capacity with age, they have not been without controversy. One issue has been whether the findings are compatible with some kind of learning model (e.g. Stigler, Nusbaum, & Chalip, 1988; but see also Kail, 1988b, 1990, 1991a). The global nature of the processing speed factor has also been challenged by Ridderinkhof and van der Molen (1997), who argue that process-specific factors may be involved. There is also a cause-and-effect question: does increased speed cause an increase in processing capacity, or the reverse? A possible answer comes from neural net models. Increased capacity reduces processing time in some neural nets because it reduces the number of cycles required for the net to settle into the solution that best fits the parallel-acting constraints. Alternatively it is possible that higher processing speed permits more information to be processed before activation decays. This issue seems likely to remain active for some time (see e.g., Cowan, 1998; Halford, Wilson, & Phillips, 1998a). These controversies notwithstanding, the discovery of a global processing speed factor must be considered one of the major achievements in the field. Processing speed has emerged as a major factor in cognitive development across the lifespan (Cerella & Hale, 1994; Kail & Salthouse, 1994; Salthouse, 1996), and it has found application in a number of other contexts (Kail, 1997, 1998, 2000; Kail & Hall, 1999).

Further issues have been raised by Anderson (1992), who proposes that individual differences reflect processing efficiency, whereas cognitive development depends on knowledge elaboration and maturation of modules. He reviews evidence that individual differences in intelligence are stable over the course of development, and are related to measures of processing speed such as inspection time, which is the exposure duration required to detect which of two vertical lines is longer. This has been found to correlate with intelligence (Nettelbeck, 1987).

Cognitive development, on the other hand, is considered to be heavily dependent on maturation of specialized modules that are functionally independent, complex processes of evolutionary importance that are independent of general intelligence. Anderson proposes that there are modules for perception of three-dimensional space, phonological encoding, syntactic parsing, and theory of mind. The mechanisms that enable us to see in three-dimensional space are specialized for processing visual information, and are complex, but do not correlate with intelligence. Although it is not possible to resolve this controversy here, it does not seem likely that cognitive development and individual differences in intelligence exist in separate, watertight compartments. It seems more likely that differences in processing efficiency affect both intelligence and cognitive development, and that while modular processes are undoubtedly important, cognitive development also depends on acquisition of domain-general processes, such as memory storage and retrieval functions, and analogical reasoning.

Cognitive Complexity

The orderly interpretation of findings in cognitive development depends on having a metric for cognitive complexity. That is, we need some way of specifying how complex a particular task is. If complexities of tasks cannot be compared, then questions such as whether young children's performance on a given task is precocious are inherently unanswerable. What appears to be precocious might be performance of a simpler task. Neo-Piagetian theories have provided partial answers to this problem.

Another approach, which has its origins partly in the neo-Piagetian approach, is to define complexity in terms of relations that can be processed in parallel (Halford, Wilson, & Phillips, 1998b; see also commentary and reply). The essential idea is that each argument of a relation represents a source of variation, or a dimension, and an *n*-ary relation is a set of points in *n*-dimensional space. Thus relations of higher arity are more complex, so a unary relation is less complex than a binary relation, which is less complex than a ternary relation, and so on. Processing load increases with relational complexity, and empirical evidence indicates that quaternary relations are the most complex that adults can process in parallel. This is consistent with limitations in short-term memory capacity (Cowan, 2001). Normative data suggest that unary relations are processed at a median age of 1 year, binary relations at 2 years, ternary relations at 5 years and quaternary relations at 11 years.

Concepts too complex to be processed in parallel are handled by *segmentation* (decomposition into smaller segments that can be processed serially) and *conceptual chunking* (recoding into less complex relations, but at the cost of making some relations inaccessible). For example, $v = st^{-1}$ (velocity = distance/time) is a ternary relation, but can be recoded to a unary relation, a binding between a variable and a constant. However, this makes relations between velocity, distance, and time inaccessible (e.g., if velocity is represented as a single variable, we cannot answer questions such as how speed is affected if the distance is doubled and time held constant).

Complex tasks are normally segmented into steps, each of which is of sufficiently low relational complexity to be processed in parallel. The steps are processed serially. Expertise is important for devising strategies that reduce the complexity of relations that have to be processed in parallel, though a lower limit is usually imposed by the structure of the task. The effective relational complexity of a task is the most complex relation that has to be performed in parallel, using the most efficient strategy available. Complexity analyses are based on principles that are common across domains and methodologies.

We can illustrate relational complexity with the class inclusion task, discussed earlier, comprised of wooden beads, most of which are red, while the remainder are blue. Children are asked: "Are there more wooden beads or more red ones?" Young children tend to say there are more red ones. The possible causes of error have been the subject of much controversy (Breslow, 1981; Bryant & Trabasso, 1971; Halford, 1993; Hodkin, 1987; Markovits, Dumas, & Malfait, 1995; McGarrigle, Grieve, & Hughes, 1978; Pears & Bryant, 1990; Siegel, McCabe, Brand, & Matthews, 1978; Thayer & Collyer, 1978), but when allowance is made for these, we still have a complexity factor that influences performance. The problem is that in order to determine which class is the superordinate and which are the subclasses, children must consider the relations among the superordinate class and the two subclasses. A class such as wooden beads is not inherently a superordinate, and its status is defined by its relations to the subordinates. That is, wooden is a superordinate because it includes red and blue beads. All three sets and the relations between them are necessary to understand that the subclasses are included in the superordinate class. This entails a ternary relation. If the task is represented as a series of separate binary relations that are not integrated, then the full implications of the entire relational structure among the classes (e.g., that the superordinate class is necessarily more numerous than the major subclass) will be missed.

Relational complexity can be manipulated independently of other factors, and substantial effects have been produced (Andrews & Halford, 1998). A number of unequivocal developmental predictions have been made in advance using relational complexity theory (Halford, 1993). For example, 2-year-olds should be able to discriminate either weight or distance, but not both, on the balance scale, which has been confirmed by Halford, Andrews, Dalton, Boag, and Zielinski (submitted). It was also predicted that structural complexity would be a factor in concept of mind (Halford, 1993), which was confirmed by Davis and Pratt (1995), Frye, Zelazo, and Palfai (1995), Gordon and Olson (1998), Halford, Andrews, and Bowden, (1998), and Keenan, Olson, and Marini (1998). Ability to process relations has been linked to the frontal cortex (Christoff et al., submitted; Robin & Holyoak, 1995; Waltz et al., 1999), which suggests that maturation of the frontal lobes may be a factor in growth of processing capacity.

Levels of Cognitive Functioning

Levels of cognitive function have been defined by a number of writers, including Campbell and Bickhard (1986) and Karmiloff-Smith and her collaborators (Clark & Karmiloff-Smith, 1993; Karmiloff-Smith, 1992, 1994). The most influential at present is probably that of Karmiloff-Smith, based on the implicit–explicit distinction. I will try to link this approach to the other information-processing approaches. Level I, or implicit knowledge, is an effective basis for performance, but is not accessible to other cognitive processes, and cannot be modified strategically. It is *knowledge in the system* but not *knowledge to the system*. There are three levels of explicit knowledge. Level E1 is accessible and modifiable, but not available to consciousness and verbal report; Level E2 is accessible to consciousness, but not verbal report; Level E3 is accessible to both. Explicit or Level E knowledge is a reduced and abstracted version of Level I, produced by a process of representational redescription. The theory is not a stage theory like the Piagetian and neo-Piagetian models, but representational redescription tends to occur independently in each domain, and is not age- or stage-linked. Nevertheless representational redescription has features in common with, and attempts to integrate, both Piagetian constructivism and Fodor's (1983) concept of innate knowledge.

The nature of representational redescription has been only partly specified. Phillips, Halford, and Wilson (1995, July) proposed that the implicit–explicit distinction can be captured by the distinction between associative and relational knowledge. Karmiloff-Smith (1994) has speculated about neural net models that might make the transition from one level to another. However, much remains to be done to address this fundamental issue.

Process Models of Cognitive Development

A number of information-processing models of concept acquisition have been developed. The Q-SOAR model of Simon and Klahr (1995) applied Newell's (1990) SOAR architecture to Gelman's (1982) study of number conservation acquisition. Children are shown two equal rows of objects, asked to count each row in turn and say how many each contains, then to say whether they are the same or different. Then one row is transformed (e.g., by spacing objects more widely, thus increasing the length of the row without adding any items) and the child is asked whether each row still contains the same number, and whether they are the same or different.

The preconserving child cannot answer this question. This is represented in Q-SOAR as an impasse. The model then searches for a solution to the problem, using a procedure based on the work of Klahr and Wallace (1976). This entails quantifying the sets before and after the transformation, noting that they were the same before the transformation, that they are the same after the transformation, and finally that the transformation did not change the relation between the sets. This process uses knowledge already available, including quantifying the sets, comparing them, recalling results of quantification and comparison, and noticing the effect of transformations (both conserving and nonconserving). With repeated experience, the model gradually learns to classify the action of spacing out the items as a conserving transformation.

Following work on rule assessment (Briars & Siegler, 1984; Siegler, 1981), Siegler and his collaborators conducted an extensive study of strategy development (Siegler, 1999; Siegler & Chen, 1998; Siegler & Jenkins, 1989; Siegler & Shipley, 1995; Siegler & Shrager, 1984). Two of the models were concerned with development of addition strategies in young children. When asked to add two single-digit numbers, they choose between a set of strategies including retrieving the answer from memory, decomposing the numbers (e.g. $3 + 5 = 4 + 4 = 8$), counting both sets (counting right through a set of three and a set of five, perhaps using fingers) and the *min strategy* of counting on from the larger set (e.g. 4, 5, 6, 7, 8, so $3 + 5 = 8$).

Their early strategy choice model was based on distribution of associations (Siegler & Shrager, 1984). The idea is that each addition sum is associated with answers of varying strengths so for a given sample of children $2 + 1$ might yield the answer "3" 80 percent of the time, "1" or "2" 4 percent of the time, "4" 3 percent of the time, and so on. The chance of an answer being chosen is a function of its associative strength relative to competing answers. The more peaked the distribution the more likely it will be that a single answer will occur. However, it will be adopted only if it is above the confidence criterion. If not, alternative strategies, such as counting, are sought.

In their later work Siegler and his collaborators developed the Adaptive Strategy Choice Model (ASCM, pronounced "Ask-em"). This model makes more active strategy choices. At the beginning ASCM knows only the small set of strategies typically used by 4-year-olds, but it has general cognitive skills for choosing and evaluating strategies. The model is trained on a set of elementary addition facts, then the min strategy is added to the model's repertoire. The model chooses a strategy for each problem on the basis of the past speed and accuracy of the strategy and on similarity between the current problem and past problems where a strategy has been used. Each time a strategy is used the record of its success is updated and the projected strength of the strategy for that problem is calculated. The strength of association between a problem and a specific answer is increased or decreased depending on the success of the answer. One of the strengths of the model is that it can account for variability, both between children and between different strategies used by the same child for a particular class of problems. Most importantly it provides a reasonably accurate account of strategy development in children over age.

Relational Knowledge and Analogy

One of the most fundamental problems in cognitive development is children's acquisition of relational and dimensional knowledge (see Goswami, ch. 13 this volume), yet there has been little systematic study of it. One of the most interesting research projects in this area is that by Smith, Gasser, and Sandhofer (n.d.; unpublished manuscript). Examining evidence from children's word acquisition, Smith noted that dimensional adjectives (e.g. wet, soft, big, red) are learned relatively slowly as compared with, say, nouns. Smith postulated that to learn dimension words, children must learn three kinds of mappings: between words and objects ("red" for red objects); word–word maps ("red", "blue", etc. are associated with color), and property–property maps ("They are the same color"). Smith argues that early use of relational terms is holistic, but relational terms gradually become organized into dimensions (by about 5 years of age). This enables recognition that "more than" is the opposite of "less than" and transitivity of relations (e.g., $a > b$ and $b > c \rightarrow a > c$).

Recognition of the role of analogy in cognition and cognitive development increased rapidly in the 1980s. Gentner (1983) provided a workable conceptualization of human analogical reasoning with her theory that analogy is a mapping from a familiar structure, the base, to an unfamiliar structure, the target. The mapping is validated by correspondence between the structures in base and target. Computational models of analogical mapping (e.g., Falkenhainer, Forbus, & Gentner, 1989; Holyoak & Thagard, 1989; Hummel & Holyoak, 1997) helped to clarify the nature of the process, and its role as a mechanism of cognitive development has been explored (e.g., Halford, 1993). One difficulty is that analogical reasoning has sometimes been difficult to produce in the laboratory (Gick & Holyoak, 1983) but it occurs readily in real life (Dunbar, 2001), so this difficulty might be overcome by using more naturalistic procedures.

Much of the developmental interest in analogy has centered around the age of attainment (Gentner & Rattermann, 1991; Gentner, Rattermann, Markman, & Kotovsky, 1995; Goswami, 1996; Goswami & Brown, 1989). There is no reason to doubt that simple proportional analogies of the form A is to B as C is to D can be performed by children under 5 years. Indeed, according to complexity analyses by Halford and his collaborators (Halford, 1993; Halford, Wilson, et al., 1998b) they should be possible at age 2. Analogies that require parallel processing of more complex relations are predicted to be consistent with the age norms for that level of relational complexity.

Symbolic Neural Net Models

Neural net models, considered by Thomas and Karmiloff-Smith (ch. 26 this volume), have become one of the most important types of computational models of cognitive development. However, questions about the ability of some early models to account for symbolic processes (Fodor & Pylyshyn, 1988; Marcus, 1998a, 1998b; Smolensky, 1988) have given rise to symbolic neural net models (Halford, Wilson, Guo, Gayler, Wiles, & Stewart, 1994; Hummel & Holyoak, 1997; Shastri & Ajjanagadde, 1993). I will briefly consider two attempts to build symbolic neural net models of cognitive development.

The first is a neural net implementation of the processing complexity theory of Halford, Wilson, et al. (1998b) discussed earlier. It is based on the Structured Tensor Analogical Reasoning (STAR) model of Halford, Wilson, et al. (1994). The essential idea is that the structural properties of higher cognition can be captured by the representation and processing of relations. Representation of a relation entails a symbol for the relation, plus a representation of the related entities. These must be bound together in a way that preserves the truth of the relation. Consider a simple binary relation, such as larger-than. An instance of larger-than, in predicate calculus notation, is larger-than (elephant, mouse). In our model we represent this by having a set of units representing each component, larger-than, elephant, and mouse. Each set of units corresponds to a set of activation values, or vector. The binding is represented by computing the tensor (outer) product of the vectors, producing a three-dimensional matrix. More complex relations correspond to binding more entities, and therefore to tensor products of higher rank. Thus a binary relation entails binding three entities, the symbol and two arguments, a ternary relation to binding four entities, the symbol and three arguments, and so on. Tensor product nets are shown schematically in figure 25.1, together with the approximate Piagetian stage with which each level of relational complexity is identified in the theory of Halford, Wilson, et al. (1998b).

This model is designed to represent structure with a neural net architecture. Thus the components retain their identity in the compound representation. In the Rank 3 tensor product representing larger (elephant, mouse) the vectors representing larger, elephant, and mouse, are retained. Also, any component can be retrieved, given the remaining components, a property that Halford, Wilson, et al. (1998b) call omni-directional access. The relations in a net can be modified on line, by changing the relation symbol. This is one of the properties of explicit knowledge defined by Clark and Karmiloff-Smith (1993). The model can handle higher cognitive processes such as analogical reasoning, and mathematical operations. Because the number of neural units, and therefore the computational cost, increase exponentially with complexity of relations, the model provides a natural explanation for the link between processing loads and relational complexity observed by Halford, Wilson, et al. (1998b). On the other hand, this model does not have the learning functions that are a major benefit of multi-layered net models, such as the balance scale model of McClelland (1995), and consequently does not handle the emergent properties of these models. Therefore at the present time it appears that symbolic and multi-layered net models should be seen as complementary, and the next step forward might depend on hybrids, or on models that capture the properties of both classes of nets.

Piagetian stage	No. of dimensions	Rank	Cognitive processes	Typical tasks	PDP implementation
Preconceptual	1	2	Unary relations	match-to-sample, identity position, integration, category label distinct from category	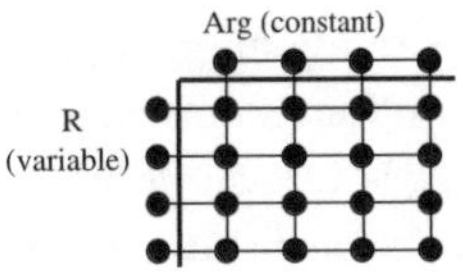
Intuitive	2	3	Binary relations Univariate functions	relational match-to sample, A not-B, complementary categories	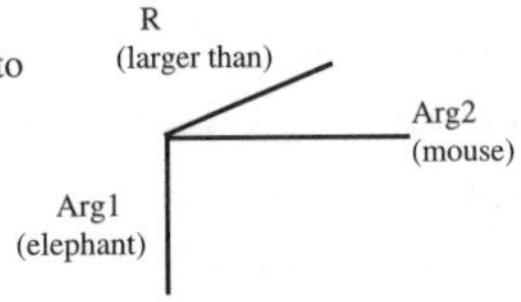
Concrete operational	3	4	Ternary relations, Binary operations, Bivariate functions	transitive inference, hierarchical categories, concept of mind	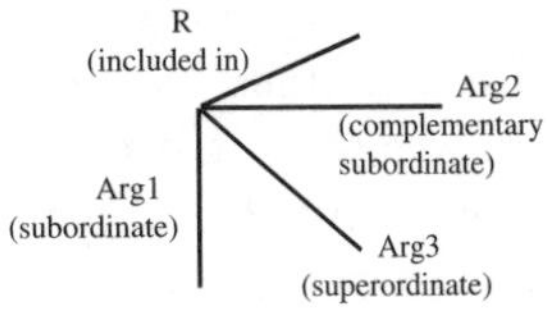
Formal	4	5	Quaternary relations Compositions of binary operations	proportion, balance-scale	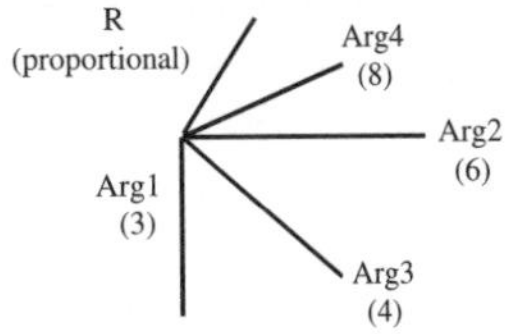

Figure 25.1 Representational ranks

The model of Smith, Gasser, and Sandhofer (n.d.) simulates children's acquisition of dimensional terms. It employs the three-layered net architecture, but can probably be categorized as a symbolic model because it specifically addresses acquisition of symbolic knowledge. An object with four perceptible attributes is coded in the input layer. There is a separate input that codes the relevant dimension, such as color. There is a further input indicating whether two successive objects are the same or different on the specified dimension. The representations in the hidden layer are copied to a perceptual buffer (analogous to the context units in the simple recurrent net: Elman, Bates, Johnson, Karmiloff-Smith, Parisi & Plunkett, 1996). The net is trained to produce the appropriate dimensional attribute (e.g., red). The training is constrained by property–property maps. If two successive objects are the same on the specified dimension, the output must be the same for both of them. The success of the model tends to support the authors' claim that culturally transmitted information about the sameness of objects on specified dimensions (e.g., "these flowers are the same color") is important for children's acquisition of dimensional terms.

Conclusion

I find it virtually impossible to provide an adequate summary of research on information-processing approaches to cognitive development, so I will content myself with a few of the observations that struck me as I was writing this chapter. The first is the extraordinary richness of both empirical and theoretical work in the field, and the ingenuity that has been displayed. The second is that information-processing approaches to cognitive development have told us a lot about the nature of the underlying processes in cognitive development. This means that we now have a lot more information about what is happening when a child is performing a task. This yields a lot of insights and offers genuinely new ways of understanding many issues. The third observation is the success with which information-processing conceptions have been linked to neuroscience and to neural net models. While no one would pretend that all problems have been solved in these areas, they certainly offer exciting possibilities for the future. The fourth observation is that a good deal of common ground has emerged from neo-Piagetian models about what constitutes conceptual complexity in cognition. This yielded a complexity metric, based on the number of related variables in a cognitive representation, that enables tasks to be compared for complexity, and tasks of equivalent complexity to be recognized, independent of domain or methodology. Furthermore it can be applied, not only to cognitive development, but to cognition generally. This is an illustration of the way cognitive development research can contribute to general cognition and cognitive science.

Note

1. It is with great regret that I note the untimely death of Robbie Case on May 19, 2000.

CHAPTER TWENTY-SIX

Modeling Typical and Atypical Cognitive Development: Computational Constraints on Mechanisms of Change

Michael S. C. Thomas and Annette Karmiloff-Smith

Introduction

Empirical studies of cognitive development usually report the abilities that children display at different ages. The cognitive mechanisms that allow the child to move from one set of abilities to a more complex set remain shrouded in mystery and have given rise to much controversy.

To take a famous example, Piaget characterized cognitive development as a process of acquiring mental representations of increasing complexity. He proposed that the mechanism of change involved a combination of three processes: assimilation, accommodation, and equilibration (Smith, ch. 23 this volume). One process interprets new experience according to existing knowledge (assimilation) while a second adjusts existing knowledge to fit with new experience (accommodation). These first two are local processes, whereas a third (equilibration) is the attempt of the whole system to find global equilibrium after multiple local changes. In this theory, successive stages of cognitive development have greater complexity and representational power than the previous stages (Piaget, 1954). However, Fodor (1980) argued that, in principle, increases in representational power could not be the consequence of a learning mechanism. This is because the achievement of such increases would require the learning mechanism to evaluate information it did not have the power to represent. Put another way, the mechanism would have to determine the truth of theories that it did not have the ability to understand. Fodor concluded that any

Many thanks to Denis Mareschal for discussions of the ideas in this chapter, and Yonata Levy for helpful comments on an earlier draft. This work was funded by MRC Project Grant no. G9809880 and MRC Programme Grant no. G9715642 to Annette Karmiloff-Smith.

increases in complexity during cognitive development are necessarily maturational and that learning is merely a process that uses experience to select among subsets of representational primitives already available to the cognitive system at that point in development.

These two theories place radically different amounts of weight on the role of learning in driving cognitive development. Which is the right account? Part of the difficulty in evaluating the relative merits of these kinds of proposals about mechanisms of change is that verbally expressed theories are often vague and ill defined. What exactly are equilibration or representational power? What do real learning mechanisms look like and what factors affect the way they learn? Computational modeling offers one method to explore questions like these with far more precision. Models provide the opportunity to establish what types of learning system can be successful in acquiring certain competencies, what constraints such systems should include to best make use of the knowledge available to them in the learning environment, and what stages of performance such systems go through before achieving mastery. Computational models provide candidate systems for the mechanisms of change that drive cognitive development.

In this chapter we examine the use of computational models for studying development from one main perspective. This is the approach that employs connectionist models, also known as artificial neural networks. Although we relate these models to other types of computational modeling, much of the chapter is taken up with considering the range of cognitive developmental phenomena to which connectionist models have so far been applied, both in typical and atypical populations. We start with a very brief introduction to the basic concepts of connectionist modeling and then consider a single model in some detail, that of children's performance in reasoning about balance scale problems. Subsequently we look at models proposed to account for the development of other aspects of reasoning in children, development in infancy, and the acquisition of language. We then pause to examine some of the theoretical issues raised by these models. In the second half, we consider a recent extension of connectionist networks to capture behavioral deficits in developmental disorders.

An introduction to connectionist networks

Connectionist models are computational systems loosely based on principles of neural information-processing. It is important to stress that in the current context, they are not intended to be models of neural circuits, but to sit at a higher level of description. Their aim is to incorporate concepts at the cognitive level so that their performance can be evaluated against behavioral data. Connectionist models are relevant to cognitive development for two main reasons. The first relates to biological plausibility. Although there is controversy over whether current connectionist models have abstracted the correct computational primitives from neural circuits, it nevertheless seems likely that computational solutions achieved in these models will be readily implementable in real neural circuits (O'Reilly, 1998). Computational modeling of any sort can be useful in clarifying theories; however, the attempt here is to build models which employ the same style of computation as the brain.

The second reason that connectionist models are relevant to cognitive development is that they are essentially learning systems. A typical model will comprise an initial network

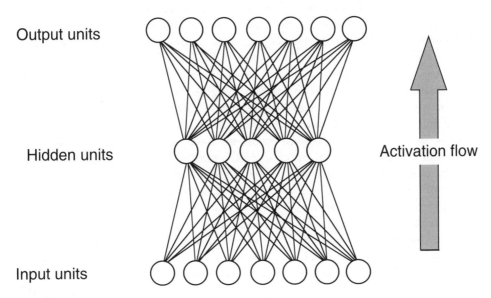

Output units

Hidden units

Activation flow

Input units

Figure 26.1   A three-layer feedforward network

structure and a training environment representing the domain to be mastered. With the application of a learning algorithm, the network alters its structure to achieve competency in the domain. In particular, through interacting with the training environment, connectionist networks develop *internal representations* or knowledge states that permit them to perform the relevant computations. Given that cognition is characterized as the progressive construction and manipulation of mental representations in the brain, together these characteristics make connectionist networks attractive systems to model processes of cognitive development (Elman, Bates, Johnson, Karmiloff-Smith, Parisi, & Plunkett, 1996; Karmiloff-Smith, 1992; Plunkett & Sinha, 1992).

A brief overview of the components of a connectionist model follows. More detailed introductions can be found in Elman et al. (1996), McLeod, Plunkett, and Rolls (1998), and Rumelhart and McClelland (1986a). Software is also available with these volumes enabling the reader to build and explore his or her own computational models.

Connectionist systems comprise simple processing units connected together into networks. Each processing unit has associated with it an activation level, analogous to the firing rate of a neuron. Units influence the activity of their neighbors depending on the strength of the connection between the units. Thus, activity on one unit may facilitate or inhibit the activity of neighboring units. A given unit determines its activation depending on the sum of facilitation or inhibition it receives from adjacent units and on the unit's decision function (functions can vary, but they usually take the form of a non-linear threshold). Networks are generally organized into layers of units, the particular configuration of which is referred to as the *network architecture*. Figure 26.1 shows a typical network architecture, with three such layers: an input layer, a layer of internal processing units (usually called "hidden" units), and an output layer. This particular network uses a *feedforward* design, in that activation only propagates in one direction up through the network, from input to output. The training environment for such a network amounts to a set of pairs of input patterns (defined in terms of the activation levels to be applied to the input units) and the corresponding desired output patterns.

Knowledge is stored in the network in terms of the strengths of the connections between the units. The strength of a connection is often referred to as its "weight." We will not use this term here to avoid confusion when we come to examine the balance scale model. Learning amounts to iteratively altering the connection strengths by tiny amounts so that ultimately, for each input pattern, the network produces the correct output pattern. A variety of learning algorithms are available, but many take the form of *gradient descent*; that is, for a given input, an "error" term is derived which gives a measure of how close the actual output is to the desired output. The connection strengths are then changed in a way that reduces the size of this disparity (or moves the network "downhill" in error space). The most common such algorithm is called *backpropagation* (Rumelhart, Hinton, & Williams, 1986).

Although each processing unit is computationally very simple, networks of units can compute complex functions. Indeed, in theory a three-layer network such as that shown in figure 26.1 can learn any arbitrarily complex relation between a set of input-output pairs so long as it is given sufficient "hidden" units over which to develop its internal representations (Cybenko, 1989). Besides the feedforward network, there is a range of other architectures. For instance, some include loops of connections so that activation can cycle round within the network. In such *attractor* networks, for a given input the network must gradually settle into a stable state that forms the output, such that further cycling produces no change in output activations. Cycling activation can be used to provide the network with a memory of previous inputs. This enables it to process sequences of inputs, in so-called *recurrent* systems. Finally, networks can be used merely to form concise representations of a given set of input patterns. Here, there is no desired output supplied during training. Instead, the network *self-organizes* its representations to form a concise description of the input set across a small set of abstract features.

Connectionist Models of Normal Development

An example model: the balance scale task

To illustrate the use of connectionist models for exploring cognitive development we begin by looking at one model in some detail. The model attempts to capture the development of children's problem-solving abilities in balance scale problems. The balance scale was one of a set of problems which Piaget's collaborator, Inhelder, put forward as demonstrating the stages of development through which children pass, each stage representing a more complex understanding (Inhelder & Piaget, 1958). Siegler (1981) demonstrated that children's performance on this task at different stages of development could be characterized by four rules (although see Wilkening & Huber, ch. 16 this volume). In the first rule, 4- to 5-year-olds only considered the number of weights on each side of the scale: the side with the greater number will go down. In the second rule, focus is still on the number of weights, but when the weights are equal, the child will then take into account their distance from the fulcrum – the side with the weights further away will drop. The third rule is more sophisticated, always taking weight and distance into account; but if one side has more weight while the other has its weights farther away, the child simply guesses. By age 8, children were generally using rule 2 or 3, and by 12, most children had settled on rule 3. The fourth rule establishes the torque on each side of the scale, with the side with the greater torque predicted to descend. This rule is not reached by everyone: in Siegler's sample, most 20-year-olds continued to use rule 3, although 30 percent were now using rule 4.

McClelland (1989) proposed a connectionist model of the development of problem-solving in the balance scale task (see also McClelland & Jenkins, 1991). The structure of this model is shown in figure 26.2a. The input layer is split into two channels, one representing information about the number of weights on each side of the scale, the other representing information about their distance from the fulcrum. Particular configurations can be presented to the model as a pattern of activation over the input units, with four units active and 16 units inactive. For each input pattern, the model must determine the side which will drop by turning on one of the two output units and turning off the other. If the scale balances, both output units should be half-activated (as in figure 26.2a). Notice, then, that this domain has been converted into pairs of input-output activation patterns. Note also that the network is oblivious to any information about weights and

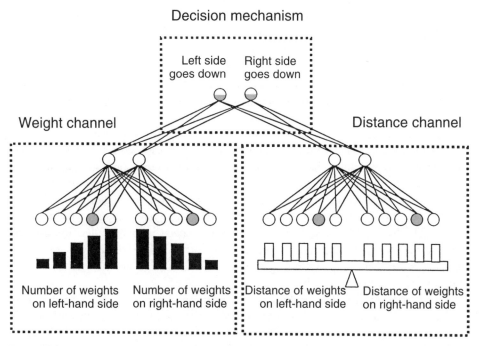

Figure 26.2a Structure of McClelland's (1989) balance scale model, with separate channels for processing weight and distance information. Left side of scale: four weights on second peg out. Right side of scale: two weights on fourth peg out. Scale should balance (both output units half-activated)

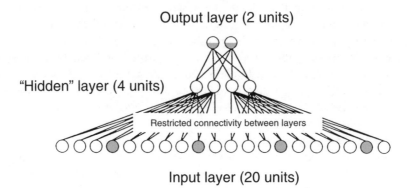

Figure 26.2b   "Uninterpreted" structure of the balance scale model – a three-layer network with restricted connectivity between input and hidden layers

distances *per se*. While figure 26.2a includes information to help us understand the model's structure in relation to the task, figure 26.2b provides a better idea of the model in its uninterpreted form: this is simply a three-layer feedforward network with a restriction on which input units are connected to which hidden units.

Prior to training, the strengths of the connections between the units are randomized within some small range around zero. In this state, the network will perform badly on the balance scale problem because, prior to training, it has no knowledge. However, we will later argue that it does have a sort of knowledge even at this initial stage. For the moment, suffice it to say that it has no knowledge of the *content* of the problem it is facing (Elman et al., 1996). The model is now exposed to the training set. For each configuration of weights and distances, the network produces an output. This is compared to the correct response, and the connection strengths are altered to bring the network's response closer to the correct output. Connection strengths are altered by only a small amount for each individual problem, and the network is exposed to the set of balance scale problems many times. The consequence is that it converges on a solution where its performance is optimized on the full task. However, in reaching this solution, it goes through phases where it performs well only on subsets of the individual problems. Indeed, McClelland (1989) demonstrated that it passes through the *same four stages of performance* that the children exhibited and that Siegler characterized with his rules. Importantly, although the four stages appear to be qualitatively different types of behavior, the model moved between these stages via a single mechanism of continuous and gradual changes to its set of connection strengths.

How does the model simulate this stage-wise pattern of behavior during development? We have already seen one built-in assumption of the model, that weight and distance information are processed separately. However, a second assumption was built in to the model, this time in terms of the training set. The training set was constructed to reflect the supposition that children have a bias to focus more on weight rather than distance. This was achieved by giving the network more training trials where the distance of the weights either side of the fulcrum was equal; only the number of weights varied. As a result of these extra items, the network initially came to rely more on weight than distance as a reliable predictor of the outcome.

Once these two biases are built in, the emergence of the four stages can be explained as follows. Because of the biased training set, the weight channel of the network initially develops more quickly than the distance channel (rule 1). With additional training, the distance channel also begins to develop, but is initially only sufficient to drive the network response when the weight channel does not overrule it (rule 2). With yet more training, the distance channel now starts actively to contribute to the solution, but when weight and distance conflict, the network produces erroneous responses (rule 3). Finally the network finds the appropriate way to combine weight and distance information, effectively discovering the law of torque (rule 4). McLeod, Plunkett, and Rolls (1998) provide a detailed analysis of the connection strengths at each stage within the network. As in the human case, performance of rule 4 is unstable within the model. For the McClelland model, this is because the law of torque requires a precise calibration of the connection strengths. By contrast, Shultz, Mareschal, and Schmidt (1994) have shown that a slightly different model can learn stable rule 4 behavior, as well as accounting for other empirical effects. Theirs was a *generative* model, an idea that we will encounter shortly.

In sum, McClelland's model delivers a concrete example of a *single mechanism of change* in which there is an accumulation of very gradual increases in connection strengths inside the network, but which nevertheless produces behavior that shifts through stages of qualitatively different performance corresponding to developmental data from children.

Connectionist models of logical development

Seriation is another Piagetian task taken to illustrate distinct stages of transitive reasoning development (Piaget, 1965). Children are initially presented with a random array of sticks of different lengths, and asked to sort the sticks in order of increasing length. Four stages of performance have been identified during development: random sorting, sorting of small subgroups, sorting of the entire array but by trial and error, and finally efficient sorting, e.g., by always choosing the smallest stick in the remaining to-be-sorted array.

Mareschal and Shultz (1999) demonstrated how a connectionist network, which once again gradually fine-tuned the strength of its connections, could exhibit a progression of behavior according to these four stages. Like the balance scale model, Mareschal and Shultz built in an assumption constraining the way in which the model could process the information. They built two sub-networks into the model, one of which was given feedback about which stick to select for moving, while the second was given feedback about where to move the stick. The combination of the development of the "which" and "where" sub-networks eventually led to success on the seriation task. Moreover, the model predicted that performance would be better when the array was further from its correctly ordered state. The novel prediction was subsequently confirmed by Mareschal and Schultz in testing with young children.

This model differed from the balance beam model in one key respect: during training, the seriation model changed not just the strength of its connections but also its architecture. The seriation model sought to capture the process of development not only by adjusting connection strengths, but also by adding further hidden units when learning faltered. Using an algorithm called *cascade correlation* (Fahlman & Lebiere, 1990), new hidden units were added not at random but specifically to advance learning when it plateaued. Such an approach is referred to as *generative connectionism.*

Shultz (1998) also used a generative connectionist approach to model children's performance on conservation tasks. These tasks represent a widely used technique for examining children's knowledge of those physical attributes that remain invariant under various sorts of transformation, such as number, weight, and volume (Piaget, 1954, 1965). Shultz constructed a network model of number conservation that was presented with information about two rows of items. The network was told the length and density of each row, with values coded as the activation level of a single input unit for each dimension. This information was presented twice, once describing the rows before a transformation had been performed, and a second time after the transformation had been performed. In addition, the network was given information about which of the two rows had been transformed and about the type of transformation carried out. Two transformations preserved the attribute of number in a row (elongation, compression) while two others altered it (addition, subtraction). The network was trained to indicate whether the rows had the same number of items or, if not, which row had the greater number.

As the model altered its connection strengths and added hidden units during training, it simulated a number of the effects exhibited by children. At first, the network failed to conserve number. However, midway through training, the system showed an abrupt shift to conserving number across the relevant transformations. The model also captured the fact that in children, correct conservation judgments emerge for small quantities before they emerge for larger quantities (the problem size effect). Lastly, when the network failed to conserve number appropriately, it tended to choose the longer of the two rows as having more items, just as children do (the length bias effect). The network exhibits the length bias because, in the training set, length tends to be a better predictor of number than density does. Length varies across elongation, compression, subtraction, and addition, while density varies only across elongation and compression (since item spacing is kept constant for subtraction and addition). When the network fails to conserve, it is erroneously employing this "perceptual" information. The problem size effect in the network is ascribed to the use of continuously valued representations of length and density. With continuous representations, small sizes are easier to discriminate since differences are proportionally larger (e.g. 3 is greater than 2 by 50 percent but 8 is greater than 7 by only 14 percent). The continuous coding scheme contrasts with the use of discrete units to code weight and distance values in the balance scale model. In a continuous scheme, three (out of a maximum five) might be represented by turning on a single unit which normally varies from 0 to 1 to a level of 0.6; in a discrete scheme, three might be represented by fully activating the third unit in a row of five. This contrast illustrates how modelers make different decisions in converting a cognitive domain into a set of activations to be presented to a network.

Lastly, why does the model exhibit an abrupt change from failure to success at this conservation task? Shultz characterizes the performance of the network as undergoing a shift from solutions that initially rely on "perceptual" information to an increasing focus on the identity of the transformation ("cognitive" information), and finally to a focus on the impact of particular transformations. Shultz attributes the abrupt shift in performance not to incremental changes in connection strengths, but specifically to the addition of extra hidden units. Indeed, some researchers claim that incremental connection changes alone cannot produce discontinuities in development (Raijmakers, van Koten, & Molenaar, 1996) and that changes in architecture are a necessary precondition. However, others argue that the non-linearity of the decision functions within processing units does provide the condition for abrupt changes in performance, even when a network architecture is held constant and its connections gradually changed during training (e.g., Elman, et al., 1996; Plunkett, Sinha, Moller, & Strandsby, 1992).

The models so far described illustrate the broad approach to producing mechanistic computational models of important Piagetian tasks used in exploring childhood development. However, this is not the limit of connectionist models. They have also been used to examine a variety of other developmental phenomena: discrimination shift learning (Sirois & Shultz, 1998), the understanding of the relationship between velocity, time, and distance (Buckingham & Shultz, 1994), the development of concepts (Schyns, 1991), and the development of strategy use in external memory tasks (Bray, Reilly, Villa, & Grupe, 1997).

Connectionist models of infant development

Infant behavior is more closely tied to perceptual-motor skills, and the development of knowledge in infants typically must be explored by indirect means. These include the use of preferential looking and habituation techniques, where infants are found to direct more attention to unfamiliar or unexpected events, as well as the study of search behaviors such as reaching for objects. When a ball passes behind an occluder, do infants look to see whether the ball reappears from the other side of the screen? Are they surprised if the ball does not reappear? If the ball remains behind the screen, do the infants reach behind the screen to recover it? The empirical data here suggest a disparity between the different indices of measuring infant knowledge. While infants younger than 7.5 to 9 months fail to reach for the ball when it is hidden behind the occluding screen (Piaget, 1954), infants as young as 3.5 months display surprise in terms of their looking behavior if the ball does not reappear from behind the screen (e.g., Baillargeon, 1993). If reaching behavior and looking behavior disagree, at what age would we want to claim that infants have a mental representation of the hidden object?

Two connectionist models tackled this phenomenon by employing recurrent network architectures. Munakata, McClelland, Johnson, and Siegler (1997) designed a network to predict the motion of objects across the retina. As the system was given increasing experience with the trajectory of moving objects, an internal representation of a temporarily hidden object could eventually be maintained in the memory loop long enough to drive an expectancy that it would reappear. The model suggests that the concept of the (out of view) object is gradually built up through experiences of object trajectories, rather than taking the form of an all-or-nothing understanding of object permanence. Again, performance relies on the fact that knowledge in the network is built up via the gradual strengthening of connections during training. The disparity between expectancy and reaching behavior is accounted for by showing that the developing representation of the hidden object corresponds to activation patterns which are at first only strong and unambiguous enough to drive expectancy. Further training is required for the representation to be sufficiently robust to drive reaching as well.

Mareschal, Plunkett, and Harris (1999) took a more neurophysiologically motivated approach to the same problem, again using recurrent networks. However, they split processing in the model into an object knowledge module (a "what" channel) and an object location module (a "where" channel), based on evidence of such a functional split in the brain (e.g., Milner & Goodale, 1995). A further reaching module had the task of integrating knowledge from both the "what" and "where" channels. In this model, the expectancy/reaching disparity was accounted for because expectancy (e.g., looking to where the object might reappear) was driven by one of the lower modules, while reaching required integration of both lower-level modules and so took longer to develop (see Mareschal, 2000, for a review of this research). This explanation predicts that, prior to showing reaching behavior, infants can generate expectancies based only on information in one of the lower-level modules, relating either to the object's motion or its identity but not both simultaneously. Subsequent empirical evidence has supported this prediction (e.g. Leslie, Xu, Tremoulet, & Scholl, 1998; Wilcox, 1999).

The contribution of models of infant development has been to question the legitimate inferences that should be drawn from the indirect measures of infant knowledge currently in use. Thus far, connectionist models have pointed to the importance of considering graded internal representations, and of considering that certain behaviors may index individual systems while others may require that the cognitive system integrates across separate processing modules and so exhibit developmental lags. While these models have explained high-level conceptual knowledge (categories, representations of hidden objects) in terms of predominantly perceptual information (visual features), they do not imply that there are no such things as high-level concepts, and indeed these models have not provided explanations of the development of conceptual categories. They do however caution against ignoring simpler, low-level explanations of the infant behavior revealed in current paradigms.

Connectionist models of language development

A great deal of research has employed connectionist models to investigate processes of language development (see Plunkett, 1998 for review). There is insufficient space to review this work here, other than to give an indication of its scope. Models have employed self-organizing networks to explore processes of early phonological development in learning to categorize speech sounds (Nakisa & Plunkett, 1998; Schafer & Mareschal, in press). They have used recurrent architectures in models of the development of segmentation of the speech stream into discrete words (Christiansen, Allen, & Seidenberg, 1998) and the acquisition of syntax structure from sequences of words (e.g. Elman, 1993). Generative networks have been employed to model the acquisition of personal pronouns (Shultz, Buckingham, & Oshima-Takane, 1994). Feedforward networks and attractor networks have been used in models of the development of vocabulary (Gasser & Smith, 1998;

Plunkett, Sinha, Muller, & Strandsby, 1992), as well as in two of the most heavily researched areas, the development of inflectional morphology, including past tense and pluralization (e.g. Daugherty & Seidenberg, 1992; Forrester & Plunkett, 1994; Hahn & Nakisa, in press; MacWhinney & Leinbach, 1991; Plunkett & Juola, 1999; Plunkett & Marchman, 1991, 1996; Plunkett & Nakisa, 1997; Rumelhart & McClelland, 1986b), and the development of reading (Harm & Seidenberg, 1999; Plaut, McClelland, Seidenberg, & Patterson, 1996; Zorzi, Houghton, & Butterworth, 1998a).

Theoretical implications

We now turn to consider some of the theoretical issues raised by the use of connectionist networks to model processes of normal cognitive development. The chapter began by pointing out that mechanisms of change in cognitive development were poorly understood, and that verbal theories of such mechanisms, such as Piaget's notions of assimilation and accommodation, were vaguely defined and therefore hard to evaluate. The process of building computational models of development in domains such as conservation and the balance scale task demands that both the task environment and the mechanisms be precisely specified and, in turn, allows us to generate candidate realizations of vague theoretical terms.

There have been at least two (contrasting) attempts to use connectionist models of development to offer computational interpretations of Piaget's mechanisms of change. McClelland (1989) suggested that, for networks with a fixed architecture, the activation caused in the network by the presentation of an input might be viewed as assimilation, the interpreting of experience according to existing knowledge. The alteration of connection strengths during learning could then be viewed as accommodation, the adjustment of knowledge structures to fit with new experience. An alternative interpretation of these concepts was offered for generative networks that add additional hidden units during learning. Here assimilation is viewed as the gradual change in connection strengths that occurs during training, while accommodation is viewed as the change in network structure caused when the network adds hidden units to move from a plateau in its learning performance (e.g., Mareschal, 1991; Shultz, 1998).

With concrete definitions of these notions in hand, we can then move on to consider some of the wider theoretical debates. For example, at the beginning of the chapter we saw how Fodor (1980) had downplayed the role of learning in development, arguing that increases in representational power are due to maturation and cannot be a consequence of learning. Learning itself only involves selecting among subsets of pre-existing representational primitives. However, it turns out that Fodor's conception of limited learning is entirely consistent with the learning that goes on in networks with fixed architectures. On the other hand, generative networks that change their structure during learning may indeed be seen as systems that increase their representational power during development as a direct consequence of learning. How can we reconcile the notion that fixed architecture networks are essentially learning systems with the apparently nativist Fodorian notion that learning is a process of merely selecting amongst pre-existing representational primitives? And how is it that generative networks escape this limitation?

To answer these questions, we must consider a description that is often ascribed to connectionist models of development. This is that they are *tabula rasa* learning systems. If this were true, such models would necessarily fall within a strongly empiricist view of development. However, this characterization ignores the fact that networks are highly constrained in what kinds of problems they can learn (Karmiloff-Smith, 1992). These constraints are defined by the design decisions that the modeler makes in constructing the network with regard to the initial state of the network, the number of units, layers, connections, and the pattern of connectivity, as well as the way that activation propagates through the network, the learning algorithm, the input and output representations, and the regime of training that the network will undergo. Initial network constraints thus define the full set of representational primitives that the system possesses, and the process of learning selects a particular set. It is in this sense that fixed networks conform to Fodor's nativist notion (Quartz, 1993).

Despite this apparent weakening of the role of learning, the balance scale model illustrates that connectionist networks still manage to give a powerful account of the stage-wise acquisition of problem-solving in children. Moreover, this account is consistent with Piaget's *constructivist* conception of development, as an interaction between pre-existing structures, domain-general learning mechanisms (i.e., principles of neural computation), and the environment. Thus the use of connectionist networks as models of development offers the opportunity of a rapprochement between the apparently divergent views of Piaget and Fodor. Furthermore, these models suggest a view of the nature of innate knowledge. Networks clearly distinguish between knowledge of content, derived through learning, and knowledge based on the constraints that will shape learning. In a connectionist formulation, only the second of these types of knowledge is a realistic candidate for knowledge given to the system in advance of development (Elman et al., 1996).

Although static networks fit Fodor's notion of development, it has been argued that generative networks are examples of systems that can increase their representational power through learning, with the addition of hidden units to improve performance (Quartz, 1993). Thus generative networks seem to be well fitted to model the increase in complexity of cognition during development. However, a caveat must be introduced: to some extent, the claim that generative networks increase their representational power is a matter of frame of reference. From the point of view of the task-specific network, the representational power indeed increases. However, if hidden units are seen as analogous to neurons (or clusters of neurons or cell assemblies or neural circuits), these must have been available in the cognitive system to begin with, albeit not pre-committed to a specific problem. The representational power of the overall system would only change if new hidden units were "grown from scratch." On the other hand, if one described a generative network as initially containing a large set of hidden units which it chooses to use only later on in learning (Marcus, 1998a), then the network's representational power would be fixed by this total number of units.

Two other theoretical issues are now briefly considered. The first relates to whether connectionist models are actually sufficiently powerful learning devices to explain the acquisition of the competencies we witness in humans. The second relates to the developmental origin of the network architectures that we see presented for each model. Where do task-specific networks come from?

Learning within any system at all must employ *biases* to get off the ground (a basic axiom within theories of machine learning; see Mitchell, 1997). The biases contained in connectionist systems correspond to the constraints listed above, and serve just this role of determining what theories the network will consider in learning about a given domain. In a sense, the constraints are the "helping hand" that the system receives to enable it to succeed at learning. Of course, whether learning is ultimately successful depends not just on this "helping hand" but also on the complexity of the problem to be learned. For example, a network with too few hidden units may fail to learn a complex set of input–output mappings but be effective in learning a simpler problem. A number of theorists have suggested that certain capacities that humans display could not be learned given the information available in the environment and the constraints typically built into the connectionist networks we have considered (see e.g. Fodor & Pylyshyn, 1988). These capacities usually involve situations characterized by the use of rules, for example in high-level reasoning and language. Rules are hard for connectionist systems to learn because such networks derive their knowledge of content through exposure to associations between inputs and outputs. While networks can extend this knowledge to novel situations, these situations must be similar in some respects to those previously encountered, whereas rules imply generalization to situations without such similarity. Since humans successfully acquire abilities in rule-based domains such as language, many theorists maintain that the constraints available in network models are insufficient and that these models will require a pre-existing rule-based processing system; the system will initially contain blank rules and then sets the content of these rules through learning (Marcus, 1998b).

Although this view may ultimately be right, three kinds of problems arise. Firstly, current networks can often produce behavior that looks as if the model were following rules, as if it were simulating a rule-based system (e.g., McClelland, 1989). Secondly, it is not uncontroversially established that humans themselves use rules in cognition. Thirdly, non-connectionist, rule-based computational models of development have great difficulty in accounting for mechanisms of change. By contrast, the very strength of connectionist models is that they are plausible candidates for mechanisms of change in cognitive development. When connectionist networks have been applied to the domain of language, where the case for rule-based representations of syntactic structure appears strongest, recent models of sentence-processing have produced an interesting finding. Recurrent connectionist networks that attempt to acquire this rule-based behavior are only partially successful. However, it turns out that the limitations the networks display conform to similar limitations shown by people when processing sentences (Christiansen & Chater, in press). The current connectionist/rule-based models debate is unlikely to be resolved until either connectionist network models are put forward that convincingly demonstrate the acquisition of apparently rule-based behaviors, or rule-based computational models are put forward that incorporate plausible mechanisms of change.

Lastly in this section, we consider the origin of the architectures proposed to explain performance in each domain. It is a standard assumption in cognitive psychology that the adult cognitive system can be decomposed into specialized components or modules, but some developmentalists claim on neuroconstructivist grounds that high-level modules are more likely the gradual product of development than reflecting the innate structure of the brain (Johnson, 1999; Karmiloff-Smith, 1992, 1998). However, all of the computational models of development we have seen so far focus on explaining only one domain – that is, they assume a module dedicated to learning the computations in a given domain prior to exposure to the training set (see discussion in Karmiloff-Smith, 1992). There is a model for balance scale problems, a model for seriation, and so on, each with input and output representations encoding information specific to its domain. In the broader picture, there is a step missing in connectionist theories of cognitive development. If development itself produces such modules, what is the nature of the developmental process that produces modules? Connectionist work is beginning to address this issue (see Jacobs, 1999, for a review). The basic idea is that although areas of the neocortex may not initially be specialized to particular cognitive domains, they will differ in their computational properties (i.e. in terms of the constraints we discussed earlier). A given set of computational properties equips a given area to be particularly effective in processing a given domain (e.g., recurrent connections would equip a network to process sequences). Areas might thus have *domain-relevant* rather than *domain-specific* properties (Karmiloff-Smith, 1998). Their content is not fixed, and in principle, they could be used to acquire other domains for which they are less well suited, although performance would then be sub-optimal. Apart from this computational heterogeneity, areas would also be distinguished by the input and output systems to which they are initially connected. A process of competition between different areas would lead to specialization and the emergence of modular structure. Thus Jacobs, Jordan, and Barto (1991) showed how specialization to perform "what" and "where" processing in a model of visual object recognition could emerge from a network which at the outset only contained components differing in their computational properties. Work of this nature is a necessary step for connectionist models of development, so that the field can consider some of the more high-level aspects of development, such as strategy formation, the interaction between modules (such as between modalities), and phenomena thought to require "representational re-description" (Karmiloff-Smith, 1992).

Connectionist Models of Atypical Development

Developmental disorders can be classified into four groups: genetic disorders caused by well-understood genetic abnormalities (e.g., Fragile X syndrome, Down's syndrome, Williams syndrome, Turner's syndrome); disorders defined by a behavioral deficit (e.g., developmental dyslexia, Specific Language Impairment, autism); mental retardation of unknown etiology; and disorders resulting from environmental factors (e.g., an impoverished environment, fetal alcohol syndrome). The first and last of these groups distinguish the locus of initial causality in terms of a nature/nurture distinction. The middle two groups tell us about the current understanding of the field of such disorders. For example, disorders like SLI and autism appear to have a genetic component but the genes involved are not yet identified (Bishop, North, & Donlan, 1995; Pennington & Smith, 1997; Simonoff, Bolton, & Rutter, 1998).

The first research aim of the field of developmental cognitive neuropsychology has been to characterize the strengths and weaknesses exhibited in each disorder, i.e.

to describe its *behavioral phenotype*. Temple (1997, p. 5) outlined two further aims. The first is to use developmental disorders to inform and expand our current understanding of normal development. For example, if in a certain disorder, ability A develops in the absence of ability B, one might claim that ability B is not necessary for the development of A. The second aim is to identify what Temple describes as "intact subsystems" within a disorder, which might then be utilized in an educational or remedial context.

Despite the apparent simplicity of these aims, the terminology of "intact subsystems" is in fact controversial, and highlights a current debate in the field. The identification of intact and damaged components of the cognitive system is an approach that originates in research on adults with brain damage. In the field of adult cognitive neuropsychology, patterns of preserved and impaired abilities in adults with different types of brain damage have been used to identify the structure of specialized components within the cognitive system. But Bishop (1997) and Karmiloff-Smith (1997) amongst others have argued that this approach is inappropriate for the study of developmental disorders. Most obviously, using the adult system as a model for a developing infant or child system offers no explanatory role for *development* in developmental disorders. Use of the adult model in this context relies on two assumptions, both of which are unlikely to be true. The first is that the specialized components found in the adult system are present in the infant system. However, in the previous section we saw that specialized components are most likely an outcome of development rather than a precursor to it (Karmiloff-Smith, 1992). Second, the adult model needs to assume that if a specialized component is initially damaged in a developmental disorder, the rest of the cognitive system can nevertheless develop normally around it. However, such independence between components does not seem to be a characteristic of normal cognitive development where, early on, interactivity is more typical (Bishop, 1997).

The alternative to the adult brain damage model is to view developmental disorders as the outcome of a long development process occurring in a system in which there are different initial computational constraints (Elman et al., 1996; Karmiloff-Smith, 1998; Oliver, Johnson, Karmiloff-Smith, & Pennington, 2000). Causes are seen not as the failure of high-level specialized cognitive components for, say, language or reasoning about mental states, but in terms of low-level deficits in neural connectivity or the firing properties of particular neurons. These deficits may initially be small, but become exaggerated by the process of development so that marked behavioral deficits are apparent in the adult state. This perspective predicts that atypical systems could show strengths as well as weaknesses, perhaps even demonstrating behavior at a higher level than typically developing individuals. Even where behavior appears normal in a given developmental disorder, it may have atypical cognitive processes underlying it (Karmiloff-Smith, 1998).

Connectionist models of cognitive development are an ideal framework within which to explore this latter view of developmental disorders because, as we have seen, such models throw a particular spotlight on the role of initial computational constraints in development (Karmiloff-Smith & Thomas, in press). The ability of a model to acquire information from a given domain is limited by its initial architecture, activation dynamics, learning algorithm, and the representations with which the domain is depicted. In connectionist models of typical development, such design decisions are justified as far as possible via empirical evidence. A model is then judged successful if it captures the endstate competencies of the system as well as the developmental trajectory through which it passes. The opportunity here is to demonstrate that theoretically motivated alterations to the initial constraints of a normal model can capture both the atypical trajectory and endstate behavioral deficits found in a particular developmental disorder.

Connectionist models of behavioral phenotypes

Developmental dyslexia.   Perhaps the largest body of work in this area has been dedicated to the investigation of the possible computational causes of developmental dyslexia. A number of connectionist models have attempted to simulate the reading process in adults, a process characterized in this context as learning to map between representations of the orthographic and phonological properties of word forms, and their corresponding meanings (see also Snowling, ch. 18 this volume). The general computational framework postulates that hidden units mediate the mappings between these three sources of information, and that processing is both bottom-up and top-down (Seidenberg & McClelland, 1989). In the usual case, however, only a portion of this framework is implemented within a working model. While few current models constitute serious attempts to capture the developmental processes of early reading acquisition (see Zorzi et al., 1998a, for an exception), these models do commence with randomized connection strengths and use training on large word sets to acquire the adult processing structures. On this basis, several attempts have been made to alter initial constraints in these models such that at the end of training, the network exhibits the behavioral features of dyslexia. The target is to capture two particular clusters of deficits. In *phonological dyslexia*, children and adults predominantly show difficulties in reading novel words. In *surface dyslexia*, there is a difficulty in reading words whose pronunciations form exceptions to the usual way letters map onto sounds.

With regard to surface dyslexia, an impairment in reading exception words is simulated by altering any initial constraints that reduce the general ability of the network to learn. Exception words will be the first to suffer from this degradation, since they are inconsistent with most of the knowledge gained from exposure to reading words. Constraints that have this effect have included a reduction in the initial number of hidden units in the network mapping between orthography and phonology (Bullinaria, 1997; Harm & Seidenberg, 1999; Plaut et al., 1996; Seidenberg & McClelland, 1989; Zorzi, Houghton, & Butterworth, 1998b), a less efficient learning algorithm (Bullinaria, 1997), less training (Harm & Seidenberg, 1999), and a slower learning rate (Harm & Seidenberg, 1999).

Phonological dyslexia represents a case of developing an insufficiently general function relating orthography to phonology. This could derive from input and output representations that themselves are insufficiently general (Brown, 1997; Plaut et al., 1996; Seidenberg & McClelland, 1989), or network constraints that prevent a general function being learnt even when given appropriate initial representations (Harm & Seidenberg, 1999; Zorzi et al., 1998a). Since reading assumes a large pre-existing spoken vocabulary, some researchers have focused on the development of phonological representations in isolation, following the hypothesis that problems with phonology precede the attempt to relate visual word forms to pronunciations. For example, Harm and Seidenberg (1999) separately manipulated weight change algorithms and architectural constraints in a model of the development of phonology, to explore what initial alterations would generate insufficiently general representations at the end of training.

It is notable that several manipulations have been proposed to simulate each form of dyslexia. To the extent that these manipulations are mutually successful, one might infer that there are many ways to produce the same behavioral deficits. This is a point to which we will return shortly. In terms of dyslexia, the next research step will be to determine which of these manipulations are computationally equivalent accounts and which are sufficiently distinct to generate different empirically testable predictions.

Specific language impairment.   In Specific Language Impairment (SLI), there is a serious limitation in language ability without associated impairments in hearing, low IQ, or neurological damage (Leonard, 1998; see also Dodd & Crosbie, ch. 21 this volume). It has been proposed that these individuals show relatively greater deficits in using grammatical rules than in accessing lexical items. Problems with inflectional morphology are often cited as an example. For instance, in English past tense formation, individuals with SLI fail to show the usual advantage of regular past tense formation (talk-talked) over irregular (creep-crept), and fail to inflect the root form in many cases, producing "unmarking" errors (e.g., van der Lely & Ullman, 2001). Hoeffner (1992) constructed a connectionist model of inflectional morphology designed to learn the mappings between the meanings of verbs and their phonological forms under a variety of inflections, including past tense, third person –s and progressive –ing suffixes (e.g. [jump] → jump, jumped, jumps, jumping). Hoeffner and McClelland (1993) then altered the initial constraints under which the model was trained in order to simulate SLI. Their aim was to test the hypothesis that SLI is associated with impairments in the processing of speech which affect the development of phonological representations and in turn, cause knock-on effects in learning morphology and syntax (see Leonard, 1998). On the grounds that children with SLI have difficulty in processing low phonetic substance inflections in English, Hoeffner and McClelland systematically degraded the phonological representations of their model such that the network's ability to represent word-final stops and fricatives (including /t/, /d/, and /s/) was particularly impaired.

The model showed slower and more error-prone learning, with differential deficits across the inflection types. Its final performance displayed a dramatic increase in the number of errors where the verb stem was unmarked, as well as difficulty applying the past tense rule to verbs and, to a lesser extent, in producing irregular past tense forms – all characteristics of SLI. Moreover, just as in SLI, the model showed an impairment on morphemic phonemes (e.g., the final /d/ in died) but not phonologically identical phonemes which were non-morphemic (e.g., the final /d/ in need). This is because during training, "die" was often presented in contexts other than with the final /d/, such as in "dies" and "dying." On the other hand, since neither "nees" nor "neeing" existed in the training corpus, "nee" was always presented in the context of a final /d/. "Need" was therefore learned as a single output, while "died" was learned as a stem with an optional (and vulnerable) affix. This result is important because it establishes the viability of a perceptual deficit account that can preferentially target morphemic phonemes.

Despite some impressive features, this model has limitations. Ullman and Gopnik (1999) point out that the model was unable to capture the low performance on irregular as well as regular verbs reported by themselves and by van der Lely and Ullman (2001). Furthermore, the perceptual deficit account of SLI on which it is predicated remains controversial.

Autism. Autism represents a behavioral phenotype with a much wider range of impairments. The disorder is characterized by a central triad of deficits in social interaction, communication, and imagination (see Baron-Cohen et al., ch. 22 this volume). In addition, there are other associated features, including a restricted repertoire of interests, an obsessive desire for sameness, savant abilities, excellent rote memory, a preoccupation with parts of objects, improved perceptual discrimination, and an impaired ability to form abstraction or generalize knowledge to new situations (see Happé, 1994, for a review).

Cohen (1994) suggested that simple categorization networks could capture the fact that in some cases, children with autism have trouble acquiring simple discriminations and attend to a restricted range of stimuli, while in others children have good discrimination and indeed very good memory but seem to rely on representing too many unique details of stimuli. Cohen concluded that evidence from neuropathological investigations of the brains of affected individuals was suggestive of abnormal wiring patterns in various brain regions. In comparison with the normal brain, the structural deficits were consistent with too few neurons in some areas, such as the cerebellum, and too many neurons in other areas, such as the amygdala and hippocampus. Cohen showed that simple classification networks with too few hidden units showed a failure to learn, while those with a surfeit of hidden units showed very fast learning, but subsequently generalization became poor, and the network increasingly responded according to particular details of the training set. Interestingly in this case, neuropathological evidence was used to motivate alterations to initial constraints in a cognitive model, such that the performance of the network made contact with behavioral deficits of the disorder (see Mareschal & Thomas, in press, for detailed discussion of this model).

Gustafsson (1997) has argued that alterations to the dynamics of learning in low-level sensory features maps could also account for differences in perceptual discrimination in autism. Gustafsson proposed that the relevant atypical computational constraint would be the level of inhibition existing between units in self-organizing feature maps. In these maps, units compete with each other to represent particular aspects of the input. If the competition is too fierce, the argument goes, units will end up defending too small a territory – that is, they will come to represent too fine a level of detail in the sensory input to support robust categorization, although perceptual discrimination will be facilitated. This idea has yet to be tested in a direct implementation, although Oliver et al. (2000) have explored related ideas (see Thomas, 2000).

O'Loughlin and Thagard (2000) have proposed that a similar idea applied to a very much higher-level (and less developmental) model may also account for difficulties in theory-of-mind reasoning in autism. Their model exhibited a deficit in reasoning about false beliefs, produced by high levels of inhibition between representations of concepts in a hand-wired interactive network. The system reasons by settling into a stable activation state. Cycling activation is constrained by the inhibitory and facilitatory connections that represent the consistency between beliefs, each belief being represented by a single unit. With heightened inhibition, however, the network falls into a stable state before it has time to integrate all aspects of its knowledge. In particular, there is insufficient time for knowledge about false beliefs to override information about the state of the world directly fed from the perceptual system. The attempt to link low- and high-level models of autistic characteristics via alterations to a similar computation constraint is novel. One might question the validity of attempting to link such disparate levels of description, and the theory-of-mind model certainly sheds much developmental and biological validity. However, together these proposals represent one of the few exceptions to the current trend in this field of addressing the behavioral deficits of a disorder in isolation.

Modeling a developmental disorder with clear genetic cause: Williams syndrome

Williams syndrome (WS) is a rare neurodevelopmental disorder, caused by a micro-deletion on one copy of chromosome 7 (Tassabehji et al., 1999). It results in specific physical, cognitive, and behavioral abnormalities (Karmiloff-Smith, 1998). The syndrome has been of particular interest to cognitive scientists because individuals with WS exhibit an uneven cognitive-linguistic profile, together with mental retardation (Howlin, Davies, & Udwin, 1998). Full IQ scores, typically between 50 and 70, mask differences in specific cognitive abilities: individuals with WS frequently display relatively good verbal abilities alongside deficient visuo-spatial abilities (e.g. difficulties in constructing patterns, drawing, etc.). While this is the most salient disparity, there are others. People with WS often perform within the normal range on certain standardized tests for face recognition (Bellugi, Wang, & Jernigan, 1994; Udwin & Yule, 1991), and show relatively good performance on theory-of-mind tasks (Karmiloff-Smith, Klima, Bellugi, Grant, & Baron-Cohen, 1995). By contrast, they exhibit difficulties in numerical cognition (Karmiloff-Smith et al., 1995), and in problem-solving and planning (Bellugi et al., 1994).

The dissociation of cognitive abilities in WS has led to the use of this syndrome to support arguments concerning the independence of certain cognitive abilities during development, in particular the developmental independence of general cognition and language (see Dodd & Crosbie, ch. 21 this volume). However, it has also been used to attempt a fine-scaled fractionation of the language system itself. Thus, Pinker (1994, 1999) and Clahsen and Almazan (1998) have claimed that individuals with WS have intact mental representations of grammatical knowledge but an impairment to the system which stores knowledge about individual words. The genetic nature of the syndrome then leads to the claim that dissociations found in the language abilities of individuals with WS can serve to reveal the innate structure of the language system – for instance, that the distinct processing of grammatical rules versus word knowledge is built into the cognitive system prior to birth.

The experimental evidence put forward to support this picture once again comes from the acquisition of the English past tense, where it has been claimed that individuals with WS show a specific difficulty in producing irregularly inflected past tense forms (Clahsen & Almazan, 1998). Theoretical arguments are based on a particular (verbal) model of the acquisition of past tense formation (Pinker, 1994). Pinker proposed that the acquisition of the past tense involves two mechanisms, one that learns the grammatical rule (add –ed to the verb stem), the other that learns about individual words that are exceptions to the rule. (This is a good example of a theoretical approach wishing to ascribe an innate rule-processing mechanism to the cognitive system to permit it to learn rule-based behavior.) If separate mechanisms indeed underlie formation of regular and irregular past tense forms, then it is assumed that difficulties in inflecting one of these forms can be taken as revealing impairments to the respective mechanism. In WS, then, the evidence would imply a deficit to the mechanism processing irregulars. We saw earlier the claim that individuals with SLI have difficulties forming *regular* past tenses. By the same logic, SLI would imply a disorder with a deficit to the regular rule mechanism. Taken together, Pinker (1999) has argued that these two disorders represent a "genetic double dissociation" of two mechanisms in the language system (p. 262).

Three points are of interest here. Firstly, Pinker's theory is not the only one that seeks to explain the acquisition of inflectional morphology. A number of neural network models have been proposed seeking to explain how this partially regular domain might be acquired (e.g., Plunkett & Marchman, 1991; Plunkett & Juola, 1999). These models have demonstrated that a neural network learning the relationship between phonological representations of verb stems and past tense forms, can successfully acquire both regular and irregular forms in the same network, as well as extend the "add –ed" rule to novel exemplars (see Pinker, 1999; Thomas & Karmiloff-Smith, 2001a, for discussions). These models make no a priori division in their architecture between processing structures for regulars and irregulars. In contrast to the verbal theory offered by Pinker, these connectionist systems are working computational models of typical development, evaluated both against the type and quantities of errors they make during learning and against their success in acquiring the domain. We will shortly see this alternative model used to explore atypical language development in WS.

Secondly, the argument that deficits in WS relate to damage to particular processing structures in a model of adult performance represents a classic example of an attempt to extend a brain damage approach to a developmental disorder. As an illustration, here is the claim made by Clahsen and Almazan on the basis of poor WS performance on irregular past tense formations: "[the] computational [rule-based] system for language is *selectively spared*, yielding excellent performance on syntactic tasks and on regular inflection, whereas the lexical system and/or its access mechanism required for irregular inflection are *impaired*" (1998, p. 193, italics added). The explanation of the behavioral deficit is couched in terms of damage to an adult system – an impairment to lexical memory – alongside other components which are claimed to be spared or intact. The proposal contains no role for development, and the "intact" component is assumed to have reached its normal endstate. This explanatory framework becomes obvious when Pinker directly compares the behavior of individuals with Williams syndrome to past tense deficits shown by patients with Alzheimer's disease and aphasia (Pinker, 1994).

Thirdly, the initial data collected to support this claim had limitations, both in the small number of participants with WS involved in the study and in the nature of the control data against which their performance was compared. Subsequent to these initial findings, the largest study to date (Thomas, Grant, Barham, Gsödl, Laing, Lakusta, Tyler, Grice, Paterson, & Karmiloff-Smith, 2001) suggested that the performance of individuals with WS is in fact best captured by three characteristics. Firstly, children and adults with WS are delayed in their production of past tense forms, showing a level of accuracy demonstrated by much younger typically developing children. This is consistent with other findings that language development in WS is often delayed (e.g., Harris, Bellugi, Bates, Jones, & Rossen, 1997). Secondly, while individuals with WS do show poorer performance on exception verbs than on regular verbs, this appears to be in step with their delayed performance, since younger children also find exception verbs harder than regular verbs. There is no *specific* deficit for irregular verbs. Thirdly, individuals with WS are significantly less willing to generalize what they know about existing verbs to novel verbs, for instance in extending the regular rule (crog–crogged).

Thomas and Karmiloff-Smith (2001a) set out to explore whether alterations to the initial constraints of a connectionist model of past tense development could account for these three features of the WS data. The past tense network mapped from verb stem to past tense form in the presence of semantic information. Various claims have been made that there are in fact subtle deficits in the language system of individuals with Williams syndrome. These include the proposals that their phonological representations may be atypical and perhaps rely on sensitive auditory processing (Karmiloff-Smith, Grant, Berthoud, Davies, Howlin, & Udwin, 1997; Majerus, Palmisano, van der Linden, Barisnikov, & Poncelet, 2001; Neville, Mills, & Bellugi, 1994;), that their semantic representations may be atypical (Rossen, Klima, Bellugi, Bihrle, & Jones, 1996; Temple, Almazan, & Sherwood, in press), or that semantic information about words may be poorly integrated with phonology (Frawley, in press; Karmiloff-Smith et al., 1998). In order to explore the viability of these different accounts to explain the pattern of performance in the past tense task, Thomas and Karmiloff-Smith altered the initial constraints of the network model to implement each type of deficit.

They found the following results. First, a manipulation of the phonological representations that reduced their similarity and redundancy was sufficient to reproduce the delay for regular and irregular past tense forms, as well as the reduction in generalization. Second, the pattern could also be produced when noise was added to the information coming from the semantic system during the acquisition of the past tense. Third, elimination or weakening of the semantic contribution produced a pattern inconsistent with the WS data, including a selective delay for irregular verbs and no reduction in generalization. Lastly, slowed learning failed to produce a reduction in generalization, suggesting that delayed development alone was insufficient to explain WS performance, and atypical computational constraints are involved. This modeling work was therefore able to test the viability of several competing hypotheses on the causes of language impairments in Williams syndrome. Manipulations to phonology or to the integration of phonology and semantics were able to simulate the past tense data; manipulations to semantics alone or delayed development were not.

What if the WS data *had* shown a selective deficit on irregular verbs – could the model have shown this pattern? In addition to impoverishing semantic information, performance on irregular verbs could be preferentially delayed either by employing a two-layer network which restricted the complexity of the function that the network could learn between verb stems and past tense forms, or by a calibrated reduction in the plasticity of the learning algorithm. However, none of these three manipulations resulted in an impairment to irregular verbs at the end of training. Endstate deficits on irregular verbs only emerged if training was terminated earlier than usual or if the network was forced to learn at a slower rate, so that by the end of training, regular verbs had reached ceiling but irregular verbs had not. In this latter case, a selective deficit for irregular verbs would then be apparent.

Although not necessarily relevant to Williams syndrome, the potential of the past tense model to produce a selective developmental deficit in irregular past tense formation leads to an important theoretical point. When Thomas and Karmiloff-Smith's findings are taken in combination with Hoeffner and McClelland's (1993) model of past tense formation in SLI, it is evident that alterations in initial constraints are sufficient to produce either selective impairments in regular or irregular past tense formation at endstate. Compared to Pinker and Clahsen and Almazan's static explanation based on selective damage to an *adult* model of the past tense system, these computational developmental models give a more plausible explanation of deficits in developmental disorders. In addition, the two models imply that developmental double dissociations should not automatically be taken to reveal structure within the cognitive system: neither of these models employed a structural distinction between components for processing regular and irregular verbs, yet regular and irregular verb performance could be selectively dissociated by different changes to the initial network constraints.

Modeling implications for atypical development

We will use the Thomas and Karmiloff-Smith model to focus on a number of theoretical issues. The first issue addresses how easy it is to produce a given pattern of developmental impairments in these models. A number of connectionist models of developmental disorders have simply demonstrated that manipulating one network constraint is sufficient to capture some target atypical data. But how many other network constraints did the researchers test? What if many possible manipulations applied to the model at the start of training successfully simulate the target data? Then the simulations would be consistent with many different theoretical accounts of the impairment. The model would fail to usefully constrain the theory (unless, of course, the theory was that a given impairment had many causes). When a model with a single altered constraint simulates a pattern of atypical data, how can we be confident that we have the right explanation for the emergence of a behavioral deficit?

In addition to their theoretically driven manipulations, Thomas and Karmiloff-Smith (2001a) systematically explored a range of other manipulations to the initial state of the model, including varying the number of hidden units, varying the architecture, and varying the learning algorithm, adding noise to processing, and altering the threshold function in the processing units. When they compared the results, they found that the three features of the WS data were in fact generated by very few manipulations. However, interestingly, many of the manipulations produced one or two of the three features. A single endstate deficit might be the result of a number of different initial network manipulations, whereas patterns involving several features were harder to come by. One might take this result as offering a cautionary note for disorders that are defined on the basis of narrow behavioral impairments (e.g., "grammatical" SLI; van der Lely, 1997). The modeling work suggests a high risk that such disorder groups will contain individuals for whom the computational cause of the impairment is different. How can we avoid this? Simulations generate a possible solution. Groups of individuals who share the same underlying cause are likely to show smaller levels of variance across other related behavioral measures, and across longitudinal testing, compared to groups of heterogeneous cause (see Thomas & Karmiloff-Smith, 2001b).

We have encountered the theoretical debate that adult brain damage models are inappropriate for explaining behavioral deficits in developmental disorders. Here again, developmental connectionist models can help us evaluate this claim. Connectionist models of adult performance have been widely used to simulate cognitive breakdown under brain damage (see e.g., Reggia, Ruppin, & Berndt, 1996). Now we can straightforwardly compare the deficits in performance of a network model that experiences the same damage prior to training (as in a developmental disorder) with one that experiences it at the end of training (as in adult brain damage). Are the behavioral deficits the same in each case? Thomas & Karmiloff-Smith (2001c) carried out this comparison for several forms of damage in the past tense network: the elimination of network connections, the addition of noise to unit activations, and alterations to the ability of units to discriminate activation levels (i.e., the sharpness of their activation thresholds).

The results showed a highly complex pattern relating adult (endstate) and developmental (startstate) deficits. Sometimes damage at the two points produced the same effect (eliminating connections) but to different degrees (removing connections in the endstate was far more damaging, since the network could no longer reorganize around the damage). Sometimes deficits appeared in one case but not in the other (higher discrimination produced deficits only when applied to the endstate; noise produced deficits only when applied to the startstate). Sometimes the effect of a manipulation was selective (higher discrimination only impaired performance on exception verbs), whereas sometimes it was global (noise caused a deficit for regulars, exceptions, and in generalization). Given that the startstate and the endstate are separated by a dynamic developmental process, it is perhaps unsurprising to find in this model that the relationship between them is so complex. This modeling work does, however, tend to support the contention that adult deficits are unlikely to serve as a reliable analogy to developmental deficits.

Finally, in this chapter we have encountered modeling work that seeks to explain two types of variation: the variation in cognitive performance as individuals get older, and the variation between individuals who are developing typically compared to those who are developing atypically. There is a third type of variation, however, that of individual differences of intelligence. There is insufficient space here to describe the initial connectionist work on modeling intelligence. However, it is worth mentioning that it is an open question whether each type of variation should be explained in these cognitive models by manipulating similar computational parameters, or whether each type of variation should be explained by appeal to different parameters. Indeed, there is a further debate about whether learning and development should themselves be ascribed to different mechanisms of change. Thomas and Karmiloff-Smith (in press) recently compared connectionist models of the three types of variation. They concluded that thus far, similar manipulations have been used to model each type of variation (a popular candidate being alterations in the number of hidden units). However, this similarity may be an artefact of the infancy of the respective fields, and explanations for sources of variation may well diverge as time goes on.

Conclusion

In this chapter we have discussed the use of computational models for exploring possible mechanisms of change in cognitive development, focusing in particular on connectionist modeling. We have seen how these neurally inspired models of cognition can learn complex cognitive abilities when exposed to a training environment. Importantly, in theoretical terms, we have shown how these systems are not blank sheets, but contain constraints that shape the content that they can learn. We also explored how differences in the initial constraints under which a network develops can provide hypotheses about the causes of behavioral deficits in developmental disorders such as developmental dyslexia, autism, Specific Language Impairment, and Williams syndrome. This theoretical approach to explaining developmental deficits was contrasted with an earlier approach attempting to conceive of such deficits as equivalent to cases of adult brain damage. We finish the chapter with two final points.

First, it is important to clarify an idea that may have become obscured in the discussion of the many models outlined in this chapter. In any modeling endeavor, the aim is not solely to produce a model that can simulate human behavior, whether typical or atypical. The aim is to derive an explanation of the target behavior. Explanations based on connectionist models tend to be in terms of particular learning systems being exposed to cognitive domains with particular (statistical) structures, as we saw in the case of the balance scale and conservation models. However, they must be clearly specified and empirically testable. It is not sufficient merely to point to a working model or list a set of connection strengths! Models allow the viability and coherence of theoretical ideas to be tested and, in so doing, drive theory forward. They also provide the opportunity to unify disparate empirical phenomena in a unified (and implemented) explanatory framework. But since models can be run in novel conditions, they also play an essential role in generating new, testable empirical predictions, as we saw in the case of the models of seriation and of infants' expectancies concerning occluded objects.

Second, two major challenges remain for connectionist models of development in the future. The first challenge we alluded to earlier, in the need for more detailed accounts of the emergence of modules, and the need for simulations that address behavior arising from cross-module interaction. The second challenge relates to training environments. The construction of a developmental model requires not just modeling the relevant cognitive system but also modeling the environment to which the system is exposed. The way in which connectionist models of development have focused attention on the exact nature of the environment has been one of their great strengths. However, the majority of current network models are passive recipients of their environment. In contrast, children are agents who, to a greater or lesser extent, control and seek out their learning environment. The next step for modeling will be to address the active nature of the child in development. This is of course a very complex issue. "Dynamical" network systems, whose current performance affects their exposure to future training experiences, are liable to lapse into unstable, fluctuating states of temporary knowledge. It is probable that multi-component learning systems will be required to protect the system from this danger and create a relatively stable trajectory of development (see e.g. McClelland, McNaughton, & O'Reilly, 1995, for initial work on this idea).

Much work remains to be done in the modeling of development. However, connectionist networks provide an exceptionally useful tool for studying cognitive change – a tool that, as a servant of empirical investigation, can finally allow us to gain significant purchase on the role of the constraints of the mind and constraints of the environment in jointly driving cognitive development.

CHAPTER TWENTY-SEVEN

Individual Differences in Cognitive Development

Robert J. Sternberg

Janet and Jeannette are identical twins. At 10 years of age, they look almost identical and people sometimes mix them up. Once they tried to fool their teachers by showing up for each other's classes, and succeeded until one of the teachers inferred from the laughing of children in the class that something was amiss. Janet and Jeannette are similar in many ways beside physical appearance. Their performance in school is quite similar and even their patterns of strength and weakness are quite similar – strong performance in language arts and not so strong performance in mathematics, for example. Neither is musically inclined, but both are athletically inclined, and they compete in the same sports, including with each other. They are each other's fiercest competitors in tennis and they also play against each other in school sports.

Jamie and Johnny are also twins, but they are fraternal twins. At 7 years of age they are rather similar in appearance, although no one is likely to confuse Jamie for Johnny, or Johnny for Jamie. Jamie is two inches taller than Johnny, and weighs at least 20 pounds more than Johnny. His hair is also a much darker brown than Johnny's. The twins are also similar in some of their interests. But they are as notable for their differences as for their similarities. Jamie is reading two years beyond grade level, whereas Johnny is barely reading at grade level. Jamie is doing well in arithmetic, but Johnny is struggling just to

Preparation of this chapter was supported by Grant REC-9979843 from the National Science Foundation and by a grant under the Javits Act Program (Grant No. R206R950001) as administered by the Office of Educational Research and Improvement, US Department of Education. Grantees undertaking such projects are encouraged to express freely their professional judgment. This article, therefore, does not necessarily represent the position or policies of the Office of Educational Research and Improvement or the US Department of Education, and no official endorsement should be inferred.

get by. Johnny, on the other hand, already has shown considerable skill on the piano, whereas Jamie has so far shown no special musical talents at all. Johnny also has had his artwork exhibited in a special section of his classroom because it is so distinguished. Jamie also has shown no special talent for art.

What is it that leads children to be similar in some ways but different in others, whether they are identical twins, fraternal twins, ordinary siblings, or simply two children of the same age? This chapter will deal with this question. The focus of the chapter will be on cognitive skills, although, of course, children can be similar and different with respect to many other kinds of skills as well.

Paradigms for Understanding Individual Differences in Cognition and Cognitive Development

Several different paradigms have been proposed for understanding individual differences. Seven of the main paradigms are the psychometric paradigm, the learning paradigm, the Piagetian paradigm, the Vygotskian paradigm, the information-processing paradigm, the biological paradigm, and the systems paradigm (Sternberg, 1990; see also Sternberg, 2000; Sternberg & Powell, 1983).

The psychometric paradigm seeks understanding of development through the use of psychometric theory and tests. Cognitive development might be understood partly in terms of differentiation of cognitive factors, with the sources of individual differences underlying task performance becoming more specific over age. Individual differences might derive, in part, from more differentiation at a given age, or from higher scores on factors representing greater degrees of facility in an ability. For example, one child might have a higher verbal comprehension factor score than another, signifying greater ability to understand verbal materials.

The learning paradigm (see Sternberg & Powell, 1983) provides understanding of cognitive development in terms of mechanisms of classical and instrumental conditioning, and possibly social learning as well. Individual differences derive from rates of reinforcement and from the discriminative value of the reinforcements. For example, a child who is reinforced frequently and only (or largely) for using English correctly might develop better verbal skills than would a child who receives less reinforcement or who is reinforced for using poor English. More recently, learning paradigms have encompassed connectionist models of cognitive development (Thomas & Karmiloff-Smith, ch. 26 this volume).

The Piagetian paradigm (Piaget, 1972a; Smith, ch. 23 this volume) provides understanding of cognitive development through the mechanism of equilibration, by which children balance assimilation and accommodation in understanding new concepts. Individual differences are not emphasized in this paradigm. Nevertheless, it is quite plausible to think about individual differences within Piaget's framework. For example, a child might first assimilate many new animals into the schema for dog, only later making accommodations by which new categories are formed that differentiate, say, wolves from dogs.

The Vygotskian paradigm (Vygotsky, 1978; Rowe & Wertsch, ch. 24 this volume) provides an understanding of cognitive development through mechanisms such as internalization – by which concepts that are first learned in a social context are made a part of one's individual cognitive repertoire. Individual differences can arise through more rapid or more effective internalization. Vygotsky (1978) also proposed a zone of proximal development, which represents the difference between what one can learn on one's own and what one can learn with mediation and guidance (see also Feuerstein, 1979). Individual differences in the zone of proximal development might arise if one child is better able to make use of adult guidance than is another child.

The information-processing paradigm (Halford, ch. 25 this volume; also Chen & Siegler, 2000b; Klahr, 1992; Sternberg, 1984; see also Deary, 2000; Lohman, 2000) provides an understanding of cognitive development through specification of how knowledge, mental representations, mental processes, and strategies develop with age. Individual differences are understood in terms of differences in the effectiveness of these elements. For example, one child might be able to execute a set of mental processes more quickly than does another child, or might be able to choose a strategy for solving a problem that is a better strategy than that chosen by another child.

The biological paradigm (Grigorenko, 2000; Vernon, Wickett, Bazana, & Stelmack, 2000) seeks an understanding of cognitive development through an understanding of mechanisms of genetic transmission of characteristics, synaptogenesis, neural conduction, and so forth. Individual differences might be understood, for example, in terms of different genetic patterns inherited by two different children. Most biological researchers conceptualize biological effects as occurring in interaction with the environment. In other words, biological mechanisms affect the child's adaptation to the environment, but the environment also affects how biological mechanisms unfold.

The systems paradigm (e.g., Gardner, 1999; Sternberg, 1997; Thelen, 1992; Thelen & Smith, 1998) seeks an understanding of cognitive development in terms of the interactions of a dynamic system with many interacting elements. Individual differences arise when certain elements of the system are more effective than others, resulting in better performance of the system as a whole. For example, someone who is better at recognizing when he or she has a problem will be more likely to develop mechanisms for solving that problem than will be someone who does not recognize that the problem exists.

In sum, there are a variety of paradigms for understanding cognitive development and individual differences in such development. In the first part of this chapter, I will discuss at some length two paradigms for understanding individual differences in cognition: the psychometric paradigm and the systems paradigm. I will focus on these two because most of the other paradigms described above are discussed in other chapters in this handbook (although not primarily from the standpoint of individual differences, e.g., Smith, Rowe & Wertsch, Halford, this volume). In the second part of the chapter, I will discuss origins and stability of individual differences, in particular, issues of heritability and modifiability of cognitive skills. In the third part of the chapter, I will discuss extremes in individual differences: giftedness and retardation in cognitive skills. In the fourth and last part of the chapter, I will discuss group differences and their relationship to individual differences in cognitive skills.

Two Key Paradigms for Studying Individual Differences in Cognition

The psychometric paradigm

Psychometric theories are unique among the seven paradigms mentioned above in relying primarily upon individual differences both in their formulation and in their verification (or falsification). Psychometric researchers use techniques of data analysis to discover common patterns of individual differences across cognitive tests. These patterns are then hypothesized to emanate from latent sources of individual differences, namely, cognitive abilities.

The Galtonian paradigm

The earliest psychometric theory of note was that of Galton (1883). Galton proposed the existence of two general qualities that he believed to distinguish the more from the less intellectually able. The two sources of individual difference are energy, or the capacity for labor, and sensitivity to physical stimuli. For seven years (1884–90), Galton maintained a laboratory at the Natural History Museum in London where, for a small fee, visitors could have themselves measured on a variety of psychophysical tests allegedly measuring these two sources of individual differences (primarily the second – sensitivity to physical stimuli). Examples of such tests were the ability to discriminate the weights of two objects and sensitivity to various pitches.

Galton's beliefs were introduced to the United States by J. M. Cattell (1890). Cattell proposed a series of psychophysical tests to measure individual differences in cognitive abilities. These tests included dynamometer pressure (greatest possible squeeze of one's hand), rate of arm movement over a distance of 50 cm, the distance on the skin by which two points need to be separated for them to be felt separately, and letter span in memory. Underlying all tests was the assumption that psychophysical tests measure cognitive abilities. For example, Cattell (1890) commented that "the greatest squeeze of the hand may be thought by many to be a purely physiological quantity. It is, however, impossible to separate bodily from mental energy" (p. 374).

The views of Galton and Cattell were dealt a blow by research done by Wissler (1901). This research suggested that the tests in Cattell's battery correlated neither with each other nor with college grades at Columbia University. But the Galtonian approach has never quite disappeared. Indeed, some current research derives from work on individual differences in cognition done by Hunt, Frost, and Lunneborg (1973), which the authors viewed as deriving from the Galtonian tradition in the study of cognitive abilities. Hunt and his colleagues did not use precisely the same tests as Galton or Cattell used. Rather, they shared these early investigators' views of the importance of relatively simple cognitive processes for understanding individual differences in complex processes. In other words, they suggested that complex processing is nothing more than the accretion and accumulation of diverse kinds of simple processing.

The Galton–Cattell view remains influential in some views of cognitive development and individual differences in such development. Anderson (1992) and Jensen (1998), for example, have proposed that attributes of neural architecture and functioning contribute to the development of individual differences in speed, efficiency, and capacity of information-processing systems. These investigators use simple tasks, such as choice reaction time or inspection time to determine which of two lines is longer (see Deary, 2000), to measure neural efficiency.

The Binetian paradigm

Researchers in the tradition of Binet do not believe that complex cognitive processing can be reduced to the accretion and accumulation of simple processing. Alfred Binet and Theodore Simon, commissioned in 1904 by the Minister of Public Instruction in Paris to create a test that would insure that mentally retarded children would receive an adequate education, took a different tack from that of Galton. To these investigators, the core of individual differences in cognitive development is to be found in judgment, or good sense. Binet and Simon pointed out that Helen Keller (see Waxman, ch. 5 this volume) would have done quite poorly on Galton's tests, yet was intelligent in any meaningful sense of the word.

Binet and Simon (1916) proposed a theory consisting of three distinct elements: direction, adaptation, and criticism. These elements, under other names (such as *metacognition*), today still are viewed as important to individual differences in cognition. Direction consists in knowing what has to be done and how it is to be accomplished. When children are required to add two numbers, for example, they give themselves a series of instructions on how to proceed and these instructions form the direction of thought. Adaptation refers to children's selection and monitoring of their strategy during the course of task performance. For example, in solving a mathematics problem, there may be several alternative strategies children can use (see e.g. Siegler, 1996; Siegler & Jenkins, 1989), and adaptation would be involved in deciding which strategy to select. Criticism or control is the ability to criticize one's own thoughts and actions. For example, after solving a mathematical word problem, a child might wish to evaluate the solution to make sure it is sensible.

The ideas of Binet and Simon were brought to the United States by a professor of psychology at Stanford University, L. M. Terman, who was involved in the construction of early versions of what has come to be called the Stanford–Binet Intelligence Test. The tasks on this test were very different from those used by Cattell in his tests. Examples of tests would include verbal absurdities, which requires recognition of why each of a set of statements is foolish; similarities and differences, which requires children to say how each of two objects is the same as, and different from, the other; comprehension, which requires children to solve practical problems of the sort encountered in everyday life; and naming the days of the week. The most recent version of this test is still widely used (Thorndike, Hagen, & Sattler, 1986).

The ideas of Binet are strongly linked to current notions about metacognition, that is, children's knowledge and control of their cognitive processing (e.g., Demetriou,

Efklides, & Platsidou, 1993; Flavell, 1992; Gopnik & Meltzoff, 1997; Goswami, 1996). In a sense, Binet was the first or certainly one of the first metacognitive theorists, recognizing the importance of children's understanding of their own behavior for their cognitive development. Indeed, mentally retarded children, who have low IQs, are distinguished largely for their lack of adequate metacognitive functioning (Borkowski & Cavanaugh, 1979; Butterfield & Belmont, 1977; Campione, Brown, & Ferrara, 1982).

Because intelligence tests have been central to the measurement of individual differences in the development of cognitive skills, it is worth saying something about how they are interpreted.

Intelligence Testing as a Means of Assessing Individual Differences in Cognition

Intelligence tests contain a wide variety of contents, as the examples above indicate. Originally, these tests were designed to yield a mental age, which refers to a child's level of intelligence in comparison to the "average" child of a given age. If, for example, a child performs at a level comparable to that of an average 12-year-old, the child's mental age will be 12, regardless of the child's chronological (physical) age. The tests were designed to yield an intelligence quotient, or IQ, which is the ratio between mental age and chronological age multiplied by 100. A score of 100 signifies that mental age is equivalent to chronological age. The IQ of 100 is thus the average IQ. A score above 100 indicates above-average intelligence and a score below 100 indicates below-average intelligence.

For a variety of reasons, the concept of mental age proved to be problematical. For example, it implied a kind of continuous mental development that was found not to exist, and it implied that mental age would keep increasing indefinitely, which it did not. As a result, IQs in recent years have been computed on the basis of relative performance within a given age group. The IQs derived from this procedure are commonly referred to as *deviation IQs*, to distinguish them from the *ratio IQs* obtained by the older method. Deviation IQ scores are set to have a mean of 100 and a standard deviation of 15 or 16. The most widely used test for children is the Wechsler Intelligence Scale for Children, third edition (WISC-III; Wechsler, 1991). (There is also a Wechsler test for preschool children, the Wechsler Preschool and Primary Scale of Intelligence – WPPSI). The WISC-III measures individual differences in cognitive abilities through two main scales – a verbal scale and a performance scale. The verbal scale includes tests such as similarities, which requires an indication of a way in which two different objects are alike; arithmetic, which requires solution of arithmetic word problems; vocabulary, which requires definition of common English words; and comprehension, which requires understanding of common societal customs. The performance scale includes tests such as picture completion, which requires identification of a missing part in a picture of an object, and picture arrangement, which requires rearrangement of a scrambled set of cartoon-like pictures into an order that tells a coherent story.

Factor theories

Galton, Binet, and Wechsler grounded their work in tests of intelligence. Other researchers used tests, but grounded their work in theories of intelligence. The researchers tested children with tests based on their theories and then analyzed their data. One technique of data analysis they used is factor analysis, which analyzes correlations or covariances among cognitive tests in order to produce a set of hypothetical underlying factors (abilities). Psychometric theories generally have been grounded in the factor as the basic unit of individual differences in cognitive abilities.

The earliest such theory was that of Spearman (1904, 1927), a theory that is still widely accepted today (see e.g. Brand, 1996; Herrnstein & Murray, 1994; Jensen, 1998). According to Spearman, underlying all individual differences in cognitive abilities is a general factor, or *g* factor, which Spearman believed to be due to differences in mental energy. This factor was alleged to permeate performance of all cognitive tests. Spearman also posited specific factors, or *s* factors, which were each specific to single tests.

Not all theorists have accepted the idea of a single factor as responsible for most individual differences in cognition. Thurstone (1938) suggested that seven primary mental abilities underlie individual differences in cognition. The seven factors in Thurstone's theory are verbal comprehension, measured by vocabulary tests; number, measured by tests of computation and simple mathematical problem-solving; memory, measured by tests of picture and word recall; perceptual speed, measured by tests that require the test-taker to recognize small differences in pictures or to cross out the "a"s in strings of letters; space, measured by tests requiring mental rotation of pictures or other objects; verbal fluency, measured by speed with which one can think of words beginning with a certain letter; and inductive reasoning, measured by tests such as analogies and number-series completions.

In recent times, many psychometric theorists have settled on hierarchical models as useful characterizations of individual differences in cognitive abilities. These models combine the general factor of Spearman with the primary kinds of mental abilities of Thurstone by suggesting that the abilities are related hierarchically. One such model, developed by R. Cattell (1971), proposes that general intelligence – at the top of the hierarchy – comprises two major subfactors: fluid ability and crystallized ability. Fluid ability represents the acquisition of new information, or the grasping of new relations and abstractions regarding known information, as required in inductive reasoning tests such as analogies and series completions. Crystallized ability represents the accumulation of knowledge over the lifespan of the child and is measured, for example, in tests of vocabulary, of general information, and of achievement. Subsumed within these two major subfactors are other, more specific factors.

A more detailed hierarchical model, based on a reanalysis of many data sets from hundreds of studies, has been proposed by Carroll (1993). At the top of the hierarchy is general ability; in the middle of the hierarchy are various broad abilities, such as learning and memory processes and the effortless production of many ideas. At the bottom of the hierarchy are many narrow, specific abilities such as spelling ability and reasoning speed. Other similar hierarchical models have been proposed as well (e.g., Gustafsson,

1988; Horn, 1994; Vernon, 1971). According to psychometric theorists, children differ from each other intellectually primarily by virtue of differences in their abilities as revealed by scores on the underlying factors of intelligence. Herrnstein and Murray (1994), among others (e.g., Jensen, 1998), have argued that children with low levels of *g*, or general intelligence, are handicapped both in school and in life, and are less capable of succeeding in a wide variety of life activities, including school performance, getting along with others, and, later in life, performance on the job. Many, although certainly not all psychometric theorists tend to emphasize the role that genes play in the development of intelligence, and tend to view levels of intelligence as relatively fixed rather than as modifiable (e.g., Bouchard, 1998).

The systems paradigm

Systems theories attempt to go beyond psychometric methods and static factors in explaining the development of individual differences in cognitive abilities. Two such theories are the theory of multiple intelligences and the triarchic theory of intelligence.

The theory of multiple intelligences.   Gardner (1983, 1993, 1999) does not view individual differences in cognition, or even intelligence, as singular. Nor does he ever speak of multiple cognitive abilities. Rather, he speaks of multiple intelligences. According to his theory, there are eight (or possibly ten) distinct multiple intelligences. These intelligences are (a) linguistic intelligence, which is used when a child reads a book, writes a paper, or even speaks to a friend; (b) logical-mathematical intelligence, which is used when a child solves a school mathematics problem, or counts change, or tries to make a logical argument in speaking to an authority figure; (c) spatial intelligence, which is used when a child needs to get from one place to another, reads a map, or needs to fit his or her clothes in a trunk when preparing for a camping trip; (d) musical intelligence, which is used when a child sings a song, plays the trumpet, or reads music; (e) bodily-kinesthetic intelligence, which is used when a child dances, plays basketball, runs a race, or throws a ball; (f) interpersonal intelligence, which is used when a child relates to other people, such as when he or she tries to understand his sibling's behavior, motives, or emotions; (g) intrapersonal intelligence, which is used when a child tries to understand him- or herself; and (h) naturalist intelligence, which is used when a child tries to understand patterns in the natural world, such as the kinds of places where trees can and cannot grow. Gardner has also speculated that there may be an additional intelligence, existential intelligence, relating to understanding of matters of existence and one's place in the universe.

Gardner has used converging operations to gather evidence to support his theory of the multiple sources of individual differences in cognition. The base of evidence used by Gardner includes (but is not limited to) the distinctive effects of localized brain damage on specific kinds of intelligences, distinctive patterns of development in each kind of intelligence across the lifespan, evidence from exceptional individuals (from both ends of the spectrum), and evolutionary theory.

Gardner's view of the mind is modular. Modularity theorists believe that different abilities – such as Gardner's intelligences – can be isolated as emanating from distinct portions or modules of the brain. Thus, a major task of existing and future research on intelligence would be to isolate the portions of the brain responsible for each of the intelligences. Gardner has speculated as to at least some of these relevant portions, but hard evidence for the existence of the separate intelligences has yet to be produced: the theory is in need of predictive empirical verification.

There may be multiple kinds of intelligence beyond those suggested by Gardner. For example, Salovey and Mayer (1990; see also J. Mayer, Salovey, & Caruso, 2000) have suggested the existence of *emotional intelligence*, which involves the child's ability to understand and regulate one's emotions (see also Goleman, 1995), and which appears to be relatively distinct from intelligence as it is conventionally conceived. For example, a child who, upon feeling frustrated, inappropriately gets angry and throws temper tantrums might be viewed as having a lower level of emotional intelligence than another child who reacts to frustration in a more prosocial way. Other investigators have discussed a concept of *social intelligence*, which is a form of intelligence used in interacting effectively with other people (Cantor & Kihlstrom, 1987; Ford, 1994; Kihlstrom & Cantor, 2000). For example, a child who effectively relates to other children in the playground might be viewed as effective in social intelligence. Still other investigators have suggested a concept of *practical intelligence*, or the ability to function effectively in everyday life (Sternberg et al., 2000; Wagner, 2000). A child high in practical intelligence, for example, would know how to allocate time in order to get his or her homework done on time. Clearly, psychological concepts of intelligence are becoming much broader than they were just a few years ago. At the same time, not all psychologists accept these broader conceptions.

The triarchic theory of intelligence.   Whereas Gardner emphasizes the separateness of the various aspects of intelligence, I have tended to emphasize the extent to which these aspects work together in the triarchic theory of human intelligence (Sternberg, 1985, 1988, 1997, 1999a, 1999b). According to the triarchic theory, intelligence comprises three aspects, which deal with the relation of intelligence (a) to the internal world, (b) to experience, and (c) to the external world. Intelligence draws on three kinds of information-processing components: (1) metacomponents – executive processes used to plan, monitor, and evaluate problem-solving; (2) performance components – lower-order processes used for implementing the commands of the metacomponents; and (3) knowledge-acquisition components – the processes used for learning how to solve the problems in the first place. Individual differences in cognition derive largely from individual differences in the execution of these three kinds of components. The components are highly interdependent.

Suppose a child was asked by his parents to justify their buying him a toy he wants. To succeed the child would need to draw on all three types of components. The child would use metacomponents to decide on a line of argument (e.g., that the toy is highly educational), plan the line or argument, monitor the argument to see whether it is winning over his parents, and evaluate how well the finished product succeeds in accomplishing his goals (i.e., do his parents buy the toy for him?). The child would draw on past uses of knowledge-acquisition components to know what kinds of arguments do and do not work with his parents. The child would also use performance components for the actual argumentation. In practice, the three kinds of components do not function in isolation. For example, if monitoring the argument reveals that it is not working, the child may then use performance components to initiate another line of argument. The child also stores the knowledge learned about kinds of arguments that do not work with his parents.

These three kinds of components all contribute to three relatively distinct aspects of intelligence. In this "triarchy" of intelligence, analytical abilities are used to analyze, evaluate, critique, or judge, as when a child decides whether to hand over a toy to his sister that the sister argues she has a right to play with. A metacomponent, such as that of planning, might be used by the sister analytically to devise a strategy to convince her brother to let her play with the toy. Creative abilities are used to create, invent, discover, and imagine, as when a child invents novel arguments why he really needs a toy (e.g., that he may see a way to improve on it and thereby start his own line of toys to be sold on the internet). Practical abilities are used to apply, utilize, and implement ideas in the real world, as when the child realizes that despite his wonderful arguments, his parents just are not going to buy him the toy and it is time to quit arguing and wait for another day. Research suggests that the three types of abilities – analytical, creative, and practical – are statistically relatively independent (Sternberg, 1985; Sternberg et al., 2000; Sternberg, Grigorenko, Ferrari, & Clinkenbeard, 1999; Sternberg & Lubart, 1995).

According to the triarchic theory, children may apply their intelligence to many different kinds of problems. For example, some people may be more intelligent in the face of abstract, academic problems, whereas others may be more intelligent in the face of concrete, practical problems. The theory does not define an intelligent child as someone who necessarily excels in all aspects of intelligence. Rather, intelligent children know their own strengths and weaknesses and find ways to capitalize on their strengths and either to compensate for or to correct their weaknesses. For example, a child strong in verbal skills but not in quantitative skills might choose to become a writer rather than an accountant. The point is to make the most of one's strengths and to find ways to improve upon, or at least to live comfortably with, one's weaknesses. Some children are extreme in their strengths and weaknesses, and we consider such children next.

Heredity, Environment, and Modifiability

Since ancient times, people have speculated on the extent to which individual differences among people are due to nature – or heredity – and the extent to which they are due to nurture – or environment. The ancient nature–nurture controversy continues in regard to cognitive skills (Sternberg & Grigorenko, 1997). However, today the large majority of psychologists believe that differences in cognitive skills result from a combination of hereditary and environmental factors.

The degree to which heredity contributes to individual differences in cognitive skills is often expressed in terms of a heritability coefficient, a number on a scale from 0 to 1, such that a coefficient of 0 means that heredity has no influence on variation among children, whereas a coefficient of 1 means that heredity is the only influence on such variation. This coefficient can be applied to cognitive skills or to any other attributes, such as height, weight, or running skills.

It is important to remember that the heritability coefficient indicates variation in measured attributes. The heritability coefficient can tell us only about genetic effects that result in individual differences among children. It tells us nothing about genetic effects where there are no, or only trivial, differences. For example, both how tall you are and how many fingers you have at birth are in large part genetically preprogrammed. But we can use the coefficient of heritability only to assess genetic effects on height, where there are large individual differences. We cannot use the coefficient to understand number of fingers at birth because there is so little variation across children.

It is also important to realize that heritability tells us nothing about the *modifiability* of cognitive skills. A trait can be heritable and yet modifiable. For example, height is highly heritable, with a heritability coefficient greater than .9 in most populations. Yet the height of Europeans and North Americans increased by over 5 cm between 1920 and 1970 (van Wieringen, 1978). Consider, as another example, attributes of corn. Many attributes of corn, including height, are highly heritable. But if one batch of corn seeds was planted in the rich fertile fields of Iowa, and another similar batch was planted in the Mojave desert, the batch planted in Iowa undoubtedly would grow taller and thrive better, regardless of the heritability of the attributes of the corn. In this case, environment would largely determine how well the corn grew (Lewontin, 1974).

These issues apply not just to corn, but also to children! Ramey and his colleagues have shown that it is possible to take children with relatively low IQs, place them in an educational environment that enriches their cognitive functioning, and thereby substantially increase their cognitive skills as measured by tests of IQ and other kinds of cognitive tests (Ramey & Ramey, 1998, 2000). Similar children, lacking such interventions, show no comparable gains. In other words, two children with similar genetic predispositions can show very different cognitive performances depending on the environments in which they find themselves.

Current estimates of the heritability coefficient of various cognitive skills are based almost exclusively on performance in conventional tests of intelligence. The estimates can be no better than the tests, and we have already seen that the tests define intelligence somewhat narrowly. Among Gardner's intelligences, for example, they measure primarily linguistic, logical-mathematical, and perhaps spatial intelligences. In Sternberg's terms, they measure only analytical abilities.

How can we estimate the heritability of cognitive skills (at least that portion of them measured by the conventional tests)? Several methods have been used. The main ones are studies of separated identical twins, studies of identical versus fraternal twins, and studies of adopted children (Mackintosh, 1998; Sternberg & Grigorenko, 1997).

Separated identical twins

Identical twins, such as Janet and Jeannette, who are discussed at the beginning of the chapter, have identical genes. No one knows exactly why identical twinning occurs, but we do know that identical twins result when a sperm fertilizes an egg, and then the newly formed embryo splits in two, resulting in two embryos with identical genes. Suppose that a set of identical twins is born, and then one of the twins is immediately whisked away to a new environment, chosen at random, so that no relationship exists between the environments in which the two twins are raised. The two twins would have identical genes, but any similarity between their environments would be due only to chance. If we then created a number of such twin pairs, we would be able to estimate the contribution of heredity to individual differences in intelligence by correlating the measured intelligence of each child with that of his or her identical twin. The twins would have in common all their heredity but none of their environment (except any aspects that might be similar due to chance).

Although, of course, purposely creating such a group of separated twins is unethical, sometimes real-life circumstances have created instances in which twins have been separated at birth and then raised separately. In studies of twins reared apart, the various estimates tend to fall within roughly the same heritability-coefficient range of 0.6 to 0.8 (e.g., Bouchard & McGue, 1981; Juel-Nielsen, 1965; Newman, Freeman, & Holzinger, 1937; Shields, 1962).

These relatively high figures must be interpreted with some caution, however. In many cases, the twins were not actually separated at birth, but at some point afterward, giving the twins a common environment for at least some time before separation. In other cases, it becomes clear that the supposedly random assortment of environments was not truly random. Placement authorities tend to place twins in environments relatively similar to those the twins had left. These tendencies may inflate in some degree the apparent contribution of heredity to variation in measured intelligence, because variation that is actually environmental is included in the correlation that is supposed to represent only the effect of heredity.

Identical versus fraternal twins

Another way to estimate heritability is to compare the correlation of IQs for identical versus fraternal twins. The idea is that, whereas identical twins share identical genes, fraternal twins, such as Jamie and Johnny, discussed at the beginning of the chapter, share only the same genes as would any brother or sister. On average, fraternal twins share only 50 percent of their genes. To the extent that the identical and fraternal twin pairs share similar environments due to age, we should not get environmental differences due merely to variations in age among sibling pairs. If environments are nearly the same for both twins, differences in the correlation of intelligence scores between fraternal and identical twins should be attributable to heredity. According to a review by Bouchard and McGue (1981), these data lead to a heritability estimate of about 0.75, again suggesting a high level of heritability. More recent estimates are similar, although quite variable (Mackintosh, 1998).

These data may be affected by the fact that fraternal twins often do not share environments to the same extent that identical ones do, particularly if the fraternal twins are not same-sex twins. Parents tend to treat identical twins more nearly alike than they do fraternal twins, even to the extent of having them dress the same way. Moreover, the twins themselves are likely to respond differently if they are identical, perhaps seeking out more apparent identity with their twin. Thus, once again, the contribution of environment may be underestimated to some extent.

Adoption

Yet another way to examine hereditary versus environmental contributions to intelligence is by comparing the correlation between the IQs of adopted children with those of their biological parents, on the one hand, and their adoptive parents, on the other. Biological parents provide adopted children with their genes, and adoptive parents provide the children with their environments. So, to the extent that heredity matters, the higher correlation should be with the intelligence of the biological rather than the adoptive parents; to the extent that environment matters, the higher correlation should be that with the intelligence of the adoptive rather than the biological parents. In some families, it is also possible to compare the IQs of the adopted children to the IQs of either biological or adoptive siblings.

Many psychologists who have studied intelligence as measured by IQ believe the heritability of intelligence to be about 0.5 in children, and somewhat higher in adults (Mackintosh, 1998; Plomin, 1997), for whom the early effects of the child-rearing environment have receded. However, there probably is no one coefficient of heritability that applies to all populations under all circumstances. Indeed, changes in distributions of genes or in environments can change the estimates. One way of changing the environment is through concerted efforts to modify cognitive skills.

Modifying cognitive skills

At one time, it was believed that cognitive abilities are fixed, and that we are stuck for ever with whatever level of cognitive abilities we have at birth. Today, many researchers believe that cognitive abilities are malleable – that the skills deriving from these abilities can be shaped and even increased through various kinds of interventions (Bransford & Stein, 1993; Detterman & Sternberg, 1982; Grotzer & Perkins, 2000; Halpern, 1996; Mayer, 2000; Perkins & Grotzer, 1997; Sternberg & Spear-Swerling, 1996). For example, the Head Start program was initiated in the 1960s as a way of providing preschoolers with an edge on cognitive skills and accomplishments when they started school. Long-term follow-ups have indicated that by mid-adolescence, children who participated in the program were more than a grade ahead of matched controls who were not in the program (Lazar & Darlington, 1982; Zigler & Berman, 1983). Children in the program also scored higher on a variety of tests of scholastic achievement, were less likely to need remedial attention, and were less likely to show behavioral problems. Although such measures are not truly measures of intelligence, they show strong positive correlations with intelligence tests. A number of newer programs have also shown some success in environments outside of the family home (e.g., Adams, 1986).

Support for the importance of home environment was found by Bradley and Caldwell (1984) in regard to the development of cognitive skills in young children. These researchers found that several factors in the early home environment, before children start school, may be linked to high IQ scores: emotional and verbal responsivity of the primary caregiver and the caregiver's involvement with the child, avoidance of restriction and punishment, organization of the physical environment and activity schedule, provision of appropriate play materials, and opportunities for variety in daily stimulation. Further, Bradley and Caldwell found that these factors more effectively predicted IQ scores than did socioeconomic status or family structure variables. Note, however, that the Bradley–Caldwell study pertained to preschool children, and children's IQ scores do not begin to predict adult IQ scores well until about age 4. Moreover, before age 7, the scores are not very stable (Bloom, 1964).

Perhaps the best evidence for the modifiability of cognitive skills comes from research by Flynn (1987, 1998; see also Neisser, 1998). This research suggests that ever since record-keeping began early in the twentieth century, IQ scores have been increasing roughly nine points per generation (every 30 years). This result is sometimes referred to as the *Flynn effect*. From any point of view, this increase is large. No one knows exactly how such large increases have occurred, although the explanation must be environmental, because the period of time involved is too brief for genetic mutations to have had an effect. If psychologists were able to understand the cause of the increase, they might be able to apply what they learned to increasing the intellectual skills of children within a given generation.

Altogether, evidence now indicates that environment, motivation, and training can profoundly affect cognitive skills. Heredity may set some kind of upper limit on how cognitively skillful a child can become. However, we now know that for any attribute that is partly genetic, there is a reaction range – the broad limits within which a particular attribute can be expressed in various possible ways, given the inherited potential for expression of the attribute in a particular child. Thus, each child's cognitive skills can be developed further within this broad range of potential skills. We have no reason to believe that children now reach the upper limits in the development of their cognitive skills. To the contrary, the evidence suggests that, although we cannot work miracles, we can do quite a bit to help children become more cognitively adept.

Extremes in Cognitive Skills

Intellectual giftedness

Psychologists differ in terms of how they define the intellectually gifted (Callahan, 2000; Winner, 1997). Some use an exclusively IQ-based criterion. For example, many programs for the gifted screen largely on the basis of scores on conventional intelligence tests, taking children in perhaps the top 1 percent (IQ roughly equal to 135 or above) or 2 percent (IQ roughly equal to 132 or above) for their programs. Others also supplement the assessment of IQ as a basis of giftedness with other criteria, such as school or career achievements or other measures of gifted performance.

Probably the most well-known studies of gifted children were conducted by Terman. Terman conducted a *longitudinal study*, research which followed particular individuals over the course of their lifespan (Terman, 1925; Terman & Oden, 1959). The study has continued even after Terman's death. In his sample of the gifted, Terman included children from California under age 11 with IQs over 140, as well as children in the 11- to 14-year age bracket with slightly lower IQs. The mean IQ of the 643 research participants selected was 151; only 22 of these participants had IQs lower than 140.

The accomplishments in later life of the selected group were extraordinary by any criterion. For example, 31 men from the study were listed in *Who's Who in America*. There were numerous highly successful businessmen, as well as individuals who were successful in all of the professions. The sex bias in these references is obvious. Most of the women became housewives, so it is impossible to make any meaningful comparison between the men (none of whom were reported to have become househusbands) and the women. As with all correlational data, it would be difficult to assign a causal role to IQ in accounting for the accomplishments of the successful individuals in the study. Many factors other than IQ could have contributed to the success of Terman's sample, among the most important of which is familial socioeconomic status and the final educational level achieved by these individuals.

Today, many, if not most, psychologists look to more than IQ for the identification of the intellectually gifted. (See Sternberg & Davidson, 1986, and Winner, 1996, for descriptions of a variety of theories of giftedness.) For example, Renzulli (1986) has suggested that high motivation, or commitment to tasks, and high creativity are important to giftedness, in addition to above-average (although not necessarily outstanding) cognitive abilities. Perhaps gifted children are children who are good at something – sometimes just one thing – but who find a way of capitalizing on that something to make the most of their capabilities (Sternberg, 1985). All of these theorists are in agreement that there is more to giftedness than a high IQ. Indeed, children can be creatively or practically gifted, and not even show up as particularly distinguished at all on an IQ test (Sternberg, 1997).

In one set of studies, high school students from all around the United States and some other countries were identified in terms of analytical, creative, and practical giftedness (Sternberg & Clinkenbeard, 1995; Sternberg, Ferrari, Clinkenbeard, & Grigorenko, 1996). In many cases, students who were gifted in one of these kinds of abilities were not gifted in others. The identified students were then taught a college-level course that emphasized analytical, creative, or practical forms of instruction. Some students were in an instructional condition that matched their pattern of cognitive skills. Other students were taught in a way that mismatched their pattern of cognitive skills. Students' achievement was also evaluated in all three ways. It was found that students achieved at higher levels when they were taught in a way that matched their pattern of cognitive skills. In general, the best teaching is teaching that enables students both to capitalize on their strengths *and* to correct or compensate for their weaknesses (Sternberg, Torff, & Grigorenko, 1998).

These findings raise a potentially important issue. Research suggests that intelligence tests are not *biased* in a narrow statistical sense: they do not tend, on average, falsely to predict criterion performance for particular groups (Mackintosh, 1998). For example, lower intelligence test scores tend to be associated with lower school achievement for children from a variety of groups. But if intelligence tests measure a somewhat narrow set of skills and schools also tend to value this narrow set of skills, then there is a possibility that both the predictor (such as an intelligence test) and the criterion (such as school grades) share the same bias. Statistical analyses would fail to detect bias because both the predictor and the criterion that is predicted share the same bias. The bias is not in the predictor (the test) per se, but in the entire system of prediction (the test, the measure of achievement, and their interrelation). Perhaps if intelligence tests and schools both valued creative and practical abilities as well as analytical abilities, children now identified as relatively lacking in intelligence would be viewed as more intelligent.

In sum, the tendency today is to look beyond IQ to identify intellectually gifted individuals. There are many ways to be gifted, and scores on conventional intelligence tests represent only one of these ways. Indeed, some of the most gifted adult contributors to society, such as Albert Einstein or Thomas Edison, were not top performers either on tests or in school during their early years. Einstein did not even speak until he was 3 years old, and many other remarkably gifted people have even shown particular characteristics that some have regarded as indicating mental retardation. We might then wonder how we can identify truly retarded intellect.

Mental retardation

Mental retardation refers to low levels of intelligence, including low adaptive competence (Detterman, Gabriel, & Ruthsatz, 2000; Detterman & Thompson, 1997). But how should we determine a precise definition of mental retardation and whom we should label as being mentally retarded? Different viewpoints lead to different conclusions.

The American Association on Mental Retardation (1992) includes within its definition of mental retardation two components: low IQ and low adaptive competence, the latter of which refers to how a child (or an adult) gets along in the world. In other words, to be labeled as retarded, a child not only would have to perform poorly on an intelligence test but also would have to show problems adapting to the environment. A child whose performance was normal in every way except for low IQ would not, by this definition, be classified as mentally retarded. Adaptive life skills are judged in a variety of domains, such as communication (as in talking to someone or writing them a letter), self-care (as in dressing oneself or using the toilet), home living (as in preparing meals), and social interaction (as in meeting the expectations of others).

It is not always easy to assess adaptive competence, however, as the following example (Edgerton, 1967) shows. A retarded man (who had scored low on tests of intelligence) was unable to tell time – an indication of some kind of cognitive deficit. However, the man employed a clever compensatory strategy. He wore a nonfunctional watch, so that whenever he wanted to know the time, he could stop, look at his watch, pretend to notice that his watch did not work, and then ask a nearby stranger (who would have observed his behavior) to tell him the correct time. How should we assess this man's adaptive competence – in terms of his strategy for determining the time or in terms of his inability to tell time by looking at a watch? Was the man mentally retarded, and if so, why?

Zigler (1982; see also Hodapp & Dykens, 1994) believes that some mentally retarded children simply develop mentally at a slower rate than do children with normal intelligence. Most investigators, however, seek not only to look at quantitative differences in rates of development but also at qualitative differences in performance. A key qualitative difference centers on metacognitive skill. There is fairly widespread agreement that mentally retarded children have difficulties with the executive processes of cognition, such as planning, monitoring, and evaluating their strategies for task performance (Campione, Brown, & Ferrara, 1982). An example would be their planning to rehearse lists of words they are asked to memorize (A. L. Brown, Campione, Bray, & Wilcox, 1973). To what extent might such difficulties be based on hereditary factors and to what extent on environmental factors?

Both environmental and hereditary factors may contribute to retardation (Grigorenko, 2000; Sternberg & Grigorenko, 1997). Environmental influences before birth may cause permanent retardation – for example, retardation resulting from a mother's inadequate nutrition or ingestion of toxins such as alcohol during the child's prenatal development (Olson, 1994). A child exposed to an impoverished environment or denied opportunities for even basic instruction in the home might display retardation. Even a brief trauma, such as from a car accident or a fall, can injure the brain, causing mental retardation.

Although we do not understand the subtle influences of heredity on intelligence very well at present, we do know of several genetic syndromes that clearly cause mental retardation. For example, one of the more common genetic causes of mental retardation is Down's syndrome, once called "mongolism." This syndrome results from the presence of extra chromosomal material on one of the chromosomes. The extra material disrupts the normal biochemical messages and results in retardation and other features of this syndrome.

Sometimes, hereditary factors interact with environmental ones to produce mental retardation. Although we cannot yet prevent the inheritance of these diseases, we can try to block the environmental contribution to the retardation. For example, we now know how to minimize the likelihood of mental retardation in phenylketonuria (PKU), a rare hereditary disease that results in mental retardation if environmental intervention is not imposed. Essentially, children with this disease do not produce an enzyme needed for properly metabolizing the amino acid phenylalanine. As a result, if PKU is not quickly discovered after birth, and the infant consumes foods containing complete proteins or other sources of phenylalanine, by-products of the incomplete metabolism of this amino acid will accumulate in the bloodstream. These by-products will cause progressively more severe brain damage and permanent retardation. In PKU, the interactive roles of nature and nurture are clear, and we can clearly specify these roles. Typically the nature of the interactive roles is not so clear, however. In looking at group differences, these roles are particularly muddy.

Group Differences in Cognitive Abilities

Cultural and societal analyses of cognitive skills render it particularly important to consider carefully the meaning of group differences in measured IQ (Fischer et al., 1996; Loehlin, 2000). For example, on average, African Americans score somewhat lower than Caucasians on conventional standardized tests of intelligence (Herrnstein & Murray, 1994); but it is important to remember that Italian American scores used to be considerably lower than they are now. Scores of groups can fluctuate. Scores of African Americans have been showing an increasing pattern over time, just as have scores for other groups.

Available evidence to date suggests an environmental explanation for these group differences (Nisbett, 1998). For example, in one study, offspring of American servicemen born to German women during the Allied occupation of Germany after the Second World War revealed no significant difference between IQs of children of African American versus white servicemen (Eyferth, 1961). This result suggests that given similar environments, the children of the two groups (African American and white) of servicemen performed equally on tests of intelligence. Another study found that children adopted by white families obtained higher IQ scores than did children adopted by African American families, again suggesting environmental factors contributing to the difference between the two groups (Moore, 1986). Another way of studying group differences has been through transracial adoption studies, where white parents have adopted African American children (Scarr & Weinberg, 1976; Scarr, Weinberg, & Waldman, 1993; Weinberg, Scarr, & Waldman, 1992). The results of these studies have been somewhat difficult to interpret, in that both white and African American children who were adopted in the study showed decreases in IQ after a ten-year follow-up on their performance.

Group differences may thus originate from a number of factors, many of which change over time. The result is that group differences are not immutable: a group that scores, on average, lower than another group at one given time may score, on average, lower, the same, or even higher at another time.

An example of a change in the nature of group differences is that with regard to sex. Overall, boys and girls do about the same on cognitive ability tests, although differences have been noted on specific ability tests. Analyses of trends over time suggest that sex differences in scores on these cognitive ability tests have been shrinking over the years (Feingold, 1988). Nevertheless, there do appear to be some differences that remain. In particular, boys, on average, tend to score higher on tasks that require visual and spatial working memory, motor skills that are involved in aiming, and certain aspects of mathematical performance. Girls tend to score higher on tasks that require rapid access to and use of phonological and semantic information in long-term memory, production and comprehension of complex prose, fine motor skills, and perceptual speed (Halpern, 1997). These differences refer only to averages, and there are many children of one sex who do better than children of the other sex, regardless of the particular skill measured by a given test. In any case, these score differences are not easily interpretable. Steele (1997), for example, has found that when boys and girls take difficult mathematical tests, boys often do better. But when the two groups are told in advance that a particular test will show no difference, on average, scores of boys and girls converge, with girls' scores increasing and boys' scores actually decreasing.

There are a number of mechanisms by which environmental factors such as poverty, undernutrition, and illness might affect intelligence (Sternberg et al., 2000). One mechanism is through resources. Children who are poor often do not have the resources in the home and school that children from more affluent environments have. Another mechanism is through attention to and concentration on the skills being taught in school. Children who are undernourished or ill may find it hard to concentrate in school, and therefore may profit less from the instruction they receive. A third mechanism is the system of rewards in the environment. Children who grow up in economically deprived environments may note that the children who are most rewarded are not those who do well in school, but rather those who find ways of earning the money they need to survive, whatever these ways may be. It is unlikely that there is any one mechanism that fully explains the effects of these various variables. It is also important to realize that whatever these mechanisms are, they can start in utero, not just after birth. For example fetal alcohol syndrome results in reduced IQ, and has its effects prenatally, before the child even enters the world outside the mother's womb.

The preceding arguments with respect to culture and group differences may make it clear why it is so difficult to come up with what everyone would consider a culture-fair test – a test that is equally appropriate for members of all cultures and that comprises items that are equally fair to members of all cultures. If members of different cultures have different ideas of what it means to be intelligent, then the very behaviors that may be considered intelligent in one culture may be viewed as unintelligent in another. Indeed, there is abundant evidence that members of different cultures in fact do have different conceptions of intelligence (Berry, 1974; Greenfield, 1997; Grigorenko et al., in press; Sternberg & Kaufman, 1998).

Consider, for example, the concept of mental quickness. In many cultures, quickness is usually associated with intelligence. To say a child is "quick" is to say that the child is intelligent, and indeed, most group tests of intelligence are quite strictly timed.

There can be no doubt that sometimes it is important to be fast. When one has not yet started studying for a test that is to occur the next day, it is definitely adaptive to be quick. If a child is trying to find an excuse for bad behavior, the child had better be fast if he wants to avoid after-school detention. In many cultures of the world, however, quickness is not at a premium. In these cultures, people may believe that more intelligent children do not rush into things. In fact, early in the twentieth century, a leading psychometric theoretician of intelligence, Thurstone (1924), defined intelligence as the ability to withhold an instinctive response. In other words, the smart child is one who does not rush into action but thinks first. So, is it culturally fair to include a speed or timing component in an intelligence test?

Almost everyone would like to construct only culture-fair tests. Unfortunately, at present and for the foreseeable future, there exist no perfectly culture-fair tests of intelligence. Even among the tests devised to date, performance on those tests that have been labeled as "culture-fair" seems to be influenced in some degree by cultural factors, such as years of schooling and academic achievements (e.g., Ceci, 1996). In sum, one must be careful about drawing conclusions regarding group differences in intelligence (Greenfield,

1997; Loehlin, 2000) that may appear to be justified on the surface but that represent only a superficial analysis of group differences.

The development of culture-fair tests based on each culture's own definition of intelligence may be an unrealistic goal, but it is possible to provide culture-relevant tests. Culture-relevant tests employ skills and knowledge that relate to the cultural experiences of the test-takers. Content and procedures are used in testing that are appropriate to the cultural context of the test-takers. For example, 14-year-old boys performed poorly on a task when it was couched as a cupcake-baking task but performed well when it was framed as a battery-charging task (Ceci & Bronfenbrenner, 1985). Brazilian maids had no difficulty with proportional reasoning when hypothetically purchasing food but had great difficulty with it when hypothetically purchasing medicinal herbs (Schliemann & Magalhües, 1990). Brazilian children whose poverty had forced them to become street vendors showed no difficulty in performing complex arithmetic computations when selling things but had great difficulty performing similar calculations in a classroom (Carraher, Carraher, & Schliemann, 1985; Ceci & Roazzi, 1994; Nuñes, 1994).

To summarize, the causes as well as the manifestations of individual and group differences in cognitive skills are complex. At times, superficial comparisons are made between individuals or groups with little attempt to gain serious insight into either the causes or the modifiability of these differences. The study of individual differences in cognitive development needs to concentrate not just on cataloguing such differences, but rather, on understanding their causes. Intervention efforts need to focus on modification with the view that cognitive skills almost always can be increased, at least to some degree.

If there is a lesson in understanding these differences, it is that children differ not only in a series of fixed attributes, but also in how they capitalize on strengths and compensate for or correct weaknesses. A child may have many strengths, but if he or she does not exploit them, they may serve little purpose in the child's life. Thus, we need not only to help children develop abilities, but to help them develop facility in using these abilities effectively.

References

Abell, F., Happé, F., & Frith, U. (in press). Do triangles play tricks? Attribution of mental states to animated shapes in normal and abnormal development. *Cognitive Development, 15,* 1–16.

Abelson, R. P. (1959). Modes of resolution of belief dilemmas. *Journal of Conflict Resolution, 3,* 343–352.

Abu-Lughod, L. (1993). *Writing women's worlds: Bedouin stories.* Berkeley: University of California.

Acredolo, C. (1989). Assessing children's understanding of time, speed, and distance interrelations. In I. Levin & D. Zakay (Eds.), *Time and human cognition: A life-span perspective* (pp. 219–257). Amsterdam: North-Holland.

Acredolo, C., & Schmid, J. (1981). The understanding of relative speeds, distances, and durations of movement. *Developmental Psychology, 17,* 490–493.

Acredolo, L. P. (1978). Development of spatial orientation in infancy. *Developmental Psychology, 14,* 224–234.

Acredolo, L. P. (1981). Small- and large-scale spatial concepts in infancy and childhood. In L. S. Liben, A. H. Patterson, & N. Newcombe (Eds.), *Spatial representation and behavior across the life span: Theory and application* (pp. 63–81). New York: Academic Press.

Acredolo, L. P., & Evans, D. (1980). Developmental changes in the effects of landmarks on infant spatial behavior. *Developmental Psychology, 16,* 312–318.

Adair-Hauk, B., & Donato, R. (1994). Foreign-language explanations within the zone of proximal development. *Canadian Modern Language Review, 50,* 532–557.

Adams, J. L. (1986). *The care and feeding of ideas: A guide to encouraging creativity.* Reading, MA: Addison-Wesley Publishing Company.

Adey, P., & Shayer, M. (1994) *Really raising standards.* London: Routledge.

Adolph, K. (1997). Learning in the development of infant locomotion. *Monographs of the Society for Research in Child Development, 62* (3, Serial No. 251).

Aguiar, A., & Baillargeon, R. (1998). 8.5-month-old infants' reasoning about containment events. *Child Development, 69,* 636–653.

Aguiar, A., & Baillargeon, R. (1999). 2.5-month-old infants' reasoning about when objects should and should not be occluded. *Cognitive Psychology, 39,* 116–157.

Aguiar, A., & Baillargeon, R. (2000). Perseveration and problem solving in infancy. In H. W. Reese (Ed.), *Advances in child development and behavior* (Vol. 27, pp. 135–180). San Diego: Academic Press.

Aguiar, A., & Baillargeon, R. (2001). Perseverative responding in 6.5-month-old infants in a violation-of-expectation task. Manuscript under review.

Aguiar, A., & Baillargeon, R. (in press). Developments in young infants' reasoning about occluded objects. *Cognitive Psychology* (accepted pending revisions).

Ahl, V. A., Moore, C. F., & Dixon, J. A. (1992). Development of intuitive and numerical proportional reasoning. *Cognitive Development, 7*, 81–108.

Allen, G. L. (1999). Spatial abilities, cognitive maps, and wayfinding. In R. G. Golledge (Ed.), *Wayfinding behavior: Cognitive mapping and other spatial processes* (pp. 46–80). Baltimore: Johns Hopkins University Press.

Allen, G., & Courchesne, E. (2001). Attention function and dysfunction in autism. *Frontiers in Bioscience, 6*, d105–119.

Allen, J. G. (2001). *Interpersonal trauma and serious mental disorder.* Chichester: Wiley.

Allen, M. J., Wittig, M. A., & Butler, K. (1981). Comments on Thomas and Jamison's "A test of the x-linked genetic hypothesis of sex differences on Piaget's water-level task." *Developmental Review, 1*, 284–288.

American Association of Mental Retardation (1992). *Mental retardation: Definition, classification, and systems of support* (9th ed.). Washington, DC: AAMR.

American Psychiatric Association. (1994). Diagnostic and statistical manual of mental disorders (4th ed., DSM-IV). Washington, DC: Author.

American Psychiatric Association (2000). *Diagnostic and statistical manual of mental disorders: DSM B IV* (4th ed., text revision). Washington, DC: Author.

Amsel, E., & Brock, S. (1996). The development of evidence evaluation skills. *Cognitive Development, 11*, 523–550.

Amsel, E., Goodman, G., Savoie, D., & Clark, M. (1996). The development of reasoning about causal and noncausal influences on levers. *Child Development, 67*, 1624–1646.

Amsterdam, B. (1972). Mirror self-image reactions before age two. *Developmental Psychobiology, 5*, 297–305.

Anderson, J. R. (1991). The adaptive nature of human categorization. *Psychological Review, 3*, 409–429.

Anderson, J. R. (1995). *Cognitive psychology and its implications* (4th ed.). New York: Freeman.

Anderson, M. (1992). *Intelligence and development: A cognitive theory.* Oxford, UK: Blackwell.

Anderson, N. H. (1983). Intuitive physics: Understanding and learning of physical relations. In T. J. Tighe & B. E. Shepp (Eds.), *Perception, cognition, and development: Interactional analyses* (pp. 231–265). Hillsdale, NJ: Erlbaum.

Anderson, N. H. (1996). *A functional theory of cognition.* Mahwah, NJ: Erlbaum.

Anderson, N. H., & Wilkening, F. (1991). Adaptive thinking in intuitive physics. In N. H. Anderson (Ed.), *Contributions to information integration theory: Vol. 3. Developmental* (pp. 1–42). Hillsdale, NJ: Erlbaum.

Anderson, S. W., Damasio, H., Jones, R. D., & Tranel, D. (1991). Wisconsin card sorting performance as a measure of frontal lobe damage. *Journal of Clinical and Experimental Neuropsychology, 13*, 909–922.

Andersson, B. (1990). Pupils' conceptions of matter and its transformation (age 12–16). *Studies in Science Education, 18*, 53–88.

Andrews, G., & Halford, G. S. (1998). Children's ability to make transitive inferences: The importance of premise integration and structural complexity. *Cognitive Development, 13*, 479–513.

Anooshian, L. J. (1997). Distinctions between implicit and explicit memory: Significance for understanding cognitive development. *International Journal of Behavioral Development, 21,* 453–478.

Antell, S. E, & Keating, D. P. (1983). Perception of numerical invariance in neonates. *Child Development, 54,* 695–701.

APA (1994). *DSM-IV diagnostic and statistical manual of mental disorders* (4th ed.). Washington, DC: American Psychiatric Association.

Aram, D., Morris, R., & Hall, N. (1993). Clinical and research congruence in identifying children with specific language impairment. *Journal of Speech and Hearing Research, 36*(3), 580–591.

Aram, D. M., & Nation, J. E. (1975). Patterns of language behaviour in children with developmental language disorders. *Journal of Speech and Hearing Research, 18,* 229–241.

Archibald, S. J., & Kerns, K. A. (1999). Identification and description of new tests of executive functioning in children. *Child Neuropsychology, 5,* 115–129.

Arnold, R., Yule, W., & Martin, N. (1985). The psychological characteristics of infantile hypercalcaemia: A preliminary investigation. *Developmental Medicine and Child Neurology, 27,* 49–59.

Arsenio, W. (1988). Children's conceptions of the situational affective consequences of sociomoral events. *Child Development, 59,* 1611–1622.

Arsenio, W., & Kramer, R. (1992). Victimizers and their victims: Children's conceptions of the mixed emotional consequences of victimization. *Child Development, 63,* 915–927.

Arsenio, W., & Lover, A. (1995). Children's conceptions of socio-moral affect: Happy victimizers, mixed emotions, and other expectancies. In M. Killen & D. Hart (Eds.), *Morality in everyday life* (pp. 87–130). New York: Cambridge University Press.

Arterberry, M. E. (1993). Development of spatiotemporal integration in infancy. *Infant Behavior and Development, 16,* 343–363.

Arterberry, M. E. (1997). Perception of object properties over time. In C. Rovee-Collier & L. P. Lipsitt (Eds.), *Advances in infancy research* (Vol. 11, pp. 219–268). Greenwich, CT: Ablex.

Aslin, R. N., Jusczyk, P. W., & Pisoni, D. B. (1998). Speech and auditory processing during infancy: Constraints on and precursors to language. In D. Kuhn & R. S. Siegler (Eds.), *Handbook of child psychology* (5th ed.): *Cognition, perception, and language* (pp. 147–198). New York: Wiley.

Asperger, H. (1944). Die "Autistischen Psychopathen" im Kindesalter. *Archiv fur Psychiatrie und Nervenkrankheiten, 117,* 76–136.

Astington, J. (1993). *The child's discovery of the mind.* Cambridge, MA: Harvard University Press.

Astington, J. W., & Jenkins, J. M. (1995). Theory of mind development and social understanding. *Cognition and Emotion, 9,* 151–165.

Astington, J. W., & Jenkins, J. M. (1999). A longitudinal study of the relation between language and theory of mind. *Developmental Psychology, 35,* 1311–1320.

Atran, S. (1999). Itzaj Maya folkbiological taxonomy: Cognitive universals and cultural particulars. In D. L. Medin & S. Atran (Eds.), *Folkbiology* (pp. 119–213). Cambridge, MA: MIT Press.

Au, T. K., Dapretto, M., & Song, Y. K. (1994). Input vs constraints: Early word acquisition in Korean and English. *Journal of Memory & Language, 33*(5), 567–582.

Au, T. K., & Markman, E. M. (1987). Acquiring word meanings via linguistic contrast. *Cognitive Development, 2*(3), 217–236.

Au, T. K., & Romo, L. F. (1999). Mechanical causality in children's "folkbiology." In D. L. Medin & S. Atran (Eds.), *Folkbiology* (pp. 119–213). Cambridge, MA: MIT Press.

Au, T. K., Romo, L. F., & DeWitt, J. E. (1999). Considering children's folkbiology in health education. In M. Siegal & C. C. Petersen (Eds.), *Children's understanding of biology and health* (pp. 209–234). New York: Cambridge University Press.

Ausley, J. A., & Guttentag, R. E. (1993). Direct and indirect assessments of memory: Implications for the study of memory development during childhood. In M. L. Howe & R. Pasnak (Eds.), *Emerging themes in cognitive development* (pp. 234–264). New York: Springer.

Avis, J., & Harris, P. (1991). Belief-desire reasoning among Baka children: Evidence for a universal conception of mind. *Child Development, 62*, 460–467.

Bachevalier, J. (1992). Cortical versus limbic immaturity: Relationship to infantile amnesia. In M. R. Gunnar & C. A. Nelson (Eds.), *Developmental behavioral neuroscience: The Minnesota symposia on child psychology* (Vol. 24, pp. 129–153). Hillsdale, NJ: Erlbaum.

Bachevalier, J., & Mishkin, M. (1994). Effects of selective neonatal temporal lobe lesions on visual recognition memory in rhesus monkeys. *The Journal of Neuroscience, 14*, 2128–2139.

Bachevalier, J., Brickson, M., & Hagger, C. (1993). Limbic-dependent recognition memory in monkeys develops early in infancy. *Neuroreport, 4*, 77–80.

Backscheider, A. G., & Gelman, S. A. (1995). Children's understanding of homonyms. *Journal of Child Language, 22*, 107–127.

Backsheider, A. G., Shatz, M., & Gelman, S. A. (1993). Preschoolers' ability to distinguish living kinds as a function of regrowth. *Child Development, 64*, 1242–1257.

Baddeley, A. (1986). *Working memory.* Oxford: Clarendon Press.

Baddeley, A. (1992). Working memory. *Science, 255*, 556–559.

Baddeley, A. (1996). Exploring the central executive. *Quarterly Journal of Experimental Psychology: Human Experimental Psychology* [Special Issue]: *Working Memory, 49A*, 5–28.

Baddeley, A. D. (1990). *Human memory: Theory and practice.* Needham Heights, MA: Allyn & Bacon.

Baddeley, A., & Hitch, G. (1974). Working memory. In G. H. Bower (Ed.), *The psychology of learning and motivation: Advances in research and theory* (Vol. 8, pp. 47–89). New York: Academic Press.

Baddeley, A. D., & Hitch, G. J. (2000). Development of working memory: Should the Pascual-Leone and the Baddeley and Hitch models be merged? *Journal of Experimental Child Psychology, 77*(2), 128–137.

Baddeley, A. D., Thomson, N., & Buchanan, M. (1975). Word length and the structure of short-term memory. *Journal of Verbal Learning and Verbal Behavior, 14*, 575–589.

Baenninger, M., & Newcombe, N. (1989). The role of experience in spatial test performance: A meta-analysis. *Sex Roles, 20*, 327–344.

Bahrick, L. E., Hernandez-Reif, M., & Pickens, J. N. (1997). The effect of retrieval cues on visual preferences and memory in infancy: Evidence for a four-phase attention function. *Journal of Experimental Child Psychology, 67*, 1–20.

Bahrick, L. E., & Pickens, J. N. (1995). Infant memory for object motion across a period of three months: Implications for a four-phase attention function. *Journal of Experimental Child Psychology, 59*, 343–371.

Bahrick, L. E., & Watson, J. S. (1985). Detection of intermodal proprioceptive-visual contingency as a potential basis of self-perception in infancy. *Developmental Psychology, 21*, 963–973.

Bailey, A., Phillips, W., & Rutter, M. (1996). Autism: Towards an integration of clinical, genetic, neuropsychological, and neurobiological perspectives. *Journal of Child Psychology and Psychiatry, 37*, 89–126.

Bailey, T., Le Couteur, A., Gottesman, I., Bolton, P., Simonoff, E., Yuzda, E., & Rutter, M. (1995). Autism as a strongly genetic disorder: Evidence from a British twin study. *Psychological Medicine, 25*, 63–77.

Baillargeon, R. (1986). Representing the existence and the location of hidden objects: Object permanence in 6- and 8-month-old infants. *Cognition, 23*, 21–41.

Baillargeon, R. (1991). Reasoning about the height and location of a hidden object in 4.5- and 6.5-month-old infants. *Cognition, 38,* 13–42.

Baillargeon, R. (1993). The object concept revisited: New directions in the investigation of infants' physical knowledge. In C. Granrud (Ed.), *Visual perception and cognition in infancy. Carnegie Mellon symposia on cognition* (pp. 265–315). Hillsdale, NJ: Lawrence Erlbaum Associates.

Baillargeon, R. (1994). How do infants learn about the physical world? *Current Directions in Psychological Science, 3,* 133–140.

Baillargeon, R. (1995). A model of physical reasoning in infancy. In C. Rovee-Collier & L. P. Lipsitt (Eds.), *Advances in infancy research* (Vol. 9, pp. 305–371). Norwood, NJ: Ablex.

Baillargeon, R. (1998). Infants' understanding of the physical world. In M. Sabourin, F. Craik, & M. Robert (Eds.), *Advances in psychological science* (Vol. 2. pp. 503–529). London: Psychology Press.

Baillargeon, R. (1999). Young infants' expectations about hidden objects: A reply to three challenges [article with peer commentaries and response]. *Developmental Science, 2,* 115–163.

Baillargeon, R. (2000a). How do infants learn about the physical world? In D. Muir & A. Slater (Eds.), *Infant development: The essential readings. Essential readings in development psychology* (pp. 195–212). Malden, MA: Blackwell.

Baillargeon, R. (2000b). Reply to Bogartz, Shinskey, and Schilling; Schilling; and Cashon and Cohen. *Infancy, 1,* 447–462.

Baillargeon, R. (in press). Infants' physical knowledge: Of acquired expectations and core principles. In E. Dupoux (Ed.), *Language, brain, and cognitive development: Essays in honor of Jacques Mehler.* Cambridge: MA: MIT PRess.

Baillargeon, R., & Brueckner, L. (2000, July). 3.5-month-old infants' reasoning about the width of hidden objects. Paper presented at the biennial International Conference on Infant Studies, Brighton, UK.

Baillargeon, R., DeJong, G., & Sheehan, J. (2001). Teaching infants physical concepts. Manuscript in preparation.

Baillargeon, R., & DeVos, J. (1991). Object permanence in 3.5- and 4.5-month-old infants: Further evidence. *Child Development, 62,* 1227–1246.

Baillargeon, R., Fisher, C., & DeJong, G. (2000, July). Teaching infants about support: What data must they see? Paper presented at the biennial International Conference on Infant Studies, Brighton, UK.

Baillargeon, R., & Graber, M. (1987). Where's the rabbit? 5.5-month-old infants' representation of the height of a hidden object. *Cognitive Development, 2,* 375–392.

Baillargeon, R., Graber, M., DeVos, J., & Black, J. (1990). Why do young infants fail to search for hidden objects? *Cognition, 36,* 225–284.

Baillargeon, R., Kotovsky, L., & Needham, A. (1995). The acquisition of physical knowledge in infancy. In D. Sperber, D. Premack, & A. Premack (Eds.), *Causal cognition: A multidisciplinary debate.* Oxford: Clarendon Press.

Baillargeon, R., Needham, A., & DeVos, J. (1992). The development of young infants' intuitions about support. *Early Development and Parenting, 1,* 69–78.

Baillargeon, R., Spelke, E. S., & Wasserman, S. (1985). Object permanence in 5-month-old infants. *Cognition, 20,* 191–208.

Baird, J. A., & Baldwin, D. A. (in press). Making sense of human behavior: Action parsing and intentional inference. In B. Malle, L. Moses, & D. Baldwin (Eds.), *Intentionality: A key to human understanding.* Cambridge, MA: MIT Press.

Baird, P., & Sadovnik, A. (1988). Life expectancy in Down's syndrome adults. *Lancet, 2*(8624), 1354–1356.

Baker-Ward, L., Hess, T. M., & Flannagan, D. A. (1990). The effects of involvement on children's memory for events. *Cognitive Development, 5*, 55–70.

Baker-Ward, L., & Ornstein, P. A. (1988). Age differences in visual–spatial memory performance: Do children really out-perform adults when playing Concentration? *Bulletin of the Psychonomic Society, 26*, 331–332.

Balaban, M. T., & Waxman, S. R. (1997). Do words facilitate object categorization in 9-month-old infants? *Journal of Experimental Child Psychology, 64*(1), 3–26.

Baldwin, D. A. (1992). Clarifying the role of shape in children's taxonomic assumption. *Journal of Experimental Child Psychology, 54*, 392–416.

Baldwin, D. A., & Baird, J. A. (1999). Action analysis: A gateway to intentional inference. In P. Rochat (Ed.), *Early social cognition: Understanding others in the first months of life* (pp. 215–240). Mahwah, NJ: Lawrence Erlbaum Associates.

Baldwin, D. A., & Markman, E. M. (1989). Establishing word–object relations: A first step. *Child Development, 60*(2), 381–398.

Baldwin, D. A., & Moses, L. J. (1994). Early understanding of referential intent and attentional focus: Evidence from language and emotion. In C. Lewis & P. Mitchell (Eds.), *Children's early understanding of mind: Origins and development* (pp. 133–156). Hillsdale, NJ: Erlbaum.

Baldwin, D. A., & Moses, L. J. (1996). The ontogeny of social information gathering. *Child Development, 67*, 1915–1939.

Baldwin, D. A., Markman, E. M., & Melartin, R. L. (1993). Infants' ability to draw inferences about nonobvious object properties: Evidence from exploratory play. *Child Development, 64*(3), 711–728.

Baldwin, J. M. (1902). *Social and ethical interpretations in mental development* (3rd ed.). New York: Macmillan.

Ball, W., & Tronick, E. (1971). Infant responses to impending collision: Optical and real. *Science, 171*, 818–820.

Bandura, A. (1991). Social cognitive theory of moral thought and action. In W. Kurtines & J. Gewirtz (Eds.), *Handbook of moral behavior and development: Vol. 1. Theory* (pp. 45–104). Hillsdale, NJ: Erlbaum.

Banks, M. S., & Salapatek, P. (1983). Infant visual perception. In M. Haith & J. Campos (Eds.), *Handbook of child psychology: Vol. 2. Infancy and developmental psychology.* New York: Wiley.

Baressi, J., & Moore, C. (1996). Intentional relations and social understanding. *Behavioral and Brain Sciences, 19*, 107–154.

Barden, R., Zelko, F., Duncan, S., & Masters, J. (1980). Children's consensual knowledge about the experiential determinants of emotion. *Journal of Personality and Social Psychology, 39*, 968–976.

Bargh, J. A. (1990). Goal ≠ intent: Goal-directed thought and behavior are often unintentional. *Psychological Inquiry, 1*, 248–277.

Barkley, R. A. (1997). Behavioral inhibition, sustained attention, and executive functions: Constructing a unifying theory of ADHD. *Psychological Bulletin, 121*, 65–94.

Barkley, R. A., Grodzinsky, G., & DuPaul, G. J. (1992). Frontal lobe functions in attention deficit disorder with and without hyperactivity: A review and research report. *Journal of Abnormal Child Psychology, 20*, 163–188.

Barnat, S. B., Klein, P. J., & Meltzoff, A. N. (1996). Deferred imitation across changes in context and object: Memory and generalization in 14-month-old children. *Infant Behavior and Development, 19*, 241–251.

Baron-Cohen, S. (1987a). Perception in autistic children. In D. Cohen (Ed.), *Handbook of autism and pervasive developmental disorders.* New York: Wiley & Sons.

Baron-Cohen, S. (1987b). Autism and symbolic play. *British Journal of Developmental Psychology*, 5, 139–148.

Baron-Cohen, S. (1988). Social and pragmatic deficits in autism: Cognitive or affective? *Journal of Autism and Developmental Disorders*, 18, 379–402.

Baron-Cohen, S. (1989a). Are autistic children behaviourists? An examination of their mental–physical and appearance–reality distinctions. *Journal of Autism and Developmental Disorders*, 19, 579–600.

Baron-Cohen, S. (1989b). The autistic child's theory of mind: a case of specific developmental delay. *Journal of Child Psychology and Psychiatry*, 30, 285–298.

Baron-Cohen, S. (1989c). Perceptual role-taking and protodeclarative pointing in autism. *British Journal of Developmental Psychology*, 7, 113–127.

Baron-Cohen, S. (1991a). Do people with autism understand what causes emotion? *Child Development*, 62, 385–395.

Baron-Cohen, S. (1991b). Precursors to a theory of mind: Understanding attention in others. In A. Whiten (Ed.), *Natural theories of mind*. Oxford, UK: Blackwell.

Baron-Cohen, S. (1994). How to build a baby that can read minds: Cognitive mechanisms in mindreading. *Cahiers de Psychologie Cognitive/Current Psychology of Cognition*, 13, 513–552.

Baron-Cohen, S. (1995). *Mindblindness: An essay on autism and theory of mind*. Boston: MIT Press/Bradford Books.

Baron-Cohen, S. (1997). Are children with autism superior at folk physics? In H. M. Wellman & K. Inagaki (Eds.), *The emergence of core domains of thought: Children's reasoning about physical, psychological, and biological phenomena* (pp. 45–54). San Francisco: Jossey-Bass.

Baron-Cohen, S., Bolton, P., Wheelwright, S., Short, L., Mead, G., Smith, A., & Scahill, V. (1998). Autism occurs more often in families of physicists, engineers, and mathematicians. *Autism*, 2, 296–301.

Baron-Cohen, S., & Goodhart, F. (1994). The "seeing leads to knowing" deficit in autism: The Pratt and Bryant probe. *British Journal of Developmental Psychology*, 12, 397–402.

Baron-Cohen, S., & Hammer, J. (1997a). Is autism an extreme form of the male brain? *Advances in Infancy Research*, 11, 193–217.

Baron-Cohen, S., & Hammer, J. (1997b). Parents of children with Asperger Syndrome: What is the cognitive phenotype? *Journal of Cognitive Neuroscience*, 9, 548–554.

Baron-Cohen, S., Jolliffe, T., Mortimore, C., & Robertson, M. (1997). Another advanced test of theory of mind: Evidence from very high functioning adults with autism or Asperger Syndrome. *Journal of Child Psychology and Psychiatry*, 38, 813–822.

Baron-Cohen, S., Leslie, A. M., & Frith, U. (1985). Does the autistic child have a "theory of mind?". *Cognition*, 21, 37–46.

Baron-Cohen, S., Leslie, A. M., & Frith, U. (1986). Mechanical, behavioural and Intentional understanding of picture stories in autistic children. *British Journal of Developmental Psychology*, 4, 113–125.

Baron-Cohen, S., O'Riordan, M., Stone, V., Jones, R., & Plaisted, K. (1999). Recognition of faux pas by normally developing children and children with Asperger Syndrome or high-functioning autism. *Journal of Autism and Developmental Disorders*, 29, 407–418.

Baron-Cohen, S., Tager-Flusberg, H., & Cohen, D. (Eds.). (1993). *Understanding other minds: Perspectives from autism*. Oxford, UK: Oxford University Press.

Baron-Cohen, S., & Wheelwright, S. (1999). Obsessions in children with autism or Asperger Syndrome: A content analysis in terms of core domains of cognition. *British Journal of Psychiatry*, 175, 484–490.

Baron-Cohen, S., Wheelwright, S., & Hill, J. (2001). The "Reading the mind in the eyes" test revised version: A study with normal adults, and adults with Asperger Syndrome or High-Functioning autism. *Journal of Child Psychiatry and Psychiatry, 42,* 241–252.

Baron-Cohen, S., Wheelwright, S., & Jolliffe, T. (1997). Is there a "language of the eyes"? Evidence from normal adults and adults with autism or Asperger syndrome. *Visual Cognition, 4,* 311–331.

Baron-Cohen, S., Wheelwright, S., Scahill, V., Lawson, J., & Spong, A. (in press). Are intuitive physics and intuitive psychology independent? A test with children with Asperger Syndrome. *Journal of Developmental and Learning Disorders.*

Baron-Cohen, S., Wheelwright, S., Stone, V., & Rutherford, M. (1999). A mathematician, a physicist, and a computer scientist with Asperger Syndrome: Performance on folk psychology and folk physics test. *Neurocase, 5,* 475–483.

Baron-Cohen, S., Wheelwright, S., Stott, C., Bolton, P., & Goodyer, I. (1997). Is there a link between engineering and autism? *Autism: An International Journal of Research and Practice, 1,* 153–163.

Barr, R., Dowden, A., & Hayne, H. (1996). Developmental changes in deferred imitation by 6- to 24-month-old infants. *Infant Behavior and Development, 19,* 159–170.

Barr, R., & Hayne, H. (1996). The effect of event structure on imitation in infancy: Practice makes perfect? *Infant Behavior and Development, 19,* 253–257.

Barr, R., & Hayne, H. (2000). Age-related changes in imitation: Implications for memory development. In C. Rovee-Collier & L. P. Lipsitt (Eds.), *Progress in infancy research* (pp. 21–67). Mahwah, NJ: Erlbaum.

Barrelet, J.-M., & Perret-Clermont, A.-N. (1996), *Jean Piaget et Neuchâtel.* Lausanne: Payot.

Barrett, S. E., Abdi, H., Murphy, G. L., & Gallagher, J. M. (1993). Theory-based correlations and their role in children's concepts. *Child Development, 64,* 1595–1616.

Barsalou, L. W. (1983). Ad hoc categories. *Memory & Cognition, 10,* 82–93.

Bartsch, K., & Wellman, H. M. (1989). Young children's attribution of action to beliefs and desires. *Child Development, 60,* 946–964.

Bartsch, K., & Wellman, H. M. (1995). *Children talk about the mind.* New York: Oxford University Press.

Bates, E., Benigni, L., Bretherton, I., Camaioni, L., & Volterra, V. (1979). Cognition and communication from 9–13 months: Correlational findings. In E. Bates (Ed.), *The emergence of symbols: Cognition and communication in infancy.* New York: Academic Press.

Bates, E., Bretherton, I., Snyder, L., Shore, C., & Volterra, V. (1980). Vocal and gestural symbols at 13 months. *Merrill-Palmer Quarterly, 26,* 407–423.

Bateson, G. A. (1955/1972). A theory of play and fantasy. In G. A. Bateson (Ed.), *Steps to an ecology of mind* (reprinted from American Psychiatric Association Research Reports, 1955, II, 39–51). New York: Chandler.

Bauer, P. J. (1992). Holding it all together: How enabling relations facilitate young children's event recall. *Cognitive Development, 7,* 1–28.

Bauer, P. J. (1993). Identifying subsystems of autobiographical memory: Commentary on Nelson. In C. A. Nelson (Ed.), *Memory and affect in development: The Minnesota Symposium on Child Psychology* (Vol. 26, pp. 25–37). Hillsdale, NJ: Erlbaum.

Bauer, P. J. (1995). Recalling past events: From infancy to early childhood. *Annals of Child Development, 11,* 25–71.

Bauer, P. J. (1996). What do infants recall of their lives? Memory for specific events by 1- to 2-year-olds. *American Psychologist, 51,* 29–41.

Bauer, P. J. (1997). Development of memory in early childhood. In N. Cowan (Ed.), *The Development of Memory in Childhood* (pp. 83–111). Hove, East Sussex: Psychology Press.

Bauer, P. J., & Dow, G. A. A. (1994). Episodic memory in 16- and 20-month-old children: Specifics are generalized, but not forgotten. *Developmental Psychology, 30,* 403–417.

Bauer, P. J., & Fivush, R. (1992). Constructing event representations: Building on a foundation of variation and enabling relations. *Cognitive Development, 7,* 381–401.

Bauer, P. J., & Hertsgaard, L. A. (1993). Increasing steps in recall of events: Factors facilitating immediate and long-term memory in 13.5- and 16.5-month-old children. *Child Development, 64,* 1204–1223.

Bauer, P. J., Hertsgaard, L. A., Dropik, P., & Daly, B. P. (1998). When even arbitrary order becomes important: Developments in reliable temporal sequencing of arbitrarily ordered events. *Memory, 6,* 165–198.

Bauer, P. J., Hertsgaard, L. A., & Wewerka, S. S. (1995). Effects of experience and reminding on long-term recall in infancy: Remembering not to forget. *Journal of Experimental Child Psychology, 59,* 260–298.

Bauer, P. J., Kroupina, M. G., Schwade, J. A., Dropik, P., & Wewerka, S. S. (1998). If memory serves, will language? Later verbal accessibility of early memories. *Development and Psychopathology, 10,* 655–679.

Bauer, P. J., & Shore, C. M. (1987). Making a memorable event: Effects of familiarity and organization on young children's recall of action sequences. *Cognitive Development, 2,* 327–338.

Bauer, P. J., & Thal, D. J. (1990). Scripts or scraps: Reconsidering the development of sequential understanding. *Journal of Experimental Child Psychology, 50,* 287–304.

Bauer, P. J., & Travis, L. L. (1993). The fabric of an event: Different sources of temporal invariance differentially affect 24-month-olds' recall. *Cognitive Development, 8,* 319–341.

Bauer, P. J., Van Abbema, D. L., & de Haan, M. (1999). In for the short haul: Immediate an short-term remembering and forgetting by 20-month-old children. *Infant Behavior and Development, 22,* 321–343.

Bauer, P. J., Wenner, J. A., Dropik, P. L., & Wewerka, S. (2000). Parameters of remembering and forgetting in the transition from infancy to early childhood. *Monographs of the Society for Research in Child Development, 65* (4, Serial No. 263).

Bauer, P. J., & Wewerka, S. S. (1995). One- to two-year-olds' recall of events: The more expressed, the more impressed. *Journal of Experimental Child Psychology, 59,* 475–496.

Bauer, P. J ., & Wewerka, S. S. (1997). Saying is revealing: Verbal expression of event memory in the transition from infancy to early childhood. In P. van den Broek, P. J. Bauer, & T. Bourg (Eds.), *Developmental spans in event comprehension and representation: Bridging fictional and actual events* (pp. 139–168). Mahwah, NJ: Erlbaum.

Bauer, P. J., Wiebe, S., Waters, J. M., & Bradley, S. K. (in press). Reexposure breeds recall: Effects of experience on 9-month-olds' ordered recall. *Journal of Experimental Child Psychology.*

Bayles, K. A., Tomoeda, C. K., & Trosset, M. W. (1990). Naming and categorical knowledge in Alzheimer's disease: The process of semantic memory deterioration. *Brain and Language, 39,* 498–510.

Bayley, N. (1993). *The Bayley Scales of Mental and Motor Development* (revised). San Antonio, TX: The Psychological Corporation.

Bearison, D., & Zimiles, H. (1986). Developmental perspectives of thought and emotion: An introduction. In D. Bearison, & H. Zimiles (Eds.), *Thought and emotion: Developmental perspectives* (pp. 1–10). Hillsdale, NJ: Erlbaum.

Bechara, A., Damasio, A., Damasio, H., & Anderson, S. (1994). Insensitivity to future consequences following damage to human prefrontal cortex. *Cognition, 50,* 7–15.

Bechara, A., Damasio, H., & Damasio, A. R. (2000). Emotion, decision making and the orbitofrontal cortex. *Cerebral Cortex.* [Special Issue]: *The mysterious orbitofrontal cortex, 10,* 295–307.

Beebe, B., Jaffe, J., Feldstein, S., Mays, K., & Alson, D. (1985). Interpersonal timing: The application of an adult dialogue model to mother–infant vocal and kinesic interactions. In T. Field & N. Fox (Eds.), *Social perception in infants* (pp. 217–247). Norwood, NJ: Ablex.

Behl-Chadha, G. (1996). Basic-level and superordinate-like categorical representations in early infancy. *Cognition, 60,* 105–141.

Beilin, H. (1992). Piaget's enduring contribution to developmental psychology. *Developmental Psychology, 28,* 191–204.

Beilin, H., & Fireman, G. (2000). The foundation of Piaget's theories: Mental and physical action. *Advances in Child Development and Behaviour, 27,* 221–246.

Bell, J. A., & Fox, N. A. (1992). The relations between frontal brain electrical activity and cognitive development during infancy. *Child Development, 63,* 1142–1163.

Bellagamba, F., & Tomasello, M. (1999). Re-enacting intended acts: Comparing 12- and 18-month-olds. *Infant Behavior & Development, 22,* 277–282.

Bellugi, U., Bihrle, A., Jernigan, T., Trauner, D., & Doherty, S. (1990). Neuropsychological, neurological and neuroanatomical profile of Williams syndrome. *American Journal of Medical Genetics, 6,* 115–125.

Bellugi, U., Lai, Z., & Wang, P. (1997). Language, communication and neural systems in Williams syndrome. *Mental Retardation and Developmental Disabilities Research Reviews, 3,* 333–342.

Bellugi, U., Marks, S., Bihrle, A., & Ssabo, H. (1988). Dissociation in language and cognitive functions in Williams Syndrome. In D. Bishop and K. Mogford (Eds.), *Language development in exceptional circumstances.* London: Churchill Livingstone.

Bellugi, U., Wang, P., & Jernigan, T. L. (1994). Williams syndrome: An unusual neuropsychological profile. In S. Broman and J. Grafman (Eds.), *Atypical cognitive deficits in developmental disorders: Implications for brain function* (pp. 23–56). Hillsdale, NJ: Erlbaum.

Bem, S. L. (1983). Gender schema theory and its implications for child development: Raising gender-aschematic children in a gender-schematic society. *Signs, 8,* 598–616.

Bem, S. L. (1993). *The lenses of gender: Transforming the debate on sexual inequality.* New Haven, CT: Yale University Press.

Benedict, H. (1979). Early lexical development: Comprehension and production. *Journal of Child Language, 6,* 183–200.

Berry, J. W. (1974). Radical cultural relativism and the concept of intelligence. In J. W. Berry & P. R. Dasen (Eds.), *Culture and cognition: Readings in cross-cultural psychology* (pp. 225–229). London: Methuen.

Bertenthal, B., & Fisher, K. (1978). Development of self-recognition in the infant. *Developmental Psychology, 14,* 44–50.

Bertenthal, B. I., & Clifton, R. K. (1998) Perception and action. In W. Damon (Series Ed.), D. Kuhn, & R. S. Siegler (Vol. Eds.), *Handbook of child psychology: Vol 2. Cognition, perception, and language* (5th ed., pp. 51–102). New York: Wiley.

Bertenthal, B. I., Proffitt, D. R., Kramer, S. J., & Spetner, N. B. (1987). Infants' encoding of kinetic displays varying in relative coherence. *Developmental Psychology, 23*(2), 171–178.

Bertenthal, B. I., Proffitt, D. R., Spetner, N. B., & Thomas, M. A. (1985). The development of infant sensitivity to biomechanical motions. *Child Development, 56,* 531–543.

Berzonsky, M. D. (1987). A preliminary investigation of children's conceptions of life and death. *Merrill-Palmer Quarterly, 33,* 505–513.

Berzonsky, M. D., Miller, P. H., Woody-Ramsey, J., & Harris, Y. (1987). The relationship between judgments of animacy and sentiency: Another look. *Journal of Genetic Psychology, 149,* 223–238.

Besner, D., Twilley, L., McCann, R. S., & Seergobin, K. (1990). On the association between connectionism and data: Are a few words necessary? *Psychological Review, 97*(3), 432–446.

Bettelheim, B. (1968). *The empty fortress.* Chicago: The Free Press.

Beveridge, M., & Davies, M. (1983). A picture-sorting approach to child animism. *Genetic Psychology Monographs, 107*, 211–231.

Bhatt, R. S., & Bertin, E. (2001). Pictorial cues and three-dimensional information processing in early infancy. *Journal of Experimental Child Psychology, 80*, 315–332.

Bhatt, R. S., & Rovee-Collier, C. (1997). Dissociation between features and feature relations in infant memory: Effects of memory load. *Journal of Experimental Child Psychology, 67*(1), 69–89.

Bialystok, E. (1999). Cognitive complexity and attentional control in the bilingual mind. *Child Development, 70*, 636–644.

Bickhard, M. (2002). The biological emergence of representation. In T. Brown & L. Smith (Eds), *Reductionism and the development of knowledge*. Mahwah, NJ: Erlbaum.

Bigelow, A. E. (2000). Discovering self through other: Infant's preference for social contingency. In G. Gergely, P. Fonagy, & J. G. Allen (Eds.), *Contingency perception and attachment development in infancy. Bulletin of the Menninger Clinic* [Special Issue].

Bigelow, A. E., & DeCoste, C. (2000). Infants' sensitivity to contingency in social interactions with familiar and unfamiliar partners. Submitted.

Binet, A., & Simon, T. (1916). *The development of intelligence in children*. Baltimore: Williams & Wilkins. [1st published 1905].

Bíró, S., Gergely, G., Csibra, G., & Koós, O. (1996). Inferring hypothetical state of affairs on the basis of the rationality assumption in infancy. Poster presented at the 10th International Conference on Infant Studies (ICIS), Providence, RI.

Bisanz, J., & Lefevre, J.-A. (1992). Understanding elementary mathematics. In J. I. D. Campbell (Ed.), *The nature and origins of mathematical skills* (pp. 113–136). Amsterdam: Elsevier Science Publishers.

Bisanz, J., Vesonder, B., & Voss, J. (1978). Knowledge of one's own responding and the relation of such knowing to learning. *Journal of Experimental Child Psychology, 25*, 116–128.

Bishop, D. (1989). *Test of reception of grammar*. Manchester: University of Manchester.

Bishop, D. (1997). *Uncommon understanding: Development and disorders of language comprehension in children*. East Sussex: Psychology Press.

Bishop, D., Carlyon, R., Deeks, J., & Bishop, S. (1999). Auditory temporal processing impairment: Neither necessary nor sufficient for causing language impairment in children. *Journal of Speech, Language and Hearing Research, 42*, 1295–1310.

Bishop, D., & Rosenbloom, L. (1987). Childhood language disorders classification and overview. In W. Yule & M. Rutter (Eds.), *Language development and disorders* (Vol. 101/102, pp. 16–41). Oxford: Mac Keith Press.

Bishop, D. V. M. (1997). Cognitive neuropsychology and developmental disorders: Uncomfortable bedfellows. *Quarterly Journal of Experimental Psychology, 50A*, 899–923.

Bishop, D. V. M., North, T., & Donlan, C. (1995). Genetic basis of specific language impairment. *Developmental Medicine & Child Neurology, 37*, 56–71.

Bissex, G. L. (1980). *GNYS at work: A child learns to write and read*. Cambridge, MA: Harvard University Press.

Bjorklund, D. F. (1985). The role of conceptual knowledge in the development of organization in children's memory. In C. J. Brainerd & M. Pressley (Eds.), *Basic processes in memory development* (pp. 103–142). New York: Springer.

Bjorklund, D. F. (1997). The role of immaturity in human development. *Psychological Bulletin, 122*, 153–169.

Bjorklund, D. F., & Coyle, T. R. (1995). Utilization deficiencies in the development of memory strategies. In F. E. Weinert & W. Schneider (Eds.), *Memory performance and competencies: Issues in growth and development* (pp. 161–180). Hillsdale, NJ: Erlbaum.

Bjorklund, D. F., & Douglas, R. N. (1997). The development of memory strategies. In N. Cowan (Ed.)., *The development of memory in children* (pp. 201–246). Hove, UK: Psychology Press.

Bjorklund, D. F., Miller, P. H., Coyle, T. R., & Slawinski, J. L. (1997). Instructing children to use memory strategies: Evidence of utilization deficiencies in memory training studies. *Developmental Review, 17*, 411–442.

Bjorklund, D. F., & Schneider, W. (1996). The interaction of knowledge, aptitude, and strategies in children's memory performance. In H. Reese (Ed.), *Advances in Child Development and Behavior* (Vol. 26, pp. 59–89). San Diego: Academic Press.

Black, B. (1992). Negotiating social pretend play: Communication differences related to social status and sex. *Merrill-Palmer Quarterly, 38*(2), 212–232.

Blades, M. (1991). The development of the abilities required to understand spatial representations. In D. M. Mark & A. V. Frank (Eds.), *Cognitive and linguistic aspects of geographic space* (pp. 81–116). Dordrecht: Kluwer Academic Press.

Blades, M., Hetherington, D., Spencer, C., & Sowden, S. (1997, April). *Can young children recognize aerial photographs?* Paper presented at the biennial meeting of the Society for Research in Child Development, Washington, DC.

Blades, M., & Spencer, C. (1994). The development of children's ability to use spatial representations. In H. W. Reese (Ed.), *Advances in child development and behavior* (Vol. 25, pp. 157–199). New York: Academic Press.

Bloom, B. S. (1964). *Stability and change in human characteristics.* New York: Wiley.

Bloom, L. (1993). *The transition from infancy to language: Acquiring the power of expression.* New York: Cambridge University Press.

Bloom, P. (1993). Overview: Controversies in language acquisition. In P. Bloom (Ed.), *Language acquisition: Core readings* (pp. 5–48). Cambridge, MA: MIT Press.

Bloom, P. (2000). *How children learn the meanings of words.* Cambridge, MA: MIT Press.

Bloom, P., & Markson, L. (1998). Intention and analogy in children's naming of pictorial representations. *Psychological Science, 9*, 200–204.

Bluestein, N., & Acredolo, L. (1979). Developmental changes in map-reading skills. *Child Development, 50*, 691–697.

Blythe, P. W., Todd, P. M., & Miller, G. F. (1999). How motion reveals intention: Categorizing social interactions. In G. Gigerenzer, P. M. Todd, & the ABC Research Group (Eds.), *Simple heuristics that make us smart* (pp. 257–285). New York: Oxford University Press.

Boas, F. (1966). Introduction. In *Handbook of American Indian languages.* Lincoln: University of Nebraska Press.

Bock, R. D., & Kolakowski, D. (1973). Further evidence of sex-linked major gene influence on human spatial visualizing ability. *American Journal of Human Genetics, 25*, 1–14.

Boden, M. (1979). *Piaget.* Brighton: Harvester Press.

Boehm, A. (1986). *Boehm Basic Concepts-Preschool.* London: Psychological Corporation.

Bogartz, R. S., Shinskey, J. L., & Speaker, C. J. (1997). Interpreting infant looking: The event set X event set design. *Developmental Psychology, 33*, 408–422.

Bolton, P., MacDonald, H., Pickles, A., Rios, P., Goode, S., Crowson, M., Bailey, A., & Rutter, M. (1994). A Case-Control Family History Study of Autism. *Journal of Child Psychology and Psychiatry, 35*, 877–900.

Bomba, P. C. (1984). The development of orientation categories between 2 and 4 months of age. *Journal of Experimental Child Psychology, 37*, 609–636.

Bomba, P. C., & Siqueland, E. R. (1983). The nature and structure of infant form categories. *Journal of Experimental Child Psychology, 35*, 294–328.

Bond, T. (1997). Measuring development: examples from Piaget's theory. In L. Smith, J. Dockrell, & P. Tomlinson (Eds), *Piaget, Vygotsky, and beyond.* London: Routledge.

Bond, T. (2001). Building a theory of formal operational thinking: Inhelder's psychology meets Piaget's epistemology. In A. Typhon & J. Vonèche (Eds), *Working with Piaget: Essays in honour of Bärbel Inhelder*. Hove: Psychology Press.

Boole, G. (1958). *An investigation of the laws of thought*. New York: Dover.

Borghi, R. (1990). Consonant phoneme and distinctive feature error patterns in speech. In D. Van Dyke, D. Lang, F. Heide, D Van Dduyne, & M. Soucek (Eds.), *Clinical perspectives in the management of Down's Syndrome* (pp. 147–152). New York: Springer.

Borkowski, J. G., & Cavanaugh, J. C. (1979). Maintenance and generalization of skills and strategies by the retarded. In N. R. Ellis (Ed.), *Handbook of mental deficiency, psychological theory, and research* (2nd ed., pp. 569–617). Hillsdale, NJ: Erlbaum.

Bornstein, M. H. (1981). Psychological studies of color perception in human infants: Habituation, discrimination and categorization, recognition and conceptualization. In L. P. Lipsitt (Ed.), *Advances in Infancy Research* (Vol. 1, pp. 1–40). Norwood, NJ: Ablex.

Bornstein, M. H. (1984). A descriptive taxonomy of psychological categories used by infants. In C. Sophian (Ed.), *Origins of cognitive skills* (pp. 313–338). Hillsdale, NJ: Erlbaum.

Borovsky, D., & Rovee-Collier, C. (1990). Contextual constraints on memory retrieval at six months. *Child Development, 61*, 1569–1583.

Bouchard, T. J. (1998). Genetic and environmental influences on adult intelligence and special mental abilities. *Human Biology, 70*, 257–279.

Bouchard, T. J. Jr., & McGue, M. (1981). Familial studies of intelligence: A review. *Science, 212*, 1055–1059.

Bourchier, A., & Davis, A. (2000). The influence of availability and affect on children's pretence. *British Journal of Developmental Psychology, 18*, 137–156.

Bowerman, M. (1996a). Learning how to structure space for language: A crosslinguistic perspective. In P. Bloom, M. A. Peterson, L. Nadel, & M. F. Garrett (Eds.), *Language and space* (pp. 385–436). Cambridge, MA: MIT Press.

Bowerman, M. (1996b). The origins of children's spatial semantic categories: Cognitive versus linguistic determinants. In J. J. Gumperz & S. C. Levinson (Eds.), *Rethinking linguistic relativity. Studies in the social and cultural foundations of language, No. 17* (pp. 145–176). Cambridge, UK: Cambridge University Press.

Bowers, P. G., & Wolf, M. (1993). Theoretical links among naming speed, precise timing mechanisms and orthographic skill in dyslexia. *Reading & Writing, 5*, 69–85.

Bowey, J. A. (1996). On the association between phonological memory and receptive vocabulary in five-year-olds. *Journal of Child Psychology, 63*, 44–78.

Bowey, J. A., & Underwood, N. (1996). Further evidence that orthographic rime usage in nonword reading increases with word-level reading proficiency. *Journal of Experimental Child Psychology, 63*, 526–562.

Bowlby, J. (1969). *Attachment and Loss: Vol. 1. Attachment*. London: Hogarth Press and the Institute of Psycho-Analysis.

Boyd, R. N. (1985), Lex orandi est lex credendi. In Churchland & Hooker (Eds.), *Images of science: Scientific realism versus constructive empiricism*. Chicago: University of Chicago Press.

Boyd, R. N. (1993), Metaphor and theory change (2nd version). In A. Ortony (Ed.), *Metaphor and thought* (2nd ed.). New York: Cambridge University Press.

Bradley, L., & Bryant, P. E. (1983). Categorising sounds and learning to read – causal connection. *Nature, 301*, 419–421.

Bradley, R. H., & Caldwell, B. M. (1984). 174 Children: A study of the relationship between home environment and cognitive development during the first 5 years. In A. W. Gottfried (Ed.), *Home environment and early cognitive development: Longitudinal research*. San Diego, CA: Academic Press.

Brady, S. A. (1997). Ability to encode phonological representations: An underlying difficulty for poor readers. In B. Blachman (Ed.), *Foundations of reading acquisition and dyslexia: Implications for early intervention.* Mahwah, NJ: Lawrence Erlbaum Associates.

Brainerd, C. J. (1995). Children's forgetting, with implications for memory suggestibility. In N. L. Stein, P. A. Ornstein, B. Tversky, & C. J. Brainerd (Eds.), *Memory for everyday and emotional events.* Hillsdale, NJ: Erlbaum.

Brainerd, C. J., & Reyna, V. F. (1993). Domains of fuzzy-trace theory. In M. L. Howe & R. Pasnak (Eds.), *Emerging themes in cognitive development* (pp. 50–93). New York, Berlin, & Heidelberg: Springer.

Brainerd, C. J., Reyna, V. F., Harnishfeger, K. K., & Howe, M. L. (1993). Is retrievability grouping good for recall? *Journal of Experimental Psychology: General, 122,* 249–268.

Brand, C. (1996). *The g factor: General intelligence and its implications.* Chichester, UK: Wiley.

Bransford, J. D., & Stein, B. S. (1993). *The ideal problem solver: A guide for improving thinking, learning, and creativity* (2nd ed.). New York: W. H. Freeman.

Braten, S. (1988). Dialogic mind: The infant and the adult in protoconversation. In M. Carvallo (Ed.), *Nature, cognition, and system* (Vol. 1, pp. 187–205). Dordrecht: Kluwer Academic Publishers.

Braten, S. (1992). The virtual other in infants' minds and social feelings. In H. Wold (Ed.), *The dialogical alternative* (pp. 77–97). Oslo: Scandinavian University Press.

Braten, S. (Ed.). (1998). *Intersubjective communication and emotion in early ontogeny.* Paris: Cambridge University Press.

Braun, I. E., Balaban, M. T., Booth, A. E., & Waxman, S. R. (2001). *Parental input to infants regarding individual objects, categories of objects, and naming.* Poster presented at the Society for Research in Child Development Biennial Meeting, Minneapolis, MN.

Bray, N. W., Reilly, K. D., Villa, M. F., & Grupe, L. A. (1997). Neural network models and mechanisms of strategy development. *Developmental Review, 17,* 525–566.

Brazelton, T. B., Koslowski, B., & Main, M. (1974). The origins of reciprocity: The early mother–infant interaction. In M. Lewis & L. Rosenblum (Eds.), *The effect of the infant on the caregiver* (pp. 49–76). New York: Wiley.

Brazelton, T. B., & Tronick, E. (1980). Preverbal communication between mothers and infants. In D. R. Olson (Ed.), *The social foundations of language and thought* (pp. 299–315). New York: Norton.

Bremner, J. G. (1978). Egocentric versus allocentric coding in nine-month-old infants: Factors influencing the choice of code. *Developmental Psychology, 14,* 346–355.

Bremner, J. G. (1985). Object tracking and search in infancy: A review of data and a theoretical evaluation. *Developmental Review, 5,* 371–396.

Bremner, J. G. (1993). Spatial representation in infancy and early childhood. In C. Pratt & A. F. Garton (Eds.), *Systems of representation in children* (pp. 67–89). New York: Wiley.

Bremner, J. G., & Bryant, P. E. (1977). Place versus response as the basis of spatial errors made by young infants. *Journal of Experimental Child Psychology, 23,* 162–171.

Brentano, F., von. (1874/1970). *Psychology from an empirical standpoint.* London: Routledge & Kegan Paul.

Breslow, L. (1981). Reevaluation of the literature on the development of transitive inferences. *Psychological Bulletin, 89,* 325–351.

Bretherton, I. (Ed.). (1984). *Symbolic play: The development of social understanding.* Orlando: Academic Press.

Bretherton, I. (1989). Pretense: The form and function of make-believe play. *Developmental Review, 9,* 383–401.

Bretherton, I., Bates, E., McNew, S., Shore, C., Williamson, C., & Beeghly-Smith, M. (1981). Comprehension and production of symbols in infancy: An experimental study. *Developmental Psychology, 17*, 728–736.

Bretherton, I., & Beeghly, M. (1982). Talking about internal states: The acquisition of an explicit theory of mind. *Developmental Psychology, 18*, 906–921.

Bretherton, I., McNew, S., & Beeghly-Smith, M. (1981). Early person knowledge as expressed in gestural and verbal communication: When do infants acquire a "theory of mind"? In M. Lamb & L. Sherrod (Eds.), *Social cognition in infancy* (pp. 333–373). Hillsdale, NJ: Erlbaum.

Brewer, W., & Samarapungavan, A. (1991). Children's theories vs. scientific theories: Differences in reasoning or differences in knowledge. In R. Hoffman & D. Palermo (Eds.), *Cognition and the symbolic processes* (pp. 209–232). Hillsdale NJ: Erlbaum.

Briars, D., & Siegler, R. S. (1984). A featural analysis of preschoolers' counting knowledge. *Developmental Psychology, 20*, 607–618.

Brooks, P. J., Frye, D., & Samuels, M. C. (1996). The comprehension and production of deception for self and other. Unpublished manuscript.

Brooks, R. (1999). Infant understanding of seeing as a referential event. Unpublished doctoral dissertation, Boston University.

Brooks, R., & Meltzoff, A. N. (2002). The importance of eyes: How infants interpret adult looking behavior. *Developmental Psychology, 38*, 958–966.

Brown, A. L. (1978). Knowing when, where, and how to remember: A problem of metacognition. In R. Glaser (Ed.), *Advances in instructional psychology* (pp. 77–165). Hillsdale, NJ: Erlbaum.

Brown, A. L. (1989). Analogical learning and transfer: What develops? In S. Vosniadou & A. Ortony (Eds.), *Similarity and Analogical Reasoning* (pp. 369–412). Cambridge: Cambridge University Press.

Brown, A. L. (1990). Domain-specific principles affect learning and transfer in children. *Cognitive Science, 14*, 107–133.

Brown, A. L., & Campione, J. C. (1990). Communities of learning and thinking, or a context by any other name. *Human development, 21*, pp. 108–125.

Brown, A. L., Campione, J. C., Bray, N. W., & Wilcox, B. L. (1973). Keeping track of changing variables: Effects of rehearsal training and rehearsal prevention in normal and retarded adolescents. *Journal of Experimental Psychology, 101*, 123–131.

Brown, A. L., & Ferrara, R. A. (1985). Diagnosing zones of proximal development. In J. V. Wertsch (Ed.), *Culture, communication, and cognition: Vygotskian perspectives* (pp. 273–305). New York: Cambridge University Press.

Brown, A. L., & Kane, M. J. (1988). Preschool children can learn to transfer: Learning to learn and learning by example. *Cognitive Psychology, 20*, 493–523.

Brown, A. L., Kane, M. J., & Long, C. (1989). Analogical transfer in young children: Analogies as tools for communication and exposition. *Applied Cognitive Psychology, 3*, 275–293.

Brown, G., & Deavers, R. (1999). Units of analysis in nonword reading: evidence from children and adults. *Journal of Experimental Child Psychology, 73*, 208–242.

Brown, G. D. A. (1997). Connectionism, phonology, reading, and regularity in developmental dyslexia. *Brain and Language, 59*, 207–235.

Brown, J. R., Donelan-McCall, N., & Dunn, J. (1996). Why talk about mental states? The significance of children's conversations with friends, siblings, and mothers. *Child Development, 67*, 836–849.

Brown, J. R., & Dunn, J. (1991). "You can cry, mum": The social and developmental implications of talk about internal states. *British Journal of Developmental Psychology, 9*, 237–256.

Brown, L., Sherbenou, R., & Johnsen, S. (1997). *Test of nonverbal intelligence-3*. Austin: Pro-Ed.

Brown, R. (1958). *Words and things*. Glencoe, ILL: Free Press.

Brown, R. (1973). *A first language.* Cambridge, MA: Harvard University Press.

Brown, T. (1996). Values, knowledge, and Piaget. In L. Smith (Ed.), *Critical readings on Piaget.* London: Routledge.

Brown, T. (2001). Bärbel Inhelder and the fall of Valhalla. In A. Typhon & J. Vonèche (Eds.), *Working with Piaget: Essays in honour of Bärbel Inhelder.* Hove: Psychology Press.

Bruck, M. (1990). Word recognition skills of adults with childhood diagnoses of dyslexia. *Developmental Psychology, 26,* 439–454.

Bruck, M. (1992). Persistence of dyslexics' phonological awareness deficits. *Developmental Psychology, 28,* 874–886.

Bruck, M., & Ceci, S. J. (1999). The suggestibility of children's memory. *Annual Review of Psychology, 50,* 419–439.

Bruck, M., Genesee, F., & Caravolas, M. (1997). A cross-linguistic study of early literacy acquisition. In B. Blachman (Ed.), *Foundations of reading acquisition and dyslexia: Implications for early intervention.* Mahwah, NJ: Lawrence Erlbaum Associates.

Bruner, J. (1983). *Child's talk: Learning to use language.* New York: Norton.

Bruner, J. (1990). *Acts of meaning.* Cambridge, MA: Harvard University Press.

Bruner, J. S. (1999). The intentionality of referring. In P. D. Zelazo, J. W. Astington, & D. Olson (Eds.), *Development of intention and intentional understanding in infancy and early childhood* (pp. 329–339). Mahwah, NJ: Erlbaum.

Bruner, J. S., Goodnow, J. J., & Austin, G. A. (1956). *A study of thinking.* New York: Wiley.

Bruner, J. S., Olver, R. R., & Greenfield, P. M. (1966). *Studies in cognitive growth.* New York: Wiley.

Brunswik, E., Goldscheider, L., & Pilek, E. (1932). Untersuchungen zur Entwicklung des Gedächtnisses [Studies on the development of memory]. In W. Stern & O. Lippmann (Eds.), *Beihefte zur Zeitschrift für angewandte Psychologie* (Vol. 64). Leipzig: Ambrosius Barth.

Bryant, P. (1995). Children and arithmetic. In L. Smith (Ed.), *Critical readings on Piaget.* London: Routledge.

Bryant, P. (1997). Mathematical understanding in the nursery school years. In T. Nuñes & P. Bryant (Eds.), *Learning and teaching mathematics.* Hove, UK: Psychology Press.

Bryant, P. (2001). Learning in Geneva: The contribution of Bärbel Inhelder and her colleagues. In A. Typhon & J. Vonèche (Eds.), *Working with Piaget: Essays in honour of Bärbel Inhelder.* Hove, UK: Psychology Press.

Bryant, P., Christie, C., & Rendu, A. (1999) Children's understanding of the relation between addition and subtraction: Inversion, identity and decomposition. *Journal of Experimental Child Psychology, 74,* 194–212.

Bryant, P., & Squire, S. (2001). Children's mathematics: Lost and found in space. In M. Gattis (Ed.), *Spatial Schemas and Abstract Thought* (pp. 175–200). Cambridge, MA: MIT Press.

Bryant, P. E. (1992). Arithmetic in the cradle. *Nature, 358,* 712–713.

Bryant, P. E., & Bradley, L. (1980). Why children sometimes write words which they do not read. In U. Frith (Ed.), *Cognitive processes in spelling* (pp. 355–370). London: Academic Press.

Bryant, P. E., & Trabasso, T. (1971). Transitive inferences and memory in young children. *Nature, 232,* 456–458.

Buckingham, D., & Shultz, T. R. (1994). A connectionist model of the development of velocity, time, and distance concepts. *Proceedings of the sixteenth annual conference of the Cognitive Science Society* (pp. 72–77). Hillsdale, NJ: Erlbaum.

Buckingham, D., & Shultz, T. R. (2000). The developmental course of distance, time, and velocity concepts: A generative connectionist model. *Journal of Cognition and Development, 1,* 305–345.

Bühler, K. (1930). Die Erinnerungen des Kindes [Memories of children]. In K. Bühler (Ed.), *Die geistige Entwicklung des Kindes* (6th ed., pp. 318–329). Jena: Gustav Fischer.

Bullinaria, J. A. (1997). Modelling reading, spelling, and past tense learning with artificial neural networks. *Brain and Language, 59,* 236–266.

Bullock, M. (1979). Aspects of the young child's theory of causation. Unpublished doctoral dissertation, University of Pennsylvania, 1979.

Bullock, M. (1991). Scientific reasoning in elementary school: developmental and individual differences. Paper presented at the Biennial Meetings of the Society for Research in Child Development, Seattle, WA.

Bullock, M., & Gelman, R. (1979). Preschool children's assumptions about cause and effect: Temporal ordering. *Child Development, 50,* 89–96.

Bullock, M., Gelman, R., & Baillargeon, R. (1982). The development of causal reasoning. In W. F. Friedman (Ed.), *The developmental psychology of time* (pp. 209–245). London: Academic Press.

Bullock, M., & Lütkenhaus, P. (1988). The development of volitional behavior in the toddler years. *Child Development, 59,* 664–674.

Burns, J. M., & Richgels, D. J. (1989). An investigation of task requirements associated with the invented spellings of 4-year-olds with above average intelligence. *Journal of Reading Behavior, 21*(1), 1–14.

Butler, S. C., Caron, A. J., & Brooks, R. (2000). Infant understanding of the referential nature of looking. *Journal of Cognition and Development, 1,* 359–377.

Butterfield, E., Nelson, T., & Peck, J. (1998). Developmental aspects of the feeling of knowing. *Developmental Psychology, 24,* 654–663.

Butterfield, E. C., & Belmont, J. M. (1977). Assessing and improving the cognitive functions of mentally retarded people. In I. Bialer & M. Sternlicht (Eds.), *The psychology of mental retardation: Issues and approaches.* New York: Psychological Dimensions.

Butterworth, B. (1999). *The Mathematical Brain.* London: Macmillan.

Butterworth, G. (1991). The ontogeny and phylogeny of joint visual attention. In A. Whiten (Ed.), *Natural theories of mind: Evolution, development and simulation of everyday mindreading* (pp. 223–232). Oxford: Basil Blackwell.

Butterworth, G. (1995). An ecological perspective on the origins of the self. In J. Bermudez, A. Marcel, & N. Eilan (Eds.), *The body and the self.* Cambridge, MA: MIT Press.

Butterworth, G., & Cochran, E. (1980). Towards a mechanism of joint visual attention in human infancy. *International Journal of Behavioral Development, 3,* 253–272.

Butterworth, G., & Hicks, L. (1977). Visual proprioception and postural stability in infancy: A developmental study. *Perception, 6,* 255–262.

Butterworth, G., & Jarrett, N. (1991). What minds have in common is space: Spatial mechanisms serving joint visual attention in infancy. *British Journal of Developmental Psychology, 9,* 55–72.

Büttner, G. (in press). Ist Output-Interferenz eine bedeutsamere Determinante von Gedächtnisleistungen als Strategiegebrauch? [Is output interference more important for recall than strategy use?]. *Zeitschrift für Entwicklungspsychologie und Pädagogische Psychologie.*

Byrne, B. (1996). The learnability of the alphabetic system: children's initial hypotheses about how print represents spoken language. *Applied Psycholinguistics, 17,* 401–426.

Byrne, B. (1998). *The foundation of literacy: The child's acquisition of the alphabetic principle.* Hove: Psychology Press.

Byrne, B., & Fielding-Barnsley, R. (1989). Phonemic awareness and letter knowledge in the child's acquisition of the alphabetic principle. *Journal of Educational Psychology, 81,* 805–812.

Byrne, B., Fielding-Barnsley, R., Ashley, L., & Larsen, K. (1997). Assessing the child's and the environment's contribution to reading acquisition: What we know and what we don't know. In

B. Blachman (Ed.), *Reading acquisition and dyslexia: Implications for early intervention*. Hillsdale, NJ: Lawrence Erlbaum Associates.

Cain, K., Oakhill, J. V., & Bryant, P. E. (2000a) Investigating the causes of reading comprehension failure: The comprehension matched design. *Reading and Writing, 12*, 31–40.

Cain, K., Oakhill, J. V., & Bryant, P. E. (2000b) Phonological skills and comprehension failure: A test of the phonological processing deficit hypothesis. *Reading and Writing, 13*, 31–56.

Call, J., & Tomasello, M. (1996). The effect of humans on the cognitive development of apes. In A. E. Russon, K. A. Bard, & S. T. Parker (Eds.), *Reaching into thought* (pp. 371–403). Cambridge: Cambridge University Press.

Call, J., & Tomasello, M. (1999). A nonverbal false belief task: The performance of children and great apes. *Child Development, 70*, 381–395.

Callahan, C. M. (2000). Intelligence and giftedness. In R. J. Sternberg (Ed.), *Handbook of intelligence* (pp. 159–175). New York: Cambridge University Press.

Callanan, M. A. (1985). How parents label objects for young children. *Child Development, 56*, 508–523.

Campbell, B. A. (1984). Reflections on the ontogeny of learning and memory. In R. Kail & N. E. Spear (Eds.), *Comparative perspectives on the development of memory*. Hillsdale, NJ: Erlbaum.

Campbell, J. (1997). The structure of time in autobiographical memory. *European Journal of Philosophy, 5*, 105–118.

Campbell, R. L., & Bickhard, M. H. (1986). *Knowing levels and developmental stages*. Basel: Karger.

Campione, J. C., Brown, A. L., & Ferrara, R. (1982). Mental retardation and intelligence. In R. J. Sternberg (Ed.), *Handbook of human intelligence* (pp. 392–490). New York: Cambridge University Press.

Campos, J. J. (1980). Human emotions: Their new importance and their role in social referencing. *Research & Clinical Center for Child Development. Annual Report*, 1–7.

Campos, J., Hiatt, S., Ramsay, D., Henderson, C., & Svejda, M. (1978). The emergence of fear on the visual cliff. In M. Lewis & L. Rosenbloom (Eds.), *The development of affect*. New York: Plenum.

Cantor, N., & Kihlstrom, J. F. (1987). *Personality and social intelligence*. Englewood Cliffs, NJ: Prentice-Hall.

Caramazza, A., & Shelton, J. R. (1998). Domain-specific knowledge systems in the brain: The animate–inanimate distinction. *Journal of Cognitive Neuroscience, 10*, 1–34.

Caravolas, M., & Bruck, M. (1993). The effect of oral and written language input on children's phonological awareness: a cross-linguistic study. *Journal of Experimental Child Psychology, 55*, 1–30.

Caravolas, M., Hulme, C., & Snowling, M. J. (2001). The foundations of spelling skill: Evidence from a longitudinal study. *Journal of Memory and Language, 45*, 751–774.

Carey, S. (1978). The child as a word learner. In M. Halle, J. Bresnan, & G. A. Miller (Eds.), *Linguistic Theory and Psychological Reality* (pp. 264–293). Cambridge, MA: MIT Press.

Carey, S. (1985). *Conceptual Change in Childhood*. Cambridge, MA: MIT Press.

Carey, S. (1991). Knowledge acquisition: Enrichment or conceptual change? In S. Carey & R. Gelman (Eds.), *The epigenesis of mind: Essays on biology and cognition* (pp. 257–291). Hillsdale, NJ: Erlbaum.

Carey, S. (1995). On the origins of causal understanding. In S. Sperber, D. Premack, & A. Premack (Eds.), *Causal cognition: A multi-disciplinary debate* (pp. 268–308). Oxford: Clarendon Press.

Carey, S. (1999). Sources of conceptual change. In E. K. Scholnick, K. Nelson, S. A. Gelman, & P. H. Miller (Eds.), *Conceptual development: Piaget's legacy* (pp. 293–326). Mahwah, NJ: Erlbaum.

Carey, S., & Spelke, E. S. (1994). Domain specific knowledge and conceptual change. In L. Hirschfeld & S. Gelman (Eds.), *Mapping the mind: Domain specificity in cognition and culture* (pp. 169–200). Cambridge, UK: Cambridge University Press.

Carey, S., & Spelke, E. S. (1996). Science and core knowledge. *Journal of Philosophy of Science, 63,* 515–533.

Carlson, S. M., & Moses, L. J. (2001). Individual differences in inhibitory control and children's theory of mind. *Child Development, 72,* 1032–1053.

Carlson, S. M., Moses, L. J., & Hix, H. R. (1998). The role of inhibitory processes in young children's difficulties with deception and false belief. *Child Development, 69,* 672–691.

Carlson, S. M., Taylor, M., & Levin, G. (1998). The influence of culture on pretend play: The case of Mennonite children. *Merrill-Palmer Quarterly, 44,* 538–565.

Caron, A. J., Caron, R. F., & Carlson, V. R. (1979). Infant perception of the invariant shape of objects varying in slant. *Child Development, 50,* 716–721.

Carpendale, J. I., & Chandler, M. J. (1996). On the distinction between false belief understanding and subscribing to an interpretive theory of mind. *Child Development, 67,* 1686–1706.

Carpenter, G. C., Tecce, J. J., Stechler, G., & Friedman, S. (1970). Differential visual behavior to human and humanoid faces in early infancy. *Merrill-Palmer Quarterly, 16,* 91–108.

Carpenter, M., Akhtar, N., & Tomasello, M. (1998). Fourteen- through 18-month-old infants differentially imitate intentional and accidental actions. *Infant Behavior and Development, 21,* 315–330.

Carpenter, M., Nagell, K., & Tomasello, M. (1998). Social cognition, joint attention, and communicative competence from 9 to 15 months of age. *Monographs of the Society for Research in Child Development, 63.*

Carraher, T. N., Carraher, D., & Schliemann, A. D. (1985). Mathematics in the streets and in schools. *British Journal of Developmental Psychology, 3,* 21–29.

Carroll, J. B. (1993). *Human cognitive abilities: A survey of factor-analytic studies.* New York: Cambridge University Press.

Carruthers, P. (1996). *Language, thought and consciousness. An essay in philosophical psychology.* Cambridge: Cambridge University Press.

Carver, L. J., & Bauer, P. J. (1999). When the event is more than the sum of its parts: Nine-month-olds' long-term ordered recall. *Memori, 7,* 147–174.

Carver, L. J., & Bauer, P. J. (2000). The dawning of a past: The emergence of long-term explicit memory in infancy. Manuscript in review.

Carver, L. J., Bauer, P. J., & Nelson, C. A. (2000). Associations between infant brain activity and recall memory. *Developmental Science, 3,* 234–246.

Case, R. (1972). Validation of a neo-Piagetian mental capacity construct. *Journal of Experimental Child Psychology, 14,* 287–302.

Case, R. (1977). Responsiveness to conservation training as a function of induced subjective uncertainty, M-space and cognitive style. *Canadian Journal of Behavioral Sciences, 9,* 12–25.

Case, R. (1978). Intellectual development from birth to adulthood: A neo-Piagetian interpretation. In R. S. Siegler (Ed.), *Children's thinking: What develops?* (pp. 37–81). Hillsdale, NJ: Erlbaum.

Case, R. (1985a). *Intellectual development: A systematic reinterpretation.* New York: Academic Press.

Case, R. (1985b). *Intellectual development: Birth to adulthood.* New York: Academic Press.

Case, R. (1992a). *The mind's staircase: Exploring the conceptual underpinnings of children's thought and knowledge.* Hillsdale, NJ: Erlbaum.

Case, R. (1992b). The role of the frontal lobes in the regulation of cognitive development. *Brain and Cognition, 20,* 51–73.

Case, R. (1999). Conceptual development in the child and in the field: A personal view of the Piagetian legacy. In E. Scholnick, K. Nelson, S. Gelman, & P. Miller (Eds.), *Conceptual development: Piaget's legacy*. Mahwah, NJ: Erlbaum.

Case, R., & Kurland, M. (1979, March). Operational efficiency and the growth of M-space. Paper presented to the conference of the Society for Research in Child Development, San Francisco.

Case, R., Kurland, M., & Goldberg, J. (1982). Operational efficiency and the growth of short-term memory span. *Journal of Experimental Child Psychology, 33*, 386–404.

Case, R., Okamoto, Y., Griffin, S., McKeough, A., Bleiker, C., Henderson, B., & Stephenson, K. M. (1996). The role of central conceptual structures in the development of children's thought. *Monographs of the Society for Research in Child Development, 61*(1–2, Serial No. 246).

Casey, M. B. (1996). Understanding individual differences in spatial ability within females: A nature/nurture interactionist framework. *Developmental Review, 16*, 240–261.

Cassel, W. S., & Bjorklund, D. F. (1995). Developmental patterns of eyewitness memory and suggestibility: An ecologically based short-term longitudinal study. *Law & Human Behavior, 19*, 507–532.

Cassel, W. S., Roebers, C. E. M., & Bjorklund, D. F. (1996). Developmental patterns of eyewitness responses to increasingly suggestive questions. *Journal of Experimental Child Psychology, 61*, 116–133.

Cassirer, E. (1950). *The problem of knowledge*. New Haven: Yale University Press.

Cataldo, S., & Ellis, N. (1988). Interactions in the development of spelling, reading and phonological skills. *Journal of Research in Reading, 11*, 86–109.

Cattell, J. M. (1890). Mental tests and measurements. *Mind, 15*, 373–380.

Cattell, R. B. (1971). *Abilities: Their structure, growth and action*. Boston: Houghton Mifflin.

Cavanaugh, J. C., & Perlmutter, M. (1982). Metamemory: A critical examination. *Child Development, 53*, 11–28.

Cazden, C. (1988). *Classroom discourse: The language of teaching and learning*. Portsmouth, NH: Heinemann.

Ceci, S. J. (1996). *On intelligence . . . more or less* (expanded ed.). Cambridge, MA: Harvard University Press.

Ceci, S. J., & Brofenbrenner, U. (1985). Don't forget to take the cupcakes out of the oven: Strategic time-monitoring, prospective memory and context. *Child Development, 56*, 175–190.

Ceci, S. J., & Bruck, M. (1993). Suggestibility of the child witness: A historical review and synthesis. *Psychological Bulletin, 113*(3), 403–439.

Ceci, S. J., & Bruck, M. (1998). Children's testimony: Applied and basic issues. In I. Sigel & K. A. Renninger (Eds.), *The Handbook of Child Psychology* (5th edn, Vol. 4, pp. 714–774). New York: Wiley.

Ceci, S. J., & Roazzi, A. (1994). The effects of context on cognition: postcards from Brazil. In R. J. Sternberg & R. K. Wagner (Eds.), *Mind in context: Interactionist perspectives on human intelligence* (pp. 74–101). New York: Cambridge University Press.

Cerella, J., & Hale, S. (1994). The rise and fall in information-processing rates over the life span. *Acta Psychologica, 86*, 109–197.

Chaminade, T., Meltzoff, A. N., & Decety, J. (in press). Does the end justify the means? A PET exploration of the mechanisms involved in human imitation. *NeuroImage*.

Chandler, M. (1997). Stumping for progress in a post-modern world. In E. Amsel & K. Renninger (Eds.), *Change and development*. Mahwah, NJ: Erlbaum.

Chandler, M., Fritz, A. S., & Hala, S. (1989). Small scale deceit: Deception as a marker of 2-, 3-, and 4-year-olds early theories of mind. *Child Development, 60*, 1263–1277.

Chapa, C., & Wilcox, T. (1999, April). Object experience and individuation: Infants' use of color information. Paper presented at the biennial International Conference on Infants Studies, Albuquerque, NM.

Chapman, L., & Chapman, J. (1967). Genesis of popular but erroneous diagnostic observations. *Journal of Abnormal Psychology, 72,* 193–204.

Chapman, L., & Chapman, J. (1969). Illusory correlation as an obstacle to the use of valid psychodiagnostic signs. *Journal of Abnormal Psychology, 74,* 271–280.

Chapman, M. (1987). Piaget, attentional capacity, and the functional limitations of formal structure. *Advances in Child Development and Behaviour, 20,* 289–334.

Chapman, M. (1988). *Constructive evolution.* Cambridge: Cambridge University Press.

Chapman, M. (1990). Cognitive development and the growth of capacity: Issues in NeoPiagetian theory. In J. T. Enns (Ed.), *The development of attention: Research and theory* (pp. 263–287). Amsterdam: Elsevier Science Publishers.

Chapman, M. (1992). Equilibration and the dialectics of organization. In H. Beilin & P. Pufall (Eds.), *Piaget's theory: Prospects and possibilities.* Hillsdale, NJ: Erlbaum.

Chapman, M., & Lindenberger, U. (1989). Concrete operations and attentional capacity. *Journal of Experimental Child Psychology, 47,* 236–258.

Chapman, M., & McBride, M. (1992). Children's class inclusion strategies. In L. Smith (Ed.), *Critical readings on Piaget.* London: Routledge.

Charman, T., & Baron-Cohen, S. (1992). Understanding beliefs and drawings: a further test of the metarepresentation theory of autism. *Journal of Child Psychology and Psychiatry, 33,* 1105–1112.

Charman, T., & Baron-Cohen, S. (1995). Understanding models, photos, and beliefs: a test of the modularity thesis of metarepresentation. *Cognitive Development, 10,* 287–298.

Chelune, G. J., & Baer, R. A. (1986). Developmental norms for the Wisconsin Card Sorting Test. *Journal of Clinical and Experimental Neuropsychology, 8,* 219–228.

Chen, Z. (1996). Children's analogical problem solving: The effects of superficial, structural, and procedural similarity. *Journal of Experimental Child Psychology, 62,* 410–431.

Chen, Z., & Klahr, D. (1999). All other things being equal: Children's acquisition of the control of variables strategy. *Child Development, 70,* 1098–1120.

Chen, Z., Sanchez, R. P., & Campbell, T. (1997). From beyond to within their grasp: Analogical problem solving in 10- and 13-month-olds. *Developmental Psychology, 33,* 790–801.

Chen, Z., & Siegler, R. S. (2000a). Across the great divide: Bridging the gap between understanding of toddlers' and other children's thinking. *Monographs of the Society for Research in Child Development, 65* (Serial No. 261).

Chen, Z., & Siegler, R. S. (2000b). Intellectual development in childhood. In R. J. Sternberg (Ed.), *Handbook of intelligence* (pp. 92–116). New York: Cambridge University Press.

Cheng, P. W., & Holyoak, K. J. (1985). Pragmatic reasoning schemas. *Cognitive Psychology, 17,* 391–416.

Chi, M. T. H. (1978). Knowledge structure and memory development. In R. Siegler (Ed.), *Children's thinking: What develops?* (pp. 73–96). Hillsdale: Erlbaum.

Chi, M. T. H., & Ceci, S. J. (1987). Content knowledge: Its role, representation, and restructuring in memory development. In H. W. Rees (Ed.), *Advances in child development and behavior* (Vol. 20, pp. 91–142). New York.

Chi, M. T. H., Feltovich, P., & Glaser, R. (1981). Categorisation and representation of physics problems by experts and novices. *Cognitive Science, 5,* 121–152.

Chiat, S. (2000). *Understanding children with language problems.* Cambridge: Cambridge University Press.

Chinn, C. A., & Brewer, W. F. (1998). An empirical test of a taxonomy of responses to anomalous data in science. *Journal of Research in Science Teaching, 35,* 623–654.

Chodorow, N. (1978). *The reproduction of mothering.* Berkeley: University of California Press.

Choi, S. H. (1992). Communicative socialization processes: Korea and Canada. In S. Iwasaki, Y. Kashima, & L. Leung (Eds.), *Innovations in cross-cultural psychology* (pp. 103–122). Amsterdam: Swets & Zeitlinger.

Choi, S., & Gopnik, A. (1995). Early acquisition of verbs in Korean: A cross-linguistic study. *Journal of Child Language, 22*(3), 497–529.

Chomsky, N. (1986). *Knowledge of language: Its nature, origins and use.* New York: Praeger.

Christiansen, M. H., & Chater, N. (in press). Toward a connectionist model of recursion in human linguistic performance. *Cognitive Science.*

Christiansen, M. H., Allen, J., & Seidenberg, M. S. (1998). Learning to segment speech using multiple cues: A connectionist model. *Language and Cognitive Processes, 13,* 221–268.

Christoff, K., Prabhakaran, V., Dorfman, J., Kroger, J. K., Holyoak, K. J., & Gabrieli, J. D. E. (submitted). Role of the prefrontal cortex in processing relational complexity during reasoning: An event-related study.

Cicchetti, D., & Toth, S. L. (Eds.). (1994). *Disorders and dysfunctions of the self. Rochester Symposium on Developmental Psychopathology, Vol. 5.*, Rochester, NY: University of Rochester Press.

Clahsen, H., & Almazan, M. (1998). Syntax and morphology in Williams Syndrome. *Cognition, 68,* 167–198.

Clark, A., & Karmiloff-Smith, A. (1993). The cognizer's innards: A psychological and philosophical perspective on the development of thought. *Mind and Language, 8*(4), 487–519.

Clark, C. D. (1995). *Flights of fancy, leaps of faith.* Chicago: University of Chicago Press.

Clearfield, M. W., & Mix, K. S. (1999). Number vs contour length in infants' discrimination of small visual sets. *Psychological Science, 10,* 408–411.

Clifton, R., Rochat, P., Litovsky, R. Y., & Perris, E. E. (1991). Object representation guides infants' reaching in the dark. *Journal of experimental psychology: Human perception and performance, 17,* 323–329.

Cohen, I. L. (1994). An artificial neural network analogue of learning in autism. *Biological Psychiatry, 36,* 5–20.

Cohen, J. (1988). *Statistical power analysis for the behavioral sciences* (2nd ed.). Hillsdale, NJ: Lawrence Erlbaum.

Cohen, L. B., & Oakes, L. M. (1993). How infants perceive a simple causal event. *Developmental Psychology, 29,* 421–433.

Cohen, L. B., & Younger, B. A. (1983). Perceptual categorization in the infant. In E. Scholnick (Ed.), *New trends in conceptual representation: Challenges to Piaget's theory?* (pp. 197–220). Hillsdale, NJ: Erlbaum.

Colby, A., & Kohlberg, L. (1987). *The measurement of moral judgment: Vol. 1. Theoretical foundations and research validation; Vol. 2. Standard issue scoring manual.* New York: Cambridge University Press.

Colby, A., Kohlberg, L., Gibbs, J., & Lieberman, M. (1983). A longitudinal study of moral judgment. *Monographs of the Society for Research in Child Development, 48* (Serial No. 200).

Cole, M. (1985). The zone of proximal development: Where culture and cognition create each other. In J. V. Wertsch (Ed.), *Culture, communication, and cognition: Vygotskian perspectives.* Cambridge: Cambridge University Press.

Cole, M. (1996). *Cultural psychology: A once and future discipline.* Cambridge, MA: Harvard University Press.

Cole, M., & Engeström, Y. (1993). A cultural-historical interpretation of distributed cognition. In G. Salomon (Ed.), *Distributed cognitions: Psychological and educational considerations.* Cambridge: Cambridge University Press.

Cole, M., Gay, J., Glick, J. A., & Sharp, D. W. (1971). *The cultural context of learning and thinking.* New York: Basic Books.

Coley, J. D. (1993). Emerging differentiation of folkbiology and folkpsychology: Similarity judg-ments and property attributions. Unpublished doctoral dissertation, University of Michigan, Ann Arbor.

Colombo, J., McCollam, K., Coldren, J. T., Mitchell, D. W., & Rash, S. J. (1990). Form catego-rization in 10-month-olds. *Journal of Experimental Child Psychology, 49*, 173–188.

Colombo, J., Mitchell, D. W., Coldren, J. T., & Atwater, J. D. (1990). Discrimination learning during the first year: Stimulus and positional cues. *Journal of Experimental Psychology: Learning, Memory, and Cognition, 16*, 98–109.

Coltheart, V., & Leahy, J. (1992). Children's and adult's reading of nonwords: Effects of regular-ity and consistency. *Journal of Experimental Psychology: Learning, Memory and Cognition, 18*, 718–729.

Connell, P., & Stone, C. A. (1994). The conceptual basis for morpheme learning problems in chil-dren with specific language impairment. *Journal of Speech and Hearing Research, 37*, 389–398.

Connellan, J., Baron-Cohen, S., Wheelwright, S., Ba'tki, A., & Ahluwalia, J. (2001). Sex differ-ences in human neonatal social perception. *Infant Behavior and Development, 23*, 113–118.

Connerton, P. (1989). *How societies remember.* Cambridge: Cambridge University Press.

Connolly, J. A., & Doyle, A. (1984). Relation of social fanatasy play to social competence in preschoolers. *Developmental Psychology, 20*, 597–608.

Connor, J. M., & Serbin, L. A. (1977). Behaviorally based masculine and feminine activity pref-erence scales for preschoolers: Correlates with other classroom behaviors and cognitive tests. *Child Development, 48*, 1411–1416.

Conti-Ramsden, G., & Botting, N. (1999). Classification of children with specific language impair-ment: Longitudinal considerations. *Journal of Speech, Language, and Hearing Research, 42*, 1195–1204.

Conti-Ramsden, G., Crutchley, A., & Botting, N. (1997). The extent to which psychometric tests differentiate subgroups of children with SLI. *Journal of Speech, Language, and Hearing Research, 40*, 765–777.

Cooley, C. H. (1912). *Human nature and the social order.* New York: Scribner.

Cooper, R. G. (1984). Early number development: Discovering number space with addition and subtraction. In C. Sophian, *The origins of cognitive skill* (pp. 157–192). Hillsdale, NJ: Lawrence Erlbaum.

Cooper, R. P., & Aslin, R. N. (1990). Preference for infant-directed speech in the first month after birth. *Child Development, 61*, 1584–1595.

Corcoran, R., Mercer, G., & Frith, C. (1995). Schizophrenia, symptomatology and social infer-ence: Investigating "theory of mind" in people with schizophrenia. *Schizophrenia Research, 17*, 5–13.

Corkum, V., & Moore, C. (1995). Development of joint visual attention in infants. In C. Moore & P. J. Dunham (Eds.), *Joint attention: Its origins and role in development* (pp. 61–83). Hillsdale, NJ: Erlbaum.

Cornell, E. H., & Hay, D. H. (1984). Children's acquisition of a route via different media. *Environment and Behavior, 16*, 627–642.

Cornell, E. H., Heth, C. D., & Broda, L. S. (1989). Children's wayfinding: Response to instruc-tions to use environmental landmarks. *Developmental Psychology, 25*, 755–764.

Cornell, E. H., Heth, C. D., & Rowat, W. L. (1992). Wayfinding by children and adults: Response to instructions to use look-back and retrace strategies. *Developmental Psychology, 28*, 328–336.

Correa, J. (1994). Young children's understanding of the division concept. Unpublished D.Phil. thesis, Oxford University.

Correa, J., Nuñes, T., & Bryant, P. (1998). Young children's understanding of division: the relationship between division terms in a noncomputational task. *Journal of Educational Psychology*, *90*, 321–329.

Cosmides, L., & Tooby, J. (1994). Origins of domain specificity: The evolution of functional organization. In L. A. Hirschfeld & S. A. Gelman (Eds.), *Mapping the mind*. New York: Cambridge.

Cossu, G. (1999). Biological constraints on literacy acquisition. *Reading and Writing*, *11*(3), 213–237.

Cossu, G., Shankweiler, D., Liberman, I., Katz, L., & Tola, G. (1988). Awareness of phonological segments and reading ability in Italian children. *Applied Psycholinguistics*, *9*, 1–16.

Courage, M. L., & Howe, M. L. (1998). The ebb and flow of infant attentional preferences: Evidence for long-term recognition memory in 3-month-olds. *Journal of Experimental Child Psychology*, *70*, 26–53.

Cowan, N. (1997). The development of working memory. In N. Cowan (Ed.), *The development of memory in childhood* (pp. 163–200). Hove, UK: Psychology Press.

Cowan, N. (1998). What is more explanatory, processing capacity or processing speed? *Behavioral and Brain Sciences*, *21*(6), 835–836.

Cowan, N. (2001). The magical number 4 in short-term memory: A reconsideration of mental storage capacity. *Behavioral and Brain Sciences*, *24*(1).

Cowan, N., Nugent, L., Elliott, E., Ponomarev, I., & Saults, J. (1999). The role of attention in the development of short-term memory: Age differerences in the verbal span of apprehension. *Child Development*, *70*, 1082–1097.

Cowan, R., & Daniels, H. (1989). The children's use of counting and guidelines in judging relative numbers. *British Journal of Educational Psychology*, *59*, 200–210.

Coyle, T. R., & Bjorklund, D. F. (1997). Age differences in, and consequences of, multiple- and variable-strategy use on a multitrial sort-recall task. *Developmental Psychology*, *33*(2), 372–380.

Crawley, S. B., & Sherrod, K. B. (1984). Parent–infant play during the first year of life. *Infant Behavior & Development*, *7*, 65–75.

Crépault J. (1979). Influence du repérage sur la durée: Etude génétique des inférences cinématiques. *L'Anée Psychologique*, *79*, 43–64.

Cromer, R. (1991). Language and thought in normal and handicapped children. London: Blackwell.

Crystal, D. (1979). *Working with LARSP*. New York: Elsevier North Holland Publishing.

Csibra G., & Gergely, G. (1998a). The teleological origins of mentalistic action explanations: A developmental hypothesis. *Developmental Science*, *1*(2), 255–259.

Csibra, G., & Gergely, G. (1998b). Beyond least effort: The principle of rationality in teleological interpretation of action in one-year-olds. Poster presented at the Swansong Conference of the Medical Research Council Cognitive Development Unit, London, September 1998.

Csibra G., Gergely, G., Bíró, S., & Koós, O., & Brockbank, M. (1999). Goal-attribution without agency cues: The perception of "pure reason" in infancy. *Cognition*, *72*, 237–267.

Csibra, G., Gergely, G., Brockbanck, M., Biró, S., & Koós, O. (1998). Twelve-month-olds can infer a goal for an incomplete action. ICIS, 11th Biennial International Conference on Infant Studies, Atlanta, Georgia, April 2–5, 1998.

Cunningham, A., & Stanovich, K. (1991). Tracking the unique effects of print exposure in children: Associations with vocabulary, general knowledge, and spelling. *Journal of Educational Psychology*, *83*, 264–274.

Custer, W. L. (1996). A comparison of young children's understanding of contradictory representations in pretense, memory, and belief. *Child Development*, *67*, 678–688.

Cybenko, G. (1989). Approximation by superpositions of a sigmoidal function. *Mathematics of Control, Signals, and Systems*, *2*, 303–314.

Dale, N. (1989). Pretend play with mothers and siblings: Relations between early performance and partners. *Journal of Psychology and Psychiatry, 30,* 751–759.

Damasio, A. (1994). *Descartes' error: Emotion, reason, and the human brain.* New York: Grosset/Putnam.

Damasio, H. (1996). Human neuroanatomy relevant to decision-making. In A. R. Damasio, H. Damasio, & Y. Christen (Eds.), *Neurobiology of decision-making* (pp. 1–12). Berlin: Springer-Verlag.

Damon, W. (1977). *The social world of the child.* San Francisco: Jossey-Bass.

Damon, W. (1980). Patterns of change in children's social reasoning: A two-year longitudinal study. *Child Development, 51,* 1010–1017.

Dan, N., Omori, T., & Tomiyasu, Y. (2000). Development of infants' intuitions about support relations: Sensitivity to stability. *Developmental Science, 3,* 171–180.

D'Andrade, R. (1987). A folk model of the mind. In D. Holland & N. Quinn (Eds.), *Cultural models in language and thought* (pp. 112–148). Cambridge: Cambridge University Press.

Daugherty, K., & Seidenberg, M. S. (1992). Rules or connections? The past tense revisited. In *Proceedings of the fourteenth annual conference of the Cognitive Science Society* (pp. 259–264). Hillsdale, NJ: Lawrence Erlbaum.

Davidson, D. (1980). *Essays on actions and events.* Oxford: Clarendon Press.

Davidson, P., Turiel, E., & Black, A. (1983). The effect of stimulus familiarity on the use of criteria and justifications in children's social reasoning. *British Journal of Developmental Psychology, 1,* 46–65.

Davis, H. L., & Pratt, C. (1995). The development of children's theory of mind: The working memory explanation. *Australian Journal of Psychology, 47*(1), 25–31.

Davison, K. K., & Susman, E. J. (in press). Are hormone levels and cognitive ability related during early adolescence? *International Journal of Behavioral Development.*

Dawson, G., Carver, L. J., Meltzoff, A. N., Panagiotides, H., & McPartland, J. (in press). Neural correlates of face recognition in young children with autism spectrum disorder, developmental delay, and typical development. *Child Development.*

Dawson, G., & McKissick, F. C. (1984). Self-recognition in autistic children. *Journal of Autism and Developmental Disorders, 9,* 247–260.

Dawson, G., Meltzoff, A. N., Osterling, J., & Rinaldi, J. (1998). Neuropsychological correlates of early symptoms of autism. *Child Development, 69,* 1276–1285.

De Haan, M., Bauer, P. J., Georgieff, M. K., & Nelson, C. A. (2000). Explicit memory in low-risk toddlers born between 27–42 weeks of gestation. *Developmental Medicine and Child Neurology, 42,* 304–312.

De Jong, P. F., & Van der Leij, A. (1999). Specific contributions of phonological abilties to early reading acquisition: Results from a Dutch latent variable longitudinal study. *Journal of Educational Psychology, 91,* 450–476.

De Ribaupierre, A., & Bailleux, C. (1994). Developmental change in a spatial task of attentional capacity: An essay toward an integration of two working memory models. *International Journal of Behavioral Development, 17*(1), 5–35.

De Ribaupierre, A., & Bailleux, C. (2000). The development of working memory: Further note on the comparability of two models of working memory. *Journal of Experimental Child Psychology, 77*(2), 110–127.

Deacon, T. W. (1997). *The symbolic species: The co-evolution of language and the brain.* New York: Norton.

Deary, I. J. (2000). Simple information processing and intelligence. In R. J. Sternberg (Ed.), *Handbook of intelligence* (pp. 267–284). New York: Cambridge University Press.

DeCasper, A. J., & Fifer, W. P. (1980). On human bonding: Newborns prefer their mothers' voices. *Science, 208,* 1174–1176.

DeCasper, A. J., & Spence, M. J. (1986). Prenatal maternal speech influences newborns' perceptions of speech sounds. *Infant Behavior and Development, 9,* 133–150.

Decety, J. (in press). Is there such thing as a functional equivalence between imagined, observed, and executed action? In A. N. Meltzoff & W. Prinz (Eds.), *The imitative mind: Development, evolution, and brain bases.* Cambridge: Cambridge University Press.

Decety, J., Chaminade, T., & Meltzoff, A. N. (in press). A PET exploration of the neural mechanisms involved in imitation. *NeuroImage.*

Decety, J., & Grèzes, J. (1999). Neural mechanisms subserving the perception of human actions. *Trends in Cognitive Sciences, 3,* 172–178.

Decety, J., Grèzes, J., Costes, N., Perani, D., Jeannerod, M., Procyk, E., Grassi, F., & Fazio, F. (1997). Brain activity during observation of actions: Influence of action content and subject's strategy. *Brain, 120,* 1763–1777.

Dehaene, S. (1997). *The number sense.* London: Penguin.

DeJong, G. (1988). An introduction to explanation-based learning. In H. Shrobe (Ed.), *Exploring artificial intelligence* (pp. 45–81). San Mateo, CA: Morgan Kaufmann.

DeJong, G. (1993). *Investigating explanation-based learning.* Boston, MA: Kluwer Academic Press.

DeJong, G. (1997). Explanation-based learning. In A. Tucker (Ed.), *Encyclopedia of computer science* (pp. 499–520). Boca Raton. FL: CRC Press.

Delis, D. C., Squire, L. R., Bihrle, A., & Massman, P. (1992). Componential analysis of problem-solving ability: Performance of patients with frontal lobe damage and amnesic patients on a new sorting test. *Neuropsychologia, 30,* 683–697.

DeLoache, J. S. (1987). Rapid change in the symbolic functioning of very young children. *Science, 238,* 1556–1557.

DeLoache, J. S. (1989). Young children's understanding of the correspondence between a scale model and a larger space. *Cognitive Development, 4,* 121–129.

DeLoache, J. S. (1991). Symbolic functioning in very young children: Understanding of pictures and models. *Child Development, 62,* 736–752.

DeLoache, J. S. (1995a). Early symbol understanding and use. In D. Medin (Ed.), *The psychology of learning and motivation: Vol. 33* (pp. 65–114). New York: Academic Press.

DeLoache, J. S. (1995b). Early understanding and use of symbols: The model model. *Current Directions in Psychological Science, 4,* 109–113.

DeLoache, J. S. (1999, March). *The role of inhibitory control in early symbol use.* Paper presented at the Society for Research in Child Development, Albuquerque, NM.

DeLoache, J. S. (2000). Dual representation and young children's use of scale models. *Child Development, 71,* 329–338.

DeLoache, J. S., & Brown, A. L. (1979). Looking for Big Bird: Studies of memory in very young children. *The Quarterly Newsletter of the Laboratory of Comparative Human Cognition, 1,* 53–57.

DeLoache, J. S., & Brown, A. L. (1983). Very young children's memory for the location of objects in a large scale environment. *Child Development, 54,* 888–897.

DeLoache, J. S., & Burns, N. M. (1994). Early understanding of the representational function of pictures. *Cognition, 52,* 83–110.

DeLoache, J. S., DeMendoza, O. A. P., & Anderson, K. N. (1999). Multiple factors in early symbol use: The effect of instructions, similarity, and age in understanding a symbol-referent relation. *Cognitive Development, 14,* 299–312.

DeLoache, J. S., Miller, K. F., & Pierroutsakos, S. L. (1998). Reasoning and problem solving. In D. Kuhn & R. Siegler (Eds.), *Handbook of child psychology* (5th ed.): *Vol 2. Cognition, perception, & language* (pp. 801–850). New York: Wiley.

DeLoache, J. S., Kolstad, V., & Anderson, K. N. (1991). Physical similarity and young children's understanding of scale models. *Child Development, 62,* 111–126.

DeLoache, J. S., Miller, K. F., & Rosengren, K. S. (1997). The credible shrinking room: Very young children's performance with symbolic and non-symbolic relations. *Psychological Science, 8,* 308–313.

DeLoache, J. S., Pierroutsakos, S. L., Uttal, D. H., & Rosengren, K.S., & Gottlieb, A. (1998). Grasping the nature of pictures. *Psychological Science, 9,* 205–210.

DeLoache, J. S., & Plaetzer, B. (1985). Tea for two: Joint mother–child symbolic play. Paper presented at Bienniel meeting for the Society for Research in Child Development, Toronto.

DeLoache, J. S., & Smith, C. M. (1999). Early symbolic representation. In I. E. Sigel (Ed.), *Development of mental representation: Theories and applications* (pp. 61–86). Mahwah, NJ: Lawrence Erlbaum.

DeLoache, J. S., Strauss, M. S., & Maynard, J. (1979). Picture perception in infancy. *Infant Behavior and Development, 2,* 77–89.

Demetriou, A. (1998). Nooplasis: 10 + 1 postulates about the formation of mind. *Learning and Instruction, 8,* 271–287.

Demetriou, A., Doise, W., & van Lieshout, C. (Eds.). (1998). *Life-span developmental psychology.* Chichester: John Wiley & Sons.

Demetriou, A., Efklides, A., & Platsidou, M. (1993). The architecture and dynamics of developing mind: Experiential structuralism as a frame for unifying cognitive developmental theories. *Monographs of the Society for Research in Child Development, 58* (5, Serial No. 234).

Dempster, F. N. (1981). Memory span: Sources of individual and developmental differences. *Psychological Bulletin, 89,* 63–100.

Dempster, F. N. (1985). Short-term memory development in childhood and adolescence. In C. J. Brainerd & M. Pressley (Eds.), *Basic processes in memory development: Progress in cognitive development research.* New York: Springer.

Dempster, F. N. (1992). The rise and fall of the inhibitory mechanism: Toward a unified theory of cognitive development and aging. *Developmental Review, 12,* 45–75.

Denckla, M. B., & Reiss, A. L. (1997). Prefrontal-subcortical circuits in developmental disorders. In N. A. Krasnegor, G. R. Lyon, & P. S. Goldman-Rakic (Eds.), *Development of the prefrontal cortex: Evolution, neurobiology, and behavior* (pp. 283–293). Baltimore, MD: Paul Publishing.

Denham, S. A. (1986). Social cognition, prosocial behavior and emotion in preschoolers. *Child Development, 57,* 194–201.

Dennett, D. C. (1987). *The intentional stance.* Cambridge MA: Bradford Books, MIT Press.

Dennett, D. C. (1991). *Consciousness explained.* Boston: Little, Brown.

Dentici, O. A., Grossi, M. G., Borghi, A., DeAmbrosis, A., & Massara, C. I. (1984). Understanding floating: A study of children aged between six and eight years. *European Journal of Science Education, 6,* 235–243.

Desforges, A., & Desforges, G. (1980) Number-based strategies of sharing in young children. *Educational Studies, 6,* 97–109.

Detterman, D. K., Gabriel, L. T., & Ruthsatz, J. M. (2000). Intelligence and mental retardation. In R. J. Sternberg (Ed.), *Handbook of intelligence* (pp. 141–158). New York: Cambridge University Press.

Detterman, D. K., & Sternberg, R. J. (Eds.). (1982). *How and how much can intelligence be increased?* Norwood, NJ: Lawrence Erlbaum.

Detterman, D. K., & Thompson, L. A. (1997). IQ, schooling, and developmental disabilities: What's so special about special education? *American Psychologist, 52,* 1082–1091.

DeVries, R. (1986). Children's conceptions of shadow phenomena. *Genetic, Social and General Psychology Monographs, 112,* 479–530.

DfEE (2000). *National Curriculum*. London: DfEE. website <www.nc.uk.net>.

Diamond, A. (1985). Development of the ability to use recall to guide action, as indicated by infants' performance in AB. *Child Development, 56*, 868–883.

Diamond, A. (1990). Developmental time course in human infants and infant monkeys, and the neural bases, of inhibitory control in reaching. In A. Diamond (Ed.), *The development and neural bases of higher cognitive functions. Annals of the New York Academy of Sciences, 608*, 637–676.

Diamond, A. (1991). Neuropsychological insights into the meaning of object concept development. In S. Carey & R. Gelman (Eds.), *The epigenesis of mind: Essays on biology and cognition* (pp. 67–110). Hillsdale, NJ: Erlbaum.

Diamond, A., & Goldman-Rakic, P. S. (1989). Comparison of human infants and rhesus monkeys on Piaget's A-not-B task: Evidence for dependence on dorsolateral prefrontal cortex. *Experimental Brain Research, 74*, 24–40.

Diamond, A., Prevor, M., Callender, G., & Druin, D. P. (1997). Prefrontal cortex cognitive deficits in children treated early and continuously for PKU. *Monographs of the Society for Research in Child Development, 62*(4) (Whole No. 252).

Dias, M. G., & Harris, P. L. (1988). The effect of make-believe play on deductive reasoning. *British Journal of Developmental Psychology, 6*, 207–221.

Dias, M. G., & Harris, P. L. (1990). The influence of the imagination on reasoning by young children. *British Journal of Developmental Psychology, 8*, 305–318.

Dias, R., Robbins, T. W., & Roberts, A. C. (1996, March 7). Dissociation in prefrontal cortex of affective and attentional shifts. *Nature, 380*, 69–72.

Dienes, Z., & Perner, J. (1999). A theory of implicit and explicit knowledge. *Behavioral and Brain Sciences, 22*(5), 735–808.

Diesendruck, G., & Gelman, S. A. (1999). Domain differences in absolute judgments of category membership: Evidence for an essentialist account of categorization. *Psychonomic Bulletin & Review, 6*, 338–346.

DiLalla, L. F., & Watson, M. W. (1988). Differentiation of fantasy and reality: Preschoolers' reactions to interruptions in their play. *Developmental Psychology, 24*, 286–291.

Diwadkar, V. A., & McNamara, T. P. (1997). Viewpoint dependence in scene recognition. *Psychological Science, 8*, 302–307.

Dixon, J. A., & Moore, C. F. (1996). The developmental role of intuitive principles in choosing mathematical strategies. *Developmental Psychology, 32*, 241–253.

Dixon, J. A., & Tuccillo, F. (2001). Generating initial models for reasoning. *Journal of Experimental Child Psychology, 78*, 178–212.

Dockett, S., & Degotardi, S. (1997). Some implications of popularity at age four. *Journal of Australian Research in Early Childhood Education, 1*, 21–31.

Dodd, B. (1995). *Differential diagnosis and treatment of children with speech disorder*. London: Whurr.

Dodd, B., & Cockerill, H. (1985). Phonologically disordered children's spelling abilities. In J. E. Clark (Ed.), *The cultivated Australian. Beitrage zur Phonetik und Linguistik*, 48 (pp. 404–415). Hamburg: Helmut Buske.

Dodd, B., & Gillon, G. (1997). The nature of the phonological deficit underlying disorders of spoken and written language. In C. K. Leong and R. M. Joshi (Eds.), *Cross-language studies of learning to read and spell* (pp. 53–70). Dordrecht: Kluwer Academic.

Dodd, B., Gillon, G., Oerlemans, M., Russell, T., Syrmis. M., & Wilson, H. (1995). Phonological disorder and the acquisition of literacy. In B. Dodd (Ed.), *Differential diagnosis and treatment of speech disordered children*. London: Whurr.

Dodd, B., McCormack, P., & Woodyatt, G. (1994). An evaluation of an intervention program: The relationship between children's phonology and parents' communicative behaviour. *American Journal on Mental Retardation, 98,* 632–645.

Dodd, B., & Thompson, L. (in press). Speech disorder in children with Down syndrome. *Journal Intellectual Disability Research.*

Dodd, B., Zhu Hua, & Shatford, C. (2000). Does speech disorder spontaneously resolve? In *Child language seminar 1999 proceedings.* London: City University Press.

Dodge, K. A., & Frame, C. L. (1982). Social cognitive biases and deficits in aggressive boys. *Child Development, 53,* 620–635.

Dolgin, K., & Behrend, D. A. (1984). Children's knowledge about animates and inanimates. *Child Development, 55,* 1546–1650.

Donaldson, M. (1978). *Children's minds.* London: Fontana.

Donaldson, M. (1982). Conservation: what is the question? *British Journal of Psychology, 73,* 199–207.

Douglas, M. (1986). *How institutions think.* Syracuse, NY: Syracuse University Press.

Dow, G. A., & Pick, H. L. (1992). Young children's use of models and photographs as spatial representations. *Cognitive Development, 7,* 351–363.

Downs, A. C. (1990). Children's judgments of televised events: The real versus pretend distinction. *Perceptual and Motor Skills, 70,* 779–782.

Downs, R. M. (1981). Maps and mappings as metaphors for spatial representation. In L. S. Liben, A. H. Patterson, & N. Newcombe (Eds.), *Spatial representation and behavior across the life span: Theory and application* (pp. 143–166). New York: Academic Press.

Downs, R. M. (1985). The representation of space: Its development in children and in cartography. In R. Cohen (Ed.), *The development of spatial cognition* (pp. 323–345). Hillsdale, NJ: Lawrence Erlbaum Associates.

Downs, R. M., & Siegel, A. W. (1981). On mapping researchers mapping children and mapping space. In L. S. Liben, A. H. Patterson, & N. Newcombe (Eds.), *Spatial representation and behavior across the life span: Theory and application* (pp. 237–248). New York: Academic.

Downs, R. M., & Stea, D. (1977). *Maps in minds.* New York: Harper & Row.

Driver, R. (1985). Beyond appearance: The conservation of matter. In R. Driver, E. Guesne, & A. Tiberghien (Eds.), *Children's ideas in science* (pp. 145–169). Milton Keynes, UK: Open University Press.

Dufresne, A., & Kobasigawa, A. (1989). Children's spontaneous allocation of study time: Differential and sufficient aspects. *Journal of Experimental Child Psychology, 47,* 274–296.

Dunbar, K. (2001). The analogical paradox: Why analogy is so easy in naturalistic settings, yet so difficult in the psychological laboratory. In D. Gentner, K. J. Holyoak, & B. K. Kokinov (Eds.), *The analogical mind: Perspectives from cognitive science.* Cambridge, MA: MIT Press.

Duncan, G. (1996). Space, place, and the problem of race: Black adolescent discourse as mediated action. *Journal of Negro Education, 65*(2), 133–150.

Duncan, L. G., Seymour, P. H. K., & Hill, S. (1997). How important are rhyme and analogy in beginning reading? *Cognition, 63,* 171–208.

Duncker, K. (1945). On problem solving. *Psychological Monographs, 58* (Whole No. 270). Washington, DC: American Psychological Association.

Dunkeld, J., & Bower, T. G. (1980). Infant response to impending optical collision. *Perception, 9,* 549–554.

Dunn, J. (1988). *The beginnings of social understanding.* Cambridge, MA: Harvard University Press.

Dunn, J., Brown, J., & Beardsall, L. (1991). Family talk about feeling states and children's later understanding of others' emotions. *Developmental Psychology, 27,* 448–455.

Dunn, J., Brown, J., Slomkowski, C., Tesla, C., & Youngblade, L. (1991). Young children's under-standing of other people's feelings and beliefs: Individual differences and their antecedents. *Child Development, 62*, 1352–1366.

Dunn, J., & Cutting, A. L. (1999). Understanding others, and individual differences in friendship interactions in young children. *Social Development, 8*, 201–219.

Dunn, J., & Dale, N. (1984). I a daddy: 2-year-olds collaboration in joint pretend play with sibling and with mother. In I. Bretherton (Ed.), *Symbolic Play* (pp. 131–158). London: Academic Press.

Dunn, J., & Wooding, C. (1977). Play in the home and its implications for learning. In B. Tizard & D. Harvey (Eds.), *Biology of play*. London: Spastics International.

Dunn, L., Dunn, L., Whetton, C., & Burley, J. (1997). *British picture vocabulary scale III*. Windsor: NFER-Nelson.

Dunn, M., Flax, J., Sliwinski, M., & Aram, D. (1996). The use of spontaneous language measures as criteria for identifying children with specific language impairment: An attempt to reconcile clinical and research incongruence. *Journal of Speech and Hearing Research, 39*(3), 643–654.

Durgunoglu, A. Y., & Oney, B. (1999). A cross-linguistic comparison of phonological awareness and word recognition. *Reading and Writing, 11*, 281–299.

Eacott, M. J., & Crawley, R. A. (1998). The offset of childhood amnesia: Memory for events that occurred before age 3. *Journal of Experimental Psychology: General, 127*, 22–33.

Ebbinghaus, H. (1885). *Über das Gedächtnis*. [On memory]. Darmstadt: Wissenschaftliche Buchgesellschaft.

Edelman, G. (1989). *The remembered present: A biological theory of consciousness*. New York: Basic Books.

Edelman, G. M. (1987). *Neural Darwinism*. New York: Basic Books.

Edgerton, R. (1967). *The cloak of competence*. Berkeley: University of California Press.

Edwards, S., Flether, P., Garman, M., Hughes, A., Letts, C., & Sikra, I. (1997). *Reynell Developmental Language Scales III*. Windsor: NFER-Nelson.

Ehri, L. (1985). Sources of difficulty in learning to spell and read. In M. L. Wolraich & D. Routh (Eds.), *Advances in developmental and behavioural paediatrics*. Greenwich, CT: Jai Press.

Ehri, L. C. (1992). Reconceptualising the development of sight word reading and its relationship to recoding. In P. B. Gough, L. C. Ehri, & R. Treiman (Eds.), *Reading acquisition* (pp. 107–143). Hillsdale, NJ: Erlbaum & Associates.

Ehri, L. C. (1995). Phases of development in learning to read words by sight. *Journal of Research in Reading, 18*, 116–125.

Ehri, L. C. (1997) Learning to read and learning to spell are one and the same, almost. In C. A. Perfetti, L. Rieben, & M. Fayol (Eds.), *Learning to spell: Research, theory and practice across languages* (pp. 237–270). Mahwah: NJ.

Eibl-Eibesfeldt, I. (1989). *Human ethology*. New York: Aldine de Gruyter.

Eifermann, R. R. (1971). Social play in childhood. In R. E. Herron & B. Sutton-Smith (Eds.), *Child's play*. New York: Wiley.

Eimas, P. D. (1994). Categorization in early infancy and the continuity of development. *Cognition, 50*, 83–93.

Eimas, P. D., & Miller, J. L. (1990). Infant categories and categorization. In G. M. Edelman, M. Cowan, & E. Gall (Eds.), *Signal and sense: Local and global order in perceptual maps* (pp. 433–449). New York: Wiley-Liss.

Eimas, P. D., & Quinn, P. C. (1994). Studies on the formation of perceptually based basic-level categories in young infants. *Child Development, 65*, 903–917.

Eisenberg, N. (1986). *Altruistic emotion, cognition and behavior*. Hillsdale, NJ: Erlbaum.

Ekman, P. (1992). Facial expression of emotion: an old controversy and new findings. In V. Bruce (Ed.), *The Face*. Oxford, UK: Oxford University Press/Royal Society.

Elbro, C. (1998) When reading is "readn" or somthn. Distinctness of phonological representations of lexical items in normal and disabled readers. *Scandinavian Journal of Psychology, 39*, 149–153.

Eliot, J. (1987). *Models of psychological space, psychometric, developmental, and experimental approaches.* New York: Springer.

Elliot, C. D. (1983). *British Ability Scales.* Windsor: NFER-Nelson.

Ellis, N. C., & Cataldo, S. (1990). The role of spelling in learning to read. *Language and Education, 4*, 1–28.

Ellis, N. C., & Large, B. (1987). The development of reading: As you seek so shall you find. *British Journal of Psychology, 78*, 1–28.

Ellis, N. R., Katz, E., & Williams, J. E. (1987). Developmental aspects of memory for spatial location. *Journal of Experimental Child Psychology, 44*, 401–412.

Elman, J. L. (1993). Learning and development in neural networks: The importance of starting small. *Cognition, 48*, 71–99.

Elman, J. L., Bates, E. A., Johnson, M. H., Karmiloff-Smith, A., Parisi, D., & Plunkett, K. (1996). *Rethinking innateness: A connectionist perspective on development.* Cambridge, MA: MIT Press.

Emde, R., Birigen, Z., Clyman, R., & Openheim, D. (1991). The moral self of infancy: Affective core and procedural knowledge. *Developmental Review, 11*, 251–270.

Emler, N., Palmer-Canton, E., & St. James, A. (1998). Politics, moral reasoning and the Defining Issues Test: A reply to Barnett et al. (1995). *British Journal of Social Psychology, 37*, 457–476.

Emler, N., & Stace, K. (1999). What does principled moral versus conventional moral reasoning convey to others about the politics and psychology of the reasoner? *European Journal of Social Psychology, 29*, 455–468.

Enright, R., Franklin, C., & Manheim, L. (1980). Chidren's distributive justice reasoning: A standardized and objective scale. *Developmental Psychology, 16*, 193–202.

Epstein, H. T. (1986). Stages in human brain development. *Developmental Brain Research, 30*, 114–119.

Ericsson, K. A., Krampe, R., & Tesch-Roemer, C. (1993). The role of deliberate practice in the acquisition of expert performance. *Psychological Review, 100*, 363–406.

Eslinger, P. J., Biddle, K. R., & Grattan, L. M. (1997). Cognitive and social development in children with prefrontal cortex lesions. In G. R. Lyon & N. A. Krasnegor (Eds.), *Attention, memory, and executive function* (pp. 295–335). Baltimore, MD: Paul Brookes.

Espy, K. A., Kaufmann, P. M., McDiarmid, M. D., & Glisky, M. L. (1999). Executive functioning in preschool children: Performance on A-not-B and other delayed response format tasks. *Brain and Cognition, 41*, 178–199.

Esterly, J. B., & Barbu, M. (1999). The role of size, weight, density, and material in children's developing understanding of buoyancy. Poster presented at the Biennial Meetings of the Society for Research in Child Development, Albuquerque, NM.

Estes, D., Wellman, H. M., & Wolley, J. D. (1989). Children's understanding of mental phenomena. In H. Reese (Ed.), *Advances in child development and behavior* (pp. 41–87). New York: Academic Press.

Eyferth, K. (1961). Leistungen verschiedener Gruppen von Besatzungskindern im Hamburg-Wechsler Intelligenztest für Kinder (HAWIK). *Archiv für die gesamte Psychologie, 113*, 222–241.

Fadiga, L., Fogassi, L., Pavesi, G., & Rizzolatti, G. (1995). Motor facilitation during action observation: A magnetic stimulation study. *Journal of Neurophysiology, 73*, 2608–2611.

Fagan, J. F. (1973). Infants' delayed recognition memory and forgetting. *Journal of Experimental Child Psychology, 16*, 425–450.

Fahlman, S. E., & Lebiere, C. (1990). The cascade-correlation learning architecture. In D. S. Touretzky (Ed.), *Advances in neural information processing systems 2* (pp. 524–532). Los Altos, CA: Morgan Kaufmann.

Falkenhainer, B., Forbus, K. D., & Gentner, D. (1989). The structure-mapping engine: Algorithm and examples. *Artificial Intelligence, 41*, 1–63.

Fantz, R. L. (1956). A method for studying early visual develoment. *Perceptual and Motor Skills, 6*, 13–15.

Fantz, R. (1963). Pattern vision in newborn infants. *Science, 140*, 296–297.

Fantz, R. L. (1964). Visual experience in infants: Decreased attention to familiar patterns relative to novel ones. *Science, 164*, 668–670.

Fantz, R. L., Fagan, J. F. III, & Miranda, S. B. (1975). Early visual selectivity as a function of pattern variables, previous exposure, age from birth and conception, and expected cognitive deficit. In L. B. Cohen & P. Salapatek (Eds.), *Infant perception: From sensation to cognition: Vol. 1. Basic visual processes* (pp. 249–345). New York: Academic Press.

Farroni, T., Johnson, M. H., Brockbank, M., & Simion, F. (2000). Infant's use of gaze direction to cue attention: The importance of perceived motion. *Visual Cognition, 7*, 705–718.

Farver, J. A. M. (1999). Activity setting analysis: A model for rexamining the role of culture in development. In A. Goncu (Ed.), *Children's engagement in the world: Sociocultural perspectives* (pp. 99–127). New York: Cambridge University Press.

Farver, J. A. M., & Wimbarti, S. (1995). Paternal participation in toddler's pretend play. *Social Development, 4*, 17–31.

Farver, J. M., & Howes, C. (1993). Cultural differences in American and Mexican mother–child pretend play. *Merrill-Palmer Quarterly, 39*, 344–358.

Fay, A., & Klahr, D. (1996). Knowing about guessing and guessing about knowing: Preschoolers' understanidng of indeterminacy. *Child Development, 67*, 689–716.

Fechner, B. (1965). Zur Psychologie des Gedächtnisses III [On the psychology of memory]. *Zeitschrift für Psychologie, 170*, 1–22.

Fein, G. G. (1975). A transformational analysis of pretending. *Developmental Psychology, 11*, 291–296.

Fein, G. G. (1981). Pretend play in childhood: An integrative review. *Child Development, 52*, 1095–1118.

Fein, G. G. (1989). Mind, meaning, and affect: Proposals for a theory of pretense. *Developmental Review, 9*, 345–363.

Fein, G. G., Moorin, E. R., & Enslein, J. (1982). Pretense and peer behavior: An intersectoral analysis. *Human Development, 25*, 392–406.

Feingold, A. (1988). Cognitive gender differences are disappearing. *American Psychologist, 43*, 95–103.

Feinman, S. (1982). *Social referencing in infancy. Merrill-Palmer Quarterly, 28*, 445–470.

Feinman, S. (Ed.). (1992). *Social referencing and the social construction of reality in infancy.* New York: Plenum Press.

Feldman, J. (2000). Minimization of Boolean complexity in human concept learning. *Nature, 407*(6804), 630–632.

Feldman, J. A., & Ballard, D. H. (1982). Connectionist models and their properties. *Cognitive Science, 6*, 205–254.

Feldman, M. J., & Drasgow, J. (1951). A visual-verbal test for schizophrenia. *Psychiatric Quarterly Supplement, 25*, 55–64.

Felton, M., & Kuhn, D. (in press). The development of argumentive discourse skills. *Discourse Processes.*

Fenson, L., Cameron, M. S., & Kennedy, M. (1988). Role of perceptual and conceptual similarity in category matching at age two years. *Child Development, 59*(4), 897–907.

Fenson, L., Dale, P. S., Reznick, J. S., Bates, E., et al. (1994). Variability in early communicative development. *Monographs of the Society for Research in Child Development, 59*(5), v–173.

Fenson, L., & Ramsay, D. S. (1981). Effects of modeling action sequences on the play of twelve-, fifteen-, and nineteen-month-old children. *Child Development, 52,* 1028–1036.

Ferguson, T. J., Stegge, H., & Damhuis, I. (1991). Children's understandings of guilt and shame. *Child Development, 62,* 827–839.

Fernald, A. (1992a). Human maternal vocalizations to infants as biologically relevant signals: An evolutionary perspective. In J. H. Barkow, L. Cosmides, & J. Tooby (Eds.), *The adapted mind: Evolutionary psychology and the generation of culture* (pp. 391–428). New York: Oxford University Press.

Fernald, A. (1992b). Meaningful melodies in mothers' speech to infants. In H. Papousek, U. Jurgens, & M. Papousek (Eds.), *Nonverbal vocal communication: Comparative and developmental approaches. Studies in emotion and social interaction* (pp. 262–282). New York: Cambridge University Press.

Ferretti, R. P., & Butterfield, E. C. (1986). Are children's rule-assessment classifications invariant across instances of problem types? *Child Development, 57,* 1419–1428.

Ferretti, R. P., Butterfield, E. C., Cahn, A., & Kerkman, D. (1985). The classification of children's knowledge: Development on the balance-scale and inclined-plane tasks. *Journal of Experimental Child Psychology, 39,* 131–160.

Feuerstein, R. (1979). *The dynamic assessment of retarded performers: The Learning Potential Assessment Device, theory, instruments, and techniques.* Baltimore, MD: University Park Press.

Field, T. (1979a). Differential behavioral and cardiac responses of 3-month old infants to a mirror and peer. *Infant Behaviour and Development, 2,* 179–184.

Field, T. M. (1979b). Visual and cardiac responses to animate and inanimate faces by young term and preterm infants. *Child Development, 50,* 188–194.

Field, T., Goldstein, S., Vaga-Lahr, N., & Porter, K. (1986). Changes in imitative behavior during early infancy. *Infant Behavior and Development, 9,* 415–421.

Field, T. M., Woodson, R., Cohen, D., Greenberg, R., Garcia, R., & Collins, E. (1983). Discrimination and imitation of facial expressions by term and preterm neonates. *Infant Behavior and Development, 6,* 485–489.

Field, T. M., Woodson, R., Greenberg, R., & Cohen, D. (1982). Discrimination and imitation of facial expressions by neonates. *Science, 218,* 179–181.

Fiese, B. H. (1990). Playful relationships: A contextual analysis of mother-toddler interaction and symbolic play. *Child Development, 61,* 1648–1656.

Filipek, P. A., Semrud-Clikeman, M., Steingard, R. J., Renshaw, P. F., Kennedy, D. N., & Biederman, J. (1997). Volumetric MRI analysis comparing subjects having attention-deficit hyperactivity disorder with normal controls. *Neurology, 48,* 589–601.

Fischer, C. S., Jankowski, M. S., & Lucas, S. R. (1996). *Inequality by design: Cracking the Bell Curve myth.* Princeton, NJ: Princeton University Press.

Fischer, K. W. (1980). A theory of cognitive development: The control and construction of hierarchies of skills. *Psychological Review, 87,* 477–531.

Fischer, K. W., & Bidell, T. R. (1998). Dynamic development of psychological structures in action and thought. In W. Damon & R. M. Lerner (Eds.), *Handbook of child psychology: Vol. 1. Theoretical Models of Human Development* (5th ed., pp. 467–561). New York: John Wiley & Sons.

Fischer, K. W., & Rose, S. P. (1996). Dynamic growth cycles of brain and cognitive development. In R. W. Thatcher, G. R. Lyon, J. Rumsey, & N. Kresnegor (Eds.), *Developmental neuroimaging: Mapping the development of brain and behavior* (pp. 263–283). San Diego: Academic Press.

Fivush, R. (1984). Learning about school: The development of kindergartners' school scripts. *Child Development, 55,* 1697–1709.

Fivush, R. (1988). The functions of event memory. In U. Neisser & E. Winograd (Eds.), *Remembering reconsidered: Ecological and traditional approaches to the study of memory* (pp. 277–282). New York: Cambridge University Press.

Fivush, R. (1991). Gender and emotion in mother–child conversations about the past. *Journal of Narrative and Life History, 1,* 325–341.

Fivush, R. (1997). Event memory in early childhood. In N. Cowan (Ed.), *The development of memory in childhood* (pp. 139–161). Hove, UK: Psychology Press.

Fivush, R., & Fromhoff, F. A. (1988). Style and structure in mother–child conversations about the past. *Discourse Processes, 8,* 177–204.

Fivush, R., & Hamond, N. R. (1989). Time and again: Effects of repetition and retention interval on 2 year olds' event recall. *Journal of Experimental Child Psychology, 47,* 259–273.

Fivush, R., Hudson, J. A., & Nelson, K. (1984). Children's long-term memory for a novel event: An exploratory study. *Merrill-Palmer Quarterly, 30,* 303–316.

Fivush, R., & Schwarzmueller, A. (1998). Children remember childhood: Implications for childhood amnesia. *Applied Cognitive Psychology, 12,* 455–473.

Flavell, J. H. (1963). *The developmental psychology of Jean Piaget.* New York: Van Nostrand.

Flavell, J. H. (1971). First discussant's comments: What is memory development the development of? *Human Development, 14,* 272–278.

Flavell, J. H. (1988). The development of children's knowledge about the mind: From cognitive connections to mental representations. In J. Astington, P. Harris, & D. Olson (Eds.), *Developing Theories of Mind* (pp. 244–267). New York: Cambridge University Press.

Flavell, J. H. (1992). Cognitive development: Past, present, and future. *Developmental Psychology, 28,* 998–1005.

Flavell, J. H. (1999). Cognitive development: Children's knowledge about the mind. *Annual Review of Psychology, 50,* 21–45.

Flavell, J. H. (2000). Development of children's knowledge about the mental world. *International Journal of Behavioral Development, 24,* 15–23.

Flavell, J. H., Flavell, E. R., & Green, F. L. (1987). Young children's knowledge about the apparent–real and pretend–real distinctions. *Developmental Psychology, 23,* 816–822.

Flavell, J. H., Flavell, E. R., Green, F. L., & Moses, L. J. (1990). Young children's understanding of fact beliefs versus value beliefs. *Child Development, 61,* 915–928.

Flavell, J. H., Green, F. L., & Flavell, E. R. (1986). Development of knowledge about the appearance–reality distinction. *Monographs of the Society for Research in Child Development, 51*(1) (Serial No. 212).

Flavell, J. H., Green, F. L., & Flavell, E. R. (1993). Children's understanding of the stream of consciousness. *Child Development, 64,* 387–398.

Flavell, J. H., Green, F. L., & Flavell, E. R. (1995). Young children's knowledge of thinking. *Monographs of the Society for Research in Child Development* (Serial No. 243).

Flavell, J. H., Green, F. L., & Flavell, E. R. (1998). The mind has a mind of its own: Developing knowledge about mental uncontrollability. *Cognitive Development, 13,* 127–138.

Flavell, J. H., Green, F. L., Flavell, E. R., & Grossman, J. B. (1997). The developemnt of children's knowledge about inner speech. *Child Development, 68,* 39–47.

Flavell, J. H., Miller, P., & Miller, S. (1993) *Cognitive development* (3rd ed.). Engelwood Cliffs, NJ: Prentice Hall.

Flavell, J. H., & Wellman, H. M. (1977). Metamemory. In R. V. Kail & J. W. Hagen (Eds.), *Perspectives on the development of memory and cognition.* Hillsdale: Erlbaum.

Flynn, J. R. (1987). Massive IQ gains in 14 nations. *Psychological Bulletin, 101,* 171–191.

Flynn, J. R. (1998). WAIS-III and WISC-III gains in the United States from 1972 to 1995: How to compensate for obsolete norms. *Perceptual & Motor Skills, 86,* 1231–1239.

Fodor, J. A. (1980). Fixation of belief and concept acquisition. In M. Piattelli-Palmarini (Ed.), *Language and learning: The debate between Chomsky and Piaget* (pp. 143–149). Cambridge, MA: Harvard Press.

Fodor, J. A. (1983). *Modularity of mind: An essay on faculty psychology.* Cambridge, MA: MIT Press.

Fodor, J. A. (1987). *Psychosemantics: The problem of meaning in the philosophy of mind.* Cambridge, MA: Bradford Books/MIT Press.

Fodor, J. A. (1992). A theory of the child's theory of mind. *Cognition, 44,* 283–296.

Fodor, J. A., & Pylyshyn, Z. W. (1988). Connectionism and cognitive architecture: A critical analysis. In S. Pinker & J. Mehler (Eds.), *Connections and Symbols* (pp. 3–71). (*Cognition, 28* [Special Issue]). Cambridge, MA: MIT Press / Bradford Books.

Foley, E. J., & Berch, D. B. (1997). Capacity limitations of a classic M-Power measure: A modified dual-task approach. *Journal of Experimental Child Psychology, 66,* 129–143.

Foley, M. A., Harris, J. F., & Hermann, S. (1994). Developmental comparisons of the ability to discriminate between memories for symbolic play enactments. *Developmental Psychology, 30,* 206–217.

Foley, M. A., & Ratner, H. H. (1998). Children's recoding memory for collaboration: A way of learning from others. *Cognitive Development, 13,* 91–108.

Folstein, S., & Rutter, M. (1977). Infantile autism: A genetic study of 21 twin pairs. *Journal of Child Psycholology and Psychiatry, 18,* 297–321.

Fonagy, P. (1996). The significance of the development of metacognitive control over mental representations in parenting and infant development. *Journal of Clincial Psychoanalysis, 5,* 67–86.

Fonagy, P., & Target, M. (1997). Attachment and reflective function: Their role in self-organization. *Development and Psychopathology, 9,* 679–700.

Fonagy, P., Target, M., & Gergely, G. (2000). Attachment and borderline personality disorder: A theory and some evidence. *Psychiatric Clinics of North America, 23*(1), 103–123.

Fontaine, R. (1984). Imitative skills between birth and six months. *Infant Behavior and Development, 7,* 323–333.

Forbus, K. D. (1984). Qualitative process theory. *Artificial Intelligence, 24,* 85–168.

Ford, M. E. (1994). A living systems approach to the integration of personality and intelligence. In R. J. Sternberg & P. Ruzgis (Eds.), *Personality and intelligence* (pp. 188–217). New York: Cambridge University Press.

Forrester, N., & Plunkett, K. (1994). Learning the Arabic plural: The case for minority default mappings in connectionist networks. In A. Ramand & K. Eiselt (Eds.), *Proceedings of the sixteenth annual conference of the Cognitive Science Society* (pp. 319–323). Mahwah, NJ: Erlbaum.

Fowler, A. (1990). Language abilities of children with Down's syndrome: Evidence for a specific syntactic delay. In D. Cicchetti and Beeghly (Eds), *Children with Down's Syndrome. A developmental perspective* (pp. 302–328). New York: Cambridge University Press.

Fowler, A. (1991). How early phonological development might set the stage for phoneme awareness. In S. A. Brady & D. P. Shankweiler (Eds.), *Phonological processes in literacy: A tribute to Isabelle Liberman* (pp. 97–117). Mahwah, NJ: Erlbaum.

Fox, R., & McDaniel, C. (1982). The perception of biological motion by human infants. *Science, 218,* 486–487.

Frawley, W. (in press). Control and cross-domain mental computation: Evidence from language breakdown. *Computational Intelligence.* Hiusdale: Erlbaum.

Freeman, F. N. (1916). *The psychology of the common branches.* Boston: Houghton Mifflin.

Freeman, K. E., & Sera, M. D. (1996). Reliance on visual and verbal information across ontological kinds: What do children know about animals and machines? *Cognitive Development, 11,* 315–341.

Freeman, N. H. (1993). Drawing: The representation of public representations. In C. Pratt & A. F. Garton (Eds.), *Systems of representation in children* (pp. 113–132). New York: Wiley.

Frege, G. (1972). *Conceptual notation and related articles.* Oxford, UK: Clarendon Press.

Frege, G. (1979). *Posthumous papers.* Oxford, UK: Blackwell.

Freud, S. (1911). Formulation on the two principles of mental functioning. In J. Strachey (Ed.), *The standard edition of the complete psychological works of Sigmund Freud* (Vol. 12, pp. 215–226). London: Hogarth Press.

Freud, S. (1946). Formulations regarding the two principles in mental functioning. In *Collected Papers, Vol. IV* (pp. 13–21). London: Hogarth. [1st published 1911].

Freud, S. (1953). Three essays on the theory of sexuality. In J. Strachey (Ed.), *The standard edition of the complete psychological works of Sigmund Freud* (Vol. 7, pp. 135–243). London: Hogarth Press. [1st published 1905].

Freud, S. (1966). *Introductory lectures on psychoanalysis.* Trans. and ed. J. Strachey. New York: Norton. [1st published 1916–1917].

Friedman, W. (1990). *About time: Inventing the fourth dimension.* Cambridge, MA: MIT Press.

Frith, C. D. (1992). *The cognitive neuropsychology of schizophrenia.* Hillsdale, NJ: Erlbaum.

Frith, C., & Frith, U. (2000). The physiological basis of theory of mind: Functional imaging studies. In S. Baron-Cohen, H. Tager-Flusberg, & D. J. Cohen (Eds.), *Understanding other minds: Perspectives from developmental cognitive neuroscience* (2nd ed., pp. 334–356). Oxford, UK: Oxford University Press.

Frith, U. (1970). Studies in pattern detection in normal and autistic children: I. Immediate recall of auditory sequences. *Journal of Abnormal Psychology, 76,* 413–420.

Frith, U. (1985). Beneath the surface of developmental dyslexia. In K. Patterson, M. Coltheart, & J. Marshall (Eds.), *Surface dyslexia: Neuropsychological and cognitive studies of phonological reading* (pp. 301–330). London: Erlbaum.

Frith, U. (1989). *Autism: Explaining the enigma.* Oxford, UK: Basil Blackwell.

Frith, U. (1991). *Autism and Asperger's Syndrome.* Cambridge: Cambridge University Press.

Frith, U. (1997). Brain, mind and behaviour in dyslexia. In C. Hulme & M. Snowling (Eds.), *Dyslexia: Biology, cognition and intervention.* London: Whurr.

Frith, U., & Snowling, M. J. (1983). Reading for meaning and reading for sound in autistic and dyslexic children. *British Journal of Developmental Psychology, 1,* 329–342.

Frith, U., Wimmer, H., & Landerl, K. (1998). Differences in phonological recoding in German and English speaking children. *Scientific Studies of Reading, 2*(1), 31–54.

Frydman, O., & Bryant, P. E. (1988). Sharing and the understanding of number equivalence by young children. *Cognitive Development, 3,* 323–339.

Frye, D., Braisby, N., Lowe, J., Maroudas, C., & Nicholls, J. (1989). Young children's understanding of counting and cardinality. *Child Development, 60,* 1158–1171.

Frye, D., Zelazo, P. D., & Palfai, T. (1995). Theory of mind and rule-based reasoning. *Cognitive Development, 10,* 483–527.

Fuson, K. C. (1988). *Children's counting and concepts of number.* New York: Springer.

Fuster, J. (1989). *The prefrontal cortex: Anatomy, physiology and neuropsychology of the frontal lobe* (2nd ed.). New York: Raven.

Gale, E., deVilliers, P., deVilliers, J., & Pyers, J. (1996). Language and theory of mind in oral deaf children. Paper presented at the Boston University Conference on Language Development, Boston, MA.

Galili, I., & Bar, V. (1997). Children's operational knowledge about weight. *International Journal of Science Education, 19,* 317–340.

Gallagher, A., Frith, U., & Snowling, M. J. (2000). Precursors of literacy-delay among children at genetic risk of dyslexia. *Journal of Child Psychology and Psychiatry, 41,* 23–213.

Gallistel, C. R., Brown, A. L., Carey, S., Gelman, R., & Keil, F. C. (1991). Lessons from animal learning for the study of cognitive development. In S. Carey & R. Gelman (Eds.), *The epigenesis of mind: Essays on biology and cognition. The Jean Piaget Symposium series* (pp. 3–36). Hillsdale, NJ: Lawrence Erlbaum.

Gallup, G. G. Jr. (1970). Chimpanzees: Self-recognition. *Science, 167*, 86–87.

Gallup, G. G. Jr. (1991). Towards a comparative psychology of self-awareness: Species limitations and cognitive consequences. In G. R. Goethals & J. Strauss (Eds.), *The self: An interdisciplinary approach* (pp. 121–135). New York: Springer.

Gallup, G. G. Jr., & Suarez, S. D. (1986). Self-awareness and the emergence of mind in humans and other primates. In J. Suls and A. G. Greenwald (Eds.), *Psychological perspectives on the self* (Vol. 3, pp. 3–26). Hillsdale, NJ: Erlbaum.

Galton, F. (1883). *Inquiry into human faculty and its development.* London: Macmillan.

Gardner, D., Harris, P. L., Ohomoto, M., & Hamazaki, T. (1988). Japanese children's understanding of the distinction between real and apparent emotion. *International Journal of Behavioral Development, 11*, 203–218.

Gardner, H. (1983). *Frames of mind: The theory of multiple intelligences.* New York: Basic Books.

Gardner, H. (1993). *Multiple intelligences: The theory in practice.* New York: Basic Books.

Gardner, H. (1999). *Intelligence reframed: Multiple intelligences for the 21st century.* New York: Basic Books.

Garvey, C., & Berndt, R. (1975). Organization in pretend play. Paper presented at Paper presented at the meeting of the American Psychological Association, Chicago.

Gaskins, S. (1999). Children's daily lives in a Mayan village: A case study of culturally constructed roles and activities. In A. Goncue (Ed.), *Children's engagement in the world: Sociocultural perspectives* (pp. 25–60). New York: Cambridge University Press.

Gasser, M., & Smith, L. B. (1998). Learning nouns and adjectives: A connectionist account. *Language and Cognitive Processes, 13*, 269–306.

Gathercole, S. E. (1998). The development of memory. *Journal of Child Psychology & Psychiatry & Allied Disciplines, 39*, 3–27.

Gathercole, S. E., & Baddeley, A. (1989). Evaluation of the role of phonological STM in the development of vocabulary in children: A longitudinal study. *Journal of Memory and Language, 28*, 200–213.

Gathercole, S. E., & Baddeley, A. (1990a). The role of phonological working memory in vocabulary acquisition: A study of young children learning new names. *British Journal of Psychology, 81*, 439–454.

Gathercole, S. E., & Baddeley, A. (1990b). Phonological memory deficits in language disordered children: Is there a causal connection? *Journal of memory and language, 29*(29), 336–360.

Gattis, M. (Ed.). (2001). *Spatial schemas and abstract thought.* Cambridge, MA: MIT Press.

Gauvain, M. (1993). The development of spatial thinking in everyday activity. *Developmental Review, 13*, 92–121.

Gazzaniga, M. S., Ivry, R. B., & Mangun, G. R. (1998). *Cognitive neuroscience: The biology of the mind.* New York: W. W. Norton.

Gee, J. P. (1999). *An introduction to discourse analysis: Theory and method.* New York: Routledge.

Geertz, C. (1984). From the natives' point of view: On the nature of anthropological understanding. In R. A. Shweder & R. Levine (Eds.), *Culture theory* (pp. 123–136). Cambridge, UK: Cambridge University Press.

Gelman, R. (1982). Accessing one-to-one correspondence: Still another paper about conservation. *British Journal of Psychology, 73*, 209–220.

Gelman, R. (1990). First principles organize attention to and learning about relevant data: Number and the animate–inanimate distinction as examples. *Cognitive Science, 14*, 79–106.

Gelman, R. (1991). Epigenetic foundations of knowledge structures: Initial and transcendent constructions. In S. Carey & R. Gelman (Eds.), *The epigenesis of mind: Essays on biology and cognition. The Jean Piaget Symposium series* (pp. 293–322). Hillsdale, NJ: Lawrence Erlbaum.

Gelman, R., & Baillargeon, R. (1983). A review of some Piagetian concepts. In J. H. Flavell & E. M. Markman (Eds.), *Handbook of child psychology: Vol. 3. Cognitive development* (pp. 167–230). New York: Wiley.

Gelman, R., Durgin, F., & Kaufman, L. (1995). Distinguishing between animates and inanimates: Not by motion alone. In D. Sperber, D. Premack, & A. J. Premack (Eds.), *Causal cognition: A multidisciplinary debate* (pp. 150–184). Oxford, UK: Clarendon Press.

Gelman, R., & Gallistel, C. R. (1978). *The child's understanding of number.* Cambridge, MA: Harvard University Press.

Gelman, R., & Meck, E. (1983). Preschoolers' counting: principles before skill. *Cognition, 13,* 343–360.

Gelman, R., Meck, E., & Merkin, S. (1986). Young children's numerical competence. *Cognitive Development, 1,* 1–30.

Gelman, R., Spelke, E. S., & Meck, E. (1983). What preschoolers know about animate and inanimate objects. In D. Rogers & J. A. Sloboda (Eds.), *The acquisition of symbolic skills* (pp. 297–324). New York: Plenum.

Gelman, R., & Williams, E. M. (1999). Enabling constraints for cognitive development and learning: A domain-specific epigenetic theory. In D. Kuhn & R. Siegler (Eds.), *Handbook of Child Psychology: Vol. 5. Cognition, perception, and language, Vol. 2.*

Gelman, S. A. (1988). The development of induction within natural kind and artifact categories. *Cognitive Psychology, 20*(1), 65–95.

Gelman, S. A. (1996). Concepts and theories. In R. Gelman & T. Kit-Fong (Eds.), *Perceptual and cognitive development. Handbook of perception and cognition* (2nd ed., pp. 117–150). San Diego: Academic Press.

Gelman, S. A., & Coley, J. D. (1990). The importance of knowing a dodo is a bird: Categories and inferences in 2-year-old children. *Developmental Psychology, 26,* 796–804.

Gelman, S. A., Coley, J. D., & Gottfried, G. M. (1994). Essentialist beliefs in children: The acquisition of concepts and theories. In L. A. Hirschfeld & S. A. Gelman (Eds.), *Mapping the mind: Domain specificity in cognition and culture* (pp. 341–365). New York: Cambridge University Press.

Gelman, S. A., Coley, J. D., Rosengren, K. S., Hartman, E. E., & Pappas, A. S. (1998). Beyond labeling: The role of parental input in the acquisition of richly structured categories. *Monographs of the Society for Research in Child Development, 63*(1), v. 148 (Serial No. 253).

Gelman, S. A., Croft, W., Fu, P., Clausner, T., & Gottfried, G. (1996). Why is a pomegranate an apple? The role of shape, taxonomic relatedness, and prior lexical knowledge in children's overextensions of apple and dog. *Journal of Child Language, 25,* 267–291.

Gelman, S. A., & Diesendruck, G. (1999). A reconsideration of concepts: On the compatibility of psychological essentialism and context sensitivity. In E. K. Scholnick, K. Nelson, S. A. Gelman, & P. H. Miller (Eds.), *Conceptual development: Piaget's legacy* (pp. 79–102). Mahwah, NJ: Erlbaum.

Gelman, S. A., & Ebeling, K. S. (1998). Shape and representational status in children's early naming. *Cognition, 66,* 35–47.

Gelman, S. A., & Gottfried, G. (1996). Children's causal explanations of animate and inanimate motion. *Child Development, 67,* 1970–1987.

Gelman, S. A., & Hirschfield, L. (1994). *Mapping the mind.* Cambridge: Press Syndicate, University of Cambridge.

Gelman, S. A., & Hirschfeld, L. A. (1999). How biological is essentialism? In D. L. Medin & S. Atran (Eds.), *Folkbiology* (pp. 406–443). Cambridge, MA: MIT Press.

Gelman, S. A., & Markman, E. M. (1986). Categories and induction in young children. *Cognition, 23*, 183–209.

Gelman, S. A., & Markman, E. M. (1987). Young children's inductions from natural kinds: The role of categories and appearances. *Child Development, 58*, 1532–1541.

Gelman, S. A., & Medin, D. L. (1993). What's so essential about essentialism? A different perspective on the interaction of perception, language, and conceptual knowledge. *Cognitive Development, 8*(2), 157–167.

Gelman, S. A., Rodriguez, T., Nguyen, S., & Koenig, M. (1997, April). *Children's spontaneous talk about kinds: Domain-specificity in use of generics.* Paper presented at the Society for Research in Child Development. Washington, DC.

Gelman, S. A., & Tardif, T. Z. (1998). Generic noun phrases in English and Mandarin: An examination of child-directed speech. *Cognition, 66*, 215–248.

Gentner, D. (1982). Why nouns are learned before verbs: Linguistic relativity versus natural partitioning. In S. Kuczaj (Ed.), *Language development: Language, thought, and culture* (Vol. 2, pp. 301–334). Hillsdale, NJ: Erlbaum.

Gentner, D. (1983). Structure-mapping: A theoretical framework for analogy. *Cognitive Science, 7*, 155–170.

Gentner, D. (1989). The mechanisms of analogical learning. In S. Vosniadou & A. Ortony (Eds.), *Similarity and analogical reasoning* (pp. 199–241). London: Cambridge University Press.

Gentner, D., & Boroditsky, L. (in press). Individuation, relativity, and early word learning. In M. Bowerman & S. Levinson (Eds.), *Language acquisition and conceptual development.* New York: Cambridge University Press.

Gentner, D., & Namy, L. (1999). Comparison in the development of categories. *Cognitive Development, 14*, 487–513.

Gentner, D., & Rattermann, M. J. (1991). Language and the career of similarity. In S. A. Gelman & J. P. Byrnes (Eds.), *Perspectives on language and thought: Interrelations in development.* Cambridge: Cambridge University Press.

Gentner, D., Rattermann, M. J., Markman, A., & Kotovsky, L. (1995). Two forces in the development of relational similarity. In T. J. Simon & G. S. Halford (Eds.), *Developing cognitive competence: New approaches to process modeling* (pp. 263–313), Hillsdale, NJ: Erlbaum.

Gentner, D., & Toupin, C. (1986). Systematicity and surface similarity in the development of analogy. *Cognitive Science, 10*, 277–300.

Gentner, D., & Waxman, S. R. (1994). Perceptual and conceptual bootstrapping in early word meaning. Paper presented at the Meeting of the International Conference on Infancy Studies, Paris.

Gentry, J. R. (1982). Analysis of developmental spelling skills in GNYS AT WRK. *The reading teacher, 36*, 192–200.

Gerber, R. (1981). Young children's understanding of the elements of maps. *Teaching Geography, 6*, 128–133.

Gerber, R. (1984). The development of competence and performance in cartographic language by children at the concrete level of map-reasoning. *Cartographica, 21*, 98–119.

Gergely, G. (1994). From self-recognition to theory of mind. In S. Parker, R. Mitchell, & M. Boccia (Eds.), *Self-awareness in animals and humans: Developmental perspectives* (pp. 51–61). Cambridge University Press.

Gergely, G. (2000). Mahler reapproached: New perspectives on normal autism, symbiosis, splitting and libidinal object constancy from cognitive developmental theory. *Journal of the American Psychoanalytic Association, 48*(4).

Gergely, G., & Csibra, G. (1997). Teleological reasoning in infancy: The infant's naive theory of rational action. A reply to Premack and Premack. *Cognition, 63*, 227–233.

Gergely, G., & Csibra, G. (1998). La interpretacion teleologica de la conducta: La teoria infantil de la accion racional [The teleological interpretation of behaviour: the infant's theory of rational action]. *Infancia y Aprendizaje, 84*, 45–65 [*Journal for the Study of Education and Development:* Special Issue on The Physical Mind and the Social Mind ed. J. C. Gómez and M. Nunez].

Gergely, G., & Csibra, G. (2000). The teleological origins of naive theory of mind in infancy. Paper presented at the Symposium on Origins of theory of mind: studies with human infants and primates. 12th Biennial International Conference on Infant Studies (ICIS), 16–19 July 2000, Brighton, UK.

Gergely, G., & Watson, J. (1996). The social biofeedback model of parental affect-mirroring. *International Journal of Psycho-Analysis, 77*, 1181–1212.

Gergely, G., & Watson, J. S. (1999). Early socio-emotional development: Contingency perception and the social-biofeedback model. In P. Rochat (Ed.), *Early social cognition: Understanding others in the first months of life* (pp. 101–136). Mahwah, NJ: Erlbaum.

Gergely, G., Koós, O., & Watson, J. S. (2000). Contingency perception and the role of contingent parental reactivity in early socio-emotional development: Some implications for developmental psychopathology. In J. Nadel & J. Decety (Eds.), *Imitation, action et intentionnalité.* Paris: Presses Universitaires de France.

Gergely, G., Magyar, J., & Balázs, A. (1999). Childhood autism as "blindness" to less-than-perfect contingencies. Poster presented at the Biennial Conference of the International Society for Research in Childhood and Adolescent Psychopathology (ISRCAP), Barcelona, 16–20 June, 1999.

Gergely, G., Nádasdy, Z., Csibra, G., & Bíró, S. (1995). Taking the intentional stance at 12 months of age. *Cognition, 56*, 165–193.

Gerken, L., & McIntosh, B. J. (1993). Interplay of function morphemes and prosody in early language. *Developmental Psychology, 29*(3), 448–457.

German, D. (1989). *German test of word finding.* Austin: Pro-Ed.

German, T. P., & Defeyter, M. A. (2000). Immunity to "functional fixedness" in young children. *Psychonomic Bulletin & Review, 7*, 707–712.

Gerstadt, C. L., Hong, Y. J., & Diamond, A. (1994). The relationship between cognition and action: Performance of children $3^1/_2$–7 years old on a Stroop-like dayight test. *Cognition, 53*, 129–153.

Gibbon, F., Dent, H., & Hardcastle, W. (1993). Diagnosis and therapy of abnormal alveolar stops in a speech-disordered child using electropalatography. *Clinical Linguistics & Phonetics, 7*(4), 247–268.

Gibson, E. J., & Walk, R. D. (1960). The "visual cliff." *Scientific American, 202*, 64–71.

Gibson, E. L. (2000). Commentary on perceptual and conceptual processes in infancy. *Journal of Cognition and Development, 1*, 43–48.

Gibson, J. J. (1979). *The ecological approach to visual perception.* Hillsdale, NJ: Lawrence Erlbaum.

Gibson, J. J., & Gibson, E. J. (1955). Perceptual learning: Differentiation or enrichment? *Psychological Review, 62*, 32–41.

Gick, M. L., & Holyoak, K. J. (1983). Schema induction and analogical transfer. *Cognitive Psychology, 15*, 1–38.

Giffin, H. (1984). The coordination of meaning in the creation of shared make-believe play. In I. Bretherton (Ed.), *Symbolic play* (pp. 73–100). Orlando: Academic Press.

Gillberg, C. (1991). Clinical and neurobiological aspects of Asperger syndrome in six family studies. In U. Frith (Ed.), *Autism and Asperger Syndrome.* Cambridge: Cambridge University Press.

Gillette, J., Gleitman, H., Gleitman, L., & Lederer, A. (1999). Human simulations of vocabulary learning. *Cognition, 73*(2), 135–176.

Gilligan, C. (1982). *In a different voice: Psychological theory and women's development.* Cambridge, MA: Harvard University Press.

Gilligan, C., & Wiggins, G. (1987). The orgins of morality in early childhood relationships. In J. Kagan & S. Lamb (Eds.)., *The emergence of morality in young children* (pp. 277–305). Chicago: University of Chicago Press.

Gladstone, R. (1969). Age, cognitive control and extinction. *Journal of Experimental Child Psychology, 7*, 31–35.

Gladstone, R. (1976). On the ability of young children to use significant cues intelligently. *The Journal of Genetic Psychology, 129*, 311–316.

Gleitman, L. (1990). The structural sources of verb meanings. *Language Acquisition: A Journal of Developmental Linguistics, 1*(1), 3–55.

Gleitman, L. R., & Wanner, E. (1988). Current issues in language learning. In M. H. Bornstein & M. E. Lamb (Eds.), *Developmental psychology: An advanced textbook* (2nd ed., pp. 297–356). Hillsdale, NJ: Lawrence Erlbaum.

Glenn, S. M., Cunningham, C. C., & Joyce, P. F. (1981). A study of auditory preferences in non-handicapped infants and infants with Down's Syndrome. *Child Development, 52*, 1303–1307.

Goffman, E. (1974). *Frame analysis: An essay on the organization of experience.* Cambridge, MA: Harvard University Press.

Goldberg, E. (1995). Rise and fall of modular orthodoxy. *Journal of Clinical and Experimental Neuropsychology, 17*, 193–208.

Golden, C. J. (1981). The Luria-Nebraska children's battery: Theory and formulation. In G. W. Hynd & J. E. Obrzut (Eds.), *Neuropsychological assessment and the school-aged child* (pp. 277–302). New York: Grune & Stratton.

Goldfield, B. A., & Reznick, J. S. (1990). Early lexical acquisition: Rate, content, and the vocabulary spurt. *Journal of Child Language, 17*(1), 171–183.

Goldin-Meadow, S. (1997). When gestures and words speak differently. *Current Directions in Psychological Science, 6*, 138–143.

Goldin-Meadow, S., Seligman, M. E., & Gelman, R. (1976). Language in the two-year-old. *Cognition, 4*(2), 189–202.

Goldman, A. I. (1992). In defense of simulation theory. *Mind & Language, 1*, 104–119.

Goldman, A. I. (1993). The psychology of folk psychology. *Behavioral and Brain Sciences, 16*, 15–28.

Goldman, A. I. (2001). Desire, intention, and the simulation theory. In B. F. Malle, L. J. Moses, & D. A. Baldwin (Eds.), *Intentions and intentionality: Foundations of social cognition* (pp. 207–224). Cambridge, MA: MIT Press.

Goldman, P. S., & Alexander, G. E. (1977, June 16). Maturation of prefrontal cortex in the monkey revealed by local reversible cryogenic depression. *Nature, 267*, 613–615.

Goleman, D. (1995). *Emotional intelligence.* New York: Bantam Books.

Golinkoff, R. M., Harding, C. G., Carlson, V., & Sexton, M. E. (1984). The infant's perception of causal events: The distinction between animate and inanimate objects. In L. L. Lipsitt & C. Rovee-Collier (Eds.), *Advances in infancy research* (Vol. 3, pp. 145–165). Norwood: Ablex.

Golledge, R. G. (Ed.). (1999). *Wayfinding behavior: Cognitive mapping and other spatial processes.* Baltimore: Johns Hopkins University Press.

Golledge, R. G, Smith, T. R., Pellegrino, J. W., Doherty, S., & Marshall, S. P. (1985). A conceptual model and empirical analysis of children's acquisition of spatial knowledge. *Journal of Environmental Psychology, 5*, 125–152.

Golomb, C., & Kuersten, R. (1996). On the transition from pretence play to reality: What are the rules of the game? *British Journal of Developmental Psychology, 14*, 203–217.

Goncu, A. (1993). Development of intersubjectivity in the social pretend play of preschool children. *Human Development, 36*, 185–198.

Goncu, A., Tuermer, U., Jain, J., & Johnson, D. (1999). Children's play as cultural activity. In A. Goncue (Ed.), *Children's engagement in the world: Sociocultural perspectives* (pp. 148–170). New York: Cambridge University Press.

Goodman, N. (1976). *Languages of art: An approach to a theory of symbols* (2nd ed.). Indianapolis, IN: Hackett Publishing.

Goodnight, J. A., & Cohen, R. (1985). The social cognition of spatial cognition: Regulating personal boundaries. In R. Cohen (Ed.), *The development of spatial cognition* (pp. 257–276). Hillsdale, NJ: Lawrence Erlbaum.

Goodwin, B. (1982). Genetic epistemology and constructionist biology. *Revue Internationale de Philosophie, 142–143*, 527–548.

Gopnik, A. (1993). How we know our minds: The illusion of 1st-person knowledge of intentionality. *Behavioral and Brain Sciences, 16*, 1–14.

Gopnik, A., & Astington, J. W. (1988). Children's understanding of representational change and its relation to the understanding of false belief and the appearance–reality distinction. *Child Development, 59*, 26–37.

Gopnik, A., & Graf, P. (1988). Knowing how you know: Young children's ability to identify and remember the sources of their beliefs. *Child Development, 59*, 1366–1371.

Gopnik, A., & Meltzoff, A. N. (1986). Relations between semantic and cognitive development in the one-word stage: The specificity hypothesis. *Child Development, 57*, 1040–1053.

Gopnik, A., & Meltzoff, A. N. (1987). The development of categorization in the second year and its relation to other cognitive and linguistic developments. *Child Development, 58*, 1523–1531.

Gopnik, A., & Meltzoff, A. N. (1997). *Words, thoughts and theories*. Cambridge, MA.: MIT Press.

Gopnik, A., Meltzoff, A., & Kuhl, P. (1999a). *How babies think*. London: Weidenfeld & Nicolson.

Gopnik, A., Meltzoff, A. N., & Kuhl, P. K. (1999b). *The scientist in the crib: Minds, brains, and how children learn*. New York: Morrow Press.

Gopnik, A., & Wellman, H. (1994). The theory theory. In L. A. Hirschfeld & S. A. Gelman (Eds.), *Mapping the mind: Domain specificity in cognition and culture* (pp. 257–293). New York, NY: Cambridge University Press.

Gopnik, M. (1990). Feature blindness: A case study. *Language Acquisition, 1*(2), 139–164.

Gordon, A. C. L., & Olson, D. R. (1998). The relation between acquisition of a theory of mind and the capacity to hold in mind. *Journal of Experimental Child Psychology, 68*(1), 70–83.

Gordon. R. M. (1986). Folk psychology as simulation. *Mind and Language, 1*, 158–171.

Goren, C. C., Sarty, M., & Wu, P. Y. K. (1975). Visual following and pattern discrimination of face-like stimuli by newborn infants. *Pediatrics, 56*, 544–549.

Gorenstein, E. S., Mammato, C. A., & Sandy, J. M. (1989). Performance of inattentive-overactive children on selected measures of prefrontal type function. *Journal of Clinical Psychology, 45*, 619–632.

Goswami, U. (1988). Orthographic analogies and reading development. *Quarterly Journal of Experimental Psychology, 40A*, 239–268.

Goswami, U. (1991). Analogical reasoning: What develops? A review of research and theory. *Child Development, 62*, 1–22.

Goswami, U. (1992). *Analogical Reasoning in Children*. Hillsdale, NJ: Lawrence Erlbaum.

Goswami, U. (1996). Analogical reasoning and cognitive development. In H. Reese (Ed.), *Advances in child development and behaviour, 26* (Vol. 26, pp. 91–138). San Diego, CA: Academic Press.

Goswami, U. (1999) Phonological awareness and orthographic representation. In M. Harris & G. Hatano (Eds.), *Learning to read and write: A cross-linguistic perspective* (pp. 134–156). Cambridge: Cambridge University Press.

Goswami, U. (2001). Analogical reasoning in children. In D. Gentner, K. Holyoak, & B. Kokinov (Eds.), *Analogy: Interdisciplinary Perspectives* (pp. 437–470). Cambridge, MA: MIT Press.

Goswami, U. (in press). Inductive and deductive reasoning. In U. Goswami (Ed.), *Blackwell handbook of child cognitive development.* Oxford, UK: Blackwell.

Goswami, U., & Brown, A. L. (1989). Melting chocolate and melting snowmen: Analogical reasoning and causal relations. *Cognition, 35,* 69–95.

Goswami, U., & Brown, A. L. (1990). Higher-order structure and relational reasoning: Contrasting analogical and thematic relations. *Cognition, 36,* 207–226.

Goswami, U., & Bryant, P. E. (1990). *Phonological skills and learning to read.* London: Erlbaum.

Goswami, U., & East, M. (2000). Rhyme and analogy in beginning reading: Conceptual and methodological issues. *Applied Psycholinguistics, 21,* 63–93.

Goswami, U., & Mead, F. (1992). Onset and rime awareness and analogies in reading. *Reading Research Quarterly, 27,* 153–162.

Gottfried, G. M. (1997). Comprehending compounds: Evidence for metaphoric skill? *Journal of Child Language, 24,* 163–186.

Goubet, N., & Clifton, R. K. (1998). Object and event representation in 6.5-month-old infants. *Developmental Psychology, 34,* 63–76.

Goudena, P. (1982). Social aspects of private speech of young children during cognitive tasks. Paper presented at the Tenth World Congress of Sociology, Mexico City.

Goudena, P. (1983). Private speech: An analysis of its social and self-regulative functions. Dissertation, University of Utrecht.

Goudena, P., & Leenders, F. H. R. (1980). Exporatief onderzoek naar aspekten van private taal. [Exploratory research on aspects of private speech]. Utrecht: Internal report, IPAW.

Gough, P. B., & Hillinger, M. (1980). Learning to read: An unnatural act. *Bulletin of the Orton Society, 30,* 179–196.

Gough, P. B., & Tunmer, W. E. (1986). Decoding, reading and reading disability. *Remedial and Special Education, 7,* 6–10.

Grant, D. A., & Berg, E. A. (1948). A behavioral analysis of degree of reinforcement and ease of shifting to new responses in a Weigl-type card-sorting problem. *Journal of Experimental Psychology, 38,* 404–411.

Grant, J., Karmiloff-Smith, A., Berthoud, I., & Cristophe, A. (1996). Is the language of people with Williams syndrome mere mimicry? Phonological short term memory in a foreign language. *Cahiers de Psychologie Cognitive, 15,* 615–628.

Gratch, G. (1976). A review of Piagetian infancy research: Object concept development. In W. F. Overton & J. M. Gallagher (Eds.), *Knowledge and development: Advances in research and theory* (pp. 59–91). New York: Plenum.

Greco, P. (1962) Quantité et quotité: Nouvelles recherches sur la correspondance terme-à-terme et la conservation des ensembles. In P. Greco and A. Morf, *Structures numériques élémentaires: Etudes d'epistemologie genetique* (Vol. 13, pp. 35–52). Paris: Presses Universitaires de France.

Greenfield, P. M. (1997). You can't take it with you: Why abilities assessments don't cross cultures. *American Psychologist, 52*(10), 1115–1124.

Greenwald, C., & Leonard, L. (1979). Communicative and sensorimotor development of Down's syndrome children. *American Journal of Mental Retardation, 84,* 296–303.

Gregory, R. L. (1970). *The intelligent eye.* New York: McGraw-Hill.

Grigorenko, E. L. (2000). Heritability and intelligence. In R. J. Sternberg (Ed.), *Handbook of intelligence* (pp. 53–92). New York: Cambridge University Press.

Grigorenko, E. L., Geissler, P. W., Prince, R., Okatcha, F., Nokes, C., Kenny, D. A., Bundy, D. A., & Sternberg, R. J. (in press). The organization of Luo conceptions of intelligence: A study of implicit theories in a Kenyan village. *International Journal of Behavioral Development*.

Gross, D., & Harris, P. L. (1988). Understanding false beliefs about emotion. *International Journal of Behavioral Development, 11*, 475–488.

Grotzer, T. A., & Perkins, D. A. (2000). Teaching of intelligence: A performance conception. In R. J. Sternberg (Ed.), *Handbook of intelligence* (pp. 492–515). New York: Cambridge University Press.

Guajardo, J. J., & Woodward, A. L. (2000). *Using habituation to index infants' understanding of pointing.* Paper presented at the XIIth Biennial Meeting of the International Society for Infant Studies, Brighton, UK.

Gustafsson J. E. (1988). Hierarchical models of the structure of cognitive abilities. In R. J. Sternberg (Ed.), *Advances in the psychology of human intelligence* (Vol. 4, pp. 35–71). Hillsdale, NJ: Erlbaum.

Gustafsson, L. (1997). Inadequate cortical feature maps: A neural circuit theory of autism. *Biological-Psychiatry, 42*, 1138–1147.

Gutheil, G., & Gelman, S.A. (1997). Children's use of sample size and diversity information within basic-level categories. *Journal of Experimental Child Psychology, 64*, 159–174.

Gutheil, G., Vera, A., & Keil, F. C. (1998). Do houseflies think? Patterns of induction and biological beliefs in development. *Cognition, 66*, 33–49.

Guttentag, R. E. (1984). The mental effort requirement of cumulative rehearsal: A developmental study. *Journal of Experimental Child Psychology, 37*, 92–106.

Haden C. A. (1998). Reminiscing with different children: Relating maternal stylistic consistency and sibling similarity in talk about the past. *Developmental Psychology, 34*, 99–114.

Haden, C. A., Haine, R. A., & Fivush, R. (1997). Developing narrative structure in parent–child reminiscing across the preschool years. *Developmental Psychology, 33*, 295–307.

Hagen, M. A. (1985). There is no development in art. In H. H. Freeman & M. V. Cox (Eds.), *Visual order* (pp. 59–77). Cambridge: Cambridge University Press.

Hahn, U. & Nakisa, R. C. (in press). German inflection: Single route or dual-route? *Cognitive Psychology*.

Haidt, J., Koller, S. H., & Dias, M. G. (1994). Affect, culture, and the morality of harmless offenses. *Journal of Personality and Social Psychology, 65*, 613–629.

Haight, W. L., & Miller, P. J. (1993). *Pretending at home.* Albany: SUNY Press.

Haight, W. L., Wang, X.-l., Fung, H. H.-t., Williams, K., & Mintz, J. (1999). Universal, developmental, and variable aspects of young children's play: A cross-cultural comparison of pretending at home. *Child Development, 70*, 1477–1488.

Haith, M. M., & Benson, J. B. (1998). Infant cognition. In W. Damon (Series Ed.) and D. Kuhn & R. Siegler (Vol. Eds.), *Handbook of child psychology: Vol. 2. Cognition, perception, and language development* (5th ed., pp. 199–254). New York: Wiley.

Halford, G. S. (1984). Can young children integrate premises in transitivity and serial order tasks? *Cognitive Psychology, 16*, 65–93.

Halford, G. S. (1993). *Children's understanding: The development of mental models.* Hillsdale, NJ: Lawrence Erlbaum.

Halford, G. S. (in press). Information-processing models of cognitive development. In U. Goswami (Ed.), *Blackwell handbook of child cognitive development.* Oxford, UK: Blackwell.

Halford, G. S., Andrews, G., & Bowden, D. (1998, July 1–4). *Complexity as a factor in children's theory of mind.* Paper presented at the XVth Biennial Conference of the International Society for the Study of Behavioral Development, Berne, Switzerland.

Halford, G. S., Andrews, G., Dalton, C., Boag, C., & Zielinski, T. (submitted). Young children's performance on the balance scale: The influence of relational complexity.

Halford, G. S., Brown, C. A., & McThompson, R. M. (1986). Children's concepts of volume and flotation. *Developmental Psychology, 22,* 218–222.

Halford, G. S., Maybery, M. T., O'Hare, A. W., & Grant, P. (1994). The development of memory and processing capacity. *Child Development, 65,* 1338–1356.

Halford, G. S., & Wilson, W. H. (1980). A category theory approach to cognitive development. *Cognitive Psychology, 12,* 356–411.

Halford, G. S., Wilson, W. H., Guo, J., Gayler, R. W., Wiles, J., & Stewart, J. E. M. (1994). Connectionist implications for processing capacity limitations in analogies. In K. J. Holyoak & J. Barnden (Eds.), *Advances in connnectionist and neural computation theory: Vol. 2. Analogical connections* (pp. 363–415). Norwood, NJ: Ablex.

Halford, G. S., Wilson, W. H., & Phillips, S. (1998a). Authors' response: Relational complexity metric is effective when assessments are based on actual cognitive processes. *Behavioral and Brain Sciences, 21*(6), 848–864.

Halford, G. S., Wilson, W. H., & Phillips, S. (1998b). Processing capacity defined by relational complexity: Implications for comparative, developmental, and cognitive psychology. *Behaviorial and Brain Sciences, 21*(6), 803–831.

Hall, D. G., & Graham, S. A. (1999). Lexical form class information guides word-to-object mapping in preschoolers. *Child Development, 70*(1), 78–91.

Hall, D. G., & Waxman, S. R. (1993). Assumptions about word meaning: Individuation and basic-level kinds. *Child Development, 64*(5), 1550–1570.

Hall, D. G., Waxman, S. R., & Hurwitz, W. M. (1993). How two- and four-year-old children interpret adjectives and count nouns. *Child Development, 64*(6), 1651–1664.

Halpern, D. F. (1996). *Thought and knowledge: An introduction to critical thinking* (2nd ed.). Mahwah, NJ: Lawrence Erlbaum.

Halpern, D. F. (1997). Sex differences in intelligence: Implications for education. *American Psychologist, 52,* 1091–1102.

Hamond, N. R., & Fivush, R. (1991). Memories of Mickey Mouse: Young children recount their trip to Disneyworld. *Cognitive Development, 6,* 433–448.

Han, J. J., Leichtman, M. D., & Wang, Q. (1998). Autobiographical memory in Korean, Chinese, and American children. *Developmental Psychology, 34,* 701–713.

Hanley, J. R., Tzeng, O., & Huang, H.-S. (1999). Learning to read Chinese. In M. Harris & G. Hatano (Eds.), *Learning to read and write: A cross-linguistic perspective* (pp. 173–195). Cambridge: Cambridge University Press.

Hanna, E., & Meltzoff, A. N. (1993). Peer imitation by toddlers in laboratory, home, and day-care contexts: Implications for social learning and memory. *Developmental Psychology, 29,* 702–710.

Happé, F. (1993). Communicative competence and theory of mind in autism: A test of Relevance Theory. *Cognition, 48,* 101–119.

Happé, F. (1994). *Autism: An introduction to psychological theory.* UCL Press.

Happé, F. (1995). The role of age and verbal ability in the theory of mind task performance of subjects with autism. *Child Development, 66,* 843–855.

Happé, F. (1996). Studying weak central coherence at low levels: children with autism do not succumb to visual illusions. A research note. *Journal of Child Psychology and Psychiatry, 37,* 873–877.

Hardiman, P. T., Pollatsek, A., & Well, A. D. (1986). Learning to understand the balance beam. *Cognition and Instruction, 3,* 63–86.

Hardwick, D. A., McIntyre, C. W., & Pick, H. L. (1976). The content and manipulation of cognitive maps in children and adults. *Monographs of the Society for Research in Child Development, 41*(3) (No. 16615).

Harm, M. W., & Seidenberg, M. S. (1999). Phonology, reading acquisition, and dyslexia: Insights from connectionist models. *Psychological Review, 106*, 491–528.

Harmon, G. (1986). *Change in view: Principles of reasoning.* Cambridge, MA: MIT Press/Bradford Books.

Harnishfeger, K. K., & Bjorklund, D. F. (1990). Children's strategies: A brief history. In D. F. Bjorklund (Ed.), *Children's strategies: Contemporary views of cognitive development* (pp. 1–22). Hillsdale, NJ: Erlbaum.

Harnishfeger, K. K., & Bjorklund, D. F. (1993). The ontogeny of inhibition mechanisms: A renewed approach to cognitive development. In M. L. Howe & R. Pasnak (Eds.), *Emerging themes in cognitive development: Vol 1. Foundations* (pp. 28–49). New York: Springer.

Harnishfeger, K. K., & Brainerd, C. J. (1994). Nonstrategic facilitation of children's recall: Evidence of triage with semantically related information. *Journal of Experimental Child Psychology, 57*, 259–280.

Harris, M., & Hatano, G. (Eds.). (1999). *Learning to read and write: A cross-linguistic perspective.* Cambridge: Cambridge University Press.

Harris, N. G., Bellugi, U., Bates, E., Jones, W., & Rossen, M. (1997). Contrasting profiles of language development in children with Williams and Down's syndromes. *Developmental Neuropsychology 13*, 345–370.

Harris, P. L. (1987). The development of search. In P. Salapatek & L. B. Cohen (Eds.), *Handbook of infant perception* (Vol. 2, pp. 155–207). New York: Academic Press.

Harris, P. L. (1991). The work of the imagination. In A. Whiten (Ed.), *Natural theories of mind* (pp. 283–304). Oxford, UK: Basil Blackwell.

Harris, P. L. (1992). From simulation to folk psychology: The case for development. *Mind & Language, 7*, 120–144.

Harris, P. L. (2000). *The work of the imagination.* Oxford, UK: Blackwell.

Harris, P. L., Brown, E., Marriot, C., Whithall, S., & Harmer, S. (1991). Monsters, ghosts and witches: Testing the limits of the fantasy–reality distinction in young children. *British Journal of Developmental Psychology, 9*, 105–124.

Harris, P. L., Johnson, C. N., Hutton, D., Andrews, G., & Cooke, T. (1989). Young children's theory of mind and emotion. *Cognition and Emotion, 3*, 379–400.

Harris, P. L., & Kavanaugh, R. D. (1993). Young children's understanding of pretense. *Monographs of the Society for Research in Child Development, 58*(1) (Serial No. 231).

Harris, P. L., & Leevers, H. J. (2000). Reasoning from false premises. In P. Mitchell & K. J. Riggs (Eds.), *Children's reasoning and the mind*, pp. 67–86. Hove, UK: Psychology Press.

Harris, P. L., & Nunez, M. (1996). Understanding of permission rules by preschool children. *Child Development, 67*, 1572–1591.

Hart, C. (1989). *Without reason.* New York: Harper & Row.

Hart, K. (1981) *Children's understanding of mathematics: 11–16.* London: John Murray.

Hart, K. (1988). Ratio and proportion. In J. Hiebert & M. Behr (Eds.), *Number concepts and operations in middle grades* (pp. 198–219). Hillsdale, NJ: Erlbaum.

Hart, K. (1994). *Ratio: Children's strategies and errors. A report of the strategies and errors in secondary mathematics project.* Windsor: NFER-Nelson.

Hart, R. A. (1981). Children's spatial representation of the landscape: Lessons and questions from a field study. In L. S. Liben, A. H. Patterson, & N. Newcombe (Eds.), *Spatial representation and behavior across the life span: Theory and application* (pp. 195–233). New York: Academic Press.

Hart, R. A., & Berzok, M. (1982). Children's strategies for mapping the geographic-scale environment. In M. Potegal (Ed.), *Spatial abilities: Development and physiological foundations* (pp. 147–169). New York: Academic Press.

Harter, S. (1999). *The construction of the self: A developmental perspective.* New York: The Guilford Press.

Harter, S., & Buddin, N. (1987). Children's understanding of the simultaneity of two emotions: A five-stage developmental acquisition sequence. *Developmental Psychology, 23,* 388–399.

Haryu, E., & Imai, M. (1999). Controlling the application of the mutual exclusivity assumption in the acquisition of lexical hierarchies. *Japanese Psychological Research, 41*(1), 21–34.

Hasebe, Y., Nucci, L., & Nucci, M. S. (2001). Parental overcontrol of the personal domain and adolescent psychopathology. Unpublished Manuscript, University of California, Berkeley.

Hasselhorn, M. (1992). Task dependency and the role of category typicality and metamemory in the development of an organizational strategy. *Child Development, 63,* 202–214.

Hasselhorn, M. (1995). Beyond production deficiency and utilization inefficiency: Mechanisms of the emergence of strategic categorization in episodic memory tasks. In F. E. Weinert & W. Schneider (Eds.), *Memory performance and competencies: Issues in growth and development.* Hillsdale, NJ: Erlbaum.

Haste, H. (1993). Morality, self, and socio-historical context: The role of lay social theory. In G. Noam & T. Wren (Eds.), *The moral self: Building a better paradigm* (pp. 175–208). Cambridge, MA: MIT Press.

Hatano, G., & Inagaki, K. (1991). Sharing cognition through collective comprehension activity. In L. Resnick, J. Levine, & S. Teasley (Eds.), *Perspectives on socially shared cognition* (pp. 331–348). Washington, DC: American Psychological Association.

Hatano, G., & Inagaki, K. (1994). Young children's naïve theory of biology. *Cognition, 50,* 171–188.

Hatano, G., Siegler, R. S., Richards, D. D., Inagaki, K., Stavy, R., & Wax, N. (1993). The development of biological knowledge: A multi-national study. *Cognitive Development, 8,* 47–62.

Hawkins, J., Pea, R.D., Glick, J., & Scribner, S. (1984). "Merds that laugh don't like mushrooms": Evidence for deductive reasoning by preschoolers. *Developmental Psychology, 20,* 584–594.

Heath, S. B. (1983). *Ways with words: Language, life, and work in communities and classrooms.* Cambridge: Cambridge University Press.

Heaton, R. K. (1981). *Wisconsin Card Sorting Test (WCST).* Odessa, FL: Psychological Assessment Resources.

Hecht, S. A., Burgess, S. R., Torgesen, J. K., Wagner, R. K., & Rashotte, C. A. (2000). Explaining social class differences in growth of reading skills from beginning kindergarten through fourth-grade: The role of phonological awareness, rate of access, and print knowledge. *Reading and Writing, 12*(1–2), 99–127.

Heibeck, T. H., & Markman, E. M. (1987). Word learning in children: An examination of fast mapping. *Child Development, 58*(4), 1021–1034.

Heider, F., & Simmel, M. (1944). An experimental study of apparent behavior. *American Journal of Psychology, 57,* 243–259.

Heimann, M., & Meltzoff, A. N. (1996). Deferred imitation in 9- and 14-month-old infants: A longitudinal study of a Swedish sample. *British Journal of Developmental Psychology, 14,* 55–64.

Heimann, M., Nelson, K. E., & Schaller, J. (1989). Neonatal imitation of tongue protrusion and mouth opening: Methodological aspects and evidence of early individual differences. *Scandinavian Journal of Psychology, 30,* 90–101.

Heimann, M., & Schaller, J. (1985). Imitative reactions among 14–21-day-old infants. *Infant Mental Health Journal, 6,* 31–39.

Heit, E. (2000). Properties of inductive reasoning. *Psychonomic Bulletin & Review, 7,* 569–592.

Held, R., & Hein, A. (1963). Movement-produced stimulation in the development of visually guided behavior. *Journal of Comparative & Physiological Psychology, 56*(5), 872–876.

Helwig, C., Tisak, M. & Turiel, E. (1990). Children's social reasoning in context: Reply to Gabbenesch. *Child Development, 61,* 2068–2078.

Hepper, P. G. (1992). Fetal psychology: An embryonic science. In J. G. Nijhuis (Ed.), *Fetal behaviour: Developmental and perinatal aspects* (pp. 129–156). Oxford, UK: Oxford University Press.

Herman, J. F., Norton, L. M., & Klein, C. A. (1986). Children's distance estimates in a large-scale environment. *Environment and Behavior, 18,* 533–558.

Hermelin, B., & O'Connor, N. (1970). *Psychological experiments with autistic children.* London: Pergamon Press.

Herrenkohl, L., & Guerra, M. (1998). Participant structures, scientific discourse, and student engagement in fourth grade. *Cognition and Instruction, 16,* 431–473.

Herrnstein, R. J., & Murray, C. (1994). *The bell curve.* New York: Free Press.

Hespos, S. J. (1998, April). Infants' physical reasoning about containment and occlusion: A surprising décalage. Paper presented at the biennial International Conference on Infant Studies, Atlanta, GA.

Hespos, S. J. (2000, July). Tracking individual objects across occlusion and containment events in 6.5-month-old infants. Paper presented at the biennial International Conference on Infant Studies, Brighton, UK.

Hespos, S. J., & Baillargeon, R. (2001a). Infants' knowledge about occlusion and containment events: A surprising discrepancy. *Psychological Science, 12,* 140–147.

Hespos, S. J., & Baillargeon, R. (2001b). Knowledge about containment events in very young infants. *Cognition, 78,* 204–245.

Hewlett, N., Gibbon, F., & Hardcastle, W. (1998). When is a velar an alveolar? Evidence supporting a revised psycholinguistic model of speech production in children. *International Journal of Language and Communication Disorders, 33,* 161–176.

Hewson, M. G. (1986). The acquisition of scientific knowledge: Analysis and representation of student conceptions concerning density. *Science Education, 70,* 159–170.

Heyes, C. (1998). Theory of mind in nonhuman primates. *Behavioral and Brain Sciences, 21,* 101–148.

Heyman, G. D., & Gelman, S. A. (2000). Preschool children's use of trait labels to make inductive inferences. *Journal of Experimental Child Psychology, 77,* 1–19.

Heyman, G., Phillips, A. T., & Gelman, S. A. (2000). Animacy effects on children's reasoning about physics. Unpublished data, University of Michigan.

Hickling, A. (1996). The emergence of causal explanation in everyday thought: Evidence from ordinary conversation. Ph.D. dissertation, University of Michigan, Ann Arbor.

Hickling, A. K., & Gelman, S. A. (1995). How does your garden grow? Evidence of an early conception of plants as biological kinds. *Child Development, 66,* 856–876.

Hickling, A. K., Wellman, H. M., & Gottfried, G. (1997). Preschoolers' understanding of others' mental attitudes toward pretend happenings. *British Journal of Developmental Psychology, 15,* 339–354.

Hill, W. L., Borovsky, D., & Rovee-Collier, C. (1988). Continuities in infant memory development. *Developmental Psychobiology, 21,* 43–62.

Hilton, D. (in preparation). Commonsense and scientific thinking about causality: Cognitive and social bases or reasoning. In P. Carruthers, S. Stich, & M. Siegal (Eds.), *The cognitive basis of science.* Under review.

Hines, M. (2000). Gonadal hormones and sexual differentiation of human behavior: Effects on psychosexual and cognitive development. In A. Matsumoto (Ed.), *Sexual differentiation of the brain* (pp. 257–278). Boca Raton, FL: CRC Press.

Hitch, G. J., & Towse, J. (1995). Working memory: What develops? In F. Weinert & W. Schneider (Eds.), *Memory performance and competencies. Issues in growth and development* (pp. 3–22). Mahwah, NJ: Lawrence Erlbaum.

Ho, C. S. H., & Bryant, P. E. (1997). Phonological skills are important in learning to read Chinese. *Developmental Psychology, 33*(6), 946–951.

Hobson, R. P. (1989). On sharing experiences. *Development and Psychopathology, 1*, 197–203.

Hobson, R. P. (1993). *Autism and the development of mind.* Hove: Lawrence Erlbaum.

Hodapp, Robert M., & Dykens, Elisabeth M. (1994). Mental retardation's two cultures of behavioral research. *American Journal on Mental Retardation, 98*, 675–687.

Hodkin, B. (1987). Performance model analysis in class inclusion: An illustration with two language conditions. *Developmental Psychology, 23*, 683–689.

Hoeffner, J. (1992). Are rules a thing of the past? The acquisition of verbal morphology by an attractor network. In *Proceedings of the 14th Annual Meeting of the Cognitive Science Society.* Hillsdale, NJ: Erlbaum.

Hoeffner, J. H., & McClelland, J. L. (1993). Can a perceptual processing deficit explain the impairment of inflectional morphology in developmental dysphasia? A computational investigation. In E. V. Clark (Ed.), *Proceedings of the 25th Child language research forum.* Stanford University Press.

Hofer, B., & Pintrich, P. (1997). The development of epistemological theories: Beliefs about knowledge and knowing and their relation to learning. *Review of Educational Research, 67*, 88–140.

Hoffman, M. L. (1981). Is altruism part of human nature? *Journal of Personality and Social Psychology, 40*, 121–137.

Hoffman, M. L. (1983). Affective and cognitive processes in moral internalization. In E. Higgins, A. Ruble, & W. Hartup (Eds.), *Social cognition and social development: A sociocultural perspective* (pp. 236–274). Cambridge: Cambridge University Press.

Hoffman, M. L. (2000). *Empathy and moral development: Implications for caring and justice.* Cambridge: Cambridge University Press.

Hofstaeder, D. (1979). *Godel, Escher, Bach: An eternal golden brain.* New York: Basic Books.

Holland, V. M., & Rohrman, N. L. (1979). Distribution of the feature [+animate] in the lexicon of the child. *Journal of Psycholinguistic Research, 8*, 267–378.

Hollos, M., Leis, P., & Turiel, E. (1986). Social reasoning in Ijo children and adolescents in Nigerian communities. *Journal of Cross-Cultural Psychology, 17*, 352–376.

Holyoak, K. J., Junn, E. N., & Billman, D. O. (1984). Development of analogical problem-solving skill. *Child Development, 55*, 2042–2055.

Holyoak, K. J., & Thagard, P. (1989). Analogical mapping by constraint satisfaction. *Cognitive Science, 13*(3), 295–355.

Holyoak, K. J., & Thagard, P. (1995). *Mental Leaps.* Cambridge, MA: MIT Press.

Hood, B. M. (1995). Gravity rules for 2- to 4-years-olds? *Cognitive Development, 10*, 577–598.

Hood, B., & Willatts, P. (1986). Reaching in the dark to an object's remembered position: Evidence of object permanence in 5-month-old infants. *British Journal of Developmental Psychology, 4*, 57–65.

Hood, B., Willen, J., & Driver, J. (1997). An eye-direction detector triggers shifts of visual attention in human infants. Unpublished manuscript, Harvard University.

Horn, J. L. (1994). Theory of fluid and crystallized intelligence. In R. J. Sternberg (Ed.), *The encyclopedia of human intelligence* (Vol. 1, pp. 443–451). New York: Macmillan.

Hornick, R., Risenhoover, N., & Gunnar, M. (1987). The effects of maternal positive, neutral, and negative affective communications and infant responses to new toys. *Child Development, 58*, 937–944.

Horton, M. S., & Markman, E. M. (1980). Developmental differences in the acquisition of basic and superordinate categories. *Child Development, 51*, 708–719.

Howe, M. L. (1991). Misleading children's story recall: Forgetting and reminiscence of the facts. *Developmental Psychology, 27*, 746–762.

Howe, M. L. (2000). Historical and future trends in studying the development of long-term retention. Commentary on Bauer et al., *Monographs of the Society for Research in Child Development, 65*(4) (Serial No. 263).

Howe, M. L., & Brainerd, C. J. (1989). Development of children's long-term retention. *Developmental Review, 9*, 301–340.

Howe, M. L., & Courage, M. L. (1993). On resolving the enigma of infantile amnesia. *Psychological Bulletin, 113*, 305–326.

Howe, M. L., & Courage, M. L. (1997). The emergence and early development of autobiographical memory. *Psychological Review, 104*(3), 499–523.

Howe, N., Petrakos, H., & Rinaldi, C. (1998). "All the sheeps are dead. He murdered them." Sibling pretense, negotiation, internal state language, and relationship quality. *Child Development, 69*, 182–191.

Howes, C., & Matheson, C. C. (1992). Sequences in the development of competent play with peers. Social and social pretend play. *Developmental Psychology, 28*, 961–974.

Howes, C., & Rodning, C. (1992). Attachment security and social pretend play negotiations. In C. Howes, O. Unger, & C. C. Matheson (Eds.), *The collaborative construction of pretend: Social pretend play functions* (pp. 89–98). Albany, NY: State University of New York Press.

Howes, C., Unger, O. A., & Matheson, C. C. (1992). *The collaborative construction of pretend: Social pretend play functions*. Albany, NY: State University of New York Press.

Howlin, P., Davies, M., & Udwin, O. (1998). Cognitive functioning in adults with Williams syndrome. *Journal of Child Psychology and Psychiatry, 39*, 183–189.

Huang, H. S., & Hanley, J. R. (1994). Phonological awareness and visual skills in learning to read Chinese and English. *Cognition, 54*, 73–98.

Huber, S., Krist, H., & Wilkening, F. (in press). Judgment and action knowledge in speed adjustment tasks: Experiments in a virtual environment. *Developmental Science*.

Hudson, J. A. (1990). The emergence of autobiographical memory in mother–child conversation. In R. Fivush & J. A. Hudson (Eds.), *Knowing and remembering in young children* (pp. 166–196). Cambridge, MA: Cambridge University Press.

Hudson, J. A. (1991). Learning to reminisce: A case study. *Journal of Narrative and Life History, 1*, 295–324.

Hudson, J. A. (1993). Reminiscing with mothers and others: Autobiographical memory in young two-year-olds. *Journal of Narrative and Life History, 3*, 1–32.

Hudson, J. A., & Fivush, R. (1991). As time goes by: Sixth graders remember a kindergarten experience. *Applied Cognitive Psychology, 5*, 346–360.

Hudson, J.A., & Sheffield, E. G. (1998). Déjà vu all over again: Effects of reenactment on toddlers' event memory. *Child Development, 69*, 51–67.

Huettel, S. A., & Needham, A. (2000). Effects of balance relations between objects on infants' object segregation. *Developmental Science, 3*, 415–427.

Hughes, C. (1998a). Finding your marbles: Does preschoolers' strategic behavior predict later understanding of mind? *Developmental Psychology, 34*, 1326–1339.

Hughes, C. (1998b). Executive function in preschoolers: Links with theory of mind and verbal ability. *British Journal of Developmental Psychology, 16*, 233–253.

Hughes, C., & Dunn, J. (1997). "Pretend you didn't know": Preschoolers' talk about mental states in pretend play. *Cognitive Development, 12*, 381–403.

Hughes, C., & Russell, J. (1993). Autistic children's difficulty with mental disengagement from an object: its implication for theories of autism. *Developmental Psychology, 29,* 498–510.

Hughes, M. (1981). Can preschool children add and subtract? *Educational Psychology, 3,* 207–219.

Hughes, M. (1986). *Children and number.* Oxford, UK: Blackwell.

Hull, C. L. (1920). Quantitative aspects of the evolution of concepts. *Psychological Monographs* (Whole No. 123).

Hulme, C., & Mackenzie, S. (1992). *Working memory & severe learning difficulties.* Lawrence Erlbaum.

Hulme, C., & Snowling, M. J. (1992). Deficits in output phonology: An explanation of reading failure? *Cognitive Neuropsychology, 9,* 47–72.

Hulme, C., Thompson, N., Muir, C., & Lawrence, A. (1984). Speech rate and the development of spoken words: The role of rehearsal and item identification processes. *Journal of Experimental Child Psychology, 38,* 241–253.

Hume, D. (1748/1988). *An Enquiry Concerning Human Understanding.* Illinois: Open Court.

Hume, D. (1973). *A Treatise of Human Nature,* ed. L. A. Selby-Bigge and P. H. Nidditch (2nd ed.). Oxford, UK: Oxford University Press.

Hummel, J. E., & Holyoak, K. J. (1997). Distributed representations of structure: A theory of analogical access and mapping. *Psychological Review, 104,* 427–466.

Hunt, E., Frost, N., & Lunneborg, C. (1973). Individual differences in cognition: A new approach to intelligence. In G. Bower (Ed.), *The psychology of learning and motivation* (Vol. 7, pp. 87–122). New York: Academic Press.

Hunt, E., & Lansman, M. (1982). Individual differences in attention. In R. J. Sternberg (Ed.), *Advances in the psychology of human intelligence* (Vol. 1, pp. 207–254). Hillsdale, NJ: Lawrence Erlbaum.

Hunter, W. S. (1917). Delayed reaction in a child. *Psychological Review, 24,* 74–87.

Hupbach, A., Mecklenbräuker, S., & Wippich, W. (1999). Implicit memory in children: Are there age-related improvements in a conceptual test of implicit memory? In M. Hahn & C. Stoness (Eds.), *Proceedings of the twenty first annual conference of the Cognitive Science Society.* Mahwah, NJ: Erlbaum.

Huston, A., & Wright, J. (1998). Mass media and children's development. In I. E. Sigel & K. A. Renninger (Eds.), *Handbook of child psychology* (5th ed.). *Vol. 4. Child psychology in practice.* New York: Wiley.

Huttenlocher, J., & Higgins, E. T. (1978). Issues in the study of symbolic development. In W. A. Collins (Ed.), *Minnesota Symposia on Child Psychology* (Vol. 11, pp. 98–140). Hillsdale, NJ: Erlbaum.

Huttenlocher, J., Levine, S. C., & Jordan, N. (1994) A mental model of early arithmetic. *Journal of Experimental Psychology – General, 123,* 284–296.

Huttenlocher, J., Newcombe, N., & Sandberg, E. H. (1994). The coding of spatial location in young children. *Cognitive Psychology, 27,* 115–148.

Huttenlocher, J., Newcombe, N., & Vasilyeva, M. (1999). Spatial scaling in young children. *Psychological Science, 10,* 393–398.

Huttenlocher, J., & Smiley, P. (1987). Early word meanings: The case of object names. *Cognitive Psychology, 19*(1), 63–89.

Huttenlocher, P. R. (1990). Morphometric study of human cerebral cortex development. *Neuropsychologia, 28,* 517–527.

Iacoboni, M., Woods, R. P., Brass, M., Bekkering, H., Mazziotta, J. C., & Rizzolatti, G. (1999). Cortical mechanisms of human imitation. *Science, 286,* 2526–2528.

ICD-10. (1994). *International classification of diseases.* (10th ed.). Geneva, Switzerland: World Health Organisation.

Imai, M., & Gentner, D. (1993). Linguistic relativity vs. universal ontology: Cross-linguistic studies of the object/substance distinction. In *Proceedings of the Chicago Linguistic Society.*

Imai, M., Gentner, D., & Uchida, N. (1994). Children's theories of word meaning: The role of shape similarity in early acquisition. *Cognitive Development, 9*(1), 45–75.

Inagaki, K., & Hatano, G. (1987). Young children's spontaneous personification as analogy. *Child Development, 58*, 1013–1020.

Inagaki, K., & Hatano, G. (1991). Constrained person analogy in young children's biological inference. *Cognitive Development, 6*, 219–231.

Inagaki, K., & Hatano, G. (1993). Young children's understanding of the mind–body distinction. *Child Development, 64*, 1534–1549.

Inagaki, K., & Hatano, G. (1996). Young children's recognition of commonalities between animals and plants. *Child Development, 67*, 2823–2840.

Inagaki, K., & Sugiyama, K. (1988). Attributing human characteristics: Developmental changes in over- and under-attribution. *Cognitive Development, 3*, 55–70.

Inhelder, B. (2001). The experimental approach of children and adolscents. In A. Typhon & J. Vonèche (Eds.), *Working with Piaget: Essays in honour of Bärbel Inhelder.* Hove, UK: Psychology Press.

Inhelder, B., & Piaget, J. (1958). *The growth of logical thinking from childhood to adolescence: An essay on the construction of formal operational structures.* New York: Basic Books.

Inhelder, B., & Piaget, J. (1963). Itération et récurrence. In P. Gréco, B. Inhelder, B. Matalon, & J. Piaget, *La Formation des raisonnements récurrentiels.* Paris: Presses Universitaires de France.

Inhelder, B., & Piaget, J. (1964). *The early growth of logic.* London: Routledge & Kegan Paul.

Inhelder, B., & Piaget, J. (1980). Procedures and structures. In D. Olson (Ed.), *The social foundations of language.* New York: Norton.

Isaacs, N. (1951) Critical notice: *Traité de logique. British Journal of Psychology, 42*, 185–188.

Isabella, R. A., & Belsky, J. (1991). Interactional synchronoy and the origins of mother–infant attachment: A replication study. *Child Development, 62*, 373–384.

Ittelson, W. H. (1996). Visual perception of markings. *Psychonomic Bulletin & Review, 3*(2), 171–187.

Jacobs, R. A. (1999). Computational studies of the development of functionally specialized neural modules. *Trends in Cognitive Science, 3*, 31–38.

Jacobs, R. A., Jordan, M. I., & Barto, A. G. (1991). Task decomposition through competition in a modular connectionist architecture: The what and where vision tasks. *Cognitive Science, 15*, 219–250.

Jacobson, C. F. (1936). Studies of cerebral functions in primates: I. The functions of the frontal association areas in monkeys. *Comparative Psychology Monographs, 13*, 1–30.

Jacques, S., & Zelazo, P. D. (2001). The Flexible Item Selection Task (FIST): A measure of executive function in preschoolers. *Developmental Neuropsychology, 20*(3).

Jacques, S., Zelazo, P. D., Kirkham, N. Z., & Semcesen, T. K. (1999). Rule selection versus rule execution in preschoolers: An error-detection approach. *Developmental Psychology, 35*, 770–780.

Jaffe, J., Beebe, B., Feldstein, S., Crown, C., & Jasnow, M. D. (2001). Rhythms of dialogue in infancy: Coordinated timing in development. *Monographs of the Society for Research in Child Development, 66*(2) (Serial No. 265), 1–132.

Jaffee, S., & Hyde, J. (2000). Gender differences in moral orientation: A meta-analysis. *Psychological Bulletin, 126*, 703–726.

Jäger, S., & Wilkening, F. (2001) Development of cognitive averaging: When light and light make dark. *Journal of Experimental Child Psychology, 79*.

James, W. T. (1890). *The principles of psychology.* New York: Henry Holt.

James, W. T. (1950). *The principles of psychology.* New York: Dover. [1st published 1890].

Jammer, M. (1954). *Concepts of space.* Cambridge, MA: Harvard University Press.

Janke, B. (1995). Entwicklung naiven Wissens über den physikalischen Auftrieb: Warum schwimmen Schiffe? *Zeitschrift für Entwicklungspsychologie und Pädagogische Psychologie, 27,* 122–138.

Jansen, B. R. J., & van der Maas, H. L. J. (1997). Statistical test of the rule assessment methodology by latent class analysis. *Developmental Review, 17,* 321–357.

Jarrold, C., Baddeley, A., & Hewes, A. (1998). Verbal and nonverbal abilities in the Williams syndrome phenotype: Evidence for diverging developmental trajectories. *Journal of Child Psychology and Psychiatry and Allied Disciplines, 39,* 511–523.

Jeannerod, M. (1997). *The cognitive neuroscience of action.* Oxford, UK: Blackwell.

Jeannerod, M. (1999). To act or not to act: Perspectives on the representation of actions. *The Quarterly Journal of Experimental Psychology, 52A*(1), 1–29.

Jenkins, J. M., & Astington, J. W. (1996). Cognitive factors and family structure associated with theory of mind development in young children. *Developmental Psychology, 32,* 70–78.

Jensen, A. R. (1998). *The g factor: The science of mental ability.* Westport, CT: Praeger/Greenwood.

Joanisse, M., & Seidenberg, M. (1998). Specific language impairment: A deficit in grammar or processing? *Trends in Cognitive Sciences, 2*(7), 240–247.

Johansson, G. (1973). Visual perception of biological motion and a model for its analysis. *Perception and Psychophysics, 14,* 201–211.

Johnson, C., & Harris, P. L. (1994). Magic: Special but not excluded. *British Journal of Developmental Psychology, 12,* 35–51.

Johnson, K. E., Mervis, C. B., & Boster, J. S. (1992). Developmental changes within the structure of the mammal domain. *Developmental Psychology, 28,* 74–83.

Johnson, M. H. (1998). The neural basis of cognitive development. In W. Damon (Gen. Ed.), D. Kuhn & R. S. Siegler (Vol. Eds.), *Handbook of child psychology* (5th ed.): *Cognition, perception, and language* (Vol. 2, pp. 1–49). New York: Wiley.

Johnson, M. H. (1999). Cortical plasticity in normal and abnormal cognitive development: Evidence and working hypotheses. *Development and Psychopathology, 11,* 419–437.

Johnson, M. H., & Morton, J. (1991). *Biology and cognitive development: The case of face recognition.* Oxford, UK: Basil Blackwell.

Johnson, M. K., Hashtroudi, S., & Lindsay, D. S. (1993). Source monitoring. *Psychological Bulletin, 114,* 3–28.

Johnson, S. C. (2000). The recognition of mentalistic agents in infancy. *Trends in Cognitive Sciences, 4,* 22–28.

Johnson, S. C., Slaughter, V., & Carey, S. (1998). Whose gaze will infants follow? The elicitation of gaze following in 12-month-olds. *Developmental Science, 1,* 233–238.

Johnson, S. P., & Aslin, R. N. (2000). Infants' perception of transparency. *Developmental Psychology, 36,* 808–816.

Johnson-Laird, P. N., Legrenzi, P., & Sonino-Legrenzi, M. (1972). Reasoning and a sense of reality. *British Journal of Psychology, 63,* 395–400.

John-Steiner, V. (1985). *Notebooks of the mind: Explorations of thinking.* Albuquerque: University of New Mexico Press.

Johnston, J., & Ellis-Weismer, S. (1983). Mental rotation abilities in language-disordered children. *Journal of Speech and Hearing Research, 26,* 397–403.

Jolliffe, T., & Baron-Cohen, S. (1997). Are people with autism or Asperger's Syndrome faster than normal on the Embedded Figures Task? *Journal of Child Psychology and Psychiatry, 38,* 527–534.

Jolliffe, T., & Baron-Cohen, S. (2001). A test of central coherence theory: Can adults with high-functioning autism or Asperger syndrome integrate objects in context? *Visual Cognition, 8,* 67–101.

Jolliffe, T., & Baron-Cohen, S. (in press). A test of central coherence theory: Can adults with high-functioning autism or Asperger syndrome integrate fragments of an object? *Cognitive Neuropsychiatry.*

Jones, S. S., & Smith, L. B. (1993). The place of perception in children's concepts. *Cognitive Development, 8,* 113–139.

Joyner, M. H., & Kurtz-Costes, B. (1997). Metamemory development. In N. Cowan (Ed.), *The development of memory in childhood* (pp. 275–300). London: London University College Press.

Juel-Nielsen, Niels (1965). *Individual and environment: A psychiatric-psychological investigation of monozygotic twins reared apart.* New York: Humanities Press.

Jusczyk, P. W., & Aslin, R. N. (1995). Infants' detection of the sound patterns of words in fluent speech. *Cognitive Psychology, 29*(1), 1–23.

Jusczyk, P. W., & Kemler Nelson, D. G. (1996). Syntactic units, prosody, and psychological reality during infancy. In J. L. Morgan & K. Demuth (Eds.), *Signal to syntax: Bootstrapping from speech to grammar in early acquisition* (pp. 389–408). Mahwah, NJ: Lawrence Erlbaum.

Kahneman, D., Slovic, P., & Tversky, A. (Eds). (1982). *Judgment under uncertainty: Heuristics and biases.* Cambridge, UK: Cambridge University Press.

Kail, R. (1986). Sources of age differences in speed of processing. *Child Development, 57,* 969–987.

Kail, R. (1988a). Developmental functions for speeds of cognitive processes. *Journal of Experimental Child Psychology, 45,* 339–364.

Kail, R. (1988b). Reply to Sigler, Nusbaum, and Chalip. *Child Development, 59,* 1154–1157.

Kail, R. (1990). *More evidence for a common, central constraint on speed of processing.* Amsterdam: North Holland.

Kail, R. (1990). *The development of memory in children* (3rd ed.). New York: W. H. Freeman.

Kail, R. (1991a). Controlled and automatic processing during mental rotation. *Journal of Experimental Child Psychology, 51,* 337–347.

Kail, R. (1991b). Developmental change in speed of processing during childhood and adolescence. *Psychological Bulletin, 109,* 490–501.

Kail, R. V. (1991c). Processing time declines exponentially during childhood and adolescence. *Developmental Psychology, 27*(2), 259–266.

Kail, R. V. (1993). The role of a global mechanism in developmental change in speed of processing. In M. L. Howe & R. Pasnak (Eds.), *Emerging themes in cognitive development: Vol. 1. Foundations* (pp. 97–119). New York: Springer.

Kail, R. (1994). A method for studying the generalized slowing hypothesis in children with specific language impairment. *Journal of Speech and Hearing Research, 37,* 418–421.

Kail, R. (1995). Processing speed, memory, and cognition. In F. E. Weinert & W. Schneider (Eds.), *Memory performance and competencies: Issues in growth and development* (pp. 71–88). Mahwah, NJ: Erlbaum.

Kail, R. (1997). Phonological skill and articulation time independently contribute to the development of memory span. *Journal of Experimental Child Psychology, 67*(1), 57–68.

Kail, R. (1998). Speed of information processing in patients with multiple sclerosis. *Journal of Clinical and Experimental Neuropsychology, 20*(1), 98–106.

Kail, R. (2000). Speed of information processing: Developmental change and links to intelligence. *Journal of School Psychology, 38*(1), 51–61.

Kail, R., & Hall, L. K. (1999). Sources of developmental change in children's word-problem performance. *Journal of Educational Psychology, 91*(4), 660–668.

Kail, R., & Park, Y. (1992). Global developmental change in processing time. *Merrill-Palmer Quarterly, 38*(4), 525–541.

Kail, R., & Salthouse, T. A. (1994). Processing speed as a mental capacity. *Acta Psychologica, 86*, 199–225.

Kaiser, M. K., Proffitt, D. R., & McCloskey, M. (1985). The development of beliefs about falling objects. *Perception and Psychophysics, 38*, 533–539.

Kalish, C. W., & Gelman, S. A. (1992). On wooden pillows: Multiple classification and children's category-based inductions. *Child Development, 63*(6), 1536–1557.

Kanner, L. (1943). Autistic disturbance of affective contact. *Nervous Child, 2*, 217–250.

Kant, I. (1781/1787). *Critique of pure reason.* London: Macmillan (1963).

Kant, I. (1933). *Critique of pure reason* (2nd ed.). London: Macmillan.

Karmiloff-Smith, A. (1992). *Beyond modularity: A developmental perspective on cognitive science.* Cambridge, MA: MIT Press.

Karmiloff-Smith, A. (1994). Precis of Beyond modularity: A developmental perspective on cognitive science. *Behavioral and Brain Sciences, 17*, 693–745.

Karmiloff-Smith, A. (1997). Crucial differences between developmental cognitive neuroscience and adult neuropsychology. *Developmental Neuropsychology, 13*, 513–524.

Karmiloff-Smith, A. (1998). Development itself is the key to understanding developmental disorders. *Trends in Cognitive Sciences, 2*, 389–398.

Karmiloff-Smith, A., Grant, J., Bellugi, U., & Baron-Cohen, S. (1995). Is there a social module? Language, face-processing and theory of mind in William's syndrome and autism. *Journal of Cognitive Neuroscience, 7*, 196–208.

Karmiloff-Smith, A., Grant, J., Berthoud, I., Davies, M., Howlin, P., & Udwin, O. (1997). Language and Williams syndrome: How intact is "intact"? *Child Development, 2*, 246–262.

Karmiloff-Smith, A., & Inhelder, B. (1974). If you want to get ahead, get a theory. *Cognition, 3*, 195–212.

Karmiloff-Smith, A., & Thomas, M. S. C. (in press). Developmental disorders. In M. A. Arbib (Ed.), *The Handbook of brain theory and neural networks* (2nd ed.). Cambridge, MA: MIT Press.

Karmiloff-Smith, A., Tyler, L. K., Voice, K., Sims, K., Udwin, O., Howlins, P., & Davies, M. (1998). Linguistic dissociations in Williams syndrome: Evaluating receptive syntax in on-line and off-line tasks. *Neuropsychologia, 36*, 343–351.

Karplus, R., & Peterson, R. W. (1970). Intellectual development beyond elementary school II: Ratio, a survey. *School-Science and Mathematics, 70*, 813–820.

Karplus, R., Pulos, S., & Stage, E. K. (1983). Proportional reasoning of early adolescents. In R. Lesh & M. Landau (Eds.), *Acquisition of mathematics concepts and processes* (pp. 45–90). London: Academic Press.

Katz, L. F., & Gottman, J. M. (1991). Marital discord and child outcomes: A social psychophysiological approach. In J. Garber & K. Dodge (Eds.), *The development of emotion regulation and dysregulation* (pp. 129–153). New York: Cambridge University Press.

Kavanaugh, R. D., Whittington, S., & Cerbone, M. J. (1983). Mother's use of fantasy speech to young children. *Journal of Child Language, 10*, 45–55.

Keenan, T., Olson, D. R., & Marini, Z. (1998). Working memory and children's developing understanding of mind. *Australian Journal of Psychology, 50*(2), 76–82.

Keil, F. C. (1979). *Semantic and conceptual development: An ontological perspective.* Cambridge, MA: MIT Press.

Keil, F. C. (1989). *Concepts, kinds, and cognitive development.* Cambridge: MIT Press.

Keil, F. C. (1991). The emergence of theoretical beliefs as constraints on concepts. In S. Carey & R. Gelman (Eds.), *The epigenesis of mind.* Hillsdale, NJ: Erlbaum.

Keil, F. C. (1994). The birth and nurturance of concepts by domains: The origins of concepts of living things. In L. A. Hirschfeld & S. A. Gelman (Eds.), *Mapping the mind: Domain specificity in cognition and culture* (pp. 234–254). New York: Cambridge University Press.

Keil, F. C. (1995). The growth of causal understandings of natural kinds. In S. Sperber, D. Premack, & A. Premack (Eds.), *Causal cognition: A multi-disciplinary debate* (pp. 234–262). Oxford, UK: Clarendon Press.

Keil, F. C., Smith, W. C., Simons, D. J., & Levin, D. T. (1998). Two dogmas of conceptual empiricism. *Cognition,* 103–135.

Kelemen, D. (1999a). Function, goals and intention: Children's teleological reasoning about objects. *Trends in Cognitive Sciences, 12,* 461–468.

Kelemen, D. (1999b). The scope of teleological thinking in preschool children. *Cognition, 70,* 241–272.

Keller, H. (1904). *The Story of My Life.* New York: Doubleday, Page.

Keller, M., Eckensberger, L., & von Rosen, K. (1989). A critical note on the conception of preconventional morality: The case of stage 2 in Kohlberg's theory. *International Journal of Behavioral Development, 12,* 57–69.

Keller, M., & Edelstein, W. (1990). The emergence of morality in interpersonal relationships. In T. Wren (Ed.), *The moral domain: Essays in an ongoing discussion between philosophy and the social sciences* (pp. 255–282). Cambridge MA: MIT Press.

Kelley, K. (1990). Language intervention for children with Williams syndrome. National Williams Syndrome Conference, Boston, MA.

Kellman, P. J. (1995). Ontogenesis of space and motion perception. In W. Epstein & S. Rogers (Eds.), *Perception of space and motion* (pp. 327–364). San Diego: Academic Press.

Kellman, P. J., & Arterberry, M. E. (1998). *The cradle of knowledge: Development of perception in infancy.* Cambridge, MA: MIT Press.

Kellman, P. J., & Banks, M. S. (1998). Infant visual perception. In W. Damon (Series Ed.) and D. Kuhn & R. S. Siegler (Vol. Eds.), *Handbook of child psychology: Vol 2. Cognition, perception, and language* (5th ed., pp. 103–146). New York: Wiley.

Kelly, M. H., & Keil, F. C. (1985). The more things change . . . Metamorphoses and conceptual structure. *Cognitive Science, 9,* 403–416.

Kemler Nelson, D. G., Hirsh-Pasek, K., Jusczyk, P. W., & Cassidy, K. W. (1989). How the prosodic cues in motherese might assist language learning. *Journal of Child Language, 16*(1), 55–68.

Kemps, E., De Rammelaere, S., & Desmet, T. (2000). The development of working memory: Exploring the complementarity of two models. *Journal of Experimental Child Psychology, 77*(2), 89–109.

Kempton, S., Vance, A., Maruff, P., Luk, E., Costin, J., & Pantelis, C. (1999). Executive function and attention deficit hyperactivity disorder: Stimulant medication and better executive function performance in children. *Psychological Medicine, 29,* 527–538.

Kennedy, J. M. (1974). *A psychology of picture perception.* San Francisco: Jossey-Bass.

Kernan, K. (1990). Comprehension of syntactically indicated sequence by Down's syndrome and other mentally retarded adults. *Journal of Mental Deficiency Research, 34,* 169–178.

Kerr, A., & Zelazo, P. D. (2001, April). The development of affective decision-making in preschoolers. Poster presented at the Biennial Conference of the Society for Research in Child Development, Minneapolis, MN.

Kiernan, B., Snow, D., Swisher, L., & Vance, R. (1997). Another look at nonverbal rule induction in children with SLI: Testing a flexible reconceptualization hypothesis. *Journal of Speech, Language and Hearing Research, 40,* 75–82.

Kihlstrom, J., & Cantor, N. (2000). Social intelligence. In R. J. Sternberg (Ed.), *Handbook of intelligence* (pp. 359–379). New York: Cambridge University Press.

Kim, I. K., & Spelke, E. S. (1999). Perception and understanding of effects of gravity and inertia on object motion. *Developmental Science, 2*, 339–362.

Kimura, D. (1992, September). Sex differences in the brain. *Scientific American*, 119–125.

Kimura, D. (1999). *Sex and cognition.* Cambridge, MA: MIT Press.

Kirkham, N., Cruess, L., & Diamond, A. (in press). Helping children apply their knowledge to their behavior on a dimension-switching task. *Cognition.*

Kitcher, P. (1993). *The advancement of science.* New York: Oxford University Press.

Klaczynski, P. (2000). Motivated scientific reasoning biases, epistemological beliefs, and theory polarization: A two-process approach to adolescent cognition. *Child Development, 71,* 1347–1366.

Klahr, D. (1992). Information processing approaches to cognitive development. In M. H. Bornstein & M. E. Lamb (Eds.), *Developmental psychology: An advanced textbook* (3rd ed.). Hillsdale, NJ: Erlbaum.

Klahr, D. (1999). The conceptual habitat: In what kind of system can concepts develop? In E. Scholnick, K. Nelson, S. Gelman, & P. Miller (Eds.), *Conceptual development: Piaget's legacy.* Mahwah, NJ: Erlbaum.

Klahr, D. (2000). *Exploring science: The cognition and development of discovery processes.* Cambridge MA: MIT Press.

Klahr, D., & Dunbar, K. (1988). Dual space search during scientific reasoning. *Cognitive Science, 12,* 1–48.

Klahr, D., Fay, A., & Dunbar, K. (1993). Heuristics for scientific experimentation: A developmental study. *Cognitive Psychology, 25,* 111–146.

Klahr, D., & Robinson, M. (1981). Formal assessment of problem solving and planning processes in preschool children. *Cognitive Psychology, 13,* 113–148.

Klahr, D., & Siegler, R. S. (1978). The representation of children's knowledge. In H. W. Reese & L. W. Lipsitt (Eds.), *Advances in child development* (Vol. 12, pp. 61–116). New York: Academic Press.

Klahr, D., & Simon, H. (1999). Studies of scientific discovery: Complementary approaches and convergent findings. *Psychological Bulletin, 125,* 524–543.

Klahr, D., & Wallace, J. G. (1976). *Cognitive development: An information processing view.* Hillsdale, NJ: Lawrence Erlbaum.

Klapp, S. T., Marshburn, E. A., & Lester, P. T. (1983). Short-term memory does not involve the "working memory" of information processing: The demise of a common assumption. *Journal of Experimental Psychology: General, 112,* 240–264.

Klein, P. J., & Meltzoff, A. N. (1999). Long-term memory, forgetting, and deferred imitation in 12-month-old infants. *Developmental Science, 2,* 102–113.

Klein, R. P., & Jennings, K. D. (1979). Responses to social and inanimate stimuli in early infancy. *Journal of Genetic Psychology, 135,* 3–9.

Klewitz, E. (1989). *Zur Didaktik des naturwissenschaftlichen Unterrichts vor dem Hintergrund der genetischen Erkenntnistheorie Piagets.* Mühlheim, Germany: Westarp.

Klibanoff, R. S., & Waxman, S. R. (2000). Basic level object categories support the acquisition of novel adjectives: Evidence from preschool-aged children. *Child Development, 71*(3), 649–659.

Klin, A., Volkmar, F., Sparrow, S., Cicchetti, D., & Rourke, B. (1995). Validity and neuropsychological characterization of Asperger Syndrome: Convergence with nonverbal learning disabilities syndrome. *Journal of Child Psychology and Psychiatry, 36,* 1127–1140.

Knapp, A. G., & Anderson, J. A. (1984). Theory of categorization based on distributed memory storage. *Journal of Experimental Psychology: Learning, Memory, & Cognition, 10,* 616–637.

Kochanska, K. (1993). Toward a synthesis of parental socialization and child temperment in early development of conscience. *Child Development, 64,* 325–347.

Kohlberg, L. (1958). The development of modes of moral thinking and choice in the years ten to sixteen. Unpublished doctoral dissertation, University of Chicago.

Kohlberg, L. (1969). Stage and sequence: The cognitive-developmental approach to socialization. In D. Goslin (Ed.), *Handbook of socialization theory and research* (pp. 347–480). Chicago: Rand McNally.

Kohlberg, L. (1984). *Essays on moral development: Vol. 2. The psychology of moral development.* San Francisco: Harper & Row.

Kohlberg, L., & Kramer (1969). Continuities and discontinuities in childhood and adult moral development. *Human Development, 12*, 93–120.

Kohlberg, L., Levine, C., & Hewer, A. (1983). Moral stages: A reformulation and a response to critics. *Contributions to Human Development, 10*, 104–166.

Kohlberg, L., Yaeger, J., & Hjertholm, E. (1968). Private speech: Four studies and a review of theories. *Child Development, 39*, 691–736.

Kohn, A. S. (1993). Preschoolers' reasoning about density: Will it float? *Child Development, 64*, 1637–1650.

Kolb, B., Forgie, M., Gibb, R., Gorny, G., & Rowntree, S. (1998). Age, experience and the changing brain. *Neuroscience and Biobehavioral Reviews, 22*, 143–159.

Konow, A., & Pribram, K. H. (1970). Error recognition and utilization produced by injury to the frontal cortex in man. *Neuropsychologia, 8*, 489–491.

Koriat, A., Goldsmith, M., Schneider, W., & Nakash-Dura, M. (in press). The credibility of children's testimony: Can children control the accuracy of their memory reports? *Journal of Experimental Child Psychology.*

Koslowski, B. (1996). *Theory and evidence: The development of scientific reasoning.* Cambridge MA: MIT Press.

Koslowski, B., Barnett, S., Masnick, A., Thompson, S. (in preparation). Evaluating explanations by relying on a network of collateral information. Manuscript in preparation.

Koslowski, B., & Maqueda, M. (1993). What is confirmation bias and when do people have it? *Merrill-Palmer Quarterly, 39* (1). Invitational issue entitled *The development of rationality and critical thinking,* 104–130.

Koslowski, B., Spilton, D., & Snipper, A. (1981). Children's beliefs about instances of mechanical and electrical causation. *Journal of Applied Developmental Psychology, 2*, 189–210.

Koslowski, B., & Thompson, S. L. (in preparation). Theorizing is important, and collateral information constrains how well it is done. In P. Carruthers, S. Stitch, & M. Siegal (Eds.), *The cognitive bases of science: Multidisciplinary approaches.* Cambridge: Cambridge University Press.

Koslowski, B., & Winsor, A. P. (1981). Preschool children's spontaneous explanations and requests for explanations: A non-human application of the child-as-scientist metaphor. Unpublished manuscript, Department of Human Development, Cornell University, Ithaca, NY.

Kosslyn, S. M., Pick, H. L., & Fariello, G. R. (1974). Cognitive maps in children and men. *Child Development, 45*, 707–716.

Kotovsky, L., & Baillargeon, R. (1994). Calibration-based reasoning about collision events in 11-month-old infants. *Cognition, 51*, 107–129.

Kotovsky, L., & Baillargeon, R. (1998). The development of calibration-based reasoning about collision events in young infants. *Cognition, 67*, 311–351.

Kotovsky, L., & Baillargeon, R. (2000). Reasoning about collision events involving inert objects in 7.5-month-old infants. *Developmental Science, 3*, 344–359.

Koziol, M. K., & Klahr, D. (2000, August). If robots make choices, are they alive? Children's judgments of the animacy of intelligent artifacts. Poster presented at the Proceedings of the Society for Cognitive Science, Philadelphia, PA.

Kozulin (1990). *Vygotksy's psychology: A biography of ideas.* Brighton, UK: Harvester Wheatsheaf.

Krist, H. (1992). Development of naive concepts of motion: The lower the angle, the further the throw? *Zeitschrift für Entwicklungspsychologie und Pädagogische Psychologie, 24,* 171–183.

Krist, H. (2001). Development of naive beliefs about moving objects: The straight-down belief in action. *Cognitive Development, 15,* 397–424.

Krist, H., Fieberg, E. L., & Wilkening, F. (1993). Intuitive physics in action and judgment: The development of knowledge about projectile motion. *Journal of Experimental Psychology: Learning, Memory, and Cognition, 19,* 952–966.

Krist, H., Loskill, J., & Schwarz, S. (1996). Intuitive physics in action: Perceptual-motor knowledge about projectile motion in 5–7-year-old children. *Zeitschrift für Psychologie, 204,* 339–366.

Kuczaj, S. A. (1981). Factors influencing children's hypothetical reference. *Journal of Child Language, 8,* 131–137.

Kuczinski, L., Kochanska, G., Radke-Yarrow, M., & Girnius Brown, O. (1987). A developmental interpretation of young children's non-compliance. *Developmental Psychology, 23,* 799–806.

Kugiumutzakis, J. (1985). *Development of imitation during the first six months of life* (Uppsala Psychological Reports No. 377). Uppsala, Sweden: Uppsala University.

Kuhl, P. K. (1991). Human adults and human infants show a "perceptual magnet effect" for the prototypes of speech categories; monkeys do not. *Perception & Psychophysics, 50,* 93–107.

Kuhn, D. (1989). Children and adults as intuitive scientists. *Psychological Review, 96,* 674–689.

Kuhn, D. (1991). *The skills of argument.* New York: Cambridge University Press.

Kuhn, D. (1993). Science as argument: Implications for teaching and learning scientific thinking. *Science Education, 77,* 319–337.

Kuhn, D. (1995). Microgenetic study of change: What has it told us? *Psychological Science, 6,* 133–139.

Kuhn, D. (1999). Metacognitive development. In C. Tamis-LeMonda (Ed.), *Child psychology: A handbook of contemporary issues.* Philadelphia, PA: Psychology Press.

Kuhn, D. (2000a). Does memory development belong on an endangered topic list? *Child Development, 71,* 21–25.

Kuhn, D. (2000b). Why development does (and doesn't) occur: Evidence from the domain of inductive reasoning. In R. Siegler & J. McClelland (Eds.), *Mechanisms of cognitive development: Neural and behavioral perspectives.* Mahwah NJ: Erlbaum.

Kuhn, D. (2001). How do people know? *Psychological Science, 12,* 1–8.

Kuhn, D., Amsel, E., & O'Loughlin, M. (1988). *The development of scientific thinking skills.* Orlando, FL: Academic Press.

Kuhn, D., Black, J., Keselman, A., & Kaplan, D. (2000). The development of cognitive skills that support inquiry learning. *Cognition and Instruction.*

Kuhn, D., Cheney, R., & Weinstock, M. (in press). The development of epistemological understanding. *Cognitive Development.*

Kuhn, D., Garcia-Mila, M., Zohar, A., & Andersen, C. (1995). *Strategies of knowledge acquisition.* Society for Research in Child Development Monographs, 60(4) (Serial no. 245).

Kuhn, D., & Lao, J. (1996). Effects of evidence on attitudes: Is polarization the norm? *Psychological Science, 7,* 115–120.

Kuhn, D., & Pearsall, S. (1998). Relations between metastrategic knowledge and strategic performance. *Cognitive Development, 13,* 227–247.

Kuhn, D., & Pearsall, S. (2000). Developmental origins of scientific thinking. *Journal of Cognition and Development, 1,* 113–129.

Kuhn, D., & Phelps, E. (1982). The development of problem-solving strategies. In H. Reese (Ed.), *Advances in child development and behavior* (Vol. 17). New York: Academic Press.

Kuhn, D., Schauble, L., & Garcia-Mila, M. (1992). Cross-domain development of scientific reasoning. *Cognition and Instruction, 9*, 285–332.

Kuhn, D., Shaw, V., & Felton, M. (1997). Effects of dyadic interaction on argumentive reasoning. *Cognition and Instruction, 15*, 287–315.

Laboratory of Comparative Human Cognition. (1983). Culture and cognitive development. In P. Mussen (Ed.), *Handbook of child psychology: history, theory, and methods: Vol. 1.* New York: Wiley.

Lagattuta, K. H., Wellman, H. M., & Flavell, J. H. (1997). Preschoolers' understanding of the link between thinking and feeling: Cognitive cueing and emotional change. *Child Development, 68*, 1081–1104.

Lahey, M., & Edwards, J. (1996). Why do children with specific language impairment name pictures more slowly than their peers? *Journal of Speech and Hearing Research, 39*, 1081–1098.

Laing, E., & Hulme, C. (1999). Phonological and semantic processes influence beginning readers' ability to learn to read words. *Journal of Experimental Child Psychology, 73*, 183–207.

Lalonde, C. E., & Chandler, M. J. (1995). False belief understanding goes to school: On the social-emotional consequences of coming early or late to a first theory of mind. *Cognition and Emotion, 9*, 167–185.

Landau, B. (1994). Object shape, object name, and object kind: Representation and development. In D. L. Medin (Ed.), *The psychology of learning and motivation: Advances in research and theory* (Vol. 31, pp. 253–304). San Diego, CA: Academic Press.

Landau, B., Gleitman, H., & Spelke, E. (1981). Spatial knowledge and geometric knowledge in a child blind from birth. *Science, 213*, 1275–1278.

Landau, B., & Jackendoff, R. (1993). "What" and "where" in spatial language and spatial cognition. *Behavioral and Brain Sciences, 16*, 217–238.

Landau, B., Jones, S., & Smith, L. (1992). Perception, ontology, and naming in young children: Commentary on Soja, Carey, and Spelke. *Cognition, 43*(1), 85–91.

Landau, B., Smith, L. B., & Jones, S. S. (1988). The importance of shape in early lexical learning. *Cognitive Development, 3*(3), 299–321.

Landau, B., & Spelke, E. S. (1985). Spatial knowledge and its manifestations. In H. M. Wellman (Ed.), *Children's searching* (pp. 27–52). Cambridge, MA: Harvard University Press.

Lang, P. J. (1984). Cognition in emotion: Concept and action. In C. E. Izard, J. Kagan, & R. B. Zajonc (Eds.), *Emotions, cognition, and behavior* (pp. 192–228). Cambridge: Cambridge University Press.

Langer, S. K. (1942). *Philosophy in a new key.* Cambridge, MA: Harvard University Press.

Langley, P. (1987). A general theory of discrimination in learning. In D. Klahr, P. Langley, & R. Neches (Eds.), *Production system models of learning and development* (pp. 99–161). Cambridge, MA: MIT Press.

Lapsley, D. (1982). The development of retributive justice in children. Unpublished doctoral dissertation, University of Wisconsin, Madison.

Lapsley, D. (1996). *Moral psychology.* Boulder, CO: Westview.

Lassaline, M. E., & Murphy, G. L. (1996). Induction and category coherence. *Psychonomic Bulletin & Review, 3*(1), 95–99.

Laurendeau, M., & Pinard, A. (1962). *Causal thinking in the child: A genetic and experimental approach.* New York: International Universities Press.

Laurendeau, M., & Pinard, A. (1970). *The development of the concept of space in children.* New York: International Universities Press.

Lave, J., & Wegner, E. (1991). *Situated learning: Legitimate peripheral participation.* Cambridge: Cambridge University Press.

Lawson, A. E. (1976). M-space: Is it a constraint on conservation reasoning ability? *Journal of Experimental Child Psychology, 22*, 40–49.

Laxon, V., Masterson, J., & Coltheart, V. (1991). Some bodies are easier to read: the effect of consistency and regularity on children's reading. *Quarterly Journal of Experimental Psychology, 43A*, 793–824.

Lazar, I., & Darlington, R. (1982). Lasting effects of early education: A report from the consortium for longitudinal studies. *Monographs of the Society for Research in Child Development, 47*(2–3) (Serial No. 195).

Le Couteur, A., Bailey, A., Goode, S., Pickles, A., Robertson, S., Gottesman, I., & Rutter, M. (1996). A broader phenotype of autism: The clinical spectrum in twins. *Journal of Child Psychology and Psychiatry, 37*, 785–801.

Leach, E. (1964). Anthropological aspects of language: Animal categories and verbal abuse. In E. H. Lenneberg (Ed.), *New directions in the study of language* (pp. 23–63). Cambridge, MA: MIT Press.

Lechuga, M. T., Marcos-Ruiz, R., & Bauer, P. J. (in press). Episodic recall of specifics and generalization coexist in 25-month-old children. *Memory*.

Lécuyer, R. (1993). A propos de l'erreur A non B. *Psychologie Française, 38*, 63–74.

Lécuyer, R., & Durand, K. (1996, August). The use of interposition and perspective in a two-dimensional object permanence situation by 4-month-old infants. Paper presented at the biennial meeting of the International Society for the Study of Behavior and Development, Quebec, Canada.

Lee, D., & Aronson, E. (1974). Visual proprioceptive control of standing in human infants. *Perception and Psychophysiscs, 15*, 529–532.

Leekam, S., & Perner, J. (1991). Does the autistic child have a "metarepresentational" deficit? *Cognition, 40*, 203–218.

Leevers, H. J., & Harris, P. L. (1999). Persisting effects of instruction on young children's syllogistic reasoning with incongruent and abstract premises. *Thinking & Reasoning, 5*, 145–173.

Leevers, H. J., & Harris, P. L. (2000). Counterfactual syllogistic reasoning in normal 4-year-olds, children with learning disabilities and children with autism. *Journal of Experimental Child Psychology, 76*, 64–87.

Lefly, D. L., & Pennington, B. F. (1996). Longitudinal study of children at high family risk for dyslexia: The first two years. In M. L. Rice (Ed.), *Toward a genetics of language*. Hillsdale, NJ: Lawrence Erlbaum.

Legerstee, M. (1991). The role of person and object in eliciting early imitation. *Journal of Experimental Child Psychology, 51*, 423–433.

Legerstee, M. (1992). A review of the animate–inanimate distinction in infancy: Implications for models of social and cognitive knowing. *Early Development and Parenting, 1*, 59–67.

Legerstee, M., Pomerleau, A., Malcuit, G., & Feider, H. (1987). The development of infants' responses to people and a doll: Implications for research in communication. *Infant Behavior and Development, 10*, 81–95.

Lehrer, R., & Romberg, T. (1996). Exploring children's data modeling. *Cognition and Instruction, 14*, 69–108.

Lehrer, R., & Schauble, L. (2000). Inventing data structures for representational purposes: Elementary grade students' classification models. *Mathematical Thinking and Learning, 2*, 51–74.

Lehrer, R., Schauble, L., & Petrosino, A. (2001). Reconsidering the role of experiment in science education. In K. Crowley, C. Schunn, & T. Okada (Eds.), *Designing for science: Implications from everyday, classroom, and professional settings* (pp. 251–277). Mahwah NJ: Erlbaum.

Lempert, H. (1989). Animacy constraints on preschool children's acquisition of syntax. *Child Development, 60*, 237–245.

Lenneberg, E. (1967). *Biological foundations of language*. New York: Wiley.

Leonard, L. (1995). Functional categories in the grammars of children with specific language impairment. *Journal of Speech and Hearing Research, 38*(6), 1270–1283.

Leonard, L. (1998). *Children with Specific Language Impairment.* Cambridge, MA: MIT Press.

Leont'ev, A. N. (1981). The problem of activity in psychology. In J. V. Wertsch (Ed.), *The concept of activity in Soviet psychology.* Armonk, NY: M. E. Sharpe.

Leslie, A., & Keeble, S. (1987). Do six-month old infants perceive causality? *Cognition, 25*, 265–288.

Leslie, A., Xu, F., Tremoulet, P., & Scholl, B. (1998). Indexing and the object concept: Developing "what" and "where" systems. *Trends in Cognitive Sciences, 2*, 10–18.

Leslie, A. M. (1982). The perception of causality in infants. *Perception, 11*, 173–186.

Leslie, A. M. (1984). Infant perception of a manual pick up event. *British Journal of Developmental Psychology, 2*, 19–32.

Leslie, A. M. (1987). Pretense and representation: the origins of "theory of mind." *Psychological Review, 94*, 412–426.

Leslie, A. M. (1994). ToMM, ToBy, and Agency: Core architecture and domain specificity. In L. A. Hirschfeld & S. A. Gelman (Eds.), *Mapping the mind: Domain specificity in cognition and culture* (pp. 119–148). New York: Cambridge University Press.

Leslie, A. M. (1995). A theory of agency. In D. Sperber, D. Premack, & A. J. Premack (Eds.), *Causal cognition: A multidisciplinary debate* (pp. 121–149). Oxford, UK: Clarendon Press.

Leslie, A. M. (in press). How to acquire a "representational theory of mind." In D. Sperber & S. Davis (Eds.), *Metarepresentation. Vancouver studies in cognitive science, Vol. 10.* Oxford, UK: Oxford University Press.

Leslie, A. M., & Frith, U. (1988). Autistic children's understanding of seeing, knowing, and believing. *British Journal of Developmental Psychology, 6*, 315–324.

Leslie, A. M., & Happé, F. (1989). Autism and ostensive communication: the relevance of metarepresentation. *Development and Psychopathology, 1*, 205–212.

Leslie, A. M., & Thaiss, L. (1992). Domain specificity in conceptual development: Evidence from autism. *Cognition, 43*, 225–251.

Levin, H. S., Culhane, K. A., Hartmann, J., Evankovich, K., Mattson, A. J., Harward, H., Ringholz, G., Ewing-Cobbs, L., & Fletcher, J. M. (1991). Developmental changes in performance on tests of purported frontal lobe functioning. *Developmental Neuropsychology, 7*, 377–395.

Levin, I. (1977). The development of time concepts in young children: Reasoning about duration. *Child Development, 48*, 435–444.

Levin, I. (1982). The nature and development of time concepts in children: The effect of interfering cues. In W. J. Friedman (Ed.), *The developmental psychology of time* (pp. 47–85). New York: Academic Press.

Levine, M., Marchon, I., & Hanley, G. (1984). The placement and misplacement of You-Are-Here maps. *Environment and Behavior, 16*, 139–158.

Levit, A. G., & Utman, J. G. A. (1992). From babbling towards the sound systems of English and French: A longitudianl two-case study. *Journal of Child Language, 19*, 19–49.

Lewis, C., Freeman, N. H., Hagestadt, E., & Douglas, H. (1994). Narrative access and production in preschoolers' false belief reasoning. *Cognitive Development, 9*, 397–424.

Lewis, C., Freeman, H., Kyriakidou, C., Maridaki-Kassotaki, K. M., & Berridge, D. M. (1996). Social influences on false belief access: Specific sibling influences or general apprenticeship? *Child Development, 67*, 2930–2947.

Lewis, C., & Osborne, A. (1990). Three-year-olds' problems with false belief: Conceptual deficit or linguistic artifact? *Child Development, 61*, 1514–1519.

Lewis, M., Allessandri, S. M., & Sullivan, M. W. (1990). Violation of expectancy, loss of control and anger expressions in young infants. *Developmental Psychology, 26*(5), 745–751.

Lewis, M., & Brooks-Gunn, J. (1979). *Social cognition and the acquisition of self.* New York: Plenum Press.

Lewontin, R. (1974). The analysis of variance and the analysis of cause. *American Journal of Human Genetics, 26*, 400–411.

Liben, L. S. (1981). Spatial representation and behavior: Multiple perspectives. In L. S. Liben, A. H. Patterson, & N. Newcombe (Eds.), *Spatial representation and behavior across the life span: Theory and application* (pp. 3–36). New York: Academic Press.

Liben, L. S. (1988). Conceptual issues in the development of spatial cognition. In J. Stiles-Davis, M. Kritchevsky, & U. Bellugi (Eds.), *Spatial cognition: Brain bases and development* (pp. 167–194). Hillsdale, NJ: Lawrence Erlbaum.

Liben, L. S. (1991a). Environmental cognition through direct and representational experiences: A life-span perspective. In T. Garling & G. W. Evans (Eds.), *Environment, cognition, and action* (pp. 245–276). New York: Oxford University Press.

Liben, L. S. (1991b). The Piagetian water-level task: Looking beneath the surface. In R. Vasta (Ed.), *Annals of Child Development* (Vol. 8, pp. 81–143). London: Jessica Kingsley.

Liben, L. S. (1997). Children's understanding of spatial representations of place: Mapping the methodological landscape. In N. Foreman & R. Gillett (Eds.), *A handbook of spatial research paradigms and methodologies* (pp. 41–83). Hove, UK: Psychology Press.

Liben, L. S. (1999). Developing an understanding of external spatial representations. In I. E. Sigel (Ed.), *Development of mental representation: Theories and applications* (pp. 297–321). Mahwah, NJ: Lawrence Erlbaum.

Liben, L. S. (2001a). Thinking through maps. In M. Gattis (Ed.), *Spatial schemas and abstract thought* (pp. 44–77). Cambridge, MA: MIT Press.

Liben, L. S. (2000b). Map use and the development of spatial cognition: Seeing the *bigger* picture. *Developmental Science, 3*, 270–274.

Liben, L. S., et al. (2002). The effects of sex steroids on spatial performance: A review and an experimental clinical investigation. *Developmental Psychology* [contingent, pending revisions].

Liben, L. S., & Downs, R. M. (1989). Understanding maps as symbols: The development of map concepts in children. In H. W. Reese (Ed.), *Advances in child development and behavior* (Vol. 22, pp. 145–201). New York: Academic Press.

Liben, L. S., & Downs, R. M. (1991). The role of graphic representations in understanding the world. In R. M. Downs, L. S. Liben, & D. S. Palermo (Eds.), *Visions of aesthetics, the environment, and development: The legacy of Joachim Wohlwill* (pp. 139–180). Hillsdale, NJ: Lawrence Erlbaum.

Liben, L. S., & Downs, R. M. (1992). Developing an understanding of graphic representations in children and adults: The case of GEO-graphics. *Cognitive Development, 7*, 331–349.

Liben, L. S., & Downs, R. M. (1993). Understanding person–space–map relations: Cartographic and developmental perspectives. *Developmental Psychology, 29*, 739–752.

Liben, L. S., & Downs, R. M. (1994). Fostering geographic literacy from early childhood: The contributions of interdisciplinary research. *Journal of Applied Developmental Psychology, 15*, 549–569.

Liben, L. S., & Downs, R. M. (2001). Geography for young children: Maps as tools for learning environments. In S. L. Golbeck (Ed.), *Psychological perspectives on early childhood education* (pp. 220–252). Mahwah, NJ: Lawrence Erlbaum.

Liben, L. S., Dunphy-Lelli, S., & Szechter, L. E. (2001). Children's and adults' interpretations of aerial photographs: The role of viewing distance and viewing angle. Unpublished manuscript, Penn State.

Liben, L. S., Moore, M. L., & Golbeck, S. L. (1982). Preschoolers' knowledge of their classroom environment: Evidence from small-scale and life-size spatial tasks. *Child Development, 53,* 1275–1284.

Liben, L. S., Patterson, A. H., & Newcombe N. (Eds.). (1981). *Spatial representation and behavior across the life span: Theory and application.* New York: Academic Press.

Liben, L. S., & Yekel, C. A. (1996). Preschoolers' understanding of plan and oblique maps: The role of geometric and representational correspondence. *Child Development, 67,* 2780–2796.

Libet, B. (1985). Unconscious cerebral initiative and the role of conscious will in voluntary Action. *Behavioral and Brain Sciences, 106,* 237–255.

Lien, Y., & Cheng, P. (2000). Distinguishing genuine from spurious causes: A coherence hypothesis. *Cognitive Psychology, 40,* 87–137.

Light, P. H., Buckingham, N., Robbins, A. H. (1979). The conservation task as an interactional setting. *British Journal of Educational Psychology, 49,* 304–310.

Lillard, A. S. (1993). Pretend play skills and the child's theory of mind. *Child Development, 64,* 348–371.

Lillard, A. S. (1998). Playing with a theory of mind. In O. Saracho & B. Spodek (Eds.), *Multiple perspectives on play in early childhood education* (pp. 11–33). New York: SUNY Press.

Lillard, A. S. (2000). Pretend play as twin earth. Unpublished manuscript, University of Virginia.

Lillard, A. S. (in press). Pretending, understanding pretense, and understanding minds. In S. Reifel (Ed.), *Play and culture studies* (Vol. 3). New Jersey: Ablex.

Lillard, A. S., & Flavell, J. H. (1990). Young children's preference for mental state versus behavioral descriptions of human action. *Child Development, 61,* 731–741.

Lillard, A. S., & Witherington, D. (2000). Parent behavior during pretense episodes with young children. Unpublished manuscript, University of Virginia.

Lillard, A. S., Zeljo, A., Curenton, S., & Kaugars, A. S. (2000). Children's understanding of the animacy constraint on pretense. *Merrill-Palmer Quarterly, 46,* 21–44.

Lillard, P. P. (1996). *Montessori Today.* New York: Schocken.

Linell, P. (1998). *Approaching dialogue: Talk, interaction, and contexts in dialogical perspectives.* Amsterdam: John Benjamins.

Linn, M. C., & Petersen, A. C. (1985). Emergence and characterization of sex differences in spatial ability: A meta-analysis. *Child Development, 56,* 1479–1498.

Lins-Dyer, T. (1999). Northeastern Brazilian mothers' and daughters' views of everyday social conflicts. Paper presented at the biennial meeting of the Society for research on Adolescence, Chicago.

Lipton, P. (1991). *Inference to the best explanation.* London: Routledge.

Locke, J. (1959). *An essay concerning human understanding: Vol. 2.* New York: Dover [1st published 1671].

Locke, J. L. (1993). *The child's path to spoken language.* Cambridge, MA: Harvard.

Loehlin, J. C. (2000). Group differences in intelligence. In R. J. Sternberg (Ed.), *Handbook of intelligence* (pp. 176–193). New York: Cambridge University Press.

Logan, G. D. (1994). On the ability to inhibit thought and action: A users' guide to the stop signal paradigm. In D. Dagenbach, & T. H. Carr (Eds.), *Inhibitory processes in attention, memory, and language* (pp. 189–239). San Diego: Academic Press.

Lohman, D. F. (2000). Complex information processing and intelligence. In R. J. Sternberg (Ed.), *Handbook of intelligence* (pp. 285–340). New York: Cambridge University Press.

Looft, W. R. (1974). Animistic thought in children: Understanding of "living" across its associated attributes. *Journal of Genetic Psychology, 124,* 235–240.

Loose, J. J., & Mareschal, D. (1997). When a word is worth a thousand pictures: A connectionist account of the percept to label shift in children's inductive reasoning. In *Proceedings of the nineteenth annual conference of the Cognitive Science Society* (pp. 454–459). London: Erlbaum.

Lourenço, O., & Machado, A. (1996). In defense of Piaget's theory: A reply to 10 common criticisms. *Psychological Review, 103*, 143–164.

Lovell, A. (1978). *In a summer garment.* London: Secker & Warburg.

Luciana, M., & Nelson, C. A. (1998). The functional emergence of prefrontally-guided working memory systems in four- to eight-year-old children. *Neuropsychologia, 36*, 273–293.

Luck, S. J., & Vogel, E. K. (1997). The capacity of visual working memory for features and conjunctions. *Nature, 390*(6657), 279–281.

Luhrman, T. M. (1989). *Persuasions of the witch's craft.* Cambridge, MA: Harvard University Press.

Lukes, S. (1977). Methodological individualism reconsidered. In S. Lukes (Ed.), *Essays in social theory.* New York: Columbia University Press, pp.177–186.

Lundberg, I. (1999) Learning to read in Scandanavian. In M. Harris & G. Hatano (Eds.), *Learning to read and write: a cross-linguistic perspective* (pp. 157–172). Cambridge: Cambridge University Press.

Lundberg, I., Olofsson, A., & Wall, S. (1980). Reading and spelling skills in the first school years predicted from phonemic awareness skills in kindergarten. *Scandinavian Journal of Psychology, 121*, 159–173.

Luo, Y. (2000, July). Young infants' knowledge about occlusion events. Paper presented at the biennial International Conference on Infant Studies, Brighton, UK.

Luo, Y. (2001, April). Infants' knowledge about transparency in occlusion and containment events. Paper presented at the biennial meeting of the Society for Research in Child Development, Minneapolis, MN.

Luo, Y., & Baillargeon, R. (2001a). Developments in young infants' ability to determine what are expected and unexpected occlusion events. Manuscript under review.

Luo, Y., & Baillargeon, R. (2001b). Infants' reasoning about transparency in occlusion and containment events. Manuscript in preparation.

Luo, Y., & Baillargeon, R. (2001c). Qualitative but not quantitative reasoning about height information in occlusion events in 5-month-old infants. Manuscript in preparation.

Luo, Y., & Baillargeon, R. (2001d). Young infants' responses to events involving transparent occluders. Manuscript in preparation.

Luria, A. R. (1966). *Higher cortical functions in man* (2nd ed.). New York: Basic Books. (Original work published in 1962).

Luria, A. R. (1973). *The working brain: An introduction to neuropsychology,* trans. B. Haigh. New York: Basic Books.

Luria, A. R. (1977). *Cognitive development: Its cultural and social foundations.* Cambridge, MA: Harvard University Press.

Luria, A. R. (1979). *The making of mind: A personal account of soviet psychology.* Cambridge, MA: Harvard University Press.

Luria, A. R. (1982). *Language and cognition.* New York: John Wiley & Sons.

Lutchmaya, S., Baron-Cohen, S., & Raggett, P. (submitted). Foetal testosterone and eye contact at 12 months. University of Cambridge.

MacIntyre, A. (1984). *After virtue.* (2nd ed.). Notre Dame, IN: University of Notre Dame Press.

Mackintosh, N. J. (1998). *IQ and human intelligence.* Oxford, UK: Oxford University Press.

Macnamara, J. (1994). Logic and cognition. In J. Macnamara & G. E. Reyes (Eds.), *The logical foundations of cognition. Vancouver studies in cognitive science, Vol. 4* (pp. 11–34). New York: Oxford University Press.

MacWhinney, B., & Leinbach, J. (1991). Implementations are not conceptualizations: Revising the verb learning model. *Cognition, 40*, 121–157.

Madden, T. (1992). Cultural factors and assumptions in social reasoning in India. Unpublished doctoral dissertation, University of California, Berkeley.

Madole, K., & Oakes, L. (1999). Making sense of infant categorization: Stable processes and changing representations. *Developmental Review, 19*, 263–296.

Mahler, M. S., Pine, F., & Bergman, A. (1975). *The psychological birth of the human infant.* New York: Basic Books.

Maier, N. R. F. (1931). Reasoning in humans II: The solution of a problem and its appearance in consciousness. *Journal of Comparative Psychology, 12*, 181–194.

Majerus, S., Palmisano, I., Van der Linden, M., Barisnikov, K., & Poncelet, M. (2001). An investigation of phonological processing in Williams syndrome. *Journal of the International Society, 7*(2), 153.

Malatesta, C. Z., & Izard, C. E. (1984). The ontogenesis of human social signals: From biological imperative to symbol utilization. In N. A. Fox & R. J. Davidson (Eds.), *The psychobiology of affective development* (pp. 161–206). Hillsdale, NJ: Erlbaum.

Malle, B. F., Moses, L. J., & Baldwin, D. A. (Eds.). (2001). *Intentions and intentionality: Foundations of social cognition.* Cambridge, MA: MIT Press.

Malt, B. C. (1995). Category coherence in cross cultural perspective. *Cognitive Psychology, 29*, 85–148.

Mandler, J. M. (1988a). How to build a baby: On the development of an accessible representational system. *Cognitive Development, 3*, 113–136.

Mandler, J. M. (1988b). The development of spatial cognition: On topological and Euclidean representation. In J. Stiles-Davis, M. Kritchevsky, & U. Bellugi (Eds.), *Spatial cognition: Brain bases and development* (pp. 423–432). Hillsdale, NJ: Lawrence Erlbaum.

Mandler, J. M. (1990). Recall of events by preverbal children. In A. Diamond (Ed.), *The development and neural bases of higher cognitive functions* (pp. 485–516). New York: New York Academy of Science.

Mandler, J. M. (1992). How to build a baby: II. Conceptual primitives. *Psychological Review, 99*(4), 587–604.

Mandler, J. M. (1997). Development of categorisation: Perceptual and conceptual categories. In G. Bremner, A. Slater, & G. Butterworth (Eds.), *Infant development: Recent advances* (pp. 163–189). Hove, UK: Psychology Press.

Mandler, J. M. (1998). Representation. In W. Damon (Series Ed.) and D. Kuhn & R. Siegler (Vol. Eds.), *Handbook of child psychology: Vol. 2. Cognition, perception, and language* (5th ed., pp. 255–308). New York: Wiley.

Mandler, J. M. (2000a). Perceptual and cognitive processes in infancy. *Journal of Cognition and Development, 1*, 3–36.

Mandler, J. M. (2000b). What global-before-basic trend? Commentary on perceptually based approaches to early categorization. *Infancy, 1*, 99–110.

Mandler, J. M., & Bauer, P. J. (1988). The cradle of categorization: Is the basic-level basic? *Cognitive Development, 3*(3), 247–264.

Mandler, J. M., Bauer, P. J., & McDonough, L. (1991). Separating the sheep from the goats: Differentiating global categories. *Cognitive Psychology, 23*(2), 263–298.

Mandler, J. M., & McDonough, L. (1993). Concept formation in infancy. *Cognitive Development, 8*(3), 291–318.

Mandler, J. M., & McDonough, L. (1995). Long-term recall of event sequences in infancy. *Journal of Experimental Child Psychology, 59*, 457–474.

Mandler, J. M., & McDonough, L. (1996). Drinking and driving don't mix: Inductive general-ization in infancy. *Cognition, 59*(3), 307–335.

Mandler, J. M., & McDonough, L. (1998a). On developing a knowledge base in infancy. *Developmental Psychology, 34*, 1274–1278.

Mandler, J. M., & McDonough, L. (1998b). Studies in inductive inference in infancy. *Cognitive Psychology, 37*, 60–96.

Mandler, J. M., & Robinson, C. A. (1978). Developmental changes in picture recognition. *Journal of Experimental Child Psychology, 26*, 122–136.

Manis, F., & Morrison, F. (1985). Reading disability: A deficit in rule learning? In L. Siegal & F. Morrison (Eds.), *Cognitive development in atypical children: Progress in cognitive development research*. New York: Springer.

Manis, F. R., Seidenberg, M. S., Doi, L. M., McBride-Chang, C., & Petersen, A. (1996). On the bases of two subtypes of developmental dyslexia. *Cognition, 58*, 157–195.

Maratos, O. (1982). Trends in the development of imitation in early infancy. In T. G. Bever (Ed.), *Regressions in mental development: Basic phenomena and theories* (pp. 81–101). Hillsdale, NJ: Erlbaum.

Marcus, G. F. (1998a). Can connectionism save constructivism? *Cognition, 66*, 153–182.

Marcus, G. F. (1998b). Rethinking eliminative connectionism. *Cognitive Psychology, 37*(3), 243–282.

Marcus, G. F., Pinker, S., Ullman, M., Hollander, M., Rosen, T. J., & Xu, F. (1992). Overregu-larization in language acquisition. *Monographs of the Society for Research in Child Development, 57*(4) (Serial No. 228).

Marcus, R. B. (1993). *Modalities: Philosophical essays*. New York: Oxford University Press.

Mareschal, D. (1991). Cascade-correlation and the Genetron: Possible implementations of Equi-libration. *Technical Report 91–10–17*. McGill Cognitive Science Center, McGill University, Montreal, Canada.

Mareschal, D. (2000). Infant object knowledge: Current trends and controversies. *Trends in Cognitive Science, 4*, 408–416.

Mareschal, D. & French, R. M. (2000). Mechanisms of categorization in infancy. *Infancy, 1*, 59–76.

Mareschal, D., Plunkett, K., & Harris, P. (1999). A computational and neuropsychological account of object-oriented behaviours in infancy. *Developmental Science, 2*, 306–317.

Mareschal, D., & Shultz, T. R. (1996). Generative connectionist networks and constructive cognitive development. *Cognitive Development, 11*, 571–603.

Mareschal, D., & Shultz, T. R. (1999). Development of children's seriation: A connectionist approach. *Connection Science, 11*, 153–188.

Mareschal, D., & Thomas, M. S. C. (in press). Self-organization in normal and abnormal cogni-tive development. In A. F. Kalverboer and A. Gramsbergen (Eds.), *Brain and Behavior in human development: A source book*. Dordrecht: Kluwer Academic Publishers.

Marini, Z. A. (1992). Synchrony and asynchrony in the development of children's scientific rea-soning. In R. Case (Ed.), *The mind's staircase: Exploring the conceptual underpinnings of children's thought and knowledge* (pp. 55–73). Hillsdale, NJ: Erlbaum.

Markman, E. M. (1989). *Categorization and naming in children: Problems of induction*. Cambridge, MA: MIT Press.

Markman, E. M. (1994). Constraints on word meaning in early language acquisition. *Lingua, 92*, 199–227.

Markman, E. M., & Hutchinson, J. E. (1984). Children's sensitivity to constraints on word meaning: Taxonomic versus thematic relations. *Cognitive Psychology, 16*(1), 1–27.

Markovits, H., Dumas, C., & Malfait, N. (1995). Understanding transitivity of a spatial relation-ship: A developmental analysis. *Journal of Experimental Child Psychology, 59*, 124–141.

Marler, P. (1991). The instinct to learn. In S. Carey & R. Gelman (Eds.), *The epigenesis of mind: Essays on biology and cognition*. Hillsdale, NJ: Lawrence Erlbaum.

Marlier, L., Schaal, B., & Soussignan, R. (1998). Neonatal responsiveness to the odor of amniotic and lacteal fluids: A test of perinatal chemosensory continuity. *Child Development, 69*, 611–623.

Marr, D. (1982). *Vision*. New York: Freeman.

Marsh, G., Friedman, M., Welch, V., & Desberg, P. (1981). A cognitive development theory of reading acquisition. *Reading research: Advances in theory and practice* (Vol. 3). New York: Academic Press.

Marzolf, D. P., & DeLoache, J. S. (1994). Transfer in young children's understanding of spatial relations. *Child Development, 64*, 1–15.

Marzolf, D. P., & DeLoache, J. S. (1997). Search tests as measures of cognitive development. In N. Foreman & R. Gillett (Eds.), *Interacting with the environment: A handbook of spatial research paradigms and methodologies* (pp. 131–152). Hove, UK: Lawrence Erlbaum.

Marzolf, D. P., Pascha, P. T., & DeLoache, J. S. (1996). Transfer of a symbolic relation by young children. Poster presented at the International Conference on Infant Studies, Providence, RI.

Mash, C., Quinn, P. C., Dobson, V., & Narter, D. B. (1998). Global influences on the development of spatial and object perceptual categorization abilities: Evidence from preterm infants. *Developmental Science, 1*, 85–102.

Masnick, A. M. (1999). Belief patterns and the intersection of cognitive and social factors. Unpublished doctoral thesis, Cornell University.

Masnick, A. M., Barnett, S. M., Thompson, S. L., & Koslowski, B. (1998). Evaluating explanations in the context of a web of information. In M. A. Gernsbacher & S. J. Derry (Eds.), *Proceedings of the twentieth annual conference of the Cognitive Science Society* (pp. 663–668). Mahwah, NJ: Lawrence Erlbaum.

Masonheimer, P. E., Drum, P. A., & Ehri, L. C. (1984). Does environmental print identification lead children into word reading? *Journal of Reading Behaviour, 16*, 257–271.

Massey, C., & Gelman, R. (1988). Preschoolers decide whether pictured unfamiliar objects can move themselves. *Developmental Psychology, 24*, 307–317.

Matsuda, F. (1994). Concepts about interrelations among duration, distance, and speed in young children. *International Journal of Behavioral Development, 17*, 553–576.

Matsuda, F. (1996). Duration, distance, a speed judgments of two moving objects by 4- to 11-year-olds. *Journal of Experimental Child Psychology, 63*, 286–311.

Maurer, D. (1985). Infants' perception of facedness. In T. N. Field & N. Fox (Eds.), *Social perception in infants* (pp. 73–100). Norwood, NJ: Ablex.

Mayer, J. D., Salovey, P., & Caruso, D. (2000). Emotional intelligence meets traditional standards for an intelligence. *Intelligence, 27*, 267–298.

Mayer, R. (2000). Intelligence and education. In R. J. Sternberg (Ed.), *Handbook of intelligence* (pp. 519–533). New York: Cambridge University Press.

Mayer, R. E. (1992). *Thinking, Problem Solving, Cognition* (2nd ed.). New York: W. H. Freeman.

Mayringer, H., & Wimmer, H. (2000). Pseudoname learning by German speaking children with dyslexia: Evidence for a phonological learning deficit. *Journal of Experimental Child Psychology, 75*, 116–133.

Mays, W. (2000). Piaget's sociology revisited. *New Ideas in Psychology, 18*, 261–278.

McCall, D. (2001, April). Perseveration and infants' sensitivity to cues for containment. Paper presented at the biennial meeting of the Society for Research in Child Development, Minneapolis, MN.

McClelland, J. L. (1989). Parallel distributed processing: Implications for cognition and development. In R. G. M. Morris (Ed.), *Parallel distributed processing: Implications for psychology and neurobiology* (pp. 9–45). Oxford, UK: Oxford University Press.

McClelland, J. L. (1995). A connectionist perspective on knowledge and development. In T. Simon & G. S. Halford (Eds.), *Developing cognitive competence: New approaches to cognitive modelling* (pp. 157–204). Hillsdale, NJ: Erlbaum.

McClelland, J. L., & Jenkins, E. (1991). Nature, nurture, and connections: Implications of connectionist models for cognitive development. In K. van Lehn (Ed.), *Architectures for intelligence* (pp. 41–73). Hillsdale, NJ: LEA.

McClelland, J. L., McNaughton, B. L., & O'Reilly, R. G. (1995). Why there are complementary learning systems in the hippocampus and neocortex: Insights from the successes and failures of connectionist models of learning and memory. *Psychological Review, 102*, 419–457.

McCloskey, M. (1983). Intuitive physics. *Scientific American, 248*(4), 122–130.

McCune-Nicolich, L. M. (1977). Beyond sensorimotor intelligence: Assessment of symbolic maturity through analysis of pretend play. *Merrill-Palmer Quarterly, 23*, 89–99.

McCune-Nicolich, L. M. (1981). Toward symbolic functioning: Structure of early use of pretend games and potential parallels with language. *Child Development, 52*, 785–797.

McDonough, L., Mandler, J. M., McKee, R. D., & Squire, L. R. (1995). The deferred imitation task as a nonverbal measure of declarative memory. *Proceedings of the National Academy of Sciences, 92*, 7580–7584.

McGarrigle, J., & Donaldson, M. (1974). Conservation accidents. *Cognition, 3*, 341–350.

McGarrigle, J., Grieve, R., & Hughes, M. (1978). Interpreting inclusion: A contribution to the study of the child's cognitive and linguistic development. *Journal of Experimental Child Psychology, 26*, 528–550.

McGee, M. (1979). Human spatial abilities: Psychometric studies and environmental, genetic, hormonal, and neurological influences. *Psychological Bulletin, 86*, 889–918.

McKee, R. D., & Squire, L. R. (1993). On the development of declarative memory. *Journal of Experimental Psychology: Learning, Memory, and Cognition, 19*, 397–404.

McLaughlin, G. H. (1963). Psycho-logic: A possible alternative to Piaget's formulation. *British Journal of Educational Psychology, 33*, 61–67.

McLeod, P., Plunkett, K., & Rolls, E. T. (1998). *Introduction to connectionist modelling of cognitive processes.* Oxford, UK: Oxford University Press.

Mead, G. H. (1934). *Mind, self, and society.* Chicago: University of Chicago Press.

Mead, G. H. (1955). *Mind, self & society from the stand-point of a social behaviorist,* ed. C. W. Morris. Chicago: University of Chicago Press.

Medin, D. (1989). Concepts and conceptual structure. *American Psychologist, 44*, 1469–1481.

Medin, D. L., & Heit, E. (Eds.). (in press). *Categorization.* San Diego: Academic Press.

Medin, D. L., & Ortony, A. (1989). Psychological essentialism. In S. Vosniadou & A. Ortony (Eds.), *Similarity and analogical reasoning* (pp. 179–195). Cambridge: Cambridge University Press.

Meins, E., & Fernyhough, C. (1997). Linguistic acquisitional style and mentalising development: the role of maternal mind-mindedness. Unpublished manuscript, University of Cambridge.

Meins, E., Fernyhough, C., Russell, J., & Clark-Carter, D. (1997). Security of attachment as a predictor of symbolic and mentalising abilities: a longitudinal study. Unpublished manuscript, University of Cambridge.

Meins, E., & Russell, J. (1997). Security and symbolic play: the relation between security of attachment and executive capacity. *British Journal of Developmental Psychology, 15*, 63–76.

Meltzoff, A. N. (1985). Immediate and deferred imitation in fourteen- and twenty-four-month-old infants. *Child Development, 56*, 62–72.

Meltzoff, A. N. (1988a). Infant imitation after a 1-week delay: Long-term memory for novel acts and multiple stimuli. *Developmental Psychology, 24*, 470–476.

Meltzoff, A. N. (1988b). Infant imitation and memory: Nine-month-olds in immediate and deferred tests. *Child Development, 59*, 217–225.

Meltzoff, A. N. (1990a). Foundations for developing a concept of self: The role of imitation in relating self to other and the value of social mirroring, social modeling, and self practice in infancy. In D. Cicchetti & M. Beeghly (Eds.), *The self in transition: Infancy to childhood* (pp. 139–164). Chicago: University of Chicago Press.

Meltzoff, A. N. (1990b). The implications of cross-modal matching and imitation for the development of representation and memory in infants. In A. Diamond (Ed.), *The development and neural bases of higher cognitive functions* (pp. 1–37). New York: New York Academy of Science.

Meltzoff, A. N. (1995a). Understanding the intentions of others: Re-enactment of intended acts by 18-month-old children. *Developmental Psychology, 31*, 838–850.

Meltzoff, A.N. (1995b). What infant memory tells us about infantile amnesia: Long-term recall and deferred imitation. *Journal of Experimental Child Psychology, 59*, 497–515.

Meltzoff, A. N. (1996). The human infant as imitative generalist: A 20-year progress report on infant imitation with implications for comparative psychology. In C. M. Heyes & B. G. Galef (Eds.), *Social learning in animals: The roots of culture* (pp. 347–370). New York: Academic Press.

Meltzoff, A. N. (1999). Origins of theory of mind, cognition, and communication. *Journal of Communication Disorders, 32*, 251–269.

Meltzoff, A. N., & Decety, J. (2003). What imitation tells us about social cognition: A rapprochement between developmental psychology and cognitive neuroscience. *Philosophical Transactions of the Royal Society: Biological Sciences, 358*, 491–500.

Meltzoff, A. N., & Gopnik, A. (1993). The role of imitation in understanding persons and developing a theory of mind. In S. Baron-Cohen, H. Tager-Flusberg, & D. J. Cohen (Eds.), *Understanding other minds: Perspectives from autism* (pp. 335–366). New York: Oxford University Press.

Meltzoff, A. N., & Moore, M. K. (1977). Imitation of facial and manual gestures by human neonates. *Science, 198*, 75–78.

Meltzoff, A. N., & Moore, M. K. (1983). Newborn infants imitate adult facial gestures. *Child Development, 54*, 702–719.

Meltzoff, A. N., & Moore, M. K. (1989). Imitation in newborn infants: Exploring the range of gestures imitated and the underlying mechanisms. *Developmental Psychology, 25*, 954–962.

Meltzoff, A. N., & Moore, M. K. (1992). Early imitation within a functional framework: The importance of person identity, movement, and development. *Infant Behavior and Development, 15*, 479–505.

Meltzoff, A. N., & Moore, M. K. (1994). Imitation, memory, and the representation of persons. *Infant Behavior and Development, 17*, 83–99.

Meltzoff, A. N., & Moore, M. K. (1995). Infants' understanding of people and things: From body imitation to folk psychology. In J. Bermúdez, A. J. Marcel, & N. Eilan (Eds.), *Body and the self* (pp. 43–69). Cambridge, MA: MIT Press.

Meltzoff, A. N., & Moore, M. K. (1997). Explaining facial imitation: theoretical model. *Early Development and Parenting, 6*, 179–192.

Meltzoff, A. N., & Moore, M. K. (1998a). Infant intersubjectivity: broadening the dialogue to include imitation, identity and intention. In S. Braten (Ed.), *Intersubjective communication and emotion in early ontogeny* (pp. 47–62). Paris: Cambridge University Press.

Meltzoff, A. N., & Moore, M. K. (1998b). Object representation, identity, and the paradox of early permanence: Steps toward a new framework. *Infant Behavior and Development, 21*, 201–235.

Meltzoff, A. N., & Moore, M. K. (1998c). Persons and representation: Why infant imitation is important for theories of human development. In J. Nadel & G. Butterworth (Eds.), *Imitation in infancy* (pp. 9–35). Cambridge, MA: Cambridge University Press.

Meltzoff, A. N., & Prinz, W. (2002). *The imitative mind: Development, evolution, and brain bases.* Cambridge: Cambridge University Press.

Melville, H. (1964). *Moby-Dick.* New York: Bobbs-Merrill [1st published 1851].

Menzel, E., Savage-Rumbaugh, E. S., & Lawson, J. (1985). Chimpanzee (*Pan troglodytes*) spatial problem solving with the use of mirrors and televised equivalents of mirrors. *Journal of Comparative Psychology, 99*, 211–217.

Mervis, C. B. (1987). Child-basic object categories and early development. In U. Neisser (Ed.), *Concepts and conceptual development* (pp. 201–233). Cambridge: Cambridge University Press.

Mervis, C. B., & Bertrand, J. (1997). Developmental relations between cognition and language: Evidence from Williams syndrome. In L. B. Adamson & M. A. Romski (Eds.), *Research on communication and language disorders: Contributions to theories of language development* (pp. 75–106). New York: Brookes.

Mervis, C. B., & Crisafi, M. A. (1982). Order of acquisition of subordinate-, basic-, and super-ordinate-level categories. *Child Development, 53*(1), 258–266.

Mervis, C. B., & Rosch, E. (1981). Categorization of natural objects. *Annual Review of Psychology, 32*, 89–115.

Messerly, J. (1996). *Piaget's conception of evolution.* Lanham, MD: Rowman & Littlefield.

Metcalfe, J., & Mischel, W. (1999). A hot/cool-system analysis of delay of gratification: Dynamics of willpower. *Psychological Review, 106*, 3–19.

Metsala, J. L., Stanovich, K. E., & Brown, G. D. A. (1997). Regularity effects and the phonological deficit model of reading disabilities: A meta-analytic review. *Journal of Experimental Psychology, 90*(2), 279–293.

Michie, S. (1984) Why preschoolers are reluctant to count spontaneously. *British Journal of Developmental Psychology, 2*, 347–358.

Middleton, D., & Edwards, D. (Eds.). (1990). *Collective remembering.* London: Sage Publications.

Millar, S. (1994). *Understanding and representing space.* Oxford, UK: Clarendon Press.

Miller, J. (1988). Developmental asynchrony of language development in children with Down syndrome. In L. Nadel (Ed.), *Psychobiology of Down syndrome* (pp. 167–198). Boston: MIT Press.

Miller, J., & Bersoff, D. M. (1995). Development in the context of everyday family relationships: Culture, interpersonal morality, and adaptation. In M. Killen & D. Hart (Eds.), *Morality in everyday life: Developmental perspectives* (pp. 259–282). Cambridge, UK: Cambridge University Press.

Miller, J. L., & Bartsch, K. (1997). The development of biological explanation: Are children vitalists? *Developmental Psychology, 33*, 156–164.

Miller, J. L., & Eimas, P. D. (1996). Internal structure of voicing categories in early infancy. *Perception & Psychophysics, 58*, 1157–1167.

Miller, K. (1984) The child as the measurer of all things: measurement procedures and the development of quantitative concepts. In C. Sophian, *Origins of cognitive skills* (pp. 193–228). Hillsdale, NJ: Erlbaum.

Miller, P., & Garvey, C. (1984). Mother–baby role play: Its origins in social support. In I. Bretherton (Ed.), *Symbolic play* (pp. 101–158). London: Academic Press.

Miller, P. H. (1994). Individual differences in children's strategic behavior: Utilization deficiencies. *Learning and Individual Differences, 6*, 285–307.

Miller, P. H. (2000). How best to utilize a deficiency: A commentary on Waters' "Memory strategy development." *Child Development, 71*, 1013–1017.

Miller, P. H., & Seier, W. L. (1994). Strategy utilization deficiencies in children: When, where, and why. In H. W. Reese (Ed.), *Advances in child development and behavior* (Vol. 25, pp. 107–156). San Diego: Academic Press.

Millikan, R. G. (1998). A common structure for concepts of individuals, stuffs, and real kinds: More mama, more milk, and more mouse. *Behavioral and Brain Sciences, 21*, 55–100.

Milner, A. D., & Goodale, M. A. (1995). *The visual brain in action.* Oxford, UK: Oxford University Press.

Minick, N. (1987). Introduction. In Vygotsky, L. S., *Thinking and speech*. New York: Plenum.

Mischel, W., Ebbesen, E. B., & Zeiss, A. M. (1972). Cognitive and attentional mechanisms in delay of gratification. *Journal of Personality and Social Psychology, 21*, 204–218.

Mischel, W., Shoda, Y., & Rodriguez, M. L. (1989, May 26). Delay of gratification in children. *Science, 244*, 933–938.

Mitchell, R. W. (1993). Mental models of mirror self-recognition: Two theories. *New Ideas in Psychology, 11*, 295–325.

Mitchell, T. M. (1997). *Machine learning*. McGraw-Hill: New York.

Miura, I. T., Kim, C. C., Chang, C.-M., & Okamoto, Y. (1988). Effects of language characteristics on children's cognitive representation of number: Cross-national comparisons. *Child Development, 59*, 1445–1450.

Miura, I. T., Okamoto, Y., Kim, C. C., Chang, C.-M., Steere, M., & Fayol, M. (1994). Comparisons of children's cognitive representation of number: China, France, Japan, Korea, Sweden and the United States. *International Journal of Behavioural Development, 17*, 401–411.

Mix, K. S., Levine, S. C., & Huttenlocher, J. (1997). Numerical abstraction in infants: Another look. *Developmental Psychology, 35*, 423–428.

Mix, K. S., Levine, S. C., & Huttenlocher, J. (2001). *Quantitative development in infancy and early childhood*. New York: Oxford University Press.

Molenaar Raijmakers, M. (2000). A causal interpretation of Piaget's theory of cognitive development: Reflections on the relationship between epigenesis and nonlinear dynamics. *New Ideas in Psychology, 18*, 41–55.

Moll, I. (1994). Reclaiming the natural line in Vygotsky's theory of cognitive development. *Human Development, 37*, 333–342.

Montangero, J. (1979). Les Relations du temps, de la vitesse et de l'espace parcouru chez le jeune enfant. *L'Année Psychologique, 79*, 23–42.

Moore, C. (1999). Gaze following and the control of attention. In P. Rochat (Ed.), *Early social cognition: Understanding others in the first months of life* (pp. 241–256). Mahwah, NJ: Erlbaum.

Moore, C., Barresi, J., & Thompson, C. (1998). The cognitive basis of future-oriented prosocial behavior. *Social Development, 7*, 198–218.

Moore, C., & Corkum, V. (1994). Social understanding at the end of the first year of life. *Developmental Review, 14*, 349–372.

Moore, C., & Corkum, V. (1998). Infant gaze following based on eye direction. *British Journal of Developmental Psychology, 16*, 495–503.

Moore, C. F., Dixon, J. A., & Haines, B. A. (1991). Components of understanding in proportional reasoning: A fuzzy set representation of developmental progression. *Child Development, 62*, 441–459.

Moore, C., & Dunham, P. J. (Eds.). (1995). *Joint attention: Its origin and role in development*. Hillsdale, NJ: Erlbaum.

Moore, E. G. J. (1986). Family socialization and the IQ test performance of traditionally and transracially adopted black children. *Developmental Psychology, 22*, 317–326.

Moore, G. E. (1903). *Principia ethica*. Cambridge: Cambridge University Press.

Moore, M. K., & Meltzoff, A. (1999). New findings on object permanence: A developmental difference between two types of occlusion. *British Journal of Developmental Psychology, 17*, 563–584.

Morais, J. (1991). Metaphonological abilities and literacy. In M. S. M. Thomson (Ed.), *Dyslexia: Integrating theory and practice*. London: Whurr.

Morgan, J. L., & Demuth, K. (Eds.). (1996). *Signal to syntax: Bootstrapping from speech to grammar in early acquisition*. Mahwah, NJ: Lawrence Erlbaum.

Morison, P., & Gardner, H. (1978). Dragons and dinosaurs: The child's capacity to differentiate fantasy from reality. *Child Development, 49*, 642–648.

Morris, A., & Sloutsky, V. (1998). Understanding of logical necessity. *Child Development, 69,* 721–741.

Morris, S. C., Taplin, J. E., & Gelman, S. A. (2000). Vitalism in naïve biological thinking. *Developmental Psychology, 36,* 582–595.

Morrongiello, B. A., Timney, B., Humphrey, G. K., Anderson, S., & Skory, C. (1995). Spatial knowledge in blind and sighted children. *Journal of Experimental Child Psychology, 59,* 211–233.

Morton, J., & Johnson, M. H. (1991). CONSPEC and CONLEARN: A two-process theory of infant face recognition. *Psychological Review, 98,* 164–181.

Morton, J. B., Trehub, S. E., & Zelazo, P. D. (2000). Representational inflexibility in children's interpretation of emotion in speech. Manuscript under review.

Moser, P. K. (1995). Epistemology. In R. Audi (Ed.), *The Cambridge dictionary of philosophy* (2nd ed.). Cambridge: Cambridge University Press.

Moses, L. J. (1993). Young children's understanding of belief constraints on intention. *Cognitive Development, 8,* 1–25.

Moses, L. J., & Flavell, J. H. (1990). Inferring false beliefs from actions and reactions. *Child Development, 61,* 929–945.

Moshman, D. (1998). Cognitive development beyond childhood. In W. Damon (Ed.), *Handbook of child psychology* (5th ed., Vol. 2). New York: Wiley.

Muir, D. W., & Hains, S. M. J. (1993). Infant sensitivity to perturbations in adult facial, vocal, tactile, and contingent stimulation during face to face interactions. In B. de Boysson-Bardies, S. de Schonen, P. Jusczyk, P. McNeilage, & J. Morton (Eds.), *Developmental neurocognition: Speech and face processing in the first year.* Dordrecht: Kluver.

Muir, D. W., & Hains, S. (1999). Young infants' perception of adult intentionality: Adult contingency and eye direction. In: P. Rochat (Ed.), *Early social cognition* (pp. 155–187), Mahwah, NJ: Erlbaum.

Mullen, M. K. (1994). Earliest recollections of childhood: A demographic analysis. *Cognition, 52,* 55–79.

Mullen, M. K., & Yi, S. (1995). The cultural context of talk about the past: Implications for the development of autobiographical memory. *Cognitive Development, 10,* 407–419.

Müller, U., & Carpendale, J. (2000). The role of social interaction in Piaget's theory. *New Ideas in Psychology, 18,* 139–156.

Müller, U., Sokol, B., & Overton, W. (1998). Reframing a constructivist model of the development of mental representation: The role of higher-order operations. *Developmental Review, 18,* 155–201.

Müller, U., Sokol, B., & Overton, W. (1999). Developmental sequences in class reasoning and propositional reasoning. *Journal of Experimental Child Psychology, 74,* 69–106.

Muma, J., & Muma, D. (1979). *Muma assessment program.* Lubbock, TX: Natural Child Publishing Company.

Mumme, D. L., Fernald, A., & Herrera, C. (1996). Infants' responses to facial and vocal emotional signals in a social referencing paradigm. *Child Development, 67,* 3219–3237.

Munakata, Y., McClelland, J. L., Johnson, M. N., & Siegler, R. S. (1997). Rethinking infant knowledge: Towards an adaptive process account of successes and failures in object permanence tasks. *Psychological Review, 104,* 686–713.

Munakata, Y., & Yerys, B. E. (in press). All together now: When dissociations between knowledge and action disappear. *Psychological Science, 12,* 335–337.

Mundy, P., & Crowson, M. (1997). Joint attention and early social communication. *Journal of Autism and Developmental Disorders, 27,* 653–676.

Murphy, G. L. (1982). Cue validity and levels of categorization. *Psychological Bulletin, 91,* 174–177.

Murphy, G. L., & Lassaline, M. E. (1997). Hierarchical structure in concepts and the basic level of categorization. In K. Lamberts & D. Shanks (Eds.), *Knowledge, concepts, and categories* (pp. 93–131). Cambridge, MA: MIT Press.

Murphy, G. L., & Medin, D. L. (1985). The role of theories in conceptual coherence. *Psychological Review, 92*(3), 289–316.

Murphy, G. L., & Smith, E. E. (1982). Basic-level superiority in picture categorization. *Journal of Verbal Learning and Verbal Behavior, 21*, 1–20.

Murray, L., & Trevarthen, C. (1985). Emotional regulation of interactions between two-month-olds and their mothers. In T. M. Field & N. A. Fox (Eds.), *Social Perception in Infants* (pp. 177–198). Norwood, NJ: Ablex.

Muter, V., Hulme, C., Snowling, M., & Taylor, S. (1998). Segmentation, not rhyming, predicts early progress in learning to read. *Journal of Experimental Child Psychology, 71*, 3–27.

Muter, V., & Snowling, M. J. (1998). Concurrent and longitudinal predictors of reading: the role of metalinguistic and short-term memory skills. *Reading Research Quarterly, 33*, 320–337.

Muter, V., Snowling, M. J.. & Taylor, S.(1994). Orthographic analogies and phonological awareness: Their role and significance in early reading development. *Journal of Child Psychology & Psychiatry, 35*, 293–310.

Myers, N. A., Clifton, R. K., & Clarkson, M. G. (1987). When they were very young: Almost-threes remember two years ago. *Infant Behavior and Development, 10*, 123–132.

Myers, N., & Perlmutter, M. (1978). Memory in the years from two to five. In P. A. Ornstein (Ed.), *Memory development in children.* Hillsdale, NJ: Erlbaum.

Mynatt, C. R., Doherty, M. E., & Tweney, R. D. (1977). Confirmation bias in a simulated research evironment: An experimental study of scientific inference. *Quarterly Journal of Experimental Psychology*, 85–95. Excerpts reprinted in P. N. Johnson-Laird & P. C. Wason (Eds.), *Thinking: Readings in cognitive science* (pp. 315–325). Cambridge: Cambridge University Press.

Nadel, L. (1990). Varieties of spatial cognition: Psychological considerations. In A. Diamond (Ed.), *The development of neural basis of higher cognitive functions* (pp. 613–636). New York: New York Academy of Sciences.

Nagel, T. (1997). *The last word.* New York: Oxford University Press.

Nakisa, R. C., & Plunkett, K. (1998). Innately guided learning by a neural network: the case of featural representation of speech language. *Language and Cognitive Processes, 13*, 105–128.

Nass, M. L. (1956). The effects of three variables on children's concepts of physical causality. *Journal of Abnormal and Social Psychology, 53*, 191–196.

Nation, K., Marshall, C. M., & Snowling, M. J. (2000). Phonological and semantic contributions to children's picture naming skill: Evidence from children with developmental reading disorders. *Language and Cognitive Processes, 16*, 241–259.

Nation, K., & Snowling, M. J. (1998a). Individual differences in contextual facilitation: Evidence from dyslexia and poor reading comprehension. *Child Development, 69*(4), 996–1011.

Nation, K., & Snowling, M. J. (1998b). Semantic processing and the development of word recognition skills: Evidence from children with reading comprehension difficulties. *Journal of Memory and Language, 39*, 85–101.

Nation, K., & Snowling, M. J. (1999). Developmental differences in sensitivity to semantic relations among good and poor comprehenders: Evidence from semantic priming. *Cognition, 70*(1) B1–13.

Neale, M. (1988) *Neale Analysis of Reading Ability–revised.* Hawthorn: Australian Council for Educational Research.

Needham, A. (1998). Infants' use of featural information in the segregation of stationary objects. *Infant Behavior and Development, 21*, 47–76.

Needham, A. (1999). The role of shape in 4-month-old infants' segregation. *Infant Behavior and Development, 22,* 161–178.

Needham, A. (in press). The development of object segregation during the first year of life. To appear in R. Kimchi, M. Behrmann, & C. Olson (Eds.), *Perceptual organization in vision: Behavioral and neural perspectives.* Mahwah, NJ: Erlbaum.

Needham, A., & Baillargeon, R. (1993). Intuitions about support in 4.5-month-old infants. *Cognition, 47,* 121–148.

Needham, A., & Modi, A. (2000). Infants' use of prior experiences in object segregation. In H. W. Reese (Ed.), *Advances in child development and behavior* (Vol. 27, pp. 99–133). New York: Academic Press.

Neisser, U. (1988). Five kinds of self-knowledge. *Philosophical Psychology, 1,* 35–59.

Neisser, U. (Ed.). (1998). *The rising curve.* Washington, DC: American Psychological Association.

Nelson, C. A. (1995). The ontogeny of human memory: A cognitive neuroscience perspective. *Developmental Psychology, 31,* 723–738.

Nelson, C. A. (1997). The neurobiological basis of early memory development. In N. Cowan (Ed.), *The development of memory in childhood* (pp. 41–82). Hove, UK: Psychology Press.

Nelson, C. A., & Collins, P. F. (1991). Event-related potential and looking time analysis of infants' responses to familiar and novel events: Implications for visual recognition memory. *Developmental Psychology, 27,* 50–58.

Nelson, C. A., & Collins, P. F. (1992). Neural and behavioral correlates of recognition memory in 4- and 9-month-old infants. *Brain and Cognition, 19,* 105–121.

Nelson, C. A., & Ludemann, P. M. (1989). Past, current, and future trends in infant face perception research. *Canadian Journal of Psychology, 43,* 183–198.

Nelson, D. G. K. (1995). Principle-based inferences in young children's categorization: Revisiting the impact of function on the naming of artifacts. *Cognitive Development, 10*(3), 347–380.

Nelson, K. (1973). *Structure and strategy in learning to talk. Monographs of the Society for Research in Child Development, Vol. 149.* Chicago, IL: University of Chicago Press.

Nelson, K. (1993). Events, narratives, memory: What develops? In C. A. Nelson (Ed.), *Memory and affect in development: The Minnesota Symposium on Child Psychology* (pp. 1–24). Hillsdale, NJ: Erlbaum.

Nelson, K., & Gruendel, J. (1981). Generalized event representations: Basic building blocks of cognitive development. In M. E. Lamb & A. L. Brown (Eds.), *Advances in developmental psychology* (Vol. 1, pp. 131–158). Hillsdale, NJ: Erlbaum.

Nelson, K., & Gruendel, J. (1986). Children's scripts. In K. Nelson (Ed.), *Event knowledge: Structure and function in development* (pp. 21–46). Hillsdale, NJ: Erlbaum.

Nelson, K., Hampson, J., & Shaw, L. K. (1993). Nouns in early lexicons: Evidence, explanations and implications. *Journal of Child Language, 20*(1), 61–84.

Nelson, K., & Ross, G. (1980). The generalities and specifics of long-term memory in infants and young children. In M. Perlmutter (Ed.), *New Directions for Child Development – Children's Memory* (pp. 87–101). San Francisco: Jossey-Bass.

Nelson, K., & Seidman, S. (1984). Playing with scripts. In I. Bretherton (Ed.), *Symbolic play* (pp. 45–72). London: Academic Press.

Nelson, L. A. (1987). The recognition of facial expressions in the first two years of life: Mechanisms of development. *Child Development, 58,* 889–909.

Nettelbeck, T. (1987). *Inspection time and intelligence.* Norwood, NJ: Ablex.

Neville, H. J., Mills, D. L., & Bellugi, U. (1994). Effects of altered auditory sensitivity and age of language acquisition on the development of language-relevant neural systems: Preliminary studies of Williams syndrome. In S. Broman and J. Grafman (Eds.), *Atypical cognitive deficits in developmental disorders: Implications for brain function* (pp. 67–83). Erlbaum.

Newcombe, N. (1982). Sex-related differences in spatial ability. In M. Potegal (Ed.), *Spatial abilities: Developmental and physiological foundations* (pp. 223–243). New York: Academic Press.

Newcombe, N. (1989). The development of spatial perspective taking. In H. W. Reese (Ed.), *Advances in child development and behavior* (Vol. 22, pp. 203–247). New York: Academic Press.

Newcombe, N., & Bandura, M. M. (1983). Effect of age at puberty on spatial ability in girls: A question of mechanism. *Developmental Psychology, 19,* 215–224.

Newcombe, N., Bandura, M. M., & Taylor, D. G. (1983). Sex differences in spatial ability and spatial activities. *Sex Roles, 9,* 377–386.

Newcombe, N., Dubas, J. S., & Baenninger, M. A. (1989). Associations of timing of puberty, spatial ability, and lateralization in adult women. *Child Development, 60,* 246–254.

Newcombe, N., & Fox, N. A. (1994). Infantile amnesia: Through a glass darkly. *Child Development, 65,* 31–40.

Newcombe, N., & Huttenlocher, J.(2000). *Making space.* Cambridge, MA: MIT Press.

Newcombe, N., Huttenlocher, J., & Learmonth, A. (1999). Infants' coding of location in continuous space. *Infant Behavior and Development, 22,* 457–474.

Newcombe, N., & Liben, L. S. (1982). Barrier effects in the cognitive maps of children and adults. *Journal of Experimental Child Psychology, 34,* 46–58.

Newell A. (1990). *Unified theories of cognition.* Cambridge, MA: Harvard University Press.

Newell, A., & Simon, H. A. (1972). *Human problem solving.* Englewood Cliffs, NJ: Prentice-Hall.

Newman, F., & Holzman, L. (1993). *Lev Vygotsky: Revolutionary scientist.* London: Routledge.

Newman, H. H., Freeman, F. N., & Holzinger, K. J. (1937). *Twins: A study of heredity and environment.* Chicago: University of Chicago Press.

Newsome, M., & Jusczyk, P. (1994). Infants' ability to learn and parse words. Paper presented at the 127th Meeting of the Acoustical Society of America, Cambridge, MA.

Nguyen, S., & Gelman, S. A. (2000). Children's understanding of death: The case of plants. Unpublished data, University of Illinois.

Nicolich, L. M. (1977). Beyond sensorimotor intelligence: Assessment of symbolic maturity through analysis of pretend play. *Merrill-Palmer Quarterly, 23,* 89–99.

Nikolopoulos, D. S. (1999). *Cognitive and linguistic predictors of literacy skills in the Greek language. The manifestation of reading and spelling difficulties in a regular orthography.* London: University College London.

Ninio, A., & Bruner, J. (1978). The achievements and antecedents of labeling. *Journal of Child Language, 5,* 1–15.

Nisan, M. (1987). Moral norms and social conventions: A cross-cultural comparison. *Developmental Psychology, 23,* 719–725.

Nisbett, R. E. (1998). Race, genetics, and IQ. In C. Jencks & M. Phillips (Eds.), *The Black-White test score gap* (pp. 86–102). Washington, DC: Brookings Institution.

Norman, D.A. (1988) *The psychology of everyday things.* New York: Basic Books.

Norman, D.A. (1993) *Things that make us smart: Defending human attributes in the age of the machine.* Reading, MA: Addison-Wesley.

Norman, D. A., & Shallice, T. (1986). Attention to action: Willed and automatic control of behavior. In R. J. Davidson, G. E. Schwartz, & D. Shapiro (Eds.), *Consciousness and self-regulation* (Vol. 4, pp. 4–18). New York: Plenum.

Nucci, L. (1996). Morality and the personal sphere of actions. In E. Reed, E. Turiel, & T. Brown (Eds.), *Values and knowledge* (pp. 41–60). Hillsdale, NJ: Lawrence Erlbaum.

Nucci, L. (2001). *Education in the moral domain.* Cambridge, UK: Cambridge University Press.

Nucci, L., Camino, C., & Sapiro, C. (1996). Social class effects on Northeastern Brazilian children's conceptions of areas of personal choice and social regulation. *Child Development, 67,* 1223–1242.

Nucci, L., & Smetana, J. (1996). Mothers' concepts of young children's areas of personal freedom. *Child Development, 67,* 1870–1886.

Nucci, L., & Turiel, E. (2000). The moral and the personal: Sources of social conflicts. In L. Nucci, E. Turiel, & G. Saxe (Eds.) *Culture, thought and development* (pp. 115–140). Mahwah, NJ: Erlbaum.

Nucci, L., & Weber, E. K. (1995). Social interactions in the home and the development of young children's conceptions within the personal domain. *Child Development, 66,* 1438–1452.

Nuñes, T. (1994). Street intelligence. In R. J. Sternberg (Ed.), *Encyclopedia of human intelligence* (Vol. 2, pp. 1045–1049). New York: Macmillan.

Nuñes, T., & Bryant, P. (1996) Children doing mathematics. Oxford, UK: Blackwell.

Nuñes, T., Bryant, P., & Bindman, M. (1997). Morphological spelling strategies: Developmental stages and processes. *Developmental Psychology, 33,* 637–649.

Nuñes, T., Schliemann, A.-L., & Carraher, D. (1993). *Street mathematics and school mathematics.* New York: Cambridge University Press.

Nunner-Winkler, G., & Sodian, B. (1988). Children's understanding of moral emotions. *Child Development, 59,* 1323–1338.

O'Connell, B., & Betherton, I. (1984). Toddler's play, alone and with mother: the role of maternal guidance. In I. Bretherton (Ed.), *Symbolic Play* (pp. 337–368). London: Academic Press.

O'Connor, N., & Hermelin, B. (1991). A specific linguistic ability. *American Journal of Mental Retardation, 95,* 673–680.

O'Keefe, J., & Nadel, L. (1978). *The hippocampus as a cognitive map.* Oxford, UK: Clarendon Press.

O'Loughlin. C., & Thagard, P. (2000). Autism and coherence: A computational model. *Mind & Language, 15,* 375–392.

O'Reilly, R. C. (1998). Six principles for biologically based computational models of cortical cognition. *Trends in Cognitive Sciences, 2,* 455–462.

O'Sullivan, L. P., Mitchell, L. L., & Daehler, M. W. (1999). Representation and perseveration: Influences on young children's symbolic functioning. Unpublished manuscript.

Oakes, L. M. (1994). The development of infants' use of continuity cues in their perception of causality. *Developmental Psychology, 30,* 869–879.

Oakes, L. M., & Cohen, L. B. (1990). Infant perception of a causal event. *Cognitive Development, 5,* 193–207.

Oakes, L. M., Coppage, D. J., & Dingel, A. (1997). By land or by sea: The role of perceptual similarity in infants' categorization of animals. *Developmental Psychology, 33,* 396–407.

Oakes, L. M., Madole, K. L., & Cohen, L. B. (1991). Object examining: Habituation and categorization. *Cognitive Development, 6,* 377–392.

Oakes, L. M., Plumert, J. M., Lansink, J. M., & Merryman, J. D. (1996). Evidence for task-dependent categorization in infancy. *Infant Behavior & Development, 19,* 425–440.

Ochs, E., & Schieffelin, B. (1984). Language acquisition and socialization. In R. Shweder & R. LeVine (Eds.), *Culture Theory.* Cambridge: Cambridge University Press.

Okin, S. (1996). The gendered family and the development of a sense of justice. In E. Reed, E. Turiel, & T. Brown (Eds.), *Values and knowledge* (pp. 61–74). Hillsdale, NJ.: Lawrence Erlbaum.

Oliver, A., Johnson, M. H., Karmiloff-Smith, A., & Pennington, B. (2000). Deviations in the emergence of representations: A neuroconstructivist framework for analysing developmental disorders. *Developmental Science, 3,* 1–23.

Olson, D., & Astington, J. (1993). Thinking about thinking: Learning how to take statements and hold beliefs. *Educational Psychologist, 28*, 7–23.

Olson, D., & Campbell, R. (1993). Constructing representations. In C. Pratt and A. F. Garton (Eds.), *Systems of representation in children: Development and use* (pp. 11–26). New York: John Wiley & Sons.

Olson, D. R. (1970). *Cognitive development: The child's acquisition of diagonality.* New York: Academic Press.

Olson, D. R. (1994). *The world on paper: The conceptual and cognitive implications of writing and reading.* Cambridge: Cambridge University Press.

Olson, D. R., & Bialystok, E. (1983). *Spatial cognition: The structure and development of mental representations of spatial relations.* Hillsdale, NJ: Lawrence Erlbaum.

O'Neill, D. K., & Gopnik, A. (1991). Young children's ability to identify the sources of their beliefs. *Developmental Psychology, 27*, 390–397.

Oney, B., & Goldman, S. (1984) Decoding and comprehension skills in Turkish and English: effects of the regularity of grapheme–phoneme correspondences. *Journal of Educational Psychology, 76*, 557–568.

Onishi, K. H. (2000, July). Infants can reason about the support of 2 but not 3 stacked boxes. Paper presented at the biennial International Conference on Infant Studies, Brighton, UK.

Opfer, J. E. (2000). Developing a biological understanding of goal-directed action. Unpublished doctoral dissertation, University of Michigan, Ann Arbor.

Opfer, J. E., & Gelman, S. A. (1998). Children's and adults' models of teleological action: From psychology- to biology-based models. Paper presented at the Jean Piaget Society Conference, Chicago, IL.

Osterlaan, J., Logan, G. D., & Sergeant, J. A. (1998). Response inhibition in ADHD, CD, comorbid ADHD + CD, anxious, and normal children: A meta-analysis of studies with the stop-task. *Journal of Child Psychiatry and Psychology, 39*, 411–426.

Ottosson, T. (1987). Map-reading and wayfinding. *Göteborg Studies in Educational Sciences, 65* [whole issue].

Overman, W. H., Bachevalier, J., Schuhmann, E., & McDonough-Ryan, P. (1997). Sexually dimorphic brain-behavior development: A comparative perspective. In N. A. Krasnegor & G. R. Lyon (Eds.), *Development of the prefrontal cortex: Evolution, neurobiology, and behavior* (pp. 337–357). Baltimore, MD: Paul H. Brookes Publishing Co.

Overton, W. F. (1998). Developmental psychology: Philosophy, concepts, and methodology. In W. Damon (Series Ed.) & R. M. Lerner (Vol. Ed.), *Handbook of child psychology, Vol 1. Theoretical models of human development.* (5th ed., pp. 107–188). New York: Wiley.

Oyen, A.-S., & Bebko, J. M. (1996). The effects of computer games and lesson contexts on children's mnemonic strategies. *Journal of Experimental Child Psychology, 62*, 173–189.

Ozonoff, S., & Jensen, J. (1999). Brief report: Specific executive function profiles in three neurodevelopmental disorders. *Journal of Autism and Developmental Disorders, 29*, 171–177.

Ozonoff, S., Pennington, B., & Rogers, S. J. (1990). Are there emotion perception deficits in young autistic children? *Journal of Child Psychology and Psychiatry, 31*, 343–363.

Ozonoff, S., Pennington, B. F., & Rogers, S. J. (1991). Executive function deficits in high-functioning autistic individuals: Relationship to theory of mind. *Journal of Child Psychology and Psychiatry, 32*, 1081–1105.

Ozonoff, S. (1995). Executive functions in autism. In E. Schopler & G. Mesibov (Eds.), *Learning and cognition in autism.* New York: Plenum Press.

Ozonoff, S., & Strayer, D. L. (1997). Inhibitory function in nonretarded children with autism. *Journal of Autism & Developmental Disorders, 27*, 59–77.

Ozonoff, S., Strayer, D. L., McMahon, W. M., & Filloux, F. (1994). Executive function abilities in autism: An information processing approach. *Journal of Child Psychology and Psychiatry, 35,* 1015–1031.

Pacherie, E. (1997). Motor-images, self-consciousness, and autism. In J. Russell (Ed.), *Autism as an executive disorder* (pp. 215–255). Oxford, UK: Oxford University Press.

Palincsar, A. S., & Brown, A. L. (1984). Reciprocal teaching of comprehension-fostering and comprehension-monitoring activities. *Cognition and Instruction, 1,* 117–175.

Palincsar, A., & Magnusson, S. (in press). The interplay of first-hand and second-hand investigations to model and support the development of scientific knowledge and reasoning. In S. Carver & D. Klahr (Eds.), *Cognition and instruction: Twenty-five years of progress.* Mahwah, NJ: Erlbaum.

Papousek H., & Papousek, M. (1974). Mirror-image and self-recognition in young human infants: A new method of experimental analysis. *Developmental Psychobiology, 7,* 149–157.

Papousek, H., & Papousek, M. (1987). Intuitive parenting: a dialectic counterpart to the infant's integrative competence. In J. D. Osofsky (Ed.), *Handbook of infant development* (pp. 669–720). New York: Wiley.

Park, C. (1967). *The siege.* London: Hutchinson.

Parker, S. T., Mitchell, R. W., & Boccia, M. L. (Eds.). (1994). *Self-awareness in animals and humans: Developmental perspectives* New York: Cambridge University Press.

Parkin, A. J. (1993). Implicit memory across the life-span. In P. Graf & M. Masson (Eds.), *Implicit memory: New directions in cognition, development, and neuropsychology* (pp. 63–131). Amsterdam: Elsevier.

Parkin, A. J. (1997). The development of procedural and declarative memory. In N. Cowan (Ed.), *The development of memory in childhood* (pp. 113–137). Hove, UK: Psychology Press.

Parten, M. B. (1932). Social participation among preschool children. *Child Development, 27,* 243–269.

Parten, M. B. (1933). Social play among preschool children. *Journal of Abnormal & Social Psychology, 28,* 136–147.

Pascual-Leone, J. A. (1970). A mathematical model for the transition rule in Piaget's developmental stages. *Acta Psychologica, 32,* 301–345.

Pascual-Leone, J. A. (1978). Compounds, confounds, and models in developmental information processing: A reply to Trabasso & Foellinger. *Journal of Experimental Child Psychology, 26,* 18–40.

Pascual-Leone, J. A. (2000). Reflections on working memory: Are the two models complementary? *Journal of Experimental Child Psychology, 77*(2), 138–154.

Pascual-Leone, J. A., & Baillargeon, R. (1994). Developmental measurement of mental attention. *International Journal of Behavioral Development, 17*(1), 161–200.

Pascual-Leone, J. A., & Smith, J. (1969). The encoding and decoding of symbols by children: A new experimental paradigm and a neo-Piagetian model. *Journal of Experimental Child Psychology, 8,* 328–355.

Pascual-Leone, J. A., & Sparkman, E. (1980). The dialectics of empiricism and rationalism: A last methodological reply to Trabasso. *Journal of Experimental Child Psychology, 29,* 88–101.

Pauen, S. (1996). Children's reasoning about the interaction of forces. *Child Development, 67,* 2728–2742.

Pauen, S. (1999). The development of ontological categories: Stable dimensions and changing concepts. In W. Schnotz, S. Vosniadou, & M. Carretero (Eds.), *New perspectives on conceptual change* (pp. 15–31). Amsterdam: Elsevier.

Pauen, S., & Wilkening, F. (1997). Children's analogical reasoning about natural phenomena. *Journal of Experimental Child Psychology, 67,* 90–113.

Pears, R., & Bryant, P. (1990). Transitive inferences by young children about spatial position. *British Journal of Psychology, 81*(4), 497–510.

Peirce, C. S. (1903). Logic as semiotic: The theory of signs. In J. Buchler (Ed.), *The philosophical writings of Peirce* (1955) (pp. 98–119). New York: Dover Books.

Penner, D. E., & Klahr, D. (1996). The interaction of domain-specific knowledge and domain-general discovery strategies: A study with sinking objects. *Child Development, 67,* 2709–2727.

Pennington, B. F. (1997). Dimensions of executive functions in normal and abnormal development. In N. A. Krasnegor, G. R. Lyon, & P. S. Goldman-Rakic (Eds.), *Development of the prefrontal cortex: Evolution, neurobiology, and behavior* (pp. 265–281). Baltimore: Paul H. Brooks Publishing Co.

Pennington, B. F., van Orden, G. C. V., Smith, S. D., Green, P. A., & Haith, M. M. (1990). Phonological processing skills and deficits in adult dyslexics. *Child Development, 61,* 1753–1778.

Pennington, B. F., & Ozonoff, S. (1996). Executive functions and developmental psychopathology. *Journal of Child Psychology and Psychiatry, 37,* 51–87.

Pennington, B. F., Rogers, S., Bennetto, L., Griffith, E., Reed, D., & Shyu, V. (1997). Validity test of the executive dysfunction hypothesis of autism. In J. Russell (Ed.), *Executive functioning in autism.* Oxford, UK: Oxford University Press.

Pennington, B. F., & Smith, S. D. (1997). Genetic analysis of dyslexia and other complex behavioral phenotypes. *Current Opinion in Pediatrics, 9,* 636–641.

Perfetti, C., Beck, I., Bell, L., & Hughes, C. (1987). Phonemic knowledge and learning to read are reciprocal: A longitudinal study of first grade children. *Merrill-Palmer Quarterly, 33,* 283–319.

Perkins, D. N., & Grotzer, T. A. (1997). Teaching intelligence. *American Psychologist, 52,* 1125–1133.

Perner, J. (1991). *Understanding the representational mind.* Cambridge MA: MIT Press.

Perner, J. (2000a). Memory and theory of mind. In E. Tulving and F. I. M. Craik (Eds.), *The Oxford handbook of memory* (pp. 297–312). Oxford, UK: Oxford University Press.

Perner, J. (2000b). About + Belief + Counterfactual. In P. Mitchell & K. J. Riggs (Eds.), *Children's reasoning and the mind* (pp. 367–401). Hove, UK: Psychology Press.

Perner, J., & Lang, B. (1999). Development of theory of mind and cognitive control. *Trends in Cognitive Science, 3,* 337–344.

Perner, J., Leekam, S. R., & Wimmer, H. (1987). Three-year-olds' difficulty with false belief. *British Journal of Developmental Psychology, 5,* 125–137.

Perner, J., Ruffman, T., & Leekam, S. R. (1994). Theory of mind is contagious: You catch it from your sibs. *Child Development, 65,* 1228–1238.

Perner, J., & Wimmer, H. (1985). "John thinks that Mary thinks that . . .": Attribution of second-order beliefs by 5–10 year old children. *Journal of Experimental Child Psychology, 39,* 437–471.

Perron-Borelli, M., & Misès, R. (1974). *Epreuves différentielles d'efficience intellectuelle.* Issy-les-Moulineaux, France: Editions Scientifiques et Psychologiques.

Peterson, C. C., & Rideout, R. (1998). Memory for medical emergencies experienced by 1 and 2-year-olds. *Developmental Psychology, 34,* 1059–1072.

Peterson, C. C., & Siegal, M. (1995). Deafness, conversation and theory of mind. *Journal of Child Psychology and Psychiatry, 36,* 459–474.

Peterson, C. C., & Siegal, M. (1997). Domain specificity and everyday biological, physical, and psychological thinking in normal, autistic, and deaf children. *New Directions for Child Development, 75,* 55–70.

Pettersen, L., Yonas, A., & Fisch, R. O. (1980). The development of blinking in response to impending collision in preterm, full-term, and postterm infants. *Infant Behavior and Development, 3,* 155–165.

Phelps-Terasaki D., & Phelps-Gunn, T. (2000). *Test of Pragmatic Language.* London: Psychological Corporation.

Phillips, A. T., & Wellman, H. M. (submitted). Infants recognize goal directed actions.

Phillips, A. T., Wellman, H. M., & Sootsman, J. L. (2000). Infants' understanding of object-directed action. Manuscript submitted for publication.

Phillips, A. T., Wellman, H. M., & Spelke, E. S. (in press). Infants' ability to connect gaze and emotional expression to intentional action.

Phillips, S., Halford, G. S., & Wilson, W. H. (1995, July). The processing of associations versus the processing of relations and symbols: A systematic comparison. Paper presented at the Proceedings of the Seventeenth Annual Conference of the Cognitive Science Society, Pittsburgh, PA.

Piaget, J. (1918). *Recherche.* Lausanne: La Concorde.

Piaget, J. (1923). La psychologie des valeurs religieuses. In Association Chrétienne d'Etudiants de la Suisse Romande (Ed.), *Sainte-Croix 1922* (pp. 38–82).

Piaget, J. (1928). *Judgment and reasoning in the child.* London: Routledge & Kegan Paul.

Piaget, J. (1929). *The child's conception of the world.* London: Routledge & Kegan Paul [published in 1951, Savage, MD: Littlefield Adams].

Piaget, J. (1932). *The moral judgment of the child.* New York: Free Press.

Piaget, J. (1941). Le Mécanisme du développement mental et les lois du groupement des opérations. *Archives de Psychologie, 28,* 215–285.

Piaget, J. (1945/1962). *Play, dreams, and imitation in childhood.* New York: Norton.

Piaget, J. (1946a). *Le Développement de la notion de temps chez l'enfant.* Paris: Presses Universitaires de France.

Piaget, J. (1946b). *Les Notions de mouvement et de vitesse chez l'enfant.* Paris: Presses Universitaires de France.

Piaget, J. (1949). *Traité de logique: Essai de logistique opératoire.* Paris: Colin.

Piaget, J. (1950a). *The psychology of intelligence,* trans. M. Piercy & D. E. Berlyne. London: Routledge & Kegan Paul [1st published 1947].

Piaget, J. (1950b). *Introduction à l'épistémologie génétique: Vol. 1. La pensée mathématique.* Paris: Presses Universitaires de France.

Piaget, J. (1950c). *The psychology of intelligence.* London: Routledge & Kegan Paul.

Piaget, J. (1952a). Autobiography. In E. Boring (Ed.), *History of psychology in autobiography.* Worcester, MA: Clark University Press.

Piaget, J. (1952b). *The child's conception of number.* London: Routledge & Kegan Paul.

Piaget, J. (1952c). *The origins of intelligence in children.* New York: International Universities Press [1st published 1936].

Piaget, J. (1953a). How children form mathematical concepts. *Scientific American, 189*(5), 74–79.

Piaget, J. (1953b). *Logic and psychology.* Manchester: Manchester University Press.

Piaget, J. (1954). *The construction of reality in the child,* trans. M. Cook. New York: Basic Books; London: Routledge.

Piaget, J. (1960a). *The child's conception of physical causality.* Paterson, NJ: Littlefield, Adams.

Piaget, J. (1960b). The general problems of the psychobiological development of the child. In J. Tanner & B. Inhelder (Eds.), *Discussions on child development* (Vol. 4). London: Tavistock.

Piaget, J. (1962a). *Play, dreams and imitation in childhood.* New York: Norton.

Piaget, J. (1962b). Will and action. *Bulletin of the Menninger Clinic, 26,* 138–145.

Piaget, J. (1963). Foreword. In J. Flavell, *The developmental psychology of Jean Piaget.* New York: Van Nostrand.

Piaget, J. (1965). *The child's concept of number.* New York: Norton Library.

Piaget, J. (1967). *Logique et connaissance scientifique.* Paris: Gallimard.

Piaget, J. (1968). *On the development of memory and identity.* Barre, MA: Clark University Press.

Piaget, J. (1969). *The mechanisms of perception.* New York: Basic Books.

Piaget, J. (1970). Piaget's theory. In P. Mussen (1983). *Handbook of child psychology* (4th ed.). New York: Wiley.

Piaget, J. (1971). *Biology and knowledge.* Edinburgh: Edinburgh University Press.

Piaget, J. (1972a). *The development of intelligence.* Totowa, NJ: Littlefield, Adams.

Piaget, J. (1972b). *Insights and illusions in philosophy.* London: Routledge & Kegan Paul.

Piaget, J. (1974). *Understanding causality.* New York: Norton.

Piaget, J. (1976). *The grasp of consciousness.* Cambridge, MA: Harvard University Press.

Piaget, J. (1977). *Epistemology and psychology of function.* Dordrecht: Reidel.

Piaget, J. (1978). *The development of thought.* Oxford, UK: Blackwell.

Piaget, J. (1980). *Experiments in contradiction.* Chicago: University of Chicago Press.

Piaget, J. (1981). *Intelligence and affectivity: Their relationship during child development,* ed. and trans. T. Brown & C. Kaegi. Palo Alto, CA: Annual Reviews Monographs.

Piaget, J. (1985). *The equilibration of cognitive structures.* Chicago: University of Chicago Press.

Piaget, J. (1986). Essay on necessity. *Human Development, 29,* 301–314.

Piaget, J. (1987a) *Possibility and necessity: The role of necessity in cognitive development. Vol. 1.* Minneapolis, MN: University of Minnesota Press.

Piaget, J. (1987b) *Possibility and necessity: The role of necessity in cognitive development. Vol. 2.* Minneapolis, MN: University of Minnesota Press.

Piaget, J. (1992). *Morphisms and categories.* Hillsdale, NJ: Erlbaum.

Piaget, J. (1995a). *Sociological studies.* London: Routledge.

Piaget, J. (1995b). Commentary on Vygotsky's criticisms. *New Ideas in Psychology, 13,* 325–340.

Piaget, J. (1998). *De la pédagogie.* Paris: Odile Jacob.

Piaget, J. (2001). *Studies in reflective abstraction,* trans. R. Campbell. Hove: Psychology Press.

Piaget, J., & Garcia, R. (1989) *Psychogenesis and the history of science.* New York: Columbia University Press.

Piaget, J., & Garcia, J. (1991). *Toward a logic of meanings.* Hillsdale, NJ: Erlbaum.

Piaget, J., & Inhelder, B. (1956). *The child's conception of space.* New York: Norton.

Piaget, J., & Inhelder, B. (1966) *Mental imagery in the child.* London: Routledge & Kegan Paul.

Piaget, J., & Inhelder, B. (1974) *The child's construction of quantities.* London: Routledge & Kegan Paul.

Piaget, J., Inhelder, B., & Szeminska, A. (1960). *The child's conception of geometry.* New York: Basic Books.

Piaget, J., Kaufmann, J.-L., & Bourquin, J.-F. (1977). *La Construction des communs multiples.* In J. Piaget, *Recherches sur l'abstraction réfléchissante: Vol 1. L'Abstraction des relations logico-mathématiques* (pp. 31–44). Paris: Presses Universitaires de France.

Piaget, J., Montangero, J., & Billeter, J. (1977). La Formation des correlats. In J. Piaget (Ed.), *Recherches sur l'abstraction réfléchissante* (Vol. 1, pp. 115–129). Paris: Presses Universitaires de France.

Piaget, J., & Szeminska, A. (1939). Experiences of children in the conservation of quantities. *Journal of Normal Psychology, 36,* 36–65.

Piaget, J., & Voyat, G. (1968). Recherche sur l'identité d'un corps en développement et sur celle du movement transitif. In J. Piaget, H. Sinclair, & Vinh Bang (Eds.), *Epistémologie et psychologie de l'identité* (pp. 1–82). Paris: Presses Universitaires de France.

Pick, H. L., & Lockman, J. J. (1981). From frames of reference to spatial representations. In L. S. Liben, A. H. Patterson, & N. Newcombe (Eds.), *Spatial representation and behavior across the life span: Theory and application* (pp. 39–61). New York: Academic Press.

Pieraut-Le Bonniec, G. (1980). *The development of modal reasoning.* New York: Academic Press.

Pieraut-Le Bonniec, G. (1985). From visual-motor anticipation to conceptualization: Reaction to solid and hollow objects and knowledge of the function of containment. *Infant Behavior and Development, 8,* 413–424.

Pillemer, D. B., & White, S. H. (1989). Childhood events recalled by children and adults. In H. W. Reese (Ed.), *Advances in child development and behavior* (Vol. 21, pp. 297–340). San Diego: Academic Press.

Pillow, B. H. (1988). The development of children's beliefs about the mental world. *Merrill-Palmer Quarterly, 34,* 1–32.

Pillow, B. H. (1989). Early understanding of perception as a source of knowledge. *Journal of Experimental Child Psychology, 47,* 116–129.

Pinker, S. (1994). *The language instinct: The new science of language and mind.* London: Penguin.

Pinker, S. (1999). *Words and rules.* London: Weidenfeld & Nicolson.

Plaisted, K., O'Riordan, M., & Baron-Cohen, S. (1998a). Enhanced discrimination of novel, highly similar stimuli by adults with autism during a perceptual learning task. *Journal of Child Psychology and Psychiatry, 39,* 765–775.

Plaisted, K., O'Riordan, M., & Baron-Cohen, S. (1998b). Enhanced visual search for a conjunctive target in autism: A research note. *Journal of Child Psychology and Psychiatry, 39,* 777–783.

Plaut, D. C. (1997). Structure and function in the lexical system: Insights from distributed models of naming and lexical decision. *Language and Cognitive Processes, 12,* 767–808.

Plaut, D. C., McClelland, J. L., Seidenberg, M. S., & Patterson, K. E. (1996). Understanding normal and impaired word reading: Computational principles in quasi-regular domains. *Psychological Review, 103,* 56–115.

Plomin, R. (1997). Identifying genes for cognitive abilities and disabilities. In R. J. Sternberg & E. L. Grigorenko (Eds.), *Intelligence, heredity, and environment* (pp. 89–104). New York: Cambridge University Press.

Plunkett, K. (1998). Language acquisition and connectionism. *Language and Cognitive Processes, 13,* 97–104.

Plunkett, K., & Juola, P. (1999). A connectionist model of English past tense and plural morphology. *Cognitive Science, 23,* 463–490.

Plunkett, K., & Marchman, V. (1991). U-shaped learning and frequency effects in a multi-layered perceptron: Implications for child language acquisition. *Cognition, 38,* 1–60.

Plunkett, K., & Marchman, V. (1996). Learning from a connectionist model of the acquisition of the English past tense. *Cognition, 61,* 299–308.

Plunkett, K., & Nakisa, R. C. (1997). A connectionist model of the Arabic plural system. *Language and Cognitive Processes, 12,* 807–836.

Plunkett, K., & Sinha, C. (1992). Connectionism and developmental theory. *British Journal of Developmental Psychology, 10,* 209–254.

Plunkett, K., Sinha, C., Muller, M. F., & Strandsby, O. (1992). Vocabulary growth in children and a connectionist net. *Connection Science, 4*(3–4), 293–312.

Poag, C. K., Goodnight, J. A., & Cohen, R. (1985). The environments of children: From home to school. In R. Cohen (Ed.), *The development of spatial cognition* (pp. 71–113). Hillsdale, NJ: Lawrence Erlbaum.

Pollack, R. H. (1969). Some implications of ontogenetic changes in perception. In D. Elkind & J. H. Flavell (Eds.), *Studies in cognitive development* (pp. 365–407). New York: Oxford University Press.

Poole, D. A., & Lindsay, D. S. (1995). Interviewing preschoolers: Effects of nonsuggestive techniques, parental coaching and leading questions on reports of nonexperienced events. *Journal of Experimental Child Psychology, 60,* 129–154.

Potegal, M. (Ed.). (1982). *Spatial abilities: Development and physiological foundations.* New York: Academic Press.

Potter, M. C. (1979). Mundane symbolism: The relations among objects, names, and ideas. In N. R. Smith & M. B. Franklin (Eds.), *Symbolic functioning in childhood* (pp. 41–65). Hillsdale, NJ: Erlbaum.

Poulin-Dubois, D. (1999). Infants' distinction between animate and inanimate objects: The origins of naïve psychology. In P. Rochat (Ed.), *Early social cognition: Understanding others in the first months of life* (pp. 257–280). Mahwah, NJ: Erlbaum.

Poulin-Dubois, D., Lepage, A., & Ferland, D. (1996). Infants' concept of animacy. *Cognitive Development, 11,* 19–36.

Povinelli, D. J. (1995). The unduplicated self. In P. Rochat (Ed.), *The self in infancy: Theory and research* (pp. 161–192). Amsterdam: Elsevier.

Povinelli, D. J., & Eddy, T. J. (1996). What young chimpanzees know about seeing. *Monographs of the Society for Research in Child Development, 61*(2) (Serial No. 247).

Povinelli, D. J., Landau, K. R., & Perilloux, H. K. (1996). Self-recognition in young children using delayed versus live feedback: Evidence for a developmental asynchrony. *Child Development, 67,* 1540–1554.

Povinelli, D. J., Landry, A. M., Theall, L. A., Clark, B. R., & Castille, C. M. (1999). Development of young children's understanding that the recent past is causally bound to the present. *Developmental Psychology, 35,* 1426–1439.

Povinelli, D. J., & Prince, C. G. (1998). When self and other met. In M. Ferrari & R. J. Sternberg (Eds.), *Self awareness: Its nature and development* (pp. 37–107). New York: Guilford.

Povinelli, D. J., & Simon, B. B. (1998). Young children's understanding of briefly versus extremely delayed images of the self: Emergence of the autobiographical stance. *Developmental Psychology, 34,* 188–194.

Pratt, C., & Bryant, P. E. (1990). Young children understand that looking leads to knowing (so long as they are looking into a single barrel). *Child Development, 61,* 973–982.

Premack, D. (1990). The infant's theory of self-propelled objects. *Cognition, 36,* 1–16.

Premack, D., & Premack, A. J. (1997). Infants attribute value+– to the goal-directed actions of self-propelled objects. *Journal of Cognitive Neuroscience, 9,* 848–856.

Pressley, M., Borkowski, J. G., & Schneider, W. (1989). Good information processing: What it is and how education can promote it. *Journal of Educational Research, 14,* 857–867.

Pressley, M., & Van Meter, P. (1993). Memory strategies: Natural development and use following instruction. In R. Pasnak & M. L. Howe (Eds.), *Emerging themes in cognitive development* (Vol. 2, pp. 128–165). New York: Springer.

Presson, C. C. (1982). The development of map-reading skills. *Child Development, 53,* 196–199.

Presson, C. C., & Somerville, S. C. (1985). Beyond egocentrism: A new look at the beginnings of spatial representation. In H. Wellman (Ed.), *Children's searching: The development of search skill and spatial representation* (pp. 1–26). Hillsdale, NJ: Lawrence Erlbaum.

Preyer, W. (1982). *Die Seele des Kindes* [The mind of the child]. Leipzig: Grieben.

Prinz, W. (1997). Perception and action planning. *European Journal of Cognitive Psychology, 9,* 129–154.

Prior, M. R. (1979). Cognitive abilities and disabilities in infantile autism: A review. *Journal of Abnormal Child Psychology, 7,* 357–380.

Pugh, G. E. (1977). *The biological origin of human values.* New York: Basic Books.

Quartz, S. R. (1993). Neural networks, nativism, and the plausibility of constructivism. *Cognition, 48,* 223–242.

Quartz, S. R., & Sejnowski, T. J. (1997). The neural basis of cognitive development: A constructivist manifesto. *Behavioral and Brain Sciences, 20*(4), 537–596.

Quinn, P. C. (1987). The categorical representation of visual pattern information by young infants. *Cognition, 27*, 145–179.

Quinn, P. C. (1998). Object and spatial categorization in young infants: "What" and "where" in early visual perception. In A. M. Slater (Ed.), *Perceptual development: Visual, auditory, and speech perception in infancy* (pp. 131–165). Hove, UK: Psychology Press.

Quinn, P. C. (1999). Development of recognition and categorization of objects and their spatial relations in young infants. In C. Tamis-LeMonda & L. Balter (Eds.), *Child psychology: A handbook of contemporary issues* (pp. 85–115). Philadelphia: Psychology Press (Taylor & Francis).

Quinn, P. C. (in press-a). Categorization. In M. Lewis & A. Slater (Eds.), *Infant development.* Oxford, UK: Oxford University Press.

Quinn, P. C. (in press-b). Development of spatial categorization in young infants. In D. H. Rakison & L. M. Oakes (Eds.), *Categories and concepts in early development.* Oxford, UK: Oxford University Press.

Quinn, P. C., & Bomba, P. C. (1986). Evidence for a general category of oblique orientations in 4-month-old infants. *Journal of Experimental Child Psychology, 42*, 345–354.

Quinn, P. C., & Eimas, P. D. (1986). On categorization in early infancy. *Merrill-Palmer Quarterly, 32*, 331–363.

Quinn, P. C., Eimas, P. D., & Rosenkrantz, S. L. (1993). Evidence for representations of perceptually similar natural categories by 3-month-old and 4-month-old infants. *Perception, 22*(4), 463–475.

Quinn, P. C., & Eimas, P. D. (1996). Perceptual organization and categorization in young infants. In C. Rovee-Collier & L. P. Lipsitt (Eds.), *Advances in infancy research* (Vol. 10, pp. 1–36). Norwood, NJ: Ablex.

Quinn, P. C., & Eimas, P. D. (1997). A reexamination of the perceptual to conceptual shift in mental representations. *Review of General Psychology, 1*, 271–287.

Quinn, P. C., & Eimas, P. D. (1998). Evidence for a global categorical representation for humans by young infants. *Journal of Experimental Child Psychology, 69*, 151–174.

Quinn, P. C., & Eimas, P. D. (2000). The emergence of category representations during infancy: Are separate perceptual and conceptual processes required? *Journal of Cognition and Development, 1*, 55–62.

Quinn, P. C., & Johnson, M. H. (1997). The emergence of perceptual category representations in young infants: A connectionist analysis. *Journal of Experimental Child Psychology, 66*, 236–263.

Quinn, P. C., & Johnson, M. H. (2000). Global-before-basic object categorization in connectionist networks and 2-month-old infants. *Infancy, 1*, 31–46.

Quinn, P. C., Johnson, M. H., Mareschal, D., Rakison, D. H., & Younger, B. A. (2000). Understanding early categorization: One process or two? *Infancy, 1*, 111–122.

Quinn, P. C., Slater, A. M., Brown, E., & Hayes, R. A. (2001). Developmental change in form categorization in early infancy. *British Journal of Developmental Psychology, 19*, 207–218.

Rack, J. P., Snowling, M. J., & Olson, R. K. (1992). The nonword reading deficit in developmental dyslexia: A review. *Reading Research Quarterly, 27*, 29–53.

Raijmakers, M. E. J., van Koten, S., & Molenaar, P. C. M. (1996). On the validity of simulating stagewise development by means of PDP networks: Application of catastrophe analysis and an experimental test of rule-like network performance. *Cognitive Science, 20*, 101–136.

Rakison, D. H., & Butterworth, G. E. (1998). Infants' use of object parts in early categorization. *Developmental Psychology, 34*, 49–62.

Rakison, D. H., & Poulin-Dubois, D. (in press). The developmental origin of the animate–inanimate distinction. *Psychological Bulletin.*

Ramey, C. T., & Ramey, S. L. (1998). Early intervention and early experience. *American Psychologist, 53*, 109–120.

Ramey, C. T., & Ramey, S. L. (2000). Intelligence and public policy. In R. J. Sternberg (Ed.), *Handbook of intelligence* (pp. 534–548). New York: Cambridge University Press.

Rapin, E. (1996). Practitioner review. Developmental language disorders: A clinical update. *Journal of Child Psychology and Psychiatry, 37*(6), 643–655.

Rapin, I., & Allen, D. (1983). Developmental language disorders: Nosologic considerations. In U. Kirk (Ed.), *Neuropsychology of language, reading, and spelling* (pp. 155–180). New York: Academic Press.

Rapin, I., & Allen, D. (1987). Developmental dysphasia and autism in preschool children: Characteristics and subtypes. In J. Martin, P. Martin, P. Fletcher, P. Grunwell, & D. Hall (Eds.), *Proceedings of the first international symposium on specific speech and language disorders in children* (pp. 20–35). London: AFASIC.

Raven, J., Raven, J. C., & Court, J. (1998). *Raven's progressive matrices.* Windsor: NFER-Nelson.

Read, C. (1971). Preschool children's knowledge of English phonology. *Harvard Educational Review, 41*, 1–34.

Read, C., Zhang, Y., Nie, H., & Ding, B. (1986). The ability to manipulate speech sounds depends on knowing alphabetic writing. *Cognition, 55*, 151–218.

Reed, M. (1989). Speech perception and the discrimination of brief auditory cues in reading disabled children. *Journal of Experimental Child Psychology, 48*, 270–292.

Reed, S. K., & Evans, A. C. (1987). Learning functional relations: A theoretical and instructional analysis. *Journal of Experimental Psychology: General, 116*, 106–118.

Reese, E., Haden, C. A., & Fivush, R. (1993). Mother–child conversations about the past: Relationships of style and memory over time. *Cognitive Development, 8*, 403–430.

Reese, E., Haden, C. A., & Fivush, R. (1996). Mothers, fathers, daughters, sons: Gender differences in autobiographical reminiscing. *Research on Language and Social Interaction, 29*, 27–56.

Reggia, J. A., Ruppin, E., & Berndt, R. S. (1996). *Neural modeling of brain and cognitive disorders.* London: World Scientific.

Regier, T., & Carlson, L. (in press). Grounding spatial language in perception: An empirical and computational investigation. *Journal of Experimental Psychology: General.*

Reilly, J.. Klima, E., & Bellugi, U. (1991). Once more with feeling: Affect and language in atypical populations. *Developmental and Psychopathology, 2*, 367–391.

Renfrew, C. E., & Geary, L. (1973). Prediction of persisting speech defect. *British Journal of Disorders of Communication, 8*, 37–47.

Renzulli, J. S. (1986). The three-ring conception of giftedness: A developmental model for creative productivity. In R. J. Sternberg & J. E. Davidson (Eds.), *Conceptions of giftedness* (pp. 53–92). New York: Cambridge University Press.

Repacholi, B. M., & Gopnik, A. (1997). Early reasoning about desires: Evidence from 14- and 18-month-olds. *Developmental Psychology, 33*, 12–21.

Resnick, L. V., Levine, J. M., & Teasley, S. D. (Eds.). (1991). *Perspectives on socially shared cognition.* Washington, DC: American Psychological Association.

Resnick, S. M., Berenbaum, S. A., Gottesman, I. I., & Bouchard, T. J. (1986). Early hormonal influences on cognitive functioning in congenial adrenal hyperplasia. *Developmental Psychology, 22*, 191–198.

Rest, J., Narvaez, D., Bebeau, M., & Thoma, S. (1999). *Postconventional moral thinking: A neo-Kohlbergian approach.* Mahwah, NJ: Erlbaum.

Reyna, V. F., & Brainerd, C. J. (1995). Fuzzy-trace theory: An interim synthesis. *Learning and Individual Differences, 7*, 1–75.

Reznick, J. S. (1989). Research on infant categorization. *Seminars in Perinatology, 13*, 458–466.

Reznick, J. S., & Kagan, J. (1983). Category detection in infancy. In L. P. Lipsitt (Ed.), *Advances in infancy research* (Vol. 2, pp. 79–111). Norwood, NJ: Ablex.

Ricard, M., & Allard, L. (1993). The reaction of 9- to 10-month-old infants to an unfamiliar animal. *Journal of Genetic Psychology, 154*, 5–16.

Riccuiti, H. N. (1965). Object grouping and selective ordering in infants 12 to 24 months. *Merrill-Palmer Quarterly, 11*, 129–148.

Rice, M., Wexler, K., & Cleave, P. (1995). Specific language impairment as a period of extended optimal infinitive. *Journal of Speech and Hearing Research, 38*, 850–863.

Richards, D. D. (1982). Children's time concepts: Going the distance. In W. J. Friedman (Ed.), *The developmental psychology of time* (pp. 13–45). New York: Academic Press.

Richards, D. D., & Siegler, R. S. (1984). The effects of task requirements on children's life judgments. *Child Development, 55*, 1687–1696.

Richardson, K. (1998). *Models of cognitive development.* Hove, UK: Psychology Press.

Ridderinkhof, K. R., & van der Molen, M. W. (1997). Mental resources, processing speed, and inhibitory control: A developmental perspective. *Biological Psychology, 45*, 241–261.

Rieser, J. J. (1990). Development of perceptual-motor control while walking without vision: The calibration of perception and action. In H. Bloch & B. I. Bertenthal (Eds.), *Sensory-motor organizations and development in infancy and early childhood* (pp. 379–408). Dordrecht, Netherlands: Kluwer Academic Publishers.

Rieser, J. J., Doxsey, P., McCarrell, N., & Brooks, P. (1982). Wayfinding and toddlers' use of information from an aerial view of a maze. *Developmental Psychology, 18*, 714–720.

Rivera, S. M., Wakeley, A., & Langer, J. (1999). The drawbridge phenomenon: Representational reasoning or perceptual preference? *Developmental Psychology, 35*, 427–435.

Rizzolatti, G., Fadiga, L., Matelli, M., Bettinardi, V., Paulesu, E., Perani, D., & Fasio, F. (1996). Localization of grasp representations in humans by PET: 1. Observation versus execution. *Experimental Brain Research, 111*, 246–252.

Robbins, T. W. (1996, September 6). Refining the taxonomy of memory. *Science, 273*, 1353–1354.

Robbins, T. W. (2000). Chemical neuromodulation of frontal-executive functions in humans and other animals. *Experimental Brain Research, 133*, 130–138.

Roberts, K. (1988). Retrieval of a basic-level category in prelinguistic infants. *Developmental Psychology, 24*, 21–27.

Roberts, K., & Cuff, M. D. (1989). Categorization studies of 9- to 15-month-old infants: Evidence for superordinate categorization? *Infant Behavior and Development, 12*, 265–288.

Roberts, R. J., & Pennington, B. F. (1996). An interactive framework for examining prefrontal cognitive processes. *Developmental Neuropsychology, 12*, 105–126.

Robin, N., & Holyoak, K. J. (1995). Relational complexity and the functions of prefrontal cortex. In M. S. Gazzaniga (Ed.), *The Cognitive Neurosciences* (pp. 987–997). Cambridge, MA: MIT Press.

Robinson, E. J., Nye, R., & Thomas, G. V. (1994). Children's conceptions of the relationship between pictures and their referents. *Cognitive Development, 9*, 165–191.

Rochat, P. (1992). Self-sitting and reaching in 5- to 8-month-old infants: The impact of posture and its development on early eye–hand coordination. *Journal of Motor Behavior, 24*, 210–220.

Rochat, P., & Morgan, R. (1995). Spatial determinants in the perception of self-produced leg movements in 3- to 5-month-old infants. *Developmental Psychology, 31*, 626–636.

Rochat, P., Morgan, R., & Carpenter, M. (1997). Young infants' sensitivity to movement information specifying social causality. *Cognitive Development, 12*, 537–561.

Rochat, P., Neisser, U., & Marian, V. (1998) Are young infants sensitive to interpersonal contingency? *Infant Behavior and Development, 21*(2), 355–366.

Roebers, C. M., & Schneider, W. (in press). The impact of misleading questions on eyewitness memory in children and adults. *Applied Cognitive Psychology.*

Roediger, H. L., & McDermott, K. B. (1993). Implicit memory in normal human subjects. In H. Spinnler & F. Boller (Eds.), *Handbook of neuropsychology* (Vol. 8, pp. 63–131). Amsterdam: Elsevier.

Roediger, H. L., Rajaram, S., & Srinivas, K. (1990). Specifying criteria for postulating memory systems. In A. Diamond (Ed.), *The development and neural basis of higher cognitive function: Annals of the New York Academy of Sciences* (Vol. 608, pp. 572–595). New York: New York Academy of Sciences.

Rogoff, B. (1981). Schooling and the development of cognitive skills. In H. C. Triandis & A. Heron (Eds.), *Handbook of cross-cultural psychology* (Vol. 4). Boston: Allyn & Bacon.

Rogoff, B. (1990). *Apprenticeship in thinking: Cognitive development in social context.* Cambridge: Cambridge University Press.

Rogoff, B. (1995). Observing sociocultural activity on three planes: Participatory appropriation, guided participation, and apprenticeship. In J. V. Wertsch, P. del Río, & A. Alvarez (Eds.), *Sociocultural studies of mind* (pp. 139–164). Cambridge: Cambridge University Press.

Rogoff, B. (1997). Evaluating development in the process of participation: Theory, methods, and practice building on each other. In E. Amsel & A. Renninger (Eds.), *Change and development* (pp. 265–285). Hillsdale, NJ: Erlbaum.

Rogoff, B., & Wertsch, J. V. (1984). Children's learning in the "zone of proximal development." In B. Rogoff and J. V. Wertsch (Eds.), *New directions for child development, 23.* San Francisco: Jossey-Bass.

Rolls, E. T., Hornak, J., Wade, D., & McGrath, J. (1994). Emotion-related learning in patients with social and emotional changes associated with frontal lobe damage. *Journal of Neurology, Neurosurgery & Psychiatry, 57,* 1518–1524.

Rondal, J. A. (1994a). Exceptional cases of language development in mental retardation: The relative autonomy of language as a cognitive system. In H. Tager-Flushberg (Ed.), *Constraints on language acquisition: Studies of atypical children* (pp. 155–174). Hillsdale, NJ: Erlbaum.

Rondal, J. A. (1994b). Exceptional cases of language development in mental retardation: Natural experiments in language modularity. *Cahiers de psychologie cognitive, 13,* 427–467.

Rondal, J. A., & Edwards, S. (1997). *Language in mental retardation.* London: Whurr.

Rondal, J. A., & Lambert, J. L. (1983). The speech of mentally retarded adults in a dyadic communication situation: Some formal and informative aspects. *Psychologica Belgica, 23,* 49–56.

Ronnqvist, L., & von Hofsen, C. (1994). Neonatal finger and arm movements as determined by a social and an object context. *Early Development and Parenting, 3,* 81–94.

Rosch, E. (1978). Principles of categorization. In E. Rosch & B. B. Lloyd (Eds.), *Cognition and categorization* (pp. 27–48). Hillsdale, NJ: Erlbaum.

Rosch, E., Mervis, C. B., Gray, W. D., Johnson, D. M., & Boyes-Braem, P. (1976). Basic objects in natural categories. *Cognitive Psychology, 8*(3), 382–439.

Rose, S. A., Gottfried, A. W., Melloy-Carminar, P., & Bridger, W. H. (1982). Familiarity and novelty preferences in infant recognition memory: Implications for information processing. *Developmental Psychology, 18,* 704–713.

Rosengren, K. S., Gelman, S. A., Kalish, C. W., & McCormick, M. (1991). As time goes by: Children's early understanding of growth in animals. *Child Development, 62,* 1302–1320.

Rossen, M., Klima, E. S., Bellugi, U., Bihrle, A., & Jones, W. (1996). Interaction between language and cognition: Evidence from Williams syndrome. In J. H. Beitchman, N. J. Cohen, M. M. Konstantareas, & R. Tannock, *Language learning and behaviour* (pp. 367–92). New York: Cambridge University Press.

Rovee-Collier, C. (1989). The joy of kicking: Memories, motives and mobiles. In P. R. Solomon, G. R. Goethals, C. M. Kelley, & B. R. Stephens (Eds.), *Memory: Interdisciplinary approaches.* New York: Springer.

Rovee-Collier, C. (1997). Dissociations in infant memory: Rethinking the development of implicit and explicit memory. *Psychological Review, 104*, 467–498.

Rovee-Collier, C., & Gerhardstein, P. (1997). The development of infant memory. In N. Cowan (Ed.), *The development of memory in childhood* (pp. 5–39). Hove, UK: Psychology Press.

Rovee-Collier, C., Schechter, A., Shyi, G., & Shields, P. (1992). Perceptual identification of contextual attributes and infant memory retrieval. *Developmental Psychology, 28*, 307–318.

Rovee-Collier, C., Sullivan, M. W., Enright, M. K., Lucas, D., & Fagen, J. W. (1980). Reactivation of infant memory. *Science, 208*, 1159–1161.

Rubia, K., Overmeyer, S., Taylor, E., Brammer, M., Williams, S. C., Simmons, A., Andrew, C., & Bullmore, E. T. (2000). Functional frontalisation with age: Mapping neurodevelopmental trajectories with fMRI. *Neuroscience and Biobehavioral Reviews, 24*, 13–19.

Rubin, D. C. (1982). On the retention function for autobiographical memory. *Journal of Verbal Learning and Verbal Behavior, 21*, 21–38.

Rubin, K. H., Fein, G. G., & Vandenberg, B. (1983). Play. In E. M. Hetherington (Ed.), *Handbook of child psychology: Socialization, personality, and social development.* (4th ed., Vol. 4, pp. 693–774). New York: Wiley.

Rubinstein, S. L. (1973). Das Gedächtnis [Memory]. In S. L. Rubinstein (Ed.), *Grundlagen der Allgemeinen Psychologie* (pp. 359–409). Berlin: Volk und Wissen.

Ruffman, T., Perner, J., Naito, M., Parkin, L., & Clements, W. (1998). Older (but not younger) siblings facilitate false belief understanding. *Developmental Psychology, 34*, 161–174.

Ruffman, T., Perner, J., Olson, D., & Doherty, M. (1993). Reflecting on scientific thinking: Children's understanding of the hypothesis–evidence relation. *Child Development, 64*, 1617–1636.

Ruffman, T., Perner, J., & Parkin, L. (1999). How parenting style affects false belief understanding. *Social Development, 8*, 395–411.

Rumelhart, D. E., Hinton, G. E., & Williams, R. J. (1986). Learning internal representations by error propagation. In D. E. Rumelhart & J. L. McClelland (Eds.), *Parallel distributed processing: Explorations in the microstructure of cognition: Vol. 1. Foundations* (pp. 318–362). Cambridge, MA: MIT Press.

Rumelhart, D. E., & McClelland, J. L. (1986a). *Parallel distributed processing, Vol. 1.* Cambridge, MA: MIT Press.

Rumelhart, D. E., & McClelland, J. L. (1986b). On learning the past tense of English verbs. In J. L. McClelland, D. E. Rumelhart, & the PDP Research Group, *Parallel distributed processing: Explorations in the microstructure of cognition: Vol. 2. Psychological and biological models* (pp. 216–271). Cambridge, MA: MIT Press.

Rumelhart, D. E., & Todd, P. M. (1993). Learning and connectionist representations. *Attention and performance XIV: Synergies in experimental psychology, artificial intelligence, and cognitive neuroscience* (pp. 3–30). Cambridge, MA: MIT Press.

Russell, B. (1948). *Human knowledge: Its scope and limits.* New York: Simon & Schuster.

Russell, B. (1964). *The principles of mathematics* (2nd ed.). London: George Allen & Unwin.

Russell, J. (1996). *Agency: its role in mental development.* Lawrence Erlbaum, Howe.

Russell, J. (Ed.). (1997a). *Autism as an executive disorder.* Oxford, UK: Oxford University Press.

Russell, J. (1997b). How executive disorders can bring about an inadequate theory of mind. In J. Russell (Ed.), *Autism as an executive disorder.* Oxford, UK: Oxford University Press.

Russell, J., Mauthner, N., Sharpe, S., & Tidswell, T. (1991). The "windows task" as a measure of strategic deception in preschoolers and autistic subjects. *British Journal of Developmental Psychology, 9*, 331–349.

Russell, M. J. (1976). Human olfactory communication. *Nature, 260*, 520–522.

Rutter, M. (1978). Language disorder and infantile autism. In M. Rutter & E. Schopler (Eds.), *Autism: A reappraisal of concepts and treatment.* New York: Plenum.

Ryle, G. (1949). *The concept of mind.* Chicago: University of Chicago Press.

Saah, M. I., Waxman, S. R., & Johnson, J. (1996). The composition of children's early lexicons as a function of age and vocabulary size. Paper presented at the 21st Boston University Conference on Language Development, Boston, MA.

Sacks, O. (1985). *The man who mistook his wife for a hat and other clinical tales.* New York: Summit.

Salomon, G. (Ed.). (1993). *Distributed cognitions: Psychological and educational implications.* Cambridge: Cambridge University Press.

Salovey, P., & Mayer, J. D. (1990). Emotional intelligence. *Imagination, Cognition, and Personality, 9,* 185–211.

Salthouse, T. A. (1996). The processing-speed theory of adult age differences in cognition. *Psychological Review, 103*(3), 403–428.

Samarapungavan, A. (1992). Children's judgments in theory choice tasks: Scientific rationality in childhood. *Cognition, 45,* 1–32.

Samuels, A., & Taylor, M. (1994). Children's ability to distinguish fantasy events from real-life events. *British Journal of Developmental Psychology, 12,* 417–427.

Sander, L. W. (1970). Regulation and organization of behavior in the early infant-caretaker system. In: R. Robinson (Ed.), *Brain and early behavior.* London: Academic Press.

Sapir, E. (1921). *Language: An introduction to the study of speech.* New York: Harcourt, Brace.

Savage, P. (1982). Symbol–word correspondence learning and symbol–sound correspondence knowledge in normal and disabled readers. Unpublished doctoral dissertation. University of Minnesota, MN.

Savage, R. S. (1997). Do children need concurrent prompts in order to use lexical analogies in reading? *Journal of Child Psychology and Psychiatry, 38,* 235–246.

Saxe, G. (1979) A developmental analysis of notational counting. *Child Development, 48,* 1512–1520.

Scaife, M., & Bruner, J. (1975). The capacity for joint visual attention in the infant. *Nature, 253,* 265–266.

Scarborough, H. S. (1990). Very early language deficits in dyslexic children. *Child Development, 61,* 1728–1743.

Scarlett, W. G., & Wolf, D. (1979). When it's only make-believe: The construction of a boundary between fantasy and reality. In E. Winner & H. Gardner (Eds.), *Fact, fiction, and fantasy in childhood* (Vol. 6, pp. 29–40). San Francisco: Jossey-Bass.

Scarr, S., & Weinberg, R. A. (1976). IQ test performance of black children adopted by white families. *American Psychologist, 31,* 726–739.

Scarr, S., Weinberg, R. A., & Waldman, L. D. (1993). IQ correlations in transracial adoptive families. *Intelligence, 17,* 541–545.

Schacter, D. L. (1992). Understanding implicit memory: A cognitive neuroscience perspective. *American Psychologist, 47,* 559–569.

Schacter, D. L., & Moscovitch, M. (1984). Infants, amnesics, and dissociable memory systems. In M. Moscovitch (Ed.), *Infant memory: Its relation to normal and pathological memory in humans and other animals* (pp. 173–216). New York: Plenum.

Schafer, G., & Mareschal, D. (in press). Qualitative shifts in behavior without qualitative shifts in processing: The case of speech sound discrimination and word learning in infancy. *Infancy, 2.*

Schank, R. C., & Abelson, R. P. (1977). *Scripts, plans, goals and understanding.* Hillsdale, NJ: Lawrence Erlbaum.

Schauble, L. (1990). Belief revision in children: The role of prior knowledge and strategies for generating evidence. *Journal of Experimental Child Psychology, 49,* 31–57.

Schauble, L. (1996). The development of scientific reasoning in knowledge-rich contexts. *Developmental Psychology, 32,* 102–119.

Scheibel, R. S., & Levin, H. S. (1997). Frontal lobe dysfunction following closed head injury in children. In N. A. Krasnegor, G. R. Lyon, & P. S. Goldman-Rakic (Eds.), *Development of the prefrontal cortex: Evolution, neurobiology, and behavior* (pp. 241–263). Baltimore, MD: Paul Brookes Publishing Co.

Schlagmüller, M. (2000). Mikrogenetische Studie zur Entwicklung einer Organisationsstrategie im Grundschulalter [Microgenetic study on the development of organizational strategies]. Unpublished doctoral dissertation, University of Würzburg.

Schliemann, A. D., & Magalhües, V. P. (1990). Proportional reasoning: From shops, to kitchens, laboratories, and, hopefully, schools. In proceedings of the fourteenth international conference for the psychology of mathematics education, Oaxtepec, Mexico.

Schlottmann, A. (1999). Seeing it happen and knowing how it works: How children understand the relation between perceptual causality and underlying mechanism. *Developmental Psychology, 35,* 303–317.

Schmitt, K. L. (1997). Two- to three-year-olds' understanding of the correspondence between television and reality. Unpublished doctoral dissertation, University of Massachusetts, Amherst.

Schmuckler, M. A. (1996). Visual-proprioceptive intermodal perception in infancy. *Infant Behavior and Development, 19,* 221–232.

Schneider, W. (1998). The development of procedural metamemory in childhood and adolescence. In G. Mazzoni & T. O. Nelson (Eds.), *Monitoring and control processes in metacognition and cognitive neuropsychology* (pp. 1–21). Mahwah, NJ: Erlbaum.

Schneider, W. (1999). The development of metamemory in children. In D. Gopher & A. Koriat (Eds.), *Attention and performance XVII: Cognitive regulation of performance: interaction of theory and application* (pp. 487–514). Cambridge, MA: MIT Press.

Schneider, W. (2001). Giftedness, expertise and (exceptional) performance. In K. A. Heller, F. J. Mönks, R. J. Sternberg, & R. F. Subotnik (Eds.), *International handbook of giftedness and talent* (2nd ed., pp. 165–177). New York: Elsevier.

Schneider, W., & Bjorklund, D. F. (1998). Memory. In W. Damon (Series Ed.), D. Kuhn & R. S. Siegler (Vol. Eds.), *Handbook of child psychology: Vol 2. Cognition, perception, and language* (5th ed.). New York: Wiley.

Schneider, W., & Detweiler, M. (1987). A connectionist/control architecture for working memory. *The Psychology of Learning and Motivation, 21,* 53–119.

Schneider, W., Gruber, H., Gold, A., & Opwis, K. (1993). Chess expertise and memory for chess positions in children and adults. *Journal of Experimental Child Psychology, 56,* 328–349.

Schneider, W., & Lockl, K. (in press). The development of metacognitive knowledge in children and adolescents. In T. Perfect & B. Schwartz (Eds.), *Applied metacognition.* Cambridge, UK: Cambridge University Press.

Schneider, W., & Pressley, M. (1989). *Memory development between 2 and 20.* New York: Springer.

Schneider, W., & Pressley, M. (1997). *Memory development between 2 and 20* (2nd ed.). Mahwah, NJ: Erlbaum.

Schneider, W., Schlagmüller, M., & Visé, M. (1998). The impact of metamemory and domain-specific knowledge on memory performance. *European Journal of Psychology of Education, 13,* 91–103.

Schneider, W., & Sodian, B. (1997). Memory strategy development: Lessons from longitudinal research. *Developmental Review, 17,* 442–461.

Schneider, W., & Weinert, F. E. (1995). Memory development during early and middle childhood: Findings from the Munich Longitudinal Study (LOGIC). In W. Schneider & F. E. Weinert (Eds.), *Memory performance and competencies. Issues in growth and development* (pp. 263–279). Mahwah, NJ: Erlbaum.

Scholnick, E. (1999). Piaget's legacy: Heirs to the house that Jean built. In E. Scholnick, K. Nelson, S. Gelman, & P. Miller (Eds.), *Conceptual development: Piaget's legacy*. Mahwah, NJ: Erlbaum.

Schubert, R. E. (1983). The infant's search for objects: Alternatives to Piaget's theory of concept development. In L. P. Lipsitt & C. K. Rovee-Collier (Eds.), *Advances in infancy research* (Vol. 2, pp. 137–182). Norwood, NJ: Ablex.

Schult, C. A., & Wellman, H. M. (1997). Explaining human movements and actions: Children's understanding of the limits of psychological explanation. *Cognition, 62*, 291–324.

Schumann-Hengsteler, R. (1992). The development of visuo-spatial memory: How to remember location. *International Journal of Behavioral Development, 15*, 445–471.

Schumann-Hengsteler, R. (1995). *Die Entwicklung des visuo-räumlichen Gedächtnisses* [Development of visuo-spatial memory]. Göttingen: Hogrefe.

Schumann-Hengsteler, R. (1996). Children's and adults' visuo-spatial memory: The game Concentration. *Journal of Genetic Psychology, 157*, 77–92.

Schwartz, R. G. (1980). Presuppositions and children's metalinguistic judgments: Concepts of life and the awareness of animacy restrictions. *Child Development, 51*, 364–371.

Schwartz, S. P. (Ed.). (1977). *Naming, necessity, and natural kinds*. Ithaca, NY: Cornell University Press.

Schwartzman, H. B. (1978). *Transformations: The anthropology of children's play*. New York: Plenum.

Schwebel, D. C., Rosen, C. S., & Singer, J. L. (1999). Preschoolers' pretend play and theory of mind: The role of jointly constructed pretence. *British Journal of Developmental Psychology, 17*, 333–348.

Schyns, P. G. (1991). A modular neural network of concept acquisition. *Cognitive Science, 15*, 461–508.

Schyns, P. G., Goldstone, R. L., & Thibaut, J. P. (1998). The development of features in object concepts. *Behavioral and Brain Sciences, 21*, 1–54.

Scollon, R. (1998). *Mediated discourse as social interaction: A study of news discourse*. London: Longman.

Scott, F. J., Baron-Cohen, S., & Leslie, A. (1999). "If pigs could fly": A test of counterfactual reasoning and pretence in children with autism. *British Journal of Developmental Psychology, 17*, 349–362.

Scribner, S. (1977). Modes of thinking and ways of speaking. In P. N. Johnson-Laird & P. C. Watson (Eds.), *Thinking: Readings in cognitive science* (pp. 483–500). Cambridge, UK: Cambridge University Press.

Scribner, S., & Cole, M. (1981). *The psychology of literacy*. Cambridge, MA: Harvard University Press.

Searle, J. R. (1969). *Speech acts*. London: Cambridge University Press.

Searle, J. R. (1983). *Intentionality: An essay in the philosophy of mind*. New York: Cambridge University Press.

Seidenberg, M. S., & McClelland, J. L. (1989). A distributed, developmental model of word recognition and naming. *Psychological Review, 96*, 523–568.

Semel, E., Wiig, E., & Secord. W. (1995). *Clinical evaluation of Language Fundamentals-3 UK*. London: Psychological Corporation.

Semrud-Clikeman, M., Steingard, R. J., Filipek, P., Biederman, J., Bekken, K., & Renshaw, P. F. (2000). Using MRI to examine brain–behavior relationships in males with attention deficit disorder with hyperactivity. *Journal of the American Child and Adolescent Psychiatry, 39*, 477–484.

Serbin, L. A., & Connor, J. M. (1979). Sex-typing of children's play preferences and patterns of cognitive performance. *Journal of Genetic Psychology, 134*, 315–316.

Serbin, L. A., Zelkowitz, P., Doyle, A.-B., Gold, D., & Wheaton, B. (1990). The socialization of sex-differentiated skills and academic performance: A mediational model. *Sex Roles, 23,* 613–628.

Seymour, P. H. K. (1990). Developmental dyslexia. In M. W. Eysenck (Ed.), *Cognitive Psychology: An International Review* (pp. 135–195). Chichester: John Wiley & Sons.

Seymour, P. H. K., & Elder, L. (1986). Beginning reading without phonology. *Cognitive Neuropsychology, 1,* 43–82.

Shah, A., & Frith, U. (1983). An islet of ability in autism: A research note. *Journal of Child Psychology and Psychiatry, 24,* 613–620.

Shah, A., & Frith, U. (1993). Why do autistic individuals show superior performance on the block design test? *Journal of Child Psychology and Psychiatry, 34,* 1351–1364.

Shallice, T. (1982). Specific impairments of planning. In D. E. Broadbent & L. Weiskrantz (Eds.), *The neuropsychology of cognitive function* (pp. 199–209). London: The Royal Society.

Shallice, T., & Burgess, P. W. (1991). Deficits in strategy application following frontal lobe damage in man. *Brain, 111,* 727–741.

Share, D. L. (1995). Phonological recoding and self-teaching: Sine qua non of reading acquisition. *Cognition, 55,* 151–218.

Share, D. L. (1999) Phonological recoding and orthographic learning: a direct test of the self-teaching hypothesis. *Journal of Experimental Child Psychology, 72,* 95–129.

Share, D. L., Jorm, A. F., Maclean, R., & Matthews, R. (1984). Sources of individual differences in reading acquisition. *Journal of Educational Psychology, 76,* 1309–1324.

Sharon, T. (1999, October). Avenues into symbolic understanding: The role of intentionality. Paper presented at the meeting of the Cognitive Development Society, Chapel Hill, NC.

Sharon, T., & DeLoache, J. S. (2000). The role of perseveration in the symbolic object retrieval task. Manuscript under review.

Sharon, T., & DeLoache, J. S. (2001a). The role of intentionality in young children's performance in the symbolic object retrieval task. Research in progress.

Sharon, T., & DeLoache, J. S. (2001b). Young children's sensitivity to intentionality in the symbolic object retrieval task. Research in progress.

Sharp, K. C., Candy-Gibbs, S., Barlow-Elliot, L., & Petrun, C. J. (1985). Children's judgment and reasoning about aliveness: Effects of object, age, and cultural/social background. *Merrill-Palmer Quarterly, 31,* 47–65.

Shastri, L., & Ajjanagadde, V. (1993). From simple associations to systematic reasoning: A connectionist representation of rules, variables, and dynamic bindings using temporal synchrony. *Behavioral and Brain Sciences, 16*(3), 417–494.

Shatz, M., Wellman, H. M., & Silber, S. (1983). The acquisition of mental verbs: A systematic investigation of first references to mental state. *Cognition, 14,* 301–321.

Shayer, M., Demetriou. A., Pervez, M. (1988). The structure and scaling of concrete operational thought: Three studies in four countries. *Genetic, Social and General Psychology Monographs, 114,* 309–375.

Sheffield, E. G., & Hudson, J. A. (1994). Reactivation of toddlers' event memory. *Memory, 2,* 447–465.

Sheingold, K., & Tenney, Y. J. (1982). Memory for a salient childhood event. In U. Neisser (Ed.), *Memory observed* (pp. 201–212). San Francisco: Freeman.

Shemyakin, F. N. (1962). General problems of orientation in space and space representations. In B. G. Anan'yev et al. (Eds.), *Psychological science in the U.S.S.R.* (Vol. 1, pp. 186–255). NTIS Report TT62–11083. Washington, DC: Office of Technical Services.

Shepard, R. N., Hovland, C. I., & Jenkins, H. M. (1961). Learning and memorization of classifications. *Psychological Monographs, 75*(13) (Whole No. 517), 42.

Sherman, T. (1985). Categorization skills in infants. *Child Development, 56,* 1561–1573.

Shi, R., Werker, J. F., & Morgan, J. L. (1999). Newborn infants' sensitivity to perceptual cues to lexical and grammatical words. *Cognition, 72*(2), B11–B21.

Shields, J. (1962). *Monozygotic twins brought up apart and brought up together.* London: Oxford University Press.

Shimamura, A. P., Janowsky, J. S., & Squire, L. R. (1991). What is the role of frontal lobe damage in memory disorders? In H. D. Levin, H. M. Eisenberg, & A. L. Benton (Eds.), *Frontal lobe functioning and dysfunction* (pp. 173–195). New York: Oxford University Press.

Shue, K. L., & Douglas V. I. (1992). Attention deficit hyperactivity disorder and the frontal lobe syndrome. *Brain & Cognition, 20,* 104–124.

Shultz, T. R. (1982). *Rules of causal attribution.* Monographs of the Society for Research in Child Development, *47*(1) – serial no. 194. Chicago: University of Chicago Press.

Shultz, T. R. (1998). A computational analysis of conservation. *Developmental Science, 1,* 103–126.

Shultz, T. R., Buckingham, D., & Oshima-Takane, Y. (1994). A connectionist model of the learning of personal pronouns in English. In S. J. Hanson, T. Petsche, M. Kearns, & R. L. Rivest (Eds.), *Computational learning theory and natural learning systems: Intersection between theory and experiment* (Vol. 2, pp. 347–362). Cambridge, MA: MIT Press.

Shultz, T. R., Mareschal, D., & Schmidt, W. C. (1994). Modeling cognitive development on balance scale phenomena. *Machine Learning, 16,* 57–86.

Shultz, T. R., & Mendelson, R. (1975). The use of covariation as a principle of causal analysis. *Child Development, 46,* 394–399.

Shweder, R. A. (1990a). In defense of moral realism: Reply to Gabennesch. *Child Development, 61,* 2060–2067.

Shweder, R. A. (1990b). Cultural psychology: What is it? In J. W. Stigler, R. A. Shweder, & B. Herdt (Eds.), *Cultural psychology: Essays on comparative human development.* New York: Cambridge University Press.

Shweder, R. A., Mahapatra, M., & Miller, J. (1987). Culture and moral development. In J. Kagan & S. Lamb (Eds.), *The emergence of morality in young children.* Chicago: University of Chicago Press.

Sieg, K. G., Gaffney, G. R., Preston, D. F., & Hellings, J. A. (1995). SPECT brain imaging anomalies in attention deficit hyperactivity disorder. *Clinical Nuclear Medicine, 20,* 55–60.

Siegal, M., & Beattie, K. (1991). Where to look first for children's understanding of false beliefs. *Cognition, 38,* 1–12.

Siegal, M., & Petersen, C. (1999). *Children's understanding of biology and health.* Cambridge, UK: Cambridge University Press.

Siegel, A. W. (1981). The externalization of cognitive maps by children and adults: In search of ways to ask better questions. In L. S. Liben, A. H. Patterson, & N. Newcombe (Eds.), *Spatial representation and behavior across the life span: Theory and application* (pp. 167–191). New York: Academic Press.

Siegel, A. W., & Schadler, M. (1977). Young children's cognitive maps of their classroom. *Child Development, 48,* 388–394.

Siegel, A. W., & White, S. H. (1975). The development of spatial representations of large-scale environments. In H. W. Reese (Ed.), *Advances in Child Development and Behavior* (Vol. 10, pp. 9–55). New York: Academic Press.

Siegel, L. S., McCabe, A. E., Brand, J., & Matthews, J. (1978). Evidence for the understanding of class inclusion in preschool children: Linguistic factors and training effects. *Child Development, 49,* 688–693.

Siegler, R. S. (1975). Defining the locus of developmental differences in children's causal reasoning. *Journal of Experimental Child Psychology, 20,* 512–525.

Siegler, R. S. (1976). Three aspects of cognitive development. *Cognitive Psychology, 8*, 481–520.

Siegler, R. S. (1978). The origins of scientific reasoning. In R. S. Siegler (Ed.), *Children's thinking: What develops?* (pp. 109–149). Hillsdale, NJ: Erlbaum.

Siegler, R. S. (1981). *Developmental sequences within and between concepts.* Monographs of the Society for Research in Child Development, *46*(1) – serial no. 189.

Siegler, R. S. (1995). Children's thinking: How does change occur? In F. E. Weinert & W. Schneider (Eds.), *Memory performance and competencies: Issues in growth and development* (pp. 405–430). Mahwah, NJ: Erlbaum.

Siegler, R. S. (1996). *Emerging minds: The process of change in children's thinking.* New York: Oxford University Press.

Siegler, R. S. (1998). *Children's thinking* (3rd ed.). Upper Saddle River, NJ: Prentice Hall.

Siegler, R. S. (1999). Strategic development. *Trends in Cognitive Science, 3*(11), 430–435.

Siegler, R. S., & Chen, Z. (1998). Developmental differences in rule learning: A microgenetic analysis. *Cognitive Psychology, 36*(3), 273–310.

Siegler, R. S., & Crowley, K. (1991). The microgenetic method: A direct means for studying cognitive development. *American Psychologist, 46*, 606–620.

Siegler, R. S., & Jenkins, E. A. (1989). *How children discover new strategies.* Hillsdale, NJ: Lawrence Erlbaum Associates.

Siegler, R. S., & Liebert, R. M. (1974). Effects of contiguity, regularity, and age on children's causal inferences. *Developmental Psychology, 10*, 574–579.

Siegler, R. S., & Richards, D. D. (1979). Development of time, speed, and distance concepts. *Developmental Psychology, 15*, 288–298.

Siegler, R. S., & Shipley, C. (1995). Variation, selection, and cognitive change. In T. Simon & G. S. Halford (Eds.), *Developing cognitive competence: New approaches to process modeling* (pp. 31–76). Hillsdale, NJ: Erlbaum.

Siegler, R. S., & Shrager, J. (1984). *Strategy choices in addition and subtraction: How do children know what to do?* Hillsdale, NJ: Erlbaum.

Siegler, R. S., & Stern, E. (1998) Conscious and unconscious strategy discoveries: a microgenetic analysis. *Journal of Experimental Psychology – General, 127*, 377–397.

Sigel, I. E. (1953). Developmental trends in the abstraction ability of children. *Child Development, 24*, 131–144.

Sigel, I. E. (1970). The distancing hypothesis: A causal hypothesis for the acquisition of representational thought. In M. R. Jones (Ed.), *Miami Symposium on the prediction of behavior, 1968: Effect of early experiences* (pp. 99–118). Coral Gables, FL: University of Miami Press.

Sigel, I. E. (1978). The development of pictorial comprehension. In B. S. Randhawa & W. E. Coffman (Eds.), *Visual learning, thinking, and communication* (pp. 93–111). New York: Academic Press.

Signorella, M. L., Jamison, W., & Krupa, M. H. (1989). Predicting spatial performance from gender stereotyping in activity preferences and in self-concept. *Developmental Psychology, 25*, 89–95.

Silverman, I., & Eals, M. (1992). Sex differences in spatial abilities: Evolutionary theory and data. In J. H. Barkow, L. Cosmides, & J. Tooby (Eds.), *The adapted mind* (pp. 543–549). New York: Oxford University Press.

Simon, T., & Klahr, D. (1995). A computational theory of children's learning about number conservation. In T. Simon & G. S. Halford (Eds.), *Developing cognitive competence: New approaches to process modeling* (pp. pp. 315–353). Hillsdale, NJ: Erlbaum.

Simonoff, E., Bolton, P., & Rutter, M. (1998). Genetic perspectives on mental retardation. In J. A. Burack, R. M. Hodapp, & E. Zigler (Eds.), *Handbook of mental retardation and development* (pp. 41–79). Cambridge, UK: Cambridge University Press.

Simons, D. J., & Keil, F. C. (1995). An abstract to concrete shift in the development of biological thought: The "insides" story. *Cognition, 56*, 129–163.

Sirois, S., & Shultz, T. R. (1998). Neural network modelling of developmental effects in discrimination shifts. *Journal of Experimental Child Psychology, 71*, 235–274.

Sitskoorn, S. M., & Smitsman, A. W. (1995). Infants' perception of dynamic relations between objects: Passing through or support? *Developmental Psychology, 31*, 437–447.

Skinner, B. F. (1953). *Science and human behavior.* New York: Macmillan.

Skinner, B. F. (1983). *A matter of consequences.* New York: Alfred A. Knopf.

Slater, A. (1995). Visual perception and memory at birth. In C. Rovee-Collier & L. P. Lipsitt (Eds.), *Advances in infancy research* (Vol. 9, pp. 107–162). Norwood, NJ: Ablex.

Slater, A. M., Mattock, A., & Brown, E. (1990). Size constancy at birth: Newborn infants' responses to retinal and real size. *Journal of Experimental Child Psychology, 49*, 314–322.

Slater, A. M., Mattock, A., Brown, E., & Bremner, J. G. (1991). Form perception at birth: Cohen & Younger (1984) revisited. *Journal of Experimental Child Psychology, 51*, 395–406.

Slater, A. M., & Morrison, V. (1985). Shape constancy and slant perception at birth. *Perception, 14*, 337–344.

Slaughter, V. (1998). Children's understanding of pictorial and mental representations. *Child Development, 69*, 321–332.

Slaughter, V., Jaakkola, K., & Carey, S. (1999). Constructing a coherent theory: Children's biological understanding of life and death. In M. Siegal & C. Petersen (Eds.), *Children's understanding of biology and health.* Cambridge, UK: Cambridge University Press.

Smedslund, J. (1961). The acquisition of conservation of substance and weight in children: III. Extinction of conservation acquired "normally" and by means of empirical controls on a balance scale. *Scandinavian Journal of Psychology, 2*, 85–87.

Smeets, P. M. (1973). The animism controversy revisited: A probability analysis. *Journal of Genetic Psychology, 123*, 219–225.

Smetana, J. G. (1995). Conflict and coordination in adolescent–parent relationships. In S. Shulman (Ed.). *Close relationships and socioemotional development* (pp. 155–184). Norwood, NJ: Ablex.

Smetana, J., & Braeges, J. L. (1990). The development of toddlers' moral and conventional judgements. *Merrill-Palmer Quarterly, 36*, 329–346.

Smolucha, L., & Smolucha, F. (1998). The social origins of mind: Post-Piagetian perspectives on pretend play. In O. N. S. B. Saracho (Ed.), *Multiple perspectives on play in early childhood education* (pp. 34–58). SUNY series *Early childhood education: Inquiries and insights.* Albany, NY: State University of New York Press.

Smirnov, A. A. (1973). *Problems of the psychology of memory.* New York: Plenum Press.

Smith, C., Carey, S., & Wiser, M. (1985). On differentiation: A case study of the development of the concepts of size, weight, and density, *Cognition, 21*, 177–237.

Smith, C., Maclin, D., Houghton, C., & Hennessey, M. G. (2000). Sixth-grade students' epistemologies of science: The impact of school science experiences on epistemological development. *Cognition and Instruction, 18*, 349–422.

Smith, C., Snir, J., & Grosslight, L. (1992). Using Conceptual Models to facilitate conceptual change: The case of weight–density differentiation. *Cognition and Instruction, 9*, 221–283.

Smith, E. E., & Medin, D. L. (1981). *Categories and concepts.* Cambridge, MA: Harvard University Press.

Smith, L. (1993). *Necessary knowledge.* Hove, UK: Erlbaum Associates.

Smith, L. (1997a). Necessary knowledge and its assessment in intellectual development. In L. Smith, J. Dockrell, & P. Tomlinson (Eds.), *Piaget, Vygotsky, and beyond.* London: Routledge.

Smith, L. (1997b). Jean Piaget. In N. Sheehy, A. Chapman, & W. Conroy (Eds.) *Biographical dictionary of psychology*. London: Routledge.

Smith, L. (1998). On the development of mental representation. *Developmental Review, 18,* 202–227.

Smith, L. (1999a). What Piaget learned from Frege. *Developmental Review, 19,* 133–53.

Smith, L. (1999b). Epistemological principles for developmental psychology in Frege and Piaget. *New Ideas in Psychology, 17,* 83–117.

Smith, L. (1999c). Eight good questions for developmental epistemology and psychology. *New Ideas in Psychology, 17,* 137–147.

Smith, L. (1999d). Necessary knowledge in number conservation. *Developmental Science, 2,* 23–27.

Smith, L. (1999e). Representation and knowledge are not the same thing. *Behavioural and Brain Sciences, 22,* 784–785.

Smith, L. (in press). *Reasoning by mathematical induction in children's arithmetic.*

Smith, L. B. (1999). Children's noun learning: How general learning processes make specialized learning mechanisms. In B. MacWhinney (Ed.), *The emergence of language* (pp. 277–303). Mahwah, NJ: Lawrence Erlbaum.

Smith, L. B., & Heise, D. (1992). Perceptual similarity and conceptual structure. In B. Burns (Ed.), *Percepts, concepts and categories: The representation and processing of information. Advances in psychology* (Vol. 93, pp. 233–272). New York and Amsterdam: North Holland.

Smith, L. B., Gasser, M., & Sandhofer, C. M. (n.d.). Learning to talk about the properties of objects: A network model of the development of dimensions. Unpublished manuscript.

Smith, L. B., Jones, S. S., & Landau, B. (1992). Count nouns, adjectives, and perceptual properties in children's novel word interpretations. *Developmental Psychology, 28*(2), 273–286.

Smith, N. V., & Tsimpli, I. M. (1995). *The mind of a savant: Language learning and modularity.* Oxford, UK: Blackwell.

Smith, P. K. (1988). Children's play and its role in early development: A re-evaluation of the "play ethos." In A. D. Pellegrini (Ed.), *Psychological bases for early education.* New York: John Wiley.

Smolensky, P. (1988). On the proper treatment of connectionism. *Behavioral and Brain Sciences, 11*(1), 1–74.

Snarey, J. (1985). Cross-cultural universality of social-moral development: A critical review of Kohlbergian research. *Psychological Bulletin, 97,* 202–232.

Snedeker, J., & Gleitman, L. (1999). Knowing what you know: Metacognitive monitoring and the origin of the object category bias. Paper presented at the 24th annual Boston University Conference on Language Development, Somerville, MA.

Snowling, M. J. (1987). *Dyslexia: A cognitive developmental perspective.* Oxford, UK: Blackwell.

Snowling, M. J. (1998). Reading development and its difficulties. *Educational and Child Psychology, 15*(2), 44–58.

Snowling, M. J., Bishop, D. V. M., & Stothard, S. E. (2000). Is pre-school language impairment a risk factor for dyslexia in adolescence? *Journal of Child Psychology and Psychiatry, 41,* 587–600.

Snowling, M. J., Goulandris, N., Bowlby, M., & Howell, P. (1986). Segmentation and speech perception in relation to reading skill: A developmental analysis. *Journal of Experimental Child Psychology, 41,* 489–507.

Snowling, M. J., & Hulme, C. (1994). The development of phonological skills. *Philosophical Transactions of the Royal Society B, 346,* 21–28.

Snowling, M. J., Nation, K., Moxham, P., Gallagher, A., & Frith, U. (1997). Phonological processing deficits in dyslexic students: A preliminary account. *Journal of Research in Reading, 20,* 31–34.

Sodian, B. (1994). Early deception and the conceptual continuity claim. In C. Lewis & P. Mitchell (Eds.), *Children's early understanding of mind.* Hove, UK: Erlbaum.

Sodian, B., & Huelsken, C. (1999, April). Young children's ability to differentiate pretense from reality. Paper presented at the Biennial Meeting of the Society for Research in Child Development, Albuquerque, NM.

Sodian, B., Huelsken, C., Ebner, C., & Thoermer, C. (1998). Children's differentiation of mentality and reality in pretense-precursor to a theory of mind? *Sprache & Kognition*, *17*, 199–213.

Sodian, B., & Schneider, W. (1999). Memory strategy development: Gradual increase, sudden insight or roller coaster? In F. E. Weinert & W. Schneider (Eds.), *Individual development from 3 to 12: Findings from the Munich Longitudinal Study* (pp. 61–77). Cambridge: Cambridge University Press.

Sodian, B., Zaitchik, D., & Carey, S. (1991). Young children's differentiation of hypothethical beliefs from evidence. *Child Development*, *62*, 753–766.

Soja, N. N., Carey, S., & Spelke, E. S. (1991). Ontological categories guide young children's inductions of word meaning: Object terms and substance terms. *Cognition*, *38*(2), 179–211.

Soja, N. N., Carey, S., & Spelke, E. S. (1992). Perception, ontology, and word meaning, *Cognition*, *45*, 101–107.

Solomon, G. E. A., & Cassimatis, N. L. (1999). On facts and conceptual systems: Young children's integration of their understanding of germs and contagion. *Developmental Psychology*, *35*, 113–126.

Solomon, T. L. (1999, April). The effect of enriched instructions on 2.5-year-olds understanding of scale models. Poster presented at the Society for Research in Child Development, Albuquerque, NM.

Sophian, C. (1988) Limitations on preschool children's knowledge about counting: using counting to compare two sets. *Developmental Psychology*, *24*, 634–640.

Sophian, C. (1997). Beyond competence: The significance of performance for conceptual development. *Cognitive Development*, *12*, 281–303.

Sophian, C., Garyantes, D., & Chang, C. (1997). When three is less than two: Early developments in children's understanding of fractional quantities. *Developmental Psychology*, *33*, 731–744.

Sorce, J. F., Emde, R. N., Campos, J. J., & Klinert, N. D. (1985). Maternal emotional signaling: Its effect on the visual cliff behavior of 1-year-olds. *Developmental Psychology*, *20*, 195–200.

Spear, N. E. (1978). *The processing of memories: Forgetting and retention*. Hillsdale, NJ: Erlbaum.

Spearman, C. (1904). "General intelligence," objectively determined and measured. *American Journal of Psychology*, *15*(2), 201–293.

Spearman, C. (1927). *The abilities of man*. London: Macmillan.

Spelke, E. S. (1993). Object perception. In A. I. Goldman (Ed.), *Readings in philosophy and cognitive science* (pp. 447–460). Cambridge, MA: MIT Press.

Spelke, E. S. (1994). Initial knowledge: Six suggestions. *Cognition*, *50*, 431–445.

Spelke, E. S. (2000). Nativism, empiricism, and the origins of knowledge. In D. Muir & A. Slater (Eds.), *Infant development: The essential readings. Essential readings in development psychology* (pp. 36–51). Malden, MA: Blackwell.

Spelke, E. S., Breinlinger, K., Macomber, J., & Jacobson, K. (1992). Origins of knowledge. *Psychological Review*, *99*, 605–632.

Spelke, E. S., & Kestenbaum, R. (1986). Les Origines du concept d'objet. *Psychologie Française*, *31*, 67–72.

Spelke, E. S., Kestenbaum, R., Simons, D. J., & Wein, D. (1995). Spatiotemporal continuity, smoothness of motion and object identity in infancy. *British Journal of Developmental Psychology*, *13*, 113–142.

Spelke, E. S., & Newport, E. L. (1998). Nativism, empiricism, and the development of knowl-edge. In W. Damon (Series Ed.) & R. M. Lerner (Vol. Ed.), *Handbook of child psychology, Vol 1. Theoretical models of human development.* (5th ed., pp. 275–340). New York: Wiley.

Spelke, E. S., Phillips, A., & Woodward, A. L. (1995). Infants' knowledge of object motion and human action. In D. Sperber, D. Premack, & A. J. Premack (Eds.), *Causal cognition: A multi-disciplinary debate* (pp. 44–78). Oxford, UK: Clarendon Press.

Spence, M. J. (1996). Young infants' long-term auditory memory: Evidence for changes in pref-erences as a function of delay. *Developmental Psychobiology, 29,* 685–695.

Spencer, C., Blades, M., & Morsley, K. (1989). *The child in the physical environment.* New York: Wiley.

Spencer, C., & Darvizeh, Z. (1981). Young children's descriptions of their local environment: A comparison of information elicited by recall, recognition and performance techniques of investigation. *Environmental Education and Information, 1,* 275–284.

Spencer, C., Harrison, N., & Darvizeh, Z. (1980). The development of iconic mapping ability in young children. *International Journal of Early Childhood, 12,* 57–64.

Sperber, D. (1994). The modularity of thought and the epidemiology of representations. In L. A. Hirschfeld & S. A. Gelman (Eds.), *Mapping the mind* (pp. 39–67). New York: Cambridge University Press.

Spinillo, A., & Bryant, P. (1991). Children's proportional judgements: The importance of "half." *Child Development, 62,* 427–440.

Spinillo, A., & Bryant, P. (1999). Proportional reasoning in young children: Part–part compar-isons about continuous and discontinuous quantity. *Mathematical Cognition, 5,* 181–197.

Spiro, M. (1993). Is the Western conception of the self "peculiar" within the context of the world's cultures? *Ethos, 21,* 107–153.

Springer, K. (1999). How a naive theory of biology is acquired. In M. Siegal & C. Petersen (Eds.), *Children's understanding of biology and health.* Cambridge, UK: Cambridge University Press.

Springer, K., & Keil, F. C. (1991). Early differentiation of causal mechanisms appropriate to bio-logical and nonbiological kinds. *Child Development, 62,* 767–781.

Squire. L. R. (1992). Memory and the hippocampus: A synthesis from findings with rats, monkeys, and humans. *Psychological Review, 99,* 195–231.

Squire, L. R., Knowlton, B., & Musen, G. (1993). The structure and organization of memory. *Annual Review of Psychology, 44,* 453–495.

Squire, S., & Bryant, P. (in press; 2002) The influence of sharing on children's initial concept of division. *Journal of Experimental Child Psychology.*

Stackhouse, J., & Wells, B. (1997). *Children's speech and literacy difficulties: A psycholinguistic frame-work.* London: Whurr.

Stanislavsky, K. (1922/1984). On various trends in the theatrical arts. In O. C. Korneva (Ed.), *Konstantini Stanislavsky: Selected works* (pp. 133–191). Moscow: Raduga Publishers.

Stanovich, K. E. (1994). Does dyslexia exist? *Journal of Child Psychology and Psychiatry, 35,* 579–595.

Stanovich, K. E., Cunningham, A. E., & Cramer, B. B. (1984). Assessing phonological awareness in kindergarten children: Issues of task comparability. *Journal of Experimental Child Psychology, 38,* 175–190.

Stanovich, K. E., & Siegel, L. S. (1994). The phenotypic performance profile of reading-disabled children: A regression-based test of the phonological-core variable-difference model. *Journal of Educational Psychology, 86,* 24–53.

Stark, R., & Tallal, P. (1981). Selection of children with specific language deficits. *Journal of Speech and Hearing Disorders, 46,* 114–122.

Starkey, P., & Cooper, R. (1980). Perception of numbers by human infants. *Science, 210,* 1033–1034.

Starkey, P., Spelke, E. S., & Gelman, R. (1990) Numerical abstraction by human infants. *Cognition, 36,* 97–128.

Stavy, R., & Stachel, D. (1985). Children's conception of changes in the state of matter: From solid to liquid. *Archives de Psychologie, 53,* 331–344.

Stavy, R., Strauss S., Orpaz, N., & Carmi, G. (1982). U-shaped behavioral growth in ratio comparisons. In S. Strauss (Ed.), *U-shaped behavioral growth* (pp. 11–36). New York: Academic Press.

Steele, C. M. (1997). A threat in the air: How stereotypes shape intellectual identity and performance. *American Psychologist, 52*(6), 613–629.

Stern, D. N. (1977). *The first relationship.* Cambridge, MA: Harvard University Press.

Stern, D. N. (1985). *The interpersonal world of the infant: A view from psychoanalysis and developmental psychology.* New York: Basic Books.

Stern, D. N. (1995). Self/other differentiation in the domain of intimate socio-affective interaction: Some considerations. In P. Rochat (Ed.), *The self in infancy: Theory and research* (pp. 419–429). Amsterdam: Elsevier.

Stern, E. (1993). What makes certain arithmetic word problems involving the comparison of sets so difficult for children? *Journal of Educational Psychology, 85,* 7–23.

Stern, W. (1910). Abstracts of lectures on the psychology of testimony and on the study of individuality, *American Journal of Psychology, 21,* 270–282.

Sternberg, R. J. (Ed.) (1984). *Mechanisms of cognitive development.* New York: Freeman.

Sternberg, R. J. (1985). *Beyond IQ: A triarchic theory of human intelligence.* New York: Cambridge University Press.

Sternberg, R. J. (1988). *The triarchic mind: A theory of human intelligence.* New York: Viking.

Sternberg, R. J. (1990). *Metaphors of mind.* New York: Cambridge University Press.

Sternberg, R. J. (1994). *Encyclopedia of human intelligence.* New York: Macmillan.

Sternberg, R. J. (1997). *Successful intelligence.* New York: Plume.

Sternberg, R. J. (1999a). Successful intelligence: Finding a balance. *Trends in Cognitive Sciences, 3,* 436–442.

Sternberg, R. J. (1999b) The theory of successful intelligence. *Review of General Psychology, 3,* 292–316.

Sternberg, R. J. (Ed.) (2000). *Handbook of intelligence.* New York: Cambridge University Press.

Sternberg, R. J., & Clinkenbeard, P. R. (1995). A triarchic model of identifying, teaching, and assessing gifted children. *Roeper Review, 17*(4), 255–260.

Sternberg, R. J., & Davidson, J. E. (Eds.). (1986). *Conceptions of giftedness.* New York: Cambridge University Press.

Sternberg, R. J., Ferrari, M., Clinkenbeard, P. R., & Grigorenko, E. L. (1996). Identification, instruction, and assessment of gifted children: A construct validation of a triarchic model. *Gifted Child Quarterly, 40*(3), 129–137.

Sternberg, R. J., Forsythe, G. B., Hedlund, J., Horvath, J., Snook, S., Williams, W. M., Wagner, R. K., & Grigorenko, E. L. (2000). *Practical intelligence in everyday life.* New York: Cambridge University Press.

Sternberg, R. J., & Grigorenko, E. L. (Eds.). (1997). *Intelligence, heredity, and environment.* New York: Cambridge University Press.

Sternberg, R. J., Grigorenko, E. L., Ferrari, M., & Clinkenbeard, P. (1999). A triarchic analysis of an aptitude-treatment interaction. *European Journal of Psychological Assessment, 15,* 1–11.

Sternberg, R. J., & Kaufman J. C. (1998). Human abilities. *Annual Review of Psychology, 49,* 479–502.

Sternberg, R. J., & Lubart, T. I. (1995). *Defying the crowd: Cultivating creativity in a culture of conformity.* New York: Free Press.

Sternberg, R. J., & Nigro, G. (1980). Developmental patterns in the solution of verbal analogies. *Child Development, 51,* 27–38.

Sternberg, R. J., & Powell, J. S. (1983). The development of intelligence. In P. H. Mussen (Series Ed.) and J. Flavell & E. M. Markman (Vol. Eds.), *Handbook of child psychology* (3rd ed., pp. 341–419). New York: Wiley.

Sternberg, R. J., & Spear-Swerling, L. (1996). *Teaching for thinking.* Washington, DC: American Psychological Association.

Sternberg, R. J., Torff, B., & Grigorenko, E. L. (1998). Teaching triarchically improves school achievement. *Journal of Educational Psychology, 90*(3), 1–11.

Stevens, T., & Karmiloff-Smith, A. (1997). Word learning in a special population: Do individuals with Williams syndrome obey lexical constraints? *Journal of Child Language, 24,* 737–765.

Stich, S. P. (1983). *From folk psychology to cognitive science: The case against belief.* Cambridge, MA: MIT Press.

Stigler, J. W., Nusbaum, H. C., & Chalip, L. (1988). Developmental changes in speed of processing: Central limiting mechanism of skill transfer? *Child Development, 59*(4), 1144–1153.

Stiles, J. (1998). The effects of early focal brain injury on lateralization of cognitive function. *Current Directions in Psychological Science, 7,* 21–26.

Stiles-Davis, J., Kritchevsky, M., & Bellugi, U. (Eds.). (1988). *Spatial cognition: Brain bases and development.* Hillsdale, NJ: Lawrence Erlbaum.

Stokols, D., & Altman, I. (1987). *Handbook of environmental psychology.* New York: Wiley.

Stothard, S., & Hulme, C. (1995) A comparison of reading comprehension and decoding difficulties in children. *Journal of Child Psychology and Psychiatry, 36,* 399–408.

Strauss, M. S. (1979). Abstraction of prototypical information in adults and 10-month-old infants. *Journal of Experimental Psychology: Human Learning and Memory, 5,* 618–632.

Strauss, M. S., & Curtis, L. E. (1981). Infant perception of number. *Child Development, 52,* 1146–1152.

Strauss, S. (Ed.). (1982). *U-shaped behavioral growth.* New York: Academic Press.

Strauss, S., & Stavy, R. (1982). U-shaped behavioral growth: Implications for the theories of development. In W. W. Hartup (Ed.), *Review of child development research* (Vol. 6, pp. 547–599). Chicago: University of Chicago Press.

Strawson, P. F. (1959). *Individuals: An essay in descriptive metaphysics.* London: Methuen.

Stroop, J. R. (1935). Studies of interference in serial verbal reactions. *Journal of Experimental Psychology, 18,* 643–662.

Stuart, M., & Coltheart, M. (1988). Does reading develop in a sequence of stages? *Cognition, 30,* 139–181.

Stuart, M., Masterson, J., Dixon, M., & Quinlan, P. (1999). Inferring sublexical correspondences from sight vocabulary: Evidence from 6- and 7-year-olds. *Quarterly Journal of Experimental Psychology, 52A,* 353–366.

Stuss, D. T., & Alexander, M. P. (2000). Executive functions and the frontal lobes: A conceptual view. *Psychological Research, 63,* 289–298.

Stuss, D. T., & Benson, D. F. (1986). *The frontal lobes.* New York: Raven Press.

Stuss, D. T., Eskes, G. A., & Foster, J. K. (1994). Experimental neuropsychological studies of frontal lobe functions. In F. Boller & J. Grafman (Eds.), *Handbook of neuropsychology* (Vol. 9, pp. 149–185). Amsterdam: Elsevier.

Stuss, D. T., Toth, J. P., Franchi, D., Alexander, M. P., Tipper, S., & Craik, F. I. M. (1999). Dissociation of attentional processes in patients with focal frontal and posterior lesions. *Neuropsychologia, 37,* 1005–1027.

Sullivan, K., & Winner, E. (1993). Three-year-old's understanding of mental states: The influence of trickery. *Journal of Experimental Child Psychology, 56,* 135–148.

Surber, C. F., & Gzesh, S. M. (1984). Reversible operations in the balance scale task. *Journal of Experimental Child Psychology, 38,* 254–274.

Swan, D., & Goswami, U. (1997). Phonological awareness deficits in developmental dyslexia and the phonological representations hypothesis. *Journal of Experimental Child Psychology, 60,* 334–353.

Swettenham, J., Baron-Cohen, S., Charman, T., Cox, A., Baird, G., Drew, A., Rees, L., & Wheelwright, S. (1998). The frequency and distribution of spontaneous attention shifts between social and non-social stimuli in autistic, typically developing, and non-autistic developmentally delayed infants. *Journal of Child Psychology and Psychiatry, 9,* 747–753.

Swiderek, M. R. (1999). Beliefs can change in response to disconfirming evidence and can do so in complicated ways, buy only if collateral beliefs are disconfirmed. Unpublished doctoral dissertation, Cornell University.

Szatmari, P., Tuff, L., Finlayson, M., & Bartolucci, G. (1990). Asperger's syndrome and autism: Neurocognitive aspects. *Journal of the American Academy of Child and Adolescent Psychiatry, 29,* 130–136.

Tager-Flusberg, H. (1993). What language reveals about the understanding of minds in children with autism. In S. Baron-Cohen, H. Tager-Flusberg, & D. J. Cohen (Eds.), *Understanding other minds: Perspectives from autism.* Oxford, UK: Oxford University Press.

Tager-Flusberg, H., Boshart, J., & Baron-Cohen, S. (1998). Reading the windows of the soul: Evidence of domain specificity sparing in Williams syndrome. *Journal of Cognitive Neuroscience, 10,* 631–639.

Talcott, J., & Stein, J. (1999) Impaired neuronal timing in developmental dyslexia – the magnocellular hypothesis. *Dyslexia, 5,* 59–77.

Tallal, P. (1976). Rapid auditory processing in normal and disordered language development. *Journal of Speech and Hearing Research, 19,* 561–571.

Tallal, P., & Piercy, M. (1973). Defects of non-verbal auditory perception in children with developmental aphasia. *Nature, 241,* 468–469.

Tallal, P., & Piercy, M. (1975). Developmental aphasia: The perception of brief vowels and extended stop consonants. *Neuropsychologia, 13,* 69–74.

Tallal, P., Stark, R., Kallman, C., & Mellitis, D. (1981). A reexamination of some nonverbal perceptual abilities of language impaired and normal children as a function of age and sensory modaliy. *Journal of Speech and Hearing Research, 24,* 351–357.

Tamis-LeMonda, C. S., & Bornstein, M. H. (1991). Individual variation, correspondence, stability, and change in mother and toddler play. *Infant Behavior & Development, 14,* 143–162.

Tamis-LeMonda, C. S., Bornstein, M. H., Cyphers, L., Toda, S., et al. (1992). Language and play at one year: A comparison of toddlers and mothers in the United States and Japan. *International Journal of Behavioral Development, 15,* 19–42.

Tanaka, J. W., & Taylor, M. (1991). Object categorization and expertise: Is the basic level in the eye of the beholder? *Cognitive Psychology, 23,* 457–482.

Tannock, R. (1998). Attention deficit hyperactivity disorder: Advances in cognitive, neurobiological, and genetic research. *Journal of Child Psychology & Psychiatry & Allied Disciplines, 39,* 65–99.

Tardif, T. (1996). Nouns are not always learned before verbs: Evidence from Mandarin speakers' early vocabularies. *Developmental Psychology, 32*(3), 492–504.

Tardif, T., & Wellman, H. M. (2000). Acquisition of mental state language in Mandarin- and Cantonese-speaking children. *Developmental Psychology, 36,* 25–43.

Tassabehji, M., Metcalfe, K., Karmiloff-Smith, A., Carette, M. J., Grant, J., Dennis, N., Reardon, W., Splitt, M., Read, A. P., & Donnai, D. (1999). Williams syndrome: Use of chromosomal micro-deletions as a tool to dissect cognitive and physical phenotypes. *American Journal of Human Genetics, 64,* 118–125.

Taylor, C. (1985) *Human agency and language: Philosophical papers I.* Cambridge: Cambridge University Press.

Taylor, M. (1996). A theory of mind perspective on social cognitive development. In E. C. Carterette & M. P. Friedman (Series Eds.), R. Gelman & T. Au (Eds.), *Handbook of perception and cognition: Vol.13. Perceptual and cognitive development* (pp. 283–329). New York: Academic Press.

Taylor, M. (1999). *Imaginary companions and the children who create them.* Oxford, UK: Oxford University Press.

Taylor, M., & Carlson, S. M. (1997). The relation between individual differences in fantasy and theory of mind. *Child Development, 68,* 436–455.

Taylor, M., & Carlson, S. M. (2000). The influence of religious beliefs on parents' attitudes about children's fantasy behavior. In K. S. Rosengren, C. N. Johnson, & P. L. Harris (Eds.), *Imagining the impossible: Magical, scientific, and religious thinking in children* (pp. 247–268). Cambridge, UK: Cambridge University Press.

Taylor, M., Esbensen, B., & Bennett, R. (1994). Children's understanding of knowledge acquisition: The tendency for children to report they have always known what they have just learned. *Child Development, 65,* 1581–1604.

Temple, C. (1997). *Developmental cognitive neuropsychology.* Hove, UK: Psychology Press.

Temple, C. M., Almazan, M., & Sherwood, S. (in press). Lexical skills in Williams syndrome: a cognitive neuropsychological analysis. *Journal of Neurolinguistics.*

Templin, M. (1957). *Certain language skills in children: Their development and inter-relationships. Child welfare monograph 26.* Minneapolis, MN: University of Minnesota Press.

Terman, L. M. (1925). *Genetic studies of genius: Vol. 1. Mental and physical traits of a thousand gifted children.* Stanford, CA: Stanford University Press.

Terman, L. M., & Oden, M. H. (1959). *Genetic studies of genius: Vol. 4. The gifted group at midlife.* Stanford, CA: Stanford University Press.

Tessler, M., & Nelson, K. (1994). Making memories: The influence of joint encoding on later recall by young children. *Consciousness and Cognition, 3,* 307–326.

Thatcher, R. W. (1992). Cyclic cortical reorganization during early childhood development. *Brain and Cognition, 20,* 24–50.

Thatcher, R. W. (1994). Cyclic cortical reorganization: Origins of human cognitive development. In G. Dawson & K. W. Fischer (Eds.), *Human Behavior and the Developing Brain* (pp. 232–266). New York: Guilford.

Thayer, E. S., & Collyer, C. E. (1978). The development of transitive inference: A review of recent approaches. *Psychological Bulletin, 85,* 1327–1343.

Thelen, E. (1992). Development as a dynamic system. *Current Directions in Psychological Science, 1,* 189–193.

Thelen, E., & Smith, L. B. (1994). *A dynamic systems approach to the development of cognition and action.* Cambridge, MA: MIT Press.

Thelen, E., & Smith, L. B. (1998). Dynamic systems theories. In W. Damon (Series Ed.) & R. M. Lerner (Vol. Ed.), *Handbook of child psychology: Vol. 1. Theoretical models of human development* (5th ed.). New York: Wiley.

Thomas, G. V., Nye, R., & Robinson, E. J. (1994). How children view pictures: Children's responses to pictures as things in themselves and as representations of something else. *Cognitive Development, 9,* 141–164.

Thomas, H. (1983). Familial correlational analyses, sex differences, and the X-linked gene hypothesis. *Psychological Bulletin, 93,* 427–440.

Thomas, H., & Turner, G. F. W. (1991). Individual differences and development in water-level task performance. *Journal of Experimental Child Psychology, 51,* 171–194.

Thomas, M. S. C. (2000). Neuroconstructivism's promise. *Developmental Science, 3,* 35–37.

Thomas, M. S. C., Grant, J., Barham, Z., Gsödl, M., Laing, E., Lakusta, L., Tyler, L. K., Grice, S., Paterson, S., & Karmiloff-Smith, A. (2001). Past tense formation in Williams syndrome. *Language and Cognitive Processes, 16*(2/3), 144–176.

Thomas, M. S. C., & Karmiloff-Smith, A. (2001a). Modelling language acquisition in atypical phenotypes. Manuscript under revision.

Thomas, M. S. C., & Karmiloff-Smith, A. (2001b). The implications of neural network models for causal explanations of behavioural impairments in cases of atypical development. Manuscript in preparation.

Thomas, M. S. C., & Karmiloff-Smith, A. (2001c). Are developmental disorders like cases of adult brain damage? Implications from connectionist modelling. Manuscript submitted for publication.

Thomas, M. S. C., & Karmiloff-Smith, A. (in press). Connectionist models of cognitive development, atypical development and individual differences. In R. J. Sternberg, J. Lautrey, & T. Lubart (Eds.), *Models of intelligence for the next millennium.* American Psychological Association.

Thompson, C., Barresi, J., & Moore, C. (1997). The development of future-oriented prudence and altruism in preschoolers. *Cognitive Development, 12,* 199–212.

Thompson, G. B., & Johnston, R. S. (2000). Are nonword and other phonological deficits indicative of a failed reading process? *Reading and Writing, 12,* 63–97.

Thompson, P. M., Giedd, J. N., Woods, R. P., MacDonald, D., Evans, A. C., & Toga, A. W. (2000, March 9). Growth patterns in the developing brain detected by using continuum mechanical tensor maps. *Nature, 404,* 190–193.

Thompson, R. A. (1998). Empathy and its origins in early development. In S. Braten (Ed.), *Intersubjective communication and emotion in early ontogeny* (pp. 144–157). Paris: Cambridge University Press.

Thorkildsen, T. A. (1989). Justice in the classroom: The student's view. *Child Development, 60,* 323–334.

Thorkildsen, T. A. (2000). Children's coordination of procedural and commutative justice at school. In W. van Haaften, T. Wren, & A. Tellings (Eds.), *Moral sensibilities and education II: The schoolchild* (pp. 61–88). The Netherlands: Concorde Publishing.

Thorkildsen, T. A., Nolen, S., & Fournier, C. (1994). What is fair? Children's critiques of practices that influence motivation. *Journal of Educational Psychology, 86,* 475–486.

Thorkildsen, T. A., & Schmall, C. (1997). Conceptions of fair learning practices among low-income African American and Latin American children: Acknowledging diversity. *Journal of Educational Psychology, 89,* 719–727.

Thorndike, R. L., Hagen, E. P., & Sattler, J. M. (1986). *Stanford–Binet Intelligence Scale: Guide for administering and scoring the fourth edition.* Chicago: Riverside.

Thurstone, L. L. (1924). *The nature of intelligence.* New York: Harcourt Brace.

Thurstone, L. L. (1938). *Primary mental abilities.* Chicago: University of Chicago Press.

Thurstone, T. G. (1962). *Primary mental abilities.* Chicago: Science Research Associates.

Tippet, L. J., McAuliffe, S., & Farah, M. J. (1995). Preservation of categorical knowledge in Alzheimer's Disease: A computational account. *Memory, 3,* 519–533.

Tisak, M. (1995). Domains of social reasoning and beyond. *Annals of Child Development, 11,* 95–130.

Todd, C. M., & Perlmutter, M. (1980). Reality recalled by preschool children. In M. Perlmutter (Ed.), *New directions for child development: Children's memory* (pp. 69–85). San Francisco: Jossey-Bass.

Tolman, E. C. (1948). Cognitive maps in rats and men. *Psychological Review, 55*, 189–208.

Tolman, E. C., Ritchie, B. F., & Kalish, D. (1946). Studies in spatial learning: I. Orientation and the shortcut. *Journal of Experimental Psychology, 36*, 13–34.

Tomasello, M. (1988). The role of joint-attentional processes in early language acquisition. *Language Sciences, 10*, 69–88.

Tomasello, M. (1993). On the interpersonal origins of the self. In U. Neisser (Ed.), *The perceived self: Ecological and interpersonal sources of self-knowledge* (pp. 174–184). Cambridge: Cambridge University Press.

Tomasello, M. (1995). Joint attention as social cognition. In C. Moore & P. Dunham (Eds.), *Joint Attention: Its origins and role in development* (pp. 103–130), New York: Erlbaum.

Tomasello, M. (1999). *The cultural origins of human cognition*. Cambridge, MA: Harvard University Press.

Tomasello, M., & Barton, M. (1994). Learning words in non-ostensive contexts. *Developmental Psychology, 30*, 639–650.

Tomasello, M., & Call, J. (1997). *Primate cognition*. Oxford, UK: Oxford University Press.

Tomasello, M., Striano, T., & Rochat, P. (1999). Do young children use objects as symbols? *British Journal of Developmental Psychology, 17*, 563–584.

Towse, J. N., & Saxton, M. (1997). Linguistic influences on children's number concepts: Methodological and theoretical considerations. *Journal of Experimental Child Psychology, 66*, 362–375.

Trabasso, T., & Foellinger, D. B. (1978). Information processing capacity in children: A test of Pascual-Leone's model. *Journal of Experimental Child Psychology, 26*(1), 1–17.

Trabasso, T., Stein, N. L., & Johnson, L. R. (1981). Children's knowledge of events: A causal analysis of story structure. In G. H. Bower (Ed.), *Learning and motivation* (Vol. 15, pp. 237–282). New York: Academic Press.

Tranel, D., Anderson, S. W., & Benton, A. (1994). Development of the concept of "executive function" and its relationship to the frontal lobes. In F. Boller & J. Grafman (Eds.), *Handbook of neuropsychology* (Vol. 9, pp. 125–148). Amsterdam: Elsevier.

Treiman, R. (1993). *Beginning to spell: A study of first-grade children*. Oxford, UK: Oxford University Press.

Treiman, R., & Breaux, A. M. (1982). Common phoneme and overall similarity relations among spoken syllables: Their use by children and adults. *Journal of Psycholinguistic Research, 11*(6), 569–598.

Treiman, R., Goswami, U., & Bruck, M. (1990). Not all nonwords are alike: Implications for reading development and theory. *Memory and Cognition, 18*, 559–567.

Treiman, R., Mullenix, J., Bijeljac-Babic, R., & Richmond-Welty, D. (1995). The special role of rimes in the description, use and acquisition of English orthography. *Journal of Experimental Psychology: General, 124*, 107–136.

Trevarthen, C. (1977). Descriptive analysis of infant communication behavior. In H. R. Schaffer (Ed.), *Studies on mother–infant interaction*. New York: Academic.

Trevarthen, C. (1979). Communication and cooperation in early infancy. A description of primary intersubjectivity. In M. Bullowa (Ed.), *Before speech: The beginning of human communication*, London: Cambridge University Press. pp. 321–347.

Trevarthen, C. (1980). The foundations of intersubjectivity: Development of interpersonal and cooperative understanding in infants. In D. R. Olson (Ed.), *The social foundations of language and thought: Essays in honor of Jerome S. Bruner* (pp. 316–342). New York: Norton.

Trevarthen, C. (1993). The self born in intersubjectivity: an infant communicating. In U. Neisser (Ed.), *The perceived self* (pp. 121–173). New York: Cambridge University Press.

Trevarthen, C., & Hubley, P. (1978). Secondary intersubjectivity: Confidence, confiding and acts of meaning in the first year. In A. Lock (Ed.), *Action, gesture and symbol: The emergence of language* (pp. 183–229). NY: Academic Press.

Triandis, H. C. (1988). Collectivism vs. individualism: A reconceptualization of a basic concept in cross-cultural social psychology. In C. Bagley & G. K. Verma (Eds.), *Personality cognition and values: Cross-cultural perspectives of childhood and adolescence.* London: Macmillan.

Tronick, E. Z. (1989). Emotions and emotional communication in infants. *American Psychologist, 44,* 112–119.

Tronick, E., Als, H., Adamson, L., Wise, S., & Brazelton, T. B. (1978). The infant's response to entrapment between contradictory messages in face-to-face interaction. *Journal of the American Academy of Child and Adolescent Psychiatry, 17,* 1–13.

Troseth, G. L. (2000). TV guide: Learning to use video as a source of information. Unpublished doctoral dissertation. University of Illinois, Urbana-Champaign.

Troseth, G. L. (2001). Getting a clear picture: Young children's understanding of a televised image. Unpublished manuscript.

Troseth, G. L., & DeLoache, J. S. (1998). The medium can obscure the message: Young children's understanding of video. *Child Development, 69,* 950–965.

Troseth, G. L., & DeLoache, J. S. (2001). Now you "see" it, now you don't: Young children's use of directly experienced versus symbol-mediated information. Unpublished manuscript.

Tudge, J. (1992). Processes and consequences of peer collaboration. A Vygotskian analysis. *Child Development, 63,* 1364–1379.

Tunmer, W. E., & Nesdale, A. R. (1985). Phonemic segmentation skill and beginning reading. *Journal of Educational Psychology, 77,* 417–427.

Turiel, E. (1974). Conflict and transition in adolescent moral development. *Child Development, 45,* 14–29.

Turiel, E. (1975). Domains and categories in social-cognitive development. In W. Overton (Ed.), *The relationship between social and cognitive development* (pp. 53–90). Hillsdale, NJ: Erlbaum.

Turiel, E. (1978). The development of concepts of social structure: Social convention. In Joseph Glick & K. Alison Clarke-Stewart (Eds.), *The development of social understanding.* New York: Gardner Press.

Turiel, E. (1979). Distinct conceptual and developmental domains: Social convention and morality. In H. Howe & G. Keasy (Eds.) *Nebraska Symposium on Motivation: 1977, Vol. 25. Social Cognitive Development* (pp. 77–116). Lincoln: University of Nebraska.

Turiel, E. (1983). *The development of social knowledge: Morality and convention.* Cambridge, UK: Cambridge University Press.

Turiel, E. (1996). Equality and hierarchy: Conflict in values. In E. Reed, E. Turiel, & T. Brown (Eds.), *Values and knowledge* (pp. 41–60). Hillsdale, NJ: Lawrence Erlbaum.

Turiel, E. (1998). The development of morality. In W. Damon (Ed.), *Handbook of child psychology* (5th ed.): *Vol. 3.* N. Eisenberg (Ed.), *Social, emotional, and personality development* (pp. 863–932). New York: Academic Press.

Turiel, E. (2000). Cultural practices as "funny things." It depends on where you sit. In W. Edelstein & G. Nunner-Winkler (Eds.), *Morality in context* (pp. 261–298). Germany: Suhrkampf.

Turner, M. (1997). Towards an executive dysfunction account of repetitive behavior in autism. In J. Russell (Ed.), *Autism as an executive disorder* (pp. 57–100). Oxford, UK: Oxford University Press.

Tyler, L., Karmiloff-Smith, A., Voice, K., Stevens, T., Grant, J., Udwin, O., Davies, M., & Howlin, P. (1997). Do individuals with Williams syndrome have bizarre semantics? Evidence for lexical organisation using an on-line task. *Cortex, 33*(3), 515–527.

Udwin, O., & Yule, W. (1991). A cognitive and behavioural phenotype in Williams syndrome. *Journal of Clinical and Experimental Neuropsychology, 13*, 232–244.

Ullman, M. T., & Gopnik, M. (1999). Inflectional morphology in a family with inherited specific language impairment. *Applied Psycholinguistics, 20*, 51–117.

Ungerer, J., Zelazo, P. R., Kearsley, R. B., & O'Leary, K. (1981). Developmental changes in the representation of objects in symbolic play from 18 to 34 months of age. *Child Development, 52*, 186–195.

Usher, J. A., & Neisser, U. (1993). Childhood amnesia and the beginnings of memory for four early life events. *Journal of Experimental Psychology: General, 122*, 155–165.

Uttal, D. H. (1996). Angles and distances: Children's and adults' reconstructions and scaling of spatial configurations. *Child Development, 67*, 2763–2779.

Uttal, D. H. (2000a). Maps and spatial thinking: A two-way street. *Developmental Science, 3*, 283–286.

Uttal, D. H. (2000b). Seeing the big picture: Map use and the development of spatial cognition. *Developmental Science, 3*, 247–286.

Uzgiris, I. C., & Hunt, J. McV. (1975). *Assessment in infancy: Ordinal scales of psychological development.* Chicago: University of Chicago Press.

Valsiner, J. (1998). *The guided mind: A sociogenetic approach to personality.* Cambridge, MA: Harvard University Press.

Van de Walle, G. A. (1997). Perceptual foundations of categorization in infancy: The animal/vehicle distinction. Unpublished doctoral dissertation, Cornell University.

Van de Walle, G., Spelke, E. S., & Carey, S. (1997, April). Concepts and categorization in infancy. Paper presented at the meeting of the Society for Research in Child Development, Washington, DC.

Van den Broek, P. (1997). Discovering the cement of the universe: The development of event comprehension from childhood to adulthood. In P. W. van den Broek, P. J. Bauer, & T. Bourg (Eds.), *Developmental spans in event comprehension and representation: Bridging fictional and actual events* (pp. 321–342). Mahwah, NJ: Erlbaum.

Van der Lely, H. (1994). Canonical linking rules: Forward versus reverse linking in normally developing and specifically language impaired children. *Cognition, 51*, 29–72.

Van der Lely, H. K. J. (1997). Language and cognitive development in a grammatical SLI boy: Modularity and innateness. *Journal of Neurolinguistics, 10*, 75–107.

Van der Lely, H. K. J., & Ullman, M. T. (2001). Past tense morphology in specifically language impaired and normally developing children. *Language and Cognitive Processes, 16*(2/3), 178–217.

Van der Maas, H. L. J., & Molenaar, P. C. M. (1992). Stagewise cognitive development: An application of catastrophe theory. *Psychological Review, 99*(3), 395–417.

Van der Molen, M. W., & Ridderinkhof, K. R. (1998). The growing and aging brain: Life-span changes in brain and cognitive functioning. In A. Demetriou, W. Doise, & C. van Lieshout (Eds.), *Life-span developmental psychology* (pp. 35–99). New York: Wiley.

Van der Veer, R., & Valsiner, J. (1991). *Understanding Vygotsky: A quest for synthesis.* Oxford, UK: Blackwell.

Van Duuren, M., & Scaife, M. (1996). "Because a robot's brain hasn't got a brain, it just controls itself": Children's attributions of brain related behaviour to intelligent artifacts. *European Journal of Psychology of Education, 11*, 365–376.

Van Geert, P. (1993). A dynamic systems model of cognitive growth: Competition and support under limited resource conditions. In L. Smith & E. Thelen (Eds.), *A dynamic systems approach to development: Applications* (pp. 265–331). Cambridge, MA: MIT Press.

Van Loosbroek, E., & Smitsman, A. W. (1990). Visual perception of numerosity in infancy. *Developmental Psychology, 26*, 916–922.

Van Wieringer, J. C. (1978). Secular growth changes. In F. Falker & J. M. Tanner (Eds.), *Human growth* (Vol 2). New York: Plenum.

Vandenberg, S. G., & Kuse, A. R. (1979). Spatial ability: A critical review of the sex-linked major gene hypothesis. In. M. A. Wittig & A. C. Petersen (Eds.), *Sex-related differences in cognitive functioning* (pp. 67–95). New York: Academic Press.

Vaughn, H. (2000). Software-supported, scientific inquiry learning in middle school, academically-at-risk students. Unpublished doctoral dissertation, Teachers College, Columbia University USA.

Vellutino, F. R., & Scanlon, D. M. (1991). The pre-eminence of phonologically based skills in learning to read. In S. Brady & D. Shankweiler (Eds.), *Phonological processes in literacy: A tribute to Isabelle Liberman.* Hillsdale, NJ: Lawrence Erlbaum.

Vellutino, F. R., Scanlon, D. M., Sipay, E., Small, S., Pratt, A., Chen, R., & Denckla, M. (1996). Cognitive profiles of difficult to remediate and readily remediated poor readers. *Journal of Educational Psychology, 88,* 601–638.

Vergnaud, G. (1982). A classification of cognitive tasks and operations of thought involved in addition and subtraction problems. In T. P. Carpenter, J. M. Moser, & T. A. Romberg, *Addition and subtraction: A cognitive perspective* (pp. 60–67). Hillsdale, NJ: Lawrence Erlbaum.

Vernon, P. A., Wickett, J. C., Bazana, P. G., & Stelmack, R. M. (2000). The neuropsychology and psychophysiology of human intelligence. In R. J. Sternberg (Ed.), *Handbook of intelligence* (pp. 245–264). New York: Cambridge University Press.

Vernon, P. E. (1971). *The structure of human abilities.* London: Methuen.

Vidal, F. (1994). *Piaget before Piaget.* Cambridge, MA: Harvard University Press.

Vinden, P. G. (1996). Junin Quechua children's understanding of mind. *Child Development, 67,* 1707–1716.

Vinden, P. G. (1999). Children's understanding of mind and emotion: A multi-cultural study. *Cognition and Emotion, 13,* 19–48.

Vinter, A. (1986). The role of movement in eliciting early imitations. *Child Development, 57,* 66–71.

Von Wright, G. H. (1983). *Practical reason.* Oxford, UK: Blackwell.

Vonèche, J.-J. (2001). Mental imagery: From Inhelder's ideas to neuro-cognitive models. In A. Typhon & J. Vonèche (Eds.), *Working with Piaget: Essays in honour of Bärbel Inhelder.* Hove, UK: Psychology Press.

Vosniadou, S., & Brewer, W. (1992). Mental models of the earth: A study of conceptual change in childhood. *Cognitive Psychology, 24,* 535–585.

Voyer, D., Voyer, S., & Bryden, M. P. (1995). Magnitude of sex differences in spatial abilities: A meta-analysis and consideration of critical variables. *Psychological Bulletin, 117,* 250–270.

Vygodskaya, G. L., & Lifanova, T. M. (1996). *Lev Semënovich Vygotskii: Zhizn', deyatel'nost', shtrikhi, i portrety* [Lev Semënovich Vygotsky: Life, activity, traits, and portraits]. Moscow: Smysl.

Vygotsky, L. S. (1934a). *Myshlenie i rech': Psikhologicheskie issledovaniya* [Thinking and speech: Psychological investigations]. Moscow and Leningrad: Gosudarstvennoe Sotsial'no-Ekonomicheskoe Izdatel'stvo.

Vygotsky, L. S. (1934b). Problema obucheniya i umstvennogo razvitiya v shkol'nom vozraste [The problem of instruction and cognitive development during the school years]. In L. S. Vygotsky, *Umstvennoe razvitie detei v protsese obucheniya* [Cognitive development in children in the process of instruction]. Moscow and Leningrad: Uchpedgiz.

Vygotsky, L. S. (1962). *Thought and language.* Cambridge, MA: MIT Press.

Vygotsky, L. S. (1978). *Mind in society: The development of higher psychological processes,* ed. M. Cole et al. Cambridge, MA: Harvard University Press.

Vygotsky, L. S. (1981a). The instrumental method in psychology. In J. V. Wertsch (Ed.), *The concept of activity in Soviet psychology* (pp. 134–143). Armonk, NY: M. E. Sharpe.

Vygotsky, L. S. (1981b). The genesis of higher mental functions. In J. V. Wertsch (Ed.), *The concept of activity in Soviet psychology* (pp. 144–188). Armonk, NY: M. E. Sharpe.

Vygotsky, L. S. (1986). *Thought and language*, trans. A. Kozulin. Cambridge, MA: MIT Press.

Vygotsky, L. S. (1994). *The Vygotsky reader*. Oxford, UK: Blackwell.

Vygotsky, L. S. (1997). Psychology and the theory of the localization of mental functions. In R. W. Rieber & J. Wollock (Eds.), *The collected works of L. S. Vygotsky* (Vol. 3, pp. 139–144), trans. R. van der Veer. New York: Plenum Press.

Waber, D. P. (1977). Sex differences in mental abilities, hemispheric lateralization, and rate of physical growth at adolescence. *Developmental Psychology, 13*, 29–38.

Wachs, T. (2000). *Necessary but not sufficient: The respective roles of single and multiple influences on individual development*. Washington, DC: APA.

Wagner, R. K. (2000). Practical intelligence. In R. J. Sternberg (Ed.), *Handbook of human intelligence* (pp. 380–395). New York: Cambridge University Press.

Wagner, R. K., Torgesen, J. K., Laughan, P., Simmons, K., & Rashotte, C. A. (1993). The development of young readers' phonological processing abilities. *Journal of Educational Psychology, 85*, 1–20.

Wainryb, C. (1991). Understanding differences in moral judgments: The role of informational assumptions. *Child Development, 62*, 840–851.

Wainryb, C., & Turiel, E. (1994). Dominance, subordination, and concepts of personal entitlements in cultural contexts. *Child Development, 65*, 1701–1722.

Wakeley, A., Rivera, S., & Langer, J. (2000a). Can young infants add and subtract? *Child Development, 71*, 1525–1534.

Wakeley, A., Rivera, S., & Langer, J. (2000b). Not proved: Reply to Wynn. *Child Development, 71*, 1537–1539.

Walden, T. A., & Ogan, T. A. (1988). The development of social referencing. *Child Development, 59*, 1230–1240.

Walker, A. S. (1982). Intermodal perception of expressive behaviours by human infants. *Journal of Experimental Child Psychology, 33*, 514–535.

Walker-Andrews, A., & Kahana-Kalman, R. (1999). The understanding of pretense across the second year of life. *British Journal of Developmental Psychology, 17*, 523–536.

Walton, K. L. (1990). *Mimesis as make-believe*. Cambridge, MA: Harvard University Press.

Waltz, J. A., Knowlton, B. J., Holyoak, K. J., Boone, K. B., Mishkin, F. S., de Menezes Santos, M., Thomas, C. R., & Miller, B. L. (1999). A system for relational reasoning in human prefrontal cortex. *Psychological Science, 10*(2), 119–125.

Walzer, M. (1995). *Pluralism, justice and equality*. Oxford, UK: Oxford University Press.

Wang, S. (2001, April). Ten-month-old infants' reasoning about weight in collision events. Paper presented at the biennial Meeting of the Society for Research in Child Development, Minneapolis, MN.

Wang, S., & Baillargeon, R. (2001a). Balancing objects on narrow supports: Developments in infants' reasoning about support events. Manuscript in preparation.

Wang, S., & Baillargeon, R. (2001b). The development of infants' ability to reason about height information in covering events. Manuscript in preparation.

Wang, S., & Baillargeon, R. (2001c). Priming infants to attend to height information in covering events. Manuscript in preparation.

Wang, S., & Baillargeon, R. (2001d). Reasoning about weight information in collision events in 10-month-old infants. Manuscript in preparation.

Wang, S., & Baillargeon, R. (2001e). Teaching infants about the variable height in covering events. Manuscript in preparation.

Wang, S., Baillargeon, R., & Paterson, S. (2001). Décalages in 9-month-old infants' reasoning about height information in events involving containers, tubes, or covers. Manuscript under review.

Wang, S., & Paterson, S. (2000, July). Infants' reasoning about containers and covers: Evidence for a surprising décalage. Paper presented at the biennial International Conference on Infant Studies, Brighton, UK.

Wapner, S., Kaplan, B., & Ciottone, R. (1981). Self–world relationships in critical environmental transitions: Childhood and beyond. In L. S. Liben, A. H. Patterson, & N. Newcombe (Eds.), *Spatial representation and behavior across the life span: Theory and application* (pp. 251–280). New York: Academic Press.

Warrington, E. K., & Weiskrantz, L. (1974). The effect of prior learning on subsequent retention in amnesic patients. *Neuropsychologia, 12*, 419–428.

Wason, P. C., & Johnson-Laird, P. N. (1972). *Psychology of reasoning: Structure and content.* Cambridge, MA: Harvard University Press.

Waters, H. S. (2000). Memory strategy development: Do we need yet another deficiency? *Child Development, 71*, 1004–1012.

Watson, J. K. (1999, April). Theory of mind and pretend play in family context. Paper presented at the biennial meeting of the Society for Research in Child Development, Albuquerque, NM.

Watson, J. K., Gelman, S. A., & Wellman, H. M. (1998). Young children's understanding of the non-physical nature of thoughts and the physical nature of the brain. *British Journal of Developmental Psychology, 16*, 321–335.

Watson, J. S. (1972). Smiling, cooing, and "the game." *Merrill-Palmer Quarterly, 18*, 323–339.

Watson, J. S. (1985). Contingency perception in early social development. In T. M. Field & N. A. Fox (Eds.), *Social perception in infants* (pp. 157–176). Norwood, NJ: Ablex.

Watson, J. S. (1994). Detection of self: The perfect algorithm. In S. T. Parker, R. W. Mitchell, & M. L. Boccia (Eds.), *Self-awareness in animals and humans: Developmental perspectives* (pp. 131–148). New York: Cambridge University Press.

Watson, J. S. (1995). Self-orientation in early infancy: The general role of contingency and the specific case of reaching to the mouth. In P. Rochat (Ed.), *The self in infancy: Theory and research* (pp. 375–393). Amsterdam: Elsevier.

Watson, J. S., & Ramey, C. T. (1972). Reactions to response-contingent stimulation in early infancy. *Merrill-Palmer Quarterly, 18*, 219–227.

Watson, M. W., & Fischer, K. W. (1977). A developmental sequence of agent use in late infancy. *Child Development, 48*, 828–836.

Waxman, S. R. (1990). Linguistic biases and the establishment of conceptual hierarchies: Evidence from preschool children. *Cognitive Development, 5*(2), 123–150.

Waxman, S. R. (1994). The development of an appreciation of specific linkages between linguistic and conceptual organization. *Lingua, 92*, 229–257.

Waxman, S. R. (1998). Linking object categorization and naming: Early expectations and the shaping role of language. In D. L. Medin (Ed.), *The psychology of learning and motivation* (Vol. 38, pp. 249–291). San Diego: Academic Press.

Waxman, S. R. (1999a). The dubbing ceremony revisited: Object naming and categorization in infancy and early childhood. In D. L. Medin & S. Atran (Eds.), *Folkbiology* (pp. 233–284). Cambridge, MA: MIT Press.

Waxman, S. R. (1999b). Specifying the scope of 13-month-olds' expectations for novel words. *Cognition, 70*(3), B35–B50.

Waxman, S. R., & Booth, A. E. (2000a). Distinguishing count nouns from adjectives: Evidence from 14-month-olds' novelty preference and word extension. In Proceedings of the 24th annual Boston University conference on language development.

Waxman, S. R., & Booth, A. E. (2000b). Principles that are invoked in the acquisition of words, but not facts. *Cognition, 77*(2), Netherlands: Elsevier Science Publishers BV.

Waxman, S. R., & Booth, A. E. (2001). On the insufficiency of domain-general accounts of word learning: A reply to Bloom and Markson. *Cognition, 78,* 277–279.

Waxman, S. R., & Booth, A. E. (in press). Seeing pink elephants: Fourteen-month-olds' interpretations of novel nouns and adjectives.

Waxman, S. R., & Braig, B. (1996). Stars and starfish: How far can shape take us? Paper presented at the Tenth Biennial International Conference on Infant Studies, Providence, RI.

Waxman, S. R., & Gelman, R. (1986). Preschoolers' use of superordinate relations in classification and language. *Cognitive Development, 1*(2), 139–156.

Waxman, S. R., & Guasti, M. T. (in preparation). Cross-linguistic differences in children's extensions of novel count nouns and adjectives: Evidence from Italian.

Waxman, S. R., & Hall, D. G. (1993). The development of a linkage between count nouns and object categories: Evidence from fifteen- to twenty-one-month-old infants. *Child Development, 64*(4), 1224–1241.

Waxman, S. R., & Markow, D. B. (1995). Words as invitations to form categories: Evidence from 12- to 13-month-old infants. *Cognitive Psychology, 29*(3), 257–302.

Waxman, S. R., & Markow, D. B. (1998). Object properties and object kind: Twenty-one-month-old infants' extension of novel adjectives. *Child Development, 69*(5), 1313–1329.

Waxman, S. R., Senghas, A., & Benveniste, S. (1997). A cross-linguistic examination of the noun-category bias: Its existence and specificity in French- and Spanish-speaking preschool-aged children. *Cognitive Psychology, 32*(3), 183–218.

Weatherford, D. L. (1985). Representing and manipulating spatial information from different environments: Models to neighborhoods. In R. Cohen (Ed.), *The development of spatial cognition* (pp. 41–70). Hillsdale, NJ: Lawrence Erlbaum.

Wechsler, D. (1991). *Manual for the Wechsler Intelligence Scales for Children* (3rd ed.). (WISC III). San Antonio, TX: Psychological Corporation.

Wegner, D. M., & Wheatley, T. (1999). Apparent mental causation: Sources of the experience of will. *American Psychologist, 54*(7), 480–492.

Weinberg, R. A., Scarr, S., & Waldman, I. D. (1992). The Minnesota Transracial Adoption Study: A follow-up of IQ test performance at adolescence. *Intelligence, 16*(1), 117–135.

Weinert, F. E. (1962). Untersuchungen über einige Bedingungen des sprachlichen Lernens bei Kindern und Jugendlichen. *Vita Humana, 5,* 185–194.

Weinert, F. E. (1986). Developmental variations of memory performance and memory-related knowledge across the life-span. In A. Sörensen, F. E. Weinert, & L. R. Sherrod (Eds.), *Human development: Multidisciplinary perspectives* (pp. 535–554). Hillsdale, NJ: Erlbaum.

Weinreb, N., & Brainerd, C. J. (1975). A developmental study of Piaget's groupment model of the emergence of speed and time concepts. *Child Development, 46,* 176–185.

Weir, C., & Seacrest, M. (2000). Developmental differences in understanding of balance scales in the United States and Zimbabwe. *Journal of Genetic Psychology, 161,* 5–22.

Weiss, C., Gordon, M., & Lillywhite, H. (1987). *Clinical management of articulatory and phonologic disorders.* Baltimore, MD: Williams & Wilkins.

Wellman, H. M. (1971). Tip of the tongue and feeling of knowing experiences: A developmental study of memory monitoring. *Child Development, 48,* 13–21.

Wellman, H. M. (1993). Early understanding of mind: The normal case. In S. Baron-Cohen, H. Tager-Flusberg, & D. J. Cohen (Eds.), *Understanding other minds: Perspectives from autism* (pp. 10–39). Oxford, UK: Oxford University Press.

Wellman, H. (Ed.) (1985). *Children's searching: The development of search skill and spatial representation.* Hillsdale, NJ: Lawrence Erlbaum.

Wellman, H. (1988). First steps in the child's theorizing about the mind. In J. Astington, P. Harris, & D. Olson (Eds.), *Developing theories of mind* (pp. 64–92). Cambridge: Cambridge University Press.

Wellman, H. M. (1990). *The child's theory of mind.* Cambridge MA: MIT Press.

Wellman, H. M., & Banerjee, M. (1991). Mind and emotion: Children's understanding of the emotional consequences of beliefs and desires. *British Journal of Developmental Psychology, 9,* 191–124.

Wellman, H., & Bartsch, K. (1988). Young children's reasoning about beliefs. *Cognition, 30,* 239–277.

Wellman, H. M., Cross, D., & Bartsch, K. (1987). Infant search and object permanence: A meta-analysis of the A-not-B error. *Monographs of the Society for Research in Child Development, 51,* 1–51.

Wellman, H. M., Cross, D., & Watson, J. (in press). A meta-analysis of false belief reasoning: The truth about false belief. *Child Development.*

Wellman, H. M., & Estes, D. (1986). Early understanding of mental entities: A reexamination of childhood realism. *Child Development, 57,* 910–923.

Wellman, H. M., & Gelman, S. A. (1992). Cognitive development: Foundational theories of core domains. *Annual Review of Psychology, 43,* 337–375.

Wellman, H. M., & Gelman, S. A. (1998). Knowledge acquisition in foundational domains. In W. Damon (Series Ed.), D. Kuhn, & R. S. Siegler (Vol. Eds.), *Handbook of child development: Vol. 2. Cognition, perception, and language* (5th ed., pp. 523–573). New York: Wiley.

Wellman, H. M., Harris, P. L., Banerjee, M., & Sinclair, A. (1995). Early understanding of emotion: Evidence from natural language. *Cognition and Emotion, 9,* 117–149.

Wellman, H. M., & Hickling, A. K. (1994). The minds "I": Children's conception of the mind as an active agent. *Child Development, 65,* 1564–1580.

Wellman, H. M., Hickling, A., & Schult, C. A. (1997). Young children's psychological, physical, and biological explanations. In H. M. Wellman & K. Inagaki (Eds.), *The emergence of core domains of thought* (pp. 7–25). San Francisco: Jossey-Bass.

Wellman, H. M., Hollander, M., & Schult, C. A. (1996). Young children's understanding of thought-bubbles and of thoughts. *Child Development, 67,* 768–788.

Wellman, H. M., & Phillips, A. T. (2001). Developing intentional understandings. In B. F. Malle, L. J. Moses, & D. A. Baldwin (Eds.), *Intentions and intentionality: Foundations of social cognition* (pp. 125–148). Cambridge, MA: MIT Press.

Wellman, H. M., & Somerville, S. C. (1982). The development of human search ability. In M. E. Lamb & A. L. Brown (Eds.), *Advances in developmental psychology* (pp. 41–84). Hillsdale, NJ: Erlbaum.

Wellman, H. M., & Woolley, J. D. (1990). From simple desires to ordinary beliefs: The early development of everyday psychology. *Cognition, 35,* 245–275.

Welsh, M., & Pennington, B. (1991). Assessing frontal lobe functioning in children: views from developmental psychology. *Developmental Neuropsychology, 4,* 199–230.

Welsh, M. C., Pennington, B. F., & Groisser, D. B. (1991). A normative-developmental study of executive function: A window on prefrontal function in children. *Developmental Neuropsychology, 7,* 131–149.

Wenner, J. A., & Bauer, P. J. (1999). Bringing order to the arbitrary: One- to two-year-olds' recall of event sequences. *Infant Behavior and Development, 22,* 585–590.

Werker, J. F., Lloyd, V. L., Pegg, J. E., & Polka, L. (1996). Putting the baby in the bootstraps: Toward a more complete understanding of the role of the input in infant speech processing. In J. L. Morgan & K. Demuth (Eds.), *Signal to syntax: Bootstrapping from speech to grammar in early acquisition* (pp. 427–447). Mahwah, NJ: Lawrence Erlbaum.

Werner, H. (1948). *Comparative psychology of mental development.* New York: International Universities Press.

Werner, H. (1953). Einführung in die Entwicklungspsychologie [Introduction to developmental psychology]. (3rd ed.). Leipzig: Barth.

Werner, H. (1957). The concept of development from a comparative and organismic point of view. In D. B. Harris (Ed.), *The concept of development: An issue in the study of human behavior* (pp. 125–148). Minneapolis: University of Minnesota Press.

Werner, H., & Kaplan, B. (1963). *Symbol formation.* New York: Wiley.

Wertsch, J. V. (1979). From social interaction to higher psychological processes: A clarification and application of Vygotsky's theory. *Human Development, 22,* 1–22.

Wertsch, J. V. (1985). *Culture, communication and cognition: Vygotskyan perspectives.* New York: Cambridge University Press.

Wertsch, J. V. (1991). *Voices of the mind: A sociocultural approach to mediated action.* Cambridge, MA: Harvard University Press.

Wertsch, J. V. (1998). *Mind as action.* New York: Oxford University Press.

Wertsch, J. V., del Río, P., & Alvarez, A. (1995). Sociocultural studies: History, action, and mediation. In J. V. Wertsch, P. del Río, & A. Alvarez (Eds.), *Sociocultural studies of mind* (pp. 1–36). New York: Cambridge University Press.

Wertsch, J. V., Hagstrom, F., & Kikas, E. (1995). Voices of thinking and speaking. In L. M. W. Martin, K. Nelson, & T. Tobach (Eds.), *Sociocultural psychology: Theory and practice of doing and knowing* (pp. 276–290). Cambridge: Cambridge University Press.

Wertsch, J. V., Tulviste, P., & Hagstrom, F. (1993). A sociocultural approach to agency. In E. A. Forman, N. Minick, & C. A. Stone (Eds.), *Contexts for learning: Sociocultural dynamics in children's development* (pp. 336–356). New York: Oxford University Press.

West, T. A., & Bauer, P. J. (1999). Assumptions of infantile amnesia: Are there differences between early and later memories? *Memory, 7,* 257–327.

Westwood, P. (1979). *South Australian Spelling Test.* Adelaide: Education Department of South Australia.

Whipple, G. M. (1909). The observer as reporter: A survey of the "psychology of testimony." *Psychological Bulletin, 6,* 153–170.

Whipple, G. M. (1911). The psychology of testimony. *Psychological Bulletin, 8,* 307–309.

Whitehurst, G. J., Falco, F. L., Lonigan, C. J., Fischel, J. E., DeBaryshe, B. D., Valdez-Menchaca, M. C., & Caulfield, M. (1988). Accelerating language development through picture book reading. *Developmental Psychology, 24,* 552–559.

Whiten, A. (1991). *Natural theories of mind.* Oxford, UK: Basil Blackwell.

Wilcox, T. (1999). Object individuation: Infants' use of shape, size, pattern, and color. *Cognition, 72,* 125–166.

Wilcox, T., & Baillargeon, R. (1998a). Object individuation in infancy: The use of featural information in reasoning about occlusion events. *Cognitive Psychology, 17,* 97–155.

Wilcox, T., & Baillargeon, R. (1998b). Object individuation in young infants: Further evidence with an event-monitoring task. *Developmental Science, 1,* 127–142.

Wilcox, T., Nadel, L., & Rosser, R. (1996). Location memory in healthy preterm and fullterm infants. *Infant Behavior and Development, 19,* 309–323.

Wilcox, T., & Schweinlee, A. (2001). Infants' use of speed of motion to individuate objects in occlusion events. Manuscript under review.

Wilkening, F. (1981). Integrating velocity, time, and distance information: A developmental study. *Cognitive Psychology, 13,* 231–247.

Wilkening, F. (1982). Children's knowledge about time, distance, and velocity interrelations. In W. J. Friedman (Ed.), *The developmental psychology of time* (pp. 87–112). New York: Academic Press.

Wilkening, F., & Anderson, N. H. (1982). Comparison of the two rule-assessment methodologies for studying cognitive development and knowledge structure. *Psychological Bulletin, 92*, 215–237.

Wilkening, F., & Anderson, N. H. (1991). Representation and diagnosis of knowledge structures in developmental psychology. In N. H. Anderson (Ed.), *Contributions to information integration theory: Vol. 3. Developmental* (pp. 45–80). Hillsdale, NJ: Erlbaum.

Wilkening, F., & Martin, C. (in press). How to speed up to be in time: Action–judgment dissociations in children and adults. *Swiss Journal of Psychology*.

Willatts, P. (1999). Development of means–end behavior in young infants: Pulling a support to retrieve a distant object. *Developmental Psychology, 35*(3), 651–667.

Willows, D. M., Kruk, R. S., & Corcos, E. (Eds.). (1993). *Visual processes in reading and reading disabilities*. Hillsdale, NJ: Lawrence Erlbaum.

Wilson, J. Q. (1993). *The moral sense*. New York: The Free Press.

Wilson, M. (1989). Saltus: A psychometric model of discontinuity in cognitive development. *Psychological Bulletin, 105*, 276–289.

Wilson, R. A., & Keil, F. C. (2000). The shadows and shallows of explanation. In F. C. Keil & R. A. Wilson (Eds.), *Explanation and cognition* (pp. 87–114). Cambridge, MA: MIT Press.

Wimmer, H. (1996). The early manifestation of developmental dyslexia: Evidence from German children. *Reading and Writing, 8*, 171–188.

Wimmer, H., & Goswami, U. (1994). The influence of orthographic consistency on reading development: word recognition on English and German. *Cognition, 51*, 51–103.

Wimmer, H., Hogrefe, J., & Perner, J. (1988). Children's understanding of informational access as source of knowledge. *Child Development, 59*, 386–396.

Wimmer, H., Hogrefe, J., & Sodian, B. (1988). A second stage in children's conception of mental life: Understanding sources of information. In J. W. Astington, P. L. Harris, & D. R. Olson (Eds.), *Developing theories of mind* (pp. 173–192). New York: Cambridge University Press.

Wimmer, H., Landerl, K., & Schneider, W. (1994). The role of rhyme awareness in learning to read a regular orthography. *British Journal of Developmental Psychology, 12*, 469–484.

Wimmer, H., Mayringer, H., & Landerl, K. (1998). Poor reading: A deficit in skill-automatization or a phonological deficit? *Scientific Studies of Reading, 2*(4), 321–340.

Wimmer, H., & Perner, J. (1983). Beliefs about beliefs: Representation and constraining function of wrong beliefs in young children's understanding of deception. *Cognition, 13*, 103–128.

Windsor, J., & Hwang, M. (1999). Testing the generalized slowing hypothesis in specific language impairment. *Journal of Speech, Language and Hearing Research, 42*, 1205–1218.

Wing, L. (1976). *Early Childhood Autism*: Pergamon Press.

Wing, L. (1981). Asperger syndrome: a clinical account. *Psychological Medicine, 11*, 115–130.

Wing, L. (1988). The continuum of autistic characteristics. In E. Schopler & G. B. Mesibov (Eds.), *Diagnosis and assessment in autism* (pp. 91–110). New York: Plenum.

Wing, L., & Gould, J. (1979). Severe impairments of social interaction and associated abnormalities in children: Epidemiology and classification. *Journal of Autism and Developmental Disorders, 9*, 11–29.

Winner, E. (1996). *Gifted children: Myths and realities*. New York: Basic Books.

Winner, E. (1997). Exceptionally high intelligence and schooling. *American Psychologist, 52*, 1070–1081.

Wise, S. P., Murray, E. A., & Gerfen, C. R. (1996). The frontal cortex–basal ganglia system in primates. *Critical Reviews in Neurobiology, 10*, 317–356.

Wiser, M. (1988). The differentiation of heat and temperature: History of science and novice–expert shift. In S. Strauss (Ed.), *Human development series: Vol. 2. Ontogeny, phylogeny, and historical development* (pp. 28–48). Norwood, NJ: Ablex Publishing Corporation.

Wissler, C. (1901). The correlation of mental and physical tests. *Psychological Review, Monograph Supplement 3*(6).

Wittgenstein, L. (1953). *Philosophical investigations*, trans. G. E. M. Anscombe. Oxford, UK: Blackwell.

Wolf, D., Goldfield, B., Beeghly, M., Waner, D., & Cardona, L. (1985, October). "There's not room enough," the baby said: A study of intertextuality in young children's discourse. Paper presented at the Tenth Annual Boston University Conference on Language Development, Boston.

Wolf, D. P., Rygh, J., & Altshuler, J. (1984). Agency and experience: Actions and states in play narratives. In I. Bretherton (Ed.), *Symbolic play*. Cambridge: Academic Press.

Wolf, M. (1997). A provisional, integrative account of phonological and naming-speed deficits in dyslexia: Implications for diagnosis and intervention. In B. A. Blachman (Ed.), *Foundations of reading acquisition and dyslexia: Implications for early intervention*. Mahwah, NJ: Lawrence Erlbaum.

Woodward, A. (1998). Infants selectively encode the goal object of an actor's reach. *Cognition, 69*, 1–34.

Woodward, A. L. (1999). Infants' ability to distinguish between purposeful and non-purposeful behaviors. *Infant Behavior and Development, 22*, 145–160.

Woodward, A. L., Markman, E. M., & Fitzsimmons, C. M. (1994). Rapid word learning in 13- and 18-month-olds. *Developmental Psychology, 30*(4), 553–566.

Woodward, A. L., Phillips, A., & Spelke, E. S. (1993). *Infants' expectations about the motion of animate versus inanimate objects*. Proceedings of the 15th annual meeting of the Cognitive Science Society. Hillside, NJ: Erlbaum.

Woodward, A. L., & Sommerville, J. A. (2000). Twelve-month-old infants interpret action in context. *Psychological Science*, in press.

Woodward, A. L., Sommerville, J. A., & Guajardo, J. J. (2001). How infants make sense of intentional action. In B. F. Malle, L. J. Moses, & D. A. Baldwin (Eds.), *Intentions and intentionality: Foundations of social cognition* (pp. 149–169). Cambridge, MA: MIT Press.

Woolley, J. D. (1997). Thinking about fantasy: Are children fundamentally different thinkers and believers from adults? *Child Development, 6*, 991–1011.

Woolley, J. D., & Bruell, M. J. (1996). Young children's awareness of the origins of their mental representations. *Developmental Psychology, 32*, 335–346.

Woolley, J. D., & Phelps, K. E. (1994). Young children's practical reasoning about imagination. *British Journal of Developmental Psychology. Special Issue: Magic, 12*, 53–67.

Wynn, K. (1990). Children's understanding of counting. *Cognition, 36*, 155–193.

Wynn, K. (1992). Addition and subtraction by human infants. *Nature, 358*, 749–750.

Wynn, K. (1998). Psychological foundations of number: numerical competence in human infants. *Trends in Cognitive Science, 2*, 296–303.

Wynn, K. (2000). Findings of addition and subtraction in infants are robust and consistent: Reply to Wakeley, Rivera and Langer. *Child Development, 71*, 1535–1536.

Xu, F. (1999). Object individuation and object identity in infancy: The role of spatiotemporal information, object property information, and language. *Acta Psychologica, 102*(2–3), 113–136.

Xu, F. (2000). Chinese immigrant children's and mothers' concepts regarding morality, social convention and children's personal autonomy. Unpublished disseration, University of Illinois at Chicago.

Xu, F., & Carey, S. (1996). Infants' metaphysics: The case of numerical identity. *Cognitive Psychology, 30*(2), 111–153.

Xu, F., Tenenbaum, J. B., & Sorrentino, C. M. (1998). Concepts are not beliefs, but having concepts is having beliefs. *Behavioral and Brain Sciences, 21*, 89.

Yakovlev, P. I., & Lecours, A. R. (1967). The myelogenetic cycles of regional maturation of the brain. In A. Minkowski (Ed.), *Regional development of the brain in early life* (pp. 3–70). Oxford, UK: Blackwell.

Yamada, J. (1990). *Laura: A case for the modularity of language.* Cambridge, MA: MIT Press.

Yasuno, F., Hirata, M., Takimoto, H., Taniguchi, M., Nakagawa, Y., Ikejiri, Y., Nishikawa, T., Shinozaki, K., Tanabe, H., Sugita, Y., & Takeda, M. (1999). Retrograde temporal order amnesia resulting from damage to the fornix. *Journal of Neurol Neurosurg Psychiatry, 67,* 102–105.

Yau, J., & Smetana, J. G. (1995). Adolescent–parent conflict among Chinese adolescents in Hong Kong. Unpublished manuscript, University of Hong Kong.

Yirmiya, N., Sigman, M., Kasari, C., & Mundy, P. (1992). Empathy and cognition in high functioning children with autism. *Child Development, 63,* 150–160.

Yonas, A., & Granrud, C. E. (1984). The development of sensitivity to kinetic, binocular, and pictorial depth information in human infants. In D. Engle, D. Lee, & M. Jeannerod (Eds.), *Brain mechanisms and spatial vision* (pp. 113–145). Dordrecht: Martinus Nijhoff.

Youngblade, L. M., & Dunn, J. (1995). Individual differences in young children's pretend play with mother and sibling: Links to relationships and understanding of other people's feelings and beliefs. *Child Development, 66,* 1472–1492.

Younger, B. A. (1990). Infants' detection of correlations among feature categories. *Child Development, 61,* 614–620.

Younger, B. A., & Cohen, L. B. (1986). Developmental change in infants' perception of correlations among attributes. *Child Development, 57*(3), 803–815.

Younger, B. A., & Fearing, D. D. (1999). Parsing items into separate categories: Developmental change in infant categorization. *Child Development, 70,* 291–303.

Younger, B. A., & Fearing, D. D. (2000). A global-to-basic trend in early categorization: Evidence from a dual-category habituation task. *Infancy, 1,* 47–58.

Younger, B. A., & Gottlieb, S. (1988). Development of categorization skills: Changes in the nature and structure of infant form categories? *Developmental Psychology, 24,* 611–619.

Yuill, N., & Oakhill, J. (1991). *Children's problems in text comprehension.* Cambridge: Cambridge University Press.

Zahn-Waxler, C., & Radke-Yarrow, M. (1990). The origins of empathic concern. *Motivation and Emotion, 14,* 107–130.

Zahn-Waxler, C., Radke-Yarrow, M., & King, R. (1979). Child rearing and children's prosocial initiations toward victims of distress. *Child Development, 50,* 319–330.

Zaitchik, D. (1990). When representations conflict with reality: The preschooler's problem with false beliefs and "false" photographs. *Cognition, 35,* 41–68.

Zajonc, R. B. (1980). Feeling and thinking: Preferences need no inferences. *American Psychologist, 35,* 151–175.

Zelazo, P. D. (1999). Language, levels of consciousness, and the development of intentional action. In P. D. Zelazo, J. W. Astington, & D. R. Olson (Eds.), *Developing theories of intention: Social understanding and self-control* (pp. 95–117). Mahwah, NJ: Lawrence Erlbaum.

Zelazo, P. D., Astington, J. W., & Olson, D. (Eds.). (1999). *Development of intention and intentional understanding in infancy and early childhood.* Mahwah, NJ: Erlbaum.

Zelazo, P. D., Burack, J., Boseovski, J., Jacques, S., & Frye, D. (in press). A cognitive complexity and control framework for the study of autism. In J. A. Burack, T. Charman, N. Yirmiya, & P. R. Zelazo (Eds.), *Development and autism: Perspectives from theory and research.* Mahwah, NJ: Lawrence Erlbaum.

Zelazo, P. D., Carter, A., Reznick, J. S., & Frye, D. (1997). Early development of executive function: A problem-solving framework. *Review of General Psychology, 1,* 198–226.

Zelazo, P. D., & Frye, D. (1996). Cognitive complexity and control: A theory of the development of deliberate reasoning and intentional action. In M. Stamenov (Ed.), *Language structure, discourse, and the access to consciousness* (pp. 113–153). Philadelphia: John Benjamins.

Zelazo, P. D., & Frye, D. (1997). Cognitive complexity and control: A theory of the development of deliberate reasoning and intentional action. In M. Stamenov (Ed.), *Language structure, discourse, and the access to consciousness* (pp. 113–153). Amsterdam: John Benjamins.

Zelazo, P. D., Frye, D., & Rapus, T. (1996). An age-related dissociation between knowing rules and using them. *Cognitive Development, 11,* 37–63.

Zelazo, P. D., & Jacques, S. (1996). Children's rule use: Representation, reflection and cognitive control. In R. Vasta (Ed.), *Annals of child development* (Vol. 12, pp. 119–176). London: Jessica Kingsley.

Zelazo, P. D., Jacques, S., Burack, J., & Frye, D. (in press). The relation between theory of mind and rule use: Evidence from persons with autism-spectrum disorders. *Infants and Young Children* [Special Issue: *Executive function and its development*].

Zelazo, P. D., & Reznick, J. S. (1991). Age-related asynchrony of knowledge and action. *Child Development, 62,* 719–735.

Zelazo, P. D., Reznick, J. S., & Piñon, D. E. (1995). Response control and the execution of verbal rules. *Developmental Psychology, 31,* 508–517.

Zhou, Z., Peverly, S. T., Boehm, A. E., & Chongde, L. (2000). American and Chinese children's understanding of distance, time, and speed interrelations. *Cognitive Development, 15,* 215–240.

Zhu Hua, & Dodd, B. (2000). Development and change in the phonology of Putonghua-speaking children with speech difficulties. *Clinical Linguistics and Phonetics, 14,* 351–368.

Zhu, S. C., & Yuille, A. L. (1996). FORMS: A flexible object recognition and modeling system. *International Journal of Computer Vision, 20,* 187–212.

Zigler, E. (1982). Development versus difference theories of mental retardation and the problem of motivation. In E. Zigler & D. Balla (Eds.), *Mental retardation: The developmental–difference controversy.* Hillsdale, NJ: Erlbaum.

Zigler, E., & Berman, W. (1983). Discerning the future of early childhood intervention. *American Psychologist, 38,* 894–906.

Zilbovicius, M., Garreau, B., Samson, Y., Remy, P., Barthelemy, C., Syrota, A., & Lelord, G. (1995). Delayed maturation of the frontal cortex in childhood autism. *American Journal of Psychiatry, 152,* 248–252.

Zimmerman, C. (2000). The development of scientific reasoning skills. *Developmental Review, 20,* 99–149.

Zinchenko, V. P. (1985). Vygotsky's ideas about units for the analysis of mind. In J. V. Wertsch (Ed.), *Culture, communication, and cognition: Vygotskian perspectives.* New York: Cambridge University Press.

Zola-Morgan, S., & Squire, L. R. (1993). Neuroanatomy of memory. *Annual Review of Neuroscience, 16,* 547–563.

Zorzi, M., Houghton, G., & Butterworth, B. (1998a). The development of spelling–sound relationships in a model of phonological reading. *Language and Cognitive Processes, 13,* 337–372.

Zorzi, M., Houghton, G., & Butterworth, B. (1998b). Two routes or one in reading aloud? A connectionist dual-process model. *Journal of Experimental Psychology: Human Perception and Performance, 24,* 1131–1161.

Index

Note: The index is arranged in word-by-word sequence; page numbers in italics refer to figures; page numbers in bold refer to tables.

DATE DUE

GAYLORD   #3523PI   Printed in USA